DEWEY TO LC CONVERSION TABLES

DEWEY TO LC CONVERSION TABLES

COMPILED AND EDITED
BY
Gerald L. Swanson

Library of Congress Catalog Card Number 72-82737
ISBN 0-8409-0305-7

CCM Information Corporation
866 Third Avenue
New York, New York 10022

CONTENTS

INTRODUCTION

The *Dewey to LC Conversion Tables* are intended as an aid for libraries in converting their collections from the Dewey Decimal system of classification to the Library of Congress classification system. The tables are not intended as a means of bypassing the use of the Library of Congress schedules but rather as a tool for a more rapid approach to the LC Classification schedules from the Dewey numbers.

The methodology used in the compilation of these tables utilized the Library of Congress MARC records which were distributed by the MARC Distribution Services during the period of 1969 to 1971, during which the 17th edition of the Dewey Decimal Classification was used by the Library of Congress. About 130,000 English-language main entries were analyzed by computer. From these bibliographic entries the computer extracted the Dewey Decimal classifications (other than "E" and "Fic") and the accompanying Library of Congress classification. The LC classification was formatted by computer to allow sorting in shelf list order. Book numbers were deleted, as were dates (which form a part of the book number). The computer deleted invalid numbers and consolidated like numbers, resulting in about 74,000 LC classifications. It should be noted that the MARC records (*MA*chine *R*eadable *C*ataloging) distributed by the Library of Congress are for English-language materials only (regardless of place of publication). About 94% of these records contain Dewey classifications.

The Library of Congress classification is that portion of the LC Call Number indicated by the MARC editor as being the classification. In the few cases of multiple LC classifications, the first has been used. The resultant manuscript has been searched for invalid numbers and any found have been deleted. An occasional invalid number is possible, specifically in the case of an error in a MARC record not caught in the manual proofreading procedure.

The Class Number is generally that part of the Call Number which gathers together all works on a given topic. In MARC, this break may occur between two Cutter numbers but not in the middle of an expanded Cutter number (such as a Cutter number representing a further breakdown of a subject which is expanded to indicate authorship). In this case, the entire Cutter is a part of the class. Dates included in LC classifications are deleted, as are the "s" suffixes appended to DDC numbers to indicate that the number is for a series. The optional truncation points in Dewey numbers have been deleted (indicated by prime signs on the printed cards) thus using the fullest DDC number in order to provide a smaller range of LC numbers under any given DDC number.

The *Dewey to LC Conversion Tables*, while containing DDC numbers from the 17th edition, can be used for conversion from previous editions of Dewey as well. There were about 800 relocations between editions 16 and 17 of the DDC and twice that number between editions 15 and 16.

Dewey Decimal Classification: History and Use

The DDC is the most widely used classification in the world. Tauber reported in 1953 that it was used in 96% of all public libraries, in 89% of college and university libraries, and in 64% of special libraries. The Library of Congress began use of the 18th edition of the DDC on January 1, 1971, although the schedules were not published until more than a year later.

The first edition of the classification of Melvil Dewey was published anonymously in Amherst, Massachusetts in 1876 and was entitled *A Classification and Subject Index for Cataloging and Arranging the Books and Pamphlets of a Library.* The next edition, seven times larger than the first, was published in 1885 under Melvil Dewey's name, entitled *Decimal Classification and Relativ Index* (simplified spelling was one of Dewey's passions).

Sixteen revised editions have since appeared, in addition to a series of nine abridged editions. Since 1957, the DDC has been edited at the Library of Congress under a contract with Forest Press, Inc., Lake Placid, New York, which owns the copyright. The 18th edition of DDC, a massive three-volume set, includes much useful information not included in previous editions. A helpful list of relocations and discontinued numbers should be noted.

Library of Congress Classification: History and Use

The Library of Congress classification was developed by a large number of subject specialists beginning in 1900 for the purpose of reclassification from the Jeffersonian Classification which was previously used (based on Thomas Jefferson's arrangement of his own collection). The LC classification, now totaling over 30 volumes, is tailored to the Library of Congress collection. New numbers are added only as new topics are added to the collection which require it. As the classification has developed, the lack of a combined index to the schedules – a massive undertaking – has been one great shortcoming.

While the DDC is hierarchical both in notation and in classification, the LCC is not. In Dewey, insertion of a new subject often requires vacating of a number, usually by relocation. The growth of science and technology and the social sciences has resulted in a great expansion within the 300's, 500's, and 600's. In some cases, DDC numbers have been extended decimally up to 22 digits.

The LCC does not suffer from this problem. New subjects can be inserted without disturbing the present notation by extension beyond the decimal point. Another advantage of the LCC is the inclusion of the number on all LC cards (except some Law). A library can adopt a policy of strict acceptance of the LC Class when it is present on the printed card, thus reducing cataloging with LC copy to a primarily clerical task.

The *Dewey to LC Conversion Tables* provide a limited index from the DDC to one or a limited range of LC numbers. With book in hand, the reclassifier should be able to quickly decide among a choice of LC numbers by consulting the *Dewey Decimal Classification Summaries* as well as the *Outline of the Library of Congress Classification.* The one-to-one conversion situation takes place in about 50% of all instances, which should enable reclassification of a large amount of material to be done with clerical workers under minimal professional supervision.

BIBLIOGRAPHY

This bibliography includes only a few basic books of use in conversion from the Dewey Decimal Classification to the Library of Congress Classification. A very extensive annotated bibliography can be found in the Matthis book.

Dewey, Melvil. *Dewey Decimal Classification and Relative Index.* Ed. 18. (Lake Placid, New York, Forest Press, 1971)

Matthis, Raimund E. & Desmond Taylor. *Adopting The Library of Congress Classification System: A Manual of Methods and Techniques for Application or Conversion.* (New York, R.R. Bowker, 1971) Annotated bibliography pp. 149-194.

Problems in Library Classification: Dewey 17 and Conversion. Edited by Theodore Samore. (New York, R.R. Bowker, 1968)

Schimmelpfeng, Richard H. & C. Donald Cook, eds. *The Use of The Library of Congress Classification.* (Chicago, American Library Association, 1968)

Tauber, Maurice F. *Technical Services in Libraries.* (New York, Columbia University Press, 1953)

LIBRARY OF CONGRESS CLASSIFICATION SCHEDULES

For sale by the Card Division, Library of Congress, Building 159, Navy Yard Annex, Washington, D.C. 20541, to which inquiries on current availability and price should be addressed.

Classes A to Z:

A General works: Polygraphy.
B Philosophy and Religion:
  Part I, B-BJ: Philosophy
  Part II, BL-BX: Religion
C History: Auxiliary Sciences.
D History: General and Old World.
E-F History: America.
G Geography, Anthropology, Folklore, etc.
H Social Sciences.
J Political Science.
K Law.
  KF: Law of the United States.
L Education.
M Music.
N Fine Arts.
P Philology and Literature:
  P-PA: Philology. Classical Philology and Literature.
  PA Supplement: Byzantine and Modern Greek Literature.
  PB-PH: Modern European Languages.
  PG: Russian Literature.
  PJ-PM: Languages and Literatures of Asia, Africa, Oceania, America; Mixed Languages; Artificial Languages.
  P-PM Supplement: Index to Languages and Dialects.
  PN, PR, PS, PZ: Literature – General, English, American. Fiction and Juvenile Literature.
  PQ, Part 1: French Literature.
  PQ, Part 2: Italian, Spanish, Portuguese Literatures.
  PT, Part 1: German Literature.
  PT, Part 2: Dutch and Scandinavian Literatures.
Q Science.
R Medicine.
S Agriculture, etc.
T Technology.
U Military Science.
V Naval Science.
Z Bibliography and Library Science.

001 ..... AZ361
..... Q176
..... QA76.5
001.2 ..... AG90.I8
..... AZ221
..... AZ361
..... AZ504
..... CB417
..... HM213
..... LA228.E53
..... PQ4507
..... PR3487
001.209174927 ..... DS36.8
001.20917496 ..... E185.82
001.2094 ..... PA85.B5
001.20942 ..... DA485
..... PN22.A2
..... PR461
001.2094281 ..... DA690.J3
001.20943613 ..... DB851
001.20947 ..... DK276
001.20973 ..... E169.1
001.2098 ..... LA543
001.3 ..... AZ361
..... LC1011
001.306273 ..... AS24
001.307 ..... CB3
..... LB2365.R4
001.3071142 ..... LB1576
001.3071242 ..... LB1576
..... LC101
001.3094436 ..... DC715
001.30975 ..... AS36.G378
001.4 ..... AZ105
..... AZ507
..... Q183
001.40216 ..... Q177
001.40973 ..... AZ507
..... Q180.U5
001.409781 ..... Q183.4.K2
001.42 ..... AZ105
..... BD241
..... P93
..... T14
001.4201 ..... B945
001.422 ..... HA37
..... HA201
001.424 ..... HD20.5
..... QA279
..... T57.6
..... T57.62
..... TA343
..... TP155.7
001.424028 ..... QA76.5
001.43309783 ..... HC107.K2
001.44 ..... AS8
..... AS118
..... AS911.F6
..... LB2285.E35
..... LB2336
..... Q180.U5
..... Z1375
001.4402542 ..... AS911.A2
001.440922 ..... E176.8
001.440973 ..... HV89
001.4409769 ..... LB2336
001.5 ..... HE151
..... P90
..... P91
..... P92.U5
..... P98
..... P106
..... PE1585
..... Q223
..... T10.5
001.501 ..... B820
..... P91
001.50202 ..... P90
001.50208 ..... P93.5
001.5072 ..... P91
001.508 ..... P87
001.509 ..... P90
001.50922 ..... P92.5.A1
001.50924 ..... P92.5.M3
001.50954 ..... P92.I7
001.51 ..... P87
001.53 ..... AS36
..... E105
..... Q180
..... Q295
..... Q300
..... Q310
..... Q315
..... Q327
..... Q365
..... QA9
..... QA402
..... QP475
..... T57.6
..... T385
..... TA168
..... TL521.3.C6
..... Z663.23
001.5301 ..... B809.8
001.5308 ..... Q295
..... Z663.23
001.532 ..... QH508
001.533 ..... Q327
..... TK5
..... TK7895.O6
001.535 ..... Q335
..... Q335.5
001.539 ..... JN301
..... Q180.A1
001.539 ..... Q360
..... QA268
..... QA404.5
..... T57.95
..... TK5102.5
001.53902462 ..... Q360
001.53903 ..... Q360
001.5509 ..... HE152
001.550947 ..... P92.R9
001.551460028 ..... Z6004.P6
001.553 ..... TK7895.O6
001.6 ..... QA76
..... T57.5
001.64023 ..... QA76.25
001.6402574 ..... QA76.5
001.6402578 ..... QA76.5
001.642 ..... QA76.5
001.6424 ..... QA76
..... QA76.5
..... QA76.8.I12
..... QA267.3
001.6443 ..... Q180.A1
..... QA76
..... TL521.3.C6
001.9 ..... CB160
..... QL89
..... TL788.7
..... TL789
..... TL789.3
001.90924 ..... Q143.F67
001.94 ..... AG243
..... GC28
..... GR825
..... QL89
..... TL789
..... TL789.3
001.95 ..... CC140
..... G530.C95
..... Z1024
001.96 ..... AZ999
..... BF1775
..... GR615
010 ..... Z1001
..... Z1002
010.28 ..... Z1001
..... Z1008
..... Z7161
010.8 ..... Z1005
010.924 ..... Z1004.N29
010.968 ..... Z3601
011 ..... AG600
..... BS432
..... Z881
..... Z881.A1
..... Z921
..... Z997.W24
..... Z1019
..... Z1033.U6
..... Z1035
..... Z1039.P8
..... Z2001
..... Z5346
..... Z5347
..... Z5811
..... Z6620.G7
..... Z7164.A2
..... Z7164.E15
011.02 ..... Z711
..... Z733.C82
..... Z1035.1
011.08 ..... Z881
012 ..... Z6616.D5
..... Z8130.3
..... Z8136.2
..... Z8231.5
..... Z8341.3
..... Z8455.8
..... Z8514.6
..... Z8757.134
013.37764888 ..... Z5055.U5S63397
013.3779474 ..... Z5055.U5
013.94972 ..... Z2957.C7
013.954 ..... Z7405.R4
013.955 ..... Z6621.B86P43
013.973 ..... Z1361.N39
013.976391 ..... Z5055.U5L8266
013.976714 ..... AS36
013.9914 ..... Z955
..... Z5055.P47
014.1 ..... Z1065
015.4 ..... Z1014
015.41 ..... Z2051
015.41815 ..... Z2037
015.42 ..... CD1042
..... Z921.C72
..... Z1028
..... Z2001
..... Z2002
..... Z2009
015.44 ..... Z2162
015.45 ..... Z2342
015.489 ..... Z2562
015.4923 ..... Z999
015.51 ..... Z881
015.515 ..... Z6621
015.52 ..... Z881
015.54 ..... Z3201
015.545 ..... Z3207.P8
015.549 ..... Z3191
015.561 ..... Z881
015.591 ..... Z3216
015.593 ..... Z3237
015.595 ..... Z3246
015.6 ..... Z3504
015.667 ..... Z3785
015.67 ..... Z3585
015.71 ..... Z1365
015.7291 ..... Z6954.C9
015.73 ..... HD8051
..... Q180.A1
..... Z473
..... Z1035.9
..... Z1215
..... Z1223.A12
..... Z1223.Z7
..... Z1224
..... Z5348
..... Z6951
..... Z7164.C81
015.7413 ..... Z1292.B3
015.7419 ..... Z1292.P6
015.743 ..... Z1343
015.744 ..... Z1223.5.M35
015.7443 ..... Z1296.W9
015.74485 ..... Z1296.N4
015.745 ..... Z1331
015.7463 ..... Z1266.H3
015.7467 ..... Z1266.H3
015.7468 ..... Z1266.N4
015.747 ..... Z1223.5.N57
015.74743 ..... Z232.M923
015.74768 ..... Z1318.A8
015.74789 ..... Z1318.R67
015.748 ..... Z1223.5.P4
015.74966 ..... Z1314.T8
015.74967 ..... Z1314.P7
015.74974 ..... Z1314.M8
015.751 ..... Z1267
015.752 ..... Z1293
015.756 ..... Z1319.L28
015.757915 ..... Z1334.C47
015.759 ..... Z1223.5.F5
015.762 ..... Z1301
015.768 ..... Z1223.5.T4
..... Z1337
015.77157 ..... Z1324.C67
015.77576 ..... Z473.A68
015.794 ..... Z1223.Z7
..... Z1261
015.8 ..... Z1609.G7
015.81 ..... Z1679.M4
015.861 ..... Z1739
015.9 ..... Z5055.N65
015.931 ..... Z4101
015.941 ..... Z4435
015.944 ..... Z4019
015.9611 ..... Z4651
016 ..... Z1009
016.0013 ..... Z5579
016.00153 ..... Z7405.C9
016.0019 ..... Z5064.F5
016.01 ..... Z1002
016.011 ..... Z1009
016.015 ..... Z1002
016.01547 ..... Z1002
016.01571 ..... Z1313
016.01573 ..... Z1002
016.016 ..... Z1002
016.016.093 ..... Z240.A1
016.01605 ..... Z1002
016.01615 ..... Z7201
016.0165 ..... Z7401
016.016620135 ..... Z5063
016.01662913 ..... Z5063.A1
016.01682 ..... Z2011
016.01686 ..... Z2691
016.0169 ..... Z6201
016.01691 ..... Z6001
016.016914031 ..... Z6203
016.016914203 ..... Z1002
016.0169168 ..... Z3601.A1
016.0169173097496 ..... Z1361.N39
016.016918 ..... Z1601.A2
016.0169191403 ..... Z3291.A1
016.0184 ..... Z999
016.02 ..... Z666
..... Z721
016.02018 ..... Z678.9.A2
016.0205 ..... Z666
016.0207 ..... Z668
..... Z669.5.A25
016.020711 ..... Z668
016.02072 ..... Z721
016.02100973 ..... Z731
..... Z732.I2
016.02460973 ..... Z713.5.U6
016.025 ..... Z678
016.02502 ..... Z688.5
016.025171 ..... Z6620.G7
016.0254 ..... Z696
016.0256 ..... Z1009
016.0276251 ..... Z1037
016.0277 ..... Z666
016.02770924 ..... Z720.M4
016.028 ..... Z1035.9
016.0281 ..... Z883
..... Z1035
016.02852 ..... Z1037
..... Z1037.A1
016.0297 ..... TL521.3.C6
..... Z699.2
016.03 ..... Z7004.D5
016.05 ..... AS8
..... Z5073
..... Z6653
..... Z6941
..... Z6945
..... Z6951
016.051 ..... Z6944.S8
..... Z6951
..... Z6952.N6
016.052 ..... Z6945
..... Z6955
..... Z6956.G6
016.0561 ..... Z1419.M46
016.0571 ..... Z6956.R9
016.05786 ..... Z6956.C9
016.0587 ..... Z7913
016.05995 ..... Z6945
016.059951 ..... Z6958.C5
016.06 ..... Z6461
016.0684 ..... Z2000
016.07 ..... CD3358.L5
..... Z6940
..... Z6945
..... Z8970.9
016.07041 ..... Z8735.4
016.070573 ..... Z1002
016.070924 ..... Z6616.M53
..... Z8971.5
016.071 ..... Z6944.N39
016.07148 ..... Z6952.P4
016.07918 ..... Z6947
016.07994 ..... AI21.S85
016.091 ..... Z997.S26
..... Z6605.H4
..... Z6620.A8
016.0910945 ..... Z6623
016.091097468 ..... Z6604
016.094 ..... Z1008
016.1 ..... Z5873
..... Z7125
016.13390924 ..... Z8828.4
016.1427 ..... Z7128.E9
016.15 ..... BF80.3
..... Z3508.P8
..... Z7201
016.1505 ..... Z7203
016.1506 ..... Z3508.P8
016.150947 ..... Z7201
016.152 ..... Z7204.V5
016.153 ..... Z7204.P67
016.15312 ..... Z7204.M4
016.15315 ..... LB1059
016.1539 ..... Z7204.I5
016.15524 ..... Z7201
016.15761 ..... Z7721
016.15794 ..... Z7254
016.181.4 ..... Z7129.I5
016.18111 ..... Z7129.C5
016.191 ..... Z8228
016.192 ..... Z8513.45
016.193 ..... Z8460
..... Z8628.85
016.194 ..... Z8784.44
016.195 ..... Z8941.8
016.199492 ..... Z8268
016.199931 ..... Z8713.564
016.2 ..... Z7751
016.200 ..... Z7751
016.21170924 ..... Z8438
016.22 ..... Z7770
016.2207 ..... Z7770
016.22143 ..... Z7771.M3
016.2265 ..... Z7772.M1
016.229108 ..... Z5781
016.24690971 ..... Z1395.P6
016.25019 ..... Z7204.R4
016.2548 ..... DA689.C5
016.2618 ..... Z7164.S6
016.2620342 ..... CD1041
016.2625 ..... Z7838.C7
016.266 ..... BV2361
016.26600968 ..... Z7817.B86
016.26636 ..... Z7817
016.2665268 ..... Z7817
016.271.509 ..... BX3701
016.27179 ..... CD2000.M3
016.2771 ..... CD3626
016.2834241 ..... CD1068.G55
016.2858 ..... Z8255.5
016.287 ..... Z8967
016.2898 ..... Z7845.S5
016.2899 ..... Z7845.P5
016.2960947 ..... Z6373.R9
016.2970924 ..... Z8019.4
016.297122 ..... Z6623
016.3 ..... H61
..... Z716
..... Z6461
..... Z7161.A1
..... Z7164.E2
..... Z7164.S66
016.30005 ..... Z7163
016.30018 ..... Z7165.U5
016.3005 ..... Z7164.C81
016.3007 ..... Z7161
016.300712 ..... Z7161
016.300924 ..... Z8978.46
016.3009519 ..... Z3316
016.301 ..... Z7164.S68
016.301018 ..... Z7164.S68
016.3010924 ..... Z8173.9
..... Z8195.43
016.3011 ..... Z7164.S66
..... Z7204.A5
..... Z7294.S67
016.3011091724 ..... Z7164.U5
016.301154 ..... Z1245
..... Z7204.S67
016.3012 ..... Z8522.5
016.30124 ..... Z7405.H6

016.30124	Z7914.T25
016.30129	Z5111
016.301294	Z5117
016.30130942	Z7164.N3
016.30131	Z5118.A5
	Z5853.P7
016.30132	Z1361.N39
	Z5942
	Z7164.B5
	Z7164.F7
016.30132951	Z7164.D3
016.30134	Z7164.C842
016.301340973	Z7164.S66
016.30135095	Z7165.J3
016.301364096	Z7165.A42
016.3013640973	JK8501
	Z7165.U5
016.301364097526	
	Z7165.U6M36
016.30136409795	Z7164.U7
016.30141	Z7164.S42
016.301412096	Z3507
016.301415	Z7164.S42
016.30142	Z5118.F2
016.301420971	Z5118.F2
016.301420973	Z7164.M2
016.301426	Z7164.B5
016.301427	Z5814.C52
016.301431	Z5814.C5
016.3014350971	Z673
016.3014350973	Z7165.U5
016.30144	Z7164.S64
	Z7164.Y8
016.301441	S21
016.30145	Z7164.I3
016.301450942	Z2021.R3
016.301450973	Z1236
	Z1361.N39
	Z7164.R12
016.301451	Z1361.N39
	Z7164.R12
016.301451.96073	Z1361.N39
016.3014516073	Z1361.M4
016.301451924073	Z6373.U5
016.30145196	Z1361.N39
016.30145196073	Z1361.N39
016.301451963	AS611
016.3014522	Z1251.S7
016.301453	Z2021.R3
016.301453073	Z1361.M4
016.3014768588	Z6677
016.301476861	Z7721
016.301476863	Z7164.N17
016.30154	TH7
	Z7164.H8
016.301540973	HD7293.A49
016.309	Z7164.E15
	Z7164.U5
016.3091	HX15
016.3091046	Z6204
016.30914	Z7165.E8
016.30914585	Z7165.M29
016.3091495	Z7165.G83
016.309151	Z3108.A5
016.3091561	Z7165.T9
016.3091661	Z3553.M3
016.309173	Z7165.U5
016.30918	Z7165.L3
016.309212	Z7164.E15
016.30925	Z7164.O7
016.3092509713	Z7165.C2
016.3092509746	Z7165.U5
016.30926	Z5942
016.31	Z7551
	Z7554.G7
016.3113973	Z7554.U5
016.312	Z7554.U5
016.314	Z7553.C3
016.3142	Z7554.G7
016.316	Z7554.A34
016.32	Z7161
016.320072	Z7165.U5
016.32009595	Z7165.M28
016.320158	Z7164.N2
016.320944	Z2180.3
016.32096	DT1
	Z3501
	Z3871
016.320967	Z7165.A42
016.320973	Z1223
016.3209744	Z7165.U5
016.3209794	Z1261
016.3231196076149	Z7164.R4
016.3232	Z7164.P19
016.32344	Q180.A1
	Z7164.L6
016.3241	Z7165.U5
016.32421	Z7165.U5
016.325345096	Z2361.C7
016.325346098	Z2709
016.327	Z6461
016.32742	CD1051
016.32742051	CD1051
016.32743	Z2247.R4
016.327561	Z2857.R4
016.32794	Z4030.3
016.3284201	Z2009
016.32873	Z7165.U5
016.329020973	Z7165.U5
016.3298	Z7165.U5
016.32998	Z7165.L3
016.33	HF5030
	Z5055.C2
	Z7164.E2
016.33	Z7164.S84
	Z8398.67
016.3309415	Z7165.I68
016.33094391	Z7165.H9
016.330952	Z7165.J3
016.3309549	Z7165.P3
016.330973	Z7165.U5
016.3309767	HC107.A8
016.3309795	Z7165.U5
016.331	Z7164.L1
016.3310922	Z6616.B46
016.3310942	Z7165.G8
016.33111	Z7164.L1
016.3311120971	Z7165.C2
016.3311120973	Z1223.Z7
	Z7164.L1
016.331113	Z7164.L1
016.331116813621	Z7164.T7
016.331127	Z7164.L1
016.3311330973	Z7165.U5
016.331137	Z7164.U56
016.3311808	Z7164.L1
016.3311942	Z7165.G8
016.3311954	Z7165.I6
016.331230973	Z7165.U5
016.33140973	KF3555
	Z5814.T4
016.33163	HD5715.2
016.331702	HD8051
	HF5381
	Z1035
	Z7164.C81
016.33188	Z7164.T7
016.331880942	Z7165.G8
016.331880944	Z7164.T7
016.332	Z7164.F5
016.333	Z7164.N3
016.333320963	Z7164.L3
016.33333	Z7164.C81
016.3333360973	Z7165.U5
016.33376	Z7165.G8
016.33378	Z6827
	Z7511
016.33391	Z7164.W2
	Z7935
016.335	Z7164.S67
016.33500973	Z6616.H57
016.335430951	DS777.55.H8152
	Z7165.C6
016.33543096	Z7164.S67
016.335430973	Z7164.S67
016.336180973	Z7164.F5
016.336185	Z7164.F5
016.336200973	HJ2385
016.33624	Z7164.T23
016.338	Z7164.O7
016.33809	Z7164.L9
016.3380942	Z7164.L1
016.338094274	Z7165.G8
016.3381	L5074.E3
	Z5074.E3
	Z7295
016.3381094	Z5075.E8
016.3381096	Z5075.A4
016.338109713	Z5076
016.3381759	Z5996.F55
016.338176	Z881.U4
016.33819	Z7164.F7
016.338409549	Z7165.P3
016.3384730155	Z7914.B9
016.3384733210954	Z7165.I6
016.3384762148	Z5160
016.33847664	Z7164.F7
016.33847670994	Z7165.A8
016.33847677216	Z5701
016.338479170453	Z6004.T6
016.33852	Z7164.P94
016.33864	JX1977
	Z7164.C81
016.3389	Z7164.E15
	Z7164.O7
016.33890091724	Z7164.U5
016.338900956	Z3013
016.33891	Z7164
016.33891171242	Z7164.O7
016.338914201724	Z7164.U5
016.338942	Z7165.G8
016.339	Z7164.C81
016.33923	Z7164.E2
016.3394	Z7164.C81
016.34	KF1
	KF4
	RA569
016.340115	KF1
016.340605	Z6672.J9
016.3411	Z6464.Z9
016.34113	Z6481
016.34277309	KFI1602
016.3430973	KF9223
016.343740973	KF9444
016.3477	KF1539
016.35000018	Z7164.A2
016.350000954	JA37
016.350722	Z7164.F5
016.352000973	Z5942
016.3520009749	Z7165.U6N37
016.35200730973	JS411
	Z7164.L8
016.35204274	CD1067.S27
016.3520975537	Z1223.5.V5
016.353001	Z7164.C81
016.3530072	CD3026
016.35300722	Z7165.U5
016.353007222	Z7165.U6
016.35300823	Z7164.N3
016.3530085	Z7405.P8
016.353008777	Z5065.U5
016.35304025	Z7165.U5
016.3531	Z6465.U5
016.35371	Z7165.C2
016.35386	Z7164.T8
016.3539293	JK2408
016.3539758	Z1273
016.3539794008	AS36.C2
016.3539797	CD3574.W38
016.35442	CD1051
016.35451	Z7165.C6
016.354549	Z7165.P3
016.354669	Z7165.N5
016.354710085	Z7405.P8
016.355000947	Z6725.R9
016.355000973	KF7250
016.35500947	Z6725.R9
016.35503	Z6724.A9
016.35522	Z6724.M3
016.355310973	CD3022
016.3584142	Z6724.A38
016.35900942	Z6835.G7
016.35900973	Z1249.N3
	Z6835.U5
016.3593310924	Z6616.S37
	Z6616.S4
	Z6616.S58
016.3593320922	Z6616.S6
016.35996	CD3022
	Z6724.A8
016.3616	Z6677
016.361942	Z7164.C4
016.361973	Z7164.C4
016.362	RA440.5
016.3621	Z6658
	Z7164.I7
016.36210973	Z6673
016.3622	Z6664.N5
	Z6677
016.362220973	Z6677
016.36224	Z6664.N5
016.3623	Z6677
	Z6677.B74
016.3624	Z7254
016.36241	Z5346
016.3625	Z7164.C4
016.36250973	Z7165.U5
016.362580973	KF336
016.3627	Z7164.C5
016.36271	Z7164.C5
016.362783	Z6677
016.362830973	Z7164.I25
016.3632	Z7164.P76
016.36335	Z6724.C6
016.36362	Z881.U4
016.364	Z5118.C9
	Z7164.P76
016.3641	Z1251.W5
016.364135	Z6016.P6
	Z8455.57
016.364143	Z7165.U5
016.3641522	Z7615
016.36415240924	Z8462.8
016.3644	Z5118.C9
016.36462	Z5118.C9
016.364973	Z5118.C9
016.368400973	Z7164.L1
016.3694	Z7164.Y8
016.37	LB1044.Z9
	Z5811
	Z5816.D8
	Z5819
	Z6945
016.37011	Z5811
016.37015	Z5811
	Z5814.P8
016.370184	Z5814.T3
016.37019	Z5814.F5
016.3701934	Z5814.D5
016.37019348	Z5814.U8
016.370196	Z5814.E23
	Z5814.S88
016.3705	Z5813
016.3707	Z5814.A85
	Z5814.T3
016.37071	LB1044.Z9
	Z5811
	Z5814.T3
016.370924	Z6616.A55
016.370942	Z5815.G5
016.3709485	Z5814.R4
016.370952	Z5815.J3
016.37096762	Z7165.A42
016.370973	Z5815.U5
016.370994	Z5815.A8
016.3711	Z5814.T33
016.3711412	Z5814.T3
016.371200973	Z5814.M26
016.371254	Z5814.N6
016.37126	Z5814.P8
016.37127	Z5814.P8
016.3713	Z5814.T3
016.3713078	Z5817.2
016.37133	Z5814.V8
016.371330942	Z5815.G5
016.371335	Z5814.V8
016.37133523	LB1044.Z9
	Z5814.M8
016.3713358	Z5814.T45
016.3713944	LB1028.7
016.37139445	Z5814.A85
016.3714	Z5814.P8
	Z5814.V8
016.37148	Z5814.P8
016.37162	L13
016.37167	Z5814.A85
016.371716	Z881.U4
016.37194	Z5814.C52
016.37196	Z5811
	Z5814.C52
016.37197	Z5815.R5
016.37198	Z1361.S7
016.3721	Z5814.M26
016.37213209798	Z5817
016.37214	Z5814.P8
016.37237	Z6673
016.3725	Z7911
016.37283	Z7161
016.37313209798	Z5817
016.373246	Z5814.T4
016.374	L136
	Z5814.A24
016.37401	Z5814.A24
016.3744	Z5814.C82
016.374943	Z5815.G3
016.374975	Z7165.U5
016.375	Z5814.C9
016.3755	Z7405.A6
016.378	Z5814.U7
016.378005	Z5813
016.3780091724	Z5814.U7
016.37810570973	Z5814.U7
016.37812	Z5814.T3
016.378196	Z5943.U5
016.37819810973	Z5814.U7
016.3782420976365	Z5055.U5
016.3783	Z5814.S35
016.378713	Z5814.U7
016.37875437	Z5055.U5
016.37877595	Z5055.U5
016.3801456640094	Z7164.F7
016.3805	Z5704
	Z5942
	Z7164.T8
016.3805097	Z7164.T8
016.38050973	Z7164.T8
016.38052	Z5853.T7
016.381410973	HD1751
016.38141750973	Z5074.E3
016.382	Z7164.C8
016.3820954	Z7164.C8
016.38209549	Z7165.P3
016.3824	Z7164.C81
016.38245660007	HD9656.A1
016.3826	Z7164.C8
016.385	Z7231
016.3850942	Z7236.Z9
016.387702573	Z5065.U5
016.387742	Z5064.A27
016.388109755	Z7295
016.38831	Z7164.T81
016.388833	Z5170
016.389152	QC100
	Z7144.W4
016.390	Z5115
016.391	Z5691
016.39100967	Z5694.A4
016.3944	Z1249.P7
016.398096	Z3785
016.3980971	E78.C2
016.3985	Z2014.C4
016.4	Z7001
016.403	Z7405.D5
016.407	Z5814.L26
016.4094	Z7006
016.41	Z7001
016.418	Z7006
016.423	PE1689
016.42824	Z5814.E59
016.4284	Z5814.R25
016.428408	Z5814.R25
016.42843	Z5814.R25
016.43	Z883
016.443	Z2175.D6
016.4791	Z7031
016.4951	Z699.5.C53
	Z7059
016.496	Z7106
016.4963	Z965
016.5	Q181
	Q223
	Z7401
	Z7402
	Z7405.H6
	Z7407.P7
	Z7409
016.5009	Z7408.U6C34
016.5025	Z7405.D55
016.503	Z7401
016.505	QC100
	Z7403
	Z7409
	Z7913
016.507	Z7405.A6
016.5072	Q223
016.509024	Z7405.H6
016.50954	Q11
	Z1009
	Z7407.C5
	Z7407.I4
016.50999	Z6005.P7
016.51	Z6651
	Z6654.N8
016.51286	Z6654.F5
016.513	Z6654.A7

Dewey	LC
016.5138	Z6654.G4
016.517382	Z6654.D45
016.52	Z5151
	Z8463
016.5238903	Z5151.5
016.5268	Z6027.A5
016.5269	Z5853.S89
016.526907	Z5853.S89
016.5300212	QC100
016.53009	QC7
016.5300973	Z7143.5
016.5325	TJ898
016.533293	Z5064.S5
016.536401	QC100
016.5375344	Z5838.L3
016.5375352	Z5834.R7
016.537622	QC100
016.538	TA1
016.539	QC100
	Z5160
016.53914	QC100
016.5397	QC792
	Z5160
	Z7144.I8
016.53970222	QC792
016.53973	Z663.23
016.53975	Z5524.R5
016.53976	QC770
016.53977	Z7144.R2
016.54	QD8.5
	Z5521
016.540924	Z8219.7
016.54137	Z5524.E43
016.54138	QC100
016.54492	Z5524.C55
016.54532	Z5524.E36
016.545822	QC100
016.5464	Z6679.R3
016.546751	TN295
016.546755	Z5524.X4
016.54734	Z5524.E43
016.547411	QC100
016.54968	Z6033.F4
016.55	QE75
	Z6034.U49
016.550	QE1
016.551	QC801.3
016.551.576	Z6683.C6
016.5510222	QE75
016.551345	GB1615
016.55146	Z6004.P6
016.551465	Z6004.P6
016.55148	Z6004.H9
016.5514909747	GB1025.N7
016.5515	QC851
	Z6681
	Z6684.N4
016.551522	QC100
016.551576	Q180.A1
016.55516	Z6683.C5
016.55160963	Z6683.C5
016.55160971	QC985
016.55160973	Z6685
016.551609771	Z6683.C5
016.55169437	Z6683.C5
016.55169599	Z6683.C5
016.551696771	Z6683.C5
016.55309792	Z6034.U5
016.5534109685	Z6738.G7
016.5537909781	QE113
016.55485	QE282
016.55714	Z6034.C19
016.55755	HD9506.U63
016.55773	QE105
016.55777	Z6034.U5
016.5598	Z6005.P7
016.56	Z6033.P2
016.561	QE75
016.5643	QE75
016.5648097	Z6033.P2
016.5699	Z5118.A6
016.5730947	Z5115
016.574	QH303
	Z8430.5
016.574028	Z5524.C38
016.57405	Z6945.A2
016.5741915	Z5322.I8
016.574192	Z5321
016.5745	Z5322.E2
016.5745091692	Z5322.E2
016.57492	Z5322.M3
016.57495981	Z7408.S8
016.57605	Z5180
016.57664	Z5321
016.58	Z5351.A1
016.5805	Z5353
016.581	Z881.U4
	Z5358.A4
	Z5360
016.58146	QE993
016.581959	Z5358.A82
016.58332	Z5356.M4
016.58355	Z881.U4
016.58398	SD433
016.5849	QK495.G74
016.5852	SD11
016.5892	Z5356.F97
016.5893	Z5356.A6
016.58995	Z5185.R5
016.59	Z6676
016.59109771	Z7998.U5
016.59112	Z6663.R46
016.5913	Z7994.A5
016.5915	Z7991
016.595122	SH1
016.5957	QL461
016.596	Z8420.17
	Z8704.14
016.59755	SH11
016.59810972	QL31.D83
016.5982994	SK577
016.5997357	Z7996.M3
	Z7997.E5
016.599745	SK361
016.6	T65.5.M6
	Z7164.E2
	Z7911
016.61	R100
	R835
	Z6658
	Z6660
	Z6664.A1
	Z6676
016.61018	Z6675.E2
	Z6675.E4
016.6105	Z6676
	Z7403
016.6106	Z6658
016.610690973	Z6675.N7
016.61073	RT73
	Z6675.N7
016.6109549	Z6661.P3
016.61201	Z5322.P4
016.6120144	Z663.23
	Z6664.4
016.612015	R793
016.61281	Z5524.E5
016.61288	Z6663.N5
016.613	RA440.5
	RA790
016.6130222	RA440.5
016.61307	Z5814.H9
016.61337	Z6121
016.61383	HV5808.5
	Z7164.N17
016.613830973	Z7164.N17
016.613943	Z7164.B5
016.614	RA440.5
	Z6675.G7
016.6140222	RA440.5
016.61408	Z6673
016.61409789	Z6673
016.61458	Z6664.N5
016.6148	HV677.C22O57
016.61483	Z7144.R17
016.6148505	Z7164.A17
016.614862	Z7164.T81
016.615	Z6665.P3
016.6151	Z6665
	Z6675.P5
016.615323962	Z7164.N17
016.6157883	RM315
016.615837	ML128.M77
016.615851	Z6664.N5
016.615925663	Z7891.M4
016.616855	Z6675.S55
016.616858842	Z6664.N5
016.61689	RA790
	Z6664.N5
016.6168915	Z6664.N5
016.6169	Z663.23
016.61692	Z663.23
016.616963	Z6664.S33
016.616992	Z6664.C2
016.61699200724	RC267
016.616994	Z6664.C2
	Z6673
016.6171028	Z6667.W6
016.61711	Z6667.W6
016.6173	Z6667.O8
016.617481	Z6666
	Z6667.N4
016.6176	Z6668
016.617601	Z6668
016.6177	Z6669
016.6177005	Z6669
	Z7144.O6
016.61789	Z6663.H4
016.61795	Z6667.T7
016.61796	RD82
016.61833	Z6672.J9
016.62	TL521.312
016.6201123	Z5853.E38
	Z5853.M38
016.6201124	Z5853.S85
016.6201127	Z7914.U4
016.62016	Z663.23
016.620176	Z6333.B7
016.620197	Z7914.C3
016.6204	Z5160
016.6208	QC100
016.621130947	Z7235.G7
016.6213	Z5832
016.6213193	Z5834.C6
016.62138	QE33
016.62138152	QC100
016.62148	Z5160
016.62148335	QC770
016.621902	Z5853.M2
016.6228	Z6738.S3
016.6238	V393
016.6238728	AS36
016.62405	TH4
016.62415	Z5853.S6
016.6241513	Z5853.S6
016.625143	Z1009
016.6257	Z7295
016.6258	Z6738.A48
016.6270973	Z7935
016.62754	Z881.U4
016.628167	TC7
016.628168	TC424.T4
	Z5853.S22
	Z6004.P6
016.62816809146	Z5853.P7
016.62836	Z5074.I7
016.628445	Z5853.S22
016.6285	Z5354.P57
	Z5853.S22
	Z6673
016.6285028	QC100
016.62850973	Z5853.P7
016.62851	Z5853.P7
016.628542	Z6673
016.629	Z5064.S3
016.6291	Z5060
016.629132304	Z5064.N6
016.6291366	Z5064.T7
016.629222	Z5170
016.6292222	Z5170
016.6293232	Z6683.T8
016.6294	KF27.S3
016.63	Z1035
	Z5071
016.6302	S531.5
016.630715	Z5074.E8
016.630951	Z881.U4
016.6309549	Z5075.P3
016.630973	Z5071
	Z5075.U5
016.63295	Z5321
016.6329509759	Z5074.P397
016.632951	Z881.U4
016.633895	Z6297
016.6345	S21
016.63475	Z5996.S8
016.6349	Z5991
	Z5991.U566
016.634909711	Z5991
016.63490974	SD11
016.6349285	SD11
016.63496180973	Z5991
016.63498	Z5991
016.635	SB445
	Z5996
016.6364	Z1009
016.6367089393	Z7997.D7
016.6392	SH223
	SH317
	SK361
	Z5971
016.63920947	Z5974.R9
016.6393	Z1009
016.639543	Z1009
016.64071	Z5814.T4
016.64072054	Z5775
016.64073	Z7164.C81
016.6411	Z5776.N8
016.6413	Z5776.F7
016.6415	Z5777
016.64159763	Z5776.G2
016.65	HD31
	Z7164.C81
016.6518	QA76
	Z1035
	Z6654.C17
016.6552	Z2027.P3
016.65528	Z253.3
016.6553120944	Z117
016.65570924	Z8592.72
016.65576	Z733
016.657	Z7164.C81
016.658	HD20.15.P3
	Z7164.C81
	Z7164.O7
016.658022	Z7164.C8
	Z7164.C81
016.6581	U15
016.6581145	KF6495.L4
016.658155	Z7914.I55
016.6583	Z7164.C81
016.6583124	Z5814.T4
016.6584	Z7164.C81
	Z7963.E7
016.6585	Z7164.O7
016.658501	Z7914.M27
016.658502	Z791.A2
	Z1009
	Z7164.O7
016.6588	Z7164.M18
016.65880005	HF5415
016.65880009797	HF3161.W2
016.658809637	Z5706.A1
016.65883	Z7164
	Z7164.C81
016.65883973	HF5415.1
016.65887	Z7164.C8
	Z7164.C81
016.65887007	Z7164.C81
016.6588700942	HF5429.6.G7
016.6588700973	Z7164.C81
016.658873	Z7164.C81
016.658875	Z7164.C81
016.658878	Z1009
016.6589130154	Z7164.O4
016.6589133333	HD268.S4
	Z7164.L3
016.66142	Z5524.N55
016.66274	Z5991
016.66632	Z7951
016.664	Z5776.F7
016.66407	Z6663.S57
016.66412	Z7609
016.66475	Z5776.B15
016.66493	Z5074.P8
016.66494	Z5973.F5
016.666	TA1
016.6676	Z7914.P15
016.669142	Z6331
016.66973	Z5063.A2
016.66995	QC100
016.6712	Z7914.F7
016.67156	Z7914.B5
016.671733	Z6679.C7
016.672	Z6331
016.674134	Z7914.W8
016.674808	Z5991
016.67484	Z5991
016.67612	Z7914.W8
016.6762	Z7914.P2
016.67623	Z7914.P2
016.68	Z7914.A6
016.685	Z7914.L27
016.69	TH165
	Z7144.W4
	Z7164.H8
	Z7914.B9
016.690018	Z7914.B9
016.6900222	TH151
016.6900973	Z7164.H8
016.698124	Z7164.C81
016.7	N7225
	Z674
	Z2014.D7
016.700	Z5931
016.700947	Z2501
016.707	Z5814.A8
016.709	Z8174
	Z8735.4
016.709174924	Z5956.J4
016.70951	Z5961.C5
016.70971	Z1401
016.7114	Z5942
016.71140973	Z7164.O7
016.71157	Z5814.U7
016.711590973	Z7164.U7
016.712	Z881.U4
016.72	Z1035
	Z5941
016.720924	NA737.R5
	Z5942
	Z8986.3
016.7211	QC100
016.7275	Z7405.L3
016.7309669	Z5954.N5
016.7374954	Z6869.I5
016.73837	Z8961.8.H4
016.7410922	NC993
016.74164	Z1023
016.7416420922	NC965
016.741942	Z8730.33
016.741973	NC139.P8
016.744.424	NA2605
016.7455	Z1035
016.74550973	Z1209
016.7464	Z1009
016.74643	Z5956.L2
016.757	N7620
016.75913	E51
016.7695	Z5956.P6
016.76956	HE6224
016.769922	NE1112.B48
016.769924	Z8414.935
016.769973	NE2303
016.77	Z7144.H6
016.7781	Z7136.P5
016.778352	Z6028
016.78	ML113
	ML118
	ML128.J3
	ML128.M8
	ML128.S25
	ML136
	ML136.N52
	ML136.U5
016.7805	ML128.P24
	ML128.P24L6
016.7808	ML128.M8
016.780924	ML141.L6B5
016.78157	ML128.J3
016.781716	ML120.A35
016.78172924	ML128.J4
016.78172960973	ML120.N49
016.781751	ML120.C5
016.7835	ML102.C45
016.785	ML128.O5
016.78542	ML128.J3
016.7863	ML132.P3
016.78761	ML128.G8
016.78805543	ML128.C4
016.789912	ML111.5
	ML156.4.M6
016.7902	Z6935
016.791.438	Z5784.M9
016.79143	PN1998
	Z5784.M9
016.7914302320924	PN1998.A3
016.792	Z5781
016.792098	Z1609.D7
016.7933196	ML120.A35
016.79374	Z6654.M3
016.796	Z7511
	Z7514.O8
	Z7516
016.796352	Z7514.G6

016.796358 ... Z1009
016.796420942 ... Z7514.T8
016.7971 ... Z7514.B6
016.7972 ... Z7631
016.80802 ... Z6514.S8
016.808383 ... Z7164.Y8
016.8088 ... ML156.2
... Z999
... Z2014.T7
016.808803 ... Z6514.C5O44
016.8088193 ... Z2014.P7
016.80882 ... Z5781
016.8088293 ... Z6520.C5
016.8088381 ... Z5917.H6
016.80883872 ... Z5917.D5
016.809 ... Z6514.C7
... Z6514.C97
... Z8405
016.8092 ... Z5781
016.809933 ... Z5865
016.81 ... Z1225
... Z1231.F5
... Z7118
016.810 ... Z1225
016.8108032 ... Z1261
016.81080917496 ... Z1361.N39
016.8109 ... Z1225
016.8109003 ... PS201
016.8113 ... Z8699
016.8114 ... Z8230.5
016.81140803 ... PS261
016.81152 ... Z1231.P7
... Z8035.6
... Z8198.1
... Z8574.87
... Z8709.3
... Z8842.7
... Z8998.8
016.81154 ... Z8130.4
016.812 ... Z1231.D7
016.812008 ... Z5784.N4
016.8121 ... Z1231.D7
016.8123 ... Z1231.D7
016.81252 ... Z6616.A6
016.813 ... Z1231.F4
016.813.52 ... Z8504.38
016.81308 ... Z1231.F4
016.8132 ... Z1231.F4
... Z8191.7
016.8133 ... PS2386
... Z8393
... Z8562.58
016.8134 ... Z8024.8
... Z8388.65
... Z8633
016.81352 ... PS3523.E94
... PS3537.T3533
... Z8165.2
... Z8241.7
... Z8288
... Z8301.2
... Z8324.15
... Z8385
... Z8396.3
... Z8705.7
... Z8980.45
016.8135209 ... Z1231.F4
... Z8405
016.81354 ... Z1361.N39
... Z8532.383
... Z8544.57
... Z8913.85
016.8143 ... PS1642.B6
... Z8265
016.8174 ... Z8176
016.81752 ... Z8878.4
016.818.5208 ... Z8395.52
016.818.5209 ... Z8977.5
016.818108 ... Z8313
016.818208 ... Z8315
016.818209 ... Z8439.7
016.818308 ... Z8873
016.818309 ... PS2635.V3
016.818409 ... Z8198.2
016.8185209 ... Z8563.5
... Z8976.44
016.82 ... Z2010
... Z2011
... Z2012
... Z2013
... Z4021
016.820 ... Z1009
... Z2011
016.820.99174924 ... PR151.J5
016.8208 ... Z2012
016.8208005 ... Z2013
016.8208096 ... Z3508.L5
016.8209 ... Z2014.C5
016.8209007 ... Z2013
016.820900914 ... Z2057
016.82093 ... Z7164.R12
016.821 ... Z8301.4
... Z8834.15
... Z8992
016.821.912 ... Z8260.5
016.8214 ... Z8578
016.821408 ... Z2014.P7
016.8215 ... Z8704
016.8216 ... Z8368.9
016.8217 ... PR4453.C6
016.8218 ... Z8044.5
... Z8415.6
... Z8866
016.821912 ... Z921

016.821912 ... Z8005.5
... Z8260.5
... Z8784.5
... Z8870.5
016.82191208 ... Z8870.5
016.822 ... Z2014.D7
... Z2039.D7
... Z5784.J6
016.822.33 ... Z8811
016.8223 ... Z2012
... Z2014.D7
016.822308 ... Z2014.D7
016.82233 ... Z8811
016.8224 ... Z2014.D7
016.822509 ... Z2014.D7
016.823 ... Z2039.F4
... Z8355.9
... Z8547.6
... Z8592.6
... Z8665.2
... Z8757.25
016.82303 ... Z2014.F4
... Z2014.F5
016.8230872 ... Z5917.D5
016.8230876 ... Z5917.S36
016.8236 ... Z2014.F4
... Z8822.5
016.8237 ... Z8802
016.8238 ... PR4585
... Z921
... Z2014.F4
... Z8230
... Z8314.42
... Z8386.5
016.823809 ... Z2013
... Z8122
016.823912 ... PR6005.R517
... Z8189.7
... Z8368.987
... Z8533.75
... Z8555.3
... Z8647
... Z8883.45
... Z8947.46
... Z8979.5
016.823914 ... Z8025.45
... Z8976.485
016.824709 ... Z8393.4
016.8248 ... Z8147
016.8268 ... Z8386.5
016.8275 ... Z8856
016.828 ... Z8602.9
016.828.809 ... Z8234.8
016.828309 ... Z8368.988
016.828709 ... Z8802
016.828808 ... PR4433
... Z8137.8
016.828809 ... Z8226
... Z8234
... Z8234.8
... Z8465
... Z8595
016.82891208 ... Z8089.34
016.82891209 ... Z8166.5
016.82891409 ... Z8503.8
016.829 ... Z2012
016.8293 ... Z2012
... Z2012.A1
016.83 ... Z7036
016.832 ... Z2234.D7
016.833.912 ... Z8884.96
016.833912 ... Z1033.B3
016.84009 ... Z7033.T7E56
016.8408015 ... Z5939
016.848809 ... Z8079.3
... Z8756.9
016.84891209 ... Z8924
016.84891409 ... Z8086.37
016.85 ... Z2354.T7
016.8514 ... Z2354.P7
016.86 ... PQ6014
... Z1609.L7
... Z1621
016.8608 ... Z1609.T7
016.8609 ... Z1609.L7
016.861 ... Z8713.55
016.8633 ... Z8158
016.86905 ... Z1685
016.88 ... Z1011
... Z7018.T7E87
... Z7018.T7S73
016.880 ... Z7016
016.88401 ... Z8692.3
016.8912 ... Z6621.G3
016.8916 ... Z2037
016.8917 ... Z2501.A1
016.891730876 ... Z2504.F5
016.892426 ... Z7070
016.8924908 ... Z7070
016.894511 ... Z2148.L5
016.895 ... Z8947.4
016.89573 ... Z3319.L5
016.9 ... Z6201
... Z6205
016.9019 ... Z5579
... Z6201
... Z7401
016.907 ... Z6208.M5
016.9090971242 ... Z2021.C7
016.90982 ... Z6461
016.91 ... Z1236
... Z6001
... Z6009
016.910 ... Z6011

016.9100018 ... G77.5
016.91003174927 ... Z3013
016.91009171242 ... Z2021.C7
... Z6621
016.9104 ... Z921
... Z6011
016.9107 ... Z5814.G34
016.910924 ... Z8191
016.911 ... Z6022
... Z6022.R5
016.912 ... GA193.U5
... GA317
... Z6003
... Z6028
016.9121551609597 ... Z6683.C5
016.912196652 ... Z6027.N54
016.91242 ... Z6003
016.9124212 ... Z6003
016.9124258 ... Z6003
... Z6027.H4
016.91252 ... Z6003
016.912597 ... Z6027.V5
016.9126 ... Z6027.A2
016.912678 ... Z6027.T3
016.91271 ... Z6027.C21
016.912713 ... Z6027.O5
016.912716 ... Z6027.N85
016.9127292 ... Z6003
016.91272981 ... Z6003
016.912748 ... Z6027.P4
016.91277434 ... Z6027.D45
016.91294 ... Z6003
... Z6027.A89
016.912944 ... Z6003
016.9130305 ... Z6202
016.913031 ... Z5131
016.91336 ... Z2027.A8
016.9133803 ... Z5579
016.914 ... Z2000
016.9140025 ... Z5771
016.914031 ... Z6203
016.9140321 ... Z6207.R4
016.9140974918 ... Z7041
016.91415 ... Z2041
... Z5055.I73
016.9141503 ... Z1035
016.9142 ... Z2016
... Z2023
016.914203 ... CD1069.5
... Z2016
... Z2021.C7
... Z2027.A8
016.9142038 ... Z2019
016.91420381 ... Z2019
016.914225 ... CD1069.A7
016.914227 ... Z2024.S65
016.914238 ... Z2024.B25
016.9142720025 ... Z5771.4.G7
016.91427203 ... Z2023
016.914274 ... Z2024.Y6
016.91427403 ... CD1065.Y6
016.914281 ... Z2024.G37
016.9143 ... Z2483
016.91437 ... Z2136
016.9143863 ... Z2526
016.9144949 ... Z2191
016.914503 ... Z2356
016.9146 ... Z2681
016.9147 ... Z2491
... Z2506
016.9147007 ... DK18
016.914703 ... Z2491.5
016.914704 ... Z2491
016.914771 ... Z2514.U5
016.91478 ... Z3409
016.91495 ... Z2309
016.9149503 ... Z2281
016.91496 ... Z2831
016.914977 ... Z2896
016.91498 ... Z2921
016.915 ... DS2
... Z1009
... Z3001
016.9151003 ... Z3109
016.915103 ... Z3001
... Z3106
016.91519034 ... Z3316
016.9152 ... Z955.T6413
016.915281 ... Z3307.R9
016.915293 ... Z3306
016.9153 ... Z3026
016.915303 ... Z6605.S85
016.91536 ... Z3453.P33
016.9154 ... Z1009
... Z3185
... Z3208.A4
... Z3221
016.9154503 ... Z3207.P3
016.915455 ... Z3197.P8
016.91549 ... Z1035
016.91549033 ... Z3191
016.91549603 ... Z3207.N4
016.915497 ... Z3207.S53
016.9155 ... Z3366
... Z3453.K8
016.915503 ... Z3366
016.9156033 ... Z3013
016.9156103 ... Z2831
016.915694 ... Z3476
016.9159 ... Z3221
016.915903 ... Z1009
... Z3221
... Z3316
016.91595 ... Z3246

016.915951 ... Z6605.M28
016.91597 ... Z3228.M43
... Z3228.V5
016.916 ... Z3501
... Z3509
016.916005 ... Z3503
016.91603 ... E184.7.Z9
016.916033 ... DT4
... Z3501
016.9161 ... Z3501
016.916303 ... Z3524.H5
016.916625035 ... Z3507
016.91667 ... Z3785
016.9166703 ... Z3785
016.91669 ... Z3553.N5
016.91669008 ... Z965
016.91669031 ... Z3553.N5
016.9167 ... Z3501
... Z3509
... Z7165.A42
016.916703 ... Z3503
016.91676 ... Z3516
016.916803 ... Z3501
... Z3609
016.91681 ... Z7165.A42
016.9168303 ... Z3607.S9
016.91687 ... Z3563.P6
016.91687034 ... CD2457.C3
016.916906957 ... Z4708.K6
016.917 ... Z1201
... Z1207
... Z6016.T74
016.917.3097496 ... Z1361.N39
016.9171 ... Z1365
016.917103 ... Z997
016.91711 ... Z1392.B73
016.9171503 ... CD3645.N4
016.9172 ... Z1595
016.91729 ... Z1501
016.9172981 ... Z1561.B3
016.9173 ... Z1361.C6
016.917303 ... Z1035.9
... Z1236
... Z1361.S7
016.9173032 ... Z1249.F9
016.9173036 ... Z1236
016.91730696 ... Z1361.N39
... Z6611.N4
016.91730696073 ... Z1361.N39
016.917309746 ... Z1361.M4
016.91730974893 ... Z1361.G7
016.91730974924 ... Z6366
016.9173097496 ... Z1361.N39
016.917309749992 ... Z1361.B3
016.9174 ... Z1237
016.9174103 ... F16.5
016.9174497 ... Z1296.N3
016.91748 ... Z1329
016.917503 ... Z6621.N8
016.9175044 ... Z1251.S7
016.91756 ... Z1319
016.9175603 ... L184.B2
016.91761 ... F323
016.9176303 ... Z1289
016.91766031 ... Z1325
016.9176803 ... Z1337
016.9176903 ... Z1287
016.917693 ... Z1288.L5
016.91774097496 ... Z1361.N39
016.91775 ... Z1351
016.9178 ... Z1251.W5
016.9178032 ... Z6616.R86
016.91781032 ... Z1285
016.9179103 ... Z1257
016.91794035 ... E175.5.R7
016.9179409154 ... Z1251.S8
016.91794097495 ... Z1261
016.91796 ... Z1275
016.91797097496 ... Z1347
... Z1347.W36
016.91798 ... Z1255
016.918 ... CD1692.A2
... Z1601
... Z1610
016.91803 ... Z1601
016.918033 ... Z1610
016.918043 ... Z1601
016.919 ... Z4001
... Z4501
016.91935 ... Z4980.S33
016.9194 ... Z997
... Z4011
016.91942903 ... Z4161
016.91945 ... Z4394.M4
016.9195 ... Z4811
016.919504 ... DU740
016.91961 ... DU600
... Z4651
016.91965 ... Z4980.W3
016.919681 ... Z4671
016.91969 ... Z4701
016.919699 ... Z4980.J6
016.9199 ... Z7405.E9U63
016.91996 ... Z4501
016.92 ... Z5301
016.920 ... Z5301
016.92003 ... Z5301
016.9291 ... Z5313.U5
... Z5313.U6V8
016.9291097 ... Z5311
016.92910973 ... Z5313.U5
016.92920942 ... CD1069.5.L3
... Z5313.G69
016.9293 ... CD3648.A1

016.9293 CS1
CS482
F187.G2
F525
Z5313.G69
Z5313.G69S6
Z5313.U5
Z5313.U6
016.9293094212 CD1068
016.9296 Z5312
016.93 Z6202
016.938070924 Z8025.65
016.94 Z6204
016.9401 Z6203
016.9405308 U27
016.940540973 Z6725.U5
016.941 D16.2
016.9415 Z2041
016.942 CD1064
DA690.P37
Z2016
Z5055.G6
016.9420072 Z2016
016.94202 Z2017
016.942073 Z2024.M16
016.9420810924 Z8347
016.9420820924 Z6616.H25
Z8169.45
016.94225 CD1069.5.P4
016.94267 DA670.E7
016.94274 Z2024.W26
016.94281 CD1067.G3
016.94285 Z2024.C87
016.94297 Z7165.G8
016.943905 Z2148.A5
016.9439102 Z8442
016.944.03 Z2177.5
016.947 Z2506
016.947084 Z2510
016.947085 Z2510.3
016.95 Z3001
016.951 Z3109
016.951026 Z3106
016.951050924 DS778.M3
016.9519042 Z3319.K6
016.954 CD2081
Z3221
016.954040924 Z8617.3
016.9597 Z1009
016.959704 Z3228.V5
016.963 Z3521
016.9664 Z3553.S5
016.969 Z6620.U6H32
016.97 Z998
016.9701 Z1209
Z1210.M65
016.9703 Z1209
Z1210.C5
016.9704281 Z1208.G8
016.970463 Z1209
016.970494 Z1209
016.9713 Z1392.O6
016.9729 Z1502.B5
016.97291063 Z1525
016.97291064 Z1525
016.973 Z1236
Z6621
016.97308 Z1223
016.973180922 Z8140
016.9732 Z1237
016.9733 Z1238
Z6616.E87
016.973460924 E302
Z8136
016.973510924 E302
016.97356 Z8443
016.97362 Z1241
016.9737 Z1242
016.97370924 Z8505
016.973752 Z733
016.97391 Z1244
016.9739110924 Z6616.R73
Z8757.3
016.9739170924 Z6616.L45
016.9739210924 Z8246.85
016.9739220922 Z5315.K4
016.9756 Z1319
016.9757 Z1333
016.976303 F372
016.9769020924 Z8109
016.9778 Z1303
016.978 Z1251.W5
016.9789 Z1315
016.9794 Z1261
016.981 Z1699
016.991403 Z3298
016.994 Z6621.S98
016.99691 Z4706
016.999 Z6005.P7
017.1 Z881.H832
Z921
Z977
Z1035.1
Z3316
017.1097444 Z7011
017.2 Z999
Z6621.S45G73
017.5 Z881
Z881.N66356
Z881.S785
Z6004.P6
017.50952135 Z955
017.509768 Z881.A12T47
017.6 Z6623.B37
017.7 Z4039
018 Z1225
Z6004.P6
Z7817
018.1 DS61.9.L48
Z240
Z881
Z921
Z975
Z1029
Z1215
018.1094125 Z240
018.10976347 CD3269.L31
018.2 Z725.F5
Z732.V8
Z921
Z997
018.2094297 Z792.G27
019.1 Z881
020 Q223
Z665
Z673
Z699
Z721
Z1001
020.18 Z678.9
Z678.9.A1
Z699
020.207 Z682.5
020.23 Z665
Z682
Z845.P5
020.25549 Z720.A46P36
020.28 Z678.9
020.285 Z674
020.6173 KF27.E335
Z673.A1
020.62241 Z673
020.62345456 Z673
020.6234757 Z673.A1
020.6234762 Z673
020.6234793 Z673
020.7 Z665
Z668
Z669.3
Z669.5.C6
Z681.5
020.71 Z668
Z673
020.711 Z668
Z674
020.71173 Z668
020.71177589 Z669.W62
020.72 Z669.7
020.7401471 Z673.5
020.7402 Z717
020.75 Z987
Z989
Z992
Z1000
Z8699
020.7508 Z987
020.750922 Z989.A1
020.76 Z668.3
Z670
020.77 Z670
020.8 Z665
Z674
020.922 Z720.A4
020.924 E185.97.M16
Z720.P2
020.942 Z665
020.9421 Z791.L6
020.944 Z797.A1
020.954 Z845.I4
020.9545 Z845.I5P86
020.971 Z673
020.972 Z739.A1
021 Z673
Z675.U5
Z717
Z721
021.0018 Z678.9
Z678.9.A1
021.00202 Z710
021.00212 Z672
021.002541 Z79.S35
Z791.S35
021.002542 Z791.A1
021.0025425 Z791.A2
021.00254274 Z791.A2Y63
021.00255487 AS468
021.0025549 Z845.P28
021.0025676 Z857.E3
021.00256891 Z857.R45
021.0025746 Z732.C8
021.0025747 Z732.N7
021.0025774 Z732.M6
021.0028 Z678
021.00285 Z678.9
021.006 Z672
021.009 Z721
021.00941 Z791.S35
021.0094141 Z791.G8
021.00942 Z791
Z791.A1
021.00943 Z801
021.0094436 Z797.P2
021.00947 Z819
021.009485 Z827.A1
021.00954 Z845.I5
021.0095487 Z674
021.00971 Z673
021.00971 Z735
021.009713541 Z735.A2T65
021.00973 Z731
021.009744 Z732.M41
021.0097462 Z732.C82
021.009748 Z732.P42
021.009749 Z732.N6
021.009764 Z732.T25
021.009768 Z732.T2
021.00977 Z732.I2
021.009786 Z732.M9
021.009791 Z732.A68
021.009793 Z732.N38
021.009797 Z732.W2
021.009798 Z732.A3
021.0098 Z738.A1
021.4 Z665
Z682
Z711.92.S6
Z721
021.609797 Z732.W28
021.63 Z732.T25
021.64 AS722.A8
DT1
Z674.5.P5
Z675.P3
Z678.2
Z713.5.U6
Z732.I16
Z732.S72
Z733
Z881.A1
021.6408 Z718
021.6409729 Z753
021.640973 Z678.2
021.64097471 Z732.N7
021.6409773 Z678
021.6409795 Z732.P34
021.6478685 Z732.M92M93
021.70994 Z716.3
021.82 Z681.5
021.820973 Z681.5
021.8309747 Z732.N7
022 CD981
022.3 Z674
Z675.S3
Z679
Z679.5
Z732.N6
022.7 Z680
022.9 Z684
023 Z682
023.5 Z675.S3
Z733.M6232
023.7 Z675.S3
Z675.U5
024.6 Z678.8.C3
024.60971 Z713.5.C3
024.60973 Z674
Z713
024.609747 Z713.5.U6
024.60977434 Z713.5.U6
024.609931 Z713.5.N4
025 Z675.A2
Z823
025.02 Z674
Z675.U5
Z732.F6
Z732.N7
025.02018 Z699
025.020975662 Z675.S3
025.1 Z673
Z675.U5
Z678
Z678.3
Z681.5
Z682
Z732.I2
Z733.M621
025.1015199 Z699
025.10186 Z678
025.11 Z703.5
025.129 Z681
025.17 Z688.N6
025.170186 Z675.S3
025.171 CD950
025.171094281 CD1065.D8
025.172 Z691
025.173 Z692.S5
Z1223.Z7
025.176 Z692.M3
025.177 Z717
025.1770973 Z675.S3
025.178 ML111
ML111.5
025.179 Z265
025.2 Z663.285
Z675.G7
Z689
Z3001
025.2018 Z689
025.21 Z665
Z689
Z711.4
Z718.1
Z1035.A1
025.2108 Z689
025.210951 Z689
025.23 Z689
025.3 Z693
Z695
Z699
025.30202 Z693
Z881.C81
025.307 Z693
025.32 Z672
Z694
Z695
Z695.C693
Z695.1.P4
Z1001
025.3209 Z695
025.33 Z695
Z695.92
025.3300077 Z695
025.330285 Z695.1.C6
025.33331 Z695.1.L12
025.3334 KF209
Z695.1.L3
025.33340091767 Z695.1.L3
025.3337 Z695.1.E3
025.3354 Z695.1.C5
025.336 Z695.1.S3
025.3361 Z695.1.M48
025.336411 Z695.1.N84
025.336655 Z695.1.P43
025.33778315 Z695.62
025.34 Z695.66
025.341 Z695.74
025.343 Z695.7
025.346 Z695.6
025.347 Z695.66
025.35 Z695
025.37 Z736.B72
025.4 Z695
Z695.98
Z696
Z696.D51955
Z696.U4O
Z697.C9
Z697.P545
025.43 Z696
Z696.D6
025.46001553 Z695.66
025.4634 Z697.L4
025.463400973 Z697.L4
025.46341 Z697.I5
025.46352008 Z697.M8
025.46359 Z696
025.4661 Z697.M4
025.4662 Z697.T4
025.466381 Z697.B4
025.4665 Z697.B9
025.4669 Z697.B8
025.467 Z696.U5N
025.4670494 Z697.A8
025.467114 Z697.C53
025.4678 ML111
025.4678094 ML111
025.4691945 Z697.B7
025.5 Z710
Z711.2
025.50973 KF27.E335
025.509749 Z732.N6
025.52 Z711
025.52077 Z711.2
025.6 Z675.M4
Z711.3
Z712
Z713.5.C3
Z714
025.7 Z700
Z701
025.8 Z701
025.81 Z698
025.84 Z701
026 Z675
Z675.A2
026.00025714281 Z735.M82
026.00025788 Z732.C6
026.0002591 Z845.I6
026.00025931 Z870.N47
026.000994 Z870
026.0043155 Z675.A8
026.01451924 Z792.P3
026.34 KF209
026.3805 Z675.T7
026.380502573 Z675.T7
026.6 Z675.T3
026.60942 Z675.T3
026.61 KF26.L354
Z675.H7
Z675.M4
026.6102542 Z675.M4
026.6102573 Z675.M4
026.61073 Z675.N8
026.610973 Z675.M4
026.69 Z699.5.B8
026.7 Z675.A85
026.7914309747 Z717
026.82233 Z792.B61
026.912 GA193.C3
026.91202573 GA193.U5
026.914703 Z2483
026.915002542 Z3001
026.9150302542 Z3001
026.973 CD3023
027 Z791
Z875
027.0025595 Z845.M3
027.009 Z721
Z723
027.04254 Z791.L4
027.073 Z675.R45
027.0969 Z875.A1
027.1075 Z992
027.14183 Z6623.B37
027.179493 Z733.S25

027.2421 ..... Z792.M84
027.24274 ..... Z792
027.34237 ..... Z792.P42
027.4 ..... Z671
..... Z673
..... Z673.A1
..... Z678
..... Z686
..... Z716.2
..... Z716.4
..... Z721
..... Z735.A1
..... Z791.A1
027.40182 ..... Z674
027.408 ..... Z665
..... Z671
027.409 ..... Z721
027.40924 ..... Z720.B89
027.40941 ..... Z791.S35
027.409756 ..... Z732.N8
027.409775 ..... Z732.W8
027.442 ..... Z673
..... Z675.C8
..... Z791
027.44252 ..... Z792.N923
027.44267 ..... Z792.C42
027.4549183 ..... Z845.K3
027.45492 ..... Z845.E3
027.468 ..... Z857
027.4687 ..... Z858.S69
027.4711 ..... Z720.M69
027.473 ..... Z731
027.47331 ..... Z733.S662
027.474423 ..... Z733.A55
027.4746 ..... Z732.C8
027.4747 ..... Z732.N7
027.474723 ..... Z671
027.474731 ..... Z733.T96
027.474771 ..... Z733.C82
027.474921 ..... Z733.T243
027.475271 ..... Z733.B142
027.477311 ..... Z733.C5255
..... Z733.C531
027.4774 ..... Z732.M6
027.4781 ..... Z732.K2
027.478229 ..... Z686
027.478868 ..... Z733.F677
027.479452 ..... Z732.C3S65
027.479488 ..... Z733.B126
027.479493 ..... Z732.D3
027.479625 ..... Z733.W495
027.479686 ..... Z732.I16
027.479755 ..... Z733.S46
027.494 ..... Z870
027.4944 ..... Z871.N54
027.4945 ..... Z871.E82
027.5 ..... Z675.G7
..... Z675.I6
027.50942 ..... Z791
027.50973 ..... Z675.G7
027.509749 ..... Z675.I6
027.509771 ..... Z675.I6
027.50994 ..... Z870
027.542 ..... Z792.B86
..... Z792.B863
027.5429 ..... Z792
027.54321 ..... Z802.L44913
027.54391 ..... Z794.B943
027.54551 ..... Z810.F64
027.54891 ..... Z824.C78
027.573 ..... Z733
027.57444 ..... KF27.G623
027.574743 ..... Z733.N645
027.5753 ..... Z733.U63
027.5759 ..... Z732.F6
027.5772 ..... Z733
027.579537 ..... Z733
027.5947 ..... Z871
027.6 ..... Z711.92.P5
..... Z711.92.S6
027.625 ..... Z711.92.S6
..... Z718.1
027.62509747 ..... Z718.1
027.626 ..... Z718.5
027.63 ..... Z711.92.S6
027.65 ..... Z675.M5
027.6609759 ..... Z675.I6
027.662 ..... Z675.H7
027.6620941 ..... Z675.H7
027.6620971331 ..... Z675.H7
027.6630973 ..... HV1731
027.67 ..... CD1581
..... Z675.C5
..... Z791
027.67094223 ..... Z725.S23
027.67094244 ..... Z792.H497
027.6709794 ..... Z732.C2
027.68 ..... Z675.F7
..... Z729
..... Z733.U45
027.69 ..... HD70.G7
..... Z675.F3
027.7 ..... Z674
..... Z675.P3
..... Z675.U5
..... Z679.9
027.70285 ..... Z678.9
027.70942 ..... Z675.U5
027.70973 ..... Z675.R45
..... Z675.U5
027.709756 ..... LA340.5
027.74183 ..... Z792
027.742 ..... Z675.P3
027.74257 ..... Z792.O938
027.74259 ..... Z792
027.7444 ..... Z733
027.773 ..... Z674
027.77471 ..... Z733.N7598
027.77554252 ..... Z733.W686
027.775655 ..... Z733.R147A5
027.77643 ..... Z733.L986
027.776992 ..... Z733.M93
027.777152 ..... Z733.K379
027.777157 ..... Z733
027.777435 ..... Z733
027.777589 ..... Z733.H26
027.7781 ..... Z675.U5
027.779173 ..... Z733
027.779467 ..... Z674
027.779534 ..... Z733.O6557
027.779686 ..... Z733
027.8 ..... Z675.S3
027.80202 ..... Z675.S3
027.80971 ..... Z675.S3
027.809711 ..... Z675.S3
027.809749 ..... Z675.S3
027.809756 ..... Z675.S3
027.809771 ..... Z675.S3
027.809777 ..... LB3044
027.809786 ..... Z675.S3
027.809796 ..... Z675.S3
027.809969 ..... Z675.S3
027.82208 ..... LB3044
027.8222 ..... Z675.S3
027.82220973 ..... Z675.S3
027.8223 ..... Z668
..... Z675.S3
027.824216 ..... Z675.S3
027.827426 ..... Z733.E995
027.82794 ..... Z675.S3
027.8294 ..... Z675.S3
028 ..... LB1632
..... Z710
..... Z1003
..... Z1035.9
..... Z1039
..... Z1039.H7
028.074 ..... Z716.3
..... Z717
028.1 ..... Z1035.A1
..... Z1037.A1
028.10973 ..... Z1035.A1
028.5 ..... PN1009.A1
..... PN1009.R8
..... PN1009.Z6
..... PS3545.E6
..... Z473.R8
..... Z688.C47
..... Z718.1
..... Z992
..... Z1037
028.508 ..... PN1009.A1
..... Z1037
028.509 ..... PN1009.A1
..... Z987
028.50922 ..... PN452
028.50942 ..... LB518
..... Z718.1
028.50973 ..... PN1009.A1
028.50994 ..... PN1009.A1
028.52 ..... L184
..... PN452
..... PN1009.A1
..... Z037
..... Z718.1
..... Z720
..... Z1003
..... Z1035
..... Z1037
..... Z1037.A1
..... Z1037.1
..... Z1037.9
..... Z1039.S5
..... Z1277
..... Z1361.N39
028.520922 ..... PN452
028.520942 ..... Z921
028.7 ..... AS5
..... HD9710.U52
..... HF5353
..... Z675.M93
..... Z675.S3
..... Z699
..... Z710
..... Z718.1
..... Z732.M38
..... Z732.M6
..... Z1037.1
..... Z7164.E15
028.702454 ..... QD8.5
028.708 ..... Z1003
028.7091732 ..... Z716.2
028.709794 ..... Z1003.3.C3
028.8 ..... Z1003
028.9 ..... PN5510
..... Z284
..... Z1003
028.90942 ..... Z1003.5.G7
..... Z1035.4
029 ..... AS36
..... HF1041
..... KF242.A1
..... P309
..... QD9
..... T10.63
..... T10.65.S6
..... Z699.5.B8
..... Z699.5.M25
029 ..... Z5167
029.5 ..... QC100
..... Z695.9
..... Z695.92
029.7 ..... AS36
..... H62
..... KF27.S383
..... Q223
..... QA76
..... R835
..... RA790.6
..... T10.63
..... T20
..... T174.3
..... T174.5
..... TL521.3
..... Z678.9
..... Z693
..... Z695
..... Z695.9
..... Z699
..... Z699.A1
..... Z699.3
..... Z699.4.M2
..... Z699.5.A4
..... Z699.5.C5
..... Z699.5.E6
..... Z699.5.I5
..... Z699.5.M35
..... Z699.5.M39
..... Z699.5.P5
..... Z699.5.S3
..... Z699.5.S65
..... Z1001
029.70245 ..... T10.65.E8
029.703 ..... Z1006
029.954 ..... Z699.5.C5
029.961 ..... Q180.A1
..... Z699.5.M39
029.96157042 ..... RS53
030 ..... AE5
030.924 ..... E748.B337
031 ..... AE5
..... AE6
..... AG5
..... AG105
..... AG195
031.02 ..... AG5
..... AG6
..... AG105
..... AG106
..... AG195
..... AG600
032 ..... AE5
..... AG5
032.02 ..... AG105
050 ..... PN4720.L4
..... Z6944.C5
..... Z6945.A2
050.148 ..... Z6945.A2
051 ..... AP2
..... AY31.A1
..... E169.1
..... F46
..... HF6122.L5
..... JK1
..... PN4877
..... PN4899.P48
..... PN4900.M28
..... PN4900.U5
051.09 ..... PN4832
052 ..... AP4
..... PN5124.W6
..... PN5130.Y4
..... Z6958.I4
060 ..... AS4.U8
..... AS4.U82
..... AS4.U83
..... AS6
..... E184.B67
..... HD2421
..... HD2425
..... HV97
..... JC362
..... JX1950
..... KF31.F6
060.254 ..... AS911.A2
061.3 ..... HS17
..... HV97.A3
061.55 ..... AS911
061.73 ..... AS404
061.764 ..... BX6346.5
061.94 ..... HD2428.C3
063 ..... AS182.M53
068.4 ..... JN94
068.51 ..... AS452.C49
069 ..... AM1
..... AM5
..... AM7
..... AM9
..... F906
..... Z5940
069.018 ..... AM133
069.0256 ..... AM80.A2
069.02568 ..... AM80.S6
069.02571 ..... AM21.A2
069.0924 ..... CT788.B752
069.09421 ..... AM101.B87
069.0954 ..... AM73.I5
069.0973 ..... AM11
069.0974743 ..... AM101
069.0974966 ..... AM101.N524.5
069.09787 ..... AM12.W9
069.1 ..... LB3291
069.2 ..... F74.B9
069.20979357 ..... AM101
069.4 ..... CC75
..... CC135
069.5 ..... AM101.H25
..... CC135
069.53 ..... AM151
..... DA655
070 ..... HE8700.7.P6
..... PN4775
..... PN4784.F6
..... PN5510
070.0202 ..... PN4783
070.023 ..... HF5381
..... PN4797
070.02574 ..... Z6952.N52
070.043 ..... PN4714.A1
070.0601 ..... PN4712.I534
070.08 ..... PN4722
070.1 ..... N4738
..... PN4784.T4
..... PN4888.T4
070.10942 ..... HX11
070.11 ..... JK518
..... PN4738
070.4 ..... PN4731
..... PN4775
..... PN4778
..... PN4834
..... Z253.5
070.40922 ..... PN5122
070.40924 ..... CT275.S4296
..... E415.9.G8
..... E664.P15
..... PN4874.A5
..... PN4874.B56
..... PN4874.B63
..... PN4874.C32
..... PN4874.H4
..... PN4874.R3
..... PN5123.F63
..... PN5123.M35
..... PN5596.H6
070.41 ..... PN4775
..... PN4778
..... PN4783
070.410924 ..... PN4874.D3
..... PN4874.H224
..... PN4874.H48
..... PN4874.M363
..... PN4874.M46
..... PN4913.M24
..... PN5376.S7
070.43 ..... PN4731
..... PN4736
..... PN4739.W5
..... PN4781
..... PN4784.I6
..... PN4784.R2
..... PN4841
..... PN5111.R4
070.430973 ..... PN4855
070.44 ..... PN4781
..... PN4784.S6
..... Q225
070.4420973 ..... PN4858
070.48 ..... PN4731
..... Z7403
070.4820942 ..... PN5124.R45
070.484 ..... PN4914.F62
070.4840973 ..... PN4884
070.486 ..... PN4784.A3
..... PN4784.C7
070.5091724 ..... Z278
070.50924 ..... Z325
070.50942 ..... Z323
070.5097444 ..... Z209.C3
070.5097471 ..... Z479
070.509753 ..... Z232.U6
070.572 ..... Z479
070.9 ..... PN4736
..... PN4815
070.922 ..... PN4823
..... PN4855
..... PN4888.N4
..... PN5114
..... PN5130.P8
070.924 ..... CT275.B313
..... CT275.M755
..... CT275.R6
..... CT788.C89
..... CT2918.C3
..... D413.M28
..... DU396
..... E185.97.R89
..... E302.6.B14
..... E415.9.G8
..... E415.9.W37
..... E664.G73
..... GV915.D82
..... PN1991.4.A4
..... PN4784.S6
..... PN4797
..... PN4874.A56
..... PN4874.B24
..... PN4874.B27
..... PN4874.B66
..... PN4874.B67
..... PN4874.C59
..... PN4874.G535
..... PN4874.H222
..... PN4874.L3
..... PN4874.L45
..... PN4874.M89

070.924 PN4874.P8
PN4874.S46
PN4874.S687
PN4874.S7
PN4874.S78
PN4874.S786
PN4874.W52
PN4913.S8
PN5123.C48
PN5123.E3
PN5123.H56
PN5123.M35
PN5123.S83
PN5123.W18
PN5476.H6
PN5510
PN5526.L4
PS1302
PS2014.H5
PS2243
PS3531.A5855
Z720.S38
070.942 PN5122
071 PN4888.T3
071.1 Z674.M57
071.1312 PN4919.F62
071.14281 PN4920.F3
071.3 PN4722
PN4724
PN4738
PN4855
PN4857
PN4867
PN4884
PN4888.C5
PN4888.C594
PN4888.N4
PN4888.P6
PN4888.U5
Z6367
Z6951
071.4 PN4861
Z6952.N52
071.4461 PN4899.B6
071.463 PN4899.H35
071.47 PN4885.Y5
071.471 AI21.N47
PN4899.N42
PN4899.N42W62
071.4886 PN4899.P56P64
071.5 PN4893
071.53 PN4872
071.5771 PN4899.C555
071.58231 PN4899.A75
071.63355 PN4899.N32
071.6773 PN4899.L55
071.77 PN4897.I7
071.89 PN4897.N54
071.9177 PN4899.T85T85
071.9494 PN4899.L64
072 PN5111.I63
PN5114
PN5115
PN5118
072.1 PN5130.P8
072.565 PN5129.B37T53
073.7 PN5355.C95
074.436 PN4899.N42H44
079.4121 PN5139.I53
079.497 PN5355.Y8
079.51 PN5362
079.52 PN5369.P43J43
079.54 PN4748.I6
PN5372
PN5374
079.5479 PN5378.M32
079.6 Z6959
079.67 PN4712.I558
079.931 PN5510
PN5594
079.93127 PN5599.W43
079.94 PN5510
PN6231.B8
080 AS122
AS244
AS591
AS622
AS622.A7
AS722
PN621
PN6361
PR1293
081 AC5
AC8
AM101
AS36
B828
BX4705.S612
BX7260.B3
E173
E660
E757
E839
E840.8.K4
F1052
GT150
JC177
KF27.A3
KF373
LB1025
LD5332.2
PN4874.A36
PN4874.L76
PR13
081 PR1367
PR6001.L4
PR6007.I63
PR6013.R44
PR6023.A97
PR6025.A794
PR6025.O4
PR6025.U8
PR6052.O92
PS508.N3
PS551
PS688
PS1101.B8
PS1292
PS1449.C74
PS2017
PS2545.P4
PS2835
PS2930
PS3117
PS3157.W4
PS3503.O87
PS3503.R7
PS3509.A85
PS3511.E17
PS3511.I683
PS3513.R25
PS3515.A363
PS3519.O2
PS3521.I715
PS3525.O2
PS3527.E917
PS3527.O2
PS3527.O45T5
PS3531.A5855
PS3535.E923
PS3535.I65
PS3537.H693
PS3545.O717
PS3557.R275
PS3558.O3478
PS3561.A867
QB638
TA140.F9
TS1440.S64
082 AC5
AC7
AC8
AC146
AS122
AS122.B4
AS622
AS722
B29
BX891
BX5199.G73
CT788.B8683
CT2808.L94
DA27
DA447.H2
DA490
DA566.9.B5
DS481.G3
DS481.N35
DS481.S5525
E169.12
PE1121
PN761
PN5426.R6
PN6014
PN6081
PR973
PR1125
PR1149
PR1365
PR1366
PR1367
PR3519.J12
PR4115
PR4606
PR4759.H4
PR4787
PR5227.R7
PR6003.A67
PR6003.E45
PR6003.U13
PR6007.E59
PR6009.L8
PR6013.A35
PR6013.A6
PR6013.R735
PR6015.A48
PR6015.U83
PR6019.O2
PR6021.O4
PR6023.U24
PR6023.Y42
PR6025.E4
PR6025.U8
PR6031.A7
PR6031.O87
PR6035.E24
PR6037.A519
PR6045.O75
PR6060.E9
PR6073.E75
PS688
PS1229.B6
Q143.W5
Z42
083.1 AC35
B3118.E5
B3213.B84
083.1 BF173
084 PQ2386.R37
084.1 PQ2603.A82
086.1 AC12
089.15 P911.K5
089.9143 PK2098.D53
089.943 PL1
090 ML3178.S5
Z1021
Z6621.C77H44
090.922 Z989
090.9415 Z8.I78
091 ML96.4
PA47
PJ5208
PN6245
Z105
093 PQ4619
Z240
Z241.S31
Z242.C7
Z6517
093.0943 Z147
094 Z240
094.4 E221
Z2014.F5
095 Z276
095.0924 Z269.5
095.0942 Z268
096 Z725.M44
096.1 ND3148.M6
ND3174.M3
ND3363.B5
Z1023
Z2014.C4
096.108 Z1023
096.10942 Z250
096.10943613 ND2898
097 Z1029
098 Z1019
098.1 Z1019
098.12 HQ454
098.3 PN171.F6
Z1024
099 AY754
100 B11
B29
B53
B105.E9
B832
B840
B945
B945.C53
B1201
B1201.G53
B2430
B5244.N55
BD21
BD23
BD31
BD331
BH39
BL90
BP565
101 B53
BD21
101.4 B49
103 B41
108 B21
B29
B808.5
B905
B945
B1618
B1618.A93
BD21
BD31
109 AC5
B72
B77
B823.3
110 B105.U5
B765.J3
B816
B840
B931
B1348
B1854
B2949
BD21
BD111
BD113
BD131
BD171
BD215
BD313
BD331
BD416
BD431
BD450
BP567
110.0924 B1618.B74
110.8 BD111
110.9 BD111
110.924 B3999
110.94 B801
111 AC8
B66
B105
B105.I3
B105.U5
B731
B818
B945.C164
111 B1034.C43
B2430.M379
B2794
B2918.E5M5
B3279
B4279.U73
BD190
BD236
BD311
BD331
BD394
BD396
BD581
BL226
111.014 BD311
111.1 B105.E65
B3279
B3279.H48S467
BD331
111.10922 B2430.S34
111.8 B825.2
BD331
111.820924 B2430.T374
111.83 BD161
BD171
BD417
111.84 BD431
BJ1401
BJ1409
111.85 B945
B1674.W354
BH39
BH41
BH181
BH201
BH203
BH221.G34
N75
111.8508 BH39
111.85094 BH131
112 BC172
BD241
113 B2430
B2918
BD331
BD511
113.2 BD581
113.6 BD645
114 BD621
BD632
115 B187.T55
BD638
115.08 BD638
116 B818
117 BD648
119 BF1623.P9
120 BD161
BD171
BD175
121 B132.K6
B655.Z7
B808.5
B816
B823.3
B1294
B1297
B1349.P4
B1485
B1533
B1645
B1645.H4
B2430.M44
B2784
B2808
B3279.H48
B3583
B5134
BD143
BD161
BD181
BD201
BD215
BD236
BF111
BR100
121.08 B2430
BD161
BD181
121.0924 B1647.M74
B1649.R94
QC6
121.5 B837
121.6 B3376.W563
BC91
BD171
BD215
121.8 BD232
BR53
121.80924 B1674
122 BD591
123 B29
B824.4
BJ1451
BJ1461
BJ1462
124 B2799.T3
126 AC8
B63
B132.A8
B1647.M133
B1925.E5
BD331
BD450
BF311

126 ..... BF697
127 ..... AS262.T87
128 ..... B187.M25
..... B765.B663
..... B820
..... B2043.D33
..... BD431
..... BD450
..... BF111
..... BJ1470
..... BL290
..... BL627
..... BP565
128.08 ..... BD450
128.0922 ..... B2177
128.1 ..... BD421
..... BD450
..... BL290
..... BT741
128.108 ..... BD419
128.2 ..... B749
..... B2043
..... BC199.I5
..... BD236
128.20924 ..... B1618.C74
..... B1649.N474
128.3 ..... B105.E95
..... B398.P9
..... B415
..... B2430
..... B2430.T273
..... B2430.T373
..... BD450
..... BD450.H675
..... BF161
..... BF697
..... BL465
128.308 ..... BD450
128.3091821 ..... BF81
128.30924 ..... B689.Z7
128.30938 ..... B187.M25
128.30951 ..... BD450
128.5 ..... BD444
..... BL85
129 ..... BL535
..... BP565
129.4 ..... BL515
129.6 ..... BL530
129.608 ..... BL530
130 ..... BF1999
131 ..... BD701
..... BF171
..... BJ1581.2
131.3 ..... BF637.S8
..... BF723.P25
..... BJ1533.C7
..... BJ1533.F8
..... BJ1581.2
..... BJ1610
..... BJ1611
..... BJ1611.2
..... BJ1691
..... BP565
..... HF5386
..... R154.S823
131.30207 ..... PN6231.P785
131.3076 ..... BF637.S8
131.30924 ..... BF1027.P64
131.32 ..... BF575.L8
..... BF637.C5
..... BF637.S8
..... BF639
..... BF1411
..... BF1999
..... BJ1581.2
..... BJ1611
..... BJ1611.2
..... BX9890.U5
..... HF5386
131.33 ..... BJ1487
131.35 ..... BP605.S2
133 ..... AC8
..... BF161
..... BF637.S8
..... BF1021
..... BF1028.5.E8
..... BF1031
..... BF1411
..... BF1421
..... BF1429
..... BF1434.U6
..... BF1561
..... BF1611
..... BF1775
..... BF1999
..... BL518
..... BL1490.L6
..... BL2015.K3
..... BP605.U75
..... BR115.O3
..... DA784.5
..... GR580
133.03 ..... BF1407
133.062 ..... BL35
133.072 ..... BF1031
133.08 ..... BF1023
..... BF1031
..... BF1261.2
..... BF1598.A3
133.09 ..... BF1411
133.0973 ..... BF1434.U6
133.1 ..... BF1461
..... GR580
133.10924 ..... BF1461
133.10942 ..... BF1475
133.12942 ..... BF1461
..... GR580
133.12973 ..... BF1461
..... GR580
133.14 ..... BF1045.A6
133.3 ..... BF1751
..... BF1861
133.309 ..... BF1791
133.30922 ..... BF1812.U6
133.30924 ..... BF1283.D48
133.32 ..... BF1791
..... CB161
133.320924 ..... BF1815.G32
133.322 ..... BF1325
133.323 ..... BF1628
133.3232 ..... GB1005
133.324 ..... BF1773
..... BF1861
133.32424 ..... BF1879.T2
133.32429 ..... BF1878
133.33 ..... BF1770.C5
133.333 ..... BF1779.I4
133.335 ..... BF1623.P9
133.3359 ..... BF1623.P9
133.35 ..... HQ734
133.4 ..... BF1410
..... BF1521
..... BF1531
..... BF1565
..... BF1566
..... BF1567
..... BF1569.A2
..... BF1575
..... BF1576
..... BF1577.P4
..... BF1581
..... BF1584.W5
..... BF1589
..... BF1591
..... BF1593
..... BF1611
..... BF1612
..... BF1623.R6
..... BL2620.H3
..... GR530
133.408 ..... BF1563
133.409 ..... BF1589
133.40904 ..... BF1571
133.40924 ..... BF1408.2.S25
133.409415 ..... BF1581
133.40942 ..... BF1581
..... BF1623.R7
133.4095951 ..... BF1622.M3
133.409678 ..... BF1584.A53
133.40972 ..... BF1584.M6
133.409729 ..... BF1584.W5
133.42 ..... BF1521
..... BF1581
133.422 ..... BF1548
..... BL480
133.426 ..... BF1555
133.43 ..... BF1558
..... BF1572.R4
..... BF1601
..... BF1623.R6
..... BF1995
..... BM525
133.44 ..... BF1561
133.5 ..... BF1674
..... BF1679.8.A3
..... BF1701
..... BF1713
..... BF1714.C5
..... BF1714.H5
..... BF1714.M6
..... BF1715
..... BF1725
..... BF1729.M8
..... BF1729.P8
..... BF1729.S4
..... DX155
133.503 ..... BF1655
133.509 ..... BF1671
133.50972 ..... F1435.3.A8
133.52 ..... QB803
133.520207 ..... PN6231.A73
133.53 ..... BF1701
133.54 ..... BF1701
..... BF1727
..... BF1727.2
..... BF1727.25
..... BF1727.3
..... BF1727.35
..... BF1727.4
..... BF1727.45
..... BF1727.5
..... BF1727.6
..... BF1727.65
..... BF1727.7
..... BF1727.75
..... BF1728
..... BF1728.A2
133.548 ..... BF1701
..... BF1728.O5
133.56 ..... BF1714.H5
133.5830142 ..... BF1729.L6
133.58411 ..... BF1674
133.586491 ..... BF1729.C45
133.589 ..... BF1711
133.6 ..... BF921
133.7 ..... AZ999
133.8 ..... BF1023
..... BF1029
133.8 ..... BF1031
..... BF1041
..... BF1171
..... BF1311.E75
..... BF1321
..... BF1325
..... BF1389.A7
133.808 ..... BF1321
133.80922 ..... PN2205
133.80924 ..... BF1027.C3
..... BF1027.V3
..... BF1031
133.82 ..... AS36
..... BF1171
..... BF1321
..... BF1411
133.84 ..... BF1261
..... BF1325
133.9 ..... BF1031
..... BF1042
..... BF1261
..... BF1261.2
..... BF1301
..... BF1311.E43
..... BF1311.F8
..... BF1311.N4
..... BF1389.A7
..... BF1461
..... BF1999
..... BL515
..... BR115.P85
133.901 ..... B2793.E5
133.909 ..... BF1241
133.90924 ..... BF1283.K55
..... BF1286
..... BX5995.P54
133.90973 ..... BF1241
133.91 ..... BF1286
..... BF1288
..... BF1290
..... BF1311.F8
..... BF1999
133.91014 ..... BF1311.L25
133.9108 ..... BF1235
133.910922 ..... BF1281
133.910924 ..... BF1283.C49
..... BF1283.G29
..... BF1283.G7
..... BF1378
133.92 ..... BF1381
..... BF1385
..... BF1389.A7
133.93 ..... BF1031
..... BF1290
..... BF1301
..... BF1347
135.3 ..... BF1091
135.4 ..... B127.I2
..... BD701
..... BF1611
..... BF1623.R7
..... BF1623.S9
..... BF1879.T2
..... BF1999
..... BM723
135.40924 ..... B759
135.43 ..... BF1612
..... BF1623.R7
135.4308 ..... BF1623.R7
137 ..... BF458
137.7 ..... BF891
138 ..... BF798
..... BF851
138.0938 ..... Q11
139 ..... BF871
139.4 ..... BP573.R5
140 ..... B819
141 ..... B517
..... B823
..... B905
..... B945.R63
..... B1133.C2
..... B2948
141.3 ..... B905
141.305 ..... B905
141.30973 ..... B905
141.5 ..... B828.5
141.6 ..... PN603
142.7 ..... B105.E9
..... B819
..... B829.5
..... B2430.S34
..... B3279
..... B3279.H93I33
..... BD312
..... BD436
142.70924 ..... B3279
..... B3279.H94
144 ..... B821
..... CB353
..... PK1725
144.3 ..... B818
..... B832
..... B5134.G32
144.308 ..... B832
144.30973 ..... B832
144.6 ..... B1571
146 ..... B828.2
..... B945.C54
146.3 ..... B809.8
..... B825
146.4 ..... B808.5
..... B816
..... B824.6
146.4 ..... B2223
146.6 ..... B1809.M3
147 ..... BP561.S43
..... BP565
..... BP565.A77
..... PR4484
149.1 ..... B731
149.2 ..... B835
..... B839
..... Z7128.R4
149.3 ..... B799
..... B828
..... B4249.G84
..... BL625
..... BL627
..... BL2015.K3
..... BP595
..... BV4501
..... BV5070.F73
..... BV5083
149.7 ..... BL2703
..... BL2750
149.73 ..... B779
149.8 ..... B187.F3
..... B828.3
149.9 ..... B808.5
..... B841.4
149.94 ..... B808.5
..... B809.15
..... B820
..... B824
..... B840
..... B3376.W563
..... B3376.W564
149.9408 ..... B820
..... B840
149.940924 ..... B945.Q54
150 ..... B829.5
..... BF20
..... BF21
..... BF38
..... BF111
..... BF121
..... BF121.M8
..... BF123
..... BF131
..... BF139
..... BF145
..... BF149
..... BF161
..... BF181
..... BF319.5.F4
..... BF323.E8
..... BF575.S75
..... RT86
150.1 ..... BF161
..... BF204.5
150.15 ..... BF39
150.151 ..... BF39
150.1519 ..... BF39
150.18 ..... BF76.5
..... BF319.5.R4
150.182 ..... BF21
..... BF39
150.184 ..... BF39.5
150.19 ..... BF38
..... BF57
..... BF95
150.192 ..... BF41
..... BF149
..... BF171
..... BF204.5
150.1943 ..... BF319
150.19434 ..... BF319.5.R4
150.1944 ..... RC458
150.195 ..... BF21
..... BF173
..... BF173.R36
..... RC509
150.19508 ..... BF731
150.19509 ..... BF1569
150.1950924 ..... BF109.E7
..... BF173
150.1952 ..... BF173
..... BF173.F85
150.195203 ..... BF173
150.19520922 ..... BF173.F85
..... BF173.R376
150.19520924 ..... BF173.F85
150.1953 ..... BF173
..... BF175
150.1954 ..... BF173
..... BF173.J85
..... BF175
150.195408 ..... BF23
150.19540924 ..... BF173.J85
150.1957 ..... RC506
150.1982 ..... BF173
..... BF203
..... RC480.5
150.19820924 ..... HM251
150.202 ..... BF141
150.2461073 ..... RT86
150.28 ..... BF80
150.3 ..... BF31
150.72 ..... BF76.5
..... BF77
..... BF575.A6
150.8 ..... BF21
..... BF21.A1
..... BF149
..... BR110
..... BV4012
150.9 ..... BF81

150.91766 .... BF51
150.924 .... BF109.L3
..... BF109.P6
..... BF149
..... BF698
..... BF940.W6
150.947 .... BF108.R8
152 .... BF76.5
..... BF79
..... BF181
..... BF207
..... BF210
..... BF319.5.O6
..... BF323.V5
..... BF685
..... PZ8.3.B6487
..... QP355
..... QP355.2
..... QP356
152.018 .... BF39
152.0182 .... QP356
152.0184 .... BF39
152.08 .... BF181
..... QP355
152.1 .... B1533
..... BF292
..... BF311
..... BF320
..... BF321
..... PZ10
..... TL521.3.C6
152.14 .... BF241
..... BF311
..... BF367
..... BF471.C5
..... QP495
152.1408 .... BF241
152.1409 .... BF241
152.142 .... BF21
..... BF241
152.1423 .... BF241
..... Z663.23
152.1425 .... BF723.M6
152.143 .... BF21.A1
152.145 .... BF698.8.L8
152.148 .... BF241
152.15 .... BF205.N6
..... BF1040
152.166 .... BF21
152.182 .... QP435
..... TL521.3.C6
152.1824 .... BF515
..... RB127
152.3 .... BF205.M6
..... BF295
..... BF323.C8
152.3224 .... BF319
152.32240924 .... QP26.P35
152.334 .... LB1067
152.384 .... BF637.C45
152.3842 .... BF319.5.V4
..... BF455
152.4 .... BF319.5.E4
..... BF319.5.P8
..... BF511
..... BF531
..... BF575.F16
..... BF575.L3
..... BF575.S75
..... BF575.S9
..... BH301.C7
..... BJ1471.5
..... QP401
152.42 .... BF591
..... QP401
152.432 .... BF575.A3
..... BF575.L8
..... BF692
152.434 .... BF575.A6
..... BF575.E5
..... BF575.E65
..... BF575.L3
152.442 .... PN6147
152.444 .... BF515
152.452 .... BF323.C5
..... BF773
152.5 .... BF575.F14
..... BF683
..... LB1065
152.508 .... BF683
152.52 .... BF323.E8
..... BF575.A3
..... BF575.F7
..... BF683
152.8 .... BF39
..... BF237
152.82 .... Z7204.R35
152.83 .... BF317
153 .... BF161
..... BF311
..... BF319.5.V4
..... BF335
..... BF433.B6
..... BF455
..... BF469
..... BF637.C45
..... LB1103
153.0924 .... BF431
153.1 .... BF371
..... LB1051
..... LB1059
..... QP406
153.108 .... QP406
153.12 .... BF371
153.122 .... BF371
153.123 .... BF371
153.14 .... BF385
153.15 .... AS36
..... BF319.5.F4
..... BF319.5.R4
..... BF321
..... LB1051
..... LB1057
..... LB1064
..... LB1065
..... LB2846
153.1501 .... LB1051
153.152 .... LB1049
153.15208 .... Z663.23
153.1522 .... LB1063
153.1526 .... BF1
..... LB1064
153.1532 .... BF323.L5
153.22 .... BF365
153.3 .... BF367
..... BF408
153.32 .... BF367
153.35 .... BF408
..... BF411
..... BF1021
153.3507 .... LB1062
153.35077 .... BF411
153.4 .... BF311
..... BF455
..... BF637.C45
..... BF723.I6
153.42 .... BF455
..... LB1055
153.420184 .... Q335
153.43 .... BF435
..... BF441
153.45 .... BF773
153.46 .... BF21.A1
153.54 .... BF1701
153.63 .... BF1091
153.7 .... BF311
153.73 .... BF321
153.733 .... BF321
153.75 .... TL507
153.752 .... BF241
153.753 .... BF468
..... QP481
153.8 .... BF621
153.83 .... AS36
..... BF441
153.85 .... BF634
153.852 .... BF637.P4
153.9 .... BF39
..... BF431
..... LB1131
153.908 .... BF431
153.93 .... BF431
..... JV6601.C5
153.932 .... BF431
153.9323 .... BF431
153.94 .... BF431
153.94355 .... UB147
153.944 .... LB1059
..... LB1139.L3
153.9462 .... BF433.M4
153.9478 .... ML3832
..... ML3838
153.98 .... BF412
..... D810.E8
154 .... BF175
..... BF207
..... BF311
154.2 .... BF23
..... BF175
154.22 .... BF173
..... BF175
154.24 .... BF575.F7
154.6 .... PZ10.S688
..... QP425
154.63 .... BF1078
..... BF1091
..... GN453.A8
154.634 .... BF1078
..... BF1091
154.7 .... BF1141
..... BF1142
..... BF1156.S8
..... BF1156.S83
154.709 .... BF1125
154.76 .... BF1141
155 .... BF175
..... BF341
..... BF701
..... BF703
..... BF717
..... BF721
..... BF724.8
155.2 .... BF175
..... BF335
..... BF697
..... BF698
..... BF698.9.B5
..... BF701
..... BF723.S4
..... BJ1610
..... BV4012
..... BX903
..... JA74
..... LB775.G22
155.208 .... BF698
155.23 .... BF323.D6
155.23 .... BF698
155.25 .... LB3609
155.264 .... BF698
..... BF798
155.28 .... BF698.4
..... BF698.5
..... RC467
155.28018 .... BF698.5
155.282 .... BF891
155.283 .... BF431
..... BF698.8.M5
..... BF698.8.S5
155.284 .... BF463.M4
..... BF697
..... BF698.8.B4
..... BF698.8.D7
..... BF698.8.H6
..... BF698.8.T4
..... BF698.8.W6
..... BF698.8.Z8
155.284072 .... BF698.7
155.2842 .... BF698.8.R5
155.2844 .... BF145
..... BF698.8.T5
155.3 .... BF692
..... HQ21
..... PN1949.S7
..... RC560.M3
155.31 .... BF692
155.33 .... BF724.3.S4
155.333 .... BF692
155.4 .... BF717
..... BF721
..... BF723.D7
..... BF723.I6
..... BF723.M56
..... BF723.P25
..... BF723.P4
..... BF723.R3
..... HQ772
..... HQ784.W6
..... HV9069
..... LB1051
..... LB1103
..... LB1139.P3
..... LB1140
155.40186 .... BF722
155.408 .... BF721
155.40924 .... BF721
155.41 .... BF698.8
..... BF701
..... BF721
..... BF723.D7
..... LB1103
..... Q60
..... RJ131
155.410922 .... BF721
155.412 .... BF723.M6
155.413 .... BF21.A1
..... BF311
..... BF671
..... BF721
..... BF723.C5
..... BF723.C7
..... BF723.E4
..... BF723.M4
..... BF723.S63
..... BF723.S75
..... BF723.T6
..... LB1139.L3
..... LB1140
155.4130924 .... BF721
155.415 .... BF723.C5
155.418 .... BF710
..... BF721
..... BF723.A35
..... BF723.A4
..... BF723.C57
..... BF723.E8
..... BF723.I4
..... BF723.M35
..... BF723.P25
..... BF723.P4
..... BF723.S25
..... BF723.S75
..... BJ1408.5
..... LB1117
..... RJ499
155.41808 .... BF721
155.42 .... RJ131
155.422 .... BF698.9.B5
..... BF722
..... BF723.I6
..... BF723.P25
..... RJ131
155.423 .... BF723.I6
..... HQ769
155.424 .... BF721
..... HQ769
155.433 .... GT2540
155.44 .... BF721
155.443 .... BF723.B5
155.444 .... CT9998.B7
155.446095694 .... HQ792.P3
155.45 .... BF575.D35
..... BF723.P25
..... LC3951
155.45120926 .... HV2395
155.453 .... HQ773
155.454 .... BF723.P25
..... RC514
155.5 .... BF724
..... HQ796
155.50186 .... BF724
155.502436 .... HV43
155.508 .... BF724
155.50973 .... HQ796
155.532 .... BF724
155.6 .... BF724.5
155.633 .... HQ1206
155.646 .... HQ734
155.6463 .... HQ759
155.67 .... BF724.8
..... HQ1060
155.7 .... BF698.9.C8
155.8094 .... BF731
155.81 .... GN451
155.82 .... BF431
..... BF755.C3
155.8496 .... E185.625
..... GN651
155.9 .... BF353
..... BF431
..... BF575.S75
..... BF698.9.C8
..... PN1995.5
..... PN1995.9.C45
155.91 .... GA1
155.916 .... BF727.P57
155.92 .... BF575.S75
..... BF698
155.93 .... BF683
..... BF723.D3
..... BF789.D4
..... BJ1487
..... HQ784.D4
..... RC49
155.936 .... BF789.D5
155.96 .... BF469
155.966 .... RC1080
156 .... BF671
..... BF673
..... BF701
..... QL751
..... QL785
..... QL785.5.D7
..... QL785.5.M7
156.2 .... BF207
..... BF723.I6
156.208 .... QP355
156.2143 .... QL785
156.235 .... BF319.5.A9
156.252 .... QL775
156.28 .... QP357
156.3 .... QL785.5.H7
156.315 .... BF319.5.O6
..... QL763
..... QP351
156.31528 .... QL785
157 .... BF173
..... HV6080
..... RC450.G7
..... RC454
..... RC467
..... RC574
157.08 .... RC454
..... RC455
157.282 .... BF21
..... RC514
..... RC574
157.28208 .... RC514
157.282092 .... RC465
157.33 .... RC555
157.6 .... RC566
157.61 .... HV5035
157.63 .... RC454
157.65 .... HV5727
157.7 .... BF515
..... RC555
157.735 .... HQ79
157.739 .... HQ21
..... HQ71
157.744 .... B828.5
..... BF789.D4
..... HV6546
157.9 .... AS36.G378
..... BF637.B4
..... BF637.C6
..... BF698.8.R5
..... RC458
..... RC465
..... RC467
..... RJ50
157.9023 .... BF76
157.908 .... RC467
157.92 .... RC467
158 .... BF123
..... BF636.A1
..... BF637
..... BF637.B4
..... BF637.C6
158.1 .... BF515
..... BF637.P3
..... BF637.S8
..... BF697
..... BF789.D4
..... BF1031
..... BJ1611.2
..... H91
..... HF5386
..... LB1051
158.2 .... BF145
..... BF637.C6
..... BF637.N4
..... BF637.S8
..... RC488
158.26 .... HF5549.5.C6
158.3 .... BF637.I5

Dewey	LC
158.4	BF637.L4
	BF698
158.6	BF636
	BF698.9.O3
	HF5381
158.7	HD57
	HF5386
	HF5500.2
	HF5548.B
	HF5548.8
	HF5549
	T59.7
158.708	HF5548.8
160	B132.N8
	B133
	B749
	B808.5
	B809.7
	B1674.W53
	B2799.T7
	B2942
	B3279.H94
	BC25
	BC50
	BC51
	BC55
	BC57
	BC61
	BC71
	BC73
	BC91
	BC101
	BC108
	BC122
	BC151
	BC173
	BC177
	BC199.C56
	BC199.E93
	BC199.M6
	BX890
	PA3265
160.2434	BC151
160.77	BC59
160.8	BC51
	BC71
	Q175
160.9	BC15
160.924	B441
	B765
	B3279.H94
	BC181
161	B945.P44
	BC91
162	BC71
162.076	BC177
164	BC126
	BC135
	Q180
	QA3
	QA9
	QA76
	QA248
164.03	QA9
164.0924	BC135
165	BC175
	BC199.P2
166	B440
	B945
	BC185
168	BC177
170	AS36
	B105.O7
	B831.3
	B945.J21
	B1500
	BD232
	BD431
	BF311
	BF637.C5
	BF723.E8
	BJ21
	BJ37
	BJ41
	BJ47
	BJ51
	BJ59
	BJ71
	BJ319
	BJ604
	BJ1005
	BJ1008
	BJ1011
	BJ1012
	BJ1031
	BJ1063
	BJ1251
	BJ1311
	BJ1401
	BJ1451
	BJ1581.2
	BJ1595
	BJ1601
	BT736.6
	HF5387
	HM216
	LB2321
	LB2331
	LB3609
	R724
170.19	BF175
170.202	B3118.E5
	B5134.K75
	BD431
170.202	BJ21
	BJ1012
	BJ1185.J3
	BJ1548
	BJ1581
	BJ1581.2
	BJ1597
	BT1595
	LB1044.Z9
	PS1585
170.2020951	BJ117
170.20222	BJ1631
170.202220926	BJ1408.5
170.20223	BJ1611
	BJ1661
	LB3605
170.202232	BJ1678.P3
170.3	BJ63
170.6273	BJ10.E8
170.8	B1667.S251
	BJ21
	BJ1012
170.922	B1499.E8
170.924	B1499.E8
	B2430
	B2799.E8
	BJ604.P7
170.942	BJ602
170.952	BJ972
170.954	BJ122
170.973	HN59
171	B945.J24
	B2766
	B2766.E6
	B2949.E8
	BJ1390
	BP605.S2
171.09	BJ311
171.0942	BJ601
171.0947	BJ1390
171.1	BX9833.6.B68
	HB72
171.2	B1501
	B2799.E8
	BJ1360
171.4	BJ1491
171.5	BJ21
171.6	BJ1471
171.7	BJ1008
	HM106
171.8	BJ1474
172	BJ10.M6
	JA79
172.08	JK1051
172.2	JF1525.E8
	JK271
172.4	HM278
	JX1946.K33
	U21.2
	U22
173	BJ1661
	HQ21
	HQ734
	HQ744
174	BJ1725
174.2	AS36
	BL65.M4
	HQ751
	Q11
	R149
	R723
	R724
	R725.5
	RD120.7
174.208	R724
174.24	R726
174.3	KF306
	KF6320
174.30973	KF305
	KF305.A2
	KF306
174.309759	KFF76.5
174.4	HD59
	HD1375
	HF3826.5
	HF5387
174.40942	HD60
174.907	KF32.I555
	PN4888.E8
174.9070973	PN4888.E8
174.90713	PN4867
174.9355	U408.3
174.937	LB1779
174.93712	LB2806
174.95	Q125
174.96	T14
174.9623	Q125
174.96234072	Q125
174.9657	HF5616.U5
174.9657023	HF5616.U5
174.96570942	HF5616.G7
175	BJ1498
175.1	PN1995.5
175.2	PN2047.C62
176	HQ31
	HQ32
	HQ35
	HQ35.2
	HQ63
	HQ76
	HQ460
176.808	HQ471
176.809489	HQ471
177.1	BJ1601
177.3	BJ1421
	BJ1422
177.5	E446
	E449
	HT1091
177.7	BJ1581
178	HV5035
178.062781	HV5297.K2
178.1	HV5015
	HV5066
	HV5258
178.10924	HV5060
178.10973	HV5292
178.1097463	HV5298.H3
178.7	HV5770.G8
178.70207	PN6231.C44
178.8	HV5825
179	BJ1535.C7
179.3	HV4705
	HV4708
	HV4711
	HV4806
179.409	HV4915
179.6	G530
179.7	D810.J4
	HQ767
179.8	BF575.E65
179.9	BJ1431
	BJ1523
180	B56
	B171
181	B20
	B121
181.043	B162
	B3148
	BL1475.P7
181.044	B162.5
181.07	B744.3
	B753
	B753.I24
181.09512	B128.C8
	B5244
	PL2473.Z7
181.11	B128
	CT1828.H8
181.12	B5241
	B5244
181.3	B156
	B759.M34
	B3213
	BM723.B755
181.308	BM43
181.4	B131
	B133.S5
	B5132
	B5134.A232
	B5134.G32
	B5134.K75
	B5134.T28
	BJ1581.2
	BL1175.S3
	BL1175.S36
181.41	B132.S3
181.44	B132.V2
	BL1245.V3
181.45	B132
	B132.Y6
	B5134
	BD21
	BL1175.G47
	BL1175.P28
	BL1270.G4
	BP605.S43
181.452	B132.Y6
181.48	B132.V3
	B5134.R3652
181.4808	B132.V3
181.482	B132
	B132.A3
	B133.S5
	BL1135.P34
181.483	BL1130
	BL1171
181.5	BP189
182	B171
	B188
	B543
182.2	B243
182.4	PA3998
182.5	B218.Z7
182.8	B205.Z7
183.1	B288
183.2	B316
	B317
184	B358
	B377
	B380
	B385.A5
	B393
	B395
	B398.A6
	B491
184.08	B395
185	B467.A8
	B485
185.08	B485
186	B525
186.4	B693.E53
187	B512
	B573
	PA3970.E2
188	B528
	B563
188	BJ214.S4
	PA6661
189	B720
	B721
	B765.B24
189.2	BR128.G8
	BR1720.G7
189.4	B659.C2
	B721
	B734
	B765
	B765.A24
	B765.L84
	B765.T54
	BX4705.A2
	PR1549
189.5	BV5080
190	B21
	B29
	B53
	B72
	B158.7
	B775
	B790
	B791
	B801
	B802
	B803
	B804
	B804.A1
	B3279.H49
	BR100
	CT119
190.8	B29
	B802
	B945.C272
	BD31
190.9046	AS722.A8
191	B29
	B53
	B131
	B804
	B851
	B873
	B921
	B921.J24
	B945
	B945.B773
	B945.D41
	B945.F24
	B945.F43
	B945.H24
	B945.H64
	B945.J24
	B945.L454
	B945.M2984
	B945.P44
	B945.R64
	B945.S21
	BJ1012
	BP525
	BP585.B6
	CT3990.J6
	LB875.D5
	PS169.T7
	PS1613
	PS3042
	PS3503.R526
191.08	B935
192	B29
	B68
	B1153
	B1155
	B1197
	B1198
	B1246
	B1247
	B1253
	B1296
	B1297
	B1299
	B1300
	B1303
	B1331
	B1348
	B1435
	B1455
	B1485
	B1497
	B1498
	B1533
	B1574
	B1574.B31
	B1574.B34
	B1583.Z7
	B1589.H23
	B1606
	B1607
	B1612.T352
	B1615
	B1618
	B1618.A41
	B1618.A84
	B1618.C74
	B1626
	B1647
	B1647.M74
	B1649
	B1649.N473
	B1649.R94
	B1653
	B1656
	B1667
	B1674.W354

Dewey	LC
192	B1674.W563
	B1875
	B3376.W564
	BD431
	BD450
	BF1581.2
	BJ1005
	BL2790.C5
	PR2322
	Q171
192.08	B1674.W563
193	B2521
	B2558
	B2597
	B2741
	B2758
	B2779
	B2798
	B2799.G6
	B2847
	B2908
	B2929
	B2947
	B2948
	B2973
	B3086
	B3118.E5
	B3138.E5
	B3147.W3
	B3213.B84
	B3216.D84
	B3245.F24
	B3263.W45
	B3279
	B3279.H49
	B3279.J34
	B3305
	B3305.M74
	B3312.E5
	B3313.J43
	B3313.W53
	B3316
	B3317
	B3329.S52
	B3329.S64
	B3376
	B3376.W563
	B3376.W564
	B4568
	B4815.L84
	BJ1483
	BP595
193.	B2798
194	B29
	B792
	B1837
	B1848.E5
	B1854
	B1873
	B1875
	B1903
	B1911
	B1925.E5
	B2022.E5
	B2145
	B2172.E5
	B2177
	B2185
	B2328
	B2430
	B2430.B43
	B2430.B585
	B2430.M33
	B2430.M34
	B2430.M378
	B2430.M38
	B2430.M44
	B2430.S34
	B2430.T374
	BX4735.P26
	PQ2105
	PQ2605.L2
	QA29.A4
195	B783.Z7
	B785.C24
	B3583
	B3614.C74
196	B4568.O74
196.1	B785.V63
197.2	B4238.C49
	B4238.C52E5
	B4259.S52
	BD116
198.5	B29
	BX8711.A25
198.9	B4377
199.437	B821
	B4805.M374
199.4391	B4815.L84
199.492	B785
	B785.E64
	B3997
	B3998
	PA8518
199.495	B3501
199.498	AC25
199.72	B1016
199.82	B1034.I64
199.94	B5700
200	AC8
	BJ1470
	BL48
	BL50
200	BL55
	BL65.S4
	BL80
	BL80.2
	BL85
	BL87
	BL240.2
	BL444
	BL515
	BL560
	BL2775
	BL2775.2
	BL2790.A35
	BR41
	BR115.I7
	BR118
	BR124
	BR125
	BR135
	BR1155
	BR1640
	BS543
	BS1192.5.A1
	BS1198
	BS2395
	BT10
	BT21.2
	BT27
	BT28
	BT60
	BT77
	BT78
	BT83.7
	BT303
	BT769
	BT772
	BT1102
	BV4801
	BX6.W77
	BX320
	BX890
	BX1751
	BX1755
	BX4827.H7
	BX7260.B3
	BX8065.2
	BX8080.B75
	BX8080.N8
	BX8219
	BX9869.N4
	E185.7
200.1	B56
	B799
	B921.J24
	B2799.E8
	BD111
	BD215
	BD573
	BF717
	BL48
	BL50
	BL51
	BL53
	BL60
	BL95
	BL2747.6
	BR252
	BT701.2
	HX807
200.14	BL65.L2
200.19	BL51
	BL53
	BL65.D7
200.3	BL31
200.4	BL25
	BL304
	BL310
200.403	BL311
200.66	BS511.2
200.7	BL41
200.71	BV1471.2
200.722	BL41
200.8	BL27
200.9	BL48
	BL50
	BL80
	BL80.2
200.904	BL48
200.922	BL72
200.932	BL2455
200.937	BL802
200.9421	BR764
200.947	BR936
200.951	BL1801
	BL1802
200.95125	BL1950.H6
200.952	BL2202
	Z7834.J3
200.956	BL1600
200.9597	BL2055
200.96	BL2400
	BL2466
200.9669	BL2470.N5
200.96781	BL2470.Z35
200.968	BR1450
200.972	BR600
200.973	BR516.5
	BR525
	BR563.N4
200.9861	BR685
200.9931	BR1480
200.9969	BR555.H3
201	B56
	B667
201	B921
	B2430
	B2430.T374
	BL51
	BL51.M33
	BL60
	BL65.L2
	BL237
	BL2775.2
	BR50
	BR83
	BR85
	BR95
	BR100
	BR100.N5
	BR115.P85
	BR118
	BR121
	BR121.2
	BR128.G8
	BR525
	BR1616
	BR1705
	BR1725.H69
	BS511
	BS543
	BS612
	BT27
	BT28
	BT50
	BT60
	BT90
	BV600.2
	BV4319
	BX891
	BX1395
	BX1747
	BX1751.2
	BX4735.P26
	BX4811
	BX4827.B57
	BX4827.K5
	BX8143.M5
	BX8639.S57
	LB475.C6
201.1	BP567
	BS2397
	BT80
	BX1747
	BX1751.2
	BX4700.F85
	BX4827.N47
	BX5199.D66
	BX9420
	BX9422.2
201.108	BR50
201.109	BT21.2
201.10924	BX4705.G45
201.4	BL65.L2
	BR96.5
201.9	BR110
202.07	PN6149.M6
	PN6231.C5
	PN6328.C5
203	BR95
207	BV656.3
	BV1464
	BV1471
	BV1471.2
	BV1473
	BV1475.2
	BV4030.T48
	BX7619
207.1	BR129
	BV1475.9
207.11	BV2030
	BV4011
	BV4080
207.112	LB375.L6
207.1120945632	BX920.R76
207.122	BV1475.9
207.2024	BX5199.H85
207.22	BR138
207.42965	BV4160.T7
207.6668	BV3625.I8
207.67	BV4140.A4
207.71233	BV4140.C3
207.73	BL41
	BV4030
	BV4080
207.74	BV1467
207.7445	BV4070.A56
207.7471	BV4070.G46
207.763355	BV4070.N4356
207.77311	BV4070.M76
	BV4070.6
207.8	BV4140.L3
208	BL25
	BL50
	BL87
	BR67
	BR85
	BR115.H5
	BR121.2
	BR123
	BR479
	BR783
	BT15
	BT75.2
	BX9
	BX880
	BX890
	BX5037
	LC283
208.	PQ2032
	PS3531.H4
209	BR67
	BR123
	BR141
	BR145.2
209.015	BR170
209.04	BL48
	BR115.W6
	BR121.2
	BR121.2.G363
	BR123
	BR124
	BT28
	BT77.3
	BT771.2
	BT1102
209.046	BT60
209.22	BR1450
	BR1700
	BR1700.2
	BR1702
	BR1713
	BS571
	CT3203
209.42	D70
209.42132	BV2865
209.437	BR1050.C9
	BX4827.H7
	BX4854.C9
209.47	BR936
209.5	BR1065
209.52	BL2202
	BR1307
209.73	BR515
	BR520
209.935	GN473
210	AC8
	BF637.P3
	BL51
	BL180
	BR85
	BR100
	BT28
	BV4639
	BV4908.5
	BX4705.N5
	BX4827.T53
	PQ6412.L8
210.38	B187.T5
210.8	BT50
211	BL205
	BT102
211.08	BT102.A1
211.0922	B188
211.3	B132.N8
	BL51
	BL200
	BT98
	BT102
211.4	BL2775
	BL2775.2
	PS3503.R526
211.40944	B1815
211.50922	BL2785
211.6	B780.M3
	BD450
	BL2747.8
	BR100
	BT1210
	BX7732
211.60924	BL2790.B8
211.60973	BR517
211.8	BL2747.3
211.80740745	BL2780
211.808	BL2747.3
211.809	BL2751
211.80904	BL2747.3
211.80954	BL2765.I5
212	BT102
	BT175
212.5	B398.G6
	BP561
	BP565
	BP567
	BP573.G6
	BP573.P3
	BP605.C5
213	B818
	BL263
	BS650
	BS651
	BS659
	BT695
213.09	BT695
213.5	BS659
215	B56
	B2430
	BL240
	BL240.2
	BL241
	BL245
	BL254
	BS650
	BS657
	BX7732
	Q125
215.09	BL245
215.0924	B2430.T374
215.0942	BL245
215.2	BL254
215.9	BL65.M4
218	BT912

Dewey	LC
220	BS475.2
	BS483.5
	BS511
	BS617
	BS1140.2
	BS2387
220.0202	BS592
220.07	BS417
	BS600.2
	BS603
	BS605.2
220.08	BS531
220.09	BS445
220.1	BS475.2
	BS480
	BS513.2
220.13	BS480
220.1309	BS480
220.15	BF1099.B5
	BS647.2
	BS649.J5
220.2	BS425
	BS432
220.3	BS440
220.4	BS445
220.48	BS744
220.5	BS391.2.B7
220.52	BS185
	BS192
	BS192.A1
	BS391.2
	BS455
	BS537
	BS560
	BX8630.A2
220.5201	BS170
220.5203	BS185
	BS186
	BS191
	BS391.2
220.5204	BS191.A1
	BS195
	BS391.2
	BS895
220.5205	BS192.3.A1
220.6	BS475.2
	BS476
	BS480
	BS511.2
	BS512.2
	BS514.2
	BS530
	BS540
	BS605.2
	BS2387
	BX2350.2
220.63	BD241
	BS476
220.630974	BS500
220.64	BS534
	BS537
220.66	BS511
	BS511.2
	BS533
220.68	BS534
	BS655
220.7	BS491
	BS491.2
220.77	BS491.2
220.8	BS1245.2
220.8262	BV600
220.8301412	BS575
	BT704
220.8301422	BS1235.2
220.8301431	BS576
220.83014522	E449
220.83317	BS680.O3
220.8337	BS680.O3
220.85	BS650
220.85231	BS651
220.8529	BS680.T54
220.8549	BS667
220.8574	BS660
220.858	BS665
220.859	BS663
220.861	R135.5
220.8616998	R135.5
220.86413	BS680.F6
220.89292	BS569
220.9	BS621
	BS630
	BS635.2
	BS637.2
220.91	BS630
220.92	BS570
220.922	BS570
	BS572
220.93	BS621
	DS621
220.95	BS635
	DS119.2
	DS121.6
220.9500202	BS637.2
220.950093947	BS635
220.9505	BS550.2
	BS551.2
	BS635.2
221	BS410
	BS540
	BS571
	BS1140.2
	BS1192
	BS1192.5
221.06	BS1171.2
221.08	BS1192
221.4	BM487
221.42	BS709.4
221.44	BS1136
221.52	BS892.A1
	BS1151.5
221.5203	BS185
	BS1091
221.6	BR333
	BR333.5.B5
	BS410
	BS625
	BS1140.2
	BS1171.2
	BS1192
	BS1192.5
	BS2387
221.60903	BS1160
221.64	BS478
221.8115	BS1199.T5
221.82361	BS1199.D34
221.83014522	HT915
221.92	BS580.D2
221.922	BS575
	BS580.D3
	BS580.E4
	BS1198
221.924	BS580.D3
	BS580.S6
	BS1286.5
221.93	PJ3185
221.95	BM107
	BS1151.2
	BS1180
	BS1194
	BS1197
	DS110.G57
	DS121.65
221.9505	BS551.2
222	BS621
	BS1203
	BS1309.A2
222.09505	BS551.2
222.1	BM612.5
	BS1226
222.1007	BS1227
222.1042	BS1223
222.1044	BS718
222.1052	BS1223
222.106	BS410
	BS1225.2
	BS1227
222.1066	BS1225.4
222.107	BM724
222.1077	BS1225
222.1082966	BS1199.P7
222.10924	BS580.M6
222.11	BS573
	BS580.M6
	BS658
	BS1233
	BS1235.4
	BS1239
222.11052	N8027
222.1106	BS1235.2
	BS1235.5
222.11066	BS1235.5
222.11068	BS1235.5
222.11077	BS1235.4
222.110922	BS580.I67
222.110924	BS580.A3
	BS580.J6
222.1109505	BS580.N6
222.1207	BS1245.3
222.1209505	BS680.E9
222.14	BS580.B3
222.14077	BS1265.3
222.1506	BS1275.2
222.1507	BS1275.3
222.16	BV4655
222.2	BS1295.2
222.3	BS1305.3
222.35	BS1315.2
222.3507	BS1315.3
222.406	BS1325.2
222.5077	BS1335.3
222.509505	BS551.2
222.706	BS1355.2
223	BS1415.2
	BS1455
223.106	BS1415.2
223.1066	BS1415.2
223.1077	BS1415.3
223.2	BS1423
	BS1430.2
	BS1430.3
	BS1430.4
	BS1445.S6
	BS1450
223.200222	BS1423
223.2007	BS1430.5
223.202	BX5946
223.2052	BS1422
	BS1440.W4
223.206	BS1430
	BS1430.2
223.2066	BS1430.2
	BS1430.2.A5
223.208815	BS1430.2
223.252	BS1421
223.7	BS1465.4
	BS1467
223.7077	BS1465.3
223.9	BS1483
223.905203	BS1483
223.9077	BS1483
224	BS1198
	BS1505.3
224.007	BS1506
224.044	BS1286
224.06	BS1198
	BS1505.2
224.1	BS410
	BS1199.S4
	BS1515.3
	BS1520
224.1044	BS1515.2
224.1066	BS1585.2
224.107	BS1515.2
224.1077	BS1515.3
224.406	BS1545.2
224.407	BS1545.3
224.4077	BS1545.3
224.507	BS1555.3
224.5077	BS1555.3
224.606	BS1565.2
224.6077	BS1565.3
224.707	BS1575.3
224.806	BS1585.3
224.807	BS1585.3
224.8077	BS1585.3
224.9	BS1595.3
224.907	BS1560
224.91	BS1595.3
224.92	BS580.J55
224.9206	BS1605.2
224.9209505	BS580.J55
224.9506	BS1635.2
225	BS2330.2
	BS2370
	BS2397
225.0202	BS2525
225.052	BS2025
225.07	BS2535.2
225.08	BS2395
225.4	BS2325
225.48	BS1939
	BS1965
225.52	BS2092.A1
	BS2095
	BS2095.N36
	BS2317
225.5203	BS2085
225.5204	BS2095
	BS2097
225.591660924	PB2109.S2
225.6	BS2330.2
	BS2361.2
	BS2370
	BS2395
	BS2397
225.63	BS2331
225.67	BM170
225.68	BS2378
225.7	BS2341.2
225.77	BS2341.2
225.82341	BT768
225.8262	BV597
225.826413	BV228
225.83014284	HQ824
225.834	BS2417.L3
225.9	BS633
225.91	BS2410
225.922	BS2440
225.924	BS2505
	BS2506
	BS2506.5
225.93	BS2375
225.95	BS2330.2
	BS2400
	BS2407
	BS2410
225.9505	BT302
226	BS2465
	BS2551.A2
	BS2555
	BS2555.2
	BS2555.3
	BT297
	BT299.2
226.04	BS2555.2
226.048	BS2555
226.052	BS2553
226.06	BS2363
	BS2555.2
226.066	BR60
	BS2555.2
	BS2555.5
	BT202
226.067	BS2555.2
226.077	BS2555.3
226.08933	BS2545.J4
226.093	BS2375
226.09505	BS2430
226.1	BT299.2
226.106	BS2555.2
226.2	BS2545.W45
	BS2575.2
	BS2675.4
	BT380
	BT380.2
	BT382
226.2052	BS2577
226.2066	BS2575.2
226.2077	BS2341.2
226.3066	BS2585.2
226.3067	BS2585.2
226.307	BS2585.3
226.3077	BS2585.3
226.4	BS2589.A3
	BS2595.2
226.4048	BS2591
226.406	BS2465
	BS2595.2
226.4077	BS2341.2
226.5	BS2615.2
226.501	BS2615.2
226.5047	BS2612
226.506	BS2615.2
226.5066	BS2615.2
226.5067	BS2601
226.507	BS2615.3
	BS2615.4
226.5077	BS2615.3
226.6	BS2625.3
226.606	BS2625.2
226.6066	BS2625.2
226.6067	BS2625.2
226.6077	BS2341.2
	BS2625.3
226.60924	BS2506
226.8	BT375.2
226.8007	BT377
226.806	BT375.2
226.900222	BV232
226.906	BV232
226.93	BT382
227	BM487
	BS2651
	BS2665.3
	BS2705.5
227.048	BS2641.7
227.052	BS2633
227.06	BS2651
227.066	BS2506
227.07	BS2650.3
227.08326	BS2655.S55
227.1	BS2665.3
	BS2665.4
	BS2675.2
	BS2675.3
227.1066	BS2665.3
227.107	BS2665.2
	BS2665.3
227.1077	BS2665.3
227.2	BS2675.2
227.207	BS2675.4
227.307	BS2675.3
227.3077	BS2675.3
227.406	BS2650.2
227.4077	BS2341.2
	BS2685.3
227.5077	BS2341.2
227.6	BS2705.4
227.6077	BS2705.3
227.8	BS2735.2
	BS2735.3
227.81	BS2725.3
227.8107	BS2725.3
227.83048	BS2745.2
227.83077	BS2341.2
	BS2735.3
227.87007	BS2775.5
227.870071	BS2775.5
227.87014	BS2775.2
227.87077	BS2341.2
227.9	BS2795.3
227.91	BS2785.4
227.9106	BS2785.2
227.9107	BS2785.3
227.91077	BS2785.3
227.92	BS2795.3
227.9207	BS2795.3
227.92077	BS2341.2
	BS2795.3
227.94066	BS2805.2
227.9407	BS2805.2
	BS2805.3
227.94077	BS2805.3
228	BS2825.2
228.06	BR185
	BS2825.2
228.066	BS2825.2
228.07	BS2825.3
228.077	BS2825
	BS2825.3
	BX8712
229.052	BS1692
229.806	BS2840
229.913	BS1830.E6
229.92043	BS2870.S9
230	B765
	B765.A81
	BF175
	BL182
	BR65.A9
	BR85
	BR100
	BR115.H5
	BR115.W6
	BR121.2
	BR123
	BR124
	BS478
	BS543
	BS1192.5
	BS2397
	BS2545.F7
	BS2651
	BT10
	BT15
	BT19

Dewey	LC
230	BT25
	BT28
	BT60
	BT65
	BT75
	BT75.2
	BT77
	BT82
	BT83.5
	BT83.53
	BT83.6
	BT83.7
	BT98
	BT135
	BT695
	BT703
	BT771.2
	BT1102
	BT1105
	BV603
	BV4637
	BX6.W775
	BX885
	BX1747
	BX4805.2
	BX4827.K5
	BX4827.T53
	BX6495.N59
	BX9721.2
230.01	BT10
	BT40
230.03	BR95
230.076	BR96
230.08	BT10
	BT15
	BX7117
230.09	BR65.A9
	BT19
	BT21.2
	BT80
230.09031	BR301
230.0904	BL65.L2
	BR121.2
	BS543
	BT28
230.09042	BT82.3
230.0922	BR525
	BR569
	BT28
230.0924	B2430.T374
	B4377
	BR115.H5
	BR326
	BR350.B93
	BV600.2
	BX4827.B3
	BX4827.B78
	BX4827.K5
	BX4827.N47
	BX4827.N5
	BX4827.T53
	PR3332
	PR4487.R4
230.0942	BT28
230.0973	BT30.U6
230.130922	BR1720.T3
230.14	BR63
230.140924	BR65
	BR65.A9
	BR1720.A7
230.19	BX320
230.2	B2430.T373
	BR115.H5
	BS543
	BS543.A1
	BT19
	BT21
	BT60
	BT75.2
	BT77
	BT80
	BT202
	BT993.2
	BX830
	BX1749
	BX1751.A1
	BX1751.2
	BX1751.2.A1
	BX1752
	BX1753
	BX1754
	BX1767
	BX3503
	BX4705.N5
230.208	AC8
230.20924	B2430
	BT126
	BT126.5
	BT751.2
	BT761.2
	BX1396
	BX4700
	BX4705.L7133
	BX4735.P26
230.3	BR85
	BT77
230.308	BX7117
230.30922	B1133.C2
230.30924	B1674.W3483
	BX8066.T46
230.4	BT30.G3
	BX4827.T53
230.40924	BX4827.B3
	BX4827.R5
230.41	BR336
	BX8065
230.410924	BR333.2
	BR333.5.B5
	BX4827.B57
	BX4827.B78
	BX8066.T46
	BX8080.B47
230.420924	BX9418
230.5	BR85
	BT80
230.5808	BX7117.E33
230.5908	BX9315
230.6	BT77
	BX6225
230.61	BT1102
	BV4870
	BX6333.S45
230.66	BX7321
230.67	BT75.2
230.7	BR85
230.70924	BX8495.W5
230.76	BT77
230.8	BX9869.P3
230.91	BX9940
230.924	PR1578
230.93	BX8635
	BX8635.2
230.930924	BX8635.2
230.933	BX8674
230.94	BX8721.2
	BX8748
230.96	BX7731.2
	BX7732
230.973	BX8129.H8
230.98	BX9771
230.99	BR85
	BR126
231	BS543
	BT77
	BT83.5
	BT98
	BT102
	BT111.2
	BT175
	BT180.N2
	BX9418
231.07	BT99
231.0924	BT83.5
	BT100.T4
	BT102
	BX4827.T53
231.3	BR65
	BS2615.2
	BT121
	BT121.2
	BX1751.2.A1
231.4	BT102
	BT124
	BT124.5
	BT912
231.5	BT135
231.6	BT140
	BV4639
231.7	BR65.A64E5
	BS649.J5
	BS2417.K5
	BT94
	BT155
231.73	BS511.2
	BT97
	BT97.2
	BX2167.A5
231.74	BT102
	BT126.5
	BT127
	BT127.2
	BT140
231.8	BJ1401
	BT160
	BV4905.2
	BV4909
232	BR333.5.C4
	BS2430
	BS2555
	BT198
	BT200
	BT201
	BT202
	BT205
	BT232
	BT254
	BT264
	BT270
	BT297
	BT303.2
	BT304.96
	BT307
	BT308
	BT590.N2
232.	BT202
232.09	BT198
232.09015	BS2615.2
232.1	BT220
	BT232
232.12	BS647.2
232.3	BT450
232.309	BT263
232.5	BT870
232.6	BT886
232.8	BT200
	BT202
	BT215
232.9	BT301
232.9	BT301.2
	BT301.9
	BX1747.5
232.901	BT198
	BT299.2
	BT301
	BT301.2
	BT302
	BT303
	BT306.3
232.90108	BT306.5
232.9030924	BT304.2
232.908	BT303.2
	BT303.8
232.91	BT638
	BT640
	BT645
232.913	BS2595.3
232.92	BT310
232.921	BT315.2
232.929	BT320
232.932	BT690
232.94	BS2456
232.95	BT366
232.954	BS2261
	BS2415
	BS2416
	BT306
	BT380.2
	BT382
232.96	BT431
	BT453
	BV4298
232.961	BS2460.J8
232.962	BT430
	BT440
232.963	BT456
	BX2040
232.9635	BT456
232.97	BT481
233	BD431
	BD450
	BF1791
	BR128.H8
	BS680.S2
	BT700
	BT701.2
	BT703
	BT725
	BT736.6
	BV1610
233.0922	BT701.2
233.0924	BT701.2
233.1	BS661
233.11	BT695
233.14	BT710
233.2	BT715
	BT720
233.21	BV4626
233.7	BT810.2
234	BS680.E9
	BT205
	BT262
	BT753
	BT759
	BT766
	BV4501.2
	BX2350.2
	BX8495.W5
234.01	BR128.G8
234.1	BT123
	BT761.2
	BT769
	BX5995.B394
	BX7233.E3
	Z7798
234.160924	BV800
234.163	BX2215.2
234.1630924	BX2220
234.165	BT706
	BX2250
234.2	BS1199.H65
	BT771.2
	BV4310
	BV4637
234.20922	BT771
234.20924	BR333.2
234.3	BT775
234.4	BT795
234.5	BT795
	BV4509.5
234.8	BT766
	BT767
234.9	B765
	BJ1461
	BT810.2
	BX6195
235.2	BR1710
	BX1765
	BX4662
235.3	BT966.2
235.4	BF1520
	BT980
	BT981
235.47	BT981
236	B4238
	BS647.2
	BT75.2
	BT821.2
	BT823
	BT870
	BT875
	BT876
	BT902
236	BV4638
236.08	BT825
236.0924	B4238.B44
236.1	BD444
	BT825
	BX5133.D6
236.2	BT101.A1
	BT823
	BT901
	BT904
	BX8729.F8
236.22	BT921.2
	BT923
236.220924	BR65.A9
236.23	BT930
236.24	BT846.2
236.25	BT836.2
236.3	BT891
	DG737.97
238	BT1031.2
	BX9428
238.11	BT993.2
238.2	BX926
	BX1751.2
	BX1961
	BX1965
	BX1966.D8
238.3	BX5137
238.41	BR332
	BX8070.L77
238.42	BX9429
238.5	BX9184
238.58	BX9184.A5
239	BL2775.2
	BT1101
	BT1102
	BT1105
239.009	BT1106
239.00904	BT1102
239.3	BR60
239.8	BT1105
240	BV4501.2
241	BJ1031
	BJ1225
	BJ1249
	BJ1251
	BJ1275
	BJ1451
	BJ1459
	BJ1533.F8
	BJ1581.2
	BJ1661
	BR85
	BT706
	BT708
	BT738
	BV4647.C5
	BX1758.2
	BX4827.B3
	E449
	HQ35
	HQ63
	HQ766.3
	HQ767
	HV5186
241.019	BJ1249
241.07	BV1471.2
241.071	BJ1200
241.08	BJ1193
	BJ1251
241.1	BJ1471
	BV4615
241.3	BV4625
	BV4626
241.4	BR85
	BT767
	BV4630
	BV4638
	BV4639
	BX2350.5
	BX7233.E3
241.5	BJ1191
241.52	BV4655
241.699	BV4638
	BV4639
242	BJ1548
	BJ1581.2
	BS483.5
	BT107
	BT382
	BT732.5
	BT769
	BV210.2
	BV213
	BV233
	BV245
	BV255
	BV260
	BV280
	BV4510.2
	BV4531.2
	BV4638
	BV4655
	BV4801
	BV4811
	BV4813
	BV4832.2
	BV4850
	BV5091.C7
	BX2170.C55
	BX2170.F3
	BX2182.2
	BX2184

Dewey	LC
242	BX2185
	BX2350.2
	BX6123
	BX6333.H345
	BX6333.P4
	BX8066.H583
	BX8495.W5
	PN6084.R3
	PS3552.R63
	QK84
242.019	BF1091
242.08	BV4801
	BV4818
	PN6081
242.09	BV4818
242.0904	BV4501.2
242.1	BR65
	BR65.A9
	BV4818
	BV4821
	BV4829
	BX2179.F8
242.2	BS390
	BV245
	BV4501
	BV4810
	BV4811
	BV4832.2
	BV4850
242.3	BV30
	BX2170.C55
242.33	BV40
	BX2182.2
242.34	BX2170.L4
242.4	B785.C33
	BJ1581.2
	BV199.F8
	BV245
	BV270
	BV4832.2
	BV4905.2
	BV4907
	BV4909
	BV4910
	PN6084.C57
242.62	BV4870
242.63	BV4850
242.64	BV835
	BV4596.M3
242.643	BV283.M7
	BV4844
242.65	BV4501.2
	BV4580
242.68	BV4588
242.694	BV4813
242.72	BV245
242.722	BV230
242.8	BL560
	BV245
	BV280
242.802	BV245
242.803	BR124
	BV245
	BV260
242.8041	BV245
	BV260
242.807	BV245
242.82	BV245
	BV4870
242.83	BV210.2
	BV283.Y6
242.84	BV4845
242.842	BV245
242.843	BV4844
242.88	BV280
	BV283.C7
242.892	BV4830
245	BT453
245.0922	BV325
245.2	ML3170
246	BL65.C8
	BX4700.C57
246.5	BV825.52
	BX2310.R7
246.55	BL604.H6
246.9	BM654
	BT660.C34
247	BX5975
247.7	BX5975
248	BJ1499.S6
	BJ1581.2
	BL53
	BL624
	BR85
	BR112
	BR115.C45
	BR115.H5
	BR1608.C66
	BR1725.J64
	BT732.7
	BT1102
	BT1105
	BV772
	BV4490
	BV4500
	BV4501.2
	BV4510.2
	BV4513
	BV4515.2
	BV4517
	BV4638
	BV4740
	BX2350
	BX2350.2
248	BX4705.G415
	BX5995.S346
	BX9420.A32
	BX9890.U5
	ML420.B7
248.0924	BR1725.R47
	BX7260.W48
	E457.2
248.10924	BX4827.B57
248.2	BJ1548
	BL53
	BL54
	BR125
	BR1700.2
	BR1725.R63
	BV5095
	BX2350.2
	BX8763
248.20924	BT732.5
	BV4935.B77
248.22	B2430.T373
	BF639
	BV5075
	BV5077.G3
	BV5080.C6
	BV5080.M29
	BX155
	F152.2
248.2208	BX890
248.220922	BV5077.G7
248.220947	BV5077.R8
248.24	BV4916
	BX5199.A75
	BX6193.L4
248.242	BX4668.A1
248.246	BV2623.A1
	BV2623.T66
	BV2626.3M54
	BV4922
	BV4925
	BV4930
	BX4668.A495
	GV964.C3
248.25	BJ10.M6
248.250924	BJ10.M6
	CT275.S5228
248.29	BR60
	BX2323
248.3	BL627
	BV205
	BV210.2
	BV213
	BV284.G6
	BV4517
	BV4813
	D839.7.H3
248.4	BF575.L8
	BJ1533.C4
	BJ1581.2
	BJ1595
	BJ1597
	BJ1611
	BR121.2
	BV4490
	BV4501.2
	BV4639
	BV4647.C5
	BV4647.P5
	BV4832.2
	RC530
	RC537
248.42	BJ1571
	BJ1581.2
	BJ1611.2
	BT1102
	BV4500.F47
	BV4501.2
	BV4509.5
	BV4510.2
	BV4637
	BX2182.2
	BX2350.2
248.482	BJ1468.5
	BJ1583
	BJ1595
	BR121.2
	BV4501.2
	BX2250
	BX2350.2
	BX2435
248.48208	BV210.2
	BV4501.2
	BX2350.5
248.4820967	BX2351
248.483	BJ1251
248.4851	BV4501.2
248.4857	BV4511
248.4858	BV4501.2
	BX7233.K6
248.486	BV4501.2
	BV4510
248.4861	BV4501.2
	BV4509.5
248.48673	BV4501.2
248.487	BV4501.2
248.4893	BJ1251
	BJ1611.2
248.4896	BV4501.2
	BX7607.N4
248.4897	BV4501.2
248.4899	BF575.L8
	BX9890.U5
248.5	BV4520
248.8	BV4911
248.82	BJ1249
	BV1475.2
	BV1475.8
248.820207	PN6328.C5
248.83	BJ1251
	BJ1661
	BV639.C6
	BV652.1
	BV1485
	BV1561
	BV2390
	BV4447
	BV4501.2
	BV4531.2
	BX2355
	BX8643.Y6
248.830212	BV4531.2
248.832	BJ1671
248.84	BT706
	BV835
	BV4526.2
	BV4596.S5
	BV4832.2
	BX2250
	HQ10
248.843	BJ1610
	BV4527
248.85	BV4580
248.86	BV4905.2
	BV4909
248.860924	RC263
248.88	BV4515.2
248.89019	BX2380
248.894	BV4518
	BX1912
	BX2350
	BX2385
	BX2435
	DA670.L19
248.894019	BX2440
248.89408	BX2435
248.894094	BX2470
248.8940942	BS2592
	BX2470
248.8942	BX1912.5
248.89425	BX2440
248.89428	BV4408
	BX3004
248.8943	BX4205
248.8943019	BX4205
248.89432	BX4210
248.92	BX2350.2
248.9208	BV4501.2
250	BV600.2
	BV652.2
	BV660.2
	BV705
	BV4011
	BV4017
	BV4319
250.19	BV4011
250.207	PN6231.C5
250.904	BV601.8
251	BV4207
	BV4210
	BV4211.2
	BV4222
	BV4307.D5
	BX4827.B3
	BX9334.2
251.009	BV4207
251.00922	BV4207
251.00924	BV4207
	BX7077.Z8K45
251.00942	BV4208.G7
	BX9333
251.00973	BR563.N4
	BV4208.U6
251.02	BV4223
	BX1756.Q5
251.08	BV4225.2
252	BV3797
	BV4241
	BV4253
	BX9727.C65
252.008	BV4241
252.00973	BV3797
	BV4241
252.0242	PR1119
252.03	BX5133.B87
	BX5133.N4
252.0308	BX5133
252.041	BR1608.R8
	BX8066
	BX8066.G7
	BX8066.H46
	BX8066.H583
252.04143	BV4244
252.05	BX9178.M172
	BX9178.R367
252.051	BX9178.F79
	BX9178.J59
	BX9178.M363
252.052	BV4253
252.05241	BX9178
252.058	BT738
	BX7233.M32D36
252.06	BV3797
	BX6333
	BX6333.C58
	BX6333.L3953
	BX6333.W27
252.0608	BX6333.C77
252.061	BX6333
252.061	BX6333.A1
	BX6333.F568
	BX6333.H345
	BX6333.P394
	BX6495.L43
252.06132	BX6333.A1
252.063	BX7077.Z6
252.066	BX7327.A1
252.0663	BV4253
	BX7077
252.07	BV4515.2
	BX8333.A67
	BX8333.W425
252.076	BX8333.G65
252.08	BX9843
	BX9843.B288
252.093	BX8639
	BX8639.C7G6
252.099	BX6198.A7
	BX6510.B676
252.52	BV4315
252.53	BV4315
252.55	BV4310
252.6	BV652.7
	BX6333.F568
252.61	BV4254.5
252.62	BS1235.4
	BV4277
	BV4298
252.6208	BX8333.L43
252.68	F229
252.9	BR60.F3
	BV199.I5
253	BR63
	BV660.2
	BV672.5
	BV4010
	BV4011
	BV4012
	BV4017
	BV4165
	BV4423
	BX1912
	BX1913
	BX7326
	PR3507
253.019	BV4012
253.0207	PN6231.C5
253.023	BV660.2
253.0924	BR1720.A9
	BX1912
253.2	BR517
	BV660.2
	BV672.5
	BV676
	BV4390
	BV4395
	BX4669
253.20207	NC1760.J4
253.20924	BX4705.L717
253.5	BL53
	BV652.2
	BV1610
	BV2695.W6
	BV4012
	BV4012.2
	BV4165
	DA670.Y59
	HQ728
	R726.5
253.50186	BV4012.2
253.5019	BV4012
253.508	BV4012.2
253.50926	BV4012.2
253.7	BV3755
	BV3790
	BV3793
	BX6495.E4
253.78	BV2082.R3
254	BV600
	BV600.2
	BV650.2
	BV652.2
	BV652.9
	BV664
	BV705
	BV777
254.02	BV652.9
254.2	BV1610
254.240975	BV638
254.3	BV656
254.4	BV653
	BV2369
254.50974	BX9353
254.6	BV652.1
	BV652.9
254.7	BV604
	BV652.7
	CS435
255	BX2410
	BX2434
255.5	BX3704
255.79	BX3825
255.9	BX4210
258	BV4012.3
	BV4470
	HV530
	RA790.6
259	BV652.2
	BV1610
	BV1630
	BV1650
	BV2656.S9
	BV4377

259 BV4438
BV4447
BV4464.5
BV4470
260 BR50
BR115.W6
BR121.2
BR123
BT28
BT83.7
BT265.2
BT738
BT759
BT1102
BV598
BV600
BV600.2
BV601.8
BV601.9
BV603
BV652
BV1643
BV3795
BV4400
BX6
BX6.W77
BX1746
BX2347.8.W6
BX4805.2
BX6333
BX8937
HN39.L3
260.207 PN6231.C35
260.27 BV4
260.3 BR95
BR96.5
260.7 BL65.N3
260.8 BX1746
260.83 HN39.U6
260.901 BM535
260.904 BV600.2
261 BL60
BL65.P7
BL2747.8
BR115.W6
BR121.2
BR123
BR124
BR128.A8
BR479
BR1700.2
BT83.7
BT703
BT738
BV600.2
BV601.8
BV625
BV1473
BV1534.5
BV4208.U6
BV4509.5
BX891
BX946
BX1395
BX1404
BX1426.2
BX1685
BX6225
BX7615
261.0712 BV1561
261.08 BX830
261.0924 BX9886.Z8
BX9886.Z8B43
261.0942 BR757
261.0973 BT738
261.0994 BT738
261.1 BV601.8
HT151
261.2 BL220
BM535
BR127
BR128.B8
BR128.H5
BV2170
261.5 BJ59
BL241
BR115.C8
BS659
BV1610
261.7 BJ1459
BR115.P7
BR115.W6
BR516
BV741
BX1396.4
BX1401.A1
BX1793
E297
HN373
261.709021 BX1790
261.70924 BV630.2
261.709436 AS36
261.72 BR757
BV741
BX4931.2
261.7208 BV740
261.720942 BV741
261.7209436 Q11
261.720946 BR1023
261.720973 BR516
261.8 BL65.C8
BL485
BR85
BR115.P7
BR115.W6
BR121.2
BR1642.U5
BS1505.4
BT38
BT77
BT736.15
BT736.6
BT738
BT738.3
BV600.2
BV601.8
BV602
BV625
BV637
BV639.C6
BV2105
BV3797
BX1405
BX5093
BX5195.C6
BX7321.2
BX7648.N8
BX8381
E169.12
E446
E449
GF80
HN18
HN31
HN37.C3
261.808 BT738
261.80924 BX4705.P439
BX4827.E5
261.83 BJ59
BJ1249
BJ1661
BR115.W6
BR121.2
BR525
BT706
BT708
BT732
BT734
BT734.2
BT736.15
BT738
BT738.3
BV637
BV639.C6
BV4470
BV4531.2
BX835
BX1753
BX2250
BX4705.L795
BX6193.W5
BX6480.M23
BX7748.R3
BX8641
DA125.A1
E185.615
E446
E446.B77
E449
E449.H793
HM136
HN37.C3
HN37.F9
HN39.U6
HQ32
HQ76
HQ766.3
HT871
HT1521
HV645
JC585
261.8308 BV4647.B7
261.830922 HN385
261.830975 BX8237
261.83098 HN39.L3
261.83417 HQ766.3
261.834493 E449
HT917.M4
261.834510420973 BT734.2
261.85 BC2695.M5
BR115.E3
BV639.P6
BV2695.M5
S912
261.850902 BR115.E3
261.85094297 BV625
261.87 BR115.I7
BR115.W6
BX7606.5
261.873 BL2780
BT736.2
BT736.4
HJ2305
JX1963
262 BV600.2
BV639.W7
BV640
BV649
BV1471.2
BV4415
BX830
262.001 BR121.2
BR123
BR744
BR764
BV600
BV600.2
262.001 BV603
BV652
BV720
BV3793
BX6
BX6.W77
BX6.W78
BX6.5
BX6.9
BX8.2
BX8.2.A1
BX9
BX9.5.C5
BX809.F6
BX830
BX1746
BX1751.2
BX1765.2
BX4817
BX5129.8.P7
BX8495.W5
BX9211.H22
262.00924 BV598
BX9418
262.02 BT810.2
BX1802
262.0209 BX1802
262.02415 BX1503
262.0273 BX833
262.02914 DS689.M15
262.03 BX5021
262.0342 BR759
BX5150
262.041748 BX8061.S63
262.05241 BX9078
262.05242 BX9053
262.06 BX6346
262.06132 BV652.1
BX6340
262.076 BX8388
262.07601 BX8.2
262.07673 BX8388
262.096 BX7678.L6
262.1 BS2618
BV648
BV652.1
BV660.2
BX540
262.12 BX1751.2
BX1905
BX8065.2
262.120942 BX4666
262.13 BV720
BX955.2
BX957
BX1805
262.1309 BR162
262.1309023 BX1270
262.1309034 BX955.2
262.130922 BX955.2
BX957
BX1365
262.130924 BX1187
BX1226
BX1323
BX1355
BX1378
BX1378.2
BX1378.3
262.135 BX4664
262.1350922 BX4665.U5
262.1350924 BX4705.S74
262.14 BV676
BX1912
BX5165
BX5965
262.140922 BR563.N4
262.140942 BR747
262.15 BV680
BV687
BX1912
BX1920
262.150715 BV652.1
262.15091734 BV638.8
262.150924 BX4705.N5
262.22 BX1913
BX8675
262.220942 BR747
262.3 BX5106
262.30922 BX5195.H4H45
262.3094281 DA20
262.4 BX220
BX4705.R45
BX8968.O7
BX9478
262.5 BR200
BX6.W77
BX830
BX838
BX1765.2
262.7 BT83.7
BV598
BV601.8
BX1390
BX1746
262.70924 BV598
262.70973 BV600.2
262.72 BV601.6.I5
BV601.8
BX324.5
262.8 BT90
BT91
BX1751.2.A1
BX1802
262.80901 BT91
262.9 BR750
262.90973 KF4865
263 BV111
BV125
263.042788 F777
263.3 BM685
BV130
263.92 BV85
264 BS1435
BS2940.T5
BV10.2
BV15
BV25
BV26
BV176
BV199.D3
BV199.O3
BV1522
PN49
264.0014 BV15
264.011 BV185
264.019 BX350
BX350.A5
BX360.A5
BX375.E75
BX375.H6
BX375.K3
BX375.L4
BX375.M37
BX375.O3
BX5927
264.02 BV170
BX830
BX1970
BX2169
BX4711.663
BX4711.665.H6
264.02009 BX1970
BX5141
264.020094281 BX2015.7
264.0206 BV199.O3
264.0209 BX2045.P65
264.022 BX2032.A3S34
264.023 BV825.5
BX2015
BX2015.A2
BX2015.A4
BX2015.8.H6
BX2037
BX2169
BX2230.2
BX4773
BX5142
BX5143
Z241.M67
264.024 BX2000
264.0272 BV55
264.0274 BX2040
264.03 BX5141.A25
BX5145
BX5945
264.03009 BX5141
264.031 BV85
264.035 BV199.F8
BV199.I5
BX5149.B2
264.038 ML3166
264.070942 BX8337
264.097 BV10.2
264.1 BV210.2
BV213
BV228
264.107 BV214
264.13 BT670.T5
BV245
BV280
264.2 BV315
BV350
BV467.5.R6
264.3 BX2230.2
264.3094372 BX4933.M6
264.7 BV29
265 BT202
BV800
BX9.5.S2
BX2200
BX2205
265.1 BV803
BV811.2
BX5141
265.12 BV813.2
265.2 BV815
BX5149.C7
BX5949.C7
BX8074.C7
265.3 BR121.2
BV823
BV825.2
BV825.5
BV4257.5
BX9.5.I5
BX2220
BX5949.C5
265.309 BV823
265.4 BX2031.R5
BX2240
265.5 BX2250
265.6 BV840
BX2260
265.609 BV840
265.62 BV845
BX2265.2
BX2266.C5

Dewey	LC
265.62019	BV845
266	BT891
	BV2061
	BV2070
	BV2073
	BV2360.B48
	BV2369
	BV3793
266.001	BV2063
266.007	BV2090
266.008	BV2035
266.009	BR141
	BV2100
266.00952	BV3445
266.00968	BV3555
266.00978	E99.D1
266.0098	BV2831
	BV3777.L3
266.0099	BR1490
266.009921	BV3365
266.00994	BV2470.A8
266.0220924	BV2657.W35
266.02209944	BV2656.S9W35
266.023	BV2061
	BV2073
	BV2093.C66
	BV3625.R53
266.02306273	BV2360.A5
266.023091724	BV2061
266.0230922	BV2360.O7
	BV3503
	BV3680.H4
	BV3700
	BV3703
266.0230924	AS36
	BR1725.G94
	BV3317.B7
	BV3427.A9
	BV3427.T3
	BV3555
	BV3625.A6
	BV3625.C63
	BV3625.K42
	BV3625.M2
	BV3625.M22P4
	BV3667.W6
	BV3680.H4
	BX6495.K357
	DT776.M7
266.0230952	BV3445.2
266.0230954	BV2410
	BX9743.S55
266.0230956	BV3160
266.02309597	BV3325.A6
266.023096	BV3500
266.023096652	BV3625.G814
266.0230967	BV3500
	BV3520
266.0230968	BV3550
266.02309729	BV2845.2
266.023098611	BV2853.C7
266.02309911	BV3345
266.023099112	BV3345
266.0234	BV3625.S4
266.0236711	BV3625.C29
266.025	R722
266.0250924	CT1098.S45
	R722
266.025095	R722
266.09	BV3630.K3
266.1947	BV2857.S68
266.2	BV2160
	BV2180
	BX1746
	R722
266.2025	BV2178
266.20922	BX4705.B18
266.20924	BV3269.T67
	BV3271.C58
	BV3462.S35
	BX4705.L4
	BX4705.L413
266.209689	BV2290.A5
266.2096891	BV2290
266.20971317	F1030.7
266.209763	BV2803.L8
266.2594	BV3325.L3
266.273	E98.M6
266.279498	F869.S22
266.28	BX1461
266.285	BV2300.P3
266.2931	BX1685
266.294	BV3650
	BX3048.A1
266.2941	BV3660.K5
266.30924	BV2653
	BV3457.R8
	BV3625.U4
	BV3667.K4
	BX5620.I74
	BX5720.5
	CT275.F824
266.354	BV3265.2
266.36	BV3625.N82
266.363	BV3625.S8
266.3666	BV3625.L5
266.36694	BV3630.I2
266.367	BV3530
266.3686	BV3625.K3
266.3687	DT846.K2
266.37	BV2500.A6
266.37297	H31
266.395	BV3680.N5
266.41	BV2540
	BV2540.A536
266.410924	BV2853.D9
	BV3667.S84
266.415412	BV3280.S3
266.4195	BV3680.N5
266.46701	AS36.G378
266.46729722	BV2848.V5
266.510924	BV3415.2
	BV3457.G7
	E98.M6
266.513309675	BV3625.C6
266.5136	BV2835.2
266.51519	BV3460
	HV1559.K8
266.5181	BX9042.B66
266.520924	BV3625.N6
266.5209941	BV3660.W4
266.52681	R722
266.526897	BV3520
	BV3625.N8
	BV3625.N82
266.570924	BV3427.D35
266.5806273	BV2360.A5
266.5809684	BV3625.Z8
266.6	BV2520
	BV3265.2
	BV3425.H6
266.607	BV2090
266.60922	BV3427.H24
266.60924	BV2853.B7
266.610924	BV2848.C92
	BV3202.R6
	BV3269.A67
	BV3427.B38
	BV3427.L44
	BV3427.M55
	BV3457.A9
	BX6495.J95
266.610954162	BV3280.A8
266.6132	BV2520
266.61320951249	BV3450.F7
266.613209569	BV2625
266.614	BX6275
266.615695	BV2087
266.61701	E98.M6
266.6173	BV2766.B5
266.670924	BV3271.T45
	BV3342.Y65
	BV3427.S63
	BV3557.A6
	BV3680.F6
	BV3680.S62
	BX6193.G6
266.673	BV3680.N5
266.6730924	R154.R96
266.673099611	BV3680.F5
266.67519	BV2087
266.675991	BV3380
266.678	BV2087
266.6781	BV2853.B6
266.70924	BV3269.S375
	R722
266.709969	BX8248.H38
266.71685	BV3625.O7
266.71688	BV3625.S65
266.716891	BV1651
266.760924	BV2853.B5
	BV2853.B7
	BV3462.K58
	BX8495.W584
	R608.S92
266.7673	BV2766.M7
266.935	BV3151
266.9375	BX8661
266.96	BX7748.I65
266.960924	BV2803.A4
266.970924	BV3427.B36
266.976694	BV3625.N5
266.99	BV3317.J6
	BV3625.C6
	BV3625.S352
267	BV4408
267.10924	BV4487.L3
267.1309753	BX8076.W3C65
267.15	BX9722
	Z232.S18
267.150922	BX9741
267.150924	BX9743.B37
	BX9743.B6
	BX9743.B63
	BX9743.W45
	BX9743.Y3
267.15095	HV4432
267.23	BV4520
	BX8128.W4
267.3951	BV1060.C6
267.4	BV199.I5
267.59	BV1340
267.6	BV1610
267.61	BV1430.Y6
	BV4427
267.610924	BX5199.B873
267.622	BX809.Y62
267.626	BX6207
267.6261	BX6205.B27
268	BV1471.2
	BV1521
	BV1533
	BV1615.M37
	BV1615.M4
268.01	BV1464
	BV1475
268.01	BX4827.T53
268.019	BV1471.2
268.0202	BV1471.2
268.07	BV1534
268.0712	BX926
268.08	BV1473
	BV4319
268.09	BV1465.K5
268.093	BV1465
268.09427	BR759
268.0973	BV1521
	LC2751
268.09746	BV1468.C8
268.1	BS600.2
	BV1585
268.174	BX6239
268.4	BV1475.2
	BV1534
	BX9714
268.43	HM271
268.432	BV1475.2
	BV1475.8
	BV1534
	BV1536
	BV1539
	BV1540
	BV1546
	BV1559
	BV1615.M4
	BV4870
	BX929
	BX930
268.433	BT108
	BV1485
	BV1534
	BV1549.2
	BV4511
	BX930
	BX6225
	BX8015
	BX8124
268.434	BV1488
	BV4511
	BX930
	BX5875
	BX8015
268.6	BS592
	BV1470.J3
	BV1471.2
	BV1473
	BV1558
	BV1559
	BV1615.S6
	BX1968
	BX5049
268.6019	LB1067
268.61	BV1471.2
	BX930
	BX6225
	HQ772
268.635	BV1535.Z9
268.67	BV1534.4
	PS351
268.817	BV1470.E8
268.82	BV1471.2
	BX921
268.8208	BV1473
268.8373	BX5850
268.86132	BV4520
268.87673	BX8223
269	BV3790
	BV4400
269.2	BR195.E9
	BV3775.A5
	BV3777.G6
	BV3785.H346
	BV3790
	BV3795
	BX6154
269.20924	BV3785.A43
	BV3785.F49
	BV3785.G69
	BV3785.J59
	BV3785.M7
	BV3785.R58
	BV3785.S56
	BV3785.S6
269.20942	BV3790
269.2095	BV3755
269.209669	BV3777.N54
269.2097293	BV3777.D6
269.20973	BR520
269.209769483	BV3775.W5
269.63	BX2376.S7
270	BL2775.2
	BR138
	BR141
	BR145
	BR145.2
	BR146
	BR148
	BR162.2
	BR252
	BR1700
	BR1710
	BV600.2
	BX4651
	BX4654
	BX4655.2
	BX4658
	BX4659.G7
	BX4659.I7
270.1	BR67
	BR160.A2
270.1	BR165
	BR168
	BR170
	BR195.C5
	BR1700.2
	BR1710
	BT308
270.1072	BR138
270.108	BR63
	BS2650
270.10922	BR195.C5
	BR1706
270.10924	BR1720.P28
270.2	BR162.2
270.20924	BX4700.C8
	BX4700.I78
	BX4700.P3
270.5	BR252
	BR270
	BX1301
	PR1999
270.50924	BX4905
270.6	BR280
	BR305
	BR305.2
	BR309
	BR430
270.608	BR430
270.60922	BR315
	BR350.O36
270.60924	BR325
	BR331.E5
	BR345
	BR350.V34
270.60942	BR375
270.82	BR121.2
	BX6.5
271	BV4405
	BX2461.2
	BX4272
271.008	BX2432
271.009	BX2432
271.009415	BX2600
271.0097	BX2440
271.1	BX3460
271.10924	DC89.7.S8
271.1094241	BX2596.P7
271.1094255	DA670.N69
271.10994	BX3048.A9
271.12	BX4700.B5
271.120924	BX4700.E7
271.1209449	BX2615.L46
271.20924	BX4705.C76
	DG737.97
271.20973	BX3508
271.3	BX3653.U6
	BX4700.F6
271.30922	F864
271.30924	BX4700.F6
271.36	BX3115
271.5	BX3705.A2
	BX3706.2
271.5073	BX3708
271.50924	B2430.T374
	BX4700.L7
	BX4705.B3845
	BX4705.P72
271.5095482	BV3280.M35
271.509794	BX3712.L6
271.530924	BX4700.C25
271.750924	BX4705.C737
271.780994	BX3060.Z5A84
271.79	BX2970
	BX3653.U6
	BX4705.B3846
	BX4705.M72
	CR4723
	CR4731.P7
	CR4731.R9
271.8	BV4408
271.9	BX4225
271.91	BX4457.Z5C57
	BX4467
271.93	BX4705.M4236
271.950924	BX4705.S6138
271.9710924	BX4323.8
	BX4705.M41235
	NX652.T4
271.9720924	BX4705.W66
271.9730924	BX4354
271.9760924	BX4210
271.977	BX4511
271.979	BX4700.B6
	BX4705.H383
	BX4705.M41134
	BX4705.R424
272	BR1601.2
	BR1608.R8
272.09	BR1601.2
272.1	BR1604
272.2	BX1711
272.20946	BX1735
272.20972	BX1740.M6
272.6	BR1607
272.7	BX1492
272.8	BR1608.R85
272.9	BR1608.R8
	BR1608.U45
273	BT1313
273.09021	BT1315.2
273.4	BT1350
273.5	BT1450
273.60924	F67.H92

273.9 ... BT109
274 ... BR200
... BX1304
274.15 ... BX4659.I7
274.2 ... BR350.T8
... BR375
... BR746
... BR748
... BR750
... BR757
... BR759
... BX4705.W477
... DA375
... PR1578
... PS858.W2
274.20922 ... BR767
274.219 ... DA690.E315
274.225 ... BR377.5.S9
274.235 ... BR763.D6
274.37 ... DB205
274.38 ... BR952
274.771 ... BR937.U4
275.1 ... BR1288
275.4 ... BR1155
276 ... BR1440
276.1 ... BR1390
276.67 ... BR1463.G5
276.7 ... BR1360
276.78 ... BR1443.T35
277.1 ... BR570
277.1274 ... BR580.S7
277.3 ... BR515
... BR516
... BR520
... BR563.N4
... BV601.9
... BV637
... BV637.7
277.4 ... BR520
277.469 ... F102.F2
277.47 ... F122.1
277.9562 ... BR560.T5
277.97 ... BR555.W3
278 ... BR600
279.14 ... BR1260
279.22 ... BR1235
280.09174397 ... BR563.S8
280.0973 ... BR516.5
280.4 ... BT82.2
... BX4811
280.40922 ... BR569
... BR1700.2
280.40947 ... BX4849
280.4097281 ... BX4834.G9
280.40973 ... BR515
... BR520
280.40977866 ... BR560.S2
280.4098 ... BR600
281.108 ... BR60
281.2 ... BR166
281.30922 ... BR1706
281.4 ... BR60
... BR65.A52
... BR205
281.5 ... BT1375
... BX166.2
281.62 ... BX126
... BX126.2
281.7 ... BX133
281.809 ... BX153
281.9 ... BX290
... BX320
... BX320.2
281.909 ... BX290
281.90924 ... BX597.S37
... BX653
... E184.U5
281.93 ... BX290
... BX410
281.9472 ... BX601
281.94771 ... BX324.3
281.954 ... BX163.2
281.963 ... BX143.2
281.973 ... BX738.U45
281.97471 ... BX591.N57
282 ... BV600.2
... BX930
... BX945.2
... BX955.2
... BX1396
... BX1746
... BX1751.2
... BX1753
... BX8763
282.0207 ... PN6231.C22
282.08 ... BX890
... BX891
282.09 ... BX945.2
... BX1396
282.0902 ... BR252
282.0903 ... BX1330
... BX1365
... BX1396.2
282.09034 ... BX1396
282.0904 ... BX885
... BX1389
... BX1751.2
... BX1780
282.0922 ... BX4651
... BX4655
... BX4655.2
... BX4661
... BX4667

282.0922 ... BX4670
... BX4676
... BX4705.M4847
282.0924 ... BX1390
... BX4700.F35
... BX4700.K3
... BX4700.L66
... BX4700.S35
... BX4700.S7
... BX4705.B12
... BX4705.B88
... BX4705.C2625
... BX4705.E66
... BX4705.F6
... BX4705.F635
... BX4705.G484
... BX4705.H37
... BX4705.H79
... BX4705.J333
... BX4705.L3684
... BX4705.M252
... BX4705.O498
... BX4705.R286
... BX4705.S517
... BX4705.T482
... BX4705.Y56
... F864
... PQ1796
... PQ1796.J313
... PR6039.H575
282.094 ... BX1490.A2
282.41 ... BX1497
... BX1499.2
282.415 ... BX1503
282.4161 ... BX4632.G54S3
282.42 ... BR747
... BX1763
282.4274 ... BX4631.H6
282.52 ... BX1668
282.54 ... BX1644
282.716 ... BX1423.A6
282.72 ... BR610
282.7295 ... BR645.P7
282.73 ... BX1389
... BX1406
... BX1406.2
... BX1407.I7
... BX1751.2
282.748 ... BX1417.S4
282.76 ... BX1410
282.76342 ... BX4603.F67A82
282.794 ... BX1415.C2
282.798 ... BX1415.A4
282.8 ... BX1426.2
... Q180.A1
282.94 ... BX1685
283 ... BX5003
... BX5131.2
283.02542 ... BR754.A1
283.0922 ... BR1700
... BX5100
... BX5197
283.0924 ... BV3269.C6
... BV3625.N6R29
... BX4705.W3
... BX5197
... BX5199.A43
... BX5199.A545
... BX5199.B64
... BX5199.F57
... BX5199.H28
... BX5199.H5
... BX5199.H812
... BX5199.M29
... BX5199.P26
... BX5199.P33
... BX5199.S515
... BX5199.T3
... BX5199.T48
... BX5199.T49
... BX5199.W6
... BX5199.Y57
... BX5595.S9
... BX5620.S75
... BX5720.C45
... BX5995.B63
... BX5995.B66
... BX5995.B825
... BX5995.J27
... BX5995.L28
... BX5995.P54
... BX5995.P6
... BX5995.R3
... CT788.W757
... DA533
... LF724.W5
283.4148 ... BX5370.D8
283.415 ... BX5550
283.42 ... BV4400
... BX5071
... BX5093
... BX5098
... BX5100
... BX5125
... BX5129.8.M4
... BX5130
... BX5131.2
283.4216 ... BX5199.T66
283.4241 ... CD1068.G55
283.4246 ... BX5195.S69S25
... BX5195.S754S7
283.4247 ... BX5107.W8
283.4248 ... DA670.W3
283.4255 ... DA690.U65

283.429 ... BX5107.B2
283.71233 ... BX5617.E3H6
283.713 ... BX5620.S75
283.73 ... BX5880
... BX5881
... BX5930.2
283.746 ... BX5917.C8
... BX5918.C7
283.7463 ... BX5980.H37
283.748 ... BX5918.P4
283.74921 ... BX6081.T4
283.74998 ... BX5980.C23S395
283.753 ... BX5980.W3
... BX5980.W3P33
283.75551 ... BX5980.P83L95
283.75552 ... F234.N8
283.75591 ... BX5917.V8
283.756144 ... BX5980.H47C5
283.769 ... BX5918.L5
283.77427 ... BX5980.L33
283.77866 ... BX5980.S2
... BX5980.S2S25
283.93157 ... BX5720.5.A44D8
283.944 ... BX5705
... BX5717.R6S26
284 ... BX4810
... BX4818.3
... BX4931.2
284.0947 ... BX4849
284.10924 ... BR325
... BR326
... BR335
... BR403
... BR1608.R8
... BX4827.B57
... BX8080.B615
... BX8080.K68
... BX8080.U4
284.173 ... BX8011
... BX8041
... BX8055.L8
... BX8061.W6
284.1730924 ... BX8080.W3
284.174985 ... BX8076.A75S34
284.175 ... BX8042.S6
284.176425 ... BX8076.N37S3V
284.177311 ... BX8076.C5S34
284.1776519 ... BX8076.M55
284.1788 ... BX8061.M745
284.181 ... BX8063.B77
284.20924 ... BX9418
284.244 ... BX9424.5.F8
284.3 ... BX4931
... BX4946.G7
284.50924 ... BX9459.C84
284.60924 ... BX8593.B77
... BX8593.S63
285.09 ... BX8930
285.0924 ... BX9225.R715
... BX9225.T34
285.0971352 ... BX9003.H3
285.10924 ... BX9193.B7
... BX9225.C526
... BX9225.H6
... BX9225.H75
... BX9225.T64
... BX9225.W4515
285.10975743 ... BX9211.R64F57
285.131 ... BX8951
... BX8955
285.132 ... BX8952
285.173 ... BX8936
285.174946 ... BX9211.A36
285.174976 ... BX8949.F7
285.175 ... BX8941
285.1753 ... BX9211.W3N37
285.1764 ... BX8941
285.1764113 ... BX9211.C77
285.1791 ... BX8947.A7
285.181 ... BX9042.B66
285.20924 ... BX9223
... BX9225.C637
... BX9225.L485
... BX9225.W4
285.241 ... BX9072
... BX9081
285.2947 ... BX9166.C3
285.70924 ... BR1725.D38
... BX9250.Z8
... BX9593.N4
285.75 ... BX7470.S6
285.774728 ... BX9531.T3
285.774838 ... BX7481.O7O75
285.7749 ... BX9516.N5
285.777415 ... BX9531.H6T5
285.8 ... BX7230
285.809 ... BX7131
285.80922 ... BX7259
285.80924 ... BR1725.W458
... BX7077.Z8
... BX7260.A2
... BX7260.B3
... BX7260.B9
... BX7260.E3
... BX7260.H315
285.873 ... BX7232
285.87419 ... BX7255.B83F5
285.8744 ... BX7148.M4
285.87444 ... BV637.7
285.87463 ... BX7255.H4
285.877137 ... BX9886.Z7
285.87731 ... BX7255.D55F53
285.877339 ... BX7255.M69
285.878165 ... BX7255.L38

285.879541 ... BX7255.O76
285.879746 ... BX7255.C68
285.8944 ... BX7257.W6W65
285.9 ... F68
285.9014 ... BX9322
285.908 ... BX9334.2
285.90924 ... F67
285.909415 ... BR795
285.90942 ... BX9322
285.90973 ... BX9313
... BX9354.2
286 ... BX5720.5.Z7W33
286.0722 ... BX6331.2
286.0922 ... BX6201.B72
... BX6453
286.0924 ... BX6455.W47
... BX6495.M5
... E185.97
286.094258 ... BX6490.H5
286.09761781 ... BX6480.B54R78
286.09764 ... BX6248.T4
286.09795 ... BX6248.O7
286.09944 ... BX6326.N4
286.1 ... BX6331
286.10924 ... BX6495.B735
... BX6495.H267
... BX6495.T44
286.10978 ... BX6248.C57
286.109794 ... BX6455.C58
286.13109744 ... BX6248.M4
286.1320924 ... BX6495.G78
286.1330924 ... BX6455.W3
286.17520924 ... E444
286.1755496 ... BX6480.A4E4
286.1756865 ... BX6209.M66
286.1758225 ... BX6480.D37
286.1764 ... BX6248.T4
286.1764175 ... BX6480.S366F55
286.176855 ... BX6480.N3
286.17688 ... BX6209.C52
286.1769425 ... BX6480.S84
286.177252 ... BX6480.I53
286.1795 ... BX6245
286.1945 ... BX6326.M4
286.609 ... BX7315
286.60924 ... BX6793.P47
... BX7077.Z8
... BX7343.C2
286.6757 ... BX7317.S6
286.678188 ... BX6781.P6C5
286.70924 ... BX6193.B3
... BX6193.N8
... BX6193.W5
286.73 ... BX6111
... BX6154
287 ... BX8231
287.0924 ... BX8495.P548
... BX8495.S37
... BX8495.W5
287.09759 ... BX8248.F6
287.10924 ... BX8495.M625
... BX8495.W2426
287.6 ... BX8387
287.609 ... BX8231
287.60924 ... BX8277.C6
... BX8495.C6
... BX8495.G35
... BX8495.L36
... BX8495.L4
... BX8495.L452
... BX8495.V5
... E185.97
287.64253 ... BX8278.L48
287.673 ... BX8245
... E441
287.674 ... BX8239
287.6748 ... BX8248.P4
287.6752 ... BX8248.M3
287.675271 ... BX8481.B2T38
287.6753 ... BX8481
287.6755293 ... BX8481.F33
287.675662 ... BX8481.G8R45
287.6764145 ... BX8481.B35
287.677136 ... BX8481.C9
287.677175 ... BX8481.H28
287.6781 ... BX8248.K2
287.80924 ... BX8449.H4
... BX8495.C62
287.83 ... BX8443
287.87471 ... BX6480.N577C45
287.874811 ... BX8448
287.8758 ... BX8444.G4
287.920924 ... BX9883.H7
287.97 ... BV3785.B7
... BX8213
... BX9100
288.09 ... BX9843
288.0924 ... BX9869.C6
... BX9869.C8
... BX9869.G3
... BX9869.P3
288.73 ... BX9833
288.757915 ... F279.C445
289 ... BR157
289.173 ... BX9933
289.3 ... BS8628
... BX8622
... BX8628
... BX8635.2
289.30202 ... BX8675
289.308 ... BX8609
289.30922 ... BX8678
... BX8693
... BX8695.M27

Dewey	LC
289.30922	BX8695.S6
289.30924	BX8680.S88
	BX8695.B33
	BX8695.F57
	BX8695.H5
	BX8695.J45
	BX8695.S6
	BX8695.Y7
289.32	BX8627
	BX8628
	BX8629.P6
	BX8638
289.322	BX8623
	BX8627
	BX8627.A2
289.3220922	BX8627
289.33	BX8608
	BX8635.2
	BX8657
289.343	BX8617.G4
289.371	BX8617.C3
289.473	BX8716
289.5	BX6943
	BX6947
289.50924	BX6995
289.573	BX6943
289.6	BX7615
	BX7747
289.608	BX7617
289.609	BX7637
289.60922	BX7676.2
	BX7791
289.60924	BX7617
	BX7795.F7
	BX7795.H5
	BX7795.J55
	BX7795.S443
	PS892
289.642	BX7676
	BX7676.2
289.64219	BX7678.U9
289.64258	BX7678.H4
289.671	BX7650
289.673	BX7635
289.674821	F157.B8
289.67521	BX7649.E3
289.677264	BX7649.S65
289.6777	BX7648.I8
289.6795	BX7607.O7
289.70924	BX8143.M54
289.73	BX8129.O4
289.773	BX8117.O34
289.7748	BX8129.A6
289.774815	BX8143.W3
289.777161	BX8117.O34
289.7783	BX8129.H8
289.809033	BX9766
289.9	BF639
	BF648.D8
	BF648.H6
	BL441
	BR763.S45
	BR1608.B8
	BR1725.A77
	BX6571.2
	BX7056
	BX7230
	BX7548.A4
	BX7548.A45
	BX7990.I68M33
	BX8762.Z7C48
	BX8764.Z8
	BX9886.Z8
	BX9890.U5
289.90924	BX7548.Z8
290	BL80.2
	BL87
	BL96
	BL1802
	BR516.5
290.3	BL31
290.95	BL1035
290.973	BJ1661
291	BL27
	BL48
	BL50
	BL60
	BL80
	BL80.2
	BL98
	BL430
	BL625
	BR127
	GN470
291.03	BL31
291.042	BL430
291.071	BL41
291.08	BL85
291.0924	GN21.F65
291.1	BM585
291.13	BL304
	BL310
	BL311
	BL325.T8
	BL660
	GN8
291.1303	BL303
291.130934	BL2001.2
291.17	BL60
	BL87
291.2	BL80.2
291.211	BL65.S85
	BL205
	BL510
291.211	BL1590.R5
	BL1605.A5
	BS1216
291.212	BL325.A6
291.213	BL325.H46
	BL325.K5
291.22	BL85
	BT703
291.23	BL50
	BL510
	BL515
	BL2015.K3
291.3	BH91
291.37	BL48
	NA2543.S6
291.38	BV800
291.4	BL48
	BL624
291.42	BL624
	BL625
	BV5075
291.5	BL603
291.63	BL72
	CT9981.W53
291.630922	BL72
291.8	BL71
292.003	BL303
292.07	BL802
292.08	BL781
	BL782
	BL785
292.13	BL722
	BL782
	BL802
292.20973	CS71.L325
292.211	B1180
	BL805
	BL820.B2
	BL820.C8
	BL820.H5
	BL820.V5
292.23	BL535
292.38	BL815.T35
293	BL860
293.13	BL860
	BL863
293.211	BL860
294	BL2001.2
294.0954	BL2001
294.1	BL1115
	PK2911
294.12	BL1115
294.14	BL1115
294.15	BL1115
294.3	BL1405
	BL1424
	BL1442.S5
	BL1451
	BL1451.2
	BL1455
	BL1456.21
294.30222	BL1455
294.303	BL1403
294.30904	BL1451.2
294.30934	BL1425
294.3094	BL1446.A2
294.30947	BL1445.R9
294.3095493	BL1427
294.309593	BL2075
294.3372	BL515
	BL1440
294.34	BL1473.R4
294.342	B123
	BL1416.S33
	BL1456
	BL1456.21
	BR128.B8
294.3420924	BL1453
294.34211	BL1201
294.3423	BL1456.66
294.3442	BL625
	BL1433.3.T3
294.3443	BJ1289
	BL1433.3.T3
	BL1478.6
294.3444	BL1478.6
294.35	BJ1289
	BL1495.T3
294.361	BL1473.M54
294.363	BL1455
	BL1470
294.364	BL1442.S53
294.365	BL1442.S6
294.36570922	BL1460
294.38	BL1475.N3
294.3808	BL1410
294.382	BL1410
294.3823	BL1411.S83
294.3824	PK4541
294.39	BL1442.S585
294.392	BL1442.S5
	BL1495.T3
	BP605.I8
294.3920951	BL1430
294.3920952	BL1440
294.3923	BL1485
	BL1493
294.39230924	BL1490.L6
294.3927	B2430.B43
	BL1432.Z4
	BL1478.6
	BL1493
294.392708	BL1493
294.39270951	BL1432.Z4
294.4	BL1351.2
294.422	BD422.S7
294.45	BJ1290
294.482	BL1311.S5
294.5	BL1175.M43
	BL1202
	BL1210
	BL1226.85
294.508	BL1146.N6
	BL1210
294.509	BL1150
294.50922	BL1171
294.50924	BL1175.M43
294.5095414	BL1150
294.5172	BR128.H5
	BT304.94
294.521	BL1215.C7
294.5211	BL1215.C8
294.5212	BL1215.S6
294.523	BL515
294.53	BL1226.2
294.538	BL1226.3
294.54	B132.V3
	B132.Y6
	B5134.R37
	BL1146.P23
	BL1146.R35
	BL1146.R35A1
	BL1202
	BL1228
294.542	BL1175.A5
	BL2015.M9
	DS486.P58
294.543	B132.Y6
	BL627
	BL1226.8
294.544	BJ1290.5
	BL1146.V3E4
294.548	BL1125.A2
	BL2018.32
	BR128.H5
294.550954	BL1245.A1
294.5512	BL1171
294.551209	BL1245.V3
294.5513	BL1245.S5
294.5514	BL1245.S4
294.553	BL2017.4.A4
	BL2017.47
	BL2017.47.S3
	BL2018
	BL2018.36.D4
	BL2018.38
294.5530924	BL2017.9.G6
	BL2017.9.N3
294.555	B132.V3
	BL1270
	BL1270.R3
294.5550924	BL1270.R3
294.561	BL2017.6
294.5610924	BL1146.M322
	BL1146.R352
	BL1175.S38
	BL1175.S5
294.563	BL1245.V36
294.5630924	B133.S5
	BL1175.M4
	BL1245.V36
294.5640924	BL1175.V5
	BL1245.V3
294.565	BL1175.B7
294.59	BL1201
294.5921	BL1120
	BL1120.A3
	PK3521
	PK8506
294.5922	BL1130
	PL4758.9.K27
294.5923	GR305
	PK3633.A2
294.5924	BL1130
	BL1130.A4
	PK3631
	PK3633.B5
	PK3642.B5
294.5925	BL1135.P75
	BL1135.P775
	PK3621.B53
	PK3621.G3
	PK3798.N56
295	BL1566.J8
	BL1571
	PK6197
295.82	PK6116.E5
296	BL1650
	BM42
	BM43
	BM45
	BM205
	BM535
	BM561
	BM565
	BM570
	BM580
	BM648
	BM700
	BM729.P3
	BM755.A74
	N8197
296.01	B154
	BM560
296.0207	NC1429.L45
296.03	BM50
296.071173	BM75
296.072024	BM755.H225
296.08	BM40
	BM45
	BM205
	BM565
296.09	BM40
	BM155.2
	BM160
296.0901	BM165
296.09014	BM173
296.0904	BM601
296.0924	BM755.R44
296.095694	BM729.P3
296.0973	BM205
296.1	BM495
	BM496.5
	BM529
296.12	BM500.5
296.1206	BM503.5
296.123	BM497.5.E5
	BM506
	BM506.A23
296.124	BM498.5.E52
296.14	BM506.A23
	BM517.P4
296.14077	BM517.M43
296.16	BM525
	BM525.A412
	BM525.A6S55
	BM525.L835
	BM526
296.18	BM522.42
	BM710
	BS639
296.3	BM529
	BM545.A45
	BM590
	BM590.A1
	BM601
	BS680.M4
296.30924	BM755.H37
	BM755.N5
296.311	BL221
	BM529
	BM610
296.32	BM627
296.38	BM565
296.385	BJ1281
	BJ1285
	BJ1287.A25
	BM723
	HQ32
296.38508	BJ1279
296.387	BM565
296.3872	BM176
	BM535
296.3875	BM538.S3
296.4	BM295.S7
	BM654
	BM656
	BM657.A1
	BM660
	BM667.S6
	BM669
	BM675.D3
	BM690
	BM700
	BS680.S2
	NK1672
296.41	BM685
296.42	BM740
	BM740.2
	BM745
296.43	BM666
	BM690
	BM745
296.437	BM675.P4
	BM675.P4G52
	BM675.P45
296.44	BM707.4
296.445	BM712
296.610207	PN6268.J4
296.610924	BM755.R348
	BM755.R545
	BM755.S2
	BM755.S6
	BM755.W53
296.7	BF723.D3
296.71	BM723
296.72	BM724
296.73	BM710
296.74	BJ1581.2
	BM545.A45
	BM723
296.8	BM440.E8
296.81	BM175.E8
	BM177
296.83208	BM565
296.8320942	BM292
296.833	BM198
	BM532
	BM755.I8
296.8342	BM225.N5B63
296.834408	BM197.7
296.8346	BM197
	BM522.36
296.83460924	BM755.H47
297	BP88
	BP88.M7823
	BP130
	BP161.2
	BP165
	BP170
	BP170.5
297.008	BP163

297.09 BP50
297.0922 BP63.I4
297.0954 BP63.I4
297.096 BP64.A1
297.122 BP132
BP169
D199.3
PJ6696.Z8
297.12252 BP109
297.124052 BP135.A3
297.197 BP52
BP134.S6
297.1972 BP172
297.1977 BP163
DS299
297.19785 BP173.75
297.2 BP88
BP88.P324
BP130
BP170
BP189
BP195.A5
297.23 BP134.D35
297.4 BP189
GR75.B6
297.42 BP189
297.43 BP183.3
297.5 BJ1291
297.610924 BP80.M8
297.63 BP75
BP166.55
DS38.3
297.65 BP10
297.8 BP10.P48
BP165
297.822 BP195.A8
297.87 BP223
297.89 BP365
BP370
297.8901 BP365
297.8935 BP310
297.898 BP360
299 GN470
299.16 BL910
BL980.I7
299.2 BL1600
BL1615
299.21 BL1625.A8
299.26 BL1671
299.31 BF1598
BL2441
BL2441.2
BL2450.B2
PA4368
299.4511 BL2370
299.51 BL1801
299.512 BL1851
DS721
299.51264 B128.C8
299.5128 PL2478
299.514 BL1900.H8
299.5142 BL1930
299.5144 BL1923
299.51482 PL2478
299.56 BL2202
BL2215.R9
BL2228.S4
299.5619 BL2222.O4
299.6 B5305
BL205
BL2400
BL2465
BL2480.B3
BL2480.M3
BL2480.N8
BL2490
BT10
BT98
GN470
GN475.8
299.60966 BL2465
299.6096692 BL2480.Y6
299.7 BL325.C7
E59
E59.R38
E98.R3
E99.A6
E99.H7
E99.K9
E99.N3
E99.P25
E99.W7
F863
299.9 BL2130
BL2615
BL2620.M4
GN671.N5
GR385.H3
300 AG6
BF121
H33
H35
H61
H62
H81
H83
H91
HC110.D4
HD82
HD4861
HM51
HM55
HM221
HM251
300 HN17.5
HN389
HX86
LT305
300.1 B132.V3
B945.S24
B3317
H61
JA36
300.15 H61
300.18 H31
H61
H62
HM24
300.182 H31
H61
HA29
HA33
300.183 H62
300.184 H61
300.185 HA33
300.202 H83
300.23 H62.5.U5
300.2465 BF121
300.3 DT1
JN118
300.7 H62
H62.5.C22
LB1050
LB1530
LB1584
Q183.8.I6
300.71 H62
300.71142 H62
300.712 H62
300.71273 H62
300.71274 H62.5.U5
300.712762 L166
300.71294 H62.5.A8
300.72 BF76.7
H62
H62.5.U5
HF1103
HM24
HM48
Q180.5
300.72042 HM48
300.720489 H62
300.72054 H62.5.I5
300.720729 H62
300.72073 H62
H62.5.U5
300.722 H61
300.76 H62
300.8 AC8
DS557.A76
E302
H31
H35
H62.5.U5
H83
H91
HX11
LD6098
300.9 H61
300.922 H57
300.924 B1607
E185.97.D73
PK1729.V5
300.94 HC240
300.947 H53.R9
300.972 HC135
300.973 H53.U5
300.9742 HC107.N4
301 BD175
BF173.M3566
CB195.G7
DC149
F574.D4
GN400
GV320
H83
HB199
HM5
HM13
HM15
HM19
HM22.U5
HM24
HM51
HM57
HM66
HM68
HM101
HM131
HM136
HM221
HM251
HM278
HM281
HM291
HN16
HN17
HN17.5
HN18
HN40.H5
HN57
HN59
HN64
HN90.V5
HN103.5
HN400.V5
HN690.5.A8
JC328.5
301 JX1930.W6
301.01 B53
BD175
HM22.F8
HM24
HM26
HN28
301.018 H61
HM24
HM48
HM131
301.0182 HA29
301.0184 HM24
301.0202 HM51
301.0207 PN6231.S633
301.03 HM17
301.0422 E185.615
301.071142 HM47.G7
301.072 H62
301.072042 HM48
301.08 AC8
H62.P29
HM15
HM24
HM51
HN17.5
HN18
HN381
301.09 HM19
HM22.U6S483
HM24
301.0922 HM19
HM22.U6B62
301.0924 H59.L4
HM15
HM22.F8C73
HM22.G3
HM22.G3W454
HM22.G3W485
HM22.U6C65
HM22.U6S634
HM59.P35
HV28.B6
301.0942 HM22.G7
301.0947 HM22.R9
301.0954 HM22.I5
HN40.H5
301.1 BD175
BF323.C5
BF365
BF437
BF441
BF455
BF575.A3
BF575.L3
BF636
BF698
BF701
BF723.R3
BF789.D5
BX8635.2
GN273
HD6483
HD7255
HM101
HM131
HM132
HM133
HM136
HM251
HM253
HM271
HM278
HM291
HN18
HN57
HN59
HN800.Z32
HQ460
HQ783
JC585
Q180
301.1018 HM251
301.10724 HM251
301.108 BF731
HM251
HM291
RC455
301.11 HM132
301.110184 HM132
301.114 BF365
301.12 JC323
301.15 BF121
BF632.5
BF698
BF701
DD232
HM131
HM132
HM133
HM251
HM291
HN773
HQ783
JC330
JC585
301.150184 HM291
301.1515 HM141
301.152 PN1994.A5
301.1523 HM263
P96.C4
PN4731
301.153 D421
E743
301.153 E839.8
HM101
HN13
HN57
301.15308 HN13
301.1530922 HN385
301.1530924 E185.97.D73
HM22.U6B42
PS1928
301.1530973 HN57
HN59
301.15309748 HN79.P4
301.1530975 HN79.A13
301.154 BF323.C5
BV2495
DB215.6
DC140.9
DK274
DK274.3
DS557.A68
E169.12
E183.8.R9
E469.8
E743.5
GN37.G743
HD1691
HD4148
HD6483
HE8697.A8
HE8700.8
HG8535
HM261
HM263
HQ1031
HT393.C8
HT409
JF223
JK468.A8
JX1974
KF4770
L142
LB41
LB2844.1.N4
LC191
LC5051
P93
RC455
TL789.8.U5
301.15409438 HM261
301.154320973 CT216
301.1543301451 HT1581
301.15433216 E210
301.15433310947 HD4904
301.1543339 HD9506.B64A83
301.15436168588 RC570
301.1543629132304 TL521.3.C6
301.15439701 E76.6
301.154398 F1414.2
301.155 BF637.N4
HM136
HM141
HM271
HV1441.A8
HV8141
JS341
301.1550954 HN683.5
301.155097 E185.96
301.155208 HM271
301.15708 HM291
301.16 HE8689
HE8689.7.P6
HE8689.8
HM15
HM101
HM258
HN133.5
HQ784.M3
P87.5
P90
P96.V5
301.1608 HM258
P91
301.1609495 P92.G75
301.160954 P92.I7
301.160973 P92.U5
Q180.A1
301.161 HM258
P90
301.1610973 P92.U5
P96.V5
301.18 BJ1533.F8
HD6483
HM131
HM132
HM133
HN57
HV41
301.1808 HM131
HM251
301.182 GV715
HM283
301.183 AS6
HM131
HQ1903
LC6519
301.18308 HM131
301.1832 HD5875
HM131
301.185 F548.9.N3
HM132
HM133
HQ799.A9
301.2 AS36
AS36.C2

Dewey	LC
301.2	B3279
	BD175
	BF637.N4
	BF731
	BF1581
	BJ57
	BJ1012
	BL2120.B2
	BL2202
	CB19
	CB59
	CB427
	DA118
	DA135
	DA152
	DD256.5
	DK750
	DS379
	DS423
	DS430
	DS646.36
	DS666.S8
	DT15
	DT434.E242
	DT443
	DT737
	DT764.B8
	DT864
	DU374
	DU397.5
	DU580
	DU740
	E58
	E78.C2
	E78.I18
	E99.C6
	E169.12
	E185.615
	F129.B8
	F200
	F394.H8
	F869.L8
	F1027
	G58
	GN2
	GN3
	GN6
	GN8
	GN21.L4
	GN24
	GN29
	GN315
	GN320
	GN325
	GN345
	GN473
	GN491
	GN575
	GN665
	GV173
	HD4843
	HM73
	HM101
	HM106
	HM107
	HM131
	HM132
	HM136
	HM251
	HM278
	HM291
	HN57
	HN59
	HN90.V5
	HN380.Z9S63
	HN385
	HQ796
	HV6477
	HX632
	KF9428
	P41
	P91
	P106
	P123
	PJ5119.U5
	PM4068.7
	Q125
	Q127.G7
301.201	CB19
301.2018	CC75
	GN33
301.208	GN2
	GN325
	HM101
301.20954	HN683
301.21	GN345
301.24	BD450
	BL2600
	CB151
	CB425
	CB440
	CB478
	E51
	E839
	GN405
	GV706
	HC51
	HC110.A9
	HC610.A9
	HD45
	HD59
	HD60
	HD60.5.U5
	HD320.5
301.24	HD6331
	HD6971
	HD9521.5
	HE5623
	HM101
	HM221
	HM278
	HM281
	HN16
	HN17.5
	HN59.U6
	HN690.C55
	HN980
	JX1255
	JX1395
	P92.U5
	P94
	PN6231.E4
	Q125
	Q127.C5
	Q127.G4
	Q175
	QA76
	QA76.5
	QH315
	RA418
	RC455
	T174.3
	T174.5
	T212
	TD180
	TL789.8.U5
301.2408	HM101
301.2409	HM101
301.24098	HD8110.5
301.242	HM283
301.24203	H41
301.243	Q180.A1
301.245	HM101
301.246	RC455
301.29	AS2.5
	AS4.Z9
	E169.12
	E185.615
	GF51
	GN4
	GN6
	GN8
	GN27
	GN400
	HM258
	QH1
301.29.91153	DS646.3
301.2902	CB353
301.2904	D1065.U5
301.29171301717	CB199
301.291717067	DT1
301.2917491804	BR253
301.291749240174927	DS119.7
301.29174927	DS153.5
301.2917492704	DS63.2.E8
301.29174933	DT313
301.29174943	GN4
301.2917496	E448
	GN652.S8
301.29174972	E99.A6
301.2917498	F2520.1.Y3
301.291749912	DU744
301.291749915	DU120
	HN850.D8
301.2924	GN21.K7
	GN21.L4
301.294051	DS706
301.294073	CB358
	D843
	D1055
	D1065.U5
301.29410438	DA765
301.29415	GF561
301.29415042	DA950
301.2942	DA592
301.2942044	AS122.B4
301.2942052	DA47.9.J3
301.2942056	DS63.2.G7
301.294205694	DS126.5
301.294205951	HF3800.6.Z7G77
301.294206	DT32
301.2942071	F1029.5.G7
301.2942073	E183.8.G7
301.29431047	DD261.4
301.29437047	DB205.7
301.2943704771	DK508.57.C95
301.29437054	DB205.8.I5
301.29437071	DB205.8.C2
301.29438047	DK418.5.R9
301.2943910495	DB926.3.B9
301.294391073	E184.H95
301.294429	DU120
301.2946073	DP75
301.29469	JV4235
301.29470497	DR367.R9
301.2947054	DS450.R8
301.2947073	DR48.5
	E183.8.R9
301.29485	HN572.5
301.29496	GN2
301.295	DS33.2
301.295073	DS518.1
301.2951	DS740.4
301.295101821	DS740.4
301.295104	DS821
301.29510597	DS740.5.V5
301.2951073	E183.8.C5
	E743.5
301.295201821	DS821.5.A1
301.295205	DS849.E3
301.2952059	DS849.A84
301.295365	DS247.B24
301.2954	DS430
	GN387
	HN683.5
301.29540174927	DS63.2.I5
301.295405496	DS450.N3
301.295412	HN690.R36
301.2954165	DS432.N3
301.29544	DS432.L63
301.295475	DS485.G8
301.295481	DS491.L3
301.295484	HN690.K63
301.2956	DS119.7
301.2956042	DS63.2.G7
301.2956073	DS63.2.U5
301.295694	DS126.5
301.2956940174927	DS119.7
301.295694073	DS132
301.29586	DK928
301.29593	HN750.5
301.295953	DS646.33
301.29597	DS538
301.296	DT6
	GN645
301.296073	DT31
	DT38
301.29624	DT132
301.2964073	E183.8.M65
301.2966704	HF3899.G64
301.29669	DT513
	GN653
301.296695	DT515.42
301.2967	DT19.8
	DT351
	DT365.42
	DT530
	GN645
301.29672	DT530
301.296721	DT546.142
301.29673	DT611.42
301.29675	DT650
301.29676	DT432
301.29676.2	DT1
301.296761	DT434.U242
	GN659.L3
301.296762	DT1
	DT429
	DT434.E242
301.29678	DT1
	DT443
301.296782	DT443
	GN475.8
301.2968	DT737
	DT761
	DT763
301.29680681	DT779.7
301.2968073	DT733
301.29682	DT920
301.29683	DT971
301.29684	DT878.Z9
301.29686	DT786
301.296894	DT955
301.296897	DT864
301.29691	DT469.M31
301.297	E20
301.29701	E77.2
	E78.A3
	E99.E7
	E99.F7
	F1435
301.2971073	E183.8.C2
	F1034
301.2971134	E99.S2
301.297124	F1071
301.29713073	F1058
301.2972	HQ562
301.2972073	KF27.F646
301.29727	F1221.T9
	HN120.A4
301.297294	AZ541
301.2973	E169.1
	E169.12
	E175.8
	E744
	E840
	HN64
	JK274
	PN1582.U6
301.2973072	F975
301.297308	F1401
	F1408.4
	F1418
301.2973094	E183.8.A8
301.2975818	HN79.G4
301.29764	F386
301.2977641	HN80.B52
301.2977677	F612.M36
301.298	F1408
	HN110.5
301.29801	F2519.1.A6
301.2981	F2519
301.2985	HN350.Z9E46
301.29852	HN350.A6
301.29861	HN303.5
301.298615	HN310.S27
301.29914	DS665
301.299145	DS666.S85
301.299149	DS665
301.29931096	DU421
301.2993504	GN671.S6
301.29936	DU553
301.29936	DU740
301.2994	DU120
	GN665
301.29941	DU120
301.29942	DU397.5
301.29946	DU473
301.2995	DU744
301.29951	DU744
	DU744.5
301.29953	DU740
301.2996	DU510
	DU600
301.29966	DU568.P7
301.299683	DU710
301.29969	DU624.7.A1
301.3	CB161
	CB478
	GF3
	GF8
	GF23
	GF33
	GF37
	GF41
	GF51
	GF80
	HB871
	HC68
	HC107.C23E55
	HC107.N73E58
	HC110.A4
	HC110.E5
	HD1773.A5
	HM206
	JX1977
	KF26.P825
	KF26.P868
	KF27.F648
	KF27.G636
	KF27.M445
	KF31.P8
	KF32.E3
	KF32.G636
	KF32.S382
	KF3786
	NC1420
	QH77.G7
	QH311
	QH368
	QH541
	QH541.14
	QP82
	S942
	T48
	TD177
	TD180
	TX341
301.307	KF27.E335
301.308	QH541
	QH541.13
	TD176.7
301.30913	GF895
301.30942	HB1951
	HC260.E5
	QH77.G7
301.3094272	TH6010
301.31	GF43
	HC68
	HC79.E5
	HC110.E5
	KF26.I5
	TD174
	TD175
	TD180
301.31025	HC68
301.3108	QH311
301.3109798	HD9567.A4
301.32	AS36
	DU120
	E185.8
	E185.9
	F90.A1
	F597
	GF51
	HA37
	HA747.O6
	HB849
	HB851
	HB863
	HB871
	HB881
	HB883
	HB885
	HB891
	HB903.F4
	HB1780.5.A5
	HB1951
	HB1965
	HB1989
	HB1990.N4
	HB2049
	HB2100.5
	HB2126.G5
	HB3583
	HC440.5
	HD9000.6
	HN690.U8
	HQ763
	HQ763.6.I5
	HQ766
	HQ766.3
	HQ766.5.I5
	HQ766.5.K4
	HQ766.5.P3
	HQ766.5.U5

Dewey	LC
301.32	HT361
	JV6035
	JV6080
	JX1977
	KF26.G646
	Q180
	QL752
301.320212	JX1977
301.3207	HM206
301.32071254	HB850.5.I4
301.3208	HB871
	HB885
	HB1951
	HM206
301.3209	HB851
301.32095456	HB3640.D4
301.320955	HB3653
301.32096	HB3661
301.32409793	F850.A1
301.3260979493	F868.L8
301.3291724	HB849
301.3294	HB3581
301.32942	HB3583
301.329471	G23
301.3295	HB3635
301.32951249	HQ766.5.F6
301.32952	HB3651
301.3295412	HB3640.B44
301.3295487	HB3640.B33
	HQ766.5.I5
301.329549	HB3640.5
	HC440.5
301.3295493	HB3636.8
301.3295496	HB3659.N4
301.3296762	HB2126.K4
301.329713541	HB3530.T6
301.329715	HB3530.M32
301.329729	JV7322
301.32973	HA37
	HB849
	HB3505
	HT123
	KF27.B387
301.3297454	HN80.W23
301.32975	HD207
301.3297511	HB3527.W5
301.329754	HA706
301.32977677	HT393.M6
301.329776771	HB3525.M62
301.329792	HB3525.U8
301.329794	HQ766.5.U5
301.329797	HB2195.W2
301.3298	HB1360.5
301.32981	HB3563
301.32991	HB3647
301.32991153	HB3644.6
301.329914	HB3649
301.32995	DU740
301.34	AS36.M48
	DT352.42
	HC59
	HN17.5
	HN683.5
	HT55
	HT65
	HT166
	HV41
	HV88
	JX1950
	KF27.B344
301.3401	HT65
301.340624248	HT110
301.3407152	HN683.5
301.3408	HT65
301.340942	HT169.G7
301.340954	HN683
	HN683.5
	HN690.Z9
	HN690.Z9C67
301.34095413	HN690.O7
301.340954792	HN690.M33
301.3409549	HN690.5
301.340954923	HN690.5.C66
301.340973	HC110.P63
	HN57
	HN58
	HN90.C6
	Z5942
301.3409786	HT393.M9
301.340994	JS8001
301.35	HD111
	HD1407
	HD1491.M38
	HM101
	HN17.5
	HN690.A45
	HT411
	HT421
	JC35
301.35072	H31
301.3508	HT431
301.350942	HN385
301.35094221	HN385
301.350945753	HN488.C25
301.3509468	HN590.A5
301.3509489	HN543.5
301.350951	DS721
301.350951249	HN680.5
301.350952	SD225
301.350954	HN683
	HN683.5
301.35095412	DS485.B51
301.3509542	HN690.U8
301.350954792	HN690.M33
301.3509549	HN690.5
301.35095492	HN690.5.A8
301.350954923	HN690.5.C66
301.3509597	HN700.V5
301.3509678	HN814
301.35096789	HD1516.T3
301.3509686	HN800.L4
301.350971	HN103.5
301.350973	HN57
	HN59
	HT415
	HT431
301.350977	HN79.A172
301.3509853	HN350.P8
301.3509861	HN303.5
301.3509914	HN712
301.35099141	HN720.L8
301.352	HD211.N6
301.3520942	JC43
301.36	HB2161
	HE148
	HT151
	HT155
	HT166
	HT330
301.3608	HT151
301.3609	HT111
301.360942	HT133
301.3609429	HT133
301.360954	HN683.5
301.36095414	HN690.B4
301.3609714281	HN10.M7
301.360973	HT123
	HT167
301.3609749	HT167.5.N42
301.3609764	HT123.5.T4
301.3609944	HC638.H8
301.3610184	HT394.B6
301.362	HT351
301.3620954	HT147.I5
301.3620973	HT351
301.363	HV4028
301.3630904	JS341
301.3630973	HN90.P6
301.364	BS680.C5
	GN2
	HB2161
	HD7325.B6
	HF1025
	HN57
	HN398.S85
	HT107
	HT111
	HT119
	HT133
	HT151
	HT153
	HT155
	HT166
	HT169.G7
	HT169.H8
	HT371
	HV8
	JS422
	SB481
301.364018	HT153
301.3640184	HT153
301.364072073	HT109
	HT110
301.36407273	HT110
301.36408	HT108
	HT151
	HT321
301.36409034	HT119
301.364091724	HT169.5
	HT371
301.364091767	D199.3
301.364094141	HC258.P3
301.3640942	HT133
301.364094272	TH6010
301.36409429	HT133
301.3640944	HT169.F
301.3640947	HT145.R9
301.3640954	HN683.5
301.36409669	DT513
	HT148.N5
301.3640967	HT148
301.36409684	HT148.S6
301.3640971	HT127.C3
301.36409715	HT395.C32M372
301.3640972	HT127.M4
301.3640973	HT123
	HT123.W17
	HT167
	HT175
	HT334.U5
301.36409744	J87
301.3640974461	HN80.B7
301.36409747	HT123.5.N7
301.364097471	F128.9.J5
301.3640977	HT123.5.M53
301.36409944	HN850.Y6
	HT149.A8
301.36409945	HN850.M4
301.372094711	G23
301.37209783	HD1775.S8
301.37209797	HT393.W3
301.3770973	HN59
301.4	GN488
	HM107
	HM131
	HQ13
301.400991	GN490
301.402	Q180
301.405	HD31
	HM131
301.4099613	GN670
301.41	BF575.L8
	BF692
	HN103.5
	HQ12
	HQ18.G7
	HQ18.U5
	HQ21
	HQ27
	HQ29
	HQ31
	HQ32
	HQ35
	HQ36
	HQ56
	HQ57.5.C5
	HQ58
	HQ60
	HQ462
	HQ734
	HQ801
	HQ964
	HQ1154
	PN6231.S54
301.410207	PS3501.R55
	PS3558.U38
301.41076	HQ21
301.4108	HQ5
301.411	HQ800
	HQ1067
301.412	E51
	E185.86
	HD6097
	HQ759
	HQ800
	HQ814
	HQ1106
	HQ1121
	HQ1122
	HQ1154
	HQ1201
	HQ1206
	HQ1221
	HQ1423
	HQ1426
	HQ1593
	HQ1596
	JF851
	JK1885
	JX1977
	PN6071.W7
301.4120207	PN6231.W6
301.4120222	E185.86
301.41206242	HQ1593
301.41208	HQ1206
	HQ1426
301.41209	HQ1121
	HQ1154
	HQ1426
301.4120917496	E185.86
301.412091766	HQ1172
301.4120922	HQ759
	HQ1412
301.4120924	BR1725.R27
	DS135.G5
301.4120942	HQ1593
	QH1597
301.41209438	HQ1665.7
301.4120947	HD6166
	HQ1662
	HQ1663
301.41209485	HQ1687
301.412095	HQ1106
301.4120951	DS734
301.4120952	HQ1762
301.4120954	DS422.W8
	HQ1742
301.41209549	HQ1745.5
301.412096694	DT515.4
	DT515.42
301.412096762	HQ1799.K4
301.4120973	E161
	HQ1403
	HQ1410
	HQ1420
	HQ1426
	LC1402
301.41209746	HQ1438.C8
301.4120975	HQ1416
	HQ1418
	HQ1420
301.41209773	HQ1438.I3
301.41209776	HQ1438.M6
301.41209782	HQ1438.N2
301.41209786	HQ1438.M85
301.41209795	HQ1438.O7
301.4120994	HQ1822
	HQ1823
301.41209953	DU740
301.412109	HQ1150
301.41210924	HQ1413.R6
301.41210947	HQ1663
301.4122	BV4527
301.41220973	HD6095
301.4129	HQ1106
301.414	BF636
	HQ10
	HQ801
301.4140207	NC1429.B659
	PN6231.L6
301.415	HQ12
301.415	HQ27
	HQ31
	HQ71
	HQ76
	HQ79
	HQ111
	HQ117
	HQ144
	HQ151.A5
	HQ184
	HQ186
	HQ240.B6
	HQ247.T6
	HQ460
	HQ462
	HQ471
	HQ806.N46
	PN6231.S54
301.4150973	HQ18.U5
	HQ806
301.4152	HQ999.U6
301.41530973	HQ18.U5
301.41540977311	HQ146.C4
301.417	HQ31
301.418	HQ31
	HQ56
301.42	BX9334
	E185.86
	HB1125
	HQ7
	HQ10
	HQ31
	HQ518
	HQ535
	HQ536
	HQ670.5
	HQ728
	HQ734
	HQ759
	HQ802
	HQ1040
	HQ1221
	RC514
301.420222	HQ744
301.4208	HQ518
	HQ536
	HQ728
	HQ734
301.420924	BX5199.J66
301.420942	BX9334
	HQ613
	HQ728
301.4209421	HQ614
301.420944	HQ792.F7
301.420954792	HQ669
301.42095487	HQ669
301.420973	HN57
	HQ535
	HQ536
301.42097445	F74.A6
301.42097448	HQ557.P5
301.420975	S445
301.4209914	HQ679
301.420994	HQ705
301.420996	HQ724
301.421	HQ518
301.421095125	HQ667
301.422	BX8641
	DU740
	E185.62
	GN237
	HQ525.J4
	HQ557.N5
	HQ724
	HQ997
301.423	E184.J5
	HN59
	HQ669
	HQ728
301.4230968	DT751
301.4230971	HQ560
301.4230977311	HQ728
301.426	AS36
	HQ21
	HQ31
	HQ46
	HQ728
	HQ734
	HQ763
	HQ763.I63
	HQ766
	HQ766.3
	HQ766.5.I5
	HQ766.5.U5
	HQ767
	HQ802
301.4260207	PN6231.W5
301.427	BF723.B5
	BF723.P25
	HQ10
	HQ535
	HQ586.5
	HQ734
	HQ769
	HQ773
	HQ773.7
	HQ784.H3
	HQ796
	HQ799.5
	HQ1062
	LB3609
301.428	HQ814
	HQ1058.5.G7
	HQ1058.5.U5

301.428 .... HQ1221
301.4284 .... HQ769
..... HQ814
301.42840942 .... HQ876
301.42840973 .... HQ834
301.42840994 .... HQ960
301.431 .... HQ775
..... HQ784.H3
..... KF3869
..... RJ131
301.4310625694 .... HQ799.I7
301.43106273 .... HQ796
301.43108 .... HQ768
301.4310942 .... HQ792.G7
301.431095694 .... HQ792.P3
301.4310968 .... HQ792.S6
301.4310973 .... HQ772
..... HQ796
301.4310977866 .... E185.86
301.43109945 .... HQ799.A82V53
301.43109953 .... HQ799.N44P64
301.4314 .... HQ772
..... HQ781.5
..... HQ784.Q4
..... HQ790
301.43140207 .... PN6328.C5
301.43140222 .... HQ781.5
301.43140947 .... HQ799.R9
301.431409492 .... PZ9.B773
301.4315 .... HQ793
..... HQ796
..... HQ798
..... HQ799.G53
..... HQ799.2.M3
301.431506394 .... HQ799.A8
301.4315094 .... HQ799.E9
301.43150942 .... HQ799.G7
301.4315094215 .... HQ799.G72B48
301.431509431 .... HQ799.G33
..... HQ799.8.G43
301.43150947 .... HQ799.R9
301.431509471 .... GR1
301.43150951 .... HQ799.C55
301.43150954 .... HN683.5
301.4315095694 .... HQ799.I7
301.43150968 .... HV5840.S6
301.43150972983 .... HQ799
..... HQ799.T7
301.43150973 .... HN59
..... HQ796
..... HQ799.7
301.431509747 .... HQ796
301.431509748 .... HQ792.U52P36
301.431509764 .... HQ796
301.43150976686 .... HQ796
301.431509794 .... HQ796
301.43150979461 .... HQ799.73.S3
301.43150994 .... HQ799.A8
301.434 .... HQ1061
301.435 .... GN485
..... HQ1060
..... HQ1061
..... HQ1062
..... R707
301.435025 .... HV1450
301.435025773 .... HQ1064.U5
301.4350715 .... HQ1062
301.43508 .... HQ1061
301.4350944381 .... HQ1064.F7
301.4350971 .... HV1475.A2
301.4350973 .... HQ1064.U5
..... KF26.5.A3
301.43509742 .... HV1468.N4
301.4350974811 .... HQ1064.U5
301.43509751 .... HV1468.D4
301.43509764 .... HQ1064.U6T516
301.4350978225 .... HQ1064.U6N15
301.43509786 .... HQ1064.U6M95
301.4350994 .... HV1490.A1
301.44 .... AS36.C2
..... BF698.9.C8
..... DS422.C3
..... DS432.J25
..... DT1
..... GN490
..... HM141
..... HN58
..... HN64
..... HN263
..... HN682
..... HN843.5
..... HN850.Z9S65
..... HQ796
..... HQ799.7
..... HT609
..... HT621
..... HT720
..... HT1521
..... HV6762.U5
..... Q180
301.4401 .... HT609
301.440440973 .... HN90.S65
301.4408 .... HM146
..... HT609
301.440942 .... DA118
301.4409485 .... HN573
301.440954 .... DS422.C3
301.44095482 .... DS485.M277
301.4409549 .... HN690.5.A8
301.44096 .... HN773
301.440968 .... DT763
301.440971 .... HN103.5
301.440973 .... E185.615
..... HN57
301.440973 .... HT609
301.440985 .... HN343
301.4409922 .... HN710.J3
301.440994 .... HN843.5
301.441 .... HC108.S2
..... HC110.P6
..... HC110.P63
..... HC110.W4
..... HC260.P6
..... HD8391
..... HN80.N5
..... HN363.5
..... HQ557.C5
..... HT653.G7
..... HT690.G7
..... HV245
..... HV885.N49
..... HV4046.N6
..... HV4046.O45
..... HV4488
..... HV4504
..... HV4505
301.441094 .... HT653.E9
301.4410942 .... HN385.5
301.441094551 .... HF416
301.442 .... DA28.1
..... GN2
..... GN480
..... HQ614
..... HT653.F7
..... HT653.I4
..... HT657
301.4420951 .... HQ667
301.4420954 .... HQ670
301.442095475 .... HN690.G8
301.444 .... DF78
..... HB2581
..... HD156
..... HD639.H9
..... HD644
..... HD654
..... HD1126
..... HD1525
..... HD4901
..... HD5841.N5
..... HD6955
..... HD7051
..... HD8039.M62U53
..... HD8039.M62U65
..... HD8039.M72G73
..... HD8039.R52I54
..... HD8072
..... HD8391
..... HN113.5
..... HT687
301.44420977434 .... HD8085.D6
301.4443 .... HD1527.C2
301.445 .... HB915
..... HD6095
..... LB3605
301.4450941 .... LB1131
301.445096 .... LA1503.7
301.447 .... HT1521
301.448 .... E184.S75
301.44809429 .... JN1153.5.L3
301.4493 .... E446
..... E449
..... HT863
301.44930924 .... E444
301.4494 .... HQ796
..... HQ799.73.S3
301.45 .... BF575.P9
..... CB195
..... DA125.A1
..... DS509.5.A1
..... E168
..... E173
..... E184.J5
..... E185.61
..... F73.5
..... F391.2
..... GN387
..... HM131
..... HM276
..... HT1505
..... HT1521
..... HT1523
..... JC311
..... JV6450
..... JV6455
..... JV6465
..... JV7626
..... JX235
..... JX1977
..... P380
301.4508 .... HT1521
301.450924 .... DA591.P64
301.450941435 .... DA890.G5
301.450942 .... DA120
..... DA125.A1
..... DA591.P64
301.450942565 .... DA690.B4
301.450947 .... DK33
301.450954 .... DS430
..... HN683.5
..... JC311
301.450973 .... BF575.P9
..... E169.1
..... E184.A1
..... E185.61
..... E185.86
..... HT1521
..... KF26.G648
301.4509781 .... F690.A1
301.45098 .... F1419.A1
301.451 .... BF723.R3
..... BF731
..... E184.A1
..... E185.61
..... F128.9.A1
..... F128.9.N3
..... F215
..... F216.2
..... GN320
..... HT1505
..... HT1521
301.45104208 .... HT1501
301.451072073 .... KF27.E333
301.45108 .... HT1521
301.4510942 .... DA120
301.4510947 .... DK33
301.45109593 .... DS569
301.4510969 .... DU624.7
301.4510973 .... E184.A1
..... E185.61
..... E450
..... HT1521
..... PQ2613.A58
301.451097451 .... HB3037.W85
301.45109794 .... F870.A1
301.45151079461 .... F869.S3
301.45160747 .... F130.P85
301.451679073 .... E184.M5
301.4516872073 .... E184.M5
301.4519179 .... F1035.U5
301.451918506273 .... AS23
301.451924 .... DS102.4
..... DS112
..... DS119
..... DS141
..... HN40.J5
301.451924042 .... DS135.E5
301.451924043 .... DS135.G332
..... DS141
..... DS146.G4
301.45192404385
..... DS135.P62C865
301.451924044 .... DS124
..... DS135.F83
301.45192404436 .... DS135.F83
301.451924047 .... DS135.R9
..... DS146.R9
..... H35
301.4519240495 .... DS124
301.4519240561 .... BM755.I16
301.45192405694 .... JV8749.P3
301.451924062 .... DS135.E4
301.451924073 .... DS146.U6
..... E184.J5
301.451924094 .... DS135.A88
301.451926043 .... DS135.G31
301.4519260749 .... F145.J5
301.4519270569 .... DS113.7
301.451948105412 .... DS432.O7
301.451951073 .... E184.C5
301.4519510794 .... N7344
301.4519549 .... DS485.N4
301.45196 .... E185
..... E185.6
..... E185.61
..... E185.62
..... E185.96
..... E185.97.L5
..... E441
..... E449
..... F2659.N4
..... GN645
..... HT1521
..... HT1581
..... HT1589
301.45196006273 .... E185
301.45196024 .... E185.86
..... E185.97
..... E185.97.E795
..... E185.97.G3
..... E185.97.G795
..... E444
..... E444.M39
..... HD8039.A4
301.45196042 .... DA125.A1
..... DA125.W4
..... DU780
301.451960421 .... DA689.N4
..... DA689.W3
301.4519604272 .... HQ799.G72L54
301.4519606 .... DT15
301.4519606273 .... E185.5
301.45196067 .... DT429
301.45196068 .... DT737
..... DT763
..... DT763.5
..... DT834
301.4519606822 .... DT944.J66
301.4519607 .... E29.N3
301.451960713 .... E450
301.451960729 .... E449
..... F1629.N4
301.4519607291 .... F1789.N3
301.45196072983 .... F2119
301.45196073 .... E184.A1
..... E184.5
..... E184.6
..... E184.7
..... E185
..... E185.5
..... E185.5.N276
..... E185.6
..... E185.61
301.45196073 .... E185.615
..... E185.62
..... E185.8
..... E185.86
..... E185.9
..... E185.96
..... E185.97.C6
..... E185.97.D73
..... E185.97.G3
..... E185.97.L5
..... E185.97.L75
..... E185.97.S5
..... E443
..... E448
..... E449
..... E457.8
..... E458.2
..... E668
..... F215
..... JV6895.N44
..... PE1122
..... PN6231.R25
301.451960737 .... E185.61
301.45196074 .... F128.9.N3
301.45196074461 .... E185.615
..... F73.9.N4
301.451960745 .... E185.93.R4
301.4519607468 .... F104.N6
301.4519607471 .... E185.93.N56
..... F128.68.H3
..... F128.9.N3
301.45196074723 .... E185.97
301.451960748 .... E185.93.P41
301.45196074811 .... E185.93.P41
..... F158.9.N3
301.45196074886 .... F159.P6
301.45196075 .... E185
..... E185.6
..... E185.61
..... E185.86
301.451960753 .... F205.N4
301.451960755 .... E185.93.V8
301.451960756 .... E185.93.N6
301.45196075779 .... F277.O5
301.45196075799 .... E185.93.S7
301.4519607624 .... E185.93.M6
301.451960764141 .... F394.H8
301.451960771 .... E185.93.O2
301.45196077178 .... F499.C5
301.451960773 .... F550.N3
301.45196077311 .... F548.9.N3
301.45196077434 .... F574.D4
301.451960777 .... E185.93.I64
301.451960778411 .... F474.K2
301.451960778 .... E185.93.P41
301.451960797 .... F900.N4
301.45196081 .... F2659.N4
301.451960924 .... E185.61
..... E185.97
..... E444
301.451960968 .... DT15
301.451960973 .... E449
301.4519675 .... E185
301.45197 .... E77
..... F1411
..... GN2
301.4519707123 .... E78.C2
301.45197076 .... E98.S7
301.4519915 .... BX7615
..... DU120
301.4519915094 .... DU120
301.45199150941 .... DU374
301.4519920595 .... DS595
301.451994 .... DU423
301.4519940931 .... DU422.5
301.4522 .... E185
..... E185.93.S7
..... E185.97
..... E441
..... E443
..... E444
..... E444.L26
..... E445.D6
..... E446
..... E448
..... E449
..... E449.E49
..... E449.H792
..... E450
..... F160.R3
..... F1871
..... HT855
..... HT861
..... HT867
..... HT869.E6
..... HT871
..... HT1031
..... HT1033
..... HT1048
..... HT1091
..... HT1162
..... HT1394.C3
..... PE1152
301.4522075 .... E444
301.4522208 .... E446
301.452209 .... E446
..... HT861
..... HT975
301.45220922 .... E444
..... E450
301.45220924 .... E185.97.T48
..... E444
..... E444.H526
..... E444.L26

Dewey	LC
301.45220924	E449
	E450
301.45220937	HT863
301.45220942	HD604
301.45220961	HT1345
301.45220966	HT1381
301.452209687	HT1394.C3
301.452209729	HT1091.S7
	HT1092
	HT1093
301.4522097291	F1783
301.4522097292	F1886
301.45220973	AC8
	E185
	E440.5
	E441
	E444
	E446
	E449
	E450
	E451
	E458.4
	PS535
301.45220975	E441
	E444
	E449
	E449.R32
301.452209755	E444
	E445.V8
301.452209763	E445
301.452209769	E445.K5
301.452209773	E445.I2
301.452209778	E444
301.452209946	HD6664
301.4523	E185.86
	HC110.P6
301.452309421	HV4088.L8
	HV4548.L7
301.45230973	HC110.P6
301.452309756	HC107.N83P615
301.452309757	HD1751
301.452309764	F395.S75
301.452770914	DS666.M7
301.4528	BR517
	BX5671.I53
	DS135.G72
301.4528095691	BR1110
301.452824231	BX1494.W5
301.4528273	BX1406.2
301.452896748	F152
301.452945	HQ1742
301.45296	HN40.J5
301.452960973	E184.J5
301.45296833	BM198
301.45297	BP163
301.45297046	DP104
301.45297054	DS463
301.453	GF101
	JV6450
301.453071	F1035.P6K6
301.4534073	JV6465
301.453416073	E184.S4
301.45343073	E184.G3
301.453437073	E184.B67
	F674
301.453438073	E184.P7
301.45345073	E184.I8
301.4534507468	F104.N6
301.45345077311	F548.9.I8
301.45345751073	JV6455
301.4534607895	F805.S75
301.453469074	F15.P8
301.45347073	E184.R9
301.4534771	DK508.8
301.4534771073	E184.U5
301.45348073	E184.S18
301.453481073	E184.S2
301.4534810777	CT275.N668
301.453495073	E184.G7
301.4535073	E184.O6
301.45351073	JV6876.E2
301.4535109112	DS646.3
301.453510991	DS632.C5
301.453515054	DS432
301.45352073	E184.J3
301.453540595	DS595
	HD8700.6
301.4535406	DT16.E17
301.453540684	HN800.N3
301.4535406982	DT469.M4
301.453676206761	HN800.U353
	HN800.U353K36
301.45372073	E184.M5
	F1208.5
	JV6798.M6
301.453720791	F790.M5
301.453720794	F870.M5
301.45373	E184.2
301.453730729	F1629.N4
301.453914073	JV6891.F54
301.4596073	E185.5
301.4768	HQ773
301.4768588	RC570
301.476858809794	HV897.C3
301.476861	HV5009
	HV5035
	HV5132
	HV5135
301.4768610979777	HV5298.S43
301.476863	HV5801
	HV5822.M3
	HV5822.M5
	HV5825
	HV5840.S8
301.476863	J87
301.4768630942	HV5840.G7
301.4768630973	HV9103
301.47689	R438
301.477712	HV1598
	HV1796.N7
301.47771209542	HV2095.L8
301.47771209776579	
	HV1796.M66
301.4778	HV2395
	HV2716
301.4778097526	HV2561.M3
301.5	AS36
	BD444
	BF575.S35
	BL60
	DT1
	GN221
	H31
	HC79.C6
	HD1741.L6
	HD2117
	HD6096.O7
	HM136
	HQ767
	HV5135
	JA74
	JA76
	JC330
	JF1001
	JF2051
	KF27.5.C7
	R131.A1
	RA418
	RA965
	U21.5
	U766
301.51	GN489
	HC21
	HC107.I32
	KF562
301.54	E185.89.H6
	F264.R1
	GN414.A1
	HD60.5.U5
	HD1751
	HD5707
	HD7286
	HD7287
	HD7287.5
	HD7287.6
	HD7287.9
	HD7289.A3
	HD7289.U6
	HD7289.U7
	HD7293
	HD7293.A3
	HD7304.C4
	HD7304.I5
	HD7304.N5
	HD7332
	HD7334
	HD7363.6.S5
	HT123
	KF27.P868
	KF581
	Q180.A1
	TH7
	TX911
	Z7164.H8
301.540186	HD7287
301.54094	JX1977
301.540941	HD7335
301.540942	HD7333
	HD7333.A3
	TH6010
301.54094274	TH6010
301.54094281	HD7333.S78
301.54094788	HD7303.N7
301.54095125	HD7371.H6
301.54095414	HD7361.C3
301.54095456	HA1719
301.54096782	HD7376.T3
301.540968	HD7374.S6
301.5409684	HD7374.D8
301.54096897	HD7374.M33
301.540971	HD7286
	HD7305
	HD7305.A3
301.5409711	HD7305.B7
301.5409711633	HD7305.M55
301.54097292	HD7317.T7
301.54097295	HT178.P82
301.540973	E185.89.H6
	HD7289.U6
	HD7293
	HD7293.A3
	HD7304.N5
	HM261
	HT123
	KF25.E277
	KF26.B353
	KF27.B344
301.5409744	HD7303.M4
301.54097446	HD7304.B7
301.5409745	HD7303.R4
301.5409746	HD251
301.54097468	HD7304.N37
301.5409747	HD7303.N7
301.54097471	HD7303.N7
	HD7304.N5
	HT177.N5
301.5409748	HD7303.P4
301.540974811	HD7304.P5
301.5409749	HD7303.N5
301.5409752	HD7303.M3
301.54097526	HD7304.B2
301.5409753	HD7304.W3
301.5409754	HD7303.W4
301.540976229	HD7304.V47
301.540976813	HD7304.U6
301.5409771	JK5574
301.540977311	HD7304.C4
301.540979412	HD7303.C2
301.540979498	HD7304.S28
301.5409798	HD7303.A4
	HD7304.M65
301.54098	HD7305.5
301.540983	HD7324
301.540994	HD7379.A3
301.5409969	JQ6103
301.55	HD20
	HD20.3
	HD60.5.U5
	HD60.5.U52R67
	HD69.S5
	HD2956
	HD4904
	HD4904.7
	HD6305.N4
	HD6331
	HD6490.S6
	HD6961
	HD6971
	HD7262.5.U6
	HD8039.S4
	HD8039.T42G78
	HD8072
	HF5547
	HF5548.8
	PN4748.G7
	Q147
301.5508	HD6961
301.55094274	HD9521.7.Y6
301.5509544	HD8690.K62
301.550973	HD3616.U47
	HD8072
301.550974885	HD8085.H63
301.56	LA632
301.57	BJ1498
	E185.93.D6
	GV14
	GV14.5
	GV182
	GV433.G72
	GV1624.5.C5
	HB199
	HD4904.7
	HQ784.T4
	PN1995.9.S6
	SB482.A4
301.570942	HX11
301.570947	HD4904.7
301.570973	GV53
	SB482.A4
301.5709762	GV54.M7A26
301.5709969	GV54.H3A44
301.58	AS36.G378
	BF1261.2
	BL48
	BL60
	BL85
	BR157
	BX4811
	GV605
301.580942	BR749
	BR759
301.5809519	BT738
301.58096891	BL2480.M3
301.580973	BR515
	BT738
301.592	JA66
	JA76
301.6	HM291
	HN90.R3
301.63	HM136
	HQ796
301.632	HM278
301.633	HN90.V5
	KF9223
301.6330973	HN90.V5
301.63330924	HM281
306.142	HN385.5
309	HC54
	HD4841
	HN13
	HN15.5
	HN17.5
	HN18
	HN28
	HN64
309.018	JA73
309.1	AC5
	CB195
	D443
	D727
	HC21
	HN14
	HN18
	HT391
	TD892
	Z3107.K9
309.101	HN8
	HQ504
309.102	HN11
309.104	CB427
	D421
	HC59
309.104	HD82
	HN16
	HN17.5
	HN18
309.1043	D442
309.1046	HN18
309.1047	CB425
309.1171242	HC246.W64
309.11724	HC59.7
	HD82
	HN980
	JF60
309.1173541	HN110.T6
309.1174927	DS36.8
	DS135.T8
309.117496	E185
309.117497	E99.P9
309.11767	HN40.M6
309.124	HN40.H5
	PS3556.I34
309.133	DS109.912
309.137	DG254.2
309.1376	PA25
309.138	DF82
309.14	D443
	D1053
	D1060
	HC240
	HC241
	HC241.2
	HD8380.5
	HN373
	HN373.5
	JF51
309.141445	DA890.E3
309.1415	DA960
	HC257.I6
309.141509	HC257.I6
309.142	DA198.5
	DA533
	DA535
	DA566.7
	DT844.5
	HB3583
	HC253
	HC254
	HC254.4
	HC254.5
	HC255
	HC256.5
	HC256.6
	HD8384
	HN383
	HN385
	HN385.5
	HT169.G7
	JN137
	JN234
	JS3111
309.142082	DA566.9.S5
309.1421	HV4088.L8
309.14237	HC254.3
309.14246	HN398.S78
309.14252	HC258.N8
	HN398.N62
309.1426	HN398.E3
309.14264	HN398.S84
309.14271	HC258.C7
309.14272	HC258.L5
309.14274	HD8039.M62
309.14282	DA670.N8
309.143	DD17
	DR1
	HC286.6
	HN445.5
	JN3971.5
309.1431	DD261
	HC287.A2
309.14363	HN418.H3
309.1437	DB215.5
	DB215.6
309.14371	DB212
	DB917
309.1438	DK411
	HN537.5
309.144	DC17
	DC133.8
	HC276.2
	HN425.5
309.1441	HN438.P5
309.145	HC304
309.1455	DG737.4
309.14585	HN660.5.M32
309.146763	HD1741.S82V34
309.147	DK267
	DK268.3
	DR1
	DR48.5
	HC333
	HC335
	HN373.5
	HN523
	HN523.5
	HN525
	HN532.5
309.147084	DK267
	JN6515
309.1471	DK459
309.14735	DK651.V525
309.1474	DK511.B3
309.14741	HQ1665.3
309.148	HN540
309.1485	DL658.8
	HD7199

Dewey	LC
309.1485	HN573.5
	JV8221
309.148505	HC375
309.1489	DL159
	HN546
309.14912	DL326
309.1495	DF852
309.149512	HN470.A8
309.1497	HC407.Y6
	JN9670
309.14977	HC407.B9
	JN9609.A8
309.1498	HC407.R8
309.15	DS35
	DS515
	DS703.4
	DS777.55
	HC412
	HN663.5
309.151	DS706
	DS721
	DS777.55
	DS778.C593
	DS806
	HN673
309.151225	HN680.C55
309.151245	DS793.L515
309.15125	HN761.H6
309.15173	DS798
309.1518	DS783
309.1519	DS901
	DS917
	HN730.5.A8
309.152	DS801
	DS811
	DS889
	HC462.9
	HN723
309.1538	DS248.M4
309.154	DS407
	DS421
	DS425
	DS428
	DS430
	DS432.A55
	DS480.84
	DS480.85
	HC435.2
	HM278
	HN682
	HN683
	HN683.5
	HN690.D36
	HT720
309.15404	HN690.B6
309.15412	HN690.C55
309.15414	DS485.B41
	HN690.B4
	HN690.C2
309.154162	GN635.I4
	HN690.A8
309.1543	HN690.S17
309.15475	HC438.A35
309.154792	HC437.M32
	HN690.M33
309.1548	JQ215
309.15482	DS432.T3
309.15484	DS485.A55
	HN690.P3
309.1549	HC440.5
	HN690.5
	HN690.5.A8
309.1549105	DS485.M74
309.1549142	HN690.5.R35
309.15492	HN690.5.E3
309.154922	HC440.5.Z7
309.155	DS266
309.156	DS44
	HN660.8
	JX1977
309.1561	DR417
	HC405
	HC408.T7
309.1564	HD2037
309.1567	HN764.I7
309.1569	DS97
309.15691	DS93
309.15694	DS113.7
	DS119.7
	HN761.P3
	HN761.P32
309.1569405	DS126.5
309.15695	DS153
309.1584	HC487.C4
309.159	DS503.4
	DS511
309.1591	DS485.B81
309.1593	DS586
	HN750.5.A8
309.15951	DS596.5
309.16	DT1
	DT30
	DT30.2
	DT38
	DT352.4
	H62.5.A34
	HC502
	HN773
	HN773.5
309.1611	DT245
	HN810.T82S513
309.1612	DT215
309.162	HN783
309.1629	DT135.M6
309.166	DT524
309.1664	HC517.S5
309.1669	DT515.42
	HN800.N5
309.167	DT14
	DT30
	DT351
	DT353
	DT434.E262
309.1675	HC591.C6
	HN820.S7
	JS7715.9.K5
309.16761	DT434.U22
	HN800.U353
309.16773	DT401
309.16782	DT443
309.1679	DT459
309.168	DT763
	DT779.7
	HD6867
309.16808	DT779
309.1681	DT791
309.16822	DT944.J66S68
	HN800.S63J6
309.1684	DT872
309.1687	HC517.S72C42
309.16891	DT955
	DT962
	HC517.R43
309.16894	DT963
309.17	HN57
309.1701	E78.C15
	E98.E2
	E99.D1
	E99.O3
	E99.P25
	F1219.3.S6
309.171	F1027
	F1034.2
	HN103.5
	HN107
309.17121	HC117.Y8
309.171233	SB484.C2
309.17124	JL303
309.17127	HC117.M3
309.1713	HN110.O5
309.1713133	HC118.S9
309.171352	JS1721.O58
309.171353	HN110.B9
309.1713541	F1059.5.T68
309.1714	F1027
309.171635	HN110.H32
309.171695	HC117.C3
309.1718	HC117.N4
309.17188	HN250.S2
309.172	E1234
	F1233.5
	F1405.5
	HC135
	HN113
	HN113.5
309.1722	JS2120.E62
309.1727	F1221.C56
309.1728	HC125
309.17281	HN143
	HN143.5
309.1729	F2131
	HN244
309.17291	F1765.2
	HN203
	HN203.5
309.17292	F1871
	F1895.W65
	HN222
	HN223.5
309.17293	HN217.5
309.172973	F2033
309.173	BR516.5
	DK268.3
	E165
	E168
	E169.02
	E169.12
	E185.615
	E185.86
	E301
	E338
	E660
	E661
	E741
	E742
	E743
	E784
	E801
	E806
	E839
	E840
	E846
	E855
	F210
	H53.U5
	H83
	HC105
	HC106
	HC106.3
	HC106.5
	HC106.6
	HC110.P6
	HN18
	HN56
	HN57
	HN57.W45
	HN58
309.173	HN59
	HN64
	HN65
	HQ796
	HT107
	HT123
	HT334.U5
	JA84.U5
	JK216
	JK271
	JK274
	KF373.A7
	PR6058.O27
	PS688
	PS3552.E75
309.1730918	JC330
309.173092	E839.5
309.1730922	E839.5
309.1730923	JS341
309.1730924	E855
	JK261
309.174	HN79.A13
309.1741	F19
309.17446	HN80.B7
309.1745	F85
309.1746	HN79.C8
309.1747	HC107.N7
309.17471	HN80.N5
	HQ146.N7
	JS1228
309.1747275	HN80.N5
309.174811	F158.52
	HN80.P5
309.174992	DS646.36
309.175	F106
	F209
	F213
	F215
	F216
	F216.2
	HC107.A13
	HN79.A13
	HT123.5.S6
309.1752	HC107.A12
309.1753	HN80.W3
309.175404	LC144.W4
309.1755	F229
	HT123.5.V5
309.1757	F273
309.1758	HC107.G4
	HN79.G4
309.1759	HN79.F6
309.175921	HN80.D32
309.1763	F373
309.1763355	F379.N557
309.1768	HC107.T33P617
	HN79.A135
309.1769	HC107.K4
	HN59.U5
	HN79.A13
309.17692	F456
309.17702	F479
309.1771	HC107.O3
309.177157	HN80.C7
309.177178	F499.C5
309.177274	F534.F7
309.177311	F548.5
	F548.52
309.177327	HN80.S545
309.1775	HB3525.W6
	HN79.W6
309.177583	HV98.W6
309.177595	HN80.M58
309.1781	F686
309.178961	HC107.N63P67
309.1792	HC107.U8
309.1793	HC107.N3
309.1794	JK8725
309.179493	F869.W3
309.179494	HN80.L7
309.1795	HC107.O7
309.179523	HC107.O72
309.1797	HN79.W2
309.179755	HC107.W22Y35
309.179777	HN80.S54
309.1798	HC107.A45
309.17984	HC107.A45
309.18	F1406.7
	F1408
	F1408.2
	F1414
	F1414.2
	HC125
	HN110.5
	HN110.5.A8
	JX1977
309.181	F2510
	HC187
309.1813	HN283.5
309.1814	HV195.S2
309.182	JL2026
309.183	F3099
	HN293.5
309.185	F3448
	HN343.5
309.1852	HN350.I23
309.1853	HN350.P8
309.1861	HN303.5
	HN307
309.18612	HC198.B8
309.187	F2308
	HN363.5
309.1881	HC207
	HN330.L4
309.19	DU28
	GN662
	HC601
309.191	DS615
	HC447
	HN703
309.1914	DS685
	HC455
	HM51
	HN713
309.19145	HN720.P3
309.1922	HN710.M6
309.1931	DU400
	HC665
	HN930.5
	JQ4015
309.1935	AS281
309.194	HC605
	HN847
309.1941	HC652
	HN930.N4
309.19429	DU397.H3
309.1943	HD4393
309.1944	DU178
	HC638.H8
309.1945	HN843
309.195	DU740
	HC687.P3
309.1951	DU744.5
309.1961	HN940.F5
309.19611	DU600
309.19614	AS36
309.19681	DU615
309.1969	HC107.H3
309.1977	E179.5
309.199	DU740
309.2	HD38
	HM15
	HN470.A8
	HN683.5
	HT391
309.2071173	JF1338.A2
309.2091724	HC59.7
309.20944	HT395.F7
309.20954	HC435.2
309.209717	HC117.P7
309.2120183	HT166
309.22	HC59.7
	JX1977
	KF26.F6
	KF27.G6594
309.220996	DU29
309.223	F1414.2
	F1418
	HC59.7
	HC60
	HC125
	HC435.2
	HC438.R6
	HC443.V5
	HC502
	HD107
	HF1455
	KF26.F6
	KF27.F6
	KF4668
309.2230943	HC60
309.22309931	HC60
309.2232	HC60
	HC60.U42
309.22321812	HC125
309.223373	HC60
309.2235	HC60.5
309.223573	HC60
	HC60.5
	KF26.F6
	KF27.F6
	KF4689
309.223573097292	HC60.5
309.22357309965	HC60
309.2235861	HC60.5
309.223594	HC412
309.23	HT107
309.230942	HC256.C48
	HN383.5
309.2309438	HT391
309.230945	HN537.5
	HN573.5
309.230947	HN523.5
	JN6598
309.23095	Q127.A65
309.230951249	HD870.5
309.230952	AS4.U8
309.230954	HC440.P63
	HV392
309.230954792	HC437.M32
309.2309549	HC440.5
309.2309667	HD989.G6
309.2309669	JQ3083
309.2309688	DT703
309.230971	D829.C2
309.230973	HC106.5
	HC110.E5
	HC110.P63
	HN53
	HN58
	HN59
	HV696.F6
	KF26.B353
	KF27.E374
	KF31.L3
309.2309749	HV1468.N5
309.230994	DU120

Dewey	LC
309.25	HT390
	HT391
309.25025764	HT393.T48
309.2508	HT390
309.25091732	HD259
309.2509412	HT395.S32M66
309.2509422	HC256.6
309.2509423	HC257.S6
309.2509425	HT395.G72N65
309.2509426	HT395.G72
	HT395.G72E215
309.250945	HT395.I8
309.2509542	HN690.U8
309.250954792	HT395.I52M38
309.2509669	HT395.C32N54
309.25096781	HN814.T3
309.250967891	HN814.T3
309.250971	HM13
309.250971221	HT395.C32
309.25097131	HT395.C32O57
309.250971338	HT395.C32N52
309.250973	HT392
	HT394.W3
	KF25.E277
	KF26.P828
309.250974	HT394.N5
309.2509744	HT393.M4
309.250974461	HT394.B6
309.25097463	HT394.H3
309.2509747	HT167.5.N5
309.25097472	HT394.N5
309.2509748	HT393.P43
309.25097488	HT393.P43
309.2509749	HC107.N53P633
309.250975284	HT393.M38M645
309.250975529	HD211.V8
309.2509759	HT393.F5
309.2509764	HT393.T48
309.250976858	HT393.T42D82
309.250976879	HT393.T42
309.2509771	HT393.O4
309.2509775	HN79.W6
	HT393.M6
309.250977829	HN80.I35
309.2509792	HT393.U8
309.250979438	HT393.T3
309.25097946	HT394.S25
309.25099147	HN720.M5
309.250994	HT395.A92N43
309.26	HC107.T3
	HC108.C4
	HN17.5
	HT166
	HT169.I52B68
	HT175
	HT177.V5
	HT390
	HT391
	JS323
309.26018	HC106.5
	HC107.A45
	HT167
309.26025	JX1977
309.26025769	HC107.K43P634
309.2606374461	HT177.B6
309.2607	HT167
309.26072073	HT109
309.26091724	HT169.5
309.260942	HC251
	HT169.G7
	HT175.G7
309.2609421	HT169.G72L646
309.26094237	HT395.G72
309.260942965	HT169.W32B72
309.260954	HT169.I5
309.2609555	DS325.K43
309.260971314	HT177.T5
309.260971317	HT169.C32B35
309.260971352	HN110.H28
309.260971691	HT169.C32
309.26097296	HT169.B32
309.260973	AS36.C2
	HF5006
	HN59
	HT123
	HT151
	HT167
	HT169.U5
	HT175
	HT175.U6
	HT334.U5
	JK2408
309.26097448	HT168.D8
309.26097468	HT177.N37
309.26097471	HT168.N5
	HT177.N5
309.2609748	HT123.5.P4
309.260974886	HC110.P63
309.2609753	HT168.W3
309.2609755	HT167.5.V8
309.2609763355	HT168.N4
309.260976428	HN80.D25
309.260977252	HT168.I5
309.260977311	HT168.C5
	HT177.C5
309.2609773794	HT168.C4
309.260977434	HT177.D4
309.2609778	HC107.M83
309.2609791	HT167.5.A7
309.26097946	HT394.S25
309.260979466	HC108.O3
309.260979494	HN80.L7
309.260979772	HT168.B8
309.2609815	HT169.B72G87
309.2609941	HT395.A93P46
309.262	HT123
309.2620184	HT166
309.2620973	HT167
309.26209753	HT168.W3
309.2620975965	HT168.T3
309.2620976823	HT168.H8
309.26209776579	JS1140
309.2917496	GN645
309.29540594	DS450.L3
309.5409742277	HD7304.O86
309.714281	HN110.M63
309.7284	F1405.5
310	HA29
	HA42
310.08	HA1503
310.0954	HA37.I4
310.09969	HA37.U7
	HA37.U7H3
310.246584	HA29
310.8	HA29
310.9	HA19
311	HA29
	QA276.16
311.076	JK717.S67
311.2	HA29
	HA37
	JX1977
311.20942	HA37.G7
311.21	HA37.U55
	JX1977
311.2108	HA31.2
311.22	RG107.5.E9
311.23	HA29
	HB881
	RA409
311.25	HA31.3
311.26	HA31
	QA90
311.28	HF5415.3
311.39416	HA1147.N6
311.3973	HA37
	HA37.U55
311.39744	HA37.U7M4
311.39747	HA37.U7
311.39758	HA37.U7G46
312	HA37
	HA262
	HB881
	HB885
	HG8784.U6
312.018	HB881
312.0182	HB881
	RA409
312.03	HB879
312.08	HB881
	HC331
312.09	HA36
	HB881
312.0941	HA1152
312.094112	HB3588.O7
312.0942	CS421
	HA1121
	HA1125
	HB3583
312.0943	HA1235
312.09438	HB3608.7
312.095125	HA1950.H6
	HB3659.H6
312.0954	HB3639
312.095414	HB3640.B42
312.09549	HA37.P27
	HA1730.5
	HB3640.5
	HC440.5
312.095492	HC440.5
312.0954923	HB3640.5
312.09593	HB3656.5
312.096692	HA1977.N5
312.0968	HB2126.S6
312.09682	DT763
312.09683	HA1977.S9
312.096891	HA1977.R5
312.096894	HB3666.R4
312.096897	HB3666.M3
312.097124	HB3530.S3
312.09713	HB3530.O5
312.0973	HA37
	HA37.U54
	HA211
	HB915
	HB3505
	RA407.3
312.09741	HA414
312.0974461	HB3527.B7
312.09747	HB3506.N4
	HB3525.N7
312.0974842	F157.A2
312.09752	HA426
312.09754	HB3525.W4
312.09756	HB3525.N8
312.09764	F385
312.097699	F457.J23
312.09771	HB3525.O3
312.09772	HB3525.I6
312.09773	HA346
312.09776	HA453
312.09791	F810
312.09794	HB3525.C2
312.0979463	HB3525.C2
312.0979466	HB3527.O45
312.0983	HB3565
312.09934	HA4008.V5
312.1	HB891
312.1	HB915
312.1701	E78.C6
312.173	HA211
312.1794	HA38.C2
312.2	HB1415
312.209437	HB1422.C95
312.20952	HB1481
312.209549	HC440.5
312.2095492	HB1470.5
312.209701	E78.N65
312.20973	HB915
	RA409
312.209768	HB1355.T2
312.2342	HB1323.I4
312.23492	HB1323.I4
312.2373	RJ59
312.23754	RJ59
312.23776	HB1323.I4
312.23786	RG631
312.26	G58
	RA407.4.A7
312.26994	RC277
	RC277.P4
312.2699409748	RC277.P4
312.27	HB1323.A2
312.270971	HB1323.A2
312.27609794	HV7571.C3
312.3	HV1553
	RA8
312.30942	RG530
312.30971	RA407.5.C2
312.30973	RA407.3
312.3097471	RA407.4.N7
312.309768	RA447.T2
312.346209485	RC660
312.380942	RC450.G7
312.3809973	PA407.3
312.3855	RC423
312.389	RC448
312.3994	RC277
312.3994009746	RC277.C6
312.3994009781	RC277.K2
312.3994097295	RC279.P8
312.4	HV675
312.40973	RA407.3
312.43	TN295
312.44	HE5614.3.W9
312.4409747	HE5614.3.N5
312.4409776	HE5614.3.M5
312.5	HA211
312.6	RA407.3
312.8	HB2047
312.80954792	HB3640.B5
312.9	E78.A3
	E185.6
	E185.88
	HA211
	HA1125
	HA1152
	HB2619
	HB3507
	HB3525.W6
	HB3617
	HC440.5
	HV1475.A2
	JV6455
	JV7626
312.9096761	HA1977.U35
312.909753	HV1471.W42D47
314	HA1107
314.1	HC257.S4
314.2	DA190.D7
	HB3583
	HC256.6
	HN385.5
314.7	HA1435
315.125	HA1950.H6
315.4	HA1727
315.414	HA1729.C3
315.49	HA1730.5
316.3	HA1967.B3
316.773	HB3670.S582A47
316.78	HA37
317.020973	LC49
317.27	LB3051
317.3	HA37
	HA37.U52
	HA201
	HA215
	HA217
	HC105
317.44	HA432
317.471	HA730.N5
317.51	HA294
317.54	HA706
317.55	HA686
317.552	HA686
317.56	HA553
317.58	HA37.U7G42
317.73	F536.I34543
317.86	HA483
	HA484
317.87	HA726
317.92	HA664
	HA666
318.77162	LD3141.M23
319.5	HA4007.P323
319.69	HA329.1
320	DA592
	JA28
	JA66
	JA71
	JC177
	JC179.M8
320	JC181
	JC211
	JC212
	JC213
	JC223
	JC252
	JC257
	JC258
	JC330
	JF51
	KF4770
	PR5403
320.01	DG731.5.M4
	E176.1
	GN1
	HC256.6
	HM213
	JA66
	JA71
	JA74
	JA76
	JA79
	JA83
	JA84.U5
	JC143
	JC143.M4
	JC153
	JC179.R9
	JC212.C66
	JC229.P8
	JC251
	JC251.L55
	JC273
	JC330
	JC507
	JC571
	JF51
	JN231
320.015128	Q180.A1
320.018	JA71
	JA73
320.0182	JA73
320.0184	JA73
320.019	JA74
	JA74.5
320.0207	PN6231.P6
320.03	JA61
320.0627471	JS1239
320.07	JA86
	JA88.U6
	JK271
	LB1584
320.071173	JA88.U6
320.072	JA86
320.072024	E415.9.L7
320.072042	JA88.G7
320.0720753	JA88.U6
320.076	JA66
320.08	D521
	DA500
	HT167.5.P4
	JA36
	JA38
	JA41
	JA66
	JA71
	JK271
320.09	JA38
	JA81
	JA84.G7
	JA84.U5
	JF51
320.0924	DA585.C34
	JA83
320.0934	JC50
	JQ200
320.0942	JN239
	JN318
	JN321
320.09437	JN9670
320.095	DS33.3
320.0951	DS777.55
320.0952	JQ1626
320.0954	JQ215
	JQ298.8
320.09549	JQ543
320.09597	DS557.A5
320.096	DT18
320.0966	JQ2998
320.0967	JA84.A33
320.096891	JQ2923
320.0971	JL187
320.0973	JA84.U5
	JK271
	JK274
320.09756	F260
320.09778	JK5425
320.09789	JK8031
320.098	JA84.L3
320.0991	JA84.I45
320.09914	JQ1410
320.1	DG738.14.M2
	HC179.M8
	JC11
	JC71.A7
	JC143
	JC251
	JC258
	JC273
	JC330
	JC501
	JC571
320.10924	DG552.8.M3
	JC233.H46

320.11	JC336
320.110924	JC179.R9
320.12	HB99.3
	JC319
320.1209471	DK459.45
320.1209474	JX1552.5.Z7R93
320.120951	DS706.5
320.12096	DT23
320.13	JC311
	JX4054
320.15	JC153
	JC153.H66
	JC257
	JC325
	JC328
320.155	JC365
	JC423
	JF60
320.15509	E208
320.1550967	DT353
320.157	JC327
320.1570985	JL3400
320.158	DA42
	E277
	JC311
	JC329
	JF60
320.158094	D359
320.1580941	DA765
	DA821
	DA824.S35
	JN1213
320.1580942	DA821
320.1580943	DD76
320.15809436	DB77
320.1580945	DG545
320.1580947	DR37
320.158094771	DK508.8
320.15809481	DL441
	H31
320.158094984	DB739
320.1580954	DS421
	DS446.3
320.158095694	DS119.7
320.1580959	DS518.1
320.158095952	JC311
320.158096	DT31
320.158096657	DT613.62
320.15809669	DT515.62
320.1580967	DT475
	JX1631
320.1580971	F1033
320.1580973	E169.12
	E185
320.15924	DT504.J64
320.1594	D1060
320.1596	DT21
	DT30
320.15961	DT204
320.1597	F1418
320.3	HC517.G6
	JF51
	JN234
	TN234
320.3018	JF51
320.306054	JF51
320.307	JF130
320.308	JF51
320.3094	JF51
	JN12
	JN94.A3
320.3095	JQ5
320.3098	JF51
320.473	JK274
320.4761	JK274
320.5	B802
	B945
	B2948
	BF175
	BJ1431
	CB195
	DA565.B7
	DT764.E3
	E183
	E855
	GN320
	HN17
	HN90.R3
	HV6278
	HX846.C4
	JA71
	JA76
	JA81
	JA83
	JA84.U5
	JC153.H66
	JC177
	JC179.M25
	JC179.M8
	JC330
	JC423
	JC491
	JK271
	JK316
	JN234
	JX1977
320.5072043	JA86
320.508	AC8
	JA71
320.509	JA81
320.50901	JA82
320.50922	JC571
320.50924	B2923
	DS481.G3
320.50924	JC153.V32
	PQ2012
320.50947	JN6526
320.50951	BL1925
320.50954	BL2001.2
	DS427
	JA84.I4
320.50973	E839.5
320.51	DA522.C27
	JC571
	JN216
320.510207	PN6231.L47
320.510924	JC178.V2
320.51094	HM276
320.510942	JN234
320.510954	JA84.I4
320.510973	HM276
	JA84.U5
320.5130973	E806
320.52	BR115.P7
	DD238
320.520942	HX11
320.520944	DC252
320.520954	JC571
320.520973	E855
	JA84.U5
	JC251
320.531	DA410
	HX11
	HX44
	HX828
320.5310924	HX263.B56
320.5310942	HX246
320.5310994	HD8848
320.5315	PL2908.O17
320.532	D847
	HX518.R4
	JC474
320.5320924	DS481.R6
320.5320947	DK267
320.533	JC481
320.533019	JC481
320.533094	D410
	D424
320.5330944	DC33.6
320.54	E185
	JC311
320.54095	DS33.1
320.540973	E301
320.7	LB1059
320.712	JA88.G7
320.9	D3.U6
	D445
	D842.5
	D843
	D849
	D849.5
	DK265.9.I5
	E839.3
	JA37
	JA81
	JA83
320.90207	PN6231.C612
320.904	D450
320.909729	JL602
320.9171242	DA18
	JN234
	JN276
	JV1027
320.91724	D843
	JF60
320.9174927	JA84.A6
320.91822	U162
320.922	DA585.A1
320.924	E835
320.93	JC85.C7
320.935	DS73.2
320.9376	AS122.B4
	DG279
320.938	JC73
320.9385	DF277
	JC79.A8
	PA25
320.94	AS36
	D105
	D289
	D363
	D397
	D443
	D727
	D1060
	DC192.H5
	JA81
	JF51
	JN15
	JN94
	SF51
320.9415	DA913
	DA950
	DA950.2
	DA957
	DA960
	DA962
	JN1405
	JN1415
320.9416	DA990.U46
	JS4411.F4
320.942	BX6276
	D742.G7
	DA42
	DA395
	DA499
	DA505
	DA508
320.942	DA535
	DA565.B846
	DA565.C4
	DA566.7
	DA570
	DA576
	DA585.M38
	DA591.N3
	HC256.6
	HN385
	JA66
	JA84.G7
	JN101
	JN118
	JN185
	JN212
	JN216
	JN223
	JN231
	JN234
	JN237
	JN321
	JN329.P7
	JN371
	JN521
	JN550
	JN675
	PN5130.Q4
320.943	DD112
	DD197.5
	DD210
	DD232
	DD237
	DD247.B67
	DD247.H5
	DD253
	DD256.3
	DD256.5
	DD257.25
	DD257.4
	DD259.4
	DD259.7.B6
	DD261.4
	DD343.8
	DD881
	DK254.T6
	JN3425
	PT2625.A44
320.943084	DD231.S35
320.9431	DD261.4
320.9436	DB47
320.9437	DB215.6
320.94391	DB955
	DB956
320.944	DC252
	DC340
	DC369.O8
	DC404
	DC412
	E744
	JA84.F8
	JN2429.R4
	JN2562
	JN2594.2
	JN2597
320.945	DG552.5
	DG555
320.94535	JN5269
320.9458	JN5289
320.946081	DP257
320.947	DK260
	DK266.I69
	DK272.5
	DK274
	DK274.3
	E744
	JN96
	JN6515
320.9485	JN7825
	JN7995.A1
320.949	JN5700.A3
320.9493	JS6006
320.9495	DF852
320.9497	DR370
	JN9662
320.94977	DR90
320.9498	DR250
	DR267
320.95	D463
	DS35
	DS518
	DS518.1
320.951	DS753
	DS775
	DS777.55
	DS778.M3
	JA84.C6
	JQ1502
	JQ1503
	JQ1508
	JQ1519
	JQ1519.A45
320.9510924	DS778.T77
320.951249	DS895.F75
320.95127	DS796.C2
320.9515	DS786
320.9518	DS784
320.952	DS845
	DS888.5
	DS889
	JQ1611
320.954	AS36
	DK265.17
	DS447
320.954	DS450.C5
	DS451
	DS463
	DS479
	DS479.5
	DS479.7
	DS480.45
	DS480.83
	DS480.84
	DS481.G3
	DS481.J34
	DS889
	E741
	JC423
	JQ200
	JQ215
	JQ283
	JQ298
	JQ298.I5
	JQ298.8
320.954035	DS403
320.9545	DS485.P2
320.954792	DS485.B68
320.9548	DS484
320.9549	DS384
	JQ542
	JQ543
320.954904	DS384
320.95492	DS485.B492
320.95493	JQ653
320.95496	JQ1825.N4
320.955	DS79.65
	DS318
320.956	DS62.4
	DS62.8
	DS63
	KF32.F666
	U162
320.9561	DR590
	JN9715
320.9567	DS79
	DS79.65
320.9569	DS119.7
	DS126.4
320.95694	DS109.93
	DS119.7
	DS126.5
	JQ1825.P3
	JQ1825.P32
320.957	DK753
320.959	DS518.1
	JF51
320.9591	DS485.B85
320.9594	DS557.L28
320.9595	DS597
320.959504	DS597
320.9597	DS557.A5
320.96	DT30
	DT30.2
	DT31
	DT352.8
	GN490
	JQ1873
	JQ1915
320.961	JQ3189
320.9611	DT264
320.9624	JQ3981.S8
320.963	JQ3754
	JQ3760
320.964	DT324
320.96405	DT324.3.B5
320.965	DT295
320.966	DT471
	JQ2998
320.9663	JQ3396.A3
320.9664	DT516.62
	JQ3121
320.9666	DT631
	DT632
320.96668	JQ3386.A98D495
320.9667	DT511
320.9669	DT515.42
	DT515.5
	DT515.7
	DT515.8
320.96691	JS7656.9.L32
320.96695	JQ3099.N63
320.967	DT352.8
	DT353
	DT431
320.9675	DT655
320.96757	DT449.R442
320.9676	DT431
320.96762	DT434.E262
320.96782	JQ3519.S83
320.9679	DT463
320.968	BR123
	J705.K24
	JQ1915
320.9681	GN490
320.9682	DT926
320.9683	DT1
320.96891	DT962.62
	DT962.7
320.96894	DT963.8
320.97	E18
320.9701	E99.O3
320.971	F1027
	F1032
	F1034.2
	JL11
	JL27
	JL65
	JL195

Dewey	LC
320.9711	F1088
320.9712	F1060.92
320.97124	F1072
320.9713	F1058
	JL262
	JL263
320.9713541	JS1789
320.9714	F1027
	F1032
	F1053
	JL246.S8
320.971404	F1053
320.9715	F1035.8
320.972	F1235
	JL1224
320.9721	F1401
	JL1299.S73
320.9729	F2131
320.97291	F1788
320.97292	JL639.A2
320.97293	F1938.55
320.97295	F1976
	JL1043
320.973	D753
	DK274
	E165
	E169.12
	E173
	E183
	E185
	E185.615
	E211
	E301
	E302
	E338
	E341
	E357.7
	E381
	E415.7
	E440
	E457
	E458
	E459
	E467.1.T6
	E660
	E661
	E666
	E668
	E742
	E743
	E743.5
	E747
	E784
	E806
	E813
	E839.4
	E839.5
	E839.8
	E840.8.M3
	E846
	E847
	E855
320.931	F196
	H62
320.973	H83
	JA71
	JA74
	JA84.U5
	JA88.U6
	JC423
	JC571
	JC578
	JF1351
	JK11
	JK21
	JK31
	JK39
	JK136
	JK216
	JK261
	JK271
	JK274
	JK325
	JK421
	JK424
	JK469
	JK1726
	JK1965
	JK1967
	JK2261
	JK2275.N4
	JK2316
	JK8725
	JN237
	JQ1825.P3
	JS341
	PN4201
320.9730207	F866
320.97309	E742
320.9730915	E743
320.9730917	E806
320.9730923	E839.5
320.9730924	JK274
320.974	JK54
320.9742	F37
320.9744	F73.4
	JK3116
	JK3125
320.97447	F74.D3
320.9746	E302.6.I6
	JK3325
320.9747	F119
320.974886	JS1298
320.975	JK325
320.9752	H31
	JK3825
320.97526	JC330
320.9753	JK2716
	JK2725
320.9755	F231
320.9757	E384.3
	F272
	F274
	JK99.S5
320.9758	F291.2
320.9759	JK4401
320.976	F216.2
320.9761	F326
320.9764	F391.2
	JK4825
320.977	F354
320.9771	F496
320.9772	F526
320.9773	JK5725
320.977311	JS708
320.977434	JS838
320.977593	F589.O2
320.9778	F466
320.978	F591
320.9788830924	F784.D4
320.9794	F861
	F866.2
	JK8725
320.9796	F746
320.98	F1414
	F1414.2
	F1787.5
	HN110.5.A8
	JL952
320.981	F2538.2
	HC187
320.982	UA613
320.983	F3081
	F3099
	JL2669.P7
320.984	F3325
320.985	F3448
320.9866	JL3015
320.9881	J146.N15
320.9883	JL782
320.99	DS518
	DU29
	DU29.C52
320.991	DS644
	DS644.1.S8
	DS644.2
	DU744.5
	J631.H53
	J631.N3S827
	JQ763
320.9914	JQ1403
	NC1720.P6
320.99143	JQ1419.M53
320.9931	DU421
	JQ5815
320.994	DU110
	DU112
	DU114.M4
	DU117
	DU222.P4
	JQ4011
	JQ4015
	JQ4098.C6
320.9944	DU170
320.995	DU740
320.9951	DU744.5
320.9965	DU500
321	JC385
	JC3048
321.001	JF1051
	JK54
	JK3968
321.008	JA71
321.02	JC355
	JC357
321.02094	D1060
	JC355
	JN15
	JN15.A7513
321.0209729	F2134
321.03	JC359
321.0308	DA18
321.030937	DG241
321.03094	JC359
321.030942	DA18
321.04	HC241.2
	JC362
321.040924	JC71.A7
321.04094	HC240.A1
321.07	B785.M84
	HX806
	HX811
	HX811.1516
	HX833
	JC71
321.08	JC365
321.09	HM281
	HX811
	JC491
	JC494
321.0908	JC491
321.1	GN490
321.11	JN7
321.120942	JN335
321.14	DF572
321.140954	JQ620.D4
321.3	JC111
321.30952	JQ1600
321.40945	DG523
321.5	DS141
	DS145.P7
	DT1
	HB87
	JC51
321.6	JC393.B3
	JN1239
321.609922	JQ779.J32
321.72	JC393.D3
	JN351
321.720942	JN331
321.740942	HX244
321.8	DS451
	JC421
	JC423
	JC433
321.801	BX9418
	JC423
321.808	JC423
321.80924	E302.6.H2
	JC229.T8
	JK171.A3
321.80942	JC423
	JN234
321.80954	JQ215
321.80973	JK81
321.80975	JK1929.A2
321.8098	HN110.5.A8
321.809947	JQ4099.A83
321.9	D107
	JC381
	JC481
321.908	JC481
321.9097293	F1938.5
321.92	DK265
321.920943	JN3953
321.94	D726.5
	DD256.5
	JC481
321.940924	DD247.H5
321.940943	DD253
321.940945	DG571
322	DT512
	HN19
	UA23
	UA840
	UA855
322.1	BL65.N3
	BL65.P7
	BP64.E3
	BR115.P7
	BR555.C8
	BV630.A1
	BV2853.B4
	BV3625.C6
	BX1406.2
	F2651.J83
	JQ1698.K6
	LC111
322.10924	DC255.T3
	F82
322.109415	BR794
	BX5500
	BX5550
322.10942	BR750
322.10944	DC158.2
322.10945	DG799
322.10947	BX492
322.109495	BX613
322.10954	BL2003
	BL2747.8
322.1095694	BM390
322.10973	BR516
322.109861	BX1470
322.2	E185.615
322.20944	JN2652
322.20973	HD8072
322.3	HC256.2
	HD3611
	HD9515
	JK467
322.30942	HD3616.G72
322.30971	HD3616.C22
322.30973	HD3665
322.309751	HC107.D3
322.4	BR516
	CT275.T925
	D842
	DA954
	DS62.8
	DS557.A68
	DS644
	DS885.5.K52
	DT1
	E185.5
	E185.61
	E185.615
	E415.9.S79
	E441
	E445.K5
	E446
	E448
	E449
	E451
	E668
	E740.J6
	E839.8
	F444.M5
	F449
	HD8396
	HM278
	HN17.5
322.4	HQ799.5
	HQ799.7
	HT1029.C5
	HT1161
	JC328
	JC328.5
	JL3469.P7
	LA186
	LA229
	LA707
	LA1153.7
	LB3605
	LC2605
322.401	HG221
322.40924	E449
	HT1029.C5
322.409415	DA954
322.40944	HN425
	HT1176
322.40947	JN6515
322.40973	E185.615
	JK1118
322.42	D210
	E185.615
322.420924	CT2750.F3
322.44	BX1504
	LA186
322.440981	F2538.2
322.5096	DT30
323	E813
	JC328.5
	JC585
323.01	JA71
323.0973	JC585
323.098	JC328.5
323.1	JC311
323.106268	JQ1998.A4
323.111	HD9688.U52
	JC330
323.11915905691	DS94.8.K8
323.11924043	DS135.G33
323.119240437	DS135.C95
323.11924047	DS135.R9
	DS135.R9C3
	DS146.R9
323.1192705694	DS113.7
323.1196022	E185.6
323.1196024	E185.97.T75
323.1196042	DA588
323.1196068	DT779.7
	JQ1998.A4
	KF27.F625
323.119606891	DT962.42
323.1196073	E185
	E185.61
	E185.615
	E441
	F216.2
	JK1924
323.1196075	E185.92
323.11963068	DT763.5
323.119915	DU120
323.119915094	DU120
323.14	AS262
323.147	JN6520.M5
323.173	DS133
323.2	D767.63
	DS481.G3
	DS557.A68
	DT21
	DT510.6.N5
	E183
	E185.5
	E185.97.S7
	E447
	E668
	E839.4
	E839.8
	HM278
	HN18
	HN65
	HQ799.7
	HS2330.K63
	JC328.3
	JC328.5
	JC491
	JC494
	JX4541
	KF26.J832
	KF27.I548
	KF27.U5
	LD1961.G54
323.208	JC328.3
323.20924	DK254.A8
	E169.12
	E185.615
	E185.97.B87
	E185.97.C6
	E185.97.L23A3
	F891
	F2849.22.G85
323.20942	DA535
323.20943	DD256.3
323.20947	DK266.3
323.20951	HX933
323.2095951	DS597
323.20962	DT107.82
323.20973	E185.61
	E185.615
	E839.8
	JC423
	KF26.J832
	LA229
323.2098	F1414.2

323.2098 ..... F1415
323.3 ..... E185
..... E433
..... E441
..... E447
..... E449
..... E453
..... E457.4
..... E668
..... E815
..... F67
..... F685
..... HD715
..... HD8395
..... HT609
..... HT1165
..... JN6598.S6
323.30973 ..... E449
323.4 ..... AS4.U8
..... E185.6
..... E185.61
..... E185.615
..... E185.97.K5
..... HE6331
..... HN440.R3
..... HX11
..... JC311
..... JC571
..... JC585
..... JC599.L3
..... JC599.R9
..... JC599.U5
..... JK516
..... JN1129.C682
..... JX1977
..... JX5268
..... PS683.N4
323.402573 ..... JC599.U5
..... KF4755
323.4061778 ..... JC599.U52
323.406273 ..... AS911.F813
323.406373 ..... KF27.F648
323.408 ..... JC571
..... JC585
323.4091717 ..... JC474
323.40922 ..... E185.96
323.40924 ..... E185.97.K47
..... E185.97.K5
..... E185.97.W6
323.409416 ..... JC599.I66
323.40942 ..... HX11
..... JC599.G7
323.40954 ..... JC599.I4
323.409715 ..... JC599.C2
323.4097291 ..... F1405.5
323.40973 ..... E185
..... E185.6
..... E185.61
..... E185.615
..... JC571
..... JC599.U5
..... KF31.J836
..... KF4743
..... KF4750
..... KF4755
..... KF4770
323.409746 ..... JC599.U5
323.409748 ..... E185.61
323.409761 ..... E185.93.A3
323.40976284 ..... JC599.U52M638
323.409788 ..... F785.A1
323.40994 ..... JC599.A8
323.44 ..... E185.61
..... E450
..... HF5573
..... HG2121
..... HV5840
..... HV5840.G7
..... JC571
..... JC585
..... JC591
..... JC599.C2
..... JC599.U5
..... JN906
..... KF9444
..... LA635
..... PN4748.G3
323.440922 ..... JC599.U5
323.440947 ..... DK274
..... DK276
323.440973 ..... E840.8.A34
..... JC591
..... JC599.U5
..... KF1262
..... UA23.2
323.442 ..... E332.2
323.44209755 ..... BR555.V8
323.443 ..... HE8700.8
..... JC591
..... KF2801
323.4430973 ..... KF224.M57
..... KF4770
323.44309756 ..... KFN7796
323.445 ..... E449
..... PN4735
..... PN4748.G7
323.4450973 ..... KF2750
..... KF4774
323.44509744 ..... PN4739.M3
323.460973 ..... KF485
323.49 ..... JC599.U5
323.5 ..... HM146
323.50968 ..... DT763.5
323.509689 ..... DT853

323.60971 ..... H53.C3
323.60973 ..... JK1758
323.62 ..... JK1814
323.620973 ..... JK1758
323.64097281 ..... Q180.A1
323.65 ..... JC328.3
323.67 ..... KF27.P6
324 ..... JK1846
324.1 ..... KF26.J836
324.10973 ..... JK96
324.2 ..... JF1001
324.2021 ..... JF1001
324.202142 ..... JN1037
324.202154 ..... JQ294
324.20217123 ..... JL339.A15
324.2021715 ..... JL239
324.202173 ..... JK1967
..... JK1968
324.2021755 ..... JK3993
324.2021758231 ..... F294.A8
324.2021762 ..... JK4693
324.2021768 ..... JK524
324.2021783 ..... JK6501
324.2021797 ..... JK9293
324.202179777 ..... JK9293
324.20942 ..... JN956
324.20943 ..... JN3971
324.20954 ..... JQ292
..... JQ294
..... JQ298.I5
324.20973 ..... JK524
..... JK526
..... JK529
..... JK1965
..... JK1976
..... KF31.R8
324.209943 ..... JQ4792
324.21.0973 ..... JK529
324.210973 ..... JK528
..... KF26.J8
..... KF27.J8
324.24 ..... JA71
..... JF1001
324.240954 ..... JQ294
324.24095413 ..... JQ620.O765
324.240972983 ..... JL659.A5
324.240973 ..... JK2357
324.24097452 ..... JK3293
324.2409764 ..... JK4893
324.241 ..... KF27.J835
..... KF27.J8666
324.241095125 ..... JQ679.A5
324.2410973 ..... JK1924
..... KF27.R8
324.24109748 ..... JK3691
324.273 ..... JK1991
324.3 ..... JK1901
324.309 ..... JK1896
324.30922 ..... HQ1595.A3
324.30924 ..... JK1899.A6
..... JK1899.S7
324.30942 ..... JN979
324.3094219 ..... DA690.T95
324.30973 ..... JK1896
..... JK1901
324.309777 ..... JK1911.I8
324.309794 ..... JK1911.C2
324.42 ..... JN218
..... JN955
..... JN1081
324.4237 ..... DA670.C8
324.52 ..... JQ1692
324.71 ..... JL191
..... JL192
..... JL193
324.73 ..... E183
..... JK524
..... JK1923
..... JK1965
..... JK1967
324.7471 ..... JS1230
324.748 ..... JK1923
..... JK1929.P4
324.75 ..... JK1967
324.755 ..... JK1929.V6
324.759 ..... JK1963
..... JK1963.F6
324.783 ..... JK6593
324.794 ..... JK8795
324.914 ..... JQ1418
325.0212 ..... JV6029
325.1 ..... JV6217
325.10973 ..... KF27.J875
325.21095694 ..... HV640.5.A6
325.220947 ..... DK33
325.240973 ..... JV6895.J6
325.2415073 ..... JV7711.Z79U57
325.24150973 ..... E184.I6
325.242 ..... JV7604
325.242097 ..... JV6451
325.2420971 ..... F1001
325.2420994 ..... DU107
325.2430973 ..... E184.G3
325.2434309747 ..... F130.P2
325.24391 ..... DB957
325.243910994 ..... DU122.H8
325.245 ..... JV8131
325.24920973 ..... E184.D9
325.249409748 ..... F160.S9
325.2510973 ..... JV6874
325.2510985 ..... F3619.C5
325.25409171242 ..... HD8398.E3
325.254095951 ..... DS595

325.25694 ..... HV640.5.A6
325.2569409436 ..... DS135.A9
325.259709593 ..... DS570.V5
325.268709684 ..... DT773
325.2720973 ..... JV6798.M6
325.27295097471 ..... F128.9.P8
325.273096 ..... E448
325.2730966 ..... E448
325.2730967 ..... E448
325.2730971333 ..... F1059.K3
325.29140973 ..... JV6891.F54
325.294 ..... JV9126
325.3 ..... DA11
..... JV305
325.3063 ..... E448
325.308 ..... JV37
325.309 ..... JV105
325.31 ..... JV171
..... JV412
..... JV418
..... JV431
325.3109171242 ..... JV1060
325.310924 ..... DA565.B27
325.31094 ..... DT31
325.310942 ..... DT434.U262
..... E195
..... F152
..... HC445.5
..... JQ1881
..... JV1017
..... JV1060
..... JV1061
325.310954 ..... JQ224
325.31096 ..... DT32
325.310966 ..... DT502
..... JV246
325.310968 ..... JN276
325.310973 ..... E713
..... F970
..... JK2556
325.31098 ..... JV4066.I5
325.337 ..... DG87
325.342 ..... DA16
..... DA17.M2
..... DA18
..... HF1533
..... HF3025
..... JN276
..... JV12
..... JV33.G7
..... JV1012
..... JV1025
325.342054165 ..... DS485.G28
325.342073 ..... E187
325.3420924 ..... DA565.B8
..... DA822.M3
..... DT107.6
325.342094 ..... JV9227
325.342095 ..... DS33.1
325.3420954 ..... DS481.N35
325.342096 ..... DT32
..... DT515.7
..... JQ1890
325.342096694 ..... JQ3099.E23
325.342096695 ..... DT515.7
325.342096782 ..... JS7697.3.A8
325.3420968 ..... JV1037
325.342096891 ..... DT962.42
325.3420971 ..... F1032
325.3420973 ..... E188
325.34209931 ..... DU420
325.343 ..... JV2018
325.3430947 ..... DK43
325.343096711 ..... DT574
325.343096782 ..... DT447
325.343099 ..... DU29
325.344096 ..... DT33
325.3440964 ..... DT324
325.34409662 ..... DT532
325.3460985 ..... JL3426
325.3469 ..... HF3694
..... JV4211
325.3469095126 ..... DS796.M2
325.347095845 ..... DK908
325.373 ..... E713
325.373096 ..... E448
325.37309914 ..... DS685
325.42 ..... DA11
..... DA120
..... DA588
..... HB3583
..... JV7604.A8
..... JV7620
..... JV7625.5
..... JV7626
325.42096 ..... JV1062
325.43 ..... JV2017
325.54792 ..... HB3640.B5
325.5694 ..... DS126.4
..... DS149
325.6 ..... DT31
325.666 ..... E448
325.67 ..... DT731
325.73 ..... JV6415
..... JV6450
..... JV6451
..... JV6455
..... JV6461
..... JV6463
..... JV6465
..... JV6507
..... JV6543
..... JV6895.N44
..... KF27.J8

325.73 ..... KF4710
325.73096 ..... E448
325.747 ..... JV6453
325.7472 ..... JV6483
325.8 ..... KF27.F646
325.82 ..... JV7442
325.9 ..... DU29
325.931 ..... JV9262.Z8
325.94 ..... DU122.B7
..... HB1925
..... HB3675
326 ..... DT463
..... E445.I2
..... E447
..... E449
..... HT867
..... HT915
326.09171244 ..... HT1180
326.0922 ..... E449
326.0924 ..... DA522.W6
..... DT636.A8
..... E185.97
..... E449
..... E449.M93
..... E449.T18
..... HT1029.W5
..... HT1162
326.0942 ..... HT1165
326.09729 ..... E449
..... F2131
..... HT1093
326.097291 ..... HT1078
326.0973 ..... E415.6
..... E415.7
..... E441
..... E446
..... E447
..... E449
..... E449.W46
..... E453
..... F158.8.P4
326.09743 ..... E450
326.097496 ..... E445.T3
326.0975 ..... E449
326.09755 ..... H31
326.09757 ..... E445.S7
327 ..... D443
..... D839
..... D840
..... D843
..... D849
..... D8393
..... JX1291
..... JX1308
..... JX1311
..... JX1395
..... JX1417
..... JX1963
..... JX1974
..... PN1997
327.01 ..... JX1395
327.018 ..... JX1291
..... JX1417
327.0182 ..... JX1901
327.019 ..... JX1255
327.0202 ..... JX1297
327.025 ..... JX1293.U6
327.03 ..... JX1226
327.07 ..... JX1291
327.071173 ..... JX1293.U6
327.072 ..... JX1291
327.072073 ..... JX1293.U6
327.08 ..... JF331
..... JX1391
..... JX1395
..... JX4005
327.09 ..... D443
327.0904 ..... D443
..... D843
327.09046 ..... D843
327.09171242 ..... DA18
327.091713 ..... D844
..... D1060
327.09174927 ..... DS119.7
327.091767 ..... DS38
327.09474 ..... DK511.B3
327.0956 ..... DS62.85
327.09597 ..... DS550
327.096 ..... DT365.62
327.09728 ..... F2171
327.1 ..... D397
..... D421
..... D443
..... D839.3
..... D843
..... D844
..... D849
..... D1058
..... DA964.G7
..... DD261.4
..... E813
..... HF1411
..... HX518.S8
..... JC319
..... JX1395
..... JX4005
..... Z6464.Z9
327.109046 ..... D843
327.109171242 ..... DA18
327.1094 ..... D273.5
327.1095 ..... DS35
327.10956 ..... DS63.2.R9
327.11 ..... JC361
327.1109044 ..... D843

327.11094 D727
HX15
327.112094 D273
327.116 D840
D1058
JX1395
327.12 DK272.5
KF27.I548
KF32.I53
UB251.R8
UB270
UB270.I55
327.1206173 JK468.I6
327.1209 UB270
327.12091717 UB271.R9
327.120922 UB270
327.120924 DK268.G6
DS126.5
HX44
JQ298.C6
KF26.J832
UB271.F72
UB271.R92A23
UB271.R92B58
UB271.R92L54
UB271.R92P436
VB250
327.120942 UB251.G7
UB270
327.120947 DK268.P66
327.12095694 UB271.I8
327.120968 UB271.S6
327.120973 JK468.I6
UB271.U5
327.120994 HF73.A8
327.14 D450
D843
D844
JX4079.P7
327.1724 D839.3
327.2 D397
DU29
JX1662
JX1706
JX1907
JX4473
KF26.G6585
327.2018 JX1311
327.2023 JX1876.Z5
327.206273 JX1706
327.20903 JX1644
327.20922 D412
E183.8.G7
JX1807.A2
327.20924 D413.C23
D413.M23
DA483.H32
DA586
DR262.T5
DS63.1
DS63.2.U5
DS228.G7
DU105
E183.8.I4
E302.6.P5
E313
E415.9.S58
E664.P15
E748.G835
F1034.3.V3
F2846.A4815
Q11
327.2094 D217
327.20947 JX1807
327.20951 JX1837
327.20973 JX1417
JX1705
327.3431 DD232
327.4 D843
D1053
D1058
327.4044 D308
DC412
327.4045 D387
327.4047 DK67
327.4073 D1065.U5
327.415042 DA910
DA963
327.42 D273
D304
DA45
DA46.U8
DA390
DA510
DA530
DA535
DA560
DA563.5
DA564.S2
DA566.7
DA578
DA592
JN1129.L32
JX1543
JX1543.Z5
327.4204 DA47
DA331
DA499
327.42043 DA47.2
DT714
327.420437 DB205.8.G7
327.42044 D511
DA47.1
DA530
327.42047 DA47.65
DK258
327.420492 DJ182
327.4205 DA47.9.E2
327.42051 DA47.9.C6
DA47.9.G7
DS740.5.G5
DS759
DS760
327.42052 DA47.9.J3
DS518.4
DS881.3
327.420536 DS326
327.42054 DS480.83
327.420545 DS485.P3
327.42055 DS274.2.G7
327.42056 DS63.2.G7
327.420561 DR589
327.420597 DS557.A5
327.420669 DT515.63.G7
327.420682 DT926
327.4206891 DT962.63
DT962.7
327.42073 E183.8.G7
E313
327.4208 F1416.G7
327.420964 DA47.9.M8
327.43 DD240
DD259.4
DR48.5
327.43042 D394
327.430431 DD257.4
327.430436 DD120.G7
327.430438 DD801.O35
JX1901
327.43044 DC59.8.G3
327.43047 DD259.4
DD261.4
327.43052 DD120.J3
327.430561 D566
327.4305694 DS119.8.G4
327.43068 DD259.4
327.43073 D742.U5
DD257
327.4308 F1416.R8
327.43604 DB80
327.436047 DB99.1
327.437073 DB215.5
327.438047 DK418.5.R9
327.44 DC340
DC404
E183.8.F8
327.4404 D309
327.44045 DC277.33
327.44047 D397
327.4406 DT108.5
327.44073 E183.8.F8
E249
E323
327.45 DG498
DG552.5
327.450497 DB321
327.46042 JX1530.Z6F325
327.46073 E183.8.S7
327.47 D274.H3
D376.R7
DK63
DK63.3
DK197
DK264.8
DK266
DK266.5
DK273
DK274
DK274.3
DR48.5
JX1395
JX1555.Z5
JX1807
JX4041
Q180
327.4701724 DK274
327.4701822 DK186
327.4704 Q180.A1
327.4705 DS518.7
327.47051 DK68.A2
DK68.7.C5
DS740.5.R8
Q180.A1
327.47052 DS849.R7
327.47054 DK68.7.I5
DS450.R8
JX1571.Z5
327.47055 DS274.2.R8
327.47056 AS36
DS63.2
DS63.2.R9
DS127
327.4705691 DS95.6.R9
327.4705694 DS119.8.R9
327.47066 DT476.5
327.47073 DK26
DR48.5
E183.8.R9
JX1555
327.4708 JX1555.Z7L36
327.47094 DS518.7
327.471 DK451.7
327.4771047 DK265.8.U4
327.481 DL458
327.494073 DQ76.U6
327.496 DR48.5
327.4961042 DR562
327.497 DR367.A1
327.497073 E183.8.Y8
327.498 DR226
327.5 DS33.3
DS35
327.5073 DS5
DS33.4.U6
DS35
DS518.8
DS557.A63
327.50914 DS33.4.P5
327.51 DS740
DS740.4
DS740.5.I5
DS775
DS777.55
DS778.L49
327.51042 DS740.5.G5
327.51047 DS740.5.R8
327.510519 DS910.2.C5
327.51052 DS740.5.J3
DS740.63
JX1577.Z7
327.510594 DS740.5.L3
327.510597 DS740.5.V5
327.51073 E183.8.C5
JX1428.C6
KF27.F638
327.5108 F1416.C5
327.51091 DS640.C5
327.515054 DS785
327.518 DS783.7
327.519073 E183.8.K7
327.5193 DS935.5
327.52 DA47.9.J3
DS881.3
DS884.H3
DS889
327.52042 DS884.S3
327.52051 DS777
327.52073 DS888.5
E183.8.J3
E184.J3
327.52094 JA113.5.J3
327.5281 DS895.R9
327.54 DS445
DS450.C5
DS480.84
E183.8.I4
JQ298.B5
JX1569
327.540171242 DS480.84
327.54047 DK68.7.I5
327.540549 DS485.K2
327.5405496 DS450.N3
DS485.N4
327.5405694 DS450.I7
327.54073 DS480.84
DS485.K2
327.549 DS383.5.A2
327.5490561 DS383.5.T8
327.550567 DS274.2.I57
327.55073 DS254.5
E183.8.I55
327.56 DS63.2.R9
327.5606 DT23
327.56073 DS42
DS63.2.U5
327.561 CD200
327.5662073 D651.A7
327.5694 DS119.6
327.56940174927 DS119.7
327.5694043 DS119.8.G4
327.59073 DS518.8
Q180
327.593073 E183.8.T4
327.595073 DS592
327.595091 DS640.M34
327.597073 DS550
327.6 DT31
JK2356
327.61073 E335
327.62073 E183.8.E3
327.667 DT512
327.676206773 DT434.E28
327.68 DS335
DT770
DT779
DT779.7
327.6891073 KF27.F625
327.71 F1029
F1034
F1034.2
JX1515.Z5
327.710729 F2131
327.71073 E183.8.C2
F1027.5
F1032
JX1428.C2
Z6465.U5
327.7207291 F1228.5.C9
327.72073 E183.8.M6
F353
F1234
327.720862 JX1398
327.7285073 E183.8.N5
F1526.3
327.7291 F1776.3.R9
327.7291073 E183.8.C9
327.73 D843
E182
E183.7
E249
E302.6.H2
E310.7
327.73 E312.952
E661.7
E711
E713
E744
E744.5
E748.B7
E756
E761
E766
E768
E785
E801
E806
E813
E835
E840
E840.2
E855
HC110.D4
HD6490.F58
JX1395
JX1398
JX1407
JX1416
JX1417
JX1427.M5
JX1705
JX4044
KF26.J832
KF27.F6
KF27.F625
KF27.F6483
327.7301717 E183.7
JX1428.C73
327.7301822 D843
327.7301823 DU30
E182
327.7304 D849
D1065.U5
KF27.F642
KF32.F642
Z6465.U5
327.73042 E183.8.G7
E314
E398
327.73043 E183.8.G3
327.73044 E313
E469
327.73044949 E183.8.M8
327.73047 D1065.U5
E183.8.R9
E377
U162
327.730493 E183.8.B4
327.7305 DS33
DS33.4
DS33.4.U6
DS518.8
E748.J746
E840
JX1428.A7
327.73051 E183.8.C5
327.73052 AS36
E183.8.J3
327.73054 E183.8.I4
327.73056 DS63.2.U5
DS119.7
327.73059 DS518.8
KF31.F6
327.730594 E183.8.L3
327.7306 KF27.F625
327.73062 DS63.2.U5
E183.8.E35
327.730669 KF27.F625
327.73068 KF27.F625
327.73071 E183.8.C2
327.73072 E744
F786
327.730728 F1418
327.7307291 KF27.F646
327.7308 F1418
HN110.5.A8
KF26.F697
KF27.F646
327.73081 E183.8.B7
327.73085 JX1428.P4
327.730861 E183.8.C7
327.730862 E183.8.P2
327.730866 E183.8.E2
327.730914 DS685
DS686.5
327.73094 E183.8.A8
327.730965 DU647
327.8 F1228
F1415
F2235
327.82 F2833
327.91 DS638
327.931 DU421
327.94 DU113
DU116
DU117
328.023 JK3466
328.1 JF515
KF1451
328.103 JF515
328.2 JF493.U6
328.20973 KFD1215.2
328.3 JF511
328.308 JF501
328.3345 JK1982
328.334520973 KF32.P634
328.33454 JQ4067

Dewey	LC
328.3347	JF1001
328.34509943	JQ4729.I6
328.3620924	JK1261
328.365	HJ9921.Z9S35
	KF27.I548
328.366	JK1429
328.3750182	JA73
328.38	JK1118
328.401	JF501
328.415	JN1468
328.42	JN234
	JN515
	JN550
328.42008	JN521
328.4207	JN215
328.4207031	DA460
328.42071	JF541
	JN621
	JN623
328.42072	JN673
	JN675
	JN678
	JN688
	JN961
328.420734	JN539
328.4209	JN505
	JN525
	JN543
328.420922	DA566.9.A1
328.420924	DA536.M7
	DA990.U46
328.440765	JN2791
328.47	JN6554
328.52072	JQ1654
328.5405	JQ262
	JQ263.A3
328.54165	JQ620.N25
328.54505	JQ573
328.5479205	JQ620.M265
328.5479207345	JQ620.M2665
328.548605	JQ620.P65
328.5490922	DS385
328.5492	JQ559.E15
328.680747	JQ1956
328.68105	JQ2760
328.71	JL136
328.710922	JL131
328.73	JK1059
	JK1061
	JK1067
	JK1096
	JK2488
	JK2490
	JK2497
	KF27.I547
	KF32.R854
	KF4935
328.730018	JK468.A8
	KF27.G625
328.7301	E668
328.7302	JK1036
328.7304	JK1059
328.7305	JK1331
	KF4982
328.7307	E331
	JK1061
	JK1161
	JK1331
	KF27.R854
	KF4651
	KF4935
	KF4970
328.73071	E664.B2
	JK1161
	KF42.2
328.730710924	E840.8.M8
328.73072	JK468.A8
	JK1331
328.73072018	JK1316
328.730720924	E840.8.P6
328.73073	JK1012
328.730734	KF26.J836
328.73073452	JK2493
	KF32.D5
328.73074	AS36.C2
	JK1430.G6
	KF27.F6483
328.730741	JK1239
328.730746	JK573
328.73076	JK1061
	JK2356
328.730765	JK775
	JK1029
	JK1239
	JK1240.A62
	JK1240.C57
	JK1240.F5
	JK1240.I5
	JK1240.L3
	JK1430.I5
	JK1430.W32
	KF26.G655
	KF32.G6
	KF42.2
	KF4987.N8
	KF4997.E3
	KF4997.P6
	KF4997.S3
328.730766	KF27.S7
328.730768	JK1118
	JK2498
328.73077	JS308
	KF3812
	KF4945
328.73077	KF6241
	KF9395.5
	UG633
328.730775	JK1061
328.7309	E303
	E666
328.730922	E747
328.730924	E302.6.P73
	E340.H4
	E340.I5
	E415.9.B84
	E415.9.G4
	E467.1.B87
	E661
	E664.H53
	E664.N54
	E664.P41
	E748.C523
	E748.D55
	E748.D552
	E748.S24
	E748.S5154
	E840.8.C48
	E840.8.L53
	E840.8.U85
	E840.8.Y3
	F128.52
	F390
	JK1030
	JK1030.B35
	JK1030.E94
	JK1030.H6
	JK1030.M3
	JK1030.R5
	JK1030.S3
	JK1433
	KF31.5.S7
	S417.P57
328.744073452	J87
328.7440924	E840.8.B34
328.74607	JK3369
328.7470765	JK3466
328.7480768	JK3674.5
328.74905	KFN2221
328.749073452	JK3568
	KFN2220.85.A6
328.752	JK3867
328.754	KFW1621
328.75407	JK4067
328.755	E748.R656
	F229
328.755071	J87
328.7550777	JK176
328.756073452	JK4168
328.759	KFF421
328.764077	JK4801
328.7670768	JK5174
328.76901	KFK1218.2
328.77	JK2488
328.772	JK5667
328.7730768	JK5774.5
328.7730924	E840.8.R6
328.7740733	JK5857
328.775	JK6069
328.77505	KFW2821.5.R8
328.77507	KFW2821
328.777076	KFI4621
328.78303	JK6567
328.78705	JK7671
328.79	JK2484
328.791077	JK8201
328.7910922	KF355.M6
328.794073452	KFC714
328.7940768025	JK8774.5
328.795	JK9071
328.7950773	KFO2821.5
328.94	DU114.G68
328.9401	J905
	J905.L3
328.9405	J905
328.9407	JA41
328.94071	JQ4061
328.94073454	JQ4067
328.95073	JQ6513
328.953	DU740
328.965	JQ6451.A71
328.969	JK9374
329	HQ799.Y8
	JF51
	JF2049
	JS371
	JS3408
	KF26.C634
	KF27.I5538
329.00182	Q180
329.00207	JK1976
329.006273	E668
	E688
	HS2330.A6
329.009	HE8689.7.P6
329.00924	E415.9.W39
	E856
329.00942	HE8700.7.P6
	JN951
	JN1121
329.00954	JQ292
	JQ294
329.0095412	JQ620.B5265
329.0095484	JQ620.A77
329.00971	F1034.2
329.00973	E743
	JA71
	JK268
	JK524
329.00973	JK529
	JK1726
	JK1976
	JK2261
	JK2265
329.009744	E357.7
329.009752	JK1966.M3
329.009757	JK4293
329.009794	JK8725
329.01	E851
	HE8700.7.P6
329.02	E183
	E310
	JF2051
	JK2260
	JK2265
329.0209	DS35
329.02094	JN94
329.020942	JN1117
329.0209471	AS262.T84
329.02095493	JQ659
329.020973	E660
	JK2255
	JK2260
	JK2261
	JK2265
329.020994	JQ4098
329.02130973	JK2255
329.0220942	JN558
329.0221	JK2063
	JK2255
329.02210973	JK2353
329.023	E183
	E383
	E440
	F128.52
	JK1976
	KF26.C634
329.02302	NK805
329.0230922	E851
329.0230942	JN956
	JN961
329.023094274	JS3325.Y69D45
329.023095483	JQ620.K4765
329.0230973	E183
	E840.8.M3
	E851
	JK516
	JK2283
329.023097471	F128.52
329.0230994	DU117
329.02373087	JK2317
329.0240924	QC16.N7
329.025	JF2112.C28
	JK1991
	JK2255
329.0250971	JL193
329.0250973	JK1991
	JQ6103
329.02509775	JK1991
329.03	JF529
329.030973	JK1118
329.05	JK271
	JK2261
329.050943	DD228.2
329.050971133	JL438.5.V3
329.078	HX550.I5
329.1	E310
	E331
329.100974	JK2306
329.2	E310
329.3	HE8700.7.P6
	JK2316
	JK2317
	JK2318
329.30097471	JS1239.Z7
329.301	E837.5
329.30221	E185.97.P55
	E805
329.3023	E851
329.3097471	JK2319.N56
	JS1239.Z7
329.4	JK2331
329.4305694	DS119.8
329.5	JK2341.A6
329.500975	F213
329.544	JQ620.R287
329.6	E436
	E661
	F215
	JK2320.A7
	JK2357
329.601	E810
	JK2357
329.602110924	F124
329.60221	JK2353
329.60230974788	JS451.N79M68
329.6025	JK2358.F537
329.7307345	JK1343.I6
329.8	E748.L22
	F841
	JK2261
	JK2336
	JK2336.A6
	JK2374.K2
	JK2374.M6
	JK2391.D4
	JK2391.U5
329.81	HX84.T47
329.82	JK2391.C5
329.9	HX13
	HX44
329.94	JN94.A979
329.94	JQ4015
329.941	JN1371.L5
329.9415	DA960
329.942	DA578
	DA670.Y59
	DA690.N6
	HC256.6
	HD8393.H3
	JN223
	JN956
	JN1120
	JN1121
	JN1129
	JN1129.C62
	JN1129.C63
	JN1129.C7
	JN1129.C82
	JN1129.C83
	JN1129.L32
	JN1129.L33
	JN1129.L45
	JN1129.L47
	JN1129.S62
329.943	DD253.25
	DD256.5
	H31
	JN3946.S83
	JN3970.K6
	JN3971.A98N5553
329.9438	JN6769.A52
329.944	JN3007.C6
	JN3007.S6
329.945	JN5655
	JN5657.D43
329.947	JN6598.K5
	JN6598.K7
	JN6598.K7G33
329.94976	JN9679.A576
329.94977	JN9609.A8
	JN9609.A8K6
329.951	JQ1519.A5
	JQ1519.A52
329.9519	HX415.5.A6
329.952	JQ1698.J5
	JQ1698.K9
329.954	DS448
	DS480.84
	JQ298.B5
	JQ298.C6
	JQ298.C62
	JQ298.I5
	JQ299.U83
329.95493	JQ659.A8L44
	JQ659.A8L45
329.95694	JQ1825.P373
329.95952	JQ745.S573P42
329.9597	DS557.A6
	JQ898
329.9678	JQ3519.A8
329.968	JQ1998.P75
	JQ1998.U6
329.96897	JQ2941.A98M3
329.971	JL197.C6
	JL197.P67
329.983	JL2698.D4
329.991	JQ779.A598
	Q180
329.994	JQ4098.C6
	JQ4098.C65
	JQ4098.L3
329.9940924	DU114.G66
329.9944	DU172.B7
329.9946	JQ5115
330	B1608.L3
	HB34
	HB71
	HB75
	HB76
	HB161
	HB163
	HB171
	HB171.5
	HB171.7
	HB173
	HC53.2
	HC57
	HC79.I5
	HC79.T4
	HC106.3
	HC502
	HD82
	HF1007
	HX39.5
330.01	H11
	HB71
	HB74.M3
	HB75
	HB171
	HB171.5
	HB199
	PA4494
330.014	HB61
330.0151	HB74.M3
	HB171
	QA402
330.01517	HB74.M3
	HD6483
330.018	AS36
	HB74.M3
	HB75
	HB615
	HD82
	HD6331
330.0182	HA29

Dewey	LC
330.0182	HA30.3
	HA33
	HB74.M3
	HC106.5
	HD82
	HD8064
	HF5011
	QA278.5
330.0184	AS36.C2
	H374.M3
	HB74.M3
	HD6483
	Q180.A1
330.0202	HB171.5
330.03	HB61
330.0611	HC59
330.06242	HB1
330.07	H62
	H62.5.A34
	H62.5.U5
330.071	H62
330.0711549	H62
330.071273	H62
330.076	HB171.5
330.077	HB171.5
330.08	H11
	HB31
	HB33
	HB34
	HB35
	HB71
	HB171
	HB171.5
	HC106.5
	HC107.L8
	HD82
	HD3611
330.09	HB75
	HB111.A2
	HC12
	HC21
	HC25
	HC26
	HC39
	HD82
330.0922	HB119
330.0924	HB101.S7
	HB103
	HB103.B2
	HB103.S6
	HB119.C64
	HB126.I43G4
	HC255
330.0942	HC256.5
330.0947	HB113.A2
330.1	HB75
	HB87
	HB97.5
	HB99.3
	HB161
	HB171
	HB171.5
	HB171.7
	HB173
	HB199
	HB201
	HB501
	HB501.5
	HB615
	HD47
	HD82
	HD6483
	HG4521
330.108	HB34
330.109	HB75
	HC59
330.10922	HB76
	HD1313
330.12	HB99.3
	HD82
330.122	HB178
	HB221
	HB501
	HF5341
330.12208	HB501
330.1220924	HC54
330.15	HB71
	HB74.M3
	HB98
	HB171
	HB501
330.150924	HC54
330.151	HB91
	HC254.5
330.15108	HB91
330.1510944	HB91
330.153	HB75
	HB95
	HB98.2
	HB161
	HB171.5
	HB771
330.1530924	HB103.M15
	HB103.S6
330.154	HB161
330.155	AS36.C2
	HB99.3
330.156	H11
	HB71
	HB97.5
	HB99.7
	HB171.5
330.15608	HB34
	HB99.7
330.1560924	HB99.7
	HB103.K47
330.1594	HB97.5
	HB173
330.16	HB161
	HB1965
330.161	HB831
330.162	HB201
	HB203
330.163	HB301
330.17	HB701
330.8	HF5011
330.9	HB199
	HC21
	HC51
	HC54
	HC57
	HC59
	HC115
	HC253
	HC295
	HC412
	HD82
	HF1025
	HF1027
	HT391
	Z1209
330.902	HC41
330.9031	HC45
330.904	HB171.5
	HC54
	HC57
	HC59
	HD82
330.9042	HC57
330.9045	HC59
330.9046	HF499
330.9047	HC59
330.9171242	HC256.6
330.91713	HC240
330.91724	HC53
	HC59.7
	HC110.P6
	HC227
	HD82
330.91728073	F1401
330.9173	HT390
330.91732	HT151
330.9174924	DS140.5
330.917496	E185.8
330.9174960973	E185.8
330.9174994	DU423.E3
330.924	DD247.S335
	HD8073.W54
330.93	HC31
330.934	HB126.I4
	HC434
330.935	DS69.6
330.937	HC39
330.94	HA1107
	HC41
	HC240
	HC241
	HC241.2
	HF1532.92
	HN380.5
330.941	HC257.S4
330.9411	HC257.S42H58
330.94112	HC257.S42O74
330.9412	HC257.S4
330.9415	HC257.I6
330.942	HB161
	HB3717
	HC241.25
	HC251
	HC251.A1
	HC251.5
	HC253
	HC254
	HC254.3
	HC254.5
	HC255
	HC256
	HC256.5
	HC256.6
	HC2561.P62
	HD82
	HD593
	HD1925
	HD4145
	HD8388
	HD8391
	HF3507
	HX246
	JV7625
330.942083	HC256.3
330.942085	HC256.5
330.94212	HC258.L6
330.94235	DA690.T24
330.94237	HC257.E5C65
330.9425	HC257.M5
330.94267	DA670.E7
330.94272	HC258.L5
330.94274	HC258.H77
	HT395.G72H84
330.9429	BX3425
	HC257.W3
330.943	HC286.5
	HC286.6
	HD3616.G35
330.943086	HC286.3
330.9431	HC287
	HC287.A2
330.943615	HC267.S75
330.9437	HC267.B2
	HD84.5
330.9438	HC337.P7
	HD3517.7
330.944	DC25
	HC273
	HC276.2
	HD3715
	HJ1079
330.944032	HC275
330.945	DG571
	HF3586.5
330.94585	HC247.M3
330.946	HC383
	HC385
330.946082	HC385
330.9469	HC392
330.947	HC244
	HC251
	HC333
	HC334
	HC335
	HC336
	HC336.2
	HC336.23
	HG186.R8
330.947084	HC335
330.9471	HC337.F5
330.94795	HC337.G38
330.9485	HC375
330.9492	HC315
	HC325
330.9493	HC315
	HD4203
330.9494	HC397
330.949407	HC397
330.9495	HC295
	HF3576.5
330.9496	HC265
330.94965	HC407.A4
330.9497	D839
	HC407.Y6
	JN9663
330.94977	HC407.B9
330.9498	HC407.R8
330.95	HC412
	HC462.9
	HF3766.5
	JX1977
330.951	DS711
	HC427
	HC427.9
330.951249	HC430.5
330.95125	HC497.H6
330.9518	HC428.M3
330.952	HC462
	HC462.7
	HC462.9
330.95204	HC462.9
330.9535	HC497.A62T76
330.9536	HF3861.T72
330.954	HA1721
	HB126.I4
	HC434
	HC435
	HC435.1
	HC435.2
	HC440.P63
330.954031	HF3785
330.95404	HC435.2
	HD3616.I43
330.95414	HC437.B43
330.9546	HC437.K28
330.95475	HC437.G85
330.954792	HA1728.M3
	HC437.M32
330.9549	HA37.P26
	HC44.5
	HC440.5
330.9549183	HC440.5.Z7K35
330.95492	HC440.5
	HC440.5.Z7E276
330.95493	HF331.C75
330.95496	HC497.N5
330.955	HF3836.5
330.956	HC410.7
330.9567	HC497.I7
330.9569	HC410.7
330.959	HC60
	HC412
330.9593	HC497.S5
330.9595	HF3800.6.Z5
330.959504	HC445.5
330.95952	HC445.8
	HC445.8.A4
330.9597	HD2080.V5
330.96	HB171.5
	HC502
	HF3877
	JX1977
330.963	HC591.A3
330.966	HC517.W5
	HC547.W5
330.9667	HC517.G6
330.966705	HC517.G6
330.967	HC502
	HC517.E2
	HF3508.A3
330.96721	HC547.G3
330.9675	HC591.C6
	HF3919
330.96762	HA1977.K4
330.9678	DT443
	HC557.T32
330.9678	HC557.T33Z63
330.96782	HD107
330.968	HC503.S65
	HC517.S7
	HC517.S72
	JX1977
330.9684	HC517.S72
330.96894	HC517.R42
	HF3899.Z3
330.97	F1016
	HC95
	HC104
330.9701	E98.E2
330.971	HC115
	HC117.N48
	HD7129
	HG3883.C3
330.9711	HC117.B8
330.9712	HC117.P67
330.97121	HC117.Y8
330.97122	HC117.B25
330.971233	HC118.C3
	HC118.R4
330.97127	HC117.M3
330.971322	HC117.O6
330.97133	HC117.O62E7
330.971384	HC118.O75
330.9714	HC117.Q4
330.9715	HC117.M35
330.9716	HC117.N8
330.971613	HC117.N8
330.972	F1421
	HC135
	HC140.S3
330.9729	HF3362.3
330.972905	HC155
330.97291	E183.8.C9
330.97292	HC157.J2
330.972921	HC157.C32
330.97294	HC157.H2
330.97295	HC157.P8
330.9729505	HC157.P8
330.973	E169.1
	E185.6
	E185.8
	E801
	E807
	H31
	HA211
	HB172
	HC56
	HC103
	HC105
	HC106
	HC106.3
	HC106.4
	HC106.5
	HC106.6
	HC107.A12
	HC107.W2
	HC110.D4
	HC110.P63
	HC110.R4
	HD2785
	HD7125
	HF5006
	HT321
	KF26.B3
	KF26.F6
330.973091	HC106.3
330.973092	HC106
	HC110.P63
	PZ9.C367
330.974	HA218
	HC107.A11
	HC107.A13
330.9741	HC107.M2
	HC107.M23P613
	JK2874
330.9744	HC107.M4
330.974426	HC108.C47
330.97444	HC108.L9
330.97447	HC108.C27
330.9747	HC107.N7
	HF5006
330.97471	HC108.N7
330.9747103	HC108.N7
330.97472	HC107.N7
330.97475	HC107.N72F75
330.97476	HC107.N7
330.9748	E185.93.P41
	HC107.P4
330.974866	HE356.P4
330.9749	HC107.N5
330.975	E185.6
	HB119.A2
	HC107.A13
	HC107.G4
330.97523204	HC107.M32T35
330.975234	HC107.M32Q44
330.975255	HC107.M32A73
330.975271	HC107.M32B32
330.975274	HC107.M32
330.975281	HC107.M32H63
330.9754	HC107.W5
330.97546	HC107.W5
330.975499	F249.H2
330.9755	HC107.V8
330.97558	AS36
330.9756	HC107.N8
330.9756355	HC107.N8
330.975662	HC108.G85
330.975693	F262.T7

330.975697 HC107.N8
330.9757 HA626
330.975702 HC107.S7
330.9762 HC107.M7
330.9762536 HC107.M72L32
330.9763 HC107.L8
330.97633503 HC108.N4
330.9764 HC107.T4
330.976422 HC107.T42U77
330.976496 HC108.E4
330.976665 HC107.O5
330.9767 HC107.A8
330.9768 HC107.T3
HC107.T32C86
330.976844 HC107.K42B44
330.976852 HC107.T32S58
330.976855 HC108.N2
330.97686 HC107.T32C85
330.97688 HC107.T32
330.9769 HC108.L6
330.977 HC107.A14
HC107.A16
330.9771 HC107.O3
330.9773 HA344
330.9773793 HC108.M884
330.9774 HC107.M5
330.9775 HC107.W6
330.97788 HC107.M82O975
330.978 HC107.A17
HC107.M8
330.9781 HC107.K2
330.9782 HC107.N2
330.97833 HF3163.S63
330.97839 HE5006
330.9787 HC107.W9
330.978755 HC107.W92
330.9788 HC107.C7
330.978883 HC108.D37
330.9791 HC107.A165
HC107.A6
330.979177 HC110.D4
330.9793 HC101
330.9794 HC107.C2
330.979466 HC108.O3
330.979498 HC108.S65
330.9795 HC107.O7
330.97953 HC107.O72W54
330.979539 HC107.O72
330.979544 HC107.O72T56
330.979549 HC108.P87
330.9796 HC107.I2
330.9797 HC107.W2
330.97977 HC107.W22P83
330.9798 HA232
HC107.A45
330.98 AS36
F1401
HC123
HC125
330.981 HC187
HG5332
JV7462
330.9816 F2631
330.982 HC175
330.98204 HC175
330.983 HC192
330.985 HC227
330.9861 HF3426.5
330.98613 HC198.M25
330.987 HA1096
HC237
330.9881 HC207
330.991 HF3816.5
330.991153 HC445.7
330.9914 HC454
HC601
330.9931 HC622
HC623.W33
HC665
330.993122 HC668.T3
330.993127 HC667.U6
330.993157 HC668.O2
330.9936 HC687.N38
330.994 HB3717
HC601
HC603
HC604
HC605
HC605.C55
330.9941 HC652
HC653.A4
HC653.B8
HC653.G4
330.9944 HC615
HC617.H8
HC617.L3
HC618.N4
HC618.S9
HD2157
330.9945 HC647
330.9946 HC642
330.995 HC687.P3
330.9953 HC687.P3
330.99611 HC687.F5
HF4039.F5
HN940.F5
330.99614 HC687.S3
330.9969 HC107.H3
HC687.H3
331 HB171.7
HB301
HB501.5
HC110.A9
HC110.P63

331 HC287.A23A93
HD4813
HD4875.A83
HD4901
HD4946.I4
HD4976.S6
HD5650
HD5706
HD5725.T4
HD6278.J3
HD6331
HD8051
HD8072
HD8110.5
HD8384
HD8388
HD8390
HD8391
HD8396
HD8831.E8
331.01 HC110.P6
HD4904
HD8686.5
HF5549.5.J63
HX40
331.012 HF5549.5.J63
331.01209438 HF5549.5.J63
331.019 HF5548.8
331.0413636209415
HD9685.I74I73
331.041386540977
HD4966.S4U65
331.0611 HD7801
KF27.E384
331.061931 HD8013.A83
331.0621 HD4813
HD7801
HD7864
331.0631 F1405.5
331.07 HD4824
331.071273 HD5724
331.08 HD5701
HD5724
HD8102
331.09 HD4841
HD4844
331.0922 HD8073
331.0935 PJ3875
331.09415 HD8399.I6
331.0942 HD594.6.H35
HD8389
HD8390
HD8391
HN389
331.0947 HD6305.J3
HD8051
HD8526.5
331.0952 HD8724
331.0954 HD8681.C52
HD8682
HD8686.5
331.095491 HD8690.5.Z8
331.095692 HD8051
331.09593 HD8750.5
331.09595 HD6820.6
331.0968 HD8799.S73
331.097 HD8066
331.0971 HD5728
331.097293 HD8051
331.0973 HC101
HD4901
HD5701
HD6508
HD8051
HD8066
HD8072
KF3390
331.09747 HD5725.N7
331.09764 HD4973
331.0977311 HD5325.R12
331.0991 HD8051
331.0994 HD5850.A6
HD8844
HD8846
331.1 HD5726.N53
HD6961
HD6971
HD8384
HD9695.U54G436
331.101 HD6961
331.1065 HD9866.I64
331.1072073 HD6971
331.108 HD8072
331.10973 HD5724
HD8051.A9
HD8072
331.11 AS36
E185.8
HB31
HD21
HD57
HD1761
HD5110
HD5472
HD5701
HD5707
HD5724
HD5726.C4
HD5726.D4
HD6331
HD8037.U5
HD8039.M342G72
HD8051
HD8072

331.11 HD9156.J8P3533
HD9486.C2
HD9940.G8
LC66
S451.5.A1
331.11018 HD6331
331.1107 LC66
331.1108 HD5701
HD5711
331.11094 HD5764.A6
331.110942 HD5765
331.110947 HD8526.5
331.11095 HD5812.A6
331.110952 HD5724
331.110954 HD5817
HD5819
331.11096 HD5837
331.110965 HD5842.A4
331.11096773 HD5844.S6
HD5844.S63
331.1109684 HB2126.S6
331.110971 UD5701
331.1109716 HD5729.N6
331.110973 HD5701
HD5724
HD5875
KF27.E345
331.1109744 HB3525.M42P56
331.1109746 HD5725.C8
331.110974781 HD5725.N7
331.1109752 HD5725.M35
331.1109756 HD5725.N8
331.1109758 HD5725.G4
331.1109762 HD5725.M7
331.11097625 HD5725.M7
331.1109766 HD5725.O35
331.1109767 HD5725.A8
331.1109772 HD5725.I6
331.110977311 HD5726.C4
331.1109778 HD5725.M8
331.110977866 HD5726.S2
331.110978961 HD5726.A33
331.1109794 HD5725.C2
331.110979466 HD5726.O22
331.110979685 HD5726.L46
331.1109798 HD5725.A4
331.11098 HD5730.5.A6
331.1109861 HD5757
331.112 HB301
HC60
HD5706
HD5707
HD5724
HD5725.C2
HD5725.M35
HD5725.N3
HD5725.N6
HD5725.N7
HD5725.N8
HD5725.O3
HD5725.T4
HD5726.M5
HD5730.5
HD8039.R382C34
HD8039.S452
HD8051
HN58
LB2833.3.D4
LB2833.4.S35
LB2833.4.S9
QA14.G7
RA410.7
TA157
331.1120212 JX1977
331.1120720612 HD5844.L5
331.112091724 HD8051
331.1120924 HD5875.W54
331.112094259 HD7024
331.112094585 HD5811.95.M3
331.1120948 HD5798
331.1120954 HD5819
LC67.I5
331.1120954792 HD5820.B6
331.112095484 HD5820.A52
331.112095487 HD5820.M8
331.112095491 HC440.5
331.112095694 HD5835.P3
331.112095695 HD5835.J6
331.11209591 HD5812.7
331.11209593 HD5832.5
331.112096 HD8772
331.1120971 HB2583.L5
HD5727
HD5728
HD5729.N6
331.11209713 HD5729.O6
331.1120973 HA37
HD5724
HD8051
331.1120974 HD1751
331.11209743 HD5725.V5
331.11209744 HD5725.M4
331.11209746 HD5725.C8
331.112097471 HD6305.M5
HV99.N6
331.112097472 HD5725.N7
331.1120974721 HD5725.N7
331.11209748 HD5725.P4
331.11209749 HD5725.N5
331.112097492 HD5726.P35
331.1120974985 HD5726.A78
331.11209752 HD5725.M35
331.11209754 HD5725.V8
331.11209756985 HD5725.N8

331.11209757 HD5725.S6
331.11209758 HD5725.G4
331.11209759381 HD5726.M47
331.11209766 HD5725.O35
331.11209767 HD5725.A8
HD5725.G4
331.112097671 HD5725.A8
331.112097 HD8083.A4
331.1120977132 HD5726.C55
331.1120977311 HD5726.C4
331.11209774 HD5725.M5
331.112097749 HD5725.M5
331.1120977532 HD5725.W5
331.1120977563 HD5725.W5
331.1120977579 HD5725.W5
331.1120977 HD5725.I8
331.11209787 HD5725.W9
331.11209788 HD5725.F65
331.11209793 HD5725.N3
331.11209794 HD5725.C2
331.1120979465 HD5725.C2
331.11209795 HD5725.O7
331.112097952 HD5725.O7
331.1120979533 HD5725.O7
331.1120979561 HD5725.O7
331.11209796 HD5725.I23
331.11209797 HD5725.W2
331.11209798 HD5725.A4
331.11209914 HD5825
331.11209934 HD5851.N45
331.112099614 HD5851.W44
331.11209969 HD5725.H3
331.1120996931 HD5851.H32
331.113 E185.61
HD4903
HD4903.3.B92U57
HD4903.5.U58
KF26.J884
331.1130968 HD4903.5.S6
331.1130973 HD4903.5.U58
KF26.J833
KF26.L363
KF27.E343
KF31.L3
KF32.E3
KF3464
331.113097471 HD4903.5.U58
331.11309764141
HD4903.5.U6T43
331.11309775 HD4903.5.U6W52
331.11309791 HD4903.5.U58
331.114 HD5725.W9
HD6278.U5
LC66
Q149.C3
331.1140951249 HB2728.95
331.115 HD5820.M28
HD5861
HD5875
HD6274.C8
HF5381
HF5382.5.G7
HF5382.5.U5
HF5383
HF5549.5.E45
L900
LC1043
331.115095487 HD5970.M9
331.1150974899 HD5724
331.11509794 HD5725.C2
331.11509969 HD5873.H3
331.116 HD4945
HD4946.G7
HD6483
HD6508
HD6664
HD6961
HD8008
HD8008.A1
HD8051
KF27.E346
LB2842
331.116018 HD6483
331.116072073 HD6961
331.1160942 HD4946.G7
HD8391
331.1160971 HD6521
HD6524
HD6971
331.11609711 HD8109.B72
331.11609713 HD6529.O5
331.11609716 HD5508.N6
331.116097292 HD6571
331.1160973 HD5504.A3
HD6483
HD6501
HD6508
HD8057
KF3408
331.11609749 KFN2132.8
KFN2132.8.P77
331.11681020973 Z682
331.11681362109716
HD6528.H782
331.116813621109716
HD6528.H6
331.116813684300973 HD8051
331.116813711 LB2842
LB2842.2
331.11681371100973 LB2342
LB2842
LB2842.2
331.116813711009749 LB2842.2
331.1168137782 LC461

331.116813781209794 ... LB2329.5
331.116813834973 .... HE6499
331.1168138454 .... HD6515.T39
331.11681385 .... KF32.I55
331.116813850973 ..... HD6515.R1
..... KF26.L3
331.1168138750973 ... HD6515.S4
331.116813875440979
..... HD6515.L82P344
331.1168138770973 .... TL561
331.116813883240973
..... KF3409.T65
331.11682 .... HD6664
331.11682209944 ..... HD6899.M6
331.116829133340942
..... HD6668.A29
331.1168292094141 ... HD6668.A8
331.116830973 .... HD1484
331.116864900973 .... HD8072
331.1168709716 ...... HD6529.N63
331.11687820942 ...... HD6668.R9
331.11689009716 ...... HD6528.B9
331.11689009747 ...... HD8053.N7
331.12 .... HC107.L8
..... HD1527.C2
..... HD5701
..... HD8038.C6
331.120979531 .... HD5725.O7
331.1212 .... HD5718.A6
331.122 .... LB2833.3.M5
331.126 .... HC251
..... HD266.C2
..... HD6283.G7
..... LB2833
..... LB2838
331.1260942 .... HF5549.5.T8
331.12609767 .... HD5725.A8
331.127 .... HC101
..... HC240
..... HD1476.G7
..... HD5701
..... HD5706
..... HD6278.G7
..... HD8038.A1
..... HF5549.5.I5
..... Q148
331.1270184 .... HM131
331.127094 .... HD5764.A6
331.1270942 .... HD5767
331.12709428 .... HD5767
331.127094971 .... HD5811.6.B4
331.127095 .... TA157
331.1270973 .... HD5724
..... HD7123
331.12709786 .... HD5725.M9
331.12709797 .... HD5725.W2
331.128 .... HF5549.5.E45
331.13 .... HD5853
331.1330973 .... HD4903.5.U58
331.137 .... HB31
..... HD5724
..... HD7096.U6P43
..... HD8037.U5
331.1370973 .... HD5724
331.13709762 .... HD5723
331.13709786 .... HD5725.M9
331.1374099691 .... HD5725.H3
331.1377 .... HD5724
331.137804 .... HD5724
331.137815097946 .... Q149.U5
331.1378309795 .... HD1527.O7
331.1379 .... HD5706
331.137942 .... HD5706
..... HD5767
331.137954 .... HD5819
..... HD6278.I5
331.137954792 .... HD5820.B6
..... HD5820.M29
331.137971 .... HD5728
331.137973 .... HD5723
..... HD5724
..... HD8072
331.1379764141 .... HD5726.H8
331.1380973 .... HC110.D4
331.15 .... HF5549.5.G7
331.152 .... HD5650
..... HD5660.G7
..... HD5660.U5
331.152094 .... HD5660.N6
331.1520942 .... HD5660.G7
331.1520943 .... HD5660.G4
331.15209497 .... HD5660.Y8
331.155 .... HD5481
..... HD6961
..... KF3450.P8
331.15503 .... KF9085
331.1550973 .... KF3424
..... KF3544
331.1550994 .... HD6961
331.176009415 .... S21
331.18134 .... KF3369
331.181384540971 .... HD6961
331.1813850942 .... HD6668.R1
331.18138660971696
..... HD8039.L82C33
331.18238065 .... VM301.F3
331.182920942 .... HD9710.G72
331.1866394246 ...... HD8039.P82
331.18772109542
..... HD6814.C66K35
331.1878 .... HD8085.A27
331.1937 .... HD4844
331.194 .... HD6961
331.1942 .... HD8246.5

331.1942 .... HD8381
..... HD8391
331.19485 .... HD8576.5
331.19489 .... HD8546
331.19492 .... HD8514
331.195 .... HD6961
..... HD8666.5
331.1952 .... HD8726.5
331.1954 .... HD8681
..... HD8686
..... HD8686.5
331.195414 .... HD8689.B42
331.19547 .... HD8686.5
331.19548 .... HD8681
331.195484 .... HD8689.A52
331.19561 .... HD8612
331.196761 .... HD8799.U42
331.196982 .... HD8799.M32
331.1971 .... HD8101
..... HD8106.5
331.1973 .... HD4901
..... HD6483
..... HD8008
..... HD8072
..... KF3408
331.1994 .... HD8844
..... HD8846
331.2 .... HB301
..... HD4932.N6
..... HD4976.W56
..... HD5017
..... HD8072
..... KF27.P653
331.201 .... HC106.3
331.208 .... HB301
331.20973 .... HD4975
331.209931 .... HD5100.4
331.21 .... HC106
..... HD4906
..... HD4909
..... HD4945
..... HD5015
..... HD5104.G7
..... HD6961
..... HD8051.A62
331.215 .... HD4909
..... HD4918
..... HD4919.N7
..... HD4919.S6
..... HD4926
..... HD4966.A5I56
..... HD4966.L4I44
..... HD4966.M486I48
..... HD4966.O52
..... HD4966.T4I49
..... HD6524
..... HD7801
..... HD8072
..... JS7025.P8
..... KF26.P637
..... LB2842.2
331.2150942 .... HD5017
331.2150973 .... KF27.E343
331.22 .... HD4920.C2
..... KF26.P6
331.220977311 .... HD5726.C4
331.230973 .... HC110.I5
331.25 .... HC110.D4
..... HC661
..... HD4966.T4I48
..... KF27.P674
..... LB2334
..... LB2842
331.250973 .... HD7125
331.2509945 .... HD4932.N6
331.252 .... HD7106.U5
..... HD7116.A83U63
..... HD8039.A82U626
..... HQ1062
..... KF26.J844
..... KF26.L373
..... KF26.P674
..... KF27.I55
..... KF27.I5536
..... KF27.I5587
..... KF27.J8666
..... KF27.P674
..... KF32.D5
..... KF3660
331.252025773 ..... HD7106.U6I356
331.2520942 .... HD7106.G8
331.2520971 .... HD7106.C2
331.2520973 .... HD7106.U5
331.25209776 .... JK6160.P4
331.255 .... HD4932.N6
..... HD5261
..... HD5726.C4
..... HV8148.N52
..... KF26.L363
..... KF27.E336
..... LB2842
331.2550954 .... HD7748
331.259230973 .... HD7256.U5
331.281254 .... BR1450
331.28133210973
..... HD4966.B262U45
331.2813400973 .... KF26.C688
331.281352000971 .... JS1714
331.281353 .... HD8051
..... KF27.P652
331.2813530084 .... HC110.P63
331.2813621 .... RA972.5
331.28137 .... AS36
331.281370973 .... LB2842

331.2813711 .... LB2842
..... LB2844.G6
331.281371100942 ..... LA639.B78
331.2813711009769 .... LB2842
331.2813711009773 ...... LB2842.2
331.281371100978 .... LB2842.2
331.2813711009792 ...... LB2842.2
331.281374 .... LB2335.G7
331.281378110942 ..... LB2335.G7
331.281378120942 ..... LB2335.G7
..... LB3335.G7
331.281378120974 .... LB2334
331.2813781209759 .... LB2334
331.2813781209764 .... LB2334
331.2813850971
..... HD4966.R17C322
331.281388322 .... HC251
331.28150973 .... Q149.U5
331.28161 .... R728
..... R728.5
331.2816176 .... RK34.C3
331.28162 .... TA157
331.28162233 ..... HD4966.M63G77
331.28164795 .... HD8053.N7
331.2816479573 .... HD4966.R4
331.281658420973 .... HF5549
331.28165885 ..... HD4966.S35U65
331.28165887 .... HD4966.M4
331.281658870974932
..... HD4966.M4
331.28166 .... HD4966.C452I42
331.28169 .... HC251
331.2816931 .... HD4966.S72I53
331.28172 .... NA2570
331.282 .... TA157
331.282233094252
..... HD4966.M63G77
331.28223410954 ... HD4966.M72I5
331.28240973 .... HD8051
331.2830973 .... HD1751
331.283389520954 .... HD4966.R82
331.28584 .... HD4965.5U6
331.286570942 .... HC251
331.2870973 .... HD8051
331.28709758 .... HD4976.G4
331.287109767 .... HC107.A8
331.2872 .... HD4966.I5
331.28772100954 .... HD4966.T4I53
331.289 .... HD4919.D6
331.28900942 .... HC251
331.289009471 ...... HD4966.B892
331.29 .... HD5070.B43
331.291724 .... HD4967
331.2942 .... HD5017
331.2947 .... HD5046
..... Q180.A1
331.2954 .... HD5067
..... HD5069
331.295475 .... HD5070.S9
331.297 .... HD4977
331.29713 .... HD4920.C2
331.29716 .... HD4980.N6
331.2973 .... HD8051
331.2975 .... HD8051
331.29797 .... HD4973
331.2994 .... HD5100
331.31091732 .... HD6231
331.310942 .... HD6250.G7
331.310973 .... HD6250.U3
331.3109787 .... HD6250.U4W85
331.3150184 .... HG845
331.34 .... HD6270
..... HD6273
..... HD6275.C49
..... HD6276.A3
..... HD6276.E5
..... HD6276.G7
..... HQ796
331.340184 .... Q180.A1
331.3402573 .... HD6273
331.3406173 .... HD6273
..... HD6275.P5
..... KF27.E345
331.340954 .... HD5819
331.340973 .... HD6273
..... HD8051
..... HF5382.5.U5
..... HQ796
331.34097471 .... HD6275.N4
331.3409748 .... HD6274.P4
331.3409749 .... HD6274.N5
331.34097641411 ...... HD6275.H6
331.340977133 .... HD6275.G3
331.340977224 .... HD6273
331.3409773 .... HD6274
331.340977434 .... HD6275.D4
331.340977456 .... HD6275.G7
331.3409776 .... HD6274.M6
331.3409778 .... HD6274.M65
331.3409778411 .... HD6275.K3
331.340977865 .... HD6274.M65
331.340978965 .... HD6275.M4
331.340979493 .... HD6274.C3
..... HD6275.L6
331.3409795 .... HD6274.O7
331.34097975 .... HD6275.R3
331.38133300973 .... KF6075.5
331.38900977178 ..... HD5715.4.C5
331.39 .... HD6279
331.398 .... HD6279
..... HD6280
..... HQ1060
331.3980973 .... HD6280
..... HF5382.5.U5

331.39809744 .... HD6281.M3
331.4 .... HD6052
..... HD6058
..... HD6095
..... HD6096.D7
..... HD6096.P4
..... HD6097
..... HD6190.P3
..... HF5383
331.406173 .... HD6275.S25
331.406273 .... HD6050.N34
331.4091724 .... HD6223
331.40942 .... HC251
..... HD6135
..... HD6137
..... LC2052
331.40947 .... HD6166
331.40954 .... HD6189
331.409549 .... HD6190.5
..... HD6190.5.A6
331.40971 .... HD6097
..... HD6099
331.40973 .... HD6053
..... HD6053.C18
..... HD6072
..... HD6093
..... HD6095
331.40974461 .... HD6096.B7W8
331.40974886 .... HD6096.P5
331.409771 .... JK5574
331.40978961 .... HD6273
331.409794 .... HD6096.C3
331.40994 .... HD6073.M37
..... HD6220
331.42 .... HD6061
331.420942 .... HD6061
331.43 .... HD6055
..... HD6137
331.430971 .... HD6055
331.430973 .... HB915
331.430994 .... HD6220.A8
331.4810971 .... LB2371
331.481353 .... JK721
331.481353002 .... JK721
331.48135471001 .... JL111.W6
331.4816588700971 .... HD6097
331.48752 .... HD8039.L4
331.4887094775 .... HD8039.T42
331.5 .... HD5723
..... HD5724
..... HD6273
..... HV1568
331.50924 .... HD4875.U5
331.5109759 .... HV8929.F7
331.540942 .... HD4875.G7
331.5409682 .... HD4875.T8
331.5409748 .... F160.R3
331.540993 .... HD4875.P15
331.5409934 .... HD4875.A84
331.59 .... HD7255
..... HD7256.A76N43
..... HD7256.C9
..... HD7256.L5
..... HD7256.U5
..... HD8053.N7
..... HV1553
..... HV1655
..... HV3005
..... HV3018
..... JK3460.5.H35
331.590973 .... HD7256.U5
..... KF26.L352
331.6 .... HD6305.M5
..... HD6305.N4
..... HD8085.B93
331.62 .... HD8081.A5
..... JV6415.A4
..... KF27.E336
331.620942 .... HD8398.A2
331.6209729722 .... HD8241
331.620973 .... HD8081.A5
331.62510171242 .... JV8701
331.63 .... HD4903.5.U58
..... HD6305.M5
..... HD8039.H82U65
331.63924073 .... HD6305.J3
331.6396 .... E185.5
..... E185.8
..... JK4160.5.N4
331.6396073 .... E185.5
..... E185.8
..... E185.93.V8
..... HD5701
331.6396074811 .... F158.9.N3
331.639607614 .... HD1775.A2
331.63960769 .... E185.93.K3
331.6396077866 .... HD7256.U6
331.639607946 .... F868.S156
331.63960973 .... E185.5
331.660973 .... HD1525
331.6609767 .... HD1511.U5
331.67 .... KF26.L3
331.67025747 ..... HD5856.U52N69
331.67094 .... HD5856.E8
331.67096761 .... DT1
331.670973 .... KF26.L3655
331.6709749 .... HD1527.N5
331.6709764 .... HD1527.T4
..... HD5856.U52
331.6709771 .... HD1527.O2
331.6709774 .... HD1527.M5
..... HD5856.U52
331.6709775 .... HD5856.U52
331.6709794 .... HD1527.C2

331.6709794 .... HD5856.U52
331.6709797 .... HD1527.W2
331.69095412 .... HD8681
331.6997 .... E59.E3
..... E99.A6
331.7 .... CB426
..... HD8037.U5
..... JS308
331.70012 .... HB2581
331.700212 .... HD5712
331.7002571 .... HF5382.5.C2
331.700954 .... HF5382.5.I4
331.70095414 .... HB2730.B4
331.700971 .... HB2619
331.700973 .... HB2595
..... HD8051
..... HF5382.5.U5
331.7009742 .... HB2615.N4
331.700974948 .... HD5726.L3
331.7009767 .... HD5725.A8
331.7009778 .... HB2615.M8
331.7009797 .... HF5382.5.U6
331.702 .... BV4740
..... HD6059.C2
..... HD6059.G7
..... HF5381
..... HF5381.5
..... HF5381.7
..... HF5382
..... HF5382.5.B28
..... HF5382.5.R8
..... HF5382.5.U5
..... HF5549.5.E45
..... HJ4661
..... HV10.5
..... LB2343
..... LC2781
331.70201 .... HF5381
331.702019 .... HF5381
..... HF5548.8
331.70208 .... HF5381.A1
331.7020942 .... HF5382.5.G7
331.70209421 .... HF5381
331.702096762 .... HF5382.5.K4
331.7020973 .... HF5382.5.U5
331.70209773 .... HF5381
331.70209781 .... HF5382.5.U6K3
331.71 .... E185.82
..... HD8038.A4
..... HD8038.U5
..... HT687
331.71019 .... HF5548.8
331.71091724 .... HC60
331.710917496 .... LC2781
331.71095413 .... HD8038.I5
331.71095475 .... HD6278.I52G83
331.71095487 .... HD6278.I52M55
331.710973 .... HD6278.U5
..... HD8038.U5
331.710994 .... HD8038.A8
331.76 .... LA226
331.760942 .... HB2673
331.76102770973 .... Z675.U5
..... Z732.I2
331.76107 .... HD6305.M5
331.76109792 .... HD5725.U8
331.7613 .... HT687
331.761301 .... HM22.U5
331.7613013 .... KF27.I5568
331.76133210954
..... HD8039.B27I42
331.76135200023 .... JS358
331.76136463 .... HV9103
331.761371 .... LB2833
331.7613711 .... LB2832
..... LB2833.2
..... LC1042
331.7613711002573 .... L901
331.76137120120973 .... LB2842
331.761378124 .... T65.3
331.7613800994 .... HD6278.A9
331.76138464 .... HD8039.T3
331.7613850954 .... HD8039.R1
331.761387164097471
..... HD8039.L82U73
331.7613875 .... HD8039.S42U637
331.761387544 .... HD7801
..... HD8039
331.761387544095484
..... HD8039.L82I48
331.76138770954 .... HD8039.A42
331.76138774 .... KF26.P674
331.761388 .... HE243
331.7613883220942 .... HE5663
331.7615 .... HD8051
..... Q127.G4
331.76150954 .... Q149.I5
331.76150973 .... HD8051
..... Q149.U5
..... TA157
331.761550973 .... QE34
331.76155364 .... HD8039.F422I54
331.76161 .... RA410.7
331.7616107309768 .... JK5274
331.761610971 .... RA410.9.C2
331.761610993 .... R99
331.76164720973
..... HD8039.D52U69
331.76164790971
..... HD5718.H82C33
331.76164795763
..... HD8039.H82U623
331.7616518 .... HD9696.C63
331.761658400942 .... HF5500.2
331.76179209747 .... HD4903.3.M6
331.762009514 .... HD8039.M22I522
331.7620095487 .... HD8039.M22I57
..... TA157
331.7620994 .... TA157
331.76210954 .... HD8039.M22I55
331.762233 .... HD8039.M62I425
..... HD8039.M72
331.762233094274
..... HD8039.M62G745
331.7622330973
..... HD8039.M62U66
331.76223309769
..... HD8039.M62U6465
331.762234 .... HD8039.M6
331.7622342 .... HD8039.M74A94
331.76238200954
..... HD8039.S512I53
331.76240954 .... HD8039.B92I45
331.76251 .... HD8039.R3152G74
331.76252094231 .... HD8039.R1
331.762570973 .... HD4903.3.R6
331.763 .... HD1511.A3
..... HD1521
..... HD2072
331.763094 .... HD1531.5
331.7630942 .... HD1534
331.7630947 .... HD8039.A20
331.7630954 .... HD1537.I4
331.76309542 .... HD1537.I4
331.7630973 .... HD1525
..... HD1751
..... KF26.L363
331.76309794 .... HD1527.C2
..... KF228.D5
331.763180954 .... HD8039.F422I56
331.7633720954 .... HD1537.I4
331.76337209549 .... HD1537.P2
331.7633730954 .... HD8039.R92I52
331.7634 .... HD1751
331.76347 .... HD1527.O7
331.76349820924
..... HD8039.L92U53
331.766 .... HD8039.C45
..... HD9650.5
331.7660009763 .... HD5725.L8
331.766410954 .... HD8039.S86I52
331.766550954 .... HD8039.P42I52
331.766630954 .... HD8039.P672I54
331.76691 .... HD8039.I52U52
331.767028 .... TA158
331.76709763 .... HD5725.L8
331.7672 .... HD8039.I5
..... HD8039.I52
..... HD8039.I52G75
..... HD8051
331.76720974886 .... HD8039.I52
331.76752 .... HD8039.L4
331.76760954 .... HD8039.P34I44
331.7676320973 .... HD8051
331.7677 .... HD8039.T4
331.76770091724 .... HD8039.T4
331.767700973 .... HD5718.T42U53
331.7677130954 .... HD8039.J82I53
331.7677180954
..... HD8039.C642I56
331.7677390922 .... HD8393.A1
331.76900942 .... HD8039.B92
331.76900973 .... HD8051
331.7696476 .... HD8053.N7
331.7940942 .... HD2346.G7
..... HD8395
331.79409543 .... HD5820.M25
331.8 .... HD6490.S5
..... HD8055.A5
331.80973 .... HD8072
331.81 .... HD5115.2.I5B63
331.81813850973 .... KF27.I55
331.819711 .... HD5130.5.B7
331.86 .... HC412
..... HC557.T32
..... HD4885.U5
..... HD5701
..... HD5715
..... HD5715.3.M5
..... HD5723
..... HD5724
..... HD5725.F6
..... HD5725.N7
..... HD6274.C6
..... HD7255
..... HD7256.U6I25
..... HD8039.S4
..... HD8051
..... HD9560.5
..... HF5383
..... HF5531
..... HF5549.5.T7
..... HV3005
..... TT166.I4
331.860184 .... Q180.A1
331.860943 .... HD2346.G3
331.860954 .... HD5819.D4
331.86095492 .... HD5820.5.E2
331.86095695 .... LC5057.J6
331.8609612 .... LC5058.L5
331.860971 .... LC1047.C2
331.8609729725 .... HD5715.5.B7
331.860973 .... HD60.5.U5
..... HD5715.2
..... HD5723
..... HD5724
..... HD6273
..... HD7256.U5
331.860973 .... HF5549.5.T7
..... HV85
..... LC1042
331.8609745 .... HD5725.R4
331.86097468 .... HD5726.N37
331.8609747 .... HD5715.3.N7
331.8609749 .... HD5715.3.N38
331.8609753 .... HD5726.W3
331.8609759121 .... HD5715.4.J3
331.86097731 .... HD5726.C4
331.860977433 .... HD5725.M5
331.860977684 .... HD5725.M6
331.8609778 .... HD5725.M8
331.860977865 .... HD5726.S2
331.86097787 .... HD5725.M8
331.860978225 .... HD5715.4.O4
331.8609786 .... HD7256.U6
331.8609789 .... HD5715.3.N39
331.860979173 .... HD5725.A6
331.860979493 .... HD5725.C2
331.860979494 .... HD5726.L77
331.861 .... E185.8
..... HD4885.C3
..... HD4885.U5
..... HD4903.5.U6
331.861094227 .... HD4885.G7
331.86109747 .... HD4885.U5
331.86109931 .... HD4885.N4
331.8610994 .... HD4885.A8
331.863 .... HD8051
331.8630942 .... HC60
331.86309701 .... E93
331.8630973 .... HD5724
331.86309747 .... HD5725.N7
331.868 .... HD7255
..... HD7255.A2
..... HD7256.U6
..... HV3005
331.86808 .... HD7255
331.8680943 .... HD7256.G3
331.868094976 .... HD7256.Y8
331.86809567 .... HD7256.I7
331.868096 .... HD7255.A2
331.868096761 .... HD7256.U4
331.8680971 .... HD7256.C3
331.868097281 .... HD7256.G8
331.86809729722 .... HD7256.V5
331.8680973 .... HD6274.M4
..... HD7255
..... HD7256.U5
..... KF26.L354
331.86809744 .... HD7256.U6M425
..... HD7256.U6M427
331.86809745 .... HD7256.U6R44
331.86809754 .... HD7256.U6W44
..... HD7256.U6W472
331.8680975437 .... HD7256.U6
331.8680975471 .... HD7256.U6
331.86809755 .... HD7256.U6V47
331.86809757 .... HD7256.U5
331.86809758 .... HD7256.U6G42
331.86809769 .... HD7256.U6K44
..... HD7256.U6K47
331.86809776 .... HD7256.U6M65
331.8680977658
..... HD7256.U6M615
331.86809786 .... HD7256.U6
331.86809789 .... HD7256.U6N62
331.86809792 .... HD7255
331.86809793 .... HD7256.U6
331.86809794 .... HD7256.U6
331.8680979463 .... HD7256.U6
331.86809795 .... HD7256.U6O727
331.86809797 .... HD7256.U6W24
..... HD7256.U6W242
331.8680981 .... HD7256.B7
331.88 .... HD6475.A1
..... HD6476
..... HD6483
..... HD6490.S5
..... HD6508
..... HD7395.R4
..... HD8055.A5
..... HD8398.E3
331.88001 .... HD6812
331.880025716 .... HD6523
..... HD6529.N63
331.88002594 .... HD6891
331.8800621 .... HD6475
331.880062485 .... HD8572.L34
331.88007206762 .... HD4824
331.8801 .... HD6483
331.88025769 .... HD6517.K4
331.88091 .... HD6475
..... HD6475.M4
..... HD6475.T7
..... HD7801
..... HD8055.I5
331.880922 .... HD6509
331.880924 .... HD6665.C6
..... HD8073.G6
..... HD8073.H55
..... HD8799.S73
331.88094 .... HD6660.5
331.8809416 .... HD6669.I7
331.880942 .... HD6664
..... HD6668.M4
..... HD8391
..... HX544
331.880947 .... HD6732
331.8809481 .... HD8566
331.8809497 .... HD6785.5
331.88095 .... HD6802
331.880951 .... HD6807
331.880954 .... HD6812
..... HD8682
331.88096 .... HD6857
331.8809669 .... HD6870.N5
331.8809678 .... HD6877.T35
331.88096782 .... HD6877.T35
331.880968 .... HD6870.A35
331.880971 .... HD8102
331.8809716 .... HD6529.N63
..... HD6529.N65
331.880973 .... E185.8
..... HD6486
..... HD6490.R3
..... HD6508
..... HD6511
..... HD8051
..... HD8055
..... HD8055.A5
..... HD8055.I5
..... HD8055.L4
..... HD8073.J6
..... HD8076
331.8809861 .... HD6622
331.8809931 .... HD8013.N52
331.8809969 .... HD6517.H3
331.881102 .... Z733.P53
331.881136320942 .... HV8195
331.88113711 .... L13.U483
331.8811371100942 .... L18.N5
331.881137110097471 .... L13.U483
..... LC233.N72
331.88113850954 .... HD6814.R1
331.8811387109421 .... HD6668.L8
331.881138710954 .... HD6814.L8
331.8811387509931 .... HD6904.S4
331.88113883240924
..... HD6515.T3
331.8812000994 .... HD6894.E52A42
331.881220924 .... HD6509.H3
331.8812233 .... HD5325.M62
..... HD6869.M616N57
331.88122330924 .... HD6509.L4
..... HD8073.L4
331.881223309754 .... HD5325.M62
331.8812380973 .... HD6515.S5
331.881240973 .... HD5324
331.881292 .... HD5325.A82
..... HD6515.A82
331.8812920924 .... HD8073.R4
331.8813 .... F866.2.C5
331.881309794
..... HD6515.A292C35
331.881348850924 .... HD5325.A29
331.881353 .... HF5549
331.881600954 .... HD8039.C46I45
331.8816330973 .... HD6515.L75
331.881720924 .... HD8073.M2
331.881760979 .... HD6515.P26W44
331.8817721094272 .... HD6668.T42
331.881853100973 .... HD6515.B7
331.88187100973 .... HD6515.T2
331.881900942 .... HD6668.B9
331.881960973 .... HD6515.P6
331.8860973 .... HD8055.I5
331.89 .... HD6515.R1
..... HD6664
..... HD6961
331.89041350000973 .... HD8008
331.89041350109759 .... HD8011.F6
331.890421309969
..... HD6515.E372H36
331.890947 .... HD8526.5
331.890971 .... HD6524
331.890973 .... HD6483
..... HD6508
331.892 .... HD5324
331.8922 .... HD5306
331.8927 .... KF27.E346
331.89281354542006
..... HD8013.I47U86
331.8928137110097471
..... LA339.N4
..... LB2842
..... LB2842.2
331.89281385 .... HD5325.R12
331.8928138710924
..... HD6665.D28
331.8928169 .... HD8051
331.892820004609415
..... HD5367.B8
331.892822330974879
..... HD5325.M63
331.8928223309754 .... HD5326.W4
331.892822330977337
..... HD5325.M63
331.892822342 .... HD5325.M8
331.89282234309791
..... HD5325.M73
331.8928250973 .... HD5325.R12
..... KF27.I55
331.892825230977311
..... HD5325.R12
331.8928292 .... HD9710.G74F66
331.892830973 .... KF26.A3534
331.8928348809794
..... HD5325.A29
331.89283488509794
..... HD5325.A29
331.89286910973 .... HD5325.I5
331.8928720973 .... HD5325.I5
331.89287700975653
..... HD9860.P3
331.892942 .... HD5366

331.89294274 DA535
331.892971 HD5327
331.8929713 HD5330.O5
331.892973 HD5324
HD8072
KF3425
331.892978858 HD5325.M8
331.893 HD5325.A82
331.894 HD5448.B92
331.898 KF26.L3
331.8980973 KF3369
331.91009756 HD1694.N8
332 HB501
HB539
HC79.S3
HC120.I6
HD6483
HF1755
HG136
HG153
HG171
HG173
HG174
HG175
HG184.N5
HG186.E8
HG186.G7
HG186.P7
HG188.C4
HG221
HG221.5
HG229
HG255
HG521
HG527
HG538
HG2473
HG2705
HG3308
HG4517
HG4572
HG5131.B8
332.01 HB171
HG173
332.0184 HG221
332.024 HG179
KF27.D5644
U133
332.024076 HG179
332.02573 HG181
332.0414 HD52
332.04154098 HG185.L3
332.0621 HG3729.E92
332.08 HG181
HG2565
HJ257
332.0922 HG181
332.0924 DT929.8.B3
HC132.5.S3
HG172.G7
332.0954 HG188.I6
HG1232
332.09593 HG188.T45
332.09595 HG188.M26
332.09664 HG3399.S5
332.09676 HG188.A4
332.0973 HC105
HG153
HG181
HG538
HG2461
HG2473
HJ241
332.09744 HG513.M4
332.0994 HG188.A8
332.1 HG181
HG221
HG1521
HG1572
HG1586
HG1588
HG1601
HG1611
HG1616.M3
HG2406
HG2980.5.A7
332.101 HG1591
332.1018 HG1709
332.10202 HG219
332.1025421 HG3000.L82
332.1028 HG1709
332.103 HG151
HG1601
332.1065 HG2463.C25
HG2525
332.108 HG221
332.10924 F566.W58
HG1552.H8
HG2463.L28
HG2463.P7
HG2613.S5
HG3000.L84R66
HJ251
332.10942 HG186.G7
HG2988
HG2990
HG2992
332.10945 HG3080
332.109494 HG3204
HG3205
332.10954 HG3284
HG3289.R3
332.10959 HG188.A7
332.10971 HG2704
332.109714 HG185.C2
332.1097295 HG2834
332.10973 E386
HG153
HG181
HG221
HG538
HG1601
HG2406
HG2461
HG2472
HJ251
332.109772 HG2611.I4
332.1097731 HG2613.C4
332.10977311 HG2613.C4
332.109782 HF1134
332.109953 HG1490.P3
332.11 HG1811
HG1851
HG2562.D5
HG2563
332.11065 HG3286
HG3338.B3
332.1108 HG1811
332.11094 HG2976
332.110942 HG1656.G8
HG2994
332.1109429 HG950.W3
332.110943 HG3054
332.110954 HG3286
332.11096 HG1811
332.1109714281 HG2710.M
332.110973 HG2525
HG2535
HG2543
HG2563
332.110978136
HG2613.A67E813
332.110994 HG3446
332.12 HG2461
HG2481
HG2613.S54B38
HG2613.W64F615
HG5123.B3
332.12065 HG3450.S94N47
332.120924 HG172
332.12094212 HG3000.L84
332.12097295 HG2834
332.120973 HG2461
HG4342
332.1209747 HG2613.N54
332.120974766
HG2613.S94M415
332.120974811
HG2613.P54G5315
332.120974814
HG2613.C364D44
332.1209757915
HG2613.C34S75
332.15 HC101
HC431
HD69.I7
HG136
HG255
HG3881
HG3883.G7
HG3883.U7
HG4517
KF26.F6
KF27.B3
KF31.F6
KF32.B3
332.150962 HG3384
332.152 HC101
HG136
HG255
HG3881
HG3883.G7
HG3883.P4
HG3883.T3
HG3883.U7
HG4517
KF25.E255
332.1520954 HG3883.I4
332.1520973 HG3883.U7
332.153 HG3881
HG4517
JX1907
KF26.F6
KF27.B3
KF27.F646
332.15306581 HG2888.B35
332.154 HC101
332.154065 HG4910
332.1540942 HG3754.G7
332.15409753 KF27.B3
332.16 AS36
HG1616.B7
HG2990
KF27.B3
KF31.B3
332.170285 HF5566
332.175 HG1616.I5
HG1660.U5
HG2051.I4
HG2051.U5
HG2611.M8
HG3444
HG3450.S94N48
HG3729.U5
KF27.B3
332.1750973 HT390
332.178 HG1616.L6
HG2611.M3
332.178 HG4315
KF26.B345
332.2 HD6476
HG3000.L47L43
332.2018 HG1881
332.2065 HG2613
332.20973 HB31
332.2097413 HG2613.B34P315
332.31 HG2051.U5
332.31065 HG2051.U5
332.310954 HG2051.I4
332.32 HG2126
332.320212 HG2150
332.32065 HG2626.S28
HG3000.Z6
332.320942 HG2156.G8
332.320968 HG2156.A32
332.320973 HG2151
332.3209757 HG2153.S6
332.320977157 HG2626.C7
332.320979173 HG2626.P55
332.320979494 HG2626.L6
332.32098 HG2156.L3
332.350977289 HF5569
332.4 HG136
HG221
HG221.3
HG221.5
HG229
HG231
HG235
HG249
HG255
HG289
HG291
HG363
HG527
HG538
HG935
HG938
HG939.5
HG1210.5.M3
HG3811
HG3881
Z323
332.401 HB201
HC1660.U5
HG221
HG521
HG538
HG939.5
HG1235
HG1660.U5
HG2563
KF25.E2
332.40212 HG219
332.4095496 HG1311.N4
332.41 HB235.U6
HG538
332.41091723 HG1496
332.413 HB221
HG538
HG1235
HG1311.P3
332.4130954 HG1235
332.4130973 HG538
332.414 HD8051
HG229
HG501
HG538
HG937
HG999
KF26.B367
332.42 HG255
HG395
HG538
HG555
HG933
332.422 HG289
HG293
HG297
HG301
HG555
332.4220942 HG939
332.423 HG407
HG556
HG562
HG942
332.45 HC101
HG136
HG3821
HG3826
HG3851
HG3863
HG3865
HG3881
HG3883.G3
HG3943
332.450151 HG3851
332.4509 HG3811
332.450942 HG3851
HG3943
332.4509597 HG3973
332.450971 HG3883.C3
332.450973 HG3883.U7
332.4509861 Q180.A1
332.454 HG3881
332.46 HG289
HG939.5
KF27.B3
332.4609 HG265
332.460942 HG939.5
332.49 HG221
HG231
332.49 HG253
HG527
332.4938 HG237
332.494 HG930.5
332.4942 HB3783
HG935
HG936
HG938
HG939
HG939.5
332.49492 HG1043
332.497 HG508
332.49701 E59.M7
332.4973 HC106.6
HD6483
HG508
HG525
HG529
HG538
HG3883.U7
332.4981 HG834
332.4994 HG1392
332.509946 HG1457
332.528 HB225
332.53 HG506
HG817
332.530942 HG938
332.530944 HG978.2
332.530973 HG591
HG605
332.5309747 HG513.N5
332.56 HG355
332.6 HC120.C3
HD1375
HD1379
HD7105
HD7106.U5
HG172.Y67
HG181
HG4028.C4
HG4513
HG4521
HG4572
HG4636
HG4910
HG5432
HG5438
HG6041
HJ3833
KF1434
332.60151 HG4539
332.6025549 HG5740.5
332.6076 HG4910
332.608 HG4521
HG4921
332.60924 CT275.S3442
E184.J5
HC102.5.A3
HG4530
HV6769
332.60973 HG181
HG4521
HG4556.U6
HG4910
HG4921
332.6097471 HG4572
332.61 HG4521
HG4551
HG4553
HG4575
332.6102542 HG4556.G7
332.6109421 HG4577
332.610943 HG5492
332.610973 KF27.I5536
332.6109747 HG4572
332.62 HG4621
HG4910
332.63 HC652
HG4028.C4
HG4521
HG4916
HG5434
332.630973 HG4910
332.632 HG5123.I6
332.6322 HG5123.I6
HG5893
332.63220207 PN6231.S73
332.6322077 HG4539
332.63220973 HG4915
HG4921
332.63223 HG4661
332.632230942 HG5434
332.632230971 HG5158
332.632230973 HG4521
332.632230994 HG5892
332.6323 HG1621
HG4517
HG4963
332.63230212 HG4537
332.6324 HD1375
HD1379
332.632409794 HD266.C2
332.6327 HG179
HG4530
HG4930
KF26.B3
KF1078
332.63270971 HG5154.5
332.63270973 HG4930
332.6328 HD9235.S62U52
332.64 HB3717
HG4521
HG4910
HG6046

Dewey	LC
332.640973	KF27.I5536
332.642097471	HG4575
332.6420994	HG5892
332.6430973	HG4910
332.644	HG6046
	HG6047.G8
332.645	HG4636
	HG6015
	HG6036
	HG6041
	HG6051.U5
332.645065	HG6008
332.6450924	HG6007
332.660973	HG4963
332.67	HD7361.C3
	HE6184.I5
	HG4521
	HG4921
	HG5128.F6
	HG5892
	JX1977
332.670182	HG4028.C4
332.670212	HG4537
332.67091724	HG4517
332.672	E185.8
	HD7105
	HD7106.U5
	HG3729.P32
	HG3729.U5
	HG4539
	HG5123.I6
	HG5899.M4
	HJ3835.I38
	JS308
	KF25.E247
	KF27.I5587
332.6720971	HC120.C3
332.673	HD9536
	HF5006
	HG188.C6
	HG4538
	HG5332
	HG5582
	HG5780.5.A3
	HG5850.W4
	KF27.F644
332.67308	HG4538
332.673091724	JX1977
332.6730945	HG5522
332.6730947	HG5572
332.6730954	HG5732
332.673095952	HG5750.6.S5
332.673096	HC502
	HG5822
332.6730961	HG5860.N6
332.6730971	HD2809
	HG5152
332.673098	HC125
332.6730991	HC447
332.6730994	HC601
	HG5892
332.67312	HG179
332.673373083	TA7
332.67373	HG4538
332.6737301724	HG4517
332.6737304	HG5422
332.673730492	HG5542
332.6737305	HF3766.5
332.67373051249	HG5730.5.A3
332.67373098	HG4538
332.678	HF5681.B2
	HG4521
	HG4551
	HG4921
	HG4963
	HG5432
	HG5435
	HG6021
	HG6041
332.6780942	HG5432
	HG5435
332.678095694	HG5811.P32
332.6780973	HG4521
	HG4921
332.6780994	HG5894
332.6794	HG5892
332.6809415	HG6188.I7
332.7	HG1641
	HG3701
	HG3729.U5
	KF1040
332.70184	HG1641
332.70954	HG3729.I42
332.71	HD9483.I42
	HG2041
	KF26.A3533
332.7109492	HG2051.N3
332.710954	HD1741.I29
	HG2051.I4
332.71095492	HG2051.P12
332.710954923	HG2051.P12
332.71096762	HG2051.K4
332.710973	HD1751
	HG2041
	HG2051.U5
332.710994	HG2051.A8
332.72	H11
	HD251
	HG1634
	HG2040
	HG2040.5
	HG2040.5.G7
	HG2040.5.U5
	HG2040.5.U5A5
332.72	HG2040.5.U6
	HG2040.5.U6C34
	HG2040.5.U6H33
	HG2040.5.U6N43
	HG2051.U5
	HG5095
	KF26.B353
	KF26.F584
	KF27.V446
	KF7749.H6
	UB357.A52
332.720973	KF26.B3
332.7209794	HG2040.5.U6C33
332.720979483	HF5006
332.742	HG3729.U5
	HG3729.U6M48
	HG3754.I4
	HG3754.U5
	JX1977
	KF27.B3
332.74209493	HG3754.B4
332.74209549	HG3729.P32
332.7420973	HG4061
332.74209769	HC107.K43I542
332.74209798	HC107.A47I534
332.743	HF5568
	HG3755
	KF1040
332.7430973	KF26.B345
	KF1040
332.754	KF26.J8354
332.7540973	HG3766
	KF27.J8666
332.76	HG1691
332.760973	HG355
332.7609763	HG2611.L6
332.77	HG3745
332.8	HB539
	HG1621
	HG4936
	KF27.B3
332.80973	HJ8119
332.809753	KF27.D5644
332.82	H11
	HG1621
	HG5095
	HG8790
	KF27.A3226
332.820973	HB545
	HG1623.U5
	KF26.B345
332.8309	HB531
332.84	HG1652.G7
333	HC68
	HD105
	HD111
	HD211.C2
	HD211.N5
	HD251
	HD257
	HD313
	HD9557.A32
	S537
333.003	HF1051
333.0072	HC55
333.008	HD107
333.009415	HD625
333.00942	HC253.5
	HD594.6
333.00946	HD775
333.00947	HD586
333.00951	HD863
333.00951249	HD870.5
333.00954	HC433.5
	HD876
333.009543	HD879.M2
333.0095493	HD2065.8
333.009595	JX1977
333.0095951	HD890.6.Z8M35
333.0096	HD963
333.00967	HC517.E2
333.009681	HD990.B6
333.00971	HC113.5
	HD316
	JL187
333.0097124	HC117.S3
333.00971622	HD320.H3
333.00973	HC110.E5
	NA9000
	S930
333.009744	HD211.M4
333.0097482	HD210.M5
333.009759	HC107.F6
333.009764	S451.T4
333.00976496	F786
333.009769	HC107.K4
333.00977677	HD268.D75
333.00977781	G1433.M2
333.00977783	G1433.M3
333.00979544	HD211.O7
333.00979788	G1488.C7
333.009798	HD211.A4
333.00981	S239
333.00983	HD505
333.0099	HC725
333.00993122	HD1120.5.Z8O53
333.00993125	HD1120.5.Z8G55
333.00994	HC603.5
333.071	S946
333.0910978716	S131
333.095484	HD879.H9
333.0981	HD496
333.1	F181
	HD1045
333.1	KF26.I547
	LB2827
333.10973	HD181.G8
	HD197
	HD216
	KF26.I547
	KF27.A3
	KF27.A348
	KF5601
	KF5605
333.109791	HD243.A7
333.10979497	KF26.I5
333.109795	HD184
333.109798	E78.A3
	KF27.I527
333.109969	JQ6103
333.11	HD243.O7
	HD1751
333.1120977556	HD5725.W5
333.13	KF27.P8
333.130973	TE7
333.14	BX1428.2
333.160934	HD879.B4
333.160973	KF5675
333.1609755	F225
333.1609758	F290
333.1609771	HD211.O3
333.160978953	KF26.I527
333.1609794	HD211.C2
333.160994	HD1116
333.16099429	HD1066
333.2	HD715
333.2094253	HD594.6
333.3	HD833
	HD835
	HD865
	HD1301
333.309415	HD623
333.30942	DA499
333.30954792	HD879.M444
333.30971	JL41
333.30973	HD194
333.3099611	HC687.F5
333.32	HC440.5
333.320917497	KF5660
333.320943	HD728
333.320947	HD715
333.320954	HD873
	HD875
333.32095483	HD879.K4
333.320963	HD1021.E83A73
	HD1021.E83G35
	HD1021.E83S53
	HD1021.E83T53
	HD1021.E83W25
	HD1021.E83W34
333.320966	HD981
333.32096891	DT1
333.320973	HD205
333.320984	HD486
333.32099	DU1
333.320993123	HD1059.T3
	HD1120.5.Z8T35
333.320994	HD1036
333.3209953	DU740
333.3220942	HC254.3
333.322094228	HD599.W48
333.32209425	HD594
333.322094267	HC254.3
333.3220944	HD644
333.323097482	HD7303.P4
333.3230981	HD496
333.324	HD1511
333.33	HD600.L6
	HD876
	HD1375
	HD1379
	HD1381
	HD1394
	HD4605
	HD7287.8
	HD7287.9
	HD7293
	HD7304.N5
	HD7333
	KF6540
	Q180.A1
333.3303	HD1375
333.33062764	HD251
333.33307	HD1381
333.330711	HD1381
333.330924	HD205
333.330942	HD598
	HD7333.A3
333.3309457	HD676
333.330948	HD7346
333.330973	HD257
	HD1375
333.3309764	HD266.T4
333.3309776	KFM5512
333.3309794	KFC446.R3
333.3309796	HD266.I2
333.330983	AS36
333.332	AS36
	HD1387
	HT123
	KF27.B343
	QC945
333.3320968	HD989.S6
333.3320971145	HD319.B8
333.33209778	HD211.M8
333.33209931	HD1387
333.3320993127	HD1387
333.33209944	HD1393
333.333	HD1379
333.3330973	HD7293
333.33409746	HD7287.9
333.33409747	HD7303.N7
333.335	HD107
	HD594.6
	HD1387
	HD1393
	HD1476.G7
	HD1481.P4
	HD1753
	JX1977
333.335023	HD9428.A82
333.335065	KF27.A3226
333.33509415	HD625
333.33509437	HD639.C8
333.335097124	HD319.S3
333.3350974811	HD268.P5
333.3350981	HD496
333.33509842	HD107
333.3350985	HD556
333.33509942	HD1089.S8
333.33509944	HD1049.M8
333.33509947	HD1079.B4
333.336	HF5430.3
	TN27.O4
333.337	HD251
	HD268.C4
	HD596
	HD1391
	HD7287.6.U5
	HF5429.3
	HT123
	KF27.P868
	KFC144.5
	TE7
333.33709729	HD403.2
333.33709931	HD1387
333.339	HD1395
333.38	HD257
333.38095951	HD890.6
333.43	RA410.9.G7
333.476697	HD9539.A2
333.509747	HD7303.N7
333.53095412	HJ4387.B5
333.540974932	HD7304.N6
333.7	DA731
	GF31
	HC55
	HC107.A45
	HD111
	HD1120.5.Z8
	HE336.E3
	HE355.8
	HT166
	JK5574
	KF26.I547
	KF27.M445
	QH76.5.M3
	S21
	S591
	S916.M4
333.7018	GA51
333.7023	QE185
333.7071273	S21
333.7091724	JX1977
333.70942	HT395.G7
333.709422	HT395.G73L66
333.7094281	HT395.G72
333.7094698	HD789.A8
333.70954	HC55
333.7095695	HD954.J6
333.709667	HD989.G6
333.70973	HD205
	KF26.I5
	SK353
333.70974	HD211.N7
333.7097442	HD211.M4
333.709746	HC107.C8
333.7097479	F123.E394
333.7097612	HD211.A2
333.709776	GV54.M6
333.709789	KF26.I527
333.709794	HD211.C2
	S932.C3
	S946
333.709798	KF26.P8
333.70993153	S478.5.N45
333.70994	HD1090.A3
	S934.A8
333.709944	S934.A8
333.709969	HD211.H3
333.72	HC68
	HC103.7
	HC110.P55
	HT166
	KF27.G636
	QH75
	QH77.E9
	S930
	S936
	S938
	S942
333.7206173	KF26.I5
333.7207	S946
333.72071	S946
333.720941	S954.G7
333.720942	S942
333.720971359	S934.C3
333.72097295	HC157.P83E54
333.7209729841	QH77.D6
333.720973	HD171
	S930
	S938

Dewey	LC
333.720973	S942
333.7209741	S624.M2
333.7209743	HC107.V53E55
333.7209744	S932.M35
333.72097444	QH77.U6
333.72097462	HT393.C8
333.7209774	S932.M4
333.7209775	S932.W6
333.7209786	HC107.M93E533
333.7209787	S932.W8
333.7209793	S916.N68
333.720979412	KF32.I5
333.72097946	KF32.G6
333.73	GB611
	KF26.I549
	S605
333.730942	QH77.G7
333.730945	HD1671.A85
333.74	HD241
333.7409676	SF55.A34
333.75	HD9757
	KF26.I547
	SD397.D7
	SD421
	SD428.A2I35
	SD565
	SD568.O5
	SD601
333.750913	SD393
333.750942	SD45
	SD601
333.7509422	SD180.W4
333.75094255	DA670.N69
333.750947	HD9765.R9
	SD629
333.750973	SD565
333.7509742	SD413.N4
333.75097719	SD11
333.7509781	SD11
333.7509786	KF31.I5
333.7509789	SD11
333.7509794	SD397.R3
333.7509795	SD393
333.76	HD111
	HD594.6
	HD1033
	HD1415
	S21
	S433
	S439
	S478.A1
333.7609411	HC257.S42H55
333.760942	HD594
	HD596
333.76094391	G56
333.760952	S471.J3
333.760954	HD876
	HD1516.S76
333.760955	HD926
333.760962	HD976
333.76096761	DT1
333.76096762	DT1
	HD1516.K4
333.76096782	HD2137.T2
333.760973	KF27.A3226
	S624.A1
333.7609748	HD211.P4
333.7609789	S451.N554
333.760979578	HC107.O72G72
333.76098	HD320.5
	HD1516.L3
333.760983	HD506
333.7609881	F2380.1.W25
333.7609914	HD906
333.7609945	HD1109.G5
333.760995	HC687.P3
333.77	HD257
	HD259
	HD1393.5
	HD7293
	HT167
	KF27.D5644
	KF27.G669
	QH75
333.770182	HD111
333.7709713	HD319.O5
333.770973	HD257
	HD7287
	HT166
	HT175.U6
333.770975594	HT168.L8
333.770976453	HD211.T42
333.7709944	HC638.H8
333.78	GV53
	GV54.C2
	GV54.C2D43
	GV54.F6
	GV54.M6
	GV54.M7
	GV54.W2
	GV182.2
	GV423
	H31
	KF26.C6
	KF26.C645
	KF26.I547
	KF27.A348
	KF27.M445
	KF32.I5
	QH76.5.T4
	QH77.U6
	S914
	SB481
	SB482.A4
333.78	SB484.C2
	SD11
333.78023	SB482.A4
333.780924	SB482.A4
333.780942	GV75
	NA9053.G7
333.780947	SB484.R9
333.780971	SB481
	SB484.C2
333.780971233	SB484.C2
333.780973	KF26.I542
	KF26.I547
	KF27.I537
	KF31.I5
	S970
	SB482
333.7809742	GV54.N4
333.78097449	KF31.I5
333.7809749	GV54.N5
	SB482.N5
333.7809752	GV54.M3
333.78097539	KF26.I5
333.7809755	HT393.V6
333.780975928	KF31.I5
333.780975939	S972.F58
333.780976	KF27
333.7809767	GV54.A7
333.780977324	GV54.I3
333.7809774	GV54.M5
333.7809775	GV54.W6
	KF26.I542
333.78097751	F612.S2
333.7809776	GV54.M6
	KF27.I537
333.7809788	KFC1820
333.780979173	SB482.A7
333.7809792	KF26.I542
333.7809794	GV54.C2
	GV54.C2
	GV54.C2A53
333.780979438	GV54.C2
333.7809795	SB481
333.780979521	F882.R6
333.78097967	KF27.I537
333.780979676	F752.S35
333.7809797	GV54.W2A578
333.78097977	GV54.W2
333.7809798	GV54.A4
333.780994	GV145
	QH77.A8
333.7809945	SB484.A9
333.8	HD9540.4
	HD9545
	HD9554.C29
	HD9554.C292
	HD9560.5
	KF26.I534
	TK1193.U5
	TN19
333.80973	KF26
	KF26.I547
	KF27.I536
	KF27.I5538
333.809769	HC107.K4
333.809773	TN24.I3
333.8097732	TN24.I3
333.8097736	TN24.I3
333.8097737	TN24.I3
333.80977399	TN24.I3
333.809794	TN24.C2
333.809931	TN121
333.80994	TN122.A8
333.82	KF26.B375
	TD883.2
333.82094	HD9555.A23
333.85	HD9213.C42
333.9	F859.3
	HD9540.5
	HD9545
	KF26.I542
	KF27.M445
	QH76.5.C2
	QH77.A8
	QH77.U6
	QL88
	QL737.M35
	S914
	S962
	S964.A8
	SD111.N7
	SH11
	SH318.W4
	SH333
	SH348
	SH351.C4
	SK297
	SK463
	SK471.B7
	TC424.C2
	TD224.C3
	TD425
	TJ153
333.909943	QH95.55.G7
333.91	F868.T92
	GB661
	GB1625.A7
	GC58
	HD1691
	HD1694
	HD1694.I3
	HD1694.K2
	HD1695.S66
	HD1698.I4
	HD1698.P3
333.91	KF5569
	QE125
	TC558.A35
	TC801
	TD224.T4
	TD225.B63
	TD225.C35
	TD225.M76
	TD423
333.9100182	HD1691
333.910072073	KF27.I529
333.91007673	KF27.P846
333.9100791	TD224.A7
333.91008	HD1694
	HD1694.C8
333.9100942	HD1697.G7
	TD257
333.910094274	TD258.Y65
333.9100951	TC901
333.9100954	HD1698.I4
333.910095414	TC504.D3
333.91009543	HD1698.I42
333.910095452	S934.I4
333.910095695	HD1699.J6
333.9100959	TD313.S6
333.91009597	HC60
333.91009667	TC558.G62A44
333.9100971	GB707
	HD1696.C2
333.9100971145	HD1694
333.9100973	HD1694
	HD1695.S37
	HD3881
	KF27.I537
333.9100974	HD1695.N45
	HD1695.N6
333.91009754	TC424.W4
333.91009756	HD1694.N8
	TD224.N8
333.9100975646	HD1694.N8
333.9100975688	HT393.N8
333.91009757	HD1694.S6
333.91009759	TC424.F6
333.91009762	HD1694.M7
333.91009764	HD1694.T4
	TD24.T4
	TD224.T4
333.9100976449	TD224.T4
333.91009766	TD224
333.910097668	TK24.O5
333.91009768	HN79
	HN79.A135
	TD224.T2
333.9100977	HD1694
333.91009773	TD224.I3
333.9100977439	TD224.M5
333.91009775	TD224.W6
333.91009776	TD224.M6
333.910097767	TD224.M6
333.91009783	TC424.S8
333.910097887	KF27.I529
333.91009789	HD1694.N6
333.91009791	TD224.C3
333.91009792	HD1695.S43
333.91009793	S900
333.910097935	TD224.N2
333.910097941	TD224.C3
333.9100979424	TC424.C2
333.9100979432	TD225.S108
333.910097946	HD1695.S37
	KF27
	TD225.S252
333.9100979492	HD1694.C3
333.910097959	GB705.O7
333.9100979694	KF27.I529
333.91009797	KF27.I529
333.9100981	HD1696.B84S35
333.910099141	TD313.P6
333.910099147	TD313.P6
333.9100994	HD1700
333.91009944	TC522.M3
333.9102	F472.E4
	F752.C62
	F802.R5
	HD1698.M4
	KF26.I542
	KF27.A3226
	KF27.P893
	TC522.S6
	TD225.D28
333.91020972	KF27.F646
333.91020973	KF27.P893
	TD223
333.910209744	TC424.M4
333.9102097473	KF26.I549
333.9102097496	GB1025.C2
333.910209755	TC424.V8
333.91020975635	HD1694.N8
333.9102097581	KF27.P846
333.910209759	KF26.P846
333.91020977	GC1
	HD1694.A2
333.91020977191	TD224.O3
333.91020977342	TD224.I3
333.91020977583	S932.W6
333.910209782	KF27.I529
333.910209787	KF26.P846
333.9104	HD1694
	TC423.9
	TC424.L8
333.91040973	GB1015
333.91040976413	TD224.T4
333.9104097759	TC424.W6
333.91094	QH87.3
333.91094245	TD927
333.9109549	HD1698.P3
333.9109549[3]	HD1698.C4
333.91097	TD227.O5
333.910971	TD226
333.910971142	TD370
333.910973	KF26.I549
	KF27.P893
333.91097687	F457.C9
333.9109781	HC107.K2
333.910978463	KF26.I549
333.9109794	HD1694.C2
333.910979493	TD225.S32
333.910979495	TD225.S29
333.91099141	TD313.P6
333.910996924	GB832.H4
333.912	TD224.G4
	TD224.I3
	TD224.M65
	TD224.T4
	TN295
333.9120942	HD4465.G7
333.9120942[2]	TD257
333.91209753	KF26.D5
333.9120975684	TD225.N46
333.91209794	HD1694.C2
	TD224.C3
333.9120979465	TD224
333.913	HC440.5
	HD1741.I3A55
	S613
	TC558.A75
333.91309542	S616.I4
333.91309593	HD1741.T5
333.9130977543	S599.W5
333.9130978	KF27.I529
333.91309781155	HD1695.M5
333.9130978617	S616.U6
333.913097887	KF27.I529
333.9130978982	KF27.I529
333.9130979521	KF27.I529
333.91309796	KF26.I549
333.9130979694	HD1740.R3
333.914	KF27.I529
	KF31.I5
	QH76.5.N5
333.914097411	TC424.M2
333.91409755	KF26.P8
333.914097961	KF26.I549
333.9140979731	HD1740.C6
333.91409798	KF26.I549
333.916	GC1015
	HD9698
	KF26.C663
	KF26.I549
	KFC790
333.9160973	GC1015
333.9160974	HC107.A11
333.917	HT393.W6
333.9170916612	KF26.G6443
333.9170942	HT395.G7
333.9170973	KF27.M473
	KF27.P869
333.91709749	KFN1923.W2
333.91709751	HT393.D3
333.91709774635	KF27.I537
333.9170977512	KF31.I5
333.9170977513	KF27.I537
333.9170979462	KF27.I537
333.9180973	KF27.J878
333.91809943	QE566.G7
333.92	HC110.A4
	QC861.2
333.920977177	TD883.2
334	HC412
	HD2956
	HD2961
	HD2965
	HD3271
	HD3538
	JX1977
334.06242	HD3488
334.06291	HD3544.A4
334.07	HD2955
	HD3545.A4
334.08	HD2961
334.091724	HD3575
334.0942	HD3486
	HD8388
334.09497	HD3531.6
334.094977	HD3531.5
334.095	HD3532
334.0954	HD3538
334.095487	HD3540.A3M927
334.095492	HD3540.5
334.0954923	HD3540.5
334.0955	HD3549.A4
334.096894	HD3561.A6Z24
334.0971	HD3448
334.0973	HD3444
	KF1470
334.0974	HD3444
334.0991	HD3544
334.09914	HD3545
334.1	HD7287.7.A3
	HD7287.7.U5
334.109485	HD7287.7.S8
334.2	HG2035
	HG2039.A78
	HG2039.I4
	HG2051.I4
334.20954	HG2039.I4
	HG2051.I4
334.20954792	HG2051.I5B643

334.5 HD2961
HD3522
HD9016.I42
334.5094252 HD3488.L6
334.509437 HD3332.A3C9383
334.50947 HD3355
334.509664 HD3561.A6S46
334.5096692 HD3561.A6
334.6 HD2961
334.609437 HD3492.A3
334.60954 HD3538
334.638 HD1491.A3
334.683 HD1491
HD1491.I39
HD1491.U6F65
334.6830917242 HD1491.G7
334.68309429 HD1491.G72W38
334.68309437 HD1496.C8
334.6830954 HD1491.I39
334.6830954162 HD1491.I392A8
334.6830954923 HD1491.P22
334.68309591 HD1491.B95
334.6830973 HD1484
HD1491.U5
334.68309969 HD2199
334.6833 HD9016.I42
334.68331109544 HD9049.W5I65
334.68340409794 HD1484
334.6835095493 HD1491.C4
334.687700954 HD9866.I63B4
334.68817 HD9486.C24
334.70942 HS1510.R94
335 DS481.G3
HB711
HD84.5
HN18
HX86
HX87
HX246
HX276
HX457.T3
335.00184 HD84.5
335.008 HX36
335.009 HX21
HX35
HX36
HX86
335.00917165 HX434
335.00922 HX243
335.00924 HX84.T47
335.0094 HX39
335.009415 HX40
335.00954 HX394
335.0096 HX439
335.00973 HX86
HX89
335.0330994 UA830
335.1150973 UB357
335.12 HX696.O9
335.120924 HX696.O9
335.14 HX246
335.140924 D15.U84
335.2 HX704.F9
335.20924 HX653
HX704.F9
335.223 UB343
335.3 HX811
335.30924 HX84.D3
335.4 HB97.5
HQ799.R9
HX36
HX44
HX314
HX696
335.401 HB97.5
HX541.5
335.40202 HX19
335.408 DK254
DK254.L3
HB97.5
HX39.5
HX314
335.409 HX36
HX40
335.40922 HX39.5
335.40924 HX39.5
HX44
HX273.L3
HX273.L83
HX276
HX276.E6
HX276.L3
HX276.L86
335.40954 HX392
335.4097291 HX159
335.40973 HX86
335.41 HB501
HX39.5
JC491
335.410924 HX39.5
335.411 B809.8
HB501
HX39.5
HX314
HX392
HX437
335.413 HD4854
HX40
HX44
HX314
JC474
335.42 HX11.I5
HX44
HX312
335.42094 HX237
335.43 D839
D844
DK254.L3
DK265.95
DS586
DS778.M3
F1405.5
HB97.5
HD4851
HX13
HX36
HX40
HX44
HX244
HX312
HX314
HX542
JN3007.C6
335.4307 HX86
335.4308 HD4869
335.4309 HX40
335.430917165 HX434.A6
335.430924 CT275.K832
DK254.L4
DK254.L46
DS778.L49
HX40
HX84.D28
HX84.W53
HX288.G7
HX312.L43
HX312.R3
HX314
335.43094 HX237
HX239.Z7
335.430942 HX249
335.4309431 HX280.A2
335.430947 DK274
DR48.5
HC335
HC336.2
HD8526
HX44
HX312
HX313
HX314
HX314.Z7
335.43095 HX384
335.430951 DS33.3
DS777.55
DS778.M3
HX387
HX389.
335.430954 HX392
HX393.5
335.4309584 HC487.C4
335.4309597 HX400.V5
335.430968 HX450.S6
335.43097291 F1788
HX157
335.430973 HX86
HX653
KF27.I548
335.43098 HX110.5
HX110.5.A6
335.430991 DS644
335.432 HX13.C63
HX518.S8
335.434 HX389
335.435 DS796.S2
335.437 HB301
HC59
HD82
HX518.S8
JC474
335.4382 HX536
335.43820924 HX536
335.4383 HX541.5
335.438301 HM291
HX542
335.438301412 HX546
335.4383014121 HX546
335.438320158 HX550.N3
335.438320973 DK254.L3
335.438331 HD7791
335.43833188 HX544
335.438331880973 HD6508
335.43833332309597 HD889.V5
335.4385 HX541
335.43895105 DS777.55
335.44 HS17
HX11.I5
HX44
HX387
335.5 HX273
335.501 HX339
335.50924 HX84.S53
335.50943 HX273
335.509485 HX339
335.820944 HD6684
335.83 B945.M2983
HX828
HX833
HX844
HX914
HX915
JC571
335.8309 HX828
335.830924 HX843
335.830973 HX844.P68
335.9 HX635
HX811
335.95694 HD1491.P3
335.95694 HD1516.P18
HX765.P3
335.96 HD1516.A34
335.973 HX653
HX656.H2
335.974461 HX656.B8
335.974764 HX656.O5
335.977234 HX656.N5
335.982 HD1516.A7
336 HJ119
HJ141
HJ2005
HJ8013
HJ9105
336.0242 HJ1028
HJ9427
336.0273 HJ2381
336.02759 HJ2400
336.02794 HJ2395.A7
336.02798 HJ2392
336.1 HD594
336.16 HE5633.S8
336.170942 HG6185
336.18 HJ135
336.185 HB31
HC107.P43
HJ275
HJ389.55
HJ505.A42
HJ635
HJ665
HJ793
HJ795.A1
HJ2438
HJ4655
JK5574
JS308
KF27.G663
KF6733
KFA1687.F3
336.1850973 HJ275
HJ2381
JK2408
JS308
336.18509773 HJ405
336.18509797 HJ755
336.2 HC335
HJ2305
HJ2321
HJ2337.U6
HJ2381
HJ2385
HJ4120
HJ4661
HJ4707
HJ5703
HJ9297
KF26.G655
KF6275
KF6335
KF6452
336.200942 HJ2305
HJ2605
HJ2619
HJ9427
336.2009485 HJ2835
HJ2837
336.200951 HJ2970
336.200954 HJ2928
HJ2929
HJ9551
336.20095475 HJ2934.G8
336.20096 HJ2999.5
336.2009666 HJ3099.L5
336.20097 KF6289
336.200971 HJ2449
336.2009713 HJ2460.O5
336.200971622 HJ9353.H3
336.200972 HJ2466
336.200973 HF5006
HJ257.2
HJ2369
HJ2381
HJ2385
KF25.E247
KF27.W3
KF6335
KF6355.5
KF6386
KF6495.P8
KF6720
336.2009748 HJ2430.A7
336.200975274 F187.H2
336.2009753 HJ9216
KF26.D545
KFD1670
336.2009756 HJ2412.A7
336.2009758 HJ2401
336.2009759 HJ2400
336.2009767 HC107.A8
336.2009786 HJ2418.A7
336.200979 HJ2429
336.2009792 HJ2436
336.2009861 HF5688
336.2009914 Z7164.T23
336.2009969 KFH470
336.204 HD2753.A3
336.20420932 HJ3093
336.2044 HJ2351
336.211 HJ3241
336.22 HJ3343.2
HJ4181
HJ4182.A6
HJ4225
336.22 HJ4277
HJ4338.A6G75
HJ4387.R3
HJ4442
LB2817
336.220942 HJ4337
336.2209543 HJ4387.M29
336.220971 HJ4291
336.220973 HD1751
HJ4120
HJ4181
HJ4209
KF6535
336.2209747245 HJ4121.N76
336.220974765 HD1295.U5
336.2209749 KFN2291.R4
336.2209768 HJ2434
336.220977386 HJ4121.I32
336.2209776 HJ4231
336.2209797 HJ4121.W2
HJ4279
336.23 HJ2419
HJ4120
HJ4165
HX11
336.230973 HD1751
336.24 HF5630
HJ4629
HJ4653.C7
HJ4653.C73
HJ4653.R45
HJ4655.A1
HJ5905
KF26.F5
KF6297
KF6330
KF6355
KF6369
KF6379
KF6385
KF6389
KF6415
KF6443
KF6535
336.240942 HJ40
HJ9427
336.240954 HJ4761
336.240973 HD1775.N8
HJ4652
HJ4652.A5
HJ4656
KF26.F5
KF32.W3
KF6335
KF6355.5
KF6368
KF6369
KF6369.6
KF6369.8.E9
KF6370
KF6415
KF6450
336.2409774 KFM4691.I5
336.242 HJ4653.G5
HJ4661
KF26.C6
KF26.5.A3
KF27.I5587
KF6355
KF6355.5
KF6369.8.E3
KF6385
KF6388
KF6394
KF6425
KF6443
KF6449
336.2420942 HJ2323.G7
HJ4707
336.2420973 HJ4653.G5
KF31.C6
KF6369.3
KF6415
336.243 HD2753.N4
HG1768.U5
HG8913.M38
HJ4708.A7
KF6386
KF6419
KF6449
KF6452
KF6458
KF6464
KF6477
KF6482
KF6491
KF6495.B2
KF6499.M4
336.2430942 HD2753.G7
336.2430973 HD2753.A3
HD2753.U6A4
KF6464
336.26 HF5489.G65
336.26094271 DA670.L19
336.264 HB31
HJ9552.A5
336.26409549 HC440.5
336.2650954 HF2326
336.2666213173 HF2651.E36A83
336.266629248 HF2651.A8A85
336.26662927 HF2651.T28A83
336.26663134 HF2651.S45A82
336.26664648 HF2651.G53A85
336.2666610732

Dewey	LC
336.2666610732	HF2651.C553A83
336.2666655	KF6482
336.26667183	HF2651.P5A79
336.26667721	HF2651.B45A82
336.2666817	HF2651.S97A84
336.266683820994	HF2651.C98A94
336.266747	HF2651.F58A82
336.271	HJ5715.U6
336.271091724	HJ2351
336.2711	HJ5715.U6
336.2713	HJ5715.E9
336.271320942	HJ5715.G7
336.27132095475	HJ5715.I4
336.271320973	HJ5715.U6
336.27209945	HJ5505
336.2730973	JV6416
336.27309768	JK5274
336.27309768885	HJ5623.T2
336.274	HJ5815.I4
336.276	KF6388
	KF6449
	KFI3482
336.2760973	KF6443
	KF6571
	KF6572
336.2783310942	HJ5627.G7
336.2783321	KFN2280.5.B3
336.278333760954	HD1295.I5
336.2783805	KF26.C688
336.27838050973	HE197.U5
336.2783877	KF27.W3
336.27838770973	KF6614.A9
336.27838830973	HE5623
336.278630954	HD1295.I5
336.29	HJ3604.C4
336.294	HJ2321
	HJ4182.A27
	HJ4206.6.A27
	KF6449
336.2943	HD9855
	HG181
	HJ4653.C7
	KF26.B3
336.2943094	HD2753.E8
336.29430973	HJ2337.U6
	KF6449
336.294309744	HD2753.U7
336.2944	BV777
	HJ2337.U6
	HV97
	HV97.A3
	KF6388
	KF6449
336.2950971	HJ4661
336.3	KF27.W3
336.3091724	HJ192
336.30973	HJ257
	HJ2381
	KF26.F5
336.31	HG4952
	JK5274
	KF1070
	KF1439
336.31094	HG5424
336.34	HJ8119
336.3401	HJ8036
336.3409797	HJ8227
336.3431	HJ9129
	Z732.I2
336.343209789	HG4948.N4
336.34330942	HJ8623
336.34330973	HJ8101
336.3435	KF27.G6594
336.343509931	HC621
336.344	KF32.G6
336.3460973	HJ8119
	KF26.F5
	KF6245
336.363	KF32.G6
336.368	HJ8224
336.36809762	HJ8372
336.39	HC79.I5
	HJ2052
	HJ7461
	HJ7766
336.390942	HJ7766
336.390973	HJ131
336.42	HJ40
	HJ40.S4
	HJ1011
	HJ1019
	HJ1023
	HJ2096
	HJ4707
336.437	HG186.C9
336.44	HJ1079
336.495	HJ2737
336.54	HJ1313
	HJ9927.I4
336.543	HJ1320.M27
336.54792	HJ1320.B6
	HJ1320.M33
	HJ9552.N652
336.5493	HJ1334
336.595	HJ1337
336.630973	HG4556.U5
336.669	HJ1609.N5
336.68	HJ9587
336.686	HJ1589.L4
336.71	HJ793
	HJ2449
336.7281	HJ822
336.73	HG605
	HJ241
	HJ247
	HJ249
	HJ255
	HJ257
	HJ257.2
	HJ275
	HJ2052
	HJ2385
	HJ8109
	HJ9145
336.741	HJ475
	HJ2053.M2
336.743	HJ731
336.7434	HJ9328.M6
336.746	HJ345
336.748	HJ2053.P4
336.751	HJ2053.D3
336.752	HJ485
336.754	HJ760
336.755	HJ2438.A3
336.764	HJ713
336.767	HJ315
336.76819	HJ9319.M4
336.773	HJ405
336.774	HJ9257
	HJ9863.A3
336.788	HJ9206
336.794	HJ9203
336.795	HJ2053.O7
336.797	HJ4121.W2
336.798	HJ2392
336.914	HJ9927.P3
336.969	HJ389.55
338	F1401
	HB51
	HB74.M3
	HB171.5
	HD31
	HD2346.I5
	HD2741
	HD3616.U47
	HF1051
	HF1052
	HF5429.6.N63
	JK421
	JX1977
338.001	HB171.5
	HD38
338.0012	HA40.I6
	JX1977
338.0018	JX1977
338.00182	HB74.M3
	HD82
338.0025	HD2346.I5
	HF3731
338.002573	E185.8
	HD3858
338.0025798	HC107.A45
338.0029	T12
338.006242	HC251
338.00724	HC79.R4
338.01	DT1
	HB171
	HD49
338.012091724	HC79.S3
338.013	HB199
	HD47
338.016	HB201
338.018209774	HC107.M53D65
338.0183	HC79.T4
	HC257.I6
	HD82
338.0183071142	HD82
338.0185	HB201
338.0186	HD45
338.02	HF1040.7
338.04	E185.8
338.06	HD6331
338.060973	HC110.T4
338.064	HC517.S73A95
	HD6331
338.09	HC25
	HC51
	HC240
	HD21
	HD57
	HD58
	HD69.C3
	HD1751
	HD2326
	HF1025
	HT391
	JX1977
338.091724	HC59.7
	JX1977
338.091732	HD58
	HT321
338.0922	CT105
	HC106.5
	HC375
	HF3023
	HG181
338.094	HC240
	HC241.2
338.0942	HC254.5
	HC256.6
	HC260.D5
	HD70.G7
	HD4145
338.094223	HC257.E5K43
338.094241	HC257.E5B73
338.09427	HC256.6
	HC257.N5
338.094274	HC257.E5H825
	HF5547
338.09429	DA731
338.0943	HC285
	HD3616.G45P85
338.09431	HC287.A2
338.09434	HC288.R7
338.09437	HD84.5
338.09438	HC337.P7
338.094391	HC267
338.0947	HC244
	HC333
	HC335
	HC336.23
338.094741	HC337.E7
338.09481	HC365
338.09482	HD9685.I43T3
338.09485	HC375
338.09492	HC325
338.09494	HC397
338.095	DS10
338.0951	DS727
	HC427.8
	HC427.9
	Q180.A1
338.0952	HC462.9
338.0954	HA1719
	HC435.2
	HC437.B43
	HC440.D5
	HD2899
338.095413	HC437.D7
338.095414	HA1729.D8
338.0954162	HC437.A8
338.09542	HC437.A73
338.095475	HC437.G85
338.095479	HC437.M32
338.0954792	HC437.K57
	HC437.M32
338.095484	HC437.A73
338.095487	HC437.C52
	HC437.M8
338.09549	HA40.I6
	HC440.5.Z9D53
338.0954918	HC440.5
338.0954923	HC440.5.Z7C64
338.095496	HC497.N5
338.095952	HG5750.6.S5
338.09597	HC443.V5
338.09667	HC517.G6
338.09669	HC517.N48
338.0967	HC502
	HC517.E2
338.09676	HC517.E2
338.09678	HC557.T32
338.0968	HC517.S73D55
338.09682	HC517.S72
338.09687	HC517.S72C36
338.0971	HC115
	HC120.I53
	HD2809
	HD9734.C25
338.097113	HC117.C317
338.09713	HC117.O6
338.0971554	HD58
338.0972	HD3616.M43
338.0973	E98.E6
	HA37
	HB31
	HC102.5.A2
	HC103
	HC104
	HC106.5
	HC106.6
	HC110.D4
	HC110.D5
	HC110.I53
	HF5415.1
	HG181
	KF26.5.S656
	LC66
338.0974	HC107.A12
338.09742	HD5725.N4
338.09744	HC107.M4
	HC107.M43D45
338.097444	HD6068
338.09747	HC107.N7
	HC107.N73
338.09748	HC107.P4
338.09749	HC107.N5
338.097557	HC107.V8
338.0975867	HC108.S72
338.09761	HC107.A43I533
338.09767	HC107.A8
338.09768	HC107.T3
	HC107.T33
338.09769	HC107.K4
338.09771	HC107.O323
338.09772	HC107.I63I532
	HC107.I63I533
338.09774	HC107.M53I535
338.09775	HC107.W6
338.0977564	HC108.N24
338.09778	HC107.M8
	HD58
338.09782	AS36
338.09789	HD2753.U6
338.09792	HC107.U8
338.09795	HC107.O7
	HC107.O73I533
338.09796	HC107.I23P634
338.09798	HC107.A45
338.09798	HC107.A47I533
338.098	HC125
	JX1977
338.0981	HD3616.B83
338.09816	HC188.S3
338.0985	HC227
338.099311	HC668.A8
338.09936	HC687.N38
338.0994	HC605
	T177.A8
338.09941	HC652
338.09943	HC632
338.09944	HC118.N6
338.09945	HC608.M4
	HC650.I53
338.1	GB841
	HC440.5
	HD1405
	HD1407
	HD1411
	HD1415
	HD1417
	HD1714
	HD1741.I27
	HD1753
	HD1761
	HD1775.O7
	HD2071
	HD2073
	HD2075.T7
	HD2083
	HD2130.R6
	HD2146.M6
	HD2157
	HD2192
	HD9000.1
	HD9000.5
	HD9006
	HD9255.I52
	HE356.M85
	HE375
	KF26.A35334
	KF27.A3
	QC929.D8
	S439
	S441
	S477.J26
	S493
	S564
338.10182	HD1425
338.10212	HD1425
	HD9000.4
338.1023	HD9005
338.1025	HD1761
338.102573	HD1751
338.103	HD1410
338.10611	S401.U63
338.1072	S541
338.1072079495	S544
338.108	HD1407
	HD1411
	HD1751
	HD1775.S6
	HD9016.J42
	S21
	SB205.S7
338.109	HD1411
338.1091724	HD1417
338.1091812	HD1415
338.10924	CT275.G294
338.1092453	S457.L5
338.1094	HD586
	HD1411
	HD1491.E9
	HD1916
	HD1917
	HD1920.5
338.10941	S459
338.109415	HD1930.I6
338.1094163	S462.D6
338.10942	HD1534
	HD1925
	HD1927
	HD1930.E5
	S455
338.1094225	S457.S85
338.1094235	S457.D5
338.1094247	S457.W6
338.1094253	S457.L5
338.1094257	S457.O8
338.10942575	HD1930.B8
338.1094264	S457.S8
338.1094271	S457.C45
338.1094272	S457.L3
338.109429	HD1930.W3
	HF1930.W3
338.109437	HD1940.C92
338.1094391	HD1492.H8
338.10944	HD1945
	S463
338.1094585	HD2060.4.M3
338.10947	HD1411
	HD1992
	HD1993
	S469.R9
338.109485	HD2018
338.109489	HD2002
338.109492	HD1986
	HD9015.N42
338.109493	HD9015.B42
338.109497	HD2045.5
338.1094977	HD2042
338.1095	DU740
	S470.A1

338.10951 H31
HD2066
HD2067
HD2068
HD2070.H6
338.10951249 HD870.5
HD1411
338.10952 HD2092
338.10954 HD1476.I4
HD2071
HD2072
HD2073
S471.I3
S471.I4
338.1095412 HD2075.B5
338.1095414 HD2075.B4
338.109543 HD2075.M33
338.109544 HD1741.I29
338.10954792 HD2075.K35
HD2075.S6
338.10954799 HD2075.G6
338.1095483 HC437.K4
338.1095484 HD2075.A5
338.1095487 HC437.T8
S471.I32
338.109549 HD2075.5
338.1095492 HD2075.5
HD2075.5.Z9
338.1095496 HD2111.N52
338.109581 HD2065.6.Z9H47
338.109593 HD2105.5
338.1096 S472.A1
338.109624 HD2146.S82
338.10963 HD2146.E82
HD2146.E84C5
338.10966 HD2130.W5
S760.I88
338.109669 HD2130
HD2130.N5
338.10967 HD2117
HD2130.E2
338.1096711 HD2137.C34W43
338.1096762 DT1
H31
HD2130.K4
338.10968 HD2130.S6
338.1096891 AS36
338.10969 HD1775.H3
338.1097 HD1750
338.10971 HD1781
HD1785
HD9014.C3
SD13
338.109711 S141
338.1097123 HD1407
HD1790.A6
338.1097124 HD1790.S3
338.109713 HD1790.O6
S451.5.O5
338.109715 HD1790.M5
338.109716 HD1790.N6
338.10972 HD1792
338.109728 HD1797
338.1097281 HD1807
338.109729 HD1855.7.Z9B78
338.1097295 HD1852
338.10973 HD201
HD1411
HD1753
HD1761
HD1765
HD1773.A5
HD9475.U52
KF31.A35
KF31.5.S6
S21
338.109747 HD1775.N8
S95
338.10975 F209
HC107.A13
HD1773.A5
338.109755 AS36
338.1097552 AS36
338.109759 S49
338.1097644 HD1751
338.10976819 HD1775.T2
338.10977 HD1751
338.109771 HD1775.O3
338.109774 HD1775.M5
338.109777 S451.I8
338.10978 HD1773.A3
338.109786 HD1775.M9
338.109791 HD1775.A6
338.109797 S451.W2
338.1097983 HD1775.A4
338.1098 HD1790.5
338.10981 HD1872
338.10982 HD1862
S475.A7
338.10983 HD1877
338.10985 HD1902
338.109861 HD1411
338.1098615 HD9014.C72
338.10987 HD1917
338.109895 HD1907
338.109931 HD2195.5
338.10994 HD2152
338.109969 HD184.H32
338.12 HD1753
338.12091717 S469.R
338.120942 HD1921
338.13 HC440.5
HD1407
HD1411
338.13 HD1741.I3
HD1751
HD1759
HD1773.A5
HD1872
HD4966.A292A87
HD9004
HD9006
HD9014.C3
HD9046.I4
HD9066.L52
HD9075
HD9198.I42
HD9421.6
HD9433.U4
HG6047.C7
KF27.G676
S279
S562.G7
338.130182 HB221
338.130954 HD9016.I42
S567
338.1309549 HB235.P25
HD2075.5
338.130973 HD9004
338.1364009756 HD9435.U6
338.15095412 HD9016.I43
338.16 HD1751
338.16094 S671
338.1609543 HD2075.M17
338.17 HD9019.S432J34
338.17110994 HD9049.W5A87
338.173 HD9036
SB208.I5
338.17300976483 SB187.U6
338.1731 HD1411
HD9030.5
HD9046.I4
338.17310954 HA1719
338.17310971 HE199.5.G7
338.17311 S21.A72
SB191.W5
338.1731108 HD9049.W3
338.173110947 HD1407
338.173110971 HD9049.W5
HD9049.W5C199
338.1731109712 SB191.W5
338.1731109788 HD9049.W5
338.1731109794 KF27.A365
338.17315096762
HD9049.C8K44
338.173150981 HD1411
338.173174 SB317.B8
338.17318 HD1751
HD9066.I62
338.1731809593 HD9066.T52
338.1731809664 HD9066.S52
338.173180975 HD9066.U46
338.1731809883 S239
338.1732009411 HD1407
338.17334 HD9235.S62
HD9235.S62U68
338.1733710973 HD1773.A5N67
338.17341 HD1751
338.173491 HD9016.I43
HD9235.P82G78
338.1734910994 HD9235.P82A
338.17350966 HD9155.W42
338.17351 HD9070.5
HD9870.5
HD9881.5
338.1735106273 HD9079.C65
338.173510954 HD9086.I45
338.17351095455 HD9086.I5
338.173510973 S445
338.173510975 HD9075
HD9877.A2
338.17352 HD9155.U4
338.1735409549
HD9156.J8P3534
HD9156.J8P38
HD9156.J8P57
338.17360973 HD1751
338.17361 HD9114.M32M623
HD9116.I4
338.173610954 SB229.I4
338.173610994 HD9118.A8
SB229.A
338.17371 AS36
S21
338.1737106275566 HD9131
338.173710942 HD9141.1
338.173710952 HD9146.J2
338.173710973 HD1751
HD9135
338.173720954 HD9198.I42
338.17372096762 DT1
338.17373 HD9199.T32
SB269
338.1738 QK567
338.17382 HB31
338.17383096982
HD9210.M32L92
338.17385 SB299.R2
338.1738952 HD9161.S53B87
338.173895209595 HD9161.M32
338.174 HD1759
S21
338.17411 SB363
338.17413 SB373
338.17422 HD1407
338.1743 HD9259.C54A82
338.174309759 HD9259.C54
338.174772 HD9259.B2
338.1748856 HD1759
338.1749 HC107.A45
SD393
338.1749015192 SD381.5
338.17490769 SD11
338.174908 SD110
338.17490954 SD223
338.17490954792 SD393
338.1749095493 SD87
338.1749097 HD9764.C3
338.174909715 SD14.M37
338.17490973 HD9755
SD393
338.17490974 L113.A6
338.174909756 HD9757.A2
338.174909768 SD144.A17
338.174909769 SD11
338.17490977515 F589.S55
338.174909795 HD9757.A5
338.17490977982 HC107.A45
338.17490994 SD665
338.1749809747 HD9757.N7
338.1749809762 SD433
338.1749809796 HD9757.I28
338.1749809798 HD9757.A7
338.17498309795 HD9757.O6
338.175091822 HD9000.1
338.1750942 SB319.G7
338.175095492 SB320.8.P3
338.175096761 SB320.8.U3
338.17534 HD9235.C32U54
338.17535 SB333
338.1753609794 HD1759
338.175520979476 HD1759
338.175642 SB349
338.1757 HD9210.U4
338.17590973 HD1751
338.176 HD1751
HD9440
338.176009931 S21
338.176085 HD9044.C25
338.17608830971 HD9433.C2
338.17608830973 HD9433.U4
338.17609429 HD9421.7.A7
338.1760973 HD1751
338.176097982 SF51
338.1762 HD1751
SF196.I4
338.176200978735 SF196.U5
338.176213094 SF207
338.17621309728 S21
338.17621309941 HD9433.A83
338.176213099429
HD9433.A83N6
338.17621409943 SF233.A
338.176294 HC107.A45
338.1763009412 HD1407
338.1763009716
HD9436.C23N63
338.176300994 HD9436.A82
338.17630994 HD9908.A82
338.176349 KF26.A3576
338.1764009757 HD1775.S6
338.1765009797 SF487.8.W3
338.177 HD9282.A2
338.1770942 HD9282.G7
338.17709429 HD9275.G82W3
338.177097286 HD9275.C82
338.1770973 HD1751
KF27.A3
338.1770977 HD9275.U7M57
338.17710942 HD9282.G7
338.1771095414 SF258.C3
338.17710971428
HD9275.C3M66
338.17710973 HD1751.A5
338.1771097472
HD9282.U5N727
338.17754109748 S451.P4
338.17816 HD1751
338.17820954792 HD9926.I7B66
338.17911 HD9944.C22
338.1792 SH317
338.17920973 S914
338.1847 HD1993
338.1854 HD2073
338.1883 HD506
338.19 HD1445
HD9000
HD9000.1
HD9000.5
HD9000.6
HD9006
HV630
S439
S537
TA7
TX345
TX355
338.190212 HD9000.4
338.190611 HD9000.6
338.1909415 HC257.I6
338.1911 TX360.A72
338.1917242 HD9000.5
338.194 HD9015.E82
338.195 HD9016
338.1951 HC430.F3
338.1952 HD1411
338.1954 HD2073
HD9016.I42
338.195412 HD2075.B5
338.1954792 HD9016.I43M288
338.19577 HD9015.R93O54
338.196 TX360.A3
338.1973 HD9000.5
HD9006
KF27.A3
TX345
TX360.U6
338.1975 HD9007.A13
338.198 HD9014.A15
338.1983 HD9014.C52
338.1991 HD9016.I42
338.2 HD8039.M6
HD9506
HD9506.K62
HD9506.U62
TN24.N7
338.202571 TN26
338.2028 TN210
338.2065 TN26
338.208 HD9506.C2
338.20942 TN57
338.2094237 HD9506.G73
HD9506.G73C63
338.209495 TN75
338.2097124 TN27.S3
338.20973 KF26.I534
TN145
338.209771 HD9506.U63O32
338.209773 QE105
338.2097738 TN24.I3
338.209789 HD9506.U63N36
338.20979691 HD9506.U63I25
338.209798 HC107.A45
338.209831 TN44.N6
338.20994 HD9506.A72
QE340
TN121
338.209941 TN122.W5
338.23 HD1739.C6
HD1741.I3
HD9560.4
HD9560.6
HD9560.65
338.25 KF26.I534
338.26 HD9565
338.2710954 TN103
338.272 HD7801
338.2720924 HD9570.D4
338.2720941 HD9551.7.A3
338.2720942 HD9551.1
HD9551.5
338.272094282 HD9551.7.N6
338.272094293 TN808.G8
338.2720973 HD8039.M615
338.27209944 HD9558.A84N34
338.2721 TN837
338.272809498 HD9575.R82
338.27280971 TN873.C2
338.27280973 KF1852.A4
338.272809781 QE113
338.272809789 TN24.N6
338.27282 HC107.K2
HD9560.5
HD9565
HD9566
HD9567.C2
HD9576.I44I38
HD9578.A55
HG4821
QE113
338.27282023 HD9565
338.27282025 HD9560.5
338.27282091724 HD9560.5
338.272820922 HD9565
338.272820924 CT275.F582
HD9570.M25
338.272820956 HD9576.N36
338.2728209669 HD9577.N52
338.272820971 HD9574.C22
338.27282097124 TN873.C22
338.272820973 HD9565
KF26.J835
338.2728209748 HD9567.P4
338.2728209764 HD9570.C83
338.2728209798 KF26.I532
338.272820987 HD9574.V42
338.272820994 G58
HD9578.A82
338.2728209945 HD9568.V5
338.27285094 HD9581.E82
338.272850973 KF26.I534
338.2728509945 HD9581.A86V54
338.273 JX1977
338.273094274 TN405.G72E54
338.2730947 HD9525
338.2730971 HD9506.C2
338.274094237 HD9506.G73C63
338.274210978838 TN295
338.2743 TN445.G7
338.274309774 HD9539.C7U54
338.274530984 HD9539.T6B656
338.2747 HD9539.A83I4
338.27493 TN490.U7
338.2751 HD9621.U6I54
338.27636 HD9660.P7C38
TN919
338.2764 HD9483.I42
TN914.W4
338.27668 HD9585.S84T46
338.276680973 HD9585.S83U54
338.2767 HD9585.M53I54
338.277 KF27.I529
TC5
TD224.O7
338.2770976819 TD225.M5
338.2778 KF27.P846

338.2782 HD9677.A2
338.283071142 S535.G7
338.31 HE372.K18
338.322065 HE5623.Z7G746
338.372 HC110.P63
338.372097121 F1091.A1
338.37241 SH255
338.3727 SH333
SH334
338.37270916612 SH1
338.37270916653 SH323
338.3727092 S914
338.37270947 SH283
338.3727095483 HD8039.F66I43
338.3727096695
HD9467.N53Y42
338.37270968 HD9467.A472
338.372709715 SH224.M36
338.37270973 S914
338.372755 SH224.B6
338.372758 SH319.H3
338.3728209416 SH262.N4
338.3729509 SH383
338.4 DK448.5
G23
HA1719
HC106.3
HD2346.U52
HD9666.56
HD9720.5
HD9982.8.L6
HF5843
PZ9.B363
TS103
338.4018 HC106.5
338.40254274 DA690.S54
338.4025774 E185.93.M5
338.4025942 HC637
338.4025944 HD9738.A83
338.4072094 HD20.3
338.4091724 HC59.7
338.4094 HC240
338.40941 T26.G75
338.409415 HC257.I6
338.40942 HC256
HC256.3
HC256.6
HD2356.G7
T26.G7
338.4094272 HC257.L33
338.40943 HC286.6
338.409481 HC365
338.409494 HC396
338.40954 HA1719
HC435
HC435.2
338.40954792 HC437.M32
338.4095483 HC437.K4
338.409549 HC440.5
338.4095492 HD2346.P32E34
338.409682 HC517.S7
338.40971 HC115
338.409728 HC141
338.40973 HC106.5
HD9724
338.409755 HC107.V8
338.40976944 F459.L8
338.409771 HD9981.7.O2
338.409773 HC107.I3
338.409791 HC107.A6
338.409796 HD9727.I2
338.409798 HC107.A45
338.40982 HC175
338.40994 HC605
338.409941 HC653.K9
338.409942 HC637
338.409945 HC647
338.43 HB235.C2
HC106.6
HD251
HD259
HD1751
HD6483
HD8051
HD9490.A82
HD9515.3
HD9524.C22
HD9578.A82
HD9622.C23
HD9622.I52
HD9666.4
HD9685
HD9685.U5
HD9698.A1
HD9698.U52
HD9710.U52
HD9715
HD9715.U52
HD9724
HD9755
HD9835
HE736
HG939.5
HV873
KF27.M445
Q127.G4
Q180.A1
Q180.U5
R728
RA410
RA410.5
RA971.3
RA981.P4
TD224.N7
338.43 TD478.6.I75
TK435
TL152
TL712
TP155
TP1122
Z253.3
338.430705730942 Z1000
338.4337782 LC501
338.43610973 RA407.3
338.45 HD6331
338.4540954 HC440.A9
338.45610253 Z675.H7
338.45621313 HD9695
338.45629287 TL152
338.4566320094 HD9382.5
338.4567125 TS233
338.45672098 HD9524.L32
338.4567612 HD9769.W52
338.4567614 TS1174.I5
338.456770973 HD9855
338.45677310994 HD9908.A82
338.4568531009744 HD9787.U5
338.46 HE4718.E2
338.46091724 HD82
338.460971 HD9985.C32
338.4609747 HC107.N7
338.47 TL787
338.470690973 AM7
338.473321 HG2611.N7
338.4733210954 HG3284
338.47332130942 HG2987
338.4733216 HG2491
338.473322 HG1891
338.4733220942 HG1926
338.4733222096761 HG1956.U4
338.47332320968 HG2040.5.S6
338.47332320973 HG2151
338.473323209783 HF5006
338.473326327 KF27.I5536
338.473326409764 HG5128.T4
338.47332710994 HG2051.A8
338.473338 TN295
338.473339 TJ23
338.4734167 HC110.D4
HD9705.U62
HF5006
338.47355000973 UC267
338.47355070973 HC110.D4
338.4735580994 UC265.A8
338.47361609744 HJ275
338.47362 HE5614.2
338.473621 HD7123
RA981.A2
338.4736210973 RA410.7
338.473621976 RK11.G
338.4736261110973 RA412.5.U6
338.473635 HD3881
338.4736360973 HD2766
338.4736362096762
HD9685.K42
338.47363620973 HD9685.U5
338.473636209944
HD9685.A83N4
338.47368009415 HG8604
338.4736800942 HG8597
338.47368942 HG8051
338.47368973 HG8535
338.4737 LB2824
338.47370954 LB2947
338.473710109793 LB2826
338.47378100973 LB2825
338.473840954 HE9424
338.473877 HE9786
338.473881 TE145
338.47388109786 HE356.M85
338.4738831 HE5614.3.I4
338.4738833 HE370
338.4753005 QC5.45
338.4753973 QC786
338.4753976 HD9698.A2
338.476 TJ1175
338.4761 HD7102.U4
RA407.3
RA410.7
RA427
338.4761072 RA410.5
338.4761073 RT73
338.47610730971 RT6
338.47610942 RA410.9.G7
338.47610973 HD1751
RA410.A1
RA410.5
338.4761304 G155.E7
338.476147109746
HC107.C83A42
338.4761486 HE5614
338.47615 HD9665.5
338.476150255493 RS76.C48
338.476151 HD9671
RS189
338.4761510942 HD9667
338.4761519 HD9666.5
338.4761519002573 HD9666.3
338.476151900952 HD9672.J32
338.476151900973 HD7103.5.U5
338.47615191 HD9665.5
338.4761519109561 HD9672.T92
338.476151910973 HD9666.5
338.476154 HD9666.5
338.4761591 JX1977
338.476176 RK58
338.476176002573 KK58
338.4762 TA217
338.47621 HD9705.I72
338.47621209416 TC459.3.U4
338.476213 HD9695.U54W35
TA177.4
338.4762131 HD9685.U5
HD9695.I44H38
338.476213109415 HD9685.I72
338.47621310951 HD9685.C62
338.47621310973 HD9685.U5
338.476213109747 HD9695.U53
338.4762131910979 TK447
338.47621320954 HD9684.I52
338.4762132139 KF26.I534
338.47621381 TK7835
338.476213810254 HD9696.A2
TK7805
338.476213810942
HD9696.A3G75
338.476213810973
HD9696.A3U58
338.4762138109758
HC107.G43I536
338.4762138109786
HD9696.A3U564
338.4762138195 HD9696.C62
QA76.5
338.4762138195025 TK7885
338.47621381950973
HD9696.C63U518
338.4762148 HD9698.A2
HD9698.U52
JX1974.7
KF25.A827
TK9145
338.47621480942 HD9698.G72
TK9057
338.476214809549 HD9698.P32
338.47621480973 HD9698.U52
338.47621483 HC108.H29
HD9698.A2
338.4762148335 HD9698.U52
338.47621809416 HD9705.I72
338.4762180973 HD9705.U62
338.47621900973 HD9703.U5
KF27.5.S676
338.47621912 HD9773.U6N355
338.4762193 TJ1170
338.47622342 TN295
338.47622348 HD9539.N52A85
338.476223493 F830
338.476234091821 UF530
338.4762344065 TS533.4.G7
338.4762382 VM23
VM105
VM121
VM298.5
338.476238200973 KF27.M464
338.4762382075 VM23.5
338.47623820952 VM105
338.47623820971 HF1762
338.47623823 VM139
338.476238245 VM301.A5
338.476251 HE2791.U55
338.476257 TE7
338.4762712 TC458.W35
338.4762713 F127.E5
338.476274 TC425.R25
338.4762752 KF26.I549
TC904.P3
338.476278 TC425.P8
338.47628167 JX1977
338.47628168 TD741
338.476281680971 HC120.P55
338.476281683 TN321
338.476283 HD4475
338.476291 HD9711.5
TL521
TL686.M25
338.4762910942
HD9711.G74B74
338.476291300924 CT275.H6678
338.476291300973 HD9711.U6
338.476292 HD9710
HD9710.C22
HD9710.U52
KF26.C626
338.47629202473 TL159
338.476292091724 HD9710.A2
338.4762920942 HD9710.G72
338.4762920954 HD9710.I42
338.4762920973 HD9710.U52
338.4762922029 TL160
338.47629222 HD9710.U52
338.476292220973 HD9710.U57
338.4762922602573
HD9715.7.U62
338.47629244 TL261
338.476294094 TL787
338.47636089 SF779.7
338.47636200978 SF196.U5
338.47639209718 SH226
338.476413 HD9000.5
HD9005
338.47641336 SB217
338.47643 HD7395.M6
338.476456 HD9999.L38
338.476479 TX911
338.4764794 TX911
338.47647940924 TX910.5.E65
338.476479442 TX910.G7
338.476479473 TX911.3.F5
338.4765129 HD9829.U75
338.4765129 HF5371
338.47655 Z122
338.47655095125 Z464.S5
338.47655142 Z244.5
338.476554 Z468.N5
338.47655454 Z284
338.47655494 Z533
338.47655572 Z286.S4
338.47655573 LB2851
338.476555730942 Z151.4
Z325
Z716.6
338.4765557309498 Z445
338.4765709786 HF5616.U5
338.476583124 HF5549.5.T7
338.47658570942 T177.G7
338.47658785 HD9075
338.476588 HF5429.6.G7
338.476588700942565
HF5429.6.G7
338.476588710971
HF5465.C4E254
338.476591 HF5821
338.4765910942 HF5813.G7
338.4766 HD9235.G82I45
HD9651.7
HD9657.I44P93
338.4766002571 TP12
338.4766002573 HD9651.3
338.47660091724 HD9650.5
338.476600922 TP139
338.476600943 TP130
338.476600947 HD1993
338.476600974888 TP24.P4
338.4766009758 HD9651.7.G4
338.476609282 TP58.T9
338.476609438 HD9556.P652
338.47660973 HD9651.4
338.476610094 HD9656
338.4766100943 HD9654.5
338.4766100973 HD9651.5
338.4766143 HD9484.P5C56
338.47661804 TP690.2.U6
338.4766260994 HD9558.A82
338.47662622109776
HD9559.P5U66
338.476632 HD9377.O7
338.476633 TP573.G7
338.47663420973 HD9397.U52
338.4766352 HD9395.A2
TP605
338.47663520941 TP605
338.4766400942 HD9011.3
338.47664009497 HD9015.Y82
338.4766400973 HD9004
HD9321.5
338.4766400994 HD9018.A7
338.476640285 HD9005
338.476641 HD9105
338.4766410954 HD9116.I4
338.4766412209931
HD9118.N44
338.4766432 SF268
338.476644095492 HD9213.P23
338.47664725 HD9049.O2
338.476647520942 HD9057.G75
338.4766492 HD9435.G72
338.47664920285 HD9410.5
338.47664920924 TS1971.C5
338.47664922 HD9440.G72
338.476649310975 S445
338.4766494 HD9455
SH367.C2
338.476655 HD9567.A18
338.4766550954 HD9576.I44I37
TP690.2.I4
338.47665509741 HD9567.M3
338.47665538 HD9560.1
338.4766553840973 KF26.B375
338.47665709421 TP733.G7L83
338.4766573 KF27.I536
338.4766577 HD9565
338.47666095694 JX1977
338.4766610973 HD9623.U45
338.476666094246 HD9612.7.S8
338.4766673091724 JX1977
338.47666890973 HD9622.U52
338.476669409549 HD9622.P32
338.4766812095496
HD9999.S73
338.476681209711 HD9999.S73
338.476684 HD9661.A2
338.476684025762 TP1112
338.4766840947 HD9661.R92
338.47668409497 HD9661.Y82
338.4766840952 HD9661.J32
338.4766860254 HD9656.A2
338.4766862 HD9483.A2
HD9483.I42
S633
338.4766862091724 JX1977
338.4766862095484
HD9483.I43A55
338.4766862095491
HD9483.P23W48
338.47668620956 HD9483.I72
338.47668622097 S633.2
338.47668620973 HD9483.U52
338.47668624 JX1977
338.47668625 HD9483.N36
338.4766865 HD1751
338.4766865094 HD9660.P33
338.47668654 HD9660.P33
338.4766910971 HD9524.C22

338.476691420981 HD9524.B82
338.4766972209776
HD9539.A63U545
338.4766982 TN295
338.4767 HC257.N57
HD9710.U52
HD9780.U52
338.476700973 HD9724
338.476702543 HF3099
338.476702573 HD9724
338.476709 TS15
338.476709542 HC437.U6
338.47670971 HD9734.C3N57
338.47670973 HC106.5
HD9724
338.476709772 HD9727.I6
338.476709791 HD9727.A6
338.47671 TS283
338.4767102571 TS26
338.4767109471 T12.5.F5
338.476710973 HD9506.U62
338.4767120973 HD8051
338.47672 HD9510
HD9510.5
HD9526.I62
HF2651.S76U52
TS229.5.I4
338.476720212 HD9510.4
338.47672023 HD9515
338.476720621 HD9510
338.476720924 TN140.H74
338.4767209437 HD9525.C92
338.476720947 HD9525.R9
338.476720954 HD9526.I62
338.476720973 TN704.U5
338.4767209748 TS303
338.476720974892 HD9518.E6
338.47672820942 HD9521.5
338.4767283 HD9529.P53C33
338.476733 HD9539.C6
338.47673722 HD9539.A63U54
338.47674 HD9757.A2
338.4767400994 HD9768.A7
338.476740968 HD9767.S72
338.476740973 HD9754
338.4767480947 HD9765.R9
338.47674834095483
HD9769.P63
338.47674834095496
HD9769.P63N43
338.476752025543
HD9780.I64M33
338.47675209581 HD9780.A45
338.476760954 HD9836.I42
338.4767609711 HD9764.C4B66
338.4767609747 HD9757.N7
338.476762 HD38
HD9820.5
338.4767620954 HD9836.I42
338.4767620973 HD9824
338.47676288 HD9839.P33N33
338.47677 HD9854
HD9866.N43B56
338.4767700942 HD9861.1
HD9969.K7G75
338.476770094272
HD9861.7.L35
338.4767700954 HD9866.I62
338.476770095492
HD9866.P33E23
338.476770095691 HD9866.S92
338.476770954 HD9886.I42
338.476771109411
HD9930.G73S27
338.476771309549
HD9156.J8P377
338.47677180954
HD9156.C63I52
338.4767721 HD8039.T42G72
HD9881.7.L2
TS1565.U6
338.47677210942 HD9861.5
338.47677210954 HD9886.I42
338.47677210954792
HD9886.I43
338.476772109764 TS1575
338.476772109922
HD9886.I53J35
338.476773 HD9895
HD9901.5
338.47677309429 HD9901.7.A7
338.47677731 HD9909.T93H45
338.4767731094117
HD9909.T93H45
338.47677310942 HD9901.5
338.47677310952 HD9908.C6
338.47677310977 HD9897.A3
338.47677390922 HD8393
338.47677390924 CT275.T5734
338.47677390951 HD9926.C62
338.476774 HD9929.5.E82
338.4767740954 HD9929.5.I4
338.4767740994 HD9929.5.A82
338.4767762 HD9839.F43C35
338.4767776430994 HD9937.A92
338.476776530924 TS140.H4
338.4767765309424 TS1782
338.476776610942
HD9969.K7G75
338.47677671 HD9156.C63I48
338.4767771 HD9156.J8
338.47678 HD9161.I42
338.476780942 HD9161.G72
338.4767832 HD9161.U52

338.47679609415 HD9999.B84
338.4767973 HD9149.C4
338.47679730973
HD9149.C42U68
338.4768 TT95.C9
338.4768114 HD9999.B9
338.476817 Q185
338.476834029 TS534.7
338.476838309931 HC621
338.476841 SD541
338.476841009415 HD9773.I7
338.4768470973 HD9999.C3
338.4768509747
HD9780.U53N68
338.476853100954 HD9787.I52
338.4768531000973 KF26.B375
338.476870942 HD9940.G8
338.4768709493 HD9940.B42
338.476870973 HD9940.U4
338.4768711 HD9940.U4
338.476871109415 HD9940.I72
338.4768712 TT555
338.4768730254 HD9969.K7
338.476873094 HD9969.K7E85
338.4768730942 HD9969.K7G72
338.4768732095496 HD9969.H8
338.4768872 TS2301.N55
338.4769 HD9715.U53
JX1977
338.476900182 HD9715.G72
338.476900254 JX1977
338.4769002573 TH12
338.4769003 HD9715.A2
338.476900942 HD9715.G72
338.47690094235 HJ9779.G7
338.4769009497 TH95.Y8
338.4769009676 HD9715.A52
338.47690097292 HD9715.J152
338.476900973 HB31
HD9715.U52
338.4769009771
HD9715.U53O36
338.476900994 HD9715.A82
338.4769025789
HD9715.U53N435
338.47690511 JK1618
338.4769051109753 JK1618
338.47690594 KF27.F638
338.4769060938 DF261.E6
338.4769071 LB2826.P4
338.4769080973 HD7293
338.4769082 HD7287.6.U5
338.47690942 TH435
338.4769106273 HD9715.U52
338.4769397 HD9715
338.4769793 TH7687
338.476980973 HD7293
338.477 N6512
NX26.S2
NX711.U5
338.477392 HD9747.G72
338.477455 HD2341
338.47745509729843
HD2346.S17
338.47746 HD9866.P33R35
338.4775 N8675
338.4775029 N4035.K28
338.4776902573 NE1850
338.47774044 G155.U6
338.47778315 Z48
338.4778 ML36
338.4778991 ML1055
338.477900973 GV53
HD4904.7
338.4779009775 GV54.W6
338.4779143 PN1993.5.U65
PN1994
PN1999.T7
338.477914309415 PN1993.5.I85
338.477914309549 PN1993.5.P3
338.477920942 PN2595
338.47798400942 SF335.G7
338.4791 G155.A1
G155.P25
KF26.C6
338.4791410481 G155.S27
G155.S356
338.4791412504 G155.S356
338.4791414 G155.S356
338.4791420485 G155.G7
338.479142304 TX910.G7
338.4791489045 G155.C64
338.4791549604 TL500
338.47915694045 G155.I78
338.479170453 G155.U6
338.47917304 G155.U6
338.4791754044 HC107.W5
338.4791755 G155.U6
338.4791757044 G155.U6
338.4791758 G155.U6
338.479176804 G155.U6
338.4791776 G155.M67
338.4791776045 G155.U6
338.47917836604 G155.U6
338.4791791045 HC107.A6
338.4791793043 G155.U6
338.4791931 G155.N5
338.4791969044 G155.U6
338.49 HD9685
338.5 HB31
HB3723
HF1436
S97
338.501 HB201

338.50182 HB201
338.50973 HF5681.R25
338.52 HB221
HC435.2
HF5417
KF27.G659
338.5208 HB221
HB235.U6
338.520946 HB235.S75
338.520947 HB235.E8
338.520954 HB235.I4
338.520971 HB235.C2
338.520973 HB235.U6
KF25.E2
338.521 HB221
338.522 HD6483
KF26.J835
338.5220971 HF1480
338.523 HD2735
338.526 HF5415.1
338.5260973 HC110.W24
338.528 HB31
HB235.J3
JX1977
338.54 H11
HB3711
HB3716
HB3717
HB3726
HB3743
HB3783
HC105
338.540184 HD82
338.5409 HB3716
338.540942 HC256.5
338.540973 HB3717
HB3743
HC106.5
338.542 HB3711
338.5420973 HC106.3
338.544 HB74.M3
HB3730
HC101
338.544018 HB3730
338.5440184 HB3730
338.54430943 HC286.6
338.6 HD5660.Y8
338.6042 HD58
338.60420184 HD58
338.60420974 HC107.A11
338.60480973 HF5006
338.60942 HC255
338.60954 HD2346.A75
HD2900
338.63 HD2346.I5
TT690
338.630954 HD2346.I5
338.63095492 HD2346.P32
338.6309681 HD2346.B63
338.630995 DU740
338.64 DS126.5
HA1719
HD1516.G7
HD2073
HD2346.J3
HD6460
HD6461.F55
HD6461.S6
HD6462.B7
HD6462.D8
HD6462.L7
HD9866.P33
HD9866.P33E22
KF26.S6
KF1659
338.6408 Z7164.C8
Z7164.C81
338.64091724 HD2341
338.640942 HD2346.G7
HD6460
338.6409544 HD2346.I52R36
HD2346.I52R37
338.64095475 HC437.B79
338.64095492 HD2346.P32
338.640973 HG3729.U5
KF26.B375
KF27.5.S6762
338.6409773 HD2346.U52
338.642 JX1977
KF31.5.S6
338.6420973 HC110.P63
KF26.5.S625
338.65019 HD2351
338.650942 HD2356.G7
TS1357
338.650947 HD2356.R9
338.7 E185.8
HC253
HD31
HD41
HD2791
HD5660.G7
338.70942 HC253
HC256
338.7097 HC106.3
338.70973 HD2795
338.70974 HC107.A11
338.709755692 HC107.V82H53
338.709955 DU740
338.74 HD69.I7
HD2741
HD9539.Z6A84
338.740207 PN6231.C63
338.740924 HC432.5.S5

338.740942 HD2847
338.740943 HD2859
338.740973 HD2785
338.7409764 HG5128.T4
338.740994 HD2927
338.761 HD9705.G48B34
338.7612673 BV1040
338.761301415 HQ146.N4
338.761333330977 F517
338.7613337609764
HD275.P6T43
338.7613636 HD9685.U7I565
338.76136361 HD4464.H25
338.7613636209762
HD9685.U7M55
338.7613636209772
HD9685.U7P863
338.761363630976199
HD9581.U53
338.761368 HG8511.N7
338.76136800971
HG8551.Z9D63
338.7613683 HG8540.B8
338.7613683009747
HG8963.M87
338.761368320097419
HG8963.U62
338.761368320924 HG172.M28
338.76138 HF486.L5
338.76138450942 HE8699.G7
338.7613846 HE8846.A55
338.7613846094891 HE8240.S8
338.761387542073
HE601.U6W534
338.7613884 HE4491.D45D445
338.76161540978393 HF6201.D6
338.761641 HD9321.9.G7
338.7616479578 TX945.5.H35
338.76165180924 HD9999.B94
HD9999.B94I54
338.76165547471 Z473.C98
338.761655474811 Z473.C98
338.7616576 HF5616.U5
338.76165886
HD9999.H724A427
338.7616588700942 HC252.5.D4
338.7616588702 HD9322.9.S23
338.7616591 HF5813.U6
338.7617950924 HV6722.G86
338.762 HD9695.U54H5
HD9705.U64W42
338.7620922 HD9710.U52
338.762113094282 TJ625.S828
338.76213 HD9729.L4
338.762131 HD9695.U54C53
338.76213109669
HD9685.N54E42
338.762131099141
HD9685.P54M45
338.762132 HD9685.U7H38
338.76213810974 HD9696.G7
338.7621436094272
HD9705.G48G74
338.76218 HD9486.G74
HD9680.I54H43
HD9705.G48R48
HD9705.U64W4
338.762180977132
HD9710.U54E15
338.762180993122
HD9705.N44P73
338.76218330979461
HD9705.U64W46
338.76219097462 HD9745.U5
338.7621944097463
HD9745.U5S78
338.762209774985
HD9539.C7U546
338.76223328 HD9569.S63
338.7622342 HD9536.U4H634
338.7622361 HD9592.9.E5
338.762345 UF533
338.762382 F72.P7
338.762382040972185
VM301.H6
338.7623820941435 VM301.F3
338.7623862 VM791
338.7625733 HD9710.G74E34
338.7629133 HD9711.N44K64
338.7629133340974854
TL724.5.P5
338.762920924 CT275.S5233
HD9710.G72
338.762920942 TL140.R58
338.762920977289
HD9710.U54S85
338.763 HD1992
338.7630924 HD9036
338.7630947 HD1992
338.763094977 HD1492.B8
338.7630954 HD2073
338.763097292 HD1471.J3
338.7630973 HD2785
338.76311 F1060.8
338.76313 HD9486.C24
338.763498 HD9759.G4
338.763498209797 HD9759.B6
338.7635965094258 SB89
338.763911 F1060
338.7641 HD9010.P38
HD9057.U62N25
338.76479478856 F784.C7

Dewey	LC
338.76554	Z473
	Z473.C98
338.765547471	Z473.H27
338.765557074	Z232.S75
338.7658785	HF5489.I54
338.76588700942	HD9961.9.M3
338.76610971	HD9623.C24C65
338.7661519	RS68.A3
338.766352	HD9395.U47B75
338.7663520942	HD9395.G72
338.7663520976944	HD9395.U47B735
338.766362	HD9349.C6
338.76655	HD9571.9.B73
338.766570993122	TP738
338.766588730924	HF5465.U6
338.766840942	HD9661.G74B72
338.766842094255	HD9660.R44S33
338.7668651	HD9660.P33
338.7672	HD9519.B65
	HD9521.9.S3
338.76720924	CT275.C3
	HD9520.G3
338.7672094245	HD9521.9.C6
338.767283094255	HD9521.9.S8
338.7674	HD9759.K4
338.767409931	HD9768.N44
338.7675209421	TS957.G7
338.76760982	HD9834.A74
338.7677	HD9868.N44R65
338.76770094235	HD6961
338.76770285	HD9859.S3
338.76770974	HD9859.S8
338.767721097443	HD9859.W48
338.767731	HD9908.A84E46
338.767731094274	HD9861.9.B68
338.76774	HD9929.5.G74C67
338.7677626	HD9861.9.C5
338.7677626094257	HD9901.9.C47
338.7681130977311	LB1043.5
338.768114	HD9999.B94V53
338.768140025771	HD9743.U7
338.76817	HD9486.G74T35
338.7683	HD9745.G74
	HD9745.G74K43
338.7683309421	HD9999.S29
338.76841	TS880
338.7684100993157	HD9773.N49B82
338.7687	HD9787.U6G45
338.769	HD9715.U54B36
338.7690094258	HD9715.G74F67
338.769054	HD9715.N24C63
338.769612095483	HD9529.P53I54
338.8	HB31
	HD2741
	HD2791
	HD2810
	HD2848
	HD9695.G73G46
	HD9710.U54S76
338.80942	HD2847
	PN1999.R37
338.80973	HD2795
338.82	HD2731
338.8208	HD2731
338.820942	HD2848
338.820954	HD2900
338.820973	HC106.3
	HD2785
	HD2791
338.82610713	KF27.J835
	KF27.J8666
338.8264674	TT954.G7
338.826661520942	HD9623.G72
338.85	HD2795
338.850973	HD2785
338.860924	HC102.5.T46
338.860973	HD2795
338.88	HD69.I7
	HD9560.5
	HG5422.H4213
338.88091821	HD69.I7
338.9	HD82
	HD2321
	HD3611
	HD3842
	HD3847
	HJ275
	HT391
	JC507
	T65.3
338.9001	HB31
	HD82
338.9001724	HD82
338.90018	HD82
338.900182	HD82
338.900184	HD82
	HD6483
	HT391
338.90072	HD82
338.90072094	Q180.A8
338.9008	HD82
338.90091717	HC704
338.90091724	HB31
	HC59.7
	HD82
	HD5724
338.900954	HC435.2
338.91	AS36
338.91	HC54
	HC59.7
	HC60
	HD82
	HD2953
	HF1408
	HF1411
	HF1413
	HF4050
	HG3881
	JX1977
338.9100993155	HD1701.N42M36
338.9101	HF3698.G7
338.910184	HF1411
338.9102097887	KF26.I549
338.910611	HC241
338.91171242	HC241.25.G7
	HF1411
338.911717	HF1411
	HF4050
338.91171701724	HC59.7
338.91172201724	HC59.7
338.911724	HC59.7
	HC60
	HD69.I7
	HF1410
	HF1411
338.914	HC60
	HC240
	HC241
	HC241.2
	HC241.25.G7
	HF1532.92
338.914042	HC241.25.G7
338.914073	HF1456.5.E8
338.9142	HC60
	HF1533
	JN248
338.914201724	HC60
	TA57
338.914204	HC241.25.G7
338.9142054	HC412
338.9143	HC60
338.914301724	HG4517
338.914306897	DD259.4
338.91439101724	HF3549.H8
338.9147	HC59
	HC60
338.914701724	HC60
338.914705	HC412
338.9147051	Q180
338.9148	DL1
338.9149401724	HC60
338.91497	HF1578.5
338.91497701724	HF1577
338.915	HC412
	HC440.5
	HD69.I55
338.915073	HF1456
338.915195073	HC467
338.9152054	HF1590.15.J3
338.9154	HC435
	HC435.2
338.91540549	HF1590.15.P3
338.915406	HF1590.15.A3
338.9154073	HC60
	HC440.5
	HF1590.15.U5
338.91549071	HF1590.5.C2
338.915493043	HF1546.5.C4
338.91569404	AS36.M48
338.91569406	HC502
338.915694073	HC60
338.91581047	HC417
338.9159	HC412
338.916	HC502
338.9167	HC517.E2
338.917101724	HC60
338.91728	JA37
338.9173	HC60
	HC60.U6
	HC101
	HC110.P63
	HF1455
	HV640.4.U54
	KF4668
338.917301724	HC60
338.9173043	HC286.5
338.91730597	HC60.U6
338.917306	HC502
338.917306668	HC547.I8
338.917306762	HC517.K4
338.91730728	HC141
338.917308	HC60
	HC125
	HC141
	HF1456.5.L3
338.91730861	HC197
338.918	HC125
338.91931	HF1642.5
338.9194	HC60
338.919405	HC412
338.94	HC240
	HC241
	HC241.2
	HC241.25.G7
	HC241.4
	HC256.6
	HD82
338.941	HC652
338.9415	HC257.I6
	HC257.I65
338.942	H11
338.942	HC60
	HC256
	HC256.6
	HD1415
	HD3616.G72
	HD4141.A5
	HD4145
	HT395.G7
	PR3404
338.9431	HC287.A2
338.9437	HC267.B2
338.9438	HC337.P7
338.944	HC276.2
338.946	HC385
	Q127.S7
338.947	HC244
	HC335
	HC335.4
	HC336.2
	HF5601
	Q180
338.9481	HA1503
	HC365
338.9495	HC295
338.9497	HC407.Y6
338.94977	HC407.B9
338.9498	HC407.R8
338.95	HC440.5
	HD30
338.95195	HC467
338.95335	HC497.F3
338.954	HC431
	HC435
	HC435.2
	HC440.P63
	HC4351.2
	HD82
	HD4293
	HG4517
	HT395.I5
	HV392
338.95413	HC437.O7
338.954162	HC437.A8
338.954165	HC437.N25
338.9542	HC437.A73
	HC437.U6
	HN690.U8
	HT395.I52K35
338.9543	HC437.M28
338.9544	HC437.R3
338.95452	HC437.H5
338.95455	HC437.H29
338.9546	HC437.K28
338.95475	HC437.G85
338.954792	HC437.C45
	HC437.M32
	HC437.N28
	HC437.R37
	HC437.S17
338.954799	HC437.G6
338.95482	HC437.M3
	HC437.T24
338.95483	HC437.K4
338.95484	HC437.A73
338.95487	HC437.M8
338.9549	HC440.5
	HC440.5.Z7E273
338.95496	HC497.N5
338.956	JX1977
338.9561	HC405
338.95694	HC497.P2
338.959	HC412
338.9593	HC497.S5
338.9595	HC445.5
338.9597	HC443.V5
338.96	HC502
338.962	Q180
338.963	HC591.A3
338.9667	HC517.G6
338.9669	HC517.N48
338.967	HC517.E2
338.96762	HC517.K4
338.96773	HC567.S7
338.9678	HC557.T3
338.9683	HC517.S9
338.96894	DT1
	HC517.R42
338.971	HC115
338.971477	HC117.Q4
338.9716	HJ795.N68
338.972	HC135
	HT395.M6
338.9728	HC141
338.973	E744
	HB119.A2
	HC60.U6
	HC106
	HC106.3
	HC106.3.A52
	HC106.4
	HC106.5
	HC106.6
	HC110.D4
	HC110.P6
	HC110.P63
	HC110.R4
	HD60.5.U5
	HD1773.A5
	HD3616.U46
	HD3616.U47
	HD5724
	HJ275
	HT167
	JX1974
338.973	KF25.E2
	KF25.E235
	KF26.F6
	KF26.L3
	KF26.P8
	KF26.P828
	KF27.B3
	KF27.G659
	KF27.P8
	KF27.P836
	S21
338.974	H31
	HC107.A133.P637
338.9744	HT393.M4
338.97441	HC107.M42B453
338.9746	HC107.C83D44
338.9747	HC107.N7
	HJ605
338.97471	HC108.N7
338.975244	HC107.M32C284
338.9756	HC107.N8
338.9757	HC107.S7
338.9758	HC107.G4
338.97672	HC107.A8
338.9768	HC107.T3
338.976812	HC107.T32L35
338.976844	HC107.T32D52
338.9773	HJ405
338.977311	HC108.C4
338.977456	HD6275.G7
338.9775	HC107.W6
	HJ775
338.97768	HC107.M63P632
338.9777	HC107.I7
338.9778411	HC107.M83P6352
338.9784	HC107.N9
338.9786	HC107.M9
338.978841	HC107.C72G85
338.9789	HC107.N6
338.979173	HC108.P55
338.979175	HC107.A63P636
338.9794	HD3890.C2
338.9795	HC107.O7
	HC107.O73P633
	HC107.O73P634
338.98	HC125
	HG660.5
338.981	HC187
338.984	HC182
338.9876	HC238.B6
338.991	HC446
	HC447
338.9914	HC455
338.9931	HC665
338.994	HC605
	HD3616.A83
338.9941	HC651
	HC653.P5
338.9944	HT395.A92M33
	HT395.A92N45
338.9945	HC648.M8
338.9946	HC643.F5
338.995	HC687.P3
338.9951	JX1977
338.9969	HC107.H3
339	H11
	HB151
	HB171
	HB171.5
	HB601
	HB3730
	HC51
	HC79.I5
	HC106.3
	HC106.6
	HC107.I33I53
	HC256.3
	HC260.I5
	HD82
	HD8051
	HF5635
	HG221
	HG229
	JK1673
	JX1977
339.018	JX1977
339.0182	HB171
339.0184	HB98.2
	HD82
339.077	HB171.5
339.08	HB171
339.091724	HC59.7
339.0942	HC260.I5
339.09437	HB601
339.0947	Q180.A1
339.094977	HC407.B93I545
339.0954	HC435
339.097161	HC117.N8
339.0972	HC135
339.09771	HC107.O3
339.1520942	QC91
339.2	HB715
	HB771
	HC79.I5
	HC103
	HC110.I5
	HD2037
339.20184	HA1503
339.208	HB601
339.2091734	HD1761
339.20942	HC260.I5
339.20947	Q180.A1
339.2095412	HC4337.B47
339.209715	HC117.M35

339.20973 ..... HC105
..... HC106
..... HC110.I5
339.20982 ..... JX1977
339.20987 ..... HC239.5.I5
339.210952 ..... HT390
339.23 ..... HB74.M3
..... HD1785
..... TN295
339.230942 ..... HC256.5
339.2309549 ..... HC440.5
339.23097476 ..... HC107.N7
339.2309754 ..... HC107.W5
339.230979482 ..... HF5006
339.26095694 ..... HG188.P45
339.3 ..... HC79.I5
..... HD9540.4
339.3091724 ..... HC59.7
339.342 ..... HC260.I5
..... HG939.5
339.347 ..... HC340.I5
..... Q180.A1
339.35125 ..... HC428.H6
339.354 ..... HC440.I5
339.354162 ..... HC437.A8
339.35482 ..... HC437.T24
339.3549 ..... HC440.5.Z9I498
339.35492 ..... HC440.5
339.3593 ..... HC497.S53I515
339.3595 ..... HC445.5.Z9I52
339.371 ..... HC120.I5
339.37292 ..... HC157.J2
339.373 ..... HC105
..... HC110.I5
339.3777 ..... HA40.I5
339.3793 ..... HC107.N33I55
339.394 ..... HC610.I5
339.4 ..... HB171.5
..... HB601
..... HC28
..... HC68
..... HC79.C6
..... HC110.C6
..... HC110.C63
..... HC120.C6
..... HC340.C6
..... HC465.C6
..... HD6993.O3
..... HD7051.5
..... HD9724
..... JX1977
..... KF32.G6
339.4019 ..... HC260.C6
..... HF5415.3
339.40973 ..... HC110.C6
..... HC110.P6
339.409944 ..... HD7070
339.41 ..... HC110.I5
..... HC437.P8
..... HD1759
..... HD7123
..... KF27.G659
..... S445
339.410182 ..... HC110.I5
..... Q180.A1
339.410942 ..... HC260.I3
339.4109492 ..... HC329.5.I5
339.410969 ..... HC107.H33I514
339.410971 ..... HC120.I5
339.4109713 ..... HD1790.O6
339.410973 ..... HC110.I5
339.410974 ..... HC107.C83I55
339.4109754 ..... HC107.W5
339.4109768 ..... HC107.T33I513
..... HC107.T33I514
339.4109787 ..... HC107.W9
339.4109796 ..... HC107.I23I52
339.410985 ..... HC227
339.42 ..... HD6979
..... HD8051
..... HV244
339.42094 ..... HD7022
339.420942 ..... HD7023
339.42094391 ..... HD7027
339.420954799 ..... HD7051
339.4209712 ..... HC111
339.420973 ..... HC110.C6
..... HD6983
..... HD8051
..... KF27.B342
339.42097471 ..... HD6994.N5
339.430952 ..... HC465.S3
339.430973 ..... HB31
..... HC110.S3
339.46 ..... AS36.C2
..... HC79.P6
..... HX11
339.46019 ..... HC79.P6
339.46072042 ..... HC260.P6
339.46072073 ..... AS36.C2
339.460973 ..... AS36.C2
..... HC110.P6
..... HC110.P63
..... HD8051
..... HD9006
..... HV4043
339.4609769 ..... HC107.K4
339.4609775 ..... HC107.W63P625
..... HC107.W63P63
339.4609783 ..... HF5006
339.460979355 ..... JK8501
339.460994 ..... HC610.P6
339.47 ..... HC110.C63
..... HC120.C6
339.47 ..... HC437.A73
339.470942 ..... HC110.C6
339.483621 ..... RA971.8
..... Z6675.H75
339.48362110973 ..... RA971.8
339.48616 ..... RA407.3
339.4863 ..... HD1751
339.4864130091724 ..... HD9000.5
339.486626 ..... HD9555.R92
339.4866260942 ..... TP317.G7
339.486696 ..... HD9539.T5
339.486740097731 ..... HD9758.C4
339.48677210973 ..... HD9874
339.49764 ..... HC107.T4
339.49775 ..... S932.W6
339.50973 ..... HC110.W24
339.53 ..... HJ8011
339.530973 ..... HG538
339.860976428 ..... HD5726.D25
340 ..... DF902
..... E78.P4
..... E78.W3
..... E94
..... E450
..... HB31
..... HC107.M4
..... HD1411
..... HD8051
..... HD9506.A72
..... HD9999.C73G76
..... HE965
..... HE6311
..... HF5616.U5
..... HJ2381
..... HJ4629
..... HT123
..... HV86
..... HV5089
..... HV5309.B7
..... HV9105.W6
..... J87
..... JK274
..... JK3360.P4
..... JK3688.M7
..... JK4401
..... JK5274
..... JN321
..... JQ6103
..... JX636
..... JX1977
..... JX4292.R4
..... KF8
..... KF25.A8
..... KF26.A35
..... KF26.A3534
..... KF26.B3
..... KF26.B345
..... KF26.B372
..... KF26.B375
..... KF26.C6
..... KF26.C634
..... KF26.C636
..... KF26.C645
..... KF26.C652
..... KF26.C688
..... KF26.D5
..... KF26.D545
..... KF26.F5
..... KF26.F6
..... KF26.I5
..... KF26.I542
..... KF26.I549
..... KF26.J8
..... KF26.J835
..... KF26.J836
..... KF26.J837
..... KF26.J855
..... KF26.J8747
..... KF26.L3
..... KF26.L334
..... KF26.L335
..... KF26.L343
..... KF26.L354
..... KF26.L363
..... KF26.L373
..... KF26.P825
..... KF26.P846
..... KF26.P866
..... KF26.R885
..... KF27
..... KF27.A3226
..... KF27.A3326
..... KF27.A3327
..... KF27.A365
..... KF27.B3
..... KF27.D5644
..... KF27.E335
..... KF27.F6
..... KF27.F646
..... KF27.F648
..... KF27.H645
..... KF27.I529
..... KF27.I537
..... KF27.I5536
..... KF27.I5538
..... KF27.I5568
..... KF27.I5587
..... KF27.J8
..... KF27.J8666
..... KF27.M436
..... KF27.M445
..... KF27.M464
..... KF27.P674
..... KF27.P876
340 ..... KF27.S387
..... KF27.V428
..... KF27.W3
..... KF30.A8
..... KF30.C57
..... KF30.C65
..... KF31.A35
..... KF31.C6
..... KF31.D5
..... KF31.I5
..... KF31.J8
..... KF31.J847
..... KF31.L3
..... KF32.A3
..... KF32.B3
..... KF32.E3
..... KF32.G6
..... KF32.I55
..... KF32.M4
..... KF32.P6
..... KF32.W3
..... KF210
..... KF213.B8
..... KF228.T43
..... KF311
..... KF338
..... KF390
..... KF390.W6
..... KF390.5
..... KF390.5.P6
..... KF412
..... KF478
..... KF644
..... KF665
..... KF729
..... KF730
..... KF740
..... KF846.3
..... KF849
..... KF850
..... KF865
..... KF902
..... KF0390
..... KF1040
..... KF1068
..... KF1070
..... KF1080
..... KF1083
..... KF1146
..... KF1164
..... KF1289
..... KF1290
..... KF1296
..... KF1297.A8
..... KF1321
..... KF1439
..... KF1477
..... KF1600
..... KF1609
..... KF1616.I5
..... KF1649
..... KF1652
..... KF1657.C6
..... KF1657.T7
..... KF1681
..... KF1709.A315A2
..... KF1715
..... KF1870
..... KF1916
..... KF1975
..... KF1978
..... KF2009
..... KF2023
..... KF2138
..... KF2181
..... KF2187
..... KF2210
..... KF2212
..... KF2230
..... KF2254
..... KF2400
..... KF2426
..... KF2661
..... KF2750
..... KF2801
..... KF2803.36
..... KF2905
..... KF2913.F3
..... KF2915.N8
..... KF2915.N83
..... KF2915.P4
..... KF2920.3
..... KF2980
..... KF2994
..... KF2995
..... KF3095
..... KF3113
..... KF3125.C5
..... KF3139
..... KF3145
..... KF3181
..... KF3305
..... KF3310
..... KF3314
..... KF3315
..... KF3318
..... KF3319
..... KF3368
..... KF3369
..... KF3402
..... KF3404
..... KF3450
..... KF3465.A25
..... KF3467
340 ..... KF3484
..... KF3552
..... KF3555
..... KF3570
..... KF3574.C65
..... KF3574.S4
..... KF3608.A4
..... KF3643
..... KF3643.5
..... KF3643.8
..... KF3644
..... KF3675
..... KF3720
..... KF3735
..... KF3738
..... KF3775
..... KF3786
..... KF3787
..... KF3812
..... KF3813
..... KF3821
..... KF3825
..... KF3828
..... KF3869
..... KF3885
..... KF3890
..... KF3891.M2
..... KF3894.B5
..... KF3924.D3
..... KF3945
..... KF3989
..... KF4107
..... KF4118
..... KF4119
..... KF4120
..... KF4136
..... KF4137
..... KF4150
..... KF4155
..... KF4159
..... KF4162
..... KF4175
..... KF4225
..... KF4234
..... KF4242
..... KF4243
..... KF4280.O3
..... KF4280.S7
..... KF4315
..... KF4545.S5
..... KF4606
..... KF4651
..... KF4668
..... KF4689
..... KF4744
..... KF4748
..... KF4757
..... KF4774
..... KF4829
..... KF4842
..... KF4865
..... KF4881
..... KF4885
..... KF4886
..... KF4933
..... KF4935
..... KF4945
..... KF5060
..... KF5102
..... KF5155
..... KF5300
..... KF5336
..... KF5346.A3
..... KF5375
..... KF5390
..... KF5402
..... KF5406
..... KF5407
..... KF5417
..... KF5505
..... KF5532
..... KF5569
..... KF5594
..... KF5599
..... KF5605
..... KF5698
..... KF5701
..... KF5723.5
..... KF5724
..... KF5729
..... KF5730
..... KF5750
..... KF5753
..... KF5840
..... KF5865
..... KF6051
..... KF6200
..... KF6275
..... KF6275.5
..... KF6276
..... KF6297
..... KF6301
..... KF6320
..... KF6329
..... KF6335
..... KF6355
..... KF6355.4
..... KF6355.5
..... KF6356
..... KF6356.53
..... KF6368
..... KF6369
..... KF6369.3
..... KF6386

Dewey	LC
340	KF6443
	KF6449
	KF6450
	KF6465
	KF6477
	KF6482
	KF6495.I5
	KF6495.M5
	KF6535
	KF6566
	KF6571
	KF6572
	KF6584
	KF6614.A9
	KF6635
	KF6653
	KF6653.5
	KF6654
	KF6708.D8
	KF6730
	KF7263
	KF7265
	KF7274
	KF7680
	KF7704
	KF7710
	KF7710.Z95
	KF8228.N313
	KF8700
	KF9066.A5
	KF9242
	KF9444
	KF9445
	KF9710
	KFA1590
	KFA1590.A3
	KFA1640
	KFA4075
	KFC80
	KFC111.M5
	KFC111.W6
	KFC162
	KFC270
	KFC300
	KFC385
	KFC474.5
	KFC512
	KFC524.P5
	KFC545
	KFC547.E61
	KFC592
	KFC600.2
	KFC605
	KFC648
	KFC811
	KFC879.I5
	KFC1820
	KFC2145
	KFC2190
	KFC3897.8
	KFC3954
	KFC3975
	KFC4077
	KFD1503
	KFD1640
	KFF297
	KFF363
	KFF440
	KFF446
	KFF450
	KFF599.O8
	KFF599.P3
	KFG137
	KFG446
	KFH330
	KFH470
	KFI1337
	KFI1496
	KFI1497
	KFI1659.3
	KFI1660
	KFI1702
	KFI3080
	KFI3336.C6
	KFI3380.5.S7
	KFI3399
	KFI4439
	KFI4590
	KFI4592
	KFK1227
	KFK1385
	KFL234
	KFL331
	KFL450
	KFL599.S25
	KFM185
	KFM354
	KFM375
	KFM380.I6
	KFM380.5.S7
	KFM484
	KFM1542
	KFM1635.5
	KFM1799.B32
	KFM1799.C5
	KFM1799.P69
	KFM2523.W2
	KFM2756
	KFM2790
	KFM2835
	KFM2858
	KFM2859
	KFM2871.5
	KFM2877
340	KFM4531
	KFM4542
	KFM4545
	KFM4590
	KFM4640
	KFM5790
	KFM5885.T6
	KFM8142
	KFM8165
	KFM9420
	KFN875
	KFN896
	KFN926.5.P42
	KFN995.9.H3
	KFN999
	KFN1020
	KFN1044
	KFN1385
	KFN1551.D6
	KFN1584
	KFN2097
	KFN2097.6
	KFN2149
	KFN2153
	KFN2165
	KFN2190
	KFN2258
	KFN2275
	KFN4031
	KFN5568.P8
	KFN5590
	KFN5648
	KFN5750
	KFN5806
	KFN5813
	KFN7523.W2
	KFN7697
	KFN7790
	KFN7796
	KFN7820
	KFO297
	KFO381
	KFO390
	KFO435
	KFO470
	KFO2585
	KFO2765
	KFO2781
	KFO2844
	KFP137
	KFP196
	KFP272.D2
	KFP329.E6
	KFP332.8.P77
	KFP375
	KFP384
	KFP432
	KFP459
	KFP459.7
	KFP484
	KFR332
	KFR349
	KFR390
	KFS2253
	KFS3123.W2
	KFS3165
	KFT444
	KFT508
	KFT599.S8
	KFT1365
	KFT1435
	KFT1556
	KFT1568
	KFT1620
	KFV2732
	KFV2756
	KFV2853
	KFW349.2
	KFW356
	KFW380.A8
	KFW399
	KFW2420
	KFW2835
	KFW4590
	KFW4644
	KFX1061.A4
	KFX1066.A48
	KFX1068.A74
	KFX1068.A76
	KFX1096
	KFX1096.A78
	KFX1098.B3
	KFX1123
	KFX1123.B37
	KFX1123.B38
	KFX1124.B43
	KFX1154.B7
	KFX1181.B76
	KFX1211.C3
	KFX1216.C27
	KFX1216.C3
	KFX1218.C33
	KFX1218.C4
	KFX1281.C55
	KFX1311.C54
	KFX1317.C6
	KFX1319.C6
	KFX1341.C55
	KFX1341.C57
	KFX1341.C58
	KFX1341.C6
	KFX1343.D3
	KFX1401.D5
	KFX1401.D57
340	KFX1401.D6
	KFX1403.D8
	KFX1403.D85
	KFX1405.E2
	KFX1405.E3
	KFX1405.E54
	KFX1407.E43
	KFX1407.E5
	KFX1443.F3
	KFX1446
	KFX1446.G27
	KFX1446.G3
	KFX1449.G37
	KFX1449.G46
	KFX1449.G6
	KFX1449.G64
	KFX1449.G7
	KFX1449.G72
	KFX1454.G75
	KFX1454.H27
	KFX1454.H3
	KFX1483.H28
	KFX1486.H62
	KFX1511.H58
	KFX1515
	KFX1546.J32
	KFX1572
	KFX1601
	KFX1601.K47
	KFX1601.L27
	KFX1601.L3
	KFX1601.L33
	KFX1603.L3
	KFX1608.L37
	KFX1751.L6
	KFX1813.M3
	KFX1817.M37
	KFX1846
	KFX1909
	KFX1909.M62
	KFX1935.N3
	KFX2080
	KFX2109.O2
	KFX2109.O25
	KFX2109.O3
	KFX2112.O7
	KFX2112.O73
	KFX2112.O86
	KFX2112.P33
	KFX2112.P34
	KFX2112.P35
	KFX2116
	KFX2119.P38
	KFX2119.P4
	KFX2173.P5
	KFX2179.P6
	KFX2263.R59
	KFX2266.S27
	KFX2277.S3
	KFX2289.1.A3
	KFX2301.S3
	KFX2371.S33
	KFX2375.S2
	KFX2375.S3
	KFX2377.S4
	KFX2382.S5
	KFX2382.S53
	KFX2382.S6
	KFX2384.S6
	KFX2384.S63
	KFX2396.S78
	KFX2428.T6
	KFX2501.T8
	KFX2503
	KFX2503.V4
	KFX2536.W36
	KFX2536.W37
	KFX2536.W47
	KFX2541.W5
	KFX2546.W47
	KFX2546.W5
	KFX2549.W5
	KFX2549.W53
	KFX2593.Z5
	KFZ2875
	L142
	L152
	LB2342
	Q11
	Q101
	QE81
	RA11.B19
	S541
	S544
	TD180
	TL526.G7
	VK371
340.01	AS9
	B1574
	JC181
	KF380
	KF382
340.018	KF240
	KF242.A1
	KF580
340.0202	KF319
340.023	KF297
	KF298
340.02461073	KF2915.N8
340.0246513	KFT1277
340.025749	KF192.N4
340.03	KF156
340.0627471	KF334.N4
	KF334.N4A845
340.07	KF275
	KFN5078
340.071	KF281
340.071142	HX11
340.071173	AS122.B4
	KF385
340.0711753	KF292.G4
340.071176184	KF292.A5
340.071273	KF281
	KF281.F7
340.072073	KF240
340.076	KF388
340.08	KF389
340.0924	KF368.C4
	KF368.M3
	KF368.P44
340.0942	KF380
	KF385
340.0973	KF211
	KF213
	KF213.B4
	KF213.H33
	KF292.H35
	KF352
	KF361
	KF379
	KF384
	KF386
	KF387
	KF394
	KF412
	KF888
	KF8700
	KFT1281
340.09747	KFN5080
	KFN5081
340.09749	KFN1881
340.09753	KFD1281
340.09755	KFV2430.5
340.09759	KFF15.2
	KFF81
340.09764	KFT1281
340.09769	KFK1227
340.09773	KFI1281
340.09778	KFM7881
340.09791	KFA2478
340.099141	DS666.I15
340.1	JC153
	JC571
	KF380
340.10924	KF373
340.11	KF8700.Z9
340.4	KF224.N4
340.570922	KF299.J4
340.6	AS122
	E842.9
	KF2905.3
	KF9242
	RA1016
	RA1051
	RA1151
	RD120.7
340.608	RA1053
341	DS126.5
	HX11
	J74.A36
	JC319
	JX41
	JX68
	JX235.9
	JX1248
	JX1249
	JX1395
	JX1398
	JX1582
	JX1971
	JX1977
	JX1979
	JX1995
	JX3091
	JX3110
	JX3110.C6
	JX3140
	JX3160
	JX3180
	JX3185
	JX3225
	JX3695.C35
	JX3695.H9
	JX3695.I5
	JX4003
	JX4053
	JX4084.S32
	JX4173
	JX5268
	KF26.F633
	KF6074
	KF6075
	S962
341.0186	JX68
341.0202	JX1297
	JX3160.N4
341.026	JX1977
341.02603	JX1226
341.026644073	JX235
341.026673	JX235.9
341.0904	JX68
341.0947	JX1555
	JX1555.Z5
341.097303	KF26.J837
341.1	D839.3
	JC363
	JX1930
	JX1937

Dewey	LC
341.1	JX1944
	JX1948
	JX1950
	JX1952
	JX1953
	JX1961.U6
	JX1963
	JX1974
	JX1995
	JX3091
341.1072	JX1961.I5
341.108	JX1977
341.10924	JX1962.B7
	JX1962.C6
341.11	JX1954
	JX1995
341.11094	D234
341.110973	JX1950
341.12	D727
	JX1937
	JX1975
	JX1975.5.U5
	JX1977
341.120924	D727
341.12948	JX1975.5.S29
341.12954	JX1975.5.I4
341.13	E744
	JX1952
	JX1974
	JX1977
	JX1977.E393
	JX1977.Z8
	JX1977.2.A1
	JX1977.2.U5
	JX1977.8.P85
	KF27.F648
	KF32.F6
341.1301519	JX1977
341.13029	JX1977
341.1308	JX1977
341.1309	JX1977
341.132	JX1976.4
	JX1977
341.133	JX1907
	JX1977.A48
	JX1977.A48U6
341.135	JX1977
341.137	JX1977
341.1370924	D839.7.H3
341.139	JX1981.P7
	JX4027
341.13942	JX1977.2.G7
341.13951	E183.8.C5
341.13954	JX1977.2.I47
341.13954670	JX1977.2.K38
341.13954913	DS485.K2
341.13956	D839.3
	JX1977.2.N4
	JX1977.2.P34
341.1395694	JX1977.2.P34
341.139612	DT236
341.1396891	JX1977.2.R5
341.13971	JX355
341.13973	JX1977.2.U5
	JX1981.P7
341.18	JX1930.I75
	JX1979
341.1816612	UA646.3
341.181713	JN94
341.181812	F1402
	F1405.5
	JX1404
	KF27.F646
341.181821	D845
	JX1954
	UA646.3
341.184	D351
	D1060
	HC241.2
	JN24
	JX1979
341.186	JX1582
	JX1582.C4
341.18729	JX1979
341.1896	KF27.F648
341.2	D460
	J74
	JX68
	JX120
	JX171
	JX234
	JX234.A23
	JX235
	JX235.7
	JX235.9
	JX235.9.A32
	JX238
	JX626
	JX640.I7
	JX959
	JX1974
	JX1977
	JX4165
	JX5810
	KF26.F6
	KF26.F643
341.22	TX1975
341.23	JX1977
341.2394	JV5318
341.24	JX626
341.2415	JX640.I7
341.242	JX636
341.242073	JX235.9
341.24209612	JX637
341.243073	JX235.9
341.2431	DD261.4
341.2438073	JX235.9
341.244073	JX235.9
341.244949073	JX235.9
341.245073	JX235.9
341.247052	DS517.7
341.247073	JX235.9
341.2481073	JX235.9
341.2485073	JX235.9
341.2489073	JX235.9
341.24912073	JX235.9
341.2492073	JX235.9
341.2493073	JX235.9
341.24935073	JX235.9
341.2494073	JX235.9
341.2497073	JX235.9
341.2498073	JX235.9
341.251	JX1570
341.251073	JX235.9
341.25195073	JX235.9
341.252073	JX235.9
341.2538073	JX235.9
341.254073	JX235.9
341.2549073	JX235.9
341.25491073	JX235.9
341.255073	JX235.9
341.2561073	JX235.9
341.2581073	JX235.9
341.2593073	JX235.9
341.25952073	JX235.9
341.2597073	JX235.9
341.26	DS149
341.2611073	JX235.9
341.264073	JX235.9
341.2661073	JX235.9
341.26651073	JX235.9
341.2666073	JX235.9
341.2667073	JX235.9
341.271073	JX235.9
341.271083	JX235.9
341.272073	JX235.9
341.27283073	JX235.9
341.27293073	JX235.9
341.272973073	JX235.9
341.272983073	JX235.9
341.273	JX235.9
	JX236
	JX1407
	JX4165
	KF8205
341.273042	JX235.9
341.273043	JX235.9
341.2730437	JX235.9
341.273044	JX235.9
341.273046	JX235.9
	KF26.F6
341.273047	JX235.9
341.2730471	JX234.A23
341.2730497	JX235.9
341.2730519	JX235.9
341.27305195	JX235.9
341.273052	JX235.9
341.27305493	JX235.9
341.2730561	JX235.9
341.2730581	JX235.9
341.2730597	JX235.9
341.2730611	JX235.9
341.2730664	JX235.9
341.27306681	JX234.A23
341.27306741	JX235.9
341.27306894	JX235.9
341.273071	JX235.9
	KF6669.M6
341.273072	JX235.9
341.27307293	JX235.9
341.273072983	JX235.9
341.273081	JX235.9
341.273082	JX235.9
	JX235.9.A32
341.273083	JX235.9
	JX235.9.A32
341.273084	JX235.9
341.273085	JX235.9
341.2730861	JX235.9
341.2730862	JX235.9
341.2730892	JX235.9
341.273091	JX235.9
341.2730914	JX235.9
341.2730931	JX235.9
341.273094	JX235.9
341.27309614	JX235.9
341.2914	JX1576
341.294	JX1165.9
341.3	AS4.U8
	D361
	JX4521
	JX5313.G7
	KF27.I5536
341.31	JX4275
	JX4481
	JX6731.W3
341.33	JX5141
341.3509	JX5371
341.36	JX1295
	JX5261.U6
341.39	JX238
341.4	JX6731.W3
341.46	JX5771
341.5	J74
	JX628
	JX4093
	JX4143
	KF26.C6
341.5	KF26.F663
	KF26.I539
341.52	JX1952
	JX5124
	JX5810
	TL507
341.55	JX5486.F7
341.57	F1405.5
	HF345
	JX636
	JX1977
	JX4143
	JX4408
	JX4419
	JX4425
	JX5763.I53
	KF26.C652
	KF6708.D8
	TL500
341.58	JX1977
341.59	JX4131
	KF410
	KF412
341.590973	KF412
341.6	F2691.C4
	JX1952
	JX1981.P7
	JX4473
	JX4475
	UA11
341.63	DX1981.P7
	JX68
	JX238
	JX238.P6
	JX1952
	JX1977
	JX1981.P7
	KF31.F6
341.65	F1034
	JX1246
	JX4481
341.67	JX1907
	JX1974
	JX1974.5
	JX1974.7
	JX5135.C5
	KF26.A784
	KF27.F6
	KF32.F663
	UG447
341.670947	DK54
341.672	JX1907
	JX1974
	JX1974.7
	KF26.F627
	U162
	UF767
341.6720943	JX1974.7
341.675	JX1974
341.7	JX1570
	JX1577
	JX1683.F6
	JX1705
	JX1706
	JX1995
	JX4173
	JX4263.P7
	KF26.F6
341.73	JX1974
	JX1974.7
341.8	JX234
342	JF36
	KF1262
	KF4748
342.24	KF4550
342.41029	JN1411
342.42	JN147
	JN237
342.42029	JN118
342.4209	JN118.S9
	JN121
	JN128
342.42909	JN1152
342.49409	DQ55
342.49509	JN5016
342.49709	JN9662
342.5409	JQ211
	JQ215
342.54909	JQ543
342.549309	JQ652
342.6809	JQ1911
	JQ1918
342.7	JK54
342.71	JL15
342.7101	JL61
342.7109	JL15
	JL65
342.72972202	KFZ5201
342.73	E211
	E441
	E441.S764
	E680
	J11
	JV6455
	JX1407
	KF26.J837
	KF27.R8
	KF32.J8
	KF4530
	KF4541
	KF4549
	KF4550
	KF4600
	KF4651
342.73	KF4748
	KF4749
	KF4755
	KF4757
	KF9625
342.7301	JK146
	JK161.M4
	JK169
	JK176
	JK271
	KF31.R8
	KF3920
	KF4550
	KF4558
	KF4748
	KF4757
	KF4893
	KFC680
342.7302	JK141
	JK146
	JK3925
	KF4510
342.73024	JK34
	JK161
342.73029	E210
	KF4575
342.7303	JK216
	KF213.M3
	KF4541
	KF4549
	KF4550
	KF4555
	KF4600
342.7304	JK261
342.7305	JK1356.A2
	KF27.S7
	KF4905
	KF4935
	KF4935.A25
342.7306	KF26.D555
342.73062	JK558
	KF5060
342.73066	KF26.G655
342.7307	KF4756
342.7308	JK171
342.73085	E93
	KF4545.S5
	KF4749
	KF4750
	KF4757
	KF4783
342.7309	JK31
	JK39
	JK166
	JK171
	JK171.A1
	JK216
	JK268
	JK273
	JK310
	JK371.I6
	JK2413
	KF4514
	KF4528
	KF4541
	KF4541.B2
	KF4550
	KF4744
342.74401	KFM2801
342.74402	KFM2801
342.74702	JK3425
	KFN5680
342.74802	KFP401
342.748042	KFP87.Z9L4
342.74903	KFN2201
342.75101	KFD401
342.75102	KFD401
	KFD1601
342.75201	KFM1601
342.75202	KFM1601
342.7525109	KFM1799.P69
342.755	KFV2801
342.75502	JK3925
342.755020922	F230
342.75601	KFN7801
342.75603	KFN7801
342.757	KFS2201
342.758	JK4316
342.759	KFF401
342.75901	KFF401
342.75909	JK4425
342.764	KFT1601
342.76601	KFO1601
342.76802	JK5225
342.77301	KFI1670
342.77302	JK5725
342.77303	KFI1601
342.77309	KFI1601.5
342.77501	KFW2801
342.77701	KFI4601
342.77801	KFM8201
342.783	KFS3401
342.788	KFC2201
342.793	KFN1001
342.794	KFC680
342.79401	KFC680
342.79402	JK8725
342.79403	KFC680
342.79709	JA37
342.9409	DU115
342.96902	KFH401
343	JX1977
	KF27.J8666
	KF9218

Dewey	LC
343	KF9223
	KFD1766.5
	KFZ2968.F75
343.0924	HV6555.A8
	KF373.F6
	KF373.H64
	KF373.L45
343.0973	K9223
	KF32.J8
	KF4765
	KF9217
	KF9218
	KF9219
	KF9219.3
	KF9223
	KF9350
	KF9618
	KF9625
	KF9646
	KF9710
	KF9750
343.097303	HV8073
	KF26.J837
	KF31.J8
	KF220
	KF9219
	KF9219.3
	KF9223
	KF9223.5
	KF9614
	KF9618
	KF9619
	KF9619.3
	KF9625
	KF9630
	KF9640
	KF9642
	KF9650
	KF9655
	KF9662
	KF9710
	KFM5975
343.0974103	KFM575
343.09742	KFN1761
343.09744	KFM2961
343.0974403	KFM2992
343.09746	KFC4162
343.09747	KFN6100
343.0974701	KFN6100
343.0974703	KFN6155
343.097471	KFX2007.35
343.0974803	KFP575
343.09749	KFN2361
343.0974903	KFN2380.5.W5
343.0975203	KFM1775
343.09753	KF32.D5
	KFD1762
343.0975303	KED1639
	KF27.D5644
343.0975803	KFG510
	KFG576.5
343.0975903	KFF583
343.09763	KFL561
343.0976303	KFL575
343.0976403	KFT1775
	KFT1780.5.E9
343.0976903	KFK1227
343.0977303	KFI1766.5
	KFI1783.A65
343.0977603	KFM5979
343.097803	KF9619.3
343.09783	KFS3578
343.0978603	KFM9575
343.09787	KFW4271.5
343.09793	KFN1192
343.09794	KFC1100
343.0979401	KFC1100
343.0979403	KFC1100
	KFC1165
	KFC1171
	KFC1194
343.0979404	KFC1100
343.0979501	KFO2961
343.0979504	KFO2975
343.09798	KFA562
343.1	HV6446
	KF9625
	KF9666.5
	KFC1155
343.10973	KF8920
343.209769	KFK1227
343.31	DB215.5
	DS135.R95K63
	KF223.Z4
	KF224
	KF224.H3
	KF224.N37
	KF224.S45
343.310924	KF223.B8
343.310926	KF224.S5
	KF224.S62
343.33	KF6334
343.331	KF223.V4
343.332	KF5075
343.34	KF8782.C5
343.43	F2384
	KFC666
	Q11
343.430977311	KF224.D37
343.457	KF224.S6
343.5	E450.L4
343.520924	KF373
343.523	E215.4
	HV6534.A6
343.523	HX84
	KF224
	KF224.M6
	KF224.T45
343.5230922	KF224
	KF224.S2
343.5230924	DA787.A1
	KF223
	KF224.B7
343.5230926	KF224
343.5230973	KF221.M8
343.5230977311	KF223.S5
343.524	E842.9
343.5250973	KF228
343.53	KF224.G5
	KF9328.S6
	KF9448
343.54	E450
343.55	KF224.D4
	KF9315
	KFC1121
	KFN6121
343.56	KF1266
343.570973	KF3890
	KF3890.A25
343.64	KF224.B4
343.7301	KF26.J8
343.73025	KF27.V424
343.73036	KF27.D5644
343.7304	KF6297
	KF6320
	KF6355
	KF6369
	KF6369.8.F3
343.73040269	KF26.J855
343.7305	KF6335
343.73050262	KF6335
343.73052	KF6368
	KF6369.6
	KF6452
343.73053	KF6572
343.73055	KF6600
	KF6614
	KF6616
343.73066	KF1439
343.7307	KF1600
343.730720269	KF1610
343.73074	KF27.F6
	KF1659
343.730873510262	KF26.A35334
343.73088	KF593.C6
343.73096	KF1104
343.730964	KF26.C688
343.7309640262	KF27.I5587
343.730994	KF26.C634
	KF27.I5538
343.74	KF26.P6
	KF9444
	KFN2371.O2
343.740973	KF27.J8666
	KF9444
343.78	KF27.A365
	KF27.I5568
344	KF5063
344.273084	JX235.9
344.49301	HD8051
344.7301110262	KF32.E3
344.73013980262	KF26.L334
344.7301890264	KF3408
344.7303892632	KF3720
344.73041	KF26.C636
	KF27.I5568
344.73046	KF26.C645
	KF27.P874
344.730463	KF26.C645
344.7305330262	KF27.J8666
344.730545	KF3890
344.73063635	KF27.P874
344.73074	KF4225
344.7470542	KFN5645
344.753054102632	KFD1575
344.753079112	KF32.E3
344.767078	KFA3993
345.1	KF2138
345.11	KF51
	KF4748
	KF7721
	KF8839
345.12	KFC3615.2
	KFL15.2
	KFL312
	KFM4215
	KFV2425.2
	KFW2420
345.22	KF5313
	KFC30.5
	KFC30.5.W4
	KFC455
	KFC3630
	KFH30
	KFI1230
	KFK1230
	KFM4230
	KFM5430
	KFN39
	KFS3030
345.32	KF209
	KFM4215.2
	KFO2425.5
345.4	KF105
	KF213
345.42	KFC47.2
	KFD59
	KFI4239
345.42	KFK1239
	KFN59
	KFN5045.2
	KFW479.5
345.5	KF135.N72
	KF604
	KF5735
345.51	KF125.C51
	KF4545.S5
	KF4549
	KF5375
345.52	KFK1259
	KFM2445
345.73	KF9219.6
345.730247	KF2231
345.7302523	KF224.R63
345.7302570262	KF3890
345.730274	KF9444
345.7305	KF220
	KF9619.3
345.73050262	KF25.E243
345.73052	KF9223
	KF9630
345.7307	KF224.F7
345.747075	KF224.B67
345.748	KFP561
345.75305	KFD1762
345.756052	KFN7976.Z9
345.78883	JK7845
345.794	KFC1100
345.79406	KFC1030
345.7950802648	KFO2986
346.42052	CR3899
346.73002462	KF902
346.73002477	KF2042.P45
346.73012	KF479
346.73026	TA180
346.7303	KF1107
	KF1423
346.73045	KF5698
346.73046	KF27.I5554
346.7304678	KF26.I538
	KF31.I5
346.73046780262	KF31.I5
346.730469170262	KF26.I542
346.730488	KF3178.4
346.73064	KF27.J8666
	KF2901
	KF4234
346.73065	HD255
346.7306520262	KF27.B3
346.73066	KF1414
346.7307	KF879.514
346.73074	KF27.I5536
346.73077	KF1024
	KF9246
346.7308	KF26.B355
346.73086	KF1290.A9
346.73092	KF1439
346.73096	KF957
346.739162	KF27.J8666
346.744070269	KFM2480
346.747033	KFN5317
346.74705	KFN5205
346.74803	KFP195
	KFP539.P4
346.748045	KFP458
346.748066	KFP210
346.7525104502633	
	KFM1799.P7
346.753064	KF27.I537
346.771059	KFO147
346.7730450269	KFI1658
346.77503	KFW2595
346.777066	KFI4280
346.7880437	KFC2082.R4
347	E99.C5
	KF27.F648
	KF385
	KF390.5.D6
	KF390.5.P6
	KF526
	KF604
	KF886
	KF1190
	KF1251
	KF1388
	KF1414
	KF1609
	KF1657.C6
	KF2094
	KF2661
	KF2750
	KF2980
	KF8992
	KFK329.E61
	KFM2610
	KFM2697
	KFM9305
	KFN3897.4
	KFN5339
	KFO305
	KFP213
	KFS3329.E61
	KFT1352
	TL152.55.G7
	TL152.55.S6
347.0973	KF387
	KF412
347.09771	KFO80
347.09773	KFI1281
347.1	E185.93.V8
	E450
	KF479
347.1	KF4757
	KF9709
347.2	JK5274
	KF26.I5
	KF581
	KF590
	KF636
	KF661
	KF662
	KF665
	KF670
	KF695
	KF730
	KF1865
	KF5599
	KFC2082.R4
	KFN1917
	KFN5171
	KFO126
	KFW2817
347.20973	KF560
	KF570
347.209741	KFM112
347.209747	KFN5140
	KFN5446.R3
347.209752	KFM1277
347.209771	KFO112
347.209775	KFW2512
347.209794	KFC140
347.22	KFK1230
347.3	KF1049
	KF4545.S5
347.30973	KF705
347.4	HG2999.S4
	KF801
	KF1017
	KF1078
	KF1080
	KF1244
	KF1530.R3
	KF2023
	KF5735
	KF6738.B2
	KFC270
	KFC1066
	KFI1385
	KFO196.3.A8
	KFW4330
	S21
347.40973	KF801
347.409748	KFP150
347.409763	KFL150
347.42	KFC267
	KFD1376.C6
347.420923	KF915
347.420973	KF915
347.5	KF561
	KF1215
	KF1249
	KF1250
	KF1257
	KF1266
	KF2915.N83
	KF3825
	KF3825.3
	KF8925.A9
	KF8925.P4
	KFC310
	KFC547.A73
	KFC1028.P4
347.50973	KF445
	KF1249
	KF1250
	KF1285
	KF8925.P4
347.509763	KFL195
347.509774	KFM4396
	KFM4740.5.N4
347.509776	KFM5595
347.6	HQ811
	KF510
	KF526
	KF535
	KF537
	KF1466
	KFC126
	KFG91.M5
	KFI1300
	KFK1294
	KFN1900
	KFV2500
347.60973	KF505
347.609794	KFC115
347.609795	KFO2494
347.65	HF3023.K35
	KF750
	KF755
	KF759.K5
	KF778
	KF1173.4
	KF1175
	KF1466
	KF6297
	KF6572
	KF6585
	KFF140
	KFI1340
	KFI1347
	KFM5547
	KFN100
	KFN1940
	KFN5201
	KFN5210
	KFP142

347.65 KFP482
347.650922 KF758
347.650973 KF755
347.6509752 KFM1347
347.6509759 KFF137
347.6509771 KFO80
KFO142
347.6509773 KFI1340
347.6509774 KFM4344
347.6509776 KFM5544
347.6509778 KFM7947
347.7 HC251
KF27.A3336
KF27.I5536
KF593.C6
KF890
KF957
KF975
KF977
KF1008
KF1024
KF1039
KF1040
KF1045
KF1048
KF1049
KF1068
KF1070
KF1071
KF1078
KF1296
KF1344
KF1345
KF1365
KF1366
KF1375
KF1413
KF1414
KF1414.3
KF1416
KF1436
KF1439
KF1440
KF1448
KF1477
KF1501
KF1521
KF1524
KF1544
KF1627
KF1645
KF1649
KF1659
KF2023
KF6075
KF6400
KFC270
KFD213
KFF175
KFI3179
KFK1365
KFM7979
KFN2013
KFN5345
KFP213
KFT1525.5
KFV2565
KFW213
347.7016 KF890
347.70973 KF26.F5
KF879
KF888
KF889
KF889.3
KF890
KF4606
347.709747 KFN5340
347.709758 KFG213
347.709771 KFO152
347.709781 KFK30
347.709791 KFA2552
347.709793 KFN752
347.73075 KF8915
347.732234 KF373.H37
347.7324 KF8752
347.7326 KF213.F68
KF8748
347.732634 KF32.J848
347.7364 KF8964
347.7372 KF8900
347.746 KFC4130
347.74806 KFP540
347.74905 KFN2330
347.75 KF32.J8
KF1103
KF1105
KF1121
347.750973 KF26.C652
KF1104
347.76405 KFT1280
347.771 KFO80
347.77105 KFO529
KFO530.M3
347.77305 KFI1730
347.77605 KFM5480
347.80973 KF400
347.809794 KF400
347.9 KF5130
KFW2620
347.91 KF8984
KF9632
KFN542
347.92 KFN6050
347.93 KFC860
347.93 KFM5477
347.930973 KF170
347.9309747 KFN5068
347.9309771 KFO68
347.9309772 KFI3080
347.94 KF27.J8666
KF8934
KF8935
KF8964
KF9664
KFM2480
347.940973 KF32.J8
KF8934
KF8935
347.9409747 KFN6030
347.95 KF9052
KFI1755
347.950973 KF9050
347.96 KF26.J855
347.99 KF8742
347.990924 E664.L2
347.9922 KF8744
347.9924 CT275.P5557
E415.9.C96
J74.A36
JK4401
KF26.J8
KF26.J858
KF31.J8
KF32.J848
KF213.K4
KF363.W9
KF368.K4
KF368.P36
KF373
KF8745
KF8745.B67
KF8745.C3
KF8745.D6
KF8745.E4
KF8745.F5
KF8745.H3
KF8745.J27
KF8745.M3
PS1981
347.9942 DA670.B29
347.9973 CD3041.S8
E447
KF26.J8
KF26.J833
KF26.J835
KF26.J855
KF26.J874
KF27.J8666
KF30.C65
KF31.J846
KF32.J8
KF220
KF281
KF380
KF384
KF2232
KF4155
KF4549
KF4550
KF4575
KF5130
KF5599
KF8700
KF8719
KF8720
KF8735
KF8742
KF8748
KF8750
KF8781
KF8815
KF8816
KF8820
KF8839
KF8840
KF8841
KF8858
KF8870
KF8900
KF8915
KF8925.P4
KF8935
KF8968
KF8984
KF9050
KF9052
KF9057
KF9223
KF9618
KF9619
KF9625
KF9709
KF9710
KF9756
KFC992
347.99741 KFM530
347.99743 KFV529
347.99744 J87
KFM2821
KFM2929
347.99745 KFR80
KFR510
347.99746 KFC3678
347.99747 KFN5979
KFN5990
KFN5995
KFN6012
347.99748 KFP530
347.9974891 KF355.B8
347.99749 KFN2329
347.99752 KFM1715
KFM1730
347.99753 KF27.D5644
347.99755 KFV2920
KFV2937
347.997554 KFV2478
347.99756 KFN7910
347.99759 KFF529
KFF529.A2
KFF537
KFF538
347.99761 KFA512
KFA575
347.99762 KF26.J8
KFM6665
347.99763 KFL529
347.99764 KFT1729
347.99768 KFT529
KFT586
347.99771 KFO530
KFO538
347.99772 KFI3080
KFI3528
347.99773 KFI1268
KFI1708
KFI1729
KFI1730
KFI1738
347.99774 KFM4280
KFM4729
KFM4730
347.99776 KFM5929
KFM5938
KFM5975
347.99777 KFI4729
347.99778 KFM8325.5.N6
KFM8329
KFM8340
KFM8342
347.99788 KFC1820
KFC2342
347.99793 KFN1129
347.99794 KF209
KFC30
KFC592.1
KFC950
KFC985.S4
KFC992
KFC1010
KFC1030
KFC1047
KFC1177
347.99796 KFI20
347.99797 KFW80
KFW529
KFW529.A2
347.99969 KFH515
348.4 KF1070
348.7346 KF4547.8
348.755 KFV2430
348.771047 KFO59
348.795027 KFO2439
348.795047 KFO2459
349.37 AS122
350 AS36
JF1351
JF1621
JQ224
JX1977
350.00018 JF1525.A8
JK468.A8
JS344.E4
350.000186 JF1338
JF1351
350.000207 PN6231.P79
350.000711 JF1338
350.000715 JF1338
350.0007152 JF1338.D27
350.00072073 JF1338.A2
350.0008 JF1351
JK9201
350.0009 JF1341
350.001 JF1351
350.0030922 D849
350.007 JF1525.E8
350.0092 HD4295.5
350.0914 CD3026
350.10018 JK468.A8
350.1008 JF1001
JF1601
350.102 HV7936.S8
350.150973 HF5549.5.T7
350.170973 HD8008
HD8008.A1
350.1740973 HD8008
350.6096 JQ1892
350.71 RA968
350.721 HJ236
350.722 JX1977
350.7232 E97
350.724 JX1977
350.7242 HD1393
350.7246 JX1977
350.74 HV7936.R4
350.7520601 JX1977
350.755 UA926
350.756 HV8055
350.823 HD1411
350.85 Q127.U6
350.864 HE333
350.87 HE193
350.87103 TD224.C3
350.877503 HE741
350.895 JC328.3
350.9 JF1525.E8
351.00094 JF1351
351.00095 JQ5
351.0092 HD3850
351.1 JF1601
351.15091724 JX1977
351.3 JK716
351.309747 JK3458
351.4 JK716
351.721094 HJ236
351.77 HD7260
351.83 HD6097
351.87 HE148.5
351.895098 Q180
352 AS36.C2
BV4327
JS78
JS425
JX1977
352.00018 JS344.E4
JS344.E42
352.0002542 JS3137
352.0008 JS78
352.0009 JS78
JS3111
352.000924 DA676.8.A1
F534.G2
F548.52
352.000941 JS4115
JS4133
352.0009416 JS4403
352.000942 HC260.C63
JF1351
JS3045.P3
JS3095
JS3111
JS3113
JS3137
JS3158
JS3270
LA635
352.0009424 HJ9423
352.000943 JS3111
352.000951 JS7352
352.000954 JS7005
JS7008
352.00095414 JS7025.W4
352.000954792 JS7025.M35
352.0009549 JS7092
352.0009561 JS6952
352.000966 JQ1879.W4
352.0009678 JS7697.2
352.000968 JS7639.2
352.000971613 HD4610.P5
352.000972 JS2108
352.000973 JS308
JS331
JS345
JS408
352.0009744 JS451.M44
352.00097467 JS451.C85
352.0009747 JS451.N75
352.0009749 JS451.N5
JS451.N55
352.0009756 JS451.N85
352.0009757 JS451.S65
352.0009758 KFG430
352.0009758794 JS1536.W516
352.0009759 JS451.F65
352.0009773 JS451.I3A5
JS451.I35
352.00097756 JS451.W65
352.0009777 JK7501
JS451.I85
352.0009783 JS451.S8
352.0009788 KFC2230
352.0009795 JS451.O75
352.000983 JS2458
352.0009941 JS8192
352.00220973 JS345
352.00291 JS674.A15053
KFP198.M8
352.0030973 KF5313
352.00309746 JS451.C85
352.00309752 KFM1631.5
352.005 HD8051
JK7501
JS148
TH439
352.0050942 JS3175
352.0050954 JS7014.A2
352.005095492 JS7094
352.0050971 JS1714
352.00509744 J87
352.00509753 KF27.D5644
352.005170973 HD8008.A1
352.006 JS344.A5
352.007 JS3095
352.0070954 JS7008
352.007095496 JQ1825.N4
352.0072073 JS331
352.0072497 JN9663
352.007309549 HC440.5
352.007309756 JS451.N85
352.007309768 JS451.T35
352.007309789 JS451.N65
352.007309796 JK7501
352.007309797 JS451.W25
352.008 HT151
JS78
JS345
JS346

352.008	JS423
	JS8273.F7
352.00808	JS308
352.0080922	JK2752
352.0080942	JS7.G58
	JS3025
	JS3041
352.0080952135	AS9
352.0080954	JS7001
	JS7008
352.00809543	JS7025.S3
352.008095492	JS45
352.008095496	JQ1825.N4
352.0080968	JS7532
352.0080971	JS1708
352.008097127	JS1721.M3
352.0080973	AS36.C2
	JS323
	JS331
	JS341
	JS356
	JS422
	KF5300
	KF5305
352.00809749	JS451.N55
352.00809756	JS451.N85
352.00809774	JS451
352.0080977447	JS593.B565
352.00809775	JS451.W65
352.00809789	JS451.N65
352.00809794	AS36.C2
352.00809796	JK7501
352.00809944	JS8293.N6
352.00840973	JS344.C5
352.0085496	JQ1825.N4
352.0090954	JS7008
352.009095493	JS7123.A3
352.00909745	JS451.R45
352.00909769	JS451.K45
352.00909781	JS451.K25
352.00909795	KFO2830
352.00920954792	HC437.M32
352.00940973	JS422
352.009409748	HD4606.P4
352.042	JS3095
	JS3111
	JS3200
352.0421	JS3325.L5L57
	JS3600
	JS3711.H35
352.04246	JS3970.W6
352.04274	JS3918
352.0429	JS4012.L7
352.05414	JS7052
352.0643	JS7809.9.C35
352.0713541	JS1789
352.07462	JS344.E43G53
352.07468	F104.N6
352.0747	JS451
352.07471	F128.52
352.0747277	JS451.N79W735
352.0753	KF27.D5644
	KF32.D5
352.0758277	JS751.C812
352.075843	JS883.9.F6
352.0758794	JS1536.W515
352.0769	JS451
352.077178	JS738
352.0773	JS451.I3
352.077481	JS541.A6
352.078958	F804.L6
352.0794	JS451.C25
352.079432	JS721.C43
352.079461	F869.S3
	JS451.C28S37
352.079549	HD4606.G7
352.0852	JS2678.L52
352.093127	JS8392
352.0944	JS8278
352.0945	JS8181
352.0947	JQ4099.A83
352.0954	JS7008
352.095456	DS486.D3
352.096894	JS7642.9.L82
352.097135	JS1721.O58
352.0974854	JS999.L28
352.1	HJ9105
352.1018	AS36
352.10942	HJ9041
	HJ9423
352.1095455	HJ9066.H35
352.109748	HJ9306.7
352.10974811	HD3858
352.109773	HJ9227
352.109796	HJ9224
352.12	HJ9111
	HJ9423
352.1209749	HJ9011.N5
352.1209768	HC107.T3
352.1209771	JK5574
352.13	HE5663
352.130954792	HJ3604
352.1309772	JF495.I4
352.1309773	KFI1691.R4
352.13109746	KFC4078
352.16	HD205
	JK8049.R4
352.16409768	JK5249.R4
352.17	HJ9733
352.1709753	KF27.G676
352.1709756	HJ9885.A3
352.2	HV7595.D5
	HV8001
	HV8138
352.20942	HV8195
352.20973	HV7991
	HV8138
	JA37
352.30979494	TH9505.L804
352.509753	KF26.D5
	KF27.P868
352.6	JS451.W45
352.6094281	TD564.D3
352.75	HC251
352.75097471	HD7304.N5
	TX960
352.7509753	KF26.D5
352.92023	TH439
352.9423	KF26.D5
352.944	HV751.A6
	KF27.D5
	KF27.G659
352.944094272	HN398.L3
352.94409753	HV8328
352.945	LA635
352.950954	HD8039.R462I52
352.96	NA9000
352.96025748	HT167.5.P4
352.96025771	HT393.O4
352.96028	HD111
352.960942	JS3111
352.96094259	HT169.G72
352.960943	HT395.G4
352.960973	HT123
	JS341
	KF5698
352.960974776	NA9000.B53
352.9609774	HD1751
352.96097953	HD211.O7
352.961	KF5698
352.9610973	HT123
	HT166
	HT167
352.96109744	J87.M4
352.96109748	HE356.P4
352.96109753	KF32.D5
352.980973	KF9223
352.98097526	KFX1117
352.9809753	KF27.D585
353	E846
	HE18
	HJ10.C7
	HJ10.F4
	JF1351
	JK34
	JK271
	JK325
	JK421
	JK649
	KF25.E243
	KF26.G6443
	KF26.G655
	KF26.J833
	KF27.G659
	KF27.G663
	KF27.J8666
353.00018	JK468.A8
353.000202	JK274
353.0007	KF5753
353.0008	Z7165.U5
353.001	JK718
	JK2462
	KF26.F6
	KF26.L363
	KF26.P6
	KF26.P637
	KF27.E336
	KF27.P653
	KF5336
353.00100202	JK635
353.0011232	KF26.P637
353.0012	HD5876.G4
	JK775
	KF27.P636
	KF27.P653
	KF27.P66
353.00122	KF27.P666
	KF5375
353.00123	JK775
	KF26.P6
	KF27.J8
	KF27.P636
	KF27.P653
353.001232	JK775
	KF27.P636
353.001320924	E839.8.O8
353.00145	JK775
353.0015	JF1338
	JK718
353.001622	KF27.E345
	RA395.A3
353.001623	KF27.G659
353.001625	HD5875
	KF26.5.A384
353.00164	KF27.P653
353.0017	HD8008
353.00172	HD8008
353.00173	HD8008
353.00174	HD8008
	HD8051
	KF26
353.0017408	HD8008
353.00182	JK791
	KF27.P674
	KF31.P6
353.002	JK661
353.003	JK9
	JK716
353.005	JK791
	JK791.A54
	JK850.A3
	KF26.P674
353.006	JK691
	JK730
	JK765
353.006012	JK775
353.0060924	JK649
353.007	HJ10.B37
	HV40
	JK468.P76
	KF26.J837
	KF1444
	KF3720
353.0071	HC106.6
	HJ9802
	JK1661
	JK1672
	KF25.E243
	KF849
353.00710924	JK1672
353.00711	HD3858
	JK1677.A8
	KF27.G662
	KF32.J8
	KF849
	KF850
	KF865
	Q180.U5
	TT305
353.007110212	HD3858.2
353.00712	HC60.U6
	HD2346.U5
	HD5873
	HD7378.L52B72
	HD9698.U52
	HE5623
	HE6331
	HE9803.A4
	JK1672
	JK1673
	JK1677.O4
	JK1677.T4
	KF26.G6
	KF26.G655
	KF26.P866
	KF27.G668
	KF27.G674
	KF27.5.S646
	KF31.G655
	KF32.G6
	KF843.5
	TL521.312
	UC267
353.00713	HV85
	JK1661
	JK1677.M7
	KF26.A758
	KF26.G645
	KF27.A7655
	KF27.G662
	KF27.G676
	Q183.3
	UC263
353.00714	JC599.U5
353.0072	KF25.E243
353.00721	HG538
	KF25.E247
353.00722	HJ10
	HJ257.2
	HJ2051
	HJ2052
	KF26.A6
	KF26.A755
	KF26.F6
	KF27.A6
	KF27.A646
	KF27.A648
	KF27.A654
	KF27.A664
	KF27.A667
	KF27.A674
	KF27.G674
	KF6221
353.007222	HJ2052
353.007224	HJ10
	HJ10.B8
	HJ10.B83
	HJ2051
	KF26.A6
	KF26.F6
	KF27.A6
	KF27.A664
	KF27.P846
	KF32.A6
353.00723	HJ9802
353.007230924	KF26.G6
353.007231	HJ10
	HJ10.R49
	HJ9802
	KF26.B367
	KF26.G644
	UA23.3.A422
353.007232	E78.A7
	E78.M7
	E97
	E744.5
	GA406
	HC60
	HC60.U6
	HC110.P63
	HC443.V5
	HD1694
353.007232	HD5873
	HD6275.C49
	HD7293
	HD8051.A9
	HD9000.9.U5
	HD9106
	HE355.A3
	HE1063
	HE5614.2
	HE6331
	HE6432
	HF73.U5
	HG3729.U5
	HG9397.5.I8
	HJ9803
	HN79.A135
	JK550
	JK775
	JK794.H4
	JK1613
	JK1672
	KF8754
	LB1027.5
	LB2338
	LB2340
	LC5081
	RA967
	TD223
	TD746
	TE250
	TK9203.B7
	TL781.5.S3
	TL4020
	TS168
	TX531
	U716
	UB373
	UC267
	UG633
	UH83
	Z232.U6
353.00724	HJ5018
	KF27.I5587
	KF27.W3
353.00724011	KF6419
353.00724076	HJ268
353.007242	HT123
353.00724202	KF27.G659
353.007244	HJ4653.R45
	KF27.P868
	KF6419.A25
353.007246	KF27.P868
353.007247	KF31.F5
353.00724711	HJ2337.U6
353.00725	HJ275
	KF26.G655
	KF27.G659
353.0074	KF26.J838
	KF26.P866
353.00740924	KF26.J8
353.0075	E743.5
	KF26.F5
	KF27.P667
	KF27.W3
	KF31.J8
	KF4850
	UA23
353.00751	KF5753
353.00752	KF26.J833
353.00753	KF3941
353.00754	HG3729.U5
	KF26.P827
	KF27.P846
	KF32.P8
	UA927
353.00755	UA927
	UA929.95.T5
353.00756	UH723
353.00761	HV5289
353.00765	AS36.C2
	HV5801
	HV5825
	KF26.J8747
	KF27.5.C7
353.0077	HC110.E5
	HD9666.4
	KF31.G674
353.0077025	RA11.D5
353.00783	HE1618
	KF26.L3
353.008	HC107.M83
	HC110.P63
	HD3616.U46
	HD6274.M65
	HF73
	HT393.G7
	JS308
	KF25.A8
	KF26.C6
	KF26.P6
	KF27.E333
	KF27.G659
	KF27.P634
	KF27.S383
	KF32.P634
	KF485
	PN4874.R64
	Q180.U5
	QC801
353.0081	HA37
353.0082	HC60
	HC106.6
	HC110.P63
	HD3616.U46

353.0082 .... HD9049.W5U4286
..... HF1756
..... HG3729.U5
..... HT393.A6
..... JK1671
..... KF26.G6443
..... KF26.P8
..... KF26.5.S6
..... KF27.5.S6
..... KF1611
353.00822 .... HC60.U6G4
353.00823 .... E173
..... HC110.E5
..... HD1725
..... HD1761
..... HD9106
..... HD9546
..... HD9698.A3U55
..... KF25.A35
..... KF26.C645
..... KF26.I5
..... KF26.I55
..... KF26.P825
..... KF26.P846
..... KF27.A3328
..... KF27.G636
..... KF27.I5568
..... KF32.G6
..... S623
..... S932.V5
..... SB482.A3
..... SD551
..... SH11
353.008232 .... HD181.G8
353.008238 .... KF26.I534
353.00824 .... KF26.R8
..... KF27.5.S6762
..... KF32.M4
353.008242 .... KF26.C6
353.00825 .... HG1662.U5
..... HG2040.5.U5
..... HG2040.5.U6J58
..... HG2051.U5
..... HG2406
..... HG2613.W34E835
..... HG4556.U5
..... HG4910
..... HG8535
..... HG9970.M6
..... JK730
..... KF26.B3
..... KF26.C6
..... KF27.A3226
..... KF27.B3
..... KF27.B333
..... KF27.G636
..... KF31.B3
..... KF32.B354
353.008250924 .... HG2040.5.U5
..... KF26.B3
353.00826 .... HD2795
353.00827 .... HD9006
..... HF1756
..... HG3883.U7
..... KF26.J833
..... KF1975
353.0083 .... HC110.P63
..... HD4903.5.U58
..... HD5325.G8
..... HD5725.I6
..... HD5725.M5
..... HD5725.M8
..... HD6273
..... HD6274.A6
..... HD8051.A9
..... KF26
..... KF26.J8
..... KF26.L3
..... KF26.L345
..... KF26.P6
..... KF27.P836
..... KF4755
353.00830924 .... HD8051
353.0084 .... E98.C6
..... HC107.I63
..... HC110.P63
..... HD1527.A6
..... HD7102.U4
..... HG2051.U5
..... HN59
..... HQ766.5.U5
..... HV85
..... HV696.F6
..... HV743.N48
..... HV1457
..... HV8756
..... KF26.I5
..... KF26.I527
..... KF26.L354
..... KF26.P643
..... KF27.E3
..... KF27.G659
..... KF27.I5568
..... KF27.J8666
..... KF27.V443
..... KF31.G6
..... KF3750
..... KF9223
..... R154.S8344
..... RA11.D5
353.00840924 .... KF26.I5
353.0085 .... E97
..... E840.2
..... GC58

353.0085 .... KF25.A8
..... KF26.C6
..... KF26.D568
..... KF26.L343
..... KF26.L354
..... KF27.A3326
..... KF27.D5644
..... KF27.E335
..... KF27.E345
..... KF27.G659
..... KF27.G663
..... KF27.S3
..... KF27.S383
..... KF32.E3
..... KF32.S382
..... L112
..... LA2317.A48
..... LA2317.M27
..... LB2338
..... LB2807
..... LC1047.8
..... Q11.U84
..... Q127.U6
..... Q180
..... Q180.U5
..... Q223
..... QE511
..... T21
..... TL521
353.00850924 .... L112.H56
353.00855 .... Q127.U6
353.0085545 .... HE8700.8
353.0086 .... HC107.A133P638
..... HC110.P63
..... HD3881
..... HD4603
..... JK865
..... KF27.G646
..... KF27.P868
..... KF27.V424
..... KF31.I5
353.00862 .... HV7565
..... JK775
..... KF26.F645
..... KF26.I5
..... KF26.P866
..... KF27.A654
..... KF27.G662
..... KF27.I5568
..... KF27.P868
..... KF31.P8
353.00863 .... GV53
..... KF26.I542
..... KF27.A3226
..... SB482
..... SB482.A3
353.00864 .... HE355.A3
..... KF26.P868
..... KF27.I55
..... KF27.P876
..... KF32.B3
..... KF5532
..... TE7
..... TE23
353.00865 .... HD255
..... HD7293
353.0087 .... HD2766
..... HD3887
..... HE199.U5
..... KF26.G644
..... KF26.G655
..... KF30.E242
353.008702 .... HD2766
353.008703 .... HD9685.U5
353.0087103 .... KF26.I549
..... KF27.A658
353.008710924 .... HN79.A135
353.008715 .... TD423
..... TD525.C58
353.00872 .... HD1694
353.008722 .... KF26.I532
353.00872203 .... HD9685.U5
353.00872208 .... GV53
..... KF27.A3
353.00872303 .... HD9581.U53A7
353.00873 .... HE6331
..... HE6425
..... HE6432
..... KF26.P6
..... KF27.P6
..... KF32.P6
353.00874 .... HE8700.8
..... KF26.C6
..... KF26.C634
..... KF27.G659
353.008745503 .... LC6576
353.00874603 .... KF26.A3533
353.0087503 .... KF27.I5587
353.00876444 .... HE537.65
353.0087736 .... HE9797.5.U5
353.008775 .... HE745
..... KF27.M464
353.00877503 .... HE745
..... KF26.C652
353.008777 .... HE9803
..... KF27.G662
..... KF2439
..... TL521
353.0087773 .... KF26.C6
353.00877736 .... HE9797.5.U52A3
353.0087774 .... HE9803
353.008778 .... KF26.A3
..... KF27.S3
..... TL521

353.008778 .... TL798.M4
..... TL862.J6
353.0087780924 .... TL521
353.00878 .... HE5623
..... KF26.C6
..... KF26.C688
..... KF31.C6
353.0087803 .... KF31.B3
353.008780924 .... HE355
353.008781 .... HE356.O3
353.00878103 .... HE355.A3
353.0087833 .... JK1677.P35
353.008784 .... HE18
..... KF27.B344
353.00878403 .... KF26.B353
353.00880924 .... KF26.J8
353.0089 .... KF4650
..... UA23
..... UB193
353.00892 .... JK851
..... JX1417
..... JX1706.A55
..... KF26.F637
..... KF26.F644
..... KF27.F646
..... KF31.F6
353.008920922 .... KF26.F6
353.008920924 .... E840.8.S5
353.00895 .... KF26.A7
..... KF26.F6
..... KF5060
..... UB193
353.008950924 .... KF26.F6
353.009 .... JK468.O6
..... JS401
..... KF27.J8666
353.0091 .... KF26.J855
353.0099 .... E183
353.00992 .... KF27.R8
353.01 .... JF1351
353.02 .... KF31.J874
353.03 .... JK421
..... JK511
..... JK516
..... JK518
..... JK643.C69
..... JK649
..... JK691
..... KF27.G659
..... PN4738
353.0318 .... E176
353.032 .... JK501
..... JK511
..... JK516
..... JK558
..... JK560
..... KF31.J8
..... KF42.2
..... KF5053
..... KF5060
..... UA23
353.035 .... E312.952
..... E660
..... E806
..... E814
..... E855
..... F1418
..... J81
..... J82
..... J82.D6
..... J82.E13
..... J82.E21
..... KF47
353.0360924 .... E666
353.04 .... JK649
..... KF26.G6443
..... KF27.G659
353.04025 .... JK464
353.07 .... JK468.E7
..... JK1261
353.09 .... E748.M64
..... HC106.5
..... HG2037
..... JK518
..... JS308
..... KF26.A6
..... KF26.A7
..... KF26.B3
..... KF26.C6
..... KF26.C663
..... KF26.G6
..... KF26.G644
..... KF26.G6443
..... KF26.I5
..... KF26.L3
..... KF26.L348
..... KF26.L363
..... KF26.L367
..... KF27.G676
..... KF27.I5568
..... KF27.J8666
..... KF27.S383
..... KF31.J874
..... Q127.U6
..... UB193
353.091 .... HD5503
..... JK901
..... KF25.A8
..... KF26
..... KF26.A7
..... KF26.L3
..... KF27.A652
..... KF2765.1
..... KF5753

353.0912 .... JK691
..... JK901
..... KF26.B3
..... KF26.C6
..... KF26.C688
..... KF27.G659
..... KF27.J8666
..... KF5406
..... KF5407
353.0913 .... KF26.C634
..... KF26.C636
..... KF26.D5
..... KF26.L3
353.0914 .... GV53
..... HC60.U6
..... HE7763
..... KF26.L343
..... KF26.L345
..... KF27.M464
353.092 .... HD3616.U47
..... HD3881
..... KF26.B372
..... KF26.B375
..... KF27.I5536
..... KF27.J8666
..... KF27.P846
353.0922 .... E841
353.1 .... E748.A15
..... HJ2052
..... JK851
..... JX1417
..... KF26.F6
..... KF26.F697
353.10922 .... KF26.F6
353.10924 .... E840.8.R5
353.2 .... HG2535
..... KF26.F5
353.3 .... JK865
..... KF26.A6
..... KF26.G644
..... KF27.A634
353.30924 .... JK865
..... KF26.I5
353.4 .... HE6331
..... JK730
..... KF27.P6
..... KF27.P667
..... KF27.P668
..... KF31.P6
..... KF32.P6
353.40922 .... HE6331
353.5 .... KF26.J8
..... KF27.G667
..... KF5107
..... KF9745
353.50922 .... KF26.J8
353.6 .... KF25.E243
..... KF26.A655
..... KF26.A7
..... KF26.A755
..... KF27.A655
..... KF27.A7
..... UA23.3
..... UA24
..... UB193
353.60922 .... KF26.A7
..... UB193
353.60924 .... KF26.A7
..... UB193
353.62 .... KF26.A7
..... KF27.P846
353.620924 .... KF26.A7
353.6212 .... UC46
353.63 .... KF26.A7
353.630924 .... KF26.A7
..... UG633
353.70922 .... VB183
353.70924 .... KF26.A7
..... VB183
353.79300122 .... HE28.N4
353.794007242130202
..... HD211.C2
353.8 .... HE206.3
..... HF73
..... KF26.G644
..... KF27.G659
353.81 .... KF26.A6
353.810922 .... KF26.A35
..... S21.Z22
353.82 .... HE18
..... HE745
..... HF73
..... HF73.U5
..... HJ6645
..... KF27.I5536
353.83 .... HD8051
..... HD8051.D9
..... KF26.L3
..... KF27.R8
353.830922 .... HD4835.U4
..... HD5503
..... HD8051
353.830924 .... HD4835.U4
..... HD8051
..... HD8051.B56
..... KF26.L3
353.84 .... HV85
..... JK468.A8
..... KF27.A652
..... LB2807
..... Q180.U5
353.840924 .... HV85
..... KF26.F5
353.85 .... HD7293.A3

353.85 HT167.2
KF26.B3
353.850922 HD7293
KF26.B3
353.850924 HT167.2
353.86 HE206.3
KF26.A6
KF26.C6
KF27.A6
353.8703 HD2766
353.9 F216.2
HJ2052
JK2408
JK2443
353.9018 JK8749.A8
353.9028 JK2445.A8
353.908 JK2403
JK2408
JS308
353.90975 JS438
353.91 JK2447
353.913 JK2447
353.9132 JK2447
353.92 JK2408
353.921 JK2477.S8
353.929 HJ275
JK325
353.9291 JK2441
JS308
353.931 KF26.G655
KF4755
353.93123 JK2474
353.931232 JK2474
353.937 HJ275
353.93712 JK1683
353.9372 JS308
353.93722 HJ2053
HJ2053.A1
353.9374 HV7965
353.938 HC103.7
353.93823 KF26.C6
353.9384 RA445
353.9385 LB2342
LC49
LC5251
353.938783422 TL285
353.939 JS403
353.954009 JQ298.8
353.97297220072 HJ9923.V6
353.974100018 JK2849.A8
353.97410008 JA37
353.974100123 JK2857
353.974100174 JK2874
353.974100754 UA928.M2
353.974100823 KFM446
353.9742 HC107.N4
353.974200722 HJ2053.N4
353.9743 JK3031
353.974300722 HJ2053.V5
353.97430085 L208.G5
353.9743035 J87.V517
353.9744 JS451.M45
353.974400018 TK3149.A8
353.974400142 JK3160.R3
353.97440083 HD7256.U6
353.97440084 HV86
353.974400864 J87
353.974404 JK3131
353.974500878105 HE356.R4
353.97470017 HD8011.N4
353.9747007222 HJ2053.N7
353.9747007232 HJ9884
353.974700725 HJ9287
KFN5906
353.974700823 HD266.N7
353.97470083 HD7256.U6N726
353.97470084 HD7102.U5
353.97470085 JK1667.N4
353.974700865 HD7303.N7
353.9747009722 HJ2053.N7
353.97472 HJ606
353.974785 LB2809.N7
353.974793 HJ9287
353.9748001 JK3655
353.9748007222 HJ2053.P4
353.9748007231 HJ9895
353.974800864 TE24.P4
353.97480087 HE28.P4
353.974804 JK3631
353.9749 JK3525
JK3538
353.9749001 JK3555
353.97490013 JK3555
353.97490072 HJ7613
353.974900755 UA928.N37
353.97490082 TD180
353.974900823 TC977.N5
353.97490083 HD7256.U6N56
353.97490084 KFN2153
353.97490085 KFN2196
KFN2199
353.9749008715 HD4479.N4
353.97490009 KFN2241.O5
353.97490912 KFN2240
353.974993 HJ9281.S54
353.97520085 LC1046.M3
353.975203 JK3831
353.9753 KF27.D5644
353.975300018 JK2749.A8
353.9753001232 KF26.D545
353.97530074 HV7619
KF27.D5
353.975300871 KF26.D5
353.975300878103 HE356.D6

353.9753008784203 KF25.D52
353.975400712 JK4088.A1
353.975400755 UA928.W4
353.97540083 HD7256.U6
353.9754008781 TE24.W4
353.9755 JK3931
353.975500018 JK3949.A8
353.9755035 F231.2
353.97560012 JK4157
353.975600755 UA928.N8
353.97560082025 JK4131
353.975700755 UA928.S5
353.975800018 JK4349.A8
353.97580008 JK4301
353.975800123 JS451.G45
353.975800153 HV9475.G4
353.975800823 HC107.G4
353.97580084 HV9475.G4
353.975804 JK4331
353.97582 HJ11
353.9758823 JK4301
353.975892 JK4331
353.9759001 JK4455
353.975900142 AS36
353.9759007231 HJ11
353.975900724 HJ2400
353.97590074 HV8145.F6
353.97598 HT167.5.F6
353.9762 JK4625
353.97620912 HD2767.M68
353.976300102 HF5549
353.97630074 HV8145.L8
353.976300864 HE356.L8
353.9764 JK4825
353.97640083 HD7256.U6T435
353.9764035 J87.T4176
353.9766001 JK7155
353.976703 JK5131
353.976800182 JK5274
353.976800722 HJ11
HJ2053.T4
353.976800724 HJ2434
353.976900018 JK5349.A8
353.976900175 JK5341
353.976900712 JK5388
353.976900724 HJ2408
353.976900823 SH11
353.9771 JK5531
353.977100172 JK5574
353.97710084 HV85
353.97710085 LB2338
353.977100864 JK5574
353.9771008764 HE395.O47
353.977200025 HC107.I63P6314
353.97720008 HC107.I6
353.977203 JK5631
353.9773 JK5725
JK5741
353.977300018 JK5749.A8
353.9773007 HV98.I15
353.9773007224 RA790.65.I4
353.97730086 JK1651.I4
353.977300874 HE7797.I55
353.977400823 HC107.M5
353.977500863 KF26.I542
353.977500874 HE7765.W6
353.97750087454 TK6548.U6
353.9776001 KFM5835
353.9776005 JK6160.P4
353.977600722 HJ2053.M6
353.97760085 L164
353.977600878103 HE356.M6
353.977604 JK6131
353.97770015 JS451.I87
353.97770088 HV7571.I8
353.9781 JK6841
353.978100823 S624.K3
353.9783 JK6525
353.97830001 JK6555
353.97830017 HD8011.S8
353.978300824 TK24.S8
353.97830083 HD4835.U4
353.97830087 HD2767.S82
353.9786007 HJ545
353.9786008 HD3630.U7
353.978800755 UA928.C6
353.97880083 JK1801
353.97880087 HD2767.C62
353.9789001 JK8055
353.97890072 HJ2053.N6
LB2817
353.9789008781 TE24.N6
353.979100724 HJ2393
353.9793001 JK8555
353.97930072421 HJ3317.2
353.979300755 UA928.N35
353.97930085 LC1046.N3
353.979300863 JK8501
353.979300878103 HE356.N37
353.9794 J87
JK8731
353.9794001 JK8760.I5
353.9794001232 JK8757
353.979400153 JK8760.I5
353.97940071 JK8788.A1
353.979400722 HJ2053.C3
353.97940074 HV7571.C3
353.979400754 UA928.C2
353.979400823 J87.C2
353.97940084 RA790.65.C2
353.97940085 LC1046.C2
353.979400863 GV54.C2
SB482.A4
353.9794008715 TD224.C3

353.9794008783 HE5633.C2
353.97940087834 HE5633.C2
353.979403 JK8731
JK8738
353.979485 LB2809.C3
353.9795 HN79.O7
JK9031
353.979500018 JK9049.A8
353.97950015 JK9060.I5
353.9795007231 HJ9893.A3
353.979500824 HD184.O75
353.97950083 HD7256.U6O726
353.979500862 HJ11
353.979503 JK9052
353.979582 HF73.U52
353.9797001 JK9255
353.979700123 JK9257
353.97970072208 HJ11
353.979700755 UA928.W2
353.979700782 HJ11
353.979700823 HJ11.W2453
SH11.W39
353.97970083 HD7256.U6
353.979700872203 HD9685.U6
353.979703 JK9252
353.979800725 HG4651
353.979800783 HE5614.3.A45
353.9969001 JK9355
353.99690015 JK9360.I5
353.996900722 HJ2053.H3
353.99690074 HV7571.H3
353.996900825 HG8059.G6
353.99690083 HD7256.U6H3
354.32002 JC66
354.34 JQ200
354.400712 JN94
354.41 HX11
JN1213
354.410084 RA395.S55
354.415006 JN1445
354.42 HC251
JN234
JN318
JN425
354.42001 HC256.5
JN421
354.4200145 HE6939.P4
354.420015 JN450.I5
354.42003 JN405
354.42006 HF5381
JN425
354.420072 CD1056
HC256.5
HC256.6
354.4200722 HF2044
354.42007246 HJ6891.A6
HJ6897
354.4200754 UA929.G7
354.4200782 HD8039.F52G75
354.42008 GA66.G7
354.4200823 SD179
354.4200826 HE4711
354.420083 HD8039.L82G7126
354.420084 RA395.G6
RA395.G6
RA986
354.4200840924 DA816.C47
354.420085 JN1129.C69
NX750.G7
354.4200865 HD7333
354.4200871 HD1697.G7
354.4200872208 TK4018
354.42008777 TL526.G7
354.4200878103 HE363.G72
354.4200892 JX1784
354.42009 JN407
354.420091 JC137
JN301
354.4203 JN371
JN2671
354.4204 JN378
JN451
354.4205 JN371
JN378
JN401
JN405
JN453.L3
354.42061 DA531.2
DA566.7
JN453.H7
JX1783
354.42062 HJ1028
HJ1030
354.42066 DA88.1.B27
UA647
354.4206873 HE6935
354.42085 LA635
354.42092 HD4141
354.43 JN3971.A2
354.43100025 DD261.63
354.431002 DD261.63
354.43700025 JN2217
354.437002 JN2217
354.438002 JN6757
354.44 JN2341
JN2728
354.440087454 HE8689.9.F7
354.450085 Q127.I8
354.47002 JN6598.K7
354.4700823 S469.R9
354.470085 LC93.R9
Q127.R9
354.4800761 HV5518
354.48100723 HJ9925.N6

354.485 JN7445
354.492008 HA37
354.4930085 Q180.B4
354.497700025 JN9604
354.498 JN9623
354.509914 HD3545
354.5100025 JQ1507
354.51002 DS778.A1
JQ1507
354.51007 HJ1412
354.52 JQ1615
354.54 DS463
DS476
JQ200
JQ220.S8
JQ224
JQ226
JQ231
JQ246
JQ298.8
JQ298.8.S45
354.540009 DS485.V6
JQ224
354.54000924 JQ224
354.54001 HD4293
HD8013.I45
JQ245
JQ246
JQ247
354.540015 JQ247
354.54001626 HV2093
354.5400175 JQ226
354.54002 JQ221
354.54007 HJ1313
JQ220.S8
354.5400722 HJ2153
354.5400724 HJ3604
HJ3604.A4
354.5400725 HJ1320
HJ1320.A1
354.54008 HC435.2
HD4294
354.540082 HC435.2
HD3616.I4
HD4294
JS7008
JX1840
354.5400823 HD2073
HD9556.I44N355
S471.I3
354.5400824 HC437.M32
354.5400825 HG3284
HG9164.Z9L52
354.540083 HD5967
HD8681
HD8686.5
354.540084 HQ766.5.I5
HQ766.5.P3
354.540085 L577.C5
354.54008722 HD9685.I42
354.5403 JQ298.8
354.5404 JQ231
354.540685 T153
354.540913 HJ7231
354.54092 HD3850
HD4293
HD4294
HD9506.I44N34
HD9526.I64H48
HD9695.I44
354.541200823 HD879.B44
354.541200992 JQ620.B5225C62
354.541300712 JQ620.O758
354.54162007242 HJ4387.A8
354.5455006 JQ572
354.5456 JQ620.D4
354.54750086 HV394.B62
354.54792 JQ620.M262
354.54792006 JQ620.M264
354.5479200712 JQ620.M2658
354.54792008 JQ620.M2625
354.547920082 3HD879.M444
354.547920085 L578.M34
354.5479204 JQ620.M263
354.5480083 HD8681
354.5482 JQ530
354.5483001232 JQ620.K474
354.5487 HD4295.M9
354.548700125 JQ620.M74
354.5487007 HJ2154.M9
354.54870086 HD4295.M9
354.549000186 JQ550
354.549006 JQ552
354.549200824 HD2346.P32E346
354.549200871 HD1698.P32E34
354.5496 JQ1825.N4
JQ1825.N42
354.5694035 DS126.6.M42
354.5810015 HF5547
354.5930083 HD8750.5
354.597006 JQ847
354.6 DT1
354.600721 HJ2999.5
354.62006 JQ3847
354.6200722 HJ2188
354.6670007152 JX1977
354.667035 DT510.6.N5
354.6690009 JQ3088
354.6690014 JQ3092
354.66900875 HE3420.N5
354.669092 HD4350.N47
354.6692 JQ3089
354.676100023 JQ2951

354.67610012 .... JQ2951.A691
354.676200871 .... HD4465.K4
354.67620087103 .... HD4465.K4
354.67730007152 .... JQ3585
354.6780082 .... HC557.T32
..... HD4357.T3
354.678106823 .... HD2130.Z2
354.6782 .... JQ3515.A1
354.68 .... DT763
..... DT962.7
354.6860012 .... JQ2740.A641
354.6891 .... JQ2922
354.68970683 .... HD8799.M27
354.7006 .... JL108
354.71 .... JL27
..... JL55
..... JL65
354.710008 .... JL108
354.71001 .... JL105
354.7100714 .... JF1521
354.7100721 .... HJ793
354.7100724 .... HJ3374
..... HJ4661
354.7100725 .... HJ793
354.7100755 .... UA929.C2
354.71008 .... Q127.C2
..... VK597.C2
354.710082 .... HC117.Q4
354.7100827 .... HD9581.C32
354.710085 .... Q127.C2
..... TL789.8.C2
354.7106108 .... F1001
354.7106823 .... S133
354.7109 .... HD9000.9.C2
354.71100722 .... HJ2056.B7
354.71240082 .... HG3729.C2S37
354.71300721 .... HJ2460.O5
354.71300725 .... HJ795.O6
354.714 .... JL27
354.71602 .... JL224.A2
354.72000922 .... F1235.5.A2
354.720085 .... LA422
354.7206871 .... HD1792
354.7291002 .... JL1007
354.7295008722 .... HD9685.P93
354.7295035 .... JL1043
354.729722 .... KF27.I547
354.79400722 .... HJ2053.C3
354.8300724 .... HJ3241
354.862001 .... HE537.65
354.863002 .... JL1676.A52
354.8630072 .... HE538.R3
354.9100722 .... HJ69
354.91035 .... J631.N3S76
..... J631.N3S768
..... J631.N3S77
..... J631.N3S835
..... J631.N3S87
..... J631.N5
354.93100023 .... JQ5845
354.93100123 .... JQ5849.S2
354.93100827 .... HJ7361
354.940084 .... HG9399.A8
354.9400863 .... SB484.A9
354.9406827 .... HF2486
354.9410077 .... RA395.A8
354.94106864 .... HE368.Z6W45
354.9440085 .... LA2109.A9
354.94404025 .... JQ4526
354.9450084 .... RA554.V5
354.945008722 .... HD9685.A83V53
354.965 .... E840.8.J6
..... JC365
354.967 .... KF26
354.969001 .... HD8011.H3
354.96900722 .... HJ2053.H3
355 .... HC110.D4
..... U17
..... U21.2
..... U101
..... U102
..... U750
..... UA10
..... UA15
355.0001 .... U21.2
355.000182 .... UA19
355.0003 .... U24
..... U25
355.0007 .... U403
..... U410.M1
..... U510
355.00071173 .... U408
..... UA23
355.0008 .... HX15
355.0009 .... D25.A2
..... U101
355.000922 .... UB433
355.000934 .... U31
355.000942 .... UA648
..... UA649
355.000943 .... UA712
355.000947 .... UA772
355.000954 .... UA840
..... UA842
355.00095694 .... UA853.I8
355.00148 .... U408.3
355.0023 .... UB147
355.003 .... U24
..... U25
355.0038 .... U33
355.0071173 .... U410.E5
355.0071174731 .... F129.W7
..... U410.L1
..... U410.M1
355.0071174731 .... U410.N1
..... U410.P1
355.00711757915 .... U430.C5
355.007174731 .... U410.L1
355.0074013 .... U13.A1
355.0074042 .... U13.A1
355.009 .... D25.A2
..... U27
355.009044 .... U102
355.00917496 .... E185.63
355.00937 .... U35
355.00938 .... DF89
..... U33
355.00942 .... DA65
..... UA649
355.00947 .... UA772
355.0095193 .... UA853.K5
355.00954 .... UA842
355.0095694 .... DS119.2
..... DS126.5
..... UA853.I8
355.00973 .... E181
..... KF27.A7
..... U173
355.02 .... U21
..... U21.2
..... U102
355.021 .... U104
..... U162
355.02108 .... UA11
355.0213 .... JX1952
..... UA23
355.02130973 .... UA23
355.0215 .... UA11
355.0217 .... UA11
..... UA23
355.02184 .... D843
..... HX110.5
..... JC328.5
..... U21.2
..... UA11
355.02184098 .... F1414.2
355.022 .... E185.63
..... U21.2
355.023 .... U395.G7
355.027 .... JX1291
..... JX1952
355.0273 .... HD82
355.03 .... UG632
355.030942 .... HX11
355.030954 .... DS480.84
..... UA840
355.030973 .... KF26.A767
..... KF26.F695
..... UA23
..... UG633
..... V858
355.030994 .... UA870
355.031 .... D844
..... D848
..... D849
..... JX1907
..... KF32.A7
..... UA646
..... UA646.3
..... UA646.5.C2
..... UA646.5.N6
..... UA646.5.U5
355.0310973 .... UA12
355.032 .... KF26.A745
..... UA12
355.032593 .... UC46
355.033 .... UA647
355.033052 .... UG635.J3
355.033091822 .... KF32.A728
355.033094 .... UA646.3
..... UA870
355.0330942 .... UA647
355.0330947 .... UA770
355.03309485 .... UA790
355.033095 .... UA830
355.0330971 .... UA600
355.0330973 .... UA23
..... UA770
355.0330994 .... UA870
355.0332 .... UA15
355.03324 .... UA646.3
355.033242 .... DA520
355.033273 .... KF32.A7
355.0335 .... UA11
..... UG630
355.03351822 .... UA23
355.033542 .... UA646
..... UA647
355.033543 .... UA710
355.033544 .... UA700
355.033547 .... UA770
355.033551 .... AS36
..... JX1974.7
355.033552 .... DS881.9
355.033554 .... UA840
355.03355694 .... DS126.5
355.033568 .... UA857.S7
355.033571 .... F1029.5.U6
..... F1034
355.033573 .... HC110.D4
..... JX1706
..... KF26.A7
..... KF27.F646
..... KF32.A7732
..... KF32.F663
..... UA23
..... UA23.3
..... UG633
355.033594 .... HX11
355.07 .... U393.5
355.0708 .... U395.S8
355.070973 .... KF26.F6
..... U393
355.1 .... E185.63
355.100937 .... U35
355.100971613 .... F1039.P6
355.10973 .... U766
355.109861 .... Q180
355.115 .... KF26.F584
..... KF27.V443
355.11506173 .... KF27.V4
355.1150973 .... E181
..... KF26.L394
..... UB357
355.1151 .... KF27.V428
355.11510973 .... F199
..... KF27.V428
..... UB373
355.1152 .... KF31.L3
355.11520973 .... KF26.L382
..... KF26.L394
..... KF27.V433
..... U408.3
355.1154 .... KF26.L382
355.11540973 .... UB357
355.1156 .... KF26.F584
..... UB369
..... UH629.3
355.1156095694 .... UB365.I75
355.11560973 .... KF27.V457
..... UB369
355.1156097949 .... KF27.V443
355.12950973 .... UB800
355.13 .... U766
355.133 .... KF7263
..... UB795.S35
355.1330924 .... F591
..... KF7652.S5
355.1330973 .... KF7625
..... UC263
355.1332 .... DA68.32.C7
..... UB856
355.13320973 .... KF7625
..... KF7639
355.1334 .... KF7606
..... KF7618.D3
355.13340924 .... KF26.G658
355.134 .... UB433
..... UB435.G8
355.1340971 .... UB435.C2
355.135 .... KF27.A774
..... KF32.A784
355.1350942 .... HC251
355.1350973 .... KF27.A778
355.14 .... UC480
..... UC535.G7
355.1409 .... UC480
355.140903 .... UC480
355.140942 .... UC485.G7
355.140943 .... DD253.65
355.140944 .... UA706.G2
..... UC485.F8
355.140973 .... Q11
355.150968 .... UC595.G7
355.17 .... UG633
355.22 .... U22.3
..... UB323
..... UB342.U5
..... UB343
355.220742 .... UB325.G7
355.220973 .... UA17.5.U5
..... UB323
..... UB343
355.223 .... UB343
..... UB345.A8
..... UB345.C2
355.2230971 .... UB345.C2
355.2230973 .... KF26.J833
..... KF7263
..... UB323
..... UB343
355.2230994 .... UB325.A8
355.2236 .... UB343
355.224 .... UB342
..... UB342.G7
355.2240924 .... UB342.U5
355.2240973 .... UB342.U5
355.2250924 .... E745.H4
355.2250973 .... KF26.A7
..... KF7263
..... UB343
355.26 .... HC106.4
355.260973 .... HC106.4
355.27 .... UC333
..... UG128.H3
355.3 .... UB337
355.30942 .... UA649
355.30951 .... UA837
355.30954 .... UA842
355.3095694 .... UA853.I8
355.30959 .... UA830
355.30973 .... UA25
355.31 .... D25.5
..... UA15
355.31096 .... UA855
355.310973 .... UA27
355.330973 .... E185.63
355.331 .... UB210
355.331018 .... TK7882.I6
355.3310202 .... UB210
355.3310924 .... DA68.32.S5
..... DD247.K45
355.3310924 .... DG262
..... E181
..... E745.M3
..... E745.P3
..... U51
..... U53.S8
..... U55.S54
..... UB275
355.3320924 .... DK268.V56
..... DS442.5
..... E83.866
..... E181
..... E745.M3
..... U55.S45
355.33552 .... UA845
355.340973 .... UA530
355.341 .... KF27.A735
..... KF27.G668
..... UC273
..... UC333
355.3410973 .... UC263
355.3430952 .... UB271.J3
355.343209 .... UB270
355.34320942 .... JN329.I6
355.34320973 .... UG633
355.34370973 .... KF27.I548
355.345 .... UH495.N4
355.3450207 .... UH490
355.34509 .... RC971
355.3450942 .... UH257
355.347 .... UH23
355.3470942 .... UH25.G7
355.3480924 .... U55.G9
355.35 .... D25.5
355.3509 .... UA15
355.3510944 .... UA709.A6
355.3510973 .... UA99
355.35109751 .... UA43.D3
355.35109773 .... UA179
355.356 .... Q180.A1
355.357 .... UA600
355.370942 .... UA661
355.37094258 .... UA661
355.37094271 .... DA690.S838
355.370973 .... UA42
355.4 .... U21.2
..... U164
..... U310
..... U408.3
355.4018 .... Q180
355.40202 .... U164
355.410973 .... UC263
355.4110924 .... HM131
355.413 .... U220
355.4130151 .... U220
355.415 .... UF700
355.42018 .... U165
355.422 .... U167.5.L5
355.42508 .... U240
355.426 .... UH723
355.43 .... U102
..... U162
..... U163
355.43008 .... U162
355.4305 .... U162
355.45 .... UA23
..... UG410
355.480942 .... DA69
355.49 .... D802.A33
355.5 .... U310
..... U860
355.50942 .... U101
355.544 .... UG400
..... UG403
355.547 .... U877
..... UF620.A2
355.6 .... UA12
..... UA943
..... UC263
..... UC267
355.613 .... UB323
355.6130973 .... UB193
355.6133 .... KF27.I5568
..... U15
..... UB323
355.61330973 .... E185.63
355.62 .... KF26.A655
355.620973 .... KF27.A736
..... UA23.3
..... UC46
355.621 .... UC263
..... UF700
..... UG633
355.6210973 .... UC267
355.6211 .... UD395.M2
355.62110973 .... HC110.D4
..... KF31.B3
..... Q180
..... UC263
..... UC267
355.6212 .... U263
..... U408.3
..... UC263
..... UD395.M2
..... UF880
..... UG633
355.62120973 .... HC110.D4
..... KF26.A7
..... KF26.J836
..... KF27.G668
..... KF32.G6
..... TE239
..... UC263
..... UC267

355.6213 JK1677.M7
KF27.A7655
KF27.G676
UA23.3
355.62130973 UA23.3
UG633
355.6220973 UA23
355.6223 TS168
UB153
355.62230973 UC267
355.640973 KF27.J8666
355.69 KF27.P668
355.7 DA660
DA690.K4
DA690.P5
DT107.83
F865
UA26.N45
UA603
355.709561 U766
355.70974948 UA26.D5
355.70975637 U294.5.B8
355.71 KF7675
UB800
355.71094227 DA690.A32
355.73 UF543.W5
355.730973 UG446.5
355.730978138 UA26.L4
355.7502573 UC263
355.750973 UC85
355.8 AS36
U168
U408.3
UC263
UC277
355.806173 UC263
355.8075 U790
355.80973 KF27.G668
UC23
UC263
355.81 AM101
355.82 KF27.A752
U800
UD384.M5
UD385.G7
UD400
UF15
UF520
UF523
UF553
UG635.G3
355.8206273 UF1.A548
355.8209 U883
355.820973 KF25.E243
355.83 KF32.A773
UC333
UG446.5
UG683
355.830943 UG685.G3
356.1 UA220
UC485.G7
356.10942 UA649
356.10943 UD233.P8
356.10973 UA29
UD160
356.11 UA652.H5
UA652.S3
UA652.S8
UC485.G7
356.110942 U55.M5
UA650
UA652.B6
UA652.C65
UA652.G55
UA652.K55
UA652.P74
UA652.R9
UA652.S65
UA652.U45
UA652.W6
356.110968 UA857.S7
356.11096891 UA857.R5
356.110971 UA602.R58
356.110973 UA29
356.15 DT23
356.150954 DS485.N4
356.160942 UA652.D814
356.166 UD480
356.1840942 UD234
356.186 UC460
356.97560012 JK4157
357.0942 UA655
UA657.5.N8
357.0968 UA857.S7
357.1 F391
UE445.G7
357.10924 U55.M38
357.10942 UA656.H8
357.10943 UE231
357.10973 UA30
357.10994 UA873.C3
357.185 UE144
357.712400723 HJ13.S2
357.7308 QE105
358.109 UF15
358.10943 UF73
358.10973 UA32
358.1209044 UF15
358.120937 U875
358.120973 UF403
358.160973 F279.C46
358.174 UG633
358.1740973 KF26.F6583
UG632

358.18 UG446.5
Z663.23
358.1809 UG446.5
358.1809041 UG446.5
358.180942 UA656.R72
UA659.K4
358.180947 UG446.5
358.20942 UG57
358.220942 UA653.5.R75
358.24 U408.3
358.240942 UG575.G7
358.25 UC275.G7
358.3 JX1977
KF27.F6483
UG447
UG447.8
358.308 UG447.8
358.3111 LB2835
358.34028 U408.3
358.3409597 UG633
358.39 UA927
UF767
358.390994 UA870
358.4 UG632
VG90
358.400148 UG633
358.400942 UG630
UG635.G7
VG95.G7
358.400943 UG633
358.40095694 UG635.I75
358.400971 UG630
358.400973 UG633
VG93
358.4009931 UG635.N45
358.403 KF32.A725
UG633
358.403097 UG633
358.4030973 UA23
UG633
358.4070973 UG633
358.40973 VG93
358.41 RC1050
358.4111540973 HD5701
358.4113320973 UG633
358.413 VA63.P37
358.41330943 UG635.G3
358.413310943 UG633
358.413370973 KF26.A774
358.413470942 UH25.G7
358.41370942 UG635.G7
358.4140942 UG635.G7
358.4140973 UG449
358.4141 VG93
358.4145 UG633
358.4145097 UG633
358.41450973 UG633
358.41550973 UG633
358.416130973 UG633
358.4161330973 UG633
358.4162 KF26.A786
U394.C3
358.41620973 AS36
358.41621 UG633
358.416212 UF553
358.4162120973 UG633
358.416223 UG633
358.4170975251 UG634.5.A415
358.41709753 UG634.5.B65
358.41750973 UG633
358.4183 TL684.3
TL685.3
TL686.N25
UG633
UG635.A8
UG635.G3
UG635.G7
UG635.J3
VG93
VG93.A687
358.43 TL685.3
358.430942 UG635.G7
358.44 UC333
358.440973 KF32.A773
358.45 KF27.A768
KF32.A775
UG633
358.450973 VA63.P4
358.8 TL862.G4
UG630
359 D27
DA88
KF25.A8
V25
359.00148 V23
359.003 V23
359.009 D362
E182
359.00902 V43
359.00903 D27
359.0091822 DE98
359.00942 DA87.1.A1
DS89
HD8039.S42G755
VA454
359.00943 VA513
359.009436 VA473
359.00944 VA503
359.00947 VA573
359.00973 DU817
E182
V19
VA56
359.00994 VK378.M45

359.03 D436
359.030973 V17
VA50
VA53
359.070973 VA58
359.09 D27
359.10924 G549
359.10942 G549
VA454
359.12 DA88
359.1334 DA690.P8
359.16 VA55
359.20922 Z6616.R5
359.30947 VA573
359.31 VG953
359.310922 V62
359.310973 E746
359.32 VA65.C68
VA454
359.320942 VA456
359.320947 VA573
359.320952 VA653
359.320973 VA61
359.325 V860
VA65.B54
VA65.T76
VA65.W24
359.3250973 VA53
VA58
VA65.C72
VB230
VK149
359.32520973 VA65.M59
VA65.N5
359.32530942 V820.5.G7
359.32530973 VA65.L65
359.3254 V830
VA65.R6
VA65.S3
VA65.W26
359.32540973 VA65.D3
VA65.G7
VA65.H4
VA65.J6
VA65.N623
VA65.R6
VA65.T38
VA65.W28
359.3255 V874
VA65.I9
VA65.Y6
359.32550973 VA65.A53
VA65.B4
VA65.C75
VA65.E5
VA65.I9
VA65.K5
VA65.R35
VA65.S33
VA65.S48
VA65.W3
359.32560973 VA65.O35
VA65.W48
359.3257 KF26.A767
V210
V857
VA65.P49
359.32570973 V858
359.32574 KF27.A762
KF32.A762
359.326 V437
VA65.M33
VA65.T39
359.32620973 VA65.C67
359.3264 VA65.N34
359.32650973 VA65
359.33 VE23
359.3310922 D27
E182
359.3310924 DA86.22.H3
DA89.1.F5
DA566.9.C5
E182.E93
GC30.M4
V63.R54
V65.L3
359.3310973 V62
359.332 VB313
359.3320924 V63.B34
V63.G55
V63.L4
359.3320973 V11.U7
VB23
359.3380973 VD430
359.341 VA65.N62
VA65.T6
359.3410973 VC263
359.3415 VA65.C55
359.34320924 VB230
359.34320973 VB230
359.345071179498 VG425.S3
359.3450973 VG123
359.3510973 VA63.P29
359.370973 VA80
359.371 VC383
359.4 DA70
V143
359.430942 VA454
359.4738 DE61.N3
359.48 D27
359.4809 D27
359.5 V245
359.6133 VG63
359.61330973 VB258

359.620973 VA60
359.62120973 VG93
359.709753 VA68.W2
359.73 KF32.A778
359.7450008 JK3201
359.81 VC373
359.82 U855
VF160
359.820973 VF23
359.83 KF26.A753
KF31.A756
359.830973 VC553
359.96 KF32.A735
VE23.25
VE25.L47
VE153
VE403
359.960924 CT275.R733
359.97 HJ6645
KF27.M436
V437
359.970973 HJ6645
KF26.C652
359.98 VA66.C6
359.98109 UF15
359.982 DS557.A655E6
VA66.C62
359.9820973 VA66
360 HV40
HV589.I54
360.0711 HV11
360.0942 HN389
360.7 HV11
360.76 HV11.5
360.942 HN389
HV248
360.973 HN59
360.97471 HV4046.N6
360.9771 HN80.N5
361 BF637.C6
HD6274.C3
HM291
HV8
HV10.5
HV13
HV31
HV40
HV41
HV88
HV95
HV245
HV248
HV393
HV4183
HV4189
KF26.L356
361.0018 HV11
361.0023 E185.82
HV10.5
HV338
HV7428
361.00255456 H31
361.006242 HV244.N43
361.007 HV11
361.0071 HV11
361.00711 HV11
361.0071173 HV11
361.00711783 HV11
361.0072 HV11
HV41
361.008 HV15
HV37
HV40
361.00973 HV91
361.02 F780
HV31
HV394.B62
HV4183
361.020257 LB2339.C3
361.020258 HV110.5
361.0209174924 HV17
361.020924 HV28.S5
361.020938 HV20.G9
361.020954 HV393
361.020973 H11
HV91
HV97
361.0209764 HV98.T5
361.0711 HV11
361.10942 RA485
361.2 HV41
JX1977
361.3 BF637.C6
HV41
HV43
HV45
361.301 HV41
HV43
361.308 HV43
361.4 BF637.C6
HM133
HV45
HV547
361.5 HV553
RA645.5
361.506 HV568
HV580.R82
361.50922 HV569.A1
361.50924 HV569.B3
HV569.D8
361.50971 HV555.C3
361.50973 HV553
HV555.U6
HV555.U62

Dewey	LC
361.509794	J87.C2
361.51	QE535
361.520954	HV610
361.5209794	KF26.P868
	KF27.P846
361.520979411	HV610
361.53	HV640.5.A6
	HV640.5.T5
	JX1977
361.530924	HV640.5.L3
361.5309494	HV640.5.J4
361.5309669	QT515.9.E3
361.53096694	KF26.J875
361.530967	HV640.5.A3
361.55095412	HD9016.I43B452
361.55096694	HV449.N5
361.58	TL553.8
361.6	HN16
	HV244
	HV245
	JX1977
	RA445
	RA790.5
	RA790.65.S6
	RA790.65.W6
	RC261
361.6072073	HV85
361.6091724	HN980
361.60942	HN385
	HV241
	HV245
	HV248
361.609421	HV250.L8
361.6094391	HD7172.H8
361.6096762	HV449.K44
361.60968	HV449.S62
361.6096982	HN800.M37
361.60971	HV105
	HV108
361.609713541	HV110.T6
361.60971384	HV110.O7
361.60973	HV85
	HV88.N62
	HV90
	HV91
	HV95
	KF32.W3
	KF3720
361.609741	HV86
361.609743	HV86
	HV98.V5
361.609744	HV86
	HV98.M39
361.609756	HV98.N8
361.609759	HV86
361.609765	HV86
361.609766	HV86
361.60977132	HV99.C54
361.609783	HV86
361.609788	JK7801
361.609794	HV86
361.610973	KF31.5.A3
361.7	BV2657.M3
	DA690.T95
	HS1510.S23
	HV25
	HV563
	HV4183
361.7025795	HV98.O7
361.706281	HV192
361.70942	HV245
361.70995	DU740
361.71	HV854
361.73	H11
	HV41
361.760627526	HV3192.B3
361.760973	HV97
361.8	HN17.5
	HN46.C2
	HV40
	HV41
	HV97.J3
	HV4183
	HV7428
361.808	HV41
361.809174924	HV3191
361.809410	HV249.N68
361.80971	HV104
361.80973	HV41
	HV4193
361.80974461	HV4196.B7S8
361.8097471	HV99.N59
361.80977311	HV4196.C4H76
361.917496	HV95
361.924	BV3192.K8
	BX8495.S753
	E185.97.E45
	E415.9.S64
	HV28.A35
	HV28.C5
	HV28.M34
	HV4196.C9
361.94	HN373.5
361.942	HV41
	HV241
	HV244
	HV245
	HX11
361.9421	HV250.L8
361.9485	HN573.5
361.95125	HV431.H6
361.954	HV12
	HV393
361.9549	HN690.5.A8
361.9549	HV395.5
361.971	HN107
	HV108
361.971384	HV13
361.9729722	HV175.5
361.973	HD7123
	HV40
	HV90
	HV91
	HV95
361.9747	HV98.N7
361.97471	HV99.N59
361.975	HV98.A13
361.9756	HV98.N8
361.979467	HD4606.B4
361.994	HV473
361.99463	HV99.H3
362	HD7255
	HD7255.A2
	HD7256.U5
	HD7256.U6N744
	HN18
	HN59
	HV547
	HV700.C3M6
	HV1553
	HV1568
	HV3011
	HV5840.A8
	KF27.I5568
	RA395.A3
	RA410.6
	RA418
	RA445
	RD795
	RM930
	RM930.A1
362.0071173	HV11
362.023	HV10.5
362.02554792	HV395.B6
362.0257	HD7256.U5
362.062795	RA421
362.09747	RM930
362.1	H31
	HD7103.5.U5
	HV244.O25
	HV687
	HV687.5.H3
	KF26.L354
	KF27.I5568
	KF3825
	PZ10.W43
	R294
	R729.5.G4
	RA11
	RA394
	RA395.A3
	RA418
	RA425
	RA645.7.C2
	RA972
	RA972.7
	RA981.H3
	RM735
	RT5.V8
	RT97
362.1023	RA440.9
362.10425	KF26.L354
362.106142	RA395.G6
362.10621	RA390.U5
362.10924	HV6248
	R489.J4
362.109416	RA987.I6
362.10942	R111
	RA395.G
	RA395.G6
362.109431	HD7102.G3
362.109471	RA418
	RA989.F3
362.109492	RA505
362.109597	R611
362.109676	R722
362.10971	RA395.C3
	RA412.5.C3
362.10971428	RA983.M6
362.10973	KF26.L354
	KF27.I5568
	KF32.I55
	RA395.A3
	RA407.3
	RA412.5.U6
	RA422
	RA445
	RA961
	RA981.A2
362.109749	KFN2141
	RA447.N57
362.109775	RA447.W6
362.109781	HC107.K2
362.109794	HV688.U55
362.109944	RA421
362.11	KF26.L354
	PZ10
	PZ10.C687
	PZ10.K128
	PZ10.W346
	PZ10.W43
	RA418
	RA965
	RA974
	RA975
	RA981.A2
	RA981.P4
	RA987.S4
362.11	RC49
	RJ242
	UB369
362.11014	R123
362.1106273	RA960
362.110941435	RA988.G5V55
362.110942	RA986
	RC450.G7
362.11094219	DA690.T95
362.11094272	RT11
362.110954	RA990.I37
362.11095493	RA390.U5
362.110973	KF26.L354
	RA407.3
	RA421
	RA971
	RA980
	RA981.A2
	RA981.A3
	UB369
362.110974461	RA982.B7
362.11097471	RA982.N5
362.110975771	KF27.V4
362.110976335	RA982.N45
362.110994	RA992.A1
362.1109941	R673.F7
362.1109942	RA992.A3R63
362.1109944	RA992.S9
	RA992.S9S34
362.1109945	RA992.M4
362.11099691	RA981.H3
362.12	RA974
	RA988.R
	RC682
362.120942	RA986
362.120973	RA395.A3
362.12097471	RA395.A4
362.120977434	RA448.5.N4
362.1209776155	RA982.R56M39
362.127471	RA395.A4
362.14	HV3003
	RT61
362.140942	HV700.G7
362.15	RA407.3
	RG12
362.150942	RG67
362.1524	E842.9
362.16	HV687
	KF27.V457
	RA976
	RA981.W2
	RA997
	RA997.5.C3
362.1602542	RA998.G
362.1602573	RA997.A2
362.160973	HV687.5.U5
	RA997
362.1609777	RA997.5.I6
362.1609797	RA997.5.W3
362.18	RA995
	RA995.5
	RA996
362.1809777	RA995.5.I8
362.19	RM930
362.196	RA1197.G
362.19612	RC682
362.196123	Q180.A1
	RA975.5.C6
362.19621094151	RE30.G
362.19639	RC620
362.196610724	RC901.7.A7
362.196610924	RC901.7.A7
362.19681	RC394.A7
362.196810924	RC388.5
362.196853	RC372
362.1968552	RC425
362.196994	RC261
362.19699400924	RC263
362.197533	RF516
362.1976	RA371
362.197600941	RK34.G72
362.1977	RA992.M4
	RE76
362.198	RG526.N38
362.1989224	RC857
362.2	RA790
	RA790.5
	RA790.65
	RA790.65.C2
	RA790.65.I4
	RC439
	RC451.A82
	RC451.4.S7
	RC455
	RC458
	RC480.5
	RC514
	RC570
	RC576
362.206173	RA11.D5
362.20942	HC251
	RC450
	RC450.G
	RC450.G7
362.209485	HV3008.S5
362.2097124	RC448.S22
362.20973	RA421
	RA790
	RA790.6
	RC443
362.209747	HV3006.N69
362.209748	RA790.65.P4
362.209752	RA790.65.M33
362.209758	RA790.65.G4
362.209761	RA790.65.A2
362.209775	RC445.W55
362.209776	RA790.65.M53
362.209781	RA790.65.K2
362.2097945	RA790.65.C2
362.2097948	RA790.65.C2
362.2099693	RA790.65.H3
362.21	BV4012
	RC439
	RC445
	RC450.G
	RC488
	RC576
362.210942	RC450
	RC514
362.21094253	RC450.G
362.21094297	RA988.C34
362.210973	HV3006
362.2109747	RC445.N68
362.2109764	RC445.T363
362.2109767	RC445
362.2109771	RC445.O28
362.2109775	RC445.W53
362.2109794	HV3006.C22
362.2109795	RC445
362.2109931	RA371
362.22	HV689
	RA790
	RA790.5
	RA790.6
	RC576
362.220942	RC450
362.220973	RA790.6
	RC439
	RC443
362.2209741	RA790.65.M3
362.2209758	RA790.65.G4
362.2209781	RA790.65.K2
362.2209797	HV86
362.230942	HV244
362.24	RC574
	RC576
362.29	HV5770.C2
	HV6713
	KF26.L335
362.290973	KF26.L335
362.292	HV5035
	HV5060
	HV5068
	HV5275
	HV5278.A78
	HV5288
	HV5292
362.292025759	HV5280.F6
362.292025764	HV5280.T47
362.2920621	HV5278.A78
362.29206273	HV5278.A78
362.292062797	HV5278
362.292071	HV5808
362.2920924	HV5447.W52
362.2920973	HV5050
	HV5279
	HV5288
	HV5292
	KF26.L335
	KF31.L3
	RC565
362.29209758	HV5280.G1
362.29209768	HV5297.T2
362.2920977866	HV5281.S3
362.29209781	HV5297.K2
362.29209794	HV5280.C3
	HV5297.C2
362.29209945	HV5675.A3V52
362.293	HV5800
	HV5800.S93
	HV5801
	HV5805.M3
	HV5822.M3
	HV5825
	HV5831.I4
	HV5831.N7
	HV5840.G
	KF26.L335
	RC566.A1
362.2930924	HV5801
362.2930926	HV5831.C2
362.2930942	HV5840.G7
362.2930973	HV5825
	KF32.I55
362.2930974	HV5825
362.29309747	HV5831.N7
362.293097471	HV5831.N7
362.29309752	HV5831.M3
362.29309769	HV5831.K4
362.29309794	HV5831
	HV5831.C2
	HV5831.C2A5
362.2930979494	HV5831.C2
362.3	HV3004
	HV3006.N7R77
	HV3008
	RA790.65.C2
	RC443
	RC576
362.3025773	HV3006.I3
362.3025776	HV3006.M58
362.3025795	HV3006.O7
362.3025945	HV901.A82V52
362.30720795	HV897.O7
362.3077	HV3004
362.30942	HV3008.G7
362.309489	HV3008.D4
362.30973	HV3006

362.30973 HV3006.A4
KF27.I55
RC439
362.309743 HV3006.V48
362.309744 HV3006.M4
362.309745 HV3006.R4
362.309746 HV3006.C7
362.309748 HV3006.P4
362.309749 HV3006.N5
HV3006.N52B64
362.309751 HV3006.D3
362.309758 HV3006.G4
362.309759 HV3006.F55
362.309761 HV3006.A57
362.309763 HV3006.L8
362.309764 HV3006.T4
362.309766 HV3006.O5
362.309768 HV3006.T35
362.309771 RA790.65.O3
362.309773 HV3006
HV3006.I3
362.30977321 HV3006.I32L58
362.309775 HV897.W6
362.30977585 HV13
362.309777 HV3006.I63
362.309778 HV3006.M8
362.309781 HV3006.K3
362.309783 HV3006.S8
362.309793 HV3006.N47
362.309794 HV3006.C2
362.309795 HV3006.O7
362.309969 HV3006.H3
362.4 HV575
HV1568
HV3022
362.4019 BF727.P57
362.4025 RM930
362.4025753 HV1555.D5
362.4072073 HV1553
362.40942 HV1559.G
HV1559.G6
362.4094215 HV1559.G6
362.409485 HV1559.S9
362.40974461 HV1555.M38
362.41 HV1598
HV1701
HV1780.S4
Q180
RJ496.S7
362.41028 HV1731
362.4106271 HV1804
362.410942 HV1945
362.410977132 HV1796.O27C62
362.410977157 HV1796.O25
362.4109794 HV1796
362.42 HV2380
HV2395
HV2452
HV2526
HV2561.N54
RJ496.D4
362.4209749 HV2561.N54
362.43 HV3018
RD755
362.43028 RD755
RD757.W4
362.430924 RC180.2
RC406.F7
362.430926 RD757.W4
362.5 BV639.P6
DA670.K3
HC101
HC107.I33P633
HC110.I5
HC110.P63
HD5715.3.T2
HG179
HV43
HV110.W5
HV250.K5P68
HV696.F6
HV1481.G55N65
HV4028
HV4194
HV4547
KF26.A35
KF26.L345
KF27.A3
TX360.U6
362.50627471 HV4046.N6
362.50942 HC255
HC260.I5
HD7167
HV245
HV4387
362.509421 HV4088.L8
362.5094219 DA690.E315
362.50971 HC120.P6
362.50973 HC110.P6
HC110.P63
HV91
HV95
HV4045
KF26.L345
362.509744 HC107.M43P637
HV98.M39
362.5097471 HV4046.N6
362.50977311 HV4046.C36
362.50977595 HC108.M6
362.50978163 HV4196.T6
362.58 HV696.F6
362.580973 KF26.J837
KF336
362.6 HD7287.9
362.6025765 HV1468.N8
362.6025945 HV1490.V5
362.60973 HV91
KF27.E335
362.609741 HV1468.M2
362.61 HD4465.S6
HV43
HV640.4.G7
HV1451
RC952
362.61023 HQ1064.U5
362.6102573 HV1465
362.61025752 HV1468.M3
362.610259969 HV1468.H3
362.6106079 HQ1064.U6
362.61072 JX1977
362.610942 HV1481.G52
HX11
362.6109485 HV1481.S82
362.610971 HV1475
362.610973 HD7102.U4
HQ1064.U5
HV1457
HV1461
KF26.5.A3
362.610977132 HD7102.U4
362.6109776 HQ1064.U6M573
362.6109781 HV86
362.6109782 RC954.5.N2
362.6109794 HV1468.C2
362.610979486 HV1468.C2
362.610994 HV1490
HV1490.V5
362.6109941 HV1490.W4
362.6109945 HV1490.V5
362.611 KF26.L334
362.61110973 RA413.7.A4
362.6114097452 RC952.5
362.6120941 RC451.4.A5
362.6121094267 RC451.4.A5
362.6123 RC439
RC451.4.A5
362.615 RA997
362.61502573 HV1465.H4
362.6150942 HV1481.G52
362.615094233 HV249.E9D653
362.61509747 RA997.5.N7
362.6150974811 RA997.5.P4
362.6206042 UB405.G7
362.7 HV391
HV697
HV703
HV713
HV741
HV742.C2
HV751
HV1421
HV1441.C3
HV9069
JX1977
LB3013.5
362.70186 HV751.A6
362.7023 HQ769
362.702542 HV751
362.7025771 HV742.O3
362.7091766 HV3191
362.70924 HV247.B
HV1150.L8
362.70942 HV751
HV751.A6
HV1441.G7
362.709421 LC145.G7
362.709485 HV790.A6
362.709489 HD7199
362.709492 HV778.A6
362.7095694 HV800.P3
362.7096 HV801.A1
362.70971 HV745.A6
362.70973 HV85
HV91
HV713
HV741
HV1431
362.709746 HV742.C8
362.709747 HV742.N7
362.70974471 HV743.N48
362.70974723 F129.B7
362.709748 HV742.P4
362.709753 HV742.D6
362.709759 HV742.F6
362.70977311 HV9106.C4
362.709776 HV742.M6
362.709777 HV742.I8
362.70994 HV1441.A8
362.71 HV851
HV854
HV857.I3
HV857.M3
HV861.C22N64
HV861.C22T69
JK5574
RA981.A2
362.7107 HV741
362.73 HV700.5
HV741
HV995.M5L33
362.73025773 HV742.I3
362.732 HV873
362.732025713 HV1009.O5
362.7320924 HV995.G72
LB775.G4785
362.7320942 HV887.G5
HV965
362.732095694 HV800.P3
362.7320976955 HV995.H62H65
362.73209773 HV742.I3
362.733 HV875
362.7330924 HV875
362.7330942 HV875
362.7330973 HV875
HV881
362.73309752 HV881
HV883.M3
362.73309758 HV875
362.73309759 HV883.F6
362.734 HV86
HV875
362.7340924 HV875
362.7340926 HV875
362.73409415 HV875
362.7340942 HV875
362.73409711 HV875
362.7340973 HV875
362.73409773 HV875
362.74209797 HQ773
362.780941 HV755.A6
362.780974461 RA564.9
362.781 RJ242
362.78110942 RC450.G7
362.7819120924 RC687
362.7819639 RJ206
362.7819689 RJ506.A9
362.781971 RD93.5.C4
362.782094228 RA564
362.78209795 RJ501.O7
362.7822 RJ504.5
362.783 HV891
RA44
362.783025741 HV897.M3
362.7830924 RJ506
362.7830973 HV894
362.78309753 HV995.W3S26
362.783099693 HV899.W3
362.784 HV888
362.784025774 HV889.M5
362.78409713 HV745.O5
362.78409749 HV905.N5
362.78409794 HV889.C3
362.7841 HV1596
362.7842 HV2395
362.7843 RJ496.C4
362.8 HD6190.A5
HG179
HG9970.A5
HV41
HV6762.A3
RA427
362.82 F128.9.N3
HD6978
HD7333
HQ10
HQ763
HQ766.5
HQ766.5.G7
HQ766.5.S3
HQ773.7
HV43
HV697
HV699
KF27.I5568
362.820924 HV28.M315
362.820942 HC260.P6
362.8209471 HV700.F5
362.82097526 HV699
362.8209758 HV742.G4
362.83 HV700.G7
HV700.5
362.830926 HQ998
362.830942 HV700.5
362.830973 HV700.5
362.8309753 HV741
362.8309794 HV700.5
362.84 E78.M25
E185.615
HC440.P63
362.840973 E185.615
362.85 HV99.N59
KF26.L354
RC965.A5
362.850924 JV8975.M5
362.8809753 KF26.D5
362.91734 HD7255.A2
362.924 HV247.S5
362.942 HV687.5.G7
362.971 HV104
362.971326 HV110.L6
362.973 AS36.C2
HD7256.U5
HN59
HN65
HV95
362.9747 HV86
HV1555.N7
362.9767 HV98.A65
362.9931 HN930.5.A8
362.994 HN16
363.2 DD256.5
HV881
HV7921
HV7923
HV7935
HV7936.P8
HV8031
HV8080.J8
HV8290
363.2018 HV7936.A8
363.2023 HV7922
HV8143
363.2028 HV7936.T4
363.206171 HV8157
363.206173 HV8141
363.207 HV7923
363.2071 HV7923
HV8148.C64
363.2071173 HV8143
363.20711758 HV7571.G4
363.20711778 HV7923
363.20711781 HV8145.K2
363.20715 HV7923
HV8145.F6
363.207152 HV7923
363.207153 HV8145.G4
363.2076 HV7923
363.2077 HV8143
363.20917496 HV8138
363.20922 JQ221
363.20924 F391
F700.H83
F801.B15
HV8148.A72
363.2094 HV7921
363.209415 HV8197.I8
363.209416 HV8195
363.20942 HV7725
HV7936.P8
HV8195
363.209421 HV8198.L7
363.2094229 HV8198.R4
363.2094258 HV8196
363.20943155 HV8210.B4
363.20944 HV8203
363.20947 HV8224
363.20952 HV7826
363.20954 HV8247
363.2095414 HV8249.W45
363.2097 HV7965
363.20971 HV8157
363.2097122 HV8157
363.20973 HV1841
HV7914
HV8138
HV8141
HV8143
KF9219.3
KF9625
363.209741 HV7571.M2
JA37
363.20974461 HV7936.C8
363.2097471 HV8148.N5
HV8148.N52
363.20974751 HV8145.N7
363.20974788 HV8145.N7
363.209751 HV7415
363.2097526 HV7576
363.209753 HV7619.D3
KF27.D584
KF27.P868
363.209754 HV7571.W4
363.209758 HV7571.G4
363.209763 HV7571.L8
363.20977311 HV8148.C4
363.20978 F591
363.20979494 HV8148.L55
363.22 HV8023
HV8093
HV8138
363.2207 KFW2420
363.22076 HV7923
363.220924 HV8249.B5
363.220973 HV8138
363.2209759 HV8145.F6
363.2209773 HV8145.I3
363.23 HV7914
HV8055
KF9223
363.232 HV8080.P2
363.2320977311 HV8148.C4
363.23209794 HV7571.C3
363.233 HE369
363.23309744 HE371.M4
363.23309794 HV7571.C3
363.234 HV8031
363.2340994 HV8280.A2
363.236 HV8080.A6
363.242 HV7936.C8
HV7936.R4
363.242028 HV7936.A8
363.2454 TS534
363.248 HV8025
363.3 HV8290
363.31 PN2091.S8
363.33 HV8059
363.34 HD2075.B5
HV553
TX7
363.3409729722 UA928
363.340973 HV555.U6
363.3409746 UA928.C8
363.3409756 UA928.N8
363.35 QC951
TL725.3.D35
UA926
UA926.5
UA927
UA928.M2
363.350202 UA927
363.3503 UA926
363.3509489 UA929.D4
363.350973 Q180
UA927
363.3509754 UA928.W4
363.3509759 UA928.F5

Dewey	LC
363.3509769	LC216
	UA928.K4
363.3509773	UA928.I3
363.3509791	UA928.A6
363.3509793	UA928.N35
363.3509796	UA928.I2
363.3509931	UA929.N45
363.350994	UA929.N45
363.351	UA927
363.3510973	UA23
363.352	KF32.G6
	UG447
363.353	UA929.6
363.35609931	UA929.N45
363.45	HV5840.I4
363.5	HC107.K2
	HD3890.P4
	HD7293
363.50954	HD4291
363.50973	HD3881
363.509747	HD3890.N7
363.60971133	HD4610.V3
363.60977	HD9685.U6
363.6099429	J905
363.61	KF5555.5
363.6102573	HD4461
363.610954	HD4465.I5
363.610959	HD1698.A1
363.6109771	HD1694.O4
363.6109791	HD1694.C2
363.62	HD9685.E82
	HD9685.U5
	HD9685.U6D47
	HD9688.U52
	TK351
363.620212	HD9685.A2
363.620954	HD9685.I42
363.6209542	HD9685.I43A45
363.6209729722	TK1233.V56
363.620973	HD9685.U5
	KF26.C6
	KF26.G655
363.620974	HD9685.U6A112
	KF27.I5566
363.620976	HD9685.U5
363.6209768	HD9685.U6T22
363.6209798	HD9685.U6A47
363.63	HD9581.C33A43
363.63025768	HD9581.U52
364	HV6021
	HV6025
	HV6028
	HV6030.W55
	HV6035
	HV6041
	HV6171
	HV6783
	HV6789
	HV8073
	HV8073.5
	HV9069
364.019	HV6105
364.06173	HV6783
364.0720713541	HV6024.5
364.08	HV6016
	HV6028
364.0973	HV8665
364.09797	HV7297.A6
364.1	CT9990
	E450
	F591
	HV5053
	HV6025
	HV6245
	HV6248
	HV6759
364.106709747	HV6793.N5
364.10922	CT9980
	F591
	HV6125
	HV6945
364.10924	DU222.K4
	HV6248.B645
	HV6248.C662
	HV6248.K36
	HV6248.R78
	HV6248.T62
	HV6452.C3V3
364.10942	HV6944
364.10973	HV6049
	HV6789
	HV6791
364.109748	KFP71.5
364.10975799	HV7911.M37
364.109763	HV6793.L6
364.109781	HV6793.K3
364.12	HV7936.R4
	HV8073
	HV8073.5
	HV8145.K2
364.1206173	HV7911.H6
	HV8138
	HV8141
364.120715	KF27.G667
364.120922	HV8073.8
364.120924	HE5903.W5
	HV6068
	HV7911.H8
	HV7914
	PR6070.H57
364.120926	HV7914
364.120942	HV8198.L7
364.1209421	HV8198.L7
364.120973	HV8073
364.120973	KF32.G6
	HV8073
364.121	HV8074
364.1210973	HV8141
364.122	HV8074
364.125	HV6074
	QC100
364.1279	HV8073
	HV8078
364.128	KFN2380.5.W5
364.13	HV6635
	HV8959.R9
364.131	DU152
	E185.97
	KF26.J832
364.1310922	HX894
364.1310924	DB215.5
	DB217.S6
	E450
	HV6248.L39
	HV9679.A2
	QC16.O62
364.13109759	E450
364.132	HV6304
364.133	HD9149.C42U58
	HJ4653.E75
	HJ5021
	HJ6619
	HJ6897
	HV6795.C4
364.1330977311	HV6795.C4
364.134	HV6457
	HV6464
364.135	HE9775
	HE9803.Z7H56
	KF26.C6
	KF27.F6
364.135091661	G535
364.1350916613	DE96
364.1350922	G535
364.1350924	G537.K5
364.135095	DS515
364.1380922	D804.G42
364.1406	DS595
	HN488.S5
	HV6452.P4
	HV6452.P4M6
	HV6789
	HV6791
364.14060973	HV6789
364.143	HV6477
	JA37
	KFV2962
364.14309542	HV6485.I52M45
364.1430973	HV6477
364.147	HE5620.D7
364.15	HQ150.5
	HV741
	KF26.J832
	KF31.J8
	PS3543.O2
364.150922	F591
	HV6245
	HV6248.B33
	HV6945
364.150924	HV6248.D5
364.150973	HV6493
	HV6789
364.1509764	F386
364.151	KF26.F639
364.1522	E185.625
	HV6545
	HV6548.G7
364.15220924	DB217.M3
364.152209701	HV6548.U5
364.1523	HV6245
	HV6499
	HV6513
	HV6515
	HV6533.C2
	HV6534.T8
	HV6541.G7
	HV6810.L8
364.15230922	HV6053
	HV6245
	HV6534.N5
364.15230924	E842.9.R8
	HV6248.G62
	HV6248.G73
	HV6248.M498
	HV6248.P26
	HV6248.S6137
	HV6248.W66
	HV6533.O7
	HV6535.A8
	HV6535.G4
	HV6555.G7
	HV6766.B4
	KF224.W54
364.15230926	HV6046
	HV6515
364.15230942	HV6499
	HV6535.G4
364.15230968	HV6535.S7
364.15230973	HV6529
364.15230976927	HV6534.A65
364.152309794	HV6533.C2
364.152309931	HV6535.N46
364.1524	E842.9
	HV6278
	HV6505
364.15240922	D412
364.15240924	DA804.1.S4
	DS126.92
	E185.97.K5
364.15240924	E840.8.K4
	E842.9
	HV6248.R39
364.15240926	HV6278
364.15240973	E842.9
	HV6278
364.153	HQ71
	HQ146.N7
	RA790.65.C2
364.1530922	HQ72.G7
364.1530942	HQ72.G7
364.1540924	DS777
364.155	F594
	HQ767
	HV6248.D26
	RA1067
364.1550924	DU222.K4
	F594
	F786.M66
364.1550977398	F549.C37
364.157	HV5822.H4
	HV5831.N5A5
	HV8079.N3
	KF27.5.C7
364.1570924	HV6248.S6138
364.157097471	HV5831.N7
364.15709753	HV5831.D5
364.15709763	HV8079.N3
364.16	HG2066
	HV6635
364.1609753	KF26.D555
364.162	HV6652
	HV7431
	HV8061
	KF27.I5587
	N8387
364.1620926	HV6791
364.16209759	HV6661.F55
364.163	AS36
	CT9980
	HV86
	HV6695
	HV6759
	HV6760.A2
	HV6766.P35
	KF26.C6
	PN181
364.16309421	HV6685.G7
364.1630973	HV6695
364.164	HV9067.V2
	SB481
364.170977311	HQ146.C4
364.172	HV6710
	HV6713
364.17208	HV6710
364.1720922	HV6710
364.1720924	HV6722.G86
	HV6722.G86L63
364.1720942	HV6722.G8
364.1720974985	HV6721.A8
364.1730942	HV5445
	HV5446
364.174	HQ460
364.1740924	HV6705
364.1740973	KF27.P667
364.2	HV6080
	HV6115
	HV6191
	HV9096.U5
	HV9148.W7
364.2018	HV9103
364.2094297	HV9146
364.24	HV6035
	HV6045
	HV6080
	HV6245
364.25	HV9069
364.250942	HV6155
364.254	HV9076.5
364.3	HV6035
	HV6080
	HV6245
	HV6441
	HV6453.G72E57
364.30922	HV6665.G7
364.30942	HV6245
364.309744	HV6049
364.30994	DU115
364.32	HV6049
364.36	HV9061
	HV9069
	HV9076.5
	HV9104
	HV9105.I3
	HV9106.S3
	HV9106.S33
	KF27.5.C7
364.36019	HV9069
364.3608	HV9069
	HV9104
364.3609	HV9065
364.360942	HV9145
364.36097123	HV9109.A55
364.3609729722	HV9069
364.360973	HV8080.J8
	HV9069
	HV9103
	HV9104
364.3609744	HV9105.M4
364.36097471	HV9105.N77
	HV9106.N6
364.360974797	HV9106.B8
364.360974811	HV9106.P5
364.36097526	HV9106.B2
364.3609759	HV9105.F7
364.3609763	HV9105.L82
364.3609768	JK5274
364.3609769	HV9105.K4
364.360977311	HV9106.C4
364.360979798	HV9105.W2
364.3609825	HV9130.C6
364.360991	HV9205
364.363	HV6080
364.363097471	HV9106.N6
364.3630974811	HV6439.U7
364.36309794	HV9076.5
364.364	HV6046
364.36409421	HV7428
364.3640973	HV6046
364.36409794	HV6793.C2
364.37	HV6046
	HV6944
364.370973	HV6046
364.4	HV7431
	HV9104
364.406374811	HV9106.P5
364.40973	JK2403
364.409744	HV7271
364.40979461	HV9106.S4
364.44	HV9103
364.440973	KF1562
364.4409747277	HV6795.N4
364.4409763	HV7268
364.4409766	HV7286
364.4409768	HV7292
364.44097739	HV9475.I3
364.4409787	HV7300.A6
364.4409793	HV7278
364.4409795	HV7287
	HV7571.O7
364.4409796	HV7261
364.6	HV8675
	HV9105.V7
	HV9278
	HV9288
	HV9304
	HV9346
	KF9685
364.601	HV8675
364.6071173	HV9304
	LA226
364.6072073	HV9304
364.608	HV8675
364.60942	HV8532.G8
	HV9644
364.60973	HV8532.U5
	HV9304
364.609757	HV8360
364.609758	HV7260
364.609773	HV9475.I3
364.61	E780
	JK7801
	KF27.I548
364.62	HV9104
	KF27.J8666
364.62076	HV9278
364.620971	HV9308
364.6209776	HV9278
364.6209794	HV9305.C3
	J87.C2
364.6209797	HV9305.W1
364.63	HV9068
	HV9146
	HV9278
	KF27.J8666
364.63076	HV9304
364.630942	HV9278
364.630973	KF9750
364.630974461	HV9106.B7
364.6309747	HV9306.N6
364.6309748	HV9093.P4
364.6309794	HV9305.C2
364.66	HV8579
	HV8694
	HV8698
364.6609	HV8694
364.660942	HV8694
364.660973	KF26.J838
364.67	HV8613
364.72	HV9069
	HV9081
	HV9145
	HV9146
	HV9278
364.720924	HV9148.D6
364.720942	HV9146
364.72095694	HV9215.I8
364.72097471	HV9105.N77
364.7209794	HV9105
364.76	HV7428
	HV9146
	HV9304
364.8	HV5825
	HV7428
	HV9068
	HV9069
	HV9081
	HV9103
	HV9104
	HV9105.I3
	HV9105.N98
	HV9110.T7
	HV9267
	HV9281
	HV9288
	HV9305.N7
	HV9345
364.808	HV9275

Dewey	LC
364.80926	HV9104
364.80942	HV9146
	HV9346
364.80973	HV9267
	HV9304
364.82	HV700.5
364.91732	HT265
364.941	HV7345
364.942	HV6018
	HV6241
	HV6944
	HV6947
	HV7431
	HV8196
364.9421	HV8198.L7
364.94223	HV6949.K4
364.94248	HV6950.B5
364.944	HV6245
	HV6965
364.954	HV7093
364.973	HV6177
	HV6197.U5
	HV6493
	HV6775
	HV6789
	HV7248
	HV8138
	HV8141
	HV9304
	KF26.J838
	KF27.5.C7
	KF32.5.C7
	KF9223
364.9744	HV271
	HV7271
364.97471	HV6795.N5
364.9748	HV7288
364.975	E185.61
364.9752	HV6793.M3
364.9753	HV6795.W3
	KF27.5.C7
364.97552	HV6793.V8
364.9757	KF27.5.C7
364.9758	KFG562
364.9763	HV7268
364.9768	HV9745.T4
364.9771	HV7285
364.977311	HV6795.C4
364.9775	HV9305.W6
364.9778	E450
364.9791	HV9305.A6
364.9797	HV86
365	HV8665
	HV8754
	HV8949
	HV9267
	HV9471
365.0184	HV9275
365.019	HV6089
365.07	HV8754
365.076	HV9470
365.3	HV8352
	HV8353
	HV8949
	HV8950.A8
	HV8950.P6
	HV8964.R8
365.4	HV8738
	HV8964.R8
	HV9679.A2
365.40924	HV8959.R9
365.42	HV9069
	HV9104
365.420973	HV9104
365.45	HV8964.R8
365.509969	HV8330.5
365.6	HV8836
365.60922	HV8956.G8
	HV9877
365.60924	DS777.55
	HV9468
	HV9475.T2
365.64	HV6089
	HV8658.B4
	HV8959.G7
365.640924	DF852
	DS777.55
	HV8956.G8
365.643	HV7231
365.647	HV9305.M6
365.65	HV9288
365.6509756	HV8929.N72
365.66	HV8833
	HV8875
	HV9106.R62
	HV9345
	HV9475.M72
365.6609713	HV9309.O5
365.6609766	HV9305.O5
365.9	HV6046
365.909781	HV9475.K3
365.924	HV6248.M253
	HV8978.F7
	HV8978.O7
	HV9272
	HV9474.A4
	HV9664
	HV9813
365.926	HV8334
365.941	HV6248.P363
365.94183	HV9650.D
365.942	HV8423
	HV8423.A6
	HV9345
365.942	HV9644
	HV9646
	HV9647
365.94214	HV8657
365.94241	HV9650.B72B74
365.954	HV9793
365.968	HV9849.S6
365.971343	HV9110.G82
365.973	HV8665
	HV9469
	HV9473
365.9741	HV8339
365.97471	HV9481.N61L8
365.9747277	HV6046
365.974768	HV9475.N72
365.9748	HV8358
365.9756	HV9475.N82
365.9758	HV8330
365.9759	HV8929.F7
365.9767	HV9475.A92
365.9772	HV9475.I6
365.9773	HV8332
	HV9475.I3
365.978	HV9475.A17
365.9781	HV9475.K3
365.978138	HV9468
365.979175	HV9475.A62F55
365.9796	HV8331.A7
366	E99.O4
	HQ1904
	HS125
366.1	HS373
	HS395
	HS425
	HS503.M38
	HS525
	HS835.6
	HS878
366.102573	HS383
366.103	HS375
366.109	HS395
	HS405
366.10922	HS509
366.1094	HS499
366.1094225	HS597.S8
366.10975775	HS539.A26A312
366.109762	HS537.M72
366.10978795	HS539.L28L316
366.109794	HS537.C22
366.109944	HS680.A7N47
366.1709752	HD859.D4
366.309714	HS1051.C22Q42
366.309769483	HS1045.N56
366.509	HS1510.E44
366.947	HS71.R8
366.966	HS317
366.9701	E99.K9
366.973	HQ1905.C2
367.9421	HS2865.L6
367.94261	HS2865.D6R625
367.94272	LF379
367.973	HS1510.W9
367.974461	HS2725.B7
367.977486	HS2725.C24B32
368	HB615
	HG8051
	HG8597
368.001519	HG8781
368.00184	HG8781
368.00202	HG8061
368.0023	HF5381
	HG8053
368.002594	HG8733
368.006242	HG8598.Z9C77
368.0065	HG8598.Z9R65
368.0076	HG8531
368.00924	HG8098
	HG8952.S7
	HG9970.A5
368.009783	HG8538.S8
368.01	HG8051
	HG8053
368.012	HG8059.R4
368.014	HG8089
368.065	HG8525
368.092	HG9970.A5
368.0920942	HG9970.A674
368.09209711	HG9970.A65C34
368.0920973	HG9970.A5
	KF1218
368.09209756	KFN7697.7
368.096	HG9970.H62
368.1	HG8053
368.1009759	HG8538.F6
368.1009794	KFC295
368.11009772	HG9769
368.11014	HG9721
368.122	HG9968.C7
	HG9970.F552
368.1400973	KF27.I5587
368.2	HE965
	HG3754.I4
	HG9903
368.220065	HE964.5.G7
368.2200973	HE964.5.U5
368.232	KF26.C6
368.2320097124	HG9970.A65C39
368.23200973	KF2219
368.232009747	HG8511.N7
368.2320973	HG9970.A5
368.3	HD7105
	HD7106.U5
368.300973	HD7106.U5
368.3009781	HG8511.K2
368.30973	HG8799
	HG8876
368.32	HG8525
	HG8771
	HG8886
368.3200151	HG8781
368.320015118	HF5695
368.32006273	HG8522
368.320065	HG8963.O25
	HG9164.Z9
368.320065756563	HG8963.N97
368.3200924	HG8952.K55
368.3200942	HG9057
368.3200968	HG9185.S6
368.3200973	HG8951
368.320954	HG9160
368.36400973	KF27.V455
	KF32.V4
	UB373
368.3700942	HG9057
368.38	HD7103.5.U5
368.3800973	HG9396
368.380973	HG9396
368.382	HB915
	HD7103.5.U5
	HD7199
368.38200621	HG9389.G7
368.3820095694	RA418
368.38200973	HD7102.U4
	HD7123
	RA412.5.U6
368.3820994	HD7102.A8
368.3822009794	RA412.5.U6
368.3823009794	RK58
368.3827009749	HG9397.5.N4
368.384	HE966
	HG9970.A5
368.38609749	HD7102.U5
368.4	HD7091
	HD7123
	KF6297
368.40018	HD7124
368.4009415	HD7167
368.400942	HD7096.G7
	HD7165
	HD7167
368.400947	HD7196
368.4009519	HD7228
368.4009567	HD7235.I7
368.4009624	HD7246.S8
368.4009667	HD7241.Z8G55
368.4009678	HD7243.Z8T36
368.40096781	HD7241.Z8Z34
368.400971	HD7127
368.400972981	HD7145.Z8B349
	HD7145.Z8B35
368.400972983	HD7145.Z8T75
368.400973	HD7091
	HD7123
	HD7125
	HJ257
	JK775
	KF26.L3
	KF27.E335
	KF27.W3
	KF3649
368.4009754	HD7123.A55
368.4009881	HD7159
368.4011	HG8793
368.41	HD7801
368.410071	HD7816.C2
368.4100973	HD7816.U6
	JK850.A3
368.41009747	HD7816.U7
368.41009769	HD7816.U7K25
368.41009969	HD7816.U7H35
368.4109969	JQ6103
368.42	HD7101
368.4200973	KF26.F5
	KF27.P674
368.42009771	JK5574
368.42009794	JK8760.H4
368.426	HD7102.U4
	HD7103.5.U5
	RA412.5.U6
368.42600973	HD7102.U4
	HD7123
	HD7125
	KF27.G663
	KF3608.A4
	RA412.5.U6
368.426009764	HD7102.U4
368.42601409794	HV3006.C2
368.4260973	KF26.F5
368.42609747	HV86
368.42609783	HD7102.U5S8
368.43	HC101
	HG9441
	KF27.E343
368.4300942	HD7106.G8
368.43009485	HD7203
368.4300973	HD7106.U5
	HD7125
368.43009793	HD5725.N3
368.4300994	HD7106.A8
368.44	HD7096.U6I32
368.440076	HD7096.U5
368.4400973	HD7096.U5
	KF26.F5
	KF27.W3
	KF3611
	KF3671
	KF3675
368.44009746	HD7096.U6
368.44009747	HD5725.N7
368.44009768	HD7096.U6T26
368.44009773	HD7096.U6I32
368.44009777	HD7096.U6I226
368.44009791	HD7096.U6
368.44009793	HD7096.U6
368.44009969	HD7096.U6H55
368.44014	HD7096.U6N22
368.4401509778	HD7096.U6M83
368.440942	HD7096.G7
368.440973	HD7123
	KF3671
368.5006273	HG8522.N315
368.500973	HG9956
368.572	HG9970.A5
368.57200973	HG9970.A5
	KF8925.T7
368.572014	KF1218
368.8	HG9968.C7
368.81	HG3729.U5
368.815	HG9970.B85
368.85200973	HG9970.M6
368.85300973	HG4538
368.854	KF26.B345
368.8700973	HG9970.C7
	KF26.B345
368.88	HG9970.T6
368.88009746	HD251
368.971	HG8550
368.973	HG8051
	S21.A6
368.9747	HG8538.N7
	HG8961.N5
368.9751	HG8511.D5
368.9771	KFO185
368.9773	HG8511.I3
368.9776	HG8101.M6
368.9794	HG8538.C2
369.1	HS1923.S63
	HV5287.U553
369.10979461	HS1914.S34
369.12	E186.99.D3
	F122
369.135	E202.5.A19
369.294	DU135
369.4	HQ793.I675
	HQ793.W643
369.402571	HQ799.C2
369.40942	HV1441.G7
369.409497	HQ799.Y8
369.40954	HQ799.I5
369.4095694	HQ799.I7
369.409945	HQ799.A8
369.43	HS3312
	HS3313.Z6
	HS3313.Z9
	HS3315.Z6
	HS3316.G7
369.430973	HS3313
	KF32.A7
369.463	HS3353.G35
369.4630971	HS3353.G36C245
369.5	HF5001.R82O22
	HF5001.R82T74
	HS2724.T4
369.509944	HF5001.A78
370	L106
	L341.H6
	LA132
	LA133
	LA410
	LB7
	LB41
	LB675
	LB695.N4
	LB875
	LB1027
	LB1028
	LB1029.C6
	LB2325
	LB2336
	LB2805
	LB2823.5
	LC4945.G7
	PR3570
370.01	LB3605
370.0938	LA75
370.0973	LB1027
370.09744	J87
370.1	B5134.G32
	BH41
	L106
	LA13
	LA25
	LA75
	LA91
	LA118
	LA132
	LA133
	LA210
	LB5
	LB7
	LB17
	LB41
	LB85.P7
	LB125
	LB475
	LB475.C6
	LB475.W2
	LB510
	LB518
	LB648
	LB675

370.1 ..... LB675.H4
..... LB775
..... LB775.L243
..... LB875
..... LB880
..... LB885
..... LB1025.2
..... LB1153
..... LC473
..... PQ2043
370.109 ..... LA11
370.10924 ..... LB85.P7
..... LB628
..... LB648
370.11 ..... L106
..... LB7
..... LB41
..... LB675
..... LB675.B56
..... LB885
..... LB1025.2
..... LB1067
..... LB1570
..... LB1705
370.1108 ..... LB41
370.112 ..... LC1011
..... LC1016
370.114 ..... BV1473
..... LB3495.G7
..... LB3609
..... LC268
..... LC283
..... LC331
370.12 ..... LA205
..... LB17
..... LB775.O82
..... LB885
370.15 ..... BF431
..... LB775.P49
..... LB1051
..... LB1055
..... LB1059
..... LB1062
..... LB1065
..... LB1067
..... LB1117
..... LB1131
..... LB1131.5
..... LB1134
..... LB3013.6
..... LB3605
..... LC203
..... LC4661
370.152 ..... LB1059
370.18 ..... LB1027
..... LB1028
..... LB1028.5
..... LB2806
..... LB2846
370.182 ..... HA29
..... LB2846
370.183 ..... LB1028
..... LB1028.2
..... LB2823
370.184 ..... LB1028
..... LB2846
370.19 ..... LA832
..... LA898
..... LB41
..... LB3605
..... LC65
..... LC67.J3
..... LC191
..... LC225
..... LC1081
..... LC2717
370.193 ..... HD6483
..... LA126
..... LA133
..... LA210
..... LB41
..... LB1028.5
..... LB1029.C6
..... LB1051
..... LB3605
..... LB3605.C84
..... LC66
..... LC189
..... LC191
..... LC1043
370.19308 ..... LC189
370.193094 ..... LC191
370.1930942 ..... LC191
370.1930954 ..... LC189
370.1930973 ..... LA210
..... LA217
..... LC191
370.19309755 ..... AS36
370.193097732 ..... LA269.C4
370.1930994 ..... LC191
370.1931 ..... LA1844.M9
..... LC215
..... LC220
..... LC230
..... LC231
..... LC232.N8
370.19334 ..... LC71
..... LC1016
..... LC1090
370.1934 ..... DT763
..... F499.C6
..... LA210
..... LA379
..... LB41
370.1934 ..... LB1028
..... LB2825
..... LC3705
..... LC4091
370.19340942 ..... LA632
370.19340973 ..... LA210
370.19341 ..... LC4091
370.19342 ..... E97.5
..... KF4755
..... LA210
..... LA245.B4
..... LA295
..... LC2801
370.193420973 ..... LA210
370.193420975 ..... LC2731
370.1934209758 ..... LA261
370.1934209763355 ..... LA297.N4
370.1934209769 ..... LA292
370.19344 ..... KF26.5.E6
..... LA209.2
..... LA244.C6
..... LB3062
370.1934409747 ..... LA337
370.1934409795 ..... LA352
370.19346 ..... LC5146
370.193460945 ..... LB1568.I8
370.193460954792 ..... LC5148.I5
370.1934609549 ..... LC5148.P35
370.19348 ..... LB2820
..... LC3115
..... LC5105
..... LC5112
..... LC5115
..... LC5119
..... LC5131
..... LC5132.I3
370.193480973 ..... LC5131
370.1934809746 ..... LC5132.C8
370.1934809797 ..... LC5132.W2
370.194 ..... LC2803.N5
370.195 ..... LA131
..... LA132
..... LA622
..... LC1090
370.1950947 ..... LA621
370.196 ..... AS4.Z9
..... CB199
..... L10.U55
..... L929
..... LB5
..... LB2283
..... LB2285.A35
..... LB2285.C55
..... LB2285.R9
..... LB2331.5
..... LB2376
..... LC1090
370.196025 ..... AS4.U8
370.196095 ..... LB2283
370.207 ..... LA23
370.23 ..... L112
..... LB1715
370.25 ..... AS4.U8
370.25798 ..... L903.A4
370.28 ..... LB1028
..... LB1028.5
..... LB1028.6
370.285 ..... LB2806
370.3 ..... LB15
370.5 ..... Z5811
370.611 ..... LA622
370.62767 ..... L13.A613
370.6277 ..... L13.N895
370.6373 ..... L106
370.7 ..... L112
..... L901
..... LA128
..... LA620
..... LB1705
..... LB1715
..... LB1731
..... LB1741
..... LC4091
370.71 ..... LB1051
..... LB1715
..... LB1719.C2
..... LB1725.G6
..... LB1725.I4
..... LB1727.C3
..... LB1727.G7
..... LB1727.S6
..... LB1731
..... LB2165
..... LB2193.I62
..... LB2198
..... LC4005
..... LC4069
370.7109744 ..... LB1772.M4
370.7109746 ..... LB1715
370.712 ..... LB1065
370.7122 ..... GV363
..... LB155
..... LB1140
..... LB1715
370.7123 ..... LB5
..... LB1737.I5
..... LB2838
370.712308 ..... LB1737.A3
370.71230954 ..... LB1737.I5
370.7124 ..... LB1738
..... LB2372.E3
370.72 ..... L901
..... LB1715
370.73 ..... LB1715
370.73 ..... LB1731
..... LB1734.5
..... LB2165
..... QD40
370.7302573 ..... L961.I4
370.730942 ..... LB1715
370.73094238 ..... LB2224.N4
370.7309543 ..... LB2251.B45
370.730973 ..... LB1715
370.732 ..... L901
370.73202542 ..... LB2173.G7
370.733 ..... LB1027
..... LB1715
..... LB1731
..... LB1740
..... LB2153
..... LB2154.A3
..... LB2157.A3
..... LB2157.U5
370.7330202 ..... LB2157.A3
370.76 ..... LB1731
370.777 ..... LB1028.5
370.778 ..... LB5
..... LB1044.7
370.78 ..... LB15
..... LB1028
..... LB2322
..... Z5814.R4
370.78042 ..... LB1028
370.7805 ..... LB1028
370.78071 ..... LB1028
370.78073 ..... L901
..... LB1028
370.780755 ..... LB1028
370.780773 ..... LB1028
370.78094 ..... LA2102
..... LA2102.A97
..... LB1028
370.784 ..... L112
..... LB1028
370.8 ..... AC8
..... LA217
..... LB5
..... LB7
..... LB41
..... LB622.E5
..... LB695
..... LB875
..... LB1051
370.9 ..... D410
..... GN488.5
..... LA11
..... LA13
..... LA25
..... LA91
..... LB575
..... LB775
370.904 ..... LA126
..... LA132
..... LB41
..... LB885
..... LB1027
..... LB1555
370.91 ..... LA13
370.912 ..... HV2534.W73
370.9171242 ..... LA631.82
370.91717 ..... LC1030
370.91724 ..... LC2605
370.91732 ..... LC219
370.91734 ..... LC2605
370.9174924 ..... LC741
370.91812 ..... LA11
370.922 ..... LA2311
..... LA2383.I6
370.924 ..... CT275.C757
..... CT275.L25
..... E332.2
..... LA206
..... LA2317.B37
..... LA2317.E53
..... LA2377.B363
..... LA2377.S48
..... LA2385.C67
..... LA2385.H8
..... LA2389.B3
..... LB125.A4
..... LB125.A8
..... LB637
..... LB639
..... LB675.F62
..... LB695.C6
..... LB695.M35
..... LB775.H788
370.93 ..... LA31
370.934 ..... LA36
370.938 ..... LA75
370.94 ..... LA13
..... LA622
370.941 ..... LA651
..... LA652
370.9415 ..... LA641.7
370.942 ..... BR758
..... L106
..... L915
..... LA11
..... LA21
..... LA116
..... LA123
..... LA631
..... LA631.3
..... LA631.7
..... LA631.8
..... LA631.82
..... LA632
370.942 ..... LA633
..... LA634
..... LA635
..... LA636
..... LB1115
..... LB2806
..... LC93.G7
..... LC191
..... LC4096.G7
..... LH631.82
370.94221 ..... LA639.W37
370.94254 ..... LH639.L4
370.94259 ..... LC4096.G
370.94274 ..... LC5056.G7
370.9438 ..... LA841
370.94391 ..... LA681
..... LA681.82
370.944 ..... LA691.8
..... LA2375.F7
370.945 ..... LA792
370.947 ..... L111
..... LA831
..... LA831.8
..... LA832
370.9481 ..... LA898
370.9485 ..... LA902
370.9492 ..... LA822
370.94965 ..... LA1040.A4
370.94977 ..... LA952
370.95 ..... LA1052
..... LA1311
370.951 ..... LA1131
370.952 ..... DS810
..... L158
..... LA1311
..... LA1312
370.95365 ..... LA1104.B3
370.954 ..... LA1151
..... LB1151
370.95479 ..... L578.M34
370.954792 ..... LA1154.C26
..... LA1154.M34
370.9549 ..... LA1156
370.95491 ..... LA1156
370.95492 ..... L106
370.95493 ..... LA1154.C3
370.95496 ..... LA1154.N4
370.955 ..... LA1351
370.9561 ..... LA942
370.95694 ..... KF32.E333
..... LA1441
370.9593 ..... LA1221
370.9595 ..... LA1271
370.95951 ..... LA1236
370.95952 ..... LA1239.5
370.96 ..... AS4.U8
..... LA1501
370.9624 ..... LA1646
370.963 ..... LB2285.E8
370.966 ..... LA1661
370.9664 ..... LA1611.S5
370.9669 ..... LA1611.N5
370.967 ..... DT471
..... LA1501
..... LA1561
370.9673 ..... LA1994.A6
370.96762 ..... L666.K4
..... LA1561
370.9678 ..... LA1841
370.96782 ..... LA1844.S9
370.968 ..... LA1501
..... LA1536
370.96894 ..... LA1596
370.971 ..... LA411
..... LA412
370.9711 ..... LA418.B8
370.9714 ..... LA418.O7
370.972 ..... LA421
..... LA422
370.973 ..... KF27.E333
..... L106
..... L154
..... LA191.82
..... LA201
..... LA205
..... LA208
..... LA209
..... LA209.2
..... LA210
..... LA212
..... LA215
..... LA217
..... LA228
..... LB41
..... LB775.G22
..... LB875
..... LB885
..... LB1025
..... LB1025.2
..... LB1027
..... LB1028
..... LB2831
..... LB3562
..... LC741
..... LC2801
..... LC5131
370.974 ..... LA206
..... LH205
370.9741 ..... L156
370.9744 ..... LA304
..... LC406.M4
370.9745 ..... L196
370.9747 ..... L182
..... LA337

370.9748 ... L194
... LA355
370.975 ... LA205
... LA209
... LC2801
370.9751 ... LA252
370.9752 ... LA301
370.9753 ... LC2853.W45
370.9754 ... L214
370.9755 ... LA379
370.9756 ... L184.C5
370.9759 ... L136
... L136.C5
370.9761 ... LA231
... LC2802.A2
370.9762 ... LA313
370.9763 ... L154
... LB2826.L8
370.9768924 ... L203.J4
370.9769 ... L152.H53
370.977178 ... LA348.C5
370.9773 ... LA267
370.9774 ... LA307
370.9787 ... LA391
370.979173 ... Z5811
370.9792 ... L206
370.9793 ... L174
370.9794 ... J87
... L124
... L124.C5
370.9795 ... L192.C5
... L192.C52
... LA352
370.9797 ... LC4032.W2
370.9798 ... LA234
370.98 ... JX1977
... LA541
370.981 ... LA556
370.9861 ... Q180.A1
370.9876 ... LA606
370.9881 ... LA578.B7
370.9931 ... LA2122
370.994 ... LA2102
370.9944 ... LA2111.7
370.9969 ... L106
371 ... LB1026
... LB1027
... LB2805
... LB2806
371.0018 ... LB2806
371.00184 ... LB2806
371.0025713 ... L906.O6
371.0028 ... LB1028.5
371.0091724 ... LC2605
371.00941 ... LB2903
371.00942 ... LA631
371.00945 ... L935
371.00973 ... LB2805
... LB2825
371.00974946 ... LA333.F7
371.00979486 ... LC2852.V56
371.00994 ... LA2102
371.01 ... L118.H5
... L124
... L183
... LB2805
... LB2822
... LB2823.5
... LC243.P4
371.01018 ... LB2846
371.0102573 ... L901
371.010973 ... LA210
... LA212
... LA216
... LC89
371.010974 ... LA215
371.010974461 ... LA306.B7
371.01097471 ... L183.N5
371.010974766 ... LA339.S8
371.010974797 ... LA339.B9
371.010974811 ... LA357.P5
371.010974988 ... LA333.C3
371.0109753 ... KF27.D585
... LA255
371.0109755 ... LA379
371.0109756 ... L184.C5
371.010975688 ... LA341.B8
371.0109764 ... L204
... LA370
371.0109769 ... L152
371.010977132 ... LA348.C6
371.010979529 ... LA354.R6
371.0109797 ... LA382
371.02 ... LC47
371.0202542 ... L915
371.0202594 ... L981
371.020973 ... LC49
371.0209743 ... LC50.V4
371.020974461 ... LA306.B7
371.020974795 ... LC6301.C5
371.020975799 ... LC2852.S32
371.020994 ... LA2105
371.1 ... LB1025
... LB1025.2
... LB1027
... LB1033
... LB1051
... LB1067
... LB1715
... LB1731
... LB1775
... LB2805
... LB2806
... LB2832
371.1 ... LB2832.4.G7
... LB2837
... LB2838
... LB2842.2
... LB2844.1.A8
... LB2844.1.N4
... LB2844.1.P3
... LC191
371.100186 ... LB1025.2
371.100202 ... LB1731
371.10023 ... LB1775
371.10062415 ... L18.I73
371.10062713 ... L13.O573
371.1006273 ... L13
371.10072 ... LB1775
371.1008 ... LB1025
... LB1025.2
371.1009 ... LA11
... LA21
371.10091732 ... LC5133.N4
371.100924 ... DA566.9.M36
... LA2311
... LA2317
... LA2317.F73
... LA2377.B36
... LA2377.D5
... LA2377.L23
... LA2377.T38
... LA2389.F7
... LB1037
... LB1602
... LC2803.P5
... LF795.W57
371.100937 ... LF330
371.100942 ... LB2901
371.100973 ... L112
... LB1775
371.1009747 ... LA2315.N7
371.1009773 ... LB2832
371.1009776 ... LB2806
371.1009944 ... LA2112
371.102 ... LB1025.2
... LB1027
... LB1033
... LB3011
... LC5115
371.103 ... LC191
... LC225
371.1030942 ... LC225
371.1108 ... LB2838
371.12 ... LB1715
... LB1725.P45
371.120971 ... LB2890
371.132 ... H62
... LB1762
371.133 ... LB1771
... LB3051
371.1330973 ... LB1771
371.13309744 ... LB1772.M4
371.13309756 ... L184
371.13309759 ... LB1772.F5
371.13309762 ... L166.B3
371.14 ... AS4.U8
... LB5
... LB1025.2
... LB1027
... LB1715
... LB1731
371.1412 ... LB2844.1.A8
371.144 ... LB1025.2
371.148 ... LB1027
371.193420976773 ... LA242.L5
371.196 ... LA637.7
... LC1090
371.2 ... JK8701
... LB1051
... LB1065
... LB2804
... LB2805
... LB2806
... LB2817
... LB2819
... LB2824
... LB2831.5
... LB2832
... LB2844.1.A8
371.2001 ... LB2806
... LB2901
371.2007 ... LB2832
371.2008 ... LB2805
371.200954 ... LB2947
371.2009678 ... LB2970.T3
371.200973 ... LB2805
371.2009744 ... LB2809.M4
371.2009943 ... L750
371.201 ... LB2806
... LB2822
371.2010973 ... LB2822
371.20109751 ... LB2831.5
371.2011 ... LB1731
371.20110924 ... LA209.2
... LA2317.B488
371.2012 ... LC225
371.2013 ... LB2805
... LB2806
371.20130973 ... LB2805
... LB2822
371.202 ... LB3013.5
... LC4019
371.204 ... LA1154.C3
371.218 ... LB2350
371.219 ... LB2846
371.21971 ... LC145.C2
371.219747 ... LC132.N7
371.219754 ... LC2802.W4
371.219769 ... LB2846
371.219771 ... L188
371.219797 ... LC132.W3
371.219969 ... LC144.H3
371.2209753 ... L134
371.2209786 ... LB2338
371.23 ... LB3034
... LB3081
371.2309751 ... LB3034
371.23209792 ... LC5752.U8
371.24 ... LC144.C6
371.25 ... LB1032
371.251 ... LB3013
371.26 ... AS36
... LB5
... LB1027
... LB1131
... LB3051
371.26013 ... LB1131
371.260942081 ... LB3056.G7
371.2609769 ... L152.B35
371.264 ... LB1117
371.2642 ... LB1067
... LB3051
... LB3056.G7
371.2642095456 ... LB1027
371.27 ... LB3051
371.271 ... LB3051
... QA43
371.271077 ... LB3051
371.272 ... LC143
371.2721 ... PE1074.5
371.2722 ... LB2846
... LB3056.G7
371.2913 ... LC142
371.29130973 ... LC143
371.291309741 ... LC144.M28
371.291309773 ... LC144.I3
371.291309788 ... LC144.C6
371.3 ... BC161.T4
... HM261
... LA243
... LB475.H76
... LB775.M8
... LB775.P49
... LB1025
... LB1025.2
... LB1026
... LB1027
... LB1028.5
... LB1029.G3
... LB1029.N6
... LB1043
... LB1051
... LB1059
... LB1062
... LB1065
... LB1715
... LB1775
... LB2157.A3
371.301 ... LB885
... LB1025
... LB1025.2
371.3018 ... LB2823
371.3028 ... LB1027
... LB1564.N55
371.30281 ... LB1047.5
... LB1049
... LB2395
371.30282 ... LB1025.2
... LB1027
... LB1032
... LB1715
... LB2806
... LB3051
371.3028209777 ... LA286
371.306277434 ... LA309.D6
371.30720747 ... LB1026
371.3078 ... LB1043
... LB3044
... Z5817.2
371.308 ... L11
... LB775.M8
371.30973 ... L13.N47645
371.309748 ... LA355
371.32 ... LB1048
371.3209769 ... Z5817
371.33 ... LB1027
... LB1028
... LB1043
... LB1043.5
... LB1044.7
... LB1131
... LB3044
... TS2301.A7
371.33019 ... LB1059
371.330202 ... LB1043
371.3305 ... LB1043
371.330973 ... LB1043
371.3331 ... LB1044.5
371.333109941 ... LC6581.A82
371.3333 ... TK7881.6
371.3333029 ... LB1044.4
371.335 ... LB1027
... LB1043.5
... LB1044
... TS171
371.3350971 ... LB1044
371.3352 ... LB1043
371.3352019 ... LB1067
371.3352029 ... LB1044.9.Z9
371.33522 ... LB1043.5
371.33523 ... LB1044
371.335230216 ... LB1044
... LB1044.Z9
371.33523029 ... LB1044.Z9
371.3352309763 ... L154
371.3356 ... LB1043.5
... LB1043.6
371.3358 ... LB1044.7
371.3358072 ... S544.5.G7
371.3358077 ... LB1044.7
371.33580941435 ... LB1043.2.G7
371.33580952 ... LB1044.6.J3
371.33580971 ... LB1044.7
371.3358097127 ... LB1044.7
371.335809713 ... LB1044.7
371.33580973 ... LB1044.7
371.335809748 ... LB1044.7
371.335809773 ... LB1044.7
371.335809787 ... LB1044.7
371.335809795 ... LB1044.7
371.36 ... LB1570
... LB2806
371.38 ... LB1026
... LB1047
371.381 ... LB1047
371.38109795 ... LB1047
371.39 ... LB1029.G3
371.394 ... LB1027
... LB1028.5
... LB1031
... LC41
371.39408 ... LB1031
371.3944 ... LB1028.5
371.3944018 ... LB1028.5
371.39440971 ... LB1028.5
371.39442 ... LB1028.5
371.39445 ... LB1028.5
... LB2846
371.4 ... L152
... LB5
... LB1027.5
... LB1028
... LB1731
... LB2846
... LC4169
371.4023 ... LB1027.5
371.40285 ... LB1027.6
371.407 ... LB1027.5
371.40720776 ... LB1027.5
371.4076 ... BF637.C6
371.408 ... LB7
... Z5814.P8
371.40947 ... BF637.C6
371.40954 ... LB1027.5
371.40974 ... LB1027.5
371.409744 ... LB1027.5
371.409769 ... L152
371.42 ... LB7
... LB1027.5
371.422 ... LB1027.5
371.425 ... HF3381
... HF5381
... HF5386
... LB1027.5
371.425023 ... LB1731
371.4250924 ... HF5381
371.4250941 ... HF5382.5.S34
371.4250973 ... LC1045
... LC2801
371.46 ... BF637.C6
... LB3013.6
371.48 ... LB1027.5
... LB1620.5
371.5 ... LB3011
... LB3013
371.59 ... LB3092
371.6 ... LB3205
... LB3209
... LB3221
... LB3222.5
... LC1048.F3
371.60954 ... LB3219.I4
371.610978883 ... LB3223
371.62 ... LB3013
... LB3235
371.6208 ... LB3219.G7
371.620973 ... LB3222
371.621 ... LB3224
371.623 ... KF26.D568
... LB3205
371.628 ... LB3241
371.67 ... LB3261
371.7 ... LB3405
... LB3409
371.709781 ... LB3409.U6
371.709795 ... LB3409.U6
371.71 ... LB3405
371.710954792 ... LB3425.B6
371.712 ... LB3405
371.71209787 ... LB3412.W9
371.716 ... KF26.A35
... KF27.A3
... KF31.A35
371.7160973 ... LB3479.U5
371.8 ... LA418.O6
371.80959 ... LA1223.7
371.81 ... LA229
371.83 ... LB3602
371.854792 ... LJ85.T58
371.872 ... LB2864
371.87209748 ... LB2864
371.87209749 ... LB2864
371.87209767 ... LB2864
371.87209773 ... L142
371.89 ... LB3605

Dewey	LC
371.890942	LB3605
371.892	GV703
371.893	LB3635
371.895	LB3015
371.897	LB3621
371.9	GV443
	GV445
	HV3005
	KF27.E333
	LB1029.R4
	LB1051
	LB1067
	LB1134
	LB2338
	LB3430
	LC198
	LC3965
	LC3969
	LC4005
	LC4015
	LC4019
	LC4025
	LC4031
	LC4032.K4
	LC4036.D4
	LC4036.G6
	LC4055
	LC4215
	LC4601
	LC4636.G
	LC4661
	LC4691
	LC5252.F5
	LD7501.M4374
	PS508.C5
	QA11
	QA135.5
371.9025	L900
371.909489	LC4036.D4
371.909492	LC4036.N4
371.90973	LC4015
371.909748	LC4032.P4
371.909755	LC4005
371.909764	LC3982.T4
	LC4032.T5
371.909771	LC4032.O3
371.909774	LC4032.M5
371.909797	LC4032.W2
371.91	GV445
	KF26.L343
	LC4019
	LC4025
	LC4215
	LC4580
371.910942	LC4005
371.910973	KFN2195.9.H3
371.910977178	LC4033.C5
371.9109795	LC4032.O7
371.911	HV1598
	HV1669
	HV1795
	LB5
	LB1050.5
371.911019	RE48.2.C5
371.9110924	HV1624.B65
	HV1624.M3
371.9110941	HV1942
371.9110942	HV1945
371.912	HV1669
	HV2353
	HV2395
	HV2417
	HV2437
	HV2440
	HV2483
	HV2487
	HV2526
	HV2537
	HV2561.I48
	HV2718
	LB1572
371.91209	HV2717.W7
371.91209775	HV2561.W6
371.91209794	HV2561.C3
371.914	LB1139.L3
	LB3454
	LC4580
371.916	LC4015
	LC4580
371.92	HV3004
	LB1029.C6
	LB1050
	LC4015
	LC4165
	LC4580
	LC4601
	LC4602
	LC4606
	LC4616
	LC4636.G7
	LC4661
	LC4692.F6
371.92025778	LC4692.M53
371.92071142	LC4625
371.9209744	HV3006.M4
371.9209754	HV3006.W4
371.9209756386	LC4041.K5
371.9209764	LC4692.T4
371.9209768	LC4182.T2
371.9209778	LC4692.M53
371.9209797	HV86.W353
371.928	LC4661
371.9282	LC4616
371.93	HV9081
371.93	LC4801
371.94	LB1139.E5
	LC4165
	RJ506.A9
371.94094259	HV9148
371.940977438	LC4182.M5
371.95	LC3969
	LC3993
371.9502573	L901
371.95094267	LB2224.B7
371.95097471	LC3995.N5
371.950975	LC3993
371.9509931	LC4000.N4
371.96	HD1525
	LA210
	LB7
	LB1047
	LB1059
	LC515
	LC1046.O3
	LC4051
	LC4055
	LC4065
	LC4069
	LC4075
	LC4085
	LC4086
	LC4091
	LC4092.C2
	LC4092.M3
	LC4092.M5
	LC4092.N38
	LC4092.N7
	LC4092.O7
	LC4094
	LC4096.G7
	LC4616
	LC5056.G7
	LC5152.N7
	LC5152.W8
371.9609747	LC1046.N5
371.967	LC4069
	LC4091
371.9675	LC5151
371.97	E78.C2
	E97
	E99.E7
	KF31.L355
	KF8210.E3
	LC2686
	LC2717
	LC2741
	LC2778.R4
	LC2803.N5
	LC2808.N5
	LC2808.S7
	LC2852.E17
	LC3501.A3
	LC3501.M3
	LC3719
	LC3731
	LC3732.V5
	LC4092.M7
	PS3505.L228
371.98	E97
	LB1529.U5
	LC2682
	LC2685
	LC2687.S6
	LC3731
	PE1128
372	LB775
	LB775.P49
	LB875
	LB1026
	LB1067
	LB1555
	LB1715
	LB2822.5
	LB3062
372.0621	L13.A683
372.07	LA418.O6
372.1	LB2822.5
372.10186	LB2822.5
372.11	LB1555
	LB1715
372.11008	LB1731
372.1100924	LB1567
372.11009767	LB1561.A8
372.110309421	LF795.L6948
372.114	LB1731
372.12	LB2822.5
	LC4093.N5
372.12009945	LB2822.5
372.12012	LB2822.5
372.120120973	LB2822
	LB2822.5
372.1254	LB1032
	LB3061
372.126	LB1050
372.12642	LB1059
	LB1131
372.127	LB3051
372.13	LB675.L3
	LB1025
	LB1715
372.130184	LB1028
372.130282	LB775.M8
	LB1059
	LB1569
	LB1715
372.130924	LB775.M8
372.133	LB1043
372.1335	LB1044.9.N4
372.13356	LB1045
372.136	LB1027
372.13810971	LB1047
372.139	LB1027
372.1394	LB1029.R4
	LB1031
372.14	LB1027.5
372.142	LB1027.5
372.16	LB3325.N8
372.162	LB3221
372.162097469	LD7501.S9
372.1712	LB1051
372.19	LB1027
	LB1523
	LB1557
	LB1569
	LB1570
	LB1715
372.190973	LB1570
372.2	LB1140
372.208	LB1140
372.21	LB1137
	LB1140
	LC143
	LC4065
	LC4091
372.21029	Z5814.P6
372.210924	LB639
372.210942	LB1117
372.210947	LB1140
372.210973	KF27.E335
	LC4091
372.2109730924	LB1140.2
372.210977389	LB1132
372.210979494	LC4092.C2
372.216	LB1140
	LB3013
	PZ9.H869
372.21609485	LB1140
372.2160954792	LB1140
372.218	LB1169
	LB1195
372.24	LA633
372.2409416	LA649.N6
372.2409748	LB1140.
372.241	LA219
	LA633
	LB1140
	LB1507
	LB1532
	LB1571
372.2410942	LB41
372.24109429	LA664
372.2410978863	LC4092.C6
372.2410994	LB1027
372.242	LB1059
372.3	LB1585
	QA135.5
372.35	L162
	LB1044.9.P5
	LB1059
	LB1532
	LB1584
	LB1585
	LB1585.3
	Q161
	Q181
	QC39
	QC171
	QC869
	QH206
	QH315
372.35044	LB1585
372.357	GV197
	QH51
372.37	HQ57.5.A3
	HV5060
	LB3405
	LB3412.W3
	RA790.5
372.3709755	LB1588.U6
372.4	LB118
	LB1050
	LB1050.5
	LB1525
	LB1573
	LB2844.1.R4
	PE1408
372.408	LB1573
372.40917496	LC2778.R4
372.41	LB1050
	LB1140.5.R4
	LB1181
	LB1525
	LB1573
	LB1576
372.412	PE112
	PE1119
	PE1121
	PZ5.F35
	PZ7.L163
372.413	LB1050
	LB1050.5
	LB1573
372.414	LB1050
	LB1573
372.4144	LB1573
372.4264	LF795.L692953
372.5	LB1140
	LB1537
	LB1591
	LB1594
	LT101
	N350
372.5	TX663
372.509747	N362
372.509764	N354.T45
372.52	N85
	N347
	N350
	N352
	N361
	NC1765
372.55	LB1140.5.A7
	TT165
372.6	L166
	LB1139.L3
	LB1140
	LB1528
	LB1573
	LB1575
	LB1575.8
	LB1576
	LB1591
	LB1631
	LC4091
	PE1066
	PE1408
	PN1101
	PZ6.G2
	PZ9
372.6044	LB1576
372.61	LB1139.L3
	LB1576
	PE1068.G5
372.62	LB1139.L3
	PE1135
372.623	LB1576
372.63	PE1145.4
372.632	LB1620
372.634	Z43
372.64	LB1042
	PN1101
372.65	LB1580.G7
	LT101
	PA2051
	PC2115
	PN3171
372.650973	LB1580.U5
372.6596	PL8016
372.66	PN3171
	PN6120.A5
372.7	LB1059
	QA11
	QA14.C3
	QA135.5
	QA139
	QA461
372.71	HV851
372.72	LB1059
	PZ10.W59
	QA135.5
	QA142
372.720968	QA135.5
372.73	LB1059
	PZ10.C374
	QA462
372.8	BV1475.2
	GV1799
	PZ9
372.83	CB59
	DA4
	DA125.H5
	DA890.G5
	DK28
	DL619
	DT352
	DU120
	E27.2
	F234.W7
	F491.3
	F581.3
	F1105.5.F7
	F1208.5
	F2508.5
	G72
	G127
	GF48
	H62
	H95
	HC108.P7
	HC251
	HQ57.3
	HT65
	HT177.S38
	L166
	LB1530
	LB1570
	LB1584
	PE1127.A6
	PE1127.T7
	PZ9.E518
372.83044	LB1530
	LB1584
372.8308	LB1584
372.830973	E178.3
	LB1584
372.832	LB1530
	LC109
	LC1091
372.86	GV224.A1
	GV362
	GV443
	GV464.5
	LB1561.M6
	LB3031
372.87	MT1
	MT3.N4

372.87 ..... MT3.U5
..... MT6
..... MT7
..... MT10
..... MT42
..... MT150
..... MT810
..... MT930
372.870182 ..... MT3.T4
372.870942 ..... MT920
372.89 ..... D756
..... DA35
..... DA130
..... DA360
..... DL65
..... E77
..... E111
..... E125.B2
..... E125.S7
..... E129.H8
..... F149.3
..... F254.3
..... F269.3
..... F326
..... F680.5
..... F864
..... F1208.5
..... G126
..... G370.P9
..... LB1582.G7
372.891 ..... DU105
..... E123
..... F106
..... F1208.5
..... G74
..... G125
..... G126
..... G127
..... G585.B8
..... GA130
372.891045 ..... G127
372.9208 ..... LC4165
372.942 ..... LA633
372.94251 ..... LC5153.G7
372.94285 ..... LF795.H37
372.95496 ..... LA1154.N4
372.9669 ..... LA1611.N5
372.96762 ..... LA1561
372.9747 ..... L182.C5
372.97471 ..... LD7501.N5
372.974812 ..... LD7251.P5
372.99312 ..... LG745.P65
372.993122 ..... LB1564.N5
372.9944 ..... LG715.B33
..... LG715.B83
..... LG745.R9
372.9945 ..... L981
373 ..... LA635
..... LB1607
..... LB1761
..... LB2822
..... LC189
..... LC5951
..... LD3512.9
373.0072203 ..... HJ2052
373.01 ..... LC268
373.0186 ..... LB1028.5
373.07201717 ..... LB1028
373.0904 ..... LB1625
373.11 ..... LB1737.A3
..... LB2901
373.1100202 ..... LB1025.2
..... LB1737.A3
373.1100924 ..... LA2317.R6
..... LB1602
373.1100942 ..... LA635
373.1102 ..... LB3013
373.110924 ..... LA2389.E4
373.12 ..... LB2822
..... LB2825
373.12012 ..... LB2804
..... LB2822
373.120120942 ..... LB2901
373.1204 ..... LB1607
373.12170942 ..... LB1627
373.12180941 ..... LB1620
373.123 ..... LC130
..... LC135.G7
373.125 ..... LB1033
373.126 ..... LB1050
..... LB3056.G7
373.1260942 ..... LB3056.G7
373.1262 ..... LB1627.7
373.1264 ..... LB1627
..... LB2353
373.12642 ..... L341
..... LB1627.7
373.127 ..... LB3051
373.1271 ..... LB3051
373.12710942 ..... LB3056.G7
373.12913 ..... LC146
373.1291309701 ..... E97
373.1291309751 ..... LC146
373.13 ..... LB1025
..... LB1062
..... LB1737.A3
373.130281 ..... LB1049
..... LB1737.A3
373.13944 ..... LB1028.5
373.14 ..... LB1027.5
..... LB1620
..... LB1620.5
..... Z5811
373.14094 ..... LB1620.5
373.140942 ..... LB1620.5
373.140973 ..... LB1620
373.142 ..... LB1620.5
..... LB2350.5
373.1422 ..... LC4092.G4
373.14220942 ..... LB1027.5
373.1425 ..... HF5381
..... LB2350
373.14250942 ..... LB1620.5
373.14250973 ..... HF5381
..... LC1043
373.142509776 ..... HF5382.5.U6
373.142509789 ..... LC1046.N45
373.16097526 ..... LD7501.B2
373.16208 ..... LB3219.G7
373.162095456 ..... LA1154.D4
373.16209581 ..... LA1082
373.16209596 ..... LA1192
373.1623 ..... LB3205
373.1710954792 ..... LB3409.I4
373.18 ..... BJ1661
..... LB1135
..... LB3605
373.1802573 ..... E154.5
373.181 ..... LA217
..... LB1135
..... LB3605
..... LB3609
..... LC2771
..... LD7501.N5
373.18108 ..... LB3605
373.1810973 ..... LA229
373.18109748 ..... LA355
373.18109771 ..... LA346
373.19 ..... LA622
..... LB1607
..... LB1628
..... LB1629.5.E9
373.1901 ..... LB41
373.19094 ..... LB1629.5.E9
373.190942 ..... LB1628
373.190954 ..... LB1629.5.I48
373.190971 ..... LB1629.5.C2
373.190973 ..... LB1628
373.190977 ..... LB1628
373.2220942 ..... HV244
..... LA632
..... LA634
..... LA635
373.22209542 ..... LG170.D373
373.2220973 ..... LB1607
373.236 ..... LB1623
373.23608 ..... LB1623
..... LB2819
373.23609773 ..... LB1623
373.23609794 ..... LB1623
373.238 ..... LB1629.7
..... LB1695
373.24 ..... LB1620
..... LC1045
373.2420924 ..... LF795.R92
373.246 ..... AS4.U8
..... HV3005
..... KF27.E333
..... LB1595
..... LC1044
..... LC1045
..... LC1046.M7
..... TT165
373.2460184 ..... LC1044
373.246072 ..... LC1043
373.246072073 ..... LC1045
373.246076 ..... LC1046.O3
373.246094 ..... HF5549.5.T7
373.2460947 ..... LC1047.R9
373.24609471 ..... LC1047.F5
373.2460954 ..... LC1047.I4
373.24609678 ..... HD2346.T3
373.2460973 ..... LC1042
..... LC1045
373.2460974 ..... L113.A6
373.24609744 ..... LC1046.M4
373.24609747 ..... LC1046.N5
373.24609748 ..... LC1046.P4
373.24609749 ..... LC1046.N4
373.2460975438 ..... HD5726.C37
373.24609764 ..... LC1046.T4
373.24609769 ..... LC1046.K4
373.24609771 ..... LC1046.O3
373.24609773 ..... LC1046.I3
373.2460977455 ..... LC1046.M5
373.24609786 ..... LC1046.M9
373.24609794 ..... LC1046.C2
373.24609795 ..... LC1046.O7
373.24609796 ..... LC1046.I2
373.24609798 ..... LC1046.A4
373.2460991 ..... T163.I6
373.246309759 ..... L136
373.246409767 ..... HD6274.A7
373.2465 ..... HF1106
..... HF5415.4
373.24650973 ..... HF1131
373.246509741 ..... HF1131
373.246509763 ..... L154.B32
373.246509767 ..... HF5415.4
373.246509793 ..... HF5415.4
373.2467 ..... HD5820.5.P8
..... T61
..... TT170
373.24670954 ..... T153
373.24670954922 ..... TT167.P3
373.246709795 ..... T74.O7
373.25 ..... LC191
373.250942 ..... LA635
..... LB2901
..... LB3061
373.42 ..... LA632
..... LA634
..... LA635
..... LB1027
..... LB1607
..... LB1629.7
..... LC3747.G7
373.4216 ..... LF795.L695
..... LF795.L7
373.4219 ..... LF795.E17
373.4231 ..... LF795.S3955
373.4237 ..... LF795.T7
373.4238 ..... LF795.B1155
373.4248 ..... LB1629.5.W3
373.4252 ..... LF795.T8
373.4254 ..... LF795.L8
373.4258 ..... LF795.A4
373.4271 ..... LF795.W3
373.4272 ..... LF795.C85
..... LF795.L692965
373.4274 ..... LF795.T38
..... LF795.Y6
373.6762 ..... LA1564.K4
..... LC55.K4
373.73 ..... L101.U6
..... LA222
..... LB5
..... LB1607
..... LC2771
373.7426 ..... LD7501.E9
373.7427 ..... LD7501.C822
373.74461 ..... LD7501.B7
373.7467 ..... LD7501.C46
373.7471 ..... LA339.N5
373.74723 ..... LD7501.N5L778
373.747275 ..... LD7501.B772
373.748 ..... LA355
373.74813 ..... LD7501.G45C477
373.74978 ..... LD7501.H13
373.75 ..... LC2801
373.75284 ..... LD7501.G314
373.76138 ..... LC2851.S575
373.773 ..... LA267
373.7731 ..... LD7501.E4
373.77311 ..... LC2803.C5
373.79473 ..... LD7501.P22
373.79733 ..... LD7501
373.81 ..... LA557
373.94 ..... LA2106
373.943 ..... LG715.B7
373.944 ..... LG715.P3
373.969 ..... LA2256
373.96931 ..... LG961.H4
374 ..... HD6870.G45
..... HD6870.Z34
..... HV2561.I22
..... L91
..... L136
..... LB1050
..... LC8
..... LC149
..... LC5056.G7
..... LC5209
..... LC5215
..... LC5219
..... LC5252.F5
..... LC5301.B87
..... LC5325.E4
..... LC6025
..... LF335
374.0025 ..... LC5201
374.008 ..... LC5215
374.01 ..... LC5251
374.0120973 ..... LC1045
374.013 ..... HD5715
..... HD6058
..... L901
..... SD144.C2
374.01302573 ..... Z5814.T4
374.013095492 ..... TT166.P3
374.01309591 ..... LB1029.C6
374.0715 ..... LB1029.C6
374.1 ..... LC31
374.2 ..... L111.A72
..... LC5219
..... LC6301.C5
..... LC6552.M4
374.21 ..... LC5057.C4
374.26 ..... LC6574
374.28094251 ..... LC5256.G7
374.2809457 ..... LC156.I8
374.402573 ..... L900
374.46 ..... LC5957.A2
374.473 ..... LC5951
374.4793 ..... LC5919
374.492 ..... LC5955.N4
374.91724 ..... LC2605
374.924 ..... LA2375.G72
374.942 ..... LC361
..... LC1043
..... LC5056.G7
..... LC5215
..... LC5256.G7
..... LF378
374.94281 ..... LC5256.G7
374.947 ..... LC5056.R9
374.948 ..... LC5256.S3
374.9485 ..... LC5256.S8
374.954 ..... LC5057.I5
374.967 ..... LC5258.C4
374.9715 ..... SD13
374.973 ..... LC5251
..... LC6301.C5
374.9747 ..... LC5252.N7
374.9759 ..... LC5252.F5
374.9762 ..... LC5252.M7
374.9764 ..... LC5252.T4
374.977386 ..... LC5253.A4
374.9778 ..... LC5252.M6
374.978 ..... LC5251
374.978883 ..... LD7501.D4
374.9794 ..... LC5252.C2
374.9931 ..... LC5259
374.994 ..... LC5259
375 ..... LB1027
..... LB1570
375.0001 ..... LB41
..... LB1570
375.00018 ..... LB2806
375.0008 ..... LC1046.I2
375.0009776 ..... LB1561.M6
375.001 ..... LA212
..... LB885
..... LB1065
..... LB1570
..... LC268
375.006 ..... LB1027
..... LB1570
375.008 ..... LB1570
375.00942 ..... LB1570
375.009713 ..... L107
375.00973 ..... LB1570
375.009747 ..... LB1563
375.0097471 ..... LB1563
375.009754 ..... L214
375.009756 ..... L184
375.009773 ..... LB1561.I3
375.009777 ..... LB1561.I8
375.23 ..... BV1559
375.3 ..... L166
..... LB1530
..... LB1584
375.30134 ..... LB2361
375.30142 ..... LC1046.I2
375.30145196 ..... E184.7
375.30145196073 ..... E184.7
375.33 ..... H62
375.33543 ..... HX19
375.355 ..... U428.5
375.37140954 ..... LB2947
375.42 ..... LB1631
375.6126 ..... HQ57.5
375.61307 ..... LB3409.U6
375.6137 ..... GV361
..... GV362
375.61383 ..... HV5808
375.616951 ..... RA644.V4
375.6292832 ..... TL152.65
375.64 ..... LB1561.M6
..... LB1629.I4
..... LC1046.I2
..... TX174.A4
375.651 ..... LC1046.I2
375.69 ..... TH165
375.8 ..... LB1575
375.9 ..... L166
375.91603 ..... DT19.95.G5
375.917303 ..... E184.7
375.91730917496 ..... E184.7
375.9196903 ..... DU625.8
375.973 ..... L166
376.08 ..... LC1446.J3
376.650973 ..... LC1663
376.7 ..... LC1601
376.922 ..... LC1752
376.924 ..... LA2317.B35
..... LC2853.W45
376.954 ..... LC1481
..... LC2322
376.974812 ..... LD7251.B85
376.974974 ..... LD7251.C74
377 ..... BX7615
..... LC111
377.08 ..... LC368
377.0973 ..... LC111
..... LC405
..... LC621
377.09755 ..... LC406.V8
377.1 ..... BV1471.2
..... LC116.G7
..... LC391
377.10942 ..... BV1470.G7
..... LC410.G7
377.10973 ..... LC111
377.10994 ..... LC119
377.8 ..... LC377
..... LC383
..... LC432.I5
377.82 ..... LC461
..... LC473
..... LC473.C37
..... LC493
..... LC501
377.8208 ..... LC487
377.820973 ..... LC461
..... LC501
377.826 ..... LC508.A2
377.8273 ..... LC501
377.8277862 ..... LC485
377.8342 ..... BX5147.S3
377.8373 ..... LC582.U53
377.852415 ..... LC625.G7
377.896 ..... LC571
377.8960942 ..... LC571
377.896748 ..... LA355

377.896749	LA331
377.96	BM103
378	AZ850
	LA133
	LA183
	LB2301
	LB2321
	LB2322
	LB2325
	LB2331
	LC171
	LC383
	LD2175
	LD6222.1
378.001	LA185
	LA226
	LA227.3
	LB885
	LB2322
	LC66
378.0018	LB1028.5
378.00207	LB2326
378.002573	L901
378.0028	LB1028.5
	LB2341
378.006	LB2301
378.0062714281	LC1761
378.0072	LB1028
378.0072094	LB1028
378.008	LB2322
	LB2325
378.00904	LB2322
378.009046	LB2322
378.00922	LD5311.T382
378.00924	E185.97
	LD2935.L85
	LD5192.7
	PQ67.B2
378.00925	E185.97
378.00938	LA75
378.01	LB41
	LB1028
	LB2321
	LB2322
	LB2325
	LC4092.C2
378.0109754	LA379.5
378.012	HD6278.U5
	LB2325
	LC1011
378.013	LC1059
378.0130942	T107
378.0130994	HD5715.5.A8
	LC1047.A7
378.02	LB2342
378.020942	LB2342
378.020971	LB2337.C3
378.020973	LB2342
378.05	LA226
378.052	LB2328
378.052097123	LB2329
378.0520973	LB2328
378.05209769	L152
378.0520978	LB2328
378.05309755	LB2329.5
378.1	KF27.E3
	LA183
	LA228
	LB2301
	LB2322
	LB2325
	LB2341
	LB2342
	LB2346
	LB2806
	LF1134.S7
	Q183.3
378.1001	LA227.3
	LB2322
	LC2851
378.10018	LB2341
	LB2846
378.100202	LB2322
378.1006273	LB2804.N373
378.1008	LB2325
378.1009	LA177
378.1009171242	LA637
378.100942	LB2325
378.100973	LA226
	LA227.3
	LB2325
	LB2329.5
	LB2341
	LB2372.E3
378.100973092	LA227.3
378.1009775	LB2329.5
378.101	LB2341
	LB2346
	LF790
378.10101	LB2346
378.1010979467	LD732.9
378.1011	LB2341
	LB2342.5
378.10110924	LG704.N5
378.101109758	L138.C5
378.102	LB2329.5
	LB2336
	Q180.U5
378.1020973	LB2336
378.102097444	LD2115
378.103	LB2321
378.1030963	LG401.A4
378.10309746	LC237
378.1030977311	LC237
378.104	LB2331.5
378.10409728	F1401
378.1040973	LB2331.5
378.105094	LA628
378.1050971	LC145.C2
378.10509747	LB1695
378.10509861	LA568
378.10560942	LB2350
	LB2351
378.10560973	LA227.3
	LB2342
	LB2351
378.105609747	LC148
378.105609755	LB2329.5
378.105609756	LA340.5
378.10560994	LB2351
378.1057	LB2350.5
	LB2351
	LB2353
378.10570942	L915
378.10570994	LB2351
378.105759	LC148
378.1059	LC148
378.1059747	L182
378.1059756	LA340.5
378.1059774	LC148
378.1059778	LC144.M8
	LC148
378.1059786	LA319.5
378.1059795	LA352
378.10709756	LD3932.9
378.11	LB2341
378.110924	DS481.S45
	E185.97
	E185.97.H8
	LA2317.A7
	LC2851.H32
	LD4291.O717
	LF624.P3
	LG169.L67
378.111	LB2341
	R740
378.1110924	E185.97.B34
	LA2317.M65
	LD3019.J6
	LF1134.E25
378.112	BV1610
	LB2331.7
	LB2341
	LB2343
378.1120924	LC2851.M72
	LD3275
	LD4672.7
	LD7212.7
378.12	JK4401
	LA228
	LB1731
	LB1738
	LB1778
	LB2331
	LB2331.7
	LB2333
	LB2335.4
	Z674
378.120202	LB2321
378.1206242	LB230
	LB2301
378.120924	E185.97.T516
	LF224.W5
378.121	KF26.J876
	LB2332
378.12109753	LB2332
378.12140973	LB2342
378.122	LB2341
378.124	LB2328
378.150973	LB2329.5
378.1540973	L106
378.15409746	LB2329.5
378.15420973	LA226
	LD5185.8
378.1543	LB2328
	LC2801
378.1543018	LB2328
378.15430973	LB2328
	LB2329
378.1544	LC5551
378.155	LB2329
	LB2341
378.1550184	LB2341
378.1550942	LA636.3
	LA637
	LF321
378.1553	LB2371
378.155302573	L901
378.15530973	LA227.3
	LA228.5
	LB2371
378.155309744	LB2371
378.155309778	LB2371
378.155309861	LA568
378.15530994	LB2371
378.15540973	LC5251
378.155409796	LC6252.I3
378.16	LC148
	LD766
378.1642	LB2353
378.166	LB2351
378.1660973	LB2353
378.1662	LB2353
378.1664	LB2367
378.16642	LB2328
378.16644	LB1131
378.1664410973	LB2367
378.166442	LB2343
378.167094274	LF347
378.1670954792	LB2367
378.1671094274	LF761
378.16710954	LB2367
378.16721	LB2371
378.1682	LA637
378.1682094248	LC148
378.169109794	LD732.9
378.169130973	LC148
378.169130977	LC148
378.16914	LB2351
378.17	AS4.U8
	LB1043
	LB1049
	LB1738
	LB1778
	LB2331
	LB2343
378.17028	LB2395
	LD743
378.170281	LB2395
378.170282	LB2331
378.17078	LB1043.2.M4
378.170973	LB1043
378.17358	LB1044.7
378.173580941	LB1043.2.S35
378.1794	LB2364
378.1794202573	L901
378.17943	LB1043
378.17944	LB1028.5
	LB1043
	LB2346
378.189	LB2346
378.1910954	LA1153.7
378.194	LB2328
	LB2343
	LB2343.5
378.194014	LB2343
378.1940954	LB2343
378.194095479	LB2343
378.1940973	LB2343
378.19409752	LB2343
378.19409766	LB2343
378.1942	LB2343.3
378.19425	LB2343
378.194250973	HF5382.5.U5
378.1942509944	LA2118
378.196	LB3223
378.19609747	LB3223.3
378.19609755	LB3223
378.19609763	LB3223
378.19609778	LB3223
378.19609786	LB3223
378.196109773	LB3223.4.I3
378.1962	T107
378.19620973	LB3223
378.196209749	LB3223.4.N5
378.196209753	LB3223.4.D5
378.196209754	LB3223
	LB3223.4.W4
378.196209778	LB3218.M8
378.196209781	LB3223
378.1962109756	LA340.5
378.19625	LB3227
378.19770942	LB3499.G7
378.198	LA229
	LA230
	LA637.7
	LA908.7
	LB2343.3
	LB2346
	LB2376
	LB3605
	LB3610
	LB3613.M3
	LD1986
	LG741.V6
378.19809174924	LB3613.J4
378.1980941435	LF1087
378.1980942	LA637
378.198094257	LF501
378.1980943	LA729.A3
378.1980954	LA1153
378.1980973	LA226
	LA229
378.1980974789	LD4721.R54
378.1980977491	LA308.N6
378.1980979467	LD760
378.1980991	LA1273.7
378.1981	AS36
	HQ35.2
	HX11
	KF26.J832
	LA186
	LA229
	LA337
	LA1153
	LB2301
	LB2341
	LB2376
	LB3605
	LB3609
	LB3610
	LC2801
	LD760
	LD1256
	RC451.4.S7
378.198108	LA186
378.19810924	LB2397
378.1981094	LB2397
378.198109421	H67.L9
378.1981094212	H67.L9
378.19810943	LA729
378.19810954	LA1153.7
378.19810971	LA417.7
378.198109714281	LC2804
378.1981097291	LA488.7
378.19810973	KF27.E336
	LA226
	LA229
	LB3609
	LC2801
378.1981097444	LD2150
	LD2153
378.1981097471	LD1250
	LD1256
378.19810974932	LD4753
378.198109753	LC2851.H84
378.19810976953	LD393
378.19810979461	LD729.C98
378.19810979467	LD760
378.19810983	LA563.7
378.1983	LD2521.4
378.19830952	LA1318.7
378.19843224	DT19.95.C3
378.198546591	HF5801.A53
378.19855	BV4647.B7
	LJ34
	LJ75.P855
378.198550973	LJ165.S55
378.198550977249	LD1621.4.L38
378.19871	LB3607
378.198710971	LB3227
378.1989	LJ85.P22
378.19897	LB3621
378.199	HD5715.2
	LB2328
	LB2361
	LB2364
	LB3609
	LC1011
	LD1233
378.199094246	HM15
378.1990973	LA226
378.19909752	LA301
378.1990977692	LD1281
378.1990994	LB2361
378.2	LB2386
378.20973	LB2381
378.24	LB1742
378.240994	LB2368
378.241	LB2391.C2
378.242	AS722.A8
378.280942	LB2389
378.3	KF27.E336
	LB2338
	LB2342
	LC2707
	LD736
	Z668
378.302573	LB2338
378.30973	LB2338
	Q180.U5
378.309744	LB2338
378.309755	LB2338
378.309773	LB2338
378.309797	HJ11
378.330973	KF27.E333
378.34	LB2338
378.340942	LB2339.G7
378.35	LB2285.P3
	LB2339.I4
	LB2376
378.350979	LB2377.6.W4
378.36202573	LB2340
378.3620942	LB2340
378.3620973	KF26.L343
	LB2340
378.365	LB1029.C6
378.4	L914.5
	LA627
	LA628
	LB2325
378.41	LA658.7
378.41445	LF1042
378.4183	LF905
378.42	H11
	L915
	LA627
	LA636.5
	LA637
	LB2224.L616
	LB2307
	LB2321
	LB2322
	LC1047.G7
	LF295
	LF419.5.B5
	Q183.8.G6
378.4225	LF55
378.4248	LF309.6
378.4252	LF484.S6
378.4257	B1649
	DA690.O98
	LF501.A7
	LF525
	LF526.E4
	LF565
378.4259	LF101
	LF797.C33
378.42965	LF1255.B73
378.43	LA727
378.431	LA728
378.4371	LF1479.5
378.4372	LF1541
378.4391	LF1693.P4
378.44	LC493
378.47	LA838

378.4795 ... LF4395
378.4933 ... LF953.L6
378.4977 ... LA958
378.54 ... L961.I4
... LA1153
... LB2301
378.5414 ... LG105
378.542 ... LG67
378.5455 ... LG125
378.552 ... LG291.T4
378.5692 ... LG351.A72
378.5694 ... LG341.J4
378.573 ... T177.R8
378.5952 ... L961.S5
378.6 ... L970
378.669 ... LA1611.N5
378.6773 ... L711
378.6822 ... LG475.J67
378.687 ... R824.S7
378.6894 ... LG469.L8
378.71 ... L905
378.71234 ... LE3.L4
378.71242 ... LE3.S72
378.71273 ... LE3.B765
378.713541 ... LE3.T499
... LE3.T538H27
... LE3.Y6
378.71372 ... LE3.Q31
378.714281 ... LE3.L72
378.73 ... AS8
... L901
... LA217
... LA226
... LA227.2
... LA227.3
... LA228
... LB1050
... LB2301
... LB2322
... LB2325
... LB2328
... LB2342
... LB2343
... LB2350.5
... LB2361
... LC501
... LC583
... LC1011
... LC2781
... LC2801
378.74 ... L901
... LA226
378.741 ... LA298
378.7423 ... LD1436
... LD1448
378.7434 ... LD2001.G4499
378.7435 ... LD3311.M32
378.74410924 ... E199.W69
378.7444 ... LB1888.F8
... LD2147
... LD2151
... LD2153
... LD2185.C5
378.74461 ... L161.B7
378.7447 ... LD7251.W498
378.746 ... LD6322
378.7463 ... LD5361.T42
378.7468 ... LD6335
378.7469 ... LD571.B467
378.747 ... KFN5666
... L182
... L182.G5
... LA337
378.7471 ... L903.N75
... LD1248
... LD1249
... LD1256
... LD1267
... LD1269.5
... LD3819.8
... LD6371.Y43
... LD7251
378.74743 ... KFN5648
... LD3840
378.74744 ... LD5481
378.74764 ... LD1083
378.74766 ... LC5301.S8
378.74771 ... LD1370
378.74785 ... LB1921.G45
378.74788 ... LB1921.B749
378.74797 ... LD791.C52
378.748 ... LA355.5
378.74811 ... LA226
378.74814 ... LB2167.P4
378.74931 ... BV4070.B66
378.74933 ... LD5491.U382
378.74942 ... LD4741
378.74967 ... LD4608
378.75 ... LA230.5.S6
378.752 ... LA301
378.753 ... HV2561.D7893
... KF27.E335
... LC2851.H82
... LD1928
378.75437 ... LC2851.W552
... U429.W4
378.75453 ... R747.W57
378.755 ... LA379
378.75541 ... LC2851.H32
378.755481 ... LD5678
378.75555 ... LC2851.H32
378.75579 ... LD7251.H722
378.75585 ... LD5873
378.756 ... L903.N3
378.756 ... LA340.5
378.75667 ... QH319.W3
378.75725 ... LD6501.A6
378.75818 ... LD1981.7
... LD1984
378.758231 ... LC2851.M72
378.75825 ... LD4701.R77
378.758563 ... LD7251.F72
378.758823 ... LD6501.G44
378.759 ... LB2329.5
378.75979 ... LD1797.5
378.76149 ... E185.97
... LC2851.T82
378.761781 ... LD4881.S1563
378.764 ... LA370
... LB2300
378.764169 ... LD4881.S1562
378.76424 ... LD5309
378.764557 ... LD271.A7
378.767 ... LA240
378.76857 ... LD3309
378.768885 ... LD3231.M852
378.769 ... LA292
378.771 ... L188.C5
378.77123 ... LD4168.3
378.77136 ... LD51.A62
378.77149 ... LD6183
378.77157 ... LD4228
378.77175 ... LD3241.M52
378.772 ... L146
378.772255 ... LD2518
378.77289 ... LD4113
378.773 ... LA267
378.77311 ... LB2167.I3
378.77339 ... LD271.A665
378.77342 ... LD2443
378.77366 ... LD2396
378.774 ... LA307
... LD5889.W42
378.77427 ... LB2193.M38
... S537.M69
378.77434 ... LD5889
378.77435 ... KFM4596.5.M5
... LD3283
378.77492 ... LD3141.M38
378.77584 ... LD6128
378.776579 ... LD271.A662
... R747.M8
378.77794 ... LD4471.P802
378.778264 ... LB2193.M67
378.77829 ... LD7251.C66
378.77844 ... LD7251.N25
378.77866 ... LD4817.S52
378.78229 ... LD3668
378.78685 ... LB3523
378.791 ... L120
378.792 ... LA373
378.794 ... LD758
... LD761
378.79461 ... LD729.C98
378.79467 ... LD758
... LD760
... LD763
378.79493 ... LD1015.C42
378.79494 ... LD781.L72
378.797 ... LA382
378.91 ... LA1273
378.9141 ... LG214.A35
378.93122 ... LG741.W3
378.93127 ... LG741.V6
378.93155 ... LG745.C45
378.93157 ... LG741.O8
378.94 ... LA2108
378.942 ... LG841.A38
378.94212 ... LF411
378.944 ... LA2109.R5
... LG715.E17
378.945 ... LG715.B8
378.946 ... T173
378.96931 ... LG961.H4
379 ... L162
... LA631.82
379.0942 ... L341
... LC93.G7
379.0973 ... KF4119.6
... LB2825
... LC71
379.10978 ... LB2301
379.12 ... L160
... LB1620
... LB2825
... LB2826.C2
379.120942 ... HX11
379.12096762 ... LB2970.K4
379.120971 ... LB2890
379.1209713 ... LA418.O6
379.120973 ... HD6483
... LB2825
379.1209746 ... LC4092.C65
379.1209747 ... LB2826.N7
379.1209756 ... LA340.5
379.1209758 ... LB2826.G4
379.1209769 ... LB2826.K4
379.1209773 ... LB2826.I3
379.1209776 ... LB2826.M6
379.1209792 ... LB2826.U8
379.121 ... KF27.E335
... LB2825
... LC5251
379.1210942 ... LB2901
379.1210973 ... KF26.L343
... KF27.E333
... LB2825
379.12109747 ... LB2826.N7
379.12109748 ... LB2826.P4
379.12109763 ... LB2826.L8
379.1212 ... KF26.L343
... KF27.E333
... L903.M2
... LC4092.N7
379.12120973 ... KF27.E3
... KF27.E333
... KF27.E368
... KF4137
... KF4151
... LB2817
... LB2825
... LC49
379.121209748 ... L194
379.121209756 ... L184
379.121209788 ... LB2826.C6
379.121209793 ... LB2826.N3
379.12122 ... LC4091
379.121220973 ... KF26.L345
... KF27.E3
... KF27.E333
379.1212209747 ... LB2826.N7
379.121220977178 ... LB2826.5.C5
379.121240942 ... LB2901
379.121240973 ... LB2825
379.1212409747 ... LB2826.N7
379.1214 ... KF27.S383
... L182
... LB2338
... LB2340
... LB2342
379.12140971 ... LB2371
379.121409715 ... LB2342.2.C3
379.12140973 ... KF27.I5568
... KF4178
... LB2338
... LB2341
... LB2342
379.121409746 ... LB2826.C8
379.121409747 ... LB2342
379.121409777 ... LB2338
379.121409794 ... LB2329.5
379.121409795 ... LB2342
... LB3223
379.121420973 ... LB2338
379.1214209794 ... LB2328
... LB2826.C2
379.122 ... HJ3241
... L124
... LB2329
... LB2329.5
... LB2338
... LB2342
... LB2824
... LB2826.I6
... LC112.M4
379.122097135 ... LB2342.2.C3
379.12209742 ... L176
379.12209747 ... LB2826.N7
379.122097474 ... L183.A3
379.12209749 ... LB2826.N5
379.12209771 ... JK5574
379.12209776 ... LB2826.M6
379.12209788 ... KFC1820
... LB2826.C6
379.12209794 ... LB2826.C2
379.12209795 ... LB2338
379.123 ... LA226
... LB2827
... LB2830
379.12309747 ... LA337
379.12309794 ... LA243
379.1309777 ... LB2826.I8
379.132 ... LB2824
379.13209748 ... LB2826.P4
379.15 ... LB1780
... LB2329.5
... LB2806.5
379.150942 ... LB2901
379.150973 ... LA210
... LB2283
379.1509792 ... LA373
379.1510942 ... LB2901
379.152 ... LB2809.C3
379.15209764 ... LC165
379.15209776 ... LB2809.M5
379.15209795 ... LB2809.O7
379.15209798 ... L118.H527
379.1521 ... LA568
... LB2809.T4
... LC1045
379.152109787 ... L218.C5
379.1522 ... LA635
379.15220954 ... LA1151
379.152209747 ... LA337
379.153 ... LB41
... LB2817
... LB3220
... LC5105
... Q180.A1
379.1530942 ... LB2901
379.15309421 ... JS3111
379.1530973 ... LB2817
379.15309767 ... LB2813
379.15309771 ... LB2817
379.1530979245 ... LA374.M5
379.15309793 ... LB2823
379.1531 ... LB2301
... LB2805
... LB2831
379.15310973 ... LB2831
379.153109747 ... LB2831
379.1535097471 ... LA339.N5
379.15350975 ... LB2817
379.153509769 ... LB2861
379.2 ... LA398
379.2097471 ... LC2803.N5
379.209759 ... L136
379.209789 ... L180
379.23 ... LC4091
379.230952 ... LC136.J3
379.230973 ... LC131
... LC4091
379.230977311 ... LC132.I3
379.2309794 ... LB1029.R4
379.24 ... LC149
379.240212 ... LC149
379.240947 ... LC156.R9
379.2409597 ... LC157.V5
379.421 ... LC145.G7
379.47 ... LA832
379.71274 ... LA419.W5
379.713 ... LB2891.O7
379.73 ... LA209.2
... LB2806
379.74 ... L113.A6
379.7471 ... LC2803.N5
379.748 ... LA355
379.756 ... LA340
379.762 ... LA313
379.764 ... L204
379.769 ... L152.C5
379.77565 ... LA390.A67
379.787 ... LA391
379.794 ... LA243
379.79474 ... Q180
379.969 ... LA2252
380 ... HE215.Z7N68
... HF1009
380.0184 ... HF1007
380.03 ... HF1002
380.06 ... HD2425
380.0621 ... HF294
380.06254 ... HF331.I4
380.076 ... HF1118
380.09 ... HE323
... HF352
380.0916612 ... HE151
380.0924 ... F82.L66
380.0942 ... HF1141
... HF3507
380.0945 ... HF3585
380.095 ... JX1977
380.0952 ... HF3826.5
380.097295 ... HE228
380.0973 ... HF3021
380.0994 ... HF4035
380.1 ... HC110.C6
... HF3505.6
... HF5006
... HF5415
... HF5415.1
380.101 ... HF5415
380.1025 ... HF54.G7
380.1025753 ... HF5429.5.W3
380.1065 ... DU740
... HF486.M25
380.108 ... HD9011.1
380.10924 ... HJ1077.C6
380.10942 ... HF3505.8
380.10943 ... DD801.H2
380.10945 ... HF411
380.1094923 ... DS135.N5A53
380.10952 ... HF3825
380.109549 ... HF5415.12.P3
380.10956 ... GN2
380.10967 ... HF3876
... HF3876.5
380.1096761 ... H31
380.10973 ... HD2791
... HF5415.1
380.109757915 ... HC108.C3
380.109773 ... HF3161.I3
380.13 ... HC440.5
380.1309171242 ... HF1534
380.141 ... KF27.A3336
380.14108 ... HD1751
... HD2075.5
380.1410952 ... HD9016.J42
380.14109549 ... HD9016.P22
380.1410973 ... KF26.A3534
380.14131 ... HD9030.6
... SB114.U6
380.141310973 ... HD9035.6
380.141318095125 ... HD9066.H72
380.1413491 ... KF26.A35334
380.1414110942 ... HD9259.A6G76
380.141498 ... HD9750.5
380.1415094 ... HD9011.1
380.14150972 ... S21
380.1416 ... HD9426.A2
380.141600973 ... HD9415.6
380.1416100924 ... CT275.K564
380.1416213096762 ... H31
380.14172 ... HD9278.N4
380.141750942 ... HD9284.G72
380.14308 ... HD9451
380.14309718 ... HD9464.C22
380.14310975 ... S445
380.1437 ... HD9450.5
380.144 ... DA565.R48
... DT378
... E185
... E442
... E446
... E449
... HT1162

380.144 HT1322
VA454
380.1440966 HT1322
380.1440973 E441
380.1440981 HT1127
380.1456292062945
HD9710.A83V52
380.1456292097 HD9710.U52
380.1456554 Z448
380.145655402542 Z327
380.145655572025 Z282
380.145676065 HD9769.W54
380.145677313023 HD9908.A82
380.14567731309931
HD9906.N452
380.145685095496 HD9780.N12
380.145778315025 Z265
380.3 KF27.S385
380.3023 HE152
380.309 HE151
380.30942 HE58
380.30973 HE7781
380.5 HC107.W5
HE148.5
HE151
HE152
HE193
HE214.C4
HE215.Z7Y85
HE243
HE554.B6
HE1049
Q180
Q180.A1
TA1005
TA1145
TE7
380.5018 HE192.5
380.50184 HE192.5
380.50212 HF151
380.5023 TA1160
380.5025756 HE9.U5
380.5065 HD9712.U54G357
380.5072 HE192.5
380.5074094 TA1006
380.508 HE131
TA1007
380.509 HE151
380.5091724 HE148.5
380.5091732 HE148
380.5094 HE242.8
380.509415 HC251.A1
HE246
380.50942 HE151
HE199.G5
HE243
HE244
380.5094227 HE244.Z7B68
380.5094238 HE437.S6
380.5094274 HE244.Z7Y67
380.509497 HE265.5
380.5095483 HE271.Z7K45
380.5095487 HE86
380.509549 HE86.5
380.5095493 HE84.8
380.50971 HE215
380.509713541 HE215.Z7T54
HE215.Z7T58
380.50973 HE18
HE203
HE206
HE206.2
KF26.C6
380.50974 HE207
380.509747 HE213.N7
HE554.N7
380.5097472 HE214.N7
380.509748 HE213.P4
380.509749 HE213.N5
380.509751 HE213.D4
380.50975473 HE213.W4
380.509759 HE213.F6
380.509774 HC107.M5
380.509794 HE213.C2
380.5097953 HE213.O7
380.509798 HE213.A4
380.509861 HE235
380.50994 HE197.A9
HE289
J905
380.509944 HE290.Z7H87
380.509946 HE295
380.50998 HE299
380.51 HE215
380.52 AS36
HD9580.U5
HE199.G5
HE199.U5
HE213.N7
HE243
HE2355
HF5770
KF27.G662
TA1215
VK235
380.53 HD9999.C743U73
TA1215
381 E78.W8
HF5465.U4
SF227.N
381.0922 CS71.W4256
381.0924 CT275.W272
E664.W24
381.094253 DA670.L69
381.0966 HF5475.W4
381.096782 HF5429.6.N9
381.0973 HF3027.3
HF5415.1
381.0974811 HF3163.P5
381.0975 HF3153
381.0975965 HF3163.T3
381.30973 HC110.P6
381.41 KF27.A3336
381.41097471 HF5472.U7
HF5472.U7N6
381.4109763 AS36
381.410979531 HD9008.E8
381.41098615 HD9014.C73C33
381.41313 S445
381.41318096762 HD9066.K42
381.4134910973 KF27.A3336
381.415 SB360
381.41509931 HD1407
381.4159 SB443
381.41612097 SF293.T5
381.41620975 S445
381.4171 HD1751
381.41710942 HD9282.G7
381.417353 HD1751
381.4220973 HD9545
381.440942 HT1162
381.440975 E442
381.45000257471 HF5068.N5
381.4500029 TS199
381.45655573 Z315
381.45665538270954
HD9576.I43
381.4566840954 HD9661.I42
381.45685065 HD9780.U54
382 HC256.5
HC498
HD69.I7
HF56
HF353
HF1005
HF1007
HF1009
HF1025
HF1408
HF1411
HF1455
HF1533
HF1590.15.R8
HF1721
HF3505.4
HG3883.U7
JX232.9
QC100
SF793
382.01 HF1007
382.0184 HF1411
382.0254 HF3496.5
382.02547 HF3493
382.025763 HF3161.L8
382.025772 HF3161.I6
382.025795 HF3161.O7
382.025922 HF3810.O54
382.025969 HF3161.H3
382.03 HF1002
382.065 HF486
HF486.E6
HF1009.5
382.08 HF1007
382.0913 HF1413
382.09171242 HF3506.5
382.0917124208 HF3540
382.09171301717 HF1411
HF1456
382.091713047 HF1411
382.091723 JX1977
382.091724 HF1413
JX1977
382.091724071 HF1413
382.091821 HF1721
382.091823 HF3762
382.0924 CT275.N63
HC602.5.L6
382.0935 HF3861.I7
382.0937 HF377
382.094 DD801.H2
382.094054 HC434
382.094056 HF3498.N4
382.09415042 HC257.I6
382.0942 HF485
HF1007
HF1533
HF3505.4
HF3505.6
HF3505.8
HF3506.5
382.09420415 HF3536.5
382.0942043 HF455
382.09420438 HF3508.G7
382.094204391 HF3549.H8
382.09420469 HF3508.P8
382.09420471 HF3632.3
382.09420481 HF3508.N7
382.09420492 HF3616.5
382.09420495 HC295
382.09420497 HF3508.Y8
382.094205 DS465
HF3508.E18
HF3766.5
382.0942054 DS465.A2
382.09420561 HF3508.T8
382.09420567 HF3861.I72
382.09420591 HF3508.B9
382.0942062 HF3508.E3
382.09420649 HF3508.C25
382.0942065 HF3909.A4
382.0942066 HF3508.A3
HF3508.A37
382.09420664 HF3508.A37
382.0942067 HF3508.A3
382.0942068 HF3899.S7
382.094207 HD6483
HF1533
382.0942071 HF3508.C2
382.0942073 HF3093
382.094208 HF3230.5.Z7G73
382.0942081 HF3408.G7
382.0942082 HF3388.G7
382.0942091 HF3508.E2
382.0942094 HF3946.5
382.09430431 Q180.A1
382.09436047 HF3548.C6
382.09437 HF3549.C95
382.09469 HF3696.5
382.09469051 HF3778.P6
382.0947051 HF3628.C45
382.0947073 HF3628.U5
382.09492 HF3616.5
382.0951 HF499
HF3774
HF3776
HF3776.5
382.0951073 HF3120
382.0952 DS871
HF3826.5
382.09520798 HF3161.A4
382.0954 HF486.E6
HF3781
382.0954047 HF1590.15.R8
382.09549 HF3790.5
382.095493 HF3770.8
382.095496 HF3861.N4
382.0956 HF1584.8
382.0956104 HF3718.E8
382.0962073 JX235.9
382.09667 HF3899.G6
382.09676 HF3896.5
382.0971 HD3616.C22
382.0971073 E183.8.C2
382.09715 HC117.M35
382.09727 HF3239.O3
382.09729101717 HD1837
382.097295 HF3356.5
382.0973 HF1455
HF1456
HF3002
HF3025
HF3031
KF1975
382.0973042 HF3025
HF3093
382.0973044 E164
382.0973047 HF3092
KF26.B3
382.0973051 HF3120
382.0973054 E183.8.I4
382.0973066 HF3134.A54
382.097308 HF3065.5
382.0974 HF3151
382.09744 HF3161.M4
382.0974461051 HF3163.B6
382.09759042 HF3161.F7
382.09794 HF3161.C2
382.09804 HF1480.55.E9
382.09931 HF4030.5
HF4030.5.Z6
382.09931094 HF3966.5
382.0994 HF3947
382.09969 HF3161.H3
382.1 HC59.7
HC120.C3
HC241.25.A3
HC241.25.G7
HC241.25.U5
HC447
HF1410
HF1558.15.C6
HG3853.F6
JX1977
382.10904 HF499
382.10954 HF5415.12.I5
382.170973 HG3883.U7
382.2 JV568
382.3 HF1007
HF1401
HF1456
HF1589
HF1721
HG221
KF6708.D8
T174.3
382.308 HF1455
382.30942 HF3506.5
382.30944 HF1543
382.30947 HF1531
382.30954 HF1589
382.309549 HC440.5
382.30971 HF1479
382.30973 HF1455
HF1456
HF3025
382.30994 HB31
382.4 HF1040.7
382.409931 HF2502
HF2570.5
382.41 HD1411
HD9000.5
HD9016.J42
382.41 JX235.9
382.41014 S21
382.41094 HD1411
HD1917
HD9015.A3
382.410942 HG3883.G7
382.410967 HD9017.E22
382.410971 HF2651.F27C3
382.410973 HD1765
HD9005.6
S21
382.410981 HD9014.B82
382.41310971 HD9044.C3A36
HD9049.W5C256
382.41311 HD9049.W5U3119
KF27.B348
382.41318 HD9066
382.41351 HD9886.J3
382.413510973 S21
382.4136 HD9105
382.41361 HD9104
382.41368 HD9052.E92
382.41371 HD9145.E22
382.4138209492 HD9210.N42
382.41383 HD9210
382.414 HD9016.I42
382.4140954 HD9256.I42
382.414550994 HF2651.A44A83
382.4149 HD9757.A5
HD9765
382.41498 SB435
382.415210994 HF2651.P76A83
382.416213094 HD9433.E82
382.4164 S21
382.417 HD9275.U6
382.4175 S21
382.4228 KF32.I525
382.42280947 HD9575.R82
382.42282 HD9490.I39
KF32.G6
382.422820973 HD9565
HD9566
KF27.I536
382.42668 HD9585.S83I53
382.43 HD9466.I52
382.43758 HD9455
382.44 HT1161
HT1162
HT1322
HT1327
382.4401 HT993
382.4409 E447
HT975
382.440924 DT515.4
HT1322
382.440942 HT1162
382.4409664 HT1334.S5
382.44096982 HT1394.M3
382.44099 HT1442
382.45 JX1977
382.4535582 HD9743.A2
382.453583 HD9743
382.4536362 HD9685.N66
382.45387744 TL500
382.455028 HF2651.S38A83
382.4561532312 HF2651.C67
382.456176909931 HF2651.P94
382.456213130973 HD9695.U52
382.45621882 HF2651.S4A82
382.456219020954 HD9703.I42
382.456292 HD9710.A2
382.456292222 HD9710.U52
382.4562989 HF2651.E372A82
382.45639110971 HD9944.C22
382.45643609538
HD9999.H83S45
382.456436538 HD9999.H83S45
382.4564674 HF2651.B327U53
382.456610393 HF2651.C25A8
382.45661824 HF2651.S7315A83
382.4566400942 HD9016.J42
382.45664363 HD9093.E84
382.4566610973
HF2651.G5U525
382.4566630994 HF2651.P8A82
382.456682 HF2651.F24A82
382.45669732 HF2651.T596
382.4567 HF1766
382.456718 HF2651.M45A83
382.45672 HD9526.I62
JX1977
382.456740942 SD1.G66
382.4567520954 HD9780.I63
382.4567721 HD9874
382.456773 HD9908.C6
382.4567731065 HD9905.S94S54
382.456783 HF2651.R92A82
382.4568113 HF2651.M7789A82
382.456812 HF2651.W3A82
382.4568160973 Z249
382.456817 HF2651.C75A92
382.456817677 HD9854
382.456831 HF2651.H18N55
382.456843 HF2651.C973A95
382.4568502554 HD9780.I62
382.456853100973
HF2651.B63U57
382.456853100994
HF2651.B63A82
382.456885 HF2651.E374A83
382.4575 KF27.I5536
382.5 HF1625
HF1630
382.5025 HF3861.L4

382.5025493 .... HF3603
382.502554 .... HF3788.H7
..... HF3788.S9
382.502598 .... HF3803
382.509415 .... HF3536.5
382.509549 .... HC440.5
382.509667 .... HF1616.9.G5
382.50967 .... HC517.E2
382.6 .... HF1455
..... HF3031
..... HF3227
..... HF3506.5
..... HF3947
..... KF27.B348
382.60182 .... HF3031
382.60202 .... HF3507
..... HF4030.5.Z6
382.602555 .... HF3837
382.6025769 .... HF3161.K4
382.606042 .... HF302
382.606242 .... HF302
382.606254 .... HF1589
382.6071 .... HF1009.5
382.6078 .... HF3782
382.6091724 .... HF1413
..... HF1431
382.60954 .... HC435.2
..... HF1589
382.609729 .... HF3312.3
382.60973 .... HF1455
..... KF26.B355
382.609762 .... HF3161.M7
382.60977866 .... HF3163.S3
382.60994 .... HF1010
..... HF3947
382.7 .... HF1713
..... HF1756
..... HJ6607
..... HJ7321.A6
382.70621 .... HJ6603
382.709 .... HF1711
382.7091724 .... AS36
382.7094 .... HJ6188
382.70951132 .... HJ7271.Z7S53
382.7095952 .... HF1044.S5
382.70973 .... HF1755
..... HF2651.W75U56
..... KF27.W3
..... KF32.W3
382.70994 .... HF2486
..... Z7164.T2
382.709941 .... HF2566
382.71 .... HF1713
..... HF1754
..... HF2046
382.7108 .... HF2043
382.7109 .... HF2043
382.7109171242 .... DA18
382.71091821 .... HF1713
382.710942 .... HF2043
382.730942 .... HF1533
..... HF2045
382.9 .... HF1721
..... JX235.9
382.91 .... JX235.9
382.911 .... HF1713
382.914 .... JN36
382.9140924 .... HF2103
382.9142 .... HC241.2
..... HC241.25.G7
..... JN30
382.914209 .... HC241.2
382.9143 .... HC241.4
382.918 .... HC125
..... HF1480.5
382.94073 .... JX235.9
382.942 .... HX11
382.9438073 .... JX235.9
382.947073 .... JX235.9
382.9494073 .... JX235.9
382.9495073 .... JX235.9
382.962073 .... JX235.9
382.973 .... KF1976
383 .... HE6371
..... HE6497.M4
..... KF27.P668
..... KF2695
383.08 .... HE6311
383.094267 .... HE6936.E75
383.09429 .... HE6184.C3
383.09743 .... HE6185.U7V47
383.0975692 .... HE6376.A1N86
383.09762 .... HE6184.C3
383.1205 .... HE6424
..... KF27.P667
383.14 .... HE7393
383.143 .... F864.T455
383.1430978 .... HE6375
383.1447095125 .... HE7311.H6
383.14470973 .... KF27.I5587
383.145 .... HE6937
383.23 .... HF5861
383.4 .... HE6376.A1
383.4942 .... HE6935
383.494289 .... HE6936.M3
383.4943 .... HE6995
383.495367 .... HE7311.K8
383.4968 .... HE6185.A43S64
383.4971 .... HE6653
383.4973 .... HE6326
..... HE6331
..... HE6371
..... HE6375
..... KF27.P667
383.4973 .... KF30.C65
383.4974185 .... HE6376.B25
383.49747 .... HE6199
383.4994 .... HE7395
..... HE7399.P4
384 .... HE7763
..... HE7775
..... HE8092
..... HE9721.U5
..... JX234.A23
..... VK391.I6
384.018 .... HE7781
384.0973 .... HE7763
384.0976 .... HE7791.G9
384.0994 .... HE8534
384.5 .... HE8689.4
..... HE9719
..... KF32.S384
..... PN1991.3.G7
..... PN1992.3.G7
..... PN1992.9
..... TK5104
384.5028 .... HE9719
384.54 .... HE8689.8
..... HE9721.C3
..... KF32.5.S633
..... PN1991.3.G7
..... PN1991.5
384.54023 .... HE8696
384.54091712 .... HE8689.9.C6
..... HE8689.9.G7
384.540942 .... HE8699.G7
..... PN1992.3.G7
384.5409438 .... HE8697.A8
384.5409549 .... HE8699.P3
384.54096 .... HE8699.A35
384.54096773 .... PN1991.3.S6
384.540971 .... HE8699.C2
384.540973 .... HE8698
..... KF27.5.S633
384.544 .... TK6554.5
384.5440973 .... HE8689.8
384.545 .... HE8700.8
..... TK6555
384.55 .... Q180
384.550994 .... HE8700.9.A8
384.554 .... HE8700.8.U5
..... PN1992.3
..... TK5104
384.554096762 .... HE8700.9.K4
384.5540971 .... HE8700.9.C2
384.5540973 .... HE8700.8
384.55409749 .... HE8700.8
384.5540994 .... HE8700.9.A8
384.5544 .... KF27.I5538
..... TK6651
384.5545 .... HE8700.8
384.555 .... HE8700.6
384.6 .... HE7631
..... KF27.A3
384.64 .... TK6397
384.6409931 .... HE7676
384.65025421 .... HE9159.L6
384.7 .... UA927
385 .... HC251
..... HD8039.R1
..... HE1031
..... HE1051
..... HE1618.A3
..... HE2705
..... HE2741
..... HE2771.N7
..... HE2791.C455
..... HE2791.U55
..... HE3008
..... HE3020.L5
..... HE3695.A72
..... HG4071.A3
..... KF26.C688
..... TA1145
..... TF20
385.009945 .... HE3538
385.023 .... HD8039.R1
385.0611 .... KF27.F646
385.065 .... HE2791.A83
..... HE2791.B63
..... HE2791.F7237
..... HE2791.M7467
..... HE2791.T32
..... HE2791.U55
..... HE2791.W312
..... HE2820.F345
..... HE3014
..... HE3020.G65
..... HE3020.G8
..... HE3020.L3
..... HE3020.L5
..... HE3020.N8
..... HE3420.N5
..... TF57
..... TF64.S58
385.091822 .... HE3009.M4
385.0922 .... TF140.S73
385.0924 .... AS36
..... HE1051
..... HE2754.H2
..... HE2754.H8
..... HE2754.J8
..... HE3018.2.B7
..... HE3020.G8
..... TF140.B63
385.0941 .... HE3037
..... HE3038
385.09411 .... TF64.H5
385.094149 .... HE3038
385.09415 .... TF59
385.094161 .... TF64.B44
385.09417 .... HE3050.S55
385.0942 .... HE243
..... HE3015
..... HE3016
..... HE3017
..... HE3018
..... HE3020.G63
..... HE3020.G8
..... HE3020.L5
..... HE3020.L75
..... HE3020.M6
..... HE3020.N8
..... HE3020.S73
..... TF57
..... TF64.G7
..... TJ603
385.094227 .... DA690.P8
385.094233 .... HE3019.D6
385.094235 .... GV1025.G7
385.094237 .... HE3019.C6
385.09424 .... TF58.M5
385.094246 .... TF64.N64
385.09425 .... TF64.S48
385.094261 .... HE3020.M6
385.09427 .... HE3020.L32
385.094272 .... HE3020.L5
385.094274 .... HE3019.Y6
..... HE3020.W45
..... TF58.W48
..... TF64.W48
385.09429 .... HE3020.C45
..... TF63
385.0942925 .... HE3821.F44
385.09458 .... HE3009.M4
385.0947 .... HE3138
385.09485 .... HE3182
385.0954 .... HE3300.N63
385.09561 .... HE3228
385.097 .... HE2751
385.0971 .... HE2810.C2
..... TF27.C3
385.0971133 .... HE2809.B7
385.09713 .... HE2809.O6
385.0973 .... E491
..... HE2721
..... HE2751
..... HE2791
..... HE2791.C455
..... HE2791.U55
..... KF2355.A4
..... TF23
385.0974 .... HE2791
385.09742 .... HE2791.C843
385.097459 .... HE2791.N215
385.0974735 .... HE2791.N653
385.09748 .... HE2771.P4
385.0975 .... HE2771.A13
..... TF25.S4
385.09756 .... HE2771.N8
385.09772 .... TF24.I6
385.09773 .... HE2791.I3
385.097731 .... HE2791.C6847
385.09774 .... HE2771.M5
385.09775 .... KFW2701
385.097772 .... HE2771.I6
385.0978 .... HE2763
..... HE2791.F7375
..... HE2791.U55
..... TF25.S68
385.0978858 .... TF25.C7
385.0979 .... HE2791.C455
385.09794 .... HE2791.C455
385.0979447 .... HE2791.Y684
385.0994 .... HE3465
..... HE3468
385.09941 .... HE3547
..... HE3548
385.09943 .... HE3508
385.09945 .... HE3538
..... TF122.V5
385.106573 .... HE2791
385.2 .... HE1783.G7
..... HE3014
385.2095491 .... HE3300.5
385.22 .... HE3014
385.220973 .... KF26.C688
..... KF27.I5587
..... TF25.C5
385.22097472 .... HE2771.N7
385.24 .... HE3479.M3
..... KF26.C647
..... KF26.C688
385.24097472 .... HE2377.N5
385.2409783 .... HE2133.S8
385.264 .... JX1977
385.3 .... TF64.N6
385.309943 .... HE3505
385.31 .... F204.U5
..... HE3014
..... HE3019.L8
..... TF308.L6
385.3109421 .... TF308.L6
385.3109941 .... HE2541
385.340973 .... HE2333
385.3610973 .... TJ603
385.5 .... HE2771.N5
..... HE2810.M6
..... HE3821.S24
..... HE3828
..... HE5428.N58
..... TF64.G7
385.5 .... TF64.I8
..... TF64.W38
..... TF675
..... TF677
385.5065 .... HE2791.C8833
..... TF64.R6
385.5094161 .... HE3049.A5
385.5094235 .... HE3020.P543
385.5094251 .... TF695
385.5094585 .... HE3010.M3
385.50954 .... TF675
385.5097111 .... TF25.W5
385.5097419 .... HE2791.B9233
385.50975288 .... HE5428.H25
385.509788 .... HE2791.D44239
385.50978825 .... HE2791
385.509794 .... HE3695.C23S67
385.50979462 .... HE3693.N6
385.6065 .... HE4071.U5
386 .... HE526
386.0942 .... HE435
..... HE663
..... TC744
386.0973 .... HE629
386.0977 .... HE630.M6
386.2 .... HE629
386.22 .... VM461
386.222 .... VM311.B3
386.224 .... VK61
386.2243 .... F42.W7
386.24 .... KF27.I5587
386.2409711 .... HE635.4.B7
386.309421 .... HE953.L8
386.309714 .... HE630.G7
386.3097581 .... HE630.S3
386.30977 .... HE627
..... HE630.O5
386.3097756 .... HE394.F6
386.3097986 .... HE630.Y8
386.4 .... HE435
386.43 .... DT154.S9
..... HE543
..... TC791
386.44 .... HE537.65
386.444 .... HE537.8
..... KF27.M475
386.460942 .... HE435
..... HE663
..... TC744
386.4609421 .... HE437.R4
386.46094227 .... HE437.B32
386.4609423 .... HE435
386.4609427 .... HE436.L35
386.46094271 .... TC664.P4
386.4609749 .... HE396.D3
386.4609771 .... TC624.O3
386.47094241 .... TC664.G55
386.47097511 .... KF27.P8
386.48 .... HE752.F55
386.480942 .... HE437.B32
..... HE664.5.W4
..... TC657
386.48094241 .... HE437.T45
386.48094272 .... HE438.B7
386.5 .... HE630.M5
386.6 .... HE5783.W3
..... HF5816
386.6094274 .... HE5814.H8
386.60971134 .... HE5785.V3
386.609716 .... HE5785.N6
386.609931 .... HE5861.C6
386.609944 .... HE5860.S9
386.8 .... VK369.6.M3
..... VK1024.N7
386.809679 .... HE560.L6
386.8097471 .... HE554.N7
386.80974743 .... HE554.A87
386.80975965 .... HE554.T3
386.809764113 .... HE554.C74
386.80993155 .... HE560.L
..... HE560.L9
387 .... HE571
..... HE945.A35
..... HF1410
..... QE75
..... VK15
387.009 .... HE571
387.0941 .... HE597.S25
387.0942 .... HE823
387.0973 .... KF27.M464
387.1 .... HE551
..... HE952.G7
387.1014 .... HE551
387.1018 .... JX1977
387.10942 .... HE557.G7
387.109421 .... HE826
387.1094241 .... DA690.B8
387.1094292 .... HE558.P56
387.1094382 .... HE558.D3
387.1094923 .... HE558.R75
387.10954 .... HE952.I5
387.1095414 .... HE560.C25
387.1095475 .... HE559.I4
387.10954792 .... HE560.B6
..... HE953.B7
387.1095482 .... HE560.C56
..... HE560.M26
387.1095484 .... HE560.V45
387.109593 .... HE560.B27
387.1096668 .... HE560.A25
387.10967 .... HE559.A36
387.109679 .... HE559.M58
387.109684 .... HE560.D8
..... HN800.N3

387.10971133 HE554.V3
387.109714281 HE945.R58
387.10974461 HE554.B6
387.1097471 HE554.N7
387.109749 HE554.D35
387.109755 HE554.A3
387.10975965 HE554.T3
387.10976318 HE554.A4
387.109764139 HE554.G3
387.10979493 HE554.L7
387.10979498 HE554.S14
387.109795 HE554
..... HE554.A6
387.1098 F1405.5
387.10991 HE559.I55
387.109931 HE559.N4
387.109944 HE559.A8
..... HE560.I4
387.109945 HE560.G4
387.109946 HE560.D4
387.13025 HF1418
387.155 VK1013
..... VK1063
387.2 G590
..... HE770
..... VM18
..... VM145
..... VM297
387.2009489 HE851
387.203 VM145
387.20924 HE569.N6
387.20942 VK145
387.2097471 HE565.U5A43
387.20977 HE565.U71
387.22 VK18
..... VK19
..... VK1255.P8
..... VM18
..... VM311.S7
..... VM351
..... VM371
..... VM395.C8
387.2209 VM150
387.220924 VM140.M3
387.23 VM615
387.232 VM464
387.2340942 HE5813.G7
387.24 HE565
387.24065 HE945.S72
387.240942 HE823
387.243 HE826
..... VM383.G7
..... VM383.O3
..... VM383.O4
387.24309414 VK61
387.24309415 HE5816
387.245 HE566.T3
387.2450216 HE566.F7
387.5 HE745
..... HE823
..... KF26.C654
..... VK18
..... VK160
387.5023 VK160
387.5065 HE945.C3
..... HE945.N74
..... VK57
387.50922 HE569
387.50924 VK140.B75
387.50942 HE564.E3G79
..... HE823
387.509423 HE826
387.50947 HD8039.S42
..... HE847
387.509481 HE855
387.50954 HF3784
387.50973 HE745
..... KF26.C652
..... KF26.C654
..... VK23
..... VM23
..... VM317
..... VM623
387.5097471 HE767.N5
387.50991 HE887
387.509931 HE932.5
387.52 HE328
..... HE745
387.522 HE327
..... VM615
387.5240969 HE752.H3
387.54 HE595.E8
..... VK24.N7
..... VK235
387.540974 HE1049
387.540994 HE915
387.544 HE199
..... HE566.T3
..... HE571
..... HE594
..... HE595.D3
..... HE596
..... HE597.G7
..... HE932.5
..... HF6201.L9
..... J905
..... JX1977
..... KF26.C654
..... VK235
..... VM311.F7
..... VM391
387.544065 HE823
387.5440973 HE745
387.54409931 TA1215
387.5440994 HE916
387.7 HE9765
..... HE9780
..... HE9783.5
..... HE9843
..... TL500
..... TL551
387.7023 TL561
387.7065 HE9768
..... HE9803.N3
..... HE9843.J4
387.708 TL500.5
..... TL526.G7
387.70924 TL540.B27
..... TL540.M225
387.70942 HE9843
387.70944 TL500
387.709497 HE9865.A3
387.70951 Q180.A1
387.70952 TL500
387.7095694 TL527.I75
387.70966 HE9882.A7W45
387.709669 HE9884.A7N52
..... HE9884.A7N54
387.709675 HE9886.7.A6
387.70971 HE9815
387.709729 HE9824.A35
387.70972972 KFZ5105.5
387.70973 HE9796.U5
..... HE9803.A3
..... HE9803.A35
..... HE9803.A4
..... HE9803.E2
..... TL521
387.709744 HE9813.M33
387.7097472 Q180
..... Q180.A1
387.709774 HC107.M5
387.709794 HE9813.C2
387.709798 TL522.A4
387.72065 HE9803.N6
387.73 HE9769.G7
387.7330947 TL526.R9
387.733097 HE9769.U5
387.7334094 HE9769.E9
387.73349 HE9770.J4
..... TL685.7
387.736 HE4491.H624
..... HE9797
..... TL696.L33
..... TL725.3.A2
..... TL725.3.P3
..... TL725.3.P5
..... TL725.3.T7
387.736025 HE9797
387.736025778 TL726.3.M5
387.73609421
..... HE9797.5.G72L635
387.7360973 KF27.I55
387.7360974 HC107.A13
387.73609753 HE9797.5.U52W37
..... HE9797.5.U52W395
..... KF26.D528
387.736097713 TL726.3.O3
387.73609782296 TL726.3.N3
387.7362 HE355.6
387.74 HE9765
..... TL500
..... TL540.Y6
..... TL725.3.I6
..... TL725.3.T7
387.74042 HE9797.5.U52
387.742 HD6073.A38
..... HD6073.A5
..... HE9768
..... HE9787
..... TL500
387.742018 Q180
387.742023 HD6073.A5
387.7420924 HD6073.A52
387.7420973 H11
..... HE9803
..... KF27.I5587
387.744 HE9783.7.U5
..... KF27.I5587
387.744028 HE9788
387.74409755 HE9788.5.U5
387.74409969 HE9813.H4
388 F387
..... HC251
..... HE192.5
..... HE206.2
..... HE214.S4
..... HE243
..... HE244.Z7
..... HE293.Z7B76
..... HE333
..... HE355
..... HE356.5.C4
..... HE356.5.D85
..... HE368.Z7M46
..... HE368.5.A8
..... HE372.B2
..... HE373.G63N66
..... HE4451
..... HE4461
..... HE4491.C45
..... HE4491.P95
..... HE4491.S624
..... HE5613
..... HE5614
..... HE5618
..... TA1205
388.091732 TA1205
388.094461 HE214.B7
388.0954792 HE4999.B62
388.0968 HE284.S7
388.09713541 HE215.Z7T5
..... HE373.C42T62
..... HE373.C42T65
388.097472 HE214.N7
388.09753 HE4491
388.09942 HE294.Z7A35
388.1 DU180.I6
..... DU740
..... HE206.2
..... HE333
..... HE336.E3
..... HE355
..... HE355.8
..... HE356.H3
..... HE356.I3
..... HE356.M2
..... HE356.M3
..... HE356.M4
..... HE356.N9
..... HE356.P4
..... HE356.U8
..... HE356.W3
..... HE356.5.M5
..... HE363.G72
..... HE367.S6
..... HE376.P9
..... HE376.R45
..... HE376.S4
..... KF5614.2
..... KF26.P868
..... KF27.P872
..... KF27.P874
..... TE7
..... TE64.W3
..... TG24.W3
..... TG122.T35
388.10151 HE370
388.1072073 TE7
388.10942 HE363.G72
388.109422 HE363.G74
388.10954 HE5691
388.1095487 HE365.I44M93
388.10955 HE365.I72
388.109713 HE357
..... HE357.Z6
..... HE357.Z6O53
388.1097295 HE359.P92
388.10973 HE355
..... KF26.P868
388.10974 HE356.A6
388.109741 HE356.M2
388.109743 HE356.V5
388.109744 HE356.M4
388.109746 HE356.C7
388.1097462 HE356.5.F33
..... HE356.5.W45
388.1097471 HE356.5.N4
388.10974789 HE356.5.R6
388.109748 HE356.P4
388.109749 HE356
..... HE356.N5
388.109751 HE356.D4
388.109752 HE356.M3
388.109753 HE356.5.W3
388.109755 HE356.V8
388.109756 HE356.N8
388.109759 HE356.F4
388.109767 TE24.A8
388.10977 HE209
388.109773 HE356.I3
388.1097732 HE214.F69
388.109776 HE356.M6
388.109786 HE356.M85
388.109787 HE356.W8
388.109789 HE356.N6
388.109791 HE356.A7
388.109793 HE356.N37
388.10979549 HE356.5.P64
388.109797 HE356.W3
388.10979751 HE356.W3
388.109798 QE75
388.109861 HE359.C44
388.10994 HE368
..... J905
388.109942 HE368.Z6S64
388.109969 HE368.5.H3
388.110973 HE355.A3
388.1109798 TE24.A4
388.120976335 HE356.5.N35
388.17372095496 HD9198.N36
388.3 HE333
..... HE5606
..... TA1205
..... TL234
388.30182 HE336.C5
388.308 HE5623.A1
388.3094274 HE244.Z7L45
388.30968 HE5704.S6
388.30971 TL26
388.30977325 HE372.J65
388.31 HE333
..... HE369
..... HE370
..... HE371.M4
..... HE371.N6
..... HE371.T2
..... HE372.C35
..... HE372.H44
..... HE372.R34
..... HE373.G62L37
..... HE5606
388.31 HE5614
..... HE5614.2
..... HE5614.3.L8
..... HE5614.3.N42
..... HE5615
..... HE5620.S6
..... Q60
..... TA7
..... TE7
388.31018 HE369
..... TE185
388.310184 HE333
..... HE369
388.3102573 HE5614.2
388.310711 HE332.5
388.3109421 HE373.G63L65
388.31094281 HE373.G63D92
388.31095487 HE373.I52M9
388.31096931 HF372
388.3109713 HE357.Z6O54
388.310971338 HE373.C42N53
388.31097423 HE356.5.H3
388.31097425 HE372.D6
388.310974426 HE372.S8225
388.31097443 HE372.W63
388.31097472 HE372
388.310974761 HE371.N7
388.310974797 HE372.B9
388.310974818 HE372
388.310974877 HE372.J6
388.31097554 HE372.H26
388.310975623 HE372.J26
388.310975643 HE372.W55
388.310975676 HE372.C365
388.310975688 HE372.A69
388.3109758 HE371.G4
388.3109764225 HE372.T95
388.310976472 HE372.S268
388.310976813 HE356.5.U6
388.310976842 HE356.5.L3
388.310976845 HE372.C58
388.3109773 HE371.I3
388.3109774 HE370
388.3109775 HE356.W5
388.3109777655 HE372.I68
388.3109778 HE371.M8
388.310978416 HE356.5.G65
388.3109786 HE371.M9
388.310978793 HE372.C27
388.310978932 HE372.P74
388.310978942 HE372.C26
388.310978952 HE372
388.3109793 HE371.N3
388.310979312 HE371.N3
388.31097946 HE372
388.314 HE369
388.32 HE5664
388.322 F593
..... HE4347
..... HE5613
..... HE5623
..... HE5635.A6
..... HE5653.A6
..... HE5664
..... TE7
388.32206 HE5663.Z7
388.322065 HE5663.Z7
..... HE5663.Z7R63
..... KF26.D545
388.3220942 HE5663
..... TL232
388.32209421 HE5664.L6
388.322094271 HE5664.W3
388.322094272 HE5664.S6
388.322094281 TA7
388.322097471 HE5634.N5
388.32209749 HE5633.N5
388.3220976819 HE372.M4
388.322097735 HE5633.I3
388.32209941 HE5717.P4
388.324 HE5613
..... HE5933.S2
..... HF5761
..... KF26.C688
..... TL230
388.3240973 HE5623
388.32409749 HE5633.N5
388.3240978 HE210.5
388.32409787 HE371.W8
388.33 HE371.M4
..... JS3551
..... TE7
..... TH9111
388.33097983 HE372.A56
388.341 HE5664
..... HE5664.E8
388.342209 TL15
388.34220994 HD9710.A82
388.342320954792 HE5691.B6
388.342330941435 TL232
388.3423309421 TL232
388.3472 GV1041
388.372709715 SH223
388.4 HE333
..... HE4491.W343
..... KF26.P868
..... TA1205
388.4042 HE4451
388.409421 HE2591.G7
388.40952135 HE5059.T65
388.40973 KF26.B353
388.409747 HE4487.N7
388.4097471 HE4491.N65
388.4097526 HE4491.B35

Dewey	LC
388.409758231	TF725.A8
388.40979777	HE4491.S624
388.413140974789	HE372.R63
388.4132	HE5634.C4
388.41321023	E185.97
388.4132209747243	HE5634.N5
388.4209421	TF847.L6
388.420974461	HE4491.B78
388.42097471	HE4491.N68
388.4209753	HE4491.W356
	HE4491.W3562
388.4209945	HE5239.M426
388.46	HE4491.S627
	HE5425.N72
	TF705
	TF755
	TF764.M3
	TL232
388.4609421	TL232
388.46094214	TF764.L6
388.46094241	HE4719.B78
388.46094272	HE4719.B55
	TL232
388.46094289	TF764.M27
388.46094297	TF764.C36
388.46094355	HE4779.R8
388.46097135	HE5430.H32H3
388.460974811	HE4450.P4F34
388.460974814	TF725.C38
388.460974816	TF725
388.460974841	HE5428.Y6
388.46097731	TF25.C55
388.460977311	HE4491.C45
388.46097949	HE5425.C2
	TF725.P4
388.4609945	HE5239.M428
388.47746109543	HD9866.I63
388.5	HD9580.U5
	TN880.5
388.5065	HD9581.C34T75
388.509798	KF26
388.7613636209669	
	HD9685.N54E43
388.954	HC435.2
	HC4351.2
389	HG221.5
	QC83
	QC88
389.1	QC89.U5
	QC94
389.10942	QC89.G8
389.10954	QC89.I4
389.10994	QC96
389.109969	QC89.U6H34
389.15	HF5715.G7
	HG219
	HG939.5
	QC91
389.152	J905
	KF27.S3
	QA1
	QC91
	QC94
	QC100
	TL521.3.C6
389.1520212	QC91
	QC94
389.15202462	QC96
389.152025674	TS835
389.1520942	HG939.5
389.1520954	QC91
389.16	QC100
389.6	TA180
389.602573	QC100
389.60611	T59
389.608	QC100
390	GN4
	GN8
	GN21.L4
	GN29
	GN33
	GN37.T553
	GN270
	GN400
	GN494
	GN670
390.00624	DT131
390.008	E78.C15
	GR1
390.0091749149	DX115
390.009174951	DS895.F75
390.00942	DA110
	GR70
390.009421	DA677.1
390.0094238	GR142.S58
390.009424	GR142.W9
390.009495	DF741
390.0094956	GR170
390.00951	DS730
390.0095414	DS432.R25
390.00954165	DS432.N3
390.009593	GR312
390.00967	DT16.B2
390.0096762	PL8545
390.00968	DT764.K2
390.009681	DT797
390.009687	DT826
390.0096894	DT963
390.00972	F1421
390.00973	E161
	GR105
390.009798	E99.E7
390.009994	DU120
390.09034	GT146
390.091749149	DX115
390.0917496	DT351
390.09174963	DT434.U2
390.09174973	E99.P98
390.09174975	E99.P25
390.091749915	DU120
390.0922	GN20
390.0924	GN21.F5
390.09376	DG90
390.094	DU120
390.0942	DA110
	DA485
	DA533
390.09421	DA688
390.09495	DF741
	GR170
390.0951	DS721
390.0952	CR6090.B8
390.09541	N7301
390.095483	DS485.K4
390.09667	DT510.42
390.09678	GN659.T3
390.099115	DS646.36
390.0993	GN668
390.09953	GN671.N5
390.177	F479
390.22	D107
	GN495.5
	GT3530
390.230942	DA115
	DA320
390.4287	GR110.P4
391	GT510
	GT518
	GT521
	GT732
	GT733
	HQ64
	PN2067
	PZ10
	Q11
	TT507
	TT515
391.003	GT507
391.009	GT510
	GT513
	GT585
	GT595
	PZ10.W148
391.009034	GT500
391.00931	DU423
391.0094	GT737
	GT1850
391.00942	GT585
	GT730
	GT732
	GT734
	GT737
391.00954	GT1460
391.00973	GT607
391.00994	GT1590
391.022	CR4480
391.0220951	GT1555
391.023	GT585
391.04094391	GT825
391.073	GT1750
391.20942	GT585
391.4	TT507
391.41	GT2120
	GT2170
	PZ10
	TS1000
391.42	GT2075
391.44	GT2210
391.4409	GT2050
391.45075	NK3670
391.5	GT2290
391.6	RA778
391.6309	GT2340
392	DK32
	GN400
	GN483
	HQ12
	HQ18.G7
	HQ801
392.09669	GN653
392.1	BV3625.T3
	GN483
392.10968	GN482
392.32	GN480
392.320924	GN480
392.32096681	GN480
392.320994	GN480
392.33	GN491
392.360463109471	S405
392.3709	GT2853.G7
	GT2860
392.370942	DA110
392.370971	TX357
392.4	GT2640
	HQ801
392.40207	PN6231.D3
392.5	GN480.8
	GR465
	GT2600
	GT2665
392.50207	PN6231.L6
392.50954	GT2776
392.50968	HQ1019.A35
392.509801	F2420.1.T7
392.50995	GT2796.N4
392.6	HQ12
	HQ16
392.60948	HQ18.S3
393	GT3150
	PL8751.7
393.09174924	BM712
393.0937	DG103
393.0946	E51
393.09624	DT132
393.2	GT3190
394	E78.M6
	E78.S7
	GR141
	GT3080
	GV1201
	TS585
394.09701	E98.R3
394.1	GT2880
	GT2910
	GT3020
	GT3843
	TP577
	TS2260
394.13	GT2880
394.14	TS2260
394.2	DA110
	DG125
	GR950.F6
	GT3930
	GT3932
	GV182.8
394.2094	TX641
394.2094289	GR142.M3
394.20952	GT4884.A2
394.2097	GT4002
394.26	GT3930
394.268	DT434.U28
	GT4935
	GT4975
	GT4985
	NC1860
	TX739
394.268282	GT4985
394.2682820941	GT4987.45
394.268296	BM695.N5
394.2691766	BM690
394.26951249	DS895.F713
394.26954	GT4876.I5
394.26971	GT4813.A2
394.2697554252	F234.W7
394.269914	GT4881
394.3	E99.P3
	GV1200
	GV1580
	GV1646.E6
	HV6710
	HV6715
	HV6722.G8
394.309701	E98.G2
394.4	DA591.A33
	DG579.S296
	E285.4.N5
	F910
394.40942	DA325
394.7	CR4557.G7
394.703	CR13
394.8	CR4595.U5
395	BJ1852
	BJ1853
	BJ1873
	BJ1874
	BJ2101
	BJ2193
	CR3515
	LB2379
	TK6167
395.09	BJ1821
395.0994	BJ1873
395.1	V736
395.122	BJ1857.B7
	BJ1857.C5
	BJ1877.C5
395.123	BJ1857.C5
395.1232	BJ1855
	BJ1857.B7
395.1233	BJ1857.G5
395.14	GT2620
395.142	BJ1855.E82
395.144	BJ1873
395.22	BJ2051
398	BL303
	BL304
	BL310
	BL311
	BL313
	GR65
	GR105
	PA8395.P36
	PE1068.S9
	PR8793.F6
398.04	BL311
398.091749691	GN653
398.0922	GR50
398.0941	GR144
	GR145.H6
398.09415	GR147
398.094259	GR142.C3
398.094391	GR158
398.09471	GR200
398.0954792	PK2412
398.096694	DT515.42
398.097	E98.F6
398.0970	PM751.6
398.0973	GR103
	GR105
	GR110.S6
	Z1209
398.09747	GR110.N7
398.0975	GR103
	GR108
398.09764	GR110.T5
398.097642	GR110.T5
398.0978	GR109
398.09791	GR109
398.098	F1408.3
398.09883	F2420
398.0994	GR365
	GR920.R3
398.2	BL304
	BL310
	BL715
	BR1711
	E98.T65
	E99.K9
	F776.6
	GN751
	GR65
	GR95
	GR108
	GR135
	GR147
	GR305
	GR350
	GR360.H3
	GR460
	GR580
	PB1347
	PG3347
	PM1641
	PN6071.S85
	PR974.A3
	PR6009.Z7
	PS3569.T334
	PZ7.M235
	PZ8.C797
	PZ8.L733
	PZ8.P661
	PZ8.1.A25
	PZ8.1.B216
	PZ8.1.B4157
	PZ8.1.B4194
	PZ8.1.D19
	PZ8.1.G455
	PZ8.1.H66
	PZ8.1.K159
	PZ8.1.L95
	PZ8.1.M372
	PZ8.1.M616
	PZ8.1.P4
	PZ8.1.P868
	PZ8.1.P9346
	PZ8.1.R858
	PZ8.1.S5384
	PZ8.1.S627
	PZ8.1.S84
	PZ8.1.W64
	PZ8.2.W5
398.2018	GR40
398.2091749149	DX157
398.209174924	GR98
398.209174963	PL8025
398.209174972	E99.T185
398.20924	PG1217.K3
398.2093	BL311
398.20935	PZ8.1.W54
398.20938	BL782
	PZ8.1.K614
	PZ8.1.L4
398.2093955	PN6120.A5
398.2094	BM107
398.209409754	GR110.W4
398.20941	GR145.H6
	PZ8.1.F484
	PZ8.1.W69
398.209415	GR147
	PZ8.1.J153
	PZ8.1.V9
398.20942	GR141
	PR1508
398.2094274	GR142.Y5
398.2094281	PR8349.D86
398.209429	GR150
398.209438	GR195
	PZ8.1.B64
398.2094391	PZ8.1.A48
398.20944	PZ8.1.C786
398.209441	PZ8.1
398.20945	GR147
398.2094551	GR177.F4
398.2094675	PZ8.1.M48
398.209469	GR235
398.20947	PG3105
	PZ8.1
	PZ8.1.D76
	PZ8.1.H999
	PZ8.1.W78
398.2094741	PZ8.1.W78
398.2094792	GR280
	PZ8.1.K954
398.20948	GR205
398.209481	PZ8.A89
398.209495	GR170
398.2095	PZ8.1.T44
398.20951	GK335
	PL2658.E8
	PR6058.S5
	PZ5.G318
398.209517	PZ8.1.O84
398.209519	GR342
	PZ8.1.W53
	PZ8.1.Y82

Dewey	LC
398.20952	GR340
398.20953	PZ8.L978
398.20954	GR305.5.A8
398.209546	GR305
398.2095694	PJ7680
398.20957	PZ8.1.G455
398.209577	GR340
398.209593	GR312
398.209597	PZ8.1.G73
398.2096	GR350
	PL8593.8
	PZ8.1.H139
	PZ8.1.R6
398.20966	GR350
	PZ8.1.D746
398.2096681	GR360.T6
398.209669	PZ8.1.C8
398.2096695	PL8234.E3
398.20967	PL8234
	PZ8.1.O54
398.209673	GR360.A5
398.209675	PZ8.1.H743
398.2096781	GR360.Z3
398.20968	GR360.K2
398.2096894	PZ8.1.S257
398.2097	E98.F6
	E98.R3
398.209701	E98.F6
	E99.A13
	E99.C5
	E99.C6
	E99.H7
	E99.K9
	E99.M77
	E99.S54
	E99.T6
	E99.T8
	F1221.T3
	PS3501.U8
	PZ8.1.A88
	PZ8.1.B38
	PZ8.1.B53
	PZ8.1.H345
	PZ8.1.N43
	PZ8.1.N432
398.20971133	E99.S7
398.209719	E78.L3
398.20972	PZ8.1.B38
	PZ8.1.S578
398.209729	GR112
398.2097295	GR121.P8
	PZ8.1.B4127
398.20973	GR1
	GR110.V8
398.20974	F4.6
	GR106
398.209741	PS3513.O852
398.20974725	F127.S9
398.209758	GR103
398.209767	GR110.M77
398.209768	GR110.T4
398.209775	E78.W8
398.209778	GR103
398.20978	F591
398.209789	GR110.N6
398.20978983	E99.Z9
398.2098	GR130
398.2099	PZ8.R248
	PZ8.1.H153
398.20991	PZ8.1.K565
398.209914	GR325
398.209931	PL6465.Z73
398.20994	BL2610
	GR365
398.20996	GR380
398.209969	BL2620.H3
398.21	PJ7737
	PT921
	PZ8
	PZ8.A854
	PZ8.C8863
	PZ8.G882
	PZ8.J19
	PZ8.K2205
	PZ8.K7
	PZ8.L15
	PZ8.L4812
	PZ8.M333
	PZ8.3.C839
398.2109	PN3437
398.210922	PD64.G7
398.210935	PZ8.O43
398.210941	PZ8.J19
398.210943	PZ8
	PZ8.G882
398.21094391	GR550
398.210944	GR161
	PZ8.D884
	PZ8.P426
398.2109441	PZ8.1
398.210947	GR550
	PZ8.1
398.2109481	PZ8.A89
398.2109495	PZ8.H295
398.210956	PZ8.S335
398.2109686	GR360.L4
398.22	BL820.A34
	BS580.E4
	DA152.5.A7
	PB1423.T3
	PR2129
	PZ8.G882
	PZ8.1.C58
	PZ8.1.H378
398.22	PZ8.1.H534
398.220938	PA3946.C3
	PZ8.1.S4575
398.2209415	GR147
398.220942	DA140
	DA152.5
	DA152.5.A7
	DA650
398.2209421	PZ8.1.L48
398.22094743	PZ8.1.R85
398.2209701	E99.N3
398.23	DF220
	DF901.T67
	GN751
	GR580
398.23094274	GR142.Y5
398.24	GR313
	GR730.S4
	PA3855
	PA3855.E5
	PA8310
	PR1119
	PZ8.1.K64
	PZ8.1.N63
	PZ8.1.T8
	PZ8.2.A254
	PZ8.2.G3
	PZ8.2.H3
	PZ10.3.C43
398.240943	PZ8.1.G878
398.240947	PZ8.1.H999
398.240966	GR350
398.240968	GR350
398.2409701	PZ8.1.M5
398.240973	PZ8.1.C462
398.32	G100
398.324	G525
398.3240973	G525
398.352	BL820.T5
	GR470
398.353	GN477.3
398.35409495	GR170
398.355	GR890
	GT450
398.362	GR625
398.36209677	QC998
398.365	GR805
398.368	GR780
	GR785
	QK83
398.37	AZ999
	BF1775
	GR525
398.37019	BF773
398.3703	BF1775
398.370917496	GR103
398.3709415	GR147
398.370974	BF1576
398.42	GN751
398.45	BF1581
	BT980
	GR525
	GR550
	PZ8.1.S7
398.468	GR785
398.469	GR825
	GR830.D7
	QL791
398.47	GR580
398.4709423	GR580
398.5	PN970
	PQ6157.A2
	PR972
	PR973
	PR8624
398.50942	PR972
398.6	PN6371.5
	PN6375
	PR1760
	PR1762
	PZ7.W637
398.730924	E748.L72
398.8	DA688
	GR485
	GR487
	GV1218.F5
	GV1797
	M1993
	PE1519
	PN6071.C5
	PN6110.C4
	PR3291.A1
	PR9554.C5
	PZ8.3
	PZ8.3.B958
	PZ8.3.G426
	PZ8.3.M418
	PZ8.3.M85
	PZ8.3.W76
398.9	PN6301
	PN6404
	PN6405
	PN6420
	PN6421
398.92	PN6421
	PN6425.S4
	PN6519.J2
398.9203	PN6421
398.927941	PN6425.S4
398.99142	PN6519.P3
398.99166	PN6425.W3
398.9924	BM530
398.9927	PN6519.A7
398.996	PN6519.A6
398.9963	PN6519.A6
398.99691	PN6519.H35
398.9992	PN6519.M26
399	U820.G7
399.4109766	HC107.O53W42
400	LB1139.L3
	P25
	P26.H33
	P90
	P101
	P106
401	B840
	BF455
	P81.F7
	P101
	P103
	P106
	P131
	PE1106
401.3	PM8563
401.9	AS36
	BF455
	BF723.C5
	LB1139.L3
	P106
	PB36
	PE1130.3.A2
402.07	P323
402.3	P60
407	P51
	P57.U7
	PB11
	PB21
	PB35
	PB36
	PB38.G5
	PB38.U6
	PB65
	U15
407.1159	PB38.A8
407.12	PB38.U6
407.2	P11.A1
407.7	PB36
407.8	PB35
	PB38.U6
409.54	JQ220.L3
409.542	JQ220.L3
409.7295	LC3735.P8
409.764	P123
410	GN31
	LB1139.L3
	P21
	P25
	P27
	P35
	P101
	P105
	P112
	P121
	P123
	P124
	P125
	P201
	P291
	P601
	PB35
	PH2101
410.0917496	E185
410.1	P23
	P33
410.18	P25
	P98
410.182	P123
410.28	P98
410.71	LB5
410.71173	L901
410.76	P201
410.8	P11
	P25
	P27
410.9	P73
410.924	P85.C47
411	AS262.T84
	P211
	Z40
411.09	P211
	Z105
412	P112
	P125
	P321
	P325
	P341
	PC123
	PE1585
413	P365
	P3611
	PE1582.A3
	PL539
413.3947	DS211
414	P217
	P325
	P599
	PB79
	PE1133
	PE1135
	PJ128
414.204850222	DA631
415	P101
	P151
	P207
	P215
	P236
	P241
	P291
415	P587
	P671
	PG1305
415.03	P29
415.09	P151
417	P1051
417.7	CN55
	P121
417.7093	P211
418	P51
	PB73
418.00712769	PB38.U6
418.00712795	PB38.U6
418.00715	PB36
418.0077	PE1128.A2
418.0078	P98
	PB36
418.02	T11.5
418.02023	P306
418.022	BS450
418.1	F2515
419	E98.S5
	HV2477
	P135
419.36	DU553.N35
420	P25
	PE25
	PE51
	PE1011
	PE1065
	PE1066
	PE1072
	PE1073
	PE1075
	PE1083
	PE1103
	PE1421
420.09	PE1101
420.7	LB1576
	LB1631
	PE66
	PE1066
	PE1068.U5
	PE1128.A2
	PE3207
420.71	LB1576
	PE1068.I4
420.711	PE1068.G5
420.71154	PE1068.I4
420.712	LB1576
	LB1631
420.71242	LB1631
420.71273	LB1631
420.76	LB1631
420.8	P25
	PE1072
	PE1574
420.9	PE225
	PE1075
	PE1101
420.954	AS122.B4
421	PE1450
	PE1450.A2
421.08	LB1576
421.5	PE1133
	PE1135
	PE1143
	PE1155
	PE1505
	PE3501
421.50924	PE1151.W57
421.52	LB1574
	PE1072
	PE1133
	PE1135
	PE1137
	PE1137.A2
	PE1142
	PE1144
	PE1150
	PE1150.A2
	PE1153
	PE1680
	PN4105
421.54	PE2815
421.5407	PE1128.A2
421.55	PE1135
421.6	PE1130.C4
	PE1139
	PE1139.5
	PN4105
422	P35
	PE1101
	PE1175
	PE1571
	PE1574
	PE1578.A2
	PE1580
	PE1583
	PE1585
	PE1599.P6
	PE2831
422.03	PE1580.A2
422.4	PE1574
422.491	PE3501
422.4924	PE1582.H4
422.4927	PE1582.A7
423	PE1617.J7
	PE1620
	PE1625
	PE1628
	PE1628.W4
	PE1670
423.1	PE1443

Dewey	LC
423.1	PE1460
	PE1584
	PE1591
	PE1628
	PE1680.A2
	PE1689
	PE1693
	PR1119
423.9144	PK1687
423.9149	PK2597
425	P151
	PC2290
	PE213
	PE1101
	PE1103
	PE1106
	PE1109
	PE1112
	PE1139.5
	PE1199
	PE1241
	PE1271
	PE1321
	PE1325
	PE1361
	PE1369
	PE1385
	PE1408
	PE1421
425.01	PE1585
426	PE1504
	PE1505
	PE1517
	PE1519
	PE1541
	PR649.I65
427	PE1667
	PN6222.A75
427.02	PE525
	PE531
	PE535
	PE664.S3
	PE1667
	PR2108.S97
427.09	D526.2
	PE1460
	PE1584
	PE3101.M5
	PE3711
	PE3721
	PE3727.N4
	PE3727.S7
427.1	PE1961
	PE1963
	PE3724.R5
	PN6222.A75
427.6	PE1887
427.64	PE2046
	PE2047
427.72	PE25
427.82	PE1997
427.9	PM7875.G8
427.9415	PB1397.V6
427.966	PM7891
427.96711	PM7891
427.97	PE2845
427.971	PE3237
	PE3243
427.97292	GR121.J2
	PE3313
427.973	PE1066
	PE2841
427.975	PE2922
427.9764	PE3101.T4
427.976819	PE1702
427.977434	PE3101.M5
427.99	PE3601
427.9914	PE3501
427.9969	P381.H3
427.9973	PE3330.T7
428	PE1106
	PE1109
	PE1115
	PE1121
	PE1128.A2
	PE1460
	PE1585
	PE1591.A2
	PE1595
	PE1689
	PN227
428.002461073	PE1116.N8
428.0028	PE1066
428.003	PE1460
428.007	PE1068.U5
	PE1128.A2
428.0071	PE1065
428.0071173	PE1128
428.0072073	PE1066
428.009	PE1072
428.018	PE1074.5
428.022	PF3498
428.1	B820
	PE835
	PE1065
	PE1129.S2
	PE1133
	PE1135
	PE1139.5
	PE1143
	PE1144
	PE1145.2
	PE1449
	PE1460
428.1	PE1574
	PE1585
428.2	LB1631
	PE1065
	PE1066
	PE1106
	PE1112
	PE1116.P6
	PE1116.V6
	PE1251
	PE1321
	PE1408
	PE1449
	PE1460
	PR6063.O8
428.202405	PE1116.J6
428.2024097	PE1116.J6
428.207	PE1065
428.24	PE1111
	PE1112
	PE1127.S3
	PE1128
	PE1128.A2
	PE1130.5.P5
	PE1161
	PE1408
	PE1460
428.2407	PE1068.A28
	PE1128
428.242	PF3420
428.243	PE1129.G3
428.24402453	Q209
428.245	PE1129.I7
428.2469	PE1129.P8
428.2496	PE1130.3.A2
428.3	PE1460
428.34	PE1128
	PE1130.5.A5
428.34071	PE1068.A28
428.343931	PE1129.D8
428.343982024646724	TT951
428.344	PE1129.F7
428.345	PE1129.I7
428.3469	PN6231.B8
428.4	LB1049
	LB1050
	LB1632
428.403	LB1050
428.407	L106
	LB1050
	LB1573
	RA409
428.4071	LB1050
428.40711	LB2365.R4
	LB2395
428.40712	LB5
	LB1632
428.40715	LC5225.R4
428.408	LB1050
428.409772	LB1573
428.42	LB1050
	LB1050.5
	LB2365.R4
	PE1065
428.4207	LB1050.5
428.420715	LC156.G7
428.43	KF280
	LB1050
	LB1050.5
	LB2365.R4
428.43077	LB1050
428.5	LB1050
428.6	DA32
	PE1116.N8
	PE1117.M235
	PE1119
	PE1120
	PE1121
	PE1122
	PE1127.H4
428.62	LC5225.R4
	PE1112
	PE1126.D4
428.64	PE1121
	PE1128
	PE1128.A2
	PE1477
	PR4567
428.643	PE1129.G3
428.643981	PE1129.S2
428.644	PE1129.F7
428.645	PE1129.I7
428.646	PE1129.S8
428.649185	B21
428.649186	PE1129.S5
428.6496	PE1130.3.A2
428.6497	PE1129.S3
429	PE135
429.17	PE26
429.2	PE161
429.20973	CS71
429.5	PE131
	PE213
430	P26
	PF3026.
430.9	PF3075
431.5	PF3135
431.6	PF3139.5
433.2	PF3640
437.01	PF3835
437.947	PJ5113
438	PF3112
438.00712	PF3066
438.1	MT883
438.242	PF3105
	PF3111
	PF3112
	PF3112.R37
	PF3420
438.342	PF3112
	PF3121
438.642	PF3115
	PF3117
	PT1105
	PT1828.B6
	PT1915.E3
	PT2259.M5
	PT2301.A4
	PT2525
	PT2528.P3
	PT2603.R397
	PT2625.A44
	PT2625.U8
	PT2678.I317
	Q213
439	PD101
439.31	PF778
439.318242	PF112
439.5	PD1514
439.78242	PD5111
	PD5115
439.78342	PD5121
439.78642	PD5117
439.827973	PD2615
439.828242	PD2623
439.828342	PD2627
439.8332	PD2691
440	PC14
	PC2026
440.9	PC2075
441.52	PC2075
442	PC2585
443.1	PC2460
443.2	PC2640
445	PC2109
	PC2111
	PC2261
	PC2271
447.01	PC2879
	PC2942
447.0103	PC2891
447.09	PC3739
448.003	PC2689
448.0077	PC2112
448.071273	PC2065
448.1	PC2137
448.2	PC2103
	PC2680
448.242	PC2111
	PC2112
	PC2117
	PC2118
	PC2121
	PC2271
	PC2420
448.2420712	PC2118
448.342	PC2111
	PC2112
	PC2121
448.642	PC2115
	PC2117
	PC2117.E75
	PC2117.F82
	PC2127.H5
	PC2127.S4
	PQ1223
	PQ1275
	PQ2637.I53
	PQ3919.2
448.6421	PC2117
449.5	PC3219
451.5	PC1101
	PC1131
453.2	PC1640
456	DS127
457.8	PC1801
458.1	MT883
458.242	PC1112
458.342	PC1121
458.642	PC1115
	PC1117
	PQ4841.I4
459.342	PC639
459.8342	PC639
460.7	PC4065
461.5	PC4131
461.52	PC4821
463	PC4628
463.2	PC4640
463.2109	PC4611
463.43	PQ7797.M225
463.98	PC4611
465	PC4315.R4
	PE1325
467.01	PC213
467.19	PC4789.C3
468.007	PC4065
468.242	PC4103
	PC4111
	PC4112
	PC4175
468.2421	PC4111
	PC4112
468.342	PC4460
468.642	PC4117
468.642	PC4127.C5
	PC4127.F3
	PQ6174.A3
	PQ6217
	PQ7297.B325
	PQ7389.M2
	T11
468.6421	PQ6601.Y3
469.071173	PC5038.U5
469.798	PC5442
	PC5444
470.09	PC1075
470.7	PA2061
	PA2063
471.7	CN510
	CN590
	Z114
472	PA2343
473	Z111
473.2	PA2365.E4
	PA2365.E5
473.70924	E415.9.C4
473.7455	E581.4.L37
475	PA2084
	PA2087
	PA6025
476.206	E668
477	PC13
478.1	PA459
478.242	PA2084
	PA2087
	PA2095
478.6	PA2095
478.642	PA2095
	PA6452
	PA6519.A6
	PA6519.M5
	PA6653.A6
479	PA2422
479.1	P25
	PC25
	PC76
479.105	Z7032
480.0924	PA85.B4
481.5	PA265
481.52	PA131
481.7	Z114
482	PA430.N6
485	PA251
	PA257
	PA337
	PA4236.Z5
	PA4273
486	PA411
	PA3553.Z7
487	PA649
	PA813
	PA881
487.109	ML800
488.242	PA257
	PA260
488.642	PA181
489.3	PA1050
491	PK1509
491.1	PK2.Z5
	PK175
	PK6103
491.2	PK409.H3
491.217	Z113
491.25	Q11
491.2824	PR663
491.357	PG7902
491.375	PK4503
491.4	P57.I4
	PK177
491.412	PK2786
491.415	PK2783
491.428242	PK2633
491.43	PK1939
491.435	PK1933
491.437	DS335
491.43802	PK1939
491.438242	PK1933
491.438342	PK1933
	PK1935
491.4392	PK1689
491.439642	PK2184
491.43981	PK1979
491.4398342	PK1973
491.4398642	PK1975
491.44	DU180.R9
491.4432	PK1687
	PK1689
491.445	PK1663
491.448242	PK1663
491.45	PK1828.Z9
491.4632	PK2375
491.467	PK2377
491.4682	PK2358
491.47242	PK1843
491.4732	PK1846
491.475	PK1843
491.485	PK2823
491.488242	PK2812
491.49	DX213
	PK2596
	PK7001
491.5	DS252.4
	PK6873
491.555	PK6233
491.558242	PK6235
491.5583421	PK6393.K3
491.59	PK6718
	PK6723

491.59 PK6901
PK6905
PK6996.T35
491.6 P381.G7
PB1013
PB1016
491.62 PB2002
491.6609031 PB2107
491.66152 PB2131
491.663 PB2195
491.6632 PB2191
491.665 PB2121
491.668342 PB2123
491.7 PG11
PG14
PG2073
491.709 PG2075
491.715 PG2135
491.7152 PG2135
491.72 P25
491.730222 PG2629
491.731 PG2625
PG2693
491.732 PG2640
491.75 PG13
PG2025
PG2211
PG2313
491.78.242 PG2112
491.78242 PG2112
PG2271
491.78342 PG2121
491.78642 PG2117
PG2127.H5
PG2127.S43
PG3365
491.798242 PG3823
491.798342 PG3827
491.8 AS281
PG53
PG441
491.818342 PE1131
491.8232 PG1376
491.825 PG1259
491.828028 PG1350.5
491.828340715 PB38.Y8
491.848022 PE1498
491.8515 PG13
491.856 PG6505
491.865 PG4369
491.8732 PG5379
491.9 PG8002
491.928642 PG8713
491.9925 PK8023
492 PJ3021
PJ4102
PJ4160
492.1 PJ3125
PJ3165
PJ3251
PJ3595.A4
PJ3711.L53
PJ3721.S4
PJ3875
PJ3885
492.4 PJ4573
PJ4845
492.409 PZ7.M549
492.4152 PJ4592
492.424927 PJ4603
492.45 PJ4645
PJ4711
492.48242 PJ4567
492.48342 PJ4573
492.49 PJ5111
492.6 P1035
492.7.242 PJ6111
492.709 PJ6075
492.715 PJ6121
492.717 PJ6690
492.77 PJ6782
PJ6823
PJ6829
PJ6901.C9
492.78007 PJ6068.U5
492.78242 PJ6307
492.78642 PJ6311
PJ6696
492.78842 PJ6111
492.8 PJ9213
PJ9239
493.117 PJ1553
PJ1681
PJ1761
PJ1771
493.17 PJ1553
493.25 PJ2095
493.5 PJ2425
PJ2531
PJ2534.A2
493.7 PL8725.5
494 PL1
494.2 PL401
PL405
PL409
494.3 PL55.U82
PL65.T3
PL383
494.358242 PL127
494.358342 PL127.3
494.5 PH1
PH14
PH2715
494.51 PH1307
494.51115 PH2131
494.51182 PH2103
494.5118242 PH2111
494.5118642 PH2117
494.54183 PH139
494.5418642 PH137
494.6 P25
494.8 PL4609
494.81 PL4791
PL4793
494.8108 PL4601
494.811 PL4751
494.81109 PL4751
494.811150924 PL4759.N33
494.811342 PL4755
494.8118242 PL4753
494.8147 PK81
494.8148642 PL4655
494.82 PL4745
494.8270924 PL4780.9.A5957
494.8272 PL4779
495 P25
495.1 PL1021
PL1279
495.1018 P98
495.1071273 PL1068.U5
495.111 PL1175
PL1185
495.115 PL1205
495.12 PL1231
495.125 QC100
495.132 PL1455
PL1481.W3
495.15 P25
PL1135
495.17 PL1703
PL1735
PL1736
495.18 PL1489
495.18016 PL1111
495.181 PL1209
495.18642 PL1117
495.4 PL3613
PL4001.K354
495.432 PL3637
495.49 AS281
PL4001.B34
PL4001.M314
495.6 PL539
495.616 PL544
495.6231 PL645
495.632 PL685
495.65 PL533
PL569
PL571
PL613
PL641
495.68242 PL535
PL537
PL539.5.A9
495.68342 PL539
495.68642 PL537
495.75 PL937.E5
495.78342 PL913
495.85 PL3931
495.87 PL4001.M314
495.9132 PL4187
495.915 PL4171
495.918342 PL4163
495.919 PL3311.M5
PL4119
PL4251.L31
PL4251.L34
495.92281 PL4379
495.9228342 PL4375
495.9328342 PL4323
495.9328642 PL4322
496 PL8005
PL8005.G73
PL8021.N5
496.3 DT963
PL8021.G5
PL8021.N5
PL8025
PL8025.3
PL8037
PL8069.4
PL8077.1
PL8147.1
PL8182
PL8201
PL8201.1
PL8261
PL8301
PL8323
PL8361
PL8577.4
PL8681
PL8689
PL8702
PL8731.4
PL8738
PL8738.4
PL8822
PL8843
496.33 PL8191
496.3325 PL8261
496.333 PL8822
496.39 PL8025
496.39282421 PL8702
496.915 PL8232
496.918242 PL8232
496.92 DT1
496.9209 PL8701
496.9232 DT1
PL8703
496.925 PL8702
496.9282407 PL8701
496.928242 PL8702
497 PM108
PM1611
PM1641
PM2019
PM2301.Z73
497.2 E51
PM2007
497.3 AS244
PM853
PM2261
QH1
497.4 PM731.Z95E5
PM1845.4
PM4176
PM4466
497.5 PM1023
PM1024.Z9T42
PM1071
497.7 P25
497.9 PM2019
PM4063
498 PM4426
PM6303
499 Q115
499.0995 PL6265
499.12 PL6621.K26
PL6621.T64
499.15 DU120
PL7002
499.2 PL5506
PL5721.Z5
499.21 PL5376
PL5571
499.21109914 PL5506
499.21132 PL6056
499.22131 PL5079
499.2215 PL5115
499.2218242 PL5073
499.2218342 PL5074
PL5075
499.222 PL5351
499.22232 PL5166
499.4 PL6409
PL6443
PL6465
PL6465.Z5
PL6515
499.5 PL6253.Z9
PL6255
PL6271.Z9
PM7891
499.92 PH5035
499.93 P943
499.95 PJ4054.N5
PJ4065.E47
499.99 PM8008
499.99232 PM8237
499.9928242 PM8213
499.9928342 PM8213
500 JX1977
KF26.A3
KF32.S3
PA6156
PZ10
PZ10.B29557
PZ10.K483
Q72
Q101
Q125
Q155
Q158
Q161
Q162
Q163
Q171
Q223
QB500
TA170
TL787
TL789.8.U5
TL791
TL796.A1
500.1 PZ10.S677
500.1071 S946
500.1072073 QH76
500.108 AS284
Q57
QH1
500.2 Q160
Q161
QC21.2
QC23
QC171
500.2028 Q183.9
QC35
500.208 AS182
AS262
AS262.T83
AS262.T84
AS281
Q60
Q62
Q171
QC71
500.5 QB500
500.9 DA670.N8
F257
F868.S136
F910
500.9 F2876
G742
GC97
PZ10
PZ10.B94
PZ10.H7958
PZ10.T9
Q11
Q171
QC801.3
QH21.E5
QH26
QH31.B18
QH31.W58
QH45
QH45.2
QH76.5.I6
QH77.U6
QH81
QH85
QH86
QH95.7
QH104.5.W4
QH105.A4
QH105.C2
QH105.F6
QH105.M55
QH105.N7
QH105.N8
QH105.S6
QH105.S8
QH106
QH111
QH125
QH137
QH138.B8
QH138.L35
QH138.N88
QH138.S4
QH141
QH144
QH151
QH169
QH184
QH186
QH197
QH197.5
QH198.H3
QH541.5.D4
QH541.5.S24
QK962.C4
SB484.G7
500.901 BL435
500.90222 QH46
500.9028 PZ10.H514
QH53
500.903 QH137
500.907 QH51
500.908 QH1
QH81
500.90924 QH31.B38
QH102
500.90941 QH141
500.909681 QH195.B6
500.90978395 QH105.S8
500.909788 QH105.C6
500.90994 QH197
500.979132 QH105.A65
500.979153 QH105.A65
501 AS348.A57
B67
B2786
Q125
Q143.P7
Q151
Q163
Q171
Q175
QC173
501.08 QA3
501.2 Q295
501.4 Q179
Q223
501.48 Q179
501.8 AC1
Q175
501.82 Q175
502.3 Q127.G4
Q149.A8
502.46649 Q181
502.554 Q145
502.8 L136
Q161
Q163
Q181
Q185
T50
TL1075
Z663.23
503 Q121
Q123
505 Q223
Z6945.A2
506.0595 Q127.P23
506.08 Q22
506.147 AS262
506.242 Q41.L85
Q127.G4
506.24259 Q41
506.2437 Q44
506.273 Q11
507 AS4.U8
AS722.W3
HM261

Dewey	LC
507	LB1584
	LB1585
	Q179
	Q181
	Q181.A1
	Q183.3
	Q223
507.1	Q180.U5
	Q181
	QA11
507.1142	LA116
	Q181
	Q181.A1
507.1173	Q183.3
	RA440.6
507.12	Q181
	Q183
507.1242	Q181
	Q183.8.G6
507.1273	Q181
507.12767	Q181
507.2	DC1
	HC79.R4
	Q125
	Q180.5
	Q223
507.2024	Q143.W38
507.204	Q180.E9
507.2042	Q125
507.2047	Q180.R9
507.2051	Q180.C6
507.2054	Q73
	Q180.I5
507.20549	Q183.43.P34
507.207295	Q180.P7
507.2073	KF26.I5
	Q180.U5
	Q183.3
	Q223
	UG633
507.2077157	Q180.U5
507.2078	Q180.U5
507.20931	Q180.N4
507.2098	Q180.P55
507.2099	G870
	Q180.U5
507.24	Q175
	Q185
507.40153	KF26.R885
507.6	Q182
507.9	Q181
508	AS283
	GN4
	Q11
	Q56
	Q60
	Q64
	Q162
	Q171
	Q180
	Q213
508.1	AS262
	AS283
	PG1418.A6
	Q11
	Q56
	Q60
	Q64
	Q111
	Q127.G4
	Q162
	Q171
	Q181
	R85.U76
	S381
508.3	QH11
508.30924	QH31.D2
508.73	E165
508.8	QH31.D2
508.9429	QH197
508.98	Q115
508.982	G743
	QH199
508.99	F3031
	G850
	G860
509	Q125
	Q181
509.03	Q125
509.032	Q125
509.034	Q125
	Q171
509.04	Q175
509.1724	Q101
509.22	Q127.U6
	Q141
	Q141.W62
	Q163
509.24	PS3551.S5
	Q125
	Q127.C5
	Q127.U6
	Q143.V3
	QC16.L54
	QH31.B26
	QH31.R79
509.3	Q125
509.38	Q127.G7
509.4	Q127.I4
509.42	Q127.G4
509.431	Q180.G42
509.44	DC26
509.51	Q127.C5
509.54	Q127.I4
509.54	Q127.T4
509.7	Q127.N6
509.71	Q127.C2
509.714	Q127.C2
509.73	Q180.U5
509.7444	Q185
509.794	Q127.U6
510	BF39
	Q60
	Q180.A1
	QA1
	QA3
	QA7
	QA9
	QA13.5.N4
	QA37
	QA37.2
	QA39
	QA39.2
	QA90
	QA93
	QA95
	QA154
	QA164
	QA166
	QA248.3
	QA303
	QA401
	TA330
510.0	QA11
510.01	QA7
	QA9
	QA248.5
510.018	QA76.5
	QC770
510.02	QA99
510.0212	QA47
	TA332
510.02433	HB74.M3
	QA37.2
	QA39
510.02453	QA37.2
510.02454	QD42
510.0246	QA39
	TA330
510.02462	QA37
	TA330
	TA332.5
510.0246213	TK153
510.02465	HF5691
510.024658	QA37.2
510.02467182	TS250
510.028	QA11
	QA76.5
510.06273	QA14.A9
510.07	DL1
	QA11
	QA13
	QA13.5.K4
	QA14.I5
510.071	QA11.A1
510.0711	QA13
510.071173	QA13
	QA13.5.N4
510.0712	LB1620.5
	QA11
	QA135.5
510.071242	QA14.G4
	QA14.G7
510.071247	QA11
510.071273	L162
510.076	QA36.5
	QA43
	QA99
	QA139
510.077	QA20.P7
510.078	QA13.5.M4
	QA20.P7
510.08	Q60
	QA1
	QA3
	QA11
	QA76
	QA171.5
510.09	QA21
510.0924	QA29.F5
	QA29.H5
	QA29.K67
510.093	QA22
510.0938	QA22
510.212	QA41
510.2462	TA330
510.71	QA11
510.71142	QA14.G7
510.712	QA11
510.78	R835
510.7823	QA73
510.9	QA21
510.924	QA29.G3
511	PZ10
	QA24
	QA107
	QA111
	QA141.3
	QA142
	QA145
	QA248
	QA248.3
511.01	QA248.3
511.02437	QA135.5
511.07	QA135.5
511.0715	QA135.5
511.076	QA139
511.1	PZ10.R85
511.1	QA141.2
511.1077	QA141
511.207809	QA75
511.23	QA76
511.3	BC135
	QA9
	QA248
511.32077	QA266
511.33	QA171.5
511.6	QA164
511.8	HB539
	HF5691
	HF5695
	QA266
	SD393
	TX335
511.80212	HG1628
	HG1634
	HG1638.E6
511.9	QA49
	QA107
512	QA39
	QA145
	QA152
	QA154
	QA155
	QA251
	QA295
512.0245	QA154
512.028	QA161
512.07	QA135
	QA159
512.077	QA154
512.1	QA37.2
	QA39.2
	QA331.3
512.13	QA154
512.2	QA3
512.21	QA76
	QA218
512.22	QA3
512.23	Q64
	QA242
512.230212	QA242
512.4	QA326
512.5	QA164
	QA166
	QA246.5
	QA251
	QA292
	QA295
512.6	QA241
512.72076	QA241
512.74	QA247
512.8	QA1
	QA3
	QA155
	QA169
	QA248
	QA248.3
	QA248.5
	QA251
	QA266
	QA269
	QA270
	T57.92
512.81	AS36
	HD6483.P8
	QA3
	QA9
	QA141
	QA241
	QA246
	QA246.5
	QA247.5
	QA248
	QA248.3
	QA255
512.813	QA247
512.815	QA3
	QA247
	QA251
512.817	QA9
	QA248
	QA326
512.82	QA3
	QA211
512.86	QA3
	QA171
	QA171.5
	QA331
	QA385
	QA387
	QA564
	TL521
512.865	QA171.5
512.87	QA3
	QA201
	QA244
512.89	QA3
	QA76
	QA169
	QA241.5
	QA251
	QA266
	QA322
	QA326
	QA387
	QA612
	T57.6
512.893	QA257
512.895	Q49.C95
	QA261
512.895077	QA261
512.896	QA1
	QA251
	QA263
	TA347.D4
	TR693
512.89602433	HB74.M3
512.897	AS283
	QA169
	QA251
	QA263
	QA326
	TL521
512.8970243	QA251
512.9	QA145
	QA154
	QA157
512.9042	QA154
512.943	QA263
513	QA32
	QA107
	QA164
	QA248
	QA445
	QA447
	QA453
	QA455
	QA465
	QA681
513.01	QA681
513.076	PZ10.H7
513.09	QA21
513.1	PZ10
	PZ10.S692
	QA31
	QA447
	QA453
	QA455
	QA482
	QA484
513.10202	QA459
513.1076	QA459
513.132	QA107
513.3	QA491
513.302	QA491
513.7	QA360
513.83	Q60
	Q180
	Q180.A1
	QA3
	QA166
	QA248
	QA322
	QA355
	QA564
	QA611
	QA611.15
	QA611.3
	QA612
	QA614
	QA614.3
513.838	QA611
513.85	QA689
513.92	QA466
514	QA531
	QA538
	QA611
514.223	QA613
514.3	QA611.A1
	QA640.7
514.32	QA611.24
514.5	QA533
514.5077	QA531
515	QA300
	QA303
515.15	QA303
515.35	QA371
	QA372
515.352	QA372
515.37	QA381
515.42	QA3
515.623	QA297
	QA372
515.63	QA261
	QA263
515.7	QA3
515.72	QA402.5
515.8	QA300
515.9	QA331
515.98	QA404
516	PZ10.P6
	QA331
	QA551
	QA553
	QA556
516.011	QP99.5.H37
516.2	Q180.A1
	QA445
	QA455
516.204	QA466
516.23	QA491
516.24	QA533
516.36	QA614.3
516.4	QA3
516.5	QA3
	QA445
	QA471
	QA564
	QA565
	QA614
	QE3
	T385
516.55	QA551
516.57	QA471
516.6	QA501

Dewey	LC
516.6	QA608
516.7	QA608
	QA641
	QA644
	QA645
	QA649
	QA689
516.74	QC174.5
516.83	QA261
	QA433
	TA347.V4
516.9	QA555
517	Q60
	QA1
	QA3
	QA37
	QA76
	QA221
	QA251
	QA292
	QA295
	QA300
	QA303
	QA331
	QA331.3
	QA402
	QA402.5
	QA425
	QA4021.3
	TL521.3.C6
517.018	QA76.5
517.02453	QC20
517.02462	TA330
	TA331
517.024621381	TK153
517.08	QA3
	QA303
	QA801
517.09	QA303
517.09033	QA300
517.2	QA306
	QA402.5
	QA431
517.21	QA295
517.29	QA305
517.3	QA273
	QA308
	QA312
	QA351
	QA355
	QA649
517.31	QA3
517.35	QA351
	QA405
517.352	QA432
517.353	QA408
517.355	QA403
	QA404
	QC174.5
517.36	QA247
517.37	Q180.A1
	QA431
	QA614
517.38	Q180.A1
	QA3
	QA269
	QA295
	QA371
	QA372
	QA381
	QA401
	QA427
	QA611.5
	QA825
517.382	QA372
	TA7
517.383	Q180.A1
	QA1
	QA374
	QA377
	TL521.3.C6
517.38302462	TA347.D45
517.4	QA3.S657
	QA315
	QA316
	QA402.5
517.5	QA1
	QA3
	QA76
	QA221
	QA297
	QA303
	QA320
	QA322
	QA329.2
	QA329.8
	QA331
	QA331.3
	QA333
	QA351
	QA402
	QA403
	QA431
	QA432
517.52	QA3
	QA300
	QA303
	QA331.5
517.6	Q180
	Q180.A1
	QA1
	QA3
	QA76
	QA212
517.6	QA214
	QA297
	QA297.8
	QA299.3
	QA371
	QA372
	QA374
	QA377
	QA401
	QA402
	QA427
	QC100
	SD11
	TL521
	TL521.3.C6
517.6018	QA76.5
517.6028	QA297
	TA345.5.I2
517.608	QA297
517.7	QA320
	QA322
	QA329.4
	QA372
	QA381
	QA432
	QC20
517.8	AS36
	Q60
	QA1
	QA3
	QA300
	QA331
	QA333
	QA351
	QA360
517.81	QA3
	QA333
517.817	QA248
517.85	QA351
517.88	QA351
517.9	QA303
519	HA29
	HD6483
	LB2846
	QA3
	QA9
	QA31
	QA263
	QA273
	QA274
	QA274.7
	QA276
	QA276.16
	QA276.25
	QA276.6
	QA277
	QA278
	QA278.2
	QA278.7
	QA278.8
	QA279.5
	QA402
	QA402.3
	QH405
	T57.4
	TA340
	TL521
519.018	QA276.4
519.0202	QA273
519.0212	QA276.25
	QH405
519.02433	HA29
	HD69.D4
519.02454	TP149
519.024574	HA29
	QH405
519.02461	RA407
519.02462	T57.35
	TA340
519.024624	TA340
519.02465	HA29
519.076	HA29
	QA276.2
519.08	QA276
519.09	QA273
519.1	AS36
	HA33
	HD6483
	Q180
	Q180.A1
	QA3
	QA273
	QA273.H67
	QA273.6
	QA274
	QA274.7
	QA274.73
	QA275
	QA276.8
	QA278.7
	QA280
	QA312
	T57.3
	T57.9
	T57.92
	T57.95
	TA340
519.10212	QA273
519.2	QA273
519.233	QA274.7
519.234	QA274.76
519.4	QA218
519.5	HA29
519.5	QA276
519.5076	QA276.2
519.53	QA278
	QA278.8
519.53077	HA29
519.54	QA276.8
	QA279.4
519.6	QA278
519.7	QA277
519.72	T57.74
519.76	Q180.A1
	T57.8
519.8	HA29
	HA33
	Q180
	Q180.A1
	QA76.5
	QA195
	QA221
	QA273
	QA275
	QA276.7
	QA276.8
	QA277
	QA278
	QA278.2
	QA278.7
	QA278.8
	QA279
	QA279.4
	QA279.5
	QA280
	QA402.5
	QE75
	TL521
519.9	HA33
	Q180.A1
	T57.9
519.92	AS36
	Q180.A1
	QA76
	QA264
	QA265
	QA316
	QA402.3
	QA402.5
	T57.7
	T57.74
	T57.8
	T57.83
519.93	QA276.6
	TS156
520	QB34
	QB41
	QB43
	QB44
	QB44.2
	QB45
	QB51
	QB64
520.03	QB14
520.0712	QB61
520.076	QB62.5
520.0924	QA29.P66
	QB36.B22
520.23	QB51.5
520.3	QB14
	TL788
520.711	QB61
520.76	QB62.5
520.8	QB1
	QB4
	QB51
520.9	QB15
	QB25
520.922	QB35
520.924	QB36.B8
	QB36.C8
	QB36.G2
	QB36.H25
	QB36.H59
	QB36.S49
520.93	AS122.B4
	QB16
520.934	QB18
520.938	QB21
520.942	QB33.G7
520.952	QB33.J3
520.954	QB18
521	QA803
	QB351
521.1	QB351
	TL521
521.16	QB410
521.3	QC1
521.54	QB355
521.8	QB175
522	QB63
	QB64
	QB145
522.0740371	QB85
522.1	QB136
522.19487	Q64
522.1979177	QB82.K55
522.2	QB64
	QB86
522.210979133	QB4
522.29753	QB4
522.2979498	QB88
522.41	PG6014
	VK583
522.56	QB461
522.6	QB47
522.67	QB470
522.78	QB41
523	QB43
	QB44
	QB45
	QB136
	QB464
	QB838
	QB860
523.002	QB67
523.00212	QB4
523.0108	QB1
	QB461
523.013	QB47
	QB461
	QB462.5
	QB464
	QB500
	QB855.5
	QB981
	QC1
	QC100
	QC485
	QC806
	TL507
523.01308	QB461
523.016	QB475
	QB479.2
	TL521.3.C6
523.1	BD511
	QB42
	QB54
	QB815
	QB981
523.10222	QB68
523.109	QB981
523.1110631	JX1977
523.112	QB46
	QB851
	QB855
	TL521
523.113	QB461
	QB819
523.1135	QB461
	QB790
	QB817
	TL521
	TL521.3.C6
523.12	QB981
523.13	QB54
523.2	QB500
	QB501
	QB501.3
	QB505
	Z5154.I5
523.3	QB581
	QB591
523.32	TL521.3.C6
523.34	QB581
	QB591
	TL799.M6
523.39	AS281
	QB585
	QB595
	TL507
	TL789.8.U6A598
523.4	QB369
	QB581
	QB601
	QB639
	TL507
523.42	QB621
	TL507
523.43	QB641
523.482	TL507
523.5	QB461
	TL521
523.51	QB461
	QB755
	QE125
	QE395
	TL507
523.51075	QB755
523.5109784	QE149
523.5109861	QE1
523.6	QB731
	TL507
523.69	QB722
523.7	QB475
	QB521
	QB524
	QB531
523.72	QB531
523.75	QB526.F6
	TL521.3.C6
	Z663.23
523.77	QB461
523.78	QB4
	QB541
	QB544.66
523.7809046	QB4
523.8	AS284
	PZ10.F714
	QB63
	QB464
	QB801
	QB809
	QB810
	QB843.D9
	QB843.N4
	QC100
523.81	QB461
523.82	QB843.M3
523.83	QB810
	QB811

523.84 ..... Q56
..... QB4
523.841 ..... QB1
..... QB4
523.8410212 ..... QB4
523.842 ..... QB4
523.844 ..... QB835
523.8442 ..... QB838
523.84425 ..... TL507
523.8446 ..... QB41
..... QB841
..... QB843.D85
..... QB895
..... QC883
523.85 ..... QB1
523.852 ..... QB4
523.855 ..... QB4
523.86 ..... Q56
..... QB801
523.87 ..... QB461
..... QB871
..... QB883
..... QC100
..... TL507
523.89 ..... QB63
523.8903 ..... QB63
..... QB65
523.8908 ..... QB1
..... QB4
..... QB6
..... QB811
523.985 ..... TL521
523.99 ..... QB175
525 ..... TL507
525.0222 ..... QB637
525.1 ..... QB1
..... QB283
..... QB410
525.38 ..... QB522
526 ..... QB279
..... QB281
..... QB296.C3
..... QB585
526.08 ..... GA1
..... QB275
..... QB280
..... QB296.F5
526.23 ..... QA402.3
526.3 ..... TL521.3.C6
526.3018 ..... GA101
526.3028 ..... QB296.N4
526.30973 ..... QB296.U89
526.309756 ..... QB296.U9
526.309982 ..... Q115
526.33 ..... QB296.N4
526.37 ..... GB275
526.6 ..... QB145
..... QB296.N4
526.7 ..... QB331
526.70976125 ..... QB335
526.70978962 ..... TN24.N6
526.8 ..... G129
..... GA9
..... GA105
..... GA110
..... GA130
..... GA135
..... GA151
..... GA203
..... GA231
..... HD107
..... Z6027.G7
526.8018 ..... GA9
..... TH7
..... Z699.5.C3
526.8028 ..... GA115
526.80611 ..... GA101
526.807 ..... G76.5.G7
526.809 ..... E121
..... G201
526.8094274 ..... GA795.Y6
526.809469 ..... GA1011
526.809718 ..... GA475.N53
526.9 ..... GA108
..... TA501
..... TA545
..... TA549
..... TA555
..... TA562
..... VG923
526.90202 ..... TA551
526.9023 ..... TA549
526.9028 ..... TA562
526.9076 ..... TA537
526.908 ..... QB280
526.90942 ..... GA66.G7
526.90954 ..... GA71.I3
526.90954792 ..... TA551
526.92 ..... TA563
526.920202 ..... TA551
526.982 ..... TA593
..... TR693
526.9823 ..... TA593
..... TR693
..... Z663.23
526.982308 ..... TA593
526.9909931 ..... VK597.N48
527 ..... VK555
527.0202 ..... VK555
527.096 ..... GN440
528 ..... QB7
528.2 ..... QB8.G7
529 ..... QB209
..... TS542
529.3 ..... CE91
529.32208 ..... CE42
529.7 ..... QB213
..... QB296.N4
..... TS542
529.709 ..... QB213
529.75 ..... KF27.I5536
..... QC100
529.750973 ..... QB223
529.78 ..... QB215
530 ..... PZ10.E6
..... PZ10.P6
..... QA402
..... QC1
..... QC16.M67
..... QC19
..... QC21
..... QC21.2
..... QC23
..... QC25
..... QC28
..... QC30
..... QC71
..... QC73
..... QC100
..... QC171
..... QC806
..... QC920
..... TL507
530.01 ..... QC6
..... QC16.N7
..... QC173
530.0202 ..... QC23
530.0212 ..... QD65
530.023 ..... QC29
530.02461073 ..... RT42
530.028 ..... PZ10.M612
..... QC33
..... QC35
..... QC37
..... QC39
..... QC53
..... TS156.8
530.05 ..... QC5.45
..... Z663.23
530.07 ..... QC61
530.0711 ..... QC31
530.071142 ..... Q149.G7
530.0712 ..... QC30
530.072 ..... QC5.45
530.072073 ..... QC30
530.0724 ..... QC51.D4
530.076 ..... Q163
..... QC32
530.08 ..... Q60
..... Q143.H98
..... QA3
..... QC1
..... QC3
..... QC21.2
..... QC71
..... QC761
530.0922 ..... QC15
530.0924 ..... QC6
..... QC16.B45
..... QC16.B48
..... QC16.B65
..... QC16.E45
..... QC16.E5
..... QC16.G5
..... QC16.M4
..... QC16.N7
..... QC16.O62
..... QC16.R3
..... QC515
..... QD22.C8
530.0938 ..... Q151
530.1 ..... QC6
..... QC20
..... QC21
..... QC75
..... QC173
..... QC174.1
530.109 ..... QC7
530.11 ..... QA1
..... QA689
..... QA808.5
..... QC6
..... QC174.1
..... QC178
530.12 ..... AS281
..... QC174.1
..... QC174.5
..... QC721
..... TL507
530.120151286 ..... QC174.5
530.120151289 ..... QC174.5
530.12076 ..... QC174.1
530.122 ..... QA3
..... QC174.3
530.123 ..... QC174.1
530.124 ..... QC174.1
..... QC174.2
..... QC231
530.13 ..... QC174.5
..... QC175.2
..... QD95
530.132 ..... Q175
..... QC175
530.133 ..... QC174.4
530.14 ..... QC174.1
..... QC174.45
530.141 ..... QC670
530.141076 ..... QC670
530.143 ..... QA1
..... QC20
..... QC174.45
..... QC721
530.1430151289 ..... QC174.45
530.144 ..... QA1
..... QC174.4
..... QC174.5
..... QC770
530.15 ..... QA401
..... QA427
..... QC20
..... QC174.5
530.15076 ..... TA333
530.15383 ..... QA612.63
530.157 ..... QC20
530.157382 ..... QA402
530.159 ..... QC20
530.1591 ..... QC20
530.16 ..... QC39
530.4 ..... QC171
..... QC176.A1
..... QC425
..... QD453
530.407 ..... LB1059
530.41 ..... Q54
..... QA3
..... QC1
..... QC100
..... QC171
..... QC174.1
..... QC174.5
..... QC176
..... QC176.A1
..... QC176.2
..... QC176.8.E35
..... QC176.8.E4
..... QC176.8.E9
..... QC176.8.M3
..... QC176.8.O6
..... QC176.8.R3
..... QC481
..... QC721
..... QD506
..... QD931
..... U395.S8
530.41072 ..... QC176
530.410924 ..... QC16.L35
530.42 ..... QC145
..... QC174.4
..... QC175.4
..... TD478
530.43 ..... QC1
..... QC175
530.44 ..... QC717.6
..... QC718
530.7 ..... QC1
..... QC107
530.8 ..... PZ10.P6
..... QC39
..... QC94
..... QC100
530.8076 ..... QC39
530.809 ..... QA465
530.924 ..... QC16.B65
..... QC16.N7
530.9544 ..... S471.I4
530.973 ..... S441
531 ..... QA611.5
..... QA801
..... QA803
..... QA808.2
..... QA821
..... QA846
..... QC21.2
..... QC125
..... QC127
..... QC131
..... QC165
..... QC173
531.01517 ..... QA261
..... QA402
..... QA805
..... QA807
531.01519 ..... QC175
531.0202 ..... QA808.2
531.076 ..... QC129
531.08 ..... QA802
531.1 ..... PZ10.B65
..... PZ10.S79
..... QB331
..... QC20
..... QC178
531.11 ..... QA871
..... QA913
..... QC100
..... QC281
..... TL521.3.C6
531.113 ..... PZ10.H473
531.163 ..... Q60
..... TL521
531.2 ..... TA351
531.2077 ..... TA351
531.3 ..... QA372
..... QA808.2
..... QA845
..... QA846
..... QA871
..... QC127
531.301 ..... QC131
531.30151 ..... QA845
531.301512 ..... TL521.3.C6
531.3077 ..... QA846
531.32 ..... QA3
531.32 ..... QA871
531.32015198 ..... TL521
531.33 ..... QA927
..... QC157
..... QC176.8.W3
531.34 ..... QA862.G9
531.38 ..... QA931
..... QA935
..... TA648.3
..... TL521.3.C6
531.382 ..... QC189
..... TL507
531.3822 ..... QA935
531.3823 ..... QA927
..... QA931
..... QA933
..... QA935
..... QC191
..... QD381
531.3823015176 ..... QA931
531.3825 ..... QC1
..... QC191
531.383 ..... QA935
531.4 ..... QC191
531.5 ..... AC1
..... QC178
531.52 ..... QC16.N7
531.54 ..... QB331
531.6 ..... TL521.3.C6
531.7 ..... QC100
531.8 ..... PZ10.R18
532 ..... QA901
..... QC145
..... QC145.2
..... QC147
..... TA357
532.00151738 ..... QA374
532.0076 ..... TA357
532.05 ..... QA911
..... QA913
..... QA925
..... QC151
..... QC168
..... QC175.3
..... QC718
..... TL507
532.05028 ..... QA911
532.057 ..... QC175.2
532.1 ..... QC145
532.5 ..... QA3
..... QA911
..... QC151
..... QC185
..... TA7
..... TC174
..... TL521.3.C6
532.51 ..... QA929
532.515 ..... QA929
532.517 ..... QA913
532.517015191 ..... QA913
532.54 ..... QC1
..... TC175
532.56 ..... QC770
532.58 ..... QA929
..... TL521
532.593 ..... QA927
..... QC174.2
532.6 ..... QA801
..... QC176.8.T5
532.7 ..... QC175.2
..... QD543
532.7028 ..... Q64
533.12 ..... QC100
..... TL500
..... TL521.3.C6
533.14 ..... QC182
533.2 ..... QA911
..... QC168
..... QC175
..... TL507
533.215 ..... TL526.G7
533.217 ..... QC243.5
..... TK9008
533.28 ..... TL521.3.C6
533.28209761395 ..... QE82.C49
533.293 ..... Q11
..... QC168
..... QC791
..... TL507
533.6 ..... QA911
533.62 ..... QA930
..... TL507
533.6217 ..... QA930
533.6275 ..... TL526.G7
533.6293 ..... TL526.G7
533.63 ..... QC185
533.7 ..... QC175
534 ..... QC157
..... QC225
..... QC225.15
..... QP461
534.208 ..... TL521.3.C6
534.23 ..... QA935
..... QC225
..... QC225.15
534.24 ..... Q180
..... Q180.A1
..... QC243
534.55 ..... QC244
..... TA367
535 ..... PZ10.A67
..... PZ10.S677
..... QC176.8.O6
..... QC353

535 QC355
QC357
QC357.2
QC360
QC361
QC446.2
535.01 QC661
535.013 QC911
535.013028 QC371
535.0140979494 QC459
535.02462 QC220
535.13 QC403
535.14 QC770
535.15 QC476.2
535.2 QC401
535.208 QC446.2
535.22 QC391
535.24 QC407
535.3 QC425
QC482
TL521
535.32 QC381
QC383
QC482
535.32028 QC385
535.323 TL521.3
535.324 TL521
535.33 QC367
QC373.L5
VG603
535.35 QC476.5
QC477
QC585
535.4 QC244.5
QC357
QC411
QC415
QC449
QC476.2
QC670
TL526.G7
535.5352 QC490
535.58 QC1
QC446.2
TJ1
TK7871.3
TK7871.35
TL521
TL521.3
Z663.23
535.5807247 Z663.23
535.6 QC495
TR210
535.601 QC495
535.8 QC448
QC451
535.84 QC100
QC373.S7
QC415
QC451
QC451.S87
QC453
QC454
QC490
QC721
QD95
535.840212 QC453
535.8409 QC451
535.8409034 QC451
535.842 QC338
QC454
QC457
QC490
QD95
535.8420212 QC457
535.846 QC176.8.E4
QC454
536 QC255
536.028 PZ10.S856
536.2 QC145
QC320
536.2001517 QC320
536.20120212 QC171
536.2014 QC185
536.23 QC176.8.T4
QC323
TL507
536.230151 QA3
536.230151738 QA401
536.25 QC100
QC320
QC327
536.33 QA491
QC171
QC331
TL507
536.401 QC1
536.412 QC165
QC286
QD181.H4
536.414 QA933
536.4140212 QC282
536.443 QC307
TD478
TK9008
536.5 QC100
QC271
QC274
536.5028 QC278
536.520212 QC100
536.56 QC284
536.56016 Z7144.L6
536.56028 QC278
536.63 QC171
536.7 QC1
QC175
QC311
QC311.5
TJ265
TL521.3.C6
536.7015191 QC1
536.70212 TN671
536.71 QC311
QC311.5
536.710922 QC311
QC311.D79
536.73 QC175
537 PZ10.S856
QC518
QC522
QC523
QC760
TK146
537.028 QC527
QC534
537.0724 QC518
537.08 QC503
537.0924 Q143.H6
QC16.F2
537.1 QC661
QC753
QC753.2
537.11 QC175
QC661
TL507
537.12 QC661
QC670
QC721
QC760
QC973
TK153
TL507
537.123 TK7876
537.125 QC661
TK4
537.16 QC320
QC717
QC717.6
QC718
QC770
QC791
TK4660
TL507
TP156.P5
Z663.23
Z663.23.A2
537.1608 QC717.6
537.21 QC581
537.24 QC585
TL521.3.C6
537.2430212 QC100
537.244 QC595
TK7872.P54
537.5 QC680
QC702
TK7835
537.508 QC680
TK7800
537.52 QC705
TL521.3.C6
537.53 QC544.C3
QC711
537.532 QC100
QC701
QC702
QC711
TK9008
537.5320212 QC100
537.534 QC453
QC454
QC661
TL521
537.5344 QC454
TK7871.4
TL521.3
537.535028 QC481
537.5352 QC176.8.E4
QC481
QC490
QC770
TA401
TK9008
537.54 QC100
QC715
537.56 QC447
QC721
QC770
TK7871.3
537.6 QC631
537.62 QC174.1
QC176.8.E4
537.622 QC100
QC612.S4
QC612.S8
QD382.S4
537.623 QC612.S4
QC612.S8
TL521.3.C6
537.624 QC100
537.627 QC612.S4
537.63 QC641
TK1141
537.64 Q54
QC39
QC631
QC680
537.65 TL521.3.C6
538 QC751
538 QC753
QC816
538.2 PZ10.M8982
538.23 QC760
QC761
538.3 QC451
QC462.F5
QC490
QC721
QC753
QC761
QC762
QC795
QD95
QD476
QD481
QD940
538.4 QC761
538.43 QC1
538.44 QC1
QC761
TL521.3.C6
538.6 Q11
Q180
QC718
TL521
TL521.3.C6
538.7 QC807.5
QC809.M35
QC971
QE185
538.70948 QB4
538.709481 QC830.N66
538.70971232 QB4
538.70971271 QB4
538.7097129 QB4
538.72 Q180
QC811
QC827
QC841
538.72094537 QE1
538.720971134 QB4
538.72097129 QB4
538.74094 QC802
538.7440998 QC835
538.748 QC809.M25
QE75
538.76 QC801
QC809.M35
TK6553
538.767 Q180
QC973
538.7675 QC485
QC801
538.768 QC971
TL507
Z663.23
538.7680999 QC972
538.78 AS4
538.7848 QB4
QC825.4
538.78931 QC801
539 AS36
Q11
QC21
QC21.2
QC100
QC173
QC174.1
QC175
QC451
QC453
QC454
QC464.C1
QC702
QC721
QD169.W3
QD461
QD471
QD501
QD547
TD478.U5
TL507
TL521.3.C6
539.03 QC772
539.07 HD9698
539.0708 QC770
539.08 QC1
QC770
539.0924 QC16.M36
QC774.M4
539.096 QC792
539.1 QC173
539.12 QC454
539.120151286 QC174.5
539.1203 QC454
539.14 QC451
QD1
539.2 QC475
539.7 Q64
QC100
QC173
QC490
QC721
QC762
QC770
QC776
QC777
QC778
QC780
QC794
QC795
QD601.A1
539.7016 Z5160
539.7028 QC1
QC338
QC786
539.703 QC772
539.7072 Q180.U5
539.7072073 QC788
539.708 HD9698
HD9698.A1
QC770
QC770.B7
QL770
539.709 TK9155
539.70924 PZ10.E6
QC16.F46
QC16.G37
QC774.K8
539.72 AS281
QA1
QC1
QC20
QC168
QC173
QC174.5
QC454
QC475
QC482
QC484.3
QC721
QC762
QC770
QC794
QC795
TL507
539.72028 QC787.C6
539.72077 QC475
539.7208 QC16.R8
539.721 QA1
QC1
QC173
QC484
QC721
QC770
QD561
TK9008
TL507
539.7210151286 QC174.5
QC721
539.7211 QC100
QC173
QC721
QC770
QD461
TL521.3.C6
539.7212 Q64
QC173
QC721
QC794
539.7213 Q180.A1
QC100
QC174.5
QC490
QC721
QC770
TK9008
539.7215 QC721
539.7216 QC490
QC721
539.7217 AS281
QC176.8.P5
539.7219 QC721
539.722 QC794
539.7222 QC481
QC482
QC490
QC795
539.7223 QC485
TL507
Z5151
539.73 QC770
QC786
QC787.P3
539.7307204945 QC770
539.733 QC100
QC787.C8
QC787.L5
539.735 QC786
539.74 QC173
QC770
539.740184 QC174.5
539.743 QC1
QC173
539.75 AS122
Q64
QA1
QC1
QC173
QC454
QC680
QC721
QC721.H367
QC762
QC770
QC772
QC794
QC795
TK9008
TL507
TL521
TL521.3
539.75018 QC1
539.752 Q64
QC795
TK9008
539.7523 Q56

Dewey	LC
539.7523	QC795
539.7524	TK9008
539.753	QC1
	QC794
	QC795
539.754	QC173
	QC490
539.756	QC100
539.76	QC490
	QC721
	QC794
539.762	QC790
539.76201519	QC790
539.76209	QC790
539.764	QC791
539.77	QC100
	QC770
	QC771
	QC786
	QC787.C6
	QC787.S55
539.772	QC787.B8
539.775	QC787.C6
539.9	QC783
540	QD1
	QD27
	QD31
	QD31.2
	QD33
	QD35
	QD37
	QD39
	QD40
540.012	HF1040.7
540.03	QD5
540.071142	Q183.8.G6
540.0712	QD40
540.1	QD13
	QD24.M3
	QD25
	QD26
540.14	QD7
	QD9.2
540.18	QD42
540.202	QD41
540.212	QD7
540.224	QD471
	QD601.2
540.23	QD39.5
540.28	QD38
	QD43
540.3	QD5
540.5	QD8.5
540.71273	QD40
540.720945	QD49.L3
540.76	QD42
540.8	QD1
	QD9
	TP1
540.85	QD1
540.89	QD1
540.9	QD11
	QD14
	QD39
540.9032	Q171
540.922	QD21
540.924	BX9869.P8
	CT275.C263
	QD3
	QD22.D2
	QD22.L4
	QD22.M43
	QD22.P8
	QD22.U75
541	QD31
	QD453
	QD453.2
	QD457
	QD461
541.028	QD457
541.09	QD461
541.2	QD453
	QD454
	QD455
	QD461
	QD471
	QD475
541.22	QD455
	QD480
541.220151222	QD461
541.222	QD461
541.224	QD95
	QD241
	QD453
	QD461
	QD469
	QD471
	QD475
	QD601.2
541.2254	QD3
541.2254015191	QD381
541.24	QD461
541.26076	QD42
541.28	QC173
	QD461
	QD462
541.3	QD453
	QD453.2
	QD454
	QD543
541.3028	QD457
541.3076	QD456
541.34	QD454
	QD541
541.341	QD541
	TD478
541.3422	QD501
	TD478
541.3423	TL521.3
541.345	QD506
	QD561
541.34513	QD549
541.3453	QC183
	QD1
	QD506
	QD547
	TP968
541.348	QD541
541.3482	QD544.5
541.35	QD601
	QD601.A1
541.36	QD501
	QD511
541.36008	QD501
541.361	QD516
541.363	QC20
	QC319
	QD181.N6
	QD501
	QD548
	TK9008
	TP1
541.363028	TN690
541.3686	QD535
541.3687	QD510
541.369	Q180.A1
	QC100
	QD501
	QD510
	TD478
	TJ270
541.3690212	QD501
541.37	QC100
	QD1
	QD453
	QD553
	QD561
	QD571
	QD585
541.372	QC100
	QD1
	QD561
	TD478
	TL521.3.C6
541.3723	QD181.N2
	QD561
541.3724	AS283
	QD561
541.378	QD475
	TL521
541.38	QD501
	QD601
	QD601.A1
	QD601.2
541.38018	QC770
541.3809	QD601.2
541.380924	QD22.H2
541.382	QD601
541.388	QD1
	QD601
541.388028	TP156.D47
541.3884	QD601
541.389381	QC490
541.389416	QC762
541.389623	QC1
	QC770
541.389634	Q60
541.389652	Q60
541.389681	QD603.C1
541.389731	QC770
541.39	QC176.A1
	QD1
	QD63.M3
	QD156
	QD471
	QD501
	TD478
541.392	QD453
	QD475
	QD501
541.392018	Q180
541.393	Q11
	QC100
	QD1
	QD63.E83
	QD63.O9
	QD181.T6
	QD501
541.394	QD501
541.3940151	QD501
541.39401519	QA273
541.395	QD1
	QD501
	TN26
	TP156.C35
541.471	GC296.A5
541.901	QD467
	QD501
541.90109	QD467
542	QD45
	QD155
	QH221
	R856
542.023	TA158
542.1	QD61
542.3	QC107
542.7	QD43
542.9	QD54.C4
543	QD73
	QD75
	QD133
	QD142
543.001	QD73
543.0018	QD73
543.0028	QD83
543.01	QD77
	QD271
543.08	QC451
	QD73
	QD117.M5
543.08028	QD73
543.085	QC437
	QD95
	QD271
543.086	QD117.T5
	QD515
543.087	QD115
543.088	TK9008
543.3	QD506
543.6	QE75
	QE438
543.8	QC451
544	TK9008
	U395.S8
544.1	QD63.S4
	QD75
544.4	QD121
544.6	QC100
	QC462.F5
	QC762
	QC770
	QD95
544.60212	QC453
544.63	QC457
544.63016	Z7144.S7
544.64	QD95
544.66	QD95
544.8	QD98
544.83	QD98
544.834	QD98
544.92	QD95
	QD117.C5
	QD271
544.923	QD117.C5
544.926	QD117.C5
	QD271
544.9260212	QD271
545	QD101
	QD101.2
545.00202	QD101
545.0028	QD101
545.2	QD111
545.24	QD111
545.32	QD115
	QD571
545.33	QC100
	QC453
545.81	QD117.F5
545.822	QC100
	QD606
545.83	QC173
	QC770
	QD117.P5
545.84	QC100
545.843	QC100
546	QD33
	QD151
	QD151.2
	QD197
	QD466
	QD477
	QD921
546.0151	QD154
546.0202	QD466
546.0212	QC100
546.028	QD45
	QD155
546.2	QD181.H1
546.21	QD461
546.22	PZ10.D274
	QD169.W3
	TD478
546.24	QD477
546.3	QD133
	QD171
546.34	QD189
546.345	QD475
	QD571
546.38225	QD181.N2
546.383	QD181.K1
546.3912	QC770
546.39324	QD181.C2
546.394	QC770
546.403	QD181.Y7
546.41	Q60
546.422	QC770
546.431	QD181.U7
546.4312	QD181.U7
546.434	QD181.P9
546.44	QD172.T7
546.512	TN693.T5
546.513	QD181.Z7
546.5242	QD181.N3
546.526	TL521.3.C6
546.5262	QD181.T2
546.6	QD172.T6
	QD475
546.6212	QD181.F4
546.623	QD181.C6
546.625	QD181.N6
546.632	QD181.R9
546.6453	QD921
546.6711	QD181.B1
546.6712	QD181.B1
546.6733	Q60
546.678	QD181.T7
546.684	QD181.G5
546.6842	QD181.G5
546.7112	QD181.N1
	QD305.N8
546.71124	Q60
	QC770
	QD181.N1
546.716	QD181.N1
546.7212	QD181.O1
546.723	QD181.S1
546.7232	QD181.C7
	QD181.S1
546.7234	SD1
546.73	QD241
	QD305.H7
	TP159.O9
546.731	QD181.F1
546.7322	QD517
546.73222	QC464.C5
546.8	QD172.R2
547	QD37
	QD154
	QD251
	QD251.2
	QD253
	QD255
	QD476
547.00212	QD291
547.0028	QD258
	QD261
547.0076	QD257
547.0077	QD251.2
547.00924	QD22.W39
547.02	QD412.F1
547.028	QD261
547.031	QD305.A2
547.035	QD305.E7
547.036	QD476
547.037	QD477
	SD1
547.038	QD305.A2
547.04	QD281.I7
	QD305.A7
	TP248.U7
547.041	QD305.N8
547.042	QD305.A7
	QD341.A8
547.044	QD305.I6
	QD305.N7
547.05	QD271
	QD411
	QD412.A7
	QD412.C15
	QD412.P3
	QD412.S7
	QD412.S7T6
547.05671	QD412.B1
547.09	QD412.A7
547.1	QD476
547.12	QD476
547.122	QD258
547.1220212	QC453
547.1222	QD481
547.12220212	QD291
547.1223	AS281
	QD381
	QD481
547.1224	QD251
	QD411
547.12254	QD281.P6
	QD381
547.128	QD461
547.13	QD255
	QD380
	QD476
547.13453	QD258
	QD506
547.13482	QD258
547.135	QD258
547.13508	QD241
547.1351	QD431
547.136	QD475
	QD511
547.1369	QD501
547.137	Q64
	QD117.E45
	QD273
547.1372	QD561
547.1377	QD476
547.138	QD603.C1
547.1388	QD601.A1
547.139	QD258
	QD305.H7
	QD476
547.139076	QD257
547.1392	QD431
547.1393	QD258
	QD262
	QD476
547.1394	QD258
547.1395	QC100
	QD501
547.2	QD241
	QD257
	QD262
	QD281.R35
	QD291
	QD341.H9
	QD476
	QD601.A1

547.2076 .... QD257
547.23 .... QD281.O9
..... QD305.A2
547.26 .... QD281.N5
547.28 .... QD281.P6
547.3 .... QD271
..... QD305.E7
..... SB951.4
..... TP1180.P8
547.30028 .... QD271
547.308 .... QD271
547.3085 .... QC453
..... QD95
547.3087 .... QD476
..... QD561
547.341 .... QD63.S4
547.346 .... QC454
..... QC762
547.346077 .... QD271
547.3463016 .... Z7144.S7
547.3464 .... QD271
547.3492 .... QD258
547.34926 .... QD139.P6
..... QD258
..... QD271
547.35 .... QD305.A2
547.3532 .... QD273
547.35330212 .... QC453
547.3583 .... QC463.B4
547.35833 .... QD139.P6
547.411 .... TL521.3.C6
547.412 .... QD305.H7
547.413 .... QD305.H8
547.42 .... QD305.H15
547.422 .... QD1
547.437 .... TP1
547.438 .... Q64
..... QD181.M6
..... QD305.E7
547.44 .... QD1
..... QD305.I6
547.441 .... QD305.N8
547.442 .... QD305.A7
547.444 .... QD305.N7
547.476 .... QP801.P45
547.5 .... QD281.R5
547.511 .... AS283
547.59 .... QD400
..... QD462
547.592 .... QD405
..... TP994
547.593 .... TN23
547.594 .... QD403
..... U395.S8
547.59593 .... TX724.5.T5
547.6 .... QC463.H9
..... QD331
..... QD369
547.61 .... QD341.H9
..... QD603.C1
547.611 .... QD281.S7
547.632 .... QD341.P5
547.635 .... QD341.E7
547.637 .... QD341.A7
547.64 .... QD401
547.644 .... QD341.N7
547.7 .... QD381
..... QD415.A1
..... QD601.A1
..... QP521
..... QP751
547.7028 .... QD415.5
547.71 .... QD416
..... QD416.A1
547.72 .... QD421
..... QD421.7
..... QK898.A4
547.7212 .... HD9698.A1I6
547.73 .... QD241
..... QD426
..... QD476
547.73014 .... QD1
547.734 .... QP801.H7
547.74 .... TX553.V5
547.75 .... QD271
..... QD431
..... QP551
..... SF221.N362
547.754 .... QP551
547.756 .... QD431.5
..... QD431.7
..... QP551
547.758 .... QD501
..... QD945
547.7580202 .... QP601
547.76 .... QD377.P4
547.78 .... QC100
..... QD321
547.782 .... QD1
..... QD321
..... QD471
547.84 .... QD139.P6
..... QD271
..... QD281.P6
..... QD380
..... QD381
..... QD382.B5
..... QD412.S6
..... QD921
..... QD945
..... TP1140
547.840151 .... AS281
547.84028 .... QD385
547.8408 .... QD380
547.8408 .... QD471
547.8432236 .... QD281.P6
..... QD381
547.85745 .... QD381
547.86 .... QD441
547.869 .... QD441
548 .... QD901
..... QD905
..... QD905.2
..... QD931
..... QD951
548.1 .... QD911
548.5 .... QC770
..... QD548
..... QD921
..... TD478
548.7 .... QD911
548.70212 .... QD911
548.8 .... QC1
..... QC176
..... QC176.8.E4
..... QC176.8.R3
..... QD921
..... QD931
548.81 .... Q60
..... QD151.2
..... QD921
548.83 .... QD945
..... QH212.E4
..... QH212.F5
548.83018 .... TN26
548.842 .... QD921
..... QD931
..... QD945
..... TP1
548.85 .... QC176.8.E35
..... QC612.S4
..... QD931
..... QD939
548.9 .... QC176.8.O6
..... QD921
..... QD941
..... TK7800
548.909669 .... QK495.G74
549 .... QE353
..... QE363
..... QE365
..... QE372
..... QE432
549.05 .... QE351
549.0740113541 .... QE364
549.0974773 .... QE175
549.1 .... QE367
..... QE392
549.1028 .... QE434
549.1145 .... QE75
549.116097122 .... QE185
549.125028 .... QE369
549.13 .... QE515
549.131 .... QE364
549.133 .... QE438
549.2 .... QE364
549.23 .... QE75
..... QE75.C5
549.27 .... TJ1193
..... TN23
549.4 .... TN24.T4
549.5 .... TN26
549.523 .... QE282
549.524 .... QE75
549.6 .... QE389.62
..... QE570
..... TP1
549.66 .... Q115
..... QE391.W66
549.67 .... TN948.P85
549.68 .... QE282
..... QE391.F3
549.72 .... QE75
549.78 .... QE471
549.94237 .... QE381.G7
549.973 .... QE392.5.U5
549.9748 .... QE375.P39
549.9791 .... QE392.5.U5
549.9794 .... TN24.C2
549.994 .... QE384
..... QE392.5.A9
550 .... Q181
..... QB591
..... QB595
..... QB631
..... QB641
..... QB661
..... QC801
..... QE1
..... QE26
..... QE26.2
..... QE28
..... QE31
..... QE33
..... QE35
..... TL507
..... TL789.8.U6A599
550.0922 .... QE21
550.1519 .... QE33
550.182 .... QE33
..... QE185
550.184 .... QE48.8
550.208 .... Q60
550.23 .... QE34
550.24624 .... TA705
550.28 .... QE33
..... QE41
..... QE48.8
550.6173 .... QC808.A1
550.71173 .... QE40
550.8 .... Q60
..... QE1
..... QE25
..... QE26.2
..... QE75
..... QE75.P9
..... QE92.C4
..... QE105
..... QE185
..... QE349.T5
..... QE605
..... QE807.A5
..... QE961
550.9 .... DU430.S57
..... QE11
550.91821 .... QE65
550.924 .... Q143.F5
..... Q143.P8
550.98 .... QE70
551 .... GB55
..... GB56
..... GB472
..... QB591
..... QC801.3
..... QC802
..... QC806
..... QC866
..... QE26
..... QE28
..... QE33
..... QE501
..... QH90
551.0182 .... QC851
551.08 .... QC801
..... QE500
551.09413 .... QE264
551.0966 .... GB355
551.0972977 .... Q57
551.0978165 .... HC107.K2
551.1 .... QE501
551.1028 .... QE185
551.11 .... QE501
..... QE509
551.12 .... QE501
551.13 .... QE75
..... QE185
..... QE511
..... TL507
551.2 .... QE501
551.21 .... QE521
..... QE522
..... QE527
..... TL521.3.C6
551.210952166 .... QE523.F8
551.2109577 .... QE527
551.21097283 .... QE1
551.210973 .... QE461
551.21097883 .... QE535
551.2109795 .... QE155
551.2109797 .... QE75
551.21099312 .... QE527
551.22 .... AS4.U8
..... QE75
..... QE340
..... QE531
..... QE534
..... QE536
..... QE538.8
..... QE539
..... TA710
..... TL521.3.C6
..... UG465.5
551.220151 .... QE534
551.22028 .... TA710
551.22094 .... QE536
551.220952 .... QE532
551.220954 .... QE537
551.220973 .... QE535
551.2209794 .... TC181
551.22097946 .... QE535
551.220979476 .... QE75
551.22097983 .... QE75
551.2209914 .... QE537
551.220994 .... QE537
551.3 .... QE75
..... QE571
551.302 .... QE570
551.303 .... QE1
..... QE75
551.30911 .... GB641
551.31 .... QE576
..... QE697
551.3103 .... GB2405
551.3109989 .... GB651
551.310999 .... AS4.U8
551.312 .... PZ10.L779
..... QE75
..... QE576
551.3120999 .... QC994.9
551.314 .... Q180.C2
..... QE282
551.343 .... GB2401
..... GB2595
551.3430916611 .... GB2595
551.3430999 .... Q180.A1
551.35 .... GB406
..... QE75.P9
551.35097961 .... QE75
551.352 .... QE571
551.353 .... GB485.A2
..... GB651
..... GC393
551.353 .... QE75
..... QE599
551.353094297 .... QE599.G7
551.35309722 .... GC398
551.35309794 .... QE75
551.36 .... QE351
..... TN24.C2
551.36097983 .... QE75
551.375 .... S599.A3
551.375097641 .... GB459.25
551.38097986 .... GB645.A4
551.4 .... GB54
..... GB55
..... GB401
..... GB406
..... GB451
..... GB457.71
..... GB459.2.C3
..... GB459.4
..... GB568.68.M4
..... GB641
..... GB661
..... PZ10.S57
..... QE26
..... QE75
551.403 .... GB10
551.4072 .... GB60
551.4084 .... GC83
551.40942 .... GB184.Y6
551.4094391 .... GB276.H9
551.40971 .... GB131
551.40973 .... GB121
551.409789 .... GB126.N4
551.40988 .... GB160
551.409945 .... HD1109.L3
551.409982 .... Q115
551.41 .... GC380
..... JX4143
..... PZ10.W148
..... QE75
..... QE505
..... QE511.5
..... TL712.5
551.42 .... QE565
551.43 .... GB501
..... GB521
..... PZ10.W148
551.4309945 .... QE347
551.44 .... GB602
..... GB604
..... GB608.46
..... GB608.89
..... QE131
551.45 .... GB578.6
551.46 .... GB451
..... GB671
..... GC1
..... GC2
..... GC3.U7
..... GC11
..... GC16
..... GC21
..... GC26
..... GC28
..... GC61
..... GC65
..... PZ10.K57
..... V396.3
551.4600202 .... GC1
551.460023 .... GC30.5
..... HD8039.S4
551.460028 .... GC57
..... GC61
551.46003 .... SH201
551.46007 .... GC10
551.460072 .... GC57
..... GC58
551.46007204 .... GC59.42
551.4600720944 .... GC872.A9
551.46008 .... GC1
..... GC26
..... GC721
551.46009 .... GC29
551.4600916612 .... GC3.U4
551.4600969 .... GC58
551.4600973 .... GC58
551.46009744 .... GC511
551.4601 .... GC32
..... GC98
..... GC178
..... GC179
..... GC299
..... SH223
551.46023 .... GC30.5
551.46025 .... GC10
551.46028 .... GC41
551.46070922 .... VK597.G72
551.46072073 .... GC58
551.4608 .... GC1
..... QE39
551.4608309729 .... QE377
551.46084 .... QE606
551.46924 .... PZ10.E25
551.46096 .... QH91
551.4609969 .... GC58
551.461 .... GC3.U7
..... GC561
..... Q64
..... QC801
551.463 .... QB280
551.465 .... GC3.U7
..... GC398
..... GC399
..... GC771

Dewey	LC
551.465	GC781
	GC791
	GC861
	SK361
551.46554	QH95.2
551.466	GC3.U7
	GC398
	SH223
551.467	GC1
	GC721
	GC741
551.468	GC3.U7
	GC401
551.469	G850
	GC461
551.4693	GC3.U7
551.47	GC201
	TC330
551.4701	GC231
	Q180
551.4701028	GC61
551.47022	TC172
551.47023	QE75
551.47024	GC221
	GC222.P3
	GC376
551.470246272	TC330
551.4708	GC211
	GC301
	PZ10.C3315
551.47080916612	GC309.E5
551.471	GC3.U7
	GC271
	GC376
551.475	GC296.P3
551.48	GB565.I8
	GB661
	GB665
	GB697
	GB811.G4
	GB1225.M6
	GB1225.V8
	PZ10.R7248
	TC801.U2
551.480212	TD351
551.480222	GB665
551.48028	GB665
	GB683
551.4808	GB755
	GB1029
	QH96
	TD201
551.4809	GB656
551.480974426	GB705.M4
551.480974721	GB1025.N7
551.480975938	QE99
551.4809762	GB705.M7
551.48097626	TD224.M65
551.480978944	GB705.N6
551.480979173	TC801
551.4809792	TD224.U8
551.4809793	GB1025.N4
551.482	GB1625.M3
	QE75
	TA1
551.4820945625	QE39.P3
551.482094891	GB1712.F82
551.482096761	GB800
551.4820971274	QE697
551.4820973	GB1615
551.4820976626	QH105.O5
551.482097694	QE115
551.4820977	QE125
551.48209774	GB1625.M5
551.48209776	TD224.M6
551.483	GB1025.N7
	GB1205
	GB1225.N8
	GB1225.V8
	QE75
	SH255
	TN24.N6
551.483094227	TD258.W4
551.48309713	GB1230.M6
551.4830974813	QE75
551.483097643	GB1225.T4
551.48309764444	GB1225.T4
551.48309764533	GB1225.T4
551.48309764544	GB705.T4
551.48309764455	GB1225.T4
551.48309764551	GB1225.T4
551.4830976467	GB1225.T4
551.48309764725	GB1225.T4
551.483097713	TC425.C94
551.48309773	GB1225.I27
551.483097731	TD225.S22
551.4830977438	GB1225.M5
551.48309777	GB1225.I8
551.48309794	GB1225.C3
551.4830979414	GB1225.C3
551.4880	TD201
551.49	GB651
	GB665
	GB705.K4
	GF51
	QE75
551.4903	GB1003
	TD201
551.490954917	GB1140
551.49097124	QE185
551.490973	GB651
551.490974813	GB1025.P4
551.490974815	GB1025.P4
551.49097514	GB1025.D3
551.49097551	TN24.V8
551.490976142	QE81
551.4909766	GB1025.O5
551.490976637	QE153
551.4909768	GB1025.T2
551.490976824	GB1025.T2
551.4909773	GB1025.I3
551.4909781	QE113
551.49097845	QE149
551.490978682	GB1025.M9
551.490978892	TC801
551.490979173	TC801
551.490979244	TC801
551.49097931	GB705.N3
551.49097946	GB1025.C2
551.498	QE75
	QE75.P9
	TD201
551.5	QB621
	QC801
	QC808.V6
	QC861
	QC861.2
	QC863
	QC871
	QC872
	QC913
	QC928
	QC981
	QE105
	TD172.5
	TL507
	Z663.23
551.5018	Z663.23
551.50202	QC871
551.5023	QC869.5
551.502462389	DC880
551.5028	QC851
	QC876
	QC973
	Z663.23
551.503	QC854
551.508	QC801
	QC851
	QC857
	QC981
	TL556
551.5085	QC851
551.509166	QC851
551.5091667	QC866
551.50942	QC857.G77
551.509493	QC851
551.5099	QC869
551.509931	QC851
	QC992.5
551.509945	QC851
551.509982	QC857.G83
551.50999	QC994.9
551.51	QB621
	QB641
	QC863
	QC880
	QC883
	TL521.3.C6
551.5112	QC879
	TL521.3.C6
551.5113	QC882
551.513	GB705.C2
	QC801
551.514	QC876
	QC879
	QC981
	TL521
551.514028	TL521.3.C6
551.51409982	QC879
551.5142	TL521
551.5145	AS36
	QC879
	QC881
	TK6553
	TL521.3.C6
551.51450182	QC100
551.5151	QC880
551.5153	Q115
	QC880
	QC933
	QE500
551.517	Q180
	QC880
	QC935
	TL507
551.517028	QC932
551.5170916611	Q180
551.517094	QC851
551.517096	QC851
551.51709789	QC851
551.518	QC851
	QC863
	QC935
	QC940.G7
551.5180182	QC851
551.51809489	QC940.D4
551.5183	QC939.T7
551.5184	QC939.M7
551.51840959	Q180.A1
551.5185	QC851
551.5185097641	QC851
551.5187	QB4
	QC851
551.52	QC921.5
551.520916611	Q180
551.5230942	QC907
551.5246	SK361
	V214
551.5248	TC424.T4
551.5248097712	QE151
551.524809786	QC909
551.5248097954	QE75
551.525028	TL521
551.52509481	QC901
551.5253	QC851
	S133
551.52530972	QC851
551.5257	TL521.3.C6
551.527	QC809.R3
	QC911
	TL521.3.C6
551.5271	Q180
	QC911
551.5271028	QC465
551.52710973	QC911
551.5271098	QC911
551.5272	TL521.3.C6
551.5273	QC175.2
	QC851
	TL521
551.5276	QC485
551.55	PZ10.B295223
	QC941
551.552	QC941
	QC945
551.552028	TL521
551.5520976	QC945
551.5520976411	QC945
	TC424.T4
551.55309748	QC955
551.55309764	QC955
551.554	QC851
551.56	QC809.E55
	QC851
	QC874
	QC975
551.561	QC916
551.563	TL507
551.5634	QC966
551.565	Q180
551.568	QC976.T7
551.57	GB671
	QC851
	QC925
551.570978	QC984.N3
551.570998	QC994.8
551.5713	QC911
551.572	PZ10.S677
	QC915
551.57209798	SD11
551.576	PZ10.R7
	Q11
	QC851
	QC921
	QC921.5
	TL507
	TL521
551.5760222	Z6685
551.5760913	QC921
551.576091667	QC922
551.57609764	TD224.T4
551.577	QC801
	QC851
551.57709481	QC801
551.577273	QC851
551.5772762	QC925.1.U8
551.5775098	QC851
551.5781	QC925
	QC925.4.G7
	QC928
551.578109595	SB290
551.57812791	QE75
551.57813	TD412
	TE7
551.57813097949	GB1225.C3
551.57841	QC929.S7
551.57846	QC985
551.57848	GB2430.B7
551.5787	QC925
551.579471	GB747.F5
551.57977	GB1615
551.579793	GB2425.N4
551.579795	GB2425.O7
551.6	G2281.C8
	QC861
	QC863
	QC884
	QC981
	QC982.5
	QC983
	QC994
	QE699
	QE993
551.60916611	QC851
551.60942	QC857.G77
551.60952	QC990.J3
551.609595	QC990.S5
551.6096	QC991.A1
551.609669	QC851
551.60971	QC985
551.6097124	QC985
551.609713	QC985
551.60973	G1201.C8
551.609764	TD224.T4
551.609774	QC984.M5
551.609881	QC851
551.609941	QC992.W4
551.609944	QC770
551.60999	G845
551.62	QC981
	QC982
	QC984.I3
551.62	QC985
551.62097644	QC984.T4
551.6209789	QC984.N6
551.63	QC875.A1
	QC995
551.6306173	QC875.U7
551.632	QC872
551.632091822	QC994.3
551.633	QC996.5
551.634	QC851
551.634028	QC996
551.635	Q180.A1
	QC973
	TL521.3.C6
551.6352	QC935
551.63520212	QC973
551.6353	QC851
551.6354	QC875
	QC879.5
	TL507
551.6362	QC996
551.6365	Q11
	QC997
551.63650973	QC997
551.64145	QC879
551.647	QC851
551.64773	GB651
551.657	QC874
551.65787	QC984.W8
	TD201
551.65931	QC992.5.A1
551.6594	QC992.A1
551.66	QC982.7
551.660947	QC989.R49
551.668	QE376.O5
551.68	QC879
	QC921.5
	QC928
	QC929.F7
	QC929.R1
	Z663.23
	Z6683.W35
551.680947	QC928
551.680978786	QC928
551.6809788	TC823.6
551.6809794	QC928
551.7	QB591
	QE33
	QE185
	QE501
	QE511.5
	QE651
	QE697
551.7001	QE1
551.7003	QE5
551.70091814	AS4.U8
551.700924	QE22.S6
551.700942	QE261
551.700994	QE758
551.701	QE508
551.701028	QC798.D3
551.709777	QE111
551.71	QE653
	QE654
	QE655
551.71097129	QE185
551.7109788	TN210
551.715	QE75
551.72	QE75
	QE662
551.72097129	QE185
551.7209758	QE101
551.7209775	QE179
551.72097789	QE131
551.72097982	QE75
551.7309711	QE185
551.730974426	QE75
551.731	QE471
551.73109748	QE662
551.74	QE75
	QE665
551.740971233	QE185
551.7409748	QE665
551.751	QE671
	QE672
	QE770
551.752	QE105
551.752094297	QE262.W2
551.75209748	QE105
551.75209754	QE674
551.752097557	QE75
551.7520977843	QE673
551.756097986	QE75
551.76	QE75
	QE675
	QE676
	QL1
551.77	QE75
	QE685
551.770976454	QE167
551.7709783	QH1
551.770979226	QE75
	QE1
551.78	QE75
	QE690
	QE691
	TN24.C2
551.780971145	QE185
551.7809791	QE85
551.7809943	QE340
551.79	QE696
551.790943	QE741
551.790975991	QE699
551.790979676	QE75

Dewey	LC
551.792	G58
	QE111
	QE131
	QE697
551.792094845	QE281
551.7920971233	QE697
551.79209748	QE697
551.792097482	QE697
551.79209773	QE105
551.79209982	Q115
551.79309486	QE699
551.8	QE36
	QE601
	TN27.O4
551.8097	QE75
551.8097895	QE75
551.81	QE340
551.87	QE75
	QE606
551.88	QE611
551.9	QC770
	QD466.5.C1
	QE75
	QE105
	QE471
	QE515
	QE516.5
	TN24.M9
551.90978681	TN24.M9
552	QB592
	QE364
552.009788	QE91
552.00979486	QE611
552.06	QE33
	QE75
	QE431.5
	QE606
	TA706.5
	TN210
552.06024624	TA705
552.0971143	QE185
552.09713	QE191
552.09761	QE365
552.09772	QE109
552.0979497	QE90.R5
552.1	QE75
	QE440
	QE461
552.10973	QE461
552.109746	QE475
552.10979487	QE75
552.2	QE131
	QE461
552.3	Q115
	QE461
	QE462.G7
552.4	Q115
	QE269
	QE281
	QE475
552.4091823	QE475
552.409482	QE281
552.40974731	QE146.G59
552.5	GC383
	QE75
	QE389.625
	QE462.O6
	QE471
	QE701
	TK9008
	TN24.N6
	TN26
	TN942
552.5028	QE472
553	QE131
	TN15
	TN24.N6
	TN113.M3
	TN146
	TN260
553.08	QE105
	TN24.N6
553.09182	JX1977
553.0954792	TN104.M29
553.09667	Z6739.G5
553.09713	TN27.Q3
553.0974	QE75
553.09752	QE121
553.0976829	TN24.T2
553.09786662	QH77.U6
553.0978844	QE75
553.0978952	TN24.N6
553.097896	QE75
553.09791	TN24.A6
553.0979316	QE75
553.09794	TN24.C2
553.0979476	QH77.U6
553.0979498	QE75
553.09795	TN24.O7
553.097967	QE75
553.097986	TN24.A4
553.0983	JX1977
553.1	QE75
	TN263
	TN265
553.1094771	TN55
553.109716	TN27.N8
553.10976157	TN24.A2
553.109764	TN24.A2
553.109786612	QE134.M4
553.109789	TN24.N6
553.10979333	QE75
553.109798	QE75.C5
553.1097986	QE75
553.16095412	QE295
553.2	QE673
	TN295
	TN800
	TN802
	TN805.M9
553.209715	TN859.C3
553.20973	QE75
553.209748	QE157
553.20974861	TN805.P4
553.20979	TN24.A6
553.21	QK956.S8
	S590
	TN837
553.2109718	TN27.N6
553.21097473	QE75
553.21097483	QE75
553.210993127	S381
553.240973	QE75
553.24097866	QE133
553.28	JX1977
553.280974867	TN805.P4
553.280974882	TN872.P4
553.28097619	QE81
553.280979221	TN210
553.2809982	TN878.2
553.282	TN863
	TN870
	TN870.5
553.282094	TN874.A15
553.2820973	TN872.A5
553.2850974899	TN881.P4
553.285097543	QE177
553.3	JX1977
	QE75
	QE185
553.3094717	Q60
553.309485	QE282
553.3095845	TN406.R92K313
553.4	QE75
	QE105
	QE389.2
553.40978795	QE75
553.40978962	QE75
553.40979332	QE75
553.4097986	QE75
553.409944	TN122.N5
553.41	QE295
553.410973	QE75
553.410975284	QE75
553.410978755	QE75
553.4109794	TN24.C2
553.4109795	QE155
553.41097983	QE75
553.41099429	QE340
553.43	TN780
553.4309714	TN444.C39
553.44	QE281
	QE516.L4
553.452094716	QE276.3
553.453	QE75
	TN470
553.462	QE185
553.465	TN799.Z5
553.492	QE75
553.493	Q115
	QE75
	TN490.T55
553.499	TN490.T5
553.5	TN953.G7
553.509416	TN953.G7
553.50973	TN295
553.51	TN967
553.6	QC770
	QE129
553.6095843	S599.45.T5
553.60972972	S599.25.V5
553.61	TA455.C55
553.6109755	TN24.V8
553.6109761	TN942
553.610979737	QE75
553.6109945	TH121
553.62	QE167
553.620916617	QE75
553.6209414	TN943.G7
553.620976923	TN939
553.63	QE75
553.64	TN24.G4
	TN948.A7
553.662	QE75
553.668	TN890
553.66809764	TN24.T4
553.67	QE75
	QE376
	TN24.N3
	TN693.T7
	TN930
553.7	GB661
	GB705.U8
	PZ10.F714
	QD169.W3
	TD223
553.7072071	GB707
553.70975225	QE121
553.70975924	QE99
553.709762	TD224.M65
553.709763	GB705.L5
553.709766	TD224.O5
553.709767	TC801
553.709773	GB705.I3
553.70978961	TC424.N6
553.709792	GB705.U8
553.709794	GB1025.C2
	TC425.S12
553.709944	TD321.N5
553.78	GB1225.A2
	QE75
553.78097141	GB1230.Q4
553.780971417	GB1230.Q4
553.780975961	QE99
553.7809761	GB1025.A2
553.780977496	TC801
553.78097954	QE75
553.7809811	QE75
553.79	GB1003
	GB1030.A64
553.790971633	TN27.N8
553.790974744	GB1025.N7
553.79097484	GB1025.P4
553.790975775	TC801
553.790975913	QE99
553.790975935	QE99
553.790976	TC424.L8
553.7909761	GB1025.A2
553.7909767	TC801
553.790977224	GB1025.I6
553.790977327	GB705.I3
553.790978195	QE113
553.7909786	GB1025.M9
553.790978638	TC801
553.79097925	TC801
553.790979334	GB1025.N4
553.790979496	GB1025.C2
553.790979498	GB1025.C2
553.790979535	GB1025.O7
553.79097956	QE75
553.790979649	TC801
553.8	GR805
	QE392
	TS752
553.8075	QE392
553.809789	QE392.5.U5
553.80994	TN986.A1
553.820994	TS753.I4
553.87	QE391.J2
	QE394.O7
	TN24.N3
554	QE260
554.018	QH405
554.117	QE261
554.139	QE261
554.2	QE261
554.221	QE261
554.223	QE261
554.23	QE262.C8
554.235	QE261
554.243	QE261
554.245	QE262.C57
	QE262.C83
554.254	QE261
554.259	QE261
554.272	QE261
554.28	QE262.L2
554.281	QE261
554.288	QE262.C74
	QE262.L2
554.292	QE261
554.38	QE276.5
554.6773	QE283
554.71	QE276.3
554.771	TA705
554.81	QE260
554.8108	Q115
554.845	Q111
554.88	QE282
555	QE289
555.2	QE304
555.3	QE75
555.367	QE291
555.4	QE295
555.5	QE307
556	QE320
556.64	QE327.S5
556.66608	QE339.L5
556.782	QE327.T3
556.8	QE325
557.108	QE185
557.11	QE185
557.111	QE185
557.1145	QE187
557.1221	QE185
557.1231	Q180.C2
557.1233	QE185
557.12408	QE194
557.1241	QE185
557.126	QE185
557.13	QE185
	QE191
557.1308	QE191
557.13133	QE191
557.1314	TN27.O4
557.1411	QE193
557.1413	QE193
557.1417	QE185
557.1425	QE193
557.1478	QE193
557.15	QE185
557.1551	QE185
557.1612	QE185
557.19	QE185
557.281	Q11
557.3	QE71
	QE75
557.308	QE75
557.4	QE78.3
	QE78.5
557.413	QE75
557.416	QE119
557.42	QE139
	QE697
557.437	QE171
557.47	QE145
557.48	QE75
557.4843	QE157
557.4861	QE158.H68
557.4872	QE158.M2
557.4882	QE158.W3
557.49	QE141
557.4946	QE75
557.4976	QE142.S9
557.5208	QE121
557.5274	QE122.H38
557.5408	QE177
557.5438	QE177
557.55	QE26.2
557.5594	QE173
557.56	QE147
557.56565	QE147
557.59	QE75
557.5981	QE99
557.6	QE81
557.61	QE81
557.6108	QE81
557.612	QE81
557.6198	QE82.L55
557.6252	QE129
557.64	QE167
557.64932	QE654
557.66	TA705
557.6708	QE87
557.673	QE75
557.6736	QE75
557.674	TN24.A7
557.6808	QE165
557.6835	QE165
557.6908	QE115
557.6913	QE115
557.6947	QE116.F39
557.7	QE75
557.7108	QE151
557.72	QE109
557.7222	QE109
557.7308	QE105
557.7337	QE105
557.74	QE125
557.74975	QE75
557.7608	QE127
557.8108	QE113
557.83	QE163
	QE694
557.86	QE133
557.8666	QE75
557.8763	QE75
557.8785	QE75
557.881	QE75
557.8812	QE79
557.8817	QE75
557.8855	QE75.B9
557.886	QE75
557.8865	QE75
557.8942	GB1025.N6
557.8943	TN24.N6
557.8952	TN24.N6
557.8962	QE75
557.8964	TN24.N6
557.9208	TN24.U8
557.9214	QE75
557.9221	QE169
557.9308	TN24.N3
557.9316	QE138.E4
557.9333	QE75.C5
557.9334	QE137
557.94	QE89
557.9408	QE89
557.9424	TN24.C2
557.9476	QE75
557.9487	TN24.C2
557.9578	QE155
557.97	GB126.W3
	QE175
	TN24.W2
557.9778	QE75
557.98	QE75
	QE75.P9
557.982	QE515
557.983	QE75
557.984	QE75
557.986	QE75
558.1	QE235
558.15	QE75
558.31	QE75
558.665	QE349.G3
559.3122	QE342
559.34	QE349.N43
559.42	QE345
559.429	QE340
559.4308	TN122
559.44	QE340
559.4408	TN122.N5
559.46	QE346
559.67	QE75
559.69	QE349.H3
559.81	QE471
559.8208	QE70
559.9	GB555
559.91	QB581
559.94	QE340
559.99	G870
560	PZ10.D274
	QE147
	QE711.2
	QE714.5

560 ..... QE719
..... QE720
..... QE765
560.17 ..... QE723
560.172 ..... PZ10.G7
..... QE841
..... QE879
560.176 ..... QE719
..... QE922
560.1760945 ..... QE347
560.178 ..... QE1
..... QE696
..... QE741
..... QE927
560.75 ..... PZ10.H84
..... QE718
560.8 ..... QE701
..... QE701.K33
560.85 ..... QE701
560.971 ..... QE185
560.97122 ..... QE185
560.9776 ..... QE718
560.978 ..... QE701
561 ..... QE75
..... QE905
..... QE911
561.074011 ..... QE908
561.0977846 ..... QE919
561.1 ..... QK658
561.13 ..... QE1
..... QE993
561.1309486 ..... QE993
561.19748 ..... QE919
561.595 ..... QE989
561.9 ..... QE1
561.92 ..... QE719
561.93 ..... QE75
..... QE282
..... QE767
..... QE955
562 ..... QE1
..... QE75
..... QE109
..... QE127
..... QE131
..... QE282
..... QE340
..... QE701
..... QE731.B73
..... QE770
563.097987 ..... QE75
563.1 ..... Q57
..... QE1
..... QE75
..... QE109
..... QE194
..... QE767
..... QE772
..... QE773
563.4 ..... QE1
563.5 ..... QE721
563.6 ..... QE75
..... QE185
..... QE778
563.60977112 ..... QE701
563.609873 ..... QE778
563.7 ..... QE779
563.7809462 ..... QE779
563.7809486 ..... QE1
563.9 ..... QE111
..... QE783.C9
563.91 ..... QE701
563.94075 ..... Q11
563.9509877 ..... QE783.E2
564.1 ..... QE75
..... QE81
..... QE340
..... QE811
..... QE812.T37
564.2 ..... QE75
564.3 ..... QE75
564.3094238 ..... QE808
564.5 ..... QE75
..... QE806
564.50976657 ..... QE701
564.53 ..... QE75
..... QE185
..... QL1
564.53097931 ..... QE75
564.5309951 ..... QE807.A5
564.6 ..... QE278
..... QE795
564.7 ..... QE1
564.8 ..... QE1
..... QE185
..... QE796
564.8094168 ..... QL461
564.809747 ..... QE75
564.809769 ..... QE75
564.809792 ..... QE75
565.32097933 ..... QE796
565.33 ..... QE75
..... QE701
..... QL444.08
565.33097665 ..... QE153
565.39309747 ..... QE821
565.39309769 ..... QE75
565.39309793 ..... QE75
565.39309798 ..... QE75
566 ..... PZ10.M455
..... QE1
..... QE340
..... QE841
566.095694 ..... QE841
566.09781165 ..... QE701
566.0978853 ..... Q11
566.09789 ..... Q11
567.0979678 ..... QE1
567.2 ..... QE852.P5
567.4 ..... QE1
..... QE185
567.409479 ..... QE852.O45
567.5 ..... QL1
567.9 ..... QE868
568.19 ..... QE862.D5
..... QE862.O65
569 ..... GN37.A8
..... QE1
569.0978889 ..... QE881
569.31 ..... Q11
..... QH1
569.33 ..... Q60
..... QH1
569.5 ..... QE1
..... QE882.C5
569.6 ..... QE882.U7
569.72 ..... GN780.J8
569.73 ..... QH1
569.74 ..... Q11
569.740979637 ..... QE882.C1
569.8 ..... QH1
569.9 ..... GN75.A2
..... R135
570 ..... GN8
..... GN27
..... QH60
..... QH308
570.8 ..... AC8
572 ..... GN3
..... GN23
..... GN29
..... GN31
..... GN310
..... GN315
..... GN320
..... GN325
..... GN330
..... GN347
..... GN350
572.023 ..... GN325
572.03 ..... GN11
572.08 ..... GN4
572.2 ..... GN771
572.3 ..... QH401
572.8 ..... GN69
572.896 ..... E185
..... HT1589.C32
572.94 ..... GN575
572.95 ..... GN625
572.951 ..... GN635.C5
572.9624 ..... DT429
572.96294 ..... DT132
572.96762 ..... GN776.K4
572.9718 ..... QH1
572.9729 ..... GN2
572.9915 ..... DU120
572.9946 ..... GN2
..... GN664.T2
573 ..... GN24
..... GN34
..... GN56
..... GN60
..... GN62
..... QH368
573.023 ..... GN33
573.0958 ..... GN58.A8
573.2 ..... GN741
..... GN743
..... GN771
..... QE707.T4
..... QH368
573.208 ..... QH368
573.21 ..... QH309
..... QH431
573.211 ..... QH431
573.2131 ..... QH431
573.22 ..... QH431
573.3 ..... GN4
..... GN738
..... GN739
573.30946 ..... GN835
573.3096 ..... GN776.A15
573.5 ..... GN197
573.6 ..... GN51
..... GN57.H8
..... GN58.U5
..... GN62
573.600917496 ..... E185.89.A5
573.6009581 ..... GN58.A3
573.609584 ..... GN58.R9
573.6097292 ..... GN237
573.677 ..... QC100
573.7 ..... GN51
573.8 ..... GN681
574 ..... KF27.S383
..... PZ10.P62
..... QH9.5
..... QH45.2
..... QH47
..... QH48
..... QH53
..... QH81
..... QH305
..... QH307
..... QH308
..... QH308.2
..... QH308.5
..... QH308.7
574 ..... QH309
..... QH315
..... QH331
..... QL48.2
..... QL50
574.01 ..... QH301
..... QH331
..... QH368
..... QH527
574.012 ..... PZ10.P6
..... QH83
574.0151 ..... QH324
..... QH331
574.01519 ..... QH405
574.01531 ..... QH324
574.018 ..... Q11
..... QH324.2
574.0182 ..... QH405
574.0184 ..... QH324.8
574.023 ..... QH314
574.028 ..... QH317
..... QH324
..... QH324.15.E26
..... QK51
..... R856
574.03 ..... QH13
574.0711 ..... QH301
574.071142 ..... QH315
574.0711747 ..... QH315
574.0712 ..... LB1059
..... QH301
..... QH315
574.072 ..... QH9.5
574.0720492 ..... QH320.N4
574.072073 ..... Q180.U5
574.0724 ..... QH305
..... QH316.5
..... QH324
..... QH324.4
574.074019177 ..... QH71.A77
574.076 ..... QH316
574.08 ..... AM101
..... Q60
..... QH1
..... QH7
..... QH9
..... QH199
..... QH302
..... QH311
..... QL1
574.09 ..... QH305
574.09152 ..... QH541.5.J8
574.0922 ..... QH26
574.0924 ..... QH31.G32
..... QH31.H88
..... QH31.H9
..... QH31.W58
..... QH91.3.C3
574.0954 ..... QL300
574.1 ..... QH527
..... QK725
..... QP31
..... QP33
..... QP43
574.10151 ..... QD415.3
574.108 ..... QP6
574.109 ..... QP21
574.109154 ..... QP82.2.H8
574.11 ..... QP101
574.13 ..... PZ10.S664
..... Q44
..... QP141
..... QP514.2
..... QP521
..... QP535.S1
574.16 ..... PZ10.C834
..... PZ10.S35
..... QH471
574.170724 ..... QH652
..... QH652.A2
574.18 ..... QH508
574.19 ..... QH345
..... QH506
574.191 ..... QD415.A1
..... QH505
..... QH543
..... QH641
..... QH651
..... R895
574.191072 ..... QH505
574.1910919 ..... KF27.S385
574.1915 ..... QC795
..... QH652
..... QP82.2.R3
574.191508 ..... Z663.23
574.19153 ..... QH651
574.1916 ..... QH653
..... QP82.2.T4
574.1917 ..... QP341
574.1919 ..... QH327
..... TL507
574.192 ..... QD381
..... QD415
..... QD415.3
..... QD476
..... QH324
..... QH345
..... QH611
..... QP501
..... QP514
..... QP514.2
..... QP516
..... QP521
..... QP551
574.192 ..... QP671
..... QP751
..... QP801.A48
..... QP801.N8
..... QP801.P68
..... QP801.S6
..... TL507
..... TL521.3.C6
574.1920202 ..... QP514
574.1920212 ..... QP516
574.192028 ..... QD415.5
574.19207204274 ..... QP518
574.192076 ..... QD415.3
574.19208 ..... QP501
574.19209 ..... QP511
574.1920924 ..... QD22.S2
574.1921 ..... QP90.5
..... QP535.C1
574.19214 ..... QP535.S1
574.19247 ..... QP751
574.1925 ..... QD601
..... QP601
574.19256 ..... QP601
574.19258 ..... QP177
..... QP601
574.1926 ..... QP601
..... QP801.P69
..... QP801.V5
574.1927 ..... QP801.H7
574.1927072 ..... QP187.A1
574.19293 ..... QH345
574.19296 ..... QP551
574.2 ..... QH545.A3
574.29 ..... QR182
574.3 ..... PZ10.Z327
..... QH431
..... QH491
..... QL955
..... QP84
574.4 ..... QL963
574.4012 ..... QH83
574.408 ..... QL801
574.5 ..... PZ10.P669
..... QH45.2
..... QH81
..... QH90
..... QH316.5
..... QH345
..... QH368
..... QH540
..... QH541
..... QH541.13
..... QH541.14
..... QH541.15.R4
..... QH541.5.C6
..... QH541.5.P7
..... QH543.6
..... QH545.P4
..... QH546
..... QK950.L3
..... TK1343
574.50151 ..... QH541
574.507 ..... LB1047
574.5071 ..... QH541.2
574.50712 ..... LB1059
574.5076 ..... QH541.2
574.508 ..... QH541
..... QH541.145
574.50913 ..... QH541.5.T7
574.509143 ..... QH541.5.M4
574.509153 ..... QH541.5.T8
574.5097 ..... QH541.5.D4
574.50973 ..... QH541.13
574.5099 ..... QH541.5.P6
574.509931 ..... QH197.5
574.50998 ..... PZ10.V37
574.52 ..... QH91
..... QH91.8.O4
..... QH95.3
..... QH95.7
..... QH138.L35
..... QH302
..... QH541.5
..... QH541.5.D4
..... QH541.5.F7
..... QH541.5.M3
..... QH541.5.M6
..... QH543
..... QH543.5
..... TC801
574.524 ..... QL752
574.53 ..... QH541.5.S3
574.55 ..... QH541
..... QH548
..... QL752
..... QL757
574.76 ..... QH316
574.8 ..... AS36
..... Q64
..... QH506
..... QH585
..... QH605
..... QP521
574.80222 ..... QH582
574.82 ..... QM563
574.82076 ..... QM553
574.87 ..... Q60
..... QH309
..... QH506
..... QH573
..... QH581
..... QH581.2
..... QH603.M35
..... QH607

574.87	QP601
	QR1
574.870184	QH581.2
574.87028	QH585
574.870724	QH585
574.873	QH302
	QH601
574.8732	QH431
	QH491
	QH591
	QH596
	QH600
	QH605
	QP551
	QP601
	RC261
574.8734	QH603.L9
	QH603.M5
	QH603.R5
	QP551
574.875	QH601
	QH603.M5
	QP88
	QR180
574.876	QH573
	QH581.2
	QH601
	QH607
	QH611
	QH631
	QH652.A2
	QH652.5
	QH653
	QH658
	QP535.C2
574.8761	QH631
574.8762	QH605
574.8764	QH302
	QH573
	QH615
574.88	QH506
574.9	QH84
574.90943	QH541.5.M65
574.90946	PZ10.D274
	PZ10.K63
	QH95.7
574.90948	QH83
574.90954	PZ10.H4828
	QH88
	TR721
574.92	QH91
	QH91.55
	QH91.75.U6
	QH95.7
	QH541.3
	QH541.5.E8
	QH541.5.S3
574.92072079498	KF27.M473
574.9208	QH91
	QH91.1.R4
574.92508	QH91
574.927	QH95.7
574.929	PZ10.G576
	QH96
574.929428	QH96
574.929773	QK105
574.942	QH137
574.9676	QH195.E2
574.9679	QH195.M6
574.974	QH81
	QH104.5.N4
574.975	QH87.3
574.978	QH104.5.R6
574.97949	QH95.7
574.97986	QH105.A4
574.98	QP1
574.994	QH197
	QK431
574.9943	QH197
575	CB68
	QH325
	QH331
	QH363
	QH366
	QH366.A2
	QH366.2
	QH367
	QH368
	QH371
	QH431
575.01	QH363
	QH369
575.016	QE707.T4
575.0162	QH31.D2
	QH311
	QH363
	QH365.O2
	QH365.O8
	QH365.Z9
	QH366
575.016208	QH31
575.01620973	QH367
575.0166	QH431
575.0182	QH431
575.08	QH366.A2
575.1	BS661
	QH405
	QH431
	QR182
575.10182	QH431
575.103	QH431
575.1076	QH431
575.108	QH431
575.109	QH431
575.10947	QH431
575.110924	QH31.M45
575.12	QH431
575.21	QH411
	QH431
	QH607
575.292	QH431
576	QH274
	QH277
	QR41
	QR41.2
	QR56
	QR57
	QR58
	QR64.5
576.012	QR81
576.028	QR65
	QR66
	QR69
576.05	QL756
576.06273	QR1.A473
576.076	QR61.5
576.1	QP601
	QR41
	QR41.2
576.1134	QR84
576.15	QR65
	QR100
576.15028	QR65
576.16	QR1
576.16028	QR65
576.163	QR115
576.16306171	S133
576.164	QR53
576.1909	QR101
	TL521.3.C6
576.192	GC1
576.1929	QR105.5
576.192947	QR105.5
576.2	QR73
	QR181
	QR181.5
	QR183
	QR185.P5
576.22	QP251
	QR180
	QR180.3
	QR181
	QR183
	QR185.A6
	QR185.T6
576.22028	QR183
576.2208	QR180
576.23	QR81
	QR181
	QR185.C6
	QR189.5.R8
576.6	E98.A55
576.64	QR82.A35
	QR360
576.640202	QR360
576.6409	QR360
576.6482	QR360
576.6483	SB736
576.6484	QR201.F63
	QR360
576.6484012	QR360
577	QH325
	QH331
	QP77
577.011	PZ10.M455
	QH325
577.0110924	Q143.P2
577.2	B1180
577.209	QP21
577.9778	QE75
578	PZ10.S677
	QH205
	QH277
578.1	QH204
	QH212.F5
578.15	QH212.E4
578.4	QH205
	QH207
	QH212.E4
578.46	QH251
578.6	QH277
578.62	QR1
578.64	QH237
578.8	QK673
579	QH60
	QH91.56
	QL123
	QL463
	QR64.5
	SB404.5
579.4	QL63
579.6	QK61
580.12	QK93
580.73	QK61
580.744	QK71
	QK73.E2
	QK445
	QK488
	SB466.G75E9
580.744025	QK96
580.8	QH7
581	QK1
	QK45
	QK45.2
	QK47
	QK49
	QK50
	QK98
581	QK725
581.0014	QK96
581.012	QK96
581.014	QK11
	QK96
581.0222	QK98
581.028	QK49
581.03	QK9
581.072	QK81
581.076	QK52.5
581.08	QH7
	QK1
581.0922	QK26
	SB404.5
581.0924	QK31.D7
	QK31.S15
581.0973	QK21.U5
581.1	QK45.2
	QK46
	QK649
	QK711
	QK711.2
	QK725
	QK865
581.108	QK711.2
581.11	QK871
581.12	QK873
581.13	QK867
	QK887
	QK898.L56
581.13342	QK882
	QK882.R29
581.1335	QK911
581.134	QK731
581.134153	S239.S2
581.15	QH406
581.158	QH406
581.16	QK827
581.1662	QK865
581.17	QK725
581.18	QK761
581.19150982	QK757
581.192	QK861
	QK898.A4
581.1927	QK745
	SB128
581.2	SB601
581.232	SB731
581.27	SB767
581.3	PZ10.B29525
	QK745
581.31	QK731
581.38	QH406
	QK653
	QK667
581.4	QK641
	QK671
581.46	QK658
581.5	PZ10.H833
	QH541.5.F6
	QK101
	QK901
	QK911.B7
	QK938.F6
	QK941.O5
	QK956.S8
581.50912	QK938.F6
581.509153	QH541.5.P7
581.50942	QK956.G7
581.5094227	QK938.F6
581.509482	QK956.N6
581.50979153	QE75
581.50979487	QE75
581.509883	QK938.P7
581.509944	QK971.N4
581.509945	QK938.F6
581.509969	SD11
581.52	QK47
581.5222	QK754
	QK870
581.522209982	Q115
581.5223	SD425
581.5223028	QK715
581.522309982	Q115
581.5226	QK929
581.526	QK955
581.5263	QK103
581.5264	QK903
	QK938.P7
581.5333	PZ10.B2952154
	QK917
581.6	QK83
	SB107
581.60974	SB108.U6
581.63	QK99
	QK489.G8
581.632	QK98.5
581.634	QK99
	QK898.A4
581.634095491	QK99
581.63409969	QK99
581.64	QK358
581.6509169	QK105
581.650973	SB612.A2
581.670954	SB617
581.69	QK100.N6
581.6909676	QK100.A55
581.8	QK725
581.82	QK725
581.87	QK725
581.876	QK725
581.90953	QK938.P7
581.90954	QK147
581.92	QH96
581.92973	QK105
581.929751	QK105
581.94251	QK306
581.94261	QK306
581.94386	QK322
581.947	QK321
581.9486	QK938.C6
581.95	QK62
581.954	QK358
581.9542	QK358
581.9544	QK358
581.95475	QK358
581.9548	QK358
581.95482	QK358
581.9575	S599.45.O5
581.96897	QK402.M28
581.96982	QK429.M3
581.97	QK110
581.9711	QK203.B7
581.971131	QK203.B7
581.973	QK115
581.97449	QK938.C6
581.9747	QK183
581.9755	QK191
581.97587	QK155
581.9764	Q180.U5
581.97671	QK125
581.97731	QK157
581.9776	QK168
581.978	QK139
	QK150
581.97884	QK150
581.979155	SD11
581.9794	G58
581.979462	QK149
581.979478	QK149
581.9795	QH1
581.979587	QH1
581.97983	AS283
581.98	QK241
581.9863	QK221
581.99141	QK368
581.9931	QK98.2
581.9945	QK459
581.9947	QK445
581.9969	SD11
582.011	QK870
582.01662	QK926
582.046	PZ10.R84
	QK652
582.0467	PZ10.C32864
	QK661
582.0498	QK644
582.0957	QK321
582.0973	QK482
582.12	QK15
582.13	PZ10.L123
	QK1
	QK50
	QK98
	QK142
	QK297
	QK306
	QK431
	QK486.B6
	QK495.A56
	QK661
	QK711.2
	QK731
	QK830
	S133
582.13041	PZ10.D274
582.13094	QK281
582.130942	QK306
582.13094289	QK306
582.1309542	QK358
582.13095479	QK358
582.13095493	QK359
582.130967	QK401
582.1309684	QK398
582.13097	QK85
	QK110
582.1309711	QK203.B7
582.1309712	QK201
582.130973	QK98
582.130974494	QK166
582.130976889	QK125
582.1309771	QK180
582.130978	QK142
	SB208.U5
582.130978652	QK484.M9
582.130979	QK143
582.130979438	QK149
582.130979462	QK149
582.130979482	QK484.C2
582.1309795	QK144
582.13097975	QK484.W3
582.13097983	QK146
582.13099	QK474.5
582.130994	QK431
582.1309946	QK457
582.14	QK396
	SB438
582.140973	QK482
582.15	QK826
582.150942	QK488
582.15096822	QK491.S6
582.1509711	QK486.B7
582.1509716	S153
582.150973	QK481
582.1509771	QK484.O3
582.150977161	QK479
582.15097736	QK484.I3
582.1509781	QK484.K2

Dewey	LC
582.150978419	QK484.N9
582.1509788	QK484.C6
582.16	PZ10
	PZ10.C834
	PZ10.S526
	PZ10.S89
	QK475
	QK477
	QK938.F6
582.1600740235	QK488
582.1601	QK711.2
582.16013	QK867
582.1601343	QK477
	QK865
582.16031	QK731
582.1604	SD534.Q8
582.160498	SD121
582.1605	QK938.F6
582.160942	SD179
582.160954	QK490.I4
582.1609543	QK490.I4
582.1609666	SD242.L5
582.1609713	QK486.C2
582.1609794	QK484.C2
582.16099	QK494
582.160994	QK492
582.17	SD11
582.17097946	QK484.C2
582.463	QK658
583	QH406
	SB13
583.012	QK97
583.0202	QK203.B7
583.09931	QK463
583.11	QK1
	QK643.R4
583.123	S239.S2
583.14	QK495.P775
583.15	QK495.A32
583.24	QK866.C59
583.28	PZ10.W22
583.3	QK495.R78
583.32	PZ10.E13
	QK1
	QK495.L52
	QK710
	S21.A72
583.397	QK495.B78
583.4	QK495.E86
	QK495.M9
583.44	QK1
583.47	QK495.C11
583.470976	QK495.C11
583.4709791	QK495.C11
583.470979248	QK495.C11
583.4709794	QK495.C11
583.48	QK1
583.55	Q60
	QK1
	QK495.C74
583.57	QK1
583.74	S239.S2
583.7480971134	QB4
583.79	QK495.S7
	QK725
	QK755
	QK898.A5
	S21
583.89	SB303.L3
583.962	QK495.M73
583.97	QK495.Q4
	SD397.A4
583.98	SD433
584	QK157
	QK484.I3
584.15	QK495.O64
584.150967	QK495.O64
584.150994	QK495.O64
584.1509944	QK495.O64
584.22	QK1
584.24	QH423
	QK1
	SB413.I8
584.32	QK495.L72
584.50968	QK495.P17
584.64	QK1
584.742	Q57
584.84	QK495.C997
584.9	QK882
584.909791	SD11
584.909942	QK495.G74
584.93	QK1
585.2	AS36
	QK495.S5
	SD1
	SD144.R6
	SD211
	SD397.P572
585.20942	QK495.C75
586	QK505
586.040222	QK673
587.09429	QK527
587.31	QE701
	QK529
587.3109768	QK525.5.T4
587.3109795	QK525.5.P33
588	QK533
588.0924	QK31.S8
588.0971	QK533
588.209481	QK544.N8
588.209541	QK545.I4
588.20974	QK541
589.1	Q64
	QK581
589.10942	QK589
589.1097	QK587
589.2	QK601
	QK603
	QK604
	QK605
589.203	QK603
589.207	QK604
589.22	QK617
	QK626
	QK629.E9
	QK629.G2
	QK629.H9
589.2210942	Z5356.F97
589.222	QK504
	QK603.5
	QK617
	QK629.A4
	QK629.H9
	QK629.P7
589.2220977	QK617
589.22209777	QK617
589.225	QK627.A1
589.23	QH605
	QK623.C53
	QK623.P4
	QK623.P9
	QK623.T3
	QK899
	QP551
	QP601
	QR151
589.24	QK625.A1
	QK625.M74
	QK625.S6
	QP601
589.25	PZ10.G653
589.252	QK621.P9
589.26	QK621.S24
589.28	QK621.M96
589.29	QK1
	QK635
589.3	QH7
	QK1
	QK103
	QK564
	QK564.5
	QK565.2
	QK566
	QK567
	QK571
	SH255
589.3091667	QK576.C3
589.30942	QK564
589.309795	QK564
589.41	QK1
	QK569.C95
589.410973	QK569.R4
589.45	GC1
589.450979	QK1
589.47	QK569.C6
	QK569.D33
589.48	QL368.F5
589.62	Q111
	QH91.57.P4
	QK564
589.79	QK495.S7
589.8	QK569.C96
589.9	QH591
	QR63
	QR82.M93
	U390
589.90014	QR81
589.901	QR84
589.9013	QR84
589.9015	QR73
589.90151	QH431
589.901592	QH431
589.901925	QD1
589.9019297	QP671
589.9038	QR73
589.9046	QR84
589.92	QR82.A35
	QR82.M9
	S21.A72
589.95	QP601
	QR75
	QR82.B23
	QR82.S7
	QR84
589.96	QR84
590	QL47
	QL89
590.744	PZ10.W349
	QL31.G64
	QL76
	QL77.T3
	QL77.5
590.744095493	QL77.5
590.74409756	QL77.N6
590.8	QL3
591	PZ10.G524
	PZ10.M455
	PZ10.R3352
	PZ10.W33
	QH408
	QL3
	QL45.2
	QL47
	QL47.2
	QL49
	QL50
	QL88
	QL791
591.012	QL99
	QL351
591.018	QP331
591.0222	QL46
591.03	QL9
591.072095	QL345.N5
591.08	QE1
	QH7
	QL1
	QL49
	QL50
591.0924	QH31.S9
	QL31.D5
591.1	QP31
	QP31.2
	QP33
	QP406
591.1028	QH324
591.108	QP71
591.11	PZ10.S664
	QP111
591.13	QP197
	QP535.N1
	QP751
591.14	QP187
	QP187.A1
	QP188.P55
591.16	PZ10.A657
	QP251
591.166	QP273
591.1662	PZ10.P6695
591.18	QL939
	QM455
	QP303
	QP321
	QP341
	QP351
	QP355
	QP361
	QP363
	QP372
	QP431
	QP475
591.1852	PZ10.P6
	QL821
591.191	QH656
591.191076	QH405
591.1915	HD9698
591.19153	QP82.2.L5
	QP475
591.1916	QP135
591.1917	QP341
591.1919	TL507
591.192	QP88.23
	QP514.2
	QP521
	QP551
	QP801.S6
	QP921.P9
591.1927	QP187
	QP187.A1
591.2	QL757
	RC261
591.3	QL955
	QP141
591.32	QL951
	QL965
591.33	QL961
591.44	QL841
591.47	PZ10.R85
	QL950.7
591.5	PZ10.B94
	PZ10.C678
	QH151
	QH541
	QH541.3
	QH546
	QL751
	QL752
	QL756
	QL758
	QL785
591.5028	QL751.7
591.508	QL85
591.5099311	QH95.7
591.51	HQ12
	PZ10.F698
	QL751
	QL751.5
	QL781
	QL791
591.51028	QL751.7
591.5108	QL751
591.52	PZ10.G529
	QL754
591.53	QP141
591.55	PZ10.A6655
	QH548
	QL124
	QL752
	QL757
	RA418
591.5509166	QL124
591.5509487	QL145
591.57	PZ10.H489
	PZ10.M455
	QL759
591.59	QL776
	QP455
591.6	QL49
	SB999.A8
591.69	QL100
591.8	Q180
	QH311
591.8	QH574
	QH581
	QL963.5
	QM555
	QM557
	QP88
	QP535.C2
591.9	QL101
591.90946	PZ10.W218
	QL121
591.90948	QL110
591.92	QH91
	QL122
	QL124
591.925	QL125
591.929	QH96
	QL141
	QL146
591.9549	QL334.P4
591.96	QL336
591.9624	QL337.S8
591.96782	QL337.T33
591.968	QL337.S8
591.972983	QL229.T7
591.994	QH95.7
	QL338
	S964.A8
591.999	QL106
592	QH91.8.P5
	QL362
	QL363
592.0074095482	QL362.5
592.014	QP187
592.018	QL1
	QL364
	QP341
	QP431
592.0192	QL364
592.033	QL958
592.04	QL363
592.05	QL758
592.092	QL3
592.0925	QL138
593.1	QL366
	QL368.D6
	TA7
593.1028	QH277
593.14	QH543.6
593.172	QL368.C5
593.19	QL368.C7
593.2973	QL676
593.4	QL1
593.46	QH1
593.7	Q115
	QL377.H9
593.9	QL381
593.93	KF31.I5
593.930947	QL384.A8
594	QL403
	QL405
	QL415.F6
594.000946	QL428
594.0012	Q11
594.0075	QL405
	QL406.5
594.096782	QL427
594.09684	QL430.4
594.097	QL404
594.0974494	QL415.M2
594.1	QC770
	QL1
	QL430.6
	QL430.7.D8
	SH365.A4
	SH379.U5
594.115	QL430.6
594.3	PZ10.S36
	QL337.C6
	QL430.5.C86
	QL430.5.C94
	QL430.5.H9
	QL430.5.V75
594.36	Q11
594.360916651	Q11
594.380942	QL430.4
594.56	Q11
	QP601
594.609727	QL421
594.7	QL396
594.8	QL395
595.08	QL461
595.1	QL386
	QL392
	QL757
595.12	QL391.P7
595.121	QL391.C4
595.122	QL391.T7
595.123	QH499
595.13	QL1
	QL391.N4
	S239.S2
595.13094776	QL391.N4
595.133	QL391.A2
595.16	QL391.O4
595.17	QL1
	QL391.P9
595.3	QH366
	QL435.A1
	QL444.A5
595.30973	QL441.1
595.30994	QL441.7
595.32	SH11
595.33	Q11
	Q115

Dewey	LC
595.33	QL444.O8
595.3309485	QL444.O8
595.34	QH91
	QL444.C7
595.35	Q11
595.3509989	QL444.C5
595.371	AS283
	Q11
	Q115
595.37109794	Q11
595.372	QL444.I8
595.382091661	QH91.A1
595.3820968	QL1
	QL444.S8
595.384	AS284
595.38409729	Q11
595.3841	HC107.F6
	QH91
	QL444.D3
595.3842	PZ10.C76
	QL444.D3
595.38420916612	QL128
595.3843	Q115
	QL444.D3
595.4	QL451
595.40968	QL457.6
595.42	QL337.C6
	QL458.A2
	QL458.H4
595.44	PZ10.H76
	QL1
	QL337.C6
595.440994	QL457.7
595.46	QL434
595.47	QL458.C5
595.61	QL449
	QL461
595.7	QL463
	QL467
	QL475.N7
	QL487
595.70012	QL468
595.700222	QL466
595.7006254	QL461
595.7008	QL461
	QL482.G8
595.700994	QL487
595.701	QL463
595.7018	QP475
595.701916	QL496
595.70222	QL466
595.7046	QL494
595.7051	QL461
	QL495
595.7052	QL496
595.70524	PZ10.D274
595.706	Q11
595.708	QR185.C4
595.7092	PZ10.M115
595.70973	QL464
595.709794	QL474.C3
595.726	QL508.A2
595.731	QH1
595.73109773	QH1
595.733	QL461
595.734	PZ10.H847
595.734097	QL513.E7
595.736	QL513.T3
595.736095	QL461
595.742	QL461
595.745094	QL517.4
595.747	QL461
595.75140974	QL503.M2
595.752	QL461
	QL523.A6
	QL523.C7
	S21.A72
595.754	QL461
595.76	Q11
	QL461
	QL577
	QL596.C9
	QL597
595.762	QL596.C2
595.764	Q11
	QH1
	QL461
	QL596.A64
	QL596.C5
	QL596.L9
	QL596.M35
	QL596.S3
595.767	QL596.M35
595.77	PZ10.S65
	Q11
	QL1
	QL535.1
	QL537.S36
595.770978	QL535.1
595.771	PZ10.A83
	Q11
	QL461
	QL536
	QL537.M7
	QL537.S4
	QL537.T6
	RA640
	SH223
	Z5858.M7
595.774	QH431
	QL482.G8
	QL537.A4
	QL537.D75
	QL537.T3
595.775	QL503.A7
595.7750995	QL503.A7
595.78	Q11
	QH1
	QL1
	QL337.C6
	QL461
	QL542
	QL548
	QL555.G7
	QL561.A34
	QL561.G6
	QL561.O6
	QL561.P9
	QL562
	QP481
595.780222	QL543
595.780942	QL555.G7
595.7809747	QL551.N7
595.789	PZ.S672
	QL461
	QL561.N9
595.789094	QL555.A1
595.7890942	SD1
595.789096	QL557
595.7890994	QL558
595.79	QL1
	QL461
	QL565
	QL568.B8
	QL568.C4
	QL568.E8
	QL568.I2
	QL568.P3
	QL569
	S21
	SD11
595.796	PZ10.H64
	QL568.F7
595.798	QL565
	QL568.V5
	QL785.5.I45
595.799	PZ10.R616
	QL461
	QL568.A6
596	PZ10.H74
	QL50
	QL77.S29
	QL88
	QL605
	QL791
596.00222	QL77.5
596.0074	QL76
	QL77.C36
596.008	QH1
	QH7
	QL605
	GC1
596.01	QP491
596.011	QL838
	QR1
596.012	QL848
596.013	QP188.P26
596.014	QL868
	QP187.A1
	QP211
596.0144	QP801.U7
596.0148	QP801.H7
596.015	QP84
596.016	QP251
596.018	QP321
	QP341
	QP363
	QP365
	QP376
	QP379
	QP431
	QP456
	QP475
	RJ252
596.01915	QH652
596.02	QL1
	RC633
596.0222	QL151
596.033	QP121
	QR182
596.038	QE841
596.04	QH301
	QL805
	QL812
	QP88.2
596.04028	QL812
596.047	PZ10.A4783
	QL821
596.05	KF26.C645
	QH546
	QL77.5
	QL88
	QL751
596.0524	QL775
596.055	QL775
596.0555	QL775
596.056	QL761
596.06	QL758
596.074	QL76
596.074086	QL77.B69
596.08	QH367
	QH574
	QH585
	QH608
	QL937
	QM551
	QP356.3
596.092	PZ10.A643
596.094	QL253
596.0942	QL255
596.095694	QL49
596.0959	QL312
596.096	QL46
	QL336
596.09676	QL337.E25
596.09681	QH195.B6
596.0973	S914
596.0994	QL338
596.09945	QL339.V6
596.2	QL391.O4
	QL613
596.3233	QP601
596.33	TL507
596.56	QL761
597	PZ10.A643
	PZ10.S557
	QL615
597.00222	QL616
597.003	QL614.7
597.01	QL639.1
597.011	QL639.1
597.018	QL639.1
597.0192	QL639.1
597.01925	U395.S8
597.02	SH171
597.047	QH1
597.05	QH1
	QL628.L6
597.055	SH333
597.059	QL639
597.06	PZ10.F43
597.09096652	QL623
597.0909667	GC1
597.092	QL137
	QL625
	QL628.F6
	QL634.P5
597.09261	SH259
597.09263	QL631.C3
597.092909761	QL628.A2
597.092966991	Q56
597.0929682	QL635.S6
597.092971	QL626
597.092973	QL625
	QL627
597.0929746	QL628.C8
597.0929748	QL628.P4
597.09297567	QL628.N8
597.094	QL633.A1
597.09415	QL633.I7
597.0968	QL635.S6
597.097	QL625
597.09711	QH71.N6
597.097296	QL621
597.31	QL638.9
597.310968	GC1
597.38	QL1
597.46	QL638.C65
597.5	Q115
	QH1
	QL616
	QL628.C2
	QL633.R8
597.5095125	QL634.H6
597.51	QL614
597.52	PZ10.S677
	Q11
	QH81
	QL1
	QL639.1
	QP121
597.53	QL638.C96
	QL638.G27
	QP471
	SH11
597.55	Q56
	Q115
	QH1
	QL628.K4
	QL638.C64
	QL638.G25
	QL638.S2
	QL639
	QL795.F7
	SH11
	SH287
	SH318.5
	SK361
597.58	Q115
	QH1
	QL1
	QL638.M2
	QL638.O2
	QL638.S35
	QL756.8
	SH259
597.6	QL971
	RC267
597.60942	QL658.G7
597.8	QH7
	QH96.A1
	QL651
	QL668.E2
	QL937
	QP321
	QP331
597.9094	QL668.C2
598.1	PZ10.A478
	PZ10.B722
	PZ10.H78
	PZ10.W728
	QL641
	QL653.P4
598.1095493	QL661
598.10972	QL655
598.109723	QL655
598.10973	QL644
598.109763	QL653.L6
598.110956	QL1
598.112	QH1
	QL1
	QL666.L2
598.12	PZ10.B656
	QH1
	QL653.C8
	QL666.O6
	QP341
598.1209713	QL654
598.13	HC107.M3
	QL1
	QL666.C5
598.2	PA10.A643
	PZ10
	PZ10.A85
	PZ10.O34
	QH1
	QL673
	QL674
	QL676
	QL676.5
	QL677.5
	QL698
	QP188.A28
598.2073	QL676.5
	QL684.F6
598.20924	QL31.A9
598.218	QL698.7
	SH1
598.22	KF27.M445
598.23	QL676
598.233	PZ10.S44
598.25	QL751
	QL785.5.B6
598.2509775	QL673
598.251	QL785.5.B6
598.252	PZ10.M455
598.255	QL775
598.256	PZ10.H643
	Q60
598.259	QL698.5
	QL765
598.26	QL676
598.2916653	QL695
598.29220968	QL692
598.29220971	QL685
598.29220974	PZ10.V615
598.29230968	QL692
598.2924094237	QL690.E5
598.29240994	QL696.A5
598.294	QL1
	QL690.A1
	QL690.G7
598.2942	QL677
	QL690.G7
598.29421	QL690.G7
598.294235	QL690.G7
598.29424	QL690.E5
598.294299	QH132
598.294585	QL690.M3
598.295	QL674
598.2954	QL691.I4
	QL691.S65
598.295492	QL691.E2
598.296761	Q11
	QL692
598.2968	QL692
598.29687	QL692
598.296894	QL692
598.297	Q11
	QL681
598.2971	QL674
598.29712	QL685
598.29714	QH1
598.2972	QL686
598.297281	QL687.G9
598.29729722	QL688.V5
598.2973	QL674
598.2974793	QH1
598.29757	QL684.S6
598.29773	QL684.I3
598.29795	QL684.O6
598.298	QL674
	QL689.A1
598.2985	QL689.P5
598.29852	QL689.P5
598.298665	QL694.G2
598.29931	QL693
598.2994	QL693
598.29941	QL693
598.29942	QL693
598.2995	QL694.N4
	SK577
598.33	PZ10.R84
	SH255
598.34	PZ10.R616
598.4	PZ10.F7147
	QL696.A5
	QL696.G2
	QL785.5.B6
	QL795.C17
	SK463
	SK465
598.42	Q11
598.44	PZ10.R616
598.443	QL696.P9
598.51	PZ10.F4
598.510968	QL696.S9

598.6097	QL696.G2
598.61	QL696.G2
	SF487
598.65	QL696.C6
	SK1
598.7	QL3
	QL696.P7
598.71	QL696.P7
598.72	QL1
598.8	QH1
	QL1
	QL696.P2
	QL785.5.B6
598.810994	QL696.P2
598.813	QL696.P2
598.842	PZ10.K1279
	QL795.B57
598.88	QL1
598.883	QH1
	QL696.P2
598.89	QL696.H3
598.899	PZ10.V75
598.9	PZ10.G532
	QL696.A2
	QL795.B57
598.91	PZ10.L855
	QL696.A2
598.97	AS622
	QL696.S8
	SK1
599	PZ10.A643
	PZ10.B294824
	PZ10.K1273
	QA64
	QL50
	QL77.5
	QL88
	QL701
	QL703
	QL706
	QL715
	QL727
	QL738
	QL751
	QL791
599.0012	QL703
599.0074086	QL77.B69
599.008	PZ10.A95
599.01	QP171
599.011	QP101
	QR185.A3
599.012	QP99.3.O9
	QP535.C1
599.013	QM601
	QP99.3.P7
	QP141
	QP551
	TX341
599.014	QP115
	QP211
599.015	QL1
	QL55
599.0151	QH431
599.0158	QH431
599.01592	QH431
599.016	QP251
	QP261
599.0160222	QL964
599.0166	QP255
	RG558
599.01662	QL265
	QP251
599.018	AS283
	QP301
	QP321
	QP341
	QP355
	QP356.3
	QP361
	QP363
	QP376
	QP385
	QP406
	QP521
	QP801.A48
599.01915	QP82.2.R3
	RA569
	RA1231.R2
599.0192	QP246
	QP514
	QP551
	QP751
	QP801.H7
	QP801.T3
599.01925	QP601
	QR185.P5
599.019256	QP801.A5
599.01926	QP801.V5
599.01927	QP187
	QP801.H7
599.019293	QP751
599.02	QL368.M5
	QR185.A4
	QR185.T6
	QR201.A3
	RA1231.R2
	RC261
599.03	QP84
	QP88
	SF95
599.033	RG600
599.038	QH367.1
599.047	QL738
	QL739
599.048	QM451
599.05	QL151
	QL706
	QL768
599.05091641	SH11
599.051	QL785.5.M3
599.078	PZ10.W728
599.08	QH581
	QH585
	QH603.M4
	QM565
	QP82.2.R3
599.092	QL713.2
599.094	QL88
599.09411	QL50
599.0942	QL727
599.096	QL731
599.09676	QL731
599.0968	QL731
599.09684	QL731
599.0971	QL791
599.09727	QH1
599.09752	QL155
599.09788	QL719.C6
599.09793	QH1
599.09794	QL719.C2
599.0985	SK351
599.0994	PZ10.W728
	QL733
599.0995	QL1
	QL735.N45
599.09969	QL719.H3
599.16	QP981.W5
599.2	PZ10.W627
	QL737.M35
	QL937
	QP93
599.3	QP378
599.31	QL368.F5
599.322	AS284
	PZ10.H847
	QL434
	QL737.L32
	QL801
	QL937
	RD701
	SK1
599.3230947	QL737.R6
599.323096	QL337.C6
599.3230966	QL737.R6
599.3232	PZ10.A655
	PZ10.R616
	PZ10.T69
	QL1
	QL737.R6
	QL737.R632
	QL737.R68
599.3233	AS284
	GN37.A8
	PZ10.F7147
	QD1
	QL737.R638
	QL821
	QL933
	QL961
	QP91
	QP145
	QP187
	QP261
	QP372
	QP535.H6
	QP801.A4
	QP801.V5
	QR185.A6
	R31
	R85
	SK463
599.3234	Q60
	QL1
	QL801
	QP88.5
	QR182
	R111
599.33	PZ10.G518
	QL737.I53
	QL937
599.4	PZ10.A655
	PZ10.P95
	Q11
	QH7
	QL1
	QL737.C5
599.40723	S914
599.40952	QL737.C5
599.40973	QL737.C5
599.409781	QL737.C5
599.5	PZ10.R616
	QL122
599.50916651	QL719.C2
599.50916653	QL715
599.509931	SH318.5
599.51	Q115
599.53	QH91
	QL737.C432
	QL737.C433
	QL737.C435
599.61	PZ10.E18
	PZ10.V62
599.7	QH431
	QL738
599.728	QL737.U63
599.734	AS284
	QL957
599.7350413	QP145
599.7357	PZ10.E18
	QK941.C6
	QL1
	QL737.U55
	QL737.U56
	SK1
599.7358	PZ10.B295245
	PZ10.W32
	QL737.U52
	QL737.U53
	QL785.5.P75
	QP96.5
	QP601
	SH11
599.740957	QL737.C2
599.7442	QL737.C22
599.74428	PZ10
	QL737.C23
	QM471
	QP156
	QP193
	QP385
	SF442
599.7443	QL737.C27
599.74442	PZ10.B29522533
	Q180.A1
	QL737.C22
	QL795.W8
	QM557
	SF422.5
	SK1
599.74443	PZ10.R617
	QL737.C27
599.74446	QL737.C27
	SK351
599.74447	QL155
	QL737.C25
	SK1
599.7446	QL737.C27
599.746	QH199
	SK361
599.748	Q60
	QL737.P6
599.8	PZ10.V25
	QL737.P9
	QL775
	QL785.5.P7
	QP91
	SF407.P7
599.80413	QL737.P9
599.8045	QL785.5.P7
599.82	QL737.P93
	QL937
	QL948
	QP385
599.88	QL737.P9
599.884	PZ10.C72
	QL55
	QL737.P93
	QL737.P96
	QL785.5.B2
	QL785.5.C5
	QL937
599.9	QH368
600	CB478
	JX1977
	PZ10.H79647
	T19
	T20
	T47
	T55.3.H3
	T185
	TA403.6
601	T14
601.2	HA40.I6
601.51	TA330
601.6	Z7913
602.00151	TA330
602.02	T49
602.5493	Q223
602.8	T57.62
603	T10
604.2	T353
604.26979	TH7683.D8
604.6	TP995.A1
606.24183	AS122
607	AS4.U8
	KF27.S383
	T62
	T65
	T73
	T107.B28
607.1	L136
	T62
	T65
	T73.A24
	T153
607.11	T62
607.1142	T107
607.114216	T173.L832
607.114231	T173.S16
607.114686	T173.E8
607.11593	T173.A7
607.11713	T77.O5
607.1173	T73
607.11743	T74.V4
607.11771	T74.O3
607.1179493	T171.C219
607.12	Q181
	T65
607.1222	T74.N7
607.1242	T107
607.125952	T163.S5
607.127	T65
607.1273	T73
607.15	T62
	T73
607.2	HC79.T4
	T10.5
	T45
	T65.3
	T174.3
	TL521.3.C6
	TL789.8.U5
607.2054	T177.I4
607.24	T177.E8
607.242	T177.G7
607.2485	T177.S9
607.25	Q183.43.A75
607.271	Q127.C2
	Q183.43.C2
607.273	KF26.5.S635
	T174.3
607.2821	T173.I827
607.34	T396
	T690.B1
607.7468	LD6337.5
607.791	T74.A6
607.8	T171
608	TJ7
608.7	T19
	T210
	T212
608.7012	T255
	T273.F6
608.709	T19
608.70904	T19
608.70942	T257.D2
608.7174960922	E185.8
608.724	T40.L46
608.773	KF3120
	T223.V2
	T339
609	T15
609.22	T39
609.3	GN429
	T16
609.4	T26
609.41	T26.G75
609.42	Q127.G4
	T26.G7
	T179
609.421	T26.G8L65
609.4235	T26.G72
	T26.G72D35
609.4241	T26.G72
609.4251	T26.G8D42
	T26.G8D45
609.42565	T26.G72B46
609.4258	T26.G72H44
	T26.G72H45
609.4272	T26.G72L33
609.428	T26.G72L264
609.71	T23
609.73	H62
	T21
	T212
609.944	Q127.A8
610	QP34
	QP40
	R106
	R111
	R114
	R117
	R128.6
	R129
	R130.5
	R135
	R149
	R705
	R706
	R708
	R895
	RC81
610.0711	R845
610.072073	RA440
610.1	QH43.5
	R723
610.12	RB115
610.14	PC4121
	R121
	R123
610.148	R123
610.1519	RA409
610.153	R895
610.18	QH405
	RA409.5
610.182	QH405
610.184	RA409
610.19	R726.5
610.207	R705
610.23	R690
610.2436	RA995
610.2461073677	RK60.5
610.28	Q11
	R856
	R895
	RA409.5
	RB37
	RM930
	TL507
610.3	R121
	R129
	RC81.A2
610.611	RA11.A3
610.6273	R15
	R15.A55
610.62944	R99

610.69 R690
R728.8
RA410.7
610.690973 HD5701
610.6909748 RA407.4.P4
610.690985 RA477
610.695 RA407.4.C6
RA445
RC455
610.6952 R692
R707
R729.5.G4
610.6952019 R690
610.69520922 R692
610.69520942 R486
610.6953 R728.8
RA410.7
RK60.5
610.6953023 R728.8
R847
RA440.9
610.696 R727.3
R729.5.G4
RC65
610.7 R737
R740
R745
R840
RA421
RA440.3
RA440.3.U5
Z675.M4
610.71 R740
R745
610.711 R737
R840
610.711171242 RA422
610.71142 R772
610.71171 R749
610.71173 R737
R745
R840
610.71174461 R747.M47
610.7117471 R747.R69
610.711756 RA410.8.N8
610.71175667 R747.B8
610.711773 RA440.3.U5
610.711776 R746.M47
610.71195 R821.P3
610.7142 R772
610.7153 R835
610.72 HA37
R850
R852
R854.U5
R860
RA8.A3
RA440.6
610.72073 R852
R854.U5
610.73 RA975
RM849
RT1
RT3
RT5.A17
RT40
RT41
RT42
RT55
RT62
RT63
RT65
RT86
RT90.5
610.7301 RT42
610.73018 RT73
610.73019 RT86
610.730202 RT52
610.73023 RA421
RT29
RT82
610.73028 RT41
RT42
610.7303 RT21
610.7306142 RT11
610.73069 RT6
RT42
610.730693 RT41
RT62
610.730693023 RT62
610.730693071173 RT62
610.730698 RT69
RT84
610.7307 LA340.5
RT3
RT71
RT73
610.730711 RT71
RT73
610.73071107471 RT81.N3
610.73071142 RT81
RT81.G7
610.73071171 RT81.C23
610.73071173 RT71
RT73
RT81
RT81.U6
610.73071175979 RT81.G25
610.730711776 R847
610.730711794 RT73
610.730711944 RT15.N44
610.73072 RT73
610.73076 RT55
RT62
610.7308 RT63
610.7309 RT31
610.730924 RT37.F4
RT37.M17
RT37.O8
610.730969 JQ6103
610.730971 RT6
610.73097123 RT6
610.730973 RA972
RT73
RT81.U6
610.7309747 RT5.N5
610.7309755 RT5.V8
610.73098 RA10
610.7343 RT4
RT61
RT97
610.73430973 RA395.A3
610.7346 RC966
610.736 RC350.5
RC674
RC874.7
RK60.5
RT3
RT41
RT42
610.7362 RJ245
RT1
610.7363 RJ245
RT1
610.7365 RC954
610.7367 RT1
610.73677 RC674
RD99
RD753
RT65
610.73678 RG951
610.7368 RC440
RC440.5
RC488
610.736807 RC440
610.7368076 RC440
610.7368094221 RC440
610.7369 RT95
610.76 RC58
610.77 R745
RB115
RT65
610.8 HQ31
R85
R85.U76
R111
R117
R708
RA8
RA418
RC81.A2
610.9 R131
R133
R145
610.902 R141
610.9032 R148
610.904 R149
610.907 RA1221
610.917496 R695
610.922 R134
R153
R154.K7
R296
R489
R489.A1
R608.A1
R626.A1
R747.S75
RA410.8.N7
UH341
610.924 DA670
DA670.L19C5
DS135.R95
E302.6.R85
QR31.B8
R117
R154.A145
R154.B14
R154.B623
R154.B77
R154.B862
R154.D236
R154.F65
R154.G6
R154.H39
R154.K265
R154.S115
R154.S24
R154.W18
R489.H9
R489.L7
R489.P38
R493
R502.B4
R512.F6
R520.C32
R654.F68
R674
R674.P68
RA454.G8
610.93 RA395.N38
610.94 R149
610.942 R149
610.952 R623
610.9549 R133
610.9701 AM101
610.973 R153
R695
610.973 RA395.A3
611 QM21
QM23
QM23.2
QM25
QM26
QM71
QM531
R126
RT69
611.0014 QM81
611.00202 QM28
QM31
611.00222 QM25
611.002461796 QM23
611.0076 QM32
611.00924 QM16.V5
611.012 QM691
RB155
RJ138
611.012012 QM691
611.013 QM601
RG591
611.014 QM81
611.018 QM55
QM551
QM555
QM569
RB27
RC692
611.0180222 QM557
611.0181 QH431
QR189.5.V5
RB125
RB131
RB155
RC882
611.0182 QP88.23
RC628
RD686
611.0185 QM197
QP94
R111
RC633
611.0186 QP535.C2
611.0188 RC347
611.1 RC687
611.13 QM191
611.24 QM261
611.31 QM311
611.314 QM311
611.314022 RK656
611.32 QM331
611.36 RC847
611.7 QM101
611.702479282 QM100
611.715 QM105
611.718 QM117
611.72 QM141
611.8 QM451
QP361
611.80222 QM451
611.81 QM455
QM611
611.810222 QM455
611.84 QM511
611.85 QM507
611.9 QM23
QM531
611.91 QM535
611.92 QM34
RB155
611.94 QM25
611.96 RG103
611.97 QM531
612 QM23
QM23.2
QP6
QP31.2
QP34
QP36
QP36.5
QP37
QP38
QP71
QP90.5
QP301
QP355.2
RB144
RT69
TL521.3.C6
612.0028 QP44
612.007 HQ35
612.0072 QM34
612.0076 QP40
612.00924 QP26.P8
QP26.Z6
612.01 QP77
612.014 QP82
612.01426 QP135
612.0144 GF51
QH543
QP1
RC1075.S53
612.014415 QP82.2.P7
612.01442 QH543
612.01444 QP481
612.01445 QP82.2.P7
612.014453 QP82.2.N6
612.01448 QH652
RA1231.R2
TL521
612.014486 TK9008
612.0145 RC1075
612.0145 TL521.3.C6
612.014532028 TL521.3.C6
612.01456 TL500
612.015 L136
QP90.5
QP93
QP521
QP551
QP671
QP701
QP801.A48
QP801.C33
QP903
QP981.F55
RB147
SK361
612.0151 QP601
612.01522 QP90.5
612.01543 QP751
612.01547 Q111
612.018 QP88
612.1 QP101
QP111
612.1028 RC74
612.11 QH585
QP92
QP94
RC633.A1
612.110222 QP94
612.111 QP96
612.1111 QP96
QP601
612.112 QP95
QR185.P5
612.115 QP93.5
RC633
612.117 QD1
QP91
QP97
612.118 QP101
612.1182 QH431
QP98
612.11822 QP98
QP551
QR180.3
QR181
QR182
QR185.C4
QR185.I5
RC633
612.11822024617 RC585
612.11825 QP98
RB45
612.12 QP99.3.P7
612.13 QP101
612.1302 QP101
612.13028 QP101
612.135 QP101
612.14 QP101
612.1825 RB145
612.2 PZ10.E4
QP121
QP121.A1
TL507
612.202461796 RD82
612.21 QM251
QP121
QP535.O1
612.215 QP121
612.22 QP121
612.3 PZ10.S637
QP26.S72
QP141
QP156
TX545
612.31 QP435
612.311 QM311
612.313 QP191
612.35 QP185
612.36 QP156
612.38 RM845
612.39 QP801.A65
QP801.S6
RG600
S445
612.392 QP141
612.3924 QP535.F4
612.397 TX560.F3
612.398 RC621
612.399 QP801.V5
RM259
612.4 QP187
QP187.A1
QP187.7.A1
RJ418
612.405 QP185
QP187
QP801.H7
RC649
612.44 QP188.T54
612.46 Q180.A1
612.461 QP211
R31
612.463 QP211
612.467 QM401
612.48336 TK9203.B6
612.492 QP188.P58
QP801.H7
612.5 QP135
612.57 QP171
612.591 QP82
612.592 QP82.2.T4
RC88.5
612.6 HQ16

Dewey	LC
612.6	HQ21
	HQ31
	HQ35
	HQ56
	HQ57
	PZ10
	PZ10.G75
	PZ10.H14729
	QP82.2.A4
	QP251
	QP255
	QP801.H7
	QP981.E7
	RG136
	RG137.5
	RG627
612.600207	PN6231.S54
612.6007	HQ21
	HQ34
	HQ35
	HQ46
	HQ51
	HQ53
	HQ56
	HQ57
	HQ57.3
	HQ57.5.A3
	HQ57.5.C3
	HQ57.5.M5
	HQ57.5.N5
	HQ59
612.60071	HQ35
	HQ57.3
612.6008	HQ21
612.61	QP255
	QP801.H7
	QP951
	RM296
612.62	HQ31
	QP261
	RG121
612.63	QM611
	QP281
	RG525
	RG558
	RG635
	RG652
612.64	QM601
612.640072	QM611
612.640183	RJ252
612.640192	QM611
612.646	QM601
612.647	RG600
	RG627
	RJ91
612.65	QP84
	QP801.H7
	RJ131
612.654	RJ131
	RJ252
612.6540212	RJ131
612.66	HQ57
612.661	RJ140
612.662	QP261
	QP265
612.664	QP246
612.665	HQ31
	RG186
612.67	HQ30
	HQ1061
	QP86
	QP88.2
612.7	BF481
	QP303
612.74	QP301
	QP321
612.75	PZ10.Z5
	QH652
	QM131
	QP88.2
	QP303
	RM849
612.76	GV481
	QP44
	QP301
	QP303
	QP311
	RC1200
	TL521.3.C6
612.760222	QP301
612.78	QP306
	QP461
612.79	PZ10.E4
	PZ10.W287
	RL87
612.791	QP82.2.U4
612.8	PZ10.B656
	QM451
	QP356.3
	QP361
	QP363
	QP376
	QP431
	QP441
612.8076	QP361
612.81	QP331
	QP363
	QP406
612.8116	QP361
612.813	QP341
	QP363
	R489.S44
612.816	TL521.3.C6
612.819	QP363
612.82	BD450
	QM455
	QP376
	QP398
612.821	QP426
	RC331
	RJ496.I6
612.822	QP376
	QP406
612.824	QP101
	QP376
612.824028	QP376
612.825	QP188.A28
	QP353
612.8255	QP475
612.826	QP376
612.827	QP379
612.84	PZ10
	QP475
	QP481
	RE46
	RE67
	RE79.E4
	RE952
	TL521.3.C6
612.846	QP476
	TL521.3.C6
612.85	QP461
	RF294
612.854	QP801.V5
612.858	QP471
	TL507
612.86	QP458
612.89	QM471
	QP368
612.902	TJ1189
613	QP36
	QP141
	QR56
	RA418.5.F3
	RA425
	RA431
	RA775
	RA776
	RA776.5
	RA777
	RA778
	RA781
	RA784
	RC480.5
	RT69
613.01	B491
613.02461073	RT67
613.07	LB3409.U6
	LB3409.U6C85
	RA440
	RA440.3.A4
	RA440.3.U5
	RA440.5
	RA440.9
613.071	RA440
613.0711	GV362
613.0712797	RA440.3.U5
613.0715	TX364
613.08	R708
613.0973	RA424
613.1	QH81
	QP82
	SK601
613.10973	HC110.E5
613.1209438	RA887.P6
613.120947	RA877.5
613.192	RA782
613.194	GV450
613.19409	GV450
613.2	KF27.I5568
	QP141
	RA784
	RC460
	RC628
	RC952.5
	RJ206
	RM216
	RM219
	RM237.9
	RM666.H55
	TX345
	TX353
	TX354
	TX355
	TX357
	TX551
613.25	RC628
	RM222.2
	RM226.5
	RM237.9
	TX360.U6
613.250207	RM222.2
613.26	TX392
613.315	S676
613.4	HV244
	PZ10.W728
	RD563
	RK61
	RK361
613.6	RA783.5
613.62	RA772.N7
	RC963.3
	RC964
	RC965.C43
	RC967
	RC969.P8
	T55.3.L5
613.6208	RC963
613.620942	RC963.7
613.6209591	HD7262.5.B8
613.6209749	RC965.A5
613.68	RC986
613.69	RC87
	UG633
613.7	B132.Y6
	GV14.5
	GV205
	GV207
	GV211
	GV224.A1
	GV225.V3
	GV288.F5
	GV333.B4
	GV341
	GV342
	GV343
	GV343.5
	GV361
	GV362
	GV363
	GV436
	GV439
	GV443
	GV445
	GV481
	GV482
	GV701
	L184
	LB1561.M6
	QP301
	RA776
	RA776.5
	RA781
	RA781.7
	RA790
613.70724	GV436
613.7077	GV361
613.71	GV461
	GV482
	GV489
	GV511
	GV1061
	RA776
	RA776.5
	RA778
	RA781
	RC682
	RC1235
613.78	RA778
	RA781
	RA781.5
613.79	RA790
613.8	HV5060
	HV5740
	HV5801
	PZ10.M4388
	RC566
613.807	HV5060
	HV5128.U5
	L116
613.80712	HV5060
613.81	HV5035
	HV5060
	HV5066
	KF27.I5568
	RC565
613.8107	HN79.M7
	HV5060
613.81071	HV5060
613.810712742	HV5060
613.810712776	HV5060
613.81077	HV5060
613.8109	HV5035
613.83	HV5800
	HV5801
	HV5816
	HV5822.A5
	HV5822.C3
	HV5822.L9
	HV5822.M3
	HV5825
	HV5840.C3
	KF26.L354
	KF32.5.C7
	RC566
	RM315
613.830208	HV5808.5
613.830222	HV5801
613.8303	HV5804
613.8307	HV5808
613.83071	HV5808
	KF26.L335
613.83071073	HV5808
613.830710783	HV5808
613.830712	HV5808
613.8308	HV5825
	RC566
613.830924	HV5825
613.830942	HV5840.G7
613.83094223	HV5840.G72L67
613.830971	HV5840.C3
613.830973	HV5825
	HV7571.C3
613.83097471	HV5833.N45
613.830974725	HV5831.N7
613.8309771	HV5831
613.8309797	HV5831.W2
613.8309931	HV5840.N44
613.8309969	HQ796
613.84	HV5800
613.85	HV5733
	HV5740
613.85	HV5748
	HV5751
	HV5760
	HV5770
	RA1242.T6
	RC567
613.8508	HV5745
613.9	RB155
613.92	RC570
613.93	QH431
	RB155
	RC620.5
	RC665
	RG626
	RJ520.P7
613.93025	QH431
613.9309973	RA395.S3
613.94	HQ766
	QH431
	QP251
613.943	HQ766
	RG136
	RG137.3
	RG137.5
613.9430711	HQ763.5
613.94309	RG136
613.9430924	HQ764.S3
	HQ766.5.U5
613.95	HQ5
	HQ31
	RC556
613.954	RG121
613.955	RG121
613.972	RJ61
613.973	RA564.5
	RA778
	RA776
613.977	RC451.4.S7
	RC952
613.979	RC952.5
614	RA8
	RA10
	RA393
	RA395.A3
	RA418
	RA422
	RA425
	RA427
	RA565
	RA569
	RA801
	RT97
	TX345
614.018	R856
	RA407.3
	RA409.
614.061797	R860
614.062747	RA121.K1
614.07	R728.8
614.07114	RA440.A1
	RA440.3.E
614.08	RA776.5
614.09174972	RA801
614.0922	R489.A1
614.0942	RA241
	RA485
614.0943	RA523.C9
614.09497	RA523.Y8
614.09498	RA523.R8
614.0954	AS9
	RA529
614.09542	RA530.M57
614.0954792	RA530
	RA530.M35
614.095496	RA751.N4
614.095694	RA751.I75
614.0967	RA784
614.096743	RA650.8.C5
614.0971	RA449
	RA565
614.09713	RA185.O5
614.0973	RA11
	RA410.7
	RA445
614.09744	RA447.M4
614.09752	RA410.8.M3
614.09753	RA447
614.0977193	RA448.B4
614.09773	RA447.I3
614.09774	RA447.M5
614.09789	RA447.N6
614.0979474	RA448.5.M4
614.09795	RA447.O7
614.120973	KF8802
614.14	RJ60.G7
614.140942	RA405.A1
614.2	KF26.D568
614.20973	KF2905.1
614.209753	KF27.D5644
614.30942	HD9000.9.G72
614.30971	TX355
614.30973	KF27.G663
614.31	HD9000.9.U5
	KF26.A3534
	KF27.A3327
	KF27.A365
	QR65
	RJ216
	TS1975
	TS1975.U59
	TX531
	TX533
	TX535
	TX537

Dewey	LC
614.31	TX571.P4
614.310973	KF27.A3327
614.32	SF254.R3
	SF259
614.33	S401
	TX553.A3
614.35	HD7273
	KF27.G663
	RM858
	RS189
614.350942	KF32.G6
614.37	KF26.C636
614.4	RA418
	RA425
	RA639
	RA642.3.W3
	RA969
	RC643
614.40182	RA409
614.408	RA422.5
614.42	RA409
614.42018	RA792
614.426743	RA949.C5
614.432	RA639.5
614.4322	RA641.F6
614.439	SF405.5
614.44	KF27.I55
	RA427
614.4409	RA424
614.48	QC770
	RA761
	RA962
614.49	HA37
	RA8
	RA649
	RA651
614.5	GB705.A8
	KF26.L354
614.50973	KF27.I5568
614.51	QR201.S25
	RA644.S15
614.511	TP368
614.521	RA8
614.532	RA644
614.542	RA644.T7
614.54209437	RC316.C95
614.542096762	RA644.T7
614.54209794	RA644.T7
614.547	HQ35
614.54707	RA644.V4
614.559	RC141.E8
614.58	RA440.9
	RA790
	RA790.A1
	RA790.5
	RA790.6
	RC574
614.58023	RA790.6
614.5807	LB3430
	RA790.6
614.580942	RA790.7.G7
614.580947	RA790.7.R9
614.58095	RA790.A
	RA790.A1
614.580973	RA790.6
614.580974461	RA790.65.M35
614.5809749	RA790.65.N5
614.5809752	RC445
614.5809755	RA790.65.V54
614.5809773	RA790.65.I4
614.5809777	RA790
614.5809781	RA790.65.K2
614.5809783	RA790.65.S8
614.58209	RC438
614.5824	RA790.5
614.58330973	RJ499
614.5846	RC969.P8
614.58467	RC969.P8
614.59123	RA645.H4
614.59136	RC692
614.5924	RA644.R4
614.59396	HD9007.N6
614.598	RC339.A2O44
614.59832	DT1
614.59851	RC389
614.59920973	RG960
614.5996	J87
	RA591.5
	RK11.G
	RK34.G7
	RK52
	Z6668
614.5996094	RK52
614.59960973	RK5
	RK52
614.5999	RC280.U8
	U15
614.6	GT3203
614.60942	GT3243
614.7	HC260.E5
	KF27.S383
	RA425
	RA569
614.7071173	KF26.L343
614.709492	RA505
614.7097471	RA447.N7
614.71	TD180
	TD883.1
614.710942	RA576
614.710974	KF31.J8
614.712	KF27
	KF31.J8
	RC965.M5
	TD885.5.S8
614.712	UG447
614.715	RA569
614.7150973	HD9698.U52
614.75	RA569
614.76	KF26.C645
	KF26.C663
	KF26.P825
	KF27.G636
614.772	GC1085
	KF26.I534
	QR105
	RA591
	TD763
614.7720973	KF26.P825
	KF27.G636
	KF32.G6
614.78	RA772.N7
	TD892
	TL725.3.N6
614.79	RA605
	RA969
614.791	TX945
614.799	RA615.1
614.8	G510
	HV675
	HV675.5
	HV676
	KF26.C636
	KF27.B344
	KF32.G6
	QD51
	S155
	TX150
614.8019	TL152.3
614.8028	T55
614.807	HV675
614.81	GV837
614.83	RA766.E8
	T55
	TP149
614.830973	KF27.G663
614.831	S21
	TS1449
614.836	RA965
	TK152
614.839	HD7269.A6
	HD7269.A62
	HD9698.U52
	KF27.I5568
	QC475
	QC770
	QC795
	RA565.A1
	RA569
	RA1231.R2
	RC78
	RC965.R25
	RM849
	TK9152
614.8390973	KF27.D5644
614.84	TH9120
	TH9148
	TH9310.5
614.8408	TH9111
	TH9115
614.840973	KF3975
614.84107	TH9124.T4
614.843	TH9310.5
614.843028	TH9114
614.84409749	KFN2181
614.847	KF32.E3
	TH9445.H7
	TH9445.T3
614.85	HD7262
	HD7269.T72I44
	HD7273
	JK1651.M4
	KF26.D568
	KF26.L363
	KF27.E343
	KF27.E345
	RA965
	RC963.7.G
	SD387.S3
	T55
	T55.A1
	TK152
	TS1630
614.850715	HD7262.5.G7
614.8509713	HD7262.5.C3
614.850973	KF26.L363
	KF3570
614.8509863	HD7265.5.C33
614.8509941	T55
614.852	HD7269.C452U5
	T55.3.L5
614.853	TX150
614.86	TA1005
	TL553.8
614.860973	HE18
	HE5614.2
614.860994	HE289
614.862	HE5614
	HE5614.2
	HE5614.5.C2
	HE5620.D7
	HF5548.8
	J87
	RA1061
	TL152.35
614.862072	TL158
614.862097124	HE5614.5.C2
614.86209715	TL152.66.C2
614.8620973	HE5606
614.8620973	HE5614.2
	KF26.P868
	KF27.I5536
	KF27.P8
614.8620974461	HE5614.4.B6
614.86209787	HE5614.3.W9
614.86209794	HE5614.3.C3
614.86209797	HE5614.3.W2
614.8620994	HE5614
614.863	HE1762
	HE1779
	HE1783.G7
	KF31.I55
614.8630973	KF26.C688
	KF27.I5587
614.864	KF27.M436
	KF32.G6
	VK1057
	VK1257.V3
	VK1359
	VK1473
614.864094267	VK1357
614.869	HE9784
	HE9784.5.U5
	TL553.5
	UC273
614.875	GB459.4
	RA645.5
614.877	KF27.E345
614.88	HV575
	HV675.5
	RC87
615	RM101
	RM300
	RM301
	RS53
	RS91
615.06273	RM1
615.09	RS158
615.1	HV5801
	HV5825
	R852
	RM84
	RM101
	RM267
	RM300
	RM315
	RM332
	RS55
	RS67.C4
	RS91
	RS122
	RS189
615.1014	RS356
615.101511	RS57
615.10154128	RS122
615.10202	RM122
	RM301
615.1023	RS122.5
615.102461073	RM125
615.1024613	RM300
615.10285	RS80
615.103	RS51
615.106273	RS1.A37
	RS1.R75
615.1062749	RS1.N519
615.1071173	RS110
615.10971	RS67.C4
615.10973	HD7103.5.U5
	RS67.U6
	RS250
615.11	RS125
615.1154	RS141.68
615.1194	RS141.8
615.13794	RS55
615.14	RM139
	RM145
615.19	HV5801
	HV5825
	QL737.P9
	RM301
	RS122
	RS189
	RS192
	RS421
	TP248.E5
615.19015	RS441
615.191	TP955
615.1910272	RS421
615.3	QP905
	RM175
	RM315
	RS160
615.313	RM666.A82
615.3142	RC628
615.32	RS441
	RX76
615.321	BF1623.R7
	E99.M44
	QK99
	RS164
	RS180.I5
615.32312	HV5816
	RM666.A4
615.32374	RM666.C94
615.3238	RM666.D5
615.323962	HV5822.M3
615.328	RM666.A79
	TP248.C93
	TP248.T55
615.329	RM267
615.32923	RM666.E8
	RS165.P38
	TP248.P43
615.32992	RM666.T3
	RS431.T4
615.35	RS190.E5
615.36	QP91
	RM291.5
615.364	RM292
615.365	QP99.3.P7
615.37	QR181
	RM279
615.372	QR189
	RC261
615.373	QP631
	QP941
615.39	RM171
615.4	RA975.5.P5
	RS91
615.40151	RS57
615.4023	RS122.5
615.40624274	RS67.G
615.43	RS201.D4
	RS201.P5
615.5	QP90
	RC48
	RM107
	RM265
615.501	AS122
615.533	RZ315
	RZ341
615.534	RZ242
	RZ255
615.5340924	RZ236
615.535	RZ440
615.537	RS164
615.6	RM101
615.63	RD78.3
	RM149
	RM170
615.63028	RA10
615.64	RM161
615.65	RB45
	RM171
	RM172
	RM175
615.6500924	PZ10.B29522535
615.6507	RM171
	RM172
615.7	RC90
	RC903
	RE48
	RM101
	RM103
	RM300
	RM301
	RS189
	RS402
	RS403
615.7042	RE48
615.71	QP551
	QP601
	RC683.5.B3
	RM345
615.711	RC684.G5
	RM666.D5
615.716	RM666.M54
615.718	RM340
615.739	QP751
	RM293
615.766	RG137.5
615.78	RA1190
	RC483
	RE48
	RM315
	RM323
615.781	RD81
	RD82
615.782	RC566.A1
	RM666.B3
615.785	RM323
	RM332
615.788	RM666.M43
615.788208	Z6665.A57
615.7883	BF209.L9
	HV5822.L9
	QP921.L9
	RC483.5.L9
	RM315
615.8	RC388.5
	RM700
	RM701
	RM930
615.82	RJ138
	RM701
	RM721
615.822	RM721
615.824	RM725
615.836	RC49
	RM161
	RM666.O8
	RM666.O83
	RZ999
615.8360202	RM161
615.837	ML3920
	RJ505.M8
615.84	RM849
	RM871
615.842	R895
	RM847
615.84208	RM859
	RM859.A1
615.8423	RM859
615.851	B819
	BF1275.F3
	RC49
	RC480

Dewey	LC
615.851	RZ999
615.8512	RC495
	RC497
	RC498
615.8515	RM735
615.8515023	RM735
615.8515076	RM735
615.852	BJ1470
	BT732.5
	RZ400
	RZ401
615.85207	BT732.5
615.8520924	RZ408.T47
615.853	RM813
	RM822.M9
615.854	RA776.5
	RC82
	RM178
	RM216
	RM219
	RM237
	RZ600
615.856	RC81
	RZ460
615.88	RS164
615.882	AG105
	R133
	RS164
615.8820942	R702
615.882094234	DA670.G9G85
615.8820959	R581
615.88209748	R133
615.88209764	R133
615.886	RC82
615.89	GN1
615.8909701	E98.M4
615.9	RA569
	RA1211
	RA1213
	RA1216
	RA1221
	RA1238
615.9.00202	RA1221
615.90019	QP941
615.900202	RA1211
615.9007	RA1196
615.902	RA1213
	RA1216
615.9072	QP941
615.91	Q11
	RA1247.C17
	RA1247.M3G7
615.92	RA1231.R2
615.9253	RA1231.M52
615.925731	RA1231.F55
615.95	RC143
615.9511	RA1242.B4
615.95233	RA1242.C84
616	R117
	R130.5
	R135
	R852
	RA11
	RA418
	RA1056.5
	RB111
	RB112
	RB131
	RB132
	RB151
	RB155
	RC39
	RC46
	RC55
	RC60
	RC73
	RC78.7.A7
	RC81
	RC332
	RC460
	RC547
	RC548
	RC941
	RD768
	RJ496.S7
	RJ550
616.0028	R895
616.01	QR46
	QR57
	QR63
616.0102461073	QR46
616.014	QR1
	QR46
	QR82.M93
	QR82.S8
616.01402461073	QR46
616.0142	QR82.M9
616.015	QR145
616.016	RC118.5
	RC119
616.016028	RC117
616.0194	QR360
	RC114.5
616.02	RC48
	RC86
	RC87
616.0212	RC81
616.024	R121
	RC81
	RC82
	RC87
616.025	RC87
616.026	R729.5.G4
	RB37
616.026	RB40
	RC46
	RC48
	RC58
	RC60
616.0260202	RB37
	RC55
616.02603	RC81
616.042	RB155
	RJ506.M4
616.07	QP87
	R117
	R135
	RB25
	RB48
	RB111
	RB113
	RB119
	RB121
	RB151
	RB153
	RB155
	RC113
	RC584
	RC585
	RC586
616.071	RB151
616.072	RB127
	RB131
	RC69
	RC268.5
	RC815
	RC944
	RE65
	RE79
	RL100
616.07203	RC82
616.075	RA642.2
	RB37
	RB48
	RC69
	RC71
	RC71.3
	RC76
	RC78.7.I5
	RE65
	TL152.35
616.075018	RC71.3
616.07502436	RC80
616.07502461073	RC71.8
616.075028	RC71
616.0754	RC65
	RC76
	RC78.7.U4
	RC815
616.0755	RB37
616.07550202	RB37
616.0756	RB36
	RB37
	RB40
	RB48
	RS403
616.0756028	RB37
616.075608	RB40
616.07561	RB45
616.07566	RB53
616.0757	R895
	RC78
	RM847
	RM849
616.0757014	RM849
616.0757023	RC78
616.075703	RM849
616.075706273	RM845
616.07572	PZ10.W43
	R852
	RC78
	RC78.5
	RC78.7.T6
616.07572028	RC78.5
616.07575	R895
	RC78.7.R4
	RM845
	RM847
616.075750222	RC78.7.R4
616.07582	RC78.7.C9
616.07583	RC78.7.C9
616.079	RC584
616.08	RC49
616.080926	RC506
616.1	RC667
	RC669
	RC672
	RC674
	RD598
616.100724	RC669
616.105	RC672
616.106	RC681.A1
616.10754	RC683
616.12	RA791
	RC672
	RC681
	RC681.A2
	RC682
	RC685.I6
	RC685.M9
	RC687
	RD598
	RM666.P85
616.12061	RC685.C6
	RM666.T65
616.120645	RC684.P3
616.120654	RC672
616.12075	RC683
616.120754	RC681.A2
	RC683.5.B3
	RC683.5.E5
616.1207540285	RC683.5.E5
616.1207572	RC683.5.R3
	RC687
616.123	RA645.H4
	RC669
	RC681
	RC685.C6
	RC685.I6
616.12306	RA975.5.C6
616.128	RC685.A65
616.1280754	RC685.A65
616.13	RC691
	RC693
616.131	RC691
	RC694
	RC694.5
616.132	RC672
	RC681
	RC685.H8
616.135	RC685.C6
	RC694.3
616.136	RC692
	RG692
616.136008	RC692
616.14	RC695
616.15	QP91
	RB45
	RB145
	RC147.G6
	RC633
	RC633.A1
	RC636
	RC641.7.H35
	RG572
	RM221.C3
616.1500222	RC636
616.15008	RC633
	RC633.A1
616.15075	RB45
	RB145
616.1507582	QP94
616.152	QP91
	RC641.7.H4
	RC641.7.H9
	RC641.7.I7
	RC641.7.M4
616.15407	TL507
616.155	RC261
	RC643
616.1550072	RC643
616.15500724	RC643
616.15500924	RJ416.L4
616.155061	RC643
616.157	QP93.5
	RC633
	RC642
	RC647.B6
616.2	QP913.N2
	RC705
	RC731
	RC732
	RC736
	RC941
616.2004622	RC87
616.2020654	RM221.A6
616.20309041	RC150.4
616.205061	RM666.A79
616.21	RE11
	RF16
	RF46
616.2100202	RF56
616.2100222	RF81
616.2100621	RF1.C63
616.2107572	RF48
616.212	RF421
616.22	RF517
616.220757	RF512
616.23	RC591
	RC736
	RC778
	RF1
616.24	HD7260
	RC685.C55
	RC711
	RC732
	RC776
	RC776.F8
	RC776.P8
	TL521.3.C6
616.24075	RC733
616.240754	QP121
616.240756	RC733
616.2407572	RC734.R3
616.2407575	RC734.R35
616.244	RC773
	RC774
616.246	RC311.1
616.248	RC685.C55
	RC776.E5
616.24806	RC776.E5
616.24807	RC732
616.3	RC799
	RC801
	RC803
	RC806
616.3075	RC803
616.30754	RC804.E6
616.307572	RC804.R6
616.307582	RC803
616.308	RC801
616.31	RC815
616.31	RK301
	RK307
616.310757	RK309
616.32	RC815.7
616.33024613	RC802
616.33075	RC803
616.3307575	RC804.R6
616.34	QR82.E6
	RC804.R6
	RC862
	RC862.D6
	RD1
	RD542
616.340757	RC804.R6
616.342	RC862.M3
	RJ23
616.343	QM345
	RC857
616.3433061	RC824
616.344	RC862.C6
	RC862.E5
616.35	RC864
	RC865
616.36	RC849
616.362	RC845
	RC847
	RC848.H4
616.3620072	QP185
616.362075	RC847
616.3620755	RC847
616.36207575	RC847
616.3623	RB125
616.3624	RM298.P5
616.37	RC857
616.38	RB144
616.39	QP801.V5
	RB144
	RB147
	RC627.P7
616.396	RA10
616.398	RC628
616.399	DA506.A2
	RC620.A1
	RC620.5
	RC629
	RC632.A5
	RC632.G3
	RC632.H87
	RJ399.P5
616.4	RB48.5
	RC48
	RC648
616.42	RC261
	RC280.L9
	RC644
	RC646
616.44	RB145
	RC655
	RC656.A1
616.44075	RC655
616.442	RA10
616.44400184	Q180
616.45	RC659
616.4507	RC659
616.462	RC660
	RC660.A1
	RE661.D5
616.462002461	RC660
616.4620072	RC660
616.4620212	RC660
616.462061	RC660
616.462075	RC660
616.466	RC662.2
616.5	RC592
	RC961.5
	RL71
	RL74
	RL110
	RL201
	RL301
	RL765
616.500202	RL74
616.50202	RL74
616.5061	RL801
616.5210019	RC585
616.546	Q57
	RL91
616.6	AS281
	RA645.K5
	RB53
	RC78
	RC556
	RC871
	RC872
	RC874.7
	RC882
616.6002461073	RC874.7
616.61	RC901.7.A7
	RC902
	RC903
	RC905
	RJ476.G5
616.610077	RC902
616.610654	RC903
	RM221.U7
616.6107	RC902.A1
	RC905
616.61075	RC904
616.62	QP251
	RC918.U5
616.62075	RC920
616.622	RC916
	RC921.V4
616.62206	RM1

616.63075 ... RC905
616.6350754 ... RC915
616.7 ... RC925
... RC933
616.71 ... RC261
... RC930
... RC931.O75
... RD684
616.710757 ... RC930
616.7107572 ... RC78
616.712 ... RC931
... RD684
616.72 ... RC927
... RC933
... RC933.A1
616.720622 ... RM719
616.720654 ... RC933
616.720754 ... RC932
616.7207572 ... RC933
616.73 ... R141
... RD533
... RD768
616.730757 ... RC400
616.74 ... RC925
... RC933.A1
616.740754 ... RC77.5
616.742 ... RC927
616.742062 ... RC927
616.744 ... RC935.M8
616.748 ... RC935.M7
616.798 ... RC154
616.8 ... QP87
... QP406
... RB155
... RC326
... RC327
... RC340
... RC341
... RC343
... RC346
... RC347
... RC348
... RC349.E5
... RC358
... RC385
... RC386
... RC386.5
... RC400
... RC429
... RC455
... RC483
... RC600
... RC936
... RD595
616.809 ... RC338
616.80922 ... R134
616.80924 ... R154.M66
616.8094285 ... RC343
616.81 ... RC386.2
... RC388.5
... RC423
... RC693
616.81062 ... RC388.5
616.810757 ... RC386.5
616.8107572 ... RC386.5
... RC388.5
616.8107575 ... RC388
... RC388.5
616.83 ... RB112
... RC385
... RC394.P7
... RC627.L5
616.83075 ... RC386.5
616.832 ... RA44
616.833 ... RC382
616.833061 ... RC382
616.835009 ... RC180.9
616.836 ... RC388.5
616.837 ... RC406.P3
616.841 ... RF260
616.842 ... RC343
616.849 ... RC547
616.85 ... BF697
... RC530
... RC562
... RC574
616.852 ... RC541
616.8522 ... BF575.A6
... RC49
... RC531
... RC535
616.8523 ... RC394.A5
616.8528 ... RC537
... RC552.N5
616.853 ... RC372
... RC372.A1
616.85307 ... RC372
616.855 ... RA790.65.C2
... RC332
... RC394
... RC423
... RC428.5
... RJ496.S7
616.8552 ... RC425
616.855200924 ... RC425
616.8554 ... RC424
616.855406 ... RC424
616.857 ... RC392
616.858 ... RC331
... RC552.H8
616.8583 ... RC555
... RC557
... RC560.C4
616.8583065 ... RC488.5
616.85834 ... RC558
616.85839 ... RC557
616.85844 ... HV6545
... RA790
... RC537
616.8588 ... HC110.P6
... RC386.2
... RC570
616.858809795 ... RC570
616.85884 ... RC386.2
... RC570
... RC1220.B6
616.858842 ... RC571
616.86 ... RC566
616.861 ... HV5035
... HV5292
... KF26.L354
... RC526
... RC565
616.86106 ... RC565
616.861061 ... RC565
616.863 ... KF27.5.C7
... RC566
616.865 ... RC567
616.87 ... RC412
616.870754 ... RC348
616.8707572 ... RC386.5
616.88 ... RC332
616.89 ... AS6
... BF173
... BF723.P25
... BF1078
... E99.M77
... R727.3
... RA790.5
... RC327
... RC331
... RC332
... RC337
... RC340
... RC343
... RC344
... RC356
... RC445
... RC451.4.P7
... RC451.4.S7
... RC454
... RC455
... RC457
... RC458
... RC460
... RC463
... RC464.B45
... RC465
... RC467
... RC480
... RC480.5
... RC481
... RC489.M67
... RC504
... RC509
... RC512
... RC528.T6
... RC534
... RJ503
... UH629
616.89001 ... RC455
616.8900202 ... RC457
616.890023 ... RC458
616.890024361 ... RC454
616.890028 ... RC336
616.89003 ... RC437
616.890071173 ... RC336
616.890072 ... RC337
616.89008 ... RC344
... RC435
... RC454
... RC455
... RC458
616.8900924 ... R154.P42
616.8900973 ... RC438
... RC443
616.8900994 ... RC438
616.89018 ... RC445.C2C35
616.8902 ... RC455
616.89023 ... RC335
616.8902461073 ... RC440
616.8903 ... RC437
616.8907 ... RC336
616.89072 ... RC423
616.89075 ... RC454
... RC467
... RC469
616.8908 ... RC458
616.8909 ... RC438
616.89092 ... RC465
616.890922 ... D107
616.890924 ... R154.N85
... R507.P5
616.8909752 ... RC445
616.891 ... BF637.C6
... RC443
... RC451.A82N43
... RC480
... RC480.5
... RC481
... RC488.5
... RC489.B4
... RC489.G4
... RJ505.B4
616.8910947 ... RC475
616.8913 ... RM719
616.8914 ... RC480
616.8914 ... RC480.5
616.891408 ... RC480
616.8915 ... RC331
... RC451.5.N4
... RC488
... RC488.5
... RC489.P7
... RJ503
616.8916 ... RC331
... RC480.5
... RC489.B4
616.89162 ... RC535
616.89165 ... RC455
616.89166 ... RC489.P6
... Z5814.R25
616.8917 ... BF173
... BF173.F85
... RC480.5
... RC489.B4
... RC501
... RC504
... RC506
... RC508
... RC509
... RC530
616.89170207 ... PN6231.P78
616.891707 ... RC502
616.891708 ... BF173
... RC454
... RC509
616.89170924 ... RC506
616.89170926 ... RC506
... RC509
616.8918 ... RM315
... RM666.L57
616.895 ... RC331
... RC483
... RC516
... RC537
616.895061 ... RM666.L57
616.897 ... RC520
616.898 ... RC514
616.8982 ... RC514
616.898200924 ... RC514
616.8982061 ... RC514
616.8982065 ... RC514
616.898207 ... RC514
616.8982092 ... RC514
616.8983 ... RC524
616.9 ... PZ10.T7
... RB37
... RC111
616.909 ... RC112
616.90942 ... RC110
616.912075 ... RC183
616.92 ... RB37
... RC114
... RC114.5
616.92061 ... RM262
616.921 ... RC137
616.922 ... QL461
616.92320094 ... RC172
616.926 ... RA10
616.927 ... RC143
616.9272061 ... RA644
616.9289 ... RJ499
616.931 ... RC203.5
616.9318 ... RC185
616.9362 ... RA644.M2
616.9362009595 ... RC164.M25
616.9362061 ... RC159.A5
616.9362075 ... RA10
616.951 ... RC200
... RC200.2
616.9510077 ... RA644.V4
616.95100973 ... RC201.5.A2
616.95107 ... RA644.V4
616.9510756 ... RC200.S4
616.9513 ... RC201
... RC201.7.N4
616.95130756 ... RC201.2
616.95150756 ... QR201.G7
616.96 ... QL392
... RC119
616.96075 ... RC119.7
616.963 ... RC182.S24
616.964 ... RC136.7
... RC184.T6
616.9652 ... RC142.5
616.9654 ... QL391.N4
... RC121
... RC186.T815
616.968 ... QL503.A6
... QL757
616.969 ... RC117
... RC120
616.97 ... RC583
... RC584
... RC585
616.973 ... RC585
... RL251
616.97300724 ... RC592
616.975 ... RM666.P35
616.98021 ... RC1050
... RC1058
... RC1075
616.9802108 ... RC1050
616.980213 ... RC1062
616.980214 ... RC1058.S6
... RC1077
... Z663.23
616.98022 ... RC1005
... RC1220.D5
616.98023 ... RC971
616.9802309 ... RC971
616.980230973 ... RC971
616.98024 ... RC986
616.98399 ... RJ390
616.988 ... R126.H6
616.9883 ... RC960
... RC961
... RC961.5
616.9894 ... TL500
616.9897 ... RA569
... RA1231.R2
... RC93
616.9897061 ... RA1231.R2
616.991 ... RC182.R4
... RC927
616.992 ... RC254.5
... RC255
... RC258
... RC261
... RC262
... RC269
... RC280.B6
... RC280.B7
... RC280.B8
... RC280.M3
... RC280.N4
... RC280.S3
... RC649
... RD661
... RD663
616.9920012 ... RC258
616.9920072 ... RC254.5
616.9920708 ... RD651
616.99207575 ... RC255
616.99261 ... RC280.K5
616.99281 ... RD663
616.99285 ... RC280.E2
616.993 ... RC261
... RD661.N6
616.994 ... RB43
... RC254.5
... RC261
... RC263
... RC265
... RC268.5
... RC269
... RC270
... RC271
... RC271.R3
... RC274
... RC276
... RC277.N8
... RG591
616.9940072 ... RC267
616.99400724 ... RC267
616.99400924 ... RC263
616.9940096 ... RC279.A38
616.994009756 ... RC277.N8
616.99400979465 ... RC277.C3
616.99406 ... RC261
... RC262
... RC271.E4
616.994061 ... QP981.A7
... RC261
... RC262
... RC271.C5
616.9940654 ... RC263
616.99407 ... RC267
... RC268.5
... RC269
616.994071 ... RC268.55
616.994075 ... RC270
616.9940754 ... RC270
616.994220642 ... RC280.T5
616.99423 ... RC280.B9
616.99424 ... RC280.L8
616.9943 ... RC280.A4
... RD1
616.99431 ... RC280.M6
616.99433 ... RC261
616.994330924 ... RC263
616.994347 ... RC280.C6
616.99435 ... RD544
616.99436 ... RC261
616.9944 ... RC261
... RC280.E55
616.99442 ... RC261
616.99444 ... RC280
... RC280.T6
... RD1
616.99449 ... RC261
... RC280.B8
616.9946 ... RC280.G5
616.99462 ... RC280.B5
616.99465 ... RC280.G5
616.99466 ... RA44
... RC280.U8
616.994718 ... RC280.U8
616.99477 ... RD655
616.99481 ... RC280.B7
616.9949 ... RC280.H4
616.99491 ... RD661
... RF1
616.995 ... RC307
... RC311
... RC313
616.995008 ... RC261
616.995061 ... RC311.3.C45
616.99542 ... RC643
616.995711 ... RC312.5.S6
616.998 ... RC154
... RC154.A1
... RC154.1

Dewey	LC
616.998	RC154.6.D4
617	QA303
	RC961.5
	RD1
	RD11
	RD31
	RD31.5
	RD37
	RD51
617.00202	RD16
	RD32
	RD37
617.002461073	RD99
617.0028	R895
	RD23
	RD73.A3
617.003	RD17
617.005	RD1
617.007	RD28
	RK71
617.0071	R489
	R489.A1
617.0071173	R745
617.008	RD1
	RD39
617.00924	R489.L4
617.01	RD1
	RM170
617.075	RD35
617.0924	R154.B26
	R154.G45
	R154.L72
	R154.N68
	R489.P28
	R608.S4
	RD598
617.1	RC87
	RC963.3
	RD30
	RD93
	RD521
	RD523
	RD536
	RD562
	RD594.3
617.1002461073	RT42
617.100922	RD131
617.1027	GV1789
	RC1200
	RC1210
	RC1220.B6
	RC1220.K3
	RD131
617.1028	HE5614.2
	HE5614.3.W5
	RC87
	RD96.6
	RZ242
617.11	RC90
	RD131
617.124	U408.3
617.14	RD58
	RD131
	RD536
	RD701
617.15	RD101
617.150724	RD701
617.156	RD526
	RE831
617.2	RD521
617.21	RB150.S5
	RD93.8
617.22	RB131
617.3	RD731
	RD732
	RD733
617.300922	RD726.U5
617.307	RD756
617.3075	RD734
617.307572	RD734
617.309	RD725
617.375	RJ482.S3
617.39	RD775
	TJ1
617.398025	RD553
617.41	QP101
	RD598
617.412	RC685.C6
	RD598
617.4120028	RC684.A7
617.41209	RD598
617.41209045	RD598
617.4120922	RD598
617.413	RD598
617.43	RD540
617.4300222	RD540
617.46	RD571
617.461	Q180
	RC901.7.A7
	RD591
	RJ466
617.462	RD581
617.472	RC933
617.477	RD520
617.48	RD593
	RD594
617.481	RC347
	RC372
	RD137
	RD594
617.48201	RD594.3
617.483	RC821
617.51	RD521
	RF46
617.52	RD523
	TS227
617.522	RC815
	RD523
	RK301
617.523	RF51
617.533	RF16
617.5395	RD1
617.54	RC941
	RD536
617.54075	RC941
617.544	RD539
617.55	RC944
	RD131
	RD540
	RD546
	RG39
	RG104
	RJ456.A3
617.55075	RC944
617.553	RD540
	RD540.5
617.55301	RD540.5
617.554	RD1
617.554509	RD542
617.5547	RC862.C6
	RD543.C6
	RD544
617.556	RD547
617.559	RD621
617.57	RD557
	RD559
	RD776
	TJ1
617.58	JX1977
	RD756
617.585	RC951
	RD563
617.5850711	RD563
617.6	RA505
	RK50
	RK51
	RK51.5
	RK52
	RK58
	RK60.5
	RK61
	RK63
	RK66
	RK305
	RK308
	RK309
	RK501
	RK701
	TR708
	VG283
617.60014	TA368
617.60023	HF5381.A1
	RK60
617.600246106953	UG633
617.60024610730698	RK60.5
617.60028	RK652
617.60062713	RK34.C3
617.60062757	RK1.S655
617.6007	RK227
617.60076	RK57
617.6009	RK29
617.601	RK61
617.601019	RK53
617.6023	RK227
617.6071171	RK98
617.630757	RK309
617.6307572	RK309
617.630942	RK34.G72
617.632	RK61
	RK281
	RK361
617.6320014	RK28
617.63207572	RK309
617.634	QD1
	RK307
	RK331
	RK351
617.63407	RK307
617.64	RK501.5
617.643	RK521
	RK523
	RK527
617.6430028	RK528.M4
617.6430976	RK5.S87
617.645	RK55.C5
	RK502
617.66	RK531
617.67	RK52
	RK501
617.675	RK652.5
617.69	RK656
617.692	RK1
	RK651
	RK656
	RK666
617.69209	RK641
617.695	RK652.5
617.7	RC1045.V5
	RE11
	RE46
	RE48
	RE51
	RE61
	RE65
	RE72
	RE79.U4
	RE80
	RE91
617.7	RE991
	RE994
617.70028	RE78
617.7008	RE1
617.7075	RE75
617.707572	RE65
617.708	RE61
617.70924	R674.G9
617.71	RE75
	RE80
	RE87
	RE96
	RE720
	RE835
	RE994
617.710222	RE79.B5
617.712	RE91
617.7120014	Q180.A1
617.7120709485	RE91
617.7120973	RA407.3
617.713	RE831
617.719	RE336
	RE906
617.72	RE351
617.73	RE79.R3
	RE80
	RE545
	RE551
	RE661.D5
617.730757	RE992.P5
617.74	RE48
617.741	RE80
	RE871
617.741075	RE871
617.742	RE451
617.746	RE501
617.75	RE925
	RE951
	RE961
617.75023	RE959
617.750624	RE30
617.752	RE962
	RE977.C6
617.7523	RE79.B5
	RE977.C6
617.755	QP476
	RE925
	RE927
617.759	RE921
617.762	RE731
	RE771
617.7622	RE925
617.771	RE155.B5
617.78	RE831.S9
617.8	RC963.3
	RF1
	RF135
	RF291
617.83	RF16
617.84	RF126
617.88	RF270
617.89	QC100
	RF294
	RF300
617.9	RA972
617.91	RD32
	RD32.3
	RD37
	RD58
617.9101	RD540
617.917	RD63
617.919	RA975
	RD58
617.95	QH431
	RC901.7.A7
	RD21
	RD118
	RD119
	RD120.7
	RD129
	RD546
	RK652.5
617.9500924	R489.M19
617.9507	RD123.5
617.9512	RD598
617.9513	RD598
617.9521	RD119
617.9531	RD523
617.9534	RD120.7
617.9536	RD546
617.9561	RC901.7.A7
	RD575
617.95716	RD526
617.9584	RE87
617.9585	RF126
617.9597	RD118
617.96	RD78.3
	RD79
	RD81
	RD82
	RD86.H3
	RG732
	RK501.5
	RK510
617.9602461073	RD81
	RT65
617.96072	RD82
617.9608	RD81.A1
617.960924	RD80.M9
617.962	RD81.A1
617.966	RD84
617.96609	RD84
617.98	RD137
617.98002461073	RD137
617.990072	RC971
618	RG101
	RG121
	RG123
	RG129.H6
618.006271	RG1
618.0202	RG103
618.02461073	RG105
618.1	RG1
	RG67.A8
	RG79
	RG101
	RG104
	RG106
618.1061	RG129
618.107	RG77
618.10754	RG39
618.107582	RG107.5.E9
618.1407582	RG310
618.15	RG104
618.17	RG103
618.172	RG163
	RG444
	RG761
618.178	RC889
	RG201
618.1907572	RG493
618.2	QM421
	RC48
	RG31
	RG520
	RG524
	RG525
	RG531
	RG556
	RG560
	RG950
	RJ60.G
618.2003	RG45
618.20076	RG531
618.22	RG527
618.24	RG500
	RG525
618.240207	RG525
618.240924	D36
	RG525
618.3	RG525
	RG571
	RG572
	RG627
618.32	RG600
	RG626
	RG627
	RG631
	RJ270
618.33019	RG734
618.397	RG649
618.4	RG525
	RG652
	RG661
618.4077	RG652
618.45	RG525
	RG652
	RG661
618.89	BF723.P3
	RC454
618.89009	RC438
618.92	RA564
	RD757.S45
	RE48.2.C5
	RE76
	RE925
	RE952
	RF122.5.C4
	RJ45
	RJ47
	RJ47.5
	RJ50
	RJ51.R3
	RJ59
	RJ61
	RJ71
	RJ101
	RJ131
	RJ496.A5
	RJ496.C4
	RJ496.D4
	RJ560
618.92000202	RJ48
618.920003	KJ26
	RJ26
618.920024	RJ47
618.920075	RJ50
618.9200754	RJ131
618.9200756028	RJ33
618.92007572	RJ51.R3
618.9201	RG626
	RJ251
	RJ252
	RJ253
618.92097522	RD523
618.92097741	RE871
618.9210012	RB115
618.9212	RC687
	RJ421
618.9213	QM261
618.9215	RJ270
	RJ411
618.922	RJ274
	RJ431
618.9224	RJ431
618.92307572	RJ51.R3
618.92342	RC862.M35
618.9239	RJ390

Dewey	LC
618.92398	RJ399.C6
618.92399	RJ390
618.924	RJ418
618.92462	RJ420.D5
618.925	RJ511
618.926	RJ466
618.92661	RC918.P9
618.92671	RJ480
618.9272	RJ520.R5
618.928	RJ255
	RJ486
618.92836	RJ496.C4
618.9283606	RJ496.C4
618.92855	RJ496.S7
	RJ499
618.9285506	RJ496.S7
618.928552	RC394.W6
	RJ496.S7
618.9285540019	RJ496.S7
618.92855406	RC427
	RJ496.S8
618.92858	RJ499
618.928588	ML3920
618.92858800973	RJ499
618.9285880926	RJ499
618.9285884	RC570
	RJ486
	RJ499
	RJ506.M4
618.92858843	RJ486
618.9289	RJ486
	RJ499
	RJ499.A1
	RJ503
	RJ504
	RJ506.A9
	Z6671.5
618.9289008	RJ499
618.928900973	RJ501.A2
618.9289092	RJ503
618.92891	LB1137
	RC489.B4
	RJ504
	RJ504.5
618.928915	RJ505.P6
618.928982	RJ506.A9
	RJ506.S3
618.92898200924	RJ506.S3
618.92898200926	RJ506.A9
618.92898206	RJ506.S3
618.928982092	RJ499
618.9297	RJ399.A4
618.929883	RC961.5
618.92992	RC281.C4
618.92995	RC312.6.C4
618.97	RA776.5
	RC451.4.A5
	RC528.S9
	RC682
	RC952
	RC952.5
	RF300
618.97007	HQ1060
618.97061	RC953.5
619	QH324.4
	QL55
620	GC1020
	QA402
	T50
	T55
	T57.85
	T212
	TA5
	TA140.F9
	TA147
	TA155
	TA157
	TA165
	TA168
	TA174
	TA192
	TA340
	TA345
	TA348
	TA349
	TA350
	TA357
	TA368
	TA410
	TA418.74
	TA705
	TA1205
	TC1505
	TC1645
	TC1660
	TJ840
	TK7870
	TL521.3.C6
	TL789.8.U5
	TS156.Q3
	TS171.A1
	TS173
	TS174
	UG465.5
620.00151	TA330
620.001512896	TA347.D4
620.0018	TA345
620.00182	T57.35
620.00184	TA167
	TA340
620.00212	TA151
620.0023	TA157
620.0025781	TA157
620.0028	TA152
620.0028	TA165
	TJ1313
	TL521
620.0045	TS174
620.0065	TR706
620.00711	AS4.U8
	T65.3
620.0071142	T107
620.0071154	T153
620.0071173	T73
620.00711747	T74.N7
620.00711758231	T171.G595
620.0071193122	T173.A9
620.0071194	T167
620.0071242	T107
620.00715	T65.3
	T74.P5
620.0072071	T177.C2
620.0072073	TA160.4
620.0076	T73
	TA153
	TA159
	TF847.N5
620.008	HC107.N9
	TA1
	TA7
	TA155
	TS176
620.009	TA15
620.00911	GB2401
	TA713
620.00922	TA139
620.00924	TA139
	TA140.E2
	TA140.M29
620.0093	TA16
620.00942	TA57
620.00954	HD5819
620.00973	TA23
620.0911	GB2401
620.1	TA350
	TA351
	TA357
	TA368
	TA403.8
	TA418.7
	TA439
	TC177
	TL574.D7
620.106	TJ840
620.1064	TA357
620.107	T62
620.11	TA401
	TA401.3
	TA403
	TA403.2
	TA403.6
	TA403.8
	TA405
	TA407
	TA418.8
	TA418.9.C6
	TS183
620.1108	TA401
620.110973	TA401.3
620.112	TA350
	TA351
	TA403
	TA403.6
	TA405
	TA407
	TA410
	TA418.4
	TA418.74
	TA658
620.112015312	TA407
620.112076	TA407.4
620.11208	QC1
620.11209497	TA417.B37
620.1121	TA418.58
620.11217	AS346
	TA418.26
	TA460
	TH460
	TL507
	TL1060
620.1122	TA409
	TA418.74
	TA460
	TA462
	TA467
	Z663.23
620.11220913	TA418.74
620.1123	TA405
	TA407
	TA409
	TA417.6
	TA418.16
	TA418.38
	TA418.78
	TA460
	TA465
	TA658.2
	TL521.3.C6
620.1123028	TL507
620.11232	QA931
	TA418
620.11233	TA418.14
	TA459
	TA460
	TL521
620.1124	TA417.7.T6
620.1126	TA409
	TA418.16
620.1127	TA417.2
	TA417.25
	TA417.4
	TS156.Q3
620.11281	TA660.B4
620.11282	QA935
	TL507
620.11283	QC100
	TA683.9
	TL521.3.C6
620.1129	QC100
	TA418.12
	TA418.5
	TA418.82
	TL507
	TL521.3.C6
	TN26
620.11297	TK454.4.M3
620.12	KF27.5.S633
	QL463
	S21
	TH1
	TS801
620.1337	TA434
620.135	TA434
	TA435
	TC7
	TE7
	TP881
	TP883
620.136	TA434
	TA439
	TA440
	TA441
	TC7
	TE7
620.13608	TA439
620.1361	TC7
620.13633	TA440
620.137	TA445
	TA472
	TA683.5.B3
	TA683.9
	TC7
620.14	QC100
	TA430
	TP790
620.144	QC100
	Z6046
620.15	TA436
	TA440
620.16	TA401
	TA459
	TA460
	TN665
620.1616	TA483
620.1617	TA418.26
620.162	TA460.S915
	TA462
	TA483
	TL521.3.C6
	TP1
620.163	TA460
620.1633	TA460
620.164	TA401
	UF535.A8
620.165	TA460
620.166	TA460
620.169	QC100
620.17	TA401
	TA485
	TS307
620.1717	TA401
	TL521.3.C6
620.172	TA459
620.18	TA483
	TN693.N6
620.182	TL507
	TL570
	TP1
620.186	TA480.A6
	TL507
	TL521.3.C6
	TN26
620.187	TA480.M3
620.188	TL521
620.189	TA455.S35
	TL521
620.1893	TA479.6
	TN700
620.18934	TL507
	TL521
	TP1
620.1896	TA467
620.19	TA409
	TA418.26
	TA455.L3
	TH4
620.191	S239
	TA710
	TC7
	TE7
	TH7
	TL521.3.C6
	TN941
620.191018	TC823.6
620.192	QC100
	QC770
	TA455.P5
	TA455.P55
	TA455.P58
	TH9446.P55
	TT297
620.193	TA462
620.195	TH1715
620.196	TA455.A7
	TA455.B5
	TA455.F55
620.197	TA418.26
	TA418.9.F5
	TL521.3.C6
	TS1449
620.198	TA418.9.C6
620.199	TA901
620.2	TA365
	TL521.3.C6
620.203	VM480.3
620.21	QC225.15
	TL521.3.C6
620.22	NA2800
620.23	TA365
	TD892
	TD893
	TD893.C2
	TL521.3.C6
	TL671.65
	U408.3
620.28	TA367
	TA417.4
620.3	QA871
	TA355
620.308	TA355
620.4	TA418.78
	TA418.8
620.4162	GC21
620.7	TA168
620.7092	QA76.2
620.8	QP303
	QR48
	R856
	T52.77
	TA164
	TA166
	TA170
	TH7
	TL507
	TL521.3.C6
	UC463
620.82	TJ211
621	TA350
	TJ7
	TJ147
	TJ840
	TT144
621.007	T74.O3
621.07	TJ160.5
621.071142	T107
	TJ1
621.08	TJ1
	TJ7
	TJ1075.A2
621.09	TJ15
	TJ153
621.1	TJ268
	TJ275
	TJ461
621.10212	QC311
	TJ270
621.10924	TA140.W3
621.110740261	TJ700
621.1109	TJ461
621.110973	TJ461
621.13065	TJ625.N58
621.130904	TJ603
621.130924	TJ140.B78
	TJ140.R53
621.130942	TJ140.S69
	TJ603
	TJ625.N58
621.1309422	TJ603
621.1309426	TF64.G64
621.130947	TJ603
621.130976	TJ625.L67
621.1309931	TJ603
621.130994	TJ605
621.1309944	TJ603
621.132	TJ603
	TJ608
	TL615
621.14	TJ700
621.140942	TJ700
621.140973	S675
621.1609	TJ461
621.1633	TA459
621.1653	TJ735
	TJ737
621.184	TJ286
	TJ289
	TJ390
621.19	TJ395
621.1972	TJ393
621.2	TC160
	TJ840
621.2002542	TJ843
621.20246289	TC163
621.209416	TC459.3.U4
621.210942	TJ859
621.24	TJ267.5.N6
621.2408	TJ870
621.252	TJ843
	TJ900
	TJ917
621.2520212	TJ901
621.26	TJ840
	TJ843
	TJ844
621.28	TC177
621.3	QC411

621.3 QC523
TA480.C7
TC1645
TK4
TK5
TK145
TK146
TK151
TK152
TK454.4.M3
TK1005
TK3201
TK3431
TK7871.15.C4
TL507
TL521
TL521.3.C6
VM473
621.300028 TK9901
621.3014 TK9
621.30151 TK153
621.30202 TK151
TK9901
621.3028 TK153
TK165
TK454.4.M3
TK7019
TL521.3.C6
621.303 TK7804
621.307 TK165
621.3071176354 TK175
621.3072042 TK415.E38
621.3076 TK168
TK169
621.308 TK1
621.309 TK15
621.30922 TK57
621.30924 Q143.J5
TK140.C7
TK140.E3
TK140.T4
621.30942 TK148
621.30973 TK6025.W4
621.31 TA1
TA177
TJ223.T7
TK152
TK1001
TK1005
TK2000
TK2181
TK2189
TK2896
TK3001
TK3401
621.310184 TK1005
621.310947 TK1193.R9
621.312 TK1041
TK1193.U5
TK1811
621.3120942 TK1257
621.312095412 TK1304.B5
621.3120973 TK1193.U5
621.31213 TK1191
TK1193.U5
Z663.23
621.312132 TJ405
621.312134 TK1425.B55
621.31213409471 TK1495.F5
621.31213409481 TK1481
621.31213409764 TD224.T4
621.312135 TC174
621.312139 TK2955
TK2970
TK2975
TK9008
621.31214 TK1541
621.3126 TK1751
621.313 TK2000
TK2189
TK2211
TK2316
TK2511
TK2514
Z663.23
621.3131 TK4057
621.3132 TK2851
621.3133 TK2761
621.3134 TK2787
621.3137 TK7871.99.T5
621.314 TK2791
TK2792
TK3335
TK3441.O5
621.315 TK7872.C65
621.316 TK2391
621.317 TK3441.S8
621.3173 TK2842
621.3178 TK2861
TK7872.R38
621.319 TK3091
TK3226
TK4001
621.3191 TK454
621.31912 TK3111
621.31913 TK168
621.3192 TK152
TK260
TK454
TK454.2
TK3221
TK3226
TK3271
TK3275
621.3192077 TK454.2
621.31921 TK454
TK3091
TK3226
621.31922 TK3144
TK3231
621.319223 TA713
621.31923 TK3251
TK3255
621.31924 TK3271
U408.3
621.3193 TK3307
621.31934 TK3226
TK3255
TK3351
TK5101
621.31937 NK5440.E4
TK3246
TK3401
TK3431
TK3441.P55
621.319370216 TK3246
621.3198 TK3226
621.32 TH7703
621.3208 TH7700.I4
621.322 S21
621.32209 PZ10.R85
621.3228 TK9921
621.323 TP746
621.32309 GT455
621.329 TK7871.3
TK7871.35
TK7871.4
TL521.3
TL521.3.C6
TL4030
Z663
Z663.23
621.35 TK2921
TP255
621.350272 TK2921
621.353 TK2921
621.354 TK2941
TL521.3.C6
621.356 TK2941
621.359 QD1
TK2931
TL521.3.C6
TN23
621.3590272 TK2931
621.36 QC100
TL521.3.C6
TR750
TS510
621.362 TK4500
621.366 TK7871.3
621.3663 TK7871.35
621.37 TK275
TK311
621.372 QC536
621.3720621 TK277
621.373 TK301
621.374 TK277
TK301
TK311
621.3742 TK311
TK7879.2
621.3743 TK7879.2
621.3747 TK7871.73
TK7878.7
621.38 HE9721.U5
Q180.A1
TA1145
TJ163
TK5
TK5101
TK5101.A1
TK5102
TK5102.5
TK5103.6
TK5104
TK5104.2.R4
TK5981
TK5982
TK6161
TK6540
TK6565.T7
TK6570.B7
TK7816
TK7845
TK7867.5
TK7868.P8
TK7870
TK7871.6
TK7872.F5
TK7881.7
TK9956
TL521
TL521.3.C6
TS510
TS2301.A7
U390
VM480.3
621.380202 TK5101
621.38028 TK5102.5
TK6565.A6
TK6590.R3
TK7871.6
TK7882.I6
621.380436 TK7867.5
621.3808 TK6540
621.381 TK146
TK275
TK454
621.381 TK7815
TK7816
TK7819
TK7828
TK7835
TK7836
TK7868.P6
TK7870
TK7871.15.C4
TK7871.15.F4
TK7871.15.P5
TK7872.F5
TK7878
TK7878.4
TK7881
TK9008
TK9965
621.3810151 TK7835
621.3810202 TK7825
TK9965
621.3810212 TK7825
TK7835
621.381028 TJ223.T7
TK275
TK7800
TK7801
TK7870
621.38103 TK7804
621.381043 TK7870
621.38107 TK7860
621.381076 TK7862
621.38108 TK7815
621.38109 TK7828
621.3811 TS173
621.3813 TK4
TK7872.F4
TK7876
621.38131 TK454
TK7876
621.38132 TA1
TK7872.O7
TK7876
621.38133 TK7871.86
621.381331 TK6565.R43
TK7871.65
TL521.3.C6
621.381336 TK7871.4
621.3813361 TK7872.M45
621.3815 TK454.2
TK7866
TK7867
TK7868.D5
TK7871.85
TK7871.9
TK7872.O7
TK7872.R4
TK8304
621.3815018 TK7867
621.381502461 TK7871.85
621.3815028 TK7867
621.38151 TK7871.7
TK7871.99.V3
621.381512021 TK6565.V3
621.38152 QC612.S4
TK7800
TK7870
TK7871.85
TK8320
TN673
621.381520202 TK7871.85
621.381520212 TK7871.85
621.38152028 TK7818
621.381522 TK7871.86
621.381528 TK7816
TK7871.2
TK7871.9
TK7871.95
TL521.3.C6
621.3815280212 TK7871.9
621.3815280216 TK7871.9
621.381528077 TK7871.9
621.38153 QA76
TK7867
TK7868.S9
TK7871.85
TK7871.9
621.381532 TK7872.F5
621.381533 TK7872.O7
621.381534 TK7868.P8
621.381535 TK7871.2
TK7871.24
TK7871.58.D46
TK7871.58.D5
621.381536 TK7835
621.3815363 TK8304
621.3815364 TK7868.P8
621.3815365 TK9180
621.381537 QA76.5
QA401
TK7867
TK7868.S9
621.38154 TK7871.15.P4
TK7871.98
TK8300
TK8304
TK9008
621.3817 AS122.B4
TK7874
TR927
621.38173 TK7868.S9
TK7871.15.F5
TK7871.85
TK7872.C7
TK7874
621.38173 TL521.3.C6
621.38174 TK7870
TK7872.P65
621.38179 TH9739
TK7882.E2
621.3819 Q327
TK7872.C7
621.38195 QA76.8.I12
QA267
TK7885
TK7887.6
TK7895.O6
TL521.3.C6
621.3819508 Z663.23
621.381950924 QA29.B2
621.381953 TK1
TK5102.5
TK7887.6
621.3819532 TK7887.5
621.3819534 TK7887.5
621.381957 QA76.4
QC770
TK7888
TK7888.3
621.381958 QA76
QA76.5
QA267.5
TK301
TK7868.S9
TK7872.C7
TK7885.A1
TK7887
TK7887.5
TK7888.3
TK7889.C2
621.3819582 TK7888.3
621.3820924 TK5243.M7
621.384 TK6550
621.384076 TK9956
621.3840924 TK5739.M3
621.3841 TK6550.7
TK7817
TK9956
621.3841076 TK5742
TK6554.5
621.38410922 TK6545.A1
621.38411 QC801
QC879
QC973
TK6553
TK6565.T73
621.3841108 Z663.23
621.38412 TK6550
TK6553
TK6560
621.38413 TK6553
621.384131 TK6561
TK9956
621.384134 TK9956
621.384135 TK6565.A6
621.3841350212 TK6565.A6
621.384151 TK6550
TK6553
TK6564.S5
TK9956
621.38415109143 TK6540
621.384152 TK6553
TK6565.F7
621.384153 TK6561
621.38416 TK6561
TK6570.C5
621.384160971 TK6548.C2
621.3841650973 TK6570.M6
621.384166 TK6554.5
TK9956
621.384166005756 TK6570.C5
621.3841660202 TK9956
621.384166076 TK6554.5
621.38417 TK6553
621.384187 TK6553
TK6563
TK6564.T7
TK6570.A8
621.384191 VK561.P3
621.3845 TK6554.5
TK6570.C5
621.3845076 TK6554.5
621.3848 TK6575
TK6580
621.38480202 TK6575
621.38481 TK6575
621.3848102854044 GB611
621.38483 TK6590.A6
621.38485 TK6580
621.385 TK6165
621.388 TK6653
621.38800202 TK6642
621.38804 TK6670
TK6670.S294
621.3883 TK6650
621.38831 TK6630.A1
621.3885 HE9719
TK6648
TK6670
621.3886 TK6680
621.38887 TK6642
TK6653
TK6670
621.38887028 TK7878.7
621.389 Q180
TK7881.4
TL521.3.C6
621.38903 TK7881.4
621.3892 TH9739

Dewey	LC
621.3893	TK7881.4
	TK7881.6
	TK7881.7
	TS2301.P3
621.38932	TK7881.6
	TS2301.P3
621.38933	TK7881.7
	TK7881.8
	TS2301.P3
621.39	TK7872.S8
621.392	TK2950
621.396	TK4601
621.4	JX1977
	TJ223.T4
	TJ250
	TJ267
	TJ267.5.N5
	TJ1063
	TK1224.C2
	TK2511
	TK2514
	TK2537
	TK2785
	TK2787
	TK2851
	TL507
621.402	TH1092
	TJ265
621.4021	TJ260
	TJ265
621.4021076	TJ265
621.4022	TJ263
	TJ265
	TJ840
	TL507
621.4023	TP315
621.4024	TH1715
621.4025	TH7140
621.4060202	TJ266
621.43	TJ1
	TJ759
	TJ785
	TJ789
621.433	TJ1
	TJ267
	TJ735
	TJ778
	TL507
	TN796
621.4332	TJ778
621.434	TJ789
	TJ790
621.435	TL782.5
621.436	TJ795
621.4360202	TJ795
621.4368	TJ795
621.45	TJ823
621.47	TJ810
621.475	TK2960
621.48	HD7269.A6
	KF26.P825
	QC100
	QC159
	QC770
	QC780
	QC795
	QD604.8
	TK5
	TK9006
	TK9146
	TK9148
	TK9151.4
	TK9152
	TK9153
	TK9185
	TK9202
	TL521.3.C6
621.48018	QC770
621.480611	HD9698.E82
	HD9698.5
621.4806191	HD9698.I56
621.4808	TK9008
	TK9202
621.4809771	TK9024.O3
621.48098	QC773.3.L3
621.483	QC1
	QC770
	QC787.N8
	TK1078
	TK1361
	TK1363.G7
	TK9008
	TK9153
	TK9202
	TK9203.H4
621.483018	QC783.4
621.483028	TK9202
621.48308	TK9203.B6
621.48309	QC787.N8
621.4831	TK9202
621.4832	QC721
	QC770
	TH4581
	TK9202
	TK9203.B7
	TK9210
621.4833	QC770
	TL507
621.48332	QC100
	TA480.Z65
	TK9202
	TL521
621.48335	QC721
	QC770
621.48335	TK9008
	TK9180
	TK9203.B6
	TK9203.H4
	TK9360
621.48336	TD353
	TK9008
	TK9203.L5
	TK9203.P7
621.48337	TK9008
621.4834	QC783.4
	TK9008
	TK9202
	TK9203.B6
	TK9203.B7
	TK9203.B9
	TK9203.G3
	TK9203.P7
	TK9360
621.4835	HD7269.A6
	TJ1
	TK9008
	TK9152
	TK9152.2
	TK9153
	TK9202
	TK9203.B6
	Z663.23
621.4835018	QC783.4
621.4837	TK9400
621.4838	HD7269.A6
	HD9698
	QC770
	QD1
	QE75
	RA569
	TD812
	TD887.R3
	TD898
621.489	KF25.A8
621.5	TP480
621.523	SB123
621.55	TJ940
	TL521.3.C6
621.5508	TL521.3.T4
621.56	TP490
	TP492
	TP495
621.5603	TP492
621.59	QC100
	TP480
	TP482
	TP482.K313
621.6	TJ900
621.63	TJ960
621.7	HF5770
	TS198.3.C6
	TS198.3.P5
621.75	TJ1160
	TJ1165
	TJ1315
	TS156.2
	TS183
621.750151	TJ1165
621.8	TJ146
	TJ148
	TJ153
	TJ159
	TJ170
	TJ243
	TJ248
621.808	TJ2
621.80924	TJ140.S29
621.809416	HD9705.I72
621.8101	TJ181.3
621.811	TJ146
	TJ170
	TJ175
621.815	TA174
	TJ230
	TJ233
621.82	TJ181
621.822	TJ1073.5
621.8220202	TJ1071
621.823	TJ1057
621.824	TJ210
621.825	TH7
	TJ1074
	TL507
	TL521.3.C6
621.83	TJ184
621.833	TA368
	TJ184
621.83309	TJ184
621.838	TJ206
621.84	TJ223.V3
	TS277
621.86	TN26
621.8608	Z663.23
621.862	TJ1350
	TJ1367
	U408.3
621.867	TJ1015
	TS180.6.B8
621.8672	TH6330
	TJ415
	TJ930
	TJ1015
621.86720202	TA492.P6
621.8672023	TH6124
621.8675	TJ1405
621.87	TJ1367
621.877	TJ1370
621.88	TA664
621.88	TJ130.P73
	TJ246
	TJ1075
621.882	TA492.B3
	TA492.B63
	TJ1340
621.884	TH7
621.885	TJ246
621.89	TA418.7
	TJ1
	TJ1073.5
	TJ1075
	TS213
	Z663.23
621.8903	TJ1075
621.9	PZ10.R614
	T48
	TA403.6
	TJ147
	TJ230
	TJ1185
	TJ1186
	TJ1188
	TJ1313
	TS850
621.902	T59.5
	TJ1185
	TJ1189
621.90209	TJ1185
621.908	VM763
621.908075	TJ1195
621.90809012	GN446.1
621.912	TJ1201.P55
621.92	TJ1280
621.93	GN799.T6
	SD211
	TJ1185
	TS851
621.94	TJ1165
621.945	TJ1260
621.95	TJ1210
621.952	JX1977
621.960212	TJ1255
621.974	TJ7
621.98	TJ1450
	TS1450
621.99	TJ1187
	TS500
622	AS36
	TN153
	TN275
622.028	TN153
622.03	TN9
622.072042	TN155
622.08	TN23
	TN23.U4
	TN24.I2
	TN26
	TN27.O4
	TN295
622.094237	HD9506.G73C68
	TN58.C7
622.094245	TN808.G62
622.096891	TN119.R4
622.097124	TN27.S3
622.0973	TN23
622.0978	TN23.6
622.0994	TN121
622.09942	TN122.S7
622.1	QE33
	QE276.3
	TN210
	TN260
	TN263
	TN269
	TN270
622.101519	QA273
622.109711	TN27.B9
622.1097124	TN270
622.12	QE75
	QE185
	TN263
622.13	TN560
622.130182	TN272
622.130982	JX1977
622.14	TN210
622.15	TN24.A4
	TN269
622.153	QE185
622.154	QE1
	QE75
	TN269
	TN270
	TN871.35
622.154028	TK7882.M4
622.159	TN269
	TN270.A1
	TN871.35
622.18	QE392
622.1828209943	TN271.P4
622.18338	TN871.35
622.1841	GE75
	QE75
622.2	TA706
	TC1505
622.2028	TN343
622.23	TA706
622.309711	TN27.B9
622.31	TN279
	TN291
622.310974	TN291
622.33	TN808.G6
	TN816
622.330942	TN802
	TN808.G6
622.335	KF27.E3
622.337	TN853
622.3382	HD9564
	TN870
	TN871.2
	TN871.3
622.3382028	TN871.5
622.33820973	TN872.A5
622.338209798	TN872.A7
622.3385	TN880.2
622.34094237	TN58.C7
622.3409428	TN58.L3
622.342	TN140.B56
	TN413.N25
	TN415.R9
	TN420
	TN423.C2
	TN424.C3B73
	TN428.W5
622.3430979157	TN443.U55
622.344094251	TN455.G7
622.3453094251	TN455.G7
622.3493	RC965.U7
622.351	QE105
622.3820957	TN994.R9
622.387	PR6073.A424
	QE394.O7
	TN997.O7
622.5	TN321
622.66	TF241
	TN337
622.7	TN500
622.708	TN500
622.752	TP1
622.8	HD7269.A6
	HD7269.M6
	KF26.L363
	TN295
	TN301
	TN311
	TN312
	TN490.U7
622.808	TN295
622.80951249	TN809.F6
622.80973	KF32.E3
	KF3574.M53
622.82	TN295
	TN315
623	UC46
623.08	UF535.A8
623.09044	UF535.G7
623.0959	KF32.A7
623.0994	UC260
623.1	DA660
623.150904	UG403
623.194391	DB906.5
623.38	TC7
623.4	U800
	UD385.G4
	UF23
	UF530
	UG632
623.4072043	UF526.5.G4
623.409	TS533
	U800
	UF535.G7
623.409044	UF520
623.40942	UG446.5
623.41	UF57
623.410942	UF57
623.410973	UF145
623.44	TS533.4.G7
	UD380
623.44029	TS535
623.44075	TS532.4
623.440973	UD383
623.4424	UF520
623.4425	KF27.A763
623.44250942	SK274
623.443	TS537
623.4430904	UD410
623.4430947	TS533.4.R9
623.444	GN799.W3
	UD400
623.45119	KF26.F6
	UF767
623.4519	KF27.F6483
	TL507
623.45194	UG632
623.4542	UF780
623.514	UF825
623.53	TD886.7
623.555	VG93
623.670947	Z663.23
623.7409044	UG680
623.746	TL685.3
	TL716
	U408.3
	UC333
	VG93
	VG95.G7
623.74607	VG93
623.7460941	TL685.3
623.7460944	TL685.3
623.7460946	TL685.3
623.7460942	TL526.G7
	TL685.3
623.7460943	TL685.3
623.74609471	UG635.F5
623.7460952	TL685.3
623.7460973	TL685.3
623.7463	TL685.3
	TL686.C58
	TL686.J8

623.746309042	TL685.3
623.746309044	TL685.3
623.74630943	TL685.3
623.7464	KF25.E243
	KF26.G658
	TL685.3
	TL686.C8
	TL686.D65
	TL686.L6
	TL686.M25
	TL686.M44
	TL686.N6
	TL686.P18
	TL686.R42
623.746409044	TL685.3
623.7464094	TL685.3
623.74640973	TL685.3
	TL686.G78
	UG633
623.747	UG680
623.74709041	UC340
623.7475	UG446.5
623.7475094	UG446.5
623.74750942	UG446.5
623.74750947	UG446.5
623.754	KF27.M473
623.8	VG923
	VM15
623.8016	Z6834.S5
623.803	V23
623.808	VM4
	VM4.D27
623.809117469	VM140.W4
623.80924	PZ10.R15
623.81	VM145
	VM149
	VM156
	VM285
623.81023	VM165
623.8108	VM1
623.817	VK543
623.8177	VM145
623.819	VM761
623.81908	VM156
	VM761
623.82	GC65
	GN440
	V857
	V858
	VM146
	VM148
	VM159
	VM287
	VM298
	VM321
	VM341
	VM351
	VM363
	VM365
	VM781
	VM981
623.82009	VM15
623.82009034	VM19
623.8200924	VM140.L5
623.8202	VM321
623.8203	VM144
	VM311.S7
623.8204	VK18
	VM615
623.8208	VM4
623.821	VA595.V3
623.8210932	VM16
623.822	VK18
	VM150
	VM298
	VM307
	VM311
	VM311.B3
	VM311.C3
	VM351
623.823	VM331
623.82310924	CT2888.H27
623.82313	VM348
623.82314	VM341
623.8232	HE592
	VM464
623.8234	VM383.E4
623.824	VM146
	VM378
	VM381
623.8243	VM381
	VM383.O4
623.8245	PZ10.Z5
	Q180
	VM317
623.825	V767
	V800
	VA40
623.82509	V750
623.8250942	VA454
	VA456
623.8250943	V765
	VA513
623.8250944	VA503
623.8250945	VA543
623.8250973	VA50
	VA58
623.8254	V895
623.82540942	VA454
623.8255	V874
623.8257	PZ10.I3
	V857
	V858
623.825709	V210
623.82572	VM365
623.826	V880
623.828	TC7
623.830973	KF27.A768
623.83097471	VM25.N5
623.84	VM148
623.8433	VM470
623.85	GC65
623.8503	TK146
	VM473
	VM474
623.856	KF27.M436
	VG77
	VK391.I6C3
	VK391.I6G7
	VM480.5.G7
623.862	VM531
	VM532
623.863	QC849
	VK577
623.865	VK1462.P7
	VK1471
623.87	VG803
	VM521
	VM951
623.87023	VM721
623.872	VM605
	VM731
623.8722	VM731
	VM741
623.87233	VM348
623.87234	VM348
623.87236	VM770
623.8728	VM776
623.873	VM761
623.88	V101
	VK391.I6
	VK543
623.88076	VK405
	VK559
623.882	VK541
623.882098	G587
623.8822	GV811
623.8882	VM533
623.89	G1413.L4
	QC994.2
	VK144
	VK555
	VK559
623.890246392	SH343.8
623.8903	V23
623.8907	VK147
623.892	VK570
623.8920212	VK563
623.89290212	VK563
623.89290973	VK993
623.892909795	VK200
623.892916612	VK988
623.89294	VK811
623.8929415	VK831
623.892951	VK909
623.892953	VK895
623.89296	VK877
623.892971221	VK808
623.8929713	VK983
623.8929714	VK988
623.892999	VK805
623.893	QC851
	VK560
623.8932	VK560
	VK561.A4
	VK561.A6
	VK561.A7
	VK561.E9
	VK561.J3
	VK561.M4
	VK561.N6
	VK561.P3
	VK561.P68
	VK561.R9
	VK561.U5
	VK572
623.89320971	VK397
623.8933	VK560
	VM480
623.8938	VK388
	VM480
623.894	VM451
623.894206242	VK1057
623.8942097473	VK1024.N7
623.894409931	VK1212
624	KF32.G677
	TA145
	TA149
	TA153
	TH95.B8
	TH153
	TH443
624.0212	TA368
624.028	TH900
624.071142	T107
624.0711763	T74.L6
624.076	TA159
624.08	QA276
	TA4
	TA7
624.09	TA15
624.09033	TA18
624.09684	TA119.N3
624.0973	TA23
624.097983	TD24.A4
624.1	QE535
	TA630
	TA658.44
624.1	TA760
624.1072073	TA638.2
624.15	QA935
	TA710.A1
	TA715
	TA775
624.151	GB2401
	GB2405
	NA9000
	TA1
	TA705
	TA706
	TA706.5
	TA710
	TA713
	TJ7
624.15108	GB384.Q4
	TA710
624.151094373	TA705
624.1510977325	TA410
624.15109798	QE75
624.1513	TA710
624.152	AS36
	GB2401
	QC792
	TA713
	TA730
	TA743
624.152028	TA735
624.154	TA710
	TA780
	TA787
624.16	TA760
	TH5281
624.17	TA645
	TA646
	TL521.3.C6
624.1701519	TA646
624.17018	TA646
624.170212	TA635
624.171	TA642
	TA645
	TA650
	TA654
624.17101512942	TA642
624.17101512943	TA642
624.1710151738	TA646
624.171018	TA642
624.1710202	TA646
624.171028	TA646
624.1713	TA640.6
624.172	TA660.T6
624.175	TA654.5
624.176	TA646
	TA658.44
	TA710.A1
	TH1094
	TL574.S55
624.17601517	TA646
624.177	TA630
	TA656.5
	TA658
	TA658.2
	TA663
	TL521.3.C6
624.177028	TA658.2
624.1772	TA651
	TA658.42
	TA660.B4
	TH1
	TL521.3.C6
624.17720212	TA660.B4
624.1773	TA652
	TA660.F7
624.1774	TH1
624.1776	QA935
	TA492.P7
	TA660.P6
	TA660.S5
	TH1
	TL507
	TL521.A3525
	TL521.3
	TL521.3.C6
	TL570
	Z663.23
624.1776015176	QA935
624.18	TA664
624.182	TA410
	TA472
	TA473
	TA652
	TA660.S5
	TA684
	TH1092
624.183	QE105
	TA434
	TA670
	TA679
	TA681
	TA681.5
	TA682.42
	TA682.5.S5
	TA683
	TA683.2
	TA683.22
	TA683.4
	TA683.5.B3
	TA683.5.F8
	TA683.5.S6
	TA683.7
	TA683.9
	TC7
	TH7
624.183	TH1461
	U408.3
624.18340228	TA680
624.184	TA666
	TH1101
624.189	TA660.S5
	TA668
	TL521.3.C6
624.19	TA712
	TA800
624.190924	TA140.B753
624.194094223	TF238.C4
624.194094224	TF238.C4
624.2	PZ10.C937
	TE7
	TE180
	TG25.M28
	TG340
	TG416
624.209	TG15
624.20942	TG57
624.2094923	TC77
624.209744	TG24.M4
624.2097471	TG25.N5
624.20974886	TG25.P59
624.209749	TG24.N5
624.209757	TG24.S6
624.209778	TG24.M5
624.20979564	TG24.O7
624.25	TA7
	TE7
	TG300
	TG416
	TG425
624.252	TG265
624.253	TG325.6
624.257	TE7
	TE278.2
	TG335
624.28	TA417.4
624.33	TG23.3
	TG265
	TG335
624.35094133	TG64.F7
624.37	TG335
	TG350
	TG425
	TG470
624.37509771	TG24.O3
624.378	TG360
624.409421	TG64.L83
624.6309494	TG140.M3
	TG155
624.92	TH2398
625	TE209
625.09781	TE180
625.1	TF147
625.10023	HD8039.R1
625.10079	TF183
625.100924	TF140.F4
625.100952	TF105
625.100973	TC623
	TF149
625.11	TA545
625.14	HE1783.G7
625.143	TF256
625.163	TF263
625.1650942	TF615
625.180973	TF300
625.19	TF197
	TJ630
625.2	TF677
625.209041	TF375
625.209042	TJ603
625.20942	TF57
625.20973	TF23
625.22	TF542
625.23	GN56
	TF459
	TF822.P4
625.230942	TF64.G7
625.240942	TF470
625.25	TF415
625.26	TF677
	TJ603
	TJ695
625.2602	TF197
	TJ630
625.260942	TJ603
625.260954	TJ608
625.261	TJ608
625.262	TF499
625.263	TK2681
625.26309	TF975
625.33097421	TF688.M66
625.4097471	TF847.N5
625.4209421	TF847.L6
625.5	TF725.S2
	TF835
625.66	TF757
625.66074019497	TF724.C2
625.660974811	TF725.P4
625.7	TE5
	TE7
	TE57
	TE145
	TE175
	TE180
	TE228
625.70212	TE180
625.7028	TE5
625.7071173	TE191
625.7072073	TE23
625.70720744	TA24.M4

625.708 TE1
TE7
625.709485 TE183
625.709691 TE24.H3
625.70971 KF27.P872
625.7097124 HE357.Z6S26
625.709744 TA24.M4
TE180
625.709746 TE24.C8
625.7097592 TE24.F6
625.709763 TE24.L8
625.709772 TE180
625.709773 TE180
625.709774 TE24.M5
625.709776 TE24.M6
625.709783 TE25.K4
625.709787 TE24.W8
625.709793 TE24.N3
625.709795 TE180
625.709796 TE24.I2
625.709797 TE24.W2
625.7097983 TE24.A4
625.7097986 TE24.A4
625.71 TE229.5
625.7109793 TE24.N3
625.72 KFM1644
TE7
TE24.P4
TE175
TE209.5
625.72028 TE209.5
625.720975572 TE24.V8
625.7209774 TE24.M5
625.72097984 HE356.A4
625.73 TA715
TE210.4
TE211
625.732 TC7
625.73209593 TC7
625.733 TE7
TE145
TE210
TE210.8
625.734 TE7
TE213
625.735 QE342
TE200
TE205
TE251
625.74 TC7
625.7409756 TE210.4
625.76 TE7
TE220
625.763 TD868
625.77 TE7
TE177
TE178
625.79 HE371.N7
TE7
TE220
TE228
625.8 TE7
TE250
TE251
TE450
625.84 TE7
TE250
TE278
625.85 TA440
TE7
TE24.C2
TE205
TE212
TE250
TE270
625.850212 TE270
627 GB665
GB683
TC5
TC405
TC409
TC424.C2
TC558.I42H58
TD392
627.0184 TC163
627.0202 TC145
627.08 GB653
GB1225.C3
GB1225.V8
TC155
TC160
TC801
TC801.U2
627.09597 TD313.M36
627.096695 TC519.N55
627.09748 TD224.P4
627.09763 TD224.L8
627.0976645 TC424.O5
627.09771 TD224.O3
627.097765 UG23
627.0978836 TC425.S187
627.09794 TC424.C2
627.1097982 QE75
627.12097759 HC107.W6
627.122 TH1
627.12509761 QE81
627.1251 TC176
627.13 TC745
627.130924 TA140.B735
627.130942 TC745
627.1310974798 TC7
627.1352 TC625.S2
627.2 TC209
627.20974725 TC224.N72P68
627.209759121 TC224.F6
627.209969 TC24.H3
627.23 TC175
627.24 TC7
TE7
627.34 VK235
627.35 TC361
627.40954 TC503
TC530
627.40973 KF26.P846
QE75
627.409742 TC424.N4
627.409752 TD224.M3
627.409763 TC425.M6
627.40977.7 TC424.I8
627.409944 TC522.M3
627.4509794 TC424.C2
627.5 S605
627.52 HD1741.A82
TC805
TC809
TC930
627.520954 TC903
627.54 S621
TC176
TH1
627.540202 TC970
627.5409492 TC345.H6
627.5409621 TC978.E3
627.5409749 TC977.N5
627.58 TC330
627.580973 TC223
627.703 VM965
627.72 VM981
627.73 TC187
627.8 TA706
TC540
627.80184 TC823.6
627.8096 TC558.A35
627.80976873 TC423.5.M4
627.809776 TC557.M6
627.809794 TC557.C2
627.80979435 TC557.C3
627.81 TC175
627.82 TC547
627.8209481 TC558.N8
627.82097295 TC557.P8
627.820979215 TC557.U82
627.83 TC543
TC557.3.S3
627.8309481 TA710
627.830954792 TC558.I42P35
627.830979228 TC557.U82
627.86 TC171
627.860973 TC801.U2
627.86097441 TD395
627.8609764555 GB705.T4
627.882 GB653
627.883097295 TC557.P82P38
627.922 PZ10.G528
627.9220924 TC140.S7
627.9220973 VK1023
627.9220975521 PZ10.F75
627.92209931 VK1122.N4
628 GC1556
TD151
TD157
TD172.5
TD365
628.028 TD153
628.03 TD9
628.08 TD227.O5
TD420
628.09744 TD524.M4
628.097983 TD24.A4
628.1 QD142
TD223
TD345
TD348
TD353
TD370
TD430
628.1042 TS835
628.10715 TD257
628.108 TD355
628.1091724 TD345
628.10924 TC140.T48
TD262.E3
628.1094231 TD264.T7
628.1095695 TD313.J6
628.10973 GB701
TD223
628.109744 J87
628.109747 TD224.N7
628.10974733 GB1025.N7
628.10974811 TD225.P52
628.109749 TD224.N5
628.109751 TD224.D4
628.109752 TD224.M3
628.1097556 TD223.5
628.109759 TD224.F6
628.10976213 TC801
628.10976496 TD225.E46
628.109771 TD224.O3
628.109794 TC424.C2
TD224.C3
TD365
628.10979445 TD224.C3
628.1097945 TD224.C3
628.1097964 TD224.I2
628.11 TD224.C3
TD405
628.11097643 TD370
628.11097743 TD224.M5
628.110979424 TD407
628.13 TD395
628.1309794 TD403
628.14 TD398
628.150971622 TD491
628.16 KF30.C65
RA121
TD223.1
TD225.R55
TD365
TD370
TD380
TD420
TD430
TD477
TD478
628.1609744 TD224.M4
628.1609756 TD370
628.1609773 TD370
628.16097731 TD370
628.1609777 TD370
628.1609791 TD370
628.160979457 TD370
628.1609797 TD370
628.166 TC1
TD468
628.167 TD429
TD478
TD479
TD479.4
TD480.2
TD480.4
TD480.7
628.16708 TD478
628.167095694 TD478.6.I75
628.1670973 KF27.I529
628.1672 TD478
TD478.U5
TD479.4
TD479.6
628.1676 TD478
628.168 KF27.M4
PZ10.O67
QH96.A1
QH541.5.F7
TC175
TD153
TD224.C3
TD303
TD420
TD425
TD427.P35
TD427.P4
TD429
TD764
TD795
628.1680182 TD420
628.168072079 TD423
628.1680916 SH1
628.16809162 TD763
628.168097124 TD227.S3
628.1680973 KF26.P825
KF27.P8
TD365
TD425
TD741
628.1680974 TD225.C74
628.168097418 TD223.15
628.16809744 J87
628.168097451 TD223.15
628.1680974725 TD224.N7
628.1680974754 TD425
628.168097492 TD225.H8
628.16809752 TD225.P74
TD225.W3
628.168097587 TD225.S37
628.1680975999 TD225.C73
628.1680976121 TD225.P46
628.168097625 TD223.4
628.16809764141 TD477
628.1680976882 TD225.C37
628.1680977 TD223.3
TD223.4
628.168097712 TD225.E7
628.168097729 TD525.C19
628.1680977299 TD525.C19
628.16809774 TD223.3
TD225.M52
628.168097749 TD223.3
TD223.31
TD225.S89
628.16809794 TD224.C3
628.16809797 TD224.W2
628.1682 GC1080
TD427.D4
TD655
TH7
628.16820973 TD223
TD523
628.1683 GC1080
GC1085
GC1311
TD427.H4
TD427.P4
TD888.M4
TD899
628.1684 RA121
TC977.C2
628.1685 TD427.R3
628.16850184 TD427.R3
628.16850942 TD427.R3
628.1686 TD370
TD423
TD427.N5
628.16860974461 TD225.B7
628.168609747 RA121
628.168609752 TD225.P74
628.1686097712 TD225.E7
628.168609969 TC1
628.168616346 TD225.N48
628.173 TD353
628.2 TD223
TD665
628.209755791 TD525.R6
628.24 TA447
TD223
TD651
TD678
628.25 TH6671.F6
628.3 TD523
TD525.S84
TD735
TD745
TD791
TD897
628.30942 TD741
TD765
628.30973 TD523
628.309744 TD524.M4
628.309776 TD741
628.35 TD8031
628.354 TD458
TD755
TD756
628.36 TD760
628.39 TD678
TD897
628.39097493 TD225.P314
628.3909776 TD524.M5
628.4 TD525.F7
TD791
628.4076 TD819.N6
628.40941435 TD62.G55
628.44 HD9517.M3
TD791
TD795
628.440943 TD795
628.440973 TD795
628.440976335 TD795
628.4409788 KFC1820
628.4420184 TD795
628.445 KF26.P825
KFN2159.R3
TD741
TD795
TD803
TD899
TP995
628.44508 TD795
628.4450973 KF31.P8
TD795
628.44509746 TD795
628.4450978661 TD795
628.5 KF27.G636
QC770
QC913
QH541
S942
TD172.5
TD174
TD175
TD176
TD180
TD370
TD881
TD887.R3
TD890
TK1078
TK9151.4
628.50973 TD178.6
TD180
628.509768 TD181.S62
628.51 TD895
TK1005
628.53 KF25.A8
QC851
TD883
TD883.1
TD884
TD885.5.S85
TD890
TL521.3C6
UG7
628.53012 TD883.1
628.53028 TD890
628.53071173 TD883.1
628.5308 TD881
628.530942 TD883.7.G7
628.530973 KF26.P825
KF31.P8
TD883.2
628.530974461 TD883.5.M4
628.530975437 TD881
628.5309755 TD883.5.V8
628.5309776 TD883.5
628.53097866 TD883.5.M9
628.5309794 TD883.5.C2
628.530994 TD883.7.A8
628.532 KF27.G674
TD881
TD883
TD883.2
TD884.5
TD885.5.S85
TD888.S7
TH7692
TN26
628.535 QC881

Dewey	LC
628.535	TD887.R3
628.54	GC1556
	QE105
	TD180
	TD380
	TD795
	TD897
	TP336
628.542	TD884
628.55	SB959
628.72	TD478
628.7209747	TD927
628.72097594	TD224.F6
628.720978652	TD224.M9
628.720979415	TD224.C3
628.720979485	TD224.C3
628.720994	TD370
628.74	TD899
628.742	TD778
628.744	TD743
628.8	TJ213
	TS156.8
628.827	GC66
628.9097526	TH9505.B2
628.92	TH9112
	TH9145
	TH9180
	TP265
	TP267
	VK1258
628.920202	TH9151
628.92028	TH9360
628.9206274728	TH9505.S8574
628.920711	TH9123
628.92076	TH9157
628.920973	TH9148
628.922	TH9445.A4
	TH9448
628.95	TE7
	TK4188
629	TA166
	TA1006
	TA1145
	TL243
	TL507
	TL521.3.C6
	VK555
	VK559
	VK560
	VK563
	VM156
629.02	TT154
629.042	KF26.C6
629.1	TA167
	TK7871.6
	TL507
	TL573
	TL589
	TL671
	TL671.2
	TL785.8.S6
629.10182	QA297
629.1028	TL500
	TL693
629.103	TL509
629.107	TL521
	TL521.312
	TL560.1
629.1072073	TL789.8.U5
629.1072079473	TL565
629.108	TL503
	TL507
	TL521
629.109	TL507
629.13	TL521.3.C6
	TL546
	TL546.7
	TL547
	TL553.5
	TL670
629.1300202	TL546.5
629.1300222	TL549
629.130023	TL561
629.13003	TL509
629.13007	TL560.1
629.130072042	TL568.F3
629.130072073	KF27.S374
	TL521
629.1300724	T178.F3
629.1300740436	TL506.P25
629.13008	TL504
	TL507
	TL526
	TL526.G7
	TL553
	TN507
629.13009	TL515
629.1300904	TL515
629.1300924	TL540.F6
	TL540.L364
	TL540.S54
629.1300973	TL521
	TL521.312
629.13009778411	TL522.M8
629.13009931	TL529
629.1308	TL504
629.1309	TL553.5
	TL721.M58
629.130911	TL659.A6
629.1309110922	TL531
629.130922	TL539
629.130924	D786
	TL532
	TL540
629.130924	TL540.A8
	TL540.B557A3
	TL540.C33
	TL540.C76
	TL540.E3
	TL540.G755
	TL540.H45
	TL540.L29
	TL540.L5
	TL540.L783
	TL540.S18
	TL540.W57
	TL685.1
	TL721.M67
629.1309798	TL522.A4
629.132	PZ10.H9
	TL710
629.1323	TL500
	TL570
	TL574.A45
	TL574.F7
	TL574.S55
	TL671.65
	TL685
629.1323008	TL570
629.132304	TL521.3.C6
	TL574.S4
	TL574.S55
	TL671.65
629.132305	TL507
	TL571
629.1323050212	TL500
629.132306	TL507
	TL574.F5
629.13232	TL507
	TL557.A5
	TL570
	TL574.B6
629.13232028	TL507
629.13233	TL507
	TL526.G7
629.13236	TL500
	TL521.3.C6
629.132362	TL574.A37
629.132364	TL526.G7
629.13237	TL500
	TL505
	TL507
	TL571.5
629.1324	QC880
	TL556
	TL557.S65
629.1325	TL553.5
629.132507	TL713
629.13250971	TL726.5.C2
629.13250973	TL710
629.13251	TL507
	TL588.5
	UG633
629.13251019	TL555
629.1325109	TL586
629.13252	TL526.G7
	TL546.5
	TL553.5
	TL556
	TL620.S58
	TL671.2
	TL710
	TL711.B6
	TL712
	TL722.1
	TL760
	TL765
	UG638
629.132520184	TL570
629.13252078	TL712.5
629.132520924	TL540.D358
629.132520973	TL710
629.13254	G2796.P6
	TL726.6.D4
629.13254096773	TL726.8.S6
629.13255	TL553.5
629.13309	TL670
629.13309041	TL670
629.1330942	TL670
629.1331	TL770
	TT154
629.13313	TL770
629.133134	TL770
629.1332	GV753
629.13322	TL616
629.13324	TL651
	TL654.P67
629.1332409	TL658.Z4
629.13330903	TL547
629.13330947	TL685.7
629.13334	TL670
	TL671.2
	TL685.7
	TL686.B7
	TL686.H24
	TL686.V4
	TL721.4
629.133340222	TL549
629.1333409	TL670
	TL685.7
629.133340942	TL686.B57
	TL724.5.M5
629.133340973	TL686.B65
629.133343	TL685.1
	TL685.3
	TL686.A44
	TL686.B36
	TL686.M53
629.133349	TK6540
	TL507
	TL521
	TL685.7
	TL686.B65
629.13335	TL570
	TL714
	TL716
629.1333509	TL714
629.134	TL671.6
	TL671.6.F67
	TL671.65
629.1342	TL698
629.13431	TL671.6
	TL699.F2
629.13432	TL507
	TL526.G7
	TL526.G7A4
629.134351	TL521
629.134352	VG93
629.134353	TJ153
	TL500
	TL507
	TL709
	TL709.5.C57
629.1343532	TL500
629.1343533	TL507
	TL709
629.134354	TL782
629.134381	TL521.3.C6
	VG93
629.134386	TL697.P5
	Z663.23
629.13443	TL521.3.C6
	TL697.S3
	TL753
	VG93
629.1345	TL507
629.13452	TL567.S4
629.1346	TL671.9
	VG93
629.1346023	TL671.9
629.135	RC965.R25
	TL521.3.C6
	TL589
	TL696.R2
	Z663.23
629.1350924	TA140.S68
629.1351	TL589.4
	TL693
	TL695
	TL697.S3
629.1352	TL507
	TL521.3.C6
	TL589.2.F5
629.1355	TL693
	TL694.A6
	TL695
	VG93
629.136	TL557.V5
	TL725
	TL725.3.N6
629.1360212	TL725.2
629.13602572	TL726.5.M4
629.136025756	TL726.3.N6
629.1360973	TL726.2
629.13609748	TL726.3.P4
629.13609781	TL726.3.K2
629.1361309755295	TL726.4W3
629.1363	TL725
	TL725.3.R8
629.13630184	TL725.3.R8
629.13634	U408.3
629.1366	TL696.R25
	TL725.3.T7
629.13660973	TL725.3.T7
629.16	TD429
629.2	KF26.C645
	TC7
	TL146
	TL147
	TL205
	TL242
	TL243
629.20202	TL208
629.203	TL9
629.209	TL15
629.20922	TL140.R63
629.20924	CT275.F68
	ML200.8.D27
	TL140
	TL140.A9
	TL140.D35
	TL140.P6
629.2094	TL55
629.20973	TL23
629.22	TL147
	TL298
629.220740153	TL7
629.220942	TL57
629.220973	TL23
629.221	TL237
629.2218	TL237
629.222	TL146
629.222075	TL7
629.22209	TL15
629.2222	TL7
	TL15
	TL23
	TL55
	TL162
	TL205
	TL215.A9
	TL215.B23
629.2222	TL215.B4
	TL215.B82
	TL215.C5
	TL215.C59
	TL215.D8
	TL215.F7
	TL215.J3
	TL215.M4
	TL215.P25
	TL215.R6
	TL215.T7
	TL215.V6
	TL236
	TL236.7
	TL242
629.22220275	TL154
629.222209	TL15
629.222209034	TL15
629.222209041	TL15
629.222209043	TL15
629.22220924	GV1032.N6
	TL140.R4
629.22220941	TL61
629.22220942	TL57
629.22220973	TL15
	TL23
629.22233	TL232
629.222330942	TL232
629.2223309421	TL232
629.223	TL230
629.224	KF27.P876
	S21.A72
	TL230
	TL295
629.2240947	Z663.23
629.226	TL297
	TL298
629.2260202	TL297
629.2272	GV1043
629.228	TL215.A35
	TL215.C6
	TL215.F7
	TL215.L67
	TL236
629.2280222	TL236
629.22809041	TL236
629.22809043	TL236
629.2280973	TL236
629.2292	TL200
629.22920924	TJ700
629.2293	TL220
629.2294	TL226
629.23	TL146
	TL240
	TL242
	TL501
	TL521.3.C6
	TL671
629.230212	TL240
629.231	TL242
	TL243
629.2310922	TL139
629.24	TL145
	TL255
629.244	TL262
	TL263
629.246	TL269
629.248	QC100
	TC7
	TE7
629.25	TL210
629.2503	TL226
629.25032	TL152
629.2504	TJ790
629.252	TL214.P6
629.253	TJ1
	TL445
629.254	TL272
	TL445
629.26	TL242
	TL255
629.271	TL273
629.276	TL159
629.277	TL271.5
629.28	GV1021
	TL152.66.C2
629.2803	TL9
629.282	TE7
	TL285
629.2820973	KF2212
629.283	TL152.3
	TL152.5
	TL152.52
629.283019	TE7
	TL152.35
629.28307	LB5
	TL152.6
	TL152.66.U5
629.283071	TL152.66.U5
629.2830712	TL152.65
629.2830712774	TL152.65
	TL152.66.U5
629.283076	TL152.4
629.283077	TL152.5
629.2830942	TL152.55.G7
629.283097124	TL152.55.C2
629.2830994	TL152.55.A8
629.28309945	TL152.55.A8
629.2832	TL152.5
629.283202434	HV8080.P9
629.283209941	TL152.55.A8
629.28333076	TL232.3
629.2843	TL230.3
629.286	TL153

Dewey	LC
629.287	TJ1
	TL152
	TL205
	TL208
	TL215.A92
	TL215.D35
	TL215.J3
	TL215.M2
	TL215.M37
	TL215.M6
	TL215.M615
	TL215.P53
	TL215.R4
	TL215.S2
	TL215.S5
	TL215.S85
	TL215.T64
	TL215.T7
	TL215.V65
	TL440
629.287023	TL147
	TL156
629.287071	TL210
629.287076	TL152
629.28722	TL215.V65
629.288	TL152
	TL215.A92
	TL215.B23
	TL215.C568
	TL215.F5
	TL215.F7
	TL215.H5
	TL215.M4
	TL215.R64
	TL215.T7
	TL215.V6
	TL448.B2
629.28822	TL152
	TL215.B25
629.28872	TL430
629.3	VM363
629.32	VM362
	VM363
629.4	KF27.S385
	PZ10.B65
	PZ10.D274
	QB500
	TL781.8.R9
	TL787
	TL793
	TL794
	TL798.S3
	TL867
	TL870
	TL3000.A1
629.40148	TL788
629.4019	TL507
629.40202	TL845
629.4023	TL850
629.403	TL509
	TL788
	TL793
629.406173	TL862.G6
629.4072073	KF32.S374
	TL789.8.U5
	TL858
629.4074	KF27.S333
629.408	TL521
	TL790
	TL859
629.409	TL781
	TL793
629.40922	TL789.85
	TL789.85.A1
	TL793
629.40924	TL781.85.G6
	TL789.8.U5
	TL789.85.O4
629.40942	TL796.5.G7
629.40947	TL789.8.R9
629.40951	Z663.23
629.40973	TL521.312
	TL787
	TL789.8.U5
	TL799.M6
629.41	TL1500
629.411	TL507
629.415	TL1060
629.4151	QC879.5
629.4152	TL507
	TL521.3.C6
629.42	TL521
	TL709
	TL781.5.S3
	TL782
629.4208	TL507
629.420924	TL781.85.T8
629.4222	TL500
	TL521.3.C6
	TL783
	TL783.3
	TL783.4
	TL785
	TL875
629.4223	TL521.3.C6
	TL783.5
	TL1102.N8
629.4225	TL783.6
	TL783.63
629.43	TL788.8.U6
	TL3250
	Z663.23
629.434	Q180.7
	TL785.8.S6
629.434	TL793
	TL796
	TL796.5.R8
	TL798.M4
	TL798.S3
	TL1050
629.4340973	TL796.5.U5
629.435	TL796
629.4352	TL798.S3
629.4353	TL521.3.C6
	TL788.5
	TL789.8
	TL789.8.U6
	TL796.5.U6
	TL799.M6
629.4353028	TL789.8.U6
629.43543	TL789.8.U6
629.437	TL521.3.C6
	Z663.23
629.44	TL521.3.C6
	TL797
629.45	TL521.3.C6
	TL787
	TL790
	TL791
	TL3260
629.450079	KF27.S353
629.4500973	TL789.8.U5
629.4501	TL788.7
629.45077	TL521.3.C6
629.450973	TL789.8.U5
629.452	TL500
629.453	QC425
	TL521.3
	TL521.3.C6
	TL787
	TL3250
	TL3260
629.454	KF26.A3
	KF27.S3
	TL789.U6
	TL789.8
	TL789.8.U5
	TL789.8.U6
	TL789.8.U6A516
	TL789.8.U6A523
	TL789.8.U6A5235
	TL789.8.U6A527
	TL789.8.U6A5338
	TL789.8.U6A536
	TL789.8.U6A539
	TL789.8.U6A577
	TL789.8.U6A5818
	TL789.8.U6A5819
	TL789.8.U6A5823
	TL789.8.U6A5855
	TL789.8.U6A588
	TL789.8.U6A5968
	TL789.8.U6A63
	TL789.8.U6S98
	TL793
	TL796.6.M6
	TL799.M6
629.455	TL788.5
	TL789.8.U5
629.4553	TL789.8.U6M344
629.457	TL521.3.C6
	TL3035
629.4588	TL1060
629.46	TL521.3.C6
	TL789.8.U6R3544
	TS198.6.C8
629.47	KF27.S353
	TL789.8.U6A533
	TL870
	TL875
	TL945
	TL3025
	TL3280
	Z663.23
629.4702	TL844
629.47028	TL1082
629.471	TL875
	Z663.23
629.472	QD380
	TL521.3.C6
	TL950
	TL953
629.474	TK454.4.M3
	TL521
	TL521.3.C6
629.4742	TL521.3.C6
629.4744	TL1100
629.4750228	TL782.7
629.475028	TL782.7
629.477	TL521
	TL521.3
	TL521.3.C6
	TL1500
	Z663.23
629.4775	TL521.3.C6
629.478	TL1495
	TL4000
	TL4024
629.4780973	TL789.8.U5
629.49	TL797
629.494	TK2921
629.8	QA402.3
	TJ212
	TJ213
	TJ217
	TJ219
	TJ840
629.8	TJ857
	TJ1189
	TK7881.2
	TL507
629.8042	TJ840
629.80947	TJ213
629.82	VM6.U62N4
629.828	VM159
629.83	TJ213
	TJ216
	TS156.8
629.831	TJ211
	TK7881.2
629.831076	TJ213.8
629.8312	QA3
	QA267
	QA267.3
	QA298
	QA402
	QA402.3
	QA402.5
	TA168
	TA331
	TJ212
	TJ213
	TJ216
	TJ1189
	TK7868.P8
	TL521.3.C6
629.83120151738	Q180.A1
629.8314	QA402
629.8315	Q327
	TS277
629.832	TJ214
629.832028	QA402.3
629.836	QA402.3
	TJ212
	TJ213
	TJ217
629.89	QA267
	QA267.5.S4
	VK555
629.892	TJ211
629.8932	VK561.A7
630	PZ10.E26
	PZ10.F445
	PZ10.M477
	S22
	S279
	S401
	S439
	S493
	S495
	S509
	S511
	S675
	S934.C3
	S934.Z3
	SB41
	SB91
	SF71
	Z5071
630.08	S21
630.110207	PN6231.C65
630.110942	S521
630.1124	CT788.M33
	PR6053.L326
	S521
630.1142	PR1111.C6
630.114235	S457.D5
630.114247	DA690.A815
630.11711	F1089.G8
630.11713	F1057
630.1173	S521
630.1194	S521
630.182	S566
630.203	S494.5
	S494.5.A4
	S534.W2
630.208	S494.5.A25
630.23	S21
	S494.5.A4
630.24	S585
630.241388	S589.5
630.25150202	QC851
630.25157	S589
630.251570956	QC851
630.2516	S600
630.2539	S494.5.R4
630.25516	S600
630.62	S531
630.62687	S17.W673
630.6273	S533.F8
630.62754	S533.F66
630.62777	HD1485.I6
630.7	S531
	S534.A2
	S535.C2
	S535.C46
	S535.G7
630.71	S217.C64
	S279
	S533
	S534.L6
	S535
	S535.G7
	S535.V5
630.711	S530.3
	S533
630.71154792	S539.I4
630.71173	S533
630.71177366	S537.I49
630.71177829	S537.M8876
630.711969	S534.H3
630.712	L341.H5
	LB1561.M6
630.715	S533
	S535.I5
	S544
	S544.3.A2
	S544.3.M4
	S544.5.A4
	S544.5.A8
	S544.5.F6
	S544.5.I5
630.717	S535
630.72024	QR31.R86
630.7204	S542.E8
630.72041445	S539.S3
630.72067	Q180.A52
630.72073	S21
630.720794	S541
630.720991	S542.I5
630.74011	S557.R73
630.74013	S549
630.8	S21
	S67
	S119
	S217
	S239.S2
	S509
	SB355
	Z5776
630.9	S421
	S494
630.901	S421
630.904	S405
630.91154	S300.B7
630.913	S471
	S481
	SB111
630.9153	S481
630.9154	S613
630.91724	S439
630.924	S417.L82
630.937	S431
630.942	S455
630.94221	S457.S85
630.94235	S457.D5
630.9426	S457.N6
630.94261	S457.N6
630.947	S469.R9
630.9471	S11
630.94973	S469.Y82S45
630.95	S470.A1
630.954	S471.I3
	S517.I
	SB87.I
630.95475	HD2075.G8
630.9549	S471.P16
630.95492	S471.P16
630.95493	DS488
	SB110
630.9552	S471.I72
630.95951	S295
	SB191.R5
630.96	S323
630.963	S473.E8
630.967	S472.A36
630.96894	S473.Z34
630.96897	S473.M3
630.971	S451.5.A1
630.9711	S451
630.971142	S142.O4
630.97127	S451.5.M3
630.9715	S451.5.N5
630.9729	HD1411
630.97291	S477.C8
630.973	S21
	S441
630.9749	S91
630.9768	S451.T2
630.9776	S451.M6
630.9777	S521
630.9784	S99
630.99315	DU430.M57
630.994	S478.A1
631.0924	PR6037.T776
631.0971272	S133
631.0973	HD191
631.2	S21
	TH4911
631.27	TH2201
631.28	TH4911
631.3	S675
	S760.R9
	TJ1480
631.3071173	S678.5
631.30942	S760.E9
	S760.G7
631.30951	S760.C55
631.309549	S471.P25
631.30971	HD1407
631.309815	S760.B7
631.315	S676
631.3720947	S760.R9
631.373	TS2010
631.4	HD209
	S133
	S590
	S591
	S598
631.4028	PZ10.S677
631.408	S591
	S950
631.4094385	S599.4.P7
631.40971	S625.C2
631.40978	S624.W4

631.409797 S624.W3
631.41 S590
..... S593
631.410947 S599.45.A1
631.410954 S599.6.I5
631.416 S587.5.T7
..... S599.7.V5
631.417 S217
..... S590
631.417097561 S599.N6
631.4209549 S599.6.P3
631.43 S591
..... S593.2
..... S598
..... TN26
631.432 S594
631.432028 S21.A72
631.44 S21
..... S591
631.440947 S598
631.440971 S591
631.45 S625.A9
631.46 QR111
631.47 S591
..... TR810
631.470978279 S599.N22
631.474223 S599.4.G7
631.474225 S599.4.G7
631.476668 S599.5.I9
631.47683 S599.5.S95
631.47729722 S599.25.V5
631.4774245 S599.N48
631.477448 S599.M35
631.4774792 S599.N43
631.4774816 S599.P4
631.4774824 S599.P4
631.4774872 S599.P4
631.4774881 S599.P4
631.4774991 S599.N5
631.477511 S599.D3
631.4775225 S599.M3
631.4775277 S599.M3
631.4775281 S599.M3
631.4775422 S599.W4
631.47755714 S599.V8
631.4775822 S599.G4
631.4775869 S599.G4
631.47758766 S599.G4
631.4775879 S599.G4
631.4775885 S599.G4
631.4776222 S599.M5
631.47762455 S599.M5
631.4776318 S599.L6
631.4776379 S599.L6
631.47764556 S599.T4
631.47764724 S599.T4
631.47764729 S599.T4
631.4776474 S599.T4
631.47764834 S599.T4
631.47764858 S599.T4
631.4776629 S599.O4
631.4776638 S599.O4
631.4776672 S599.O4
631.4776683 S599.O4
631.4776696 S599.O4
631.4776714 S599.A75
631.4776769 S599.A75
631.4776792 S599.A75
631.4776793 S599.A75
631.4776799 S599.A75
631.4776812 S599.T37
631.4776819 S599.T37
631.4776865 S599.T37
631.4776913 S599.K4
631.4776941 S599.K4
631.4776947 S599.K4
631.4776972 S599.K4
631.47771535 S599.O3
631.4777163 S599.O3
631.4777171 S599.O3
631.4777229 S599.I63
631.4777274 S599.I63
631.4777321 S599.I5
631.4777382 S599.I5
631.4777397 S599.I5
631.47773998 S599.I5
631.4777457 S599.M4
631.4777469 S599.M4
631.4777542 S599.W5
631.4777573 S599.W5
631.4777592 S599.W5
631.47776365 S599.M45
631.4777653 S599.M45
631.4777732 S599.I8
631.4777772 S599.I8
631.4777814 S599.M52
631.47778364 S599.S6
631.4778163 S599.K2
631.4778172 S599.K2
631.4778173 S599.K2
631.47782845 S599.N2
631.4778298 S599.N2
631.47784 S599.N9
631.4778458 S599.N9
631.47784844 S599.N9
631.4778874 S599.C7
631.4778876 S599.C7
631.4778894 S599.C7
631.4778963 S599.N6
631.4779154 S599.A7
631.4779313 S599.N52
631.4779314 S599.N425
631.4779431 S599.C2
631.4779475 S599.C2
631.4779492 S599.C2
631.4779493 S599.C2
631.4779521 S599.O7
631.4779654 S599.I2
631.4779737 S599.W32
631.4947 S599.45.A1
631.494971 S599.4.Y8
631.495 S599.6.A1
631.4954 S625.I47
631.49544 S625.I47
631.495452 S625.I47
..... S954.I5
631.495691 S599.6
631.49573 S599.45.S5
631.49575 S599.45.S5
631.495845 S599.R9
631.49593 S599.6.T4
631.495951 S599.6.M3
631.49684 HC517.N3
631.4973 S622
631.49747 S599.N7
631.49755785 S599.V8
631.4975729 S599.S7
631.49761 S445
631.49764835 S599.T4
631.49764879 S599.T4
631.49768464 S599.T37
631.4976861 S599.T37
631.49776579 S599.M45
631.49776651 S599.M45
631.49777 S599.I8
631.497789 S599.M52
631.49784 S599.N9
631.49786 S599.M9
631.4979227 S599.U8
631.4979257 S119
631.4979493 S599.C2
631.49931 HD1055
631.4994 S381
..... S591
..... S599.7.A1
631.49945 S625.A9
631.499982 Q115
631.5096894 S573
631.52 QK981
..... SB123
631.521 SB117
631.521095413 SB117
631.5210973 SB119
631.523 S494
..... SB123
631.542 SB125
631.544 SB415
..... SB936
631.55 S699
631.56 S133
..... SB117
631.58 S471.I3
..... S476.G9
..... S605.5
631.58109712 S451.5.P7
631.585 SB126.5
631.586 SB110
631.587 SB112
631.61 S608
631.7 S401.U6
..... S613
..... S615
..... S616.A8
..... S616.I7
..... SB112
..... TC977.C2
631.709154 S605
631.70954792 S616.I4
631.7095484 S616.I4
631.7095487 S616.I4
631.7095493 S616.C4
..... S616.I4
631.709781 HC107.K2
631.70978616 S616.U6
631.709786652 S616.U6
631.70994 S616.A8
631.709945 S616.A8
631.8 S633
631.80913 S633
631.809914 S633.5.P47
631.816 S631
631.821 S217
..... SB93
631.83 S645
631.841 JX1977
631.847 S21
631.86095484 S633.5.I4
631.8610954 TP317.I4
631.875 S661
631.8750954 S633.5.I4
632 AS122.B4
..... S21
..... S381
..... SB599
..... SB601
..... SB605.C
..... SB605.U5
..... SB731
632.08 QC770
..... SB599
632.4 SB601
..... SB733
632.43 S239
632.58 S21
..... S217
..... SB610
..... SB611
..... SH11
632.580993122 SB613.N45
632.5809944 SB613.A88
632.6 SB915
632.6513 SB998.N4
632.65130913 QL386
632.69322 SB994.R15
632.69323 SB994.R6
632.693233 SB994.R2
632.6933 SB994.M7
632.697358 SB999.N4
632.7 SB601
..... SB931
..... SB950
632.70947 SB885
632.70956 SB913.N4
632.7095694 SB815.I7
632.709676 SB605.A35
632.726 S21
..... SB945.L7
632.736 S21
..... SB945.T45
632.752 S21
632.76 SB945.J3
632.764 S21
..... TX7
632.768 S21
632.78 SD11
632.781 TX7
632.8 SB736
632.9 QD1
..... SB599
..... SB601
..... SB605.I53
..... SB936
..... SB950
632.9072073 SB950
632.908 SB599
632.90913 SB599
632.94 SB953
632.95 Q11
..... QH75
..... QH545.P4
..... RA8.A4
..... RA1270.P4
..... S914
..... SB950
..... SB951
..... SB959
..... SB978
..... SK1
..... TP248.P47
632.95016 SB951
632.950202 SB951
632.950973 HD1751
..... SB951
632.951 QH545.P4
..... RA1270.P4
..... S21.A74
..... SB951
..... SB952.D2
..... SF810.A3
632.952 SB951.3
632.954 KF26.C645
..... QK565
..... S21
..... SB614
..... SB951.4
..... SB959
..... TC801
..... Z881.U4
632.9540973 KF26.C645
632.96 S21
..... SB975
633 SB91
..... SB185
..... SB186
..... SB187.D4
..... SB731
633.00954 SB187.I6
633.00966 SB192.A35
633.00973 SB185
633.009794 SB187.U6
633.083095 SB123
633.0870954 SB187.I6
633.088709712 S133
633.0890913 SB601
633.0954 SB187.I6
633.0954792 SB187.I6
633.1 HD1751
..... S133
..... SB187.I6
..... SB189
..... SB190
..... SB192.A72
..... SB192.I4
..... SB192.U5
633.11 S588.W6
..... SB191.W5
633.1109795 SB191.W5
633.1109941 SB191.W5
633.1123 SB191.W5
633.1170954 S279
633.1170994 SB191.W5
633.13012 SB191.O2
633.139 SB608.O2
633.15 SB191.M2
633.1570222 SB191.M2
633.16 SB191.B2
633.174 SB235
633.1749951 HD1751
633.18 SB191.R5
633.180944 SB191.R5
633.180954 SB191.R5
633.18095492 SB191.R5
633.18095951 SB191.R5
633.180966 SB191.R5
633.180976 S445
633.186 KF27.A367
633.1870954 SB191.R5
633.1887095951 SB191.R5
633.1896 SB608.R5
633.1898 SB608.R5
633.2 S133
..... S239
..... SB197
..... SB199
..... SB201.L65
..... SB208.S6
633.200966 SB208.A36
633.2009791 SB197
633.200994 SB208.A8
633.208 SB199
633.2085809764 SB612.T4
633.208597 TX7
633.2095493 SB199
633.21 QH423
633.251 S21
633.2574 S21
633.31952 S21
633.32 SB205.C64
633.34 SB205.S7
633.364 S21
633.491 SB211.P8
633.49107204 SB211.P8
633.49109713 S155
633.4912 SB211.P8
633.49123 SB211.P8
633.49133028 SB211.P8
633.4915 SB211.P8
633.4917 SB211.P8
633.4919951 S21
633.51 SB245
..... SB249
633.510621 SB249
633.510947 SB251.R9
633.510954 SB251.I3
633.510975 SB249
633.515028 S695
633.517 SB19
633.5197 SB608.C8
633.52 SB261.S4
633.577 DS324.S5
..... SB261.S4
633.58 SB317.B2
633.6396 S217
633.71 SB273
..... SB275
633.716 SB276
633.7198 SB608.T7
633.7297095493 SB608.T3
633.739 SB608.C6
633.83 SB307.C5
633.88 RS164
634 S155
..... S584.N45
..... SB111
..... SB125
..... SB356
634.0952 SB354.6.J3
634.0954 SB354.6.I4
634.095484 SB357
634.0979 SB359
634.11 SB363
634.110973 S21.A6
634.110979755 SB363
634.116 S239.S2
634.119 S239
..... S239.S2
634.13 SB373
634.1309711 SB373
634.136 SB373
634.208 SB41
634.2109711 SB379.A7
634.2309711 SB379.C5
634.3 HD1751
..... S279
..... SB369
634.316 HD1751
634.37 TX7
634.370975 TX7
634.5 SB401.A4
634.51095843 SB401.W3
634.573 SB401.C3
634.61 SB401.C6
634.6109964 SB401.C6
634.6197 SB608.C58
634.620973 S21
634.71 S217
634.711 S21
..... SB608.R25
634.73709713 SB386.B7
634.75 S21
634.750979 S21
634.76 S133
634.809469 SB396.2
634.809497 SB397.Y8
634.82 S21
634.9 HD9000.1
..... SD1
..... SD373
..... SD553
634.9016 Z5991
634.90222 TA593
634.9023 SD387.F6
634.906142 SD179
634.906271133 SD433
634.9062794 SD144.C2
634.9072 S21

Dewey	LC
634.90720549	SD224.P3
634.907207123	SD255
634.9072075	SD11
634.908	SD1
	SD11
	SD11.A45792
	SD14.B7
	SD45
	SD110
	SD111.V5
	SD121
	SD211
	SD217.F5
634.9085	SD11
634.90924	SD129.F4
	SD129.L8
	SD129.P5
634.9093	SD1
634.909413	SD183
634.90942	SD179
634.9094251	SD180.P4
634.90943	SD195
634.90954	SD223
634.9095412	SD224.B5
634.9095455	SD88.H37
634.9095488	SD516.A5
634.9095491	SD235.P2
634.90959	SD527.S65
634.90971	SD373
634.909719	SD13
634.9097292	SD152.J3
634.90973	SD143
634.9097561	SD144.N8
634.909757	HD9757.A2
634.909769	SD144.K4
634.909783	SD11
634.909791	SD11
634.909931	SD666.N5
634.909942	SD111.S7
634.909945	SD111.V5
634.928	SD177
634.928094	SD1
634.928095412	SD88.B4
	SD646.B5
634.92809794	SD431
634.92809931	SD666.N5
634.9285	SD111.N7
	SD381
	SD387.A25
	SD396
	SD551
	SD555
	SD557
634.9285018	SD11
634.92850212	SD557
634.928509794	SD551
634.928509795	SD11
634.95	S598
	S954.U6
	SD399.5
	SD408
634.95028	JX1977
634.9509472	SD1
634.9509549	SD235.P2
634.956	S21
	SD111.S7
	SD399.5
	SD408
	SD425
634.95609154	QP1
634.956095694	SD409
634.95609795	SD144.O7
634.95609931	SD666.N5
634.96	SB761
	SD666.N5
634.960971	SB761
634.9618	S21
	SD11
	SD421
634.9618028	SD389.8
634.961808	SD421
634.9618097	SD421
634.961809762	SD413.M7
634.963	S21
634.9642	SD211
634.966513	SB998.N4
634.9670947	SB761
634.96709669	SD1
634.96709773	SB761
634.96709784	SB761
634.97	SD391
634.972	SD179
634.9721	QE75
634.97210947	SD397.O12
634.9722	TX7
634.9723	SD13
	SD397.P85
634.9726	SD397.B5
634.97397	SD12
634.9739809549	QK495.S16
634.9751564	AS613
634.97517	SD13
	SD111.W5
	SD211
	SD397
	SD397.P6117
	SD397.P65
	SD434
634.9752	SD13
	SD211
	SD217.F5
	SD397.S77
634.9754	SD397.D7
634.97592	SD434
634.9808	SD1
	SD14.B7
	TS800
634.9809	SD538
634.980973	KF27.A348
634.9809931	SD666.N5
634.982	SD11
	SD211
634.9820947	SD629
634.9820975	SD538.2.S68
634.98209795	SD538
634.983	SD538
	SD540
634.985025795	SD432.U6
634.987	SB299.P3
635	HD1751
	PZ10.K74
	S217
	SB16
	SB129
	SB318
	SB321
	SB322
	SB351.H5
	SB453
	SB455
	SB603.5
	SB732
	TX7
	TX537
635.0202	SB318
635.0212	S401
635.0222	SB453
635.023	SB51
635.03	SB45
635.0924	QK31.L82
635.0942	SB451
635.095487	SB320.8.I5
635.09713	S155
635.0973	SB321
	SB453
635.0974	SB451
635.09764	SB453.2.T4
635.13	SB211.C3
635.2197	S21
635.22156	SB211.S9
635.3	SB331
635.31	S21
	S217
635.35	S21
635.536	HD1751
635.6	SB324
635.611	S21
635.62	S21
635.639	SB608.C88
635.64	SB732
635.64244	SB349
635.6429	SB608.T75
635.656	S217
635.6560893	SB608.P25
635.67293	S21.A6
635.7	SB351.H5
635.77752	SB428
635.8	SB353
635.9	SB323
	SB405
	SB406
	SB453
	SB455
	SB473
	SB608.O7
635.90222	SB407
635.9023	SB472
635.903	SB45
635.9062755	SB403.Z5
635.907	SB403.5
635.909	SB404.5
635.9091814	SB453.2.S65
635.90924	SB409
635.90968	SB453.2.A45
635.90971	SB405
	SB453.3.C2
635.909711	SB453
635.90973	SB453
	SB466.U6
635.909759	SB453.2.F6
	SB466.U65
635.909969	SB453.2.H3
635.9152309	SB123
635.91531	SB453
635.92	SB608.O7
635.93	SB407
635.931	TX7
635.932	SB434
635.9331	TX7
635.93311	TX7
635.933135	TX7
635.93315	SB413.C3
635.93317	S279
635.93321	SB413.G35
635.9333	SB411
	TX7
635.93336	SB413.R47
635.93346	S239.S2
	SB413.B4
635.93347	SB413.C12
	SB438
635.933470222	SB413.C12
635.93355	SB413.C55
	SB413.D13
	TX7
635.9336	SB413.R47
635.9336	TX7
635.93381	SB413.A4
635.93415	SB409
635.934150994	SB409
635.93424	S155
	SB413.I8
	TX7
635.93425	SB413.D12
635.93432	SB413.L7
635.93730942	SB429
635.93731	SB429
635.944	SB425
635.9440222	SB425
635.952	SB421
635.955	SB454
635.96	SB45
	SB405
635.963	SB424
635.964	SB432
	SB433
	TX7
635.965	S217
	SB407
	SB418
	SB419
	SB433.5
	SB454
635.966	SB405
635.96603	SB403.2
635.967	SB417
	SB453
	SB473.2
635.9672	SB459
635.9674	SB423
	SF457.7
635.9676	SB434
635.967609941	SB439
635.97	SB435
	SB438
635.976	SB435
635.9760222	SB435
635.977	SB435
	TX7
635.977091814	SB435
635.97709759	SB404.U6
635.9770994	SD391
635.97709941	SB435
635.977348	TX7
635.98	SB417
	SB418
635.982	SB415
635.9820222	SB415
636	PZ10.A643
	PZ10.D225
	SF61
	SF71
	SF293.L5
	SF413
636.003	SF21
636.00924	SF406
636.00951	SF55.C6
636.009549	SF55.P25
636.009931	SF5
636.00994	S478.A1
636.08	SF5
	SF61
636.0811	SF115
636.082	QP251
	SF81
	SF105
636.0821	QH431
636.08210151	SF105
636.083	HV4805.R75
	KF27.A365
636.0831	SF91
	TS1960
636.085	SF95
	TP368
636.0850212	HD1751
636.085072073	SF97
636.0852	S133
	SF95
	SF97
636.0855	AS36
	SF97
636.0883	SF5
636.0885	QH324.4
	QL55
	SF77
	SF406
636.0885025	QL55
636.08850971	SF406
636.0886	SF287
636.0887	SF413
	SF981
636.0888	QL785
636.08899	QL77.5
636.089	SF605
	SF745
	SF747
	SF753
636.0890202	SF745
636.089023	HF5381.A1G73
636.08903	SF609
636.0890711	SF775
636.08908	SF604
636.0890917496	SF612
636.0890942	SF657
636.0891	SF761
636.0892	SF768
636.089239	SF1
636.0892392	SF768
636.0894432	SF810.A3
636.08944322	SF810.S3
636.089446	KF27.A365
636.0894460973	KF26.A3534
636.08945	Q143.P2
	SF793
636.08945630942	SF797
636.08951	SF915
636.089561	SF98.M4
636.08959	QP82.2.A3
	SF757.5
636.0895952	S133
	S217
636.0896	SF55.C2
	SF755
636.08960145	QR201.P75
636.089607	SF745
	SF769
636.0896075	SF771
636.08960757	SF757.8
636.089607572	SF757.8
636.0896079	SF757.2
636.08965	SF901
636.089657	QR145
636.089692	SF793
636.0896924	Q44
636.0896936	SF792
636.0896957	QR201.B8
636.0896957061	RC123.B7
636.089696	SF810
	SF810.A3
636.08969883	SF724
636.0896992	RC254.5
636.0898178	QP801.E7
636.08982	SF871
636.089833	SF871
636.0899	SF997
636.1	PZ10.R545
	SF283
	SF284.U5
	SF285
	SF285.3
	SF303
636.100202	SF285
636.1003	PZ10.R18
	SF278
636.1008	SF301
636.1009	SF283
636.100973	SF284.U5
636.10109944	SF286.A9
636.108	SF285
	SF291
	SF301
	SF309
636.10833	KF26.C645
636.10837	GT5888
	SF309.9
	SF907
636.1088	SF287
	SF301
636.10882	TH9505.S3701
636.10888	SF287
	SF309
	SF336.M36
636.108880924	SF336.B67
	SF336.J36
636.10891	SF279
636.10896	SF955
636.108960759	SF951
636.108967	SF959.L25
636.108969	SF955
636.11	SF293.A8
636.12	SF293.T5
	SF338
	SF355.K4
636.13	SF293.A7
	SF293.L5
	SF293.Q3
	SF293.T5
	SF309.5
636.130978	SF284.U5
636.15	SF311
636.16	PZ10.S7143
	SF315
636.18	SF361
	SF361.D4
636.2	SF197
	SF810.N4
636.200212	SF55.M36
636.2009931	SF55.N45
636.201	HD9433.U52
636.2010922	PS277
636.201097123	F1076
636.20109764	F391
636.2010978	F596
636.2010994	DU110
636.208	SF85
636.2081209791	SF101
636.20820954	SF196.I4
636.20820991	SF196.I45
636.208245	SF105.5
636.2084	S133
636.2085	SF95
636.208557	SF98.U7
636.20894542	SF967.T8
636.20894565	S21
636.20896	SF961
636.20896248	SF967.E5
636.20896396	SF967.M5
636.2089657	S21
636.2089673	SF967.S6
636.20896957061	SF967.B7
636.2089696	SF967.P3
636.208969944	SF967.L4
636.20898178	SF967.S75
636.210975	SF207

Dewey	LC
636.212	TH4911.G72
636.213	HD1751
	S21
	S133
	SF207
	TH4911
636.2130982	F1401
636.214	QD1
	SF203
	SF231
	TH4911
	TH4911.G72
636.222	SF199.H4
636.294	SF401.R4
636.2950994	SF401.C2
636.3	SF375
636.300971	S133
636.30097644	SF375.4.T4
636.3009943	SF375.5.A8
636.3010993122	S478.S
636.308	S21
	SF375
636.3082095455	SF375.5.I42
636.30821	SF376.2
636.3083	S21
636.30852	SF376
636.36	SF373.M5
636.368	SF373.M5
636.385	SF373.K3
636.4	QP99.3.P7
	RL251
	SF395
636.4.0822	SF396.9
636.40831	SF396.3
636.40896	SF971
636.4089696	S21
636.5	SF487
	SF510.Q2
	SF995
636.500911	SF488.T65
636.508	S21.A6
636.50821	SF492
636.50831	SF486
636.5085	SF494
636.50876	SF99.F5
636.5089	SF995
636.50892	SF487
636.50896	SF995
636.5089639	TK7803
636.5089692	SF995.6.N4
636.514	S239.S2
	SF490
636.5871	SF489.B2
636.59	SF407.J3
636.596	SF465
	SF469
636.597095484	SF505
636.6	QL795.B57
	SK321
636.68	SF512
636.686	SF461
	SF995
636.6864	SF473.B8
636.6865	SF473.P3
636.6896	SF768
636.7	PZ10.H484
	QL795.D6
	SF426
	SF427
	SF429.A1
636.70099	SF422
	SF422.5
636.708	SF427
636.7082	SF427.2
636.70833	SF427.5
636.7088	SF431
636.70886	SF428.8
	SF431
636.70887	SF427
	SF431
636.70894563	SF797
636.7089612	SF811
636.708977	SF991
636.71	SF425
	SF429.A1
636.72	SF429.D3
	SF429.P85
636.73	HV1780.S4
	SF428.2
	SF428.6
	SF429.B64
	SF429.B75
	SF429.C6
	SF429.G37
	SF429.P5
	SF429.W35
636.75	SF428.5
636.752	SF428.5
	SF429
	SF429.C55
	SF429.L3
	SF429.P7
636.753	SF429.A4
	SF429.B2
	SF429.B3
	SF429.D25
	SF429.G8
	SF429.I85
	SF429.S33
636.7530942	SF429.H6
636.755	SF429.C3
	SF429.F5
636.76	SF429.C45
	SF429.M25
636.76	SF429.P3
	SF429.P55
	SF429.P8
	SF429.P85
	SF429.S375
	SF429.T7
636.77	SF426.6
	SF430
636.8	QL795.C2
	S447
	SF442
	SF447
	SF449.A1
636.80821	SF447.5
636.808903	SF985
636.808926	SF447
636.825	SF449.S5
636.826	SF442
636.83	SF442
636.9	SF413
636.9323	SF407.R6
636.93233	PZ10.D384
	SF459.G4
636.93234	SF405.C45
636.94447	QL795.O8
636.953	QL785.5
636.974447	QL795.B2
636.9755	SK403
636.97974428	QL795.C54
636.98	QL55
	QP631
636.982	SF459.M6
637	SF275.A1
637.023	HD9275.U6
637.06273	SF232.A1
637.0924	S417.S33
637.0971	SF233.C2
637.09941	SF233.A8
637.12	S21
637.1277	S217.A6134
637.130973	SF257.U72
637.133	SF259
637.1333	SF259
637.135	SF257
	TD895
637.35	SF271
637.5	HD1751
	KF26.A35
	S133
637.83509744	HJ9861
638.08899	QL77.5
638.1	PZ10.B6557
	SF522.5
	SF525
638.10942	SF525
638.142	S217
638.15	S217
	SF538
638.2	SF553
	SF553.I4
639.1	SK223.R8
	SK421
639.109174971	E99.E7
639.11	PZ10.K425
639.11097	E98.H8
639.11097124	SK283.6.C2
639.112	SK577.5
639.117357	SH11
639.1174446	QL737.C27
639.11746	QL737.P63
	SH363
639.12861	SF510.Q2
639.144	TS959.A8
639.2	SH331
	SH344.23.E3
639.208	SH1
	SH11
	SH223
	SH259
	SH279
	SH318.5
	SH318.5.A1
639.20942	SH255
639.2094291	SH258.W2
639.20947	SH283
639.2095493	SH307.C4
639.209669	SH315.N5
639.2097	SH1
639.20971	SH223
639.20973	KF27.M445
639.20977	SH36
639.2097749	SK361
639.209795	SK361
639.209798	SH11
	SK361
639.209931	SH318.5
639.20994	SH317
639.209943	SH318.G7
639.21	S914
639.210941	SH69
639.22	G540
	RA602.S6
	SH1
	SH222.F6
	SH255
	SH344.6.S4
639.220974	SH344.6.T7
639.2755	SH1
	SH255
	SH346
	SK361
639.2758	SH351.T8
	SK361
639.28	SH381
639.28	SH387
639.280222	SH381
639.2809	PZ10.E8
639.280916611	SH383.3.N47
639.280924	SH381
639.2809722	SH381
639.280974497	SH383.3.M4
639.280994	SH381
639.29	SH363
639.3	SF457.5
	SH151
	SH171
639.3008	SH11
639.3072071	SH2231
639.3095484	SH107
639.30971317	SH572.O5
639.309758	QL628.G4
639.310975	S914
639.311	SH11
	SH159
639.312	QL628.G4
639.32	SH1
639.34	QL78
	SF457
	SF457.1
	SF458.G6
	SK361
639.3752	S21
	SH167.C35
639.3755	SH11
	SK361
639.408	SD11
639.40973	SH365.A1
639.41109711	SH223
639.41109969	SH365.H3
639.412	TS755.P3
639.4120952	SH375
639.9	KF31.C6
	QH75
	QH77.A8
	QL88
	S21
	S942
	S962
	S964.U6
	SD373
	SK354.2
	SK471.N63
639.90207	S960
639.9023	S944
639.908	SK393
639.909	S962
639.90924	SK575.Z3
639.90942	QL21.G7
639.90954	S964.I5
639.9096	S964.A3
639.90971	SK351
639.90973	KF27.M445
	SK361
639.909743	SK455
639.909759	SH11
639.909762	SK413
639.909763	SK401
639.909789	SK427
639.909791	SK369
639.909931	SK577.5
639.90993125	SK577.5
639.9209713	SK471.O5
639.93	SB950
639.96	KF26.I548
639.960924	SF613.H33
639.9761	SK421
639.977	SH1.A53
	TC801
639.97755	QL638.S2
	SH11
639.97812	SB998.R3
639.9782	QL676.7
639.978242	SF508
639.9782924	SF994.4.W3
639.97829240947	SK533
639.97829240973	SK361
639.9784	QL696.A5
639.97861	SF510.Q2
639.9797357	KF26.A6
	QH1
	QL737.U55
	SK471.B7
639.99	QK86
640	HQ1229
	TX9
	TX145
	TX147
	TX158
	TX167
	TX731
640.207	TX295
640.23	TX164
640.28	TX158
640.42	TX7
640.7	TX165
	TX173
640.711762	TX174.M7
640.7125	LB3205
640.714	TX165
	TX165.A1
	TX253
640.715	TX165
	TX167
640.72	TX5
	TX165
	TX173
640.73	HC110.C6
	HC110.C63
640.73	HD1773.A5
	HF5429.6.G7
	TX335
	TX356
640.730184	HB801
640.73097471	TX335
640.7309753	HC108.W3
640.77	TX165
640.924	TX140.C5
641	S133
	TP507
	TP546
	TP547.M35
	TP548
	TP553
	TP557
	TP559.P8
	TP605
	TX158
	TX353
	TX354
	TX355
	TX412
	TX637
641.013	TX633
	TX637
641.0130924	TP547.S5
641.0130951	TX724.5.C5
641.0202	TX652.7
641.03	TX349
	TX350
641.0924	TX649.P68
641.1	KF26.5.N358
	RM216
	TX7
	TX345
	TX353
	TX354
	TX355
	TX356
	TX360.E7
	TX360.I4
	TX360.U6A514
	TX361.C5
	TX361.Y6
	TX551
641.1018	TX357
641.10212	TX7
	TX551
641.107	TX364
641.1076	TX354
	TX357
641.1078	TX364
641.1091724	KJ206
641.10954	TX360.I4
641.1095413	TX360.I4
641.1095694	TX360.I79
641.1096	TX360.A3
641.10973	TX360.U6
641.11	TX531
641.12	TX553.P7
641.13	TX553.C28
641.130212	TX551
641.3	PZ10.P6
	PZ10.R85
	S21
	TP548
	TP548.2
	TX345
	TX354
	TX355
	TX388
	TX388.I5
641.30023	TX357
641.3003	TX349
641.30072042	TX341
641.309	GT2860
641.30973	TX360.U6
641.331	KF26.C636
641.3318	TX558.R5
641.338	TX406
641.33803	TX406
641.35	TX7
	TX801
641.3565	S21
641.35655	S21
	TX558.S7
641.36	TX7
641.362	TX7
641.371	TX379
641.375	SF490
641.4	S217
	TX7
	TX601
	TX603
	TX610
	TX611.5
641.42	TX7
641.45	TX610
641.453	TX7
641.46	TX7
641.49	HD9417.N8
	TX7
	TX749
641.4922	TX7
641.493	TX7
641.5	TX7
	TX158
	TX651
	TX652
	TX652.5
	TX663
	TX715
	TX715.R752

641.5	TX717
	TX724
	TX724.5.M5
	TX725
	TX725.A1
	TX725.A9
	TX725.N4
	TX728
	TX731
	TX737
	TX739
	TX740
	TX770
	TX830
	TX840.M7
	TX1715
641.50207	TX740
641.503	TX349
	TX715
641.509	TX645
641.50917496	TX715
641.53	TX731
	TX738
	TX740
641.54	TX737
641.55	TX7
	TX715
	TX717
	TX821
641.552	TX715
	TX728
641.56	TX652
641.561	TX652
641.563	QP141
	RC662
	RG525
	RM216
	RM219
	RM221.A6
	RM221.C3
	RM221.C4
	RM222.2
	RM237.9
	TX355
	TX715
	TX728
	TX837
641.563023	TX164
641.5635	RM222.2
641.5638	RM219
641.566	TX837
641.5676	TX724
641.5676437	TX724
641.568	TX731
	TX738
	TX739
641.57	TX820
641.570202	TX820
641.570212	TX820
641.5707	TX820
641.572	TX820
641.572023	HF5382
641.575	TX840.M6
641.5753	TX840.M7
641.578	TX823
	TX840.B3
641.58	TX825
	TX840.B5
641.586	TX827
641.59	TX725
	TX725.A1
	TX725.A7
641.594	TX719
	TX723.5
641.5941	TX717.3
	TX724.5.C5
641.59415	TX717.5
641.5942	TX705
	TX717
641.594274	TX717
641.5943	TX721
641.59436	TX721
641.59439	TX723.5.H8
641.594391	TX723.5.H8
641.5944	TX652.5
	TX719
641.5945	TX723
641.594585	TX723.5.M35
641.5946	TX723.5.S7
641.59469	TX723.5.P7
641.5947	TX723.3
641.5948	TX722.A1
641.59481	TX722.N6
641.59489	TX722.D4
641.59495	TX723.5.G8
641.595	TX724.5
	TX724.5.A1
641.5951	TX724.5.C5
641.59519	TX724.5.K65
641.5952	TX724.5
	TX724.5.J3
641.5954	TX724.5.I4
641.595493	TX724.5.C4
641.5956	TX725.N36
641.59561	TX725.T8
641.595691	TX725.S9
641.595694	TX724
641.5959	TX724.5.A1
	TX724.5.I5
641.59595	TX724.5.M3
641.596	TS725.A4
	TX725.A4
641.59669	TX725.N54
641.5968	TX725.S6
641.597	TX715
641.5971	TX715
	TX823
641.5971344	TX715
641.5972	TX716.M4
641.59729	TX716.A1
641.5973	TX715
	TX840.M6
641.5974	TX715
641.59741	TX715
641.59743	TX715
641.597444	TX715
641.597465	TX715
641.597471	TX715
641.59748	TX721
641.5975	TX715
641.59756	TX715
641.59762	TX715
641.59763	TX715
641.59763355	TX715
641.59764	TX715
641.597671	TX715
641.59768	TX715
641.59769	TX715
641.59774	TX715
641.59778	TX715
641.5978	TX715
641.59791	TX715
641.59794	TX715
641.599	TX725.S65
641.59914	TX724.5.P5
641.59931	TX725.N4
641.5994	TX725.A9
641.5996	TX724.5.P6
641.59969	TX724.5.H3
641.6	TX814.5.F5
	TX814.5.R6
	TX823
	TX837
641.6153	TX610
641.62	TX726
	TX726.3
641.63	TX558.S75
	TX808
641.631	TX765
	TX769
641.6318	TX809.R5
641.6373	TX819.C6
641.6374	TX767.C5
641.638	TX819.H4
641.6383	TX406
641.6384	TX819.C9
641.64	TX811
641.6411	TX7
	TX813.A6
641.645	TX814
641.65	TX7
	TX801
	TX837
641.650954	TX724.5.I4
641.650968	TX837
641.6521	TX7
	TX803.P8
641.6526	TX803.L4
641.6532	TX803.A7
641.65642	TX803.T6
641.65655	TX724.5.J3
641.658	TX804
641.66	TX749
641.662	TX749
641.663	TX749
641.665	TX749
641.67	S133
641.6714	TX759
641.673	TX382
	TX759
	TX825
641.675	TX745
641.69	TX747
	TX751
641.691	TX751
641.692	TX747
641.692755	TX747
641.7	TX828
	TX830
	TX840.B5
641.71	TX765
641.73	TX757
641.76	TX609
	TX840.B3
641.77	TX825
641.8	TX740
	TX757
	TX769
	TX770
	TX773
	TX825
	UG633
641.81	TX652
	TX740
	TX819.A1
	TX819.S8
	TX825
641.814	TX819.A1
641.815	TX769
641.82	TX693
	TX715
	TX825
641.821	TX693
641.8210944	TX719
641.83	TX740
	TX807
641.84	TX818
641.85	TX767.M3
641.853	TX791
641.86	TX767.C5
	TX773
	U408.3
641.862	TX795
641.863	TX795
641.865	TX773
641.86509436	TX773
641.86509489	TX765
641.8652	TX773
641.8653	TX771
641.8654	TX772
641.87	TP507
	TP548
641.872	TP507
	TP548
	TP548.2
641.873	TP577
641.87309481	TP573.N6
641.874	TX951
642.071	TX911.5
642.076	TX945
642.08	S21
642.4	TX731
642.41	TX165
	TX728
	TX731
	TX737
642.410973	TX731
642.5	TX815
642.50212	HD1751
642.560257471	TX907
642.5602579461	TX907
642.560924	TX649.F7
642.580973	LB3479.U6
642.6	TX871
642.692	TX747
642.7	TX877
643	HD1379
	TH4813
	TH4817.5
	TL297
	TT151
	TX298
	TX301
	TX307
643.03	TT155
643.0942	DA115
643.09701	E78.C2
643.3	DA670.S4
	NA2545.P5
	TH4805
	TH4816
	TX653
643.309549	TX653
643.5	TH4816
	TT153
643.6	HD9999.H83U57
	TK7019
643.6014	TX298
643.60942	NK928
643.7	TH4816
	TH4817
644.02840272	TP368
644.1	S21
645	TT323
	TX7
645.07	TX303
645.1	TS1775
645.4	TT197
	TT198
645.40202	TT195
645.997	RA407.3
646	S544
	TT507
	TT518.E7
646.0024071	RA776.5
646.023	TT507
646.15	TT525
646.2	TT705
646.2028	TJ1513
646.32	TT580
646.4	TT515
	TT520
646.404	TT515
	TT518
	TT520
	TT550
	TT705
646.404078	TT508
646.406	TT635
646.43	TT520
	TT580
646.4304	TT515
	TT518
646.434	TT515
646.4504	TT515
646.47	TT560
646.7	RA778
	RL87
	TT957
646.72	BJ1610
	HQ1219
	RA778
	TT957
646.72023	TT958
646.724	TT972
646.726	RL87
	TT957
646.74	TT960
646.7409	TT957
646.740922	TT954.5
647	SB482.A6
647.076	TX960
647.1	HD4966.T4I474
647.2	TX331
647.908	TX946
647.94	TX1105
647.94025	TX907
647.9402576	TX907
647.9402578	TX907
647.9409	GT3770
647.940924	TX910.5.G75
647.94094	TX910.A1
647.94251	TX910.G7
647.94272	TX910.G7
647.9429	TX910.G7
647.944	TX907
647.9442	DA650
	TX910.G7
647.944271	TX910.G7
647.944274	TX910.G7
647.944429	TX910.G7
647.944436	TX910.F8
647.945491	TX931
647.9468	TX910.S55
647.94715	TX910.C2
647.9477	TX909
647.9477492	TX941.G68
647.94775	TX909
647.9478	TX907
647.9478863	TX909
647.9479	TX907
647.95	TX945
	TX946
647.950924	TX910.5.S55
647.9509942	AC5
647.954212	TX635
	TX910.G7
647.95422	TX910.G7
647.954923	TX910.N4
647.955952	TX910.S48
647.95744025	TX907
647.957471	TX907
	TX945.5.C58
647.95753	KF27.5.H6
	TX907
647.9576335	TX907
647.95794	TX907
647.9579461	TX945
647.9579494	TX907
647.96	TX955
647.9651	RA972.5
647.965108	RA975.5.H6
647.96740202	TH4763
647.99	LB3235
648	U408.3
648.1	GT482
	RA960
	TS440
648.5	TX324
648.52	TH3361
648.7	S21
	TA423.7
	TX7
	TX325
648.8	TX309
648.800184	HF5415
649	BF723.I6
	HQ769
	PZ10.A646
	RJ61
	RJ101
649.0202	QP36
649.0207	PN6231.C3
649.1	CT788
	HQ769
	HQ770
	HQ772
	HQ774
	HQ792.R9
	RJ61
	RJ101
	RJ499
649.1019	BF723.I6
649.10242	RG525
649.10924	RG560
649.122	RJ61
	RJ101
	RJ253
649.123	HQ772
649.125	HQ796
649.1511	HV1598
649.1512	HV2395
649.152	LC4580
649.155	HQ773.5
649.3	RJ216
649.5	LC37
649.6	HQ769
649.7	BV1475.2
	LC37
649.8	RJ496.C4
	RT61
649.807	RA801
650	HB171.5
	HF1131
	HF5011
	HF5351
	HF5353
	HF5438
	HF5547
	HF5547.5
	HF5548.2
650.018	HF5548.2
650.0207	HF1009
650.0246655	HD9571.5
650.06273	HQ1945.N27
650.07	HF1106

650.07 ..... HF1111
..... HF1131
650.071 ..... HF1131
650.0711 ..... HF1131
..... HF1141
..... HF5429.3
650.071154 ..... HF1171.I4
650.071173 ..... HF1131
650.0711764 ..... HF1131
650.071179467 ..... HF1134.C3
650.071242 ..... HF1141
650.0715 ..... LB2844.1.P3
650.072 ..... H62
650.08 ..... HF5351
650.09 ..... HF5001
650.0922 ..... CT219
650.0924 ..... HD9506.U62W45
650.0952 ..... HC462.9
650.0954 ..... HF1171.I4
..... HF5349.I5
650.0973 ..... E185.8
650.09931 ..... HF5361
650.0994 ..... HF5351
650.1 ..... BF1611
..... HD31
..... HD38
..... HF5386
..... PS3523.O64
650.10207 ..... HF5386
650.10924 ..... HF5391
650.10926 ..... HF5386
650.7 ..... HD69.I7
651 ..... HF5547
..... HF5547.5
..... R728.8
651.0202 ..... HF5547.5
651.26 ..... HF5695
651.269 ..... T57.5
651.29 ..... HF5371
..... KF318
651.371 ..... HF5547.5
651.374 ..... JK716
651.3741 ..... HF5547
..... KF319
..... Q227
..... R728.8
651.3741023 ..... HF5547
651.3741076 ..... LB1761
651.3743 ..... HF5501
651.37430202 ..... HF5726
651.3743076 ..... JK716
651.5 ..... HF5736
..... JC599.U5
..... RA976
..... RC65
..... RC439
651.5018 ..... HF5548.2
651.51 ..... HF5736
651.53 ..... HF5736
..... LB2846
651.59 ..... S494.5.D3
651.7 ..... HF5549.5.C6
..... HF5721
..... PE1115
651.703 ..... HF1002
651.74 ..... HF5721
..... HF5726
..... PE1129.I7
651.740014 ..... HF1002
651.7402 ..... HF5547
..... PE1115
..... PE1116.S6
651.75 ..... HF5547
..... HF5721
..... HF5726
..... PE1483
651.8 ..... HD2421
..... HF5548.2
..... HF5548.5.C2
..... HF5548.5.F2
..... HF5679
..... HG939.5
..... JS3152.E4
..... Q180
..... Q180.A1
..... Q335
..... QA75
..... QA76
..... QA76.15
..... QA76.28
..... QA76.4
..... QA76.5
..... QA76.8
..... QA76.8.G2
..... QA76.8.I12
..... QA76.8.I125
..... QA76.8.R17
..... QA76.8.U6
..... QA269
..... QA402
..... QC100
..... QC770
..... QD8.3
..... T57.5
..... T385
..... TA1
..... TK7895.O6
..... TL521
..... TL521.3
..... TL521.3.C6
..... TL553
..... VC503
..... Z699
651.8023 ..... HF5548.2
651.8023 ..... QA76.25
651.803 ..... QA76.15
651.808 ..... Z678.9
651.80924 ..... HF5548.2
651.82 ..... HF5548
..... HF5679
651.82076 ..... HF5688
651.83 ..... HF5548
651.84 ..... HF5548.2
..... Q180.A1
..... QA76.5
652 ..... Z40
652.3 ..... Z49.4.B4
652.302 ..... Z49
652.3024 ..... Z49
652.307 ..... Z49.2
652.32 ..... HF5726
..... Z49
652.8 ..... PZ10.P447
..... Z103
..... Z104
653 ..... Z56
653.3023 ..... Z53
653.42 ..... Z56
653.4242 ..... Z56
653.427 ..... Z56
653.4272 ..... Z56.G833
653.428 ..... Z56
653.982 ..... SB415
655 ..... PN4855
..... Z116
..... Z122
..... Z209.C6
..... Z231.5.P7
..... Z232.U784
..... Z239
..... Z244
..... Z244.3
..... Z244.5
..... Z250.A4
..... Z464.F6
655.002 ..... Z253
655.002542 ..... Z151
655.00924 ..... ML427.A87
..... Z232.J24
655.015 ..... Z244
655.023 ..... Z122
..... Z243.U6C57
655.03 ..... Z118
655.1 ..... Z124
..... Z126.A2
..... Z232.C38
..... Z240
655.1024 ..... Z126
655.108 ..... Z276
655.14164 ..... Z232.G78
655.142 ..... Z151
..... Z232.A145
..... Z232.B2
..... Z232.C38
655.1421 ..... Z232.C36
..... Z232.P68
655.14213 ..... Z232.C65
655.14258 ..... Z232.S856
655.143 ..... Z126.Z7
655.1450924 ..... Z232.B66
655.14531 ..... Z156.V4
655.14585 ..... Z157
655.14912 ..... Z170.I3
655.154 ..... Z185
655.169 ..... Z196.M3
655.173 ..... Z205
..... Z208
..... Z258
655.1744 ..... Z209.M4
655.1747 ..... Z209.N559
655.1794 ..... Z231.5.P7
655.191 ..... Z186.I5
655.1931 ..... Z222.N5
..... Z243.N5
655.194 ..... Z221
655.1982 ..... Z170.G8
655.2 ..... NE2425
..... PN147
..... Z48
..... Z116.A3
..... Z244
..... Z244.3
..... Z247
..... Z250
..... Z250.A2
..... Z253.5
655.20627 ..... Z120.I59
655.20904 ..... Z116
655.20924 ..... Z250
655.24 ..... Z232.S777
..... Z250
..... Z250.A2
..... Z251.I7
655.25 ..... QB4
..... Z253
..... Z253.3
..... Z253.5
655.25028 ..... QC100
655.255 ..... Z254
655.28 ..... Z253.3
655.3 ..... TR657
..... Z244
655.31 ..... Z252.5.F6
655.312 ..... Z249
..... Z253
655.315 ..... Z252.5.O5
655.316 ..... TT273
655.318 ..... Z252.5.O5
655.32 ..... TR925
..... TR1010
655.325 ..... TR940
655.327 ..... TR970
..... TR975
..... TR980
655.38 ..... Z250.A4
655.382 ..... HV1668
..... HV1669
655.383 ..... GA150
..... GA150.5
..... TR835
655.384 ..... MT10
655.3840924 ..... ML427.M63
655.4 ..... PN4733
..... Z231.5.P7
..... Z473
655.4028 ..... Z476
655.403 ..... Z118
655.406242 ..... Z329.P8
655.40924 ..... PR6007.I39
655.424 ..... AS36
..... DA566.9.N7
..... PN4874.M37
..... PN4874.N39
..... Z232.H83
..... Z325
..... Z325.C96
..... Z325.M9
..... Z325.P59
..... Z325.T6
..... Z473
..... Z473.L56
..... Z542.3.R6
655.442 ..... Z278
..... Z323
655.4421 ..... Z232.O98
655.44272 ..... PR6013.R735
655.443 ..... PN5213.S7
..... Z323
655.44436 ..... Z232.B622
655.447 ..... Z366
655.448 ..... Z116.A3
655.44932 ..... Z232.P71
655.451 ..... Z462
655.452 ..... Z463
655.4549 ..... Z286.E3
655.47471 ..... Z473
655.51 ..... PN137
655.52 ..... PN151
..... PN161
655.530924 ..... Z116.A3
655.5720973 ..... PN4877
655.573 ..... PT8063.B33
..... Z116
..... Z116.A3
..... Z305.S6
655.579 ..... Z265
..... Z1033.M6
655.5794 ..... ML112
..... MT67
655.579402571 ..... ML112
655.57940922 ..... ML427.F7
655.57940924 ..... ML424.R68
..... ML427
655.5920924 ..... JA94.W6
655.593 ..... Z232.O7
655.594 ..... ML112
..... Z231.5.U6
655.5950973 ..... Z208
655.7 ..... Z269
655.70924 ..... Z269.C6
..... Z269.P34
..... Z269.W8
655.744 ..... Z701
657 ..... HF5601
..... HF5616.A8
..... HF5621
..... HF5629
..... HF5635
..... HF5657
..... HF5661
..... HF5667
..... HF5681.D5
..... HF5686.H6
657.01 ..... HF5601
..... HF5625
..... HF5657
657.018 ..... HF5667
..... HF5679
657.0202 ..... HF5635
657.0207 ..... PN6231.A24
657.024339 ..... HF5635
657.02434 ..... KF1446
657.028 ..... HF5679
657.03 ..... HF5621
657.06273 ..... HF5601
657.071173 ..... HF5630
657.076 ..... HF5635
..... HF5661
657.077 ..... HF5630
657.08 ..... HF5601
..... HF5629
..... HF5630
..... HF5635
657.09 ..... HF5605
..... HF5606
..... HF5616.U5
657.0942 ..... HF5653
657.0952 ..... HF5601
657.097124 ..... HF5616.C2
657.20712 ..... HF5630
657.3 ..... HD69.R4
..... HF5601
657.3 ..... HF5635
..... HF5657
..... HF5681.B2
..... HF5681.D5
..... HF5686.C7
657.3076 ..... HF5681.B2
657.30942 ..... HF5681.B2
657.30973 ..... HF5681.B2
657.4 ..... HF5681.B2
..... HF5681.T3
..... HF5681.V3
657.42 ..... HF5686.C8
..... HF5686.M35
657.42018 ..... HF5686.C8
657.42077 ..... HF5686.C8
657.4208 ..... HF5686.C8
657.4209 ..... HF5686.C8
657.45 ..... HE9803.A15
..... HF5667
..... KF1357
657.450186 ..... HF5667
657.4508 ..... HF5667
657.46 ..... HF5681.T3
657.48 ..... HF5635
657.6 ..... HF5667
657.609549 ..... HJ9927.P13
657.832 ..... HF5686.C3
..... HF5686.P925
..... LB2342.2.C3
..... LB2830
..... T171.B4579
657.833 ..... HF5681.L3
..... HF5686.A8
..... HG1706
..... HG1707
..... HG1707.5
657.8333 ..... HG1707
657.834 ..... KF1357.A7
..... LB2830
..... Z733.M406
657.835 ..... HJ9733
..... HJ9773
..... HJ9777.A4M42
..... HJ9777.A4N72
..... HJ9844.A23
..... HJ9927.I4
..... UB163
657.8350922 ..... HJ9843
657.83509789 ..... HJ9882
657.836 ..... HG8077
..... HG8848
657.836045 ..... HG1662.U5
657.837 ..... HF5686.H75
657.838 ..... HE4351
..... HF5686.W3
657.839 ..... HE605
..... HF5681.S3
657.86 ..... HF5686.R48
657.862 ..... HF5686.M6
657.863 ..... HD1930.M53
..... S567
..... SB443
..... SF261
657.867 ..... HF5686.P3
657.867042 ..... HF5686.S75
657.869 ..... HF5686.R6
..... HF5686.S45
658 ..... E185.8
..... HB3730
..... HD20
..... HD20.15.U5
..... HD29
..... HD30
..... HD31
..... HD38
..... HD69.D4
..... HD70.I4
..... HD2341
..... HD2421
..... HD2429.G7
..... HD2745
..... HD9711.5
..... HE5351
..... HF5343
..... HF5351
..... HF5361
..... HF5415.13
..... HF5415.15
..... HF5500
..... HF5548.2
..... HG939.5
..... HM131
..... JF1351
..... T58.6
..... T60.6
..... T174
..... T175.5
..... TS155
658.001 ..... AS36
..... HD31
..... HD38
..... HD38.A586
658.001519 ..... HA29
658.0018 ..... HD20.4
..... HD20.7
..... HD38
..... HD69.D4
..... HD70.U5
..... HF345
..... HF5386
..... HF5548.2
..... T57.5
658.00182 ..... HA29
..... HA40.I6

658.00182 ..... HD20.4
..... HF5006
658.00184 ..... HD20.4
..... HD31
658.00186 ..... HD20.5
..... HD31
..... HD38
658.00202 ..... HD31
658.00207 ..... PN6231.M2
658.0023 ..... HD20
..... HD31
658.002422 ..... BV652
658.0028 ..... HF5548.2
658.003 ..... HD19
658.006 ..... HF5415
658.006242 ..... HD70.G7
658.007 ..... HD20
..... HD20.15.U5
..... HD29
658.0071 ..... HD20.15.G7
658.0071142 ..... HD20
658.0071146 ..... HD70.S65
658.0071154 ..... HF1171.I4
658.0071173 ..... HF1101
658.00715 ..... HD20
658.0076 ..... HD31
..... JK716
658.0077 ..... HD31
..... HF5549
658.008 ..... HD30
..... HD31
..... HD38
..... HD70.U5
..... HF5500
658.00922 ..... HC102.5
658.00942 ..... HD70.G7
..... HD5660.G7
658.00943 ..... HD70.G2
658.00947 ..... HD70.R9
..... JN6598.K7
658.009493 ..... HF3607
658.00954 ..... HC435.2
..... HD70.I4
658.009549 ..... HD70.P35
658.00973 ..... HD60.5.U5
658.018 ..... HF5548.5.F2
658.0184 ..... HD20.4
658.022 ..... HB601
..... HD20
..... HD31
..... HD69.S6
..... HD2346.P32E345
..... HD2346.U5
..... HD8037.U5
..... HF5351
..... KF31.5.S6
658.0220186 ..... HF5006
658.02207 ..... HD69.S6
658.022095492 ..... HD2346.P32
..... HD2346.P32E35
658.0220971 ..... HD70.C2
658.0220973 ..... HD69.S6
..... KF27.5.S674
658.0230973 ..... HD2356.U5
658.0236 ..... HD69.I7
..... HD2826
..... HD8376.5
658.02360973 ..... HD69.I7
658.046 ..... HD2756.U5
658.047 ..... HD3271
658.05 ..... HF5548.2
658.0542 ..... T57.5
658.1 ..... HD29
..... QA76.5
..... QA76.8.I14
..... QC770
..... T385
..... TJ1
658.10943 ..... HD2859
658.11 ..... HD31
..... HD38
658.11409794 ..... KFC337
658.11410973 ..... HD8037.U5
658.1144 ..... HD2709
658.1145 ..... HD38
..... HD2741
..... HG4272
..... KF1413
..... KF1414
..... KF1414.3
..... KF2901
..... KF1525
658.11450973 ..... HD2791
658.15 ..... HC101
..... HC435.2
..... HD20.3
..... HD38
..... HD69.D4
..... HD69.I7
..... HD2984
..... HD7293
..... HD7395.M6
..... HF5006
..... HF5351
..... HF5386
..... HF5550
..... HF5601
..... HF5635
..... HF5657
..... HF5681.A3
..... HF5681.B2
..... HF5686.C7
..... HF5686.C8
..... HG173
658.15 ..... HG186.G7
..... HG3729.K62
..... HG3729.U5
..... HG4011
..... HG4026
..... HG4028.C4
..... HG4028.D4
..... HG4028.S7
..... HG4028.T4
..... HG4028.V3
..... HG4061
..... HG4062
..... HG4070.M5
..... HG4090
..... HG4135
..... HG5159.M4
..... HJ1023
..... HJ2052
..... KF1457
..... RA440.6
..... RA790.6
..... S561
..... T57.95
..... TA177.4
..... TS167
658.150182 ..... HG173
658.150184 ..... HG4026
658.150202 ..... HD31
658.15076 ..... HG4011
658.1508 ..... HC101
..... HF5550
..... HG4011
658.150942 ..... HF5550
658.1509471 ..... HB9
658.150971 ..... HG4028.C4
..... HG4358
658.150973 ..... HG4061
658.1509931 ..... HG4273.5.N45
658.151 ..... HF5603
..... HF5629
..... HF5635
..... HF5657
..... HF5679
..... HF5686.C7
..... HF5686.C8
..... HF5686.I46
..... HG4489.A8
658.1510711 ..... HF5686.C8
658.1512 ..... HF5686.C7
658.1513 ..... HF5657
..... TA177.7
658.152 ..... HD39
..... HD52
..... HD52.3
..... HG173
..... HG3701
..... HG4011
..... HG4026
..... HG4028.C4
..... HG4028.D3
..... HG4211
..... HG8059.B8
..... KF32.5.S685
658.152077 ..... HG4028.C4
658.152096761 ..... HG3729.U36
658.1520973 ..... HG4061
658.15244 ..... HG4028.C45
658.153 ..... HF5681.E9
..... HG4028.C45
..... HJ4653.D5
..... HV108
..... KF6297
..... KF6314
..... KF6464
..... TA180
658.154 ..... HD47.5
..... HF5006
..... HF5371
..... HF5429
..... HF5550
..... HG4026
..... HG4028.C4
..... HV4599.A4
..... T56.8
..... T175
..... TP155
..... TS165
..... TS168
..... Z675.S3
658.1540184 ..... HF5686.C8
658.1540954 ..... HD47.5
658.155 ..... HD36
..... HF5681.D5
..... HG4026
..... RA645.K5
658.1550186 ..... HD31
658.1552 ..... HD47.5
658.15904 ..... HF5550
658.15932 ..... H64.T9
..... LB2338
..... LB2823.5
..... LB2824
..... LB2825
..... Q180
..... Q180.U5
..... RA971.3
..... T107
658.15933 ..... HG1706
658.15934 ..... HF5686.P9A73
..... QC875.B68
658.15937 ..... HF5686.H75
658.15938 ..... TD223
658.15963 ..... S567
658.159630973 ..... HG2051.U5
658.16 ..... HD2741
..... HD2756.U5
..... HD2847
..... HF5006
..... HG4028.M4
..... KF27.J8666
..... KF1167
..... KF1475
..... KF1477
658.18 ..... HD69.I7
..... HF1009.5
..... HF5006
658.18098 ..... HD69.I7
658.2 ..... HD52
..... HD60.5.U5
..... HF5415.15
..... RA967
..... RA968
..... TA180
..... TH9445.C65
..... TP155
..... TS174
..... TS178
..... TS192
..... UF543.A3
658.202 ..... RA971
..... TH9705
..... TS192
658.2020184 ..... TS192
658.21 ..... H31
..... HC110.D5
..... HF5429
..... HF5429.6.F5
658.2109471 ..... G23
658.2109768 ..... HC107.T33D53
658.210978463 ..... HD58
658.23 ..... HF5547
658.230942 ..... HT169.G7
658.25 ..... TH7226
658.28 ..... RA965
658.3 ..... E185.8
..... HD30
..... HD38
..... HD2745
..... HD5660.N4
..... HD6971
..... HD8391
..... HF5548.8
..... HF5549
..... HF5549.2.U5
..... HF5549.5.J6
..... HF5549.5.J62
..... HF5549.5.J63
..... HF5549.5.R3
..... HF5549.5R5
..... JK765
..... LB2833.3.C2
..... RA972.7
..... RT11
..... TJ1160
658.3000954 ..... HF5548.8
658.3001 ..... HF5549.2.U5
658.30018 ..... HD21
..... HF5549
658.300186 ..... HF5549
658.30019 ..... HF5549
658.300216 ..... HF5549
658.30023 ..... HF5549
658.30071 ..... HD31
658.30072073 ..... HF5549
658.30076 ..... HF5549
658.3008 ..... HF5549
658.300924 ..... HF5549
658.300942 ..... HF5549.A2
658.300954 ..... HF5549
..... HF5549.2.I4
658.300971 ..... HF5549
658.3009931 ..... HF5549.2.N45
658.300994 ..... HF5549
658.302 ..... HF5549
..... HF5549.5.T7
..... HV11
..... HV7936.S8
..... T175.5
..... TS155.4
..... TS155.5
658.302076 ..... HE6499
658.3020973 ..... HD70.U5
658.31 ..... HD6571
..... HD8398
..... HF5549.5.C62
..... TA158
..... TX911.3.L3
658.311 ..... HF5383
..... HF5438
..... HF5549.5.I6
..... HF5549.5.R44
..... RA972.7
658.3110973 ..... HF5549.5.R44
658.3111 ..... HF5549.5.R44
..... LB2833.4.S6
..... Z602
658.3112 ..... RA410.7
658.312 ..... HF5549.5.P4
..... JF1601
..... RT11
658.3121 ..... RT89
658.3122 ..... HD5115
..... HD6065.5.C3
658.31220942 ..... HD5115.2.G7
658.3123 ..... LB2809.P4
658.3124 ..... HF5429
..... HF5549.5.T7
..... HF5630
658.3124 ..... HM133
..... HV8754
..... LB1715
..... T107
658.31240942 ..... HF5549.5.T7
658.31240973 ..... HD5715.2
..... Q180.A1
658.31243 ..... HF5549.5.T7
..... HV245
..... KFL592
658.31244 ..... HD7255
658.3125 ..... HF5549.5.J62
..... HF5549.5.P35
..... HF5549.5.R3
658.3126 ..... HD8051
658.31260186 ..... HF5549.5.P7
658.3129 ..... TF522
658.31290973 ..... HF5549.5.L3
658.3132 ..... HD6280
..... JK791
658.314 ..... HD38
..... HD8383
..... HF5548.8
..... HF5549
658.3140186 ..... HE8846.A55
658.315 ..... HD5650
..... HD8039.M4I46
..... HF5549
..... KF3365
..... RA976
658.31508 ..... HD8008
..... HF5549
658.3151 ..... HF5549.2.U5
658.3152 ..... HD5650
..... HD5660.G7
658.31520186 ..... HD5660.G7
658.31520942 ..... HD6490.S5
658.315209497 ..... HD5660.Y8
658.3152095694 ..... HD5660.I8
658.31520965 ..... HD5660.A4
658.315408 ..... HD6483
658.3155 ..... HD6490.G7
..... HF5549.5.G7
658.32 ..... HD4909
..... HD4926
..... HD4965.5.F7
..... HD4965.5.M4
658.32019 ..... HD4909
658.320942 ..... HD5017
658.321 ..... HF5564.P3
658.321018 ..... HF5564.P3
658.322 ..... HF5549.5.I5
658.3220973 ..... KF6369.8.E9
658.3222 ..... HD4906
..... HF5549.5.J62
658.32226584 ..... HD4965.5.U6
658.3225 ..... HD2984
..... HD2986
..... KF3496
..... RA410.9.G7
658.325 ..... BX6345.5
..... HD7106.U5
658.370016 ..... HF5549
658.3732720973 ..... JX1706.A59
658.373321 ..... HG1615.5
658.3736160973 ..... HV91
658.37361973 ..... HV90
658.373621097471 ..... RA972.5
658.3736211 ..... RA972.5
658.37362220973 ..... RA410.7
658.3736320973 ..... HV7991
658.37363209753 ..... HV7619
658.37363220973 ..... HV7936.S8
658.37365 ..... HV8759
658.37365973 ..... HV8754
658.37371 ..... LB1715
658.373711009762 ..... LB2833
658.373711009969 ..... KFH393
658.37378100973 ..... LB2342
658.3737812 ..... LB1028
658.376106952 ..... R496
658.3761073 ..... RT89
658.376107368 ..... RC440
658.3764709753
..... HD8039.D52U87
658.3764795 ..... TX945
658.376492 ..... HD7293
658.37651 ..... HF5547
..... HF5549
658.376588 ..... HF5549.5.T7
658.3765884 ..... HF5469
658.3779 ..... GV14.5
658.38 ..... HF5549
658.382 ..... HD7273
..... HF5549.5.A4
..... HV5831.N7
..... UA929.95.C5
658.3820973 ..... HD7262.5
658.385 ..... HD7255.5
..... HD8008
658.386 ..... HF5549.5.T7
658.386097 ..... HF5549.A2
658.4 ..... HC251
..... HD20
..... HD20.4
..... HD20.5
..... HD20.7
..... HD31
..... HD38
..... HD59
..... HD60.5.U5
..... HD69.D4
..... HD1375
..... HD2795

Dewey	LC
658.4	HD7273
	HD9940
	HF5387
	HF5500.2
	HF5548.2
	HF5549.5.T7
	HF5601
	KF3496
	LB1028
	NX710
	Q180.A1
	RA982.S24
	T55
	T56.8
	T57.35
	T57.5
	T57.95
	T58.4
	T58.6
	T174
	T174.5
	TA190
	TJ1
658.40018	HF5548.2
658.400186	HD69.D4
	HD8072
658.40019	HF5548.8
658.400207	HD38
658.40023	HD6058
658.4002437	LB2806
658.40028	HF5500.2
658.4007	HD20.7
658.40071142	HD20.15.G7
658.400715	HD20
658.4008	HD31
	HF5500.2
658.400926	HF5500.2
658.401	HD31
658.4019	HF5500.2
658.402	HD31
	HF5547
658.403	HF5548.2
	T57.95
	T58.6
658.404	T56.8
658.407	HD20
	HD20.15.G7
	HD70.G7
	HD4965.5.G7
	HF5429
	HF5500.2
	HF5549
	HF5549.5.R3
	HF5549.5.T7
658.408	HD60
658.4098614	F1401
658.42	HD31
	HD38
	HD69.D4
	HD2745
	HF5386
	HF5500.2
	HF5549
	HF5549.5.T7
	HF5630
	HV8759
	KF27.I55
	LB2831.3
	RA971
	RA972.5
658.43	HF5500.2
658.430184	HD20.5
658.430186	HF5500.2
658.430954	HF5500.3.I5
658.45	AS6
	HD21
	HD38
	HF5438
	HF5549.5.C6
	LB1028
	LB2831
658.4508	HF5549.5.C6
658.453	HD69.R4
	HF5726
658.455	Z716.3
658.46	HB119
	HD21
	HD69.C6
	HF5657
	TA157
658.46025	HD69.C6
658.4602542	HD69.C6
658.460942	HD69.C6
658.460973	HD69.C6
658.47	HD38
658.5	A190
	HD20.5
	HD30
	HD31
	HD38
	HD70.U5
	HD9565
	HF5415.7
	HF5421.5.G7
	HF5548.2
	RA971
	T56
	T56.25
	T57.6
	T58.4
	T58.6
	TA168
	TA174
	TA190
658.5	TS155
	TS155.A1
	TS156.8
	TS157
	TS167
	TS168
	TS173
	TS176
658.50018	HF5548.2
658.500182	HD20.7
658.500184	TS155
	TS183
658.500186	HD21
	HD31
658.5008	HF5415.15
658.500924	T55.85.T38
658.501	HD69.D4
	HF5548.2
	HF5601
	T58
	T58.6
	TD883.2
658.502	HD20.5
	HD4928.B6
	HD4946.G7
	LB1028.2
	RA971
	T56.8
	T57.5
	T57.6
	T57.74
	T57.85
	T58.6
	T60
	T60.8
	TA174
	TH437
	TH438
	TL789.8.U6
	TS158
658.503	HF5548.2
	JX1977
658.5032	HB221
	TS165
658.50330182	HD55
658.505	HF5548.2
	T56.4
	T57.5
	T57.62
	TS156.8
658.5053	HF5548.5.C2
658.51	HD69.P7
	RA971
	RA986
	RT42
	T57.85
	TS157.5
	TS158
658.511	HF5549.5.J6
658.512	TS180
658.5120182	HD20.4
658.5160973	KF32.5.S633
658.53	T57.85
	T59
	T60.W6
	T60.8
	TH438
	TS156.8
	TS158
	U395.S8
	Z733.B67
658.54	HF5547
	T60
	T60.W6
	T60.2
658.540924	T40.G53
	T60
658.542	S561
	T60
	T60.4
	T60.5
658.5420942	T60.2
658.56	RT5.N4
	T56
	TS155.8
	TS176
	Z244.5
658.56018	TS157
658.560184	TS157
658.561	T176.U54
	TS178.4
	TS178.5
658.562	HD9665.9.U6
	HF5371
	TJ685
	TS156
	TS156.Q3
	TS156.4
	TS173
658.5620182	TS156.Q3
658.564	HD21
	HD1751
	HF5770
	RA1216
	TS195
	TS196.2
658.57	HC79.T4
	HD20.3
	HD21
	HD45
	HD69
	HD69.N4
	HF5415.15
	KF27.A3336
658.57	KF27.A752
	KF27.I5536
	T174.3
	T175
	T175.5
	TK7807.J3
	TP155.5
	TS176
	UF543.P53
658.57025744	HD9727.M4
658.5708	T175.5
658.5709415	HC257.I63R48
658.570942	T177.G7
658.5709481	HD20.3
658.570973	HC110.T4
	T175.5
658.7	HD52.5
	HD1751
	HF5415.6
	HF5495
	HF5548.2
	RA971.3
	RA975.5.P5
	TL862.G6
	TS161
	U168
658.7018	HF5415
658.708	HD69.M35
	HF5415.7
658.72	HD52.5
	HD2381
	HD9715
	HF5437
	HF5465.U4
	HF5601
	RA968
	TL3035
658.7207	HC107.W6
658.78	HD30
	HF5415.7
	HF5681.S8
	TE24.W2
	TS161
	TS176
	TS180
	TS850
	UC263
658.780184	QA3
658.7808	HF5415.6
658.780942	HF5495
658.785	TS189.6
658.787	HD55
	HD9667.5
	HF5681.S8
	LB2830.4
	TE24.W2
	TL789.8.U6
	TS160
658.787018	HD55
	Q180
658.7870184	Q180.A1
658.788	HD58
	HF5761
	HF5780.A8
	HF5780.G7
658.7880942	HF5761
658.7880973	HF5761.K62822
658.7882028	HE5613
658.7885	HF5761
658.8	HF1009.5
	HF1025
	HF5006
	HF5415
	HF5415.1
	HF5415.12.C35
	HF5415.12.I5
	HF5415.12.I7
	HF5415.13
	HF5415.2
	HF5429.3
	HF5438
	HF5761
	HF5823
	PS3558.U37
	Z7164.R45
658.80018	HF5006
	HF5415
	HF5415.13
658.800182	HF5415
	HF5415.13
658.800184	HF5415
	HF5415.13
	HF5415.2
658.800186	HF5415
	HF5415.1
	HF5415.12.G7
	HF5415.13
658.800202	HF5415.13
658.8003	HF5415
658.80071	HF5415.1
	HF5415.4
658.80071142	HF5415
658.800712	HF5415.4
658.800715	HF5415.4
658.8008	HD31
	HD9000.5
	HF5415
	HF5415.13
658.800924	PS3553.O643
	Z350
658.80094	HF5415.12.E8
	HF5415.13
658.800942	T177.G7
658.800971	HF5415.12.C35
658.800985	HF5415.12.P4
658.80933333	HD1375
658.8093333309794	HD1379
658.80936360973	HF5006
658.8095532850994	HD9581.A85
658.80963	HD9016.P52
658.8096308	HD9433.G7
658.80963180954	HD9483.I42
658.80963180973	HD9483.U52
658.8096363140994	HD9908.A82
658.80965557	Z278
658.8096555702594	Z533.5
658.809655570974461	Z473
658.809655572025	Z286.P4
658.809655573	PS3515.A4853
	Z151
	Z278
	Z280
	Z471
	Z473
658.8096555730924	CT788.W88
658.809677	HD9850.6
658.809677310994	HD9908.A82
658.809678	HD9161.G72
658.80968712	HD9940.U4
658.8097	N8353
658.809771	HD9999.P5
658.80979143	PN1995
658.81	HF1009.5
	HF5006
	HF5438
658.8100186	HF5438
658.8100202	HF5438
658.81008	HF5438
658.812	HF5415.5
658.816	HF5415
	HF5429.6.G7
	KF25.A8
	TS756
	Z245
658.818	HF5006
	HF5415
	HF5438
658.82	HD2766
	HF5436
	HF5438
	HF6146.P75
	HF6161.D7
658.83	HB801
	HC79.C6
	HC108.O3
	HC108.S2
	HC110.C6
	HC110.C63
	HD1751
	HD6483
	HD9000.9.U5
	HF5006
	HF5415
	HF5415.13
	HF5415.2
	HF5415.3
	HF5429.3
	HF5483
	HF5770
	HG9970.A55I316
	KF26.C636
	KF27.I5536
	KF1603
	Q180.A1
	RA972
658.83018	HF5415.2
	HF5415.3
658.830186	HF5415.2
658.8303	HF5415.2
658.8308	HF5415.2
658.834	HD6483
	HE8700.8
	HF5438
658.835	HD7293
	HD9696.C62
658.838333337	HD7287.8
658.83838522	TF455
658.838633491	KF27.A3336
658.8386334910973	KF26.A35334
658.83863413	KF27.A3336
658.8386365	HD1751
658.8386367085	HC110.C6
658.838637	KF27.A3336
658.838643	HD7287.6.U5
658.838661	QD1
658.83866163	HD9660.S8U57
658.8386666	HD9617.P3
658.838672522	HD9526.I62
658.8386776430994	HD9937.A92
658.83867970942	HV572
658.8386817	AS36
658.8394	HD21
	HF5415.2
658.83942	HF5415.12.G7
	HF5415.2
658.839549	HC440.5
658.8395492	HC440.5.Z7E26
658.83971	HF5415.2
658.83973	HC110.C63
	HF5415.1
658.839745	HC107.R4
658.83977552	HC107.W6
658.839945	HC648.M4
658.84	HF5415

Dewey	LC
658.84	HF5429
	HF5429.3
	HF5470
	HF5475.E82S35
	HF5476
	KF2023
658.85	HF5421.5.G7
	HF5429
	HF5438
	HF5549
658.8508	HF5438
658.850926	HF5438
658.86	HD1751
	HD9321.5
	HF1009.5
	HF5422
658.860942	HF3505.6
658.860968	HF5421.5.S6
658.860973	HF5421
658.8609771	HF5421
658.87	HD9667.5
	HD9715
	HD9942.U42
	HF5429
	HF5429.3
	HF5429.6.G7
	HF5430.6.G7
	KF26.5.S693
	KF2023
658.8700186	HF5429
658.870023	HF5429
658.87002573	HF5429.3
658.8700715	HF5429
658.87008	HF5429
	HF5429.3
658.8700923	HF5429.3
658.8700924	DS151.A2
658.8700942	HF5429.6.G7
658.870097	HF5429.6.N6
658.8700973	HD9321.5
	HF5429.3
658.8700977	HF3155
658.87009772	HF5429.4.I6
658.8700977311	HF5429.5.C5
658.87009945	HF5429.6.A8
658.87006	HF5468
658.87070715	HD3486
658.8709495	HF5429.6.G8
658.8710973	HF5465.U4
658.872	HF5466
658.8730924	HF3023.Y6
658.875097471	HF5429.5.N5
658.878	HD9321.5
	HF5469
658.8780973	HF546
658.88	HF5566
	HG3729.C22
	HG3729.N4
	KF26.J835
658.880994	HF5568
658.883	HF5566
	KF26.B345
	KF27.B333
	KF27.P667
	KF27.5.S676
	KF31.B3
	RA971.3
658.88309769	HG3755
658.8907	PN4784.C6
658.8933333	E185.97.T73
	HD1379
658.8933333023	HD1379
658.8936832	HG8091
	HG8881
658.8937819623	LB3278.A9
658.89553421	HG307.U5
658.896359	SB443
658.896582	HD52.3
658.89684	HF5439.H78
658.89780973	ML3790
658.9102	Z678
658.910278	Z675.S3
658.9107	PN4775
658.9125	BV652
658.9126	BV652
658.9130154	JX1977
658.9133186809794	J87.C2
658.913321	HG1601.P5
	HG1615
	HG1616.I5
658.91332108	HG1615
658.9133210973	HF5011
658.91332120186	HG1615
658.9133216	HG1616.B7
658.9133260973	HG4521
658.9133272	HD1375
658.9133333	HD1375
	HD1379
	HD1383
658.913333309794	HD266.C2
658.913339100973	HD1694.A5
658.91334096894	HD3561.A6Z25
658.913341	TX960
658.91336200973	KF6320
658.913384774592	SB443
658.9134	KF318
658.913400973	KF318
658.913618	HV40
658.91362	RA790.5
658.913621	R729.5.G6
	RA971
	RA972.5
	RA975.5.P5
	RM849
658.91362107	RA972.5
658.91362109944	RA971.6
658.9136211	RA8
	RA971
	RA972
	RB36
658.913621107	RA421
658.91362160973	KF26.5.A356
658.9136320973	HV8141
658.91363242	HV7936.R4
658.9136335	UA927
658.913635	SB481
658.91368300973	HD4932.N6
658.9137	LB2805
658.9137187209771	LB2864
658.91374	LC5219
658.913781	LB2341
658.913783	LB2338
658.913805028	HF5415.6
658.913820973	HF1009.5
658.9138260994	HF1625
658.9138454	HE8698
658.91384540186	HE8689.8
658.9138454065	HE8699.G7
658.91385310973	TF662
658.91387	VK211
658.91387544018	VK235
658.9138770973	HF5006
658.91590744	QL77.T3
658.916072	T175.5
658.9161	R728
658.9161073	RT89
658.91614	RA411
658.916154	HF6201.D4
658.916154065	HF6201.D4
658.916176	RK58
658.9162576	TE7
658.91628168	RA8
658.9162892	TH9145
658.9164135	HD9251.5
658.91642	TX945
658.916472	RA960
658.916479	TX911
658.9164794	TX911
658.916479407	TX911.5
658.9164795	TX945
658.916479542	TX947
658.9164799	LB3235
658.916481	RA969
658.91651	HF5547
658.91657	HF5627
	HF5629
	HF5635
658.9165887	HF5429
	HF5429.3
	HF5430
	HF5468
	HF6201.D4
658.9165887070942	HD3486
658.9165887070954	HD3538
658.916588720973	HF5466
658.91658878	HD1751
	HF5469
658.91658896151	HF6201.D4
658.91658896360887	HF6201.P44
658.916591	HF6178
658.91659133	HF6161.M38
658.9166712	HF6201.C25
658.917114	HT166
658.9172	NA2570
658.9177	HD9999.P5
658.917830266132	MT88
658.9179	SB482
658.917914	PN1993.5.U6
658.9179143	PN1999.T8
658.917920942	PN2053
658.917960194	GV709
658.91796540973	GV198.A4
658.91796542209945	GV192
658.92	TA190
	TA194
658.922	TN274
658.92382009485	HD8039.S512S88
658.924	TA190
658.92576	TE220
658.9282	TD524.O3
658.93	S561
658.930182	S561
658.931	HD1471.U5
658.936362	TK4018
658.9385	TF505
658.94257	HD1751
658.955315	Z252.5.O5
658.96	HD31
	HD9650.1
	TP155
658.963072	S439
658.964	HD9321.5
658.96400977178	HD1751
658.966000973	HD9651.5
658.977	HD9861.5
658.97700954	TS1449
658.97700973	HD9856
658.9853104	HD9787.U45
658.987120924	TT505.S68
658.99	TH438
658.9900186	HD9715.G72
659	HG2040
659.1	HF5006
	HF5811
	HF5813.U6
	HF5821
659.1	HF5823
	HF5827
	HF5828
659.1018	HF5822
	HF5827
659.10184	HF5827
659.10202	HF5823
	HF6178
659.1023	HF5828
659.103	HF5803
659.1072	HF5415.2
659.108	HF5823
659.109	HF5811
659.10924	HF5810.C6
	HF5810.E4
659.109549	HF5821
659.10973	HF5813.U6
659.11	HF5823
	PN4784.C6
659.112	HF6178
659.1130973	HF5813.U6
659.13	HD59
	HF5813.G7
	HF5821
	HF5843
	NC997
	T325
659.130275	T325
659.130973	HF5813.U6
659.132	HF5825
659.1322	HF5825
659.1323	NC997
659.133	HF5861
659.134	HF5843
	HF6161.T67
	KF26.P868
659.13420973	HF5843.5
659.142	HF6146.R3
659.143	HF5801
	HF6146.T42
659.15	HF5845
	NC1815
	T396
659.152	HD6073.M7
	HD6073.M72U54
	TT502
659.153	DA125
659.157	HF5845
659.17	HF6146.P75
	KF27.5.S633
	KF32.5.S633
659.170973	HF6146.P75
659.1902	Z716.3
659.196152	KF27.G663
659.1962920942	HF6161.A8
659.196292222	HF6161.A8
659.19629222209	HF6161.A8
659.1963	HF6161.A3
659.19658022	HD30
659.19658871	HF5823
659.196655	HF6161.P45
659.1967973	HF6161.C35
659.19679730973	KF27.I55
659.1968383	HF6161.H75
659.197455	NK838.N37
659.2	HD59
	HD9698
	HM263
	HV85
	HV7936.P8
	HV7997
	HV8145.I3
	HV9469.2
	JF1525.P8
	JQ5849.P85
	LC1045
	RA965.5
	UA23
659.2018	HM263
659.2023	E185.97.D24
659.20924	DA3.H87
660	TP5
	TP149
660.018	TP5
660.072	TP165
660.076	TP168
660.09	TP18
660.09497	TP95.Y8
660.2	TP146
	TP155
	TP156.R45
	TP200
660.20184	TP155
660.2028	TP185
660.203	TP9
660.28	TP149
	TP155.5
660.2804	T55.3.H3
660.283	TA641
	TJ263
	TP157
660.284	TP155.7
	TP156.S55
	TP156.S8
	TP157
660.28401519	TP155.7
660.2842	TP156.D45
	TP156.F65
	TP156.S45
660.28422	TP156
660.28423	TP156.A3
	TP156.A35
	TP156.O7
660.28424	TP156.E8
660.28424	TP156.O7
660.284292	TP1
	TP156.F65
	TP156.M5
	TP157
660.284298	TP156.C7
660.28443	TP159.A5
660.28448	TP156.P6
660.28449	TP517
660.29076	TP168
660.294515	TP244.A3
660.29482	TP247.5
660.295	TP249.5
660.2963	TP156.E65
660.2969	QD501
660.297095482	TP194
660.298	TP249
660.299	TP149
	TP156.C35
	TP157
660.2995	TP156.C35
	TP159.C3
660.6	QR53
661	TD478
	TK7871.85
	TP5
	TP200
	TP201
	TP242
	TP245.O9
661.03	TA455.S35
661.07230994	TP245.S9
661.0732	TP245.C5
661.2	TP213
661.32	TP245.S7
661.332	TD478
661.34	TP223
661.43	QE113
	TP245.P5
661.8	TP145
661.802	TS921
661.804	TP690
661.808	TR280
661.814	TP248.E72
661.815	TP248.N9
661.816	TP248.P67
661.824	TP594
661.864	TP248.C6
661.894	TP248.A9
	TP248.N8
662.2	TN295
	TP270
662.20924	TP268.5.N7
662.26	QD1
	TP271
	Z663.23
662.27	TP271
662.6	TP318
	TP321
662.603	TP316
662.6229786	TP326.M9
662.623	TP328
662.6622	TN23
662.666	Z663.23
662.72	TP336
662.92	TP245.C4
662.93	QD547
	TP245.C4
663	TP505
663.2	TP548
	TP559.G7
663.2009	TP549
663.200944	TP553
663.2009444	TP553
663.20094471	TP553
663.2009794	TP557
663.200994	HD9388.A82
	TP559.A8
663.2009945	TP559.A8
663.22	TX558.G6
663.2203	TP546
663.30272	TP368
663.42	TP577
663.520942	TP533.G7
663.63	S21
663.71	SB273
663.93	TP368
663.930272	TP368
664	TL521.3.C6
	TP368
	TP370
	TP374.G8
	TP374.P7
	TX345
664.0025438	TX341
664.028	S21
	TX601
	TX611.5
664.02808	TX599
664.0282	QR115
	TX599
664.0282028	TX603
664.028450272	TP368
664.02853	TP493.5
664.0288	TX611.5
664.06	TX553.L5
664.07	TP370
	TX341
	TX511
	TX531
	TX541
	TX571.P4
664.09	HD1751
	TP373

664.095691 .... TP372.S9
664.1 .... HD9114.P82
664.103 .... TP375.4
664.12 .... TP382
664.122 .... TP380
664.1228 .... TP380
664.15 .... TX761
.... TX783
664.1530272 .... TP368
664.22 .... TP415
664.30272 .... TP368
664.32 .... SF268
.... TX560.F3
664.363095479 .... TP149
664.5 .... KF27.G663
.... S401
664.6 .... TP368
664.7 .... TS2145
664.72 .... TS2145
664.7200974 .... TJ859
664.752
.... PZ10.P643
.... TX683
.... TX763
.... TX769
.... TX773
664.7520272 .... TP368
664.755 .... TS2157
664.7560272 .... TP368
664.76 .... TS2158
664.8 .... SB360
.... TX601
664.807 .... TX553.P4
664.82 .... TX603
664.852 .... HD1751
664.9 .... TX373
664.900272 .... TP368
664.909 .... TS1973
664.92 .... QR117
.... S21
.... TP368
.... TS1955
.... TX612.M4
664.9203 .... TS1955
664.94 .... SK361
664.945 .... SH335
.... SH336.F7
.... TX612.F5
664.946 .... SH336.S6
.... SK361
665.355 .... S401.U6
665.5 .... TN870
.... TP343
.... TP355
.... TP690.2.I4
665.53 .... QD1
665.533 .... TN26
665.538 .... TA410
.... TP343
665.5382 .... TP692.2
665.53827 .... TP321
.... TP343
.... TP692.2
665.54 .... HD9565
.... TN872.A5
665.7 .... KF26.C688
.... TP703
.... TP761.L5
665.70942 .... TP751.5
665.74 .... TN880.5
.... TP757
665.75 .... TP350
665.77 .... TP754
665.772 .... TP760
665.773 .... TP751.1
.... TP761.B8
665.86 .... TN23
666 .... QC467
.... TL521.3.C6
.... TP807
.... TP810.5
666.028 .... TP809
666.08 .... TP790
.... TP815
666.1 .... TP849
.... TP857.3
666.1023 .... HD8039.G52I47
.... TP858
666.103 .... TP788
666.10740213 .... TP846.G72L65
666.12 .... TA450
.... TP857
666.13 .... TP858
666.15 .... TP862
666.19 .... NK5198.D95
.... NK5440.B6
.... NK5440.F4
.... NK5440.F7
.... NK8475.B6
666.2 .... TS700
666.3 .... TP807
.... TP808
666.30954 .... TP804.I5
666.43 .... TP808
.... TP815
666.44 .... TP794
666.45 .... TP823
666.7 .... QC770
666.72 .... TL521.3.C6
.... TN677
666.737 .... TA433
666.89 .... TC7
.... TP881
666.94 .... TP883
666.940972 .... F1219.3.A6
667.13076 .... HD8039.L32U58
667.1308 .... TT990
667.1309 .... TT998
667.2 .... TP910
667.25 .... TP913
667.252 .... TP248.P62
667.29 .... TP936
667.3 .... TP897
667.307 .... TP897
667.340272 .... TP897
667.38 .... TP930
667.3809 .... TP930
667.4 .... TS1548.5
667.5 .... TP949
.... Z247
667.6 .... TP935
.... TP936.5
.... TP937.7
667.6014 .... Z695.1.P35
667.62 .... TP935
667.75 .... TP935
667.9 .... TA357
.... TA418.76
.... TA435
.... TT305
.... U408.3
668.1 .... TP994
668.10924 .... CT275.F447
668.14 .... TP992.5
.... TP994
668.3 .... TP968
.... TS718
668.374 .... TP156.I6
668.3740272 .... TP1180.A15
668.4 .... QD1
.... TP1105
.... TP1120
.... TP1124
.... TP1125
.... TP1130
.... TT297
668.4016 .... TP1132
668.40272 .... TP1114
668.403 .... TP934.3
.... TP1110
668.41 .... TP1175.M4
668.411 .... QD1
668.413 .... TP1175.E9
668.416 .... TP1177.5.G5
668.419 .... TP1140
668.42 .... TP1105
.... TP1180.P57
.... TP1180.P66
.... TP1180.P8
668.4225 .... TP1180.P6
668.4226 .... QD1
668.4227 .... TP248.S5
668.423 .... TP1150
.... TP1180.P66
.... TP1180.P685
.... TP1180.P8
.... TP1180.T5
668.4234 .... TP1180.P67
668.4236 .... TP1180.V48
668.44 .... TP156.D45
668.49 .... TA455.P5
.... TP1114
.... TP1177
.... TP1183.F5
.... TP1183.F6
.... TS198.3.P5
668.54 .... TP983
668.5440272 .... TP983
668.55 .... RA778
.... TP983
.... TP983.A237
.... TT969
668.550272 .... TP983
668.62 .... TP963
668.625 .... TP245.P5
668.650216 .... SB951
669 .... QC1
.... TA459
.... TN7
.... TN605
.... TN665
.... TN673
.... TN675
.... TN890
.... TS205
669.0018 .... TN673
669.003 .... TN10
669.007 .... TN165
669.0071173 .... T73
669.008 .... TA459
.... TN4
.... TN7
.... TN26
669.009429 .... TN63
669.00947 .... TT205
669.0284 .... TN685
.... TN686.5.E4
669.03 .... TN10
669.08 .... TN26
669.09943 .... TN122.M6
669.1 .... TN705
669.109422 .... TS304.G7
669.10973 .... TN704.U5
669.140942 .... TN703
669.141 .... QE282
669.1413 .... TN677
669.142 .... TA479.N45
.... TA479.S7
669.142 .... TN756
669.1420202 .... TA472
669.1422 .... TN740
669.2 .... HG265
669.209 .... HG265
669.22 .... TN26
669.2209 .... TN410
669.220994 .... TN418.A2
669.23 .... TN693.S5
669.3 .... TN693.C9
.... TN780
669.3028 .... TN295
669.30947 .... Z663.23
669.309701 .... TN443.M5
669.4 .... TA480.L4
.... TN785
669.5 .... TN796
669.50282 .... TN690
669.6 .... TN793
669.7 .... TN693.P3
.... TN799.R45
669.732 .... TL507
.... TN799.T5
669.734 .... TN490.M7
669.735 .... QC770
669.8 .... TN677
669.82 .... TN677
.... TN700
669.9 .... QD131
.... TN665
669.92 .... TN27
.... TN500
669.94 .... QC176
.... TL521
.... TN673
.... TN688
.... TN690
.... TN693.H4
.... TN731
669.94028 .... TN690
669.95 .... TA459
.... TA460
.... TN690
.... TN693.H4
669.950282 .... TN690
.... TN799.V3
669.950283 .... TN690
669.951 .... TN690
669.95142 .... TN707
669.9522 .... QE75.C5
669.961 .... TN693.I7
670 .... GN2
.... TK152
.... TS156.8
.... TS176
670.973 .... HD9725
671 .... TS145
.... TS205
.... TS213
.... TS250
.... TS257
.... TS283
.... TS700
.... TT205
671.2 .... TS200
.... TS230
.... VM147
671.20621 .... TS200
671.209 .... TS229.5.A1
671.25 .... TN690
.... TS230
.... TS233
671.25023 .... TS233
671.3 .... TK5
.... TN693.H4
.... TS205
.... TS256
671.32 .... TS340
671.33 .... TJ7
.... TS253
671.34 .... TS270
671.35 .... TJ1160
.... TJ1185
.... TJ1186
.... TJ1191
671.37 .... TN695
671.5 .... TS226
.... TS227
.... TS718
671.52 .... TA492.W4
.... TS227
.... TT211
671.520202 .... TS227
671.521 .... TK4660
671.529 .... TS228.9
671.53 .... TJ1191
671.53028 .... TJ1185
671.56 .... TT267
671.73 .... TL521.3
.... TS653.A1
.... TS670.A1
671.732 .... TS670
.... TS690
671.7320272 .... TT317
671.735 .... TS695
671.739 .... TS653
671.82023 .... TS250
671.83 .... Z663.23
671.84 .... TS270
671.95 .... RC684.P3
672 .... TA479.S7
.... TN26
.... TS320
672.0212 .... TA472
672.0973 .... TN703
672.2 .... TS230
672.22 .... TN706
672.24 .... TS231
672.25 .... TA475
.... TS230
.... TS233
672.3 .... Q60
.... TS320
672.33 .... TS225
672.35 .... TA479.S7
.... TJ1185
672.36 .... TA479.S7
.... TN26
672.52 .... TA492.W4
.... TS227
672.7 .... TS653
672.732 .... TN793
672.820212 .... TA685
672.83 .... TS280
672.84 .... TS271
673.3 .... TS700
673.68 .... TS198.3.M4
673.72225 .... TS555
673.72252 .... QC770
673.72256 .... TT267
673.722732 .... TS692.C6
673.72282 .... TS195.3.F5
673.73 .... TN700
673.733 .... TS670
673.734 .... TL521
674 .... SD431
.... SD536
.... TP156.C5
674.0025776 .... TS803
674.008 .... SD45
.... SD433
.... TS801
674.0094741 .... TT180
674.08 .... TS801
674.088 .... TS801
674.0971 .... TS825.C3
674.1 .... SD435
674.134 .... TS928
674.14 .... SD536
674.22 .... TS850
674.38 .... TA424
674.384 .... TS837
674.8 .... TT185
674.83 .... SD13
674.834023 .... TS870
674.839 .... UA926.A1
675.2 .... TS965
.... TS980.U7
675.23 .... TS940
675.3 .... TS1061
676 .... TS1105
676.028 .... TS1109
676.062 .... TS1096.P3
676.08 .... SD1
.... TS1080
676.122 .... TS1176
676.183 .... TS875
676.2 .... TS1094
.... TS1109
676.209 .... TS1090
676.20973 .... TS1095.U6
676.22094223 .... TS1095.G7
676.23 .... TS1109
.... TS1117
.... Z249
676.27 .... TS1109
676.2824 .... TS1220
676.32 .... TS198.3.P3
677 .... TP930
.... TS1445
.... TS1449
.... TS1463
677.0023 .... HF5381
.... TS1463
677.003 .... TS1309
677.007401445 .... TS1306
677.009 .... TS1525
677.00924 .... TS1440
.... TS1440.C9
677.00936 .... TS1316
677.00937 .... TS1316
677.009497 .... TS1395.Y8
677.009757 .... TS1324.S6
677.022 .... HD9940.P43E36
677.028 .... TS1445
.... TS1449
677.02809 .... TS1525
677.02825 .... TP267
.... TS1512
.... TS1513
.... TS1520
677.0283 .... TS1540
677.0285 .... TT680
677.02852 .... TS1483
677.0287 .... TS1449
677.13 .... TS1485
.... TS1735
677.20942 .... TS1565.G7
677.21 .... TS1425.S52
.... TS1580
677.210924 .... CT275.A78
677.210973 .... TS1565.U6
677.213 .... S445
677.2150942 .... TS1525
677.217 .... S21
.... S445
.... TS1577
.... TS1580

677.3 HD9895
TS1625
677.303 TS1309
677.31 JX1977
677.310942 TS1625
677.4 AS122.B4
TS1548.5
677.46 TS1548.5
677.617 TS1675
677.643 TS1775
677.6610924 TS1440.L4
678 TS1890
678.03 TS1875
678.2 TS1890
678.203 TS1875
678.27 TS1892
678.29 TS1892
678.4 TS1892
678.7 TP1180.P8
678.72 TP1180.P8
678.720272 TS1925
681 TS518
681.11 TS540
TS546
681.110924 NK7497.T6
TS544.8.B3
681.11094267 TS543.G7
681.1109743 NK7110
681.113 TS545
681.11309 NK7486
TS542.5
681.113094 TS542
681.114 Z663.23
681.12 TC177
681.140924 QA29.B2
T40.B25
681.2 QC274
QC886
TL521
681.20924 T40.J58
681.4 Q180
QC371
TS510
681.40074017594 TS534.7
681.411023 RE962
681.412 QB88
TL521.3.C6
681.60272 Z249
681.6209942 AC5
681.7 QC281
RA968
TJ1480
TJ1513
TS271
TS283
TX7
681.8195 TS585
681.83 ML1050
682 TT220
682.023 TT220
682.53094212 TD884
683.32075 NK8204
683.3209 TS519.5
683.4 TS533.3.N8
TS535
UD380
UF620.T5
683.400272 TS534.5
683.400275 TS533.2
683.40029 TS534.7
683.4003 TS534.5
683.4009 TS532.4
TS533
683.400973 F591
TS533.2
683.40097845 TS533.3.P4
683.40973 UD383
683.42 TS536
UD395.W7
683.43 TS533
TS533.4.G3
TS537
683.4309 TS537
683.8 TJ1507
683.82 NK806
TJ1450
683.83 TK7018
684.08 TT180
TT185
TT325
684.08028 TT197.5.T3
684.083 TT201
684.088 TT185
684.09 TS205
TT205
684.1 TS880
TT196
TT199
684.100202 TT195
684.100924 TT140.H6
684.104 TS880
TT195
TT197
684.1043 TT199.4
684.1043023 TT325
684.1044 TT199
684.10443 TT199.4
684.105 TS408
684.106 TP1185.F8
684.12 TS880
684.12023 TT198
684.14 TS887
684.16 TT197
684.7 GT5280
684.7 TS2010
TS2020
TS2033
685 TS950
TT290
685.31 TS990
685.310072 TS1020
685.31009 GT2130
686.2 Z116
686.20924 Z674
686.20942 Z151.2
686.2255 Z254
686.284 ML112
687 PZ10.H46
TT507
687.023 HD9940.U4
TT507
687.1010922 TT502
687.11 TT590
687.12 TT518
TT520
687.15 UC485.G7
687.3209 TT685
688.4 F1895.P6
688.6 TS2003
688.72 KF26.C636
688.720740163355
NK9509.4.N44
688.7209 NK9509
688.720943 GV1200
688.724 GV1220.7
688.76 GV745
688.79 SH451
690 HD7260
KF27.E345
KF3574.C65
S381
TA417.G36
TA658
TA684
TH145
TH146
TH151
TH153
TH438
TH439
TH443
TH4815
TH7791
690.0202 TH151
690.023 HD8039.B9
HD8039.B92U647
TH159
690.028 TH435
690.03 TH9
690.07 HD5846.S8
TH165
690.076 TH438
690.08 TA435
TH1
TH7
690.0924 CT275.P5746
690.0994 TH121
690.11 S21
690.16 TH2521
690.18 TJ1370
690.202 TH153
690.28 TA151
690.51709753 F204.W5
690.521 TH9745.S7
690.5510973 RA967
690.589 TH4960
690.75614 TH4652
690.8 GC66
NA7427
TH3000
TH4811
TH4815
TX323
690.86 TH4815
690.87 TL297
690.89 TH4911
TH4916
TH4920
TH4960
TH4962
TH4965
691 TA403
TA404.5
TH1065
691.1 S21
TA666
691.12 TT325
691.2 TN967
691.3 TA440
TA681
TA683.44
TC7
691.30212 TA670
691.5 TH4
691.7 TA684
TH1651
691.8722 TA690
691.9 TH1725
691.92 TA668
692 HJ4260.A5
TH144
692.1 TH6010
692.2 TH2031
692.3 TH425
692.30942 TH435
692.5 TH7
TH435
692.503 TH9
692.8 HD9715.G72
TH425
693 TA670
693.30202 TH8531
693.5 TA439
693.544 TH4652
693.6 TH8131
693.71 TA684
693.82 TH1091
693.834 NA2800
TD892
TH7
TH1725
693.85 TA658.4
693.852 TH1095
693.854 U408.3
693.89 TH9031
693.892 TH9031
693.9 TH1099
693.91 GB2401
693.97 TH1098
TH1099
TH4812
TH4819.P7
693.970254 TH1098
693.97094 TH1000
694 HD1751
TH1101
TH4818.W6
TH5604
TH5607
694.00994 TH1101
694.0202 TH5604
694.023 TH5608
694.09 TH1101
694.094267 TH1101
694.2 TH2398
694.23 TA660.B4
695 S21
TH2431
695.6 TH2450
696 S21
TH6010
TH6021
TH6122
TH6124
TH7205
696.0202 TH6711
696.1 TH6681
696.10212 TH6125
696.1023 TH6126
696.1820924 TH140.C7
697 TH7121
TH7222
TH7223
TH7335
TH7687
697.04 TH7410
697.07 TH7466.O6
697.1 S21
TH7425
697.3 TH7466.O6
TH7601
697.4 TH7518
697.54 TH7641
697.72 TH7410
TH7434.7
697.9 TH7694
697.92 RA969
697.93 TH7222
TH7687
697.93076 TH7687
697.9315 TH7226
697.9324 TH7694
698.1 TT320
698.1076 TT305
698.124 SD433
698.3 TT325
700 DA688
DD261.2
DF78
LB1062
N25
N72.S3
N6494.K5
N6512
N7425
N7443.2
N7445
NX60
NX65
NX175
NX210
NX458
NX620
NX650.S6
PQ263
PR3519.J13
PS3553.A762
700.094 PN674
700.1 B931
BH39
BH201
BH205
BH301.S75
NX650.S6
700.17 N75
700.18 NX458
700.19 NX165
700.2573 NX22
700.25747 N6535.N5
700.5 AI3
700.6073 NX705
700.6194 NX28.A9
700.7 N365.G7
700.76 LB2367
700.79 NX730
700.8 ND623.L5
700.9 HX521
700.904 NX60
NX456
700.922 DG457
700.924 PR4146
PR4147
PR5263
PS1561
700.946 PC13
700.952 N7350
NX584
700.968 NX587
700.973 N6505
NX735
700.9748 NX510.P4
700.9749 NX510.N4
700.9764 NX50
700.9788 NX510.C6
700.98 F1408.3
700.9931 NX28.N43
700.994 NX711
701 BF408
N70
N72
N6490
N7430
N8375.L46
NX175
PN85
701.1 BH221.U54
N71
N72.S3
N7445
NX165
W70
701.10944 PQ241
701.15 BH202
BX4700.T4
N66
N70
N71
N71.O32
N6490
NX165
NX175
NX590
701.17 AC7
B829.5
B1652
BH21
BH39
BH41
BH81
BH181
BH221.U54
N62
N67
N71
N75
N6490
N7430
N7435
ND237.C493
NX165
NX210
NX556
PN81
701.1708 BH21
NX210
701.1709 N66
701.1709034 BH221.G73
701.18 N72.S6
N87
N7435
N7445
N7477
PN674
701.8 N70
N7425
N7430
N7433
ND1493.I8
701.940740164351 KF27.F648
702.02 N87
702.07 N7460
702.3 N72.S6
N8350
702.8 N7433
N8530
N8560
703 N33
N7760
704.073 N351
704.36 CT275.G399
N8410
704.360924 N5247.W95
704.94 N8217.G8
704.942 DC338
N7440
N7570
N7575
N8232
PS137
704.942095 N7260
704.9421 N73
704.9423 E377
704.94240954 N7638.I5
704.9432 N7260
N7660
704.94320740153 N7660

704.944 N5055.G85
704.946 AZ108
N7690
704.947 N6915
N7745.A5
704.948 BL603
N8180
704.9480938 N5633
704.948109495 N8189.G7
704.9482 N7830
N7832
N7880
N7987
N8080
NX650.C5
704.94820901 N7832
704.94820944 N7949
704.948209789 N7910.N6
704.9484 N8020
N8025
N8030
N8050
N8053
704.9484074094183 N7827
704.94855 N8070
704.9485507401471 N8065
704.9486 N8080
704.94897 E51
704.94930141 HQ460
N8217.E6
704.94930142 N8220
704.949301435 DF78
704.949331 N8219.L2
704.9495233 NX650.M6
704.94961 N8223
704.94978 ND3247
704.94978191 ML85
704.94979331954 GV1693
704.949796 N8250
704.9499047 NX650.W3
706 NX28.G7
706.2 NX28.G7
706.5 N5215
N8380
N8620
707 N21
N85
N87
N90
N330.V53
N345
N350
N354.W9
N362
N365.A9
NX280
707.01471 NK512.N45
707.1 N85
N87
N7433
707.11 N90
707.1173 NX280
707.12 N350
707.127471 N11.N26
707.1274886 N363
707.15 N332.B38
707.2 N380
707.2073 NX700
707.4 N5020
NK520.G7
707.40113541 N5230.C29
707.4014461 N6535.B7
707.401471 N5220
N6490
NX427.N7
707.4014966 N8219.L5
707.40153 N6490
707.4018856 N5220.L39
707.4019451 N8383
707.402 N5051
707.40318 N6490
707.4086 N8217.E6
707.5 N5200
N8386.J6
N8680
707.9 NX398
708.0013 N430
708.00924 N406.C46
N7483.R67
708.1 N5020
708.113541 N5030.T6
708.13 N510
N6490
708.134461 N521.I7
708.1444 N5220.W782
708.14461 N520
N5220
708.1471 N610
N620.F6
N5020.I5
N5020.N7
N6535.N5
PZ9.H7
708.14723 N11.B783
708.14811 N680
708.14921 N6530.N6
708.14967 N714.P65
708.1526 N515
708.153 N856
N857
708.164141 N6537.M3
708.17173 N559.D3
708.17434 N5220.T35
708.17471 N620.M9
708.17595 N5220.B77
708.176579 N582.6
708.19467 N6490.C217
708.19493 N6490
708.19498 N5220
708.2 N6761
708.21 N70
N1080
N8640
708.212 AM101
N5247.M5
708.257 AM101
708.336 N2317
N2325
708.4 N2010
708.531 N5073.V4
708.55 N2570
708.5634 N2941
708.585 N5080.V35
708.672 N3410.5
708.745 N3350
708.87 N3538
708.891 N1880
N1910
708.94125 N1185
708.941435 N25
708.941445 NK493
708.94971 N3690.Y8B397
N7823.Y8B433
708.952135 N3750.T63
708.993127 N3982
708.9945 N3948
709 N21
N5215
N5300
N5301
N5303
N5305
N7307.N4
N7430
N7440
N7445
N7454.B4
ND623.L5
NX440
709.01 N5333
709.011 DU280.C3
E59.A7
E78.N78
E78.S7
E98.A7
F1219.3.A7
F1435.3.A7
GN2
GN662
N5310
N5310.5.D5
N5311
N7397.A3
N7398
N7401
ND1942.S8
NK1496.N4
Q11
W5310
709.01109701 F1219.3.A7
709.0110973 E98.A7
709.012 N5310
N5333
709.015 N7832
709.02 N5975
N7832
709.021 N5963
709.023 N6371
709.024 N6370
N6374
N7560
709.03 N6350
N7417
NK1175
709.033 N6425.N4
709.034 N6450
N6465.A7
N6490
N7476
709.04 N70
N332.G33
N6350
N6450
N6490
N6493
N6494.F8
N6494.K5
N6494.M5
N6494.N6
N6494.O6
N6494.S8
N7445
ND6494.C8
NX600.S9
709.046 N72.S6
N6490
N6494.P6
N7476
709.174916 N6240
709.17496 N7428.5
709.1767 N6263.B55
709.22 ML300
ML390
N40
N5220
N6490
N6505
N6512
709.22 N6530.M75
N6530.U8
N6535.L6
N6535.N5
N6536
N6538.N5
N6545
N6606
N6768
N6782
N6796
N6797.U5
N6820
N7108
N7304
N7445
709.24 CT3150.G8
N722
N857.5
N5020
N5072.A55
N6490
N6537.A3
N6537.B23
N6537.D5
N6537.G68
N6537.J6
N6537.L5
N6537.P45
N6537.R27
N6537.R3
N6537.R57
N6537.S3
N6537.V35
N6537.W28
N6537.W33
N6549.P7
N6797.H3
N6797.H8
N6797.P25
N6853.B7
N6853.M4
N6888.E7
N6888.H3
N6888.N4
N6923.M27
N6923.V4
N7153.B28
N7310.S3
N7454.M6
N7593
N8375
N8375.G35
NA1053.G8
NA1123.A5
NB237.R6
NB237.S7
NB497.E6
NB553.M3
NB623.B78
NB623.M24
NB653.N5
NC139.S54
NC242.C3
NC1075.O4
ND237.P25215
ND237.S47
ND553.D3
ND553.D772
ND553.D774
ND553.P5
ND553.T7
ND623.B9
ND673.B73
ND699.C5
ND1105.S7
ND1942.G8
NK998.L5
NK1535.E7
PN3205
PR5083
PR5087.S6
PR5263
WD553.G27
709.32 DT62.T4
N3825
N5350
N7638.E35
709.34 N7307.P4
709.35 DS16
N5370
N7280
709.37 DG121
N5610
N5760
N5763
709.37094573 N2724
709.38 DF77
N5610
N5613
N5630
N5633
709.3951 N5899.S3
709.4 AS36.G378
N5963.N4M45
N5970
N6245
N6280
N6310
N6370
N6407
N6410
N6415.B3
N6465.A7
709.4 N6750
N6916
N6925
N7428.5
N7445
N7445.2
709.415 N6782
N6784
709.42 N1495
N5053
N6761
N6763
N6764
N6767
N6767.5.P7
N6797.C33
NK928
NX543
PR447
709.4267 DA670.E7
709.43 N6861
709.438 N6991
709.4391 NK944.H9
709.44 BH301.S75
N6465.A7
N6841
N6843
N6844
N6846
N7949
N8640
ND547
709.45 N6911
N6915
N6916
709.4547 N6921.R3
709.4573 N6921.N2
709.46 N910.C8
N7101
709.4619 N7962
709.469 N7124
709.47 N6981
NB699.N4
NK975
NX556.A1
W6981
709.471 N6993
709.4795 N6995.G4
709.48 N7001
709.492 NK6
709.4931 DH801.F45
N6969.F5
709.5 N6915
N7260
N7262
N7336
N7342
N8193.A5
709.5074013 N7262
709.507401468 N7336
709.509713541 N7262
709.51 N7340
N7342
N7342.W35
N7343
NX650.E7
709.515 N7346.T5
709.52 N7350
N7352
709.54 N1150
N3750.M27
N6264.I5
N7301
N7302
N7303
NX576
709.5475 NX576
709.549 N7307.P3
709.5496 N7307.N4
709.55 N7280
709.591 N7312.2.P3
709.6 N7380
N7397.W4
709.62 N7381
709.68 N7392
709.7 E59.A7
N6502
709.701 E98.A7
F1435.3.A7
709.71 E99.E7
709.710740113541 N6540
709.72 F1219.3.A7
N6553
709.7292 N6609
NX527
709.7294 BL2530.H3
709.73 E98.A7
N6490
N6494.P6
N6505
N6507
N6510
N6512
N6530.N5
N6535.W3
N6538.N5
N8640
NB237.B47
ND212
NK805
NK806
NX512.3.N5
709.74461 N6535.B7
NX511.B6

709.746 N6530.C8
709.763 N6530.L8
709.773 N6530.I4
709.789 NX510.N43
709.794 N6530.C2
709.8 N6502
W6502
709.81 NX533
709.914 N7327
709.94 N7400
709.942 N7402.S6
710.17 N75
710.994 NA9052
711 HE355.8
HT166
HT167.5.M4
HT393.M38M64
NA9031
NA9105
711.01 NA2543.S6
711.0924 F195
NA9050
NA9085.J4
711.120942 HT169.G7
711.13 NA2543.S6
711.2 HC110.E5
711.20952 NA9000
711.20967 DT1
711.3 HT391
HT393.F5
HT393.M37
711.306242 JS3121
711.3094136 HT395.S32
711.309416 HT395.I73C65
711.30942 HT395.G7
711.3094274 HT395.G73D68
711.309744 HT393.M4
711.309747 HT167.5.N5
HT393.N6
711.30974811 HT394.P5
711.30975284 HT393.M37
HT393.M38M62
HT393.M38M627
HT393.M38M63
711.30975629 HT393.N82B35
711.309773793 HT393.I42
711.30979248 HT393.U8
711.309795 HT393.O7
711.3097983 HT393.M3
711.3097984 HT393.A42B73
HT393.A42K67
711.30996931 HT394.H6
711.4 GF23
GN413
HD266.N8
HT161.H7
HT166
HT169.G7
HT390
HT391
NA9
NA2500
NA9010
NA9030
NA9031
NA9035
NA9040
NA9050
NA9052
NA9053.H6
NA9053.P55
NA9094
NA9184.M4
T57.85
TA24.M4
711.401 CC135
NA9050
711.4018 HT166
711.4060944 HT169.A87
711.408 NA9031
711.409 HT115
HT166
NA9090
711.40904 HT166
711.40921 HC251
711.40924 NA9198.P2
711.4093 NA9245.N4
711.4094 HT169.E8
711.40941445 HT169.S32E33
HT169.S32E35
711.40942 HT133
HT169.G
HT169.G7
HT177.M34
HT390
NA9185
711.409421 HT169.G72L633
HT169.G72L646
NA9188.L7
711.4094227 DA690.A36
DA690.E43
HT169.G72F55
HT169.G72L95
HT169.G72S92
HT169.G72S923
HT395.G72H34
711.4094231 HT169.G72S95
711.4094238 DA690.A96
DA690.B885
DA690.M555
DA690.N46
DA690.N755
DA690.N877
HT169.G72B322
711.409424 HC257.M5
711.4094241 HT169.G72B73
711.4094247 HT169.G72
711.4094254 HT395.G72L45
711.4094255 HT169.G72N723
711.40942565 HT169.G72
711.4094259 HT169.G72C628
HT169.G72S62
711.4094261 NA9187.Y3
711.4094271 HT169.G72C418
711.4094272 HT169.G72W34
711.4094274 DA690.Y6
HT169.G72
HT169.G72G64
HT169.G72T42
711.409429 NA9194.B8
711.4094334 HT169.G32S4613
711.40945677 HT169.I84U7313
711.40947 NA1188
711.4094745 NA9211
711.40954 HT169.I5
711.4095412 HT169.I52R34
711.40954792 HD3540.A3
HT169.I52B666
711.4095496 NA9052
711.40956 HT147.N4
711.409664 HT169.S5
711.409684 HT169.S62N33
711.4096897 HT169.M32L54
711.40971242 HT169.C32C65
711.40971244 HT169.C32
HT169.C32R63
711.40971312 HT169.C32F64
711.40971334 HT177.P67
711.409713541 HT169.C32N64
711.40971532 HT169.C32S34
711.40973 HT166
HT167
KF27.B387
NA9052
NA9105
711.4097445 HT168.S2
711.4097465 HT168.N37
HT168.N62
711.4097466 HT168.K5
711.4097468 HT110
711.409747 HT166
711.4097471 NA9127.N5
711.40974811 HT168.P43
711.40974886 HT168.P48
711.409749 HT176.N5
711.4097526 HT394.B3
711.40975284 HT168.S55
NA9126.M6
711.409753 F195
NA9127.W2
711.409755451 HT168.R5
711.409756 HT167.5.N6
711.40975627 NA735.W52
711.40975636 HT167.5.N6
711.40975655 HT167.5.N6
711.40976399 HT168.S5
711.40977 HT167.5.G7
711.40977311 HD268.C4
HT168.C5
NA9127.C4
711.40977324 HT168.V54
711.40977356 HT168.S6
711.40977394 HT168.V3
711.409773993 HT168.C7
HT168.C73
711.40977434 HT177.D4
711.409775 HT167.5.W5
711.40977617 HT168.A8
711.40977732 HT168.D4
711.40977851 NA9127.B594
711.40979466 HT168.O3
711.40979494 HT168.L6
711.40979799 HT168.P57
711.40993127 HT169.N52
711.40993311 HT169.N52
711.40994 HX11
711.409941 HT169.A82P47
711.409944 DU180.H8
HT169.A82
HT169.A82S96
HT169.A82S975
NA7470.B4
711.409945 DU230.B3
HT169.A82
711.409947 HT169.A82C34
711.4099691 HT168.H5
711.4099693 NA9284.O2
711.42 SB484.G7
711.4209775 HT167.5.W5
711.43 HT330
NA9052
711.5 NA9070
NA9127.W2
711.522 HF5429.6.S3
711.55 NA9050
711.551 JK1651.C73
NA9127.W2
711.551097416 JK1651.M26
711.55109947 JQ4079
711.552 HF5430.3
HF5430.6.D4
HF5430.6.G7
HT169.C32
NA9000
NA9053.O3
Z5942
711.552094238 HT169.G72T37
711.5520973 HT175.U6
711.5520976122 HT177.M55
711.5520977434 HT168.D45
711.557 HD7395.M6
TX1105
711.558 DA685.R43
F747
F914.V3
GV53
GV54.A11
GV54.A4
GV54.C2
GV54.D5
GV54.I3
GV54.N38
GV54.N7
GV54.T6
GV182.2
GV423
GV835.2.N73
KF27.D5644
NA9045
SB482
SB484.C2
SB484.G7
SB485.C6
TE301
U408.3
711.5580941445 SB485.E3
711.55809743 GV54.V5
711.55809749 GV54.N5
711.55809775 NA9053.R4
711.55809789 GV54.N6
711.55809797 GV54.W2
711.55809967 GV158.G8
711.57 LB3221
LB3223
LB3223.5.M3
LF953.C57
LF1134.S7
N8905
711.58 DA690.F25
DA690.G633
HD7287.6.C3
HT167
HT167.2
HT170
711.580202 TH153
711.58097526 HT168.B35
711.580976122 HT177.M55
711.5809761295 HT168.D6
711.59 F200
HD7304.B7
HD7305.T68
HT170
HT175
HT177.C67
LB3223
LG181.P35
N8850
NA9072.N48
TH7
711.59094272 HT178.G72
711.590971352 HT178.C22H35
711.590973 KF27.B344
711.590974461 HT177.B6
711.5909753 HT177.D6
711.5909763355 NA735.N4
711.7 HE151
TA1205
TE7
711.7094161 HE363.G75B36
711.70973 HE4451
711.7097418 HE372
711.709747 TE7
711.70977132 HE214.C6
711.73 HE355.8
HE356.5.B28
HE370
HE371.V8
KF27.P872
TE7
TE175
711.73094161 HE246.5.Z7
711.730942 HE363.G72
711.7309421 TE64.L7
711.73094257 TE64.O9
711.73097443 HE372.W63
711.7309755725 HE356.5.B7
711.7309776771 HE372
711.730978639 HE372.B47
711.730978967 HE372.T7
711.730979224 HE372.P95
711.730979527 HE372.B34
711.730979653 HE356.5.I3
711.7309941 HE368.Z7P48
711.74 NA9053.S7
711.75 TF300
711.750974461 HE4491.B75
711.7509746 HE2791
711.76 HE436.L6
711.760993122 HE559.N4
711.78 HE9797.5.G72L66
TL507
TL725
TL725.3.P5
711.7809421 TL671.65
TL726.6.G7
711.780973 TL725.3.P5
711.8 HD1694.N6
TD883
712 SB458
SB471
SB472
SB475
712 SB477.G7
712.023 SB476
712.076 SB469.4.A2
712.08 SB470.O5
712.094 SB465
712.0942 SB466.G7
712.5 SB472
712.50975662 E241.G9
712.6 NA9052
SB461
SB465
SB473
712.60942 SB453.3.G7
SB466.G7
712.60952 SB458
712.7 GV910
713 TE177
714 NA9400
SB473.2
715.109 SB463
719.3 SB481
719.320978 E160
719.3209786 KF26.I547
720 NA710
NA2515
NA2517
NA2520
NA2541
NA2555
NA2563
720.1 N66
NA2500
720.18 NA21
NA2570
NA2750
720.19 NA2500
720.2 TT154
720.23 NA1995
NH1995
720.28 NA2700
720.3 NA31
720.711 LB1131
720.711764 NA2125.T4
720.723 NA105
720.8 NA1
720.9 NA200
NA204
NA211
NA2560
720.91822 NA9184.M4
720.922 NA21
NA707
NA736
NA996
NH996
720.924 N6537.F55
N7483.L4
N8375.L39
NA737.B68
NA737.B8
NA737.C6
NA737.D67
NA737.E36
NA737.E4
NA737.G56
NA737.G75
NA737.K28
NA737.L27
NA737.M25
NA737.M3
NA737.R8
NA737.S68
NA737.S9
NA749.S2
NA997.A4
NA997.B7
NA997.C3
NA997.C5
NA997.G34
NA997.H3
NA997.L63
NA997.L8
NA997.M3
NA997.R45
NA997.V6
NA997.W8
NA1038.W3
NA1053.J4
NA1053.L46
NA1123.B8
NA1123.E5
NA1123.S6
NA1153.R5
NA1223.J3
NA1313.G3
NA1559.T33
NA1605.G67
NA9085.S6
NB813.M56
NC1145.M44
NK1535.W4
720.941 NA972
720.94162 NA991.L6
720.942 NA610
NA645
NA961
NA964
NA967
NA968
NA971.B2
NA988
NA1603.A4
NA2410.G7L68
NA4125

720.942	NA7328
720.9421	NA970
720.94213	DA675
720.94221	NA971.C56
720.94233	NA971.D6
720.94238	NA971.B2
720.94248	NA971.C6
720.94264	NA969.S7
720.94274	DA690.L4
720.9428	NA968
720.94282	DA670.N8
720.943	NA1068
720.9438	NA1191
720.944	NA1041
	NA1044
720.945	NA1111
	NA1115
720.945751	DG975.A274
720.946	NA1303
	NA1305
720.947	NA1181
	NA1188
720.9471	NA1193
	NA1455.F5
720.9489	NA1218
720.9494	NA1348
720.952	NA1550
	NA1555
	NA1558.J3
	NA7451
720.954	NA1501
	NA1502
	NA6001
	NB1002
720.9548	NA1502
720.9549	NA1507.P3
720.955	NA1480
	NA1483
720.9561	NA1364
720.96	NA1580
720.965	NA565
720.9667	GN414.A1
720.968	GN414.A1
	NA1592
720.971	NA745
720.971352	NA747.H3
720.972	NA750
720.973	E159
	NA705
	NA707
	NA710
	NA712
	NA737.S53
720.97449	NA707
720.974497	NA735.N2
720.9747	NA730.N4
720.97471	NA705
720.975	NA705
720.9753	NA705
	NA735.W3
720.9757915	NA735.C35
720.977176	NA730.O35
720.9794	NA730.C2
720.97946	F868.S156
720.98	NA702
720.985	NA7318.L5
720.994	NA1600
720.9942	NA1603.A4
720.9945	NA7470.V5
721	NA2610
	NA4110
	TA439
	TH151
	TH860
721.0711	T73
721.3	NA3576
721.562148	HD7269.A6
722.61	AS722
722.7	DG78
	NA295
722.8	NA600
722.91	F1219.3.A6
	F3429.3.A65
723.1	N7831
723.2	NA370
723.3	NA380
723.4	N6280
723.5	N6310
	NA440
723.501	NA440
724	NA645
	NA2500
724.23	NA600
724.9	NA642
	NA680
	NA2430
	NA2560
725	NA2545.P5
725.1	E159
725.10963	NA4377.E8
725.110943613	JN1815
725.1109753	F204.C2
725.180966	DT475
725.20942	NA6214.G7
725.21	NA6220
	Z283
725.23	NA6230
725.31	TF305
725.31094214	NA6315.G72L63
725.3109782	TF300
725.4	NA2545.P5
725.5	RA996.G
725.51	RA966
	RA967
725.51	RA987.S4
725.53	NA2545.M4
725.530973	HV3006
725.56	RA987.S4
725.560973	NA2545.A3
725.59	UH473
725.76	GV1826
725.8	NA2340
725.810977366	NA6813.U6U77
725.822	NA5470.L6
	NA6820
	NA6821
	NA6830
	NA6840.A78
	NA6845
725.9	DA687.G6
726	NA4605
726.0631	NA21
726.1	NA6001
	NA6007.T7
726.1208	NA275
726.14309596	N7315.2.A5
726.145	NA6002
726.151095484	DS485.A55
726.1709581	DS375.G37
726.209561	NA5863
726.3	NA4690
726.4	BV604
	NA5471.C15
726.5	BV604
	N6280
	NA4605
	NA4800
726.509415	NA5482
726.50942	NA440
	NA5461
	NA5467
726.5094223	BX4631.D6S45
	ML85
726.5094225	NA5469.S83
726.5094228	NA5495.W6
726.50945	NA470
	NA5613
726.509481	NA5763
726.509495	NA370
726.50963	N7988
726.509714281	NA5247.M6
726.50973	NA5212
726.50974	NA5215
726.510943613	DB859.V6
726.585174921	NA5235.B43
726.59	N7831
	NB471.L5
726.59109426	NA5461
726.597	NA2930
726.5970942	NA2930
726.6	NA4830
726.6094	NA4830
	NA5453
726.60942	BV634
	NA5461
726.6094451	NA5551.C5
726.7	NA4850
726.7094131	NA5481.R4
726.7094493	NA5551.L44
726.774	DA690.L63
726.9	NA5235.P45
727	LB3219.E9
727.08	LB3219.G7
727.10973	LB3205
727.20942575	LF795.E84
727.38	NA6602.S3
727.4000973	LC1048.F3
727.478	ML3849
	NA6880
727.553	NA6602.P5
727.709945	N3948
727.8	Z679
727.80942	Z679
727.8094257	Z792.O96
727.809969	Z675.S3
727.9	LC4041.K37
	NA4510.C7
	NA5621.F515
728	GT171
	HD7287.5
	HT175.U6
	NA2545.P5
	NA7328
	NA7451
	TH4816
728.0222	NA7126
728.094	NA7325
728.0972	NA7244
728.0973	NA7120
728.0994	NA7469
728.2	NA1479.S2
	TH4819.P7
728.209778411	NA9000
728.3	NA707
728.309753	NA705
728.370942	NA7328
728.37094274	DA690.Y6
728.370974811	NA735.C37
728.3709755	NA7235.V5
728.5	NA7800
728.5094	NA4830
728.50971	NA7850.C3
728.6	DA110
	NA7127
	NA7561
728.60223	NA7127
728.60942	NA7328
728.6094235	NA7331.D46
728.64	NA7127
	NA7238.M6
728.64094947	NA7592
728.7	NA7326.A4
	NA7574
	TH4835
728.8	NA7620
	NA7745
728.80942	NA7620
728.81094	NA7710
728.810942	NA7745
728.82	NA7580
	NA7756.G3
	NA7756.U8
728.82093918	NA279.C7
728.820945677	NA7756.U8
728.8209493	NA7725
728.82094972	NA320
728.83	F204.T8
	NA7332
728.830942	NA7620
728.83094235	NA7333.T66
728.830973	NA707
728.8309768	NA7214
728.9	NA7328
	NA8230
	PZ10.P4474
	QL676.5
729	NA2543.S6
	NA2620
	NA2750
	NA2765
	TA658.2
729.2	TH7011
729.23	NA2760
	NA2765
729.28	TH7703
	TH7725
	TH7791
729.3	NA2545.P5
	NA2840
729.31	NA9053.W3
729.320202	NA2810
729.90942	NA5461
729.91	NB490.M4
730	NB1140
730.074019494	N5311
730.0924	NB1208
730.093	N5603.N4A53
730.093915	N5899.C9
730.09669	NK1087.6.N52B46
730.096711	N7397
730.16	NB36
730.74	NB30.R6
730.74014461	N6512
730.7401471	N6512
730.74017178	NB25.C5
730.9	NB60
	NB60.C55
	NB185
730.922	N6494.M5
	N6494.S7
	N6512
	N6530.C2
	NB198
	NB205
	NB212
	NB236
	NB245
	NB467
	NB496
	NB1135
	NK9798.S3
730.924	N6536
	N6537.A5
	N6537.J3
	N6537.K29
	N6537.L48
	N6537.M34
	N6537.O4
	N6659.O35
	N6923.B9
	NA1123.B5
	NB87.P45
	NB236
	NB237.A53
	NB237.A7
	NB237.C24
	NB237.C28
	NB237.D43
	NB237.E17
	NB237.G5
	NB237.G8
	NB237.H25
	NB237.K53
	NB237.K74
	NB237.L266
	NB237.L55
	NB237.M63
	NB237.N43
	NB237.R69
	NB237.S2
	NB237.S567
	NB237.S58
	NB237.T67
	NB237.W416
	NB249.D6
	NB249.E8
	NB249.F5
	NB249.M8
	NB379.R3
	NB497
	NB497.D8
	NB497.G55
730.924	NB497.H4
	NB497.H8
	NB497.M6
	NB538.Z4
	NB553.C28
	NB553.D29
	NB553.G35
	NB553.H34
	NB553.L3
	NB553.M3
	NB553.R7
	NB588.B35
	NB588.L45
	NB623.B9
	NB623.C3
	NB623.C38
	NB623.P4
	NB623.P588
	NB623.S314
	NB653.N48
	NB699.N4
	NB773.V5
	NB813.D4
	NB813.G6
	NB853.A7
	NB893.C5
	NB893.L3
	NB933.B7
	NB953.M4
	NB979.K3
	ND623.B9
	NK7198.R8
	NK7998.L56
730.938	NB155
730.94	NB170
	NB185
730.9407401471	NB458
730.942	N6797.B37
	NB464
730.9420740241	NB468
730.9421	DA689.M7
730.944	NB543
730.94551	NB621.F6
730.946	NB803
730.9471	NB693
730.951	N7342
730.954	N7302
	N7350
	ND3247
730.9543	NB1008.S3
730.959	NB1000
730.9593	NK1015
730.9596	NB1015
730.967	NB1097.W4
730.967097471	NB1080
730.96750976428	NB1097.C75
730.9701	E59.A7
730.973	NB212
730.973074014966	N6512
730.9794	N330.C25
730.994	NB1100
731	N6494.C6
	NB1170
	NB1230
	NB1270.P5
	NK5500
	NK9704
731.2	TP808
731.4	NB198
	NB1150
	NB1170
731.452	NB1190
731.456	NB1143
	TS570
731.462	NK9704
731.463	NB1208
731.49495	CJ1229
731.549	NK835.S6
731.54909497	NA9325
731.55	NB1272
731.722	NA9406
	NA9410.C5
	NA9415.R7
731.74	N7580
	NB1309
731.75096	NB1097.W4
731.750995	N7411.S4
731.76	CC313.S2
731.76094138	NB1590.I7
731.82	NB198
	NB1293
731.82093	GN2
731.820942	NB461
731.88943095145	NB1043
731.8894309549123	NB1007.P4
731.897922	N7760
731.899178	NK7912
731.89937070924	DG12
732	N5335.N43
732.2	E59.A7
	E99.I7
	F1219.1.C54
	F1219.3.A7
	F1435.3.A7
	GN799.P4
	N5311
	N7397.A6
	N7410
	NB62
	NB1080
	NB1098
	NK9789
732.2096	NB1080
732.209701	F1219.3.A7

732.209723	F1219.3.A7
732.5	N5345
732.8	NB75
733	NB86
733.0740164	N5603
733.3	NB90
	NB94
	WB90
733.5	NB115
734.756	M1670
735	NB198
735.21	N8640
	NB185
735.24	NK5750
735.29	N6494.K5
	NB198
	NB1272
736	NK1496.M4
736.2	NK5557
	NK5565
736.2028	TS752.5
	TS756
736.20932	NK5561
736.23	TS753
736.24	NK5750
736.4	ND237.W39
	NK9704
	SK335
	TT200
	VM308
736.4074019494	NK512.L6
736.40942	NK9743
736.40973	NK9712
736.409931	NK9793
736.5	NK4646
736.50936	N5310
736.5094282	NB469
736.6	NK5825
	NK6022
	NK6050
736.68	NK6050
736.93	NK9580
736.98	TT870
737	CJ15
	CJ85
	CJ89
737.0740153	Q11
737.0934	CJ3544
	CT3530
737.095495	HG1311.M4
737.2	CJ5807
	CJ5832
	CR4801
	G246.C7
737.3	CJ4904
	CJ5056
	CJ5057
	CJ5350
	HG1480.5.Z8
737.30942	CJ5053
	CJ5056
	Z234
737.309421	CJ5058.L76
737.30943	CJ2725
737.30973	CJ4904
737.309791	E98.M7
737.309796	CJ4909.I3
737.4	CJ63
	CJ109
	CJ113
	CJ129
	CJ161.S5
	CJ969
	CJ1529
	CJ1755
	CJ1820
	CJ1836
	CJ1848.C3
	CJ2480
	CJ2485
	CJ5793.A8
737.402542	CJ63
737.403	CJ67
737.407409549143	CJ3532
737.4075	CJ36
	CJ63
	CJ81
	CJ89
737.409	CJ59
	CJ75
	HG235
737.40924	CJ62.R6
737.4098	CJ1819
737.43	CJ233
737.49094	CJ1543
737.4932	CJ1072
	CJ4134
737.4934	CJ668
737.4937	CJ233
	CJ833
737.49378	CJ1139.S9
737.4938	CJ317
	CJ335
	CJ351
	CJ385
	CJ668
	CN375.C6
737.49394	CJ3474
737.49396	CJ668
737.49415	CJ2546
737.4942	CJ125
	CJ2480
	CJ2482
	CJ2484
737.4942	CJ2485
	CJ2486
	CJ2495
	CJ5054
737.494234	CJ2498.G8
737.4948	CJ3086
737.49495	CJ2887
	HG237
737.494955	CJ437
737.4954	CJ1391
	CJ3532
	CJ3536
	CJ3545
737.495694	CJ3867
737.4972	CJ1907
737.4973	CJ1826
	CJ1830
	CJ1835
	CJ1841
737.498	CJ1819
737.49866	CJ2326
737.49931	CJ4444
737.4994	CJ4410
737.6	CD5020
738	E98.P8
	E99.P9
	F1219.3.P8
	F3429.3.P8
	NK460.C3
	NK3930
	NK4027.B4
	NK4085
	NK4162.O8
	NK4230
	NK4295
	NK4695.T6
	TP808
738.0278	NK4215
738.028	TP808
738.075	NK4230
738.0924	NK4210.B6
738.093918	NK3840
	NK3840.L4
738.094	NK4230
738.0942	NK4085
738.094246	NK4087.S6
738.0945	NK4645
738.0948	NK4113
738.0973	NK4005
	NK4008
738.097554252	NK3730.W5C65
738.1	TP808
738.13	TP808
	TP841
738.142	TP808
738.15	NK4399.L9
	NK4605
738.2	NK4210.B76
	NK4240
	NK4607
738.2075	NK4230
738.20924	NK4210.B47
	NK4210.F68
738.2094	NK4083
	NK4230
738.209437	NK4096.H6
738.2095	NK4563
738.20951	NK4165
	NK4565
738.20951245	NK4565
738.20952	NK4167
738.27	NK4087
	NK4087.S6
	NK4210.B4
	NK4210.C6
	NK4210.H44
	NK4210.M55
	NK4210.S325
	NK4335
	NK4380
	NK4390
	NK4395
	NK4399.B75
	NK4399.C3
	NK4399.C5
	NK4399.C55
	NK4399.L7
	NK4399.S9
	NK4563
	NK4565
	NK4566.F67
738.270924	NK4210.W4
738.28	N1150
	NK3670
	NK3730
738.3	E59.A7
	NK4030.B7
738.30740274	NK4085
738.30924	NK4210.W5
738.30938	NK4645
738.3093918	NK3843
738.3093939	NK685.C9
738.30942	NK4085
738.3094391	NK1035.H8
738.30951	NK4165
738.30968	QH1
738.309701	E78.S7
738.30976435	F388
738.37	F3429.3.P8
	NK3740
	NK4087
	NK4087.S6
	NK4295
	NK4335
738.37	NK4340.D4
	NK4399.S9
738.38	NK4087.S6
	NK4695.T6
738.383	TP820
738.4	NK5000
	NK5004.F8
	NK6405
738.4094	NK4999.C48M37
	NK5004.E9
738.5028	NA3750
738.6	NK4670
738.72	U856.R9
738.8	NK4680
	NK9507
739	N5899.S3
	NK6406
	TT205
739.0222	NK6410
739.0712	TT205
739.07401471	NK6402.N45
739.09	NK6406
739.13074015251	ND210
739.14	NK6530
739.15	NK5000
	TS700
739.2	NK7143
	NK7198.D5
	TS725
739.20278	NK7112
	NK7210
739.22	TS725
739.22717498	E59.A7
739.2274	NK7108
739.23	NK7110
	NK7143
739.230278	NK7210
739.230924	NK7198.D8
739.23742	NK7105
	NK7143
739.2374274	NK7250
739.23744	NK7149
739.23746	NK7162
739.23773	NK7103
	NK7111
	NK7112
739.23774	NK7112
739.2377465	NK7111
739.23776226	NK7111
739.238	NK7250
739.2382	NK7215
739.2382094247	NK7215
739.2383	NK7235
739.2384	NK7143
739.27	NK4395
	NK7304
	NK7398.D25
	NK7406
	TS740
	TS741
	TS752
739.270202	TS741
739.27023	TS741
739.27074021	NK7303
739.2709	NK7306
739.27093	NK7307
739.270932	NK7388
739.27094	NK7342
739.270942	NK7109
739.27094371	NK7415.C95
739.278	NK7503
739.3742	NK7495.G7
739.4	NK6405
	NK8205
	NK8243
739.4724	NK8298.M25
739.4742	NK8243
	NK8243.A1
739.474259	NK8244.C3
739.4774811	NK8212.P4
739.48	NK8459.S4
739.4942	CJ2490
739.4972	CJ1907
739.497294	CJ2136
739.5	NK8100
739.512	NB135
	NK8440
	TS570
739.51209	NK7906
739.5120938	NB135
739.5120951	NK7983
739.52	NB1840
	NB1842
	NK9990.C2
739.520942	NB1842
739.52094231	NB1842
739.52094259	NB1842
739.53	TT900.C4
739.531	ND621.V5
739.533	NK8412
739.5330942	NK8415.G7
739.53309421	NK8403.P4
739.5330973	NK8412
739.7	NK6602.L74
	NK6602.L74L63
	NK8475.M5
	U800
739.70941	NK6645
739.70952	NK6684
739.72	NK6684
	NK6703
	NK6750.A2
	NK6780
	U852
739.72	U855
739.720943	U820.G7
739.74	NK6949.F5
739.740740182273	NK6903.D4
739.7409	TS533
739.743	TS537
739.74409	TS533
739.744094	TS535
739.74425	SK274
739.7443	TS537
739.74430947	TS533.4.R9
739.75095	U825
739.750952	U821.J3
740.0924	PR6031.E183
740.74019491	NC15.S36
741	NK3600
	Z40
	Z43
	Z43.A3
741.07	NC650
741.074094945	NC33.S92
741.09034	NC90
741.0922	NC15.B4
	NC45
	NC249
	NC960
741.0924	NB497.G55
	NC139.P6
	NC242.B3
	NC242.C8
	NC242.D8
	NC242.M63
	NC302.A5
	NC978.5.A7
	NC1085.J3
	NC1135.C45
	NE2210.V4
741.09457307401471	NC256.N3
741.2	NC730
741.23	NC855
741.235	NC880
741.24	NC890
741.26	NC905
741.29	NC915.A35
741.4	NC730
	NC735
	NC740
	NC780
741.424	NA2700
741.5	NC1320
	NC1340
	NC1426
	NC1427.P74
	NC1429.S62
741.502573	NC1320
741.509	NC1325
	NC1340
741.5120951	NK7983
741.573	NC1420
	NC1429.B29
741.580924	NC1449.P5
741.594	NC1479.F57
741.5942	NC242.D8
	NC1429.S554
	NC1479
	NC1479.C33
	NC1479.G79
	NC1479.L47
	NC1479.M22
	NC1479.S39
	NC1479.S79
	NC1479.T55
	NC1479.T56
741.5944	DC33
	NC1499.B73
	NC1499.C63
	NC1499.D3
	NC1499.E27
	NC1499.U3
741.5954	NC1719.D37
741.5971	NC1449.M25
	NC1449.V3
741.5973	D745.2
	NC1426.3.B8
	NC1428
	NC1429
	NC1429.A25
	NC1429.B358
	NC1429.B613
	NC1429.B737
	NC1429.B772
	NC1429.C295
	NC1429.C52
	NC1429.C523
	NC1429.D36
	NC1429.D364
	NC1429.D57
	NC1429.G39
	NC1429.G46
	NC1429.G7
	NC1429.G9
	NC1429.H325
	NC1429.H39
	NC1429.H45
	NC1429.H527
	NC1429.H595
	NC1429.J42
	NC1429.J59
	NC1429.K29
	NC1429.K33
	NC1429.K68
	NC1429.L537
	NC1429.L8
	NC1429.M5395

Dewey	LC
741.5973	NC1429.N53
	NC1429.O48
	NC1429.P35
	NC1429.R6
	NC1429.R753
	NC1429.S39
	NC1429.S565
	NC1429.T78
	NC1429.U5
	NC1429.W23
	NC1429.W243
	NC1479.C65
	NC1766.C32
	NC1766.M4
741.5977	ND893.B6
741.5994	NC1750
	NC1756
741.6	NC1000
741.60922	NC975
741.64	N1150
	NC980
	Z1023
741.6409	NC960
741.640942	NC978
741.640944	NC980
741.6409946	Z232.W3
741.642	NC965
	NC1075.S74
	PN1009.A1
741.6420922	NC965
741.6709034	NC1845.A7
741.672	TT509
741.7	NC910
741.70942	N7616
	NC910
741.9	N352
	NC53
	NC915.D6
741.9074094183	NC17.I7
741.923	NC30
741.94	NC15.P7
	NC27.F7
	NC225
741.9407401468	NC225
741.94094272	NC225
741.940971384	NC225
741.941	N6797.G48
	NC242.D3
741.942	N6758
	N6797.N5
	NA997.M3
	NC15.N43
	NC139.M2
	NC228
	NC242.B55
	NC242.F57
	NC245.K568
	NC1115.L48
	NC1115.M57
	NC1115.S67
	NC1115.T47
	NC1479.L58
	NC1479.S39
741.943	NA1088.J3
	NC249
	NC251.D8
	NC251.L54
	NC1145.H66
	ND588.G7
741.9436	NC245.K8
741.9437	NC1145.T5
741.94391	NC1145.Z5
741.944	N6853.B3
	NC246
	NC248.L6
	NC248.M4
	NC248.W3
	NC1130
	NC1135.D4
	NC1135.G396
	NC1135.M25
	NC1135.M34
741.945	NC255
	NC255.E3
	NC256.T8
	NC256.V4
	NC257.B27
	NC257.C27
	NC257.F5
	NC257.L4
	NC257.T5
	NC257.Z8
	NC1045
	NC1055.B9
	NC1055.L5
	NC1055.R2
	NC1055.T47
	NC1150
	NC1155.C23
	NC1155.M6
	NC1155.S25
741.946	NC248.P5
	NC1185.G6
	ND813.D3
741.9492	NC261
	NC263.G56
	NC263.M6
	NC263.R4
741.9494	NC293.F8
741.9495	NC257.C56
741.94977	NC302.B4
741.952	NC1245.K3
	ND1059.3
741.96	NC33
741.971	NC141
	NC143.K3
	NC143.T6
741.973	F459.L8
	ML85
	NC107
	NC108
	NC139.D5
	NC139.F3
	NC139.G62
	NC139.G64
	NC139.G68
	NC139.G75
	NC139.H6
	NC139.L38
	NC139.L46
	NC139.M27
	NC139.P55
	NC139.W4
	NC312.P63
	NC860
	NC975.5.P8
	NC1075.B673
	NC1075.G88
	NC1075.M39
	NC1075.S715
	NC1075.T48
	NC1429.G42
	ND237.K8
	PN2091.S8
	TL549
741.9777	F622
741.9794	NC123
741.994	NC1260
742	NC750
	T369
743.4	NC760
	NC825.M8
	NC825.O3
743.43	NC765
743.6	NC780
743.7	NC810
743.83	NC650
743.896218	NC825.M3
743.89913031	CC77
743.899296	NC825.H4
743.921	NC1060
743.995740740254	QK98.2
744	NC740
	T11.8
	TT360
744.04	DC148
744.4	NC730
	T359
744.4071	T351.5
744.42	QH318
744.422	T11.8
	T353
	T379
744.4220202	T351.5.M55
744.42229	TL253
744.42271076	TS250
744.424	NA1088.J3
	NA2700
	TH2031
744.428	GA105
	GA203
744.45076	T363
744.5	T379
	TS250
	VG923
745	N85
	NK805
	NK835.N5
	NK1510
	TS171.T65
	TT104.C4
	TT190
745.00922	NK991
745.00944	NK1340
745.009471	NK1035.F5
745.0624247	NK12
745.09034	NK1140
745.0922	NK808
	NK841
	NK1091
745.0924	ND3150.B57
	NK942.M8
745.094391	NK944.H9
745.09475	NK976.L5
745.0956	NK1038
745.0978953	N7911.A7
745.097913	E98.A7
745.1	N8380
	N8386.J6
	NK460.N45
	NK1125
	NK9990.B6
745.10257471	NK1127
745.1029	NK1133
745.103	N40
	NK30
	NK1125
745.1074	NK1125
745.1075	N8660.S9
	NK1125
	NK1127
	PN6231.C58
745.10922	N40
745.10942	NK928
745.10973	NK805
	NK806
	NK1125
745.10974	NK810
745.109748	NK1410.P4
745.2	N6493
	N8218
	NC997
	NK1510
	NK1520
	TA166
	TS149
	TS171
	TS171.4
745.20222	TS171.6
745.2023	TS171.4
745.206242	TS149
745.2071	TS171.A1
745.20712	TS171
745.20740171	NK835.O3
745.209471	NK976.F5
745.209480994	NK979
745.20973	NK807
	TS171
745.213	TT195
745.4	NC740
	NK1484
	NK1505
	NK1510
	NK1530
	NK1535.P4
	NK1535.T3
	NK1570
	NK1585
	QA464
745.4074015655	NK814
745.441	NK1487.A3
745.444	NK1370
745.44924	NK1570
	NK8998.L3
745.44942	NK928
745.44954	NK1476
745.5	NK1047
	NK1080
	NK3665
	NK8490
	TT154
	TT155
	TT157
	TT160
	TT168
	TT169
	TT880
745.50202	TT153
745.5074	NK805
745.50942	TT18
	TT57
745.5096	TT115
745.50966	TT119.W4
745.509701	E99.C5
	TT157
745.50973	NK808
745.51	NK9604
	NK9798.P5
	NK9920
	TT154
	TT160
745.531	TT290
745.54	N6494.C6
	NK8555
	TT870
	TT871
	TT892
745.57	TT297
745.59	GV1201
	NK8475.C3
	NK8475.M5
	TT715
	TT890
	TT892
	TT896.5
	TT900.C4
	TT900.P3
745.592	NK9509
	TT157
745.5920740213	NK9509.5.G7
745.592075	NK9509
745.5922	NK4893
	NK4894.A2
	PN1972
	TS2301.T7
	TT157
	TT715
	TT870
745.5922094	N1150
745.592209701	E99.H7
745.5923	NK4893
	TT200
745.5924	GV1220.7
	TT157
745.59282	NK8475.M5
745.6	GT3910
	NK3600
745.61	NK3600
	NK3615
	NK3631.O25
	NK3640
	NK3648.D8
	Z40
	Z43
	Z43.A2
	Z43.A3M6
	Z115.E5
745.67	NC960
	ND2920
	ND2935
	ND2955
	ND2990
745.67	ND3035.P4
	ND3144.H8
	ND3239.A7
	ND3355
	ND3385.G7
	NE905
	PQ4366
	Z725.M44
745.670935	ND3399.A2
745.67096	ND3199
745.7	NK1520
745.72	NK991
	NK9530
	NK9900
745.92	SB447
	SB447.5
	SB449
	SB449.3.C3
745.9203	SB449
745.9209	SB449
745.920924	SB449
745.922	SB449
745.92252	SB449.3.D7
	SB450
745.925	SB449.3.D8
745.926	SB449.5.C4
	SB449.5.W4
745.928	SB449.3.P7
746	NK8843
	NK8943
	TT750
	TT770
	TT910
746.09923	NK8879
746.1	NK8904
	NK8907
	TT848
746.12	TS1480
746.30216	NK2985.B6
746.39	NK3000
746.3922	NK8801.N4
746.3924	N71
746.4	TT206
	TT750
	TT840
	TT880
746.41	E59.B3
	E98.B3
	TS910
	TT875
	TT877
	TT880
746.43	TT820
	TT825
746.44	F1565.3.A7
	NK9104
	NK9143.A1
	NK9276
	TT712
	TT751
	TT753
	TT770
	TT771
	TT777
	TT778.C3
	TT778.C7
746.44094	NK9242
746.4409481	TT771
746.440973	NK9203
746.445	TT750
	TT751
746.46	NK9112
	TT835
746.5	TT860
746.6	NE855
	NK8802.S8
	NK8806
	NK8843.A2
	NK8876.A2
	TP930
746.7	NK2795
	NK2808
	TT850
746.72	TT850
746.720902	NK3007
746.74	TT850
746.75	NK2808
746.751	NK2883
746.754	NK2876.A1
746.756	NK2809.I8
746.791821	NK2842
746.7942	NK2843
746.794468	TS1774.6.A8
746.9	TT507
746.92	TT505.A1
	TT507
747	NK2110
	NK2113
	NK2115
	NK2130
	NK2137
	TX301
747.0222	NK2117
747.023	NK2116
747.03	TH4816
747.0979493	NK2002
747.23	NK2002
747.294	NK1442
747.3	NK2119
747.77	NK2117.C4
747.78	NK2117
	NK2117.B33
747.797	NA2545.P5
747.88	NK2115

747.92 SB476
748 NK5104
TP857.3
TP859
TP862
748.2 NK5105.A1
NK5112
748.207401641411 NK5101.H6
748.209 NK5105
748.20977119 NK5111.F5
748.29 NK5105
NK5106
748.2904 NK5105
748.2911 NK5113
748.2913 NK5112
NK5198.W55
748.2914485 NK5198.P3
748.2914892 NK5198.P48
748.2916 AM101.N764
748.2917192 NK5112
748.292 NK5143
748.2973 NK5103
748.297554252 NK5111
748.2994 NK5142
748.4973 ML3561.J3
748.5 NK5105
748.59 NK5106
748.592 NK5104
NK5343
748.59238 NK5344.S6
748.594 NK5349.A2
748.59932 NK5188.A1
748.6 NK5198.H8
748.8 NA3750
NK5112
NK5143
NK5198.S7
NK5440.B6
NK5440.C3
NK5440.F7
NK5440.P3
NK5440.S3
748.88 NK2117
749 NK2115
NK2542
NK2542.S5
TT180
749.03 NK2205
749.07401419 BX9767
749.075 NK1125
749.2 NK1125
NK2240
NK2270
NK2350
749.202 NK2270
749.204 NK2528
TS882
749.213 NK2406
NK2408
NK2439.P5
749.2157915 NK2438.C5
749.2169 NK2435.K4
749.2177 NK2407
749.22 NK1125
NK2135
NK2528
NK2529
NK2530
NK2542.C5
NK2542.M3
NK2578
TT196
749.2951 NK2668
749.3 N1150
NK2715
749.62 NA3050
749.7 N8550
750 ND1135
750.1 ND1146
750.18 N7431
750.207 N7470
750.29 N4035
750.4 ND1260
750.74014461 W5030.N45
750.7401471 N610
N5020
N5020.B875
N6490
750.74014886 N6490
750.74014942 N588
750.740153 N856
N5220.P55
ND1471
750.74018225 N658
750.74021 N1160
N1165.U45
N5055
N5055.F7
N5056.S6
750.7405656 ND454
750.740641 N3455.M82
750.74094923 N2460
N2500
751 ND1140
ND1260
ND1262
ND1500
751.2 ND565
ND1510
751.4 NB1140
NC750
ND141
ND196.A25
ND1260
751.4 ND1263
ND1283
ND1410
ND1471
ND1500
751.42 ND1260
ND1262
WD1302
751.422 ND1260
ND2110
ND2133
ND2420
751.425 ND2460
ND2462
751.43 ND2470
751.45 ND1260
ND1262
ND1302
ND1473
751.48 NA3750
751.49 N6494.C6
751.58 N8790
ND1146
751.6 ND1530
751.7307401471 ND2550
751.730974 ND2606
751.770954 ND3247
752 ND1280
ND1285
754.1075 NK1125
754.531 TT290
755.20942 ND2728
755.209492 ND669.F5
755.209498 N8189.R8
755.2094981 ND2808.V6
755.2095645 N8189.C9
755.4 N8050
ND3356
755.52 N8050
755.6 N8080
757 ND1302
757.016 N7620
757.0942 ND1314
757.7 N7616
757.7094 ND1337.E9
757.70942 ND1337.G7
757.70973 ND1337.U5
757.9074021 N7598
757.90942 N7598
ND1314
758.1 N6505
ND1340
758.1028 ND1340
758.10740141 ND1351.5
758.10942 ND468
ND496
758.109492 ND1359.5
758.109730740172255 ND210
758.109794 ND1351.5
758.10994 ND1100
758.2028 ND1370
758.20740159381 N8240
758.30951 QL674
758.40973 ND210
758.7 N8213
ND1262
ND1349.4
759 N62
N332.B38
N515
N3310
N5247.B3
N5305
N6494.A2
ND30
ND35
ND137
ND1130
ND1130.D573
ND1135
ND1143
ND1150
ND1760
NX600.E9
NX600.S9
759.011 E98.P6
759.01109701 E99
759.02 ND143
ND150
ND2920
759.0407401471 ND456
759.05 ND192.R4
ND547
759.05074021 N6465.S9
759.06 ND195
ND196.C8
759.06074014423 N5015.A53
759.060740153 N6867
759.06074019491 N6494.S8
759.060740471 N6494.S8
759.07404797 N5020
759.0740512 N2980
759.07409491 ND195
759.1 F73.7
N8640
ND1351.4
759.11 N910.K45
N5230
N5230.C3
N6549.S5
NC139.B32
ND245
ND248
ND249.B35
759.11 ND249.C45
ND249.H28
ND249.M26
ND249.P5
ND249.R6
ND249.T5
759.13 E51
E83.866
GN1
N514.A8
N529.C15
N6512
N6512.5.P7
N6528
N6535.C3
N6536
N6537.A7
N6537.B22
N6537.L55
N6537.W28
N6537.W9
N6537.Y8
N6538.N5
N6797.R54
N7593
N8640
NA3860.S49
NC1075.P94
NC1429.N3
ND205
ND207
ND210
ND212
ND212.5.A25
ND235.N45
ND236
ND237.A4
ND237.A63
ND237.A85
ND237.B47
ND237.B6
ND237.B65
ND237.B88
ND237.C3
ND237.C485
ND237.C6
ND237.C7
ND237.C733
ND237.C846
ND237.C884
ND237.D23
ND237.D3325
ND237.D3337
ND237.D334
ND237.D46
ND237.D57
ND237.D79
ND237.D85
ND237.E15
ND237.E44
ND237.E8
ND237.F22
ND237.F35
ND237.F494
ND237.F675
ND237.F677
ND237.G8
ND237.H3
ND237.H313
ND237.H315
ND237.H4
ND237.H42
ND237.H5
ND237.H52
ND237.H58
ND237.H7
ND237.I47
ND237.I5
ND237.K47
ND237.K555
ND237.K56
ND237.K59
ND237.K83
ND237.L2
ND237.L29
ND237.L35
ND237.L53
ND237.L664
ND237.M2145
ND237.M2155
ND237.M24
ND237.M475
ND237.M78
ND237.M855
ND237.N3
ND237.N475
ND237.O5
ND237.P254
ND237.P27
ND237.P4
ND237.P47
ND237.R174
ND237.R316
ND237.R48
ND237.R53
ND237.R68
ND237.R725
ND237.S3
ND237.S32
ND237.S35
ND237.S4345
ND237.S465
ND237.S57
ND237.S59
759.13 ND237.S636
ND237.S685
ND237.S78
ND237.S8
ND237.S9
ND237.T33
ND237.T5515
ND237.T56
ND237.T8
ND237.U37
ND237.U66
ND237.W36
ND237.W6
ND237.W612
ND237.W624
ND237.W64
ND237.W93
ND497.R83
ND1059.H75
ND1839.B8
ND1839.C3
ND1839.G7
ND1839.H6
ND1839.J3
ND1839.M35
ND1839.R3
ND1839.R78
ND1839.W35
ND1998.W5
ND2606
PS875.W3
PS1449.C8
SF355.M3
WD205
759.13074 ND205
759.13074014461 N6538.N5
759.1307401452 N6512
759.1307401471 N7432.5
ND210
ND236
759.13074014797 N6512.5.M5
759.13074016638 ND217
759.13074017178 ND205
ND1805
759.13074018186 ND205
759.13074019466 ND230.C3
759.14 N6515
759.147074014748 ND238.N5
759.1471 ND1711.A43
759.147107401471 ND235.N45
759.153074015961 ND235.W3
759.2 CT788.O87
N6765
N6766
N6767
N6797.B55
N6797.H35
N6797.L47
N6797.P3
N7477
NC228
NC242.W4
ND236
ND237.W6
ND461
ND464
ND466
ND467
ND467.5.P7
ND468
ND496
ND497
ND497.A52
ND497.B6
ND497.C7
ND497.D4
ND497.G2
ND497.G66
ND497.H7
ND497.H9
ND497.L4
ND497.L48
ND497.L83
ND497.N58
ND497.R8
ND497.R83
ND497.S46
ND497.S74
ND497.S75
ND497.T8
ND497.W255
ND497.W63
ND1928
ND1942.B55
ND1942.C9
ND1942.G6
ND1942.P53
PR4144
PR5236.R9
PR5246
759.207401272 N6754
759.2074021 N467
ND468
759.20740212 ND468
759.3 N6925
ND588.A4
ND588.B37
ND588.D9
ND588.K47
ND588.R9
ND588.S42
ND1951
ND1954.N6
NX600.E9

759.3	PN1998.A3
	PT2638.W896
759.3074013	ND567
759.30740147	N6868.5.E9
759.3074017289	N6868.5.E9
759.307407595	ND1452.G3
759.36	ND538.H38
	ND538.H83
759.37	ND538.K687
759.38	ND691
	ND699.M222
759.391	N6838.M6
	N8791.H6
	ND553.V35
759.4	N332.F83P33
	N2050.J4
	N5220.A7
	N6465.N44
	N6847
	N6847.5.I4
	N6853.P48
	N8640
	NC248.D6
	ND36
	ND192.I4
	ND545
	ND546
	ND547
	ND547.5.I4
	ND548
	ND552
	ND553
	ND553.B65
	ND553.B73
	ND553.B86
	ND553.B873
	ND553.C33
	ND553.C355
	ND553.C4
	ND553.C9
	ND553.D3
	ND553.D33
	ND553.D357
	ND553.D774
	ND553.F7
	ND553.G27
	ND553.G3
	ND553.L15
	ND553.L58
	ND553.M26
	ND553.M3
	ND553.M37
	ND553.M6
	ND553.M7
	ND553.P8
	ND553.R45
	ND553.R66
	ND553.R67
	ND553.S5
	ND553.S9
	ND553.T7
	ND553.U7
	ND553.V9
	ND653.G7
	ND1947
	ND1950.P5
	QK31.R4
	WD553.C33
759.407401471	N5220.S785
	ND547.5.I4
	ND552
759.40941435	ND547
759.409431554	N2250.G4
759.4094924	ND547
759.4150207	GV1282.3
759.436	ND538.K57
759.47	ND699.B3
759.492	ND653.G7
759.5	DC412
	N25
	N6915
	N6923.B27
	ND611
	ND613
	ND615
	ND616
	ND619.T9
	ND621.V5
	ND623.A55
	ND623.A6
	ND623.B9
	ND623.C26
	ND623.C56
	ND623.F78
	ND623.G5
	ND623.G6
	ND623.J58
	ND623.L5
	ND623.L74
	ND623.M43
	ND623.M67
	ND623.R2
	ND623.T6
	ND623.T63
	ND623.T7
	ND623.U4
	ND2755
759.507401468	ND615
759.50740212	ND616
759.50740521	N2670
759.55209492	ND621.S6
759.55994	PZ9
759.59	NC1478
759.6	ND553.P5
759.6	ND804
	ND812
	ND813.D3
	ND813.G7
	ND813.G75
	ND813.M5
	ND813.V18
	ND813.V4
759.7	ND553.C355
	ND699.C5
	ND699.K3
	ND699.T35
	ND1978.C5
759.71	WD955.F5
759.93	ND75
759.931	N7407.C3
759.932	DT62.T6
	ND2863
759.94	N1250
	N1280
	N7405.R4
	N8193.Z7T38
	ND160
	ND172.M3
	ND182.B3
	ND450
	ND456
	ND1145
759.94074017252	ND450
759.940740336	N2325
759.9407403613	N1680
759.940740391	N1620
759.940740745	N3350
759.94074094923	N5072.A55
759.9409421	N1070
759.94094212	N5055.H32
759.94094336	N2325
759.940943613	N1680
759.94094512	N2980
759.94094641	N3450
759.941	ND475
	ND497.D35
759.941074041435	ND479
759.941435074021	ND481.G5
759.9415	NC242.C47
	PR6047.E3
759.9492	N6945
	N6946
	N6948
	N8375.B45
	ND625
	ND635
	ND636
	ND646
	ND653
	ND653.D64
	ND653.F4
	ND653.G7
	ND653.M76
	ND653.R4
	ND653.V43
	ND653.V5
	ND673
	ND673.R9
759.9493	ND636
	ND665
	ND669.F5
	ND673.B73
	ND673.E87
	ND673.M35
	ND673.R9
	NX600.S9
759.9494	ND588.K5
	ND853.G66
759.94961	ND142
759.94977	N7823.B93
759.95	ND197
	ND1037
	ND2955
759.951	ND1040
	ND1042
	ND1043
	ND1049.C4526
	ND1049.W18
	ND1053
	ND1366
759.952	ND1050
	ND1053
	ND1055
	ND1059.K23
	NE1325.K3
759.952074	N7352
759.954	ND1001
	ND1004
	ND1010.H85
	ND1010.M3
	ND1010.S65
	ND3247
759.9548	ND1007.S6
759.9549	ND1010.G4
759.95694	N7277
	ND979.C3
759.968	N7396.K5
759.972	ND255
	ND259.R5
	ND2644
759.972074018856	ND202
759.97294	ND306
759.98	N6502
759.98074016686	ND202
759.982	ND339.M25
759.9861	ND379.B6
759.9931	ND1107.A9
	ND1108.H6
759.99310993127	N7406
759.994	N7400
	ND1100
	ND1105.D6
	ND1105.D78
	ND1105.F6
	ND1105.G67
	ND1105.N6
	ND1105.T8
	ND2092.L5
759.9941	N7402.K5
760	E78.S65
	N6465.A7
	N8650
	NC825.P5
	NC910
	NC915.R8
	NC997
	NC998
	ND1115
	NE539.G8
	NE850
	NE1760
	NE1850
	PS3557.O25
760.023	NC1001
760.028	NC730
	NC750
	Z244
760.071	NE970
760.0740176579	N5220.J74
760.07403515	N5070.H29
760.07408165	NE42.L3
760.075	NC725
760.08	D503
760.09	NE430
760.09174924	N6886.T4
760.0922	N6530.N5
	NC95
	NC369
	QK98.2
760.0924	N6537.K55
	N6537.L5
	N6537.P4
	N6537.S6
	N6537.W25
	N6797.H57
	N6797.J6
	N6797.M6
	N6853.T6
	N6888.R6
	N7310.G6
	N7430
	NC139.M28
	NC139.O46
	NC139.P6
	NC139.R5
	NC242.B43
	NC242.C7
	NC242.W5
	NC269.C42
	NC1055.R4
	NC1075.O4
	NC1075.S713
	NC1115.T82
	NC1145.S35
	NC1429.M925
	NC1429.O35
	ND237.D8
	ND237.G6127
	ND237.H39
	ND237.K5953
	ND237.M95
	ND249.B34
	ND497.H7
	ND497.H853
	ND497.K7
	ND497.L48
	ND497.N58
	ND497.P3
	ND553.C9565
	ND553.T7
	ND588.K47
	ND623.C2
	ND653.B75
	ND653.G7
	ND653.R4
	ND893.P3
	ND1105.R4
	ND1108.M25
	ND1954.K5
	ND1954.M28
	NE45.G7
	NE539.H6
	NE539.M24
	NE539.N4
	NE539.U6
	NE642.G75
	NE650.M2
	NE654.K6
	NE674.D4
	NE2165.R5
	NE2165.S4
	NE2393
	PR4144
	PR4146
	PR4147
760.0940943613	N1670
760.09409753	N5220.B667
760.0942	N6764
	NC228
	PR3588
760.0943	N352
	NE652.S6
760.0945	N6914
760.094531	N6921.V5
760.0947	N6988
760.09493	NC1807.B4
760.09494	ND853.V3
760.0952	N7342
760.0973	N6510
	N6512
	NC999.4.P86
	NE505
760.3	Z118
760.75	NE885
761	NE850
	NE860
761.2	NE1227
	NE1265
761.209	NE1030
761.20952	NE1310
763	NE2242
	NE2420
	NE2425
763.09	NE2425
763.2409	Z265
764.8	NE1843
	TT273
764.8028	NE2236
767.2	NE2135
769	NE1
	NE42.C45
	NE53.N6
	NE400
	NE885
	NE900
	NE1215
	NE1253
769.029	NE2303.7
	NE2415.C7
769.07401.471	NC1820
769.07401526	NE2415.H58
769.0740176579	N5220.M9
769.074021	NE950
769.075	NE885
769.4260944	NE650.S27
769.434	NE953
769.436094	NE42.S3
769.44	NE628
769.46094	NE42.P7
769.496176	RK30
769.4994246	NE642.H3
769.5	D426
	DA566.4
	DC412
	HJ5404.Z7
	ML112.5
	NB1840
	NC997
	NC1807.F7
	NC1807.U5
	NC1810
	NC1877
	NC1878.E7
	NC1882
	NE965
	Z994.C2
	Z6003
769.55	HG627.N2
769.55971	HG657
769.55973	HG353.5
	HG591
	HG607
769.55991	HG1257
769.56	HE6182
	HE6183
	HE6184.C3
	HE6184.C65
	HE6185.D33F37
	HE6185.G6
	HE6185.N42
	HE6185.U6
	HE6200
	HE6215
769.56025	HE6209
769.5603	HE6196
769.5606242	HE6188
769.56075	HE6213
	HE6215
769.563	HE6183.B5
	HE6183.E4
	HE6183.J4
	HE6183.K4
769.56309438	HE6185.P62
769.5630973	HE6185.U6
769.564	HE6183
	HE6183.M3
	HE6183.M42
	HE6183.R3
	HE6185.G62
	HE6945
769.5690973	HE6185.U6
769.56942	HE6185.G62
769.569436	HE6185.A9
769.56946	HE6185.S72
769.56951	HE6185.C552
769.569519	HE6185.K7
769.56954	HE6184.C3
	HE6185.I5
769.5695484	HE6185.I53H9
769.5695694	HE6185.P14
769.56971	HE6184.C65
769.56973	HE6184.C65
	HE6185.U6
	HE6215
769.569931	HE6185.N46G78
769.56994	HE6185.A82

769.9 ..... NE400
..... NE430
..... NE957
769.9045 ..... NE490
769.922 ..... N6512
..... NC978
..... NC1340
..... NE625
..... NE1310
..... NE1315
..... NE1858
..... NE2150
..... NE2238.5.K38
769.924 ..... N527
..... N6537.C8
..... N6537.V6
..... NC251.E7
..... NC539
..... NC1135.D7
..... NC1145.E7
..... NC1499.D3
..... ND553.D774
..... NE505
..... NE539.B3
..... NE539.B85
..... NE539.D5
..... NE539.G7
..... NE539.H57
..... NE539.J57
..... NE539.P43
..... NE539.P6
..... NE539.R5
..... NE539.S2
..... NE539.S55
..... NE539.T3
..... NE539.Y8
..... NE642.B5
..... NE642.H6
..... NE642.H7
..... NE647
..... NE650.A9
..... NE650.C3
..... NE650.G3
..... NE650.G5
..... NE650.P62
..... NE650.R4
..... NE650.V5
..... NE654.N4
..... NE654.S66
..... NE674.R6
..... NE694.M8
..... NE702.G7
..... NE789
..... NE962.C7
..... NE1184.5.M37
..... NE1205.D9
..... NE1212.B5
..... NE1215.H58
..... NE1215.L37
..... NE1217.D73
..... NE1217.W8
..... NE1325
..... NE1325.S85
..... NE1334.O33
..... NE1334.W48
..... NE2012.R5
..... NE2165.R5
..... NE2195.G78
..... NE2195.P218
..... NE2210.K38
..... NE2237.5.I5
..... NE2237.5.K4
..... NE2238.5.V6
..... NE2312.H5
..... NE2312.K5
..... NE2312.L3
..... NE2312.L45
..... NE2349.5.P5
..... NE2415.B417
..... NE2415.H87
..... NE2415.R33
..... NE2415.W38
..... PR4146
..... QL31.A9
769.94 ..... NE400
769.9407401471 ..... NE625
769.942 ..... NB1842
..... NE628
..... NE962.C7
..... NE1149.A1
..... NE1280
769.944 ..... NE647
769.945 ..... NE1300.2
769.947 ..... NE625
769.9492 ..... NE1153.A1
..... NE2165.R5
769.952 ..... NE1310
..... NE1325.A5
..... NE1325.T63
769.968 ..... ND1096.T7
769.973 ..... N330.N52P36
..... N6537.R27
..... N8640
..... NE505
..... NE539.L6
..... NE1000
769.973094933 ..... NE508
769.9931 ..... ND2092.A4
770 ..... N6494.L3
..... QC244.5
..... QC449
..... TA165
..... TR145
..... TR146
770 ..... TR147
..... TR149
..... TR250
..... TR590
..... TR647.E35
770.1 ..... TR650
770.202 ..... TR146
..... TR150
770.23 ..... TR140.S33
770.232 ..... HF5381
..... TR154
..... TR581
..... TR690.2
..... Z476
770.24363 ..... TR822
770.28 ..... TR145
..... TR146
..... TR161
..... TR310
..... TR820
..... VG1013
770.282 ..... TR147
..... TR591
..... TR790
770.283 ..... TR290
770.284 ..... TR330
770.3 ..... TR9
770.74021 ..... TR6
770.9 ..... TR15
770.924 ..... PR4612
..... TR140.D3
..... TR140.J27
..... TR647.M4
..... TR690.4
770.944 ..... TR646
771.3 ..... HF6161.P5
..... TR262
771.31 ..... TR263.C58
..... TR263.E9
..... TR263.L4
..... TR263.M3
..... TR263.M47
..... TR263.N5
..... TR263.P4
..... TR263.P6
..... TR263.P7
..... TR263.R6
..... TR263.Y3
771.356 ..... TR590.5
771.5324 ..... TR283
771.534 ..... TR196
772.1 ..... TR287
772.16 ..... TR144
773 ..... TR940
773.1 ..... Z244
776.35830202 ..... GV925
778.13 ..... TR475
778.3 ..... TR706
778.311 ..... QH251
778.315 ..... TR835
..... Z265
778.324 ..... TR683
778.33 ..... QC770
..... TR750
778.35 ..... TR810
778.352 ..... TR810
778.352018 ..... TR810
778.353 ..... TL521.3.C6
778.37 ..... TR605
778.5 ..... TR850
..... TR885
778.503 ..... TR847
778.5074 ..... TR848
778.53 ..... PN1995.9.D6
..... TR850
..... TR851
..... TR852
..... TR855
..... TR880
778.530202 ..... TR850
778.5303 ..... TR847
778.5342 ..... TR853
778.5347 ..... NC1765
..... TR851
..... TR899
778.5349 ..... PN1995.8
..... TR851
..... TR852
..... TR896
778.535 ..... TR899
778.53807 ..... PN1998.A3
778.550202 ..... TR890
778.6 ..... TR510
..... TR520
..... TR545
778.620202 ..... TR510
778.66 ..... TR530
778.72 ..... TR590
778.73 ..... TR800
778.8 ..... TR656
..... TR683.5
778.92 ..... TR573
778.924 ..... TR675
778.9240924 ..... TX910.5.M334
778.93 ..... TR721
778.932 ..... TR727
778.95 ..... TR656
778.99391 ..... TR679
778.99551576 ..... QC923
778.9961 ..... TR708
778.997 ..... TR657
778.99796332640973 ..... TR821
778.99913031 ..... TR657
..... TR775
779 ..... TR1
..... TR15
..... TR650
..... TR653
..... TR654
..... TR681.F3
..... TR682
..... TR685
..... TR706
..... TR820
779.0922 ..... TR650
779.0924 ..... TR647.B7
..... TR647.B8
..... TR647.C8
..... TR647.E2
..... TR647.F5
..... TR647.K7
..... TR647.R8
..... TR647.U44
..... TR647.W46
..... TR654
..... TR656
..... TR685
..... TR721
..... TR820
779.2 ..... PZ10.B14
..... TR675
..... TR681
..... TR681.F3
779.21 ..... TR647.B76
..... TR675
779.24 ..... TR653
..... TR675
..... TR681.W6
779.25 ..... NC1429.B22
779.3 ..... TR721
779.32 ..... QL77.5
..... SF446
779.34 ..... QK98
779.37 ..... F74.D25
779.930124 ..... TR654
779.9301431509421 ..... TR654
779.968161 ..... TR654
779.99047 ..... TR140.C28
779.99796 ..... TR821
780 ..... ML37.U5
..... ML60
..... ML60.S14
..... ML60.S153
..... ML63
..... ML64
..... ML102.P66
..... ML197
..... ML410.S932
..... ML410.Y74
..... ML1015.G9
..... ML2800
..... ML2811
..... ML3545
..... ML3561.I3
..... ML3561.J3
..... ML3650
..... ML3877
..... ML3920
..... MT1
780.01 ..... MT1
780.05 ..... MT342
780.0712 ..... ML81
..... PC3304
780.073 ..... ML67
780.074 ..... ML28.P5
780.0740922 ..... ML289
780.08 ..... ML60
..... ML3849
780.0924 ..... ML410.F82
..... ML410.R23
780.1 ..... ML60
..... ML3800
780.15 ..... ML38.S87
..... ML55
..... ML60
..... ML90.K65
..... ML200.8.N52
..... ML417
..... ML427
..... ML3797.1
..... ML3800
..... ML3880
..... ML3930
..... MT3.U5
..... MT6
..... MT90
780.18 ..... ML111
780.202 ..... ML13
780.207 ..... ML65
780.23 ..... ML67
..... ML3795
780.3 ..... ML100
..... ML108
780.7 ..... MT1
..... MT3.H8
..... MT3.U5
..... MT10
..... MT170
780.72 ..... LB1629.I4
..... MT1
..... MT3.A79
..... MT3.U5
..... MT5.S89
..... MT5.S89Y44
..... MT6
..... MT936
780.72097471 ..... MT4.N5J86
780.72942 ..... MT1
780.72942 ..... MT3.G7
780.7294227 ..... MT5.W42
780.72973 ..... MT1
..... MT3.U5
780.729744 ..... MT1
780.729747 ..... MT3.U6
780.73094257 ..... ML286.8O9
780.77 ..... MT1
780.78 ..... MT1
780.79 ..... ML3795
780.7973 ..... ML37.U5
780.8 ..... ML60
..... ML90
..... MT6
780.82 ..... MT6
780.9 ..... ML60
..... ML85
..... ML160
..... ML3797.1
..... ML3930
..... MT6
780.901 ..... ML162
780.902 ..... ML189
780.9032 ..... ML193
780.9033 ..... ML60
780.9034 ..... ML60
..... ML90.K65
..... ML196
..... ML197
780.904 ..... ML197
..... ML390
780.91821 ..... ML160
780.922 ..... ML60
..... ML65
..... ML100.D5
..... ML105
..... ML106.G7
..... ML106.I5
..... ML106.R8
..... ML160
..... ML196
..... ML197
..... ML300.5
..... ML385
..... ML390
..... ML394
..... ML410.B14
..... ML410.B5
..... ML410.S4
..... ML410.W51
..... ML3930.A2
..... NA40
780.9221 ..... ML390
780.924 ..... CT788.G28
..... ML88.B22
..... ML88.H37
..... ML88.L48
..... ML88.M69
..... ML141.G83
..... ML197
..... ML390
..... ML410
..... ML410.B1
..... ML410.B275
..... ML410.B4
..... ML410.B43
..... ML410.B5
..... ML410.B566
..... ML410.B62
..... ML410.B8
..... ML410.B8447
..... ML410.B853
..... ML410.B98
..... ML410.C24
..... ML410.C327
..... ML410.C393
..... ML410.C393M9
..... ML410.C4
..... ML410.C54
..... ML410.C74
..... ML410.C754
..... ML410.D28
..... ML410.D35
..... ML410.D6
..... ML410.D99
..... ML410.E4
..... ML410.F82
..... ML410.G288
..... ML410.G295
..... ML410.G7
..... ML410.H13
..... ML410.H4
..... ML410.H52
..... ML410.H748
..... ML410.I94
..... ML410.L33
..... ML410.L42
..... ML410.L7
..... ML410.M23
..... ML410.M397
..... ML410.M41
..... ML410.M5
..... ML410.M64
..... ML410.M674
..... ML410.M84
..... ML410.M9
..... ML410.M91
..... ML410.M97
..... ML410.M973
..... ML410.O93
..... ML410.P174
..... ML410.P93
..... ML410.R12
..... ML410.R2

Dewey	LC
780.924	ML410.R68
	ML410.R89
	ML410.S15
	ML410.S221
	ML410.S283
	ML410.S3
	ML410.S4
	ML410.S436
	ML410.S53
	ML410.S54
	ML410.S63
	ML410.S7
	ML410.S93
	ML410.S932
	ML410.T452
	ML410.V3
	ML410.W1
	ML410.W3
	ML418.P2
	ML420.B84
	ML422.W86
	ML423.S3
	ML3925.M68
	ML3930.B4
	ML3930.B48
	ML3930.G8
	ML3930.H3
	ML3930.M9
	ML3930.S86
	MT92.E4
	MT92.L88
780.926	ML81
780.94	ML55
	ML159
	ML160
	ML172
	ML196
	ML240
780.941	ML288.2
780.942	ML285
	ML286
	ML286.2
780.9436	ML60
780.943613	ML60
	ML246.8.V6
780.944	ML270
	ML270.H54
	ML270.4
780.945	ML290.2
780.947	ML60
	ML300
780.954	ML338
780.954792	ML338
780.95694	ML166
780.968	ML350.8.J64
780.971	ML205
780.973	ML60.S8483
	ML120.U5
	ML200
	ML200.5
	ML3556
780.974811	ML200.8.P5
780.976496	ML200.8.E4
780.994	ML360
781	ML55
	ML171
	ML3845
	MT6
	MT10
	MT90
	PA4404.H33
781.077	MT6
781.09031	ML171
781.0904	ML197.A15
781.1	ML3805
	ML3807
	ML3817
781.15	ML60
	ML3830
	ML3920
781.2	MT6
	MT7
	MT71
	MT870
781.22	ML3807
	ML3811
	ML3830
	MT6
	MT7
781.23	ML108
781.24	ML431
781.3	ML444
	ML3003
	ML3800
	MT50
	MT58
	MT190
781.42	MT55
	MT59
781.5	ML3811
	MT58
781.55	ML3400
781.5609	ML3300
781.57	ML3561
	ML3561.J3
781.574	ML3561.J3
781.61	ML3838
	MT40
781.62	MT42
781.63	MT75
781.633	MT870
781.635	ML457
	MT85
781.66	MT68
781.7	ML315.2.A54
	ML3545
781.71	ML3547
781.72924	ML160
	ML197
781.729240947	ML3776
781.7296	ML3556
781.72960973	ML3556
781.7297	ML3557
781.7298	ML1
781.735	ML164
	ML164.G17
781.743	ML200.8.P5
781.7437	ML247
781.74391	ML248
781.7481	ML3704
781.752	ML3750
781.754	ML338
	ML338.S475
	ML3547
781.7548	ML338
781.75694	ML345.P3
781.772983	ML207.T759
781.773	ML38.B68
	ML102.J3
	ML3557
	ML3561.J3
781.7748	ML200.7.P3
781.7756	ML3551
781.91	E99.D5
	ML460
	ML462
	ML465
	ML541.J4
781.910939	ML541.N4
781.910954	ML141.N37
781.96	M1641
	PE1121
	PN6110.C5
	PR1181
781.97	ML113
	ML120.G7
	ML120.I7
	ML120.U5
	ML128.F75
	ML128.J4
	ML128.M7
	ML128.O6
	ML128.P3
	ML128.V7
	ML128.W5
	ML134.B63
	ML134.H16
	ML955
781.971	ML128.C4
	ML128.O5
	ML128.S25
781.972	ML134.H16
	ML134.S963
781.9731	ML136
	ML136.U55
781.9732	ML97.H375
781.9734	ML145.W28
782.0922	ML400
782.1	ML410.M9
	ML410.S95
	ML410.W15
	ML1700
	ML3858
782.1015	ML1700
	MT95
	MT150
782.10627471	ML1711.8.N3M4
782.1079	ML410.W2
782.109	ML1700
782.10922	ML390
	ML400
	ML410.S95
	ML420.R36
782.10924	ML410.B44O8
	ML410.B853
	ML410.M41
	ML410.M9
	ML410.P89
	ML410.R8
	ML410.V4
	ML410.W1
	ML410.W13
	ML420
	ML420.A56
	ML420.C18
	ML420.F27
	ML420.H124
	ML420.L33
	ML420.S982
	ML420.T28
	MT100.B778
	MT100.H3
	MT100.W2
782.1094	ML1700
	ML1705
782.10943613	ML1723.8.V62
	ML1723.8.V62S73
	ML1723.8.V62S83
782.109437	ML1724
782.10945	ML1733
782.10973	ML1711
782.12	ML50
	ML50.5
	ML2110
	ML3930.M45
	PR6050
782.13	MT95
782.13	MT100.P97
	MT100.V47
782.130924	MT100.J35
	MT100.V47
782.7	MT1
782.81	ML200.5
	ML1711.8.N3
782.810222	ML89
782.8107	MT955
782.810924	ML410.L42
782.8109421	ML89
	ML1731.8.L7
782.810973	ML1711
782.81097471	ML1711.8.N3
782.812	ML49
	ML50.B126P82
	ML50.C283T42
	ML50.K173
	ML50.M5712H52
	PR6070.Y6
782.813	PS3503.A923
782.85	ML2075
	MT737
782.8509	ML2075
783	ML1500
	ML3000
783.026	ML3000.D65
	ML3001
783.02609	ML3000
783.0260973	ML200
783.0262	ML36
783.0263	ML3131
783.02646	ML3172
783.0266	ML3160
783.02661	ML3160
783.07114221	MT5.L8
783.0922	ML390
	ML410.W51
	ML421.L35
	ML421.M58
783.0924	ML410.G157
	ML410.G966
	ML410.P15
	ML410.W36
783.0942	ML3131
783.0973	ML3111
783.1	MT68
783.2	ML166
783.21	ML3088
783.235	ML3080
783.30924	ML410.H13
783.4	ML3260
	ML3265
783.40627471	ML1511.8.N5
783.5	ML93
	ML3082
	MT860
783.6509	ML2880
783.6554	M1741
	ML410.G94
783.8	ML394
	ML400
	MT85
	MT875
783.80942	ML3000
	ML3131
783.9	ML200.3
	ML410.T147
	ML3186
	MT7
783.952	M2110.E43
	ML3186
784	ML1460
	ML1500
	MT820
784.023	MT820
784.09	ML3875
784.0904	ML3545
784.0922	ML55
	ML102.P66
	ML394
	ML400
	ML2811
	ML3551
	ML3561.J3
784.0924	ML54.6
	ML400
	ML410.B8
	ML410.T98
	ML410.T984
	ML410.W36
	ML420
	ML420.A6
	ML420.C22
	ML420.C265
	ML420.C473
	ML420.D44
	ML420.F78
	ML420.G253
	ML420.H25
	ML420.J76
	ML420.S43
	ML420.T96
	ML420.W55
	ML420.W554
	PR2229
784.0942	ML2831
784.0944	ML2827
784.0973	GR1
	ML156.4.P6
	ML2811
	ML3551
	ML3561.J3
	ML3930
784.09953	ML3770
784.1	MT115.M7
	MT875
784.1061	M2191.C5
784.3	ML54.6
	ML54.6.B4
	ML115.S38
784.300922	ML2831
784.3994	M1840
784.4	M1977.F5
	ML54.8
	ML3551
	ML3780
784.406	GR1
	PZ8.3.S746
784.4922	ML400
784.4924	ML420
	ML420.D98
	Z232.C36
784.494117	M1746
784.49415	ML3654
784.4942	ML403
	ML3650
	ML3652
784.494391	ML3593
784.4971	F1056
784.497292	PS3525.A24785
784.4973	M1629
	M1977
	ML200
	ML410.F78
	ML3111
	ML3551
	ML3553
	ML3561.J3
784.49741	PS548.M2
784.49755	ML3551
784.4983	ML3575.C5
784.4994	M1840.M4
784.6	M1664.A35
784.624	M2193
784.62406	M1997.R727
784.68	M1977.P4
784.687992774442	ML3652
784.7	ML54.6.B4
784.71	PN6110.N19
784.71942	ML1331
784.71973	E295
	ML3551
	ML3561.S8
784.751	E51
	ML3557
784.756	M1998
	ML2811
	ML3556
	ML3561.J3
	PS461.J6
784.756008	ML3556
784.75609	ML3556
784.903	ML108
784.93	MT820
	MT820.B125
784.932	MT820
	MT825
	MT850
	MT872
	MT882
784.934	MT892
784.962	MT1
	MT875
	MT915
	MT930
784.963	MT85
	MT88
785	ML3556
	MT130.B48
785.0284	MT70
785.062	ML1300
785.06274461	ML418.D42
785.0627468	ML200.8.N452S94
785.06274811	ML200.8.P52O74
	ML200.8.P52O744
	ML200.8.P52O749
785.06293127	ML28.W4L57
785.062944	ML76.N37P63
785.0661	ML460
	ML1211
785.0666	ML3561.J3
785.06670973	ML419.C65
785.067	MT3.U5
785.0671	ML1300
	MT733.M52
785.067107	MT733
785.067108	MT733.5
785.06710975979	ML1311
785.0672	ML3561.J3
785.07	MT170
785.0922	ML402
	ML457
	ML3561.J3
	MT125
785.0924	ML410.B26
	ML410.B8
	ML410.E44
	ML410.L7
	ML410.R23
	ML410.S53
	ML422.F92
	ML422.K7
	ML422.S324
	ML422.T67
	MT130.B72
	MT130.E6
	MT130.R28

785.095843	ML511
785.1	MT125
785.11	MT130.H4
785.11015	MT130.S5
785.1107	ML60
785.1109	ML1255
785.110924	ML410.B8
	MT130.C4
	MT130.S3
785.12	MT733
785.31	ML1156
785.41	ML3465
785.410924	ML422.C85
785.42	ML3561.J3
785.42075	ML111.5
785.4209	ML3561.J3
785.420922	ML385
785.420973	ML3561.J3
785.7	MT145.S28
785.700924	MT145.B72
	MT145.S28
785.700942	ML1131
785.747	MT145.B425
785.7471	MT145.H2
	MT145.M7
786.0924	MT145.S98
786.109	ML700
786.10922	ML397
786.10924	ML410.C54
	ML410.S196
	ML410.S5988
	ML417
	ML417.A89
	ML417.C7
	ML417.H19
	ML417.S6
	MT145.C5
786.2	ML650
	ML651
786.2109	ML652
786.210973	ML661
786.221	ML651
	ML703
786.23	ML424.S76
	ML650
	ML3809
786.3	ML60
	MT1
	MT68
	MT220
	MT222.L2
	MT228
	MT248
	MT820
786.4	ML700
	MT140
786.404	ML700
786.40410924	ML134.G68
	ML410.B8
786.40924	MT145.D4
786.41	MT145.B42
786.410924	MT145.M7
786.4254	MT145.B14
786.5015	MT145.M54
786.6	ML550
	ML557
	ML594.A1
	MT192
786.607	MT180
786.624	ML600
786.624221	ML578.8
786.6244	ML574
786.62945	ML592.A9
786.63	ML424.F65
	ML550
	ML552
	ML561
786.7	MT182
	MT224
786.88152	MT115.T29
786.923	ML597
787	ML462
	ML760
787.00902	ML760
787.01	ML750
787.010712	MT259
787.1	ML800
	ML850
787.107	MT259
	MT271
787.1071	MT260
787.109	ML1263
787.10922	ML398
	ML3930
787.10924	ML417.B23
	ML418.B69
	ML418.H22
	ML418.P2
787.12	ML424
	ML802
	ML845
787.1509	ML897
787.3071	MT300
787.30924	ML88.R774
	ML418.C4
787.5	ML501
	ML1005
787.52	ML1006
787.61	ML1015.G9
787.61071	MT580
787.610714	MT582
787.6109	ML1015.G9
787.610924	ML410.G395
787.6151	MT588
787.67	ML531
787.670924	ML531
787.9	MT634.D9
788	ML930
788.009	ML930
788.0107	MT339
788.01071	MT339
788.050712	MT339
788.1	MT440
788.20714	MT460
788.4	ML955
788.4109436	ML955
788.5102522	ML17
788.510712	MT340
788.53	ML342
788.530712	MT342
788.62	ML419.L45
788.82	ML951
788.9	ML980
789.01	ML1030
789.010284	MT70
789.0974	ML200
789.1	ML1035
789.3	ML427.E85
789.5	CC212.S6
	CC212.W5
	ML1040
789.512	NK7983
789.7	ML55
	MT41
789.71	ML597
	ML1055
789.72	ML1050
789.9	ML1092
	TK5981
789.910922	PN2287.H75
789.913	ML128.J3
	ML155.52
	ML156.2
789.9131	ML113
	ML155.59
	ML156
	ML156.2
	ML156.2.N4
	ML156.9
789.9132	ML156.5.N54
789.9136157	ML156.4.J3
	ML156.7.C58
	ML156.7.G66
	ML156.7.M65
	ML156.7.P35
	ML156.7.Y7
789.9136172960973	ML156.4.P7
789.91364	ML134.B49
	ML156.4.V7
	ML156.7.B4
789.91364756	ML156.2
789.913650671	ML156.4.B3
789.9136542	ML156.4.J3
	ML156.7.K45
789.913657	ML156.7.D4
789.9136862	ML156.4.C6
789.91374	ML156.V423
790	GV14
	GV14.5
	GV75
	GV171
	GV401
	GV1200
	GV1203
790.01	GV54.W2
	GV223
790.0135	GV75
790.019	GV54.W2
	GV183.7
790.0191	GV182.8
790.0192	GV401
	LB3608
790.01922	GV1203
	GV1205
	HQ782
790.0194	GV709
	GV711
790.0196	GV445
	LC4661
	RC489.R4
790.0207	NC1479.T54
790.0232	N8380
790.02542	GV75
790.07	GV14.5
790.071173	GV14.5
790.072	GV182.2
790.09	GV15
790.0922	GV994.A9
790.0942	GV15
790.09421	DA688
790.09471	G23.S63
790.0972	GV587
790.0973	GV53
790.09756	GV54.N8
790.09762	GV182.2
790.09763	GV54.L6
	GV182.2
790.09768	SB482.T2
790.09776	GV54.M6
790.09784	GV182.2
790.0979	GV53
790.09793	G155.N3
	GV182.2
790.09795	GV54.O7
790.09797	GV54.W2
790.2	E457.65
	GV1828
	PN1577
790.2	PN1581
	PN1586
790.2023	PN1580
790.20922	PN2285
790.2094272	GV76.M3
790.2094274	PN1582.G7
790.20947	PN1582.R8
790.2095	PN1582.A3
790.209667	PN1582.G5
790.2097463	PN1582.U6
790.209768	PN1582.U6
790.20994	PN1582
790.9775	GV54.W6
791	GV75
	PN1582.R5
	PN1993.5.A1
	PN2061
	PR635.F6
791.023	PN2055
791.02330924	PN1998.A3
791.06873	GV1835
791.076	PN1584
791.0922	PN2205
	PN2285
791.0924	PN1998.A3
	PN2287.B3
	PN2287.G38
	PN2287.K66
	PN2287.L15
	PN2287.V47
	PN2598.A65
	PN2598.C57
	PN2598.H23
	PN2598.L57
	PN2598.O55
791.0947	PN2724
791.095	GV1689
791.10924	GV1811.B3
	GV1811.K43
791.12	PN4305.N6
791.3	GV1801
791.309	GV1803
791.30903	GV1801
791.30942	GV1805.G7
791.30947	GV1805.R9
791.30973	GV1803
791.30977284	GV1803
791.330924	GV1811.P63
	GV1811.W4
791.4	E169.1
	PN1991.6
	PN1992.5
	PN1995
791.40973	PN1991.3.U6
791.43	D16.255.A8
	NC1765
	PN1993.5.A1
	PN1993.5.U6
	PN1993.5.U65
	PN1994
	PN1994.5
	PN1995
	PN1995.5
	PN1995.9.A5
	PN1995.9.E96
	PN1995.9.P7
	PN1995.9.S26
	PN1997
	PN1998.A1
	T752
	TR850
791.43.02330922	PN1995.9.W4
791.43.0909	PN1995.9.C55
791.4301	PN1993
	PN1995
	PN1995.3
	PN1995.9.E96
791.43013	KF27.I5538
	PN1994
	PN1995.5
	PN1995.9.C45
	PN1995.9.E9
791.43015	PN1994
791.43019	PN1995
791.4302	PN1994
791.43020924	PN1998.A3
791.43023	PN1995.9.E96
791.430230922	PN1998
	PN1998.A2
791.430230924	PN1998.A3
	PN1998.A3A587
	TR140.I77
791.4302320922	PN1998.A2
791.4302320924	PN1998.A3
791.430233	PN1995.9.P7
791.4302330922	PN1995.9.W4
	PN1998
	PN1998.A2
	PN1998.A3F569
791.4302330924	PN1998
	PN1998.A3
	PN1998.A3B66
	PN1998.A3E5613
	PN1998.A3F786
	PN1998.A3G6113
	PN1998.A3P276
	PN1998.A3P43
	PN2287.W456
791.43025	TR849.A1
791.43025029	PN1999.M4
791.43027	PN2068
791.43028	PN1995.9.N4
791.430280922	PN1993.5.U65
	PN1995.9.C55
791.430280922	PN1995.9.W4
	PN1998
	PN1998.A2
	PN2205
	PN2285
	PN2287.M49
	PN2297.M3
	PN2598.L27
	PN4874.G67
791.430280924	GV1785.A83
	ML420.G253
	PN1998.A3
	PN2287.A44
	PN2287.B432
	PN2287.B435
	PN2287.B48
	PN2287.C29
	PN2287.C59
	PN2287.D256
	PN2287.F45
	PN2287.F55
	PN2287.G3
	PN2287.G55
	PN2287.K4
	PN2287.L22
	PN2287.L5
	PN2287.M18
	PN2287.M69
	PN2287.N33
	PN2287.N35
	PN2287.P4
	PN2287.P5
	PN2287.R72
	PN2287.R74
	PN2287.S68
	PN2287.S9
	PN2287.T7
	PN2287.W458
	PN2598.A65
	PN2778.G3
791.430293	PN1995.9.P75
791.4303	PN1993.45
791.430711	PN1993.8.G7
791.430712	PN1993.85
791.43075	PN1995.9.C54
791.4308	PN1994
791.4309	PN1993.5
	PN1993.5.A1
	PN1993.5.U6
	PN1995
	PN1995.9.A85
	TR848
791.430909	PN1995.9.C55
791.4309091	PN1995.9.C55
791.43090916	PN1995.9.H6
791.4309093	PN1995.9.R25
	PN1995.9.R4
	PN1995.9.S26
791.4309174927	PN1993.5.A65
791.430922	PN1993.5.S8
	PN1998.A2
791.430924	PN1998.A2
	PN1998.A3
	PN1998.A3F67
791.4309353	PN1995.9.G3
791.430942	PN1993.5.G7
791.430943	PN1993.5.G3
791.430944	PN1993.5.F7
791.430947	PN1993.5.R9
791.4309492	PN1993.5.N4
791.4309497	PN1993.5.Y8
791.43094977	PN1993.5.B8
791.430962	PN1993.5.E3
791.430973	PN1993.5.U6
	PN1994
	PN1994.A4
	PN1995
	PN1995.9.C55
	PN1995.9.S3
	PN1995.9.W4
791.430979494	PN1993.5.U6
	PN1993.5.U65
	PN1998.A2
791.4323	TR858
791.435	PN1995.9.H6
	PN1995.9.S3
791.437	E846
	PN1995.9.O8
	PN1997
	PN1997.A1
	PN1997.B39413
	PR2831
791.438	DS592
	LB1044.Z9
	ML128.M7
	PN1992.8.F5
	PN1993.4
	PN1995.9.D6
	PN1995.9.E9
	PN1998
791.44	PN1991.3.U6
791.4401	HE8697.A8
791.440230924	PN1991.4.H38
791.440280922	PN1991.3.U6
791.440280924	PN1991.4.H5
791.440922	ML285.5
791.440924	PN1991.4
	PN1991.4.D4
791.443	ML406
791.445	PN1991.4.B27
791.447	LC6581
	LC6581.G
	LC6581.G7
	PN1991.3.U6

791.447 ..... PN1991.77.E3
..... PN1991.77.I5
791.45 ..... PN1992.8.P8
791.45013 ..... PN1992.6
791.450207 ..... PN1992.58
791.45023 ..... HF6146.T42
..... TK6680
791.450233 ..... PN1992.75
791.450280924 ..... PN1992.4.B7
..... PN1992.4.L9
..... PN2287.F8
791.450293 ..... HE8700.9.G7
791.4509 ..... PN1992.3.U5
791.450942 ..... PN1992.3.G7
791.450973 ..... PN1992.3.U5
..... PN1992.5
791.4509931 ..... PN1992.3.N43
791.457 ..... LC6581.G
..... PN1992.77
..... PN1992.77.P33
..... PN1992.77.R65
..... PN1992.77.T73
791.4570924 ..... PN1992.4.W3
791.5 ..... GV1218.S5
..... PN1972
..... PN1979.T6
791.53 ..... PN1972
..... PN1978.U6
..... PN1979.E4
..... PN1979.P9
..... PN1979.S5
..... PT2378.U4
791.5303 ..... PN1972
791.6 ..... GT4211.P45
791.8 ..... GV1833
791.82 ..... GV1107
791.820924 ..... GV1108.B43
..... GV1108.O7
791.8209469 ..... GV1107
792 ..... PN1655
..... PN1657
..... PN1861
..... PN2018.3
..... PN2037
..... PN2038
..... PN2039
..... PN2049
..... PN2266
..... PN2287.B4
..... PN2582.N3
..... PN6112
792.01 ..... PN2039
792.015 ..... PN1657
..... PN2021
..... PN2038
..... PN2039
..... PN2266
792.02 ..... PN1631
..... PN1657
..... PN2219.O8
..... PN2291
..... PN2924.5.K3
..... PN3175
..... PN4145
792.020924 ..... PN2598.A53
792.022 ..... PN2297.O6
792.0222 ..... PN3151
..... PN3155
..... PN4291
..... PN6120.S8
792.022302573 ..... PN2267
792.02230973 ..... PN2267
792.02260942 ..... PN2598.S53
792.0226094731 ..... PN2726.M62
792.02280976428 ..... PN2081.A7
792.023 ..... PN2053
..... PN2085
792.0230924 ..... PN2598.J25
792.0232 ..... PN2053
792.0232097471 ..... PN2291
792.0233 ..... PN2053
792.02330922 ..... PN1998.A3
792.02330924 ..... PN1998.A3
..... PN2037
..... PN2728.V3
792.025 ..... PN2091.E4
..... PN2091.S8
..... PN2590.S7
..... PN3178.S8
792.02509034 ..... PN2091.S8
792.026 ..... GT513
..... PN2067
792.0260942 ..... PR3091
792.027 ..... PN2068
792.028 ..... PN2061
..... PN2065
..... PN2071.F4
..... PN2071.I5
..... PN2080
..... PN2185
..... PN2205
..... PR3112
792.02807 ..... PN2061
..... PN3157
..... PN3171
792.028071 ..... PN2075
792.02809 ..... PN2205
792.0280922 ..... PN1998
..... PN2205
..... PN2285
..... PN2287.J5
..... PN2287.W3
..... PN2306.M6
..... PN2594
792.0280922 ..... PN2597
..... PN2598.K38
..... PR2883
..... PR3106
792.0280924 ..... DA447.G9
..... ML420.M332
..... PN2287.B5
..... PN2287.C595
..... PN2287.C8
..... PN2287.D3
..... PN2287.F4
..... PN2287.F6
..... PN2287.G52
..... PN2287.H5
..... PN2287.K25
..... PN2287.L4
..... PN2287.M2
..... PN2287.M4
..... PN2287.W46
..... PN2287.Y8
..... PN2598.A52
..... PN2598.A55
..... PN2598.C23
..... PN2598.C28
..... PN2598.D23
..... PN2598.E5
..... PN2598.F4
..... PN2598.F7
..... PN2598.G3
..... PN2598.I7
..... PN2598.J6
..... PN2598.K3
..... PN2598.K4
..... PN2598.K5
..... PN2598.L28
..... PN2598.L46
..... PN2598.M3
..... PN2598.O55
..... PN2598.P4
..... PN2598.S5
..... PN2598.S74
..... PN2598.T4
..... PN2598.T7
..... PN2598.V5
..... PN2618.M6
..... PN2638.B5
..... PN2638.R3
..... PN2688.D8
..... PN2728.S78
..... PR3112
..... PR3605.O3
..... PR4549.D5
..... PR6005.O85
..... PS2359.M42
792.02907 ..... PN2217
792.0293 ..... PN2074
792.03 ..... PN2035
792.07 ..... PN317.1
792.0711 ..... PN3171
792.0712 ..... PN3175
792.072 ..... PN2075
792.08 ..... PN2038
..... PN2083
..... PN2189
792.09 ..... PN1655
..... PN1657
..... PN1731
..... PN2037
..... PN2038
..... PN2106
..... PN2111
..... PN2189
..... PN2287.M8
..... PN2581
..... PN2728.M4
..... PQ556
792.09034 ..... PN2122
..... PN2185
792.0904 ..... PN2020
..... PN2189
792.0922 ..... PN2594
..... PN2597
..... PN2598.B75
792.0924 ..... PN1708.F6
..... PN2287.B4
..... PN2287.D254
..... PN2598.B792
..... PN2598.K375
792.0938 ..... PA3201
..... PA3202
792.09385 ..... PA3201
792.094 ..... PN1708.S6
792.09415 ..... PN2601
792.094183 ..... PN2602.D8
792.094185 ..... PN2602.D8
792.0942 ..... PN2044.G5
..... PN2044.G6
..... PN2581
..... PN2589
..... PN2592
..... PN2594
..... PN2595
..... PN2596.L6
..... PR627
..... PR719.C47
..... PR738
..... PR3095
792.09421 ..... PN1967
..... PN2589
..... PN2590.B6
..... PN2593
..... PN2595
..... PN2596.L6
..... PN2596.L7R518
792.09421 ..... PN3169.G8
792.09421.3 ..... PN2596.L6
792.094212 ..... PN2596.L6
..... PN2596.L7
792.094213 ..... PN2596.L7
792.094216 ..... PN2596.G72
792.094227 ..... DA690.S69
792.094267 ..... PN2596.S75
792.094272 ..... PN2596.L5
792.0943 ..... PN2654.D413
792.09438 ..... PN2859.P6
792.0944 ..... PN2621
..... PN2632
..... PN2635
792.094436 ..... PN2636.P3
792.0945 ..... PN2684
792.0947 ..... PN2721
..... PN2724
..... PN2728.M4
792.094731 ..... PN2726.M62
792.094977 ..... PN2821
792.0952 ..... PN2921
..... PN2924.5.K3
792.0954 ..... PN2881
792.0954792 ..... PN2885.M3
792.095694 ..... PN2919
792.096822 ..... PN2986.J6
792.09713 ..... PN2305.O5
792.0971323 ..... PR3109.C3
792.097292 ..... PN2421
792.0973 ..... E312.17
..... PN1655
..... PN2016
..... PN2037
..... PN2221
..... PN2226
..... PN2237
..... PN2248
..... PN2266
..... PN2286
..... PN2287.V35
..... PN2295.T5
792.0974461 ..... PN2277.B6
792.097471 ..... PN2266
..... PN2277.N5
..... PN2295.T5
..... PN2297.L5
..... PS3566.E6914
792.0974811 ..... PN2071.I5
..... PN2277.P52
792.0974932 ..... PN2277.N66
792.0975 ..... PN2297
792.09756565 ..... PN2297.C3
792.0977866 ..... ML1711.8.S15
792.0978162 ..... PN2277.E44W54
792.0979461 ..... PN2277.S4
792.0979777 ..... PN3185.W3
792.0993157 ..... PN3016.D82
792.1 ..... BV1534.4
..... PN3235
..... PR635.F6
792.109944 ..... MT955
792.2 ..... N7760
792.3 ..... PN1985
..... PN2071.G4
792.30942 ..... PN1985
792.7 ..... PN1949.S7
792.70978883 ..... ML200.8.D29
792.8 ..... GV1787
..... GV1788
792.80148 ..... GV1587
792.80222 ..... GV1787
792.809 ..... GV1787.5
792.80904 ..... GV1787
792.80922 ..... GV1781
792.80924 ..... GV1785.E4
..... GV1785.L5
..... GV1785.N6
..... GV1785.P3
..... GV1785.T32
792.80942 ..... GV1580
792.8094212 ..... GV1786.R6
792.80947 ..... GV1787
792.8097471 ..... GV1787
792.82 ..... GV1580
..... GV1587
..... GV1788
792.84 ..... GV1790.G5
..... GV1790.N8
..... ML3930.A3
..... ML3930.C4
..... ML3930.D4
..... ML3930.K3
..... ML3930.S235
..... ND2888.B3
793 ..... GV1203
..... GV1229
..... GV1231
..... GV1243
..... GV1471
..... GV1472
793.2 ..... GV1471
..... GV1472
793.21 ..... GV1203
793.3 ..... GV1587
..... GV1601
..... GV1618
..... GV1799
793.30148 ..... GV1587
..... GV1783
793.30222 ..... GV1595
793.307 ..... GV1799
793.308 ..... GV1580
..... GV1595
793.309 ..... GV1595
..... GV1601
793.30922 ..... GV1695
793.30924 ..... GV1785.D85
..... GV1785.S3
793.31 ..... GV1743
793.317292 ..... GV1786.N26
793.319033 ..... GV1590
793.3194 ..... GV1643
793.31941 ..... GV1646.S35
793.3194391 ..... GV1688.H8
793.31945 ..... GV1655
793.31946 ..... GV1673
793.319469 ..... GV1580
793.319481 ..... GV1669
793.31954 ..... GV1693
..... GV1694.K46
793.3195479 ..... GV1694.G8
793.3195496 ..... GV1703.N4
793.319713 ..... QH1
793.319965 ..... GV1580
793.32 ..... GV1580
..... GV1587
..... GV1743
..... GV1753.5
..... GV1781
..... GV1783
..... GV1783.5
..... GV1785.A1
..... GV1785.C85
..... GV1786.N26
..... GV1799
793.3209 ..... GV1781
793.320924 ..... DD801.B383
..... GV1785.D8
..... GV1785.H6
..... GV1785.M63
..... GV1785.S3
793.320938 ..... PA3203
793.320947 ..... GV1786.B4
793.33 ..... GV1746
..... GV1751
793.34 ..... GV1763
793.4 ..... GV1200
793.73 ..... GV1485
..... GV1493
..... GV1507.Q5
..... GV1507.W8
..... PN1009.Z6
793.732 ..... GV1507.C7
793.735 ..... GV1493
793.74 ..... GV1493
..... GV1501
..... GV1507.Q5
..... PR4611
..... QA95
793.8 ..... GV1547
..... GV1557
793.80924 ..... GV1545.G4
..... GV1545.H8
..... GV1545.S6
793.9 ..... GV1218.F5
..... PZ10.C3286
..... U310
794 ..... GV1312
..... U310
794.0942 ..... GV1227
794.1 ..... GV1445
..... GV1446
..... GV1447
..... GV1457
794.1018 ..... GV1318
794.103 ..... GV1445
794.10922 ..... GV1330.R9
..... GV1438
794.10924 ..... GV1313
..... ML410.P52
794.10947 ..... GV1330.R9
794.12 ..... GV1445
..... GV1450
..... GV1451
794.122 ..... GV1450
..... GV1450.2.B4
..... GV1450.2.C47
794.124 ..... GV1450.7
794.15 ..... GV1451.5.K5
..... GV1452
794.157 ..... GV1455
794.159 ..... GV1439.F5
..... GV1439.L27
..... GV1455
794.18 ..... GV1447
794.2 ..... GV1463
794.415 ..... GV1281
794.6 ..... GV903
..... GV907
794.60207 ..... GV905
794.72 ..... GV891
795 ..... GV1301
795.01 ..... GV1302
795.0924 ..... GV1301
795.0942 ..... GV1227
795.09793 ..... GV1301
795.1 ..... GV1303
..... GV1469.B2
795.4 ..... GV1201
795.41 ..... GV1243
795.4120973 ..... GV1251
795.413 ..... GV1281
..... GV1281.5
795.415 ..... GV1281
..... GV1282

795.415 ..... GV1282.3
795.415023 ..... GV1281
795.41503 ..... GV1282.3
795.4150922 ..... GV1282.3
795.4152 ..... GV1281
..... GV1282.3
795.4153 ..... GV1281
..... GV1282.3
795.4158 ..... GV1282.3
795.42 ..... GV1295.P17
795.43 ..... GV1261
795.438 ..... GV1549

796 ..... GV51
..... GV54.D3
..... GV54.W8
..... GV182.2
..... GV341
..... GV361
..... GV439
..... GV443
..... GV563.N273
..... GV567
..... GV701
..... GV707
..... GV722
..... GV741
..... HV675
..... SK601
796.01 ..... GV342
..... GV706
796.019 ..... GV706
796.0192 ..... GV703
796.0194 ..... GV709
796.0196 ..... GV183.5
796.0202 ..... GV361
796.02573 ..... GV182.2
796.03 ..... GV11
..... GV576
..... GV701
796.06 ..... GV391
796.068 ..... GV423
796.0680222 ..... GV424
796.068091732 ..... GV429
796.0712 ..... GV343.5
796.077019 ..... GV711
796.09 ..... GV571
..... GV576
796.09042 ..... GV576
796.0917496 ..... GV53
796.0922 ..... GV697.A1
..... GV697.B3
..... PN4874
796.09416 ..... GV605.5
796.09431 ..... GV612.A2
796.095455 ..... GV654.P8
796.0968 ..... GV667
796.0971 ..... GV585
796.0971352 ..... GV585.5.H3
796.0973 ..... GV53
..... GV182.2
..... GV565
..... GV583
796.097488 ..... GV584.P4
796.09768885 ..... GV691.M36
796.0994 ..... GV675
796.1 ..... GV1203
796.24 ..... GV1565
796.3 ..... GV1017.S58
796.3019 ..... GV861
796.31 ..... GV901
..... GV901.T73
..... GV903
..... GV909
..... GV1017.H2
796.310207 ..... GV909
796.323 ..... GV867
..... GV883
..... GV885
..... GV885.55
..... GV890.T7
796.323021 ..... GV883
796.323022 ..... GV885
796.32303 ..... GV885.1
796.3230922 ..... GV884.A1
796.3230924 ..... GV884.A4
..... GV884.B7
..... GV884.C5
..... GV884.F7
..... GV884.H8
..... GV884.R8
..... GV884.W4
..... PS3563.E78
796.3230973 ..... GV883
796.3232 ..... GV885
..... GV888
..... GV889
796.32364 ..... GV885
..... GV885.55
796.3236406273 ..... GV885.51.N37
796.323640973 ..... GV885.52.N4
796.32364097471 ..... GV884.D4
..... GV885.52.N4
..... GV885.52.N4S5
796.32378 ..... GV885.52.N4
796.3238 ..... GV885.2
..... GV886
796.325 ..... GV1017.V6
796.33 ..... GV947
..... PE3601
796.332 ..... GV938
..... GV950.5
..... GV951
..... GV951.85

796.332 ..... GV959
796.33202022 ..... GV955
796.3320222 ..... GV959
796.33203 ..... GV951
796.332077 ..... GV959
796.33209 ..... GV951
..... GV954
796.3320922 ..... GV939.A1
..... GV951
..... GV951.8
796.3320924 ..... GV939.B75
..... GV939.C3
..... GV939.C34
..... GV939.D27
..... GV939.D35
..... GV939.G27
..... GV939.G5
..... GV939.J3
..... GV939.J63
..... GV939.K7
..... GV939.L315
..... GV939.L6
..... GV939.M4
..... GV939.M62
..... GV939.N28
..... GV939.N4
..... GV939.R6
..... GV939.S16
..... GV939.S23
..... GV939.S45
..... GV939.S47
..... GV939.S7
..... GV939.S73
..... GV939.T28
..... GV939.T3
..... GV939.T45
796.3322 ..... GV951
..... GV951.1
..... GV951.8
796.33225 ..... GV951.8
796.33262 ..... GV951.1
796.3326206273 ..... KF27.J8666
796.33262097498 ..... GV951
796.33263 ..... GV955.5.S58
..... GV958.T4
796.332630973 ..... GV950
..... GV955.5.S6
796.332630975453 ..... GV958.W4
796.33264 ..... GV951
..... GV955.5.A45
..... GV956.D3
..... GV959
796.3326405 ..... GV955
796.3326406073 ..... GV937.N33
..... GV951
..... GV955.5.N35
..... GV956.G7
..... GV956.N37
..... GV959
796.3326409 ..... GV951
..... GV954
796.332640973 ..... GV950
..... GV954.2
..... GV955.5.A45
796.332640976428 ..... GV956.D3
796.3326409778411 ..... GV956.K35
796.3327 ..... GV950.7
796.333 ..... GV945
..... GV945.8.T7
796.3330207 ..... GV945.2
796.33306 ..... GV945
796.333077 ..... GV947
796.33308 ..... GV944.85
..... GV945
796.33309 ..... GV944.85
796.3330922 ..... GV944.9.A1
796.3330924 ..... GV939.J65
..... GV945
796.33309429 ..... GV945.9.G7
796.3330971 ..... GV948
796.3332 ..... GV945
796.33363094274 ..... GV945.6
796.333640968 ..... GV945.6.S6
796.33365 ..... GV945
796.333650968 ..... GV945.6.S6
796.33374 ..... GV945.6.S6
..... GV945.6.W35
796.334 ..... GV942.5
..... GV943
..... GV944.G7
..... GV944.U5
796.33403 ..... GV943
796.33406 ..... GV943.6.Q4
796.33406242 ..... GV943.55.S6
..... GV943.6.M3
796.334077 ..... GV943.8
796.33409034 ..... GV942.5
796.3340922 ..... GV944.G7
796.3340924 ..... GV942.7.B37
..... GV942.7.H34
..... GV942.7.H78
..... GV942.7.M28
..... GV942.7.W5
796.3340941 ..... GV944.S35
796.3340942 ..... GV944.G7
796.3342 ..... GV943
796.3346206 ..... GV943.6.Q4
796.3346309421 ..... GV943.6.H5
796.33463094216 ..... GV943.6.H5
796.33463094274 ..... GV943.6.L4
796.33464 ..... GV944.G7
796.33464094272 ..... GV943.6.M3
796.33464094282 ..... GV943.6.N43
796.33466 ..... GV943.5

796.33466 ..... GV943.6.M3
..... GV944.G7
796.335 ..... GV948
796.3350971 ..... GV948
796.342 ..... GV995
796.34203 ..... GV993
796.342068 ..... GV1002
796.34209 ..... GV993
..... GV999
796.3420922 ..... GV994.A1
..... GV994.A7
796.3420924 ..... GV994.A7
..... GV994.B8
796.3422 ..... GV995
796.345 ..... GV1007
796.346 ..... GV1005
796.347 ..... GV989
796.352 ..... GV963
..... GV965
..... GV967
..... NC1429.Q3
796.3520207 ..... GV967
796.35206 ..... GV969.G43
796.35209 ..... GV963
796.3520922 ..... GV964.A1
796.3520924 ..... GV964.B4
..... GV964.B6
..... GV964.C3
..... GV964.N5
796.352095952 ..... GV985.S55
796.3523 ..... GV965
..... GV979.S9
796.35264023 ..... E90.C58
796.352730975864 ..... GV970
796.35274 ..... GV970
796.355 ..... GV1017.H7
796.357 ..... GV863
..... GV867
..... GV870
..... GV873
..... GV877
..... GV885
796.3570212 ..... GV877
796.357023 ..... GV875.7
796.35703 ..... GV867
..... GV877
796.357074014774 ..... GV863
796.35709 ..... GV863
796.3570922 ..... GV865.A1
..... GV865.D5
..... GV865.J64
..... GV884.A1
796.3570924 ..... GV865.B69
..... GV865.C66
..... GV865.F45
..... GV865.F67
..... GV865.G4
..... GV865.G52
..... GV865.H28
..... GV865.H63
..... GV865.J64
..... GV865.M3
..... GV865.M335
..... GV865.M38
..... GV865.N5
..... GV865.R65
..... GV865.S4
..... GV865.W49
..... GV865.W5
796.3572 ..... GV867
..... GV873
796.35764 ..... GV875.A1
..... GV875.D6
796.357640922 ..... GV865.A1
796.35764097471 ..... GV875.N45
796.357782 ..... GV863
796.3578 ..... GV881
..... GV881.A1
796.358 ..... GV917
796.3580207 ..... GV919
796.3580624247 ..... GV921.W6
796.358068094214 ..... GV921.M3
796.35808 ..... GV917
796.35809 ..... GV913
796.3580922 ..... GV913
..... GV915.A1
..... GV915.H6
796.3580924 ..... GV915.A4
..... GV915.D3
..... GV915.D6
..... GV915.F7
..... GV915.G8
..... GV915.H27
..... GV915.H4
..... GV915.I37
..... GV915.M58
..... GV915.R5
..... GV915.S7
796.358094 ..... GV913
796.3580954 ..... GV913
796.35809549 ..... GV913
796.3582 ..... GV917
796.35822 ..... GV917
796.3586 ..... GV913
796.35862 ..... GV921.O9
796.358630942 ..... GV913
796.35863094254 ..... GV921.S53
796.35863094274 ..... GV913
..... GV921.Y6
796.35865 ..... GV913
..... GV921.N4
796.35875 ..... GV913
796.358750994 ..... GV923
796.4 ..... GV464

796.4 ..... GV483
..... GV511
..... GV706
..... GV1060.5
..... GV1060.8
796.401 ..... GV342
796.41 ..... GV461
..... GV463
..... GV464.5
..... GV481
..... GV485
..... GV505
..... GV511
..... GV546
796.42 ..... GV721.5
..... GV1060.5
..... GV1060.5.B7
..... GV1060.8
796.4207 ..... GV1060.5
796.420924 ..... GV697.K4
796.420973 ..... GV1060.5
796.426 ..... E169.02
..... GV494
..... GV1060.5
..... GV1061
..... GV1065
796.4260922 ..... GV1060.5
796.4260924 ..... GV697.O9
796.43 ..... GV697.D32
..... GV1061
..... GV1075
796.435 ..... GV1093
796.47 ..... GV545
..... GV547
..... GV551
..... GV553
796.48 ..... GV721.5
..... GV722
796.4801 ..... GV721.6
796.4809 ..... GV23
..... GV721.5
796.5 ..... G504.5
..... GV54.M84
..... GV182.2
..... SK601
796.50207 ..... SK601
796.50924 ..... SK145
796.50973 ..... GV182.2
796.509774 ..... GV54.M5
796.50994 ..... SK602.A8
796.509944 ..... G504.5
796.51 ..... G504.5
796.5106242 ..... TX931
796.5109422 ..... DA631
796.51094274 ..... DA670.Y6
796.52 ..... F859.3
796.522 ..... DA650
..... DA880.H7
..... DQ824
..... F912.D6
..... F912.M2
..... G504.5
..... G507
..... G510
..... GB511
796.52203 ..... G508
796.52206293127 ..... G505.W43
796.5220924 ..... DS486.E8
..... G510
..... G512.B6
..... G512.M6
..... G512.S45
796.5220941 ..... DA870
796.522094237 ..... DA670.C8
796.5220945383 ..... DB765
796.522094947 ..... DQ25
..... DQ841.M7
796.5220978856 ..... GV1065
796.5220979778 ..... F897.R2
796.522099315 ..... DU430.A76
..... DU430.C63
796.5220993157 ..... DU430.M49
796.525 ..... GB602
796.5250942 ..... GB602
796.54 ..... G504.5
..... GV197.H3
..... GV198.C6
..... SK601
..... SK602.G7
796.5409755 ..... SK601
796.5409774 ..... SK601
796.545 ..... GV192
796.6 ..... GV1041
..... GV1049
..... GV1051.M46
796.70904 ..... GV1021
796.70973 ..... GV1033
796.72 ..... GV1029
..... GV1029.3
..... GV1029.5
..... GV1032.A
..... TL215.M4
..... TL215.P75
..... TL236
796.720207 ..... PN6231.A8
796.720212 ..... GV1029
796.7203 ..... GV1029
796.7208 ..... GV1023
796.7209 ..... GV1029.15
..... TL236
796.7209046 ..... GV1029
796.720922 ..... GV1032.A1
..... GV1032.C27
796.720924 ..... GV1029

796.720924 .... GV1029.3
.... GV1032.A5
.... GV1032.C6
.... GV1032.F66
.... GV1032.G7
.... GV1032.H48
.... GV1032.J6
.... GV1032.K6
.... GV1032.S74
796.72094 .... TL236
796.720942 .... GV1024
.... GV1029
796.720973 .... GV1033
796.720975955 .... GV1029
796.7209931 .... GV1029
796.75 .... GV1059.5
.... GV1060
.... TL448.A2
796.7508 .... GV1059.5
796.78 .... GV1025.U6
796.780924 .... GV1032.R6
796.79 .... GV1021
.... TX910.S3
796.7909798 .... GV1024
796.8 .... GV1111
796.8095 .... GV1111
796.81 .... GV1111
796.812 .... GV1195
796.8120924 .... CT275.N6517
796.815 .... GV1111
796.8152 .... GV475
.... GV1111
796.81520712 .... GV475
796.815208 .... GV475
796.8153 .... GV476
796.8154 .... GV1111
796.8159 .... GV1111
.... GV1197
796.83 .... GV1133
796.830922 .... GV1132.D4
796.830924 .... GV1132.B35
.... GV1132.J7
.... GV1132.L3
.... GV1132.O7
.... GV1132.R6
.... GV1132.R67
.... GV1132.S7
796.85 .... GV475
796.86 .... U860
796.8609 .... U860
796.9 .... GV842
.... GV857.S6
796.90978883 .... GV584.5.D4
796.91 .... GV849
796.92 .... GV853
796.93 .... GV854
.... GV854.5.A8
.... GV854.85
.... GV854.9.C7
.... SD11
796.93025 .... GV854.A2
796.930257 .... GV854.5.N58
796.93062 .... GV854.A1K334
796.930924 .... GV854.2.G69
.... GV854.2.T6
796.93094 .... GV854.8.E9
796.93097 .... GV854.4
796.9309795 .... GV854.5.N6
796.962 .... GV847
.... GV847.25
.... GV847.7
.... GV847.8.N33
.... GV848.C3
.... GV848.C48
.... GV848.N43
796.9620222 .... GV847
796.96203 .... GV847
796.96206271 .... GV847.8.N3
796.96207 .... GV847
796.96209 .... GV847
796.9620922 .... GV847
.... GV848.5.A1
796.9620924 .... GV847
.... GV848.5.B4
.... GV848.5.D4
.... GV848.5.H6
.... GV848.5.I4
.... GV848.5.I46
.... GV848.5.M5
.... GV848.5.O7
.... GV848.5.S25
796.962097 .... GV847
796.9620971 .... GV848.T6
797 .... GV775
797.1 .... GV775
.... VK541
.... VM321
797.108 .... PN6071.B65
797.10973 .... KF27.M4
797.10979 .... GV835
797.122 .... GV783
797.123 .... GV791
797.123062421 .... GV793
797.124 .... GV811
.... GV811.O44
.... GV813
.... GV819
.... GV823.F73
.... GV826.5
.... GV829
.... SH224.N8
.... VK543
.... VK1255.C58
.... VM351
797.1240922 .... GV812.5.A1
797.1240924 .... GV822.L48
797.12409729722 .... GV817.V5
797.1250942 .... GV835.3.G7
797.12509747 .... GV835.2.N7
797.14 .... GV798
.... GV811
.... GV813
.... GV826.5
.... GV827
.... GV829
.... GV835.3.G7
.... VM331
797.1406279461 .... GV823.S19
797.1409166 .... GV813
797.140924 .... GV835
.... GV835.3.G7
797.140973 .... GV829
797.172 .... GV840.S8
797.173 .... GV840.S5
797.2 .... GV837
797.2007 .... GV837
797.21 .... GV837
797.210212 .... GV837
797.2107 .... GV445
.... GV837
797.210924 .... GV838.F3
797.23 .... GV840.S78
.... VM983
797.24 .... GV837
797.25 .... GV839
797.31071 .... GV1753.5
797.3570922 .... GV865.A1
797.5 .... GV755
797.52 .... GV757
.... GV759
797.5209 .... TL529
797.522 .... DS485.H6
797.54 .... TL711.S8
797.55 .... GV764
.... TL760
797.5509438 .... GV765.P6
798.2 .... SF285
.... SF287
.... SF295.5
.... SF295.7
.... SF309
.... SF309.5
798.209 .... SF309
798.20924 .... SF295.5
798.20968 .... SF284.A4
798.23 .... SF295.2
.... SF309
.... SF315
798.2307 .... SF310.5
798.24 .... SF295
.... SF295.2
.... SF295.7
798.240942 .... SF295.7
798.25 .... SF295.5
.... SF309.7
798.250924 .... SF295.5
798.250942 .... SF295.5
798.4 .... SF334
.... SF335.U5
.... SF338
798.400924 .... SF335.G7
.... SF359
798.400942 .... SF335.G7
798.4009945 .... SF357.M4
798.401 .... SF331
798.40207 .... PN6231.H58
798.40924 .... SF336.L6
.... SF336.S5
798.43 .... SF335.5
798.45 .... SF359
798.46 .... SF339
.... SF343.B7
798.8 .... SF469
799 .... G525
.... SK33
.... SK83
799.0968 .... SK251
799.09741 .... SK85
799.1 .... SH439
.... SH441
.... SH443
.... SK35
799.10222 .... SH439
799.102541 .... SH609
799.1028 .... SH441
799.103 .... SH411
799.108 .... SK33
799.109 .... SH421
799.10924 .... SH678
799.10942 .... SH439
799.10971 .... SH571
.... SK33
799.109718 .... SH572.N6
799.10973 .... SH441
799.109756 .... SK113
799.109795 .... SH539
799.109797 .... SH559
799.1099611 .... SH679.F5
799.11 .... SH439
.... SH441
.... SH605
799.11025748 .... SH541
799.11025756 .... SH531
799.11062788 .... SH403.W5
799.1106279549 .... SH403.D47
799.1109416 .... SH611
799.110942 .... SH605
799.1109424 .... SH605
799.1109786 .... SH517
799.1109931 .... SH678
799.12 .... SH433
.... SH439
.... SH441
.... SH451
.... SH454.2
.... SH456
.... SH457
799.1209416 .... SH611
799.120942 .... SH605
799.120994 .... SH677
799.122 .... GV783
799.16 .... SH448
.... SH456
.... SH457
.... SH457.5
799.1609426 .... SH605
799.1661 .... SH503
.... SH605
799.1663 .... SH457
799.1666 .... SH464.N6
799.1731 .... QL638.9
799.175 .... SH611
799.1752 .... SH691.R6
799.1753 .... SH691.P6
799.1755 .... SH439
.... SH451
.... SH678
.... SH685
.... SH687
.... SH691.C3
.... SH691.G7
799.1758 .... SH681
799.2 .... PZ10.K48
.... SK33
.... SK36.9
.... SK41
799.2028 .... GV1559
799.20283 .... GV1153
.... SK274
.... TS534.7
799.202832 .... SK274
799.202833 .... TS537
799.202834 .... SK37
.... SK274
799.213 .... SK31
.... SK33
.... SK37
799.23 .... SK315
799.232 .... SK25
.... SK321
799.23208 .... SK321
799.234 .... SF428.5
799.24 .... SK311
799.240924 .... SK17.H3
799.240942 .... SK311
799.244 .... SK331
799.24861 .... SK325.G7
799.24865 .... SK325.P55
799.24886 .... SK325.C7
799.25 .... SK33
799.250973 .... SK33
799.26 .... SK33
.... SK45
.... SK251
799.260222 .... SK33
799.260924 .... SK251
799.2609791 .... SK51
799.27 .... SK135
799.27.74428 .... SK305.T5
799.27735 .... SK301
799.277357 .... SK301
799.277442 .... SK305.T5
799.2774428 .... SK305.T5
799.29 .... SK21
799.2924 .... SK36
.... SK453
799.295498 .... SK237
799.296 .... SK251
799.2967 .... SK251
.... SK255.E27
799.297 .... SK33
799.29764 .... SK131
799.29794 .... QL164
799.29931 .... SK262
799.2994 .... SK261
799.299429 .... SK261
799.31 .... GV1153
.... GV1177
799.313 .... GV1181
799.32 .... GV1185
.... GV1188.J3
799.720924 .... GV1032.A5
800 .... PN45
801 .... P92.5.M3
.... PN45
.... PN72.P7
.... PR85
.... PS3553.A796
801.3 .... PN99.G7
801.45220973 .... E449
801.9 .... B829.5
.... PE1408
.... PN45
.... PN51
.... PN81
.... PN145
.... PN771
.... PN871
.... PN3331
801.92 .... PN45
801.93 .... BH221.I53
.... PN45
801.930924 .... PN45
801.95 .... P47
.... PE1471
.... PN49
.... PN81
.... PN85
.... PN86
.... PN87
.... PN98.B7
.... PN99.G7
.... PN1707
.... PN6014
.... PR67
.... PR73
.... PR4809.H15
801.9508 .... PN81
801.950924 .... PR3424
.... PR3452
.... PR6009.M7
.... PS1631
801.950942 .... PR457
801.950944 .... PN99.F82
.... PQ84
801.950973 .... PS78
801.951 .... PQ1664
801.952 .... PN1922
801.957 .... PN6149.P5
801.959 .... PA3521
.... PE1449
.... PR77
802 .... PN43
802.3 .... PN150
803 .... PN41
.... PN43
.... PN44
.... PN44.5
807 .... LB1576
.... LB1631
.... PN59
.... PN61
.... PN70
.... PN3171
.... PN4145
807.11 .... PN59
807.1173 .... PN61
.... PN70
807.6 .... PN43
808 .... PA3948.D5
.... PE1122
.... PE1408
.... PE1417
.... PE1421
.... PE1429
.... PE1431
.... PE1445.A2
.... PN45.5
.... PN175
.... PN187
.... PN203
.... PN218
.... PN3355
.... T10.5
808.0019 .... BF637.P4
808.007 .... PE1065
808.0071 .... LA2311
808.00711 .... LB2365.E5
808.00712 .... LB1631
808.008 .... PN175
.... PN203
808.00922 .... AS36
.... PS400
808.02 .... LB1631
.... LB2369
.... PE1408
.... PE1421
.... PN131
.... PN137
.... PN145
.... PN147
.... PN149
.... PN151
.... PN155
.... PN161
.... PN162
.... PN169
.... PN203
.... PN203.B313
.... PN3355
.... PR107
.... PS3551.S37
.... PS3564.O37
.... Z253
808.020202 .... PN151
808.023 .... LB2369
.... PE1429
.... PE1478
808.025 .... LB2369
.... LB3045.5
.... PN147
.... PN149
.... PS3539.U8619
.... Z253
.... Z286.H5
808.04.207 .... PE1066
808.042 .... LB163
.... LB1049
.... LB1059
.... LB2369
.... PE1068.C3
.... PE1095
.... PE1112
.... PE1121
.... PE1122
.... PE1402

Dewey	LC
808.042	PE1404
	PE1408
	PE1413
	PE1417
	PE1421
	PE1429
	PE1439
	PN147
808.0420202	PN147
808.04203	PE1460
808.04207	PE1404
	PN1085
808.042071	PE1408
808.0420712	PE1404
808.042076	PE1114
808.0427	PE1114
	PE1121
	PE1122
	PE1408
	PE1413
	PE1417
	PN6014
	PS362
808.04275	BF697
	HN17.5
	LB1631
	P87
	PE1121
	PE1121.S43
	PE1122
	PE1408
	PE1413
	PE1417
	PG3095
	PN43
	PN203
	PS688
808.04387	PA3523
808.04403	PC2680
808.047	PG2112
808.048	PA3637.R5
808.06	PN147
808.066	CT21
	HF5726
	HV41
	PE1429
	PN4778
808.0660281	LB2369
808.0660702	PN4775
808.06607043	PN4784.C65
808.0660704302	PN4783
808.066102	B52
808.0662	BR44
	PN147
808.06630002	H62
808.06633002	H62
808.06633602	PE1112
808.0663702	LB2846
808.0665	T11
808.066502	Q179
	Q223
	T11
808.0665402	T11
808.06655	QE185
808.066602	PE1478
	SK361
	T10.5
	T11
808.0666102	R119
808.06665	H62
	HD69.R4
	PE1115
808.0666502	HD69.R4
	HF5721
	HF5726
	PE1115
808.066655	Z253
808.066658	HD69.R4
808.0667914502	PN1992.7
808.066796	PE1127.S8
	PN4784.S6
808.0668	PN131
	PN145
808.06692	CT21
	CT34.G7
808.1	PK551.A534
	PK875
	PN228.M4
	PN511
	PN1031
	PN1041
	PN1042
	PN1047
	PN1064
	PN1077
	PN1085
	PN1126
	PN1136
	PN4145
	PN6101
	PR6013.R35
	PR6035.A37
	PS3505.O234
	PS3529.L655
808.101	PQ2643.A26
808.1014	PN44.5
808.107	PN1042
	PN1101
808.10712	PN1085
808.108	PE1122
	PR6003.A68
808.109	PN1042
808.10924	PR5881
808.14	PN1031
808.17	PN6231.L5
808.18	PN147
808.2	PN1623
	PN1631
	PN1657
	PN1661
	PN1664
	PR6045.H245
808.207	PN1701
808.23	PN1996
808.241	PN1661
	PN6120.A5
808.251	PN1892
808.3	PE1122
	PE1425
	PN3331
	PN3335
	PN3353
	PN3355
	PN3365
	PN3367
	PN3499
	PS41
	PS371
808.31	PE1121
	PN3373
808.32	PE1122
808.33	PN3324
	PN3353
	PN3354
	PN3355
808.385	PN3365
808.4	PE1122
	PN4500
	PR1363
808.4275	PE1122
808.5	DA564.B3
	PE1408
	PN185
	PN4061
	PN4077
	PN4086
	PN4095.G7
	PN4105
	PN4111
	PN4121
	PN4130
	PN4142
	PN4157
	PN4162
	PN6122
	PS663.N4
808.501	PN4061
808.50202	PN4092.H3
808.502437	PN4121
808.507	PN4086
	PN4092.I7
808.5071	LB1139.L3
808.508	PN4121
808.50922	E185.96
808.51	PE1407
	PN4061
	PN4105
	PN4121
	PN4124
	PN4130
	PN4193.L4
	PN6341
	PS662
808.510922	PS1799.H7
808.53	BF637.P4
	LC6515
	PN4121
	PN4181
808.5306	PN4191.S4
808.5307	LB1029.G3
808.54	PN4105
	PN4145
808.545	PE1121
	PN4145
	PN4271
808.55	PN4193.C5
	PN4305.C4
808.56	BJ2121
808.59024658	HF5549.5.C6
808.6	PE1483
808.7	PN171.C3
808.7019	PN6147
	PN6149.P5
808.8	PE1121
	PE1122
	PN43
	PN44
	PN667
	PN6013
	PN6014
	PN6110.C4
	PR1109
	PZ5
	PZ5.L965
	PZ5.M535
808.8.042	PE1408
808.8014	PN603
808.803	BJ1533.F8
	PA3136
	PE1121
	PN6071.A35
	PN6071.A4
	PN6071.B65
	PN6071.F47
	PN6071.G27
	PN6071.L7
	PN6071.W4
	PN6110.R4
808.803	PR1111.C53
	PS648.C5
	SF301
	SF426.2
808.8035	PE1122
808.81	PJ418
	PN1345
	PN6099
	PN6101
	PN6109.7
	PN6110.C4
	PN6110.C77
	PN6110.D4
	PN6110.S4
	PR1226
808.8102	PN6101
808.813	PN1323
808.814	PN6099
	PN6101
808.815	PN6101
808.817	PZ8.3.C675
808.819	PN6110.P6
808.8193	PN6110.B6
	PN6110.B85
	PN6110.C3
	PN6110.H3
	PN6110.L6
	PN6110.W28
	PN6110.W4
	PZ8.3.J138
808.82	PE1122
	PN1631
	PN4291
	PN6111
	PN6112
	PN6112.5
	PN6120.A4
808.8203	PN6112
808.82034	PN6112
808.8204	PN6112
	PR1272
808.822	PN6120.R2
808.8241	PN6112
808.8251	PN6112
808.8252	PR1251
808.8293	PN6120.R47
808.83	PN44
	PN6014
808.8304	PN6014
808.831	PE1121
	PE1122
	PN6013
	PN6014
	PN6014.A8
	PN6014.G38
	PN6014.H75
	PN6014.J5
	PN6014.W38
	PR1309
	PS643
	PS645
	PZ1.A458
	PZ1.C38
808.83104	PN6014
808.833	PN3463
808.8381	PN667
808.83872	PN6071.D45
	PN6071.S64
	PR1309.S7
	PZ1
808.839	PN6071.E7
808.8393	PN6071.G5
	PN6071.S4
	PR1309
	PR1309.R3
	Z6207.W8
808.84	PE1122
	PN6141
808.84931	PN49
808.85	PN4201
	PN6121
808.851	PN4023
808.854	PN4201
	PN4251
	PN4305.C5
	PN4305.H7
808.87	PN6081
	PN6151
	PN6153
	PN6161
	PN6231.J5
808.8793	PN6231.J5
808.88	E179
	PN6245
	PN6289
	PN6328.L3
808.882	E302
	PN6080
	PN6081
	PN6083
	PN6084.B5
	PN6084.C5
	PN6084.C57
	PN6084.F8
	PN6084.L6
	PN6084.M3
	PN6084.M6
	PN6084.N5
	PN6084.Q3
	PN6084.W35
	PN6084.W6
	PN6095.J4
	PN6231.I65
	PN6261
808.882	PN6269
	PN6271
	PN6281
	PN6319
	PN6321
	PN6331
	PN6421
	PN6511
	Z4.Z9
808.89494	PN849.S9
808.899174924	PN6067
	PN6109.5
808.89920431	PN6071.M7
808.89947	PN6014
808.8995	PJ409
808.89967	PL8013.E5
808.914	PN603
809	CT31
	NC1429.L47
	PG3358
	PL5532
	PN36
	PN51
	PN56.P93
	PN58
	PN61
	PN75.F7
	PN85
	PN171.Q6
	PN228.M4
	PN451
	PN501
	PN511
	PN511.S27
	PN521
	PN523
	PN524
	PN701
	PN710
	PN721
	PN761
	PN771
	PN803
	PN863
	PN871
	PN873
	PN883
	PN1711
	PN6231.C75
	PR13
	PR14
	PR99
	PR127
	PR2603
	PR3452
	PR4022
	PR4104
	PR5488
	PR5853
	PR6005.A4865
	PR6007.E3
	PR6035.U7
	PR6045.A323
	PR6045.A78
	PS2033
	PS2127.C7
	PS2316
	PS2696
	PS3242.L5
	PS3519.A86
	PS3525.A1435
	PS3525.I5454
	PS3525.O8638
	PS3562.I785
	PT2354
	Z1003
809.02	PN670
	PN681
	PN687.H37
809.024	PA3998.H8
809.03	PN51
	PN710
	PN721
809.031	PQ4639.A3
	PR129.I8
809.033	PN603
809.034	PN99.G72
	PN452
	PN751
	PN761
	PR5134
809.04	D410
	PN51
	PN56.I65
	PN453
	PN701
	PN710
	PN771
	PR5294
809.046	PN771
809.1	BS1405
	PN511
	PN710
	PN883
	PN1031
	PN1040
	PN1065
	PN1077
	PN1101
	PN1111
	PN1136
	PN1271
	PQ4335
	PQ4546.A1

809.1 ..... PR503
..... PR6037.I8
809.101 ..... PN1141
809.102 ..... PN811
809.104 ..... PN1271
809.12 ..... PN1301
809.13 ..... PN681
..... PN1303
809.14 ..... PN688
..... PQ207
809.15 ..... PN1077
809.19 ..... PN686.G7
809.193 ..... PN1111
..... PN1481
809.2 ..... AS591.J4
..... PN185
..... PN1625
..... PN1631
..... PN1633.R4
..... PN1661
..... PN1721
..... PN1731
..... PN1751
..... PN1785
..... PN1851
..... PN1861
..... PQ505
..... PR6045.A323
809.204 ..... PN1861
809.251 ..... PN1751
..... PN1891
..... PN1892
..... PR641
809.293 ..... PN1633.B6
..... PN1689
809.3 ..... PN3353
..... PN3448.P6
..... PN3451
..... PN3491
..... PN3503
..... PR824
809.32 ..... PN692
809.33 ..... PN3351
..... PN3451
..... PN3499
..... PN3503
..... PR881
..... PR4876
..... Z1035.A1
809.3304 ..... PN3503
809.351 ..... PN49
809.3538 ..... PN56.S53
809.38 ..... PN49
..... PN3351
809.381 ..... PN3441
809.385 ..... PN56.R6
..... PN671
809.3872 ..... PN3448.D4
809.3876 ..... PN3448.S45
809.393 ..... PN3347
..... PN3503
809.5 ..... PN4145
809.53 ..... PN4181
809.7 ..... PN6147
..... PN6149.S2
809.793 ..... PN6231.S54
809.8917496 ..... PL8010
809.894 ..... PN501
..... PN523
809.89415 ..... PB1306
809.89494 ..... PN849.S9
809.896 ..... PL8000
..... PL8010
..... PN6109.7
809.8967 ..... PL8010
809.8968 ..... PR9823
809.8973 ..... PN99.U5
809.91 ..... BH301.I7
809.912 ..... PN56.R3
809.914 ..... PN603
809.915 ..... PN56.A5
809.916 ..... PN1892
809.923 ..... PA4444
809.927 ..... PN56.D67
809.933 ..... D810.J4
..... PN49
..... PN56.H45
..... PN56.L6
..... PN56.M95
..... PN56.O7
..... PN56.R7
..... PN56.S5
..... PN56.U8
..... PN56.W67
..... PN56.5.P74
..... PN57.P7
..... PN511
..... PN685
..... PN686.T7
..... PN721
..... PN773
..... PN3347
..... PQ1543
..... PT363.B5
809.9331 ..... PN49
809.93351 ..... PN687.O7
809.9337 ..... PA57
809.9352 ..... BR85
..... BR117
809.93522 ..... BS535
..... BS1140.2
..... Z7791
809.935225 ..... BS535
809.93525203 ..... PR2248

810.202 ..... PS94
810.3 ..... PN4900.P3
..... PS21
810.5 ..... PN4897.T44
810.8 ..... PN6075
..... PN6081
..... PS507
..... PS508.C6
..... PS509.N4
..... PS535
..... PS536.2
..... PS2649.P5
..... PS3523.O46
810.8001 ..... PS533
..... PS601
..... PS703.A6
810.8002 ..... PS507
..... PS549.N5
810.8003 ..... PN4199
..... PS507
..... PS535
810.8004 ..... PS1821
810.8005 ..... PE1121
..... PE1122
..... PS508.N3
..... PS535.5
810.80052 ..... PE1121
..... PN6014
..... PS536
810.80054 ..... E169.12
..... PE1122
..... PR9235
..... PS508.N4
..... PS509.S5
..... PS536.2
810.8012 ..... PS535
810.803 ..... E647
..... PE1122
..... PS374.W6
..... PS509.A4
..... PS509.D5
..... PS509.H5
810.8032 ..... PS561
810.80352 ..... PS509.M5
810.80355 ..... PN6231.F3
810.80896 ..... PS508.N3
..... PS647.N35
810.809 ..... PS591.N4
810.809174 ..... PS508.I5
810.8091746 ..... PS508.M4
810.809174926 ..... PS508.C5
810.80917496 ..... PS508.N3
810.809282 ..... PS508.C5
..... PS508.I5
..... PZ5.F94
810.80975 ..... PS551
810.809758 ..... PS558.G4
810.809764 ..... PS558.T4
810.80978 ..... PS567
810.9 ..... F74.C8
..... PN1031
..... PR6023.A93
..... PR9111
..... PR9114
..... PS15
..... PS55
..... PS85
..... PS88
..... PS92
..... PS121
..... PS169.T5
..... PS169.W3
..... PS203
..... PS243
..... PS255.P5
..... PS261
..... PS2020
..... PS3523.E7992
..... Z1224
810.9001 ..... PS88
..... PS195.R4
810.9003 ..... CT105
..... PS121
..... PS201
..... PS285.S3
..... PS2315
..... PS2545.P4
810.9004 ..... PN761
..... PS214
810.9005 ..... PE1122
..... PN149
..... PR9153
..... PS62
..... PS121
..... PS129
..... PS221
810.90052 ..... PS129
..... PS221
..... PS221.M8
..... PS228.C54
..... PS3503.O87
810.90054 ..... PS221
..... PS508.C6
810.900952 ..... PS221
810.93 ..... PR143
..... PS169.L5
..... PS173.I6
..... PS173.N4
..... PS221
810.9896 ..... PS153.N5
..... PS508.N3
810.9917496 ..... PS153.N5
..... PS508.N3
810.992286 ..... PS166

810.9971 ..... PR9127
810.9974 ..... PS243
810.9975 ..... F209
..... PS261
810.99756 ..... PS266.N8
810.9979 ..... Z1251.N7
811 ..... PR6052.R29
..... PR6063.A92
..... PR6073.A423
811.008 ..... E98.P74
..... E185.96
..... PN6109.7
..... PR9250
..... PS305
..... PS323.5
..... PS507
..... PS548.C8
..... PS551
..... PS571.K2
..... PS586
..... PS591.N4
..... PS593.L8
..... PS595.H8
..... PS595.R4
..... PS659
..... PZ8.3.J138
811.00803 ..... E233
..... PN6110.P7
..... PS548.N7
..... PS595.B5
..... PS595.H5
..... PS595.H6
..... PS595.R4
..... PZ8.3.J138
811.009 ..... PS305
811.04 ..... PS593.L8
..... PS595.C6
811.07 ..... PZ8.3.C675
811.1 ..... PR1905
..... PS711
..... PS712
..... PS767
..... PS767.H15
..... PS866
811.108 ..... PS601
811.2 ..... F1058
..... PS704
..... PS705
..... PS739
..... PS739.Z5
..... PS757
..... PS791
..... PS866
..... PS1289
811.208 ..... PS548.C8
811.3 ..... E449
..... F104.W8
..... F1032
..... ML80.P65
..... PS744.E6
..... PS1012
..... PS1106
..... PS1181
..... PS1265
..... PS1555.D4
..... PS1764.G238
..... PS1780
..... PS1780.A2
..... PS1799.H7
..... PS1905
..... PS1908.A4
..... PS1930
..... PS1971
..... PS2018
..... PS2281
..... PS2282
..... PS2292.S3
..... PS2305
..... PS2306
..... PS2307
..... PS2331
..... PS2382
..... PS2387
..... PS2605
..... PS2609
..... PS2631
..... PS2673.R127
..... PS3054
..... PS3200
..... PS3201
..... PS3203
..... PS3204
..... PS3224
..... PS3231
..... PS3232
..... PS3238
..... PS3509.L43
811.308 ..... PS586
..... PS2859.S133
811.30803 ..... PS3250
811.309 ..... PS65
..... PS303
..... PS1292.C85
811.4 ..... PR4865.L4
..... PR6019.O3917
..... PS1059.B2
..... PS1085
..... PS1205
..... PS1260.C7
..... PS1278
..... PS1322
..... PS1541
..... PS1541.Z5
..... PS1556

811.4 ..... PS1666
..... PS1667
..... PS1900
..... PS2007
..... PS2202
..... PS2206
..... PS2216
..... PS2222
..... PS2649.P55
..... PS2704
..... PS2706
..... PS3187.W2
..... PS3231
..... PS3523.O27
..... PS3525.A235
..... PS3535.O25
..... PS3539.A89
..... PS3543.I87
..... PZ8.3.F4554
811.408 ..... E647
..... PN6110.C7
811.40803 ..... E457.9
..... PS595.C57
811.409 ..... PS310.S7
..... PS323
811.508 ..... PN6110.C7
..... PR9258
..... PS536.2
..... PS584
..... PS591.N4
..... PS613
..... PS614
..... PS615
..... PS615.P37
..... PS3235
..... PZ8.3.H776
..... PZ8.3.J138
811.50803 ..... PS595.S75
..... PZ8.3.H776
..... PZ8.3.S534
811.509 ..... PS324
811.52 ..... AS36
..... PR3512
..... PR4441
..... PR6001.U4
..... PR6003.U315
..... PR6013.L35
..... PR6013.R735
..... PR6013.U696
..... PR6021.L4
..... PR6023.I8
..... PR6031.R3
..... PR6045.A8124
..... PR6045.E43
..... PS1694.F14
..... PS2423
..... PS2428
..... PS2719.R528
..... PS2771
..... PS2812
..... PS3174
..... PS3501.B17
..... PS3501.I5
..... PS3501.L417
..... PS3501.N4
..... PS3501.N565
..... PS3501.R55
..... PS3503.A8417
..... PS3503.E39
..... PS3503.E549
..... PS3503.L165
..... PS3503.O9357
..... PS3503.R246
..... PS3503.R563
..... PS3503.U645
..... PS3505.A5317
..... PS3505.H625
..... PS3505.I27
..... PS3505.O365
..... PS3505.O735
..... PS3505.O777
..... PS3505.O8623
..... PS3505.R272
..... PS3505.R9456
..... PS3505.U287
..... PS3505.U334
..... PS3507.E2
..... PS3507.E483
..... PS3507.E69
..... PS3507.E84
..... PS3507.I28
..... PS3507.O726
..... PS3507.R55
..... PS3509.B456
..... PS3509.G53
..... PS3509.L4
..... PS3509.L43
..... PS3509.N44
..... PS3509.V23
..... PS3511.E7245
..... PS3511.R94
..... PS3513.A6315
..... PS3513.I25
..... PS3513.I75
..... PS3513.O527
..... PS3513.O614
..... PS3513.R558
..... PS3513.U45
..... PS3513.U875
..... PS3515.A2353
..... PS3515.E42
..... PS3515.O499
..... PS3515.O842

Dewey	LC
811.52	PS3515.U274
	PS3515.U4835
	PS3519.A416
	PS3519.A86
	PS3519.E27
	PS3519.O245
	PS3521.E448
	PS3521.E548
	PS3521.I7672
	PS3523.I58
	PS3523.O88
	PS3523.O89
	PS3523.O92
	PS3523.U68
	PS3525.A155
	PS3525.A1584
	PS3525.A27
	PS3525.A318
	PS3525.A83
	PS3525.E825
	PS3525.E97
	PS3525.I495
	PS3525.O5616
	PS3525.U419
	PS3525.U447
	PS3527.A637
	PS3529.P54
	PS3531.A694
	PS3531.I4155
	PS3531.O82
	PS3535.A635
	PS3535.A655
	PS3535.E75
	PS3535.E98
	PS3535.I233
	PS3535.I43627
	PS3535.I65
	PS3535.I88
	PS3535.O25
	PS3535.O55
	PS3535.U87
	PS3537.A618
	PS3537.A832
	PS3537.E24
	PS3537.I317
	PS3537.M335
	PS3537.T323
	PS3537.T42
	PS3537.T4753
	PS3539.A74
	PS3539.E15
	PS3539.R52
	PS3543.A557
	PS3543.E756
	PS3543.I325
	PS3544.R3
	PS3545.A517
	PS3545.A712
	PS3545.A748
	PS3545.H33
	PS3545.I32165
	PS3545.I544
	PS3549.U47
	PS3558.A445
	PS3558.E455
	PS3561.N49
	PS3562.E29
	PS3565.R8
	PZ8.3.A363
	PZ8.3.B42
	PZ8.3.C763
	PZ8.3.M133
	PZ8.3.M84
	PZ8.3.R88
	PZ10.A663
	Z8204.63
811.5208	PN6110.C7
	PS571.A6
	PS595.M25
	PS614
811.5209	PR9171
	PS324
	PS3523.O89
	PS3525.A83
811.54	BJ1661
	BV4832.2
	E856
	ML64
	PE1119
	PJ3771.G5
	PR6001.C65
	PR6003.R369
	PR6005.R7
	PR6015.O415
	PR6023.A97
	PR6023.I8
	PR6037.A873
	PR6037.I5
	PR6037.O8
	PR6051.T9
	PR6051.V4
	PR6052
	PR6052.A368
	PR6052.A43
	PR6052.A49
	PR6052.A78
	PR6052.I797
	PR6052.O86
	PR6052.U5
	PR6053.H37
	PR6053.O33
	PR6053.R36
	PR6053.R375
	PR6053.U44
811.54	PR6054.A94
	PR6054.I93
	PR6054.U457
	PR6055.C53
	PR6055.V4
	PR6056.I52
	PR6056.I77
	PR6056.L26
	PR6056.L36
	PR6056.O664
	PR6056.O75
	PR6057.A29
	PR6057.I24
	PR6057.I5
	PR6057.I59
	PR6057.N3
	PR6057.O76
	PR6057.R27
	PR6057.R395
	PR6058.A436
	PR6058.E49
	PR6058.E492
	PR6058.O95
	PR6058.O97
	PR6058.U39
	PR6060.O46
	PR6060.U5
	PR6061.N5
	PR6061.O56
	PR6063.A217
	PR6063.A645
	PR6063.A677
	PR6063.A92
	PR6064.E9
	PR6064.O8
	PR6064.U5
	PR6066.A72
	PR6066.E17
	PR6066.E3
	PR6066.H46
	PR6068.A335
	PR6068.E45
	PR6068.E46
	PR6068.O157
	PR6068.O195
	PR6068.O2
	PR6069.C52
	PR6069.C55
	PR6069.P33
	PR6070.A94
	PR6070.I36
	PR6070.I65
	PR6070.R6
	PR6073.A27
	PR6073.H58
	PR6073.I39
	PR6073.I4337
	PR6073.R46
	PR6075.O82
	PS301
	PS615
	PS3501.B29
	PS3501.M6
	PS3501.N565
	PS3501.R5175
	PS3501.S475
	PS3501.S57
	PS3501.U87
	PS3503.A159
	PS3503.A415
	PS3503.A5688
	PS3503.A62875
	PS3503.A7227
	PS3503.A953
	PS3503.E1435
	PS3503.E35
	PS3503.E4313
	PS3503.E734
	PS3503.E744
	PS3503.E924
	PS3503.I785
	PS3503.L268
	PS3503.L276
	PS3503.O532
	PS3503.R2736
	PS3503.R553
	PS3503.R7244
	PS3503.R759
	PS3503.R81865
	PS3503.U6875
	PS3505.A655
	PS3505.A77594
	PS3505.H678
	PS3505.O763
	PS3505.R43
	PS3507.A7346
	PS3507.E527
	PS3507.I617
	PS3507.O73277
	PS3507.R172
	PS3507.U626
	PS3507.U629
	PS3509.S62
	PS3509.V43
	PS3511.E23
	PS3511.E557
	PS3511.R425
	PS3511.R94
	PS3513.I74
	PS3513.R215
	PS3515.A3152
	PS3515.E763
	PS3515.E776
	PS3515.O2416
811.54	PS3515.O3485
	PS3515.O8415
	PS3515.O89
	PS3515.U249
	PS3515.U3
	PS3517.G53
	PS3519.O1233
	PS3519.O4545
	PS3519.U445
	PS3521.E41815
	PS3521.E4322
	PS3521.E453
	PS3521.E563
	PS3521.E88
	PS3521.O27
	PS3521.U638
	PS3523.E4583
	PS3523.E55
	PS3523.O32
	PS3523.O344
	PS3523.O742
	PS3525.A1814
	PS3525.A24235
	PS3525.A264
	PS3525.A72723
	PS3525.A854
	PS3525.A998
	PS3525.E377
	PS3525.E54
	PS3525.E588
	PS3525.E633
	PS3525.E639
	PS3525.E6645
	PS3525.E7174
	PS3525.E84
	PS3525.E976
	PS3525.I5174
	PS3525.I6772
	PS3525.O4623
	PS3525.O627
	PS3525.O8638
	PS3525.U4116
	PS3525.U716
	PS3527.A73
	PS3527.E8845
	PS3527.I6
	PS3527.O88
	PS3529.L655
	PS3529.P69
	PS3529.R48
	PS3531.A17
	PS3531.E6535
	PS3531.E6766
	PS3531.O7875
	PS3531.U426
	PS3535.A38767
	PS3535.A56274
	PS3535.A5853
	PS3535.A586
	PS3535.A846
	PS3535.O39
	PS3537.A675
	PS3537.C3278
	PS3537.C5255
	PS3537.E1884
	PS3537.H943
	PS3537.M694
	PS3537.M8693
	PS3537.N79
	PS3537.T143
	PS3537.T1815
	PS3537.T339
	PS3537.T6817
	PS3537.U46
	PS3537.U72
	PS3537.W3
	PS3537.W4786
	PS3539.E568
	PS3543.A563
	PS3543.A97
	PS3545.A345
	PS3545.A583
	PS3545.E4735
	PS3545.H117
	PS3545.H868
	PS3545.I52966
	PS3545.R58
	PS3547.E47
	PS3551.D39
	PS3551.N25
	PS3551.N366
	PS3551.N37
	PS3551.N375
	PS3551.N44
	PS3551.N47
	PS3551.R34
	PS3551.R48
	PS3551.S38
	PS3551.T6
	PS3551.U4
	PS3552.A44
	PS3552.A59
	PS3552.A614
	PS3552.A69
	PS3552.A724
	PS3552.A732
	PS3552.A736
	PS3552.A854
	PS3552.A88
	PS3552.E33
	PS3552.E35
	PS3552.E52
	PS3552.E54
	PS3552.E5457
811.54	PS3552.E7
	PS3552.E74
	PS3552.E75
	PS3552.E8
	PS3552.I78
	PS3552.L397
	PS3552.L9
	PS3552.O42
	PS3552.O48
	PS3552.O595
	PS3552.O8
	PS3552.O872
	PS3552.O93
	PS3552.R24
	PS3552.R29
	PS3552.R37
	PS3552.R48
	PS3552.R63
	PS3552.R635
	PS3552.R65
	PS3552.R658
	PS3552.R7
	PS3552.R79
	PS3552.R94
	PS3552.U4
	PS3552.U735
	PS3552.U745
	PS3552.U763
	PS3552.U78
	PS3553.A44
	PS3553.A73
	PS3553.A765
	PS3553.A769
	PS3553.A793
	PS3553.H23
	PS3553.H327
	PS3553.H35
	PS3553.H36
	PS3553.H7
	PS3553.L25
	PS3553.L29
	PS3553.L34
	PS3553.L45
	PS3553.O25
	PS3553.O3
	PS3553.O4748
	PS3553.O478
	PS3553.O482
	PS3553.O484
	PS3553.O489
	PS3553.O518
	PS3553.O55
	PS3553.O553
	PS3553.O554
	PS3553.O57
	PS3553.O593
	PS3553.O625
	PS3553.O63
	PS3553.O65
	PS3553.O73
	PS3553.O77
	PS3553.O92
	PS3553.R8
	PS3553.U44
	PS3553.U67
	PS3554.A46
	PS3554.A58
	PS3554.A915
	PS3554.A9343
	PS3554.A936
	PS3554.A94
	PS3554.A98
	PS3554.E88
	PS3554.I32
	PS3554.I323
	PS3554.I55
	PS3554.I6
	PS3554.O52
	PS3554.O67
	PS3554.O675
	PS3554.O9
	PS3554.U33
	PS3554.U43
	PS3554.U48
	PS3555.A4
	PS3555.C53
	PS3555.C6
	PS3555.D4
	PS3555.E3
	PS3555.L59
	PS3555.L6
	PS3555.M3
	PS3555.N5
	PS3555.S5
	PS3555.U2
	PS3555.V22
	PS3555.V25
	PS3556.A2
	PS3556.A35
	PS3556.A717
	PS3556.E8
	PS3556.I45
	PS3556.I48
	PS3556.I815
	PS3556.L34
	PS3556.O4
	PS3556.O69
	PS3556.O735
	PS3556.O8
	PS3556.O95
	PS3556.R326
	PS3556.R395
	PS3556.R48
	PS3557.A4114

Dewey	LC
811.54	PS3557.A417
	PS3557.A5
	PS3557.A719
	PS3557.E22
	PS3557.E34
	PS3557.E38
	PS3557.I14
	PS3557.I17
	PS3557.I19
	PS3557.I343
	PS3557.I4
	PS3557.I45
	PS3557.I53
	PS3557.I55
	PS3557.L8
	PS3557.O36
	PS3557.O37
	PS3557.O38
	PS3557.O584
	PS3557.R16
	PS3557.R19
	PS3557.R25
	PS3557.R28
	PS3557.R287
	PS3557.R293
	PS3557.R296
	PS3557.R383
	PS3557.R398
	PS3557.R434
	PS3557.R47
	PS3557.R488
	PS3557.R5
	PS3557.R69
	PS3557.U4
	PS3557.U5
	PS3558.A15
	PS3558.A175
	PS3558.A2
	PS3558.A3
	PS3558.A33
	PS3558.A337
	PS3558.A42
	PS3558.A45
	PS3558.A453
	PS3558.A478
	PS3558.A62
	PS3558.A6243
	PS3558.A6245
	PS3558.A6246
	PS3558.A6248
	PS3558.A6249
	PS3558.A625
	PS3558.A629
	PS3558.A644
	PS3558.A685
	PS3558.A72
	PS3558.A84
	PS3558.E3
	PS3558.E32
	PS3558.E35
	PS3558.E497
	PS3558.E499
	PS3558.E85
	PS3558.I357
	PS3558.I384
	PS3558.I66
	PS3558.I68
	PS3558.O335
	PS3558.O34
	PS3558.O343
	PS3558.O3435
	PS3558.O3475
	PS3558.O634
	PS3558.O89
	PS3558.O917
	PS3558.U275
	PS3558.U28
	PS3558.U446
	PS3558.U5
	PS3558.U83
	PS3559.A5
	PS3559.N3
	PS3559.R2
	PS3559.S4
	PS3560.A7
	PS3560.O2
	PS3560.O378
	PS3560.O3792
	PS3560.O3793
	PS3560.O385
	PS3560.O386
	PS3560.O3865
	PS3560.O527
	PS3560.O73
	PS3560.U6
	PS3561.A416
	PS3561.A42
	PS3561.A65
	PS3561.A77
	PS3561.A78
	PS3561.A862
	PS3561.A88
	PS3561.A89
	PS3561.E424
	PS3561.E4273
	PS3561.E67
	PS3561.E7
	PS3561.I57
	PS3561.I8
	PS3561.N6
	PS3561.N8
	PS3561.O18
	PS3561.O33
	PS3561.O43
811.54	PS3561.O6
	PS3561.O7
	PS3562.A25
	PS3562.A35
	PS3562.A42
	PS3562.A475
	PS3562.A54
	PS3562.A85
	PS3562.A87
	PS3562.A9
	PS3562.E34
	PS3562.E355
	PS3562.E37
	PS3562.E87
	PS3562.E9
	PS3562.H4
	PS3562.I85
	PS3562.O24
	PS3562.O26
	PS3562.O45
	PS3562.O54
	PS3562.O64
	PS3562.O7
	PS3562.U85
	PS3563.A23
	PS3563.A259
	PS3563.A2613
	PS3563.A2614
	PS3563.A262
	PS3563.A2623
	PS3563.A2625
	PS3563.A277
	PS3563.A294
	PS3563.A3124
	PS3563.A3179
	PS3563.A3232
	PS3563.A324
	PS3563.A326
	PS3563.A336
	PS3563.A36
	PS3563.A37
	PS3563.A39
	PS3563.A42
	PS3563.A425
	PS3563.A65
	PS3563.A67
	PS3563.A675
	PS3563.A722
	PS3563.A724
	PS3563.A743
	PS3563.A75
	PS3563.A79
	PS3563.A836
	PS3563.A837
	PS3563.A855
	PS3563.A86
	PS3563.E45
	PS3563.E49
	PS3563.E732
	PS3563.E733
	PS3563.E743
	PS3563.E75
	PS3563.I26
	PS3563.I33
	PS3563.I414
	PS3563.I48
	PS3563.I77
	PS3563.O27
	PS3563.O54
	PS3563.O8743
	PS3563.O8744
	PS3563.O8746
	PS3563.O875
	PS3563.O885
	PS3563.U45
	PS3563.U73
	PS3563.U76
	PS3563.U775
	PS3563.Y4
	PS3563.Y42
	PS3563.Y428
	PS3563.Y43
	PS3564.A25
	PS3564.A63
	PS3564.E92
	PS3564.I23
	PS3564.I46
	PS3564.O3
	PS3565.A8
	PS3565.A83
	PS3565.G38
	PS3565.L84
	PS3565.S84
	PS3565.W55
	PS3565.W6
	PS3566.A32
	PS3566.A87
	PS3566.A89
	PS3566.E23
	PS3566.E25
	PS3566.E4
	PS3566.E69
	PS3566.E6915
	PS3566.E692
	PS3566.E753
	PS3566.E8
	PS3566.H48
	PS3566.H49
	PS3566.I56
	PS3566.I6
	PS3566.L27
	PS3566.L6
	PS3566.L78
	PS3566.L8
811.54	PS3566.O55
	PS3566.O67
	PS3566.R37
	PS3566.R54
	PS3566.R58
	PS3568
	PS3568.A44
	PS3568.A495
	PS3568.A72
	PS3568.A74
	PS3568.A93
	PS3568.E36
	PS3568.E365
	PS3568.E366
	PS3568.E48
	PS3568.E88
	PS3568.E89
	PS3568.E95
	PS3568.I28
	PS3568.I32
	PS3568.I37
	PS3568.I375
	PS3568.I38
	PS3568.I8
	PS3568.O23
	PS3568.O235
	PS3568.O239
	PS3568.O249
	PS3568.O318
	PS3568.O79
	PS3568.O82
	PS3568.O84
	PS3568.O86
	PS3568.R64
	PS3568.U29
	PS3568.U35
	PS3568.U767
	PS3569.A2
	PS3569.A36
	PS3569.A4624
	PS3569.A463
	PS3569.A467
	PS3569.A468
	PS3569.A48
	PS3569.A52
	PS3569.A6
	PS3569.A72
	PS3569.C515
	PS3569.C517
	PS3569.C526
	PS3569.C54
	PS3569.C55
	PS3569.C56
	PS3569.C57
	PS3569.C69
	PS3569.C7
	PS3569.E15
	PS3569.E24
	PS3569.E38
	PS3569.H33
	PS3569.H34
	PS3569.H36
	PS3569.H37
	PS3569.H3914
	PS3569.H3936
	PS3569.H397
	PS3569.H44
	PS3569.H6
	PS3569.H7
	PS3569.H76
	PS3569.I385
	PS3569.I4725
	PS3569.I475
	PS3569.I517
	PS3569.I524
	PS3569.I8
	PS3569.L27
	PS3569.L3
	PS3569.M52
	PS3569.M537
	PS3569.M54
	PS3569.N88
	PS3569.O73
	PS3569.P55
	PS3569.T335
	PS3569.T378
	PS3569.T4555
	PS3569.T457
	PS3569.T624
	PS3569.T628
	PS3569.T69
	PS3569.T692
	PS3569.T76
	PS3569.T8
	PS3569.U5
	PS3569.U7
	PS3569.U86
	PS3569.W3
	PS3569.Y5
	PS3570.A35
	PS3570.A53
	PS3570.A75
	PS3570.A8
	PS3570.E53
	PS3570.E64
	PS3570.H35
	PS3570.H5
	PS3570.H55
	PS3570.H642
	PS3570.H643
	PS3570.H65
	PS3570.I35
	PS3570.I38
	PS3570.I55
811.54	PS3570.I8
	PS3570.O42
	PS3570.O43
	PS3570.O45
	PS3570.O78
	PS3570.O9
	PS3570.R4
	PS3570.U25
	PS3570.U57
	PS3571.P4
	PS3571.P45
	PS3572.A39
	PS3572.A423
	PS3572.A4285
	PS3572.A457
	PS3572.A458
	PS3572.A46
	PS3572.A47
	PS3572.A48
	PS3572.A87
	PS3572.E77
	PS3572.I25
	PS3572.I57
	PS3572.O43
	PS3573.A33
	PS3573.A386
	PS3573.A42
	PS3573.A4215
	PS3573.A423
	PS3573.A4234
	PS3573.A4252
	PS3573.A4253
	PS3573.A435
	PS3573.A444
	PS3573.A48
	PS3573.A792
	PS3573.E28
	PS3573.E35
	PS3573.E38
	PS3573.E48
	PS3573.E815
	PS3573.H42
	PS3573.H474
	PS3573.H495
	PS3573.H58
	PS3573.I36
	PS3573.I42
	PS3573.I446
	PS3573.I4483
	PS3573.I453
	PS3573.I4555
	PS3573.I45625
	PS3573.I457
	PS3573.I54
	PS3573.O5
	PS3573.O632
	PS3573.O64
	PS3573.R52
	PS3573.Y74
	PS3575.A77
	PS3575.O683
	PS3575.O78
	PS3576.I47
	PZ8.3.A49
	PZ8.3.B8
	PZ8.3.B81514
	PZ8.3.B823
	PZ8.3.C573
	PZ8.3.C675
	PZ8.3.F618
	PZ8.3.G15
	PZ8.3.G355
	PZ8.3.G916
	PZ8.3.H3339
	PZ8.3.H41346
	PZ8.3.H722
	PZ8.3.H776
	PZ8.3.J1348
	PZ8.3.K22
	PZ8.3.K854
	PZ8.3.K865
	PZ8.3.L4992
	PZ8.3.L972
	PZ8.3.M184
	PZ8.3.M418
	PZ8.3.M420
	PZ8.3.M4493
	PZ8.3.M55187
	PZ8.3.M576
	PZ8.3.M73
	PZ8.3.M7833
	PZ8.3.M7837
	PZ8.3.O55
	PZ8.3.P426
	PZ8.3.P9
	PZ8.3.S533
	PZ8.3.S534
	PZ8.3.S6712
	PZ8.3.S758
	PZ8.3.S793
	PZ8.3.S817
	PZ8.3.S964
	PZ8.3.W17
	PZ8.3.W5
	PZ8.3.W74
	PZ8.3.Y79
	PZ8.3.Y9
	PZ8.3.Z6
	PZ8.3.O615
811.5408	PN6110.C7
	PR9258
	PS508.C5
	PS536.2
	PS571.O3

811.5408 PS591.N4
PS591.S3
PS595.C2
PS613
PS615
PS3552.U4
PZ8.3.H776
PZ8.3.J764
811.540803 PS591.N4
PS595.D5
PS595.L5
PZ8.3.L328
811.5409 PS323.5
PS591.N4
811.54093 PS323.5
811.908 PS586
811.914 PR6069.A93
811.91408 PS591.N4
812 PR6045.A26
PR6073.A38
812.008 PN6120.A4
812.00803 PN6120.R2
812.009 PS338.N4
PS3501.N256
812.0093 PS338.S6
812.041 PN6120.A4
812.051 PS336.P3
812.2 PS721.B35
PS855.T7
PS1065.B83
PS1560
PS1561
812.208 PS625
812.3 PS2533
PS2869.S7
812.4 PN4291
PN6120.A5
PS1139.B9
PS2068.A37
PS2123
PS2359.M42
PS2989
812.408 PN4291
812.508 PN6120.A4
PN6120.T4
PS634
812.509 PS351
812.52 PN1997
PR2877
PR6025.I6233
PS3501.N256
PS3501.U8
PS3503.A842
PS3503.U645
PS3505.O4814
PS3505.U334
PS3507.R55
PS3509.P8
PS3511.A86
PS3511.R16
PS3513.E563
PS3513.O527
PS3513.R744
PS3515.E343
PS3519.E814
PS3523.O89
PS3525.I5156
PS3529.N5
PS3535.I224
PS3535.I3264
PS3535.I645
PS3535.O25
PS3537.A826
PS3537.E58
PS3537.H825
PS3537.I85
PS3537.P645
PS3537.T25
PS3537.T323
PS3545.E449
PS3545.I345
PS3545.I5365
PS3545.I6245
PS3545.O337
812.5208 PS634
812.5209 PS351
812.54 PN1997
PN6120.A5
PN6120.C5
PN6120.R4
PR6007.A814
PR6035.E247
PR6045.E77
PR6056.A46
PR6058.O3
PS3503.U1828
PS3505.A7267
PS3509.P46
PS3513.I2824
PS3513.O27
PS3515.A515
PS3515.E6325
PS3515.U83
PS3517.N265
PS3519.O4545
PS3521.O573
PS3523.E7993
PS3523.O4763
PS3525.A4152
PS3525.O627
PS3529.D46
PS3535.O7578
PS3537.A156
PS3537.I663
812.54 PS3539.A967
PS3545.E449
PS3545.I5365
PS3551.B35
PS3551.L25
PS3551.L3938
PS3551.R7
PS3552.E548
PS3552.R63
PS3552.R633
PS3552.U45
PS3552.U733
PS3553.O9
PS3553.O95
PS3553.U33
PS3554.R48
PS3554.U25
PS3555.L3
PS3556.E42
PS3556.R383
PS3556.R5
PS3557.O72
PS3557.R18
PS3558.A328
PS3558.A79
PS3558.A93
PS3558.I36
PS3558.I53
PS3558.O6
PS3558.O69
PS3559.S7
PS3561.E68
PS3562.A488
PS3563.A262
PS3563.A323
PS3563.A748
PS3563.E25
PS3563.E734
PS3563.I412
PS3563.O5
PS3564.O5
PS3566.A78
PS3566.E759
PS3566.R56
PS3567.U2
PS3568.I2
PS3568.O32
PS3569.C5
PS3569.E36
PS3569.H394
PS3569.T455
PS3569.W25
PS3570.A45
PS3570.A928
PS3570.A95
PS3570.R3
PS3570.U6
PS3572.A44
PS3572.A45
PS3573.A49
PS3573.A73
PS3573.H4
PS3573.H46
PS3573.I458
812.5408 PS634
812.540803 PN3205
812.5409 PS634
813 PR6025.I89
PR6051.N76
PR6058.O44
PR6063.A6
PR6064.I25
PS3550
PS3569.I6
813.008 PE1122
PS645
PS645.G66
PS653
PS659
PZ5
813.00803 PS509.F7
813.009 PS371
PS372
PS374.N4
813.00916 PS169.F7
813.0093 PR9207.W4
PS169.F7
PS374.H55
PS374.M5
PS374.N4
813.01 PE1122
PR9327.5
PS374.S5
PS645
PS647.N35
813.03 PS372
PS374.S2
PS377
813.0872 PN6071.D45
PS648.D4
PS3533.U4
PZ1
813.0874 PS648.W4
813.0876 PS648.S3
813.1 PS875.W3
813.2 PR1417.P6
PR2045
PR5671.T39
PS645.B75
PS707.B4
PS715.B6
PS1130
PS1293
PS1400
813.2 PS1403
PS1405.C4
PS1408
PS1418
PS1431
PS1434
PS1774.H2
PS2057
PS2081
PS2798
PS3100.T76
PZ3.B814
813.208 PS651
813.20914 PS377
813.3 E449
PN6158
PR4735.H25
PR5631
PR5913
PS839.S3
PS1006.A35
PS1019.A53
PS1025
PS1039.A77
PS1102
PS1123.B26
PS1204.B8
PS1229
PS1235.B5
PS1262.C8
PS1292.C457
PS1474.C5
PS1486
PS1525.D5
PS1567.E228
PS1567.E23
PS1586.E7
PS1659.F3
PS1679.F38
PS1744.G68
PS1779.H16
PS1850
PS1852
PS1861
PS1863
PS1868
PS1870
PS1881
PS1888
PS1919.H4
PS1929.H4
PS1934
PS1944
PS1949.H8
PS1961
PS1962
PS1999.H25
PS2048.I52
PS2150.J2
PS2191
PS2245.L4
PS2246.L363
PS2246.L8
PS2359.M176
PS2359.M647
PS2368.M4
PS2380
PS2382
PS2384
PS2384.B7
PS2384.I73
PS2384.M62
PS2384.W53
PS2386
PS2387
PS2388.B5
PS2459.N286
PS2485
PS2612
PS2614
PS2631
PS2638
PS2641
PS2672.Q34
PS2737.R55
PS2848
PS2848.B6
PS2848.C7
PS2848.G8
PS2848.S7
PS2848.V2
PS2848.W4
PS2897
PS2954
PS2954.M5
PS2954.U6
PS2957
PS3101
PS3157.W62
PS3174.W45
PS3324
PS3501.D293
PS3503.R5403
PS3537.C584
PZ3.C8398
PZ3.D929
PZ3.H318
PZ3.M498
813.308 PS551
PS653
PS1949.H8
813.309 PS377
PS2387
813.4 PS1455
813.4 BX7260.B175
HV5068
PR2927
PR3512
PR4089.B75
PR4716
PR4859.K15
PR5079
PR5282
PR6003.U23
PR6013.R272
PR6019.A565
PS12.44
PS217
PS645
PS1006.A6
PS1017
PS1025
PS1025.M2
PS1034
PS1052
PS1054.B3
PS1064.B3
PS1065.B865
PS1076
PS1086
PS1097
PS1097.Z5
PS1117
PS1139.B9
PS1202
PS1214
PS1218
PS1219.B4
PS1237
PS1244
PS1246
PS1260.C65
PS1260.C7
PS1272
PS1284
PS1292
PS1292.C22
PS1292.C27
PS1292.C6
PS1294.C63
PS1305
PS1306
PS1311
PS1317
PS1322
PS1339
PS1357.C35
PS1382
PS1392
PS1449.C85
PS1455
PS1473.C33
PS1493
PS1499
PS1515
PS1517
PS1532
PS1534.D4
PS1545.D55
PS1556
PS1569.E6
PS1570
PS1582
PS1582.E5
PS1582.H62
PS1584.E2
PS1589.E28
PS1657
PS1667
PS1687
PS1692
PS1702
PS1702.H4
PS1704.F92
PS1707
PS1707.C6
PS1708
PS1712
PS1712.S5
PS1717
PS1724
PS1727
PS1732
PS1732.M3
PS1744.G68
PS1759.G6
PS1764.G29
PS1771
PS1772
PS1772.C5
PS1787
PS1797
PS1805
PS1807
PS1819.H7
PS1824
PS1825
PS1829
PS1833
PS1847
PS1848
PS1917
PS1918
PS1922
PS1999.H44
PS2020
PS2020.F68
PS2021

Dewey	LC
813.4	PS2025
	PS2029
	PS2044.H4113
	PS2107
	PS2112
	PS2114
	PS2116
	PS2116.A53
	PS2116.A63
	PS2116.P63
	PS2116.T8
	PS2116.T83
	PS2123
	PS2124
	PS2127
	PS2127.A7
	PS2129.J5
	PS2132
	PS2147
	PS2155
	PS2157
	PS2172
	PS2177
	PS2178
	PS2179.K4
	PS2196.K45
	PS2210
	PS2248.L3
	PS2248.L8
	PS2299.L4
	PS2355.M53
	PS2359.M6448
	PS2359.M648
	PS2368.M4
	PS2372
	PS2397
	PS2404
	PS2409.M2
	PS2414
	PS2429.M8
	PS2454
	PS2471
	PS2472
	PS2472.O33
	PS2473
	PS2486.O5
	PS2495
	PS2510
	PS2514
	PS2534.P5
	PS2539.P28
	PS2545.P4
	PS2649.P4
	PS2669.P6
	PS2673.R15
	PS2695.R72
	PS2696
	PS2698.R8
	PS2719.R4
	PS2719.R665
	PS2727
	PS2731
	PS2732
	PS2736.R317
	PS2752
	PS2753
	PS2789.S36
	PS2804.S85
	PS2859.S2
	PS2859.S5
	PS2864
	PS2864.O8
	PS2897
	PS2919.S227
	PS2922
	PS2927
	PS2960
	PS2987
	PS2988
	PS3037
	PS3039.T4
	PS3087
	PS3089.T34
	PS3089.T4
	PS3089.T65
	PS3092
	PS3097
	PS3100.T18
	PS3119.V377
	PS3119.V38
	PS3142
	PS3152
	PS3272
	PS3319.W25
	PS3362
	PS3501.L4116
	PS3503.A6267
	PS3503.R937
	PS3505.A254
	PS3505.L352
	PS3505.O414
	PS3505.O42
	PS3505.R88
	PS3509.A63
	PS3509.C65
	PS3511.R337
	PS3511.U64
	PS3511.U6565
	PS3511.U6625
	PS3513.A384
	PS3513.A6376
	PS3513.R3725
	PS3515.A249
	PS3515.I13
813.4	PS3515.I35
	PS3515.O6434
	PS3515.O829
	PS3519.O6
	PS3521.E214
	PS3523.O47
	PS3523.O545
	PS3523.U49
	PS3531.E255
	PS3535.I654
	PS3535.O43
	PS3535.O674
	PS3535.Y352
	PS3537.E22
	PS3539.U43
	PS3545.A73
	PS3545.I5285
	PS3561.E8
	PZ3.A427
	PZ3.B224
	PZ3.C776
	PZ3.D836
	PZ3.H724
	PZ3.M943
	PZ3.P871
	PZ3.R284
	PZ3.S728
	PZ3.W212
	PZ7.A567
	PZ7.H242
	PZ8.J19
813.408	PS551
813.40803	PS648.R3
	PS648.S4
	PS648.S6
813.409	PS374.P7
813.4093	PS2127.M6
813.5	PR6063.A256
	PS648.W5
	PS659
	PS1774.H2
	PS3511.R4154
813.5016	Z1377.F4
813.508	PS509.P6
	PS645
	PS645.S35
	PS647.J4
	PS647.N35
	PS648.S3
	PS659
813.50803	PE1121
	PS509.W3
	PS648.D4
	PS648.S3
	PS648.W4
	PZ5.F35
813.509	PS374.N4
	PS374.W4
	PS379
813.5093	PS153.J4
	PS374.N45
813.512	PS3505.U97
813.52	HX811
	PR1127
	PR4453.C2
	PR5122
	PR5177
	PR5231
	PR6001.L678
	PR6003.I772
	PR6003.U55
	PR6005.A37
	PR6005.A77
	PR6005.H56
	PR6005.O55
	PR6005.U7
	PR6007.E34
	PR6007.I65
	PR6013.R482
	PR6013.R84
	PR6015.I415
	PR6023.E15
	PR6029.P5
	PR6031.R6
	PR6035.O76
	PR6045.A327
	PR6045.E43
	PR6061.E495
	PS648.H6
	PS1042
	PS1054.B62
	PS1064.B62
	PS1120.B5
	PS1127
	PS1284
	PS1297
	PS1499.C58
	PS1522
	PS1522.B3
	PS1535.D62
	PS1536.D33
	PS1717
	PS1732
	PS1733
	PS1762
	PS1922
	PS2044.H4
	PS2246.L18
	PS2364.M8
	PS2649.P5
	PS2719.R38
	PS2972
	PS2973
	PS3117
813.52	PS3302
	PS3345
	PS3348.W83
	PS3501.B3
	PS3501.D317
	PS3501.G35
	PS3501.L5595
	PS3501.L635
	PS3501.N4
	PS3501.N569575
	PS3501.R5654
	PS3501.R566
	PS3501.R5933
	PS3501.R64
	PS3501.T59
	PS3501.U25
	PS3501.U8
	PS3502.D215
	PS3503
	PS3503.A159
	PS3503.A413
	PS3503.A48
	PS3503.A514
	PS3503.A55138
	PS3503.A62873
	PS3503.A643
	PS3503.E1135
	PS3503.E4387
	PS3503.E4488
	PS3503.E528
	PS3503.E63
	PS3503.E7135
	PS3503.I553
	PS3503.L733
	PS3503.L984
	PS3503.O125
	PS3503.O524
	PS3503.O563
	PS3503.O857
	PS3503.O9357
	PS3503.R2215
	PS3503.R242
	PS3503.R576
	PS3503.R7834
	PS3503.R82184
	PS3503.U198
	PS3503.U548
	PS3503.U6257
	PS3503.U6258
	PS3503.U687
	PS3503.U883
	PS3505.A153
	PS3505.A3113
	PS3505.A322
	PS3505.A364
	PS3505.A763
	PS3505.A77533
	PS3505.A77825
	PS3505.A7875
	PS3505.A819
	PS3505.A842
	PS3505.A87
	PS3505.H625
	PS3505.H6428
	PS3505.L376
	PS3505.L413
	PS3505.L986
	PS3505.O14
	PS3505.O2455
	PS3505.O2578
	PS3505.O333
	PS3505.O37
	PS3505.O414
	PS3505.O48135
	PS3505.O62516
	PS3505.O655
	PS3505.O6673
	PS3505.O6693
	PS3505.O862
	PS3505.O8655
	PS3505.O9636
	PS3505.O99
	PS3505.R12
	PS3505.R2184
	PS3505.R272
	PS3505.U97
	PS3507.A475
	PS3507.A7136
	PS3507.A7343
	PS3507.E1623
	PS3507.E215
	PS3507.E2344
	PS3507.E49
	PS3507.E69
	PS3507.E867
	PS3507.E883
	PS3507.I75
	PS3507.I865
	PS3507.I93
	PS3507.O183
	PS3507.O248
	PS3507.O7373
	PS3507.O743
	PS3507.R17
	PS3507.R55
	PS3507.U143
	PS3507.U3774
	PS3507.U627
	PS3507.U6277
	PS3509.A63
	PS3509.B453
	PS3509.D472
	PS3509.L473
	PS3509.M73
813.52	PS3509.R28
	PS3511.A784
	PS3511.A8554
	PS3511.A86
	PS3511.A864
	PS3511.A87
	PS3511.A938
	PS3511.E46
	PS3511.E55
	PS3511.E56
	PS3511.E864
	PS3511.I235
	PS3511.I74226
	PS3511.I7436
	PS3511.I7438
	PS3511.I9
	PS3511.I9234
	PS3511.L26
	PS3511.L36
	PS3511.L74
	PS3511.O345
	PS3511.O356
	PS3511.O418
	PS3511.R258
	PS3513.A413
	PS3513.A6322
	PS3513.A6355
	PS3513.E46
	PS3513.E8679
	PS3513.I2823
	PS3513.I4265
	PS3513.I6364
	PS3513.I6445
	PS3513.L34
	PS3513.O527
	PS3513.R366
	PS3513.R3685
	PS3513.R3725
	PS3513.R452
	PS3513.R6545
	PS3513.R7154
	PS3513.R866
	PS3515
	PS3515.A2422
	PS3515.A363
	PS3515.A3867
	PS3515.A4347
	PS3515.A693
	PS3515.A7893
	PS3515.A79458
	PS3515.A9367
	PS3515.A9427
	PS3515.E3434
	PS3515.E37
	PS3515.E372
	PS3515.E77
	PS3515.I713
	PS3515.I955
	PS3515.O1515
	PS3515.O6447
	PS3515.O6513
	PS3515.O6583
	PS3515.O7593
	PS3515.O898
	PS3515.U773
	PS3515.U789
	PS3517.R87
	PS3519.E648
	PS3519.E714
	PS3519.O168
	PS3519.O2633
	PS3519.O445
	PS3519.O6
	PS3521.A725
	PS3521.E356
	PS3521.E412
	PS3521.E423
	PS3521.E43214
	PS3521.I338
	PS3521.I6357
	PS3521.I658
	PS3521.I696
	PS3521.R527
	PS3523.A365
	PS3523.A4235
	PS3523.A4445
	PS3523.A612
	PS3523.A7225
	PS3523.A9875
	PS3523.E113
	PS3523.E358
	PS3523.E8468
	PS3523.E94
	PS3523.I46
	PS3523.L72
	PS3523.O245
	PS3523.O46
	PS3523.O64
	PS3523.O645
	PS3523.O865
	PS3523.O46
	PS3525
	PS3525.A1772
	PS3525.A2423
	PS3525.A24573
	PS3525.A24785
	PS3525.A49
	PS3525.A6549
	PS3525.A6695
	PS3525.A67
	PS3525.A747
	PS3525.A77
	PS3525.A822
	PS3525.E6413

Dewey	LC
813.52	PS3525.I1875
	PS3525.I46
	PS3525.I486
	PS3525.I5454
	PS3525.O1157
	PS3525.O465
	PS3525.O466
	PS3525.O7446
	PS3525.O7475
	PS3527
	PS3527.E117
	PS3527.E35
	PS3527.E917
	PS3527.I865
	PS3527.O436
	PS3527.O5
	PS3527.O585
	PS3529.B45
	PS3529.G39
	PS3529.H29
	PS3529.H5
	PS3529.P6
	PS3529.R58
	PS3529.V48
	PS3531.A366
	PS3531.A3868
	PS3531.A8312
	PS3531.E255
	PS3531.E77
	PS3531.E92
	PS3531.H442
	PS3531.H5
	PS3531.O7342
	PS3531.O752
	PS3531.O7643
	PS3531.O789
	PS3531.O966
	PS3531.R248
	PS3533.U4
	PS3535.A796
	PS3535.E2666
	PS3535.E2786
	PS3535.E382
	PS3535.E399
	PS3535.H68
	PS3535.O54665
	PS3535.O798
	PS3535.U719
	PS3537.A667
	PS3537.A826
	PS3537.A832
	PS3537.A979
	PS3537.C7114
	PS3537.C76
	PS3537.C9264
	PS3537.C9265
	PS3537.C954
	PS3537.E352
	PS3537.H384
	PS3537.H8573
	PS3537.H858
	PS3537.I85
	PS3537.L38
	PS3537.M276
	PS3537.M335
	PS3537.M85
	PS3537.P7446
	PS3537.T316
	PS3537.T323
	PS3537.T3234
	PS3537.T3533
	PS3537.T733
	PS3537.T828
	PS3537.T845
	PS3537.T92516
	PS3537.U34
	PS3537.W3743
	PS3537.W4767
	PS3539.E49
	PS3539.H62
	PS3539.H94
	PS3539.H957
	PS3539.R18
	PS3539.R23
	PS3539.R857
	PS3539.R928
	PS3539.U76
	PS3539.U875
	PS3541.L39
	PS3543.A48
	PS3543.A5658
	PS3543.A579
	PS3543.A648
	PS3543.I554
	PS3545.A26
	PS3545.A4625
	PS3545.A524
	PS3545.A695
	PS3545.A726
	PS3545.A774
	PS3545.E322
	PS3545.E362
	PS3545.E5216
	PS3545.E6
	PS3545.E827
	PS3545.E8334
	PS3545.H16
	PS3545.H6
	PS3545.H6158
	PS3545.H6165
	PS3545.H617
	PS3545.H6172
	PS3545.H658
	PS3545.H75
813.52	PS3545.I343
	PS3545.I544
	PS3545.O337
	PS3545.R815
	PS3545.Y46
	PS3547.A745
	PS3547.O434
	PS3549.U47
	PS3554.E46
	PS3554.U46
	PS3557.U43
	PS3558.A6247
	PS3558.U23
	PS3562.E923
	PS3563.A28
	PS3563.E55
	PS3569.T34
	PS3572.I55
	PZ3.B2277
	PZ3.B41937
	PZ3.C107
	PZ3.C763
	PZ3.D298
	PZ3.D913
	PZ3.O3677
	PZ3.S249
	PZ3.S64803
	PZ3.S87872
	PZ3.W586
	PZ3.W5904
	PZ3.W6766
	PZ7.D989
	PZ7.W6461
	PZ10.3.H318
	SK285
813.5208	PR9276
	PS648.S3
	PS659
	PZ5.W495
813.520803	PS648.H6
	PS648.J4
	PS648.S3
813.5209	PN3448.S45
	PS221
	PS374.F27
813.53	PS3537.I85
813.54	CT275.T724
	F1060
	GV939.S2
	ML420
	NC1429
	NC1429.B613
	PE1121
	PG3476.N3
	PQ2673.O422
	PR3503.L64
	PR5326
	PR6005.A225
	PR6013.I284
	PR6013.I3335
	PR6019.O3938
	PR6021.O35
	PR6023.O2
	PR6023.O96
	PR6025.A2594
	PR6045.E78
	PR6047.O58
	PR6051.N39
	PR6051.T9
	PR6052.A313
	PR6052.R268
	PR6052.U645
	PR6053.L34
	PR6053.O35
	PR6053.O375
	PR6053.O72
	PR6053.R28
	PR6054.A69
	PR6054.A96
	PR6054.E4
	PR6054.O86
	PR6054.U66
	PR6055.A69
	PR6055.N38
	PR6056.I457
	PR6056.I48
	PR6056.O684
	PR6056.R45
	PR6056.R85
	PR6057.A6
	PR6057.A67
	PR6057.I25
	PR6057.O76
	PR6058.A6944
	PR6058.A99
	PR6058.E49
	PR6058.O428
	PR6058.O45
	PR6058.O54
	PR6058.U54
	PR6060.A22
	PR6060.A47
	PR6061.I48
	PR6061.R6
	PR6062.A8
	PR6062.A88
	PR6062.I46
	PR6062.I48
	PR6063.A167
	PR6063.A178
	PR6063.A2428
	PR6063.A243
	PR6063.A74
	PR6063.I327
813.54	PR6063.O56
	PR6063.O6
	PR6063.O673
	PR6063.O6
	PR6064.E97
	PR6064.I22
	PR6064.I25
	PR6065.B65
	PR6066.A25
	PR6066.A89
	PR6066.E73
	PR6068.I25
	PR6068.I6
	PR6068.Y4
	PR6069
	PR6069.C5
	PR6069.H26
	PR6069.H74
	PR6069.T68
	PR6069.U25
	PR6069.Y54
	PR6070.A66
	PR6073.I3
	PR6073.I4259
	PR6073.O59
	PR6075.O85
	PS558.S6
	PS648.D4
	PS1305
	PS1532
	PS3501.L419
	PS3501.L5553
	PS3501.U25
	PS3503.A6262
	PS3503.E487
	PS3503.L64
	PS3503.L718
	PS3503.O4286
	PS3503.O77
	PS3503.R167
	PS3503.R2736
	PS3503.R7246
	PS3503.R7959
	PS3503.R828437
	PS3503.U257
	PS3503.Y95
	PS3505.A59
	PS3505.A655
	PS3505.A899
	PS3505.L254
	PS3505.R89224
	PS3505.U866
	PS3507.A649
	PS3507.A7424
	PS3507.E5475
	PS3507.E8673
	PS3507.I215
	PS3507.I68
	PS3507.O662
	PS3507.O7254
	PS3507.R1723
	PS3511.A333
	PS3511.L4417
	PS3511.R416
	PS3511.U88
	PS3513.A56
	PS3513.A636
	PS3513.E288
	PS3513.E43
	PS3513.I4628
	PS3513.I6437
	PS3513.U82
	PS3515.A262
	PS3515.A757
	PS3515.I713
	PS3515.U585
	PS3517.N2
	PS3517.N265
	PS3519.O4545
	PS3521.A45
	PS3521.A7
	PS3521.E4322
	PS3523.E4583
	PS3523.E794
	PS3523.E799
	PS3523.E7993
	PS3523.I745
	PS3523.O486
	PS3525
	PS3525.A23276
	PS3525.A4152
	PS3525.A52233
	PS3525.A6694
	PS3525.A695
	PS3525.A8298
	PS3525.A8314
	PS3525.E1147
	PS3525.E278
	PS3525.E7174
	PS3525.I46
	PS3525.O2152
	PS3525.O5666
	PS3527.A15
	PS3527.A74
	PS3529.R48
	PS3529.R58
	PS3531.A837
	PS3531.E2355
	PS3531.I68
	PS3531.R14
	PS3531.U426
	PS3531.U64
	PS3533.A763
	PS3535.O1253
813.54	PS3535.O54665
	PS3535.O7493
	PS3537.C95
	PS3537.E3625
	PS3537.I54
	PS3537.M287
	PS3537.M752
	PS3537.P652
	PS3537.T2396
	PS3537.T2443
	PS3539.A68
	PS3539.A9633
	PS3539.R124
	PS3539.R455
	PS3541.R46
	PS3543.I26
	PS3545.A345
	PS3545.A565
	PS3545.A695
	PS3545.E449
	PS3545.E5425
	PS3545.E82794
	PS3545.E8315
	PS3545.E834
	PS3545.E875
	PS3545.H294
	PS3545.I365
	PS3545.I6365
	PS3545.O88
	PS3545.R834
	PS3547.A16
	PS3547.E65
	PS3550
	PS3550.V3
	PS3551.D34
	PS3551.D37
	PS3551.D38
	PS3551.D4
	PS3551.D57
	PS3551.G5
	PS3551.G55
	PS3551.L28
	PS3551.L5
	PS3551.L6
	PS3551.M2
	PS3551.M4
	PS3551.M8
	PS3551.N377
	PS3551.N378
	PS3551.N379
	PS3551.N4
	PS3551.N5
	PS3551.N7
	PS3551.N714
	PS3551.N72
	PS3551.N73
	PS3551.P6
	PS3551.R38
	PS3551.R4
	PS3551.R44
	PS3551.R45
	PS3551.R485
	PS3551.R54
	PS3551.R7
	PS3551.S37
	PS3551.S374
	PS3551.S5
	PS3551.S7
	PS3551.U78
	PS3552.A2
	PS3552.A39
	PS3552.A453
	PS3552.A455
	PS3552.A47
	PS3552.A6
	PS3552.A616
	PS3552.A618
	PS3552.A674
	PS3552.A676
	PS3552.A733
	PS3552.A734
	PS3552.A737
	PS3552.A76
	PS3552.A763
	PS3552.A79
	PS3552.A82
	PS3552.A837
	PS3552.A84
	PS3552.A85
	PS3552.E26
	PS3552.E28
	PS3552.E336
	PS3552.E34
	PS3552.E538
	PS3552.E539
	PS3552.E546
	PS3552.E57
	PS3552.E68
	PS3552.E719
	PS3552.E722
	PS3552.E723
	PS3552.E727
	PS3552.E73
	PS3552.I3
	PS3552.I34
	PS3552.I36
	PS3552.I75
	PS3552.I77
	PS3552.J6
	PS3552.L3424
	PS3552.L346
	PS3552.L365
	PS3552.L5
	PS3552.L6

813.54 ..... PS3552.L63
..... PS3552.L635
..... PS3552.L84
..... PS3552.L86
..... PS3552.O25
..... PS3552.O45
..... PS3552.O64
..... PS3552.O75
..... PS3552.O84
..... PS3552.O85
..... PS3552.O878
..... PS3552.O95
..... PS3552.R2
..... PS3552.R27
..... PS3552.R28
..... PS3552.R39
..... PS3552.R47
..... PS3552.R49
..... PS3552.R495
..... PS3552.R496
..... PS3552.R62
..... PS3552.R658
..... PS3552.R682
..... PS3552.R6853
..... PS3552.R6854
..... PS3552.R6855
..... PS3552.R6856
..... PS3552.R6857
..... PS3552.R69
..... PS3552.R76
..... PS3552.R8
..... PS3552.R85
..... PS3552.R88
..... PS3552.R89
..... PS3552.R898
..... PS3552.R9
..... PS3552.U35
..... PS3552.U46
..... PS3552.U723
..... PS3552.U725
..... PS3552.U75
..... PS3552.U76
..... PS3552.U8
..... PS3552.U82
..... PS3552.U83
..... PS3552.Y7
..... PS3552.Y73
..... PS3553.A28
..... PS3553.A38
..... PS3553.A39
..... PS3553.A4
..... PS3553.A42
..... PS3553.A425
..... PS3553.A434
..... PS3553.A48
..... PS3553.A53
..... PS3553.A58
..... PS3553.A59
..... PS3553.A64
..... PS3553.A67
..... PS3553.A76
..... PS3553.A7627
..... PS3553.A788
..... PS3553.A79
..... PS3553.A796
..... PS3553.A83
..... PS3553.A85
..... PS3553.A9
..... PS3553.A95
..... PS3553.H24
..... PS3553.H27
..... PS3553.H3
..... PS3553.H315
..... PS3553.H32
..... PS3553.H33
..... PS3553.H38
..... PS3553.H78
..... PS3553.I4
..... PS3553.L346
..... PS3553.O37
..... PS3553.O42
..... PS3553.O43
..... PS3553.O45
..... PS3553.O473
..... PS3553.O4747
..... PS3553.O477
..... PS3553.O486
..... PS3553.O487
..... PS3553.O5
..... PS3553.O515
..... PS3553.O517
..... PS3553.O518
..... PS3553.O555
..... PS3553.O557
..... PS3553.O58
..... PS3553.O62
..... PS3553.O633
..... PS3553.O64
..... PS3553.O644
..... PS3553.O645
..... PS3553.O648
..... PS3553.O69
..... PS3553.O7
..... PS3553.O88
..... PS3553.O94
..... PS3553.R2
..... PS3553.R23
..... PS3553.R29
..... PS3553.R46
..... PS3553.R48
..... PS3553.R55
..... PS3553.R57
..... PS3553.R63
..... PS3553.R78

813.54 ..... PS3553.U3
..... PS3553.U32
..... PS3553.U33
..... PS3553.U34
..... PS3553.U42
..... PS3553.U6
..... PS3553.U7
..... PS3553.O648
..... PS3554.A42
..... PS3554.A43
..... PS3554.A45
..... PS3554.A47
..... PS3554.A7
..... PS3554.A75
..... PS3554.A925
..... PS3554.A933
..... PS3554.A9335
..... PS3554.A9346
..... PS3554.A9348
..... PS3554.A935
..... PS3554.A9355
..... PS3554.A937
..... PS3554.A948
..... PS3554.E12
..... PS3554.E13
..... PS3554.E18
..... PS3554.E442
..... PS3554.E443
..... PS3554.E445
..... PS3554.E48
..... PS3554.E56
..... PS3554.I3
..... PS3554.I32
..... PS3554.I328
..... PS3554.I33
..... PS3554.I36
..... PS3554.I39
..... PS3554.I396
..... PS3554.I43
..... PS3554.I45
..... PS3554.I5
..... PS3554.I8
..... PS3554.I83
..... PS3554.I95
..... PS3554.O4
..... PS3554.O45
..... PS3554.O47
..... PS3554.O55
..... PS3554.O83
..... PS3554.O85
..... PS3554.R23
..... PS3554.R25
..... PS3554.R48
..... PS3554.R8
..... PS3554.R9
..... PS3554.U32
..... PS3554.U4
..... PS3554.U43
..... PS3554.U465
..... PS3554.U47
..... PS3555.A38
..... PS3555.A7
..... PS3555.A76
..... PS3555.B85
..... PS3555.D87
..... PS3555.D93
..... PS3555.E5
..... PS3555.L2
..... PS3555.L37
..... PS3555.L44
..... PS3555.L56
..... PS3555.L57
..... PS3555.L575
..... PS3555.L58
..... PS3555.L62
..... PS3555.L623
..... PS3555.L625
..... PS3555.L7
..... PS3555.L9
..... PS3555.M45
..... PS3555.N7
..... PS3555.R5
..... PS3555.S55
..... PS3555.S8
..... PS3555.T69
..... PS3555.V2
..... PS3555.V213
..... PS3555.V23
..... PS3556.A34
..... PS3556.A344
..... PS3556.A36
..... PS3556.A37
..... PS3556.A43
..... PS3556.A45
..... PS3556.A7
..... PS3556.A72
..... PS3556.A76
..... PS3556.A77
..... PS3556.A78
..... PS3556.E5
..... PS3556.E7
..... PS3556.E75
..... PS3556.E88
..... PS3556.I366
..... PS3556.I43
..... PS3556.I52
..... PS3556.I79
..... PS3556.I813
..... PS3556.I82
..... PS3556.I825
..... PS3556.L45
..... PS3556.L6
..... PS3556.L9
..... PS3556.O67

813.54 ..... PS3556.O696
..... PS3556.O714
..... PS3556.O722
..... PS3556.O723
..... PS3556.O73
..... PS3556.O733
..... PS3556.O744
..... PS3556.O76
..... PS3556.O94
..... PS3556.R34
..... PS3556.R35
..... PS3556.R37
..... PS3556.R38
..... PS3556.R39
..... PS3556.R43
..... PS3556.R45
..... PS3556.R5
..... PS3556.R58
..... PS3556.R77
..... PS3556.U4
..... PS3557.A25
..... PS3557.A32
..... PS3557.A4117
..... PS3557.A412
..... PS3557.A5
..... PS3557.A65
..... PS3557.A712
..... PS3557.A713
..... PS3557.A715
..... PS3557.A717
..... PS3557.A72
..... PS3557.A84
..... PS3557.A85
..... PS3557.A86
..... PS3557.E4
..... PS3557.E62
..... PS3557.I34
..... PS3557.I342
..... PS3557.I345
..... PS3557.I43
..... PS3557.I5
..... PS3557.L384
..... PS3557.L43
..... PS3557.L45
..... PS3557.L9
..... PS3557.O27
..... PS3557.O315
..... PS3557.O34
..... PS3557.O35
..... PS3557.O364
..... PS3557.O384
..... PS3557.O39
..... PS3557.O5
..... PS3557.O66
..... PS3557.O68
..... PS3557.O75
..... PS3557.O85
..... PS3557.O87
..... PS3557.R2
..... PS3557.R23
..... PS3557.R29
..... PS3557.R35
..... PS3557.R373
..... PS3557.R376
..... PS3557.R3765
..... PS3557.R378
..... PS3557.R396
..... PS3557.R438
..... PS3557.R4885
..... PS3557.R489
..... PS3557.R4894
..... PS3557.R49
..... PS3557.R53
..... PS3557.R58
..... PS3557.R74
..... PS3557.R8
..... PS3557.Y8
..... PS3557.O67
..... PS3558.A18
..... PS3558.A323
..... PS3558.A364
..... PS3558.A373
..... PS3558.A374
..... PS3558.A395
..... PS3558.A456
..... PS3558.A464
..... PS3558.A475
..... PS3558.A477
..... PS3558.A513
..... PS3558.A623
..... PS3558.A6238
..... PS3558.A624
..... PS3558.A6242
..... PS3558.A62477
..... PS3558.A628
..... PS3558.A63
..... PS3558.A64
..... PS3558.A643
..... PS3558.A645
..... PS3558.A648
..... PS3558.A657
..... PS3558.A667
..... PS3558.A672
..... PS3558.A676
..... PS3558.A73
..... PS3558.A78
..... PS3558.A82
..... PS3558.A823
..... PS3558.A88
..... PS3558.E314
..... PS3558.E4
..... PS3558.E42
..... PS3558.E43
..... PS3558.E458

813.54 ..... PS3558.E477
..... PS3558.E478
..... PS3558.E479
..... PS3558.E4827
..... PS3558.E495
..... PS3558.E55
..... PS3558.E63
..... PS3558.E75
..... PS3558.I25
..... PS3558.I36
..... PS3558.I366
..... PS3558.I3845
..... PS3558.I445
..... PS3558.I45
..... PS3558.I46
..... PS3558.J6
..... PS3558.O342
..... PS3558.O346
..... PS3558.O3464
..... PS3558.O3466
..... PS3558.O3473
..... PS3558.O348
..... PS3558.O36
..... PS3558.O39
..... PS3558.O63
..... PS3558.O687
..... PS3558.O693
..... PS3558.O728
..... PS3558.O8
..... PS3558.O865
..... PS3558.O87
..... PS3558.O875
..... PS3558.O877
..... PS3558.O89
..... PS3558.O915
..... PS3558.O947
..... PS3558.O97
..... PS3558.U27
..... PS3558.U34
..... PS3558.U464
..... PS3558.U467
..... PS3558.U48
..... PS3558.Y48
..... PS3559.A55
..... PS3559.N38
..... PS3559.N39
..... PS3560.A22
..... PS3560.A25
..... PS3560.A35
..... PS3560.A385
..... PS3560.A6
..... PS3560.A63
..... PS3560.A95
..... PS3560.E4
..... PS3560.E8
..... PS3560.E9
..... PS3560.O37
..... PS3560.O3734
..... PS3560.O376
..... PS3560.O379
..... PS3560.O3863
..... PS3560.O387
..... PS3560.O3894
..... PS3560.O394
..... PS3560.O395
..... PS3560.O44
..... PS3560.O49
..... PS3560.O494
..... PS3560.O72
..... PS3560.U58
..... PS3560.U75
..... PS3561.A414
..... PS3561.A415
..... PS3561.A417
..... PS3561.A5
..... PS3561.A55
..... PS3561.A6
..... PS3561.A62
..... PS3561.A63
..... PS3561.A67
..... PS3561.A675
..... PS3561.A68
..... PS3561.A7
..... PS3561.A75
..... PS3561.A82
..... PS3561.A863
..... PS3561.A87
..... PS3561.A9
..... PS3561.E3
..... PS3561.E335
..... PS3561.E34
..... PS3561.E375
..... PS3561.E386
..... PS3561.E392
..... PS3561.E4265
..... PS3561.E427
..... PS3561.E428
..... PS3561.E52
..... PS3561.E53
..... PS3561.E6
..... PS3561.I37
..... PS3561.I415
..... PS3561.I42
..... PS3561.I474
..... PS3561.I49
..... PS3561.I65
..... PS3561.I687
..... PS3561.L2
..... PS3561.L257
..... PS3561.L3
..... PS3561.L34
..... PS3561.L8
..... PS3561.N4
..... PS3561.N44

813.54 ..... PS3561.N55
PS3561.N68
PS3561.O3
PS3561.O39
PS3561.O46
PS3561.R2
PS3561.R25
PS3561.R6
PS3561.R8
PS3561.U5
PS3561.U7
PS3562
PS3562.A3
PS3562.A44
PS3562.A47
PS3562.A485
PS3562.A486
PS3562.A755
PS3562.A84
PS3562.E265
PS3562.E28
PS3562.E33
PS3562.E35
PS3562.E375
PS3562.E38
PS3562.E42
PS3562.E43
PS3562.E44
PS3562.E45
PS3562.E47
PS3562.E48
PS3562.E5
PS3562.E53
PS3562.E55
PS3562.E817
PS3562.E82
PS3562.E8873
PS3562.E889
PS3562.E925
PS3562.E927
PS3562.E94
PS3562.E97
PS3562.E98
PS3562.I38
PS3562.I45
PS3562.I47
PS3562.I49
PS3562.I515
PS3562.I53
PS3562.I535
PS3562.I54
PS3562.I58
PS3562.I783
PS3562.I79
PS3562.O35
PS3562.O37
PS3562.O57
PS3562.U3
PS3562.U7
PS3562.U83
PS3562.Y43
PS3562.Y44
PS3563.A24
PS3563.A253
PS3563.A255
PS3563.A257
PS3563.A26186
PS3563.A28
PS3563.A292
PS3563.A293
PS3563.A3114
PS3563.A3115
PS3563.A3116
PS3563.A3175
PS3563.A3177
PS3563.A318
PS3563.A3185
PS3563.A3188
PS3563.A319
PS3563.A3235
PS3563.A325
PS3563.A335
PS3563.A337
PS3563.A339
PS3563.A34
PS3563.A39
PS3563.A4
PS3563.A4313
PS3563.A4315
PS3563.A432
PS3563.A436
PS3563.A465
PS3563.A55
PS3563.A56
PS3563.A66
PS3563.A664
PS3563.A665
PS3563.A67
PS3563.A717
PS3563.A723
PS3563.A728
PS3563.A738
PS3563.A742
PS3563.A785
PS3563.A82
PS3563.A835
PS3563.A84
PS3563.A85
PS3563.A89
PS3563.A9
PS3563.A945
PS3563.A955
PS3563.E18
PS3563.E23

813.54 ..... PS3563.E35
PS3563.E37
PS3563.E43
PS3563.E48
PS3563.E73
PS3563.E738
PS3563.E745
PS3563.E747
PS3563.E87
PS3563.I24
PS3563.I25
PS3563.I28
PS3563.I37
PS3563.I39
PS3563.I413
PS3563.I4136
PS3563.I417
PS3563.I424
PS3563.I45
PS3563.I47
PS3563.I75
PS3563.O35
PS3563.O64
PS3563.O87145
PS3563.O8749
PS3563.O878
PS3563.O882
PS3563.O96
PS3563.U38
PS3563.U74
PS3563.U77
PS3563.U83
PS3563.U84
PS3563.Y45
PS3563.Y7
PS3564.A3
PS3564.A8
PS3564.A85
PS3564.A9
PS3564.E3
PS3564.E34
PS3564.E844
PS3564.E87
PS3564.E914
PS3564.E916
PS3564.E9165
PS3564.E95
PS3564.I35
PS3564.I4
PS3564.I9
PS3564.N375
PS3564.O39
PS3564.O65
PS3564.O9
PS3564.O97
PS3565.A8
PS3565.B66
PS3565.C55
PS3565.C57
PS3565.D59
PS3565.H3
PS3565.L35
PS3565.L54
PS3565.L8
PS3565.N45
PS3565.N5
PS3565.S85
PS3565.S87
PS3565.W55
PS3565.W6
PS3566
PS3566.A24
PS3566.A25
PS3566.A26
PS3566.A3
PS3566.A34
PS3566.A45
PS3566.A6
PS3566.A68
PS3566.A684
PS3566.A79
PS3566.A825
PS3566.E22
PS3566.E24
PS3566.E26
PS3566.E6913
PS3566.E6917
PS3566.E717
PS3566.E74
PS3566.E755
PS3566.E78
PS3566.H3
PS3566.H5
PS3566.I28
PS3566.I4
PS3566.I43
PS3566.I513
PS3566.I515
PS3566.I525
PS3566.L25
PS3566.L257
PS3566.L29
PS3566.O36
PS3566.O45
PS3566.O52
PS3566.O59
PS3566.O6
PS3566.O65
PS3566.O69
PS3566.O696
PS3566.O83
PS3566.O84
PS3566.O98
PS3566.R44

813.54 ..... PS3566.R47
PS3566.R54
PS3566.R9
PS3566.U4
PS3566.Y5
PS3566.Y8
PS3567.U25
PS3567.U3
PS3567.U35
PS3568.A27
PS3568.A3
PS3568.A43
PS3568.A48
PS3568.A79
PS3568.A8
PS3568.A89
PS3568.E25
PS3568.E35
PS3568.E365
PS3568.E367
PS3568.E43
PS3568.E46
PS3568.E49
PS3568.E53
PS3568.E58
PS3568.E75
PS3568.I343
PS3568.I36
PS3568.I365
PS3568.I4
PS3568.O238
PS3568.O248
PS3568.O28
PS3568.O29
PS3568.O315
PS3568.O34
PS3568.O46
PS3568.O76
PS3568.O763
PS3568.O77
PS3568.O785
PS3568.O853
PS3568.O857
PS3568.O87
PS3568.O88
PS3568.O887
PS3568.R28
PS3568.U2
PS3568.U24
PS3568.U28
PS3568.U4
PS3568.U75
PS3568.U757
PS3568.U765
PS3568.U77
PS3568.Y34
PS3569
PS3569.A25
PS3569.A3
PS3569.A453
PS3569.A455
PS3569.A458
PS3569.A459
PS3569.A462
PS3569.A512
PS3569.A5125
PS3569.A823
PS3569.A825
PS3569.A83
PS3569.A835
PS3569.C29
PS3569.C485
PS3569.C5175
PS3569.C528
PS3569.C553
PS3569.C566
PS3569.C593
PS3569.C62
PS3569.C63
PS3569.C7
PS3569.E33
PS3569.E35
PS3569.E4
PS3569.E7
PS3569.H317
PS3569.H334
PS3569.H392
PS3569.H3923
PS3569.H3927
PS3569.H399
PS3569.H44
PS3569.H46
PS3569.H5
PS3569.I25
PS3569.I3
PS3569.I37
PS3569.I472
PS3569.I476
PS3569.I485
PS3569.I545
PS3569.I55
PS3569.I57
PS3569.L3
PS3569.L54
PS3569.M534
PS3569.M5376
PS3569.M5378
PS3569.M538
PS3569.N6
PS3569.O7
PS3569.O8
PS3569.P25
PS3569.P42
PS3569.P43

813.54 ..... PS3569.P44
PS3569.P464
PS3569.P55
PS3569.Q4
PS3569.T15
PS3569.T2
PS3569.T32
PS3569.T333
PS3569.T3355
PS3569.T336
PS3569.T338
PS3569.T386
PS3569.T387
PS3569.T3878
PS3569.T389
PS3569.T39
PS3569.T394
PS3569.T454
PS3569.T456
PS3569.T46
PS3569.T464
PS3569.T466
PS3569.T468
PS3569.T63
PS3569.T642
PS3569.T645
PS3569.T6916
PS3569.T698
PS3569.T79
PS3569.T9
PS3569.U2
PS3569.U33
PS3569.U348
PS3569.U45
PS3569.U75
PS3569.W2
PS3569.W22
PS3569.W24
PS3569.W27
PS3569.W36
PS3569.W54
PS3570.A3
PS3570.A33
PS3570.A924
PS3570.A927
PS3570.A929
PS3570.A937
PS3570.A955
PS3570.E5
PS3570.E55
PS3570.E6
PS3570.H4
PS3570.H573
PS3570.H58
PS3570.H59
PS3570.H598
PS3570.H644
PS3570.H67
PS3570.I3
PS3570.I47
PS3570.I53
PS3570.I6
PS3570.O5
PS3570.O6
PS3570.R36
PS3570.R5
PS3570.U28
PS3570.U73
PS3570.U74
PS3570.U75
PS3570.U8
PS3570.Y45
PS3571.H6
PS3571.M5
PS3571.P35
PS3571.P4
PS3571.R3
PS3572.A416
PS3572.A424
PS3572.A429
PS3572.A435
PS3572.A44
PS3572.A53
PS3572.A55
PS3572.A76
PS3572.A85
PS3572.E7
PS3572.E75
PS3572.I7
PS3572.I83
PS3572.I85
PS3572.I88
PS3572.O3
PS3572.O46
PS3572.O5
PS3573
PS3573.A3
PS3573.A35
PS3573.A384
PS3573.A39
PS3573.A413
PS3573.A415
PS3573.A424
PS3573.A4254
PS3573.A4256
PS3573.A4257
PS3573.A4258
PS3573.A426
PS3573.A4268
PS3573.A433
PS3573.A475
PS3573.A744
PS3573.A765
PS3573.A783

Dewey	LC
813.54	PS3573.A85
	PS3573.A87
	PS3573.A9
	PS3573.E195
	PS3573.E197
	PS3573.E198
	PS3573.E385
	PS3573.E39
	PS3573.E396
	PS3573.E398
	PS3573.E43
	PS3573.E46
	PS3573.E7
	PS3573.E827
	PS3573.E9
	PS3573.E92
	PS3573.E93
	PS3573.E96
	PS3573.H44
	PS3573.H472
	PS3573.H54
	PS3573.H56
	PS3573.I2
	PS3573.I26
	PS3573.I28
	PS3573.I35
	PS3573.I39
	PS3573.I434
	PS3573.I4418
	PS3573.I4422
	PS3573.I4426
	PS3573.I4486
	PS3573.I4495
	PS3573.I456
	PS3573.I4565
	PS3573.I4567
	PS3573.I4569
	PS3573.I475
	PS3573.I4795
	PS3573.I532
	PS3573.I533
	PS3573.I534
	PS3573.I535
	PS3573.I7
	PS3573.I87
	PS3573.O4
	PS3573.O45
	PS3573.O53
	PS3573.O55
	PS3573.O565
	PS3573.O568
	PS3573.O622
	PS3573.O624
	PS3573.O645
	PS3573.O646
	PS3573.O65
	PS3573.R4
	PS3573.R49
	PS3573.R535
	PS3573.R54
	PS3573.U7
	PS3573.W3334
	PS3573.Y48
	PS3573.Y6
	PS3575.A8
	PS3575.A83
	PS3575.O68
	PS3575.O7
	PS3575.O75
	PS3575.O83
	PS3575.U7
	PS3576.A4
	PS3576.E4
	PS3576.E43
	PS3576.E45
	PS3576.I515
	PS3576.I58
	PS3576.U25
	PS3584.E84
	PZ3
	PZ3.D445
	PZ3.N121
	PZ3.V6668
	PZ3.W1426
	PZ4.B9875
	PZ4.G2315
	PZ4.L698
	PZ4.P9853
	PZ7.N4384
	PZ7.W329
813.5400975	PS261
813.5408	PS374.S7
	PS558.A5
	PS645
	PS647.N35
	PS648.S3
	PS659
	PZ5
813.540803	PS645
	PS648.S3
	PS648.W4
	PZ1
813.54083	PS561
	PS648
813.5409	DS113
	PR881
	PS261
	PS379
813.54093	PS379
813.6	PT2291
813.8	PR4753
	PS1449.C85
813.912	PS1250
	PS3515
813.912	PS3523.O46
	PS3539.O1248
813.914	PR6011.I88
	PS3557.E3
814.008	PS508.W7
	PS682
	PS683.N4
814.3	PS1025
	PS1485
	PS1602
	PS1603
	PS1608
	PS1631
	PS1638
	PS1968
	PS3107
814.4	PR4728.G7
	PS1928
	PS2353
	PS2696
	PS3152
	PS3505.O257
814.508	PS688
814.52	PR6003.U57
	PS1585
	PS3117
	PS3503
	PS3503.R7297
	PS3509.A752
	PS3515.O75935
	PS3521.R86
	PS3523.I825
	PS3525.O25
	PS3525.O71
	PS3527.O2
	PS3535.E923
	PS3537.T483
	PS3539.R99
	PS3539.O967
	PS3547.O6
	Z1035.A1
814.5208	PS682
814.54	PS3503.E932
	PS3507.U629
	PS3543.I26
	PS3558.I35
	PS3558.O334
	PS3561.O36
	PS3562.A27
	PS3568.O788
	PS3569.M53
814.912	PR6003.E45
815.01	E302.1
	PS662
	PS663.P5
815.05	PN4145
815.108	PS662
815.309	PS407
815.4	PN4271
	PS1205
	PS3341
815.509	PS661
815.54	PS3568.U45
816.008	PN6153
816.2	PS1293
816.3	PS1493
	PS2506
816.4	PS1541.Z5
	PS2123
	PS2123.A53
	PS2248.L8
816.52	PS3537.A826
	PS3539.R928
816.54	PS3535.O39
817.008	PE1121
	PN6157
	PN6158
	PN6161
	PN6162
817.009	PN6161
817.109	PS436
817.208	PN6261
817.3	PR4735.H25
	PS1142
	PS2817
	PS2876
817.4	PN6157
	PS1300
	PS1302
	PS1303
	PS1322
	PS1331
	PS1331.A3
	PS1333
	PS1336
	PS1338
	PS1342.R4
	PS1535.Z5
	PS2481
	PS2482
	PS2859.S5
817.408	PN4305.N6
817.5	PN6161
817.508	PN6231.C62
817.52	AC8
	PN4874.A45
	PN6161
	PN6162
	PR6023.E15
	PS2649.P5
	PS3503.E49
	PS3507.U6755
	PS3509.R5
	PS3513.O852
817.52	PS3513.R25
	PS3531.E6544
	PS3535.O45
817.5208	PN6161
817.54	AC8
	NC1428
	PN6162
	PN6231.G8
	PN6231.I65
	PN6231.M68
	PN6231.P79
	PR6001.L67217
	PR6027.I35
	PS3503.U1828
	PS3521.E744
	PS3551.N46
	PS3556.E42
	PS3558.E258
	PS3560.U8
817.5408	AC5
	PN6162
818.008	PE1122
818.02	E743
	PN6083
818.08	PE1121
	PS508.N3
	PS570
	PS645
818.108	PS808.M73
818.10808	PS186
818.209	PS703.A5
	PS708.B5
	PS737.C5
	PS1779.H16
	PS2088
818.302	PS3042
818.303	PS1850
	PS3039.T9
	PS3048
818.308	PS1140
	PS1141
	PS2350.L5
	PS2713
	PS2952
	PS3042
	PS3048
	PS3053
	PS3231
	PS3322
818.309	E457.92
	KF228.P6
	PQ2638
	PS263
	PS1020.F70
	PS1385
	PS1493
	PS1501
	PS1506
	PS1631
	PS1638
	PS1671
	PS1970
	PS1981
	PS2485
	PS2502
	PS2506
	PS2602
	PS2631
	PS2636
	PS2638
	PS2853
	PS2956
	PS2957
	PS2993
	PS3048
	PS3053
	PS3054
	PS3326
818.403	PS1449.C85
818.408	DC20.A2
	E175.5
	PS1074.B88
	PS1097
	PS1302
	PS1743
	PS1917
	PS1918
818.409	BX9869.J8
	E185.97.B89
	PS1773
	PS1928
	PS2033
	PS2034
	PS2037.I8
	PS2397
	PS2752
818.483	B132.A35
818.508	PS3523.E8745
818.52	PS3537.T323
	PS3545.O337
818.5203	PS1733
	PS3505.R865
	PS3509.R28
	PS3525.A1143
	PS3527.I865
	PS3537.C943
818.5208	PR6023.E15
	PS3501.N4
	PS3503.U6
	PS3505.A153
	PS3505.A87
	PS3507.A7165
	PS3507.E867
	PS3507.O743
818.5208	PS3515.E37
	PS3523.O46
	PS3527.O2
	PS3531.O82
	PS3535.O7577
	PS3537.T323
	PS3539.A74
	PS3545.I345
	PS3545.I544
	PS3545.R815
818.5209	PN6120.C5
	PR5231.Z5
	PS2425
	PS3501.G35
	PS3503.O17
	PS3503.R7297
	PS3503.U6134
	PS3505.H3224
	PS3507.A33
	PS3507.E49
	PS3511.A738
	PS3511.R13
	PS3515.A156
	PS3515.A363
	PS3525.A24785
	PS3525.E43
	PS3531.O752
	PS3537.T323
	PS3539.H94
	PS3545.A82
	PS3545.E3775
	PS3545.I544
	PS3545.I6245
	PS3545.O77
	PS3737.U47
818.54	PS3519.O4545
	PS3529.L655
	PS3552.J57
	PS3566.A32
	PS3566.I56
818.5402	PS3551.N43
	PS3573.E394
818.5403	PS3513.I74
	PS3573.I475
818.5407	PR6065.N4
	PS3568.I5
	PS3570.R46
818.5408	AC8
	PN6162
	PR6027.I35
	PR6070.R8
	PS3521.R557
	PS3537.N79
	PS3543.I26
	PS3552.A593
	PS3552.U75
	PS3554.A948
	PS3557.E8
	PS3558.A646
	PS3563.E75
	PS3563.I84
	PS3565.C57
	PS3566.A69
	PS3566.I56
	PS3568.O95
	PS3569.A525
	PS3569.A55
	PS3573.I75
818.540808	PS659
818.5409	BX4705.M542
	PN4874.K74
	PN4874.K83
	PS3509.L715
	PS3552.U75
	PS3556.A38
	PS3558.I36
	PS3558.O957
	PS3563.A339
	PS3564
	PS3564.E15
	PS3569.E15
	PS3569.E54
	PS3570.R3
	PS3573.I4563
820	PR101
	PR9471
820.008	PR1109
820.08	PR1120
820.207	PR86
820.3	PR19
	Z2012
820.7	PE1068.G5
	PR33
820.71	LB1576
820.712	LB1631
820.71242	LB1576
	LB1631
820.8	PE1121
	PE1122
	PN4199
	PN4201
	PN6175
	PR83
	PR1109
	PR1110.C3
	PR1111.A9
	PR1111.C58
	PR1111.E5
	PR1125
	PR1134
	PR1363
	PR8383
	PR8833
	PR9591.Q4

820.8 PR9797.P65
PS507
Z881
820.8001 PR1120
820.8002 PR1119
820.8004 PR1131
820.8005 PR1134
820.8008 PN6014
PR453
PR1111.H57
820.80091 PE1122
820.800912 NX600.D3
820.800914 PR33
820.801 PR1195.H8
820.803 PE1121
PE1122
PN6071.L7
PR1111.C53
PR1111.D7
PR1111.E5
PR1111.W33
PR1309.V4
PS509.C56
820.809 PR99
820.809282 PR1145
PZ8.3.W915
820.809283 PE1122
820.809287 PN6084.M6
820.8096 PR9799
820.9 PE25
PE26
PE1417
PE1421
PN165
PN452
PN501
PN511
PN6019
PN6231.B8
PR14
PR57
PR63
PR77
PR83
PR85
PR87
PR93
PR99
PR105
PR107
PR109
PR111
PR145
PR149.S7
PR401
PR403
PR414
PR441
PR447
PR473
PR830.I6
PR1109
PR1367
PR4024
PR4115
PR4453.C4
PR4606
PR4876
PR5112.O55
PR5252
PR5816
PR6003.U13
PR6009.S4
PR6015.O885
PR6023.E286
PR6023.E926
PR6023.U65
PR6025.A127
PR6031.A7
PR6033.U4
PR6045.A85
PR6073.I4678
PR8716
PR8750
PR8911
PR9080
PR9898.N5
PS88
PS92
PS121
PS124
PS221
PS3537.T246
Z1041
820.9001 PE1075
PR83
PR166
PR255
PR281
PR1120
PS530
820.9003 DA356
PR14
PR421
PR423
PR545.J2
820.9004 PR433
PR435
PR437
PR439.C4
820.9005 PR442
PR853
PR3533
820.900506 PN22.A2
820.9006 PR110.L6
PR442
PR443
PR445
PR451
PR3533
820.9007 PR451
PR453
PR457
PR915
PR4772
PR5433
PS201
820.9008 PR83
PR99
PR403
PR453
PR461
PR463
PR464
PR466
PR471
PR474
PR4437.S6
PR6013.R367
PR6025.A7955
820.9009 PR403
PR473
PS3503.O87
820.90091 PN771
PR99
PR471
PR736
PS3571.P4
820.900912 PR99
PR471
PR473
PR474
PR6037.W85
820.900914 PR471
820.90098 PR461
820.913 HX806
PN56.P25
820.914 PR99
PR146
820.93 BT550
PN56.M5
PR143
PR149.C55
PR151.S3
PR418.R6
PR439.D7
PR449.S5
PR451
PR469.S4
PR508.L5
820.933 PR149.I6
820.9913 PR9320.5
820.9920692 PN171.P73
820.99287 PR115
820.9941 PR8511
820.99415 PR8711
820.99429 PR8916
820.9954 PR9708
820.9967 PL8010
820.99914 PL5542
820.9994 PR9411
R9411
821 PR508.M9
PR4452.C725
PR4639.D37
PR4973.Z5
PR5449.S15
PR5473.S7
PR5900
PR5904.S235
PR5904.W63
PR5906
PR5907
PR5908.V4
PR6001.L6725
PR6003.R323
PR6003.R352
PR6005.H36
PR6005.O38
PR6005.O814
PR6007.O8924
PR6007.U562
PR6011.I85
PR6011.R293
PR6013.H56
PR6013.R4
PR6015.A414
PR6015.E39
PR6015.I444
PR6015.O597
PR6019.O9
PR6021.A747
PR6021.I35
PR6023.A48
PR6023.A94
PR6025.A1613
PR6025.A1626
PR6025.A218
PR6025.A22175
PR6025.A25267
PR6025.A715
PR6025.A7927
PR6027.E43
PR6029.D58
PR6029.D6
PR6031.E55
PR6035.E69
PR6035.O8
821 PR6035.U7
PR6037.A74
PR6037.C55
PR6037.M83
PR6037.T463
PR6037.T723
PR6037.T848
PR6039.H42
PR6045.E145
PR6045.E34
PR6050.A1
PR6051.D343
PR6052.A728
PR6052.A755
PR6052.E23
PR6052.E334
PR6052.L39
PR6052.R5817
PR6052.R84
PR6053.A8
PR6053.A83
PR6053.H46
PR6053.H55
PR6053.H6
PR6053.L3
PR6053.L317
PR6053.O443
PR6053.U8
PR6054.A892
PR6054.A893
PR6054.A9
PR6054.E33
PR6054.E39
PR6055.C5
PR6056.I2
PR6056.U78
PR6057.H57
PR6057.L65
PR6057.O74
PR6058.A5
PR6058.A553
PR6058.A674
PR6058.A77
PR6058.E2
PR6058.E484
PR6058.E9
PR6058.I44
PR6058.O2
PR6058.O58
PR6059.R4
PR6060.A16
PR6060.A43
PR6061.A6
PR6061.S5
PR6061.U4
PR6062.A52
PR6062.E17
PR6062.I3
PR6062.I92
PR6062.O515
PR6062.U75
PR6063.A1675
PR6063.A3
PR6063.A72
PR6063.A763
PR6063.E9
PR6063.I36
PR6063.M1693
PR6063.O48
PR6063.O5
PR6063.U74
PR6064.A4
PR6064.A5
PR6064.A9
PR6065.C8
PR6065.G7
PR6066.I9
PR6066.O83
PR6066.U75
PR6068.A27
PR6068.A33
PR6068.A94
PR6069.E365
PR6069.H3
PR6069.H33
PR6069.H48
PR6069.I59
PR6069.T29
PR6069.T44
PR6069.T48
PR6069.U38
PR6070.A97
PR6070.E38
PR6070.I25
PR6072.E7
PR6073.E45
PR6073.R53
PR8711
PS3531.E6767
PT9876.23.A3
PZ8.3.W8917
821.0016 Z2014.P7
821.003 PR19
821.008 PE1121
PE1122
PN6101
PN6110.C4
PN6110.H3
PN6110.N6
PN6231.L5
PR509.H4
PR1110.S4
PR1173
PR1174
821.008 PR1175
PR1176
PR1181
PR1184
PR1187
PR1195.B7
PR1195.H8
PR1205
PR1207
PR1225
PR8384
PR8651
PR8658
PR9086
PR9551
PR9554.C5
PR9560
PR9864
PS507
PS586
PS615
PZ8.3
PZ8.3.J6315
PZ8.3.S588
821.008022 PN1421
821.00803 GT3020
PN6110.B6
PN6110.C4
PN6110.H8
PN6110.L6
PN6110.N2
PN6110.R4
PN6110.S4
PN6110.S5
PN6231.L5
PR1184
PR1191
PR1195.A5
PR1195.H5
PR1195.P3
PR1195.R6
PR1205
PZ8.3.G726
PZ8.3.U65
821.008033 PN4305.H7
PR1175
821.0080354 PR1184
821.0087 PR1109
821.009 N7598
PE27
PE1122
PE1515
PN1031
PR14
PR65
PR66
PR99
PR106
PR109
PR143
PR408.I5
PR421
PR501
PR502
PR503
PR504.5
PR505
PR508.L3
PR509.A7
PR521
PR543
PR544
PR545.M4
PR553
PR571
PR581
PR584
PR604
PR935
PR1175
PR1175.5
PR5908.S5
PR6013.R744
PR9414
PR9471
PS2322
QR610
821.00913 PR2359
821.00914 PR509.L8
821.00915 PR14
PR99
PR1175
821.0092 PN86
821.00923 AS262
821.0093 PR508.B5
PR535.M37
821.04 PN1376
PR354
PR509.O3
PR1181
PR1195.P3
821.05 QA135.5
821.07 PN6231.L5
PR931
PR1195.H8
821.08 PR8851
821.0817 PN6231.L5
PZ8.3.C675
821.09 PR502
821.1 DA185
PB10
PR315
PR1119
PR1850

Dewey	LC
821.1	PR1852
	PR1867
	PR1868.M42
	PR1868.M6
	PR1868.P9
	PR1868.W7
	PR1874
	PR1886
	PR1895
	PR1896
	PR1905
	PR1906
	PR1924
	PR1933.A65
	PR1933.A7
	PR1939
	PR1940
	PR1964
	PR1980
	PR2011
	PR2013
	PR2015
	PR2017.R4
	PR2021
	PR2065
	PR2065.A6
	PR2065.A8
	PR2065.F63
	PR2065.G3
	PR2111
	PR2117
	PR2136
	PR2145
821.108	PR1119
	PR1203
	PR8655
821.10803	PR1119.A2
821.109	PR275.A4
	PR321
	PR351
	PR365
	PR1260
	PR1987
821.18	TJ275
821.2	PR1119
	PR2037
	PR2048
	PR2252
	PR2266
	PR2268
	PR2345
	PR2346
	PR2348
	PR2400
	PR2400.A5
	PR2403.A3
	PR8633
821.208	PR1203
	PR1205
	PR8656
821.20803	PR1184
821.209	PR531
821.3	DA358.S5
	PR535.A4
	PR1119
	PR2199
	PR2199.W63
	PR2214.B6
	PR2228
	PR2241
	PR2242.D2
	PR2245
	PR2245.A5
	PR2246
	PR2247
	PR2248
	PR2255
	PR2257
	PR2257.E63
	PR2260
	PR2263
	PR2267.T7
	PR2271
	PR2277
	PR2298
	PR2329.P85
	PR2337.R9
	PR2338
	PR2340.A5
	PR2343
	PR2349.S35
	PR2349.S5
	PR2352
	PR2356
	PR2357
	PR2358
	PR2363
	PR2364
	PR2366
	PR2366.H8
	PR2367.P7
	PR2376.P6
	PR2450
	PR2631
	PR2638
	PR2702
	PR2734
	PR2842
	PR2848
	PR2848.A2
	PR2848.A4
	PR2892
	PR3371
821.303	Z2014.P7
821.308	PR1207
821.30803	PR1207
821.309	PR525.V4
	PR534
	PR535
	PR535.S9
	PR541
	PR543
	PR549.L8
	PR2364
821.30931	PR545.R4
	PR549.R4
821.33	PR2944
821.4	DA247.W3
	DA447.R6
	N7740
	PR543
	PR1209
	PR2217.B5
	PR2294.H2
	PR2390
	PR2392
	PR2393
	PR3140
	PR3318.B5
	PR3332
	PR3339
	PR3339.C2
	PR3386
	PR3409
	PR3409.D2
	PR3412
	PR3415
	PR3416
	PR3417
	PR3418
	PR3420
	PR3423
	PR3424
	PR3506.H978
	PR3510.A5
	PR3546
	PR3551
	PR3552
	PR3555.A2
	PR3557
	PR3560
	PR3562
	PR3566
	PR3580
	PR3581
	PR3582
	PR3583
	PR3588
	PR3592
	PR3592.G4
	PR3592.M3
	PR3592.P7
	PR3592.R4
	PR3592.S3
	PR3596
	PR3605
	PR3652
	PR3736.T7
	PR3742
	PR3744
	PR3750
	PS1557
821.408	ML54.6.03
	PR1209
	PR1213
821.40803	PR1181
	PR1191
	PR1209
821.409	PR74
	PR99
	PR509.P3
	PR541
	PR544
	PR553
821.4093	PR545.R4
821.5	PR3352
	PR3473
	PR3619.P2
	PR3621
	PR3622
	PR3625
	PR3626
	PR3627
	PR3629
	PR3630
	PR3633
	PR3634
	PR3636
	PR3677
	PR3727
	PR3732
	PR3732.S5
	PR3780
	PR3782.N6
	PR3783
	Z8704
821.508	PR1175
821.509	PR509.D5
	PR571
821.5108	PR1225
821.54	PR6052.O6
	PS3569.E53
821.6	PR3310.A5
	PR3313
	PR3340
	PR3340.A5
	PR3343
	PR3346
821.6	PR3346.C8
	PR3382
	PR3383
	PR3383.A2
	PR3383.A3
	PR3448.F3
	PR3489
	PR3503
	PR3519.J12
	PR3541.L56
	PR3544
	PR3671.S3
	PR3671.S7
	PR3687.S7
	PR3991.A1
	PR4141
	PR4222
	PR4300
	PR4307
	PR4329
	PR4331
	PR4334
	PR4338
	PR4345
	PR4508.C153
	PR5189.P25
	PR5466
	PZ8.3
821.608	PR1215
	PR3579.W2
821.609	PR571
	PR3675
821.6093	PR508.M4
	PR509.D5
821.7	NX93.B55
	PN1082
	PN1082.R58
	PR583
	PR3593
	PR4056
	PR4141
	PR4142
	PR4144
	PR4144.L33
	PR4144.P63
	PR4144.S63
	PR4146
	PR4147
	PR4357
	PR4359
	PR4367
	PR4381
	PR4382
	PR4388
	PR4410
	PR4470
	PR4471
	PR4479
	PR4483
	PR4484
	PR4487.I6
	PR4513
	PR4792
	PR4796
	PR4798
	PR4830
	PR4832
	PR4836
	PR4837
	PR4870
	PR4873
	PR4874
	PR4988.M28
	PR5056
	PR5332
	PR5341
	PR5342.A2
	PR5402
	PR5403
	PR5410
	PR5416
	PR5422
	PR5422.B33
	PR5431
	PR5432
	PR5438
	PR5442.D35
	PR5442.N3
	PR5442.P5
	PR5442.P64
	PR5442.R3
	PR5466
	PR5588
	PR5849
	PR5850
	PR5852
	PR5853
	PR5858
	PR5864.A2
	PR5869
	PR5880
	PR5881
	PR5881.T5
	PR5884
	PR5885
	PR5888
	PR5892.A4
	PR5892.L5
	PZ8.3
	Z8428.2
	Z8985
821.708	PR1219
	PR1221
821.709	PR99
821.709	PR403
	PR589.L8
	PR590
	PR591
	PR4383
	PR4484
	PR5433
	PR5883
821.7093	PR575.N3
821.8	NC242.L4
	PK6513.A3
	PR1181
	PR3542.L2
	PR3991.A1
	PR4012
	PR4020
	PR4021
	PR4022
	PR4023
	PR4023.A47
	PR4024
	PR4147
	PR4149
	PR4161.B6
	PR4193
	PR4201
	PR4202
	PR4203
	PR4219
	PR4222
	PR4229.L7
	PR4231
	PR4238
	PR4242.R4
	PR4245
	PR4247
	PR4321
	PR4352
	PR4453.C6
	PR4455
	PR4456
	PR4458
	PR4483
	PR4599.D53
	PR4606
	PR4611
	PR4613.D5
	PR4713
	PR4741
	PR4750
	PR4750.D8
	PR4753
	PR4754
	PR4802.H44
	PR4803.H44
	PR4879.L2
	PR4881
	PR4970.M45
	PR4973.Z5
	PR5021.M3
	PR5074.A3
	PR5083
	PR5143
	PR5144
	PR5237
	PR5238
	PR5240
	PR5244
	PR5246
	PR5261
	PR5349.S2
	PR5473.S35
	PR5489
	PR5502
	PR5506
	PR5513
	PR5514
	PR5522
	PR5550
	PR5559.C8
	PR5560
	PR5562
	PR5581
	PR5588
	PR5592.P5
	PR5595
	PR5598
	PR5649.T4
	PR5650
	PR5651
	PR5658
	PR5820
	PR5823
	PR5906
	PR6001.L6714
	PR6027.I37
	PZ6.H842
	PZ8.3.B82
	PZ8.3.L477
	PZ8.3.R744
	Z8124.5
821.808	PR593
	PR1223
	PR1224
821.80803	PN6110.S4
	PR595.I65
821.809	PR99
	PR452
	PR461
	PR469.D4
	PR503
	PR581
	PR585.L3
	PR591

Dewey	LC
821.809	PR593
	PR4203
	PR4453.C178
821.908	PR1309.H6
	PR8964
821.909	PR610
	PS323.5
821.9108	PN6101
	PR504
	PR1175
	PR1195.N2
	PR1225
	PR1226
	PS613
	PS613.P63
	PS615
821.9108023	PR1195.N2
821.910803	PR1225
821.9109	PN1075
	PR473
	PR502
	PR603
	PR604
	PR610
821.912	AS36.G378
	DA730
	PJ5111.5.L4
	PN6110.S4
	PR4803.H44
	PR4809.H15
	PR5528
	PR6001.L6725
	PR6001.U4
	PR6003.A68
	PR6003.E45
	PR6003.E7435
	PR6003.E77
	PR6003.U36
	PR6005.A418
	PR6005.A4865
	PR6005.R58
	PR6005.R7
	PR6007.A667
	PR6007.A95
	PR6007.E3
	PR6007.O86
	PR6007.Y55
	PR6013.I23
	PR6013.R35
	PR6013.R735
	PR6013.R744
	PR6015.I466
	PR6015.U478
	PR6019.O53
	PR6021.E79
	PR6023.A93
	PR6023.E4
	PR6023.I5812
	PR6023.I58144
	PR6025.A316
	PR6025.A77
	PR6025.O35
	PR6025.O573
	PR6025.U713
	PR6027.O8
	PR6029.W4
	PR6031.A72
	PR6031.I7
	PR6031.R94
	PR6031.U3
	PR6035.A37
	PR6035.O54
	PR6035.O615
	PR6037
	PR6037.E9
	PR6037.I8
	PR6037.M43
	PR6037.P47
	PR6039.H52
	PR6039.H55
	PR6039.H58
	PR6045.A2495
	PR6045.A825
	PR6045.I45
	PR6052.A44
	PR6058.U367
	PS3509
	PS3509.L43
	PS3531.O82
	PS3571.P4
	PZ8.3.B243
	PZ8.3.B417
821.91208	PR1225
	PR1226
	PS614
821.9120803	PR1149
821.91209	PR603
	PR610
	PR6037.P47
	PS3509.L43
821.9120914	PR590
821.912093	PR508.M9
821.914	D745.2
	NC311.O2
	PR1225
	PR6001.B7
	PR6003.L26
	PR6003.R38723
	PR6005.A837
	PR6005.O396
	PR6005.O62
	PR6005.R58
	PR6007.A668
	PR6007.A95
821.914	PR6007.E55
	PR6007.I38
	PR6007.U53
	PR6009.N6
	PR6009.V37
	PR6011.R282
	PR6013.R23
	PR6013.U65
	PR6015.E24
	PR6015.O415
	PR6015.O416
	PR6021.E49
	PR6021.E626
	PR6021.I64
	PR6023
	PR6023.E76
	PR6023.E88
	PR6023.E926
	PR6023.O38
	PR6025.I25
	PR6025.O68
	PR6027.O44
	PR6031.A758
	PR6035.E38
	PR6037.C25
	PR6037.K38
	PR6037.T1615
	PR6037.W7
	PR6039.O349
	PR6039.R42
	PR6045.A249
	PR6045.A26
	PR6045.H154
	PR6045.R415
	PR6050.A1
	PR6051.D34
	PR6051.R57
	PR6051.T79
	PR6051.U8
	PR6052.A325
	PR6052.A44
	PR6052.A53
	PR6052.A62
	PR6052.E15
	PR6052.E17
	PR6052.E22
	PR6052.E4
	PR6052.I3
	PR6052.L27
	PR6052.L342
	PR6052.O38
	PR6052.O73
	PR6052.O83
	PR6052.R417
	PR6052.R446
	PR6052.R455
	PR6052.R46
	PR6052.R5813
	PR6052.R615
	PR6052.R618
	PR6052.R62
	PR6052.R96
	PR6052.U24
	PR6052.U63
	PR6052.U655
	PR6053.A683
	PR6053.A688
	PR6053.A74
	PR6053.A84
	PR6053.H28
	PR6053.H3
	PR6053.H362
	PR6053.H56
	PR6053.H8
	PR6053.L322
	PR6053.L44
	PR6053.O17
	PR6053.O4
	PR6053.O418
	PR6053.O4245
	PR6053.O46
	PR6053.O5
	PR6053.O653
	PR6053.O66
	PR6053.O88
	PR6053.R58
	PR6053.R63
	PR6053.U49
	PR6054.A4
	PR6054.A49
	PR6054.A68
	PR6054.A867
	PR6054.E49
	PR6054.E5
	PR6054.E78
	PR6054.O7
	PR6054.R3
	PR6054.U44
	PR6054.U54
	PR6055.A7
	PR6055.D93
	PR6055.L8
	PR6055.V2
	PR6055.V5
	PR6056.A5
	PR6056.E48
	PR6056.I47
	PR6056.I5
	PR6056.I8
	PR6056.L45
	PR6056.R293
	PR6056.U45
	PR6057.A7
	PR6057.I28
821.914	PR6057.I54
	PR6057.L4
	PR6057.O38
	PR6057.O72
	PR6057.O83
	PR6057.R23
	PR6057.R3
	PR6057.R5
	PR6057.R53
	PR6057.U42
	PR6058.A32
	PR6058.A434
	PR6058.A436
	PR6058.A49
	PR6058.A6925
	PR6058.A69435
	PR6058.A6948
	PR6058.A72
	PR6058.A885
	PR6058.A888
	PR6058.E495
	PR6058.E53
	PR6058.E67
	PR6058.I32
	PR6058.O2
	PR6058.O84
	PR6058.O92
	PR6058.U3
	PR6058.U35
	PR6058.U353
	PR6058.U37
	PR6059.M5
	PR6060.A2
	PR6060.A25
	PR6060.A26
	PR6060.A288
	PR6060.A29
	PR6060.A46
	PR6060.E52
	PR6060.O47
	PR6060.O49
	PR6060.O498
	PR6060.O513
	PR6060.O519
	PR6060.O524
	PR6060.O565
	PR6060.O574
	PR6060.O87
	PR6060.Q565
	PR6061.A9
	PR6061.A93
	PR6061.E679
	PR6061.E9
	PR6061.E94
	PR6061.O6
	PR6062.A36
	PR6062.E79
	PR6062.E915
	PR6062.E925
	PR6062.I2
	PR6062.I475
	PR6062.O3
	PR6062.O33
	PR6062.O45
	PR6062.U2
	PR6062.Y36
	PR6062.Y48
	PR6063.A13
	PR6063.A145
	PR6063.A157
	PR6063.A1678
	PR6063.A219
	PR6063.A237
	PR6063.A242
	PR6063.A2465
	PR6063.A255
	PR6063.A28
	PR6063.A373
	PR6063.A393
	PR6063.A62
	PR6063.A734
	PR6063.E2
	PR6063.I23
	PR6063.I377
	PR6063.I55
	PR6063.I77
	PR6063.I78
	PR6063.O54
	PR6063.O73
	PR6063.O749
	PR6063.O787
	PR6063.O794
	PR6063.U45
	PR6063.U72
	PR6063.U8
	PR6064.E4
	PR6064.E45
	PR6064.I17
	PR6064.I23
	PR6064.I85
	PR6064.O23
	PR6064.O5
	PR6064.O77
	PR6064.O9
	PR6064.Y4
	PR6065.G4
	PR6065.N43
	PR6065.R3
	PR6065.R69
	PR6066.A27
	PR6066.A715
	PR6066.A86
	PR6066.E4
	PR6066.E69
821.914	PR6066.H45
	PR6066.H49
	PR6066.I33
	PR6066.I35
	PR6066.I44
	PR6066.I52
	PR6066.I53
	PR6066.O34
	PR6066.O73
	PR6066.O75
	PR6066.R52
	PR6066.R56
	PR6066.R9
	PR6068.A82
	PR6068.A84
	PR6068.A93
	PR6068.I24
	PR6068.I36
	PR6068.I4
	PR6068.I77
	PR6068.O185
	PR6068.O187
	PR6068.O194
	PR6068.O234
	PR6068.O45
	PR6068.O55
	PR6069.E3
	PR6069.E5
	PR6069.H393
	PR6069.H8
	PR6069.I4
	PR6069.I58
	PR6069.M4
	PR6069.M48
	PR6069.M485
	PR6069.M54
	PR6069.M546
	PR6069.T36
	PR6069.T429
	PR6069.T448
	PR6069.T45
	PR6069.T55
	PR6069.T58
	PR6069.U85
	PR6070.A57
	PR6070.E2
	PR6070.H3
	PR6070.H58
	PR6070.H658
	PR6070.O67
	PR6070.O8
	PR6070.O9
	PR6070.R47
	PR6070.U4
	PR6070.U67
	PR6070.U73
	PR6070.U75
	PR6072.I55
	PR6073.A34
	PR6073.A355
	PR6073.A36
	PR6073.A38
	PR6073.A4
	PR6073.A435
	PR6073.A7218
	PR6073.A724
	PR6073.A735
	PR6073.A93
	PR6073.A95
	PR6073.E42
	PR6073.H46
	PR6073.H493
	PR6073.H515
	PR6073.H54
	PR6073.I4165
	PR6073.I432
	PR6073.I4335
	PR6073.I473
	PR6073.I84
	PR6073.R45
	PR6073.R55
	PR6073.Y3
	PR6075.O8
	PS3552.L32
	PS3552.O846
	PS3569.I53
	PZ8.3.P272
	PZ8.3.S47
	PZ8.3.Y46
821.91408	PN6110.C7
	PR1150
	PR1174
	PR1175
	PR1195.S4
	PR1225
	PR1227
	PR6052.R62
	PR6063.O787
	PR8658
	PS615
	PZ8.3.G423
821.9140803	PR1184
821.91409	PR611
822	PN1997
	PN6120.A5
	PR635.F6
	PR5042
	PR5532
	PR5533
	PR5907
	PR6003.E282
	PR6003.E417
	PR6003.R258
	PR6005.A74

Dewey	LC
822	PR6029.C33
	PR6035.U7
	PR6039.H86
	PR6045.H19
	PR6051.I33
	PR6052.U8
	PR6053.A6
	PR6053.R8
	PR6054.A755
	PR6054.E25
	PR6055.Z4
	PR6056.R5
	PR6056.U4
	PR6057.R45
	PR6059.R38
	PR6060.A43
	PR6061.A5
	PR6061.I38
	PR6061.U6
	PR6063.A4
	PR6064.A3
	PR6064.G8
	PR6066.O7
	PR6068.E32
	PR6068.I8
	PR6069.E649
	PR6069.O9
	PR6075.A9
822.003	PR623
822.008	PN6112
	PN6120.A4
	PN6120.H7
	PR1265
	PR8868
	PR8870.M8
	PR9568
	PR9797.P67
822.009	PN1623
	PN1661
	PR149.T7
	PR625
	PR627
	PR635.F6
	PR643.M8
	PR691
	PR721
	PR1271
	Z2014.D7
822.0093	PR625
	PR641.C8
822.01	PA3825
822.04	PR618
822.051	PR643.M7
	PR644.Y6
	PR1262
822.052	PR631
	PR698.C6
822.10803	PR1260
822.109	PR635.P73
	PR643.M5
	PR643.M7
	PR643.M8
	PR8585
822.1093	PR643.M8
822.2	PR2209.B2
822.208	PR1119
	PR1260
	PR1262
822.209	PR646
822.3	PR652
	PR653
	PR2279.G4
	PR2303
	PR2411
	PR2421
	PR2427
	PR2428
	PR2429
	PR2433
	PR2434
	PR2436
	PR2442
	PR2446
	PR2448
	PR2464
	PR2493
	PR2494
	PR2524
	PR2527
	PR2544
	PR2576
	PR2605
	PR2613
	PR2619
	PR2622
	PR2624
	PR2631
	PR2638
	PR2642.H4
	PR2642.M9
	PR2646
	PR2654
	PR2654.S63
	PR2659.L6
	PR2659.L9
	PR2661
	PR2664
	PR2665
	PR2666
	PR2673
	PR2674
	PR2694
	PR2697
	PR2702
822.3	PR2704
	PR2712
	PR2714
	PR2717
	PR2729.N7
	PR2734
	PR3172
	PR3184
	PR3187
	PR3188.F5
822.308	PR1248
	PR1263
822.309	PR635.H5
	PR651
	PR653
	PR654
	PR655
	PR658.M5
	PR658.S6
	PR658.T35
	PR2303
	PR2434
	PR2436
	PR2870.A2
822.30912	PR658.R4
822.3093	PR658.S8
	PR658.T5
822.33	ML80.S5
	PR1125
	PR2631
	PR2750
	PR2751
	PR2752
	PR2753
	PR2754
	PR2757
	PR2801
	PR2801.A2
	PR2802
	PR2802.A2
	PR2803
	PR2803.A2
	PR2804
	PR2805
	PR2805.A2
	PR2806
	PR2806.A2
	PR2807
	PR2807.A2
	PR2808
	PR2808.A2
	PR2809
	PR2810
	PR2810.A2
	PR2811.A2
	PR2812
	PR2814.A2
	PR2815.A2
	PR2816.A2
	PR2817
	PR2817.A2
	PR2818
	PR2818.A2
	PR2819
	PR2819.A2
	PR2820
	PR2820.A2
	PR2821
	PR2821.A2
	PR2822.A2
	PR2823
	PR2823.A2
	PR2824
	PR2824.A2
	PR2825
	PR2825.A2
	PR2826
	PR2826.A2
	PR2827
	PR2827.A2
	PR2828
	PR2828.A2
	PR2829
	PR2829.A2
	PR2830.A2
	PR2831
	PR2831.A2
	PR2832
	PR2832.A2
	PR2833
	PR2833.A2
	PR2835
	PR2836
	PR2836.A2
	PR2837
	PR2837.A2
	PR2838.A2
	PR2839
	PR2839.A2
	PR2841
	PR2870.A2
	PR2875
	PR2878.A8
	PR2878.C6
	PR2878.K4
	PR2878.K8
	PR2878.L6
	PR2878.M3
	PR2878.M5
	PR2878.T3
	PR2878.T5
	PR2890
	PR2892
	PR2893
822.33	PR2894
	PR2895
	PR2896
	PR2899
	PR2903
	PR2909
	PR2910
	PR2911
	PR2916
	PR2935
	PR2937
	PR2939
	PR2943
	PR2944
	PR2947.O9
	PR2950
	PR2951
	PR2953.W5
	PR2955.M8
	PR2955.P6
	PR2955.S6
	PR2959
	PR2965
	PR2968
	PR2969
	PR2975
	PR2976
	PR2978
	PR2981
	PR2983
	PR2987
	PR2989
	PR2991
	PR2993.F2
	PR2993.I3
	PR2995
	PR3001
	PR3004
	PR3009
	PR3011
	PR3012
	PR3014
	PR3017
	PR3034
	PR3036
	PR3037
	PR3041
	PR3047
	PR3062
	PR3065
	PR3067
	PR3070
	PR3071
	PR3072
	PR3077
	PR3081
	PR3085
	PR3091
	PR3099
	PR3109.C3
	PR4453.C8
	PR5864
	PR6045.I6138
	Z8813
822.4	PN2598.B6
	PR2439.B5
	PR2878.K2
	PR2878.K3
	PR2878.M3
	PR2878.M38
	PR2878.T4
	PR3317.Z5
	PR3364
	PR3388.C2
	PR3415
	PR3424
	PR3432
	PR3539.L2
	PR3540
	PR3607.O4
	PR3612
	PR3671.S4
	PR3671.S6
	PR3671.S8
	PR3718
	PR3737
	PR3774
	PR3776
822.408	PR1195.P7
	PR1251
	PR1266
822.409	PR3613
822.40916	PR651
822.5	E88
	PR2878.K25
	PR2878.K3
	PR2878.K9
	PR3328.B8
	PR3334.B8
	PR3454
	PR3541.L5
	PR3549.M6
	PR3605
	PR3619.P2
	PR3671.R5
	PR3699.S3
	PR3702
	PR3768.W6
822.508	PR1269
822.52	PS3537.T42
822.5409	PS351
822.6	PR2878.C6
	PR2878.W5
	PR2879
822.6	PR3393
	PR3465
	PR3605.M9
	PR3682
	PR3683
	PR5014
822.608	PR1269
822.7	PR4356
	PR4388
	PR5221.R3
	PR5408
822.8	PR4161.B2
	PR4552
	PR4713
	PR4714
	PR4876
	PR5649.T5
	PR5906
822.809	PR723
	PR736
822.9108	PN6072
822.9109	PR737
822.912	PN1997
	PN6120.A5
	PR4728.G5
	PR5360
	PR5361
	PR5363.M23
	PR5363.M34
	PR5366
	PR5367
	PR5368.W5
	PR6003.A35
	PR6003.E6
	PR6005.O85
	PR6007.R5
	PR6013.O9
	PR6015.O524
	PR6015.S5
	PR6023.A93
	PR6025.A316
	PR6025.A86
	PR6029.C33
	PR6031.R6
	PR6037.A95
	PR6039.H52
	PS3509.L43
822.91209	PR6011.R9
822.914	PN6120.A5
	PN6120.R4
	PR6003.A35
	PR6003.E5
	PR6007.E327
	PR6011.R9
	PR6013.O35
	PR6021.I275
	PR6023.A73
	PR6025.O7552
	PR6029.S39
	PR6037.I712
	PR6037.M58
	PR6039.H812
	PR6041.S73
	PR6045
	PR6045.H245
	PR6045.H28
	PR6046.H245
	PR6051.R3
	PR6052.A668
	PR6052.A762
	PR6052.E6
	PR6052.O39
	PR6052.O5
	PR6052.O58
	PR6052.O78
	PR6052.O85
	PR6052.R426
	PR6052.R5895
	PR6052.U7
	PR6053.A49
	PR6053.A856
	PR6053.A858
	PR6053.H375
	PR6053.O54
	PR6053.R45
	PR6054.E13
	PR6054.I5
	PR6054.Y4
	PR6055.V28
	PR6057.R33
	PR6058.A555
	PR6058.A673
	PR6058.O67
	PR6058.U33
	PR6058.U37
	PR6060.E5
	PR6060.O516
	PR6060.U6
	PR6062.A33
	PR6062.E6
	PR6062.E7
	PR6062.I9
	PR6062.U4
	PR6063
	PR6063.A2497
	PR6063.E7
	PR6063.O86
	PR6064.I2
	PR6065.R7
	PR6066.I53
	PR6066.L3
	PR6066.O77
	PR6068.O87
	PR6069.A9

822.914 ... PR6069.E35
... PR6069.H258
... PR6069.H39
... PR6069.H78
... PR6069.P8
... PR6069.T28
... PR6069.T6
... PR6069.T65
... PR6070.H636
... PR6070.R4
... PR6072.I5
... PR6073.E75
... PR6073.I43
... PR6073.O5
... PR6073.O57
... PR6073.O6
... PT2672.I48
822.91408 ... PR1248
... PS634
822.91409 ... PR736
823 ... HV6248.T78
... PQ7296.S5
... PR069.M45
... PR1307.B4
... PR3291
... PR4089.B75
... PR4175.B7
... PR4416
... PR4453.C75
... PR4508.C3
... PR4646
... PR4681
... PR4885
... PR5042
... PR5043
... PR5044
... PR5059.M3
... PR5189.P6
... PR5904
... PR6001.B33
... PR6001.B62
... PR6001.N24
... PR6001.R45
... PR6005.L83
... PR6005.U772
... PR6007.A822
... PR6007.A833
... PR6007.E6427
... PR6007.U83
... PR6011.U75
... PR6013.I3363
... PR6015.A568
... PR6015.A83
... PR6017.D7
... PR6019.O3985
... PR6019.O9
... PR6019.O9D874
... PR6023.A94
... PR6023.E283
... PR6023.I5815
... PR6025.A25253
... PR6025.A57
... PR6025.A644
... PR6025.A715
... PR6025.U646
... PR6027
... PR6027.A68
... PR6027.I54
... PR6029
... PR6029.B55
... PR6029.D58
... PR6031.A215
... PR6031.A384
... PR6031.A757
... PR6031.L25
... PR6031.L7
... PR6035.A425
... PR6035.O6684
... PR6035.U45
... PR6037.A814
... PR6037.M56
... PR6037.O6
... PR6037.T225
... PR6039.H42
... PR6039.H976
... PR6045.H19
... PR6050.A1
... PR6051.B3
... PR6051.C5
... PR6051.I67
... PR6051.L53
... PR6051.L57
... PR6051.L8
... PR6051.M2
... PR6051.R55
... PR6051.R64
... PR6051.S2
... PR6051.S8
... PR6051.Y6
... PR6052
... PR6052.A318
... PR6052.E314
... PR6052.E54
... PR6052.H33
... PR6052.H64
... PR6052.I97
... PR6052.O75
... PR6052.O94
... PR6052.R5894
... PR6052.U6444
... PR6053.A43
... PR6053.A685
... PR6053.A72
... PR6053.H324
823 ... PR6053.H35
... PR6053.L293
... PR6053.L315
... PR6053.O49
... PR6053.O518
... PR6053.O52
... PR6053.O96
... PR6053.R84
... PR6054.A37
... PR6054.A47
... PR6054.A48
... PR6054.A774
... PR6054.E34
... PR6054.I26
... PR6054.R8
... PR6054.Z6
... PR6055.B2
... PR6055.G33
... PR6055.R3
... PR6055.Y7
... PR6056
... PR6056.A3
... PR6056.A73
... PR6056.O682
... PR6056.O685
... PR6056.R26
... PR6056.R8
... PR6056.U44
... PR6057.A64
... PR6057.A75
... PR6057.A9
... PR6057.L43
... PR6057.O6
... PR6057.O63
... PR6057.O73
... PR6057.R24
... PR6057.R26
... PR6057.R39
... PR6057.R65
... PR6057.U45
... PR6057.U9
... PR6058.A28
... PR6058.A553
... PR6058.A69494
... PR6058.A88
... PR6058.A95
... PR6058.A97
... PR6058.I34
... PR6058.O29
... PR6058.O718
... PR6059.K4
... PR6060.E35
... PR6060.O634
... PR6061.A95
... PR6061.A97
... PR6061.E45
... PR6061.E56
... PR6061.E67
... PR6061.G6
... PR6061.I325
... PR6061.I4
... PR6061.I445
... PR6061.O58
... PR6062.E46
... PR6062.U7
... PR6063.A155
... PR6063.A165
... PR6063.A169
... PR6063.A175
... PR6063.A2415
... PR6063.A365
... PR6063.A68
... PR6063.A77
... PR6063.A86
... PR6063.E33
... PR6063.E36
... PR6063.I3
... PR6063.O745
... PR6063.O88
... PR6063.P5
... PR6064.G8
... PR6064.I4
... PR6064.O43
... PR6064.W27
... PR6064.W3
... PR6065
... PR6065.A45
... PR6065.B7
... PR6065.G45
... PR6065.G68
... PR6065.K3
... PR6065.T6
... PR6066.A4
... PR6066.A6
... PR6066.A9
... PR6066.I23
... PR6066.L84
... PR6066.O98
... PR6066.R58
... PR6066.R63
... PR6066.R93
... PR6068.A32
... PR6068.I9
... PR6068.U55
... PR6068.U85
... PR6069.A414
... PR6069.A75
... PR6069.C56
... PR6069.C595
... PR6069.E368
... PR6069.E65
... PR6069.H25
... PR6069.L33
... PR6069.M45
823 ... PR6069.M489
... PR6069.O9
... PR6070.A88
... PR6070.A95
... PR6070.H4
... PR6070.H665
... PR6070.H673
... PR6070.U8
... PR6071.U4
... PR6072.E73
... PR6072.I32
... PR6073.A25
... PR6073.E73
... PR6073.H53
... PR6073.H6
... PR6073.H64
... PR6073.I4324
... PR6073.I468
... PR9453
... PR9576
... PR9635
... PR9799
... PR9880
... PS1083.B35
... PS3515.E957
... PS3523.A914
... PS3556.A4
... PS3575.A75
... PS6073.A23
... PZ3.O32
... PZ4.M16952
... PZ4.S4886
... PZ4.W676
... PZ6
... PZ7.O4536
... PZ7.S726
823.0018 ... PR468.S8
823.008 ... PR1139
... PR1285
... PR1307
... PR1309.H6
... PR9327.5
... PR9780
... PR9881
... QL795.H7
823.008016 ... PR1309.H6
823.00803 ... DU380.K33
... GR365
... PR1111.C2
... PR1301
... PR1309.C6
... PR1309.F3
... PR1309.S3
... PS374.F27
... PS509.G5
... PS648.S3
... PZ1
823.009 ... PN1009.A1
... PR403
... PR821
... PR5301
... PR9324
... PR9503
... PR9735
... PS141
... PS371
... PS2387
823.00923 ... PR14
823.0093 ... PR830.A7
... PR830.T3
823.01 ... PE1130.J3
... PN6014
... PR1301
... PR1307.B65
... PR1309.T5
... PR8675
... PR9575
... PS645
... PS648.D4
... PS648.H6
823.03 ... PR821
... PS373
... PS374.C55
823.076 ... PR830.S35
823.081 ... PR830.H5
823.0872 ... PR1309.H6
... PS648.D4
... Z1045
823.0876 ... PN3448.S45
... PR830.S35
... PR1309.S3
... PS648.S3
823.2 ... PR2041
... PR2043
... PR2045
823.3 ... PR839.G7
... PR2244.D2
... PR2297.R7
... PR2329.P27
... PR2384.W3
... PR2490
... PR2544
... PR2574
... PR2714
... PR4716
823.309 ... PR836
... PR2541
823.33 ... PR2826.A79
823.4 ... DA396.D5
... PR3316.B37
... PR3317
... PR3330
... PR3330.A2
... PR3331
823.4 ... PR3332
... PR3605.N2
... PS2025
823.408 ... PR1295
823.409 ... AS36.G378
823.5 ... PR3349.C22
... PR3403.Z5
... PR3404
... PR3404.M63
... PR3406
... PR3454
... PR3454.H7
... PR3456
... PR3457
... PR3664.C43
... PR3666
... PR3724
823.508 ... PR1281
823.509 ... PR823
... PR851
823.52 ... PS3545.R815
823.5208 ... PS645
823.54 ... PR6068.A6
... PS3545.E449
823.6 ... PR3316.A4
... PR3348.C65
... PR3398.D3
... PR3490
... PR3494
... PR3515.H2
... PR3541.L27
... PR3543.M2
... PR3544
... PR3661
... PR3664.C43
... PR3666
... PR3667
... PR3694
... PR3696
... PR3697
... PR3710.F70
... PR3714
... PR3714.T7
... PR3714.T73
... PR3716
... PR3757.W2
... PR4091
... PR4723
... PR4735.H26
... PR5202
... PR5204
... PZ6.F36
823.608 ... PZ1
823.609 ... PR852
823.7 ... PR852
... PR4030
... PR4034
... PR4034.E53
... PR4034.M33
... PR4034.P73
... PR4034.S42
... PR4034.S43
... PR4036
... PR4037
... PR4646
... PR4699.F4
... PR4708.G2
... PR4791
... PR4891.L4
... PR5162
... PR5164
... PR5308
... PR5317
... PR5318
... PR5322
... PR5332
... PR5332.C5
... PR5333
... PR5340
... PR5341
... PR5397
... PR5398
... PZ3.S43
823.709 ... PR5341
823.7093 ... PR830.W6
823.714 ... PR6066.A93
823.8 ... ML80.D5
... NC242.D8
... PR3991.A1
... PR4057.B15
... PR4061
... PR4062
... PR4063.B3
... PR4074
... PR4084
... PR4087
... PR4104
... PR4124
... PR4132
... PR4154
... PR4154.L3
... PR4162
... PR4163
... PR4167
... PR4167.J5
... PR4167.S4
... PR4168
... PR4169
... PR4172
... PR4173
... PR4174.B56
... PR4349.B7
... PR4454.C16
... PR4494

Dewey	LC
823.8	PR4496
	PR4504
	PR4515.C45
	PR4518.C3
	PR4527
	PR4552
	PR4553
	PR4556
	PR4559
	PR4560
	PR4561
	PR4564
	PR4567
	PR4569
	PR4571
	PR4572
	PR4575
	PR4580
	PR4581
	PR4582
	PR4583
	PR4584
	PR4588
	PR4589
	PR4594
	PR4595
	PR4611
	PR4611.A73
	PR4634
	PR4639.E29
	PR4650
	PR4656
	PR4658
	PR4664
	PR4670
	PR4681
	PR4681.A3
	PR4682
	PR4688
	PR4692.E8
	PR4699.E85
	PR4706
	PR4710
	PR4710.C7
	PR4711
	PR4716
	PR4729.G5
	PR4746
	PR4747
	PR4748
	PR4750
	PR4752
	PR4753
	PR4754
	PR4757.L3
	PR4757.S4
	PR4809.H2
	PR4843
	PR4854
	PR4876
	PR4881
	PR4931
	PR4967
	PR4972.M5
	PR5005
	PR5006
	PR5013
	PR5014
	PR5014.L8
	PR5016
	PR5022
	PR5043
	PR5089.M7
	PR5112.O55
	PR5113
	PR5122
	PR5134
	PR5194
	PR5210
	PR5214
	PR5236.R27
	PR5349.S42
	PR5451
	PR5481
	PR5484.B3
	PR5484.I7
	PR5484.K5
	PR5485
	PR5486
	PR5488
	PR5493
	PR5499.S1
	PR5499.S19
	PR5499.S4
	PR5608
	PR5612
	PR5614
	PR5618
	PR5631
	PR5631.A3
	PR5632
	PR5638
	PR5684
	PR5686
	PR5687
	PR5742
	PR5782
	PR5795.W7
	PR5816
	PR5913
	PR5922
	PR6003.A527
	PR6003.A65
	PR6005.A53
823.8	PR6005.L77
	PR6013.R19
	PR6015.I4
	PR6015.O687
	PR6021
	PR6031.E4
	PR6037.T617
	PR6045.E95
	PR6045.O72
	PS1449.C7
	PS3505.R765
	PS3523.I664
	PZ3.D55
	PZ3.G45
	PZ3.H222
	PZ3.W5862
	PZ6.H836
	PZ6.T8
	PZ8.D666
	PZ8.J35
823.807	PR115
823.808	PR1297
	PR1301
	PR1309.D4
823.80803	PR1309.D4
823.80806	PR1309.H6
823.809	PN761
	PR453
	PR783
	PR871
	PR4168
	PR4169
	PR4174.B2
	PR4581
823.8093	PR868.I7
	PR871
823.90803	PR1309.H6
823.91	PR6023.O35
823.9108	PR1309.C7
	PR1309.D4
	PS535.5
	PS659
823.910803	PR1307.B8
	PS648.D4
	PS648.M6
	PS648.S3
	SF301
823.9109	PR826
	PR881
	PR888.C47
823.912	CT1218.P59
	GR580
	ML3925
	ML3925.B12M43
	ML3925.S318
	PR4074
	PR4076
	PR4099.B5
	PR4174.B6
	PR4453
	PR4454.C2
	PR4621
	PR4622
	PR4623
	PR4624
	PR4759.H37
	PR4762
	PR4787
	PR4809.H18
	PR4821.J2
	PR4825.J3
	PR4826.J58
	PR5113
	PR5177
	PR5194
	PR5365
	PR5671.T85
	PR5772
	PR5774
	PR5774.M4
	PR5774.W6
	PR5776
	PR5777
	PR5816
	PR5920
	PR5922
	PR6000.A1
	PR6001.L4
	PR6001.L72
	PR6001.M48
	PR6001.R7
	PR6001.R75
	PR6001.S42
	PR6001.U47
	PR6001.U8
	PR6003
	PR6003.A35
	PR6003.A374
	PR6003.A484
	PR6003.A525
	PR6003.A528
	PR6003.A543
	PR6003.A67
	PR6003.A679
	PR6003.A9
	PR6003.A965
	PR6003.E215
	PR6003.E23
	PR6003.E282
	PR6003.E6
	PR6003.E73
	PR6003.I2
	PR6003.L3
	PR6003.L58
823.912	PR6003.L79
	PR6003.O66
	PR6003.O6757
	PR6003.R458
	PR6003.R673
	PR6003.U13
	PR6003.U153
	PR6003.U26
	PR6003.U55
	PR6003.U63
	PR6003.Y43
	PR6005.A225
	PR6005.A486
	PR6005.A4868
	PR6005.A765
	PR6005.A83
	PR6005.H28
	PR6005.H348
	PR6005.H52
	PR6005.H66
	PR6005.H8
	PR6005.L8
	PR6005.O36534
	PR6005.O366
	PR6005.O3895
	PR6005.O4
	PR6005.O44
	PR6005.O55
	PR6005.O65
	PR6005.O85
	PR6005.R517
	PR6005.R673
	PR6005.R68
	PR6005.R7
	PR6005.O4
	PR6007.A237
	PR6007.A78
	PR6007.E3
	PR6007.E33
	PR6007.E36
	PR6007.E375
	PR6007.E635
	PR6007.E6429
	PR6007.I33
	PR6007.R3
	PR6007.U467
	PR6007.U47
	PR6007.U535
	PR6007.U554
	PR6007.U6
	PR6007.U76
	PR6009.D63
	PR6009.D7
	PR6009.R8
	PR6009.U8
	PR6009.V24
	PR6009.Y83
	PR6011.A67
	PR6011.A75
	PR6011.I49
	PR6011.I7
	PR6011.L15
	PR6011.L5
	PR6011.O56
	PR6011.O58
	PR6011.O65
	PR6011.R28
	PR6013.A5
	PR6013.A83
	PR6013.E183
	PR6013.E68
	PR6013.I233
	PR6013.I24
	PR6013.I25
	PR6013.O2
	PR6013.O35
	PR6013.O49
	PR6013.O74
	PR6013.R19
	PR6013.R25
	PR6013.R278
	PR6013.R416
	PR6013.R44
	PR6013.U64
	PR6015.A33
	PR6015.A46
	PR6015.A474
	PR6015.A48
	PR6015.A6425
	PR6015.A6723
	PR6015.E47
	PR6015.E56
	PR6015.E58
	PR6015.E795
	PR6015.I3
	PR6015.O5
	PR6015.O857
	PR6015.U35
	PR6015.U565
	PR6015.U76
	PR6015.U9
	PR6015.Y6
	PR6017.N79
	PR6017.R84
	PR6019.A2
	PR6019.A29
	PR6019.A67
	PR6019.E57
	PR6019.O3938
	PR6019.O66
	PR6019.O9
	PR6021.E65
	PR6021.E718
	PR6021.O4
823.912	PR6023.A9
	PR6023.A93
	PR6023.A935
	PR6023.E15
	PR6023.E77
	PR6023.E83
	PR6023.E926
	PR6023.E955
	PR6023.I3
	PR6023.I56
	PR6023.I5817
	PR6023.I7
	PR6023.I73
	PR6023.L47
	PR6023.O144
	PR6023.O35
	PR6023.O45
	PR6023.O95
	PR6023.O96
	PR6023.U3
	PR6023.Y43
	PR6024.A654
	PR6025.A16
	PR6025.A245
	PR6025.A2516
	PR6025.A25257
	PR6025.A2526
	PR6025.A2547
	PR6025.A438
	PR6025.A477
	PR6025.A65
	PR6025.A654
	PR6025.A77
	PR6025.A79
	PR6025.A86
	PR6025.E93
	PR6025.I832
	PR6025.I86
	PR6025.O4
	PR6025.O46
	PR6025.O7
	PR6025.U675
	PR6027.I25
	PR6027.O54
	PR6029.F5
	PR6029.M35
	PR6029.P5
	PR6029.R8
	PR6031.A49
	PR6031.E183
	PR6031.O74
	PR6031.O867
	PR6031.O87
	PR6031.O873
	PR6031.R6
	PR6031.R7
	PR6031.R76
	PR6031.O74
	PR6033.U42
	PR6035.A58
	PR6035.A9
	PR6035.A92
	PR6035.E24
	PR6035.E55
	PR6035.H96
	PR6035.I78
	PR6035.O554
	PR6035.O669
	PR6035.O78
	PR6037.A35
	PR6037.C927
	PR6037.I55
	PR6037.I73
	PR6037.I83
	PR6037.M38
	PR6037.M43
	PR6037.N58
	PR6037.T3
	PR6037.T4
	PR6037.T453
	PR6037.T454
	PR6037.T458
	PR6037.T466
	PR6037.T73
	PR6037.W85
	PR6037.Y5
	PR6037.Y57
	PR6039.H43
	PR6039.H48
	PR6039.O32
	PR6039.R35
	PR6039.U75
	PR6041.P9
	PR6043.A3
	PR6043.A85
	PR6045
	PR6045.A22
	PR6045.A327
	PR6045.A339
	PR6045.A812
	PR6045.A8143
	PR6045.A95
	PR6045.A97
	PR6045.E83
	PR6045.H127
	PR6045.H156
	PR6045.H2
	PR6045.I5
	PR6045.I55
	PR6045.O53
	PR6045.O72
	PR6045.Y46
	PR6051.U3
	PR6052.A42

823.912 PR6052.O36
PR6052.O75
PR6052.U563
PR6053.L5
PR6053.O5469
PR6055.W29
PR6056.R287
PR6057.R38
PR6058.I5
PR6060.A3
PR6062.E24
PR6063.A248
PR6063.A353
PR6065.N45
PR6068.A92
PR6068.O15
PR6069.T65
PR6070.H5
PR6070.O65
PR6072.A36
PR6072.A4
PR6073.I56
PS3507.O248
PS3513.R5772
PS3525.A2122
PS3547.O4753
PS3552.R27
PS6013.A5
PT2617.E85
PZ3
PZ3.B847
PZ3.I814
PZ3.R3494
PZ3.S6737
PZ3.W465
PZ10.3.S38514
Z8964.8
823.91208 PR883
PR1309.F3
PS645
823.9120803 PR1309.H6
PR1309.S7
823.912083 SH441
823.91209 PR881
PR883
PR6029.R8
PR6039.R38
PS3523.O335
823.912093 PR883
823.9121 PR6003.L3
823.914 PR6001.B7
PR6001.L6724
PR6001.M6
PR6003.A239
PR6003.A678
PR6003.A745
PR6003.E294
PR6003.E295
PR6003.O6957
PR6005.A7643
PR6005.L36
PR6005.L48
PR6005.L515
PR6005.O15
PR6005.O79
PR6005.R517
PR6005.R58
PR6007.E36
PR6007.U53
PR6009.H39
PR6009.K54
PR6011.I88
PR6011.L46
PR6013.I245
PR6013.I254
PR6013.O35
PR6013.R364
PR6013.T254
PR6015.I3
PR6015.I52
PR6021.I64
PR6021.N416
PR6023.E833
PR6023.E88
PR6023.I582
PR6023.I7
PR6025.A1697
PR6025.A858
PR6025.E5
PR6025.O7546
PR6027.A9
PR6029.G6
PR6031.A215
PR6031.O613
PR6035.O573
PR6037.A75
PR6037.I55
PR6037.T3
PR6037.T458
PR6037.T466
PR6037.T96
PR6037.U936
PR6037.Y46
PR6039.A928
PR6039.E53
PR6039.O8
PR6039.R518
PR6043.E74
PR6045.A249
PR6045.E763
PR6045.I577
PR6051.B5
PR6051.D33
PR6051.D335

823.914 PR6051.D337
PR6051.I35
PR6051.I36
PR6051.I65
PR6051.L28
PR6051.L3
PR6051.L36
PR6051.M3
PR6051.N39
PR6051.N45
PR6051.N48
PR6051.N77
PR6051.S4
PR6051.S45
PR6051.T5
PR6052.A315
PR6052.A319
PR6052.A32
PR6052.A364
PR6052.A37
PR6052.A46
PR6052.A57
PR6052.A648
PR6052.A66
PR6052.A723
PR6052.A725
PR6052.A727
PR6052.A75
PR6052.A83
PR6052.E19
PR6052.E45
PR6052.E545
PR6052.E65
PR6052.E75
PR6052.I4
PR6052.L25
PR6052.L33
PR6052.L34
PR6052.L343
PR6052.L345
PR6052.L5
PR6052.L6
PR6052.O48
PR6052.O65
PR6052.O7
PR6052.O78
PR6052.R24
PR6052.R2625
PR6052.R263
PR6052.R265
PR6052.R269
PR6052.R297
PR6052.R33
PR6052.R36
PR6052.R42
PR6052.R435
PR6052.R444
PR6052.R57
PR6052.R573
PR6052.R583
PR6052.R589
PR6052.R59
PR6052.R617
PR6052.R78
PR6052.R8
PR6052.U42
PR6052.U62
PR6052.U644
PR6052.U645
PR6052.U653
PR6052.U658
PR6052.U669
PR6052.U76
PR6052.U813
PR6052.U85
PR6052.U9
PR6053.A33
PR6053.A36
PR6053.A39
PR6053.A4
PR6053.A46
PR6053.A485
PR6053.A64
PR6053.A686
PR6053.A697
PR6053.A73
PR6053.A75
PR6053.E3
PR6053.H2
PR6053.H283
PR6053.H363
PR6053.H373
PR6053.H57
PR6053.H75
PR6053.H78
PR6053.L283
PR6053.L294
PR6053.L318
PR6053.L324
PR6053.L38
PR6053.L4
PR6053.L44
PR6053.L5
PR6053.L8
PR6053.O367
PR6053.O38
PR6053.O4
PR6053.O412
PR6053.O414
PR6053.O419
PR6053.O424
PR6053.O425
PR6053.O427
PR6053.O448

823.914 PR6053.O45
PR6053.O523
PR6053.O525
PR6053.O546
PR6053.O5469
PR6053.O555
PR6053.O6
PR6053.O65
PR6053.O67
PR6053.O76
PR6053.O8
PR6053.O94
PR6053.O954
PR6053.O97
PR6053.R3
PR6053.R37
PR6053.R377
PR6053.R57
PR6053.U415
PR6053.U7
PR6053.O5464
PR6054.A35
PR6054.A38
PR6054.A79
PR6054.A873
PR6054.A875
PR6054.A883
PR6054.A886
PR6054.E23
PR6054.E35
PR6054.E37
PR6054.E38
PR6054.E4
PR6054.E45
PR6054.E9
PR6054.I2
PR6054.I35
PR6054.I4
PR6054.I6
PR6054.O45
PR6054.O78
PR6054.R25
PR6054.R28
PR6054.R55
PR6054.R78
PR6054.R79
PR6054.R9
PR6054.U4
PR6054.U45
PR6054.U46
PR6054.U56
PR6054.U6
PR6054.U7
PR6054.Y4
PR6054.Y5
PR6055.A83
PR6055.A84
PR6055.D35
PR6055.D4
PR6055.D43
PR6055.D47
PR6055.D8
PR6055.D95
PR6055.G35
PR6055.L48
PR6055.L484
PR6055.L49
PR6055.N35
PR6055.S7
PR6055.V3
PR6056.
PR6056.A48
PR6056.A75
PR6056.E25
PR6056.E38
PR6056.E4
PR6056.E63
PR6056.I455
PR6056.I46
PR6056.I79
PR6056.L415
PR6056.O4
PR6056.O684
PR6056.O693
PR6056.O695
PR6056.O85
PR6056.O88
PR6056.R265
PR6056.R27
PR6056.R287
PR6056.R292
PR6056.R4
PR6056.R42
PR6056.R45
PR6056.R48
PR6056.R53
PR6056.U435
PR6057.A294
PR6057.A34
PR6057.A39
PR6057.A63
PR6057.A675
PR6057.A73
PR6057.A8
PR6057.E2
PR6057.E53
PR6057.I2
PR6057.I53
PR6057.I58
PR6057.I6
PR6057.L28
PR6057.L35
PR6057.L6
PR6057.L97

823.914 PR6057.O415
PR6057.O44
PR6057.O65
PR6057.O67
PR6057.R235
PR6057.R25
PR6057.R55
PR6057.U415
PR6058
PR6058.A438
PR6058.A444
PR6058.A547
PR6058.A552
PR6058.A554
PR6058.A58
PR6058.A59
PR6058.A676
PR6058.A6886
PR6058.A6915
PR6058.A6919
PR6058.A692
PR6058.A6949
PR6058.A698
PR6058.A73
PR6058.A79
PR6058.A8
PR6058.A82
PR6058.A98
PR6058.E25
PR6058.E493
PR6058.E52
PR6058.E68
PR6058.E69
PR6058.I25
PR6058.I35
PR6058.I45
PR6058.I5
PR6058.I52
PR6058.I54
PR6058.I55
PR6058.I7
PR6058.O24
PR6058.O5
PR6058.O88
PR6058.O98
PR6058.U2
PR6058.U36
PR6058.U365
PR6058.U53
PR6058.U7
PR6058.U85
PR6058.Y6
PR6059.R95
PR6060.E2
PR6060.E43
PR6060.O24
PR6060.O3
PR6060.O33
PR6060.O43
PR6060.O495
PR6060.O56
PR6060.O57
PR6060.O576
PR6060.O58
PR6060.O6
PR6060.O62
PR6060.O64
PR6060.U3
PR6061.A95
PR6061.E26
PR6061.E495
PR6061.E59
PR6061.E63
PR6061.E675
PR6061.I37
PR6061.I45
PR6061.I49
PR6061.I8
PR6061.N55
PR6061.N6
PR6061.O6
PR6062.A35
PR6062.A37
PR6062.A47
PR6062.A53
PR6062.A75
PR6062.A88
PR6062.E24
PR6062.E446
PR6062.E5
PR6062.E89
PR6062.E954
PR6062.E955
PR6062.I36
PR6062.I43
PR6062.I48
PR6062.I8
PR6062.L4
PR6062.O516
PR6062.O67
PR6062.O72
PR6062.O75
PR6062.O77
PR6062.O86
PR6062.O88
PR6062.Y3
PR6062.Y47
PR6062.Y5
PR6062.Y53
PR6062.Y62
PR6062.Y8
PR6062.Y85
PR6063.A163
PR6063.A1635

823.914	PR6063.A167
	PR6063.A175
	PR6063.A2176
	PR6063.A218
	PR6063.A234
	PR6063.A235
	PR6063.A239
	PR6063.A2423
	PR6063.A246
	PR6063.A2468
	PR6063.A247
	PR6063.A248
	PR6063.A249
	PR6063.A2495
	PR6063.A2498
	PR6063.A253
	PR6063.A257
	PR6063.A274
	PR6063.A278
	PR6063.A33
	PR6063.A347
	PR6063.A353
	PR6063.A375
	PR6063.A384
	PR6063.A64
	PR6063.A655
	PR6063.A675
	PR6063.A85
	PR6063.A883
	PR6063.A885
	PR6063.A89
	PR6063.E44
	PR6063.E86
	PR6063.I25
	PR6063.I33
	PR6063.I5
	PR6063.I7
	PR6063.I793
	PR6063.I8
	PR6063.O49
	PR6063.O496
	PR6063.O59
	PR6063.O68
	PR6063.O748
	PR6063.O75
	PR6063.O82
	PR6063.O9
	PR6063.U7
	PR6063.U733
	PR6064
	PR6064.A35
	PR6064.A94
	PR6064.E86
	PR6064.E92
	PR6064.F92
	PR6064.I17
	PR6064.I25
	PR6064.O2
	PR6064.O4
	PR6064.Y4
	PR6065.
	PR6065.A38
	PR6065.B7
	PR6065.C65
	PR6065.D6
	PR6065.H28
	PR6065.S17
	PR6065.S8
	PR6065.V39
	PR6066.A39
	PR6066.A45
	PR6066.E18
	PR6066.E63
	PR6066.E65
	PR6066.E756
	PR6066.H463
	PR6066.H48
	PR6066.H54
	PR6066.I38
	PR6066.L26
	PR6066.L6
	PR6066.O38
	PR6066.O5
	PR6066.O72
	PR6066.O78
	PR6066.O93
	PR6066.R55
	PR6066.R57
	PR6066.U4
	PR6067.U3
	PR6067.U35
	PR6067.U4
	PR6067.U5
	PR6067.U55
	PR6068.A25
	PR6068.A337
	PR6068.A8
	PR6068.A9
	PR6068.A93
	PR6068.A947
	PR6068.A949
	PR6068.A95
	PR6068.E25
	PR6068.E35
	PR6068.E367
	PR6068.E37
	PR6068.E42
	PR6068.E63
	PR6068.E68
	PR6068.E7
	PR6068.I244
	PR6068.I35
	PR6068.I38
	PR6068.I77
823.914	PR6068.O145
	PR6068.O15
	PR6068.O257
	PR6068.O48
	PR6068.O816
	PR6068.O82
	PR6068.O83
	PR6068.O835
	PR6068.O84
	PR6068.O98
	PR6068.U2
	PR6068.U87
	PR6068.Y35
	PR6069.A42
	PR6069.A426
	PR6069.A48
	PR6069.A515
	PR6069.A53
	PR6069.A935
	PR6069.A94
	PR6069.A96
	PR6069.C53
	PR6069.C598
	PR6069.E38
	PR6069.H38
	PR6069.H39
	PR6069.H395
	PR6069.H396
	PR6069.H42
	PR6069.H5
	PR6069.H7
	PR6069.H75
	PR6069.H8
	PR6069.I42
	PR6069.K54
	PR6069.L25
	PR6069.M52
	PR6069.M565
	PR6069.M58
	PR6069.O87
	PR6069.P48
	PR6069.T428
	PR6069.T455
	PR6069.T458
	PR6069.T46
	PR6069.T63
	PR6069.T68
	PR6069.T695
	PR6069.T78
	PR6069.U32
	PR6069.U4
	PR6069.Y4
	PR6069.Y5
	PR6070.A25
	PR6070.A56
	PR6070.A62
	PR6070.A68
	PR6070.A7
	PR6070.A75
	PR6070.A8
	PR6070.A92
	PR6070.E4
	PR6070.E5
	PR6070.H647
	PR6070.H66
	PR6070.H678
	PR6070.I4
	PR6070.I45
	PR6070.I5
	PR6070.O5
	PR6070.R34
	PR6070.R38
	PR6070.R4
	PR6070.R45
	PR6070.U22
	PR6070.U23
	PR6070.U25
	PR6070.U5
	PR6070.U75
	PR6070.U77
	PR6070.U79
	PR6070.Y4
	PR6070.Y63
	PR6070.Y8
	PR6071.N8
	PR6071.U8
	PR6072.A65
	PR6072.A76
	PR6072.I9
	PR6072.O8
	PR6073.A425
	PR6073.A427
	PR6073.A47
	PR6073.A7215
	PR6073.A723
	PR6073.A82
	PR6073.A86
	PR6073.A865
	PR6073.A93
	PR6073.E26
	PR6073.E38
	PR6073.E74
	PR6073.E76
	PR6073.H4
	PR6073.H43
	PR6073.H49
	PR6073.H494
	PR6073.H498
	PR6073.H52
	PR6073.H53
	PR6073.I415
	PR6073.I4258
	PR6073.I426
	PR6073.I4332
823.914	PR6073.I44
	PR6073.I466
	PR6073.I4678
	PR6073.I48
	PR6073.I7225
	PR6073.I77
	PR6073.O4
	PR6073.O45
	PR6073.O47
	PR6073.O58
	PR6073.O616
	PR6073.O62
	PR6073.O63
	PR6073.Y65
	PR6075.A7
	PR6076.E5
	PS3551.S5
	PS3552.E3
	PS3553.A85
	PS3556.O744
	PS3557.L6
	PS3558.E26
	PS3564.O62
	PS3569.H392
	PS3573.Y6
	PS6054.O45
	PS6069.A94
	PZ4.C9214
	PZ4.E22
	PZ4.J856
	PZ4.P883
	PZ4.R8294
	PZ4.S735
	PZ7.L7397
	PZ7.W16826
	PZ8.P555
	PZ8.1.W54
	PZ10.C5713
	SF442
823.91408	PN6110.P3
	PR1307
	PR1307.F5
	PR6039.O75
	PS374.S35
823.9140803	PR1309.G5
	PR1309.S3
	PZ5.K67
823.91409	PR881
824	PR6005.O38
	PR6025.U694
	PR6063.A175
	PR6076.E2
824.008	PR1323
	PR1363
824.0091	PR1367
824.1	PR1119
824.3	PR2206
824.4	PR3729.T2
824.5	PR925
	PR3306
	PR3621
	PR3706
824.508	PR1365
	PR3302
824.509	PR925
824.6	PA4229.L6
	PR3485.C6
	PR3487
	PR3522
824.7	PR4480
	PR4771
	PR4773
	PR4813
	PR4863
	PR5162
824.8	PR453
	PR4349.B7
	PR4433
	PR4433.A5
	PR4606
	PR4881
	PR5021.M3
	PR5136
	PR5137
	PR5138.E8
	PR5488
	PR5522
	PR5899.W9
	PR5899.Y6
	PR6025.I66
824.808	PR1366
824.908	PS688
824.9108	PR1367
824.912	AC8
	PR4099.B5
	PR4453.C4
	PR5271.R5
	PR6001.D3
	PR6001.U4
	PR6003.E4
	PR6003.E45
	PR6003.O676
	PR6005.L9
	PR6005.O4
	PR6009.L8
	PR6013.A6
	PR6013.R44
	PR6013.W8
	PR6015.U223
	PR6015.U58
	PR6015.U9
	PR6019.A24
	PR6023.U24
	PR6023.Y42
824.912	PR6025.A225
	PR6031.O87
	PR6031.R6
	PR6035.E24
	PR6035.I4
	PR6039.O35
	PR6043.I45
	PR6045.O68
825.04	HV5071
825.06	PR618
825.8	PR4854
	PR5072
825.912	PN1991.4.M8
	PR6013.R735
825.914	PS3545.I52966
826.4	DA429.T2
826.5	DA501.M7
	PR3706
826.6	PK109.J6
	PR3383.A3
826.7	PR5881
826.8	PR1343
	PR4023
	PR5238
	PR5493
826.912	PR6031.O87
	PR6039.H52
827	D10
	PN6178.A8
	PR6065.G74
827.008	PN6149.S4
	PN6153
	PN6173
	PN6175
	PN6178.S4
	PR1119
827.009	PR931
	PR932
827.28	VM451
827.3	PR2243
	PR2288
	PR2326.N3
	PR2544
	PR2694
827.308	PN6175
827.5	AS36
	PR3339.C23
	PR3724
	PR3724.G8
	PR3726
	PR3727
	PR3734
	PR6058.O28
827.509	PR935
827.6	PN6193.M8
	PR3485
827.7	PR4794.H5
827.8	PR4349.B7
	PR5812
827.9108	PN6162
827.910803	PN6231.C46
827.912	PR4821.J2
	PR6011.U55
827.914	PN6175
	PR6013.L43
	PR6037.H54
	PR6041.S73
	PR6054.O28
	PR6058.O28
827.91408	PN6175
	PN6178.B5
828	PR5299.S4
	PR5900
	PR6003.E417
	PR6005.L774
	PR6007.E6427
	PR6019.O9
	PR6029.D58
	PR6031.A384
	PR6031.A757
	PR6037.L4
	PR6043.A378
	PR6045.H19
	PR6051.T47
	PZ10.M1115
828.008	PN6071.G53
	PR9530
828.00803	PN4241
	PN6071.F3
828.02	PN6014
	PN6081
	PN6083
	PN6281
	PN6291
	PN6331
	PR509.E73
	PR1191
	PR2567
828.03	PR8610
828.08	PR1283
	PR1285
828.0808	PR1283
828.208	PR1105
	PR1293
828.209	PR2209.B2
828.308	PR2214.B4
	PR2233.C8
	PR2287
	PR2303
	PR2326.N3
	PR2544.G73
	PR2626
	PR3507
828.309	PR2298

Dewey	LC
828.309	PR2303
	PR2340.A5
	PR2544
	PR2546
	PR2631
828.403	DA447.P4
	PR3433.E5
	PR3570
828.408	B1201.B64
	BR75
	DA390.1.S4
	DA447.P4
	PR3327
	PR3329
	PR3330
	PR3331
	PR3332
	PR3338
	PR3422
	PR3594
828.409	PR3317
	PR3327
	PR3671
828.508	PR3401
	PR3408
	PR3726
828.509	PA85.B4
	PR3400
	PR3406
	PR3473
828.602	PR3522
828.603	PR3325
828.608	PR1297
	PR3325
	PR3714
	PR4023
	PR5841.W8
828.60808	PR9799
828.609	PR3325
	PR3359.C5
	PR3493
	PR3520
	PR3533
	PR3533.B7
	PR3534
	PR3541.L27
	PR3605.M6
	PR5398
	PR5841.W8
828.703	PR5056
	PR5334
	PR5849
828.708	PR3359.C5
	PR5162
	PR5233.R2
828.70808	PN6251
828.709	PR4599.D6
	PR4813
	PR4865.L8
	PR5163
	PR5331
	PR5332
	PR5338
	PR5341
828.8	PR4238
828.803	PR4193
828.808	BX4705.N5
	PQ5263
	PR4024
	PR4422
	PR4433
	PR4453.C6
	PR4536
	PR4552
	PR4825.J4
	PR5216
	PR5264
	PR5473.S6
	PR5488
	PR5811
828.809	AC1
	PR4024
	PR4062
	PR4156
	PR4263
	PR4349.B7
	PR4536
	PR4606
	PR4612
	PR4703
	PR4725.G7
	PR4754
	PR4783
	PR4784
	PR4823
	PR4850
	PR4856
	PR4886.L4
	PR5263
	PR5356
	PR5513
	PR5523
	PR5650
	PR5823
	PR5824
	PR6015.U23
828.910807	LB1631
828.912	PR4453.C4
828.91203	PR6001.C7
	PR6001.S68Z543
	PR6013.R39
	PR6023.U24
	PR6037.Y43
	PR6045.E76
828.91203	PR6072.A4
828.91208	BX4705.V33
	PQ2613.I2
	PR4759.H37
	PR4787
	PR6003.E4
	PR6007.U67
	PR6009.L8
	PR6011.O58
	PR6013.A5
	PR6013.A66
	PR6013.R19
	PR6013.R35
	PR6013.R735
	PR6023
	PR6023.U65
	PR6025.A86
	PR6025.O572
	PR6029.R8
	PR6031.O725
	PR6039.H52
828.91209	N8375.R43
	PR4076
	PR4453.C4
	PR6003.A35
	PR6003.A67
	PR6003.E4
	PR6003.E437
	PR6003.E45
	PR6003.L8
	PR6005.R7
	PR6007.U76
	PR6011.O53
	PR6011.O58
	PR6013.R35
	PR6013.R44
	PR6015.A19
	PR6015.O864
	PR6015.U9
	PR6017.N3
	PR6023.A93
	PR6023.E97
	PR6023.U24
	PR6025.A25295
	PR6025.A77
	PR6025.U8
	PR6029.R8
	PR6031.I53
	PR6031.R6
	PR6035.A7
	PR6035.E24
	PR6035.U7
	PR6037.T94
	PR6039.U64
	PR6064.O74
	PS3509.L43
828.914	PR6056.I5
	PR6064.U8
	PR6065.N6
828.91403	PR6001.L72
	PR6007.U53
	PR6052.A85
828.91408	PR6051.L3
	PR6066.R95
	PR6068.A75
	SF442
828.9140808	PS647.S4
828.91409	PR6001.N475
	PR6073.I44
829	AS262
	PR179.V4
	PR1508
	PR1530
	PR1543
	PR1545
829.09	PR173
	PR255.W8
829.1	PR173
	PR191
	PR203
	PR1508
	PR1609.A3
	PR1762
	PR1786
829.108	PR1505
829.3	PR1580
	PR1583
	PR1585
	PR1585.A2
	PR1588
829.4	PR1645.A3
829.91208	PR6005.O4
830.8	PT1105
	PT1113
830.9	AS36
	PT36
	PT91
	PT107
	PT123.G7
830.9004	PT238
830.9006	PT362
830.9007	PT341
	PT343
830.9008	PT395
830.90091	PT91
	PT405
	PT1113
	PT3705
830.900912	PT403
830.93	PT139
	PT313
830.9973	Z473
831	GR110.P4
	PT2374.Z5
831	PT2639.T28
831.008	PT1155
831.04	PT571
831.109	PT217
831.2	PT1522.F4
	PT1564.F7
	PT1575.A1
	PT1671
	PT1673
	PT1688
831.209	PT217
831.3	PT1522.F53
831.6	PT1802.A35
	PT1925
	PT1941.A1
	PT2027.A8
	PT2027.L53
	PT2051
	PT2060
	PT2139.B49
	PT2143.A2
	PT2166
	PT2177
	PT2193
	PT2328
	PT2482
831.609	PT1965
831.7	PT2316.A4
	PT2328
	PT2329.A3
	PT2340
	PT2434.Z5
831.8	PT2613.E47
831.9108	PT1174
831.912	PT2601.R7
	PT2603.E46
	PT2617.E85
	PT2635.I65
	PT2639.T67
831.91208	PT1160.E8
831.91209	PT551
831.914	PT2611.R596
	PT2621.R695
	PT2637.A4184
	PT2662.I39
	PT2662.O68
	PT2685.Y77
832	PT2617.A83
832.5	PT1734
832.6	PT1828.B6
	PT1938
	PT2026
	PT2026.F2
	PT2257
	PT2452.R25
	PT2473
	PT2473.T3
	PT2499
832.609	PT643
	PT1965
832.7	PT2253.G3
	PT2296
832.709	PT652
832.912	PN1997
	PT2603.R397
	PT2611.R814
	PT2639.T5
	PT2653.U33
	PT2667.O44
832.91208	PT1258
832.91209	PT668
832.914	PR6073.A86
	PT2607.U493
	PT2668.A5
	PT2668.O3
	PT2681.P48
	PT2685.E5
833.02	PT747.S6
	PT1338.S73
833.6	PT1982
	PT2027
	PT2293
	PT2359.H2
	PT2360
	PT2361
	PZ8
	PZ8.G882
	PZ8.H293
833.7	PT2525.H5
833.8	PT1812.A3S3
	PT2374
	PT2461.S3
833.9108	PT1338
833.9109	PT772
833.912	PR4759.H3
	PT772
	PT2607.I6
	PT2611.R23
	PT2615.A18
	PT2617.E85
	PT2621.A26
	PT2623.A81
	PT2625.A43
	PT2625.A44
	PT2627.E73
	PT2631.L6
	PT2635.E68
	PT2638.N5
	PT2640
	PT2647.A3
	PT2647.A64
	PT2653.W4
	PT3919.T7
833.91209	PT772
833.914	E59.F6
	PT2601.I26
	PT2601.N353
	PT2603
	PT2603.O13
	PT2603.O394
	PT2611.U53
	PT2613.R338
	PT2621.I76
	PT2639.I63
	PT2653.W425
	PT2662.E7
	PT2662.I3
	PT2664.E28
	PT2668.E7
	PT2668.O72
	PT2670.O36
	PT2671.R76
	PT2672.O3
	PT2673.U8
	PT2675.T8
	PT2676.A6
	PT2676.A94
	PT2676.E74
	PT2678.A84
	PT2680.N38
	PT2680.O374
	PT2685.E5
	PT2685.O36
	PZ4.G956
	PZ7.R4154
835.631	PL898.O3
836.4	PA8535
838.608	PT1824.B52
	PT2423.L4
838.609	PT2503.S7
838.709	PT1856.Z5
838.809	PT2374
838.91209	PQ2605.O15
	PT2603.E46
838.914	PT2662.U714
838.91409	PT2601.I26
	PT2603.O13
	PT2613.R338
	PT2672.I48
839	PT7077
839.0913	PJ5129.R58
839.3109004	PT5076.E5
839.311008	PT5969.N7
839.311308	PT5969.N7
839.31164	PT5881
	PT5881.25.O8
839.31364	PT5881.18.E3
839.316209	PT5180
839.32362	PT6442.O8
839.363008	PT6555
839.3634	PT6592.22.E7
	PT6592.28.A2
839.368503	CT1929
839.5	PT7083
839.509	PT7063
	PT7067
839.61	PT7233
	PT7234.E5
839.63	PT7269.L4
	PT7287.O7
	PT7287.S6
839.68	PT7220
839.6934	PT7511.L3
839.6993	PT7599.B7
839.71	PZ8.3.J265
839.715	PT9831.E5
839.726	PT9804
	PT9811.A3
	PT9814
	PT9815
839.736	PT9814
	PT9875.H2
839.7372	PT9757
	PT9767
	PT9767.D7
	PT9875.J6
	PT9875.Z4
839.7374	PT9875.H33
	PT9876.1.L46
	PT9876.14.E55
	PT9876.19.S2
	PT9876.29.J63
	PT9876.29.U5
	PT9876.33.A35
839.81172	PT8175.H365
	PT8175.J73
839.8126	PT8152.A5
839.81272	PT8175.K3
839.8127408	PT8006.E5
839.8136	PZ8.A542
839.81372	PT8175.A38
	PT8175.H33
839.81374	PT8176.12.O34
	PT8176.12.O34
	PT8176.18.O44
839.8209006	PT8363
839.8216	PT8937
839.8226	PT8854
	PT8868
	PT8876
	PT8881
	PT8890
	PT8895
839.8236	PT8811
	PT8904
	PT8913
839.82372	PT8950.A5
	PT8950.H3

Dewey	LC
839.82372	PT8950.U5
	PT8950.V42
	PT9088.V6
839.82374	PT8950.B528
	PT8951.18.A6
839.82472	PT8950.U5
839.8272	PT8950.V42
839.8336	PT8811
839.8372	PT8175.A38
840.09	PQ145.5
840.8	PQ1113
840.8004	PQ1126
840.80091	PQ1113
840.9	PQ36
	PQ53
	PQ103
	PQ118
	PQ119
	PQ139
	PQ145
	PQ146
	PQ241
	PQ2637.A82
	PR6015.U9
840.9001	PQ151
840.9004	PQ247
840.9005	PQ103
	PQ261
840.9006	PQ283
840.9007	PQ287
840.9008	PQ139
	PQ294
	PQ296
840.90091	PQ306
	PQ307.L6
	PQ2625.A93
840.900912	PQ150.C3
840.900914	PT405
840.914	PQ292
840.9352	PQ145.7.J4
840.938	PQ233
841	PQ3989.F35
	PQ3989.S47
841.008	PQ1165
	PQ1170.E6
841.09	PQ437
841.1	PB10
	PC13
	PN57.T8
	PQ203
	PQ1301
	PQ1302.E5
	PQ1445.L5
	PQ1445.Y8
	PQ1445.Y83
	PQ1448
	PQ1451
	PQ1459
	PQ1463
	PQ1475
	PQ1489.L33
	PQ1494
	PQ1521.E5
	PQ1522
	PQ1525
	PQ1528
	PQ1530
	PQ1532.R7
	PQ1537
	PR1119
	PR1989.G6
	PR2065
841.108	PQ1322
841.109	PC2864
	PC3315
	PQ155.P73
	PQ201
841.2	PQ1553.C5
	PQ1593
841.3	DG540.8.C8
	PB13
	PQ1677
	PQ1680.P6
841.309	PQ417
841.4	PN99.F82
	PQ1722
	PQ1793
	PQ1812
841.5	PQ2086
841.6	CJ5649
841.7	PQ2326
	PQ2328
841.70914	PQ434
841.7093	PQ436
841.8	PQ2191.Z5
	PQ2323.L8
	PQ2344
	PQ2344.Z5
	PQ2387.R5
	PQ2459.V9
	PQ2463
	PQ2464
841.808	PQ1170.E6
841.809	PQ438
	PQ439
	PQ1170.E6
841.80915	PQ439
841.9108	PQ1170.E6
841.9109	PQ443
	PQ1184
841.910915	PQ443
841.912	PQ2601.P6
	PQ2601.R677
	PQ2603.R35
841.912	PQ2605.H3345
	PQ2605.L2
	PQ2605.O15
	PQ2613.E54
	PQ2631.E25
	PQ2631.O643
	PQ2635.E85
	PQ2637.E33
	PQ2643.A26
	PT2613.O64
841.91209	PQ443
841.914	PQ2605.E74
	PZ8.3.F8477
	PZ24.3
842	PQ2603.E72673
	PQ2625.A6
	PQ2631.I37
	PQ3919.2.D76
	PQ3989.2.K6
842.009	PQ511
	PR8783
842.009109	PQ558
842.052	PQ566
	PQ1342.E5
842.109	PQ513
842.3	PQ1625.G2
842.4	PQ1647.M4
	PQ1745.E5
	PQ1825.E5
	PQ1827.A3
	PQ1833.A3
	PQ1834.F7
	PQ1835
	PQ1837
	PQ1852
	PQ1860
	PQ1892.A3
	PQ1904
	PQ1915.Z5
842.409	PQ526
842.5	PQ1956
	PQ1963.C57
	PQ1997
	PQ2003.Z5
842.8	PQ2154.A6
	PQ2476.V4
	PQ2619.A65
	PQ2635.O7
842.9108	PQ1223
842.9109	PQ558
842.912	PN1997
	PQ2601.N67
	PQ2601.R677
	PQ2605.L2
	PQ2605.O15
	PQ2611.E86
	PQ2613.E53
	PQ2613.I74
	PQ2637.A82
	PQ2639.A72
842.914	PQ2601.N67
	PQ2601.R65
	PQ2603.E378
	PQ2605.O7874
	PQ2617.O6
	PQ2629.B3
	PQ2637.A783
	PQ2664.U28
843	PQ1541
	PQ2193.B39
	PQ2673.A762
	PQ2679.T67
	PQ3919.T4
	PQ3949.T45
	PQ3989.O8
	PQ3989.O9
	PQ3989.2.O8
	PT9814
	PZ6
843.008	PQ3985
	PQ3985.5
843.009	PQ631
	PQ651
843.03	PQ671
843.108	PQ1391
843.20914	PN816
843.3	PQ1631
	PQ1685.E5
	PQ1694
843.4	PQ1707.U7
	PQ1805.L5
	PQ1919
843.4093	PQ145.7.A2
843.5	PQ1963.C55
	PQ1979.A663
	PQ2063
	PQ2082
	PQ2082.Z5
	PQ2105.A2
843.509	PQ648
843.7	PQ2159
	PQ2168
	PQ2170
	PQ2172
	PQ2178
	PQ2181
	PQ2227
	PQ2246.M2
	PQ2258
	PQ2285.H23
	PQ2289.T7
	PQ2435
843.709	PQ653
843.8	PC13
843.8	PQ2138
	PQ2211.C3
	PQ2216
	PQ2246
	PQ2246.M2
	PQ2246.S3
	PQ2247
	PQ2249
	PQ2254
	PQ2254.I4
	PQ2254.R6
	PQ2254.Z5
	PQ2258.Z5
	PQ2273
	PQ2309.H4
	PQ2349
	PQ2349.A4
	PQ2357
	PQ2412
	PQ2459.V8
	PQ2469
	PQ2472.Z8
	PQ2491
	PQ2496
	PQ2500
	PQ2501
	PQ2504
	PQ2518
	PQ2521.T3
	PQ2528
	PR4752
	PZ3.B666
843.809	PQ1275
843.91	PQ671
843.9108	PQ1278
843.9109	PQ671
843.912	PQ2193.B3
	PQ2364.M7
	PQ2601.P6
	PQ2601.R2
	PQ2601.U4
	PQ2601.V45
	PQ2601.Y5
	PQ2603.A435
	PQ2603.E5875
	PQ2603.O234
	PQ2605.A3734
	PQ2605.E5
	PQ2605.E55
	PQ2605.L4
	PQ2605.O15
	PQ2605.O28
	PQ2607.A558
	PQ2607.E834
	PQ2607.U53
	PQ2607.U8245
	PQ2607.U865
	PQ2611.O85
	PQ2613
	PQ2613.E53
	PQ2613.I2
	PQ2613.I57
	PQ2613.R3
	PQ2615.A25
	PQ2617.S85
	PQ2621.L6
	PQ2623.O8
	PQ2625.A716
	PQ2625.A74
	PQ2625.A93
	PQ2625.O67
	PQ2631.R63
	PQ2635.A25
	PQ2635.O1845
	PQ2635.O96168
	PQ2637.A82
	PQ2637.C63
	PQ2637.I53
	PQ2680.O782
843.91209	PQ671
843.912093	PQ150.C3
843.914	BV2623.T66
	NC1499.U3
	PQ2601.R619
	PQ2603.A74
	PQ2603.U73
	PQ2605.A3734
	PQ2605.A778
	PQ2605.L32
	PQ2605.U55
	PQ2607.E252
	PQ2607.R75
	PQ2607.U865
	PQ2613.A58
	PQ2613.O476
	PQ2613.O4767
	PQ2617.O6
	PQ2623.E3657
	PQ2623.E3849
	PQ2625.A7544
	PQ2625.E5278
	PQ2625.F5278
	PQ2625.O38
	PQ2625.O384
	PQ2631.I49
	PQ2631.O647
	PQ2631.O6476
	PQ2635.O117
	PQ2635.O573
	PQ2637.A584
	PQ2637.A783
	PQ2643.E46
	PQ2662.E5
	PQ2662.E73
843.914	PQ2662.O79
	PQ2662.U25
	PQ2663.O84
	PQ2665.T36
	PQ2667.H4
	PQ2670.U45
	PQ2672.A68
	PQ2672.E25
	PQ2673.A767
	PQ2673.I26
	PQ2673.O3
	PQ2676.R64
	PQ2678.I9
	PQ2679.C38
	PQ2679.O4
	PQ2680.O782
	PQ2680.O83
	PQ2682.I33
	PQ2683.I32
	PQ3919.B6
	PR6003.E282
	PS3557.H6
	PT2611.U436
	PT2670.A3
843.91409	PQ671
844.3	PQ1642.E5
	PQ1642.E6
	PQ1643
844.912	PQ2625
845.5	PQ1979
845.914	PQ2617.O6
846.912	B2430.T374
847.2	PQ1567
847.3	PQ1696
848.108	PR1119
848.4	DC130.T2
848.402	PQ1803.A63
	PQ1815
848.408	PQ1605.B8
848.502	PQ1963.C4
848.509	PQ2043
	PQ2057.S6
	PQ2072
	PQ2075
	PQ2099
	PQ2103.D7
	PQ2105
	PQ2105.A2
	PQ2136
848.608	PQ2431.Z5
848.609	PQ2205
	PQ2205.Z5
848.709	PQ2301
	PQ2362.Z5
	PQ2391.Z5
	PQ2436
848.808	PQ2191
	PQ2254
848.809	PQ2198.B18
	PQ2276.H7
848.91208	PQ2605.O15
	PQ2613.I2
	PQ2625.A95
848.91209	PQ2605.L2
	PQ2605.O15
	PQ2613.E53
	PQ2613.I2
	PQ2613.R3
	PQ2625.A95
	PQ2625.O45
	PQ2637.A82
	PR6003.E282
848.914	PQ2683.I32
848.91408	PQ2679.P6
848.91409	PQ2631.O643
	PR6003.E282
849.09	PC3383
849.1	PC3304
849.12	PC3330.A55
850.8	PQ4205.E5
850.9	PQ4037
	PQ4038.G3
	PQ4043
	PQ4109
850.9001	PA70.I8
850.9008	PQ4046
850.900912	PQ4087
851.009	PQ4092
	PQ4094
851.04	PQ4093
851.1	AS182
	NC1115
	PN511
	PQ4265.A62
	PQ4302
	PQ4305
	PQ4311
	PQ4311.A5
	PQ4315
	PQ4315.2
	PQ4315.4
	PQ4315.58
	PQ4335
	PQ4337
	PQ4339
	PQ4346
	PQ4349
	PQ4363.B21
	PQ4390
	PQ4406
	PQ4412
	PQ4416
	PQ4432.N3
	PQ4443

Dewey	LC
851.1	PQ4447
	PQ4451
	PQ4456
	PQ4464
	PQ4505
851.109	PQ4471.F397
851.3	PQ4587
	PQ4627.M2
851.4	PQ4615.B6
	PQ4642.E21
	PQ4646
851.7	PB13
851.9108	PQ4214
	PQ4225.E8
851.912	PQ4829.O565
	PQ4835.A846
	PQ4837.U3
	PQ4879.O443
851.91209	PQ4841.A18
851.914	PQ4879.A613
852.052	PQ4149
852.309	PQ4149
852.6	PQ4680.E5
	PQ4695.E5
852.912	PQ4835.I7
	PQ4851.A9
852.914	PQ4817.I5
853.01	PQ4254
853.1	PQ4272.E5
853.2	PQ4619.C9
853.7	PQ4714
853.8	PQ4688.F6
	PQ4734.V5
	PQ4841.C482
	PZ8.L887
853.912	PQ4809.E75
	PQ4817.A33
	PQ4817.U193
	PQ4835.A846
	PQ4835.I58
	PQ4841.I4
853.91208	PQ4250.E5
853.91209	PQ4174
853.914	D804.G4
	PQ4807.A79
	PQ4807.E815
	PQ4809.A45
	PQ4809.A682
	PQ4817.I814
	PQ4829.I52
	PQ4835.A83
	PQ4835.R385
	PQ4835.R55
	PQ4841.C4
	PQ4841.O38
	PQ4862.E816
	PQ4867.U3
	PQ4873.A42
	PQ4876.A85
	PQ4879.C54
	PQ4879.E8
	PQ4879.E82
	PZ3
854.912	PQ4835.A27
857.3	PQ4563.R2
858.109	PQ4390
858.309	PQ4627.M2
858.409	PQ4625.G6
858.6	PQ4691
858.808	PQ4841.C482
858.91203	PQ4817.U193
858.91209	PQ4835.A846
859.12	PC839.E5
859.1308	PC871.E3
859.332	PC839.S75
859.334	PC839.E38
859.9	PC959.B5
860.08	PQ7087.E5
860.0944	DP63.82.F7
860.1	PQ6014
860.8006	PQ6267.E1
860.8098	PQ7087.E5
860.9	PQ6033
	PQ6037
	PQ6059
	PQ7081
860.9004	PQ2057.S6
860.9006	F1401
860.9972	PM4068
860.998	PQ7081
861	PQ7297.G615
	PQ7297.G67
	PQ7297.P285
	PQ7384
	PQ7797.B635
	PQ8097.G6
	PQ8097.L47
	PQ8097.N4
	PQ8463.E5
	PQ8497.C5
	PQ8497.V35
	PQ8498.13.I8
861.008	PQ6176
	PQ6208.W5
	PQ6267.E2
	PQ6267.E4
	PQ7084
	PQ7258
861.00803	PQ7084
861.009	PQ7161
861.04	PQ6096.V5
861.1	PQ6374
	PQ6397.S3
	PQ6411.L32
861.3	PQ6398.H6
	PQ6419.N653
	PQ6421
	PQ9156.A2
861.62	PC13
	PQ6503.B3
	PQ6601.L26
	PQ6613.A763
	PQ6613.U5
	PQ6623.A3
	PQ6623.E8
861.6208	PQ6187
	PQ6267.E3
861.6209	PQ6085
861.64	PQ6629.I23
862	PQ7297.C2482
	PQ7439.M265
862.008	PQ7557.E5
862.3	PQ6292.V5
	PQ6300
	PQ6319.A2
	PQ6321.C7
	PQ6327
	PQ6329.A7
	PQ6429.R5
	PQ6439
862.308	PQ6459
862.309	PQ6105
862.409	PQ6119
862.40916	PQ6119
862.5	PQ6603.E6
862.6208	PQ6267.E6
862.64	PN1997.A1
862.6408	PQ6267.E6
863	PQ6625.U6
	PQ7297.F793
	PQ7297.G23
	PQ7297.G3585
	PQ7297.L67
	PQ7389
	PQ7389.C26
	PQ7389.C263
	PQ7489.F4
	PQ7499.A75
	PQ7776
	PQ7797
	PQ7797.A594
	PQ7797.B635
	PQ7797.C7145
	PQ7797.G697
	PQ7797.M74
	PQ7797.M86
	PQ7797.S214
	PQ7820.P7
	PQ8097.B36
	PQ8097.S57
	PQ8180.17.A73
	PQ8219
	PQ8259.R56
	PQ8519.B292
	PQ8549.D53
	PQ9697.P3913
863.008	PQ7535.5
863.009	PQ7081
863.0093	PQ6147.P5
863.2	PQ6277
863.3	PQ6272.Z5
	PQ6324
	PQ6329
	PQ6329.A3
	PQ6337
	PQ6341
	PQ6352
	PQ6353
	PQ6408
863.5	PQ6555
863.62	PQ6639.N3
863.64	PQ6605.E44
	PQ6613.I88
	PQ6613.O79
	PQ6623.A89
	PQ6672.E5
864.2	PQ6523.F3
864.62	PQ7297.R386
868	PQ7297.A6
	PQ7297.P285
	PQ7797.B635
	PQ7797.P665
868.1	PQ6430.A5
868.309	PQ6437.T3
868.408	PQ6523.F5
868.6209	PQ6639.N3
869.09	PQ9512
869.1	PQ9034.N4
	PQ9274.A3
869.3	PQ9697.A4
	PQ9697.A647
	PQ9697.C223
	PQ9697.M18
	PQ9697.V283
	PQ9697.V292
	PQ9697.V298
	PQ9697.V29804
869.33	PQ9261.E3
869.341	PQ9261.N22
869.342	GR235
870.9	PA6003
870.9001	BR67
	PA3081
	PA6004
	PA6007
	PA6011
871.01	PA6217
	PA6271.C3
871.01	PA6274
	PA6276
	PA6374
	PA6393
	PA6393.C9
	PA6411
	PA6484
	PA6502
	PA6519
	PA6519.M9
	PA6520.Z5
	PA6553
	PA6698
	PA6804.B7
	PA6804.G4
	PA6807
	PA6807.G4
	PA6825
	PA6826
	PA6932
	PA6945
871.0108	PA6156
871.0109	PA6050
871.02	PR1539.A4
871.0309	PA8050
871.04	Z8023
872.01	PA6568
	PA6570.A3
	PA6666.A1
	PA6756.A1
	PA6756.A5
872.0108	PA6570.A3
872.03	PA8310.D35
872.04	PA8485.D75
872.4	PA8485.C27
873.01	PA6372
	PA6374
	PA6519
	PA6519.M6
	PA6522
	PA6537
	PA6558
	PA6807.A3
	PA6807.A5
	PA6825
	PS6807
873.0109	PA6559
874.009	PA6059.E6
874.01	PA6274
	PA6274.A2
	PA6275.E5
	PA6393
	PA6393.C43
	PA6411
	PA6442
874.0209	PA8051
874.03	PR1119
875.01	PA6279
	PA6281.R44
	PA6307
	PA6307.A4
	PA6322
	PA6651
876.01	PA6156
	PA6297
	PA6393.E8
876.04	BX1308
877.01	PA6447.E5
	PA6448
	PA6556
	PA6559
877.04	PA8515
878.01	PA6205
878.0103	PA6246
878.0108	PA6498.E6
	PA6716
878.0109	PA6675
	PA6716.Z5
878.0209	PR1578
878.0309	PQ4315.6
878.04	PA8518.A1
880	PA26
	PA39
	PA3001
	PA3003
	PA4414.A2
880.09	PA3003
	PA3040
	PA4247
880.3	PA31
880.8	PA3621
880.9	PA3055
	PA3057
	PA3061
880.9001	PA3016.W7
	PA3054
	PA3061
881.009	PA3092
881.01	B235.P24
	PA3411.H3
	PA3827
	PA3873.A77
	PA4025.A5
	PA4025.H8
	PA4037
	PA4037.A5
	PA4209
	PA4275.E5
	PZ8.1.H75
881.0109	PA3020
	PA3061
	PA3092
882.009	PA3131
	PA3133
882.00916	PA3131
882.01	PA3825.P8
	PA3827
	PA3827.A8
	PA3827.C5
	PA3827.E7
	PA3827.P8
	PA3827.S4
	PA3829.S5
	PA3849
	PA3875
	PA3877
	PA3973
	PA3975
	PA3975.I6
	PA3978
	PA4245.A2
	PA4413
	PA4414
	PA4414.A7
	PA4414.E5
	PA4417
882.0109	PA3131
	PA3133
	PA3136
	PA3187
	PA3553
883.01	PA3855.E5
	PA4023.Z5
	PA4025
	PA4037
	PA4037.Z5
	PA4167
	PA4167.A2
	PA4229.L9
	PA4253.O7
	PR3635
883.0109	PA3105
	PA4037
884.009	PA3020
884.01	PA25
	PA4274
	PA4275.E5
	PA4276.Z8
884.0108	PA3622.A2
884.0109	PA25
885.01	PA3612
	PA3951.E5
	PA4214
	PA4241
885.010803	PA3634
888.002	PN6080
888.0108	PA4382
	PA4387.A2
889.08003	PA5273
889.1209	PA5250
889.132	PA5610.A6
	PA5610.P3
889.134	PA5610.S36
889.234	PA5610.K39
889.332	PA5610.M35
889.334	PA5610.S23
	PA5610.T26
	PA5610.V3
891	PK5401
	PN6071.S33
891.1	PK2978.E5
891.209	PK2903
	PK2907.E5
891.21	PK2916
	PK2917
	PK3106.A1
	PK3741.B53
	PK3791.B4
	PK3798.R77
891.2109	PK2916
891.22	PK2978.E5
	PK3796.S3
891.2209	PK2931
891.23	PK3741.S7
	PK3791.B188
891.28	PK3797
891.29	PK2903
891.4	PK5423
891.4312	PK2095.M5
891.4317	PK2098.B494
891.4336	PK2098.S7
891.4337	PK2098.Y3
891.43913	PK2198.G4
891.4391309	PK2198.M85
891.43915	BP80.I6
	PK2199.I65
891.4409	PK1701
891.441008	PK1771.E3
891.441009	PK1710
891.44104	PK1712
891.4415	PK1722.A2
	PK1723
	PK1725
891.4416	PK1718.J3
891.4417	PK1718.S418
891.4436	PK1718.B298
891.443708	PK1771.E1
891.45	PK1560
	PK1818.9.V5
891.4615	PK2418.G3
891.4634	PK2418.A58
891.49	PK2238.9.P3
891.52	P911.K5
891.5509	PK6406
891.5511	PK6480.E5
	PK6549.S3
891.551108	PK6449.E5
891.6	PB1096

891.6 ..... PB2569
891.6209 ..... PB1321
891.621 ..... PB1421
891.621008 ..... PB1424
891.62108 ..... PB1424
891.6211 ..... PB1429
891.6231 ..... PB1347
..... PB1423.C8G7
891.623109 ..... PB1327
..... PB1423.C8
891.6234 ..... PB1423.C8G7
891.631 ..... PB1648
891.661 ..... PB2273.T73
891.661008 ..... PB2369
891.6611 ..... PB2273.A73
891.661108 ..... PB2369
891.6612 ..... Z732.V8
891.6632 ..... PB2298.H83
891.708 ..... PG3213
891.709 ..... PG2933
..... PG2951
..... PG2951.W33
..... PG2991
..... PG3026.F6
..... PG3476.Z34
891.709001 ..... PG3001
891.709003 ..... BH221.R93
..... PG2951
..... PG3012
..... PG3015.5.S6
..... PG3328.Z6
891.709004 ..... PG3022
891.7090042 ..... DK266.5
891.7090044 ..... PG3026.C6
891.71008 ..... PG500
..... PG3237.E5
891.713 ..... PG3337.N4
..... PG3350
..... PG3453.B6
..... PG3460.G5
..... PG3476.M355
891.71408 ..... PG3233
..... PG3237.E5
891.7142 ..... PG3056
..... PG3476
..... PG3476.A324
..... PG3476.M3
..... PG3476.M312
..... PG3476.P27
..... PZ8.3.M28
891.7144 ..... PG3476.E96
..... PG3478.K45
891.723 ..... PG3333
..... PG3337.O8
..... PG3361.S8
..... PG3410
..... PG3421.A19
..... PG3455
..... PG3456
..... PG3456.A19
..... PG3458
..... PG3458.A5
..... PG3463
891.7242 ..... PG3476.B78
..... PG3476.P27
891.724208 ..... PG3245
891.7244 ..... PG3488.O4
891.73008 ..... PG3286.P7
891.7300803 ..... PG3276
891.7308 ..... PG3286
891.732 ..... PG3311.C5
..... PG3314
891.733 ..... AC1
..... PB13
..... PG337.G77
..... PG3325
..... PG3325.P73
..... PG3325.U5
..... PG3326
..... PG3326.I3
..... PG3326.N4
..... PG3328
..... PG3328.Z6
..... PG3328.Z7
..... PG3332.M4
..... PG3332.M5
..... PG3333
..... PG3337.G6
..... PG3337.L5
..... PG3337.P5
..... PG3343
..... PG3347
..... PG3365
..... PG3365.V6
..... PG3366
..... PG3385
..... PG3386
..... PG3390
..... PG3395
..... PG3401
..... PG3410
..... PG3420
..... PG3420.A15
..... PG3420.N6
..... PG3421
..... PG3421.D8
..... PG3421.N3
..... PG3452
..... PG3453.A8
..... PG3456
..... PG3456.A13
..... PG3456.A15
..... PG3458
..... PG3460.G3
891.733 ..... PG3463
..... PG3467.K6
..... PG3467.K8
..... PG3467.L4
..... PG3470.S75
..... PG3476.T6
..... PG3476.V6
891.73308 ..... PG3286.S75
891.73309 ..... PG2988.G4
891.7330903 ..... PG3335.Z8
891.734 ..... PG3476.T345
891.7342 ..... PG3452
..... PG3452.Z8
..... PG3463
..... PG3476.A327
..... PG3476.A637
..... PG3476.B2
..... PG3476.B425
..... PG3476.F2
..... PG3476.F4
..... PG3476.G46
..... PG3476.G53
..... PG3476.O37
..... PG3476.P22
..... PG3476.P29
..... PG3476.P543
..... PG3476.R7
..... PG3476.S52
..... PG3476.S53
..... PG3476.S58
..... PG3476.S8448
..... PG3476.V54
..... PG3476.V6
..... PG3476.Z34
..... PZ3.N121
891.7344 ..... PG3242.2.A27
..... PG3476.C34
..... PG3476.D613
..... PG3476.I8
..... PG3476.K433
..... PG3476.K94
..... PG3476.P578
..... PG3478.K7
..... PG3478.M6
..... PG3479.6.A46
..... PG3479.6.U43
..... PG3482.8.U894
..... PG3488.O4
..... PZ4.M5314
891.734408 ..... PG3276
..... PG3276.M25
..... PG3286
891.78208 ..... PG3476.O37
891.78209 ..... CT1218.L6
891.783 ..... PG1037.R29
891.78308 ..... PG2947.B5
891.78309 ..... PG3335.Z8
..... PG3337.P5
..... PG3356
..... PG3421
..... PG3465.A34
891.784203 ..... PG3476.K4
891.784209 ..... PG3476.P27
891.7909002 ..... PG3970
891.7912 ..... PG3948.S51
891.7913 ..... PG3948.D73
891.791308 ..... PG3986.E3
891.7933 ..... PG3948.S8
891.8.12 ..... PG1038.14.Z4
891.81 ..... PG1037.D54
891.813 ..... PG1037.D5
..... PG1037.K615
..... PG1037.S66
891.813008 ..... PG1145
891.8208005 ..... PG584.E1
891.8215 ..... PG1419.22.A4
..... PG1419.26.O48
891.8224 ..... PG1418.P4
891.8225 ..... PG1419
891.8235 ..... PG1418.B78
..... PG1618.K69
891.8414 ..... PG1918.P7
891.8435 ..... PG1918.C3
..... PG1918.P6
891.8509 ..... PG7012
891.8515 ..... PG7157.K7
891.8516 ..... PG7158.M5
..... PG7158.M51
..... PG7158.T8
891.8517 ..... PG7158.R63
891.8526 ..... PG7158.F7
891.8527 ..... PG7158.G669
..... PG7172.R65
..... PG7177.O94
891.8536 ..... PG7158.S4
891.8537 ..... PG7158.A7
..... PG7158.B85
..... PG7158.D913
..... PG7158.G669
..... PG7158.K6513
..... PG7158.L39
..... PG7158.T57
..... PG7158.W55
..... PG7166.R86
..... PG7170.O78
891.8608005 ..... PG5145.E1
891.8609 ..... PG5001
..... PG5002.5.R8
891.861509 ..... PG5008
891.863008 ..... PG5145
..... PG5145.E8
891.8635 ..... PG5037.2.A5
..... PG5038.C3
..... PG5039.12.E5
891.8635 ..... PG5039.16.U38
..... PG5039.17.R6
..... PG5039.21.U6
..... PG5083.N453
891.865 ..... PG5039.21.U6
891.9 ..... PH302
891.9209003 ..... PG8740
891.9312 ..... PG9048.P5
891.9333 ..... PG9048.L3
892.1 ..... PJ3771
892.4 ..... PJ5111.5.L4
892.4009 ..... PJ5016
892.408 ..... PJ5059.E1
892.409 ..... PJ5017
892.409945 ..... PJ5049.I8
892.416 ..... PJ5054.A65
892.425 ..... PJ5053.S465
892.435 ..... PJ5053.A4
892.436 ..... PJ5054.B28
..... PJ5054.B4238
..... PJ5054.C38
..... PJ5054.K326
..... PJ5054.L366
..... PJ5054.M28
..... PJ5054.M33
..... PJ5054.O75
..... PJ5054.S327
..... PJ5054.S454
..... PJ5054.T36
..... PJ5054.Y42
892.43608 ..... PZ1.R115
892.48508 ..... PJ5053.B5
892.4913 ..... PJ5129.R6
892.491308 ..... PJ5126
..... PJ5191.E3
892.4933 ..... PJ5129
..... PJ5129.A2
..... PJ5129.A5
..... PJ5129.A8
..... PJ5129.B592
..... PJ5129.G535
..... PJ5129.R2
..... PJ5129.S49
..... PJ5129.S5
..... PS3537.I8615
892.49330803 ..... PJ591.E8
892.498303 ..... PJ5129.C27
892.709 ..... PJ7510
892.711 ..... PJ7642
892.7134 ..... PJ827
892.736 ..... PJ7850.R3
..... PJ7862.A564
892.7802 ..... PJ6799.C3
..... PN6095.O7
892.783408 ..... PJ7745.J3
894.2 ..... DS798
894.3508 ..... PL271.E1
894.3509003 ..... PL248.K4
894.3513 ..... PL248.D3
894.3523 ..... PL248.T34
894.3533 ..... PL248.K43
..... PL248.K45
894.51113 ..... PH3202.A35
..... PH3281.M45
894.5113 ..... PH3281.J73
894.51133 ..... PH3241.E8
..... PH3241.F364
..... PH3281.L59
..... PH3281.M35
..... PZ3.G1784
..... PZ7.G17934
894.5411 ..... PH324.E5
894.54133 ..... PH355.S27
894.54713 ..... PH355.A54
894.81109 ..... PL4758
894.8111 ..... PL4758.9.A58
894.8111008 ..... PL4762.E3
894.81111 ..... PL4758.9
894.8111109 ..... PL4758.2
894.81209 ..... PL4718
894.81417 ..... PL4659.A25
894.82712 ..... PL4780.9
..... PL4780.9.V38
895 ..... PR6045.A265
895.1008 ..... PL2658.E3
895.108 ..... PL2659.E1
895.109005 ..... PL2302
..... PL2801.N2
..... Z1087.C6
895.11008 ..... PL2658.E3
895.11009 ..... PL2307
895.1108 ..... PL2658.E3
895.111 ..... PL2674
895.112 ..... PL2664.T75
..... PL2665.T3
..... PL2677.H3
895.113 ..... PL2677.L5
895.114 ..... PL2682
..... PL2698.K3
..... PL2735.A5
895.11408 ..... PL2658.E3
895.11409 ..... PL2362
895.11508 ..... PL2658.E3
895.125 ..... PL2923.H73
895.12508 ..... PL2658.E5
895.13008 ..... PL2658.E8
895.134 ..... PL2697.H753
895.13508 ..... PL2658.E8
895.18108 ..... PL2478
895.41 ..... PK1428.9.S2
895.6 ..... PL519
895.608 ..... PL782.E3
895.609 ..... PL717
..... PL720.5
895.609 ..... PL832.A9
895.61 ..... PR6037.T4645
895.61008 ..... PL782
..... PL782.E3
..... PZ8.3
895.61008036 ..... PL782.E3
895.6104 ..... PL782.E3
895.611 ..... PL787
895.61108 ..... PL782.E3
895.613 ..... PL794.4
..... PL794.4.Z5
..... PL797.2
..... PL797.6
895.614 ..... PL808.A35
895.62208 ..... PL782.E5
895.62209 ..... PL736
895.625 ..... PN1997
895.6308 ..... PL740
895.632 ..... PL791.2
895.63208 ..... PL790.U4
895.634 ..... PL801.K8
..... PL806.T3
..... PL812.A8
..... PL817.O4
..... PL832.A8
..... PL832.A9
..... PL838.H5
..... PZ3.N216
895.63409 ..... PL747.6
..... PL812.A8
895.635 ..... PL833.I7
..... PL840.M4
..... PL856.A8
..... PL858.E14
895.63508 ..... PL782.E5
895.63509 ..... PL747.7
895.68508 ..... PL833.I7
895.71008 ..... PL984.E3
895.71108 ..... PL984.E3
895.9221 ..... PL4378.9
896 ..... PL8010
..... PL8013.E5
..... PS153.N5
896.3 ..... PL8025.5
..... PL8593.8
..... PL8824.Z95
896.39 ..... PR6061.U5
896.5 ..... PL8041.9.B5
897 ..... PM197.E1
..... PS3501.U8
897.3 ..... PM2219
899.15 ..... PL7008.9
899.2 ..... PL5130
899.2211 ..... PL5089.A56
899.2211008 ..... PL5095.E3
899.221108 ..... PL5095.E3
899.2213 ..... PL5089.L77
899.2213008 ..... PL5095.E8
899.2221 ..... PL5158.9.T25
899.2222 ..... PN1979.S5
..... PN1980
899.334 ..... PA5610.A79
899.5 ..... PL6271.Z9
899.6609 ..... PB2227
899.95 ..... PJ4061
899.96 ..... PK9169.R8
900 ..... D3.U6
..... D13
900.7 ..... G73
901 ..... B778
..... B3216.D84
..... B4238.B44
..... BF57
..... BR115
..... BR115.H5
..... CB19
..... CB151
..... CB155
..... D15.V6
..... D16
..... D16.B65
..... D16.7
..... D16.8
..... D16.9
..... E178.6
..... PS3529.L655
901.51 ..... D16.9
901.8 ..... D16
901.82 ..... D16
901.9 ..... AC8
..... AC25
..... BP360
..... CB5
..... CB19
..... CB25
..... CB57
..... CB59
..... CB68
..... CB78
..... CB151
..... CB245
..... CB251
..... CB301
..... CB358
..... CB425
..... CB478
..... D5.5
..... D11
..... D16.7
..... D21
..... D59
..... DF78
..... G175
..... GN4

901.9 ..... GN33
..... HM101
..... JC315
901.901 ..... CB19
901.90207 ..... D10
901.90222 ..... CB13
901.9028 ..... CB245
901.904 ..... HM221
901.908 ..... AC8
901.90904 ..... CB427
901.92 ..... CB351
..... CB353
901.921 ..... CB351
..... CB354.6
..... D113
..... D121
901.922 ..... CB353
..... CB355
901.924 ..... CB427
901.93 ..... CB151
..... CB357
..... D20
901.933 ..... AZ351
901.934 ..... AZ361
..... CB415
..... D388
901.94 ..... BT902
..... CB151
..... CB161
..... CB425
..... CB426
..... CB427
..... D20
..... D720
..... G122
..... LB2301
..... PR6025.O79
..... PS3507.O743
901.94.507495218 ..... T796.7
901.94074011 ..... T752
901.940740159381 ..... KF31.F6
901.9407409521 ..... T796.7
901.94074095218 ..... T796.7
901.943 ..... D410.5
901.944 ..... CB425
..... D825
901.945 ..... CB426
..... CB427
901.946 ..... CB427
..... D421
..... PT9875.E33
901.946074011428 ..... T752
901.9460740114281 ..... T752
901.946074095218 ..... T796.7
901.947 ..... CB161
901.947074095218 ..... T796.7
901.95 ..... CB161
..... D445
902.02 ..... D11.5
..... D21
903 ..... D205
904 ..... F106
..... G162
..... G522
..... G525
..... G680
904.0904 ..... G525
904.5 ..... SB603
904.7 ..... D24
..... D25
..... D25.5
..... D27
..... D362
..... DA65
..... DA85
..... G525
..... HE1783.G7
..... TN420
..... VK1250
905 ..... D410.5
906.242 ..... DA20
907 ..... D13.2
..... D16
..... D16.2
..... D16.25
..... E175
907.12 ..... D16.4.G7
907.1242 ..... D16.4.G3
..... D16.4.G7
..... LA635
907.2 ..... D13
..... D13.06
..... D13.2
..... D16
..... D410
..... DU200
907.201767 ..... D198.2
907.2022 ..... D14
907.2024 ..... CB18.T65
..... D13
..... D15.A25
..... D15.T33
..... D521
..... DA566.9
..... DA566.9.C5
..... PS2657
907.204 ..... D13
907.2052 ..... D3.A2
907.2073 ..... E175
907.4 ..... CD28
907.6 ..... D16.2
908 ..... AC8
..... DA10
..... SF301
909 ..... D16
..... D21
..... D21.3
..... D22
..... D24
..... D25
..... D109
..... D118
..... D209
..... D210
909.002 ..... D10
909.00202 ..... CB357
909.008 ..... D5.5
909.00922 ..... D107
..... D107.3
..... D108
..... D109
909.04924 ..... DS115.5
909.07 ..... D118
..... D151
..... D159
909.08 ..... D11.5
..... D209
..... D210
909.0800202 ..... D840
909.080202 ..... D11.5
909.0971237 ..... DG209
..... DG311
909.0971242 ..... DA16
..... JV1011
909.09717 ..... D847
909.0974924 ..... DS114
..... DS117
..... DS118
..... DS145
909.0974924050924 ..... DS124
909.0974927 ..... DS38.2
..... DS223
909.0974942 ..... DS19
909.097496 ..... E185
..... E185.61
909.09767 ..... DS38.3
..... DS62
909.1 ..... CB354.6
909.5 ..... G420.M2
909.7 ..... D289
..... D308
909.8 ..... D213
..... D299
..... D360
..... D422
909.80922 ..... DC216.1
909.810207 ..... D359.7
909.810922 ..... D352.5
909.82 ..... D413.M63
..... D414
..... D421
..... D422
..... D424
..... D427
..... D443
..... D445
..... D720
..... D723
..... D842.5
..... D844
..... DK254.T6
..... JC495
909.820202 ..... D427
909.820222 ..... D840
909.82072 ..... D16.8
909.820922 ..... D25.5
..... D412.7
909.820924 ..... D720
909.821 ..... D355
..... D410.5
..... D421
909.824 ..... D840
909.825 ..... D842
909.826 ..... D840
..... JC330
910 ..... AS591.J4
..... D849
..... DT12.2
..... G58
..... G59
..... G62
..... G74
..... G80
..... G98
..... G103
..... G115
..... G122
..... G126
..... G127
..... G129
..... G133
..... G150
..... G420.D7
..... G504
..... G522
..... GA6
..... GA145
..... GF31
..... GF33
..... GF48
..... GF51
..... GF71
910.001 ..... G70
..... G522
910.00151 ..... GF23
910.0018 ..... G70
..... G105
910.00182 ..... G74
910.00182 ..... GA23
910.00222 ..... G138
910.003 ..... G105
..... G106
..... G108.A2
..... G108.E5
..... G115
910.005 ..... Z6003
910.00601 ..... G56
910.007 ..... G73
..... G126
910.0071 ..... LB1583
910.00711 ..... G58
..... G72
910.00712 ..... G74.5
910.0071294 ..... G76.5.A8
910.0072022 ..... G67
..... G99
910.007204 ..... G73
910.0076 ..... G131
910.008 ..... G58
910.02 ..... G125
..... GB55
..... GB58
..... QB55
910.020222 ..... GB60
..... QB637
910.02154 ..... GB612
910.0216 ..... GB671
910.0254 ..... GB612
910.03 ..... CB161
..... CB425
..... D20
..... G59
..... G140
..... GF71
..... H11
910.03018 ..... GF41
910.03142 ..... GR675
910.03171242 ..... TK140.S6
910.031713 ..... HN17.5
910.031724 ..... GN400
..... HF5549.5.E45
910.031732 ..... G140
910.03174 ..... GN340
910.03174911 ..... DS15
910.031749149 ..... DX115
910.03174916 ..... D70
910.0317491803 ..... D377
910.03174924 ..... BM30
..... DS102.5
..... DS102.8
..... DS112
..... DS115
..... DS135.C5
..... DS135.G3
910.03174927 ..... DS42.4
910.0317496 ..... E185
..... E185.5
..... E448
..... Z3507
910.0317499150222 ..... DU120
910.03175927 ..... Z7052
910.031767 ..... D199.3
..... DS35.6
910.031812 ..... CB357
..... E185
910.03182 ..... D973
910.031821 ..... CB5
..... CB245
..... E169.1
910.031822 ..... BR129
910.03821 ..... CB59
..... D443
910.09 ..... CB5
..... G62
..... G82
..... G95
..... G105
..... G128
..... G175
910.0901 ..... GN741
910.0904 ..... CB161
910.0911 ..... CJ6117.P6
910.09116611 ..... G650
910.0911824 ..... DS211
910.0913 ..... G515
910.09142 ..... G500
910.09143 ..... G510
910.09154 ..... GB611
910.0916 ..... G680
910.0916432 ..... G525
910.09166 ..... GC83
..... VM981
910.091661 ..... G490
..... G530
910.0916611 ..... F1060
..... G614
..... G635.P3
..... G640
..... G650
..... G665
..... G742
910.091665 ..... F851.5
910.0916651 ..... DU23
..... G420
910.0916653 ..... DS507
910.0916654 ..... G246.C7
..... GC771
910.09171242 ..... DA11
..... DA16
..... DA18
910.091732 ..... G140
..... HF5429
910.09174918 ..... D90.S46
910.09174924 ..... DS102.8
910.09174927 ..... DS223
910.0917496 ..... DT17
910.09175918 ..... DR25
910.091811 ..... G127
910.091814 ..... G496
910.091822 ..... D973
910.091824 ..... DS326.N4
910.0936 ..... G302
910.0942 ..... G240
910.0944 ..... G420
910.0946 ..... G95
910.09469 ..... G282
910.094690924 ..... G286.H5
910.09492 ..... G236.D4
910.13384 ..... HF1025
910.2 ..... G150
..... LB1047
910.202 ..... G150
..... G153
910.2573 ..... G155.U6
910.3 ..... G103
910.3174911 ..... GN539
910.4 ..... D244.8.S5
..... DA564.B3
..... DS506
..... F865
..... G160
..... G161
..... G245
..... G440
..... G463
..... G464
..... G490
..... G525
910.40207 ..... G157
910.41 ..... CT9971.G7
..... F851.5
..... G161
..... G286.M2
..... G420
..... G420.C65
..... G420.D2
..... G420.M2
..... G420.R69
..... G440
..... GV812
..... VA667.I53
910.410207 ..... G157
910.410924 ..... G420
910.45 ..... D27
..... DL291.H37
..... DS411.1
..... DU21
..... DU320
..... F1013
..... F1122
..... F2171.2
..... G161
..... G170
..... G420
..... G440
..... G464
..... G470
..... G490
..... G530
..... G540
..... G650
..... GV822.G3
..... GV822.G36
..... GV822.S95
..... GV826.5
..... VK16
..... VK18
..... VK149
910.450916612 ..... G530
910.450924 ..... G540
..... GV822.C8
910.453 ..... CC77
..... DA670.C8
..... DS335
..... DU230.W37
..... F234.W7
..... F313
..... F551
..... F2161
..... G525
..... G530
..... G530.C296
..... G530.T6
..... G530.W263
..... G535
..... G537.A8
..... G537.W3
..... G700
..... GV819
..... VK1255.C3
..... VK1291.G5
..... VK1291.V5
910.4530922 ..... G535
..... G535.W56
910.8 ..... G162
..... VK18
910.9 ..... E101
..... G96
910.91661 ..... G530
910.916612 ..... SH331
..... SH344.6.T7
910.916652 ..... DS777.55
910.91667 ..... G525
910.91821 ..... G420.C45
..... GC296.G9
910.922 ..... G175

910.922 ..... G200
..... G245
910.924 ..... CT788.C42
..... CT9971.T4
..... DT76.9.T5
..... DU20
..... E125.B2
..... G94.N5
..... G246.B5
..... G246.C7
..... G246.V3
..... G286.G2
..... G286.M2
..... G420
..... G420.C62
..... G530
..... G530.W59
..... G585.B8
..... G650
910.94 ..... G80
911 ..... D21
..... G1030
..... G1030.M84
911.42 ..... DA600
..... G1811.S1
911.54 ..... DS450.C5
911.542 ..... DS485.U64
911.5455 ..... DS485.C54
911.6 ..... DT3
..... DT21
911.64 ..... DT317
911.669 ..... DT515.62
911.6773 ..... G2516.F2
911.71 ..... F1060
911.71317 ..... F1059.S6
911.71354 ..... G1148.Y6
911.72 ..... F786
911.73 ..... G1101.S1
..... G1201.S1
..... GA405
..... Z6026.H6
911.748 ..... F157.B7
911.755 ..... F229
911.756 ..... F262.A15
911.758 ..... F286
911.772 ..... G1400
911.789 ..... G1506.S1
911.795 ..... G1491.S1
911.931 ..... G2796.F7
912 ..... G1006
..... G1007
..... G1015
..... G1019
..... G1019.R447
..... GA105
..... GA106
..... GA130
..... GA246
..... GA304.R5
..... GA315
..... PZ9.D48
..... PZ10.O43
..... QB637
912.0148 ..... GA130
..... GA871
912.071266 ..... GA130
912.071267 ..... GA130
912.075 ..... GA300
912.08 ..... GA101
..... GA193.U5
..... Z6003
912.09 ..... GA201
..... GA205
..... Z6003
912.13091421 ..... G1819.L7
912.1309156 ..... G2205
912.1309159 ..... G2362.M4
912.13091713 ..... G1146.G1
912.1309177434 ..... G1414.D4
912.1312260942 ..... RA847
912.132833450973 ..... G1201.F7
912.13300975932 ..... G1318.P2
912.133094 ..... G1796.G1
912.13309784 ..... G1441.G1
912.1333 ..... G1426.G4
912.13330097549 ..... G1298.B4
912.133300976686 ..... G1368.T8
912.133300976694 ..... G1368.R6
912.133300977159 ..... G1398.P4
912.133300977196 ..... G1398.M75
912.133300977414 ..... G1413.A5
912.133300977437 ..... G1414.F6
912.133300977559 ..... G1418.G8
912.133300977733 ..... G1433.A5
912.13330097774 ..... G1433.S5
912.1333009778325 ..... G1438.M7
912.133300977888 ..... G1438.I6
912.133300979791 ..... G1488.W2
912.133300979797 ..... G1488.M3
912.133930973 ..... G1046.G1
912.136800974811 ..... G1264.P5
912.138531 ..... TF57
912.1551465 ..... G2681.C7
912.1551543091813 ..... G1050
912.15516 ..... G1201.C8
912.155438 ..... G1951.C5
912.1621384166 ..... G1046.P8
912.16238949 ..... G1811.C787
912.163 ..... S439
912.163490974 ..... G1206.K1
912.16395430916614 ..... SK361
912.1641 ..... G1701.C7
912.17909755 ..... G1291.E63
912.17966097 ..... G1106.P2
912.1799 ..... G1437.O9
912.19159504 ..... G2381.P2
912.1917304 ..... G1201.P2
912.19174924 ..... G1030
912.196612 ..... G2806.C7
912.196614 ..... G1371.P5
912.1971242 ..... G1805
912.19813 ..... G1050
912.3 ..... G1033
912.33300977647 ..... G1428.S6
912.38 ..... G2000
912.38648 ..... G1251.P5
912.4 ..... G76
..... G1037
..... G1796.P2
912.415 ..... G1830
..... G1831.P2
912.42 ..... DA615
..... G1019
..... G1811.P2
..... G1814.A1
..... G1816.P2
912.421 ..... G1819.H6
..... G1819.L7
912.4213 ..... G1819.W54
912.4221 ..... G1818.S8
912.4225 ..... G1818.S9
912.4235 ..... G1819.E9
912.4238 ..... G1819
912.4241 ..... G1819.B7
912.4246 ..... G1819.S9
912.4252 ..... G1819.N6
912.42575 ..... G1819.W8
912.427 ..... G1817.M4
912.4272 ..... G1818.L3
..... G1819.L6
912.4274 ..... G1818.Y6
..... G1819.B65
..... G1819.H9
..... G1819.S5
912.43 ..... G1880
..... Z6003
912.51249 ..... G2344.C4
..... G2344.K5
..... G2344.T3
..... G2344.T4
..... G2344.T5
912.52 ..... G2355
912.54 ..... G2280
912.5475 ..... G2283.G8
912.551482 ..... G1817.L2
912.5694 ..... G2235
912.595 ..... G2381.P2
912.6 ..... G2445
912.667 ..... G2704.A2
912.6691 ..... G2699.L3
912.678 ..... G1540.T4
912.6782 ..... G2544.D3
912.679 ..... G2551.P2
912.6822 ..... G2562.W5
912.689 ..... G2570
912.6891 ..... G2574.B8
..... G2574.S2
912.7 ..... G1105
..... G1116.P2
..... G1201.E63
..... G1201.P2
912.71 ..... G1115
912.7123 ..... G1165
912.7124 ..... G1160
912.7129 ..... G1183.F7
912.71327 ..... G1148.L2
912.72 ..... G1545
912.7292 ..... G1629.K5
912.73 ..... G1200
..... G1201.B5
..... G1201.C2
..... G1201.P2
912.74 ..... G1210
912.744 ..... G1234.B6
912.745 ..... G1239.A1
912.7471 ..... G1254.N4
..... G1254.N42
912.747245 ..... G1253.N3
912.747277 ..... G1253.W5
..... G1254.C47
912.7473 ..... G1252.A6
912.74765 ..... G1253.O35
912.74897 ..... G1263.C8
912.749 ..... G1256.P2
912.74923 ..... G1258.P3
912.74927 ..... G1259.J5
912.74941 ..... G1258.M5
912.74948 ..... G1258.O2
912.74965 ..... G1258.M4
912.75244 ..... G1273.C2
912.75271 ..... G1273.B3
912.75284 ..... G1273.M6
912.755 ..... G1291.L1
..... Z6003
912.75523 ..... G1294.R5
912.75529 ..... G1290
912.755521 ..... G1294.N6
912.756 ..... GA442
912.758231 ..... G1314.A8
912.759 ..... G1315
912.75932 ..... G1318.P2
912.75935 ..... G1318.B8
912.76 ..... G1371.H8
912.762 ..... G1345
912.764 ..... G1371.C8
912.76414 ..... HA37.U7
912.76428 ..... G1374.D2
912.76687 ..... G1368.W2
912.77 ..... GB1627.G8
912.77131 ..... G1399.C5
912.77172 ..... G1398.M65
912.77178 ..... G1399.C4
912.772 ..... G1400
912.7731 ..... G1408.C7
912.77311 ..... G1409.C6
912.77433 ..... G1413.W3
912.77435 ..... G1413.W2
912.77475 ..... G1413.O4
912.77586 ..... G1418.G7
912.776 ..... G1425
..... G1426.P2
912.77627 ..... G1428.M8
912.77652 ..... G1428.M2
912.77662 ..... G1428.P4
912.77676 ..... G1428.L3
912.77678 ..... G1428.I8
912.77679 ..... G1428.K6
912.77697 ..... G1428.M35
912.77713 ..... G1433.S6
912.778315 ..... G1438.K6
912.77832 ..... G1438.S75
912.77833 ..... G1438.A8
912.778345 ..... G1438.L5
912.77835 ..... G1438.M35
912.77862 ..... G1438.C9
912.78 ..... G1380
912.782278 ..... G1453.N4
912.78251 ..... G1454.O4
912.78257 ..... G1453.W3
912.783 ..... G1445
912.784 ..... G1444.A1
912.78431 ..... G1443.S2
912.78436 ..... G1443.R2
912.78437 ..... G1443.C4
912.78439 ..... G1443.B4
912.78453 ..... G1443.L3
912.78454 ..... G1443.D5
912.78461 ..... G1443.B6
912.78462 ..... G1443.M2
912.78475 ..... G1443.M5
912.78478 ..... G1443.E5
912.786 ..... G1471.P2
912.79173 ..... G1513.M3
..... G1514.T4
912.794 ..... G1526.P15
912.79432 ..... G1529.P28
912.7945 ..... G1527.S3
912.79462 ..... G1528.M2
912.79469 ..... G1528.S28
912.79488 ..... G1528.K4
912.79493 ..... G1527.A58
912.79495 ..... G1528.S23
912.79496 ..... G1528.O7
912.79527 ..... G1493.J2
912.7953 ..... G1492.W5
912.79533 ..... G1493.L5
912.7963 ..... G1483.T8
912.7964 ..... F752.H8
912.79771 ..... G1488.S6
912.79777 ..... G1488.K3
912.79799 ..... G1483.C4
912.798 ..... G1530
912.9141 ..... G2394.M5
912.931 ..... G2796.P5
912.9311 ..... G2799.A8
912.94 ..... G2741.G1
912.942 ..... G2754.A3
912.943 ..... G2772.B75
912.95 ..... G2440
913 ..... CB59
..... D57
..... DE71
..... DE83
..... DF261.M2
..... G84
..... G1033
913.02 ..... GB55
913.03 ..... CB59
..... CB301
..... CB311
..... D57
..... D59
913.031 ..... CB301
..... CC73
..... CC75
..... CC80
..... CC140
..... CC165
..... E98.I4
..... GN425
..... GN446.1
..... GN738
..... GN739
..... GN775
..... GN776.M4
..... GN792.G7
..... N8237.8.R8
913.031018 ..... CC75
913.031023 ..... CC77
913.031028 ..... CC76.A3
..... CC77
..... CC80
..... GN705
..... VK1491
913.0310283 ..... CC75
913.0310285 ..... CJ233
..... DA147.L4
..... E77.9
..... GN743
..... QC798.D3
913.03103 ..... CC70
913.031072 ..... CC100
913.03107401444 ..... GN37.C353
913.03108 ..... CC65
913.03109 ..... CC100
913.09171237 ..... CB311
913.091822 ..... BR129
913.2031 ..... DT61
913.20310922 ..... DT80
913.3 ..... N5345
913.309822 ..... DE71
913.31 ..... DS721
913.3103 ..... DS723
913.32 ..... BL2441.2
..... BX133
..... DS121.5
..... DT57
..... DT60
..... DT73.K4
..... DT73.5
913.3203 ..... DT64
913.32031 ..... CB251
..... DT60
..... DT61
..... DT62.S3
913.33 ..... DS109.2
..... DS110.M5
..... DS110.R32
..... DS110.S26
913.3303 ..... DS111
..... DS117
..... DS154.9.D34
913.330308 ..... DS42.4
913.336 ..... GN792.G7
913.34 ..... DS486.B36
..... DS486.J25
..... DS486.K366
..... GN792.I3
..... Q11
913.3403 ..... DS418
913.35 ..... DS51.U7
..... DS70
..... DS135.B2
..... DS267
..... DS325.P4
913.35003 ..... DS67.8
913.3503 ..... DS57
..... DS69.5
913.3503074031554 ..... DS69
913.350308 ..... DS69.6
913.35031 ..... DS69.5
..... DS70.5.U7
..... DS72
913.35032 ..... DS69.5
913.35033 ..... DS70
913.350974924 ..... DS135.B2
913.36 ..... CC23.O929
..... CC165
..... CN590
..... DA90
..... DA142
..... DA145
..... DA146
..... DA670.E7
..... DA670.K3
..... DA670.M2
..... DA670.S2
..... DA670.S98
..... DA677.1
..... DA690.B8
..... DA690.G5
..... DA690.H24
..... DA690.R32
..... DA715
..... DA777.7.A5
..... DA920
..... DD801.R72
..... DG78
..... DK450.7
..... DL121
..... DL621
..... GN776.G7
..... GN776.I7
..... GN778.G8
..... GN780.D4
..... GN805
..... GN806.U45
..... GN826.D4
..... GT3380
913.3603 ..... DA140
..... DA145
..... GN775
913.36031 ..... DA140
913.362 ..... DA690.C729
913.3703 ..... DG77
..... DG82
..... DG83.3
..... DG209
..... DG213
..... DG312
..... DG431
913.37036 ..... DG77
..... DG79
..... DG311
913.37037 ..... DG279.
..... PA6825
913.370370924 ..... PA6716
913.375 ..... DG223
913.375031 ..... DG223
913.376 ..... DG66.5
..... DG77
..... DG97
..... DG975.C17
..... NA323
913.37603 ..... DG77
913.377 ..... DG70.P7

Dewey	LC
913.377	DG70.S9
	DG975.S337
913.37940308	F869.S22
913.38	DE5
	DF14
	DF78
913.38003	DE5
913.38008	D52
913.3803	DE57
	DE59
	DE71
	DE86
	DF14
	DF77
	DF91
	DF215
	DS155
	HD132
	N7483.W5
	PA27
	PA3061
913.380308	PA3305
913.38031	DF77
913.380311	DF77
913.38038	DF77
913.38097496	DE71
913.382	DF261.T5
913.384	DF261.E9
913.385	DF275
	DF289
913.39	GN776.A86
913.3915	DF901.T67
913.3918	DF221.C8
913.391803	DF261.C8
913.3918031	DF220
	DF221.C8
	DF261.C8
913.3918033	DF221.C8
913.392	DS51.B6
913.3923	DS156.I6
913.3937	DS54.3
	DS54.95.S2
913.393703	DS54.3
913.394	DS99.P17
	DS247.A23
913.3947	DS211
913.395	DK34.S3
913.3955	DS167
913.395503	DS156.U7
	DS171
913.396	GN855.R9
913.397	DT24
913.398	DG59.D4
913.4225	DA147.F5
913.5	DS70.5.B3
	DS261
	GN855.I7
913.5033	DS70
913.6	DC62.C2
	GN778.G8
	GN808.H8
913.61	E337.8
913.703	DG69
913.75	DG223
913.8	DF214
	DF221.M9
913.803	DF77
	DF78
	DF79
	DF214
	N5630
	PA3316
913.86	DF261.O5
913.915	DF901.T67
914	CB245
	CR4509
	D22
	D246.M33
	D410
	D907
	D909
	D910.5
	D917
	D919
	D921
	D922
	D965
	D967
	G530
	GB171
914.008	D919
914.03	CB5
	CB245
	CB357
	CB358
	CB401
	DA730
	SB466.E9
914.030712	CB20
914.031	CB245
	CB351
	CB353
	D118
	D119
914.03108	BR253
914.0314	D119
	D123
	DC73
914.0317	CB353
	CB354.6
	CR4509
914.0318	CB354.6
914.032	CB245
	CB357
914.032	CB361
	D359
914.0321	CB359
	CB361
914.032108	D113
914.0322	CB401
	D246
914.0323	BF1571
	D220
	D247
	DC113.5
914.0325	CB401
	CB411
	D273
	D273.5
914.03252	D246
	D288
914.03253	CB411
	D286
	HN373
	PR447
914.032530924	D285.8.C4
914.0327	D308
914.0328	B803
	D299
	D919
914.03287	D395
914.0350924	CT788.W318
914.0355	D907
	D922
	D1051
	D1055
914.03550202	D1050
914.037	DA530
914.04	D907
	D909
914.042	D907
914.04253	D917
914.0428	D980
914.04287	D919
914.043	D921
914.0455	D909
	D922
	DD901.O2
	G153
	GV1025.A2
914.048502465	HC240
914.09742	E184.2
914.0974918	DR25
914.1	DA867
	PB1583
914.1003	DA772
	DA869
914.103	DA760
	DA772
	DA826
	GN806.S4
914.103590924	DA822.W6
914.1037	DA812
914.10370924	BX9225.M198
914.1038	DA865
914.10381	DA826
914.103810924	CT828.K5
914.10481	DA867
	DA870
914.109692	DA867
914.11	DA880.H7
	DA978
914.1103	DA880.H6
914.110481	DA880.H7
914.111	DA890.U55
914.116	DA880.H4
	DA880.R7
914.117	DA880.H4
	DA880.I7
	DA880.S6
914.11703	DA880.H4
914.1170381	DA880.H4
914.117047	DA880.H4
914.12	DA880.G17
914.122	DA890.N3
914.125	DA890.A2
914.1250481	CT788.T9
914.131	DA890.F7
914.13204	DA880.P4
914.133	DA890.S2
914.137	DA890.C63
914.138	DA880.A85
	DA880.H4
914.139	DA880.A7
914.14	DA880.C6
914.142	DA890.T75
914.143	DA890.A4
914.143503810924	CT828.W4
914.14350481	DA890.G5
914.1445	DA890.E2
	DA890.E3
914.145	DA890.E2
	DA890.H2
	DA890.T7
914.148	DA890.M75
914.149	CT788.N417
914.15	DA911
	DA925
	DA969
	DA977
	DA978
	DA990.C24
914.15003	DA979
914.1502	GF561
914.1503	DA911
	DA925
	DA930
914.1503	DA950
	DA959.1
	PR6031.O73
914.15035	DA937
914.150359	DA925
914.150359024	CT808.L8
914.15036	DA940.3
914.15039	DA911
	DA925
	DA965.H6
	DA978
914.15049	DA978
	DA980
914.164	DA995.C56
	DA995.D45
914.17049	DA990.C6
914.173	DA990.A56
914.174	DA990.A8
914.183	DA990.D8
	DA995.D8
914.18303	DA995.D8
914.184	BR798.B33
	CT788.H263
914.189	DA995.K48
914.196	DA995.K49
914.2	D919
	DA110
	DA120
	DA170
	DA550
	DA566
	DA625
	DA630
	DA631
	DA645
	DA650
	DA655
	DA660
	DA668
	DA670.P4
	HT133
	SB466.G72E56
914.200222	DA667
914.2003	DA640
	DA645
914.2008	DA631
914.202	DA630
	DA631
914.20208	G58
914.203	BX4705.W5
	CD105
	CT777
	DA28.9
	DA30
	DA35
	DA110
	DA118
	DA125.A6
	DA130
	DA175
	DA185
	DA320
	DA472
	DA530
	DA600
	DA680
	NC1470
	PR6037.A35
	S455
914.2030922	Z2010
914.2031	DA140
	DA145
	DA152
	DA155
	GN800
	PE25
914.2032	DA185
914.20321	DA190.D7
914.203280924	CC115.A7
914.2033	DA185
	DA620
	PR457
914.203307	Z2017
914.20331	DA185
914.20337	DA185
914.20338	DA235
914.2034	DA185
914.203430924	DA247.F35
914.2035	DA317
	DA320
	DA356
914.2035208	DA331
914.20355	DA320
	DA358.A1
	PR1293
914.203550924	DA356
914.2036	DA375
	DA380
	DA447.P4
	HN385
914.203610922	DA377
914.20369	DA495
914.2037	B1301
	DA380
	DA480
	DA485
914.20370222	DA485
914.20370924	DA506.Q3
914.20373	DA485
	DA506.A9
914.203730924	CT788.C665
914.203740924	DA536.S25
914.20375	DA533
914.2038	DA566.4
914.20380924	CT788.J18
914.20381	D15.A25
	DA533
	DA550
	DA551
	HD8390
	PQ9261.E3
	PR4581
	PR4583
	PR4809.H63
914.2038108	DA533
914.203810922	BX6495.S9
	DA560
914.203810924	DA565.A17
	DA565.D6
	DA565.F7
	DA565.M78
914.20382	DA566
	DA566.2
	DA566.4
	DA570
914.203820207	DA118
914.203820924	CT788
	CT788.B8768
	CT788.D68
	CT788.H53
	CT788.M614
	CT788.S6875
	CT788.S775
	CT788.W578
	DA585.B75
914.20383	DA566.4
	DA578
914.203840924	AC8
914.20385	DA118
	DA566.2
	DA566.4
	DA592
	S455
914.203850924	CT788.H864
914.204	DA630
	DA631
	DA667
	G1808
	PR109
914.20444	DA610
914.20452	BX4827.T53
914.2046	DA380
914.20471	DA90
914.20472	DA615
914.20473	DA625
914.20481	DA625
	DA630
914.20483	DA631
914.20485	CC310
	DA630
	DA631
	DA650
	DA660
	GV1025.G7
	PR109
	SD601
914.209734	S521
914.209749149	DX127.B68
914.21	DA682
	DA684
	DA684.2
	DA685.A
	DA685.B84
914.2100207	DA684.2
914.210022	DA684.2
	DA685.A1
914.2100222	DA684
	DA684.2
914.21003	DA679
914.210222	DA684.2
	NE1334.W4
914.2103	DA676
	DA677
	DA680
	DA684.2
914.21030222	DA684.2
914.210355	PR1125
914.21036	DA681
914.21037	DA682
914.210380222	DA683
914.210381	DA683
914.21038102.22	DA683
914.2103820924	CT788.B8795
914.210384	D760.8.L7
	D811.5
914.210385	DA684.2
914.210481	DA625
914.210485	DA678
	DA679
	DA684.2
	HF5349.G7
	PR4584
914.210487	DA679
914.212	DA677.1
	DA685.A1
	NA8080
	SB466.G75L63
914.21200222	DA684.2
914.2120222	N8213
914.2120355	DA680
914.2120381	DA683
914.213	DA685.K5
	DA687.W5
914.214	BM295.H3
	DA688
914.2150485	DA685.E1
914.216	DA685.L2
	DA685.S7

Dewey	LC
914.216	DA690.G83
914.2162	DA690.W897
914.217	DA664.H4
	DA690.C8
	DA690.T95
914.2178	NA6750.L6
914.219	DA690.S912
914.22	DA670.T2
	DA690.M25
	GV1025.G7
914.2203	DA670.T2
914.221	DA685.K55
	DA690.B225
	DA690.B6375
	DA690.E895
	DA690.G56
	DA690.T385
	DA690.W62
	DS690.S563
914.2210382	PN5123.W43
914.2210485	DA670.S96
914.2210487	DA670.S96
914.223	BR765.B47
	DA664.L4
	DA664.R57
	DA685.B57
	DA690.B7686
	DA690.C458
	DA690.D7
	DA690.F27
	DA690.H13
	DA690.H398
	DA690.L534
	DA690.N84
	DA690.O83
	DA690.R76
	DA690.S934
	DA690.T638
914.22303	DA670.K3
914.2230485	DA670.K3
914.225	AM101.A22
	DA670.E2
	DA690.A368
	DA690.B5666
	DA690.B78
	DA690.C53
	DA690.C775
	DA690.E144
	DA690.F36
	DA690.L214
	DA690.M712
	DA690.P5
	DA690.S832
	DA690.W11
914.22500222	DA670.S98
914.2250485	DA670.S98
914.2250946	DA670.S98
914.227	DA670.D7
	DA670.H2
	DA670.N5
	DA670.W48
	DA685.F5
	DA690.B723
	DA690.B846
	DA690.F234
	DA690.F69
	DA690.K543
	DA690.L94
	DA690.N523
	DA690.O3
	DA690.P8
	DA690.S7
	DA690.T58
	NA5471.L984
914.2270485	DA670.H2
914.228	BX5195.B514
914.229	DA670.B4
	DA690.A14
	DA690.E1353
	DA690.H918
	DA690.M18
	DA690.N55
	DA690.T97
	DA690.W26
	DA690.W264
	DA690.W76
	DA690.W85
914.229008	DA670.B4
914.22904	DA690.W76
914.2290485	DA670.B4
914.23	DA650
914.230381	DA670.A95
914.231	DA670.P49
	DA670.W7
	DA690.C42
	DA690.C733
	DA690.C783
	DA690.D493
	DA690.P665
	DA690.S98
914.2310485	DA670.W7
914.233	DA670.D7
	GN780.G7
	PR4752
914.23303	DA670.D7
914.2330485	DA670.D7
914.234	DA670.G9
	DA670.J5
914.2340385	DA670.C4
914.2340485	DA670.C4
914.235	DA670.D49
	DA670.D5
	DA670.E9
914.235	DA670.L96
	DA690.B56
	DA690.B843
	DA690.E1322
	DA690.L296
	DA690.P14
	DA690.P7
	DA690.T24
	DA690.T68
	S523
	VK1364.L94
914.23503	DA670.D49
914.2350485	DA670.D49
	DA670.D5
914.237	DA670.C8
	DA670.L77
	DA670.S2
	VK1059
914.23700222	DA670.C8
914.23703	DA670.C8
	S523
914.237030222	DA670.C8
914.237035	DA670.C8
914.2370385	S521
914.2370485	DA670.C8
914.238	DA670.A93
	DA690.B312
	DA690.B313
	DA690.B769
	DA690.C64
	DA690.D85
	DA690.F87
	DA690.G45
	DA690.L27
	DA690.L8214
	DA690.W45
	DA690.W6137
	DA690.W637
	DA690.W77
914.2380385	DA670.S5
914.2380485	DA670.S5
914.24	DA670.M64
	DA740.B7
	DA740.O35
914.241	DA670.C83
	DA690.B8
	DA690.C594
	DA690.G5
	DA690.L36
	NA5471.H37
914.2410381	DA690.B8
914.2410485	DA670.G5
914.243	DA690.T74
	DA690.U78
914.2430485	DA670.M7
914.245	DA670.S4
	DA690.C59
	DA690.M427
	DA690.M57
	DA690.N673
914.246	DA690.B557
	DA690.N58
	DA690.W86
914.2460485	DA650
	DA670.S7
	DA690.S793
914.247	DA690.B52
	DA690.H16
	DA690.U76
	DA690.W267
	NA5471.E93
914.248	BX5195.N8N83
	DA690.B6
	DA690.R85
	DA690.W3
	HV1555
914.24800222	DA670.W3
914.24803	DA670.W3
914.2480485	DA670.W3
914.25	DA650
	DA670.F32
	DA670.F33
	DA670.M64
914.250385	HC256
914.251	DA690.E27
	DA690.R42
914.2510485	DA670.D43
914.252	DA690.B277
	DA690.B569
	DA690.E16
	DA690.N92
	DA690.O985
	DA690.W91
	HT395.G72T76
914.2520485	DA670.N9
914.253	DA670.L7
	DA690.B27
	DA690.G7
	DA690.G85
	DA690.I78
	DA690.N76
	DA690.S423
	DA690.S783
	DA690.S789
	DA690.S8
	DA690.W467
914.2530485	DA670.L7
914.254	DA664.B4
	DA690.A62
	DA690.L5
	DA690.M425
	DA690.M43
914.2540385	DA670.L5
914.2540485	DA670.L5
914.255	DA670.N7
	DA690.D44
	DA690.I7
	DA690.N8
	DA690.P47
	DA690.R24
914.25503	DA670.N7
914.2550485	DA670.N7
914.256	DA690.H93
914.2565	DA690.B4
914.256503	DA670.B3
914.25650485	DA670.B3
914.257	DA670.O9
	DA690.B22
	DA690.B55
	DA690.B644
	DA690.B842
	DA690.M4097
	DA690.O98
	DA690.P68
	DA690.W36
	DA690.W83
	DA690.W8975
914.2570485	DA670.O9
914.2575	DA670.W95
	DA690.A487
	DA690.B892
	DA690.C4525
	DA690.D29
	DA690.E75
	DA690.H597
	DA690.O5
	DA690.P34
914.257504	DA670.B9
914.25750485	DA670.B9
914.258	DA610.S25
	DA670.H5
	DA690.B734
	DA690.H428
	DA690.H57
	DA690.H715
	DA690.L633
	DA690.W47
	HT1651.L5
914.25803	DA670.H5
914.2580485	DA670.H4
	DA670.H5
914.259	DA690.C2
	DA690.C456
	DA690.W8
914.26	DA631
914.261	DA670.D4
	DA670.F33
	DA670.N59
	DA670.N6
	DA670.S986
	DA690.D74
	DA690.D743
	DA690.H436
	DA690.M466
	DA690.S5677
	DA690.T23
914.26103	DA670.N6
914.2610485	DA670.N6
914.264	DA670.S89
	DA670.S9
	DA690.A28
	DA690.D34
	DA690.H364
	DA690.L842
	DA690.T4
	DA690.W948
914.264031	GT3380
914.2640381	DA670.S9
914.2640485	DA670.S9
914.267	DA670.E7
	DA670.H25
	DA670.L57
	DA685.H28
	DA690.B28
	DA690.C7
	DA690.D818
	DA690.F67
	DA690.G816
	DA690.H184
	DA690.R27
	DA690.S1465
	DA690.T32
	DA690.T56
914.26703	DA670.E7
914.27	DA631
914.270485	DA670.P4
914.271	DA690.A318
	DA690.B34
	DA690.C472
	DA690.C72
	DA690.M12
914.2710014	DA670.C6
914.271003	DA690.C5
914.2710222	DA670.C6
914.272	BX5195.B87
	CT788.S714
	DA640.L8
	DA670.G34
	DA670.W974
	DA690.A27
	DA690.A843
	DA690.B43
	DA690.C337
	DA690.C57
	DA690.C705
	DA690.C7883
	DA690.F74
	DA690.G643
914.272	DA690.H345
	DA690.H3917
	DA690.H592
	DA690.L8
	DA690.M15
	DA690.M4
	DA690.P93
	DA690.P95
	DA690.R11
	DA690.R26
	DA690.W28
	DA690.W567
	DA690.W598
	DA690.W818
914.27200222	DA670.L2
914.27203	DA670.L2
914.27203730924	CT788.S77
914.274	DA664.F63
	DA670.Y6
	DA690.B35
	DA690.B51
	DA690.B689
	DA690.B7
	DA690.D284
	DA690.F475
	DA690.G98
	DA690.H32
	DA690.H44
	DA690.M28
	DA690.M44
	DA690.M6
	DA690.M734
	DA690.O84
	DA690.P73
	DA690.P965
	DA690.R72
	DA690.S47
	DA690.S54
	DA690.S6115
	DA690.S6116
	DA690.S813
	DA690.S855
	DA690.T45
	DA690.T63
	DA690.W35
	DA690.W534
	DA690.W563
	DA690.Y6
	HD594
	NA5471.F6
	NA7625.N48
914.274003	DA670.Y6
914.27403	DA660
	DA670.Y6
	PR4168
914.2740308	DA690.S28
914.2740485	DA662.Y6
	DA670.Y6
914.28	DA670.L1
914.280393	HD8039.M72G73
914.280485	DA670.L1
	DA670.P4
914.281	DA670.T9
	DA690.D96
	DA690.E119
	DA690.W32
914.2810485	DA670.D9
	DA670.N8
914.282	DA670.H73
	DA670.N8
	DA690.H193
	DA690.N6
	SB484.G7
914.282037	DA631
914.2820382	DA670.N8
914.2820485	DA670.N8
914.285	DA690.M713
	DA690.W599
914.28503	DA670.C9
914.2850485	DA670.L1
914.288	DA690.W72
914.29	DA731
914.2903	DA708
914.290385	DA708
	DA731
914.290485	DA731
	DA735
	GV1025.G7
914.291	DA749.T9
914.292	DA745.C3
	SB484.G7
914.2920485	DA735
914.2935	DA745.B87
	DA745.H3
914.295	DA745.C23
	DA745.T27
914.297	DA740.C19
	DA745
	DA745.B85
	DA745.C15
	DA745.C2
	DA745.L796
	DA745.N4
914.29703	DA740.G5
914.298	DA745.A25
	DA745.G85
	DA745.L67
	DA745.N46
914.299	DA740.P3
	DA745.L77
914.3	DB196
	DD17
	DD43
	DD257.4

914.3 ..... DD259
..... DD261.2
..... DD724
..... DR7
914.300222 ..... DD259
914.303 ..... DB17
..... DD61
..... DD61.3
..... DD66
..... DD112
..... DD257
914.3032 ..... DD63
914.30340924 ..... CT1098.M56
914.3037 ..... DD207.5
914.30385 ..... DD232
..... DD237
914.303860924 ..... D811.5
914.30387 ..... DD43
..... DD259
914.30487 ..... DD16
..... DD43
914.304870222 ..... DD20
914.309174924 ..... DS135.G3
..... DS135.G33
914.31 ..... DD43
..... DD261
914.3102122 ..... DD43
914.310387 ..... DD261
..... DD261.2
914.3103870922 ..... DD261.63
914.310487 ..... DD43
914.3155 ..... DD881
914.3155038 ..... DD878
914.31550387 ..... DD881
914.31550487 ..... DD859
914.317 ..... DD491.H244
..... DD901.N586
914.326 ..... DD901.M696
914.3303 ..... GN814.W8
914.332 ..... DD901.N93
914.335 ..... DD901.L72
914.336 ..... DD901.O2
914.34 ..... DD801.R73
..... DD801.R74
914.36 ..... DB785.E5
914.36.13 ..... DB857
914.3600222 ..... DB19
914.3603 ..... DB30
914.36035 ..... DB30
914.36045 ..... DB16
914.360450222 ..... DB19
914.3613 ..... DB785.W5
..... DB855
914.361300222 ..... DB847
914.361303 ..... DB847
914.3613035 ..... DB847
914.3613045 ..... DB849
914.364 ..... DB765
914.3648 ..... DB540.5
914.37 ..... DB193
..... DB199.2
..... DB215.2
..... DB879.P8
914.37032 ..... DB214
914.370340924 ..... DB215.5
914.37044 ..... DB195
914.371 ..... DB879.P8
914.38 ..... DA690.F68
..... DK404
914.380340924 ..... CT1232.G44
914.38045 ..... DK403
914.38045025 ..... DK403
914.381 ..... DD491.S54
914.382 ..... DD901.E36
..... DD901.S79
914.384 ..... DS135.P62
914.386 ..... DB345
..... DB349.2
..... DB879.K8
..... DK443.3
914.39045 ..... GV1025.H8
914.391 ..... DB864.2
..... DB877.B8
914.391035 ..... DB906.5
..... DB956
..... HQ792.H8
..... PH3381.W35
914.391045 ..... DB905
..... N8996.H8
914.4 ..... D917
..... DC17
..... DC28
..... DC29
..... DC40
914.40222 ..... DC20
914.403 ..... DC17
..... DC18
..... DC33.7
..... DC146.L3
..... DC252
..... DC252.5
..... PC3306
914.403022 ..... DC83
914.4031 ..... DC33.2
914.4032 ..... DC33.3
914.40327 ..... DC33.3
914.40328 ..... DC33.3
914.4033 ..... DC33.4
..... DC121.7
914.40332 ..... DC121.7
914.40334 ..... B1925.E5
914.403350924 ..... DC137.5.B6
914.4034 ..... PQ2025
914.40340924 ..... DC146.L3
914.4038 ..... DC33.7
..... DC365
914.403810922 ..... DC338
914.403810924 ..... PQ2625.A716
914.403816 ..... D745.2
914.403820924 ..... PR6015.E46
914.40383 ..... DC18
..... DC20
..... DC33
..... DC33.7
..... DC34
914.404 ..... DC29
914.40435 ..... DC25
914.4048 ..... PR5488
914.40483 ..... DC16
..... DC29
..... GV1025.F7
914.404830222 ..... DC20
914.41 ..... DC611.B848
914.42048 ..... DC27
914.4331 ..... CB353
914.436 ..... DC715
914.43600222 ..... DC707
914.43603 ..... DC723
..... NC139.F72
914.4360333 ..... DC729
914.436037 ..... DC278
914.4360381 ..... DC707
914.4360483 ..... DC707
..... DC708
914.44 ..... DC611.B78
914.44360483 ..... DC708
914.4490483 ..... DQ841.C4
914.45 ..... DC611.L81
914.450483 ..... DC611.L81
914.477 ..... DC611.G25
914.49 ..... DC611.P958
914.490483 ..... DC608.8
..... DC611.P958
914.492 ..... DC611.P958
..... DC801.A96
914.5 ..... D909
..... DA905
..... DA975
..... DG16
..... DG70
..... DG416
..... DG429
..... DG430
..... DG975.L2
..... DG975.T98
914.5003 ..... DG415
914.503 ..... DA920
..... DG418
914.50310924 ..... B659
914.5035 ..... CB361
..... DG431
..... DG445
..... DG533
914.50350922 ..... DG533
914.5036 ..... DG445
914.50360924 ..... DG731.5
..... DG738.14.M2
914.5037 ..... DG540
914.5039 ..... DG405
..... DG555
914.50392 ..... DG451
914.5047 ..... ML195
914.50492 ..... DG416
..... DG430
914.504920222 ..... DG430
914.509732 ..... DG417
914.518 ..... DG975.R6
914.523 ..... DG975.I63
914.531 ..... DG672
..... DG675.6
..... DG677.85
914.53100222 ..... NE42.L6
914.53103 ..... DG675.6
..... DG676.3
914.532 ..... DG975.P13
914.5414 ..... DS486.C2
914.55 ..... DG732
..... DG735.6
..... DG737
914.551 ..... DG732
..... DG737.42
914.551035 ..... DG735.6
914.5623 ..... DG975.S727
914.5630492 ..... DG806.2
914.563203 ..... DG806.2
914.5632036 ..... DG812.4
914.56320392 ..... DG806.2
914.56320492 ..... DG804
914.56504 ..... DG975.U5
914.570492 ..... DG416
..... DG821
914.573 ..... DG844.2
..... DG975.C2
914.577 ..... DG825
914.580492 ..... DG864.2
914.585 ..... DG989
..... DG999.H3
914.58504 ..... DG989
914.5904 ..... DC611.C812
914.5950391 ..... DC611.C81
914.6 ..... DP17
914.603 ..... DP17
..... DP41
..... DP42
..... DP48
..... DP91
914.6035 ..... DP48
914.6038 ..... DP41
914.60382 ..... DP357
914.603820222 ..... DP22
914.60481 ..... PR6023.E285
914.60482 ..... DP14
..... DP43
914.60974927 ..... DP103
914.641 ..... DP357
914.6520482 ..... DP302.P8
914.6603 ..... DC611.B313
914.67 ..... DP302.C6
914.672 ..... DP402.B25
914.675 ..... DP302.B26
..... DP302.B27
914.6750482 ..... DP302.B2
914.67650482 ..... DP302.A15
914.68 ..... DP302.A46
914.680482 ..... QK329
914.6820382 ..... DP402.G6
914.69 ..... DP519
..... DP538
914.6900222 ..... DP519
914.69003 ..... DP514
914.6903 ..... DP517
914.69034 ..... DP517
914.690382 ..... DP526
914.69044 ..... DP516
..... DP517
..... TF83
914.690440222 ..... DP519
914.69904 ..... DP702.A86
914.7 ..... DB199.2
..... DK4
..... DK14
..... DK16
..... DK17
..... DK18
..... DK21
..... DK23
..... DK25
..... DK26
..... DK27
..... DK28
..... DK32
..... DK274
..... DK755
..... DR10
..... DR34.8
914.700222 ..... DK28
914.7003 ..... DK18
914.70222 ..... DK18
..... DK28
914.703 ..... AC60
..... D917
..... DK4
..... DK23
..... DK25
..... DK26
..... DK32
..... DK40
..... DK189
..... DK266
..... DK267
..... DR16
914.70308410924 ..... CT1218.M257
914.7031 ..... CC105.R9
..... GN823
914.7035 ..... DK22
..... DK131
914.7036 ..... DK23
914.7037 ..... DK25
..... DK194
914.7038 ..... DK32
..... DK32.7
..... DK221
914.70380924 ..... CT1218.P587
..... CT1218.P59
..... CT1218.S354
..... DK254.S597
..... R489
914.70384 ..... DK268.3
914.703840924 ..... DK275.A4
914.7038420924 ..... DK268.3
914.70385 ..... DK28
..... DK33
..... DK266.A3
..... DK268.3
..... DK274
914.703850222 ..... DK28
914.703851 ..... DK274
914.704 ..... DK16
914.7044 ..... G161
914.704842 ..... DK28
914.70485 ..... DK16
..... DK28
914.706924 ..... DS146.E8
914.709743 ..... DK43
914.70974924 ..... DS135.R9
914.71 ..... DK450.2
914.71033 ..... DK449
914.71043 ..... DK450
..... DK450.2
..... G23.S63
914.717 ..... DL971.L2
914.71703 ..... DL971.L2
914.72 ..... DK21
914.731 ..... DK21
..... DK595
..... DK597
..... DK601.2
914.7403 ..... DK511.B25
..... DK511.B28
914.743 ..... DK511.L16
..... DK651.R5
914.74303 ..... DK511.L16
914.745 ..... DK549
..... DK552
..... DK553
..... PR6001.L72
914.7503 ..... DK511.L2
..... DK511.L212
914.750303 ..... DK511.L2
914.765 ..... DK507
..... DK507.2
914.7650385 ..... DK507.2
914.770485 ..... DK509
914.775 ..... DK511.M55
914.7750385 ..... DK511.M55
914.78 ..... DK26
914.79 ..... DK511.C1
..... DK651.S66
914.795 ..... DK511.G3
914.8 ..... DL5
..... DL11
914.8.9035 ..... DL111
914.8031 ..... DL31
914.8032 ..... DL31
..... DL65
914.8048 ..... DL4
914.809749455 ..... DL971.L2
914.81 ..... DL409
914.8103 ..... DL431
..... DL449
914.81043 ..... DL417
914.81044 ..... DL407
..... DL409
..... DL419
914.82 ..... DL581
914.85 ..... DL619
914.85035 ..... DL631
..... DL639
914.85045 ..... DL607
914.87 ..... DL976
914.89 ..... G56
914.89035 ..... DL109
..... DL113
914.89045 ..... DL107
914.891 ..... DL276
914.891045 ..... DL276.A2
914.9 ..... DH18
914.912 ..... DL305
..... DL312
..... DL314
914.91203 ..... DL313
914.912034 ..... DL314
..... DL326
914.912044 ..... DL304.I2
..... DL312
..... PR6001.U4
914.91503 ..... DL271.F2
914.92 ..... DH40
..... F521
914.9203 ..... DJ71
914.920308 ..... DJ71
914.92033 ..... DJ156
914.920370222 ..... DJ24
914.92047 ..... DH434
..... DJ16
..... DJ40
914.920470222 ..... DJ24
914.923 ..... DJ411.A53
..... DJ411.R8
914.93 ..... DH801.F45
914.9303 ..... DH418
..... DH471
914.93034 ..... DH418
..... DH434
914.93103 ..... DH801.F43
914.933 ..... DH809.7
914.935034 ..... DH905
914.94 ..... DQ17
..... DQ25
914.9400222 ..... DQ19
914.9403 ..... DQ36
914.94046 ..... DQ16
914.94047 ..... DQ16
914.943 ..... DQ851.C33
914.947 ..... DQ823
..... DQ823.5
..... DQ841.S12
..... DQ851.Z4
..... GV854.7
914.94700222 ..... DQ823.5
914.947047 ..... DQ823.5
914.95 ..... DE83
..... DF719
..... DF785
914.9503 ..... B3501
..... DF503
..... DF552
914.95031 ..... DF531
914.95035 ..... BX618
914.9503507 ..... HN463.5
914.95037 ..... DF717
..... DF741
914.950370924 ..... DF852
914.95047 ..... DF716
..... DF727
..... DF901.C9
..... DF901.I6
914.95120222 ..... DF287.A2
914.952 ..... DF901.P4
914.96 ..... DB449.2
..... HC244
914.9604 ..... GV1025.A2
914.961 ..... DR729
..... N3690.T8I7713
914.961043 ..... DR718
914.965032 ..... DR701.S5

Dewey	LC
914.97	DR10
	DR304.5
	DR305.5
914.9700222	DR305.5
914.9703	DR305
914.97032	DR305
	DR305.5
914.970320222	DR305.5
914.97042	DR304.5
	DR310
914.971	DR386.1
914.972	DB405
	DB879.R2
	DB879.Z343
	DR304.5
	DR396.P47
	DR396.S47
	DR396.S6543
	DR396.S658
	DR396.T75
914.97203	DB370.5
914.9742042	DB235
914.977	DR97
914.97703	DR55
	DR60.2
914.977033	DR55
914.977043	DR54
914.98	DR204.5
	DR210
	DR217
914.9800222	DR281.B47
914.98033	DR205
914.98043	DR204.5
914.981	DR281.P6
	DR296.J3
914.983	DR296.I8
914.984	DB735
914.99	DF901.L38
	DS52
914.996	DF901.S54
914.9960307	DS52
914.996047	DS53.R4
914.998	DF901.C8
914.998044	DF901.C8
915	CB253
	D199.3
	DK771.S2
	DK873
	DK873.W84
	DS2
	DS5
	DS10
	DS48
	DS475.2.B78
	DS504.5
	DS508.2
	DS509.3
	DS518.1
	DS786
	PS3556.L5
	Z1009
915.007	DS32.8
915.007205125	DS32.8
915.03	B121
	CB251
	DS1.5
	DS3.A2
	DS735
915.03071142	DS32.8
915.03072	DS2
915.03072047	DS32.8
915.031	BL1420
915.032	ND237.M2464
915.033	CB251
	G161
915.034	DS12
915.0341	DS508
915.0342	CB253
	DS1.5
	DS5
	DS736
915.04	DS508.2
915.041	DS6
915.042	G490
915.0442	DS4
	DS10
	DU23
	G490
915.1	DS706
	DS711
	DS721
	DS785
	GF656
915.1003	DS705
915.102	DS706
915.103	CB253
	DS703.4
	DS703.5
	DS706
	DS709
	DS721
	DS735
	DS773
915.10308	DS721
915.1032	DS721
	DS751
915.103208	DS703
915.1033	DS709
	DS760
915.10330924	DS710
915.1034	DS764
915.10340924	PR6062.I49
915.1034208	DS703.4
915.1035	DS703.4
915.1035	DS711
	DS724
	DS777.55
915.10350924	DS711
	DS778.T95
915.104	DS710
915.1043	DS709
915.1045	DS711
915.113003	Z3107.K5
915.11320330922	DS710
915.1156	DS795.8
915.1156045	DS795.A4
915.12	DS711
915.1203	DS731.H3
915.1249	GN2
	LB2376
	ND2070.L29
915.124903	DS895.F715
915.12490343	DS895.F7
915.1249035	DS895.F7
915.125	DS796.H7
915.125005	DS796.H7
915.12503	DS796.H7
915.12504	DS796.H7
915.127	DS793.H3
915.14043	DS785
915.15	DS785
	DS786
915.1503	DS786
915.17	DS793.M7
915.17003	DS798
915.170308	DS19
915.17303	DS798
915.18	DS782
915.1900222	DS902
915.1903	DS902
	DS904
915.19034	DS904
915.190343	DS902
	DS904
	DS932
915.195	DS925
915.2	DS806.3
	DS809
	DS811
	DS821
915.2024	DS806
915.203	DS821
	DS835
	DS836
	DS881.9
915.2030222	DS811
915.2031	DS835
	DS851.A2
915.20325	DS822.2
	DS836
	DS881.3
915.20331	DS821
	DS822.3
915.2033103	DS821
915.203320922	DS822.4
915.2034	CT1838.K273
	DS811
	DS821
	DS822.5
	DS881.9
	HC462.9
	SJ21
915.204250924	DS881.8
915.2044	DS805.2
	DS811
	DS822.5
	T796.7
915.213	NA6057.N5
915.2135034	DS896.5
915.2166	DS895.F9
915.219	DS897.H5
915.28103	DS895.R9
915.281031	DS895.R9
915.3	DS207
	DS244
915.3003	DS203
915.3035	DS207
915.3044	DS207
915.332	DS247.Y4
915.335	DS247.A14
915.36700222	DS247.K82
915.367035	DS247.K8
	DS247.K82
915.38	DS207
	DS248.J5
915.3803	DS248.M4
915.38044	DS207
915.4	DS335
	DS407
	DS408
	DS418
	DS421
	DS423
	DS485.H6
	DS485.K2
	N7301
915.400222	DS408
915.4008	DS503
915.402	GB301
915.403	CB253
	DS407
	DS421
	DS423
	DS436
	DS437
	DS481.R2
	DS731.M5
	Q125
915.4032	DS428
915.40325	DS411
915.4033	DS428
915.40330922	BL1265.R3
915.40335	BP80.A545
915.4033508	DS479.1.A33
915.403350924	CT1508.B43
	DS421
	DS480.6
	DS481.H78
	PK1726
915.4034	DS407
	DS414
	DS428
	DS481.D385
	DS481.G5
	DS481.N35
915.403408	DS428.2
915.4044	DS406
	DS408
	DS414
915.409742	DS463
915.409767	D199.3
915.4140329	DS485.B48
915.414034	DS485.B493
915.416	SB271
915.4162	DS432.N3
	DS485.A84
	DS485.A85
915.416203	DS485.A87
915.4165	DS432.N3
915.42	DS486.S3
	DS486.V37
915.43	DS486.K5
	GF662.B3
915.4303	DS489.15
915.44	DS485.A2
	DS485.B52
	DS485.J25
	DS485.R26
	DS486.M68
915.440325	DS485.R23
915.44034	DS485.R2
915.455	DS485.H343
915.456	DS486.L9
915.46	DS485.K2
	HQ792.I5
915.482	DS485.C24
	DS486.C7
915.483	Z3207.K4
915.484	DS485.A55
915.49	DS377
915.4903	DS379
	DS382
915.490308	DS382
915.49034	DS382
	DS384
915.49102	GB457.87
915.49103	DS425
915.492	CN1173.B4
	HC440.5.Z7
915.492034	DS485.B41
	DS485.B44
915.493	DS489
	DS489.2
915.4930025	DS490.C8
915.49303	DS489.5
915.4930320924	CT1528.M4
915.493033	HQ792.C4
915.493043	DS489
915.496	DS485.N4
915.49603	DS485.N4
915.49604	DS485.H6
915.49804	DS485.B503
915.5	DS254.5
	DS259
	F226
915.503	DS254.5
915.5035	DS254.5
915.504	DS254.5
915.5045	DS254
915.57	DS325.S52
915.595	DS325.I7
915.6	DR592.M8
	DS44
	DS48
	DS49
	DS119.7
915.603	DS37.7
	DS44
	DS62.4
915.6033	DS57
915.6034	DS119.7
915.604	DS44.5
	DS61.7.B8
915.60401	DR423
915.61	DR423
	DR429
	DR442
915.6103	DS155
915.61031	DR583
915.61033	DR432
915.61043	DR416
	DR418
	DR429
915.63	NA5871.K8
915.64	DR432
915.645044	DS54
915.66203	DS171
915.66203074095662	DS167
915.67	DS51.B3
	DS70.7
915.67034	DS70.6
915.69	G160
915.6903	DS48
915.69034	DS44
915.691	CT788.A47
915.692	DS80
	DS80.A5
915.692034	DS57
	DS80
915.692044	DS80.2
915.694	DS103.5
	DS106
	DS107
	DS107.4
	DS108.5
	DS109
	DS109.2
	DS111
	DS119.7
	DS126
915.69400222	DS109.2
915.69403	DA107.4
915.694032	N7973
915.694033	DS126.5
915.6940340924	DS125.3.S34
	DS219.B4
915.694035	DS103
	DS107.4
	DS108.5
	DS112
	DS126.5
915.6940350924	DS126.6.E4
915.694043	DS105
915.694045	DS103
	DS107.4
915.69406924	DS126
915.6940974924	DS107.4
915.695	DS109.8.G4
915.7	DK754
	DK755
	DK766
915.703	DK755
	DK771.D3
915.7033	GN855.R9
915.7037	DK755
915.70485	DK756
915.73	DK971.K5
915.7303	DK754
	GN796.R9
915.75	GN855.S5
915.77	DK771.K2
915.8	D378
	DK854
	DK873
	DK889
	DK971.M5
	DS6
	F286
915.803	DS786
915.81	AS281
915.810222	DS352
915.8103	DS352
	DS354
915.81031074	DS353
915.81034	DS354
915.81044	DS352
915.84	DK854
915.85	DK883
915.86	DK971
915.87	DK28
915.9	DS504.5
	DS505
	DS518.1
	G2360
915.903	DS508.2
	DS511
	PE1121
915.91	DS485.B81
	DS560
915.9103	DS485.B86
915.91032	DS485.B81
915.91035	DS485.B81
	DS485.B84
915.93	DS566
	DS572
915.930222	DS566
915.93032	DS564
	DS567
915.93033	DS563.5
915.93034	DS568
	DS584
915.930340924	DS568
915.93044	DS566
	DS568
915.95035	DS592
915.951	DS592
	DS595
915.9510330924	DS595.6.W5
915.952035	DS598.S7
915.9603	DS557.C24
	DS557.C25
915.96034	DS557.C2
	DS557.C22
915.97	DS557.A69
	DS557.A72
	NC1075.N5
915.9703	DS557.A5
915.97033	DS560
915.97034	DS557.A5
	DS557.A72
915.97044	DS557.A5
915.9800222	DS615
915.986	DS647.B2
916	DT3
	DT4
	DT5

Dewey	LC
916	DT6
	DT11
	DT12
	DT12.2
	DT14
	DT20
	DT25
	DT32
	DT37
	DT310
	DT351
	DT731
	DT731.L8
	DT758
	HQ1787
	JQ1881
916.00222	DT12.2
916.0071142	DT19.9.G7
916.0074	AM80.A2
916.008	DT3
916.03	DT3
	DT4
	DT14
	DT15
	DT352.4
	E448
	GN776.A15
916.0308	DT23
916.032	DT25
916.033	DT3
	DT12
	DT14
916.03307	DT19.8
916.042	DT11
916.1043	DT165.2
916.11	DT245
916.1103	DT245
916.11035	DT245
916.11045	DT244
916.12044	DT220.2.T45
916.14044	DT238.C8
916.2	DT47
	DT115
916.200222	DT47
916.203	BR1380
	DT107
916.2034	DT54
	DT117
916.2035	DT46
	DT56
916.2043	DT54
	DT135.N8
916.2044	DT55
916.2045	BF1434.E3
	DT56
916.20450222	DT47
916.21603	DT143
916.22	DT73.K4
916.24	DT121
916.24043	DT123
916.27	DT135.D2
916.2903	DT108.7
916.294033	DT135.B3
916.3	DT373
	DT377
	DT378
916.303	DT373
	DT379.5
	DT390.G2
916.303071143	DT380.85.G3
916.30330924	DT377
916.3034	DT377
916.3035	DT378
916.3043	DT377
916.3044	DT377
916.3045	DT378
916.30457	DT378
916.3403	DT379.5
916.4	DT304
916.4035	DT305
916.4044	DT310
916.4045	GV1025.M6
916.46	DT310.2
916.503	DT275
916.6	DT34
	DT333
	DT471
	DT472
	DT503
	DT513
	DT530
	GF721.W4
916.603	DT1
	DT351
	DT356
	DT360
	DT472
	DT548
916.604	DT356
	DT471
	DT472
	DT639
916.62	DT360
	DT553.T6
916.63003	DT549.2
916.64	DT516.2
	DT516.42
916.6403	DT1
	GN865.S45
916.64032	DT516
916.64043	DT516.2
	DT516.7
916.65	DT477
916.6503	DT509
916.651	DT509
916.6520330924	DT543.4
916.657003	DT613.2
916.66	DT624
	DT632
916.66003	DT623
916.6603	DT625
916.660300222	DT629
916.66032	DT624
	DT625
	DT632
	DT635
916.66033	DT629
916.668035	DT545.8
916.6703	DT510
916.67031	DT507
916.67035	DT510
	DT510.4
916.680330924	CT2750.L6
916.68035	DT541.4
916.69	DT515
	DT515.2
	DT515.3
916.6903	DT515
	DT515.2
916.69035	DT515.4
	DT515.42
	DT515.8
916.6903500222	DT515.2
916.692	DT515.9.I37
916.694	DT515.9.E3
	GN778.N5
916.695	DT515.9.A2
	DT515.9.K34
916.69503	DT515.42
916.7	DT4
	DT11
	DT36
	DT117
	DT351
	DT352
	DT352.5
	DT352.8
	DT361
	DT363
	DT423
	DT425
	DT426
	DT428.5
	DT455
	DT546
	DT611
	DT644
	DT655
	DT731
	DT731.K6
	DT731.L8
916.70071	DT352.47
916.70071273	DT352.47
916.703	DT1
	DT24
	DT351
	DT363
	DT431
916.704	DT351
	DT351.S6
	DT351.S9
	DT361
	DT363
	DT731
916.711032	DT567
916.721032	DT356
916.73042	DT611.2
916.75	DT646
	DT650
916.7503	DT639
916.75031	DT646
916.75032	DT644
	DT646
916.75042	DT646
916.7571	DT449.R9
916.7572	DT449.B8
916.76	DT117
	DT365.2
	DT425
	DT434.E22
916.7603	DT434.E22
916.761	DT117
	DT434.U242
	HC517.U22K34
916.76103	DT434.U2
	DT434.U23
916.761034	DT434.U2
916.761044	DT426
	DT434.U22
916.762	DT6
	DT434.E2
916.762034	DT434.E22
916.762044	DT434.E22
916.7703	DT403
916.78	DT438
	DT442.5
916.7803	DT438
916.781	DT434.Z3
916.781033	DT434.Z3
916.782	DT438
	DT440
	DT449.T3
	GN865.T33
916.7820310924	DT439
916.782032	DT443
916.782034	DT440
916.79	DT24
	DT453
916.79	DT465.M9
	DT731.L8
916.79003	DT452
916.8	DT729
	DT731
	DT758
	DT764.B8
	DT770
	DT773
	DT779.7
	DT848.H4
	DT921
916.800222	DT733
916.8003	DT752
916.802	G126
916.803	BV3555
	DT729
	DT731
	DT763
	DT764.B8
	DT766
916.8032	N5310
916.8033	DT763
916.8034	DT745.B2
	DT834
916.8035	CT1929.V27
916.80350924	DT779.8.G7
916.8036	DT761
	DT779
916.80360917496	DT944.J69
916.8043	DT756
916.8044	DT731
	DT757
	DT827
916.8046	DT752
916.809742	DT767
916.80974914	DT764.E3
916.80974963	DT797
	DT878.Z9
916.81	DT764.B8
	DT797
916.81034	DT791
916.81046	DT791
916.82	DT731
	DT944.J645
	DT944.J657
	QL337.T75
916.82034	SK255.T8
916.82044	DT756
916.822	DT944.J66S66
916.8304	DT971
916.84	DT878.Z9
916.8403	DT878
916.84034	DT875
	DT878.Z9
916.8404	DT875
916.84044	DT875
916.844034	DT872
916.85	DT895
916.87	DT823
	DT827
	DT848.C5
	DT848.G7
916.8700222	DT828
916.8703	DT821
	DT843
916.8704	DT823
916.87043	DT827
916.87044	DT827
916.87046	DT828
916.88	DT703
	F787
916.8804	DT703
916.88046	DT703
916.89	DT957
916.89044	DT854
916.891	DT952
	DT957
	DT958
	DT964.M4
	DT965.Z5
916.89103	DT962.4
916.891031	DT962.3
916.891044	DT962.2
916.894	DT963
	DT963.2
	DT964.B3
916.894003	DT963.2
916.89403	GN776.R5
916.894034	DT963
916.89404	DT963.2
916.897	DT858
	DT862
	DT864.
916.897003	DT857.5
916.89703	DT361
916.897032	DT862
916.9	DT468
916.9031	PR3405
916.904	DT468
916.91	DT469.M26
916.9103	DT469.M31
916.91031	DT469.M26
	DT469.M34
916.96	DT469.S4
916.982	DT469.M4
916.982033	DT469.M4
916.98204	DT469.M42
917	E41
	E166
	G1201.P2
917.044	E166
	F1013
917.0453	E169.02
917.1	F1004
	F1008.2
	F1013
	F1015
	F1016
	F1031.5
	F1060.7
	F1060.8
	HC113
917.1003	F1004
917.103	F1008
	F1021
	F1026
	PE1417
917.10303	F1006
917.1031	F1021
917.1033	F1060.8
917.1035	F1015
917.1036	F1003
917.10364	F1008
	F1016
917.103640222	F1027
917.104	F1013
917.1042	F1013
917.1043	F1013
917.1044	E167
	F1013
917.10464	F1009
	F1016
917.104640222	NC143.M34
917.109174924	F1392.J4
917.109745	F1035.I8
917.109749192	F1035.L5
917.10974924	F1035.J5
917.11	CT275.S989
	F1087
	F1090
	PM1641
917.11003	F1086.4
917.11044	F1087
917.1109761	BX7433
917.111	F1060.4
917.112	F1089.5.B25
917.113	F1089.I5
917.1131034	F1089.Q3
917.11320330924	F1060.9
917.1134	F1089.S2
	F1089.V3
	F1089.5.H3
	F1089.5.P58
	TX941.E45
917.1134033	F1089.V3
917.1142	F1089.5.A7
	F1089.5.S9
917.1145	F1089.K7
917.12	F1060.9
917.121	F931
	F1091
917.122	F880
917.122031	F1060.7
917.1220310924	F1060
917.122041	F1060
	F1060.8
917.1221	F1100.5.D5
917.123	F1079.T3
917.12303	F1079.5.B8
917.123032	F1076
	F1078
917.1230320922	F1075.8
917.1230320924	F1076.5
917.123033	F1076
917.123043	F1076
917.1231	F1079.5.B4
	F1079.5.G7
917.1233	F1071
	F1079.5.O4
	F1079.5.V4
	F1079.5.W4
	F1079.5.W48
	F1080.U5
	HC117.C32
	HC118.H33
	HC118.K5
	HC118.L3
917.1233041	F1001
917.1234	F1079.5.C36
917.124	F1070.4
917.124033	F1071
917.124043	F1071
917.1242	F1074.5.C64
	F1074.5.E9
917.1244	F1074.5.A7
917.127	E78.M25
	F1061.4
	F1062
917.1271	F1060
917.127103	E78.M25
917.1273	F1064.5.T45
917.13	F1057
	F1059.N5
917.1303	HN110.O5
917.13032	F1057
917.13033	F1057
917.130330924	CT310.C35
	F1058
917.13044	F1057
	SK602.C3
917.131	F552
	F1057
917.13133034	F1059.5.S85
917.1317	F1059.5.O7
917.1325	F1059.M6
917.1337	F1059.5.C33
917.1338	F1059.5.A35

917.1338	F1059.5.T43
	F1059.5.W18
917.133903	F127.N8
917.1342	F1059.5.A7
917.1344	F1059.5.W48
917.1351	F1059.5.S14
917.1352	F1059.5.H2
917.1352032	F1059.W4
917.1353503	F1059.P25
917.1354044	F1059.5.T68
917.1354103	F1059.5.T68
917.13541044	F1059.5.T68
917.1355	F1059.5.W44
917.1358	F1059.5.T45
917.13580330924	CT275.S442
917.1367	F1059.5.N88
917.1372	F1059.5.K5
917.1381003	F1001
917.13840464	F1057
917.14	F1050
917.1403	F1027
917.14042	F1052
917.1417	F1054.N5
917.14281	BX4605.M6
917.142810340924	PS3556.I83
917.1477031	F1054.G2
917.1543	F1044.5.O7
917.16	F1038
917.16041	F1037
917.1625	F1037
917.1634	F1039.K5
917.177	F1049.5.B4
917.18	DL65
	F1122
917.1800222	F1122
917.18042	NC139.K4
917.19	F1136
917.19032	F1136
917.2	F1208.5
	F1209
	F1216
	F1386.A4
	F1392.J4
	F1435
917.203	F1208
	F1219
	GN37.M4
917.2032	F1211
917.203208	F1227
917.2034	F1213
917.2036	F1213
917.203810924	F1234
917.20382	F1226
	HQ792.M48
917.204	F593
917.20420924	F1211.G25
917.2045	F1213
917.2046	F1213
917.20482	F1209
	F1216
917.21	F1213
	F1391.T7
917.22042	F1246
917.220482	F1246
917.2204820222	F1246
917.23	F1401
917.25	F1386
	F1386.2
917.26	F1235
	F1333
917.28	F1432
	F1434
917.28034	F1428
917.28035	F1608
917.28044	F1432
917.28045	F1429
	F1433
917.281	F1469.P4
917.28103	E51
	F1435
	F1463
917.281035	F1464.2
917.282	F1445.1.A27
917.28203	F1443
917.283	G161
917.283035	F1504
917.285035	F1523
917.286035	F1543
917.29	F1763
	F2131
	F2171
	F2171.2
917.2903	F2131
917.29033	F1610
	F2161
917.2904	G530
917.29042	F2161
917.29044	F1611
917.29045	F1609
	F2171.2
917.291	F1758
	F1763
917.29100207	F1776
917.291035	F1763
917.2910364	F1765.2
	F1788
917.291045	F1763
917.292	F1868
917.29200222	F1872
917.29203	F1871
	F1872
917.292033	F1871
917.2920334	F1871
917.292034	F1871
917.292046	F1869
917.293	F2171
917.293035	F1934
917.294	F1921
917.294034	F1931
917.294036	F1916
917.294045	F1917
917.295	F1965.2
917.29500222	F1965.2
917.29503	F1958
917.2950453	F1965.2
917.296	F1659.B55
	F1659.F7
917.29604	F1651
	F1652
917.297	F2001
917.29704	F2001
917.297203	F2136
	F2136.42
917.29722	F2136
917.2972200222	F2136.2
917.297603	F2151
917.298	F2106
917.298103	F2041
917.2982	Q11
917.2983	F2116
917.2984400222	F2061
917.29903	F1631
917.3	CT275.M6528
	E98.N2
	E155
	E158
	E159
	E160
	E161
	E163
	E165
	E166
	E167
	E168
	E169
	E169.02
	E169.1
	E173
	E178.3
	E184.S18
	E184.S6
	E184.S65
	E185.86
	F184
	F353
	F596
	NA7206
	PS2018
	SK357
917.300222	E169.O2
917.30025	E154.5
917.3003	E155
917.30076	E169.02
917.3008	E178.6
917.300924	F592
917.302	E179.5
917.30222	E168
917.30292	TL726.2
917.303	CT275.B4
	CT275.J677
	CT275.P16
	E155
	E159
	E159.5
	E161
	E162
	E164
	E165
	E166
	E168
	E169.02
	E169.1
	E169.12
	E173
	E178
	E184.C6
	E184.7
	E187
	E742
	F204.W5
	NA7205
	PS509.M5
917.303072	E169.1
917.30308	E169.1
	E173
	E178.6
917.30309176	E184.J5
917.3030922	E169.1
917.30316	E169.1
917.3032	E189
917.303208	E187
917.30327	E163
917.3033	E164
917.30330922	E302.6.F8
917.3034	E164
917.3035	E165
	E166
917.303508	E165
917.30354	E165
917.303550924	E165
	E165.T86
917.30356	E165
917.30357	E165
917.3036	E166
917.30361	E166
917.30366	E166
917.3037	E169.1
917.3038	B944.N3
917.3038	CT275.K599
	E168
	E169.1
	E661
917.30380924	CT275.B5943
	CT275.C3
	PS1013
917.30384	E168
917.30386	E168
917.30388	TS199
917.303880924	E168
917.3039	CB427
	DK254.L46
	E169.1
	E169.12
	E743
917.30390222	E161
917.30390922	CS71.D77
	E176
917.30390924	CT275.A715
	CT275.H479
	CT275.M582
	CT275.S5218
	CT275.W555
917.30391	E169
	E169.1
	E741
	E784
	E806
	LA2317.D38
	PS3545.I347
917.303910222	E161
917.303910922	E747
917.303910924	CT275.S9872
	E169.5
	E184.J5
	E185.97.Y4
917.303911	E169.1
	TS199
917.303913	E169
917.30391308	E766
917.303914	TS199
917.303915	E784
917.303916	TS2301.N55
917.303917	E806
917.30391708	E806
917.30392	D840
	E169.12
	E839
	E846
	PS659
	PS3563.U8
	PS3569.M5375
917.303920222	E185.86
	E839
917.3039208	E169.12
917.303920922	PS647.C6
917.303920924	CT275.C573
917.303921	E169.12
917.3039220924	CT275.B316
	E169.12
917.303923	E169.O2
	E169.02
	E839.4
917.3039230924	CT275.S6763
917.303924	BX930
	CT220
	CT275.T8757
	E169.12
	E839
	HV881
	PN6162
	PS3511.U6617
917.304	E161.5
917.3042	E162
917.3043	E163
	E164
917.3044	E164
917.3044108	E164
917.30443	E164
917.30448	E164
917.30451	E164
917.30454	E165
	F326
917.30456	E165
	F484.3
917.30458	E165
917.3046	E166
917.30461	E166
917.30464	E166
917.30482	E168.O332
917.304913	GV1024
917.30492	E169.02
	E839
	GV835
917.30492062	GV1027
917.304923	E27.2
	E169.02
	E169.02
	GV1065
917.3049230222	E169.02
917.304924	E158
	E169.02
917.30691992	Z232.D38
917.306924	E184.J5
917.30696	E185
917.30696073	E185.5
	E444
917.3091749162	E184.I6
917.3091749185	E184.P7
917.309174924	E184.J5
917.309732	E169
917.309743	E184.G3
917.30974397	E184.S23
917.309743982	E184.S2
917.309746	E169.1
	E184.M5
917.30974916	E184.C6
917.309749162	JV6625
917.309749163	E184.S4
917.309749182	E184.Y7
917.30974924	E184.J5
917.3097494541	E184.F5
917.3097496	E184.7
	E185
	E185.5
	E185.6
	E185.615
	E185.82
	E185.86
	PE1122
917.30974960924	E185.97.A56
917.30975956	E184.J3
917.309761	BX8530.M6
917.325	E197
917.335036	PS3565.N4
917.35	E185
917.352	F1059.5.H2
917.38	CT310.P73
917.4	E162
	F106
	F123
917.402	GB525.A6
917.403	F4.3
917.403208	E187
917.4033	F19
917.40340924	CT275.H443
	CT275.T876
917.4043	E164
	E165
	F106
917.4044	F2.3
	F106
	QE375.A67
917.40922	CT3260
917.40944	GB604
917.409743	F145.G3
917.41	F17
	F19
	F25
917.41008	F16
917.41034	S521
917.412	F27.A4
917.4125	F27.P5
	F29.P23
917.4125044	F27.P5
917.4145	S521
917.417	PN1993.5.U73
917.4195	F29.S2
917.42	F32
917.42033	F38
917.421	F44.C68
917.423044	F41.3
917.426	F44.D43
	F44.P8
917.427	F44.H77
	JK1651.N42
917.42903	F44.H43
917.43	S521
917.4300222	F50
917.430308	F49.6
917.430340924	F49
917.433	F574.H47
917.43503	F59.B85
917.44	F65
917.4400222	F71
917.4403	AM12.M4
917.44032	BF1575
	F67
	F68
917.44042	F67
917.4410330924	E444.F87
917.4426	F74.W6
917.443	F74.R97
	F74.S93
917.444	F74.C1
	F74.L67
917.445	F74.A4
	F74.E7
	F74.M63
917.4450340924	CT275.C6417
	F74.B35
917.445044	F72.E7
917.4461	F73.37
	F73.65.H3
917.4461032	F73.44
917.4461033	HN80.B7
917.4461044	F73.18
917.448	F74.N15
	F74.W28
917.449	F72.C3
917.44904	F72.C3
917.449044	F72.C3
917.4494	E78.M4
	F72.M5
917.4497034	CT275.K97
917.4503	F127.L8
917.45044	SK601
917.457	F89.N5
917.463033	HG2613.H24S6
917.46306924	F104.H3
917.466	F104.E8
	F104.P86
917.47	F117
	F122
	F123
917.47032	F122
917.471	CS71.F836

917.471 F128.37
F128.52
F128.67.O5
F128.67.T5
F128.68.G8
F128.7
917.47103 F128.44
917.471033 F128.44
917.471034 F128.47
F128.52
917.471044 F128.18
F128.5
917.47106924 F128.9.J5
917.47109745 F128.9.I8
917.4710974924 F128.9.J5
917.4710974927 F128.9.S98
917.471097496 F128.9.N3
917.472 F128.37
917.472034 PS3552.R38
917.472044 F128.18
917.472047 F128.18
917.4721 CT275.C125
F127.L8
917.472103 F127.L8
917.4723 F129.B7
917.47243 F129.J2
917.4725 F129.A47
917.472750340924 F128.68.B8
917.47277044 F127.W5
917.473 F127.H8
917.4733 F129.S613
917.4734 F129.N53
917.4737 F129.W8
917.4738044 F127.C3
917.4743097496 E185.97
917.4753 F127.A2
917.4759034 F127.L6
917.476 GV835.2.N4
917.4774 F123
F129.M78
917.47830340924 F127.S8
917.4788 F129.R94
917.4796 F129.O58
917.4797 F129.B8
917.47970340924 CT275.B4677
917.48003 F147
917.4803 F149
917.48044 F150
F155
917.4809743 F160.G3
F160.M45
917.4811 G1264.P5
917.4811033 F158.44
917.48110330924 E302.6.L67
917.4811034 CT275.R553
F158.5
917.4811044 F158.18
917.4811097496 GR103
917.4814 F159.N52
917.4815044 F157.L2
917.4816 F159.A57
F159.E95
917.4825 E78.N6
917.4827 F159.C677
917.4841 F159.Y9
917.488603 NC139.L44
917.4886034 F159.P6
917.49 F157.D4
917.49033 F138
917.49044 F132.3
917.491034 ML1711.8.N3M414
917.4923 F144.B414
917.49410340924 CT9991.B7
917.4946 F142.M63
F144.O26
917.4967044 F144.P9
917.5 CT275.H64567
F106
F210
F213
F215
F216.2
F217.B6
F351
917.503 F206
F209
F209.5
F215
917.5033 F210
F213
F216
917.50330917496 E450
917.50330924 F213
917.5034 F215
F216
917.50340924 CT275.T557
917.5043 F213
917.5044 F215
F216
917.5097496 E185.6
917.52 F186.2
F187.P8
TC625.C5
917.52003 F179
917.5203 F187.A15
917.521 F179
917.5221 F187.E2
917.5251 F187.P56
917.5255 F189.S45
917.5256044 F189.A6
917.5260340924 CT275.B4679
917.526044 F189.B1
917.5271 F187.B2
917.5284 F189.B4

917.53 BX4603.W32
F203.5.J8
F204.O4
F204.W5
KF26.I542
917.5300222 F195
917.530025 F192.5
917.5303 F200
F203.4.A1
F204.W5
917.53032 F196
F213
917.53034 F200
917.53044 F192.3
F200
ND1946.S2
917.541503 F249.W5
917.545044 SD428.M65
917.5482034 F247.P9
917.54850944 GB605.W4
917.5487 HE2791
917.55 F224
F226
F230
917.55032 F229
917.550320924 CT275.R317
917.55034 F230
917.55043 F230
917.55044 E470.2
917.5509174924 F235.J5
917.5509743 F235.G3
917.55097496 E185.93.V8
917.5515034 F232.E2
917.551803 F187.C5
917.552 F232.N86
917.5526 Q11
917.55366044 F234.F8
917.55425203 F234.W7
917.554252032 F234.W7
917.5545103 F234.R5
917.556403 F232.L9
917.55703 GN1
917.5592 F232.R7
917.5603 F440
917.560340924 CT275.S8825
917.561044 F252.3
917.56142 F264.E4
917.56155 F264.M9
917.5616 F264.W62
917.56565 NC139.P7
917.57 F277.A15
917.57033 F273
917.57034 F274
917.570696 E185.93.S7
917.5709693 PZ10.C3337
917.572 F277.R44
917.5723 F277.P5
917.573303 F277.G7
917.5789 F277.G35
917.57915033 E263.S7
917.5799 E185.93.S7
917.579903 F277.B3
917.57990696 E185.93.S7
917.5799097496 E185.93.S7
917.580330924 F290
917.5818 F294.A7
917.5823 F294.R75
917.586603 F292.O27
917.587 F291.2
917.58766 F294.S7
917.58913 F294.D4
917.59 F312
F316.2
917.5903 F311
F314
917.59036 F311.3
917.59046 F309.3
F316.2
917.5911 F129.F56
917.5932036 F317.P2
917.59381 F319.M62
917.5941 F317.E9
917.5962 F317.M2
917.59650360924 F316
917.6 F213
F296
F352
NC1135.L47
917.6043 F396
917.6100222 F327
917.61035 F326
917.6122 F334.M6
917.6134035 F332.C65
917.6147 F334.M7
917.6173 F334.H6
917.6178036 F332.J4
917.619403 F332.M4
917.6203 F440
917.62033 F341
917.622 F341
917.6226 F349.N2
917.6229 F349.V6
917.62403 E51
917.624032 F389
917.63 F367
F369
917.630350924 F213
917.630360922 F379.N5
917.63046 F375
917.63097496 E185.93.L6
917.6335503 F379.N55
917.63355046 F379.N5
917.6336 E356.N5
917.64 E169

917.6403 CT275.C684
CT275.L656
F386
F386.5
917.64036 F391.2
917.6403605 AY311.A8
917.640360924 CT275.P444
917.64046 F384.3
F391
F391.2
917.6409743 F395.G3
917.6409743982 F395.N6
917.6409753 F395.G3
917.64103 F388
917.64143 F388
917.64163 CT275.E429
917.64183 F388
917.642 F384
917.64235 F394.H8
917.6424 F392.A9
917.64245 F394.C46
917.6428 F394.D2
917.64284 F392.M2
917.643 CT275.O42
917.6435 F388
917.644 F392.P14
F790.A1
917.6444403 F392.K2
917.6446 F394.D63
917.64551036 F392.E7
917.64553 F394.B34
917.6464 F391
917.6465 F388
F394.F9
917.6468 F388
917.647503 F392.C82
917.6480360924 PN4874.G679
917.6488 E78.T4
917.64888 F394.D7
F394.W62
917.64932 F392.B53
917.649340360924 F391.M56
917.6496 CT275.H237
F394.E4
917.64960360922 CT558.B44
917.6496046 F392.E45
917.66034 F694
917.660350924 CT275.G52
917.6613 F704.B65
917.663 S521
917.6638 G1369.O6
917.6648 F704.F74
917.67 F440
917.6803 F440
917.68045 F440
917.6819 F444.M5
917.683303 F443.B4
917.6847033 F443.S9
917.6855035 F444.N2
917.688503 E78.T3
917.6889 F106
F443.G7
917.689 F436
917.6912 F106
917.692 F457.B5
917.69585 F459.A2
917.696403 F457.W4
917.6968 E185.93.K3
917.6978034 F456
917.698 F788
917.7 E166
F351
F352
F355
F479
F516
F518
F551
F606
GN2
917.7031 F544
917.7033 F351
917.7043 Z232.R76
917.71 F491
F492
917.7103 F491.3
917.7131 F499.O55
F499.S6
917.7138 F499.N55
917.7156 F499.W92
917.7178 F499.C5
917.718203 E78.O3
917.72034 F526
917.7204 F521
917.73 F539
F539.3
917.730071 F540.5
917.731 F549.K35
917.73110222 F548.37
917.731103 F548.3
917.7311034 F548.52
917.7311043 F548.18
917.7311044 F548.18
917.731109745 E184.I8
917.73380340924 CT275.N443
917.73480330922 F547.F8
917.736703 F547.P5
917.7381034 F547.C5
917.739803 F547.H3
917.74 F566
917.740022 G1411.E63
917.7403 CD3309.K3
917.740320924 CT275.H663
917.740330924 CT275.D376

917.74034 F566
917.741 F570
917.7433 F574.W34
917.7434 F574.D4
917.7446 F574.T5
917.7454 F574.P85
917.74603 F612.R42
917.747660974924 F129.S8
917.7481 CT275.M4596
917.749043 F552
917.7491 GN2
917.7492 GN2
917.7494 GN2
917.749403 GN2
917.75 E78.W8
917.75034 F581
917.7509743982 F590.N6
917.7552 F587.W9
917.7557 S521
917.7564 E78.W8
917.7569 F589.P74
917.758 F585.F5
917.7585 F589.S93
917.7586 F589.N5
917.76 E78.M7
F604
917.760022 G1426.E63
917.7603 E78.M7
917.76030922 F605
917.7609693 GV54.M6
917.76579 G1429.M5
917.76579045 F614.M6
917.7659 F612.S2
917.7703 E185.93.I64
917.77033 PZ10.M4379
917.7725 F629.R6
917.773703 F629.F53
917.7741 F629.S6
917.7752 S519
917.7766 F629.W44
917.7796 F629.D4
917.78033 F466
917.78034 F466
917.78135 F474.W52
917.7828 CT275.W3878
917.7861 F474.H5
917.786600222 F474.S2
917.786603 F474.S2
917.7874303 F472.C4
917.788 F472.C9
917.79487 F869.G78
917.8 E160
F591
F592
F592.4
F592.7
F594
F594.D627
F596
F721
F746
F865
F880
917.800222 NC139.R4
917.803 AS36
F591
F594
F595
F811
917.8032 F591
F593
F596
F800
F851
917.80320922 F591
917.80320924 F592
F596
917.80330924 CT275.B143
CT275.T7483
E185.97
917.8042 F592.4
F593
F594
F595
F721
F780
F786
917.80420924 F592
917.8043 F595.2
F721
917.804306173 F592.7
917.80696 E185.925
917.8097496 E185.925
917.81 F681
917.810330924 CT275.F6936
917.81335 F689.H7
917.8155 F689.M13
917.8168 F689.H55
917.81703 AM12.K2
917.8176 CT275.K88
917.818403 F687.K53
917.8189 F689.A72
917.8197 F689.F7
917.820330924 CT275.G352
917.83 F651.3
917.8303 E78.S63
917.832 F657.L37
917.8331 F657.L37
917.83577033 F657.J6
917.839031 F657.B6
917.8391 F657.B6
917.8393 F657.B13
917.8403 F598
917.84140320924 CT275.W3863

917.8603 F731
F731.3
F731.6
917.86032 F731
917.86033 CT275.E78
917.863703 F737.P8
917.86550330924 F731
917.8703 F761
F767.A15
917.8752 F767.T3
QH105.W8
917.875204 E160
917.8752043 F722
917.8755 F767.T3
917.88 CT275.B11
CT275.S6972
917.8803 F776
917.88032 F592
917.88043 F781.2
917.8827 E51
917.883 F780
F782.R6
917.8833 F784.P58
917.8843 F784.A7
917.8844 F784.V3
917.8855 F784.P9
917.8858 CT275.L342
F784.V6
917.8868 F782.L2
917.8869 F782.L83
917.886904 F782.R59
917.8872 F784.G7
917.8891 PS3503.O563
917.89 CT275.T287
917.8903 F796
917.89034 CT275.J757
917.89043 F800
917.89045 F801.2
917.8909746 F805.M5
917.893034 F596
917.8952 F804.T7
917.8953 F804.T2
917.895303 E78.N65
917.8956 F804.S2
917.8957 E99.C84
917.8964 F801.C3
917.8993 E78.N65
917.9 F841
F864
917.9044 F786
917.909665 F851
917.91 E125.V3
F596
F786
F799
F811
917.9100222 F815
917.9103 E99.P9
F787
F811
917.91034 F786
F811
917.9104 ND237.N447
917.91044 F811
917.91097496 E184.M5
917.9109756 F790.M5
917.913 CT275.L683
F788
917.9130074 F806.N63
917.913044 F788
917.9132 F788
917.913200222 F788
917.91320450222 F788
917.9133 F819.F57
917.913503 E99.P9
917.9137 F817.P4
917.9179032 F811
917.9203 F826
917.9227 F832.D3
917.9228 F834.R68
917.9248 F832.Z8
917.925 F832.G5
917.9254 F832.C38
917.93 F841
F843
917.9303 F839
917.93043 F841
917.9313 F849.L35
917.931603 F863
917.94 F859
F859.3
F862
F864
F865
F866
F866.2
917.9400222 F862
F866.2
917.94003 F859
F863
917.9403 F861
F865
PE1127.H6
917.94033 F864
917.94034 F865
917.940340924 F865
917.94035 CT275.A719
F861
917.94045 F859.3
F861
F862.A52
F866.2
917.9406951 F870.C5
917.940974951 F870.C5
917.94097496 E185.93.C2
917.941 F859.3
917.943 F868.S5
917.944 F859
F868.S5
917.944044 F868.S5
917.9445 F868.Y6
917.9447 F868.Y6
917.9448 F869.B65
917.94500222 F868.S173
917.9451 F869.D27
917.9452 F868.S13
917.94540340222 F869.S12
917.9457 F869.M67
917.946 F868.S156
917.94600222 F869.S3
917.946045 F868.S156
GF504.C2
917.9461 F869.F66
917.946100222 F869.S3
917.9461030222 F869.S3
917.9461035 CT275.P3872
F869.S3
917.9461045 SB483.S3
917.9462 F869.T5
917.9463 F868.C76
917.9469 G1528.S28
917.9471 F869.S723
GN37.A8
917.9473 G1528.S4
917.9476 F864
F869.B63
F869.C27
F869.M7
PS559.P3
917.9481 F868.M2
917.9486 F868.K28
917.9487 F868.D2
SD428.A48
917.949 F867
917.949035 F867
917.94904 G1526.C5
917.9491 F869.L8
917.9492 E51
917.9493 E51
F864
G1528.L6
917.94930631 F868.L8
917.94930696 F868.L8
917.94930974924 F869.L8
917.9494 F869.H74
F869.L8
917.94940340924 CT275.L795
F869.L8
917.94940350222 F869.L8
917.9495 F869.R3
917.9495008 E78.C15
917.9496 F869.L17
F869.S214
917.9498 F868.S15
F869.S22
917.9498045 F868.S15
917.95 F851.5
F851.7
F852.2
GV815
917.95044 F881.2
917.957034 CT275.N6854
917.95970022 G1493.M3
917.96043 F744.3
917.960974951 F755.C5
917.961 F752.S7
917.961045 F869.S3
917.9621 F754.S5
917.9653 E78.I18
917.9682 F752.S35
917.9686032 F752.L3
917.97 F891
917.9700222 F892
917.9703 E78.W3
917.970308 E78.W3
917.97044 GV54.W2A584
917.9737034 E78.W3
917.9748034 CT275.M719
917.975 F897.C3
917.977044 F897.P9
917.977303 F897.W57
917.9777 CT275.V563
F899.S4
917.9778 CT275.B5974
917.9792 F897.P2
917.9798044 F897.O5
917.98 F909
917.9803 F904
917.98033 F909
917.98034 CT275.R3457
917.980340924 F909
917.98035 F904
917.98045 F904
F904.3
F910
917.982 E78.W3
F912.G5
917.984 F912.R39
917.986 F914.N6
F931
918 F1401
F1408
F1409.9
F2208
HC125
918.0061 F1401
918.03 CB226
F1408.3
918.03 F1409.9
F1410
F2208.5
918.03071173 F1409.9
918.033 CT275.H354
F1408
F1408.3
F1409.9
F2224
918.043 F1409.2
F2224
918.1 F2508
F2508.5
F2510
F2515
F2520.7
F2808
918.1033 F2513
918.1035 F2510
918.1036 F2508.5
918.1044 F2513
918.1045 F3313
918.1046 F2509.5
F2516
918.11 F2546
918.11042 E125.O6
918.15 F2651.B42
918.16 F2596
F2651.S24
HN290.S33
918.2 F2217
F2808
F3058
918.203 F2217
918.2036 F2808
918.27 F2936
918.3 F3058.5
F3063
918.36 G161
918.4 F3308.5
918.403 F3314
918.4035 F3314
918.41 F3351.L2
918.5 F3408.5
F3431
918.5003 F3404
918.503 F3409.5
F3429
918.53 F3611.C9
918.61 F1401
F2258
918.6103 F2258.5
918.610363 F2258
F2264
918.610463 F2264
918.615 F2291.C15
918.62003 F1562
918.6203 GN1
918.620303 F1562
918.62032 F1564
918.62035 F1564.2
918.6303 F1569.C2
918.66 F3708
918.6603 GN1
918.66037 F3714
918.7 E2308
F2311
918.700222 F2308
918.703 F2308
918.70363 F2308.5
918.8 G161
918.81 F2368
918.8103 F2368.5
F2372
918.81032 F2371
918.8203 F2448.5
918.8303 F2408.5
918.83033 F2408.5
918.92035 F2675
918.92037 F2668.5
918.95 F2708
918.95036 F2708
F2708.5
919 DU21
DU23
DU29
G650
919.03 GN851
919.1 DS411.1
DS595
DS601
DS615
DS620
G161
919.100222 DS620
919.103 DS615
919.10322 DS615
919.1043 DS620
919.1097469 DS625
919.11033 DS646.3
919.115035 DS646.3
919.115203 DS646.33
919.1153 DS599.M4
GN780.B6
919.1204 DS646.4
919.14 DS655
DS666.G3
919.1403 DS655
919.140308 DS664
DS668
919.14031 DS661
919.140335 DS655
919.14034 DS660
919.141034 DS665
919.23 DS647.B2
919.3 DU105
DU412
DU490
PR9635
919.303 DU423
919.31 DU405
DU411
DU412
DU420
DU430.N38
919.31003 DU405
919.3102 GB381
919.3103 DU412
DU420
DU421
GN705
S521
919.31031 GN1
919.31033 CT2888.S9
DU412
DU418
DU420
919.310410924 DU410
919.31043 DU412
919.311 DU430.T47
DU430.W39
G530
919.312 GN705
919.3122 DU430
DU430.A8
DU430.C64
DU430.H2
919.3127 DU428
919.3152 DU430.B57
919.31520330924 CT2888.T6
919.3153 DU430.A2
919.3155 DU430.C3
DU430.C5
DU430.M65
919.31550310924 CT2888.T57
919.3157 DU430.D8
DU430.D85
DU430.O8
DU430.W25
919.315702 DU430.O8
919.3157033 CT2888.M25
919.315704 DU430.O8
919.3157043 DU430.O8
919.3503 GN671.S6
919.4 DU15
DU23
DU95
DU97
DU99
DU101
DU102
DU105
DU110
DU114.G5
DU115
DU116
DU222.B84
DU280.G7
DU380.N8
PR9573
SB484.A9
919.400222 DU105
919.4003 DU90
919.402 DU105
GB381
919.403 DU95
DU110
DU112
919.40306294 DU135
919.4031 GN871
919.4031028 GN665
919.4032 DU101
919.40330924 CT2808.P58
919.403350924 D811.5
919.4034 DU107
DU116
919.40340924 CT2808.C54
CT2818.P46
919.4035 CT2818.B4
DU95
DU105
DU107
ND1946.S2
919.403500222 DU93
919.40350207 DU107
919.4042 DU390
919.40420924 DU114.S8
919.4043 DU102
919.40430924 DU114.G5
919.4044 DU104
919.4045 DU23
DU93
DU95
DU105
919.40944 GB606.A94
919.409749915 DU120
919.41 DU360
DU378
DU380.K33
DU380.R68
DU380.S9
DU380.U6
TN426.A9
919.41035 DU360
919.42 CS2109.C6
DU328
DU330.B87
DU330.K35

919.42003 ..... DU305
919.4203 ..... DU320
919.42035 ..... DU310
919.429 ..... DU98.1
..... DU398.A7
..... DU398.A9
..... DU398.V5
..... GC1015
919.42900222 ..... DU395
919.43 ..... DU120
..... DU260
..... DU270
..... DU278
..... DU280.C37
..... DU280.G6
..... DU280.N65
919.4303 ..... DU260
919.43033 ..... DU270
919.430350924 ..... DU135
919.44 ..... CT2818.W5
..... DU160
..... DU161
..... DU162
..... DU178
..... DU180
..... DU180.B8
..... DU180.H3
..... DU180.J5
..... DU180.K73
..... DU180.K8
..... DU180.L47
..... DU180.M3
..... DU180.M8
..... DU180.N4
..... DU180.P62
..... DU180.S6
..... DU180.W6
..... GV1025.S95
..... LA2119.S6
..... NC1260
919.4400222 ..... DU178
919.44003 ..... DU155
919.4403 ..... PR6013.Y4
919.440330924 ..... CT2818.D3
..... CT2818.H4
919.44035 ..... DU162.N4
919.440420924 ..... DU160
919.44045 ..... DU162
919.446 ..... DU180.P62
919.45 ..... DU212
..... DU213
..... DU220
..... DU230.B4
..... DU230.B64
..... DU230.P58
..... DU230.R6
..... DU230.R8
..... DU230.T6
919.4503 ..... DU230.O54
919.45032 ..... DU102
919.45033 ..... DU220
919.4503308 ..... DU220
919.45099915 ..... DU227
919.46 ..... DU460
..... DU480.B3
..... DU480.H6
..... NC1260
919.4603 ..... DU479
919.46045 ..... GV1025.T36
919.460450222 ..... DU460
919.47 ..... DU145
919.47045 ..... DU145
919.47045025 ..... DU145
919.48 ..... DU180.N6
..... G845
919.5 ..... DU740
..... DU746.H5
..... HC687.P3
..... S381
919.500222 ..... DU740
919.503 ..... DS646.6
..... DU740
919.504 ..... DU740
919.53 ..... DU740
919.5304 ..... DU740
919.6 ..... DU10
..... DU23
..... DU510
919.603 ..... DU510
..... GN670
919.611 ..... DU23
..... DU600
919.61103 ..... DU600
919.611034 ..... DU600
919.61403 ..... GN875.S2
919.615 ..... Z4980.T6
919.618 ..... F3169
919.62 ..... DU870
919.62100222 ..... DU870
919.62103 ..... DU870
919.621100222 ..... DU870
919.621103 ..... DU870
919.621104 ..... DU870
919.622 ..... DU950.R35
919.624 ..... DU860
919.63 ..... DU510
919.66 ..... DU568.P7
919.67 ..... DU647
919.69 ..... DT515.2
..... DU625
..... GN851
919.6903 ..... DU623.2
..... DU624.5
..... GN799.P4
919.69033 ..... DU627.2
919.69034 ..... DU624.5
919.690340222 ..... DU623.2
919.69035 ..... DT515.2
919.6904 ..... DU625
919.690414 ..... DU623.2
919.69042 ..... DU622
919.69043 ..... DU623.2
919.69044 ..... DU623.2
919.6921 ..... DU628.M3
919.6931044 ..... DU629.H7
919.7304 ..... DT671.S2
919.8 ..... E99.E7
..... G606
..... G610
..... G620
..... G630.A5
..... G630.I8
..... G630.R8
..... G650
..... G665
..... G670
..... PZ10.D72
919.804 ..... G635.H45
..... G670
919.8040924 ..... G635.P4
919.81 ..... G780
919.815 ..... DU430.C63
919.82 ..... G720
..... G743
919.9 ..... G850
..... G860
..... G890.S36
919.904 ..... G850
..... G860
..... G875.S35
919.93157 ..... DU430.F5
919.94 ..... DU112
919.94035 ..... DU107
919.945 ..... DU230.W33
920 ..... CT105
..... CT3320
..... PR4382
920.003 ..... CT103
920.009034 ..... D352.5
920.00904 ..... CT119
..... CT120
920.009174924 ..... DS125.3.A2
920.00917496 ..... E185.96
920.02 ..... CT85
..... CT95
..... CT101
..... CT103
..... CT104
..... CT105
..... CT106
..... CT107
..... CT120
..... CT3230
..... D11.5
..... D107
..... D108
..... D109
..... D412
..... D412.6
..... DS35
..... DS115
..... F1026
920.0203 ..... CT103
920.03 ..... CT105
920.037 ..... DG203.5
920.04 ..... CT104
..... CT119
..... D285
..... D412.6
920.041 ..... DA880.A5
920.042 ..... CT77
..... CT106
..... CT774
..... CT781
..... CT782
..... DA28
..... DA531.1
..... DA562
..... DA566.9.A1
..... DA568.A1
..... PN761
..... PR3533.B7
920.04252 ..... DA670.N9
920.0428 ..... DA670.L1
920.04281 ..... DA690.N6
920.043 ..... DD85
920.044 ..... CT1005
..... CT1011
..... CT3420
..... DC33.3
920.045 ..... PQ4835.A27
920.046 ..... DP58
920.047 ..... CT1213
920.0481 ..... DL504.A2
920.05 ..... DS5
920.054 ..... DS434
..... DS481.A1
920.05414 ..... DS485.B46
920.0599 ..... CT1794.3
920.06 ..... DT18
920.0667 ..... DT510.6
920.068 ..... CT1924
920.07 ..... E176
920.071 ..... E89
920.071231 ..... F1079.5.H5
920.0717 ..... CT3270
920.072 ..... CT554
920.0729 ..... F2175
920.07295 ..... CT524
920.073 ..... CT107
..... CT119
..... CT213
..... CT214
..... CT215
..... CT217
..... CT219
..... CT220
..... CT3234
..... CT3260
..... CT9983.A1
..... DS115.2
..... E176
..... E176.8
..... E184.C93
..... E184.J5
..... E185.96
..... E302.5
..... E302.6.F8
..... E415.8
..... E747
..... F128.52
..... PE1121
..... PS1927
920.074 ..... CT240
920.074721 ..... F127.L8
920.075 ..... F208
920.0757 ..... F268
920.076193 ..... F334.D2
920.0764 ..... F385
920.0789 ..... F795
920.0794 ..... F860
920.079461 ..... F869.S3
920.09 ..... DU28.3
920.0914 ..... CT1793
920.094 ..... CT2803
..... DU82
920.0945 ..... DG540.8.A1
920.0969 ..... DU627.1
920.415 ..... DA948.6.A1
920.71 ..... CT774
..... DA531.2
920.72 ..... DA531.1
..... HQ1412
920.720973 ..... CT3260
923.912 ..... PR4074
929.09489 ..... DL105
929.0973 ..... CT275.S4622
929.1 ..... CS16
..... CS55
..... F148
..... F159.M5
929.1018 ..... CS15
929.10202 ..... CS51
929.103 ..... CS9
929.1072042 ..... CS415
929.10973 ..... CS51
..... CS69
929.109748 ..... CS16
929.109761 ..... F326
929.109778 ..... CS16
929.2 ..... CD3029.5.D8
..... CS44
..... CS55
..... CS69
..... CS71
..... CS71.A2
..... CS71.A674
..... CS71.B2274
..... CS71.B336
..... CS71.B6585
..... CS71.B725
..... CS71.B75
..... CS71.B75116
..... CS71.B775
..... CS71.B9433
..... CS71.C126
..... CS71.C14
..... CS71.C653
..... CS71.C6865
..... CS71.C9317
..... CS71.C9878
..... CS71.E443
..... CS71.E9512
..... CS71.F9185
..... CS71.F934
..... CS71.G481
..... CS71.G875
..... CS71.G98
..... CS71.H122
..... CS71.H243
..... CS71.H47727
..... CS71.H523
..... CS71.H647
..... CS71.H696
..... CS71.H764
..... CS71.H786
..... CS71.H8854
..... CS71.H9385
..... CS71.H993
..... CS71.J23
..... CS71.J7
..... CS71.J76
..... CS71.K16
..... CS71.K344
..... CS71.K357
..... CS71.K3915
..... CS71.K7286
..... CS71.K88
..... CS71.L18
..... CS71.L433
..... CS71.L96
..... CS71.M1144
929.2 ..... CS71.M134
..... CS71.M1745
..... CS71.M457
..... CS71.M4926
..... CS71.M738
..... CS71.M899
..... CS71.O165
..... CS71.P2515
..... CS71.P258
..... CS71.P317
..... CS71.P347
..... CS71.P366
..... CS71.P485
..... CS71.P559
..... CS71.P616
..... CS71.Q38
..... CS71.R2905
..... CS71.R52
..... CS71.R796
..... CS71.R864
..... CS71.R975
..... CS71.S189
..... CS71.S552
..... CS71.S5564
..... CS71.S688
..... CS71.S695
..... CS71.S855
..... CS71.S9727
..... CS71.T985
..... CS71.V158
..... CS71.V269
..... CS71.V5295
..... CS71.W75
..... CS71.W875
..... CS90.E85
..... CS90.M137
..... CS90.M156
..... CS90.R53
..... CS90.R62
..... CS439.A5913
..... CS439.S84
..... CS479
..... CS479.G78
..... CS494
..... CS499.B58
..... CS499.B73
..... CS629.S347
..... CS739.K3
..... CS899.O58
..... CS1520.L4
..... CS2049.L34
..... CS2109
..... CS2149.G74
..... E767
..... F160.W4
929.2073 ..... CS71.J88
929.20923 ..... CS71.J38
929.20924 ..... CS439.C692
929.20941 ..... CS71.D587
..... CS479.C88
..... CS479.F8
..... CS479.G6
..... CS479.M383
..... DA758.3.M285
..... DA880.H6
929.209415 ..... CS499.F6
929.209416 ..... CS499.M78
929.20942 ..... CS71.S854
..... CS438
..... CS439
..... CS439.C744
..... CS439.D69
..... CS439.G553
..... CS439.H3243
..... CS439.H755
..... CS439.L493
..... CS439.P64
..... CS439.S913
..... CT788.B94
..... CT788.M2167
..... DA377.2.V5
929.2094248 ..... DA670.W3
929.209429 ..... CS459.M6
929.20945 ..... CS769.D5
929.2095285 ..... CS2195.B6
929.20954 ..... CS1209.P3
929.2095493 ..... CS1209.S57
929.20968 ..... CS1612
929.20971 ..... CS71.G542
..... CS88.O6
..... CS90.B36
..... CS90.E14
..... CS90.E4
..... CS90.O66
..... CS90.S654
929.20973 ..... CS47
..... CS69
..... CS71
..... CS71.A195
..... CS71.A2
..... CS71.A225
..... CS71.A4
..... CS71.A43
..... CS71.A45
..... CS71.A4655
..... CS71.A4657
..... CS71.A467
..... CS71.A485
..... CS71.A5
..... CS71.A534
..... CS71.A55
..... CS71.A585
..... CS71.A674
..... CS71.A74

929.20973	CS71.A757
	CS71.A93
	CS71.A967
	CS71.B2
	CS71.B2553
	CS71.B288
	CS71.B3
	CS71.B3039
	CS71.B336
	CS71.B3675
	CS71.B368
	CS71.B373
	CS71.B383
	CS71.B39
	CS71.B4372
	CS71.B439
	CS71.B44054
	CS71.B466
	CS71.B469
	CS71.B512
	CS71.B526
	CS71.B629
	CS71.B6345
	CS71.B6393
	CS71.B6472
	CS71.B652
	CS71.B6704
	CS71.B688
	CS71.B698
	CS71.B726
	CS71.B7272
	CS71.B766
	CS71.B79
	CS71.B7974
	CS71.B811
	CS71.B8136
	CS71.B814
	CS71.B8336
	CS71.B8338
	CS71.B848
	CS71.B854
	CS71.B8613
	CS71.B8715
	CS71.B88
	CS71.B8844
	CS71.B886
	CS71.B944
	CS71.B986
	CS71.B99916
	CS71.B99927
	CS71.B9993
	CS71.B9995
	CS71.C128
	CS71.C129
	CS71.C19
	CS71.C3
	CS71.C312
	CS71.C332
	CS71.C352
	CS71.C442
	CS71.C454
	CS71.C487
	CS71.C528
	CS71.C541
	CS71.C5553
	CS71.C6
	CS71.C6214
	CS71.C624
	CS71.C683
	CS71.C686
	CS71.C692
	CS71.C712
	CS71.C76
	CS71.C77
	CS71.C777
	CS71.C782
	CS71.C786
	CS71.C7876
	CS71.C788
	CS71.C791
	CS71.C792
	CS71.C8525
	CS71.C869
	CS71.C8853
	CS71.C8854
	CS71.C8855
	CS71.C9
	CS71.D186
	CS71.D25
	CS71.D252
	CS71.D26
	CS71.D261
	CS71.D27
	CS71.D272
	CS71.D29
	CS71.D41
	CS71.D496
	CS71.D553
	CS71.D5696
	CS71.D5795
	CS71.D595
	CS71.D635
	CS71.D636
	CS71.D645
	CS71.D759
	CS71.D766
	CS71.D82
	CS71.D854
	CS71.D857
	CS71.D873
	CS71.D912
	CS71.D913
	CS71.D923
	CS71.D9255

929.20973	CS71.D996
	CS71.E1323
	CS71.E195
	CS71.E227
	CS71.E247
	CS71.E26
	CS71.E293
	CS71.E38
	CS71.E466
	CS71.E477
	CS71.E743
	CS71.E745
	CS71.F244
	CS71.F35
	CS71.F42
	CS71.F493
	CS71.F513
	CS71.F5317
	CS71.F532
	CS71.F533
	CS71.F567
	CS71.F612
	CS71.F688
	CS71.F695
	CS71.F736
	CS71.F756
	CS71.F856
	CS71.F8892
	CS71.F9133
	CS71.F943
	CS71.F947
	CS71.G132
	CS71.G152
	CS71.G167
	CS71.G194
	CS71.G285
	CS71.G475
	CS71.G495
	CS71.G59
	CS71.G675
	CS71.G6756
	CS71.G677
	CS71.G73
	CS71.G756
	CS71.G78
	CS71.G8
	CS71.G815
	CS71.G8172
	CS71.G81794
	CS71.G859
	CS71.G8775
	CS71.H105
	CS71.H15
	CS71.H177
	CS71.H1987
	CS71.H242
	CS71.H24894
	CS71.H25
	CS71.H263
	CS71.H27
	CS71.H326
	CS71.H343
	CS71.H394
	CS71.H418
	CS71.H423
	CS71.H435
	CS71.H46784
	CS71.H4679
	CS71.H4699
	CS71.H4735
	CS71.H476
	CS71.H519
	CS71.H55
	CS71.H567
	CS71.H619
	CS71.H63
	CS71.H633
	CS71.H637
	CS71.H64
	CS71.H6613
	CS71.H672
	CS71.H6962
	CS71.H75
	CS71.H837
	CS71.H852
	CS71.H858
	CS71.H864
	CS71.H865
	CS71.H892
	CS71.H94
	CS71.H96
	CS71.I33
	CS71.I765
	CS71.J13
	CS71.J385
	CS71.J5
	CS71.J562
	CS71.J7
	CS71.J73
	CS71.J82
	CS71.K17
	CS71.K223
	CS71.K28
	CS71.K37
	CS71.K483
	CS71.K488
	CS71.K53
	CS71.K559
	CS71.K595
	CS71.K676
	CS71.K83
	CS71.K845
	CS71.K965
	CS71.L278

929.20973	CS71.L325
	CS71.L418
	CS71.L4254
	CS71.L517
	CS71.L519
	CS71.L5397
	CS71.L675
	CS71.L7533
	CS71.L82
	CS71.L85
	CS71.L895
	CS71.L897
	CS71.L958
	CS71.L966
	CS71.L975
	CS71.M105
	CS71.M125
	CS71.M12786
	CS71.M12796
	CS71.M13
	CS71.M1323
	CS71.M1333
	CS71.M134
	CS71.M1388
	CS71.M1389
	CS71.M146
	CS71.M1618
	CS71.M1678
	CS71.M17156
	CS71.M282
	CS71.M296
	CS71.M38
	CS71.M41
	CS71.M44
	CS71.M467
	CS71.M4684
	CS71.M57
	CS71.M613
	CS71.M643
	CS71.M65
	CS71.M657
	CS71.M6578
	CS71.M6672
	CS71.M673
	CS71.M812
	CS71.M82
	CS71.M848
	CS71.M899
	CS71.M918
	CS71.M93
	CS71.M942
	CS71.M948
	CS71.M95
	CS71.M9594
	CS71.M966
	CS71.M972
	CS71.M9785
	CS71.M995
	CS71.N177
	CS71.N25
	CS71.N277
	CS71.N415
	CS71.N43
	CS71.N5
	CS71.N549
	CS71.N59
	CS71.N66
	CS71.N74
	CS71.N75
	CS71.N7512
	CS71.N92
	CS71.O122
	CS71.O127
	CS71.O315
	CS71.O34
	CS71.O395
	CS71.O469
	CS71.O47
	CS71.O575
	CS71.O814
	CS71.O87
	CS71.O9556
	CS71.O962
	CS71.P118
	CS71.P133
	CS71.P146
	CS71.P22
	CS71.P225
	CS71.P235
	CS71.P24
	CS71.P244
	CS71.P269
	CS71.P28
	CS71.P4132
	CS71.P45
	CS71.P48
	CS71.P559
	CS71.P5794
	CS71.P616
	CS71.P888
	CS71.P914
	CS71.P9484
	CS71.P949
	CS71.P955
	CS71.P995
	CS71.R145
	CS71.R228
	CS71.R2345
	CS71.R253
	CS71.R268
	CS71.R284
	CS71.R331
	CS71.R3945
	CS71.R468

929.20973	CS71.R533
	CS71.R5665
	CS71.R632
	CS71.R64
	CS71.R668
	CS71.R67
	CS71.R7
	CS71.R736
	CS71.R747
	CS71.R773
	CS71.R782
	CS71.R813
	CS71.R94
	CS71.R967
	CS71.R975
	CS71.R996
	CS71.S2194
	CS71.S223
	CS71.S282
	CS71.S336
	CS71.S449
	CS71.S53
	CS71.S532
	CS71.S543
	CS71.S544
	CS71.S552
	CS71.S5545
	CS71.S5575
	CS71.S5595
	CS71.S5602
	CS71.S56048
	CS71.S5697
	CS71.S5834
	CS71.S5836
	CS71.S614
	CS71.S615
	CS71.S6285
	CS71.S6313
	CS71.S63614
	CS71.S6392
	CS71.S643
	CS71.S647
	CS71.S654
	CS71.S656
	CS71.S678
	CS71.S7345
	CS71.S7663
	CS71.S7695
	CS71.S7835
	CS71.S7878
	CS71.S812
	CS71.S815
	CS71.S866
	CS71.S8837
	CS71.S893
	CS71.S969
	CS71.S988
	CS71.T257
	CS71.T3
	CS71.T334
	CS71.T5835
	CS71.T585
	CS71.T5984
	CS71.T599
	CS71.T634
	CS71.T6635
	CS71.T7187
	CS71.T744
	CS71.T75
	CS71.T756
	CS71.T777
	CS71.T778
	CS71.T78
	CS71.T8127
	CS71.T813
	CS71.T826
	CS71.T874
	CS71.T93
	CS71.T94
	CS71.U58
	CS71.V125
	CS71.V2196
	CS71.V2218
	CS71.V227
	CS71.V243
	CS71.V25
	CS71.V254
	CS71.V294
	CS71.V391
	CS71.V3957
	CS71.V635
	CS71.V979
	CS71.W116
	CS71.W138
	CS71.W22
	CS71.W27
	CS71.W28
	CS71.W29
	CS71.W35
	CS71.W357
	CS71.W38
	CS71.W39
	CS71.W46
	CS71.W464
	CS71.W52
	CS71.W5225
	CS71.W544
	CS71.W5487
	CS71.W552
	CS71.W56
	CS71.W574
	CS71.W585
	CS71.W614
	CS71.W616

Dewey	LC
929.20973	CS71.W642
	CS71.W671
	CS71.W675
	CS71.W68
	CS71.W684
	CS71.W72
	CS71.W75
	CS71.W774
	CS71.W795
	CS71.W875
	CS71.W914
	CS71.Y5345
	CS71.Y535
	CS71.Z64
	CS71.Z66
	CS71.024
	CS90.M52
	CT275.G6
	CT275.R726
	CT275.W664
	E99.04
	E185.97.B22
	E664.E12
	F29.B79
	F59.W6
	F93
	F148
	F285
	F419.C73
	F450
	F457.C57
	F474.F65
	F674.B28
	F868.06
	F868.T8
	GS71.G142
	TS543.U6
929.209745	F78
929.20975	CS71.D67
929.209755	CS71.P9867
929.20977839	CS71.H8583
929.209792	CS71.E715
929.209794	CS71.V183
929.20994	CS439.B254
	CS2089.L6
	CS2129.S86
	CT2858.R6
929.3	BX8076.M36
	BX8491
	BX9517.W45
	CD3524
	CS1
	CS16
	CS47
	CS68
	CS69
	CS71.A4685
	CS71.D273
	CS71.H2403
	CS71.H96
	CS71.N74
	CS71.P489
	CS411
	CS434
	CS435
	CS436.C72
	CS436.H277
	CS436.K458
	CS436.W598
	CS460
	CT213
	DA20
	DA670.N8
	DA670.Y59
	E99.C5
	E184.F89
	E184.S18
	E184.S9
	E263.S7
	E359.4
	F63
	F67
	F68
	F72.C3
	F73.25
	F74.H42
	F74.M4
	F78
	F82
	F93
	F102.M6
	F118
	F129.C525
	F129.C58
	F129.G45
	F129.H6
	F129.L73
	F129.R4
	F129.R6
	F129.S7
	F129.W9
	F133
	F138
	F148
	F152
	F153
	F172.N5
	F187.A4
	F187.A6
	F187.B2
	F187.C2
	F187.H8
	F193
929.3	F197
	F208
	F225
	F226
	F230
	F232.C93
	F247.H2
	F253
	F262.E2
	F262.N2
	F272
	F277.A2
	F285
	F292.H2
	F292.J2
	F292.J28
	F325
	F332.B5
	F332.G7
	F332.M35
	F340
	F368
	F377.E3
	F377.W6
	F379.N5
	F380.F8
	F392.B34
	F392.C3
	F392.F15
	F417.I5
	F417.J4
	F417.M35
	F419.B6
	F443.R5
	F443.W3
	F443.W7
	F450.2
	F457.C15
	F472.B4
	F472.J3
	F472.L6
	F472.S23
	F472.S28
	F474.S2
	F490
	F497.B4
	F497.D2
	F497.H6
	F497.J4
	F497.M67
	F497.P9
	F497.W7
	F499.S535
	F525
	F525.5
	F532.D8
	F532.K6
	F532.P8
	F532.W58
	F534.W33
	F540
	F547.C3
	F547.R5
	F702.K4
	F752.C35
	F861
	F868.S17
	F882.G7
	F897.W18
	F1058
	F2105
	HD243.K4
	KFV2544.8.B43
	UB373
	Z7553.C3
929.30942	CS415
929.30973	CS71.B336
	CS71.C663
	CS71.W552
	E186.5
929.374733	F129.R4
929.375646	F262.E2
929.3762536	F347.L35
929.376335	F379.N545
929.376715	F417.M3
929.376745	F417.P7
929.3767485	F417.P5
929.376777	F417.P85
929.3768	F436.H682
929.3768434	F443.H6
929.376856	F443.W7
929.376862	F443.L6
929.376974	F457.W2
929.376977	F457.T5
929.376978	F457.C55
	F459.F58
929.377226	F532.L4
929.3782276	F672.J6
929.378795	F769.F58
929.37956	F882.B2
929.4	CS2309
	CS2327.U6
	CS2367
	CS2369
	CS2375.R9
	CS2377
	CS2385
	CS2411
	CS2470
	CS2485
	CS2505
	Z1041
	Z1065
929.40934	CS3030
929.40941	CS2435
929.40942	CS2327.G7
	CS2385
	CS2501
	CS2505
929.4094261	CS2509.N6
929.40947	CS2505
929.40954	CS3030
929.40973	E184.A1
929.5	CS477.C3
	CS477.D8
	CS477.K57
	CS477.S4
	CS477.W3
	F232.F3
	F457.C25
	F472.J3
	F702.P74
	PN6291
929.5094134	CS477.K55
929.6	CJ5733
	CR21
	CR23
	CR191
	CR191.P55
	CR1179
929.603	CR13
	CR1618
929.60942	CR504
	CS410
929.609429	CR3920
929.60943	CR69.G3
929.60973	CR27
	CR1202
929.609752	CR1217.M37
929.7	CR3515
	CS55
	CS418
	D412.7
	DA758.3.S8
929.709	CR3515
929.7094	CS55
929.71	CR4513
	CR4809
929.72	CS421
	CS424
	CS425
	CS432.N7
	CS490
	DA34
	DA391
	DA555
	DA591.A33
	DA758.3.S8
929.73	DD370
929.75	DG83.3
929.769	DP632
929.79995645	CS1520.C9
929.8	CD5610
	CJ5805
	CR1200.A8
	CR1209
	CR1619
	DK421.2
929.80941	CR1658.P3
929.80942	CR1618
929.80954	CR115.I4
929.9	CR101
	CR109
	CR113
	CR115.S6
929.90973	JC346
	JC346.Z3
929.90994	JC347.A8
929.92	CR4801
930	D17
	D24
	D52
	D57
	D59
	DS61
	DS62.2
930.0202	D59
930.4	DF235.K5
930.40924	DF234
931	DS735.A2
	DS745
	DS747.2
931.1	DU420
932	DT73.D4
	DT135.N8
932.010924	DT87.2
	DT87.4
932.02	DT92
932.020924	DT92.7
933	DS117
	DS118
	DS121
	DS122
934	DS441
	DS451
934.03	DF234.6
934.030924	DS451.9.P63
934.04	DS451
934.040924	DS451.5
	DS451.9.C5
934.050924	DS451.9.K3
934.06	DS451
935	DS275
935.01	DS72
935.02	DS71
935.0308	DS68
935.06	DF234.5
	DF234.55
935.06	DS329.P2
936	DA145
	DD123
	GN803
936	DA146
936.00974916	GN549.C3
937	DG209
	DG211
	DG312
937.0072024	PA6716
	PR3476
937.008	DG211
937.01	DG233
937.02	DG231
937.040924	DG248.S3
937.05	DG268
937.050922	DG254.5
937.050924	DG254.5
	DG258
	DG260.A1
	DG260.C5
	DG261
	DG279
	PA6298
937.06	DG207
	DG270
	DG275
937.070924	DG285
	DG300
937.080924	DG315
937.6	DG210
937.604	DG254.2
937.70924	E457.2
937.8	DG55.S5
	DG866
938	DE7
	DF12
	DF208
	DF214
	DF215
	DF227
	DF285
938.007024	PA4004
938.0072	DE8
	DF211
	DF222
	PA19
938.0072022	DE8
938.0072024	DF211
	DF229.T6
	PA4004
938.00720924	PA25
938.03	DF79
	DF225.6
938.04	DF227
938.05	DF229.T55
	DF229.T6
	DF229.2
	DF229.67
938.050924	DF230.A4
938.07	DE83
938.070924	DF234
	PA3946.C3
	PA4369
938.09	DF235
938.1080924	DF237.A6
938.7	DF238.9.P55
938.9	DF261.S8
939.2	DS155
939.34	DS156.C3
939.4	DS96
939.44	DS99.J42
939.6	DS329.B2
939.7	DT167
	DT192
939.73	DT168
939.730924	DG249
940	CB59
	D21
	D102
	D103
	D147
	D209
	DR36
940.072	D13
	D14
940.1	D113
	D113.5
	D117
	D118
	D119
	D121.P53
	JN2334
940.1071	D119
940.10922	D115
940.11	D102
	D121
	D135
940.14	D148
940.14008	D113
940.1408	D113
940.17	D172
	RC172
	RC178.A1
940.18	D157
	D160
	D161.1
940.1808	D151
940.2	CB367
	D21.3
	D106
	D208
	D209
	D228

940.2 ..... D231
..... D299
..... D395
..... JN8
940.20922 ..... D108
940.21 ..... CB361
..... D228
940.210922 ..... CB361
940.22 ..... D210
940.23 ..... CB359
..... D220.F8
..... D246
..... DC113.5
940.230922 ..... BR315
940.232 ..... D221.V4
..... D228
940.24 ..... D258
940.240924 ..... D270.W19
940.25 ..... U17
940.252 ..... D246
..... D273
940.2526 ..... D281.5
940.25260924 ..... DA462.M3
940.253 ..... DA512.M6
..... DC148
940.2532 ..... D287
940.2534 ..... D297
..... E199
940.27 ..... D308
..... D351
..... D353
..... DA68.12.G75
..... DA87.5
..... DA88.5
..... DA520
..... DC148
..... DC153
..... DC198
..... DC220.2
..... DC232
..... DC235
..... DC236.55
..... DC241
..... DC241.5
..... DC242
..... DC243
940.270924 ..... DA68.12.W4
..... DA87.1.N4
..... DB80.8
..... DB80.8.G4
..... DB80.8.M57
..... DC202.1
..... DC203.4
..... DC232
..... DC239
..... DD416.N17
..... UH347.L3
940.28 ..... D299
..... D352
..... D359
..... D361
940.280922 ..... D352
..... D352.5
..... D412
940.28208 ..... D383
940.283 ..... D385
940.284 ..... D387
..... DB80.8.M57
940.287 ..... D395
940.3 ..... AC8
..... D505
..... D511
..... D523
940.3022 ..... D527.5
940.30922 ..... D507
940.30924 ..... DA566.9.P7
940.311 ..... D410
..... D511
..... D639.S6
940.3112 ..... D511
940.3113 ..... D511
940.3141 ..... D643.A7
..... D643.H9
..... D644
..... D645
..... D646
940.3142 ..... D653
940.31422 ..... D648
940.31424 ..... D465
..... D651.A4
940.3152 ..... D639.R4
940.31530145343073 ..... D620
940.316 ..... UB345.G7
940.3162 ..... UB342.U5
940.32 ..... D610
940.32273 ..... D522.42
..... D570
..... D619
940.32443 ..... D619
940.342 ..... D546
940.343 ..... DD86.7.F54
940.355 ..... DS315
940.373 ..... E780
940.4 ..... D507
..... D619
940.403 ..... D639.N4
940.40947 ..... D550
..... D764
940.40971 ..... D547.C2
940.410922 ..... D507
940.412415 ..... D547.I6
940.41271 ..... D547.C2
940.412718 ..... UA652.R826
940.41273 ..... D570
940.41273 ..... D570.33
..... UA33
940.41276246 ..... D570.32
940.412931 ..... D547.N5
940.41430922 ..... DD231.H5
940.4144 ..... D545.V3
..... D640
940.4147 ..... D559
940.4150924 ..... D568.4
..... D568.4.L45
940.416 ..... D568.7
940.42 ..... D521
940.425 ..... D568.3
940.426 ..... D568.5
940.4291 ..... D568.5
940.434 ..... D545.B4
..... D641
940.438 ..... DK265.4
940.44 ..... D600
940.441 ..... D600
940.447 ..... D545.A7
..... D570.65
940.44942 ..... D602
..... DA585.S58
940.44943 ..... D604
..... D604.R5297
..... TL540.R5
940.449430924 ..... D604
..... TL540.U3
940.44973 ..... D606
..... UG633
940.451 ..... VB230
940.45120924 ..... DD231.T5
940.454 ..... D582.F2
940.456 ..... D582.J8
940.45943 ..... D582.M6
..... D639.M82
..... VA515.C6
940.459430924 ..... D581.L87
940.45973 ..... D570.45
940.46 ..... D570.A15
940.47243 ..... D627.R8
940.4770924 ..... D638.S4
940.48173 ..... CT275.O37
..... D570.9
..... D640
..... D811
940.486 ..... D810.S2
940.48673 ..... D619.3
940.487430924 ..... D639.S8Z459
940.5 ..... D424
..... D450
..... D727
940.508 ..... D410
..... D415
940.51 ..... D726.5
940.510922 ..... D412.6
940.53 ..... D741
..... D743
..... D743.9
..... D744
..... D755
940.53022 ..... D756.5.D5
940.530222 ..... D743.2
940.5308 ..... PS3525.A27
940.531 ..... D734
..... D767.2
..... D816
..... D816.5
940.5311 ..... D727
..... D741
..... D742.G4
..... D767.92
..... D810.S7
940.53112 ..... D741
..... D753
940.53114 ..... D741
940.5314 ..... D734
..... D734.A1
..... D734.A8
..... D819.G3
..... DB215
..... DC389
940.531440959 ..... D829.E2
940.5315 ..... D810.J4
..... D811.5
..... DS135.R93
940.5315055 ..... D810.J4
940.53152960924 ..... D811.5
940.531529609438 ..... D810.J4
940.531529609489 ..... D810.J4
940.53159 ..... DS135.P6
940.53161 ..... D767.25.H6
940.531630973 ..... D769.8.A6
940.532 ..... D748
..... DG498
940.5322 ..... D753.2.R9
940.532242 ..... D750
940.5322438 ..... DK418
940.532273 ..... D753
..... E183.8.V5
..... E744
940.5322730924 ..... E807
940.533 ..... D764
940.5334 ..... DD253.27
940.53340922 ..... DD247.H5
940.5337 ..... DJ287
940.5338 ..... D763.I82A56
940.534 ..... D802
..... D810.J4
940.5342 ..... DA587
940.534234 ..... D760.8.J4
940.5343 ..... DD256.5
940.53438 ..... D802.P6
940.53438 ..... D810.J4
940.534380924 ..... D810.J4
940.5344 ..... D810.J4
940.5345 ..... D802.I8
940.5347 ..... D764
940.53492 ..... D763.N4
..... D811.5
940.53495 ..... D802.G8
940.53497 ..... D766.6
..... JX1977.2.Y8
940.5352 ..... D767.2
940.53931 ..... D767.85
940.54 ..... D743
..... E836
..... UF535.G7
940.54012 ..... D735
..... D769.2
940.5403 ..... D639.N4
..... D769.87.A4
..... D810.N4
940.5405 ..... D810.J4
940.54050943 ..... DD253.6
940.5405094384 ..... D802.P62
940.54050945632 ..... DS135.I85
940.540509492 ..... DS135.N4
940.540509520951 ..... DS777.53
940.5409438 ..... D765
940.540944 ..... D761
940.540947 ..... D764
940.5409497 ..... D766.6
940.5409498 ..... D766.4
940.540952 ..... D767.2
940.540971 ..... D768.15
940.541 ..... D743
..... D810.T8
940.5410924 ..... DA69.3.M56
940.5412 ..... D793
940.541242 ..... D736
..... D811
940.541273 ..... D769
940.5412730952 ..... D821.J3
940.541294 ..... D767.813
940.541343 ..... D757.54
..... D757.85
940.5413430924 ..... DD247.H5
940.542 ..... D756.5.N6
..... D793
940.5421 ..... D746
..... D755.6
..... D755.7
..... D756
..... D756.5
..... D756.5.A7
..... D756.5.B7
..... D756.5.D8
..... D756.5.N6
..... D756.5.S33
..... D756.5.W6
..... D757.9.B4
..... D757.9.H33
..... D759.5
..... D760.C63
..... D761
..... D762.P7
..... D763
..... D763.I82
..... D763.I82R24
..... D763.M3
..... D763.N62
..... D764
..... D764.3.M6
..... D764.3.S7
..... D766.93
..... D768.15
..... D769
..... D769.335
..... D770
..... D771
..... D772.S35
..... D780
..... D781
..... D785
..... D804.G4
..... D811
..... DA89.6.D6
..... DK268.V56
..... UG633
940.54210924 ..... D764
..... D764.3.M6
..... DA69.3.M56
..... DA89.6.D6
..... E745.P3
..... E843.K44
940.5423 ..... D766.8
..... D766.82
..... D766.84
..... D766.99.T8
..... D769.31
..... D790
940.5425 ..... D767
..... D767.5
..... D767.6
940.54250922 ..... DS890.A1
940.54250924 ..... DA69.3.W37
..... DS777.53
940.5426 ..... D767
..... D767.4
..... D767.55
..... D767.9
..... D767.917
..... D767.98
..... D767.99.G8
..... D767.99.I9
940.5426 ..... D767.99.O45
..... D769.52
..... D774.J3
..... D774.M5
..... D774.P5
..... D790
..... D792.J3
..... D811
940.54260924 ..... CT275.F4262
..... D767
..... E746.H3
940.5428 ..... D769.87.A4
940.544 ..... D760.8.L7
..... D770
..... D785
..... TL685.3
940.5440973 ..... D790
940.5441 ..... D767.2
..... D785
..... D792.J3
940.5442 ..... D785
940.544942 ..... D763.D42
..... D786
..... PR6070.R48
940.5449420924 ..... DA89.6.M35
940.544943 ..... D787
..... UG635.G3
940.5449430924 ..... TL540.H257
940.544973 ..... D745.2
..... D785
..... D790
940.5449940924 ..... D811
940.545 ..... D770
..... D774.D56
..... D807.G7
940.5450916611 ..... D771
940.5451 ..... D782.U16
940.54510924 ..... V65.P7
940.5459 ..... D771
940.545943 ..... D771
..... D772.A74
940.5459438 ..... D779.P6
940.5459481 ..... D763.N6
940.545952 ..... D777
940.545971 ..... PN6231.M5
940.545973 ..... D773
..... D774.D56
940.545994 ..... D779.A8
940.546 ..... D810.J4
940.5465438 ..... D838.P7
940.5467747277 ..... D769.85.N5
940.5472 ..... D805.A2
940.547243 ..... D804.G4
..... D805.G3
..... D810.D4
940.5472430924 ..... D805.G3
..... D810.C36G383
..... DA89.6.D3
940.5472470924 ..... D805.R9
940.547252 ..... D805.J3
..... D805.J4
..... RT37.T8
940.547273 ..... D769.8.A6
940.5475 ..... D807.U6
940.547542 ..... D806
940.547554 ..... D807.B8
940.547673 ..... D807.U722
940.54779496 ..... D769.8.A6
940.5478 ..... UH25.C2
940.5481 ..... D811.5
940.5481415 ..... D640
940.548142 ..... D759
..... D772.E9
..... D811
940.5481438 ..... D810.J4
940.548147 ..... D811
940.5481492 ..... D810.J4
940.548173 ..... D811
..... U53.H3
940.5481914 ..... D811.5
940.548243 ..... DD247.G39
..... DD247.H37
940.548245 ..... D811
..... D811.5
940.5485 ..... D742.U5
..... D802.A2
..... D802.F8
..... D810.S7
940.54860924 ..... D766.7.C7
..... D802.G8
940.548642 ..... D760.C63
..... D766.82
..... D810.S7
..... D810.S8
940.548647 ..... D810.S8
940.5486481 ..... DL532
940.548673 ..... D810.S8
940.548743 ..... D734
..... D810.S7
940.5488642 ..... D810.P7
940.5488743 ..... D810.P7
940.5488943 ..... D810.P7G3364
940.55 ..... D1051
..... D1058
941 ..... DA755
..... DA760
..... DA765
941.0072 ..... D13
941.02 ..... DA783.4
..... DA783.41
941.020924 ..... DA783.4
941.040924 ..... DA783.9.A5
941.05 ..... DA785
..... DA787.A1

941.05 DA789
941.050924 DA787
DA787.A1
941.060924 DA802.S35
941.07 DA765
DA815
941.08 DA821
941.31 DA890.D8
941.33 DA880.F4
941.37 DA890.C974
941.38 DA890.D94
DA890.O2
DA890.S84
941.42 DA890.C975
941.445 DA890.C72
941.48 DA890.D96
HE1783.G7
941.5 DA905
DA910
DA911
DA912
DA913
DA914
DA930
941.5072 AS122.B4
941.508 DA913
941.52 DA933.3
941.53152208 D810.C6
941.55 DA763
DA937
941.56 DA943
DA945
941.560924 DA940.5.O5
941.57 BX1503
DA947
DA948.5
DA949
DA949.5
941.58 DA950
DA954
941.580924 DA950.23.O4
DA952.O5
DA958.P2
DA958.S7
941.59 DA959.1
DA960
DA962
DA963
DA965.O23
DS442.6
941.590924 DA566.9.B52
DA962
DA965.C6
DA965.D4
941.6 DA990.U46
941.609 DA990.U46
941.62 DA990.L8
941.64 DA990.A82
941.68 DA990.F43
941.8359 DA962
941.94 DA995.L7
942 CD1064
D24
DA16
DA28.1
DA28.2
DA28.3
DA28.4
DA28.7
DA30
DA32
DA130
DA176
DA300
DA530
DA660
PR1322
942.007 DA4
942.0071 LB2394
942.0072 CD65
DA1
DA176
942.0072022 D14
942.0072024 DA3.L7
942.0072042 DA1
DA240
942.0074021 DA22.L6N34
942.008 DA300
942.00922 DA28.1
942.00974924 DS135.E5
942.01 DA30
DA130
DA135
DA145
DA146
DA150
DA152
DA152.5.A7
DA153
942.01072 DA3.A1
942.010922 PR1578
942.010924 DA152.5.E2
DA153
942.02 DA195
942.020924 DA154.8
DA209.T4
942.021 DA195
942.024 DA198.5
942.0240924 DA198.5
942.03 DA30
DA175
DA205
DA225
942.0308 DA175
942.0320924 DA207
942.033 DA1
942.0330924 DA208
942.0340924 DA228.M7
942.0350924 DA229
942.037 DA220
DA233
942.0370924 DA237.H4
942.038 DA30
DA235
942.04 DA245
DA250
942.04072 PR409.P7
942.041 DA255
942.0410924 DA255
942.0420924 DA256
942.0430924 DA247.M3
DA257
942.0440924 DA247.W25
942.046 DA260
942.0460924 DA260
942.05 DA30
DA315
DA317.15
DA325
DA935
942.050722 DA315
942.0508 DA20
942.050922 DA317.2
F251
942.050924 DA334.G3
DA358.B9
DA937.3
942.051 DA30
DA330
942.0510924 DA330
942.052 DA317.1
942.0520922 DA784.3.M3
942.0520924 BX4700.M717
DA332
DA333.A6
DA334
DA334.E4
DA334.G3
DA334.M8
DA334.W8
DA338
DC108
PR2322
942.0530924 DA345
942.054 DA347
942.0540924 DA347
942.055 BX1492
DA350
DA356
DA358.E7
DA360
942.0550924 D244.8.R6
DA86.22.D7
DA86.22.H3
DA86.22.N65
DA86.22.R2
DA350
DA355
DA358.T5
DA425
DA787.A1
PR2334
942.06 BX9334
DA30
DA300
DA375
DA390
DA422
DA430
E188.5
HN385
942.060924 D281.A2
DA86.1.H6
DA378.B5
942.061 DA390
DA391
DA392
942.0610924 DA391
DA391.1.A6
DA788
942.062 DA390
DA395
DA400
DA405
DA415
DA417
DA670.L5
DA690.L5
DA690.Y6
HN385
942.0620924 DA66.1.W3
DA396.S8
DA397
DA690.T95
942.063 DA425
942.064 DA426
942.0640922 DA427
942.0640924 DA426
DA428.1
942.066 DA452
942.0660924 DA445
DA447.B9
DA447.C63
DA447.G9
DA448.9
942.067 DA435
DA448.9
DA452
942.068 DA435
942.0680922 DA462.P7
942.0690924 DA495
DA497.O8
DA501.B6
942.07 DA30
DA480
DA498
DA522.C5
DA530
942.0703 DA30
942.0708 DA480
942.070922 DA28.4
DA506.F7
DA531.2
942.070924 DA68.12.W4
DA522.C5
942.071 DA480
DA499
DA814.3
942.072 DA500
DA501.A3
DA814.5
942.0720924 PR3539.K73
942.0722 DA140.G49
942.073 DA30
DA505
DA506.W2
DA521
DA690.M4
DC157
942.0730922 CT788.B434
DA87.1.N4
DA522.A1
942.0730924 DA68.12.H5
DA87.1.N4
DA483.H3
DA506.A72
DA506.B9
DA506.F7
DA506.N7
DA522.P6
DA522.S4
942.074 DA687.H7
942.0740924 DA522.C2
DA536.D96
DA536.M5
942.0750924 DA536.P3
DA565.T16
942.08 D427
DA530
DA566
942.080922 DA550
942.081 DA30
DA550
DA552
942.0810922 DA530
DA531.2
DA562
DA564.B3
DA670.J5
942.0810924 DA530
DA536.P2
DA536.R9
DA541.O3
DA552
DA554
DA555
DA557
DA563
DA563.4
DA564.B3
DA565.B8
DA565.C6
DA565.C95
G246.B8
942.082 D450
D651.G5
DA586
JN231
942.0820922 DA566.9.A1
DA566.9.L5
DA568.A1
942.0820924 DA89.1.M59
DA566.9
DA566.9.B15
DA566.9.B2
DA566.9.C5
DA566.9.H286
DA568.A2
DA574.A37
DA585
DA585.S52
DA585.T43
942.083 DA574.D35
942.0830922 DA566.9.A1
942.0830924 DA566.9.H27
DA566.9.J66
DA576
942.084 DA586
942.0840924 DA69.3.I8
DA566.9.B37
DA566.9.C5
DA581.M6
DA585.C5
942.085 DA566.3
DA566.9.M33
DA588
DA591.A33
JN1129.L32
942.0850922 DA590
DA591.A1
942.0850924 DA566.9.M33
DA585.S6
942.0850924 DA590
DA591.A33
DA591.A34
DA591.P64
942.1 DA677
DA685.C7
942.101 DA677.1
DA680
942.103 DA680
942.10384 D811.5
942.1066 DA681
942.12 BX5195.L7
DA680
DA687.S133
DA687.T7
942.1205 DA680
942.13 DA635.K5
DA685.R43
DA690.F9
942.14 DA690.H198
942.17 DA690.W233
942.177 DA690.H2
942.1795 DA690.T95
942.19 DA685.H68
942.21 DA690.W237
942.23 DA690.D33
DA690.F27
DA690.R15
942.25 DA670.S98
DA690.C53
942.27 DA690.C775
DA690.P8
942.28 DA690.R89
942.29 DA690.G617
DA690.W76
942.31 DA690.F54
DA690.M26
942.33 DA690.A25
DA690.L885
942.34 DA670.S15
942.35 DA670.D5
DA670.E9
DA690.B688
DA690.L95
942.37 DA670.S2
DA690.F53
DA690.P794
942.3705 DA670.C8
942.38 DA690.B885
DA690.S547
DA690.W955
942.41 DA690.S638
942.46 DA690.E26
DA690.S585
942.47 BX5195.C48
DA670.W9
942.48 DA670.W3
DA690.C75
DA690.L8217
DA690.O33
DA690.S569
942.53 DA690.G2
DA690.S238
DA690.S6113
942.54 DA690.L5
DA690.P11
942.55 BX5110.N6
942.565 BX5195.L85P35
942.57 DA690.B55
DA690.B845
942.575 DA690.A2
DA690.C4527
DA690.J6
942.58 DA690.B608
942.59 DA690.H347
942.61 DA670.N6
942.61062 DA670.N6
942.67 DA690.H29
DA690.P955
DA690.W25
942.71 DA690.A484
DA690.C72
DA690.K74
942.72 DA670.L2
DA690.D57
DA690.L8
DA690.M4
DA690.R133
942.74 DA670.Y6
DA690.C625
DA690.S54
942.740924 DA522.C2
942.81 DA690.S945
TN808.G6
942.82 DA483.D35
DA670.N8
942.85 HE1783.G7
942.9 DA28.3
DA708
DA714
942.9035 DA229
DA715
942.92 DA740.C35
942.93 DA745.W9
942.96503 DA740.B8
942.99 DA745.M9
943 DA687.T7
DD89
DD90
DD232
DD347
DR36
943.02 DD125
DD126

943.022 DD136
943.0240924 DD149
943.0250924 DD151
943.03 DC111
DD176
943.031 DD182
943.0310924 DD179
DD180.5
943.04 DB66
943.05 DD193
DD397
943.050924 DD402.W6
943.053 DD112
DD403
DD404
943.0530924 DB71
DD404
943.0570924 DB74
DB74.3
943.060924 DD416.S8
DD421.3
943.0610924 DA390.1.E8
943.07 DD204
DD207
DD210
JN3946.S83
943.08 DD232
943.080924 DD218
DD218.R6
943.082 DC285
DC292
DC293
943.0820924 DC285
DC293
943.084 DD228
DD228.8
943.0840924 DD228
DD229
DD231.E7
DD247.H5
943.085 D649.G3
943.0850924 DD231.R3
DD247.H5
943.086 DD247.C35
DD247.G63
DD253.6
DD256.3
DD256.5
DD257
DD259.7.L8
943.0860922 DD244
DD256.5
943.0860924 DD247.B66
DD247.G37
DD247.G6
DD247.G67
DD247.H46
DD247.H5
DD247.S63
DD247.T7
DD256.5
943.087 DD257.25
943.0870922 DD259.63
943.1087 DD261
943.155 DD878
943.1552087 DD261.2
943.3080924 DD801.B387
943.427 DD801.S13R8
943.603 DB74.3
943.604 DB80
DB80.8.M57
DB83
DG553.5.C8
943.6040924 DB80.8.M57
DB85
DB89.R8
943.605 DB91
DB96
943.7 DB200.5
943.702 DB212
943.7020924 DB208
943.703 DB215.2
DB215.3
943.704 D839.3
DB215.2
DB215.5
DB215.6
DB217.D77
943.7040924 DB215.6
DB217.D77
DB217.S55
PG5438.M57
943.705 DB215.6
943.7102 DB214
943.7303 DB679.3
943.8 DK414
DK418
943.802 D373
DK434
943.8020924 E207.P8
943.803 DK436
943.8030924 DK435.5
943.8040924 DK440.5.P5
943.805 D765.2.W3
D811.5
943.8050924 DK443
943.8302 DD491.O47
943.902 DB924
943.905 DB955
943.91 DB925.1
943.9102 DB924
943.9104 DB923.5
943.91040924 DB933.3.S8
DB937

943.9105 DB950.H6
DB955
DB956
DB957
944 DC38
DC251
DC252.5
DC611.L81
944.0072 DC36.9
944.00974924 DS135.F8
944.01 DC64
DC73.32
944.0108 DC70.A2
944.010924 DC73
DC73.32
944.022 DA197.5
944.0230924 DC90
944.025 DC96.5
DC101.5.A2
DC110
944.0260924 DC103
DC103.5
944.027 DC106
944.0270924 DC106
DC106.9
944.029 DC111
DC122.9.M6
944.0290924 DC119.8
944.03 DC36.8.B7
944.030922 DC36.2
944.031 BR845
944.0310924 DC122.8
DC122.9.M3
944.0320924 DC123.9.R5
944.033 DC125
DC129
DC129.A3
944.0330922 DC126
DC130.A2
944.0330924 DC129
DC130.L5
DC130.M2
DC130.M39
DC130.M4
DC130.R45
944.034 DC33.4
944.0340924 DC135
944.0350924 DC137.1
944.04 DC138
DC142
DC143
DC145
DC148
DC149.5
DC150
DC153
DC158.8
DC173.O62
944.040922 DC145
944.040924 DC135.D8
DC146.C8
DC146.S37
DC146.S5
DC151
ND553.D25
944.041 DC167
944.0410924 DC146.B85
DC146.L2
DC146.M7
DC146.R7
944.044 DC141
944.045 DC186.5
944.046 DC202.5
944.0460924 DC203
944.05 DC198.M2
DC240
944.050924 DC198.F7
DC203
DC211
DC239
944.063 DC266
944.07 DC270
DC272.5
DC275.2
944.070924 DC255.M3
DC269.C45
DC280
944.08 D829.F8
DC340
944.080924 DC373.G3
944.081 DC312
DC316
DC335
DC389
944.0810924 DC342.8.G3
DC373.M23
944.0815 DC389
944.0816 DC397
944.082 DC404
944.083 DC412
LA707
944.1 DC611.B856
944.10230924 DC611.B882
944.36 DC723
DC725
944.36081 DC314
944.36083 DC412
944.4 DC148
DC611.B78
944.5 DC611.L81
944.77 DC611.G25
944.9490924 DC943.G7
945 DG467
DG555

945 DG657
945.01 DG503.H693
PA6271.C4
945.05 DG463.8.B7
DG531
DG540
945.050922 DG537.8
945.050924 DG540.8.I7
DG811.6
945.06 DG551
945.060924 DG797.83
945.08 DG551
DG552
DG552.A2
DG552.6
DG658.5
DP203
945.0808 DG551
DG552.A2
945.080924 DG552.8.C3
DG552.8.G18
DG552.8.G2
DG552.8.M3
945.09 DG555
945.091 DG571
945.0910924 DG571
DG575.M8
PQ4804
945.3050924 DG677.99.G55
945.3091 DG568
945.31 DG677
945.38 DG975.V42
945.45050922 DG975.F42
945.49 DG975.S2
945.5 DG737
945.5080924 DG738.6.R5
945.51 DG737.5
DG737.55
945.510072022 DG737.55
945.5106 DG737.4
945.51092 DG738.7
945.6050922 DG463.8.B7
945.6060924 DG797.82
945.804 DG867.2
945.85 DG991
DG992.2
945.950340924 DC611.C806P37
946 DP65
DP66
DP162
946.000974924 DS135.S7
946.009 DP66
946.01 D135
DP96
946.02 DP101
DP103
DP125
946.04 D228
DP81.5
DP179
N3418
946.040924 DP175.H8
DP178
946.05 DP171
946.052 DA390.1.W6
946.055 D281.5
DP196
946.060924 DA68.12.W4
946.08 DP59
946.080924 DP240
946.081 DP63.7.J3
DP257
DP269
DP269.47.C3
DP269.47.R8
DP269.47.U6
946.0810924 DP269.9
946.082 DP270
946.0820924 DP264.F7
946.55 DP59.9
946.7 DP302.C62
946.8202 DP122
946.8203 DP122
946.89 DP302.G38
946.9 DP538
946.902 DP538
DP559
946.9020924 DP604
946.9030924 DP641
DP650
946.9040924 DP676.S25
946.99 DP702.A88
947 D147
DK35
DK37.6
DK37.8.R6
DK40
DK41
DK43
DK51.7
DK56
DR1
E178
947.003 DK36
947.01 DK71
947.02 DK70
947.03 DK90
947.04 DK106.5
DK111
DK112
DK114
947.040924 DK109
DK114.5.G6
947.05 DK22

947.05 DK133
947.050924 D285.8.B7
DK131
DK132
947.06 DK156
DK161
DK166
DK171
DK183
947.060924 DK161
947.07 D371
DK189
DK195
DK214
DK215
DK215.3
DK215.7
DK215.95
DK246
KD215.3
947.070922 DK188
947.070924 DK186
DK190.6.A8
DK191
DK201
DK210
UH347
947.0722 DK38
947.08 AS36
DK189
DK219.6.I8
DK246
DK255
DK258
DK262
DK263
DR573
947.080924 DK236.U4
DK254.S595
DK258
HX915
947.084 DK265.17
DK265.95
DK266
947.08408 DK274
DR48
947.0840924 DK254.K77
DK254.T6
DK275.K5
947.0841 D614.B6
DK5
DK265
DK265.19
DK265.2
DK265.4
DK265.42.U5
DK265.7
DK265.8.K7
DK265.8.L4
DK266.5
947.08410222 DK265.15
DK265.17
947.084108 DK265.17
947.08410924 DK254
DK254.F7
DK254.L4
DK254.L42
DK254.L44
DK254.L446
DK254.L45
DK254.L455
DK265.7
DK266.5
JN6598.K7
PG3286
947.0842 DK266.3
947.08420922 DK254.A55
947.08420924 DK254.T8
DK268
DK268.S8
947.085 DK267
947.0850924 DK274
DK275.K5
947.0974924 DS135.E8
947.1030922 DK461.M32
947.1030924 DK461.M32
947.4 DK511.B3
DL59
947.43 DK511.C6
DK511.L17
947.45 DK552
947.5 DK511.L2
947.50842 D802.L5
947.65 DK507.5
947.71 DK508.5
DK508.8
947.710841 DK265.8.U4
947.7606 NX210
947.8410924 DK254.L42
947.9 DK511.C1
947.92080924 DS195
948 DL46
948.031 DL65
948.1 DL448
948.1010924 DL467.O4
948.5 DL648
948.501 DL621
948.502 DL603
948.5020924 DL715
DL719
N3540
948.5030924 DL732
948.9 DL109
948.9010924 DL165

949 ..... DR36
949.12 ..... DL305
949.2 ..... DJ109
949.203 ..... DA47.3
..... DH185
..... DH186
..... DH186.5
..... DH187.5
..... DH188.W7
..... DH196
949.2030924 ..... DH188.W7
949.204 ..... DJ182
949.3 ..... DH418
949.303 ..... DH671
949.3030922 ..... DH514
949.32 ..... DH811.A64
949.4 ..... DQ54
949.5 ..... DF215
..... DF552.5
..... DF757
949.501 ..... PA3860.A67
949.5010924 ..... DF572
949.5030924 ..... DF605
949.5037 ..... DF727
949.504 ..... DF609
..... DF631
949.5040924 ..... DF639
949.5050924 ..... DR701.S55
949.506 ..... DF802
..... DF807
..... DF815.K64
..... DR589
949.507 ..... DF785
..... DF852
949.5070924 ..... DF850
949.55 ..... DF901.C7
949.6 ..... D374
..... D375
..... DR501
..... DR736
..... DS135.T8
949.61 ..... DF649
949.6101 ..... DF552
949.701 ..... DB48
949.70208 ..... DR370
949.7020924 ..... DR359.T5
949.71 ..... DR317
..... DR340.3.N4
..... DR359.Q5
949.72 ..... DB378
949.7202 ..... D804.Y8
949.74201 ..... D465
949.7701 ..... DR77
949.7702 ..... JX1975.5.G73
949.77030924 ..... DR93.S54
949.802 ..... DR226
949.8033 ..... DR205
949.96 ..... DS53.R4
950 ..... DS1.5
..... DS32
..... DS33
..... DS33.2
..... DS35
..... DS518
..... DU29
..... DU112.3
950.1 ..... DS33.5
950.109174943 ..... DS25
950.2 ..... DS19
..... DS22
..... DS785
950.20924 ..... DS22
950.30922 ..... G245
950.4 ..... DS518
951 ..... DS706
..... DS735
..... DS736
..... DS754
..... DS764
..... DS777.53
951.0072 ..... DS734.7
951.01 ..... DS25
..... DS749.2
951.010924 ..... DS749.3
951.026 ..... DS753
951.03 ..... DS735
..... DS754
..... DS755
..... DS757.5
..... DS759
..... DS761
..... DS772
951.04 ..... DS703.4
..... DS755
..... DS774
..... DS775
951.040924 ..... DS777
..... DS778.M3
951.0410924 ..... DS777
951.042 ..... DS777.53
951.04208 ..... E183.8.C5
951.0420922 ..... DS778.A1
951.0420924 ..... DS778.C55
..... E183.8.C5
..... E745.S68
951.05 ..... DS777.54
..... DS777.55
951.050924 ..... DS777.55
..... DS778.C5374
..... DS778.L4725
..... DS778.M3
..... PL2824.H3
..... Z8548.3
951.249 ..... DS895.F72
951.25 ..... DS796.H7
951.5 ..... DS786
951.505 ..... DS786
951.7 ..... DS783.7
951.8 ..... DS777.5
..... DS783.7.L45
951.9 ..... DS907
..... DS919
951.901 ..... DS911
951.903 ..... DS916
951.904 ..... DS917
951.9042 ..... DS918
..... DS918.2.C4
..... DS919.5
..... DS921.7
951.9043 ..... DS921.7
951.95 ..... DS925.S4
952 ..... DS835
952.03 ..... DS835
..... DS881.9
952.030924 ..... DS890.T57
952.031 ..... DS517
..... DS517.13
..... DS517.5
..... DS881
..... DS881.9
953 ..... DS37.7
953.02 ..... DS236
953.020924 ..... DS38.1
953.3205 ..... DS247.Y48
953.3505 ..... DS247.A28
953.8 ..... DS204
954 ..... DS335
..... DS435
..... DS436
..... DS452
954.007 ..... DS435.8
954.0072 ..... DS435
954.0072022 ..... DS435.5
954.008 ..... DS437
954.02 ..... DS452
..... DS457
954.0202 ..... DS433
954.0210924 ..... DS451.9.M8
954.024 ..... DS498.3
954.025 ..... DS461.1
954.02508 ..... DS461
954.0250924 ..... DS461.1
..... DS461.2
..... DS461.3
..... DS461.9.S5
954.029 ..... DS432.M2
..... DS462.5
..... DS471
..... DS472
954.0290922 ..... DS462
954.0290924 ..... DS470.M2
954.03 ..... DS463
954.030924 ..... DS475.2.P4
..... DS481.G3
954.031 ..... DS465
..... DS475.1
..... DS475.2.A2
..... DS475.3
..... DS477.1
954.0310924 ..... DS473
..... DS475.2
..... DS475.2.S37
954.035 ..... CT1508.A4
..... DS448
..... DS480.45
..... DS481.G3
954.0350922 ..... DS481.A1
954.0350924 ..... CT1508.B3
..... DS479
..... DS479.1.B29
..... DS479.1.M43
..... DS479.1.T54
..... DS479.4
..... DS480
..... DS481.B54
..... DS481.B6
..... DS481.D37
..... DS481.G3
..... DS481.G6
..... DS481.G78
..... DS481.K42
..... DS481.M6
..... DS481.N3
..... DS481.P35
..... DS481.S25
..... DS481.S35
..... DS481.S38
954.04 ..... DS384
..... DS480.45
..... DS480.84
..... DS480.85
954.0408 ..... DS480.45
954.040924 ..... DS481.G23
..... DS481.L57
..... DS481.N35
..... DS485.K2
954.12 ..... DS485.B51
954.2 ..... DS485.O94
..... DS486.A3
954.4 ..... DS432.R3
..... DS485.R2
954.503 ..... DS485.P2
954.5031 ..... DS485.P3
954.50310924 ..... DS475.2.R2
954.5035 ..... DS485.P3
954.5413092 ..... HD4295.O7
954.55 ..... DS485.H34
..... DS485.P2
954.5502 ..... DS485.P2
954.56029 ..... DS461
954.6 ..... DS485.K2
954.79 ..... DS485.B34
954.792 ..... CT1508.M32
..... DS485.D25
954.792025 ..... DS461.7
954.82 ..... DS451
954.8202 ..... DS451
954.82040924 ..... DS481.A64
954.8240924 ..... DS481.A64
954.83 ..... DS485.K4
954.870350924 ..... DS475.2.R195
954.88 ..... DS491.A5
954.9 ..... DS381
954.9008 ..... DS480.45
954.904 ..... DS384
954.90407 ..... DS376
954.9040924 ..... DS385.A93
..... DS385.J5
..... DS385.K5
954.9123 ..... DS486.P43
954.93 ..... DS489.3
..... DS489.5
954.930097494811 ..... DS489.5
954.9301 ..... DS489.5
954.930924 ..... DS489.35.G6
954.95 ..... DS485.N4
954.96 ..... DS485.N4
954.9640924 ..... DS485.N4
955 ..... DS272
955.050924 ..... DS318
955.8 ..... DS324.S5
956 ..... D198.3
..... D410
..... D463
..... D839.3
..... DS62
..... DS62.4
..... DS62.8
..... DS62.9
..... DS63
..... DS109.9
..... DS119
..... DS119.7
..... DS126.5
..... DS126.9
..... DS127
..... DS127.1
..... DS127.2
..... DS127.4.G4
..... DS127.6.O3
..... DS127.6.P8
..... DS127.7
..... DS127.85
..... DS127.9.J4
..... DS127.9.J6
..... DS143
..... DT107.83
..... KF27.F6485
..... Q180.A1
..... U162
956.002 ..... DS62.8
956.008 ..... DS62.4
956.04 ..... DS119.7
956.046 ..... DS119.7
..... DS127.6.O3
..... DS127.7
956.07 ..... DS162
956.1 ..... DR441
956.101 ..... DR473
..... DR572
..... DR584
956.102 ..... DR590.M35
956.45 ..... DS54.5
956.4502 ..... DS54.7
956.4503 ..... DS54.8
956.62 ..... DS176
..... DS186
..... DS195.5
956.703 ..... DS77
956.91 ..... DS95
956.9104 ..... DS98
956.9200222 ..... DS80.2
956.94 ..... D182
..... DS109.3
..... DS109.9
..... DS113
..... DS118
..... DS119.7
..... DS126.5
956.94001 ..... BS649.J5
..... DS119.7
..... DS126.4
..... DS145
..... DS145.P7
..... DS149
..... DS151.C63
956.9400108 ..... DS149
956.940010924 ..... DS115.9.K5
..... DS135.G5H52
..... DS151.G585
..... DS151.S9
956.9404 ..... DS119.7
..... DS125
..... DS126
..... DS126.4
956.9405 ..... DS107.4
..... DS119.6
..... DS119.7
..... DS126.4
..... DS126.5
..... DS127.6.O3
956.94050924 ..... DS125.3
956.94050924 ..... DS125.3.B37
..... DS126.6
..... DS126.6.D3
..... DS126.6.E8
..... DS126.6.M42
956.940924 ..... DS126.6.M42
957 ..... DK766
957.702 ..... F272
958 ..... DK878
..... DS785
958.1 ..... DS356
..... DS361
958.103 ..... DS363
958.408 ..... DK851
958.43 ..... DK913
958.7085 ..... DK948
959 ..... DS35
..... DS511
..... DS550
..... DS557.C28
959.1 ..... DS485.B86
959.104 ..... DS485.B89
959.105 ..... DS485.B89
959.1050924 ..... DS485.B86
..... DS485.B892
959.3 ..... DS557.C28
959.3020924 ..... DS577
959.404 ..... DS557.L25
959.5 ..... DS596
959.505 ..... DS597.2
..... DS598.S7
959.5050924 ..... DS595.6.T3
959.51 ..... DS598.N4
959.52 ..... DS598.S7
959.52050924 ..... DS595.6.L4
959.7 ..... DS542
..... DS557.A5
..... DS557.A655E58
..... DS557.C7
959.703 ..... DS550
959.704 ..... DS550
..... DS557
..... DS557.A5
..... DS557.A6
..... DS557.A61
..... DS557.A62
..... DS557.A62B55
..... DS557.A62K58
..... DS557.A63
..... DS557.A635
..... DS557.A64
..... DS557.A64A8
..... DS557.A64A845
..... DS557.A64N44
..... DS557.A645
..... DS557.A65
..... DS557.A67
..... DS557.A677
..... DS557.A68
..... DS557.A69
..... DS557.A692
..... DS557.A7
..... DS557.A72
..... DS557.C28
..... DS557.L28
..... E839.5
..... E839.8
..... E846
..... E855
..... JK339
..... JX1573
..... KF26.F6
..... KF26.J875
..... KF26.L394
..... KF27.A7
..... KF27.A764
..... KF27.F6483
..... KF27.5.A25
..... KF31.F6
..... KF32.A7
..... KF32.M436
..... KF32.5.U5
..... R611
..... RA541.V
..... UA23
..... UA853.V5
..... VA66
..... VA66.C62
959.7040207 ..... DS557.A61
959.70408 ..... DS557.A76
959.7040924 ..... DS557.A69
..... DS557.A76
..... DS557.A76H6774
..... U55.G5
..... U55.V6
959.7043373 ..... DS557.A63
..... JX1573
959.70434 ..... DS557.A6
..... DS557.C28
959.704342 ..... UA853.V48
959.70437 ..... DS557.A677
959.70438 ..... DS557.A69
959.94094212 ..... N5055.H32
960 ..... D839.5
..... DT3
..... DT5
..... DT20
..... DT21
..... DT22
..... DT30
..... DT31
..... DT32
960.071 ..... DT19.8
960.072 ..... D13

Dewey	LC
960.072	DT19
960.08	DT30
960.0971244	DT30
960.2	DT20
	DT22
	DT25
	DT29
	DT31
	DT32
960.20922	DT3
960.3	DT29
961	DT201
961.02	DT199
961.2	DT224
961.22	D194
962	DT100
	DT107
962.02	DT95
	DT96
962.020924	D198.4.S2
962.03	DT106
962.04	DT107
	DT108
962.040924	DT107.6
962.05	DT107
	DT107.83
962.050924	DT107.82
	DT107.83
962.15	DT154.S9
962.1503	DT154.S9
962.16	DT143
962.403	DT108
	DT108.1
	DT108.3
	DT108.5
962.4030924	DT108.15
	DT108.2
	DT108.3
962.903	DT361
963	DT381
	DT384
	TD381
963.03	DT384
963.030924	DT386.3
963.04	DT387.3
963.065	DT387.8
964.02	DT321
964.03	DT317
964.04	DT324
965.04	DT295
965.3	DT284
966	DT475
	DT476
	DT503
	DT534
966.008	DT503
966.3	DT549.7
966.3050924	DT549.6.S4
966.4	DT516.7
966.402	DT516.7
966.4020924	DT516.65
966.57	DT671.B9
	KF27.F625
966.5702	DT613
	DT613.7
966.6020924	CT2750.B4
966.7	DT510.42
	DT510.5
	DT511
966.701	DT511
966.703	DT511
966.705	DT510.6.N5
	DT512
966.7050924	DT510.6.N5
966.9	DT515
	DT515.5
966.9010924	DT515.6.J3
966.903	DT515.42
966.905	DT515.E3
	DT515.62
	DT515.8
	DT515.9.E3
	DT515.9N5
966.92	DT515.42
	DT515.9.B4
	DT515.9.I3
966.93	DT515.42
966.9301	DT515.9.B37
966.93030924	DT515.6.O4
966.931	DT515.9.B37
966.94	DT515.9.B6
966.9405	DT515.9.E3
966.95	DT515.42
	DT515.9.A3
	DT515.9.F8
967	DT351
	DT352.5
	DT352.6
	DT353
	DT361
	DT363
	DT365.65
967.24	DT658
	DT665.B3
967.24035	DT16.P8
967.303	DT611.7
967.5	DT655
967.501	DT652
967.502	DT655
967.5030924	DT663.L8
967.6	DT423
	DT431
967.60072	DT432
967.60974914	DT429
967.61	DT434.U25
967.62030924	DT434.E26
967.62040924	DT434.E26
967.73	DT406
	DT416
967.7303	DT406
967.8	DT444
	DT447
967.82	DT443
967.82010924	DT446.M54
967.9	DT459
968	CD2451
	DT731
	DT753
	DT766
	DT775
	DT776.A2
	DT888
968.009753936	DT888
968.03	DT731
	DT773
	DT888
968.04	DT766
	DT773
	DT777
	DT932
968.040922	DA566.9.C5
968.040924	DT776.R4
	DT776.S7
	DT777
	DT844.2.S8
968.05	DT779
	DT779.7
	DT779.8.B6
968.050924	DT779.8.B6
	DT779.8.S6
968.1	DT791
968.2	DT770
	DT927
	DT930
	DT930.A2
	DT932
	DT933
	DT934.S74
	DT935
	UB430
968.204	DT926
	DT934.S65
968.2040924	DT929.8.K8
968.20924	DT932
968.2204	TN427.S6
968.4	DT767
	DT777
	DT875
	DT878.Z9
968.404	DT777
	DT868
968.4040924	DT866
968.5040924	DT905.S7
968.6	DT782
	DT846.T7
968.6040924	DT782
968.7	DT838
	DT846.K2
	DT848.C5
968.902	DT958
968.91	DT958
	DT962.62
	DT964.M4
968.9102	DT958
	DT962.5
968.94	DT858
	DT963.5
968.9404	DT963.8
970.0072024	E175.5
970.0097496	E185.96
970.01	E57
	E111
970.03	E199
	E267
970.052	F1034
970.1	E51
	E58
	E61
	E71
	E76
	E76.6
	E77
	E77.2
	E77.4
	E77.5
	E78.G73
	E78.I18
	E78.N7
	E78.W5
	E81
	E83.869
	E87
	E88
	E98.A7
	E98.C9
	E98.M3
	E98.S7
	E99.C53
	E467.1.C99
	F517
	F598
	GN1
970.103	E77
970.10922	E89
970.13	F1246
970.2	D16
970.3	E51
	E58
970.3	E65
	E75
	E77
	E78.E2
	E78.N65
	E78.T3
	E78.T4
	E83.877
	E87
	E87.O12
	E90.B56
	E90.J8
	E90.J9
	E90.P19
	E90.R78
	E90.S45
	E90.W27
	E98.F6
	E98.M6
	E99.A16
	E99.A6
	E99.A7
	E99.B37
	E99.C18
	E99.C24
	E99.C5
	E99.C53
	E99.C6
	E99.C8
	E99.C88
	E99.D1
	E99.D2
	E99.E7
	E99.H7
	E99.H9
	E99.I7
	E99.K4
	E99.K5
	E99.K9
	E99.M3
	E99.M44
	E99.M6
	E99.M77
	E99.M8
	E99.N16
	E99.N3
	E99.P2
	E99.P25
	E99.P5
	E99.P6
	E99.P8
	E99.P9
	E99.S23
	E99.S3
	E99.S35
	E99.S4
	E99.S54
	E99.S68
	E99.T35
	E99.U8
	E99.W36
	E99.W7
	E99.Y95
	E99.Z9
	F152
	F804.S8
	F1089.N8
	F1214
	F1219
	F1221.M3
	F1221.S43
	F1221.T25
	F1221.T6
	F2520.1.T4
	F2679.2.A2
	F3430.1.A5
	GN1
	GN2
	QK477
	Z1210.F9
970.30922	E99.N3
970.30924	E90.W55
	E99.D1
	E99.S3
	E99.S35
970.401	E78.A3
970.41	E78.C2
970.412	E51
	E78.C2
970.4122	E99.E7
	F1060.92
970.4129	F1101
970.413	E78.O5
970.4131	E78.O5
970.416	E78.N9
970.42	E65
	F1216
	F1219
	F1219.3
	F1219.3.A7
	F1221.O86
970.422	E51
970.423	F1219.M55
970.4281	F1465.1.B5
970.4282	F1445.1.R5
970.4295	F1969
970.43	E73
970.4307207769	E78.I6
970.444	E78.M4
970.446	E78.C7
970.447	E78.N7
	E195
970.449	E78.N6
970.45	E51
970.45	E77
	E78.S65
970.451	F166
970.455785	E78.V7
970.457	E78.S6
970.459381	E99.M48
970.46	E78.S8
970.464	E78.T4
	F388
970.464289	E78.T4
970.464533	E78.T4
970.46648	E77.5
970.467	E78.A8
970.4671	E78.O9
970.46766	E78.A8
970.46863	E78.T3
970.47	E78.G7
970.471	E98.T7
970.472	F1346
970.474	E78.M6
970.476	E78.M7
970.47668	E78.M7
970.4778325	E77.8
970.478594	E78.M8
970.479	E78.G67
970.48	E78.W5
970.482245	E99.O4
970.48225	E99.O4
970.48355	E78.S63
970.48358	E78.S63
970.48733	F737.B5
970.48856	F776
	F782.E3
970.4898	QC884
970.49	E99.S2
970.491	E78.S7
	E98.F7
970.49133	E78.A7
970.49137	E51
970.494	E78.C15
	F863
970.4949	E78.C15
970.49491	F863
970.49492	E99.C815
970.495	E78.N77
	E78.N78
970.49637	E78.W3
970.49733	E78.W3
970.498	QH31.G36
970.5	E81
	E83
	E83.866
	E93
	E99.A6
	E99.C8
	E181.H28
970.50904	E93
970.50971	E78.C2
	E92
970.509747	E78.N7
970.509775	E78.W8
970.509776	E93
971	E99.W7
	F1026
	F1027
	F1033
	F1035.8
971.002	F1006
971.008	F1001
	F1008
971.01	E99.I7
	F1030
971.0108	F1030
971.011	E78.N7
	F1030
	F1060
971.0110924	E133.C3
971.016	F1060.7
971.018	E198
	E199
	F1030
971.02	F1032
971.024	E277
971.0240922	F1058
971.030924	F1032.B92
971.038	F1032
971.0390924	F1032
971.04	F1032
971.0490922	F1032
971.0490924	F1033
	F1033.M132
971.05	F1033
971.0508	F1033
971.050924	F1033
	F1033.M14
	F1034.B65
971.051	F1063
	F1064.R3
971.0510924	F1060.9
971.060924	F1033.K53
	F1078.P3
971.0610924	F1033.B76
971.062	F1033
971.06408	F1034.3.D5
971.0640924	F1034.3.T7
	F1034.3.V3
971.1	F1088
971.10063	F1087
971.102	F1089.C3
971.1020924	F1088.D747
971.1030922	F1086.8
971.12	F1089.B8
971.134	F1089.V3
	F1089.5.V22

Dewey	LC
971.134	F1089.5.V6
971.145	F1089.5.F4
971.2	F1060
	F1060.7
	F1062
971.201	F1060.7
971.2010924	F1060.7
	F1060.7.M2
971.22	F1100.5.Y4
	G660
971.22101	G650
971.2300922	F1079.L4
971.233	F1079.5.H8
971.234	F1079.C6
	F1079.5.C38
	F1079.5.D3
	F1079.5.G55
971.242	F1074.5.B3
	F1074.5.M48
971.242020924	F1074.S3
971.244	F1074.5.G75
971.27	F1063
971.27010924	F1063.S47
971.273	F1064.5.A7
	F1064.5.C3
	F1064.5.G7
	F1064.5.R8
	F1064.5.W3
971.274	F1064.R3
	F1064.5.D6
	F1064.5.S135
971.29010924	G660
971.3	F1058
971.302	F1032
	F1057.8
971.3020924	F1058.R9852
	F1058.S5682
971.3044	SK602.C3
971.32302	F1059.P3
971.337	F1059.5.S4
971.338	F1059.5.C8
971.351	F1059.5.S14
971.354	F1058.K56
	F1059.5.N82
	F1059.5.S33
	F1059.5.T68
971.355	F1059.5.O84
971.357	F1059.5.S45
971.361	F1059.H27
971.381	F1059.5.C27
971.383	F1059.C3
971.402	E231
	F1032
971.428	F1054.5.M857
971.4281	F1054.5.M857
971.428101	F1054.5.M8
971.5	F1035.8
971.6003	F1036.4
971.601	F1038
971.602	F1038
971.6020924	F1038.P48
971.622	F1039.5.H17
971.635	F1039.5.N4
971.64551	F394.P23
971.6901	E198
971.7	F1048
971.7020924	F1032.D47
971.9110924	E756
971.9220924	E840.8.K4
972	F1226
	F1437
972.02	F1219.3.M59
	F1230
	F1232
972.020924	F1230
	F1230.A44
	F1411
972.03	F1231.5
972.060924	F1401
972.070924	F1233
972.08	F1234
972.081	F1233.5
	F1234
	F1392.M6
972.0810924	F1233.5.D53
	F1234
972.082	F1234
972.08208	F1234
972.182	F689.M4
972.202	F1246
972.2020924	F864.K7
972.8105	F1466.5
972.9	F1411
	F1621
	F2131
	F2161
972.91	F1783
	F1787
972.9102	F1779
972.9105	F1786
972.91050924	F1783.V2546
972.91060924	BR1725.G57
972.91062	F1787
972.91063	F1787.5
972.910630924	F1787.5
972.91064	F1776
	F1788
972.910640924	F1401
	F1788
	F1788.22.C3
972.92	F1895.P6
972.9203	F1884
972.92032	F1621
972.9305	F1938.45
972.93054	E183.8.D6
	F1938.55
972.94	F1921
972.9403	F1923
972.94030924	F1923
972.9404	F1924
972.940408	F1924
972.9405	F1927
972.94060924	F1928.D86
972.95	F1981.S2
972.9502	F1958.3
972.9722	E768
	F2096
	F2105
972.98	CD3985.W5
972.981	F2041
972.982	F2081
972.983	F2120
	F2121
972.983030924	F2122.W5
972.9843	F2100
972.986	F2141
972.99	F1636
973	CD3021
	E161.5
	E172.9
	E173
	E175.8
	E176
	E176.1
	E176.2
	E178
	E178.1
	E178.2
	E178.3
	E178.4
	E178.5
	E178.6
	E179
	E179.5
	E181
	E182
	E183
	E183.7
	E184.I6
	E185.6
	E185.61
	E277
	E301
	E338
	E441
	E444
	E464
	E747
	F158.8.I3
	F591
	GF503
	HE1780
	HV6477
	J81
	N7593
973.0072	D13
	E175.7
973.01	E175.8
	E175.9
	E178.6
973.02	E174.5
973.0202	E174.5
	E175.8
	E178.2
973.0207	E178.4
973.03	E174
	E174.5
973.0496	E185
973.07	E175.8
973.070924	E664.P7
973.071242	D16.2
973.071273	E175.8
973.072	E175
	E175.1
	E175.7
	E175.8
	F1401
973.072017496	E175
973.072024	D15.P4
	E175
	E175.5
	E175.5.A1746
	E175.5.A1767
	E340.B2
973.072073	E175.45
973.0722	E175
973.074014461	E173
973.074014811	F158.15
973.074016971	E457.32
973.08	E173
	E175
	E178
	E178.6
	PE1127.H5
973.0922	E176.1
	E176.2
973.0924	E444
973.09743	E184.G3
973.09749185	E184.P7
973.0974924	E184.J5
973.097496	AG105
	E175
	E184.7
	E185
	E185.6
	E185.61
	E185.96
973.099	BR516
973.099	E99.S28O83
	E176.1
973.1	E27
	E101
	E143
	E188
973.11	E61
973.13	DL65
	E105
973.140924	E109.M3
973.15	E118
	G161
973.150924	E118
973.16	E125.N9
	E125.S7
	F1411
973.160924	E123
	E129.C1
973.17	E127
	E129.C1
	G650
973.170924	E125.B2
973.18	E131
	F1030
973.180924	E133.V5
	F1030.2
973.2	E187
	E188
	E188.5
	E191
	E195
	E209
	E302.1
	F68
	F1030.7
973.208	E18.82
	E187
	E188.5
973.20924	E302
	E302.6.F7
	E302.6.M45
	E312
	F67
	F229
973.21	F229
	F234.J3
973.22	F68
	F152
973.220922	E187.5
973.23	E191
973.24	F1030.5
973.25	E87.W732
973.26	E195
	E198
	E199
	E209
	E312.7
973.2608	E195
973.260924	E312.2
973.27	E83.76
	E83.77
973.270924	E83.76
	E195
	E302.6.A2
973.3	E173
	E203
	E208
	E209
	E210
	E230.5.O3
	E263.S7
	E267
	E301
	E303
	E312.17
973.307	E203
973.3072024	E175.5.B4
973.308	E203
	E297
973.30922	E206
	E296
	E302.5
973.30924	E207.A4
	E207.R6
	E207.W2
	E278.A7
	E278.C98
	E302
	E302.1
	E302.6.B5
	E302.6.B7
	E302.6.C3
	E302.6.D5
	E302.6.F7
	E302.6.G37
	E302.6.H2
	E302.6.H5
	E302.6.M7
	E302.6.M8
	E302.6.O8
	E302.6.S17
	E312.81
	F483
	HJ247
973.31	E203
	E209
	E216
	E277
973.3108	E210
973.310924	E302.6.P84
	E302.6.W7
973.311	E210
	E211
	E215.5
973.3111	E215.2
973.3113	E215.4
973.312	E185
	E303
973.3130922	E221
973.314	E277
	E312.25
973.315	E185.63
	E215.7
973.318	E303
973.3180924	E312.29
973.320924	E249
	E302.6.F7
	E302.6.F8
973.324	E249
	E265
973.3292072	E302.A266
973.33	E207.W65
	E221
	E230
	E230.5.S7
	E263.N6
	F128.44
	F129.W7
973.330922	E267
973.330924	E207.C5
	E207.G23
	E207.G9
	E207.P9
	E207.S3
	E207.S8
	E230
	E275
973.331	E231
973.3310924	E207.M7
973.3311	E241.L6
973.33110924	E267
	F69
973.3312	E241.B9
973.332	E230.5.V3
	E231
	E233
	E241.M9
	E241.T7
973.333	E233
	E241.B8
	E241.S2
	E275
973.3330924	E268
973.334	E241.M7
973.3341	E234
973.335	E235
973.337	E241.Y6
	E267
	E275
973.33709757	E263.S7
973.338	E238
973.34	E255
973.341	E267
973.3410922	E267
973.3410924	E267
973.342	E268
973.344	E231
	F565
973.3440924	E207.W35
973.3443	F52.A432
973.3452	E263.M3
973.345510924	E263.D3
973.3457	F273
973.3458	E263.G3
973.347	E163
	E265
973.3470924	E265
973.35	E182
	E271
	E271.C77
	E302.6.F8
973.350922	E271
973.350924	E271
	E353.1.B26
973.36	E255
	E285.3
	F155
973.375	E283
973.38	E259
	E263.N5
	E263.P4
	E263.S7
	E267
	E275
973.382	E236
	E278.A7
973.3820922	E236
973.383	E207.L47
973.3860924	E280.A5
973.4	E301
	E302.6.P6
	E310
973.408	E301
973.40922	E176
	E302.1
973.40924	E185.97.C96
	E207.S3
	E302
	E302.6.H2
	E302.6.L68
	E302.6.M7
	E302.6.R2
	E337.8
	E340.O8
	E340.W95
973.41	F279.C457
973.410924	E312
	E312.29

973.410924 ... E312.66
973.43 ... E315
973.430924 ... E312.17
973.44 ... E326
973.440924 ... E302
... E322
... E322.1
... E337.8
973.45 ... E323
973.46 ... E331
973.460924 ... E302
... E302.6.B84
... E302.6.B9
... E302.6.H2
... E302.6.M17
... E310
... E332
... E332.2
... E332.74
... E332.79
... F194.3
973.47 ... E335
973.48 ... PZ7.W458
973.480924 ... E302.6.B9
973.5 ... E83.813
... E165
... E176.2
... E337.8
... E341
... E357.7
... F592
... JK311
973.50922 ... E415.9.B63
973.50924 ... E340.B4
... E340.C3
... E340.E8
... E340.W4
... E353.1.P7
... E377
... E387
... E392
... E448.F5
... F549.A4
973.51 ... E302
973.510924 ... E342
... E342.1
973.52 ... E83.813
... E354
... E359.85
973.523 ... E354
... E355.4
... E356.D4
973.5238 ... F189.B1
... F332.T15
... F341
973.5239 ... E356.N5
... F379.N557
973.52447 ... E359.5.N6
973.52469 ... E359.5.K5
973.525 ... E354
... E360
... E360.C5
... VA65.E8
973.5254 ... E356.E6
973.528 ... E601
973.54 ... E371
... E374
973.540924 ... E371
... E372
... F279.C457
973.550924 ... E337.8.A2
... E340.P77
... E377
973.56 ... E83.83
... E337.8
... E338
... F390
973.561 ... E384.3
973.57 ... E83.835
973.570924 ... E386
... E387
973.58 ... E338
... E397
973.580922 ... E337.8
973.580924 ... AC8
... E397
973.6 ... E83.84
... E338
... E415.9.S9
... E450
973.608 ... E457.92
973.60922 ... E176
973.60924 ... E340.C15
... E415.9.C55
... E415.9.S84
... E432
... E457
... HX696.09
973.61 ... E179.5.G75
973.610924 ... E416
973.62 ... E404
973.6208 ... E404
973.621 ... E407
973.623 ... E405.1
973.6230922 ... E403
973.624 ... E409.5.I72
... F865
973.625 ... E410
973.626 ... E494
973.628 ... E411
973.630924 ... E422
973.64 ... E431
973.660924 ... E415.9.F8
... E664.M8
973.68 ... E436
973.680924 ... E415.9.D73
... E437
... E451
... E457.4
973.7 ... E453
... E458
... E468
... E468.7
... E468.9
... E487
... E505
... E609
... E649
... E661
973.7020924 ... DB217.M3
973.70922 ... E415.7
... E456
... E467
... E664.W32
973.70924 ... E83.866
... E185.97
... E415.6
... E415.9.C4
... E415.9.F4
... E415.9.H2
... E415.9.S5
... E415.9.S9
... E456
... E457
... E457.1.L53
... E457.15
... E457.2
... E457.25
... E457.32
... E457.5
... E457.5.S985
... E457.6
... E457.7
... E457.92
... E457.96
... E457.99
... E467.1.B23
... E467.1.M4
... E467.1.S55
... E467.1.S8
... E470
... E661
973.71 ... E167
... E441
... E458
... E458.Z
... E459
973.710924 ... E415.9.V2
973.711 ... E301
... E438
... E458.2
973.7110924 ... E415.9.G8
973.7113 ... E373
973.7114 ... E449
973.71140924 ... E340.B6
... E446
... E449
973.7115 ... E450
973.712 ... E469
973.713 ... E440.5
... E484
... E487
... F273
973.7130924 ... E415.9.W4
... E467.1.D26
... E487
973.714 ... E185.2
... E468
... E469.8
973.7140924 ... E457.2
973.715 ... E540.N3
... F326
973.715097 ... E609
973.7152851774 ... BX8947.M5
973.71530145196 ... E540.N3
973.72 ... E469.8
973.721 ... JX1429
973.73 ... E470
... E470.2
... E470.4
... E470.65
... E601
... E664.L83
973.73012 ... E493.5.W5
973.730120922 ... E467
973.73013 ... E551.5
973.730924 ... E467.1.B75
... E467.1.F72
... E467.1.L4
... E467.1.L55
... E467.1.S54
... E672
973.731 ... E472.18
... E472.6
973.732 ... F444.D67
973.7344 ... E475.27
973.7349 ... E475.53
973.7359 ... E470.65
973.74 ... E494
... E540.I6
973.741 ... E540.F6
973.7415 ... E492.95
... E540.N3
973.74150924 ... E185.97.S55
973.742 ... E545
973.7442 ... E520
973.745 ... E528.7
973.7455 ... E581.5
973.7456 ... F262.F8
973.7457 ... E492.94
973.746 ... E499.5
973.7463 ... E565.5
973.7464 ... E645
... F381
973.7471 ... E540.N3
973.7474 ... E514.6
973.7481 ... E508.4
973.75 ... E470.8
... E591
973.750922 ... E591
973.750924 ... E467.1.F23
... E467.1.P4
973.752 ... E473.2
973.757 ... E596
... E599.A3
973.76 ... E494
... E548
... E558.3
... E559
... E641
973.77 ... E458.8
973.7760924 ... R154.M716
973.78 ... E491
... UC483
973.781 ... E467.1.V7
... E471
... E601
973.7810924 ... E467.1.L6
... E531
... E601
973.782 ... E415.7
... E605
973.7820924 ... E415.7
973.7850924 ... E608.E26
... E608.V34
973.786 ... E470.95
... E608
973.788 ... E488.5
973.8 ... E176.1
... E185.2
... E661
... E668
... E836
... F694
973.80202 ... E661
973.808 ... E660
973.80924 ... CD3047
... E83.866
... E90.A38
... E90.G4
... E99.A6
... E99.D1
... E185.97
... E185.97.S6
... E449
... E664.A35
... E664.C4
... E664.E88
... E664.G82
... E664.H41
... E664.S39
... E664.S57
... F341.L97
973.81 ... E668
... F379.N557
973.81008 ... E185.2
973.810924 ... E415.9.J56
... E666
... E667
... F594
973.82 ... E83.866
... E83.87
... E83.876
... E661
... E671
973.820924 ... E415.9.W6
... E664.B856
... E671
... E672
973.83 ... E83.877
973.830924 ... E415.6
... E681
... E682
973.840922 ... E660.G25
973.840924 ... E687
973.850924 ... E83.88
... E660
... E697
... F566.D52
973.86 ... E83.89
... E660
973.870924 ... E664.O45
973.880924 ... E711
... E711.9
973.89 ... E715
973.891 ... E727
973.893 ... E715
... E725.45
973.8930917496 ... E725.5N3
973.8933 ... E717
... E717.1
... E729
973.8937 ... DS679
973.894 ... E725.45
973.895 ... E105
973.8950924 ... E714.6.D51
973.9 ... E741
... E742
... E743
... F200
... F204.W5
973.90922 ... E176.1
973.90924 ... E748.G53
... E748.M415
... E748.S883
... TL540.R54
973.91 ... CT275.W5518
... E743
973.910922 ... E176.1
973.910924 ... E664.B87
... E748.A15
... E748.M33
... E836
... E840.8.D5
973.9110924 ... E332
... E664.S896
... E748.B94
... E756
... E757
973.9120922 ... E757
973.9120924 ... E761
... E762
973.913 ... E660
... E780
... F1234
973.9130924 ... E748.M14
... E748.T84
973.914 ... E784
973.9140924 ... E785
... E786
973.9150924 ... E664.L16
... E748.S63
... E748.V18
... E791
973.916 ... E801
... F199
973.9160924 ... E802
973.917 ... E806
973.9170922 ... E806
973.9170924 ... E748.W23
... E807
... E807.1
... E840.8.A5
... HC102.5.R5
973.918 ... E743
... E748.M143
... E813
... J82.D792
973.9180924 ... E748.M143
... E748.M375
... E748.W54
... E813
... E814
973.92 ... E839.4
... E856
973.9208 ... E740.5
973.920922 ... E185.96
... E813
... E843
973.920924 ... E748.H46
... E856
973.9210924 ... DK266.3
... E742.5
... E748.M143
... E748.S84
... E835
... E836
973.922 ... E843
973.92207401446 ... F74.B9
973.9220922 ... E840.6
... E842
973.9220924 ... CT275.O552
... E840.8.K4
... E840.8.M35
... E842.Z9
... E842.9
... E843
... E843.K4
973.923 ... DS557.A63
... E839
... E846
... F548.52
973.9230207 ... E847
973.9230924 ... E840.8
... E840.8.K4
... E840.8.M3
... E846
... E847
... E848
973.924 ... E840.8.M3
... E856
... LD4191.O72
973.9240924 ... E840.8.A34
... E840.8.M85
... E851
... E855
... E856
973.930924 ... E767
974 ... F4.6
974.04 ... QC945
974.1008 ... F19
974.102 ... F23
974.103 ... F24
974.12 ... F29.B76
974.14 ... F29.E2
974.153 ... F29.W2
974.16 ... F29.C55
974.18501 ... F22
974.202 ... F37
974.2044 ... F40
974.230924 ... E302.6.L26
974.275 ... F44.C8
974.29 ... F44.E15
974.3 ... F52
974.302 ... F52
974.32 ... F59.D4

Dewey	LC
974.365	F59.H3
974.37	F59.S492
974.40072	F64
974.402	F67
	F68
974.403	F69
974.4030922	E277
	F69
974.4030924	E661
974.41	F74.L57
974.426	F74.S8
974.43	F72.W9
	F74.A8
974.44	F74.C8
974.45	F74.S1
974.46	F74.C4
974.4610097496	F73.9.N4
974.46102	F73.4
	F73.8.F2
974.4612	F73.4
974.47	F74.B9
	F74.F7
974.48	F68
	F74.P8
974.494040924	E840.8.K35
974.4940924	F67.M526
974.497	F72.N2
974.5	F82
974.502	F82
	F83
974.5020924	F82
974.5030922	E263.V8
974.5030924	F83.4
974.6	F95
974.602	F97
	F98
974.61	F104.K3
974.62	F104.E1
974.67	F102.T4
974.69	F104.D27
	F104.G75
	F104.S54
	F104.S75
	F104.S8
974.7	F116
	F119
	F120
	F128.3
974.702	F119
	F122
974.7020216	CD3406.S8
974.70208	F118.5
974.7020924	F122.S648
	F122.S66
	F122.1.S9245
974.703	E277
	F123
974.704	F119
974.71	F128.3
	F128.37
	F128.44
	F128.64.L6
	F128.68.H3
	F128.9.N3
974.7102	F128.4
974.7103	F128.44
974.7104	F128.47
	F128.68.H3
	F128.9.N3
974.71040924	F128
	F128.5
974.721	F127.L8
974.72303	F129.B7
974.724	E263.N6
974.7245	F129.R81
974.725	F129.S74
974.726	F127.S7
974.728	F127.R6
974.73	F127.H8
974.741	F129.T8
974.75	F127.C6
974.756	F127.S2
974.762	F129.R82
974.766	F129.S8
974.79	F556
974.7903	F129.B8
974.8	F167
974.802	F152
974.8020924	F152.2
974.8103	E450
974.811	F157.P56
	F158.3
974.81103	F158.44
974.813	F157.C4
974.815	E450
974.821	F157.B8
974.834	F157.S7
974.83403	F157.S7
974.839	F159.D2
974.843	F157.C8
	F159.S56
974.85	F157.S9
974.851	F157.L9
974.855030924	F153.L9
974.856	F157.T5
974.869	F157.C5
974.88602074014886	F159.P6
974.889	F159.M34
974.892	F159.B3
974.9	F134.3
	F157.D4
974.90097496	E185.93.N54
974.90208	F137
974.921	F142.R16
974.921	F144.D8
	F144.O5
	F144.T28
	F144.W95
974.948	F144.M241
974.971	F144.L23
974.974	F144.C49
974.981	F144.G48
974.984	F144.C37
975	E668
	F206
	F209
975.0072024	E175.5.S5
975.01	F314
975.02	F212
975.03	F206
975.0308	F209
975.04	E487
	E668
	F216
975.1	F163
975.102	F167
975.2	F181
975.202	F184
975.227	F187.D6
975.271	F189.T6
975.281	F189.E4
975.287	F189.T45
975.294	F187.A4
975.3	E457.65
	F195
	F202.G3
	F203.5.L2
	F203.7.P4
	F204.C2
975.304	E855
975.4	F241
	F241.6
975.42	F249.B85
975.457	F247.H3
975.465	F247.W37
975.47	F232.N5
975.499	E451
975.5	F217.B6
975.500712	F225.5
975.50108	G161
975.5010924	E90.P6
	F234.J3
975.502	F229
975.5020924	F229
	F229.C34
975.503	E534
975.504	F231
975.5040924	F231.3.G6
975.527502	F232.F3
975.528	F234.S62
975.529	F234.G75
	F234.M34
	F234.M8
975.5295	F234.A7
975.5296	F234.A3
975.536	F232.C2
975.5365	BX6480.S8S25
975.5416	F234.N5
975.548	F234.S3
975.55503	F232.S7
975.559	F234.B6
975.566	F232.H17
	HE1780.5.V8
975.579	F234.R6
975.589	F232.H8
975.6	CD3424
	F253
	F254.6
975.604	F259
	F274
975.6040924	E748.S84
975.6175	F262.D2
975.669	F262.D4
975.6703	E263.N8
975.676	F262.M4
975.7	F274
975.702	F272
	F279.C457
975.7020924	E302.6.R89
975.703	E185.93.S7
	F273
975.704	F274
975.7040924	F274
975.72	F272
975.771	F279.C7
975.773	SD11
975.779	F279.O6
975.789	F277.G35
975.791	F279.C46
	UA26.M6
975.7915	F279.C443
975.791502	F279.C457
975.799	E185.93.S7
975.8	F291.B7
975.802	F289
975.8020924	F289.O28
975.803	F286
975.804	F291
975.81	F277.S3
975.816	F292.E4
975.8231	F294.A8
975.835	F294.R7
975.8724	F294.S2
975.874	F294.F7
975.8876	F292.C76
975.8953	F294.A32
975.901	F314
975.9010924	F314.M54
975.903	E83.817
975.9060924	F316.2
975.918	F319.S2
975.923	F319.S3
975.932	F319.B45
975.975	F319.D8
975.977	F319.Y35
976	F396
976.02	F396
976.030924	F390.H824
976.0640924	F1034.3.L3
976.1	F326
	F326.3
976.1060924	F330.W33
976.155	F334.A83
976.174	F332.W6
976.195	F334.B7
976.2	F340.5
976.200740153	Z1301
976.205	F341
976.206	F341
976.2060924	E748.V24
976.21	F347.G9
976.26806	F347.K3
976.3009744	F380.C9
976.302	F372
	F380.G3
976.3030924	F373.G3
976.306	F375
976.3060924	E748.L86
	F376.L6
976.3355	F379.N5
976.369	F379.C6
976.4	F385
	F386
	F390
	F391
	F392.S4
976.400922	F385
976.403	F390
976.4030922	F385
976.4030924	F389
976.404	F390
	F392.B7
976.4040922	F385
	F391
976.406	F391
976.4180924	E185.97.G68
976.422705	F392.H54
976.4245	F392.W3
976.4495	UB323
976.453	CT275.V435
976.4724	F392.R75
976.4727	F394.A15
976.4843	F392.L37
976.4888	F394.M8
976.493	F392.B54
976.6	F702.A15
976.619	F704.F76
976.63	F702.C53
976.634	F704.S85
976.73	F394.A9
	F417.A7
976.732	F417.P75
976.736	F419.F6
976.742	F417.H6
976.773	F419.L7
976.8	F436
976.80072024	Z8181.95
976.8008	F436
976.812	F443.R34
976.819	F444.M5
976.82105	F443.F3
976.855	F444.N2
976.864	F443.C65
976.8885	F443.B6
976.9	F452
976.9030924	E340.C9
976.916	F199
976.92	F457.B5
976.935	F457.O2
976.9695	F457.G82
977	F479
	F482
	F516
977.01	F352
977.102	F483
977.131	F499.B35
977.132	F499.C6
977.13204	F499.C6
977.132040924	F496
977.148	F499.T76
977.178	E338
	F499.C5
977.1796	F497.B8
977.2	F526
977.2008	F526
977.252	F534.I3
977.27703	F532.D25
977.3003	F539
977.3008	F541
977.302	F544
	F545
977.3020924	F541.F3
977.3030924	F545
977.304	F546
977.3040924	F546
977.31103	F548.42
	F548.9.N3
977.311030922	HX846.C4
977.31104	F548.42
	F548.52
	F548.9.N3
	HX486.C4
977.31104	HX846.C4
977.322	F547.M14
977.348	F547.F8
977.356	F549.S7
977.358	F549.B7
977.365030922	F547.V2
977.379102	F547.E3
977.386	F549.A4
977.4	F566
977.431	F574.T4
977.434	F574.D4
977.43403	F574.D4
977.43404	F574.D4
977.439	F574.N44
977.44404	SD421
977.5	F578
977.5003	F579
977.5006	F576
977.502	F584
977.5040924	F586.L3
977.528	E587.C6
977.587	GB1225.W6
977.6	F606
977.658	F614.W45
977.6581	F614.S4
977.702	F621
	F627.A15
977.766	F629.W44
977.8	F466
977.800922	F465
977.854	F474.S8
977.865	F474.B84
977.866	F474.S2
978	E179.5
	F591
	F596
978.0072024	E175.5.G3
978.008	F591
978.02	F591
	F592.7
	F593
	F596
978.020922	F591
	F596
978.020924	CT275.J689
	F592
	F594.V6
978.1	F681
978.102	E433
	F685
978.1020924	F593.C52
978.125	F689.C74
978.1545	F689.S2
978.155	F536
978.163	F689.T6
978.176	F689.F65
978.186	F689.W6
978.193	F869.I48
978.2	F661
	F666
978.227	F666
978.287	F672.C4
978.29	GB1225.N2
978.3382009743931	F657.D7
978.393	QH105.S8
978.436	F614.F7
978.49020924	F641.M6
978.6008	F731
978.602	F739.B8
978.6663	F739.V5
978.752	KF27.J8666
978.75203	F722
978.755	F767.J3
978.793	E83.86
978.8	F776
	F776.3
978.802	F776
	F780
978.8020924	F593.G48
978.803	GB1225.C6
978.83803	F784.C795
978.84	F782.H6
978.851	F784.C9
978.858	F784.C8
978.86	F782.C6
978.863	F782.S15
978.865	F782.G7
978.9	E78.N65
	F796
978.902	E99.P9
978.9030924	E405.2
978.905	F801.2
978.9404	F804.S8
978.952	F804.T5
978.964040922	F802.L7
978.982	F802.S18
978.983	F799
979	F786
979.1	F810.5
	F811
979.100974918	F820.S6
979.101	F799
979.1030924	E90.F7
979.104	F786
	F811
979.15	F811
979.159	F817.M5
979.177050924	CT275
979.247	F826
979.3	F841
979.302	F842
979.334	F849.R5
	F849.T6
979.356	TN413.N25

Dewey	LC
979.4	F851.5
	F861
	F864
	F865
979.400974951	F870.C5
979.401	F851
	F864
979.402	F864
979.403	F864
979.404	F864
	F865
979.405	GB1225.C3
979.4050924	F866.2.R39
	KF8745.W3
979.437	F868.N5
	F869.M44
979.442	F869.J3
979.446	F868.Y6
979.448	F869.B65
979.45	F868.S13
979.453	F869.G15
979.455	F869.L68
979.46	F868.S156
979.46030924	F864.L75
979.46104	F869.S3
979.461040924	CT275.H5885
979.46105	F869.S3
979.463	F869.C56
	F869.O7
	F869.R5
979.46750222	F869.B5
979.469	F868.S19
979.473	F869.L82
979.476	F869.M7
979.4904	TN24.C2
979.491	F868.S23
979.492	F868.V5
	F869.M75
979.494	F869.L8
979.49405	F869.L8
979.495	F868.S14
	F869.U6
979.496	F868.O6
	F869.C83
979.498	F869.S22
979.49803	F868.S15
979.499	F869.F69
979.5	F852
	F876.6
	F880
979.502	F880
979.521	F884.C25
979.6	F746
	F752.B63
979.654	F752.T5
979.7	F892
979.748	F891
979.74802	F891
979.771	F899.E9
979.778	F897.A5
979.786	F899.V2
979.803	F910
979.8030924	F931
979.86	F912.Y9
980	F1408.R7
	F1410
980.007	F1409.9
980.0072024	F3444
980.008	F1410
980.01	E129.H4
	F1411
	G161
980.02	F2235
980.020922	F1407
980.020924	F2235
	F2235.3
980.030922	F1414.2
980.030924	F1788.22.G8
	F2849.22.G85
980.1	F1434
	F2230
	F2230.1.R3
980.15	MT6
980.3	F1565.2.C8
	F2520.1.Y3
	F3429
	F3430.1.C40
980.45	F3424
	GN751
981	F2521
	F2524
	F2535
981.05	F2537
981.06	F2538.2
981.060924	F2538.V33
981.1	F2546
982	F2831
	F2841
	FZ831
982.03	F2845
982.050924	F2846.S26
983	F3171
983.02	F1401
983.106	F3097.3
984.041	F3323
984.05	F3326
984.050922	F3326
984.050924	F2849.22.G85
	F3326
985	F3431
985.02	F3442
985.020924	G161
985.030924	F3444
985.063	F3448
986.1	F2271
986.101	F2272
986.10630924	F2278.T6
	Q180.A1
986.202	F2281.D2
986.3	F1569.C2
987.040924	F2323.M6
987.0610924	F2322.8
987.0630924	F2325
988.01	E129.R2
988.1020924	F2384
989.203	F2684
989.2050924	F2686
989.207	F1401
990	DU28.3
991	DS596.5
	DS634
	DS635
991.01	DS641
991.012	DS641
991.022	DS644
991.03	DS644
991.030924	DS644.1.S56
	DS644.1.S8
991.152	DS596
991.15303	DS646.36
991.153030924	DS38
991.4	DS668
	DS669
991.4007	DS673.8
991.401	DS666.C5
991.4020924	DS675.8.R5
991.40270924	DS676.8.A3
991.403	DS682
991.4031	DS679
	DS685
991.40310924	DS676.8.A3
991.4032	DS685
991.40320924	DS685
991.40350924	DS686.3
	DS686.4
991.4040924	DS685.8.R4
	DS686.6.M24
	DS686.6.M35
992.1	DS643
992.20220924	DS646.26.R3
993	DU490
993.1	DU400
	DU420
	DU427
993.101	DU420
	G477
993.1010924	DU410
993.102	DU420
993.1020924	DU422.H35
	DU422.S4
993.1030924	DU422.W25
993.12	DU430.N4
993.12202	DU430.A79
993.125	DU430.H33
993.127	DU428
	DU430.P69
993.155	DU430.C5
993.157	DU430.M54
993.5	DU850
994	DU107
	DU110
	DU115
994.0072	DU80
994.008	DU80
994.01	DU19
	DU98
	DU98.1
994.02	DU114.F6
	DU170
994.020922	DU97
994.020924	DU114.K4
	DU114.K47
994.03	DU102
	DU115
994.030924	DU114.M28
994.040924	DU114.C8
	DU114.F15
	DU114.M4
994.05	DU113
994.1	DU370
994.102	DU102
	DU370
994.2	DU330.B33
	DU330.T4
	NA6103.A3
994.2040924	DU322.P55
994.3	DU280.A7
	DU280.B34
	DU280.M27
994.303	DU270
994.4	CD2536
	D6177
	DU170
	DU178
	DU180.L4
	DU180.M57
	DU180.R47
	DU180.S85
	DU180.W3
	DU180.W32
	DU180.W4
	DU430.C7
994.4010924	DU172.R85
994.402	DU160
	S478.A1
994.4020924	CT2818.R3
994.5	D6230.H8
	DU212
994.5	DU220
	DU230.D3
	DU230.G4
	DU230.P7
	DU230.W37
	DU230.Y3
994.503	DU220
	DU230.B3
	DU230.W37
994.6	DU460
	DU473
	DU480.L3
994.6008	DU472.G7
994.602	DU473
994.8	DU180.N6
995	DU740
996	DU28.3
	DU870
996.13	DU817
996.18	G161
996.211	DU870
996.7	DU647
996.85	DU715
996.9028	DU627.2
997.1	F490
998	G620
	G635.H4
999	G850
	G860
	G870

OUTLINE OF THE
LIBRARY OF CONGRESS CLASSIFICATION

A

GENERAL WORKS. POLYGRAPHY

For works too general or comprehensive to be classed
with any particular subject, however broad

AC		Collections. Series. Collected works
	1-195	Collections of monographs, essays, etc. [For collections published under the auspices of learned bodies (institutions or societies), *see* **AS**]
	801-895	Inaugural and program dissertations
	901-995	Pamphlet collections
	999	Scrapbooks
AE		Encyclopedias (General)
AG		Dictionaries and other general reference works
	1-91	Dictionaries. Minor encyclopedias [Including popular and juvenile encyclopedias]
	103-191	General works, pocketbooks, receipts, etc.
	195-196	Questions and answers
	240-243	Wonders. Curiosities
	250	Pictorial works
	305-313	Notes and queries
	500-551	Information bureaus. Clipping bureaus. Information centers
AI		Indexes (General)
AM		Museums (General). Collectors and collecting (General)
	10-101	Museography. Individual museums
	111-157	Museology. Museum methods, technique, etc.
	200-501	Collectors and collecting. Private collections
AN		Newspapers [For history and description of individual newspapers, *see* **PN4891-5650**]
AP		Periodicals (General)
	101-115	Humorous periodicals
	200-230	Juvenile periodicals
AS		Academies and learned societies (General)
	3-4	International associations, congresses, conferences, etc.
AY		Yearbooks. Almanacs. Directories [For general works only]
	30-1725	Almanacs
	2001	Directories [For general works on theory, methods of compilation, etc.]
AZ		History of the sciences in general. Scholarship and learning
	999	Popular errors, delusions and superstitions

B

PHILOSOPHY. PSYCHOLOGY. RELIGION

PHILOSOPHY

B		Philosophy (General
		[For general philosophical treatises, *see* **BD**10-41]
	69-5739	History and systems
		[Including individual philosophers and schools of philosophy]
BC		Logic
BD		Speculative philosophy
	10-41	General philosophical works
	95-131	Metaphysics
	143-236	Epistemology. Theory of knowledge
	240-241	Methodology
	300-450	Ontology
		[Including the soul, immortality]
	493-708	Cosmology
		[Including teleology, space and time, atomism]

PSYCHOLOGY

BF		
	231-299	Sensation
	311-499	Cognition. Perception. Intelligence
	511-593	Emotion
	608-635	Will
	636-637	Applied psychology
	660-687	Comparative psychology
	683	Motivation
	698	Personality
	699-755	Genetic psychology. Child psychology
	795-839	Temperament. Character
	840-861	Physiognomy
	866-885	Phrenology
	889-905	Graphology
	908-940	The hand. Palmistry
	1001-1389	Parapsychology
		[Including hallucinations, sleep, dreams, hypnotism, telepathy, spiritualism, clairvoyance]
	1405-1999	Occult sciences
		[Including ghosts, demonology, witchcraft, astrology, oracles, fortune-telling]
BH		Aesthetics
BJ		Ethics
	1545-1725	Practical and applied ethics. Conduct of life
	1801-2195	Social usages. Etiquette

B

PHILOSOPHY. PSYCHOLOGY. RELIGION
(Cont.)

RELIGION

BL		Religions. Mythology. Rationalism
	175-290	Natural theology
	300-325	Mythology (General)
	425-490	Religious doctrines (General)
	500-547	Eschatology
	550-619	Worship. Cultus
	660-2670	History and principles of particular religions [Including Brahmanism, Hinduism, Buddhism]
	2700-2790	Rationalism [Including agnosticism, free thought]
BM		Judaism
BP		Islam. Bahaism. Theosophy
		Christianity
BR		Christianity (General)
	45-85	Collections [Including early Christian literature]
	140-1500	Church history
	1690-1725	Biography
BS		The Bible and exegesis
BT		Doctrinal theology. Apologetics
BV		Practical theology
	5-525	Worship (Public and private) [Including the church year, Christian symbols, liturgy, prayer, hymnology]
	590-1650	Ecclesiastical theology [Including the Church, church and state, church management, ministry, sacraments, religious societies, religious education]
	2000-3705	Missions
	3750-3799	Evangelism. Revivals
	4000-4470	Pastoral theology
	4485-5099	Practical religion. The Christian life
BX		Denominations and sects
	1-9	Church unity. Ecumenical movement
	100-750	Eastern churches. Oriental churches
	800-4795	Roman Catholic Church
	4800-9999	Protestantism

C
AUXILIARY SCIENCES OF HISTORY

C		Auxiliary sciences of history (General)
CB		History of civilization and culture (General) [For individual countries, *see* **D-F**]
CC		Archaeology (General) [For individual countries, *see* **D-F, GN**]
	200-260	Bells. Campanology
	300-350	Crosses
CD		Diplomatics. Archives. Seals
	931-4279	Archives [Including works on the science of archives, guides to depositories, inventories of archival material]
CE		Technical chronology. Calendar [For historical chronology, *see* **D-F**]
CJ		Numismatics
	4801-5450	Tokens
	5501-6651	Medals and medallions
CN		Epigraphy. Inscriptions
CR		Heraldry
	51-93	Crests, monograms, devices, badges, mottoes, etc.
	101-115	Flags, banners, and standards
	191-1020	Public and official heraldry
	1101-1131	Ecclesiastical and sacred heraldry
	1179-3400	Family heraldry
	3499-4420	Titles of honor, rank, precedence, etc.
	4501-6305	Chivalry and knighthood [Including tournaments, duels, orders, decorations]
CS		Genealogy
	2300-3090	Personal and family names
CT		Biography [For biography associated with a particular subject, *see* that subject]
	93-206	Collections (General. Universal)
	210-3150	National biography
	3200-3830	Biography of women

D

HISTORY: GENERAL AND OLD WORLD

Including geography and description of individual regions and countries

D		History (General)
	51-95	Ancient history
	111-203	Medieval history
	204-849	Modern history
	501-680	World War I
	731-838	World War II
	901-1075	Europe (General)
DA		Great Britain
	900-995	Ireland
DB		Austria. Czechoslovakia. Hungary
DC		France
DD		Germany
DE		The Mediterranean region. Greco-Roman world
DF		Greece
DG		Italy
DH-DJ		Belgium. Holland. Luxemburg
DK		Russia [Including Russia in Asia]
	401-443	Poland
	445-465	Finland
DL		Northern Europe. Scandinavia
DP		Spain. Portugal
DQ		Switzerland
DR		Eastern Europe. Balkan Peninsula. Turkey
DS		Asia
DT		Africa
DU		Oceania (South Seas)
	80-398	Australia
	400-430	New Zealand
DX		Gypsies

HISTORY: AMERICA

E	11-29	America (General)
	31-45	North America
	51-99	Indians. Indians of North America
	101-135	Discovery of America and early explorations
		United States (General)
	184-185	Elements in the population
	185	Negroes
	186-199	Colonial history
	201-298	Revolution
	301-453	Revolution to the Civil War
	351-364	War of 1812
	401-415	War with Mexico
	441-453	Slavery
	456-655	Civil War
	482-489	Confederate States of America
	660-738	Late nineteenth century
	714-735	Spanish-American War
	740-	Twentieth century
F	1-975	United States local history
	1001-1140	British America. Canada
	1201-1392	Mexico
	1401-1419	Latin America (General)
	1421-1577	Central America
	1601-2175	West Indies
	2201-2239	South America (General)
	2251-2299	Colombia
	2301-2349	Venezuela
	2351-2471	Guiana
	2501-2659	Brazil
	2661-2699	Paraguay
	2701-2799	Uruguay
	2801-3021	Argentina
	3051-3285	Chile
	3301-3359	Bolivia
	3401-3619	Peru
	3701-3799	Ecuador

G

GEOGRAPHY. ANTHROPOLOGY. RECREATION

G		Geography (General)
		[For geography and description of individual countries, *see* **D-F**]
	149-570	Voyages and travels (General)
		[Including discoveries, explorations, mountaineering, shipwrecks, seafaring life. For travel in special continents and countries, *see* **D-F**]
	575-890	Polar regions
		[Including exploration, history, description]
	1001-3102	Atlases
	3160-9980	Maps
GA		Mathematical geography. Cartography
	1-87	Mathematical geography
		[Including topographical surveys of individual countries]
	101-1999	Cartography
GB		Physical geography
		[Including arrangement by country]
	401-648	Geomorphology
	651-2598	Water. Hydrology
		[Including ground water, rivers, lakes, glaciers]
GC		Oceanography
	101-181	Seawater
	201-376	Dynamics of the sea
	380-399	Marine sediments
	1015-1023	Marine resources
	1080-1572	Marine pollution
GF		Anthropogeography. Human ecology
GN		Anthropology
	51-211	Physical anthropology. Somatology
	221-279	Physiological and psychological anthropology
	307-686	Ethnology and ethnography
		[Including primitive customs and institutions, individual races and ethnic groups. For purely descriptive treatment of peoples and races, *see* **D-F**]
	700-875	Prehistoric archaeology
		[Including arrangement by country]
GR		Folklore
		[For folk literature, *see* **P**]
	440-950	Folklore relating to special subjects
GT		Manners and customs (General)
		[For works limited to special countries, *see* **D-F**]
	170-482	Houses. Dwellings
	500-2370	Dress. Costume. Fashion
	2400-5090	Customs relative to private and public life
		[Including love, marriage, eating, smoking, treatment of the dead, town life, customs of chivalry, festivals and holidays]
	5320-6715	Customs relative to special classes, by birth, occupation, etc.
GV		Recreation
	192-198	Organized camping. Summer camps
	201-547	Physical training
	561-1197	Sports
	1200-1570	Games and amusements
	1580-1799	Dancing
	1800-1860	Circuses, carnivals, etc.

H

SOCIAL SCIENCES

H		Social sciences (General)
HA		Statistics [Including collections of general and census statistics of special countries. For mathematical statistics, *see* **QA276-279**]

ECONOMICS

HB		Economic theory [Including value, price, wealth, capital, interest, profit, consumption]
	848-875	Population
	879-3700	Demography. Vital statistics
	3711-3840	Crises. Business cycles
HC		Economic history and conditions. National production
HD		Land. Agriculture. Industry
	1-91	Production. Industrial management
	101-1395	Land [Including public lands, real estate, land tenure]
	1401-2210	Agricultural economics [Including agricultural laborers]
	2321-9999	Industry
	2709-2930	Corporations. Trusts. Cartels
	2951-3570	Industrial cooperation
	3611-4730	The state and industrial organization [Including state industries, public works, municipal industries]
	4801-8942	Labor [Including wages, strikes, unemployment, labor unions, industrial relations, social security, professions, state labor. For civil service, *see* **J**]
	9000-9999	Special industries and trades
HE		Transportation and communication
	331-377	Traffic engineering. Roads and highways
	381-971	Water transportation
	1001-5600	Rail transportation
	5601-5720	Automotive transportation
	6000-7500	Postal service. Stamp collecting
	7601-8688	Telecommunication. Telegraph
	8689-8700	Radio and television
	8701-9715	Telephone
	9761-9900	Air transportation
HF		Commerce
	294-343	Boards of trade. Chambers of commerce
	1701-2701	Tariff policy
	5001-5780	Business. Business administration
	5549	Personnel management
	5601-5689	Accounting
	5801-6191	Advertising
HG		Finance
	201-1492	Money
	1501-3542	Banking
	3701-3781	Credit
	3810-4000	Foreign exchange
	4001-4495	Corporation finance
	4501-6270	Stocks, investment, speculation
	8011-9970	Insurance

ECONOMICS *(Cont.)*

HJ — Public finance
- 2005-2199 Income and expenditure. The budget
- 2240-5957 Revenue. Taxation
- 6041-7384 Customs. Tariff
- 8003-8963 Public credit. Debts. Loans
- 9000-9698 Local finance
- 9701-9995 Public accounting

SOCIOLOGY

HM — Sociology (General and theoretical)
- 251-291 Social psychology

HN — Social history. Social problems. Social reform
- 30-39 The church and social problems

Social groups

HQ — The family. Marriage. Woman
- 12-449 Sexual life
- 450-471 Erotica
- 503-1064 The family. Marriage
  [Including child study, eugenics, desertion, adultery, divorce, polygamy, the aged]
- 1101-2030 Woman. Feminism. Women's clubs

HS — Societies: Secret, benevolent, etc. Clubs
  [Including Freemasons, religious societies, ethnic societies, political societies, Boy Scouts]

HT — Communities. Classes. Races
- 101-348 Urban sociology. Cities and towns
  [Including the social and economic aspects of city planning and urban renewal. For architectural aspects, *see* **NA9000-9425**]
- 390-395 Regional planning
- 401-485 Rural sociology
- 601-1445 Social classes
  [Including middle class, serfdom, slavery]
- 1501-1595 Races
  [For works on the race as a social group and race relations in general]

HV — Social pathology. Social and public welfare. Criminology
- 40-696 Charities
- 697-4959 Protection, assistance, and relief
  [Including protection of animals]
  [Arranged by special classes of persons, as determined by age, occupation, economic status, etc.]
- 5001-5720 Alcoholism. Intemperance. Temperance reform
- 5725-5770 Tobacco habit
- 5800-5840 Drug habits. Drug abuse
- 6001-9920 Criminology
  - 6251-7220 Crimes and offenses
  - 7231-9920 Penology
    [Including police, prisons, punishment and reform, juvenile delinquency]

HX — Socialism. Communism. Anarchism
- 806-811 Utopias

J
POLITICAL SCIENCE

J		Official documents
		[General serial documents only. For documents limited to special subjects, *see* the subject in **B-Z**]
	1-9	Official gazettes
		United States documents
		[For congressional hearings, reports, etc., *see* **KF**]
	80-85	Presidents' messages and other executive documents
	86-87	State documents
	100-981	Other countries
		[For documents issued by local governments, *see* **JS**]
JA		Collections and general works
JC		Political theory. Theory of the state
	311-323	Nationalism. Minorities. Geopolitics
	325-341	Nature, entity, concept of the state
	345-347	Symbolism, emblems of the state: Arms, flag, seal, etc.
	348-497	Forms of the state
		[Including imperialism, the world state, monarchy, aristocracy, democracy, fascism, dictatorships]
	501-628	Purpose, functions, and relations of the state
	571-628	The state and the individual. Individual rights. Liberty
		Constitutional history and administration
JF		General works. Comparative works
	201-723	Organs and function of government
		[Including executive branch, cabinet and ministerial government, legislative bodies]
	800-1191	Political rights and guaranties
		[Including citizenship, suffrage, electoral systems, representation, the ballot]
	1321-2112	Government. Administration
	1411-1674	Civil service
	2011-2112	Political parties
		Special countries
JK		United States
JL		British America. Latin America
JN		Europe
JQ		Asia. Africa. Australia. Oceania
JS		Local government
	3-37	Serial documents (General)
	141-231	Municipal government
	241-285	Local government other than municipal
JV		Colonies and colonization. Emigration and immigration
JX		International law. International relations
	63-1195	Collections. Documents. Cases
	101-115	Diplomatic relations (Universal collections)
	120-191	Treaties (Universal collections)
	1305-1589	International relations. Foreign relations
		[For international questions treated as either sources of or contributions to the theory of international law. For histories of events, diplomatic histories, etc., *see* **D-F**]
	1625-1896	Diplomacy. The diplomatic service
	1901-1995	International arbitration. World peace. International organization
		[Including peace movements, League of Nations, United Nations, arbitration treaties, international courts]
	2001-5810	International law (Treatises and monographs)

K
LAW

LAW OF THE UNITED STATES

KF		Federal law. Common and collective state law
KFA-KFW		Law of individual states
KFA	0-599	e.g. Alabama
	1200-1799	Alaska
KFW	0-599	Washington
KFX		Law of individual cities, A-Z
KFZ		Law of individual territories

L
EDUCATION

L		Education (General) [For periodicals, congresses, directories, etc.]
LA		History of education
LB		Theory and practice of education
	51-885	Systems of individual educators and writers
	1025-1050	Teaching (Principles and practice) [Including programmed instruction, remedial teaching, non-graded schools, audiovisual education, methods of study, reading (General)]
	1051-1091	Educational psychology
	1101-1139	Child study. Psychical development
	1140	Preschool education
	1141-1489	Kindergarten
	1501-1547	Primary education
	1555-1602	Elementary or public school education
	1603-1695	Secondary education. High schools
	1705-2286	Education and training of teachers
	2300-2411	Higher education
	2801-3095	School administration and organization
	3205-3325	School architecture and equipment
	3401-3498	School hygiene
	3525-3640	Special days. School life. Student customs
LC		Special aspects of education
	8-63	Forms of education [Including self, home, and private school education]
	65-245	Social aspects of education [Including education and the state, religious instruction in public schools, compulsory education, illiteracy, educational sociology, community and the school, endowments]
	251-951	Moral and religious education. Education under church control
	1001-1091	Types of education [Including humanistic, vocational, and professional education]
	1390-5153	Education of special classes of persons [Including women, Negroes, gifted and handicapped children, orphans, middle class]
	5201-6691	Adult education. Education extension.
		Individual institutions: universities, colleges, and schools
LD		United States
LE		America, except United States
LF		Europe
LG		Asia. Africa. Oceania
LH		College and school magazines and papers
LJ		Student fraternities and societies, United States [For other countries, *see* **LA, LE-LG**]
LT		Textbooks [For textbooks covering several subjects. For textbooks on particular subjects, *see* those subjects in **B-Z**]

M

MUSIC

M — Music

- 5-1459 Instrumental music
  - 6-175 One instrument without accompaniment
  - 177-985 Two or more solo instruments
    [Including chamber music not orchestral]
  - 1000-1365 Orchestral music
- 1495-2199 Vocal music
  - 1497-1998 Secular vocal music
    - 1500-1527 Dramatic music
    - 1530-1610 Choral music, part songs, etc.
    - 1611-1626 Songs for one voice
    - 1627-1985 Songs (Part and solo)
      - 1627-1853 National music
        [Including primitive, folk, traditional, patriotic, political, and typical music, with or without accompaniment, and with and without words]
  - 1999-2199 Sacred vocal music
    - 2000-2017 Oratorios, masses, services, etc.
    - 2018-2101 Cantatas, anthems, part songs
    - 2102-2114 Songs for one voice
    - 2115-2146 Hymn, psalm, and choral books
    - 2147-2188 Liturgy and ritual
    - 2198-2199 Temperance, revival, and gospel songs

ML — Literature of music

- 48-54 Librettos
- 111-157 Bibliography
  - 155.3-157 Phonograph records
- 159-3795 History and criticism
  [Including biographies of individual composers]
  - 460-1354 Instruments and instrumental music
    - 1100-1354 Chamber and orchestral music. Band (Military music)
  - 1400-3275 Vocal music
    - 1500-1554 Choral music (Sacred and secular)
    - 1600-2862 Secular vocal music
      [Including dramatic music, cantatas, songs (Part and solo)]
    - 2900-3197 Sacred vocal music
      [Including church music, oratorios, cantatas]
  - 3400-3465 Dance music
  - 3545-3776 National music
- 3800-3923 Philosophy and physics of music
  [Including physiology, psychology, color and music, aesthetics, ethics, therapeutics]
- 3925-3930 Fiction. Juvenile literature

MT — Music instruction and study

- 40-67 Composition
  [Including rhythm, scales, melody, harmony, modulation, counterpoint]
- 68 Improvisation
- 70-86 Orchestra and orchestration, conducting, etc.
- 90-145 Analytical guides, etc. (Hermeneutics)
  [How to listen to and how to understand special musical compositions. For historical, biographical, critical, or aesthetic works, *see* **ML410** under the composer]
- 170-810 Instrumental technics
- 820-949 Singing and voice culture
- 955-960 Production of operas. Music in theaters

N

FINE ARTS

For the arts in general, *see* **NX**

N		Visual arts (General) [For photography, *see* **TR**]
	400-4040	Art museums, galleries, etc. [Arranged by country, subarrangement by city]
	4390-5098	Exhibitions
	5200-5299	Private collections and collectors
	5300-7418	History of art
	7430-7433	Technique, composition, style, etc.
	7475-7483	Art criticism
	7575-7624	Portraits
	7790-8199	Religious art
	8555-8580	Examination and conservation of works of art
	8600-8675	Economics of art
	8700-9165	Art and the state. Public art
NA		Architecture
	200-1613	History. Historical monuments
	2700-2790	Architectural design and drawing
	2835-4050	Architectural details, motives, decoration, etc.
	4100-8480	Special classes of buildings
	9000-9425	Aesthetics of cities. City planning and beautification
NB		Sculpture
NC		Drawing. Design. Illustration
	997-1003	Commercial art. Advertising art
	1300-1766	Caricature. Pictorial humor and satire
	1800-1855	Posters
ND		Painting
	1290-1460	Special subjects [Including human figure, landscapes, animals, still life, flowers]
	1700-2495	Watercolor painting
	2550-2888	Mural painting
	2890-3416	Illuminating of manuscripts and books
NE		Print media
	1-978	Printmaking and engraving
	1000-1352	Wood engraving. Woodcuts. Xylography
	1400-1879	Metal engraving. Copper, steel, etc. [Including color prints]
	1940-2230	Etching and aquatint
	2236-2239	Serigraphy
	2250-2570	Lithography
	2800-2890	Printing of engravings
NK		Decorative arts. Applied arts. Decoration and ornament
	1135-1149	Arts and crafts movement
	1700-3505	Interior decoration. House decoration
	3600-9955	Other arts and art industries
	3700-4695	Ceramics. Pottery. Porcelain
	4700-4890	Costume and its accessories
	5000-5735	Enamel. Glass. Glyptic arts
	5800-5998	Ivory carving. Ivories
	6400-8459	Metalwork [Including armor, jewelry, plate, brasses, pewter]
	8800-9505	Textile arts and art needlework
	9600-9955	Woodwork [Including carvings, fretwork, inlaying]

N

FINE ARTS
(Cont.)

NX		Arts in general
		[Including works dealing with two or more of the fine arts media, i.e. literature, performing arts, and the visual arts. For works on any one of these subjects, *see* the subject, i.e. **GV, M, N, P, TR**]
	654-694	Religious arts
	700-750	Patronage of the arts
	800-820	Special arts centers

P

LANGUAGE AND LITERATURE

P		Philology and linguistics (General)
	87-96	Communication. Mass media
	101-409	Language (General)
	101-112	Philosophy, psychology, origin, etc. of language
	121-141	Science of language. Linguistics
	201-297	Comparative grammar
		[Including origin of the alphabet, phonetics, morphology, parts of speech, syntax]
	301	Style. Composition. Rhetoric
	306-310	Translating and interpreting
	311	Prosody. Metrics. Rhythmics
	327-361	Lexicography
	375-381	Linguistic geography
	501-769	Indo-European philology
	901-1081	Extinct (Ancient or Medieval) Asiatic and European languages
PA		CLASSICAL LANGUAGES AND LITERATURES
	227-1179	Greek philology and language
	2001-2915	Latin philology and language
		Greek literature
	3051-4500	Ancient (Classic) to ca. 600 A.D.
	5000-5665	Byzantine and modern
		Latin literature
	6001-6971	Ancient Roman
	8001-8595	Medieval and modern
		MODERN EUROPEAN LANGUAGES
PB	1-431	General works
		Celtic languages and literatures
	1201-1449	Irish
	1501-1709	Gaelic. Scottish Gaelic
	1801-1888	Manx
	2001-3029	Brythonic group
		[Including Welsh, Cornish, Breton, Gallic]
PC		Romance languages
	601-872	Romanian language and literature
	1001-1977	Italian
	2001-3761	French. Provençal
	3801-3976	Catalan language and literature
	4001-4977	Spanish
	5001-5498	Portuguese

LANGUAGE AND LITERATURE *(Cont.)*

MODERN EUROPEAN LANGUAGES *(Cont.)*

PD — Germanic languages
- 1001-1350 Old Germanic dialects
  - [Including Gothic, Vandal, Burgundian, Langobardian]
- 1501-5929 Scandinavian. North Germanic
  - 2201-2392 Old Norse. Old Icelandic and Norwegian
  - 2401-2489 Icelandic
  - 2571-2999 Norwegian
  - 3001-3929 Danish
  - 5001-5929 Swedish

PE — English

PF — West Germanic
- 1-979 Dutch
- 1001-1184 Flemish
- 1401-1558 Friesian
- 3001-5999 German

PG — Slavic. Baltic, Albanian languages and literatures
- 1-7925 Slavic.
  - 615-716 Church Slavic
  - 801-1164 Bulgarian. Macedonian
  - 1201-1696 Serbo-Croatian
  - 1801-1962 Slovenian
  - 2001-3987 Russian. White Russian. Ukrainian
  - 4001-5546 Czech. Slovak
  - 5631-7446 Polish. Sorbian
- 8001-9146 Baltic
  - 8501-8772 Lithuanian
  - 8801-9146 Latvian
- 9501-9678 Albanian

PH — Finno-Ugrian, Basque languages and literatures
- 101-1109 Finnish
  - 101-405 Finnish (Proper)
  - 601-671 Estonian
  - 701-735 Lappish
- 1201-3445 Ugrian. Hungarian
- 5001-5490 Basque

ORIENTAL LANGUAGES AND LITERATURE

PJ
- 1-995 General works
- 1001-2199 Egyptian. Coptic
- 2301-2551 Hamitic
  - 2353-2367 Libyan group
  - 2369-2399 Berber
  - 2401-2539 Cushitic
- 3001-9293 Semitic
  - 3101-4083 Assyrian. Sumerian
  - 4501-5192 Hebrew
  - 5201-5329 Aramaic
  - 5403-5809 Syriac
  - 6001-8517 Arabic
  - 9001-9293 Ethiopian

PK
- 1-6996 Indo-Iranian
  - [Including Vedic, Sanskrit, Pali, Assamese, Bengali, Hindi, Urdu, Hindustani, Sinhalese, Persian]
- 8001-8958 Armenian
- 9001-9201 Caucasian. Georgian

LANGUAGE AND LITERATURE *(Cont.)*

ORIENTAL LANGUAGES AND LITERATURE *(Cont.)*

PL		Languages and literatures of Eastern Asia, Africa, Oceania
	501-889	Japanese language and literature
	901-998	Korean language and literature
	1001-3207	Chinese language and literature
	5001-7511	Oceanic languages and literatures
	8000-8844	Africa languages and literatures
PM		
	101-7356	American Indian languages
	8001-9021	Artificial languages

LITERATURE

PN		Literary history and collections (General)
	80-99	Criticism
	101-249	Authorship
	441-1009	Literary history [Including folk literature, fables, prose romances]
	1010-1551	Poetry
	1560-1590	The performing arts. Show business
	1600-3299	The drama
	1660-1692	Dramatic composition
	1865-1999	Special types of drama [Including tragedy, comedy, vaudeville, puppet plays, pantomimes, ballet, radio and television broadcasts, motion pictures]
	2000-3299	Dramatic representation. The theater [Including management, the stage and accessories, amateur theatricals, tableaux and pageants]
	3311-3503	Prose. Prose fiction
	4001-4355	Oratory. Elocution, recitations, etc.
	4400	Letters
	4500	Essays
	4699-5650	Journalism. The periodical press, etc.
	6011-6525	Collections of general literature
	6080-6095	Quotations
	6099-6110	Poetry
	6110.5-6120	Drama
	6121-6129	Orations
	6130-6140	Letters
	6141-6145	Essays
	6147-6231	Wit and humor. Satire
	6249-6525	Miscellaneous [Including anecdotes, aphorisms, maxims, mottoes, toasts, riddles, proverbs]
PQ		Romance literatures
PR		English literature
PS		American literature
PT		Germanic literatures
PZ		Fiction and juvenile literature
	1-4	Fiction in English [Including English translations of foreign authors]
	5-90	Juvenile literature [In English and foreign languages]

Q
SCIENCE

Class	Range	Subject
Q		Science (General)
	300-380	Cybernetics. Information theory
QA		Mathematics
	8-10	Mathematical logic
	76	Computer science. Electronic data processing
	101-145	Elementary mathematics. Arithmetic
	152-299	Algebra
	300-433	Analysis
	443-699	Geometry
	611-614	Topology
	801-935	Analytic mechanics
QB		Astronomy
	145-237	Practical and spherical astronomy
	275-343	Geodesy
	351-421	Theoretical astronomy and celestial mechanics
	460-991	Astrophysics and descriptive astronomy
QC		Physics
	81-119	Weights and measures
	120-168	Descriptive and experimental mechanics
	171-197	Constitution and properties of matter. Atomic physics
	220-246	Sound. Acoustics
	251-338	Heat
	350-495	Light. Optics
	501-768	Electricity and magnetism
	770-798	Nuclear and particle physics. Atomic energy. Radioactivity
	801-809	Geophysics. Cosmic physics
	811-849	Geomagnetism
	851-999	Meteorology
QD		Chemistry
	24-26	Alchemy
	71-142	Analytical chemistry
	146-199	Inorganic chemistry
	241-449	Organic chemistry
	450-655	Physical and theoretical chemistry
	901-999	Crystallography
QE		Geology
	351-399	Mineralogy
	420-499	Petrology
	500-625	Dynamic and structural geology
	650-699	Stratigraphic geology
	701-996	Paleontology
QH		Natural history
	75-77	Nature conservation. Landscape protection
	201-278	Microscopy
	301-559	General biology
	573-671	Cytology
QK		Botany
	641-707	Morphology, anatomy, embryology, and histology
	710-899	Plant physiology
	901-987	Ecology
QL		Zoology
	750-795	Animal behavior and psychology
	801-950	Anatomy
	951-991	Embryology
QM		Human anatomy
	601-699	Human embryology
QP		Physiology
	351-499	Physiological psychology
	501-801	Animal biochemistry
	901-981	Experimental pharmacology
QR		Microbiology
	75-99	Bacteria
	180-189	Immunology
	355-484	Virology

R

MEDICINE

R		Medicine (General)
	131-684	History of medicine
	735-847	Medical education
	895	Medical physics. Electronics. Radiology, radioisotopes, etc.
RA		Public aspects of medicine
	5-418	Medicine and the state [Including medical statistics, medical economics, provisions for medical care, medical sociology]
	421-790	Public health. Hygiene. Preventive medicine [Including sanitation, disposal of the dead, transmission of disease, epidemics, quarantine, personal hygiene]
	791-954	Medical geography. Medical climatology and meteorology
	960-998	Medical centers. Hospitals. Clinics
	1001-1171	Forensic medicine
	1190-1270	Toxicology
RB		Pathology
RC		Internal medicine. Practice of medicine [Including diagnosis, individual diseases and special types of diseases, diseases of systems or organs]
	86-88	First aid
	321-576	Neurology and psychiatry
	952-954	Geriatrics
	955-962	Arctic and tropical medicine
	963-969	Industrial medicine
	970-1015	Military medicine
	1030-1097	Transportation medicine [Including automotive, aviation and space medicine]
	1200-1245	Sports medicine
RD		Surgery
	92-96	Wounds and injuries
	701-796	Orthopedics
RE		Ophthalmology
RF		Otorhinolaryngology
RG		Gynecology and obstetrics
RJ		Pediatrics
RK		Dentistry
RL		Dermatology
RM		Therapeutics. Pharmacology
	214-258	Diet therapy. Diet and dietetics in disease
	270-282	Serum therapy. Immunotherapy
	283-298	Endocrinotherapy
	300-666	Drugs and their action
	695-890	Physical medicine. Physical therapy
	845-862	Medical radiology
RS		Pharmacy and materia medica
RT		Nursing
RV		Botanic, Thomsonian, and eclectic medicine
RX		Homeopathy
RZ		Other systems of medicine
	201-265	Chiropractic
	301-397	Osteopathy
	400-408	Mental healing

S

AGRICULTURE

Class	Numbers	Subject
S		Agriculture (General)
	560-575	Farm management. Farm economics
	583-589	Agricultural chemistry and physics
	590-599	Soils
	605-621	Reclamation and irrigation of farm land [Including organic farming]
	622-627	Soil conservation
	631-669	Fertilizers and soil improvement
	671-760	Farm machinery and engineering
	900-972	Conservation of natural resources
	950-954	Land conservation
	960-964	Wildlife conservation
	970-972	Recreational resources conservation
SB		Plant culture
	110-112	Methods for special areas [Including dry-land and tropical agriculture, irrigation farming]
	114-118	Seeds
	119-125	Propagation
	183-317	Field crops
	318-450	Horticulture
	320-353	Vegetables
	354-402	Fruit culture and orchard care
	403-450	Flowers. Ornamental plants
	449-450	Flower arrangement and decoration
	451-466	Gardens and gardening
	469-479	Landscape gardening
	481-485	Parks and public reservations
	599-999	Diseases and pests [Including treatment and control]
SD		Forestry
	383-385	Description of forest trees
	391-409	Sylviculture
	411-425	Conservation and protection
	426-428	Forest reserves
	430-557	Exploitation and utilization [Including timber trees, logging, transportation, valuation]
	561-668	Forest policy and administration
SF		Animal culture
	91-92	Care and housing
	95-99	Feeds and feeding. Animal nutrition
	105-109	Breeds and breeding [Including artificial insemination, stock farms]
	114-121	Exhibitions. Judging. Stock shows
	191-275	Cattle
	221-275	Dairying. Dairy products
	277-359	Horses [Including horsemanship, racing]
	371-379	Sheep. Wool.
	381-386	Goats
	391-397	Swine
	402-405	Fur-bearing animals
	405.2-407	Laboratory animals
	411-459	Pets
	461-513	Birds [Including cage birds, pigeons, poultry, game birds]
	521-561	Insects [Including bees, silk worm, cochineal]
	600-1100	Veterinary medicine

S

AGRICULTURE

(Cont.)

SH — Fish culture and fisheries
[Including shellfish, lobsters, crabs, sealing, whaling]

- 401-691 — Angling

SK — Hunting

- 351-579 — Wildlife management. Game protection
- 601-608 — Camping. Outdoor life

T

TECHNOLOGY

T — Technology (General)

- 54-55 — Industrial safety
- 55.4-60 — Industrial engineering
  [Including operations research, systems analysis, management information systems, production efficiency, human engineering in industry, work measurement, methods engineering]
- 201-339 — Patents. Trademarks
- 351-385 — Engineering graphics. Mechanical drawing
- 391-995 — Exhibitions. World's fairs

GENERAL ENGINEERING AND CIVIL ENGINEERING GROUP

TA — Engineering (General). Civil engineering (General)

- 166-167 — Human engineering
- 168 — Systems engineering
- 177.4-185 — Engineering economy
- 329-347 — Engineering mathematics
- 349-360 — Mechanics of engineering. Applied mechanics
- 401-492 — Materials of engineering and construction
  [Including strength of materials, testing and properties of materials]
- 501-625 — Surveying
- 630-695 — Structural engineering (General)
- 705-710 — Engineering geology. Rock mechanics. Soil mechanics
- 715-787 — Earthwork. Foundations
- 800-820 — Tunneling. Tunnels
- 1001-1280 — Transportation engineering (General)

TC — Hydraulic engineering
[Including harbors and coast protective works, water-supply engineering, dams, canals, irrigation projects, drainage, ocean engineering]

TD — Environmental technology. Sanitary engineering

- 159-167 — Municipal engineering
- 172-192 — Environmental pollution
- 201-500 — Water supply for domestic and industrial purposes
  [Including water quality and pollution, treatment, saline water conversion, distribution systems]
- 511-780 — Sewage collection and disposal systems. Sewerage
- 785-812 — Municipal refuse. Solid wastes
- 813-870 — Street cleaning. Litter and its removal
- 878-893 — Special types of pollution
  [Including soil, air, noise pollution]
- 895-899 — Industrial sanitation. Industrial wastes

TE — Highway engineering. Roads and pavements

TECHNOLOGY *(Cont.)*

General Engineering and Civil Engineering Group *(Cont.)*

TF		Railroad engineering and operation [Including street railways and subways]
TG		Bridge engineering
TH		Building construction
	845-895	Architectural engineering. Structural engineering of buildings
	1061-1725	Systems of building construction [Including fireproof, wood, masonry, concrete and steel construction]
	2031-3000	Details [Including foundations, walls, chimneys, roofs, floors]
	4021-4970	Buildings: Construction with reference to use [Including public buildings, factories, dwellings, farm buildings]
	5011-5701	Construction by phase of the work (Building trades) [Including masonry, carpentry, metalworking]
	6014-7975	Environmental engineering [Including plumbing, heating, ventilation, lighting]
	9025-9745	Protection of buildings [Including dampness protection, fire prevention and extinction, burglary protection]

Mechanical Group

TJ		Mechanical engineering and machinery
	212.5-225	Control engineering
	268-740	Steam engineering [Including boilers, engines, locomotives]
	1125-1345	Machine shops and machine-shop practice [Including machine and hand tools]
	1480-1496	Agricultural machinery
TK		Electrical engineering. Electronics. Nuclear engineering
	1001-1841	Production of electric energy. Powerplants
	2000-2891	Dynamoelectric machinery [Including generators, motors, transformers]
	3001-3511	Distribution or transmission of electric power. The electric circuit
	4125-4399	Electric lighting
	5101-6720	Telecommunication
	7800-8360	Electronics
	7885-7895	Computer engineering
	9001-9401	Nuclear engineering. Atomic power
TL		Motor vehicles. Aeronautics. Astronautics
	1-390	Motor vehicles
	500-777	Aeronautics
	780-785	Rockets
	787-4050	Astronautics

T

TECHNOLOGY *(Cont.)*

CHEMICAL GROUP

TN		Mining engineering. Metallurgy [Including the mineral industries]
TP		Chemical technology
	155-156	Chemical engineering
	200-248	Manufacture and use of chemicals
	315-360	Fuel
	368-659	Food processing and manufacture [Including refrigeration, fermentation industries, beverages]
	690-692	Petroleum refining and products
	700-764	Gas industry
	785-869	Clay industries. Ceramics. Glass
	890-933	Textile dyeing and printing
	934-944	Paints, pigments, varnishes, etc.
	1101-1185	Plastics and plastics manufacture
TR		Photography

COMPOSITE GROUP

TS		Manufactures
	155-193	Production management [Including quality control, production control, inventory control, product engineering, process engineering, plant engineering]
	195-198	Packaging
	200-770	Metal manufactures. Metalworking [Including forging, casting, stamping, instrument making, firearms, clocks, metal finishing, jewelry]
	800-937	Wood technology [Including lumber, furniture, chemical processing of wood]
	940-1067	Leather industries. Tanning
	1080-1268	Paper manufacture. Woodpulp industry
	1300-1865	Textile industries
	1870-1935	Rubber industry
	1950-1981	Animal products
	2120-2159	Cereals and flour. Milling industry
	2220-2283	Tobacco industry
TT		Handicrafts. Arts and crafts
	161-169	Manual training
	180-200	Woodworking. Furniture making. Upholstering
	205-267	Metalworking
	300-382	Painting. Industrial painting
	387-410	Drapes, slipcovers, etc.
	490-695	Clothing manufacture. Dressmaking. Tailoring
	697-910	Needlework. Decorative crafts
	950-979	Hairdressing. Barbers' work
	980-999	Laundry work
TX		Home economics
	301-339	The house [Including arrangement, care, pests, finance, servants]
	341-641	Foods and food supply [Including nutrition, adulterants, preservation]
	645-840	Cookery
	901-953	Hotels, restaurants, taverns. Catering
	955-985	Building operation and maintenance
	1100-1105	Mobile home living

U

MILITARY SCIENCE

For military history, *see* **D-F**

U		Military science (General)
	750-773	Military life, manners and customs
	800-897	History of arms and armor
UA		Armies: Organization, description, facilities, etc. [Including the military situation, policy, defenses of individual countries]
UB		Military administration
UC		Maintenance and transportation
UD		Infantry
UE		Cavalry. Armored and mechanized cavalry
UF		Artillery
UG		Military engineering [Including fortification, chemical warfare, signaling, air warfare]
UH		Other services [Including medical and sanitary service, public relations, social welfare services, recreation]

V

NAVAL SCIENCE

For naval history, *see* **D-F**

V		Naval science (General)
	720-743	Naval life, manners and customs
	750-980	War vessels: Construction, armament, etc.
	990-995	Fleet ballistic missile systems
VA		Navies: Organization, description, facilities, etc. [Including the naval situation and policy of individual countries]
VB		Naval administration
VC		Naval maintenance
VD		Naval seamen
VE		Marines
VF		Naval ordnance
VG		Minor services of navies [Including communications, bands, air service, medical service, public relations, social work, recreation]
VK		Navigation. Merchant marine
	588-597	Marine hydrography. Hydrographic surveying
	600-794	Tide and current tables
	798-997	Pilot guides. Sailing directions
	1000-1249	Lighthouse service
	1250-1299	Shipwrecks and fires
	1300-1491	Saving of life and property
	1500-1661	Pilots and pilotage
VM		Naval architecture. Shipbuilding
	600-965	Marine engineering
	975-989	Submarine diving

Z

BIBLIOGRAPHY AND LIBRARY SCIENCE

BOOKS IN GENERAL

4-8	History of books and bookmaking
40-115	Writing
40-42	Autographs. Signatures
43-45	Calligraphy. Penmanship
48	Copying processes
49-51	Typewriting
53-102	Shorthand
103-104	Cryptography
105-115	Paleography

BOOK INDUSTRIES AND TRADE

116-265	Printing
266-276	Bookbinding
278-549	Bookselling and publishing

662-1000 LIBRARIES AND LIBRARY SCIENCE

679-680	Architecture and planning of the library
687-717	The collections. The books [Including acquisition, cataloging, classification, shelf-listing, information storage and retrieval systems, reference work, circulation]
719-876	Libraries [Including histories, reports, statistics of individual libraries]
881-980	Library catalogs and bulletins
987-997	Private libraries. Book collecting
998-1000	Booksellers' catalogs. Book prices
1001-8999	Bibliography
1041-1107	Anonyms and pseudonyms
1201-4980	National bibliography
5051-7999	Subject bibliography
8001-8999	Personal bibliography